# Practical Celestial Navigation

Susan P. Howell

MATERIALS NEEDED IN CONJUNCTION WITH THIS TEXT.

The basic part of this text (Chapters 1 - 13) should be used with H.O. Publication No. 229, Volume 3, Latitudes 30° - 45°, inclusive. All homework and examples use the 1976 Nautical Almanac excerpts reprinted in Appendix 2. The last part of Chapter 12 and Chapters 14, 16, 17 and 18 use tables in American Practical Navigator, H.O. Pub. No. 9, Volume II by Bowditch. The Star-Finder, 2102-D, now manufactured by Weems and Plath, Inc. is discussed in Chapter 11. Basic plotting tools (dividers and parallel rulers or two triangles) are necessary throughout the text.

REVISED EDITION ISBN 0-939510-05-7



The first printing of *Practical Celestial Navigation* was published by Susan Peterson Howell in 1979. A second revised printing was published by Mystic Seaport Museum Stores in 1987. This third printing is published by The Susan Peterson Howell Memorial Fund.

Profits from all direct sales, wholesale and retail, will be added to Sue's Memorial Fund to pay back the publishing costs and increase the principal in the fund. The Susan Peterson Howell Memorial Fund at Mystic Seaport® Museum has the two-fold purpose of: 1. Encouraging and assisting worthy individuals desiring to study navigation and sailing; 2. Supporting quality teaching of navigation, sailing and meteorology at Mystic Seaport®.

# *Table of Contents*

Winter 1979

LETTER FROM THE AUTHOR

Celestial navigation is a combination of thrills - a cool summer's evening when the brilliant stars wink at their sea reflections, the salt spray and wind dependence felt aboard a sailboat born of the coasting era, and the satisfying logic in the discipline of mathematics. After having taught over thirty-five courses in various levels of marine navigation, I have developed a very definite feeling for the type of celestial navigation study that appeals to the average sailor. He wants a straightforward approach with a minimum of theory and a maximum of practicality - and enough practice to make him feel confident when the time comes to depend on his knowledge at sea. Once this level is reached, further pursuit of theoretical concepts will be natural to the curious mind but not necessary to the competence of the navigator.

This text is aimed at building a confident knowledge. Homework is necessary, the amount dependent on the individual. Therefore, an abundant supply of practical problems is provided with explanations of methods in hopes that the student will work enough examples to make him feel at ease with each section before proceeding with the next.

There are two sections to this text. Chapters one through thirteen encompass the basic material needed in the study of celestial navigation. The last seven chapters offer additional topics that may be of interest to those wishing to acquire further knowledge.

I hope all those who use this book, either coupled with a classroom situation or a self-teaching endeavor, will find some aspect of the thrills I mentioned earlier and will enjoy safe and smooth sailing in the future.

I am indebted to the people whose talents, patience and interest contributed to the production of this book and last, but not least, to my family who endured me "resting at my desk" for too many days.

| | |
|---|---|
| Proofreading | Charles Maxwell |
| Calligraphy and sextant diagrams | Lynn Anderson |
| Typing | Nancy H. Soma & Linda Richards |
| Photography | Donald Treworgy |
| Forword, Chapter 19 & other revisions | Keith D. Palmer |
| Mechanical revisions | Mim-G Studios Inc. |
| Editor (revised edition) | Donald Treworgy |

This book is dedicated to three men whose inspiration to me in the fields of sailing and celestial navigation is invaluable. They all lived in the age when sailing ships and handling of them was a way of life, not just of pleasure, and they projected their knowledge with truth, interest and concern. I feel indeed honored to have known them so well.

Murray G. Peterson (1908 - 1974), my father. He was a naval architect, specializing in wood pleasure yachts modeled after the coasting schooners of the nineteenth and early twentieth centuries.

Frederic W. Keator (1897 - 1974), my navigation teacher. He was chief commander of the United States Power Squadron, a professor of mechanical engineering at Yale, and Director Emeritus of the Mystic Seaport Planetarium.

John F. Leavitt (1905 - 1974), my friend. His career started as a hand on the last of the coasting schooners and ended as associate curator of Mystic Seaport. He is well known as a marine artist, specializing in watercolor.

---

We further dedicate this revised edition to:

Susan Peterson Howell (1947 - 1984), navigator, teacher, author, friend, wife, mother, dreamer and builder, who has enriched our lives.

## FOREWORD

It was Susan Howell's intent to make some small revisions to Practical Celestial Navigation if demand warranted a second printing. Since the book has been well received and a second printing encouraged, we her colleagues have prepared this revised edition. In addition to making the changes Susan had indicated in the copy of the book she used for teaching, Keith Palmer has prepared the following section on nautical astronomy and revised Chapter 19. Star charts and a section of the master star list from the back of the Nautical Almanac have been added, information on magnitudes of stars and planets appears on page 118, explanatory material on the Nautical Almanac and on radio time signals has been updated. Corrections indicated on the first edition's errata sheet have been made and improvements to the H.O. 229 and H.O. 211 work forms incorporated. We have continued the use of Sight Reduction Tables H.O. 229 because celestial navigation is now supplemented by Satellite Navigation Systems and LORAN-C and for some navigators used as a means of checking the electronic fixes as well as the DR. H.O. 229 permits the reduction of sights of any of the 173 stars listed in the Nautical Almanac as well as the sun, moon and planets. This gives the broadest possible coverage of celestial objects and for sailors staying in waters between latitudes 60°N and 60°S requires only 4 volumes of sight reduction tables and no batteries!

Just as a solitary cloud can obscure the sun at local apparent noon, preventing the well planned noon sight, errors may have passed by the editor's eyes undetected. Your communication of such observations would be most appreciatively received.

- Donald Treworgy

It adds considerable interest to a course in celestial navigation if the participants have some understanding of the motions of the heavenly bodies that are under observation. For this reason it is a pleasure to write this foreword to Susan's excellent book.

- Keith D. Palmer

It is important always to specify the frame of reference from which phenomena are described. We shall examine several simpler frames of reference before arriving at our own - the mid-latitudes of the Earth's northern hemisphere.

VIEW FROM OUTSIDE THE SOLAR SYSTEM

Let us start by observing the solar system from a considerable distance out in space and from above the north terrestial pole. We see the Sun surrounded by some tiny revolving planets. The planets of interest to the navigator are from inner to outer, Venus, Earth, Mars, Jupiter and Saturn. Most of these planets have moons, but only the Earth's Moon is important to us. All of the planets revolve round the Sun in the same direction: anti-clockwise. They also revolve very nearly in the same plane. The Earth too rotates on its axis in an anticlockwise direction as seen from above the north pole and the Earth's Moon revolves in the same direction around the Earth.

NAVIGATIONAL BODIES AND THEIR REVOLUTIONS

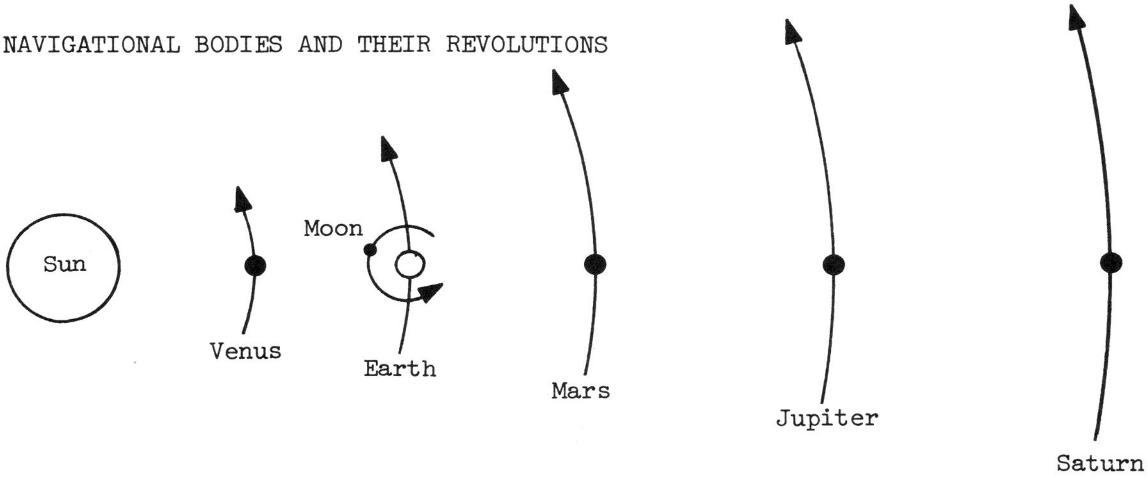


Thus in this frame of reference a person on the Earth's equator is seen to be doing two things at once. He is rotating - travelling eastward at the considerable speed of about 24,000 miles in 24 hours or 1000 mph. The sun-facing person is also travelling to his west at nearly 70,000 mph as the Earth carries him on its revolution round the Sun.

TRAVELING MAN

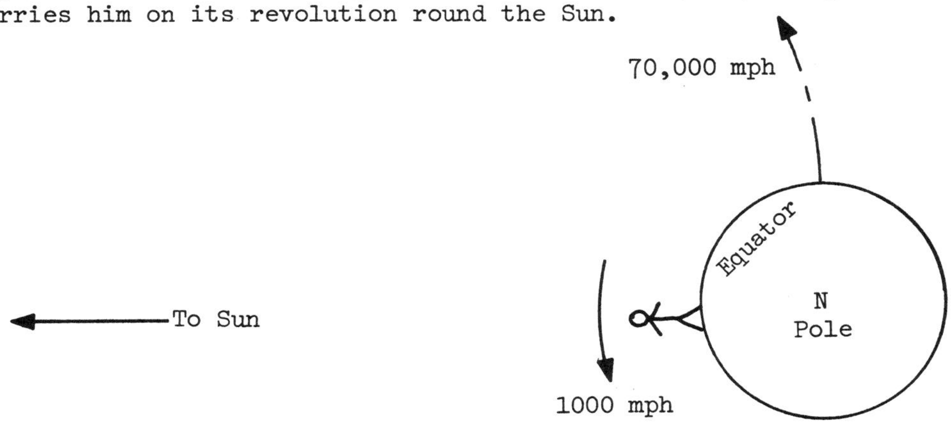

The planets revolve at different speeds round the Sun, outer planets always moving more slowly than inner. Venus takes only about eight Earth-months for one revolution with respect to the stars while Saturn takes nearly thirty Earth-years. Venus is an inner planet to the Earth while the other navigational planets are outer. We don't think that Venus takes eight months for one revolution because we ourselves have moved two thirds of a revolution in that time. In OUR frame and after eight months it appears that Venus still has a lot of catching-up to do. It takes Venus about nineteen months to again reach the imaginary line between the Earth and Sun. It is as if the finishing tape for a race around a circular track was moving round the track itself - albeit at a slower rate than the runner.

APPARENT PERIOD OF INNER PLANET

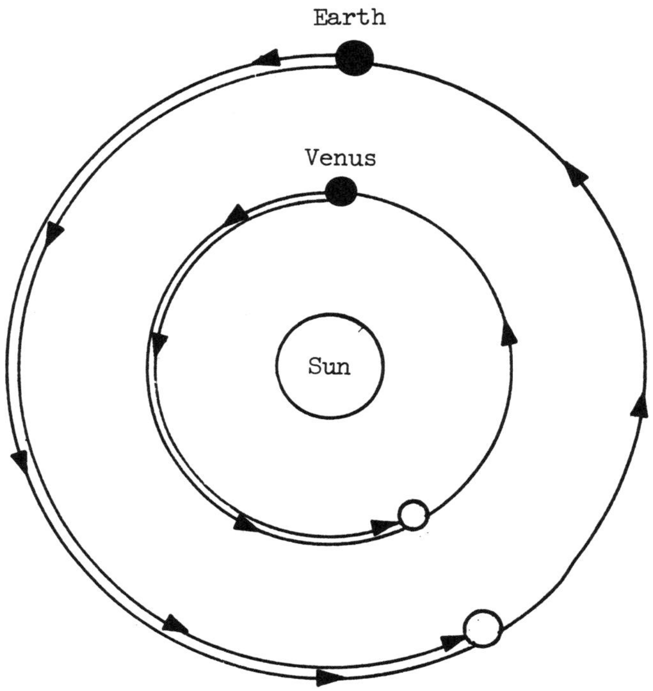


Nineteen Earth months returns Venus, Earth & Sun into alignment

APPARENT PERIOD OF OUTER PLANET

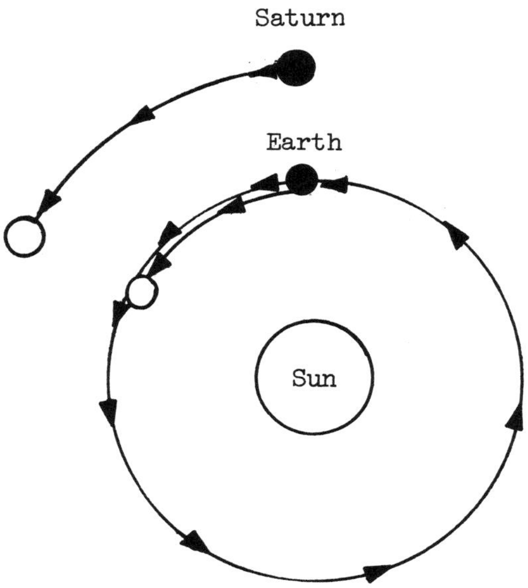

If we apply this analogy to the outer planets then they move so slowly that the finishing line (the Earth-Sun line) has gone round once and caught up with them - lapped them - before they have gone very far.

## VIEW FROM A SMALL NON-ROTATING EARTH

We now make a major change in our frame of reference. We imagine the Earth to be small only so that it doesn't obstruct our view all around us. We must introduce three important ideas. The first is that our observer imagines that he is stationary and that he sees everything else to be revolving around him.

The second idea is that of the CELESTIAL SPHERE. The observer imagines that the Universe is bounded by a sphere at the center of which he himself and his Earth are located. Let us look into this celestial sphere from one side so that north is up.

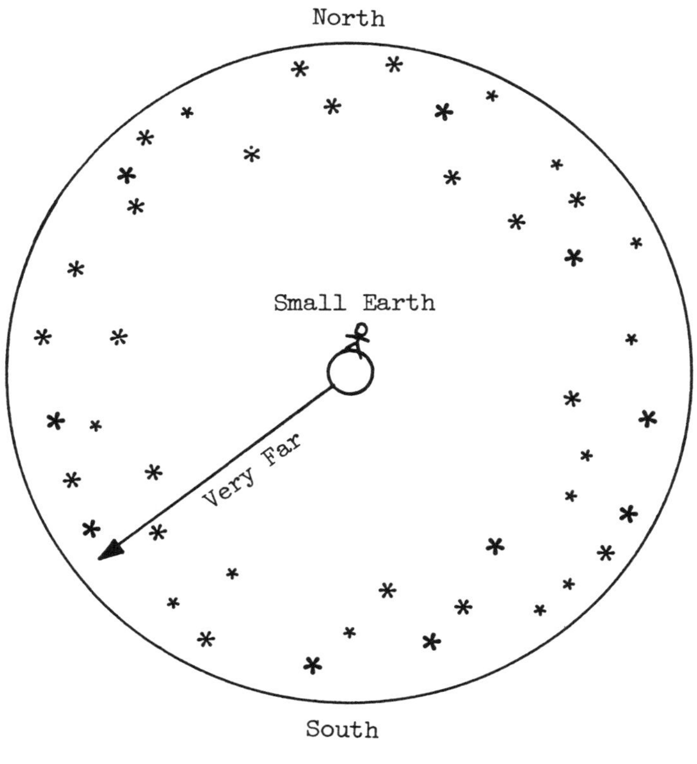


THE CELESTIAL SPHERE

The stars are all pasted in their correct positions on the inside of the sphere; note that they appear to be stationary because the Earth is not rotating. Now from this point of view you must see that the Sun, Moon and planets all appear to move. They all move to the east along roughly the same line which we will call now the ECLIPTIC. But they move at different rates. The Sun of course appears to go round the ecliptic once in the course of one year; this reduces to a rate of just under one degree per day. The Moon takes twenty-eight days for one revolution, or thirteen degrees per day. The outer planets vary in their times from twenty-three months for Mars to thirty years for Saturn.

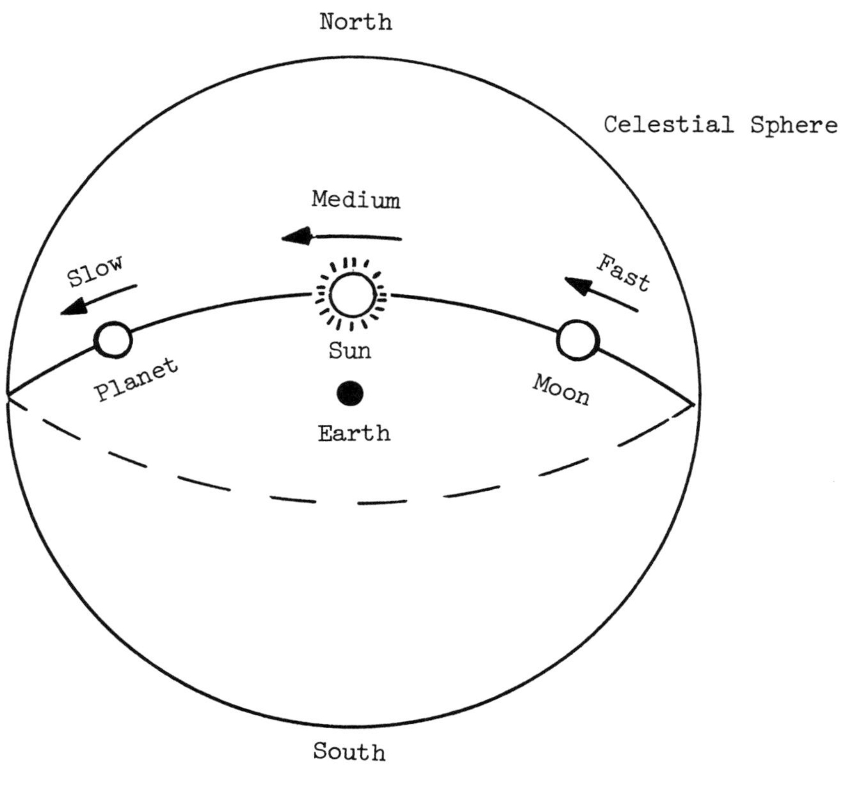


THE ECLIPITIC -
APPARENT MOTION OF THE HEAVENLY BODIES
AROUND A 'STATIONARY' EARTH

VIEW FROM AN EARTH WHICH ROTATES AND REVOLVES

Now let us incorporate into this picture what we would see if the Earth were allowed to rotate, this is the most rapid motion of all and, from the observer's frame of reference (believing himself to be stationary still) causes the other previously described motions to be perceived with some difficulty because they are relatively slow. Since the Earth is spinning to the east, all the heavenly bodies appear to move to the west, making roughly one revolution in twenty-four hours. However, since they maintain their own slower motions to the east as previously described, the Sun, Moon and planets move westward more slowly than the stars do.

Prepare for another change in our frame of reference. If we take the direction to a star as a reference line then, with respect to it, the Sun, etc. move slowly eastward. Now for the change. If we take the direction of the line to the Sun as our reference, then the stars move slowly westward with respect to the Sun and the planets move westward more slowly than the stars. Now, because of the Earth's rotation, we say in this frame that it is the Sun that revolves once a day and the stars that revolve a little bit more than once a day. In fact, one degree more. This means that in the three hundred and sixty-five days that it takes the Sun to move completely round the ecliptic once, the stars have revolved three hundred and sixty-six times. This is because the Earth has made 365 rotations and 1 revolution in that period.

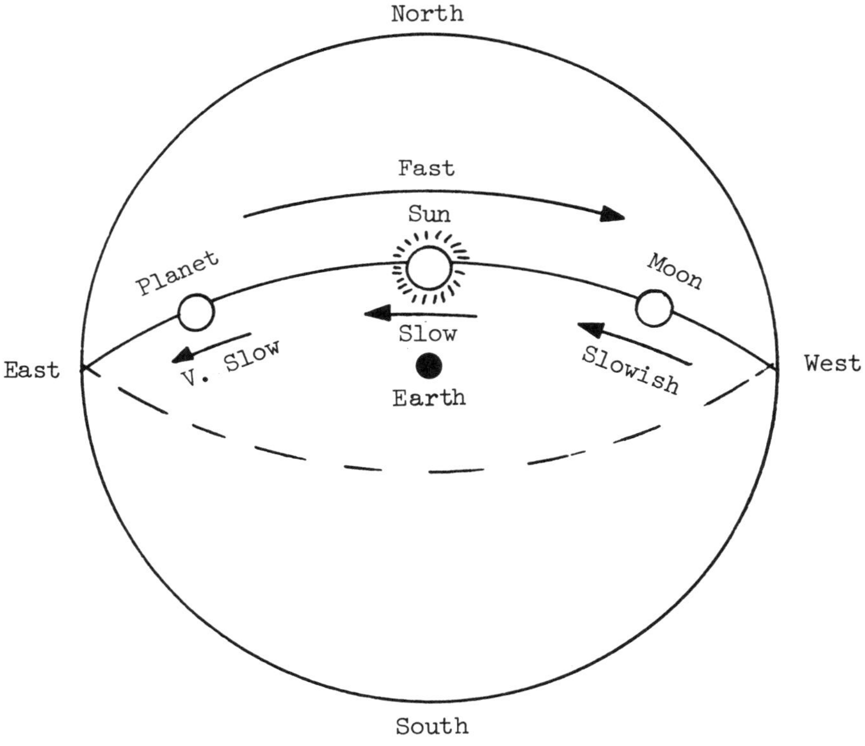


EFFECT OF EARTH'S ROTATION

How about rates? Easy - the Sun completes 360 degrees in 24 hours. This translates to:

$$360^\circ/24 \text{ hours} = 15^\circ/\text{hour}$$
$$15^\circ/\text{hour} = 1^\circ/4 \text{ minutes}$$
$$1^\circ/4 \text{ minutes} = 15 \text{ minutes of arc}/1 \text{ minute of time}$$

Sometimes we speak of the Solar day, 24 hours long by definition, and the Sidereal day of 23 hours, 56 minutes. You can see the difference: one degree of arc and four minutes of time per day, one extra rotation per year.

Having described the motion of the heavenly bodies as seen from the general location of a rotating Earth, we must now re-examine the situation as it appears from different locations on a full-sized Earth. Before we do this however, we must describe two lines - circles - on the celestial sphere. The first is nothing more than the projection upon the celestial sphere of the Earth's equator - the celestial equator. The second is the ecliptic, now to be formally defined. It is the projection upon the celestial sphere of the plane of the Earth's orbit round the Sun. You must see that - in our present frame of reference - an observer sees the Sun to move exactly along the ecliptic making of course one revolution in a year. Also see that because the solar system is so flat, the planets and the Moon also travel closely along the ecliptic. Now, if nature had been kind to navigators she would have made the axis upon which the Earth ROTATES parallel to the axis upon which it REVOLVES. That would have meant that heavenly bodies would appear to travel along the ecliptic because of the ANNUAL motion of the Earth as well as because of its DAILY motion. Unfortunately this is not the case. The Earth's axis of rotation is in fact tilted at 23 ½ degrees to its axis of revolution. This is the same as saying that the celestial equator is tilted 23 ½ degrees to the ecliptic. Earthlings consider the equator to be the reference frame and so we come to the important statement that the ecliptic is tilted 23 ½ degrees to the celestial equator.

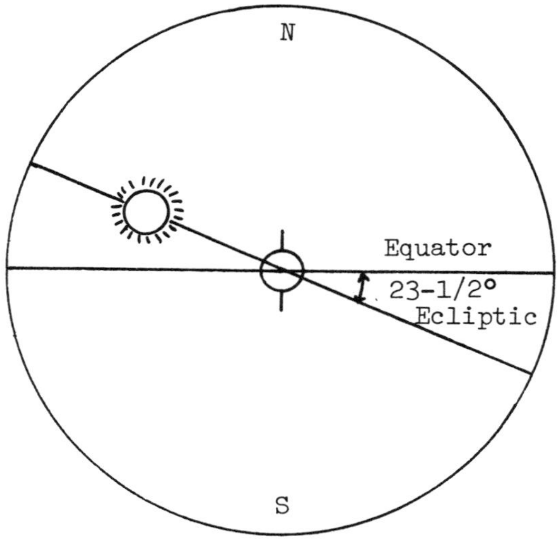


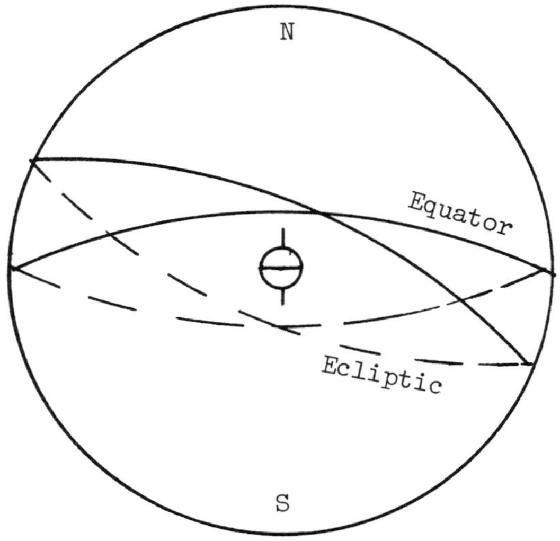


3- DIMENSIONAL VIEW

VIEW FROM THE NORTH POLE OF A FULL-SIZED ROTATING EARTH

Lastly we must discuss how these phenomena appear to observers at different places on a full-sized Earth. We will start by supposing the observer is on the North Pole. You must see that

1. The North Celestial Pole is at your zenith.
2. The heavens rotate east to west.
3. Only half the stars can be seen - those in the northern hemisphere. Southern stars are below the horizon.
4. The celestial equator coincides with the horizon.
5. Only half the ecliptic can be seen - the northern half. When the Sun is in this half of the ecliptic it is of course summer. You can see now why, at the Poles, the year has only one day and night in it.

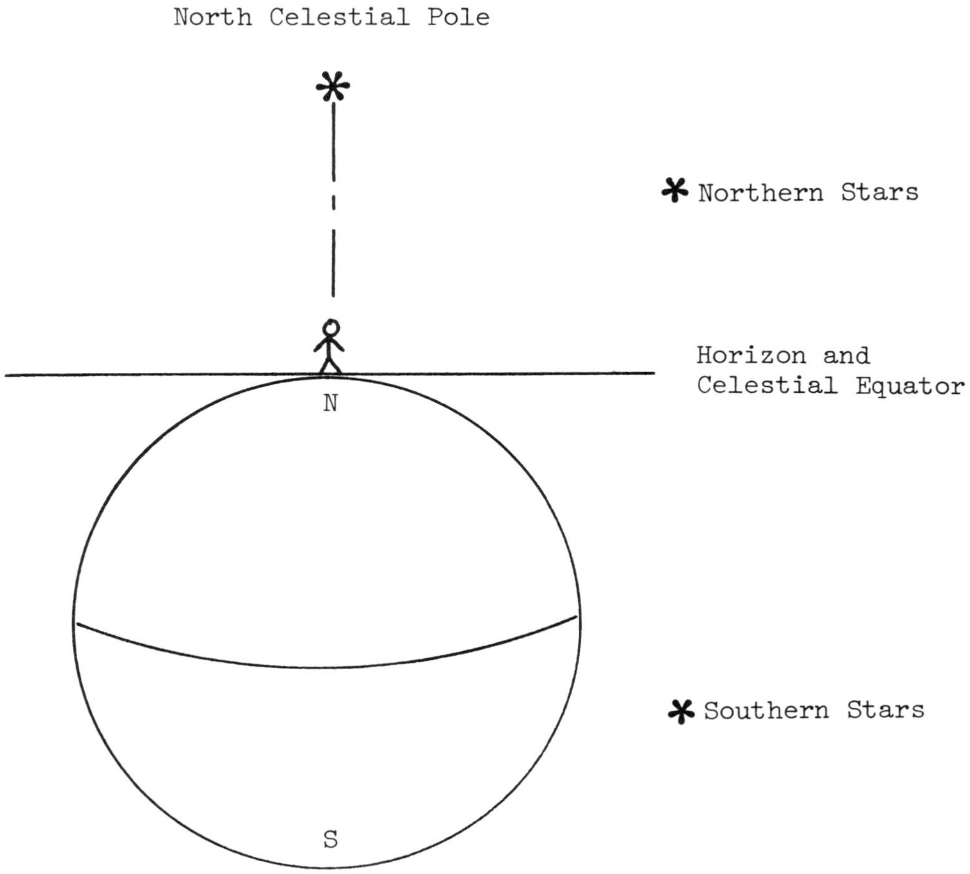


VIEW FROM THE NORTH POLE

Parenthetically, and in connection with the view from the Pole, above, DO NOT believe that, because you are well north of the equator your horizon prevents you from seeing some of the stars in the northern hemisphere that are just north of the equator. All heavenly bodies are virtually at infinity with respect to the 4000 miles of the Earth's radius and are therefore seen in exactly the SAME direction from all places on Earth. All sight lines to one star from anywhere on Earth are parallel to each other, and meet at infinity - on the celestial sphere.

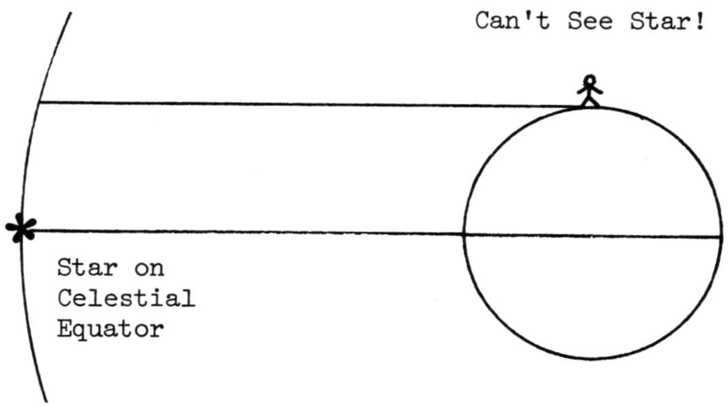


NOT TRUE

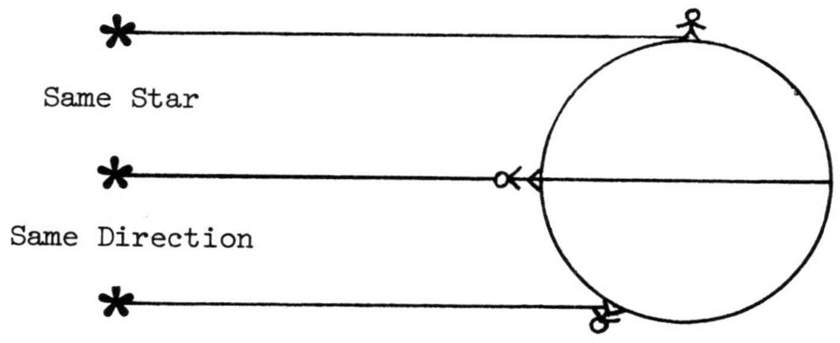


TRUE

VIEW FROM MID-LATITUDES, NORTHERN HEMISPHERE

This brings us to the last act. What do the heavens actually look like from our perspective in mid-northern latitudes?

From New England the Pole Star is about 40 degrees above the northern horizon. Realize if you will that the stars that are within 40 degrees of the Pole Star are the ones which can always be seen during the course of the day and year; they never rise or set.

Similarly, the stars that are within 40 degrees of the south celestial pole are never seen from here.

All other stars rise and set in each 24 hour period.

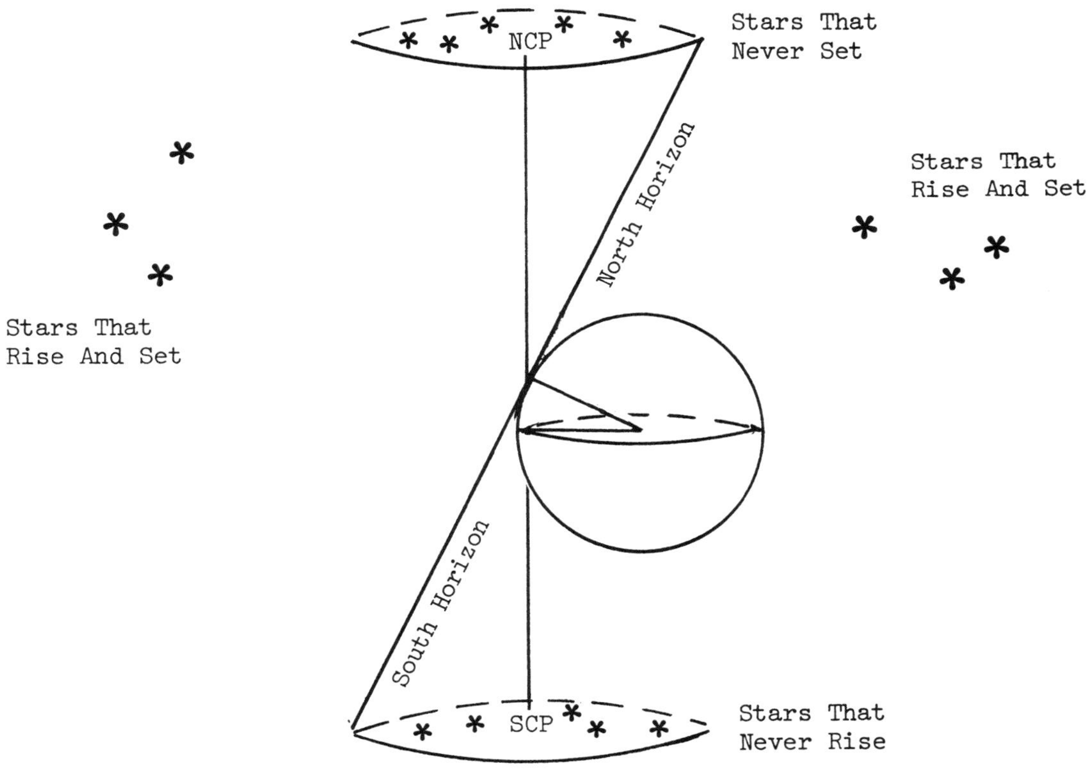


VISIBILITY OF STARS FROM 40°N

FROLIC

# Chapter 1

# Plotting, Piloting and Dead Reckoning

Celestial navigation is one of many forms of navigation involved with finding a position by means of plotting intersecting lines. This position is expressed in terms of latitude and longitude, coordinates on the earth's surface. Latitude (L) is the coordinate measured in a north or south direction using the equator as a starting point. The largest latitude possible is 90°, north or south, which would be at the poles. A location in Connecticut would have a latitude in the low forties, roughly halfway between the equator and the poles. It is an angular measurement, the vertex being at the center of the earth as drawn.

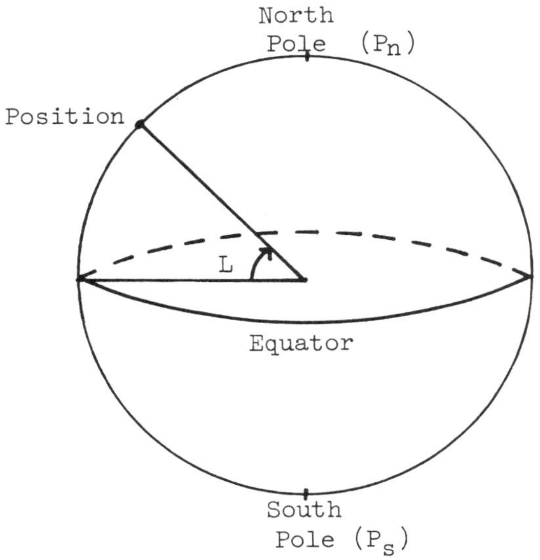

Longitude (λ) is measured along the equator in an east-west manner. However, since the equator is a great circle with no beginning or no end, a point along this circle must be established from which to measure. Meridians, great circles passing through the earth's poles and the positions in question, intersect the equator at right angles. On a Mercator projection chart or plotting sheet, meridians appear as vertical lines. Until the nineteenth century, various meridians were used as bases for longitude measurement, dependent on the country from which the ship sailed or the charts which were used. However, in 1884 the meridian through Greenwich, England, was established internationally as the prime meridian and has been used ever since. Longitude is measured east OR west from the prime meridian with maximum measurement of 180°. Increasing measurement eastward would be moving to the right on a plotting sheet or chart, increasing measurement westward would be moving to the left.

A position on the earth therefore can be uniquely defined as having a specific latitude, north or south, and a specific longitude, east or west.

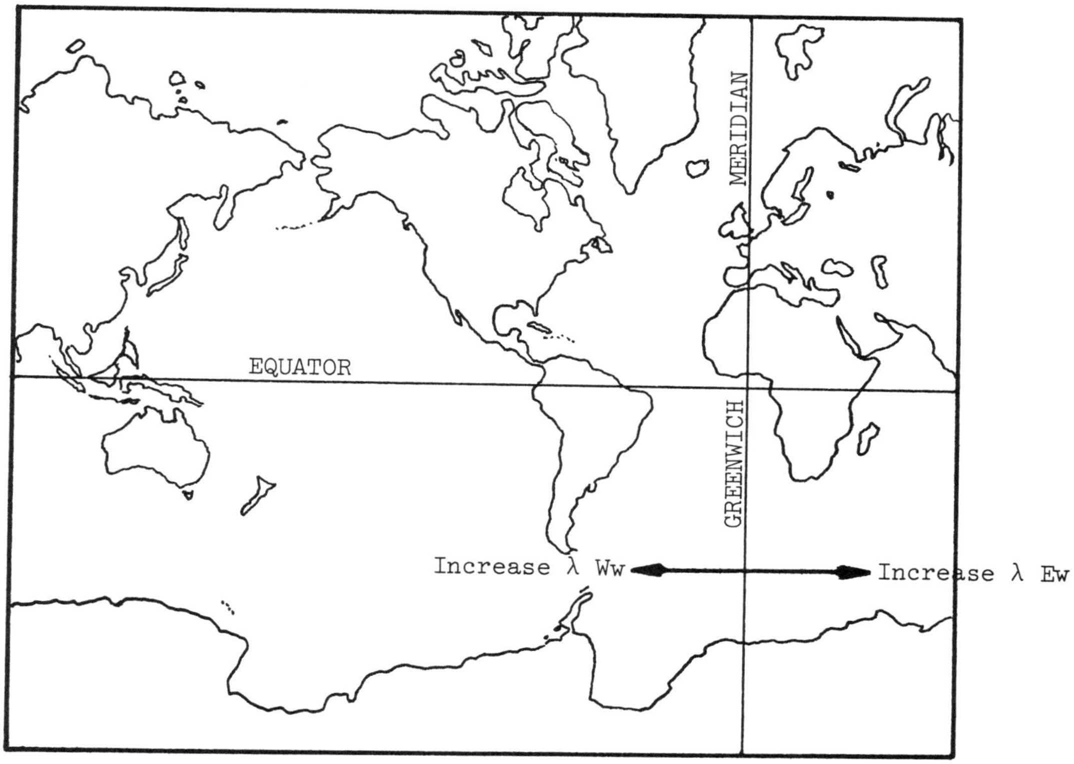

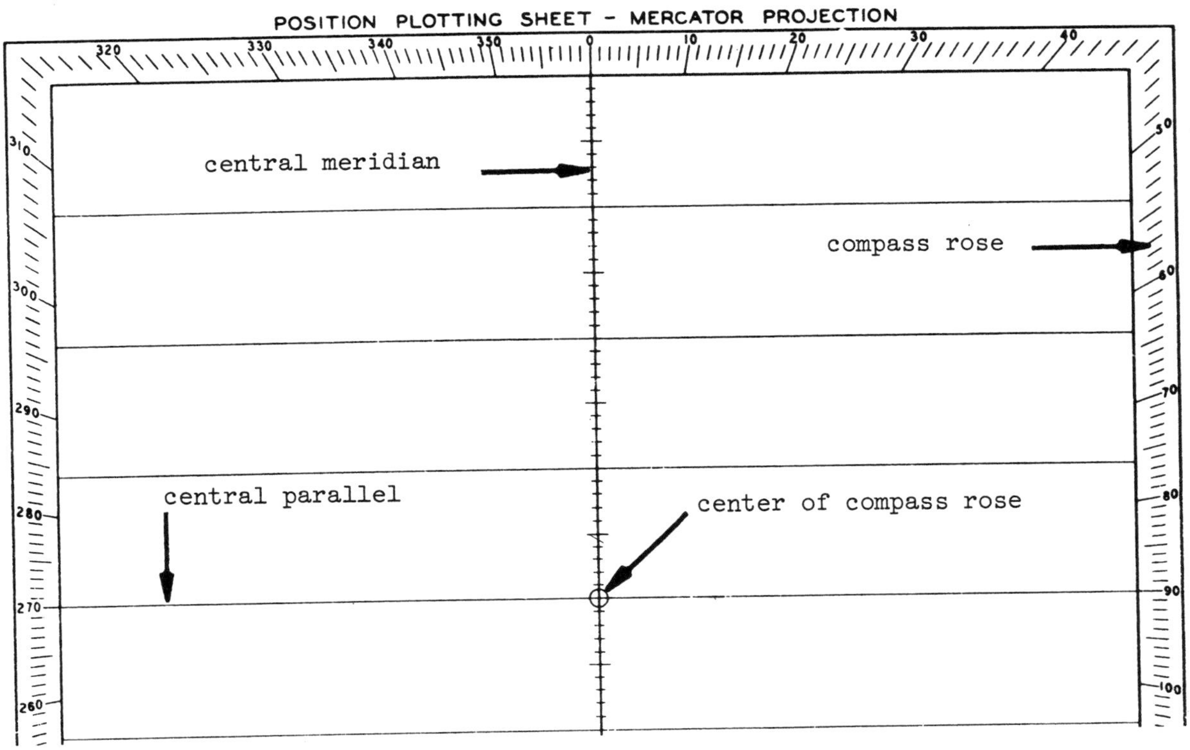


We shall use as our plotting sheets an adaption of the Coast Guard form No. 2543. On this Mercator projection, the latitude scale is fixed while the longitude scale varies depending on the latitude. The central vertical line on the sheet is the central meridian, usually established as the nearest whole or half degree of longitude to your estimated position. The central horizontal line is called the central parallel and is also usually established as the nearest whole or half degree of latitude to your estimated position. Where these two centrals cross is a small circle, the center of the compass rose which is found bordering the plotting area. To plot a course or bearing from a point on the plotting sheet, the parallel rulers or triangles should be aligned with the center of the rose and the azimuth (or direction) in question, then "walked" or slid in a parallel fashion to the point. All azimuths we will be working with in this book are true, based on true north. It is important to label lines and points consistently so we shall adopt the following method.

| | | |
|---|---|---|
| Labelling course line | C280 / S 12 | (course) / (speed) |
| Labelling bearing line | 1500 / 260 | (time) / (bearing) |

Labelling point

⊙ 1600 DR
L 20° 16!7 N
λ 45° 38!9 W

⊙ 0654 Fix
L 31° 42!5 S
λ 172° 51!0 E

Course is established to the nearest whole degree and is always written in three digits (316, 007, 068). Speed is written in units of nautical miles per hour or knots. One nautical mile (1.151 statute mile) is defined as being equal to one minute of latitude anywhere on earth. Distance, therefore, is measured on the latitude (vertical) scale of the plotting sheet. Time is referred to in the 24 hour clock manner and read as fifteen hundred (1500), eighteen twenty six (1826), twenty two thirty (2230) or zero seven nineteen (0719). For labelling purposes, time is written to the nearest minute. The diagram below will establish the conversion between conventional clock faces and the 24 hour clock face.

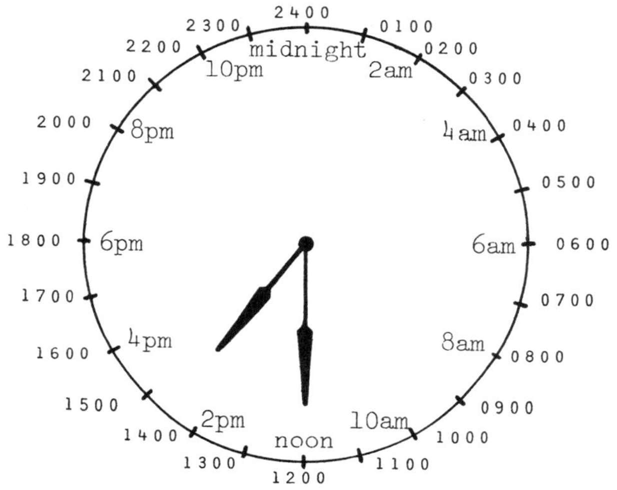


Clock now says 1430 or 2:30 p.m.

DR refers to a position established by means of course and speed alone and is called the dead reckoning position. A fix is obtained by getting bearings or distances of terrestrial objects whose positions are known. When a fix is established, the new course and speed proceed from this more accurately known point rather than the less accurate DR. All coordinates or angles will be expressed in degrees, minutes and tenths of minutes, remembering that there are sixty minutes in a degree. Examples 1 and 2 will show the method of plotting points and bearings on a plotting sheet.

If one wishes to double the scale, this will decrease the plotting area but will alleviate cramping close points and short runs. Example 3 shows a point and distance plotted on a sheet set up with double scale. Note that <u>both</u> latitude and longitude scales are doubled.

To establish a fix with piloting procedures, the navigator will choose a point at the intersection of two or more bearing lines (obtained by compass, radio direction finder, Loran, etc.), at the intersection of two or more circles of distance off (obtained by radar, or sextant altitude of the lighthouse, tower, etc. and use of Table 9 in <u>American Practical Navigator</u>, Volume II, by Bowditch), or at the intersection of a combination of these lines or circles. In Example 4, both methods are used.

Example 1. Plot the point 49° 51!3 N, 140° 17!2 W. Establish this point as the 0730 DR and from it draw a course of 110°. If the vessel travels at a speed of 12 knots, what will be the latitude and longitude of its 1030 DR?

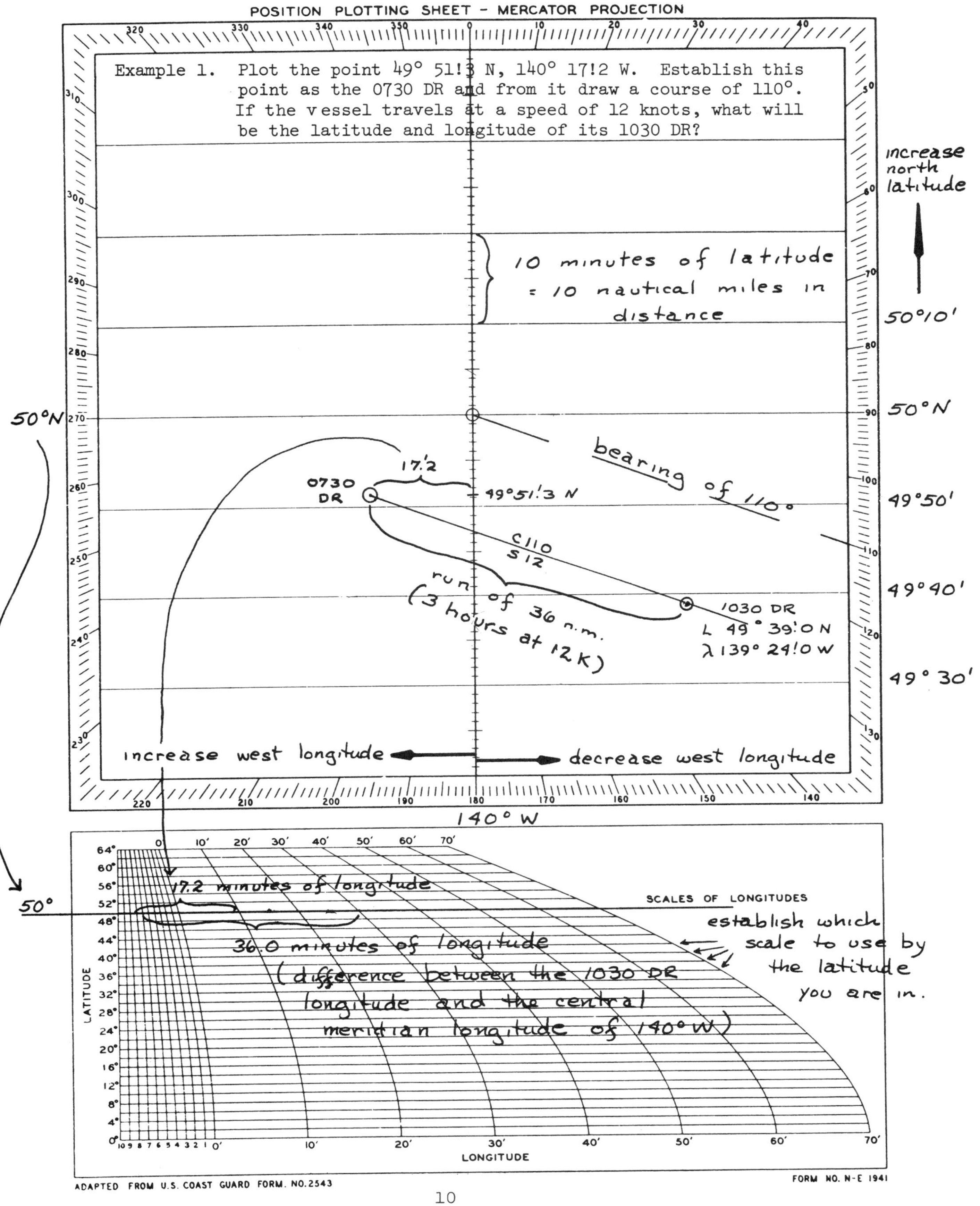

Example 2. Plot the lightship position of 27° 12!0 S, 47° 47!6 E. At 1834 a sailboat gets a bearing on the lightship of 310°. Plot and label the line of position. If it is ascertained that the sailboat is 40 nautical miles from the lightship, what would be the latitude and longitude of the 1834 fix?

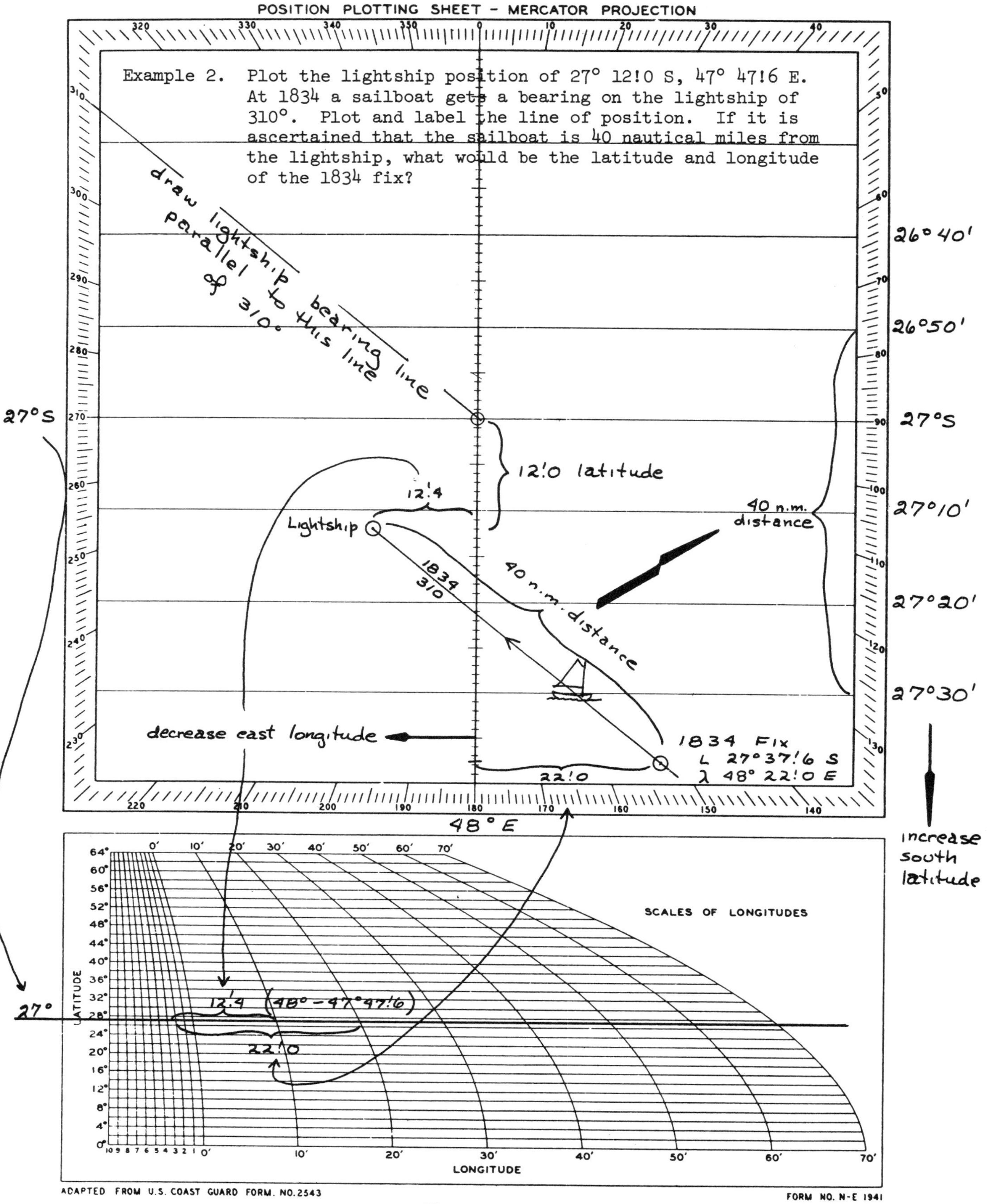

Example 3. Plot the position of Kronborg Light (Danish), 56° 02' N, 12° 38' E. Draw the circle of position of a ship that is ten miles from the light at 1013.

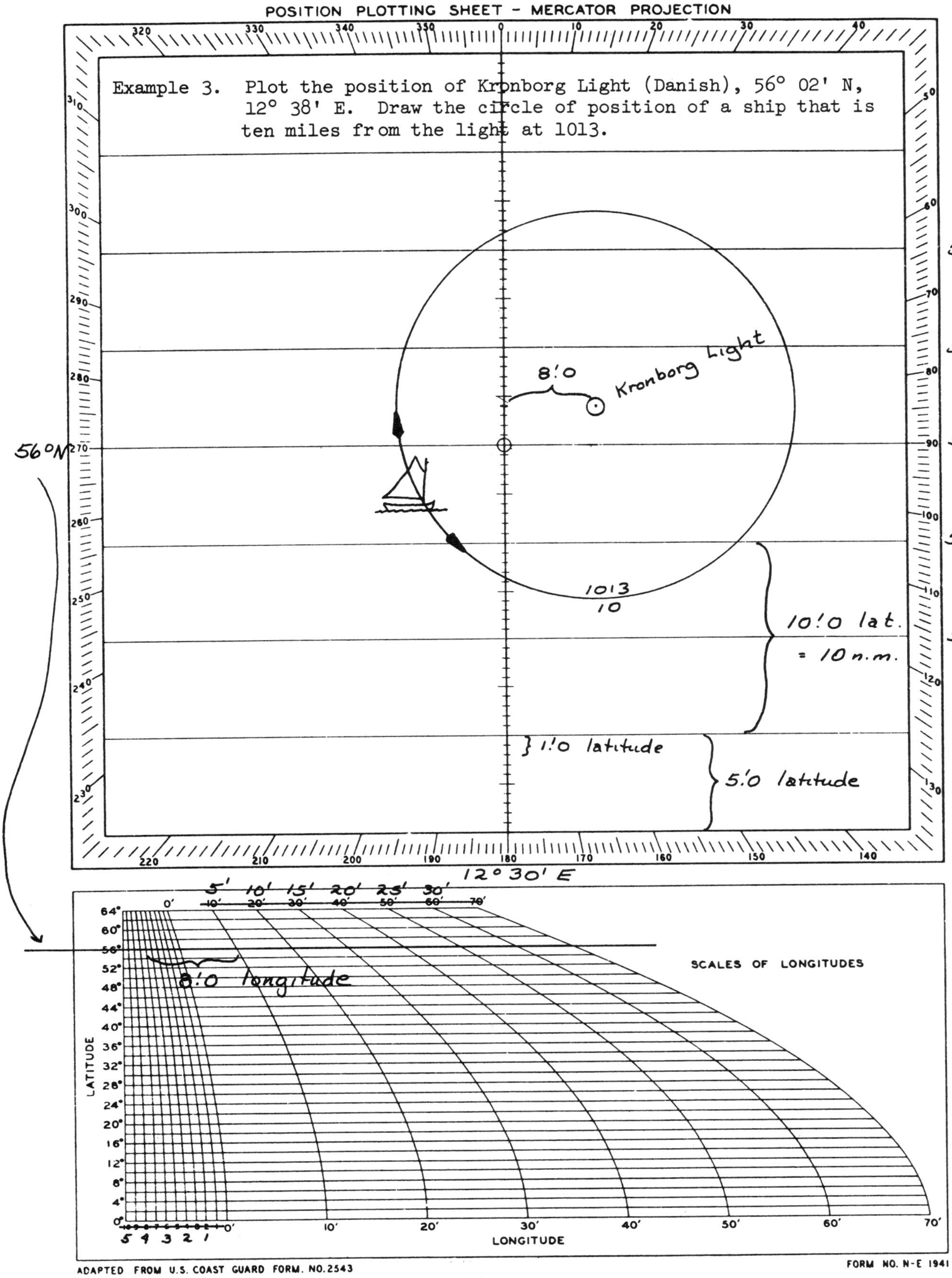

Example 4.

On a small area plotting sheet, mark the central meridian 72° W, the central parallel 41° N. Plot the following points.

| Point Judith | Race Rock | Ship's 0800 DR Position |
|---|---|---|
| 41° 21!7 N | 41° 14!6 N | 41° 00!0 N |
| 71° 28!9 W | 72° 02!9 W | 71° 50!0 W |

The ship is on course 074° at a speed of 4 knots. Plot the 1200 DR. At 1200, simultaneous bearings and distance offs of the two lights are obtained as follows.

Race Rock bears 290° true, has distance of 26.0 nautical miles from ship.
Point Judith bears 003° true, has distance of 15.5 nautical miles from ship.

Plot the 1200 fix as found by distance and as found by bearing. Record the latitudes and longitudes.

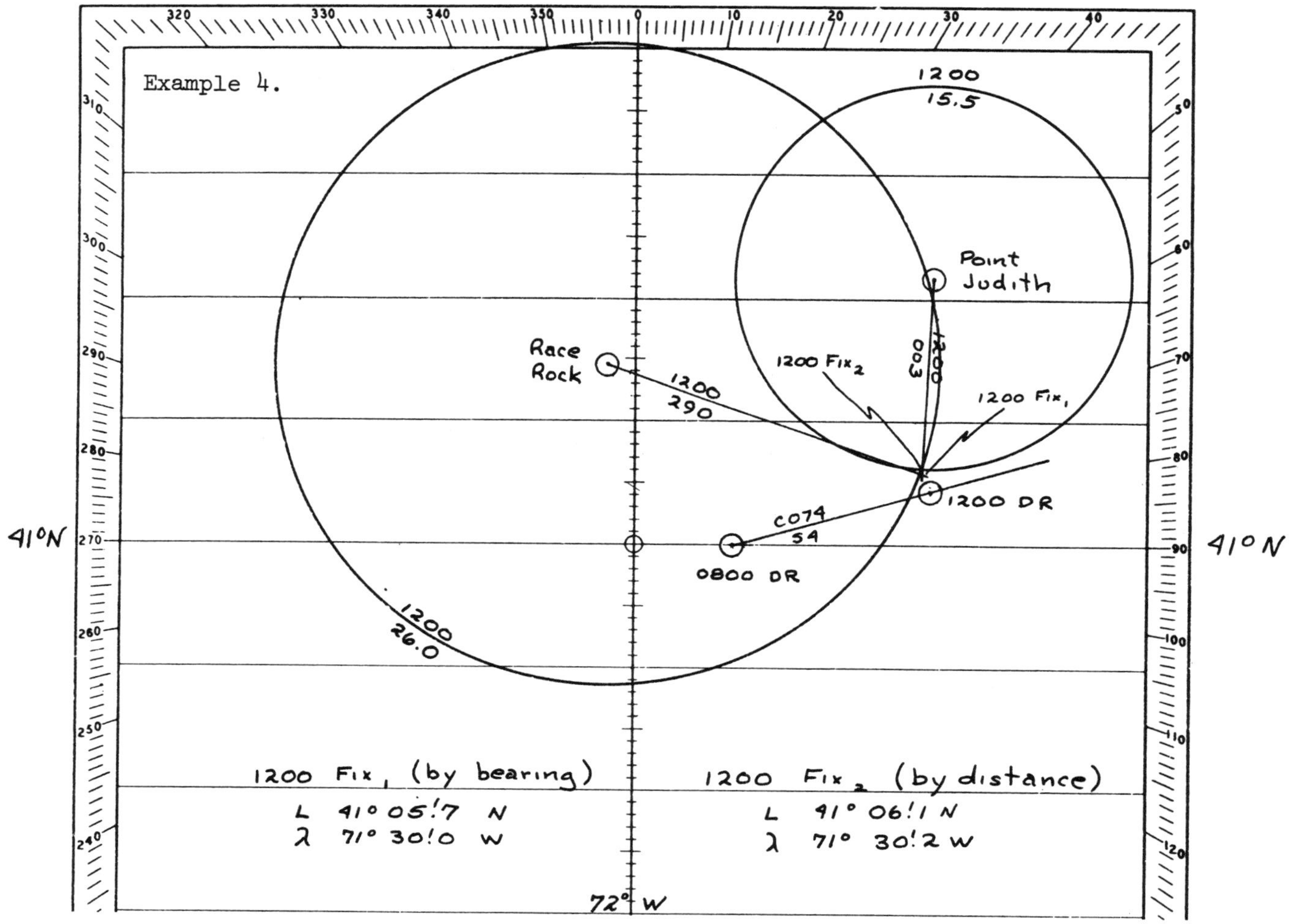

## EXERCISE 1

1. On a small area plotting sheet, mark the central meridian 70° W, the central parallel 36° N. Plot the following points.

| Light A | Light B | Ship's 1300 DR Position |
|---|---|---|
| 36° 24!5 N | 36° 18!6 N | 35° 30!0 N |
| 70° 34!3 W | 69° 49!0 W | 69° 19!0 W |

The ship is on course 305° at a speed of 8 knots. Draw the course line through the 1300 DR and extend it in the direction of travel. Measuring along the course line, mark the 1900 DR. Determine and record the latitude and longitude of the 1900 DR.

At 1900, azimuths and the distances of lights A and B are obtained from the ship.

A bears 316°, distance 30.0 nautical miles.
B bears 047°, distance 21.6 nautical miles.

Plot the 1900 fix and record its latitude and longitude. How far is the 1900 fix away from the 1900 DR?

At the 1900 fix, change course to 074° and speed to 6 knots. Plot the 0100 DR position and record its latitude and longitude.

2. On a small area plotting sheet, mark the central meridian 69° 35' W, the central parallel 43° 45' N. Double your plotting scale so that 1!0 on the scales actually equals 0!5 when you plot it.

Aboard the sloop Novice, the navigator, floundering in the Maine fog, estimates his 1915 DR to be 43° 32!2 N, 69° 24!1 W. His course is 325° and his speed 4 knots. Plot the 1915 DR and the 2045 DR.

The fog suddenly lifts to reveal two lights, a fixed one at Seguin Island and a flashing one on Pemaquid Point. Plot and label their positions.

| Seguin Island | Pemaquid Point |
|---|---|
| 43° 42!0 N | 43° 50!2 N |
| 69° 46!0 W | 69° 30!5 W |

At 2045, the navigator gathers the following data.

Seguin Island bears 284°, distance off 14.5 nautical miles.
Pemaquid Point bears 346°, distance off 12 nautical miles.

Plot the 2045 fix. Record the 2045 DR and the 2045 fix. Proceed from the 2045 fix on course 335°, speed 5 knots. Plot and record the 2257 DR.

Seeing himself near Thrumcap Island, the navigator relies on his knowledge of familiar landmarks to guide him up the Damariscotta River.

3. In the midst of the Coral Sea, three lightships suddenly appeared (L1, L2, L3) radioing to all nearby listeners their coordinates.

| L1 | L2 | L3 |
|---|---|---|
| 14° 54'.0 S | 15° 22'.7 S | 14° 48'.4 S |
| 155° 21'.0 E | 154° 51'.6 E | 154° 35'.6 E |

The sly schooner Australian Queen was bound for her home port of Brisbane but after a stormy afternoon needed a position check. With his MBM (miraculous bearing machine) the navigator obtained simultaneous bearings at 2200 of the three ships.

L1 had a bearing of 002° true.
L2 had a bearing of 257° true.
L3 had a bearing of 305° true.

On a small position plotting sheet, label the central meridian 155° E, central parallel 15° S. Plot the cocked hat fix of the Australian Queen. Assuming ship's course of 237°, speed of 11 knots, what would be the latitude and longitude of the midnight dead reckoning position?

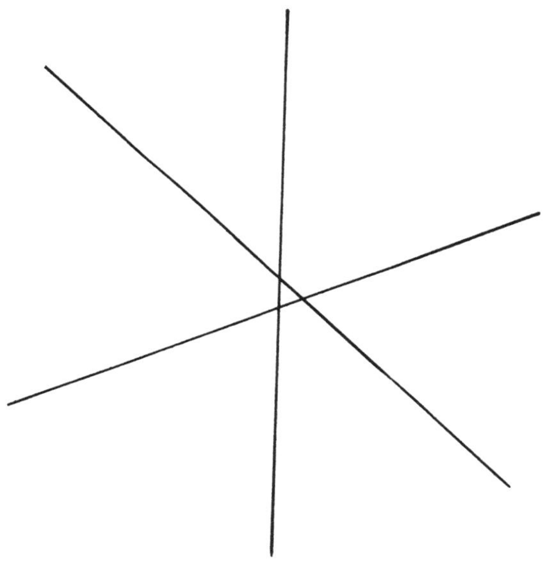

This is a cocked hat fix, a triangle.

# Chapter 2

# Celestial Position Finding

Celestial navigation, like piloting, involves plotting lines of position to establish a fix. These "lines" as we shall see are really sections of huge distance off circles whose radii would range between 900 and 4500 miles. Small pieces of the circumference of such a circle would, in effect, be a straight lines for all practical purposes.

Each celestial object can be thought of as a lighthouse since, for a specific instant of time, it stands directly over one spot on the earth. For instance, the sun will be 90° high over Honolulu for a split second this summer and therefore marks that one place much as a lighthouse would. Such a place is called the geographical position (GP) of the sun for that short time period. The Nautical Almanac lists positions (with coordinates similar to latitude and longitude) of the sun, moon, four brightest planets, and the stars which can be viewed in twilight. These positions or GPs can be figured for any day, hour, minute and second of the year with accuracy of one tenth of a minute of arc (comparable to one tenth of a mile or less). Therefore, if a lost navigator happened to observe a celestial body overhead, he would note the exact time of observation, enter his Nautical Almanac and find the "latitude" and "longitude" of the body. This position would be exactly his on the earth. This sounds like a quick and ideal way of navigating if the sky is clear but as you can imagine, there aren't enough bright celestial objects to mark every place on earth for every instant of time.

Going back to piloting procedures, you remember that we used the bearings and distances of two or three lighthouses to find position since it is very seldom that we are right underneath a lighthouse wondering where we are. Assume we have superhuman vision and can view lightships at tremendous distances. The following diagram shows our circles of position (established by knowing our distance from lights X, Y and Z) intersecting at a point which must be our location. We shall call it our geographical position or GP.

Each one of the lightships can be identified as to location (latitude and longitude). Now assume that each of the lightships has a star overhead for the moment in question. Stars also can be identified as to location, their sky coordinates being listed in the Nautical Almanac. Star X would have a geographical position of Lightship X, star Y would mark Lightship Y and star Z would be

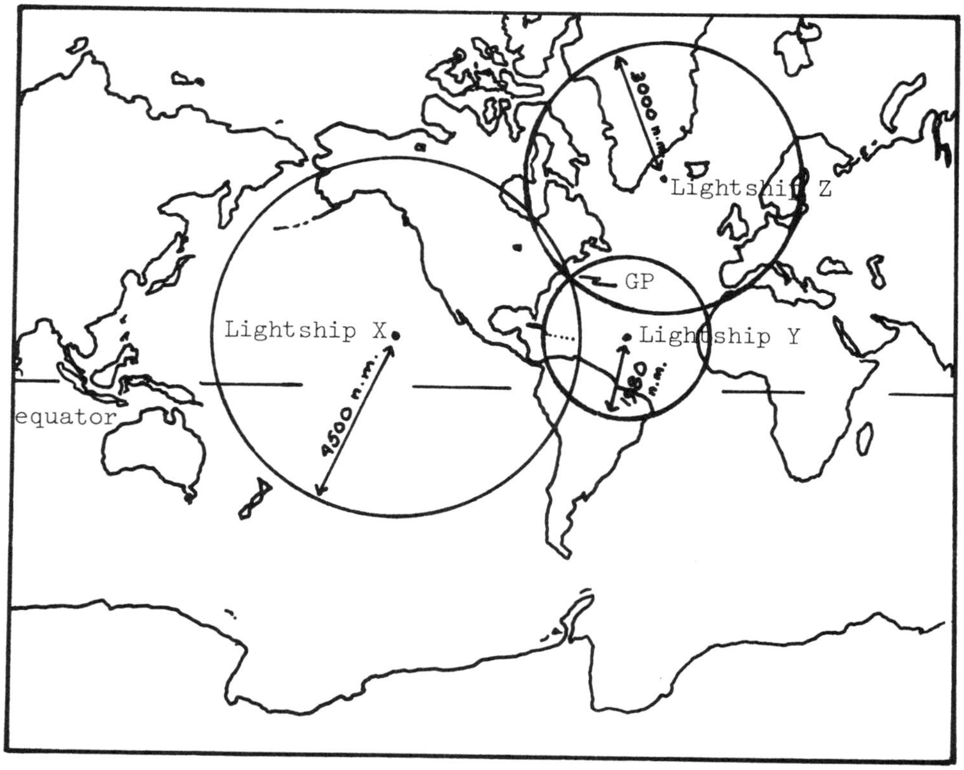


overhead for Lightship Z. If, in some way, we could find out how far our overhead point was from each of these stars, (our overhead point is the celestial counterpart to our GP), we would have an identical situation to the diagram above except now on a star map with no land or water masses.

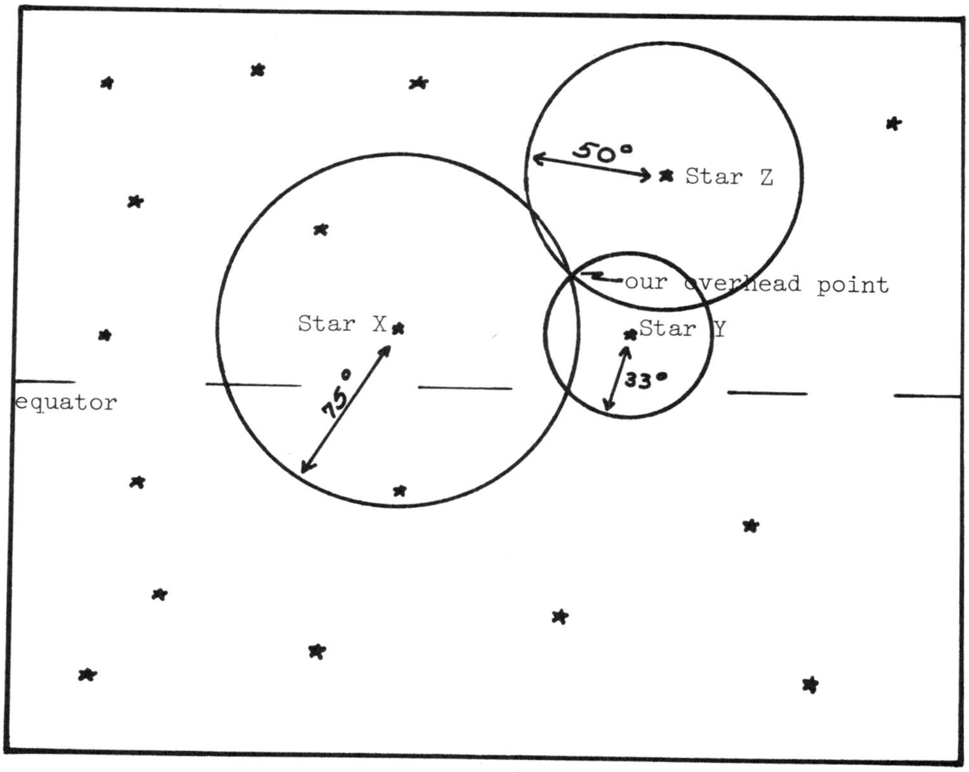

For the purpose of obtaining this distance accurately, the sextant was invented. This instrument measures the height (altitude) of celestial bodies above the horizon. Our overhead point is 90° above the horizon. Therefore, the distance between a star and our overhead point would be 90° minus the star's altitude. Of course, we aren't really measuring a distance in the sky but an angle. However, one degree or sixty minutes of altitude (angle) in the sky equals sixty nautical miles (distance) on the earth's surface. Let us look at some figures for our three stars and three lightships.

| | Distance of Lightship | Altitude of Star | 90° - Altitude | Convert to Distance |
|---|---|---|---|---|
| X | 4500 n.m. | 15° | 75° | x 60 = 4500 n.m. |
| Y | 1980 n.m. | 57° | 33° | x 60 = 1980 n.m. |
| Z | 3000 n.m. | 40° | 50° | x 60 = 3000 n.m. |

We have seen then that the coordinates of our overhead point can be found from bright celestial objects that are in the surrounding sky. Our geographical position would be directly under this overhead point and therefore have the same coordinates.

The major difficulty in the theory thus far is that we don't have a globe or chart huge enough to encompass these three distant points as well as our location. Even if we did, the vessel used to carry it would have to be a real supership. Small scale charts or plotting sheets would not allow enough accuracy of plotting such large circles. Our pencil line would be several miles wide!

To overcome such problems, sight reduction tables have been devised. Published by the United States Government, they come in several varying forms with titles such as H.O. 214, H.O. 211, H.O. 249, and H.O. 229. The latter is the table that we shall be concerned with in this book. By entering it with numbers based on our DR position and the position of the celestial body sighted, we can get information as to the corrected sextant altitude and bearing of the body from a place only a few miles from our real position. The difference between the sextant altitude at <u>that</u> place and the altitude that we obtain with our sextant gives us a distance off from that place. With a distance and a bearing, we then plot our lines of position much as you would from a lighthouse. Our problem of having huge charts is solved then because all our plotting is done from an intermediate position, one chosen fairly close to our ship.

In the following chapters we shall see step by step how a sextant altitude is obtained and corrected, how time is established, how the exact positions of celestial bodies can be found, how sight reduction tables can be used to obtain plottable numbers and lastly how to use these numbers to plot a fix.

# Chapter 3

# Use and Adjustment of the Sextant

Brief mention has been made of using a sextant to measure altitude. Much more detail of this procedure will be discussed in this chapter but first let us look into the system of coordinates involved, the horizon system.

Assuming the visible area around our ship extending to the horizon as a circular plane, we can establish the edge of this plane (the horizon) as the zero point from which to measure heights of objects in the sky. The dome of the sky is a hemisphere sitting on this plane. From one point on the horizon, up through the overhead point and down again to the horizon opposite the starting point would be an arc of 180°. The overhead point or zenith would be the highest spot from the horizon with height of 90°. Celestial bodies therefore can have angular heights of 0° to 90°. Such heights are called altitudes and are measured with a sextant or similar instrument. Sextant altitude is designated as $H_s$.

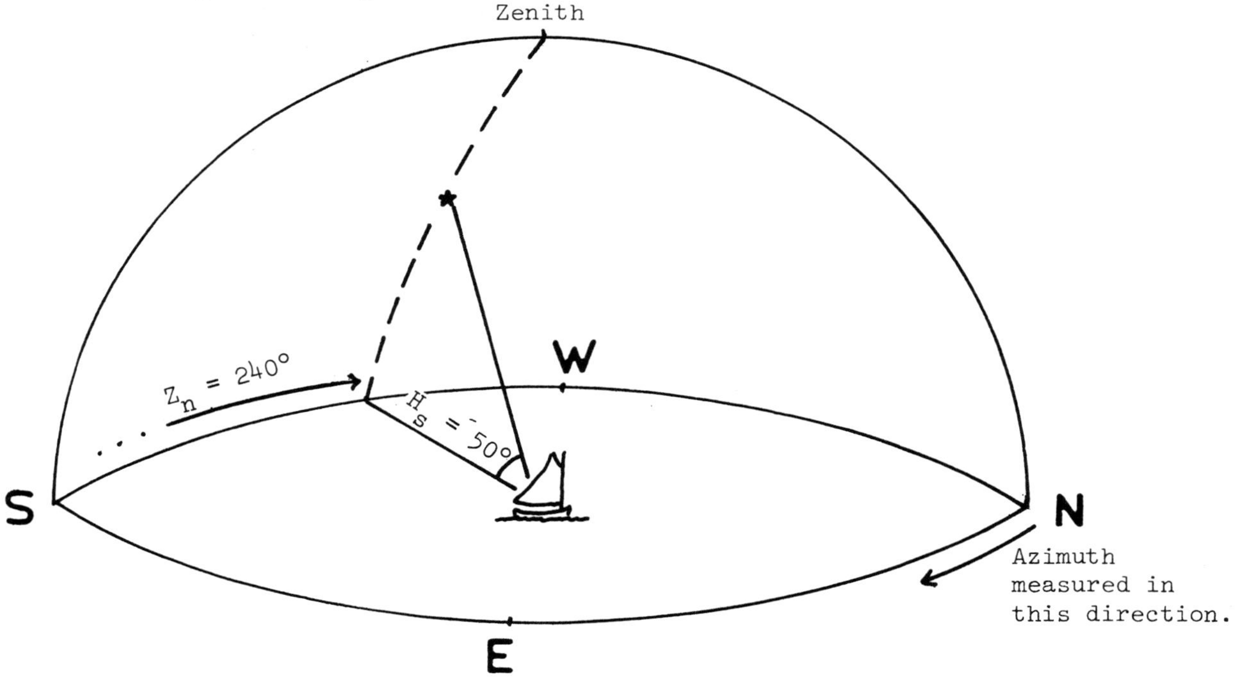

To pinpoint a body on the celestial sphere, we need more than just altitude since several bodies in different directions can have the same height. Therefore, a second coordinate is used called azimuth. It refers to direction and most often is measured from north eastward and is designated by $Z_n$. Since the horizon is a full circle or 360°, $Z_n$ can range from 0° to 360°. Later, in chapter 7, we will see reference to a "Z" which is called azimuth angle but may use south or north as its origin and may be measured in eastward or westward direction, ranging from 0° to 180° (similar to the longitude system on the earth). This Z must always be converted to $Z_n$ for use in plotting. The diagram on the preceding page illustrates altitude and azimuth. Altitude is measured with a sextant, azimuth is found in later mathematical computations.

The backstaff, cross-staff, quadrant and astrolabe were early forms of altitude measuring instruments. By the mid 1700s, the octant (one eighth of a circle in shape) had been invented which employed two mirrors to reflect the image of the celestial body and a clear glass through which to view the horizon. Today's sextant is only a perfection of the early octant with a micrometer drum to replace the older vernier, both used to measure the minutes and seconds (or tenths of minutes) of altitude. Also, as the name suggests, the shape of the frame is one sixth of a circle. Because of double reflection achieved with the two mirrors, the actual angles observed may reach 120° instead of only 60°.

In choosing a sextant, the biggest decision is quality versus purchase price. There are two basic "grades" to investigate - plastic and metal - with the corresponding retail price ranges (at time of this writing) varying from $20 to $75 for plastic and $300 to $800 for metal. The gap here is considerable as can be readily seen but after the following discussion, the buyer should be better armed to choose the side of the gap best suited to him or her.

The plastic sextant's one advantage is price. This should be weighed against several disadvantages. First, since plastic will expand and contract with varying temperatures, the index correction (instrument error) is constantly changing. This can be partially compensated for by obtaining an index correction each time a set of sights is taken. However, the navigator may find that even between the first and last sight during a twilight series, the change can be considerable. Remember, a minute of error in sextant altitude directly corresponds to one nautical mile on the plot.

Secondly, plastic sextants weigh less than a pound and some varieties offer considerable wind resistance, all making it more difficult to hold the sextant vertical when sighting in breezy conditions.

Thirdly, the quality of the components is less - the filters, the mirrors, the zero to three power viewing scopes. And lastly, the life of a plastic sextant is shorter, depending on the amount of use. Filters break off, the plastic gearing wears down, the micrometer drum develops slop.

The two manufacturers of plastic sextants at this time are Davis and EBBCO (East Berks Boat Company). I would only recommend their models with micrometer drums as the vernier models that Davis produces only read to within two minutes of arc in addition to being more difficult to achieve the "fine tuning". Any of the plastic sextants make excellent teaching aids where principle, not

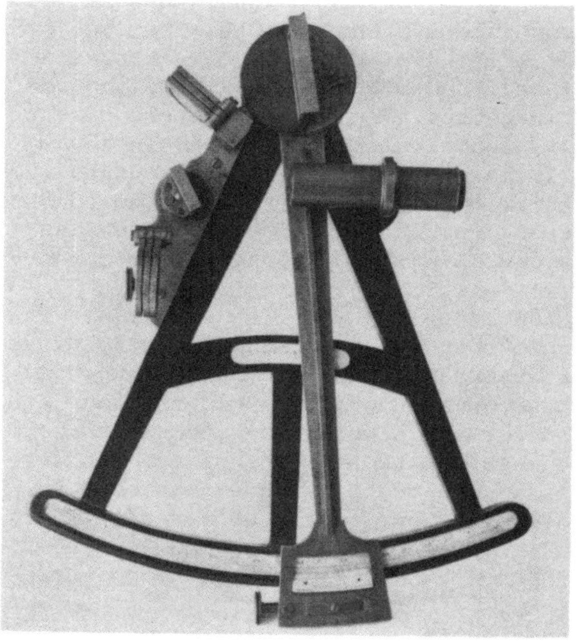

A vernier octant

A metal micrometer sextant

A metal vernier sextant

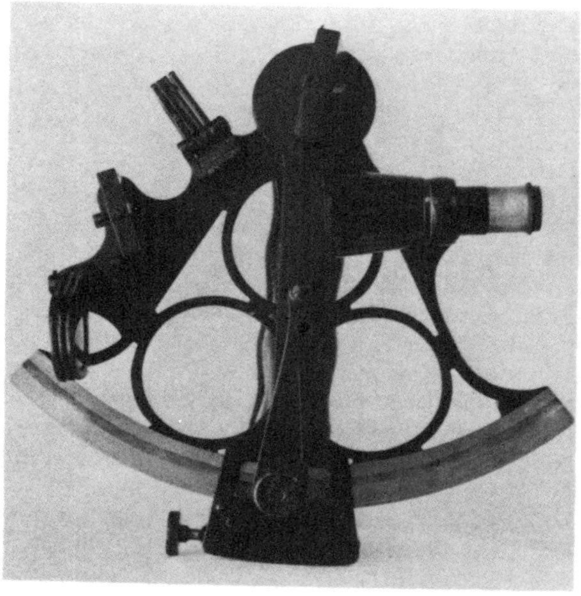

A plastic micrometer sextant

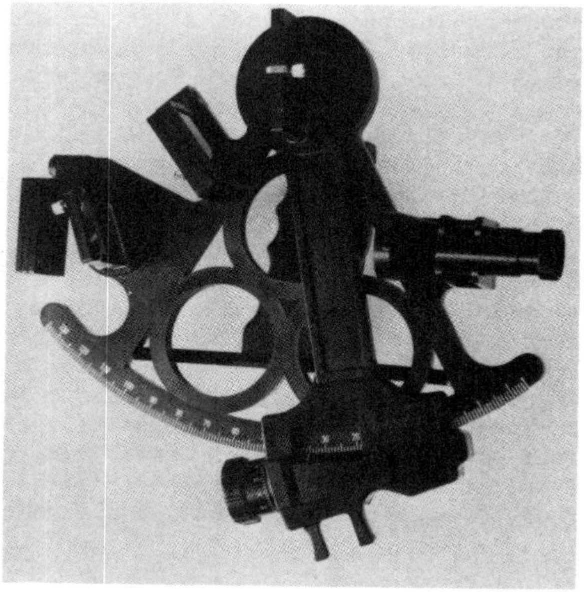

accuracy, is important. Also, as a back-up sextant, the micrometer plastic sextants can be very valuable. However, as a primary sextant when the celestial fix is important, I would strongly recommend investing in the better grade.

The advantages of a metal sextant are obvious after reading the disadvantages involved in using a plastic sextant. Index correction is always the same unless the sextant is dropped or mirror adjustments are made. The weight (2½ to 4 pounds) and openwork frame reduce windage problems, the better optics and filters give guaranteed accuracy and the life of the instrument is indefinite as long as care is exercised in usage and storage. The price range I quoted shows that a variety of manufacturers and options may be chosen. A few of these options are as follows.

The metal frame may be made of either brass or an aluminum alloy, lightening the weight from roughly four to three pounds. The size of the frame varies too, also changing the weight. I find that the lighter sextants are easier for me to hold for a length of time whereas the stronger person would prefer the heft of the larger instrument.

The telescope power varies from three to eight power, the advantage of the higher power being mainly its ability to pick up the light of a star earlier in the twilight when the naked eye still cannot see it. The disadvantage of greater power is reduced field of view - and this becomes critical when the navigator is trying to keep the celestial body in the field while bouncing around on a small vessel. A four power scope is a good compromise.

Lighting is another option. Of course this isn't needed during the day but near the end of twilight, it is convenient to press a button or turn a switch to illuminate the arc and micrometer drum. The battery case, wires and bulb socket are all subject to corrosion at sea and batteries tend to wear down when most needed so often this "luxury" is questionable. The extra cost for lighting of $80 to $100 will finance an inexhaustible supply of penlight flashlights which will clip on to clothing or store in the sextant case. Cases usually come with the sextant and are included in the price.

There are several good makers of metal sextants today including Weems and Plath, Freiberger, International Nautical Company, Tamaya, Heath, Hughes, and Cassens and Plath. Discount houses will sell some of the varieties at lower prices but be careful to assure that the return privilege applies in case of instrument defect. Second hand metal sextants are a rarity and often not much of a price bargain. Some sextants are sold as "antiques" and application of this title prices them beyond their useful value. The true antiques, the vernier sextants or octants, are nice as display items but the difficulty of reading a vernier versus a micrometer drum is a big disadvantage. Sometimes Navy surplus sextants can be found at reasonable prices. In any of these situations, instrument cleaning or mirror resilvering may be necessary but this cost will be minimal compared to the price of the instrument.

The final choice of instrument to buy comes down to how much you can afford, how essential celestial navigation is to your voyage, how comfortable the instrument is to use, and how experienced the navigator is in handling the sextant. Guaranteed accuracy ratings become less important when rough sea conditions and navigator inexperience prevail.

# THE SEXTANT AND ITS PARTS

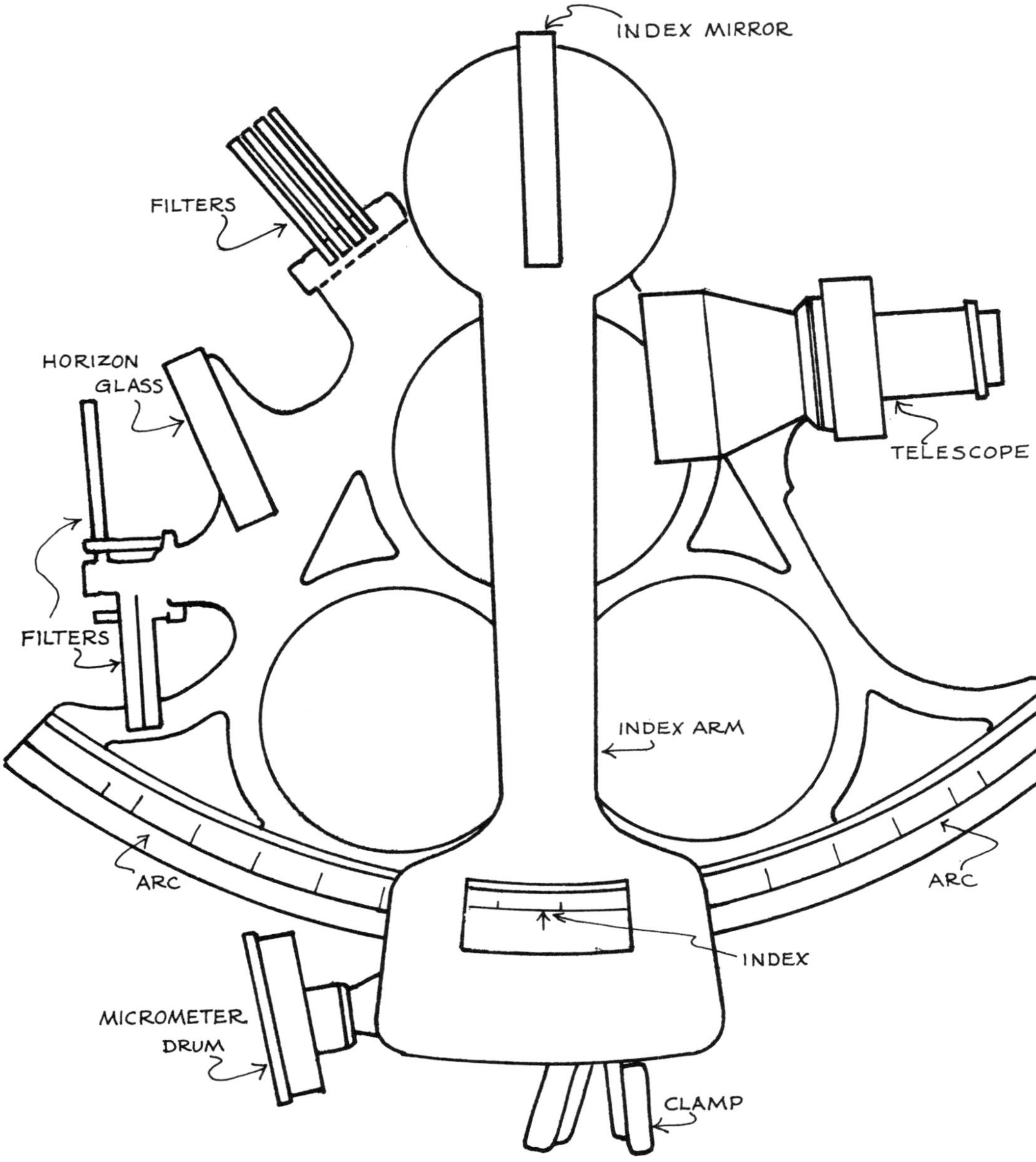

Once the sextant is obtained, adjustments to the mirrors may be necessary to reduce the index correction to a minimal amount. One or two adjusting screws are located on each mirror for this purpose. Each mirror should be perpendicular to the sextant frame and when the sextant is set at zero the two mirrors should be parallel to each other. Three tests are involved. Reference to the diagram of the sextant and its parts will aid in the following discussion.

The first test is for perpendicularity of the index mirror. Hold the sextant on its side (with handle down) and with the index arm set to 35°. Place your eye close to the sextant near the index mirror so that you can see the sextant arc in the mirror (reflected) and also just to the right of the mirror (direct). If these two images are not in a straight or continuous line, the mirror is not perpendicular to the frame. Adjusting the screw on the back of the index mirror will bring the images in line.

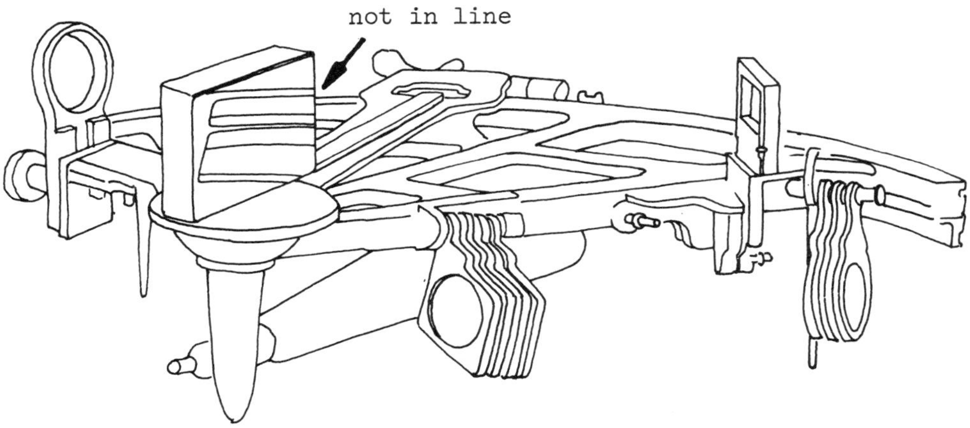


The second test is for perpendicularity of the horizon glass. Actually, the "glass" is only half glass with the right half of the frame filled with a mirror. The horizon is viewed through the glass, the reflected image of the celestial object viewed in the mirror. If this horizon glass is not perpendicular to the frame, the error is referred to as side error. If a star is viewed both in the glass and in the mirror with the sextant set near zero, by adjusting the altitude, the star should pass over itself i.e. become superimposed. If instead the reflected image of the star passes to the right of the direct image, side error exists and can be minimized by adjusting the screws on the horizon glass. Other celestial bodies may be used for this test as well as reasonably distant terrestrial objects.

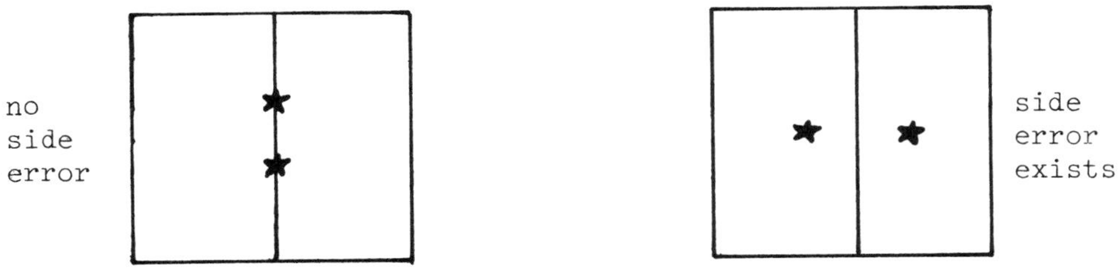

The third test is for parallelism of the index mirror and horizon glass when the index arm is set exactly at zero. If at this setting the horizon or a celestial body appear higher or lower in the mirror than in the glass, the mirrors are not parallel and should be adjusted until they are. This error is called index error and is discussed more in the next chapter.

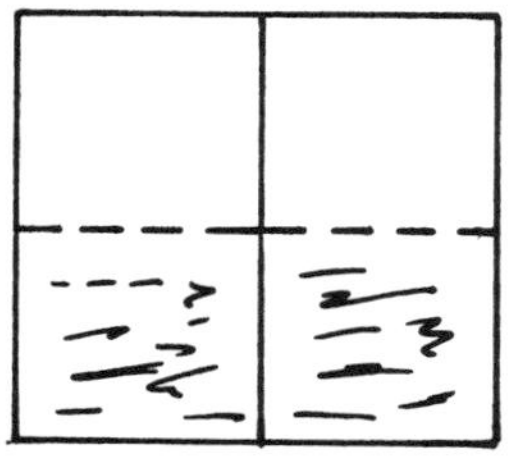


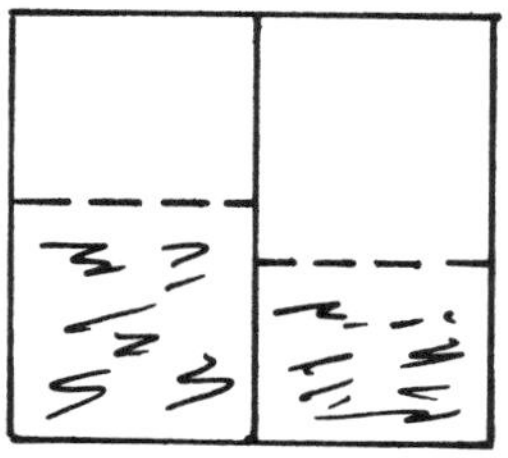


A sextant is not difficult to use but it takes practice to get a sight quickly and accurately, especially aboard a bouncing vessel. The instrument is held vertically in the right hand and the sighting is made through the telescope. The horizon is observed in the horizon glass while the celestial object is found in the mirror and positioned such that it is in line with the horizon. In the case of the Sun or Moon, the edge of the disk is placed on the horizon. If the lower edge is used, the sight is referred to as a lower limb sight. An upper limb sight is less often used with the Sun but is often necessary with the Moon since the lower edge may not actually be a circular one, depending on the phase.

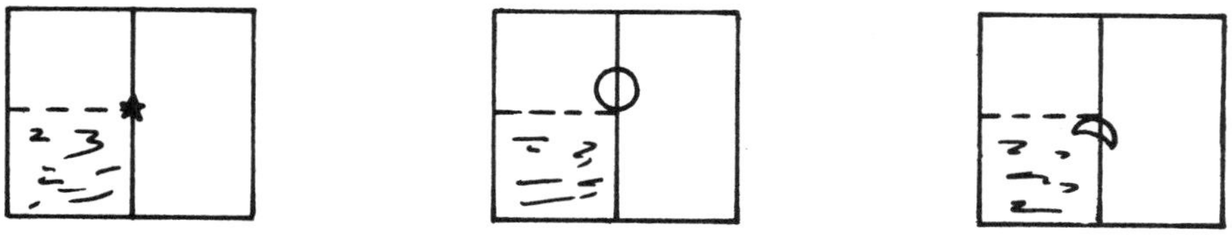

Once the body is lined up properly, the sextant is "rocked" or pivoted as if the top of the index arm were attached to the rod of a pendulum and the arc were at the bottom with the swinging action. This is done to insure that the sextant is held vertically when the sight is taken. As the rocking is done, the celestial body will seem to trace an arc with respect to the horizon. The sextant is vertical or plumb when the body is at the bottom of the arc. The sight is then "marked" i.e. the observer says "mark" to his timekeeper or observes the time himself.

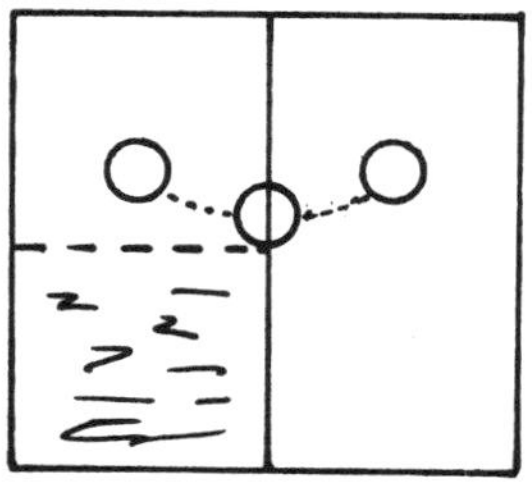

The angular height of the celestial body is read on the arc and on the micrometer drum. The arc displays the degrees whereas the drum displays the minutes and tenths of minutes (or in some cases minutes and seconds). An arrow on the index arm points to the degrees on the arc. The degree is chosen that rests just to the right of the arrow. If the arrow pointing to the micrometer drum lies between two minutes, an estimation is made as to how many tenths of the way between it is or sometimes a vernier is available on the index arm for that purpose. The following photograph shows a reading of $35^{\circ}$ 10!5.

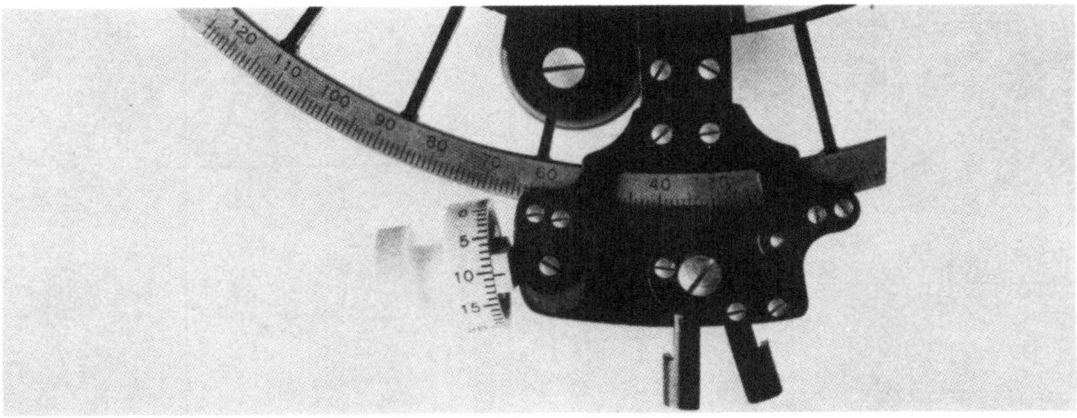


There are several techniques of getting the celestial body in the field of view, an important step in sextant use that I skipped over rather quickly a couple of paragraphs ago. In sighting the Sun, assuming reasonably good sea conditions, the observer can get the horizon under the Sun in the glass and then move the index arm back and forth, homing in on the glare surrounding the Sun until the Sun's disk is seen. Filters will be needed in front of the index mirror to protect the eye from the Sun's brightness. Also, filters may be necessary in front of the horizon glass if the Sun's sparkle on the water is too bright.

A second method is useful for non-glaring objects such as the planets, stars and daytime Moon. Hold the sextant upside down in the left hand and sight through the glass toward the celestial object. Then move the index arm until the horizon appears in the mirror. The advantage in this method is that it is easier to find the celestial object by direct observing and leave the easily found horizon line for the moving mirrors. Once the object is reasonably well lined up with the horizon, the sextant is turned right side up and the final adjustments with the micrometer drum are made.

If some mathematical calculations are made ahead of time, the rough altitude of the celestial body can be figured allowing a third method to be used. This involves presetting the sextant to the prefigured altitude and then scanning the horizon with the horizon glass until the celestial body comes into the field of view of the mirror. The rough azimuth of the body can also be prefigured so that the area of scanning can be limited. For this method, the sextant would be held right side up the whole time.

Positions of the index mirror for two different altitudes are shown in the following diagrams to give an idea of the range of the index arm.

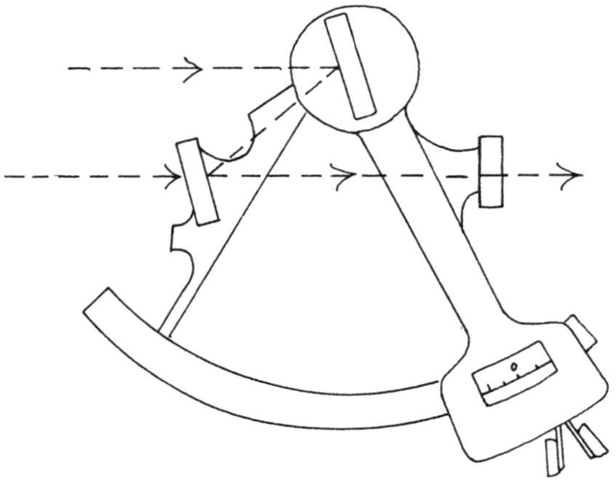


SEXTANT SET FOR ALTITUDE 0°

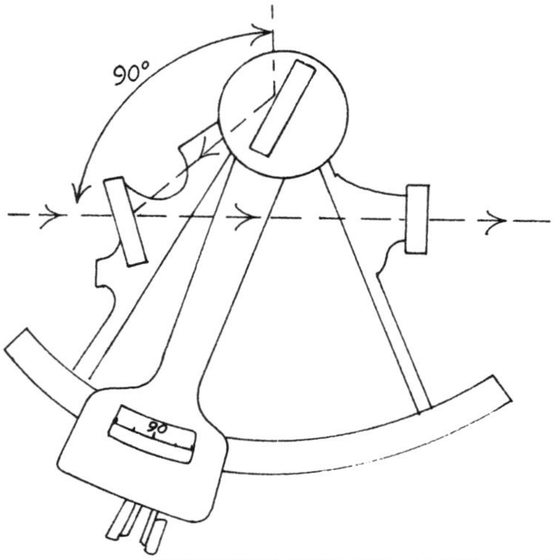


SEXTANT SET FOR ALTITUDE 90°

Some practical hints on using the sextant are in order especially if the instrument represents a considerable investment and happens to be the only sextant aboard. A lanyard attached to the sextant and to the observer saves accidental dropping of the instrument, either to be damaged on deck or to be lost to Davy Jones' Locker. Wrapping oneself around the shrouds when taking a sight over the rail saves the navigator from the same fates. If rigging and comfort allow, sitting amidships when taking the sight is the most stable position since it is the pivot point of the ship's motions. On a small vessel, the navigator has to learn to rise and fall to counteract the inevitable motion from any vantage point.

Sighting when the ship gets to the top of a wave is important to insure that the real sea horizon is used rather than the closer top of a nearby wave. The real sea horizon can vary in distance depending on the height of the observer's eye but corrections for this can be made as will be seen in the next chapter.

Lastly, from experience I can say that it is very embarrassing to not be able to find a star in the sextant when dozens of them are clearly visible to the naked eye - all because salt deposit from sea spray has not been washed off the mirrors. A sextant should be stored always in its case and wiped over after each session when a lot of spray has been flying. This will not only prolong the life of the sextant but also reduce maintenance and embarrassing situations.

A sextant can also be used in piloting. Held vertically, it can give the angular height of a light or marker above the water. In conjunction with a little mathematics or use of a numerical table, distance off of the object can be found.

A second use in piloting involves finding horizontal angles between terrestrial objects. The sextant is held horizontally while one object is sighted through the glass and another is found in the mirror. Combining two sights of three objects will give a fix. In both of these piloting situations, index correction must be applied to the reading before application.

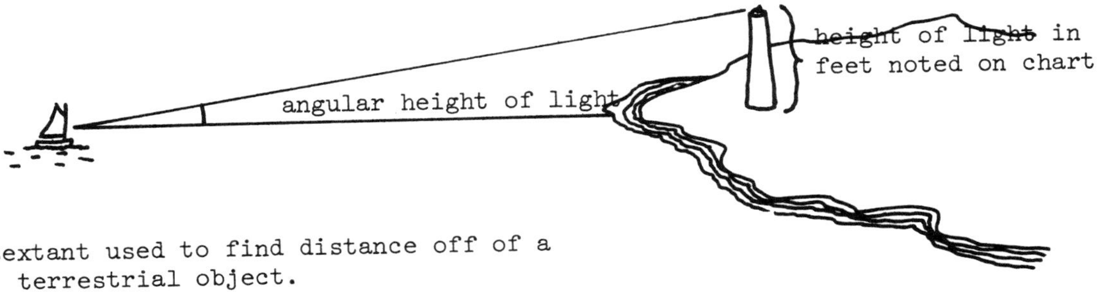


A sextant used to find distance off of a terrestrial object.

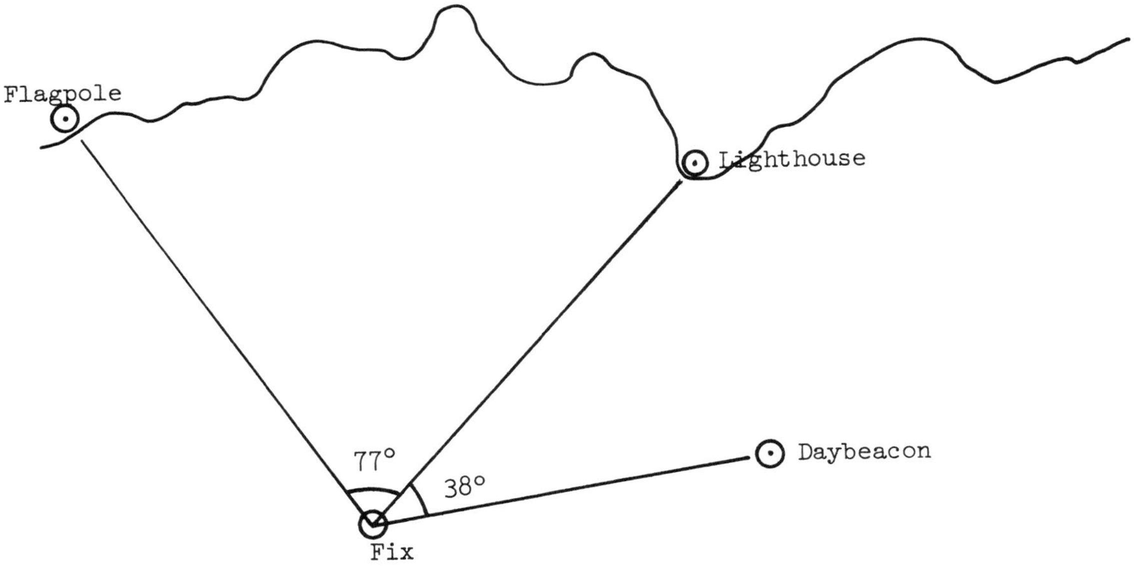


A sextant used to obtain a fix from two relative bearings of three terrestrial objects.

# Chapter 4

# Sextant Altitude Correction

Once the sextant altitude ($H_S$) is obtained, a series of corrections must be applied to compensate for inaccuracies in the instrument, the atmosphere, the diameter of the celestial body and its proximity to the observer on earth, and the height of the observer above the water's surface. We shall work with the upper right section of our sight reduction forms (page 254).

The first correction is labelled I.C. meaning index correction. This is an error in the sextant itself and can be found by setting the sextant to read exactly zero and observing the sea horizon, a distant mountain top (a reasonably flat one), or a celestial object. At zero reading, the objects observed should appear the same height in the horizon glass and mirror. See diagrams a.

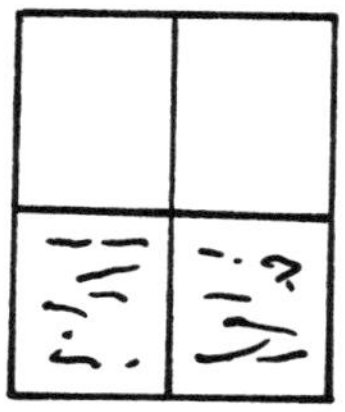

a

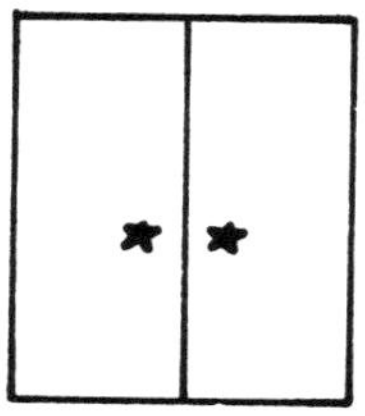

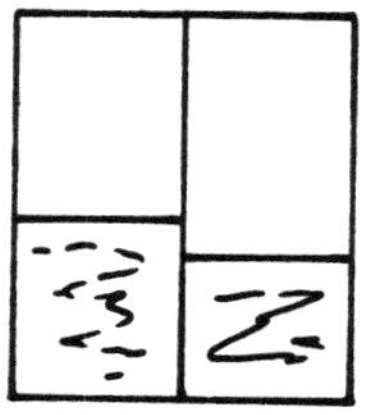

b

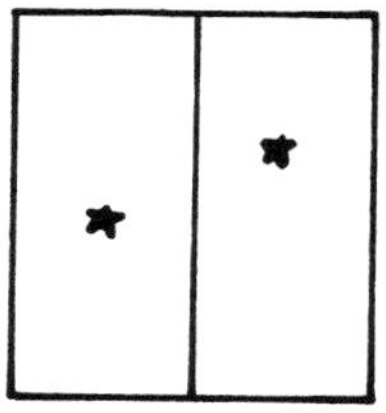

If this is not the case, in other words, if the horizon or object in one side is above or below that in the other side, see diagrams b, adjust the micrometer drum or the tangent screw until the objects are level with each other. Note the sextant reading. This is the amount of index correction. If the arrow is to the left of the zero or "on the arc", the I.C. is negative. If the arrow is to the right of the zero or "off the arc", the I.C. is positive. An easy way to remember this, though perhaps at first confusing, is to memorize - If it's on, it's off. If it's off, it's on. With a plastic sextant, the index correction should be ascertained for each set of sights since plastic will expand and contract with varying temperatures and therefore will have different instrument errors. With a brass or aluminum framed instrument, the index correction should always be the same barring tampering with the mirrors or dropping the instrument.

The next correction is called "dip". It is the angle by which the true horizon differs from the horizon at the eye of the observer so it is entirely dependent on the height of the observer's eye from the sea level.

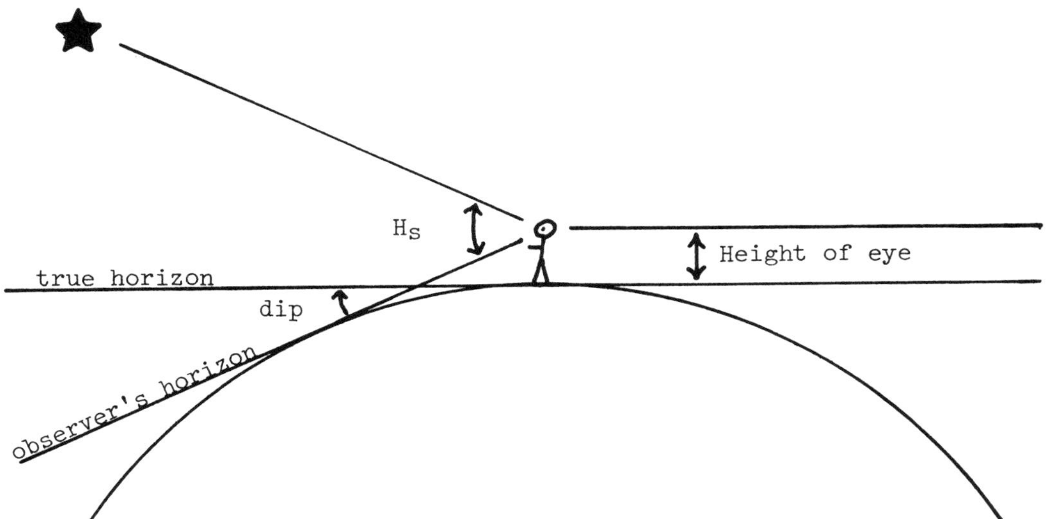


See page 203 in the text for dip table.

Since the angle measured from an eye above the surface of the earth (we are assuming that the eye is never below the water level) is always greater than that which would have been observed from sea level, the dip correction is always negative. The dip correction table is found inside the front cover of the *Nautical Almanac* with a shortened version inside the back cover. It is entered with the height of the observer's eye in feet or meters. For example, if the height of eye were 9.5 feet (between 9.2 and 9.8), the dip correction would be -3'.0. If the height were 14 meters (between 13.8 and 14.2), the correction would be -6'.6. In the case where the height of eye is a critical value, i.e. a value exactly listed in the table, the correction taken is the one toward the top of the page. For example, height of 21.0 feet would give a correction of -4'.4. For extremely high or low heights of eye, the column to the right in the table is used. Height of eye of 85 feet would give a value of -8'.9. Height of eye of 7.2 feet would give a value of -2'.6 (interpolated).

In some cases, close to land, it is impossible to use the true sea horizon. Instead, the celestial body is observed over a land horizon, where the water meets the shore of the land. This is called a dip short sight, the waterline being "short of the sea horizon". Dip can be calculated by the formula

$$\text{Dip Short} = 0.4156\,d + 0.5658\,\frac{h}{d}$$

# TABLE 22

## Dip of the Sea Short of the Horizon

| Distance | Height of eye above the sea, in feet | | | | | | | | | | Distance |
|---|---|---|---|---|---|---|---|---|---|---|---|
| | 5 | 10 | 15 | 20 | 25 | 30 | 35 | 40 | 45 | 50 | |
| *Miles* | ′ | ′ | ′ | ′ | ′ | ′ | ′ | ′ | ′ | ′ | *Miles* |
| 0.1 | 28.3 | 56.6 | 84.9 | 113.2 | 141.5 | 169.8 | 198.0 | 226.3 | 254.6 | 282.9 | 0.1 |
| 0.2 | 14.2 | 28.4 | 42.5 | 56.7 | 70.8 | 84.9 | 99.1 | 113.2 | 127.4 | 141.5 | 0.2 |
| 0.3 | 9.6 | 19.0 | 28.4 | 37.8 | 47.3 | 56.7 | 66.1 | 75.6 | 85.0 | 94.4 | 0.3 |
| 0.4 | 7.2 | 14.3 | 21.4 | 28.5 | 35.5 | 42.6 | 49.7 | 56.7 | 63.8 | 70.9 | 0.4 |
| 0.5 | 5.9 | 11.5 | 17.2 | 22.8 | 28.5 | 34.2 | 39.8 | 45.5 | 51.1 | 56.8 | 0.5 |
| 0.6 | 5.0 | 9.7 | 14.4 | 19.1 | 23.8 | 28.5 | 33.3 | 38.0 | 42.7 | 47.4 | 0.6 |
| 0.7 | 4.3 | 8.4 | 12.4 | 16.5 | 20.5 | 24.5 | 28.6 | 32.6 | 36.7 | 40.7 | 0.7 |
| 0.8 | 3.9 | 7.4 | 10.9 | 14.5 | 18.0 | 21.5 | 25.1 | 28.6 | 32.2 | 35.7 | 0.8 |
| 0.9 | 3.5 | 6.7 | 9.8 | 12.9 | 16.1 | 19.2 | 22.4 | 25.5 | 28.7 | 31.8 | 0.9 |
| 1.0 | 3.2 | 6.1 | 8.9 | 11.7 | 14.6 | 17.4 | 20.2 | 23.0 | 25.9 | 28.7 | 1.0 |
| 1.1 | 3.0 | 5.6 | 8.2 | 10.7 | 13.3 | 15.9 | 18.5 | 21.0 | 23.6 | 26.2 | 1.1 |
| 1.2 | 2.9 | 5.2 | 7.6 | 9.9 | 12.3 | 14.6 | 17.0 | 19.4 | 21.7 | 24.1 | 1.2 |
| 1.3 | 2.7 | 4.9 | 7.1 | 9.2 | 11.4 | 13.6 | 15.8 | 17.9 | 20.1 | 22.3 | 1.3 |
| 1.4 | 2.6 | 4.6 | 6.6 | 8.7 | 10.7 | 12.7 | 14.7 | 16.7 | 18.8 | 20.8 | 1.4 |
| 1.5 | 2.5 | 4.4 | 6.3 | 8.2 | 10.0 | 11.9 | 13.8 | 15.7 | 17.6 | 19.5 | 1.5 |
| 1.6 | 2.4 | 4.2 | 6.0 | 7.7 | 9.5 | 11.3 | 13.0 | 14.8 | 16.6 | 18.3 | 1.6 |
| 1.7 | 2.4 | 4.0 | 5.7 | 7.4 | 9.0 | 10.7 | 12.4 | 14.0 | 15.7 | 17.3 | 1.7 |
| 1.8 | 2.3 | 3.9 | 5.5 | 7.0 | 8.6 | 10.2 | 11.7 | 13.3 | 14.9 | 16.5 | 1.8 |
| 1.9 | 2.3 | 3.8 | 5.3 | 6.7 | 8.2 | 9.7 | 11.2 | 12.7 | 14.2 | 15.7 | 1.9 |
| 2.0 | 2.2 | 3.7 | 5.1 | 6.5 | 7.9 | 9.3 | 10.7 | 12.1 | 13.6 | 15.0 | 2.0 |
| 2.1 | 2.2 | 3.6 | 4.9 | 6.3 | 7.6 | 9.0 | 10.3 | 11.6 | 13.0 | 14.3 | 2.1 |
| 2.2 | 2.2 | 3.5 | 4.8 | 6.1 | 7.3 | 8.6 | 9.9 | 11.2 | 12.5 | 13.8 | 2.2 |
| 2.3 | 2.2 | 3.4 | 4.6 | 5.9 | 7.1 | 8.3 | 9.6 | 10.8 | 12.0 | 13.3 | 2.3 |
| 2.4 | 2.2 | 3.4 | 4.5 | 5.7 | 6.9 | 8.1 | 9.2 | 10.4 | 11.6 | 12.8 | 2.4 |
| 2.5 | 2.2 | 3.3 | 4.4 | 5.6 | 6.7 | 7.8 | 9.0 | 10.1 | 11.2 | 12.4 | 2.5 |
| 2.6 | 2.2 | 3.3 | 4.3 | 5.4 | 6.5 | 7.6 | 8.7 | 9.8 | 10.9 | 12.0 | 2.6 |
| 2.7 | 2.2 | 3.2 | 4.3 | 5.3 | 6.4 | 7.4 | 8.4 | 9.5 | 10.6 | 11.6 | 2.7 |
| 2.8 | 2.2 | 3.2 | 4.2 | 5.2 | 6.2 | 7.2 | 8.2 | 9.2 | 10.3 | 11.3 | 2.8 |
| 2.9 | 2.2 | 3.2 | 4.1 | 5.1 | 6.1 | 7.1 | 8.0 | 9.0 | 10.0 | 11.0 | 2.9 |
| 3.0 | 2.2 | 3.1 | 4.1 | 5.0 | 6.0 | 6.9 | 7.8 | 8.8 | 9.7 | 10.7 | 3.0 |
| 3.1 | 2.2 | 3.1 | 4.0 | 4.9 | 5.9 | 6.8 | 7.7 | 8.6 | 9.5 | 10.4 | 3.1 |
| 3.2 | 2.2 | 3.1 | 4.0 | 4.9 | 5.7 | 6.6 | 7.5 | 8.4 | 9.3 | 10.2 | 3.2 |
| 3.3 | 2.2 | 3.1 | 3.9 | 4.8 | 5.7 | 6.5 | 7.4 | 8.2 | 9.1 | 9.9 | 3.3 |
| 3.4 | 2.2 | 3.1 | 3.9 | 4.7 | 5.6 | 6.4 | 7.2 | 8.1 | 8.9 | 9.7 | 3.4 |
| 3.5 | 2.2 | 3.1 | 3.9 | 4.7 | 5.5 | 6.3 | 7.1 | 7.9 | 8.7 | 9.5 | 3.5 |
| 3.6 | 2.2 | 3.1 | 3.8 | 4.6 | 5.4 | 6.2 | 7.0 | 7.8 | 8.6 | 9.4 | 3.6 |
| 3.7 | 2.2 | 3.1 | 3.8 | 4.6 | 5.4 | 6.1 | 6.9 | 7.7 | 8.4 | 9.2 | 3.7 |
| 3.8 | 2.2 | 3.1 | 3.8 | 4.6 | 5.3 | 6.0 | 6.8 | 7.5 | 8.3 | 9.0 | 3.8 |
| 3.9 | 2.2 | 3.1 | 3.8 | 4.5 | 5.2 | 6.0 | 6.7 | 7.4 | 8.1 | 8.9 | 3.9 |
| 4.0 | 2.2 | 3.1 | 3.8 | 4.5 | 5.2 | 5.9 | 6.6 | 7.3 | 8.0 | 8.7 | 4.0 |
| 4.1 | 2.2 | 3.1 | 3.8 | 4.5 | 5.1 | 5.8 | 6.5 | 7.2 | 7.9 | 8.6 | 4.1 |
| 4.2 | 2.2 | 3.1 | 3.8 | 4.4 | 5.1 | 5.8 | 6.5 | 7.1 | 7.8 | 8.5 | 4.2 |
| 4.3 | 2.2 | 3.1 | 3.8 | 4.4 | 5.1 | 5.7 | 6.4 | 7.0 | 7.7 | 8.4 | 4.3 |
| 4.4 | 2.2 | 3.1 | 3.8 | 4.4 | 5.0 | 5.7 | 6.3 | 7.0 | 7.6 | 8.3 | 4.4 |
| 4.5 | 2.2 | 3.1 | 3.8 | 4.4 | 5.0 | 5.6 | 6.3 | 6.9 | 7.5 | 8.2 | 4.5 |
| 4.6 | 2.2 | 3.1 | 3.8 | 4.4 | 5.0 | 5.6 | 6.2 | 6.8 | 7.4 | 8.1 | 4.6 |
| 4.7 | 2.2 | 3.1 | 3.8 | 4.4 | 5.0 | 5.6 | 6.2 | 6.8 | 7.4 | 8.0 | 4.7 |
| 4.8 | 2.2 | 3.1 | 3.8 | 4.4 | 4.9 | 5.5 | 6.1 | 6.7 | 7.3 | 7.9 | 4.8 |
| 4.9 | 2.2 | 3.1 | 3.8 | 4.3 | 4.9 | 5.5 | 6.1 | 6.7 | 7.2 | 7.8 | 4.9 |
| 5.0 | 2.2 | 3.1 | 3.8 | 4.3 | 4.9 | 5.5 | 6.0 | 6.6 | 7.2 | 7.7 | 5.0 |
| 5.5 | 2.2 | 3.1 | 3.8 | 4.3 | 4.9 | 5.4 | 5.9 | 6.4 | 6.9 | 7.4 | 5.5 |
| 6.0 | 2.2 | 3.1 | 3.8 | 4.3 | 4.9 | 5.3 | 5.8 | 6.3 | 6.7 | 7.2 | 6.0 |
| 6.5 | 2.2 | 3.1 | 3.8 | 4.3 | 4.9 | 5.3 | 5.7 | 6.2 | 6.6 | 7.1 | 6.5 |
| 7.0 | 2.2 | 3.1 | 3.8 | 4.3 | 4.9 | 5.3 | 5.7 | 6.1 | 6.5 | 6.9 | 7.0 |
| 7.5 | 2.2 | 3.1 | 3.8 | 4.3 | 4.9 | 5.3 | 5.7 | 6.1 | 6.5 | 6.9 | 7.5 |
| 8.0 | 2.2 | 3.1 | 3.8 | 4.3 | 4.9 | 5.3 | 5.7 | 6.1 | 6.5 | 6.9 | 8.0 |
| 8.5 | 2.2 | 3.1 | 3.8 | 4.3 | 4.9 | 5.3 | 5.7 | 6.1 | 6.5 | 6.9 | 8.5 |
| 9.0 | 2.2 | 3.1 | 3.8 | 4.3 | 4.9 | 5.3 | 5.7 | 6.1 | 6.5 | 6.9 | 9.0 |
| 9.5 | 2.2 | 3.1 | 3.8 | 4.3 | 4.9 | 5.3 | 5.7 | 6.1 | 6.5 | 6.9 | 9.5 |
| 10.0 | 2.2 | 3.1 | 3.8 | 4.3 | 4.9 | 5.3 | 5.7 | 6.1 | 6.5 | 6.9 | 10.0 |

where dip is expressed in minutes of arc, d is the distance in nautical miles to the shoreline being used and h is the height of eye of the observer above the water level, expressed in feet. For convenience, Table 22 in American Practical Navigator by Bowditch can be entered with height of eye and distance to the horizon to obtain the dip correction. These values are to be interpolated when height of eye falls between the values heading the columns. Below the bold stepped line, the dip corrections are equal to those obtained with a true sea horizon. The dip short correction replaces the normal dip correction and is always negative since the land horizon will be lower than the true sea horizon.

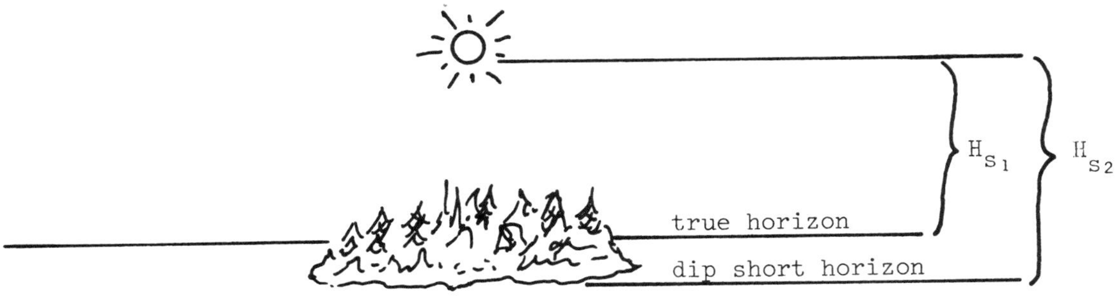


$$H_{s_2} > H_{s_1}$$

$$H_{s_1} - \text{dip} = H_{s_2} - \text{dip short}$$

The dip short table takes care of the lower land horizon as well as the height of eye. It is entered with the distance to the land horizon (in nautical miles) above which the celestial body appears and with the height of eye. To obtain the distance to the land horizon, we need a chart of the area and knowledge of the bearing of the celestial body. This bearing can be roughly obtained by a compass or more accurately obtained from the H.O. 229 tables. As we shall see later, one result of the H.O. 229 tables is $Z_n$ or true bearing of the celestial body to the nearest tenth of a degree. From our dead reckoning position, we lay off the bearing of the land and measure the distance from our DR to the intersection of land and bearing line.

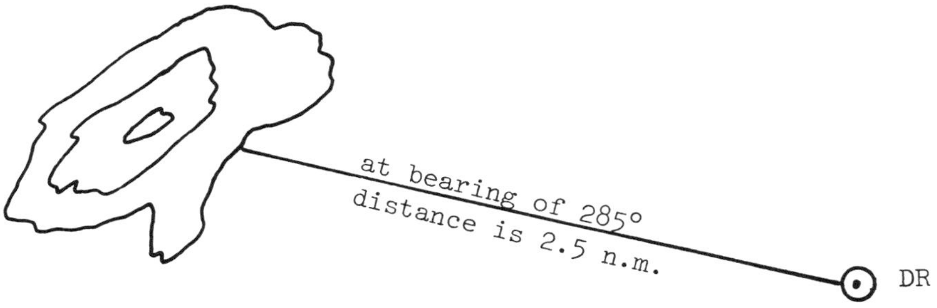

This distance to the nearest tenth of a mile is used to enter the left hand side of Table 22, the correct column is chosen by knowing height of eye. If the height of eye were 15 feet and the distance to land horizon were 2.5 nautical miles, the dip short correction would be -4.4 minutes of arc. If, however, our height of eye were 17 feet, partway between the values listed, and the distance of horizon were 2.5 nautical miles, the interpolated correction would be 2/5 of the way between 4.4 and 5.6 minutes of arc (17 is 2/5 of the way between 15 and 20).

$$5.6 - 4.4 = 1.2 \qquad 1.2 \times 2/5 = .5 \qquad 4.4 + .5 = 4.9$$

The correction then would be negative 4.9 minutes of arc.

The third correction to apply to our sextant altitude concerns air temperature and atmospheric pressure. The alteration of the atmosphere for non-standard temperatures or pressures is only significant for low altitude bodies and can be either positive or negative as indicated in the table inside the first page of the <u>Nautical Almanac</u>. Along the top of the table we find temperatures in degrees Fahrenheit or Celsius, along the side are pressures in millibars or inches. By entering the appropriate figures, we arrive at a lettered slanted zone. We continue down to the column of the same letter until we arrive at the line of altitude nearest to ours, corrected so far for index error and height of eye. If, for example, the temperature were +30° F and the pressure were 30.50 inches, the correct zone would be D. For a low altitude of 10° 15!0, the correction would be -0!4. If, in another example, the temperature were 35° C and the pressure were 980 millibars, the zone would be M. For altitude of 14° 47!8, the correction would be +0!5. See text page 205.

The last correction, entitled "main" is a combination of several factors, varying with the celestial body observed. One factor, refraction, applies to all bodies. When the light from the body enters the atmosphere (a denser medium than the near vacuum of outer space), its path is bent downward. For an observer on the earth, the celestial body will always appear higher than it really is so the refraction correction is always negative. The correction is maximum when the body is near the horizon (can be up to 34!5) and the minimum when the body is at the zenith or overhead point (0!0). See text page 203.

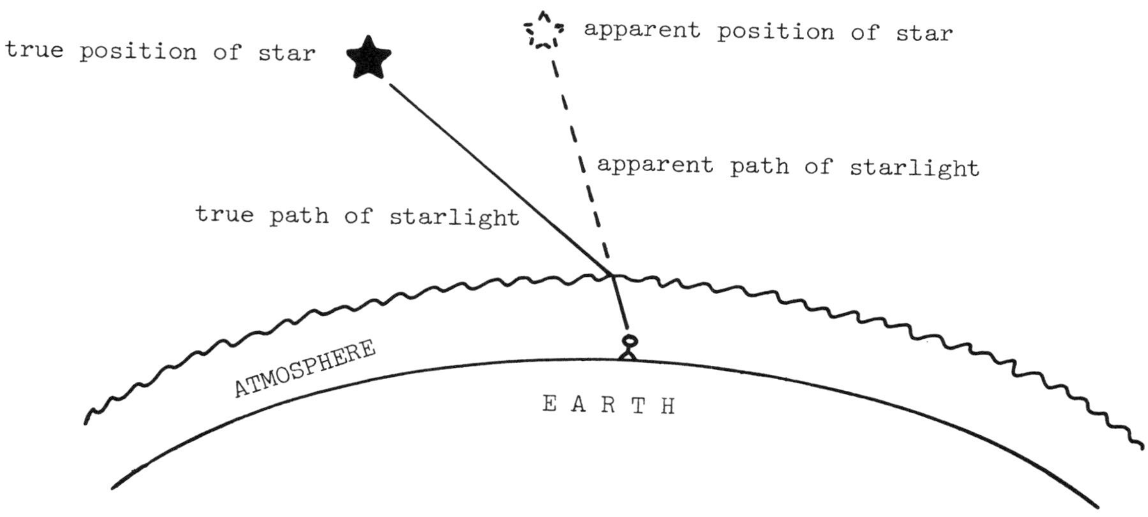

A second factor in the "main" correction is semidiameter, applicable to Sun or Moon sights. Since with these two bodies we observe either the upper limb or lower limb, we have to correct this altitude to the center of the disk. All positional figures in the Nautical Almanac are based on the disk center. The angular diameter of both the Sun and Moon is close to 30!0 but does vary slightly with the distance of the body from the earth. For instance, the Sun is closer to the earth in the northern hemisphere winter so would appear a little larger. This is apparent if we peruse the semidiameter (half diameter) figures at the bottom of the sun column in the Nautical Almanac. The S.D. varies from 15.8 to 16.3. Doing the same for the Moon, we find a variance of 14.7 to 16.8.

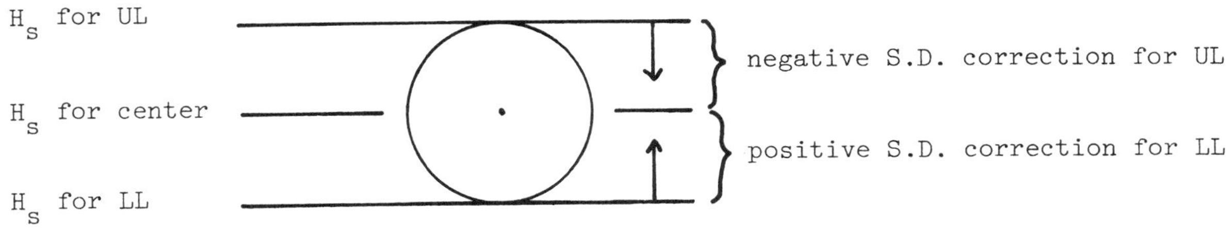


The third factor in the "main" correction is parallax, only significant for close objects such as the Sun, Moon, Venus and Mars. Since all figures in the Nautical Almanac are based on observation from the center of the earth, a correction must be made for the difference in angle from the center to the surface of the earth, our true observation point. This correction can be over a degree for the Moon, is usually less than 30 seconds for Venus and less than 9 seconds for the Sun. The parallax correction is always positive and will decrease as the altitude of the body increases. Since 1985, the parallax correction for Venus and for Mars is the sole component of the "Additional Correction" listed under "Stars and Planets" inside the front cover of the Nautical Almanac.

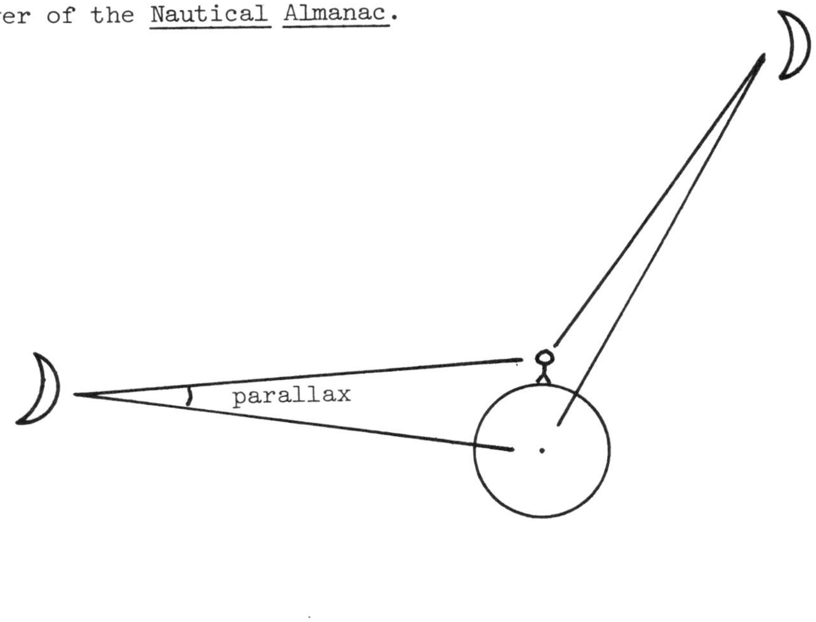

A fourth factor in the "main" correction is phase, applicable to the Moon, Venus and Mars. This correction is due to the varying of the apparent center of the lighted part of the body from its actual center. Since we observe a limb of the Moon, not its center, we do not need a phase correction here. However, for Venus and Mars, their image is so small that a limb is impossible to discern. The diagram below illustrates the problem. The phase corrections are listed in the Nautical Almanac. Since 1985 the phase corrections for Venus and Mars have been incorporated into their G.H.A.s and Declinations.

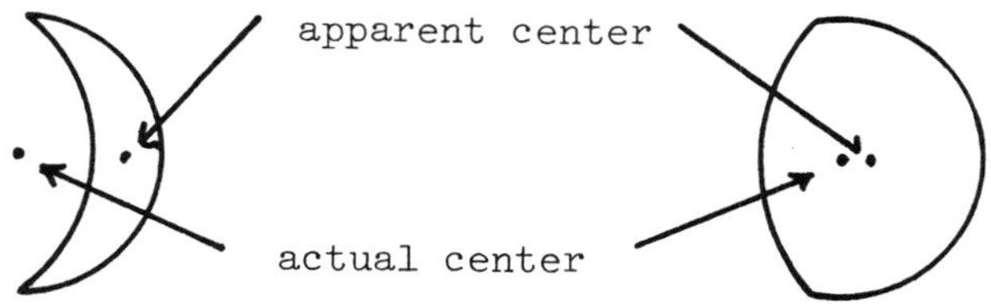


The fifth and last factor in the "main" correction is augmentation of the Moon. As the Moon increases or decreases in altitude, its distance from the center of the earth stays approximately the same, say roughly 250,000 miles. However, we are observing from the surface of the earth, not the center, and the Moon's distance from us will decrease when the Moon is higher in the sky. Therefore, the semidiameter is larger for higher altitudes since objects appear larger if they are closer to us. The change in semidiameter due to augmentation for the Moon is about 0!3 from horizon to zenith. For the Sun and planets, it is too negligible to be concerned with.

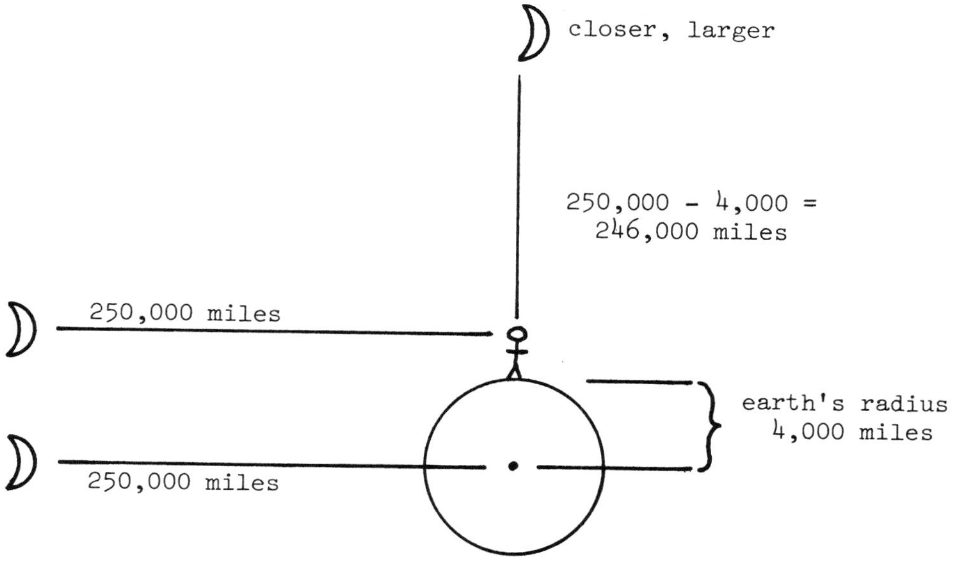

For our convenience, all of these factors except phase are lumped together in one "main" correction so we don't have to consider them individually. The corrections for the Sun and planets are found inside the front cover of the Nautical Almanac, those for the Moon inside the back cover.

In the four examples below, we will categorize the celestial bodies in the following manner - (1) stars, Jupiter, Saturn (2) Venus, Mars (3) Sun (4) Moon.

For the first category, enter the column entitled Stars and Planets with the apparent altitude of the body. If it lies between the tabular values, choose the correction that brackets the values. If the apparent altitude is one of the tabular values, choose the correction that lies toward the top of the page. Thus the correction for 12° 30' is -4!3. For 15° 30', the correction is -3!5.

For Venus and Mars, proceed as above for part one of the main correction. The second part of the correction is found in the right half of the Stars and Planets column under the sections labeled Venus and Mars. For an altitude of 25° on 13 Dec., the additional correction for Venus would be 0!2, for Mars 0!1. Both corrections are positive.

For the Sun, enter one of the two columns in the section depending on the month when sights are taken. Two corrections are available, one for upper and one for lower limb. In January, a lower limb correction for apparent altitude of 15° 20' would be +12!8. In July, the upper limb correction for apparent altitude of 11° 05' would be -20!6.

## ALTITUDE CORRECTION TABLES 10°-90°

| SUN OCT.—MAR. App. Alt. | Lower Limb | Upper Limb | SUN APR.—SEPT. App. Alt. | Lower Limb | Upper Limb | STARS AND PLANETS App. Alt. | Corrⁿ | App. Alt. | Additional Corrⁿ |
|---|---|---|---|---|---|---|---|---|---|
| ° ' | ' | ' | ° ' | ' | ' | ° ' | ' | 1976 | |
| 9 34 | +10.8 | −21.5 | 9 39 | +10.6 | −21.2 | 9 56 | −5.3 | VENUS | |
| 9 45 | +10.9 | −21.4 | 9 51 | +10.7 | −21.1 | 10 08 | −5.2 | Jan. 1 — Dec. 12 | |
| 9 56 | +11.0 | −21.3 | 10 03 | +10.8 | −21.0 | 10 20 | −5.1 | 0° | +0.1' |
| 10 08 | +11.1 | −21.2 | 10 15 | +10.9 | −20.9 | 10 33 | −5.0 | 42 | |
| 10 21 | +11.2 | −21.1 | 10 27 | +11.0 | −20.8 | 10 46 | −4.9 | Dec. 13 — Dec. 31 | |
| 10 34 | +11.3 | −21.0 | 10 40 | +11.1 | −20.7 | 11 00 | −4.8 | 0° | +0.2' |
| 10 47 | +11.4 | −20.9 | 10 54 | +11.2 | −20.6 | 11 14 | −4.7 | 47 | |
| 11 01 | +11.5 | −20.8 | 11 08 | +11.3 | −20.5 | 11 29 | −4.6 | | |
| 11 15 | +11.6 | −20.7 | 11 23 | +11.4 | −20.4 | 11 45 | −4.5 | MARS | |
| 11 30 | +11.7 | −20.6 | 11 38 | +11.5 | −20.3 | 12 01 | −4.4 | Jan. 1 — Feb. 19 | |
| 11 46 | +11.8 | −20.5 | 11 54 | +11.6 | −20.2 | 12 18 | −4.3 | 0° | +0.2' |
| 12 02 | +11.9 | −20.4 | 12 10 | +11.7 | −20.1 | 12 35 | −4.2 | 41 | +0.1 |
| 12 19 | +12.0 | −20.3 | 12 28 | +11.8 | −20.0 | 12 54 | −4.1 | 75 | |
| 12 37 | +12.1 | −20.2 | 12 46 | +11.9 | −19.9 | 13 13 | −4.0 | Feb. 20 — Dec. 31 | |
| 12 55 | +12.2 | −20.1 | 13 05 | +12.0 | −19.8 | 13 33 | −3.9 | 0° | +0.1' |
| 13 14 | +12.3 | −20.0 | 13 24 | +12.1 | −19.7 | 13 54 | −3.8 | 60 | |
| 13 35 | +12.4 | −19.9 | 13 45 | +12.2 | −19.6 | 14 16 | −3.7 | | |
| 13 56 | +12.5 | −19.8 | 14 07 | +12.3 | −19.5 | 14 40 | −3.6 | | |
| 14 18 | +12.6 | −19.7 | 14 30 | +12.4 | −19.4 | 15 04 | −3.5 | | |
| 14 42 | +12.7 | −19.6 | 14 54 | +12.5 | −19.3 | 15 30 | −3.4 | | |
| 15 06 | +12.8 | −19.5 | 15 19 | +12.6 | −19.2 | 15 57 | −3.3 | | |
| 15 32 | +12.9 | −19.4 | 15 46 | +12.7 | −19.1 | 16 26 | −3.2 | | |
| 15 59 | +13.0 | −19.3 | 16 14 | +12.8 | −19.0 | 16 56 | −3.1 | | |
| 16 28 | +13.1 | −19.2 | 16 44 | +12.9 | −18.9 | 17 28 | −3.0 | | |
| 16 59 | +13.2 | −19.1 | 17 15 | +13.0 | −18.8 | 18 02 | −2.9 | | |
| 17 32 | +13.3 | −19.0 | 17 48 | +13.1 | −18.7 | 18 38 | −2.8 | | |
| 18 06 | +13.4 | −18.9 | 18 24 | +13.2 | −18.6 | 19 17 | −2.7 | | |
| 18 42 | +13.5 | −18.8 | 19 01 | +13.3 | −18.5 | 19 58 | −2.6 | | |
| 19 21 | +13.6 | −18.7 | 19 42 | +13.4 | −18.4 | 20 42 | −2.5 | | |
| 20 03 | +13.7 | −18.6 | 20 25 | +13.5 | −18.3 | 21 28 | −2.4 | | |
| 20 48 | +13.8 | −18.5 | 21 11 | +13.6 | −18.2 | 22 19 | −2.3 | | |
| 21 35 | +13.9 | −18.4 | 22 00 | +13.7 | −18.1 | 23 13 | −2.2 | | |
| 22 26 | +14.0 | −18.3 | 22 54 | +13.8 | −18.0 | 24 11 | −2.1 | | |
| 23 22 | +14.1 | −18.2 | 23 51 | +13.9 | −17.9 | 25 14 | −2.0 | | |
| 24 21 | +14.2 | −18.1 | 24 53 | +14.0 | −17.8 | 26 22 | −1.9 | | |
| 25 26 | +14.3 | −18.0 | 26 00 | +14.1 | −17.7 | 27 36 | −1.8 | | |
| 26 36 | +14.4 | −17.9 | 27 13 | +14.2 | −17.6 | 28 56 | −1.7 | | |
| 27 52 | +14.5 | −17.8 | 28 33 | +14.3 | −17.5 | 30 24 | −1.6 | | |
| 29 15 | +14.6 | −17.7 | 30 00 | +14.4 | −17.4 | 32 00 | −1.5 | | |
| 30 46 | +14.7 | −17.6 | 31 35 | +14.5 | −17.3 | 33 45 | −1.4 | | |
| 32 26 | +14.8 | −17.5 | 33 20 | +14.6 | −17.2 | 35 40 | −1.3 | | |
| 34 17 | +14.9 | −17.4 | 35 17 | +14.7 | −17.1 | 37 48 | −1.2 | | |
| 36 20 | | | 37 26 | | | 40 08 | | | |

If the altitudes in the above three categories are too low to fit in the column, refer to inside front cover opening on the right-hand page. This table covers altitudes of less than 10° for Sun, stars and planets. For an altitude of 5° 05', corrections are circled in the table to the right. If the apparent altitude lies between tabular altitudes, interpolation is necessary. For instance, for an altitude of 5° 02!5, the correction for a star would be -9!8. For a lower limb Sun in November, correction would be +6!5. Sights with such low altitudes are not advised but sometimes are the only ones available.

## TABLES 0°–10°—SUN, STARS, PLANETS A3

| App. Alt. | SUN OCT.–MAR. Lower Limb | SUN OCT.–MAR. Upper Limb | SUN APR.–SEPT. Lower Limb | SUN APR.–SEPT. Upper Limb | STARS PLANETS |
|---|---|---|---|---|---|
| ° ′ | ′ | ′ | ′ | ′ | ′ |
| 3 30 | + 3·3 | −29·0 | + 3·1 | −28·7 | −13·0 |
| 35 | 3·6 | 28·7 | 3·3 | 28·5 | 12·7 |
| 40 | 3·8 | 28·5 | 3·5 | 28·3 | 12·5 |
| 45 | 4·0 | 28·3 | 3·7 | 28·1 | 12·3 |
| 50 | 4·2 | 28·1 | 3·9 | 27·9 | 12·1 |
| 3 55 | 4·4 | 27·9 | 4·1 | 27·7 | 11·9 |
| 4 00 | + 4·5 | −27·8 | + 4·3 | −27·5 | −11·8 |
| 05 | 4·7 | 27·6 | 4·5 | 27·3 | 11·6 |
| 10 | 4·9 | 27·4 | 4·6 | 27·2 | 11·4 |
| 15 | 5·1 | 27·2 | 4·8 | 27·0 | 11·2 |
| 20 | 5·2 | 27·1 | 5·0 | 26·8 | 11·1 |
| 25 | 5·4 | 26·9 | 5·1 | 26·7 | 10·9 |
| 4 30 | + 5·6 | −26·7 | + 5·3 | −26·5 | −10·7 |
| 35 | 5·7 | 26·6 | 5·5 | 26·3 | 10·6 |
| 40 | 5·9 | 26·4 | 5·6 | 26·2 | 10·4 |
| 45 | 6·0 | 26·3 | 5·8 | 26·0 | 10·3 |
| 50 | 6·2 | 26·1 | 5·9 | 25·9 | 10·1 |
| 4 55 | 6·3 | 26·0 | 6·0 | 25·8 | 10·0 |
| 5 00 | + 6·4 | −25·9 | + 6·2 | −25·6 | − 9·9 |
| 05 | 6·6 | 25·7 | 6·3 | 25·5 | 9·7 |
| 10 | 6·7 | 25·6 | 6·4 | 25·4 | 9·6 |
| 15 | 6·8 | 25·5 | 6·6 | 25·2 | 9·5 |
| 20 | 6·9 | 25·4 | 6·7 | 25·1 | 9·4 |
| 25 | 7·1 | 25·2 | 6·8 | 25·0 | 9·2 |

The main correction for the Moon (fourth category) involves finding a reference number in the daily pages. This horizontal parallax or H.P. is located on the right hand side of the moon column. If we observed the Moon on 5 July 1976 at 1100 Greenwich Mean Time, the H.P. would be 59!4. Remember that this is just a reference number and will not be directly added or subtracted. It has no sign.

### 1976 JULY 5, 6, 7

| | G.M.T. | SUN G.H.A. | SUN Dec. | MOON G.H.A. | MOON v | MOON Dec. | MOON d | MOON H.P. |
|---|---|---|---|---|---|---|---|---|
| | d h | ° ′ | ° ′ | ° ′ | ′ | ° ′ | ′ | ′ |
| | 5 00 | 178 53.0 | N22 47.7 | 88 32.6 | 9.4 | S 8 27.5 | 10.9 | 59.3 |
| | 01 | 193 52.9 | 47.5 | 103 01.0 | 9.3 | 8 38.4 | 10.9 | 59.3 |
| | 02 | 208 52.8 | 47.2 | 117 29.3 | 9.3 | 8 49.3 | 10.9 | 59.3 |
| | 03 | 223 52.7 | ·· 47.0 | 131 57.6 | 9.2 | 9 00.2 | 10.7 | 59.3 |
| | 04 | 238 52.6 | 46.8 | 146 25.8 | 9.2 | 9 10.9 | 10.8 | 59.3 |
| | 05 | 253 52.5 | 46.5 | 160 54.0 | 9.2 | 9 21.7 | 10.6 | 59.3 |
| | 06 | 268 52.4 | N22 46.3 | 175 22.2 | 9.1 | S 9 32.3 | 10.7 | 59.3 |
| | 07 | 283 52.3 | 46.1 | 189 50.3 | 9.0 | 9 43.0 | 10.5 | 59.3 |
| | 08 | 298 52.1 | 45.8 | 204 18.3 | 9.0 | 9 53.5 | 10.5 | 59.4 |
| M | 09 | 313 52.0 | ·· 45.6 | 218 46.3 | 9.0 | 10 04.0 | 10.5 | 59.4 |
| O | 10 | 328 51.9 | 45.4 | 233 14.3 | 8.9 | 10 14.5 | 10.4 | 59.4 |
| N | 11 | 343 51.8 | 45.1 | 247 42.2 | 8.9 | 10 24.9 | 10.4 | 59.4 |
| D | 12 | 358 51.7 | N22 44.9 | 262 10.1 | 8.8 | S10 35.3 | 10.2 | 59.4 |
| A | 13 | 13 51.6 | 44.6 | 276 37.9 | 8.8 | 10 45.5 | 10.3 | 59.4 |
| Y | 14 | 28 51.5 | 44.4 | 291 05.7 | 8.7 | 10 55.8 | 10.1 | 59.4 |
| | 15 | 43 51.4 | ·· 44.1 | 305 33.4 | 8.7 | 11 05.9 | 10.1 | 59.4 |
| | 16 | 58 51.3 | 43.9 | 320 01.1 | 8.6 | 11 16.0 | 10.0 | 59.4 |
| | 17 | 73 51.2 | 43.7 | 334 28.7 | 8.6 | 11 26.0 | 10.0 | 59.4 |
| | 18 | 88 51.1 | N22 43.4 | 348 56.3 | 8.5 | S11 36.0 | 9.9 | 59.4 |
| | 19 | 103 51.0 | 43.2 | 3 23.8 | 8.5 | 11 45.9 | 9.8 | 59.4 |
| | 20 | 118 50.9 | 42.9 | 17 51.3 | 8.5 | 11 55.7 | 9.8 | 59.4 |
| | 21 | 133 50.8 | ·· 42.7 | 32 18.8 | 8.3 | 12 05.5 | 9.7 | 59.4 |
| | 22 | 148 50.7 | 42.4 | 46 46.1 | 8.4 | 12 15.2 | 9.6 | 59.4 |
| | 23 | 163 50.6 | 42.2 | 61 13.5 | 8.2 | 12 24.8 | 9.5 | 59.5 |

Assume our apparent altitude is 37° 28' with H.P. as above. Enter the column inside the back cover which is headed by 35°-39°. Choose the section in that column that is designated by 37°. The minutes within the degree are sectioned by tens in the column to the left and to the right of the page. Our altitude rounded (interpolation may be necessary in which case the rounding is not done) to the nearest 10 minutes (37° 30') gives a correction of 55!1. (This is entered in the special box on the sight reduction sheet under the sextant altitude correction section.) Continue down the column of 35°-39° until it splits in two, one part headed with "L", one with "U". These letters refer to lower and upper limbs. If we sight the lower limb, continue down the "L" column until you come to the line designated by H.P. of 59.4. The second correction would be 6!8. Both corrections are positive and are added together for the main correction.

If we had observed an upper limb, the first correction would be found in the same manner as above. The part of the column entitled "U" would then be followed until the line for H.P. is reached. The second correction would be 4!5. The first and second corrections would be added and then 30' subtracted from the sum. If the first two corrections add to less than 30', the main correction may be negative. Remember that the Moon is roughly a ½° wide. All corrections are based on the lower limb and then adjusted for upper limb by applying the 30'. Both upper and lower limb sights have to be corrected such that we finally get the altitude of the center of the Moon. The same is true of the Sun, explaining the large difference in the altitude corrections for the two limbs there.

| App. Alt. | 35°–39° Corrⁿ | 40°–44° Corrⁿ |
|---|---|---|
| 00 | 35° 56·5 | 40° 53·7 |
| 10 | 56·4 | 53·6 |
| 20 | 56·3 | 53·5 |
| 30 | 56·2 | 53·4 |
| 40 | 56·2 | 53·3 |
| 50 | 56·1 | 53·2 |
| 00 | 36 56·0 | 41 53·1 |
| 10 | 55·9 | 53·0 |
| 20 | 55·8 | 52·8 |
| 30 | 55·7 | 52·7 |
| 40 | 55·6 | 52·6 |
| 50 | 55·5 | 52·5 |
| 00 | 37 55·4 | 42 52·4 |
| 10 | 55·3 | 52·3 |
| 20 | 55·2 | 52·2 |
| 30 | 55·1 | 52·1 |
| 40 | 55·0 | 52·0 |
| 50 | 55·0 | 51·9 |
| 00 | 38 54·9 | 43 51·8 |
| 10 | 54·8 | 51·7 |
| 20 | 54·7 | 51·6 |
| 30 | 54·6 | 51·5 |
| 40 | 54·5 | 51·4 |
| 50 | 54·4 | 51·2 |
| 00 | 39 54·3 | 44 51·1 |
| 10 | 54·2 | 51·0 |
| 20 | 54·1 | 50·9 |
| 30 | 54·0 | 50·8 |
| 40 | 53·9 | 50·7 |
| 50 | 53·8 | 50·6 |

| H.P. | L | U | L | U |
|---|---|---|---|---|
| 54·0 | 1·1 | 1·7 | 1·3 | 1·9 |
| 58·5 | 5·9 | 4·0 | 5·8 | 4·0 |
| 58·8 | 6·2 | 4·2 | 6·1 | 4·1 |
| 59·1 | 6·5 | 4·3 | 6·4 | 4·3 |
| 59·4 | 6·8 | 4·5 | 6·7 | 4·4 |
| 59·7 | 7·1 | 4·6 | 7·0 | 4·5 |
| 60·0 | 7·5 | 4·8 | 7·3 | 4·7 |
| 60·3 | 7·8 | 5·0 | 7·6 | 4·8 |
| 60·6 | 8·1 | 5·1 | 7·9 | 5·0 |

Lower limb

| | | |
|---|---|---|
| H.P. | 59!4 | Moon |
| Corr | + | 55!1 |
| Corr | + | 6!8 |
| upper limb | - | ~~30!0~~ |
| Main | ⊕ − | 61!9 |

Upper limb

| | | |
|---|---|---|
| H.P. | 59!4 | Moon |
| Corr | + | 55!1 |
| Corr | + | 4!5 |
| upper limb | - | 30!0 |
| Main | ⊕ − | 29!6 |

If the true horizon is not available such as the case when you are not near the water or when it is foggy, an artificial horizon may be used. They may be purchased inexpensively or easily put together by yourself. Fill a shallow pan with mercury, heavy oil or molasses or any liquid which is fairly viscous. Place it in a spot that is sheltered from the wind or cover it with a piece of quality plate glass. If there is a question as to whether the two sides of the glass are parallel, take two sights turning the glass 180° between the sights. Then average the two altitudes obtained. The object of the artificial horizon is to give a reflection of the celestial body off the liquid, seen through the horizon glass of your sextant. At the same time, you should observe the celestial body in the sky by means of the sextant mirrors. In the case of a planet or a star, the images are superimposed. With the Sun or Moon, the images may be superimposed or the lower limb of one image may sit tangent to the upper limb of the other image. It is considered a lower limb sight when the image in the horizon mirror is above the image in the horizon glass (or artificial horizon). For an upper limb sight, the situation is reversed.

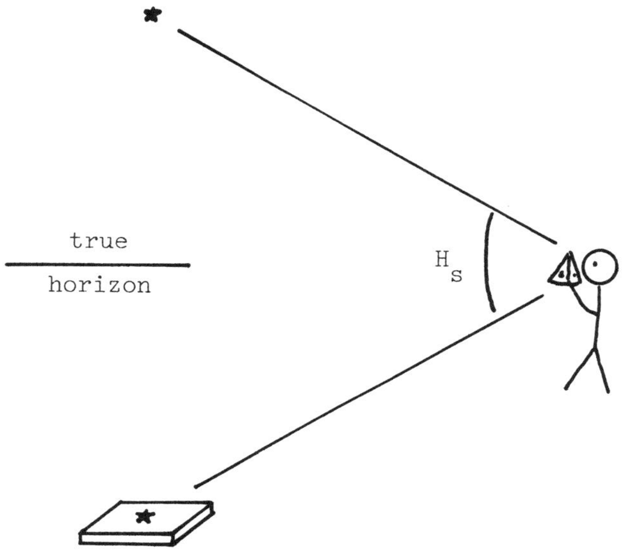


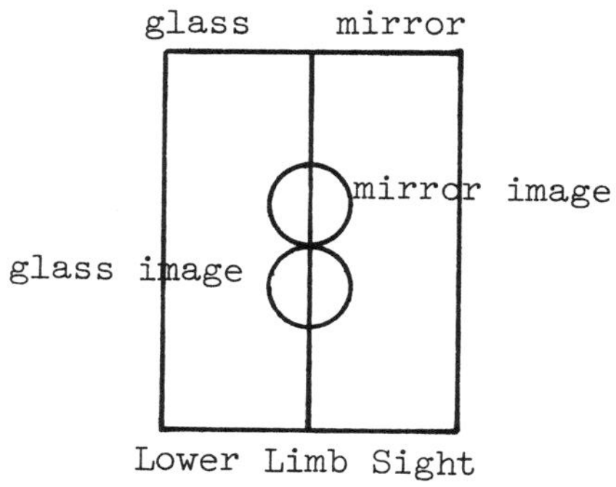


In correcting the altitude of an artificial horizon sight, first apply the index correction. There is no dip correction or temperature correction necessary. The sextant altitude with I.C. applied is then divided by two, after which the main correction is applied. The main correction is figured as for a normal sight except in the case when the Sun or Moon are superimposed upon themselves. Here, the center of the body has already been observed so there is no correction needed for semidiameter, phase or augmentation. For the Moon, there is still a parallax correction needed. The values for upper and lower limb corrections are averaged. Refraction correction is still necessary for the superimposed Sun and Moon sights, this refraction value taken from the star altitude correction table.

Therefore, for most artificial horizon sights, $H_o = \dfrac{H_s \pm I.C.}{2} \pm \text{main}$.

$H_o$ is the corrected sextant altitude.

**Example 1**
A Star, Jupiter or Saturn
Given:
$H_s$=19°47!5
I.C.=+6!5
Height of eye=6 feet

Height of eye 6 ft.

| | | |
|---|---|---|
| Body | Pollux | |
| $H_s$ | 19° | 47.5 |
| I.C. | | +6.5 |
| | 19° | 54.0 |
| Dip | | −2.4 |
| | ° | |
| Temp. Press. | | |
| App. Alt. | 19° | 51.6 |
| Main | | −2.7 |
| $H_o$ | 19° | 48.9 |

**STARS AN[D PLANETS]**

| App. Alt. | Corrn |
|---|---|
| ° ′ | ′ |
| 9 56 | |
| | −5·3 |
| 10 08 | |
| | −5·2 |
| 10 20 | |
| | −5·1 |
| 10 33 | |
| | −5·0 |
| 10 46 | |
| | −4·9 |
| 11 00 | |
| | −4·8 |
| 11 14 | |
| | −4·7 |
| 11 29 | |
| | −4·6 |
| 11 45 | |
| | −4·5 |
| 12 01 | |
| | −4·4 |
| 12 18 | |
| | −4·3 |
| 12 35 | |
| | −4·2 |
| 12 54 | |
| | −4·1 |
| 13 13 | |
| | −4·0 |
| 13 33 | |
| | −3·9 |
| 13 54 | |
| | −3·8 |
| 14 16 | |
| | −3·7 |
| 14 40 | |
| | −3·6 |
| 15 04 | |
| | −3·5 |
| 15 30 | |
| | −3·4 |
| 15 57 | |
| | −3·3 |
| 16 26 | |
| | −3·2 |
| 16 56 | |
| | −3·1 |
| 17 28 | |
| | −3·0 |
| 18 02 | |
| | −2·9 |
| 18 38 | |
| | −2·8 |
| 19 17 | |
| | −2·7 |
| 19 58 | |
| | −2·6 |
| 20 42 | |
| | −2·5 |
| 21 28 | |
| | −2·4 |

DIP

| | | |
|---|---|---|
| | −5·3 | |
| 9·2 | | 30·4 |
| | −5·4 | |
| 9·5 | | 31·5 |
| | −5·5 | |
| 9·9 | | 32·7 |
| | −5·6 | |
| 10·3 | | 33·9 |
| | −5·7 | |
| 10·6 | | 35·1 |
| | −5·8 | |
| 11·0 | | 36·3 |
| | −5·9 | |
| 11·4 | | 37·6 |
| | −6·0 | |
| 11·8 | | 38·9 |
| | −6·1 | |
| 12·2 | | 40·1 |
| | −6·2 | |
| 12·6 | | 41·5 |
| | −6·3 | |
| 13·0 | | 42·8 |
| | −6·4 | |
| 13·4 | | 44·2 |
| | −6·5 | |
| 13·8 | | 45·5 |
| | −6·6 | |
| 14·2 | | 46·9 |
| | −6·7 | |
| 14·7 | | 48·4 |
| | −6·8 | |
| 15·1 | | 49·8 |
| | −6·9 | |
| 15·5 | | 51·3 |
| | −7·0 | |
| 16·0 | | 52·8 |
| | −7·1 | |
| 16·5 | | 54·3 |
| | −7·2 | |
| 16·9 | | 55·8 |
| | −7·3 | |
| 17·4 | | 57·4 |
| | −7·4 | |
| 17·9 | | 58·9 |
| | −7·5 | |
| 18·4 | | 60·5 |
| | −7·6 | |
| 18·8 | | 62·1 |
| | −7·7 | |
| 19·3 | | 63·8 |
| | −7·8 | |
| 19·8 | | 65·4 |
| | −7·9 | |
| 20·4 | | 67·1 |
| | −8·0 | |
| 20·9 | | 68·8 |
| | −8·1 | |
| 21·4 | | 70·5 |

| ft. | ′ |
|---|---|
| 2 | −1·4 |
| 4 | −1·9 |
| 6 | −2·4 |
| 8 | −2·7 |
| 10 | −3·1 |
| See table ← | |
| ft. | ′ |
| 70 | −8·1 |
| 75 | −8·4 |
| 80 | −8·7 |
| 85 | −8·9 |
| 90 | −9·2 |
| 95 | −9·5 |
| 100 | −9·7 |
| 105 | −9·9 |
| 110 | −10·2 |
| 115 | −10·4 |
| 120 | −10·6 |
| 125 | −10·8 |
| 130 | −11·1 |
| 135 | −11·3 |
| 140 | −11·5 |
| 145 | −11·7 |
| 150 | −11·9 |
| 155 | −12·1 |

**Example 2**
Venus or Mars
Given:
$H_s$=25°17!5
I.C.=−4!0
Height of eye=25 feet
25 May 1976

Height of eye 25 ft.

| | | |
|---|---|---|
| Body | Venus | |
| $H_s$ | 25° | 17.5 |
| I.C. | | −4.0 |
| | 25° | 13.5 |
| Dip | | −4.9 |
| | ° | |
| Temp. Press. | | |
| App. Alt. | 25° | 08.6 |
| Main | +0.1 −2.1 | −2.0 |
| $H_o$ | 25° | 06.6 |

**DIP**

| Ht. of Eye | Corrn | Ht. of Eye |
|---|---|---|
| m | ′ | ft. |
| 2·4 | | 8·0 |
| | −2·8 | |
| 2·6 | | 8·6 |
| | −2·9 | |
| 2·8 | | 9·2 |
| | −3·0 | |
| 3·0 | | 9·8 |
| | −3·1 | |
| 3·2 | | 10·5 |
| | −3·2 | |
| 3·4 | | 11·2 |
| | −3·3 | |
| 3·6 | | 11·9 |
| | −3·4 | |
| 3·8 | | 12·6 |
| | −3·5 | |
| 4·0 | | 13·3 |
| | −3·6 | |
| 4·3 | | 14·1 |
| | −3·7 | |
| 4·5 | | 14·9 |
| | −3·8 | |
| 4·7 | | 15·7 |
| | −3·9 | |
| 5·0 | | 16·5 |
| | −4·0 | |
| 5·2 | | 17·4 |
| | −4·1 | |
| 5·5 | | 18·3 |
| | −4·2 | |
| 5·8 | | 19·1 |
| | −4·3 | |
| 6·1 | | 20·1 |
| | −4·4 | |
| 6·3 | | 21·0 |
| | −4·5 | |
| 6·6 | | 22·0 |
| | −4·6 | |
| 6·9 | | 22·9 |
| | −4·7 | |
| 7·2 | | 23·9 |
| | −4·8 | |
| 7·5 | | 24·9 |
| | −4·9 | |
| 7·9 | | 26·0 |
| | −5·0 | |
| 8·2 | | 27·1 |
| | −5·1 | |
| 8·5 | | 28·1 |

| Ht. of Eye | Corrn |
|---|---|
| m | ′ |
| 1·0 | −1·8 |
| 1·5 | −2·2 |
| 2·0 | −2·5 |
| 2·5 | −2·8 |
| 3·0 | −3·0 |
| See table ← | |
| m | ′ |
| 20 | −7·9 |
| 22 | −8·3 |
| 24 | −8·6 |
| 26 | −9·0 |
| 28 | −9·3 |
| 30 | −9·6 |
| 32 | −10·0 |
| 34 | −10·3 |
| 36 | −10·6 |
| 38 | −10·8 |
| 40 | −11·1 |
| 42 | −11·4 |
| 44 | −11·7 |
| 46 | −11·9 |

**[AN]D PLANETS**

| App. Alt. | Additional Corrn |
|---|---|
| **1976** | |
| **VENUS** | |
| Jan. 1—Dec. 12 | |
| 0° | +0′·1 |
| 42 | |
| Dec. 13—Dec. 31 | |
| 0° | +0′·2 |
| 47 | |
| **MARS** | |
| Jan. 1—Feb. 19 | |
| 0° | +0′·2 |
| 41 | +0·1 |
| 75 | |
| Feb. 20—Dec. 31 | |
| 0° | +0′·1 |
| 60 | |

MAIN

| | |
|---|---|
| 22 19 | |
| | −2·3 |
| 23 13 | |
| | −2·2 |
| 24 11 | |
| | −2·1 |
| 25 14 | |
| | −2·0 |
| 26 22 | |
| | −1·9 |
| 27 36 | |
| | −1·8 |
| 28 56 | |
| | −1·7 |
| 30 24 | |
| | −1·6 |
| 32 00 | |
| | −1·5 |
| 33 45 | |
| | −1·4 |
| 35 40 | |
| | −1·3 |
| 37 48 | |
| | −1·2 |
| 40 08 | |
| | −1·1 |
| 42 44 | |
| | −1·0 |
| 45 36 | |
| | −0·9 |
| 48 47 | |
| | −0·8 |
| 52 18 | |
| | −0·7 |
| 56 11 | |
| | −0·6 |
| 60 28 | |
| | −0·5 |
| 65 08 | |
| | −0·4 |
| 70 11 | |
| | −0·3 |
| 75 34 | |
| | −0·2 |
| 81 13 | |
| | −0·1 |
| 87 03 | |
| | 0·0 |
| 90 00 | |

Example 3 - Sun lower limb
Given: $H_s$ = 37° 26!5, I.C. = -1!5
Height of eye = 18 feet
1 December 1976

| DIP | | | | |
|---|---|---|---|---|
| Ht. of Eye | Corr^n | Ht. of Eye | Ht. of Eye | Corr^n |
| m | ′ | ft. | m | ′ |
| 2·4 | | 8·0 | 1·0 — | 1·8 |
| | −2·8 | | | |
| 2·6 | | 8·6 | 1·5 — | 2·2 |
| | −2·9 | | | |
| 2·8 | | 9·2 | 2·0 — | 2·5 |
| | −3·0 | | | |
| 3·0 | | 9·8 | 2·5 — | 2·8 |
| | −3·1 | | | |
| 3·2 | | 10·5 | 3·0 — | 3·0 |
| | −3·2 | | | |
| 3·4 | | 11·2 | See table | |
| | −3·3 | | | |
| 3·6 | | 11·9 | ← | |
| | −3·4 | | | |
| 3·8 | | 12·6 | m | ′ |
| | −3·5 | | | |
| 4·0 | | 13·3 | | |
| | −3·6 | | 20 — | 7·9 |
| 4·3 | | 14·1 | | |
| | −3·7 | | 22 — | 8·3 |
| 4·5 | | 14·9 | | |
| | −3·8 | | 24 — | 8·6 |
| 4·7 | | 15·7 | | |
| | −3·9 | | 26 — | 9·0 |
| 5·0 | | 16·5 | | |
| | −4·0 | | 28 — | 9·3 |
| 5·2 | | 17·4 | | |
| | −4·1 | | | |
| 5·5 | | 18·3 | | |
| | −4·2 | | 30 — | 9·6 |
| 5·8 | | 19·1 | | |
| | −4·3 | | 32 — | 10·0 |
| 6·1 | | 20·1 | | |
| | −4·4 | | 34 — | 10·3 |
| 6·3 | | 21·0 | | |
| | −4·5 | | 36 — | 10·6 |
| 6·6 | | 22·0 | | |
| | −4·6 | | 38 — | 10·8 |
| 6·9 | | 22·9 | | |
| | −4·7 | | | |
| 7·2 | | 23·9 | | |
| | −4·8 | | | |

| OCT.—MAR. SU | | |
|---|---|---|
| App. Alt. | Lower Limb | Upper Limb |
| ° ′ | ′ | ′ |
| 9 34 | | |
| | +10·8 | −21·5 |
| 9 45 | | |
| | +10·9 | −21·4 |
| 9 56 | | |
| | +11·0 | −21·3 |
| 10 08 | | |
| | +11·1 | −21·2 |
| 10 21 | | |
| | +11·2 | −21·1 |
| 10 34 | | |
| | +11·3 | −21·0 |
| ... | | |
| | +14·8 | −17·5 |
| 34 17 | | |
| | +14·9 | −17·4 |
| 36 20 | | |
| | +15·0 | −17·3 |
| 38 36 | | |
| | +15·1 | −17·2 |
| 41 08 | | |
| | +15·2 | −17·1 |
| 43 59 | | |
| | +15·3 | −17·0 |
| 47 10 | | |
| | +15·4 | −16·9 |
| 50 46 | | |
| | +15·5 | −16·8 |
| 54 49 | | |
| | +15·6 | −16·7 |
| 59 23 | | |
| | +15·7 | −16·6 |
| 64 30 | | |
| | +15·8 | −16·5 |
| 70 12 | | |
| | +15·9 | −16·4 |
| 76 26 | | |
| | +16·0 | −16·3 |
| 83 05 | | |
| | +16·1 | −16·2 |
| 90 00 | | |

Height of eye 18 ft.

| | | |
|---|---|---|
| Body | Sun LL | |
| $H_s$ | 37° | 26!5 |
| I.C. | | −1.5 |
| | 37° | 25!0 |
| Dip | | −4.1 |
| | ° | |
| Temp. | | |
| Press. | | |
| App. Alt. | 37° | 20!9 |
| Main | | +15.0 |
| $H_o$ | 37° | 35.9 |

Example 4 - Sun upper limb
Given: $H_s$ = 69° 59!0, I.C. = +2!0
Height of eye = 22 feet
13 May 1976

DIP -
see above

| JN APR.—SEPT. | | |
|---|---|---|
| App. Alt. | Lower Limb | Upper Limb |
| ° ′ | ′ | ′ |
| 9 39 | | |
| | +10·6 | −21·2 |
| 9 51 | | |
| | +10·7 | −21·1 |
| 10 03 | | |
| | +10·8 | −21·0 |
| 10 15 | | |
| | +10·9 | −20·9 |
| 10 27 | | |
| | +11·0 | −20·8 |
| 10 40 | | |
| | +11·1 | −20·7 |
| ... | | |
| | +15·0 | −16·8 |
| 45 31 | | |
| | +15·1 | −16·7 |
| 48 55 | | |
| | +15·2 | −16·6 |
| 52 44 | | |
| | +15·3 | −16·5 |
| 57 02 | | |
| | +15·4 | −16·4 |
| 61 51 | | |
| | +15·5 | −16·3 |
| 67 17 | | |
| | +15·6 | −16·2 |
| 73 16 | | |
| | +15·7 | −16·1 |
| 79 43 | | |
| | +15·8 | −16·0 |
| 86 32 | | |
| | +15·9 | −15·9 |
| 90 00 | | |

Height of eye 22 ft.

| | | |
|---|---|---|
| Body | Sun UL | |
| $H_s$ | 69° | 59!0 |
| I.C. | | +2.0 |
| | 69° | 61!0 |
| Dip | | −4.5 |
| | ° | |
| Temp. | | |
| Press. | | |
| App. Alt. | 69° | 56!5 |
| Main | | −16.2 |
| $H_o$ | 69° | 40.3 |

Example 5 - low altitude star or planet

Given: $H_s$ = 4° 55!0, I.C. = +2!0

Height of eye = 17 feet

Temperature = 90°F, Pressure + 29.50"

| App. Alt. | OCT.–MAR. SUN Lower Limb | OCT.–MAR. SUN Upper Limb | APR.–SEPT. SUN Lower Limb | APR.–SEPT. SUN Upper Limb | STARS PLANETS |
|---|---|---|---|---|---|
| ° ′ | ′ | ′ | ′ | ′ | ′ |
| 3 30 | + 3·3 | −29·0 | + 3·1 | −28·7 | −13·0 |
| 35 | 3·6 | 28·7 | 3·3 | 28·5 | 12·7 |
| 40 | 3·8 | 28·5 | 3·5 | 28·3 | 12·5 |
| 45 | 4·0 | 28·3 | 3·7 | 28·1 | 12·3 |
| 50 | 4·2 | 28·1 | 3·9 | 27·9 | 12·1 |
| 3 55 | 4·4 | 27·9 | 4·1 | 27·7 | 11·9 |
| 4 00 | + 4·5 | −27·8 | + 4·3 | −27·5 | −11·8 |
| 05 | 4·7 | 27·6 | 4·5 | 27·3 | 11·6 |
| 10 | 4·9 | 27·4 | 4·6 | 27·2 | 11·4 |
| 15 | 5·1 | 27·2 | 4·8 | 27·0 | 11·2 |
| 20 | 5·2 | 27·1 | 5·0 | 26·8 | 11·1 |
| 25 | 5·4 | 26·9 | 5·1 | 26·7 | 10·9 |
| 4 30 | + 5·6 | −26·7 | + 5·3 | −26·5 | −10·7 |
| 35 | 5·7 | 26·6 | 5·5 | 26·3 | 10·6 |
| 40 | 5·9 | 26·4 | 5·6 | 26·2 | 10·4 |
| 45 | 6·0 | 26·3 | 5·8 | 26·0 | 10·3 |
| 50 | 6·2 | 26·1 | 5·9 | 25·9 | 10·1 |
| 4 55 | 6·3 | 26·0 | 6·0 | 25·8 | 10·0 |
| 5 00 | + 6·4 | −25·9 | + 6·2 | −25·6 | − 9·9 |
| 05 | 6·6 | 25·7 | 6·3 | 25·5 | 9·7 |

Height of eye 17 ft.

| | | |
|---|---|---|
| Body | Antares | |
| $H_s$ | 4° | 55.0 |
| I.C. | | +2.0 |
| | 4° | 57.0 |
| Dip | | −4.0 |
| | 4° | 53.0 |
| Temp. + 90°F Press. 29.50 | | +1.0 |
| App. Alt. | 4° | 54.0 |
| Main | | −10.0 |
| $H_o$ | 4° | 44.0 |

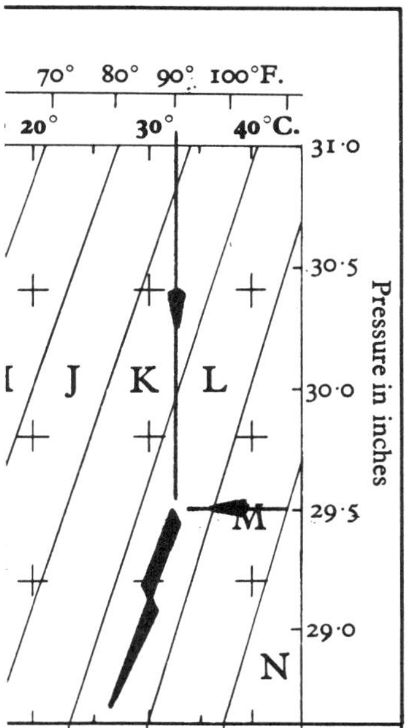


| K | L | M | N | App. Alt. |
|---|---|---|---|---|
| ′ | ′ | ′ | ′ | ° ′ |
| +3·4 | +4·6 | +5·7 | +6·9 | 0 00 |
| 2·6 | 3·5 | 4·4 | 5·2 | 0 30 |
| 2·1 | 2·8 | 3·5 | 4·3 | 1 00 |
| 1·8 | 2·4 | 2·9 | 3·5 | 1 30 |
| 1·5 | 2·0 | 2·5 | 3·0 | 2 00 |
| +1·2 | +1·6 | +2·1 | +2·5 | 2 30 |
| 1·1 | 1·5 | 1·8 | 2·2 | 3 00 |
| 1·0 | 1·3 | 1·6 | 2·0 | 3 30 |
| 0·9 | 1·2 | 1·5 | 1·8 | 4 00 |
| 0·8 | 1·1 | 1·4 | 1·6 | 4 30 |
| +0·8 | +1·0 | +1·3 | +1·5 | 5 00 |
| 0·6 | 0·9 | 1·1 | 1·3 | 6 |

Example 6 - dip short sight, low altitude sun

Given: $H_s$ = 8° 12!6, I.C. = 0!0

Height of eye = 14.0 feet

Distance to horizon = 1.1 n.m.

10 July 1976

Temperature and Pressure standard

Height of eye 14 ft.

**TABLE 22**

**Dip of the Sea Short of the Horizon**

| Distance | 5 | 10 | 14 | 15 | 20 | 25 |
|---|---|---|---|---|---|---|
| *Miles* | ′ | ′ | | ′ | ′ | ′ |
| 0.1 | 28.3 | 56.6 | | 84.9 | 113.2 | 141.5 |
| 0.2 | 14.2 | 28.4 | | 42.5 | 56.7 | 70.8 |
| 0.3 | 9.6 | 19.0 | | 28.4 | 37.8 | 47.3 |
| 0.4 | 7.2 | 14.3 | | 21.4 | 28.5 | 35.5 |
| 0.5 | 5.9 | 11.5 | | 17.2 | 22.8 | 28.5 |
| 0.6 | 5.0 | 9.7 | | 14.4 | 19.1 | 23.8 |
| 0.7 | 4.3 | 8.4 | | 12.4 | 16.5 | 20.5 |
| 0.8 | 3.9 | 7.4 | | 10.9 | 14.5 | 18.0 |
| 0.9 | 3.5 | 6.7 | | 9.8 | 12.9 | 16.1 |
| 1.0 | 3.2 | 6.1 | | 8.9 | 11.7 | 14.6 |
| 1.1 | 3.0 | 5.6 | 7.7 | 8.2 | 10.7 | 13.3 |
| 1.2 | 2.9 | 5.2 | | 7.6 | 9.9 | 12.3 |
| 1.3 | 2.7 | 4.9 | | 7.1 | 9.2 | 11.4 |
| 1.4 | 2.6 | 4.6 | | 6.6 | 8.7 | 10.7 |
| 1.5 | 2.5 | 4.4 | | 6.3 | 8.2 | 10.0 |

Height of eye above the sea, in feet

8.2
−5.6
2.6 x 4/5 = 2.1

5.6 + 2.1 = 7.7

| | | |
|---|---|---|
| Body | Sun LL | |
| $H_s$ | 8° | 12.6 |
| I.C. | | 0.0 |
| | 8° | 12.6 |
| Dip | | −7.7 |
| | ° | |
| Temp. Press. | | |
| App. Alt. | 8° | 04.9 |
| Main | | +9.5 |
| $H_o$ | 8° | 14.4 |

Example 7 - Moon lower limb

Given: $H_s$ = 29° 19!8, I.C. = +2!5

Height of eye = 13 feet

8 January 1976, 0900 GMT

1976 JANUARY 7, 8,

| G.M.T. d h | SUN G.H.A. | SUN Dec. | MOON G.H.A. | MOON v | MOON Dec. | MOON d | MOON H.P. |
|---|---|---|---|---|---|---|---|
| | ° ′ | ° ′ | ° ′ | ′ | ° ′ | ′ | ′ |
| 8 00 | 178 26.3 | S22 22.9 | 107 56.5 | 15.6 | N 3 42.2 | 10.2 | 54.3 |
| 01 | 193 26.0 | 22.5 | 122 31.1 | 15.6 | 3 52.4 | 10.2 | 54.3 |
| 02 | 208 25.8 | 22.2 | 137 05.7 | 15.5 | 4 02.6 | 10.1 | 54.3 |
| 03 | 223 25.5 | ·· 21.9 | 151 40.2 | 15.6 | 4 12.7 | 10.2 | 54.2 |
| 04 | 238 25.2 | 21.6 | 166 14.8 | 15.6 | 4 22.9 | 10.1 | 54.2 |
| 05 | 253 25.0 | 21.3 | 180 49.4 | 15.6 | 4 33.0 | 10.2 | 54.2 |
| 06 | 268 24.7 | S22 20.9 | 195 24.0 | 15.5 | N 4 43.2 | 10.1 | 54.2 |
| 07 | 283 24.4 | 20.6 | 209 58.5 | 15.6 | 4 53.3 | 10.0 | 54.2 |
| T 08 | 298 24.2 | 20.3 | 224 33.1 | 15.5 | 5 03.3 | 10.1 | 54.2 |
| H 09 | 313 23.9 | ·· 20.0 | 239 07.6 | 15.5 | 5 13.4 | 10.0 | 54.2 |
| U 10 | 328 23.6 | 19.6 | 253 42.1 | 15.5 | 5 23.4 | 10.0 | 54.2 |
| R 11 | 343 23.4 | 19.3 | 268 16.6 | 15.5 | 5 33.4 | 10.0 | 54.2 |
| S 12 | 358 23.1 | S22 19.0 | 282 51.1 | 15.5 | N 5 43.4 | 10.0 | 54.2 |
| D 13 | 13 22.8 | 18.7 | 297 25.6 | 15.5 | 5 53.4 | 9.9 | 54.2 |
| A 14 | 28 22.5 | 18.3 | 312 00.1 | 15.5 | 6 03.3 | 10.0 | 54.2 |
| Y 15 | 43 22.3 | ·· 18.0 | 326 34.6 | 15.4 | 6 13.3 | 9.9 | 54.2 |
| 16 | 58 22.0 | 17.7 | 341 09.0 | 15.4 | 6 23.2 | 9.8 | 54.2 |
| 17 | 73 21.7 | 17.3 | 355 43.4 | 15.4 | 6 33.0 | 9.9 | 54.2 |
| 18 | 88 21.5 | S22 17.0 | 10 17.8 | 15.4 | N 6 42.9 | 9.8 | 54.2 |
| 19 | 103 21.2 | 16.7 | 24 52.2 | 15.4 | 6 52.7 | 9.8 | 54.2 |
| 20 | 118 21.0 | 16.4 | 39 26.6 | 15.3 | 7 02.5 | 9.7 | 54.2 |
| 21 | 133 20.7 | ·· 16.0 | 54 00.9 | 15.3 | 7 12.2 | 9.7 | 54.2 |
| 22 | 148 20.4 | 15.7 | 68 35.2 | 15.3 | 7 21.9 | 9.7 | 54.2 |
| 23 | 163 20.2 | 15.4 | 83 09.5 | 15.3 | 7 31.6 | 9.7 | 54.2 |

| 20°–24° Corrⁿ | 25°–29° Corrⁿ | 30°–34° Corrⁿ | App. Alt. |
|---|---|---|---|
| 20° 62′.2 | 25° 60′.8 | 30° 58′.9 | 00′ |
| 62·1 | 60·8 | 58·8 | 10 |
| 62·1 | 60·7 | 58·8 | 20 |
| 62·1 | 60·7 | 58·7 | 30 |
| 61·3 | 59·5 | 57·2 | 40 |
| 61·2 | 59·4 | 57·1 | 50 |
| 24 61·2 | 29 59·3 | 34 57·0 | 00 |
| 61·1 | 59·3 | 56·9 | 10 |
| 61·1 | 59·2 | 56·9 | 20 |
| 61·0 | 59·1 | 56·8 | 30 |
| 60·9 | 59·1 | 56·7 | 40 |
| 60·9 | 59·0 | 56·6 | 50 |
| L U | L U | L U | H.P. |
| 0·6 1·2 | 0·7 1·3 | 0·9 1·5 | 54·0 |
| 0·9 1·4 | 1·1 1·5 | 1·2 1·7 | 54·3 |
| 1·3 1·6 | 1·4 1·7 | 1·5 1·8 | 54·6 |
| 1·6 1·8 | 1·8 1·9 | 1·9 2·0 | 54·9 |
| 2·0 2·0 | 2·1 2·1 | 2·2 2·2 | 55·2 |
| 2·4 2·2 | 2·4 2·3 | 2·5 2·4 | 55·5 |
| 2·7 2·4 | 2·8 2·4 | 2·9 2·5 | 55·8 |
| 3·1 2·6 | 3·1 2·6 | 3·2 2·7 | 56·1 |
| 3·4 2·8 | 3·5 2·8 | 3·5 2·9 | 56·4 |
| 3·8 3·0 | 3·8 3·0 | 3·9 3·0 | 56·7 |

| | | |
|---|---|---|
| Body | Moon LL | |
| $H_s$ | 29° | 19'.8 |
| I.C. | | +2'.5 |
| | 29° | 22'.3 |
| Dip | | −3'.5 |
| | ° | ' |
| Temp. | | ' |
| Press. | | . |
| App. Alt. | 29° | 18'.8 |
| Main | | +60'.2 |
| $H_o$ | 30° | 19'.0 |

| | | |
|---|---|---|
| H.P. | 54!2 | Moon |
| Corr | + | 59!2 |
| Corr | + | 1!0 |
| upper limb | − | 30!0 |
| Main | ± | 60!2 |

Example 8 - Moon upper limb

Given: $H_s$ = 41° 56!5, I.C. = -3!0

Height of eye = 20 feet

9 January 1976, 1300 GMT

| G.M.T. d h | SUN G.H.A. | SUN Dec. | MOON G.H.A. | MOON v | MOON Dec. | MOON d | MOON H.P. |
|---|---|---|---|---|---|---|---|
| 9 00 | 178 19.9 | S22 15.0 | 97 43.8 | 15.3 | N 7 41.3 | 9.7 | 54.2 |
| 01 | 193 19.6 | 14.7 | 112 18.1 | 15.2 | 7 51.0 | 9.6 | 54.2 |
| 02 | 208 19.4 | 14.3 | 126 52.3 | 15.2 | 8 00.6 | 9.5 | 54.2 |
| 03 | 223 19.1 | ·· 14.0 | 141 26.5 | 15.2 | 8 10.1 | 9.6 | 54.2 |
| 04 | 238 18.8 | 13.7 | 156 00.7 | 15.2 | 8 19.7 | 9.5 | 54.2 |
| 05 | 253 18.6 | 13.3 | 170 34.9 | 15.1 | 8 29.2 | 9.5 | 54.2 |
| 06 | 268 18.3 | S22 13.0 | 185 09.0 | 15.1 | N 8 38.7 | 9.4 | 54.2 |
| 07 | 283 18.0 | 12.6 | 199 43.1 | 15.1 | 8 48.1 | 9.5 | 54.3 |
| 08 | 298 17.8 | 12.3 | 214 17.2 | 15.0 | 8 57.6 | 9.3 | 54.3 |
| F 09 | 313 17.5 | ·· 12.0 | 228 51.2 | 15.0 | 9 06.9 | 9.4 | 54.3 |
| R 10 | 328 17.3 | 11.6 | 243 25.2 | 15.0 | 9 16.3 | 9.3 | 54.3 |
| I 11 | 343 17.0 | 11.3 | 257 59.2 | 15.0 | 9 25.6 | 9.3 | 54.3 |
| D 12 | 358 16.7 | S22 10.9 | 272 33.2 | 14.9 | N 9 34.9 | 9.2 | 54.3 |
| A 13 | 13 16.5 | 10.6 | 287 07.1 | 14.9 | 9 44.1 | 9.2 | 54.3 |
| Y 14 | 28 16.2 | 10.2 | 301 41.0 | 14.8 | 9 53.3 | 9.2 | 54.3 |
| 15 | 43 15.9 | ·· 09.9 | 316 14.8 | 14.9 | 10 02.5 | 9.1 | 54.3 |
| 16 | 58 15.7 | 09.6 | 330 48.7 | 14.7 | 10 11.6 | 9.1 | 54.3 |
| 17 | 73 15.4 | 09.2 | 345 22.4 | 14.8 | 10 20.7 | 9.0 | 54.3 |
| 18 | 88 15.2 | S22 08.9 | 359 56.2 | 14.7 | N10 29.7 | 9.0 | 54.3 |
| 19 | 103 14.9 | 08.5 | 14 29.9 | 14.7 | 10 38.7 | 9.0 | 54.3 |
| 20 | 118 14.6 | 08.2 | 29 03.6 | 14.6 | 10 47.7 | 8.9 | 54.3 |
| 21 | 133 14.4 | ·· 07.8 | 43 37.2 | 14.6 | 10 56.6 | 8.9 | 54.3 |
| 22 | 148 14.1 | 07.5 | 58 10.8 | 14.6 | 11 05.5 | 8.8 | 54.4 |
| 23 | 163 13.9 | 07.1 | 72 44.4 | 14.5 | 11 14.3 | 8.8 | 54.4 |
| | S.D. 16.3 | d 0.3 | S.D. 14.8 | | 14.8 | | 14.8 |

| App. Alt. | 35°–39° Corrⁿ | 40°–44° Corrⁿ |
|---|---|---|
| 00′ | 35° 56′.5 | 40° 53′.7 |
| 10 | 56·4 | 53·6 |
| 20 | 56·3 | 53·5 |
| 30 | 56·2 | 53·4 |
| 40 | 56·2 | 53·3 |
| 50 | 56·1 | 53·2 |
| 00 | 36 56·0 | 41 53·1 |
| 10 | 55·9 | 53·0 |
| 20 | 55·8 | 52·8 |
| 30 | 55·7 | 52·7 |
| 40 | 55·6 | 52·6 |
| 50 | 55·5 | 52·5 |
| 40 | 53·9 | 50·7 |
| 50 | 53·8 | 50·6 |
| H.P. | L U | L U |
| 54·0 | 1·1 1·7 | 1·3 1·9 |
| 54·3 | 1·4 1·8 | 1·6 2·0 |
| 54·6 | 1·7 2·0 | 1·9 2·2 |
| 54·9 | 2·0 2·2 | 2·2 2·3 |
| 55·2 | 2·3 2·3 | 2·5 2·4 |
| 55·5 | 2·7 2·5 | 2·8 2·6 |
| 55·8 | 3·0 2·6 | 3·1 2·7 |
| 56·1 | 3·3 2·8 | 3·4 2·9 |
| 56·4 | 3·6 2·9 | 3·7 3·0 |
| 56·7 | 3·9 3·1 | 4·0 3·1 |

| | | |
|---|---|---|
| Body | Moon UL | |
| $H_s$ | 41° | 56'.5 |
| I.C. | | −3'.0 |
| | 41° | 53'.5 |
| Dip | | −4'.3 |
| | ° | ' |
| Temp. | | ' |
| Press. | | . |
| App. Alt. | 41° | 49'.2 |
| Main | | +24'.5 |
| $H_o$ | 42° | 13'.7 |

| | | |
|---|---|---|
| H.P. | 54!3 | Moon |
| Corr | + | 52!5 |
| Corr | + | 2!0 |
| upper limb | − | 30!0 ← |
| Main | ± | 24!5 |

## EXERCISE 2

Find $H_o$ in each of the following cases. Use data from the 1976 Nautical Almanac excerpts in Appendix 2 and assume that $H_s$ is measured from the sea horizon with a marine sextant.

| | Date, GMT | Ht. of Eye | Body | $H_s$ | I.C. | Temp. Press. |
|---|---|---|---|---|---|---|
| 1. | 4 April | 17 ft. | Sun UL | 48°59!0 | +1!0 | standard |
| 2. | ------------- | 35.1 ft. | Vega | 31°02!0 | +3!1 | standard |
| 3. | 8 April, 1900 | 24 ft. | Moon LL | 53°16!9 | -2!0 | standard |
| 4. | 16 March | 11 ft. | Venus | 27°11!5 | +4!3 | +20°F, 29.7 in. |
| 5. | ------------- | 12.6 ft. | Polaris | 42°30!0 | -3!1 | standard |
| 6. | 31 July | 6 ft. | Sun LL | 37°46!3 | -2!7 | standard |
| 7. | 7 June, 2036 | 10.1 ft. | Moon UL | 17°23!1 | +6!3 | standard |
| 8. | ------------- | 31 ft. | Alpheratz | 61°00!0 | 0 | standard |
| 9. | 1 Oct. | 17 ft. | Mars | 35°01!6 | -3!3 | standard |
| 10. | ------------- | 20.1 ft. | Saturn | 8°23!6 | -4!0 | +8°F, 30.7 in. |
| 11. | 11 Dec. | 30 ft. | Sun UL | 63°51!0 | +2!8 | standard |
| 12. | ------------- | 8.4 ft. | Jupiter | 42°52!8 | -6!0 | standard |
| 13. | ------------- | 7.2 ft. | Rigel | 9°10!6 | 0 | +40°C, 1040 mb |
| 14. | 18 Oct., 0700 | 13.8 ft. | Moon UL | 71°47!9 | +3!9 | standard |
| 15. | 16 Feb. | 2 ft. | Sun LL | 7°58!2 | +4!8 | -25°C, 980 mb |
| 16. | ------------- | 57.3 ft. | Betelgeuse | 47°09!8 | -2!9 | standard |
| 17. | 30 Dec. | 85 ft. | Venus | 12°25!8 | +1!1 | standard |
| 18. | 3 Sept., 1411 | 0 ft. | Moon LL | 26°16!2 | 0 | standard |

# Chapter 5

# Time

The sextant and an accurate timepiece are the only two major instruments needed by the celestial navigator. In 1735, Englishman John Harrison developed the first chronometer that could be taken on board ship amidst the temperature changes and motion and yet tell extremely accurate time. By the end of the eighteenth century, such instruments were being constructed with more reasonable size, weight and price. By the early twentieth century, time ball signals activated by telegraph and low power audible signals in major ports enabled the navigator to check the accuracy of his chronometer.

Now, accurate and inexpensive quartz chronometers as well as short wave radio time signals make the establishment of time an easy task. One such time signal, CHU, broadcast from Ottawa, Canada on frequencies of 3.33, 7.335 and 14.67 MHz, gives Eastern Standard Time. Beeps mark the 1st through 29th, 31st through 50th seconds of each minute. The 51st through 59th seconds are filled with a voice announcement of the time, both in English and in French. The beep immediately after the voice announcement marks the beginning of the minute just announced. The only exception to this procedure is during the first minute of each hour when the 1st to 10th second beeps are omitted.

WWV broadcasts from Boulder, Colorado on 2.5, 5.0, 10.0, 15.0 and 20.0 MHz and gives Universal Coordinated Time. UTC is derived from a cesium frequency standard and differs from Greenwich Mean Time by no more than $\pm 0^{s}.7$. The seconds are marked by "clucks" except for the 29th and 59th seconds being silent. Time is announced every minute in English only. WWV can also be used for storm information. Warnings for the Western North Atlantic occur during the 8th and 9th minute of each hour, warnings for the Eastern North Pacific occur during the 10th minute of each hour.

Time and longitude are directly related. Without time, longitude by normal methods cannot be established correctly. Considering the earth to be encircled by 360° of longitude with a rotation of 24 hours of time, we find that one zone or hour of time corresponds to 15° of longitude; in other words, one hour of rotation of the earth corresponds to 15° angle of rotation of the earth. Reducing this even further, one second of time corresponds to one quarter of a minute of longitude, equal to one quarter of a mile (roughly) at the equator, less of a distance as latitude increases. An error of time, therefore, is realized in an error of longitude.

A system of time zones has been established worldwide, most zones being one hour or $15^\circ$ wide. In some cases the actual boundaries vary to coincide with state borders or island groupings. Everyone within the zone keeps the same time called zone time or ZT. The centers of each zone have longitudes evenly divisible by fifteen such as $0^\circ$, $15^\circ$, $30^\circ$, $45^\circ$, etc. The edges of the zones extend $7\frac{1}{2}^\circ$ to each side of the center. Therefore, the zone whose center is $60^\circ$ would include longitudes from $52\frac{1}{2}^\circ$ to $67\frac{1}{2}^\circ$.

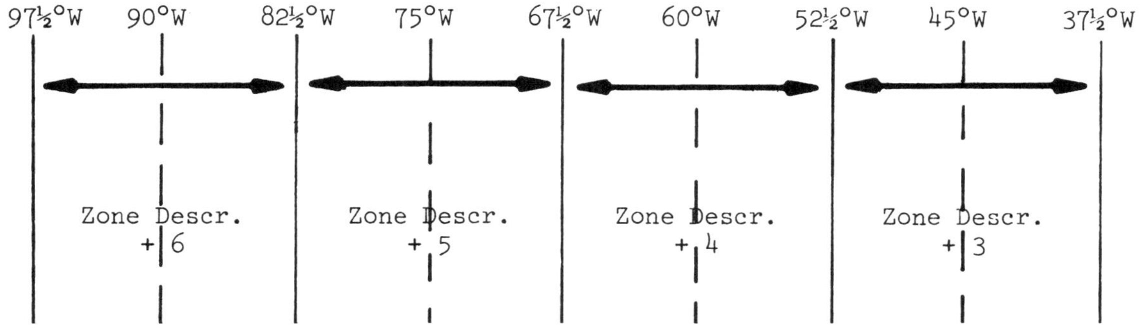


For purposes of celestial navigation, zone time must be converted to Greenwich Mean Time, time kept at the zone whose center is $0^\circ$ or the Prime Meridian. This is done by means of the Zone Description or ZD, a number obtained by dividing your longitude by 15 and rounding the answer off to the nearest whole number. If the longitude is west, the ZD is positive. If the longitude is east, the ZD is negative. For example, if your longitude were $50^\circ$ W, dividing by 15 would give 3 5/15. Rounding to the nearest whole number would give 3 as a ZD. It would be a +3 since longitude is west. This means that GMT is three hours later than your zone time. If your longitude were $129^\circ$ E, dividing by 15 would give 8 9/15. Rounding to the nearest whole number would give 9, a negative ZD since longitude is east. If addition or subtraction of the ZD to your ZT puts your GMT over $24^h$ or less than $00^h$, a date change must be made. For example, if zone time is 1500 on 3 April, ZD is +11; this makes a GMT of 0200 on 4 April. If ZT is 0400 on 7 November, ZD is -7; this makes a GMT of 2100 on 6 November. In the cases where daylight time is used instead of standard time, a negative one hour ($-1^h$) is applied to the ZD to get GMT. For example, if ZD were $8^h$ for standard time, it would be $+7^h$ for daylight time. If ZD were $-3^h$ for standard time, it would be $-4^h$ for daylight time.

Watch error or WE is the amount that your timekeeper varies from true zone time. For instance, if your chronometer is 10 seconds slow, the error should be added to the time indicated to give true zone time. A fast error should be subtracted from the chronometer reading to give true zone time. A chronometer doesn't necessarily have to tell the exact time. If its rate of loss or gain, say one second per day, is constant then the known error can be applied to get true zone time. In the absence of a chronometer, a stopwatch can be used that is set to a radio time signal. In this case, the time the stopwatch is started is added to the stopwatch reading at the time of sextant sight to obtain true zone time. The watch time or WT is the time read on your timepiece to the nearest second at the time your sextant sight is taken. For timing sextant observations, the simplest method, fraught with the least chance of reading error, is to use a digital watch which displays date and 24-hour time. Set it to Greenwich Mean Time (also called Universal Time).

The following examples show the method of correcting watch time to Greenwich Mean Time.

Given: Longitude = 142° 16!0 W
W.T. = $22^h\ 31^m\ 16^s$
W.E. = 10 seconds slow
Date = 25 June 1976

______ DR: Lat ____ ° ____ ' N/S  Lo 142° 16'.0 E/(W)
time

| | | | | | |
|---|---|---|---|---|---|
| W.T. | $22^h$ | $31^m$ | $16^s$ | Local Date | 25 June 1976 |
| W.E. | h | m | $10^s$ | (slow - add) / fast - sub | |
| Z.T. | $22^h$ | $31^m$ | $26^s$ | | |
| Z.D. | $+9^h$ | | | (W Lo +) / E Lo - | |
| GMT | $07^h$ | $31^m$ | $26^s$ | Grnch Date | 26 June 1976 |

$$15\overline{)142°16'}\ = 9,\quad 142°16' - 135 = 7°16'$$

Given: Longitude = 110° 01!6 E
W.T. = $18^h\ 41^m\ 03^s$
W.E. = 11 seconds fast
Date = 18 March 1976

______ DR: Lat ____ ° ____ ' N/S  Lo 110° 01'.6 (E)/W
time

| | | | | | |
|---|---|---|---|---|---|
| W.T. | $18^h$ | $41^m$ | $03^s$ | Local Date | 18 March 1976 |
| W.E. | h | m | $11^s$ | slow - add / (fast - sub) | |
| Z.T. | $18^h$ | $40^m$ | $52^s$ | | |
| Z.D. | $-7^h$ | | | W Lo + / (E Lo -) | |
| GMT | $11^h$ | $40^m$ | $52^s$ | Grnch Date | 18 March 1976 |

$$15\overline{)110}\ = 7,\quad 110 - 105 = 5$$

Given: Longitude = 39° 57!6 W
Stopwatch started at 04-37-47, zone time
Stopwatch reading = $14^m$ $16^s$
Date = 3 November 1976

____ DR: Lat ____ ° ____ ' . ____ N/S    Lo 39° 57'.6 E/(W)
time

| | | |
|---|---|---|
| Stopwatch Started ~~W.T.~~ | $04^h\ 37^m\ 47^s$ | Local Date 3 November 1976 |
| Stopwatch Reading ~~W.E.~~ | $14^m\ 16^s$ | slow - (add) / fast - sub |
| Z.T. | $04^h\ 52^m\ 03^s$ | |
| Z.D. | $+3^h$ | (W Lo +) / E Lo - |
| GMT | $07^h\ 52^m\ 03^s$ | Grnch Date 3 November 1976 |

$15\overline{)39}$ = $2\,\tfrac{9}{15} \rightarrow 3$
30
9

# Chapter 6

# Celestial Coordinates, the *Nautical Almanac*

In Chapter 2 we discussed finding the position of a celestial object, its latitude and longitude in the sky. The Nautical Almanac is used for this purpose, entering it with exact GMT of the sextant sight. However, to understand the meaning of the sky coordinates, we must first take a look at the celestial sphere.

Imagine a clear plastic balloon covering the earth's surface. On it we shall trace the equator, the poles and the Greenwich meridian. Now, if we expand this balloon until it imaginarily touches the sky, a view from inside this balloon shows these tracings against the sphere of stars. There is now a celestial equator directly above the earth's equator, a celestial north and south pole directly above the corresponding earth poles, and a celestial Greenwich meridian directly above the earth's prime meridian. A celestial body's coordinates can be defined exactly as ones on the earth except now we are using the expanded tracings. Sky coordinates are named differently. Sky latitude is called declination (Dec.) and is labeled north or south depending toward which pole the body is from the equator. Sky longitude is called Greenwich Hour Angle (GHA) and differs from earth longitude in that it is measured always westward from the Greenwich meridian, 0° to 360°. By establishing the GHA and Dec of a celestial body for a particular instant of time, we have found the corresponding latitude and longitude of the geographical position of that body. Since the Sun, Moon and planets change their GHA and Dec constantly as they seem to move through the sky, these coordinates are listed in the Nautical Almanac for each hour of each day of the year with additional corrections in the yellow pages in the back of the Almanac for each minute and second of the hour.

Listing the positions of these six bodies for each hour of the year is not a particularly space consuming process. Parts of two pages will cover a three day period as you can see by perusing the daily pages of the Nautical Almanac. However, there are fifty-seven navigational stars that may be easily observed during twilights and many more fainter stars which might also be picked up during this period. Therefore, to conserve space for these stars which in effect are stationary with respect to the celestial sphere, we can use another type of longitude called Sidereal Hour Angle (SHA). This is also an angular measurement along the equator but the starting point is not the

Greenwich meridian. Another arbitrary point has been chosen as the basis for SHA called the vernal equinox. Also called the first point of Aries, it is the position the Sun occupies on the first day of spring when the Sun changes from a southern declination to a northern one. At this transition point, the Sun is on the equator. The vernal equinox is designated by the sign for Aries, ♈. We can then establish a permanent longitude of stars with respect to the celestial sphere and are only left with the problem of relating this longitude to the Greenwich meridian which changes its position on the sphere as the earth rotates. To solve this problem, we need to find the GHA of the vernal equinox. Add to this the SHA of the star and you have the GHA of the star.

GHA ♈ + SHA star = GHA star

The following diagram may make this clearer.

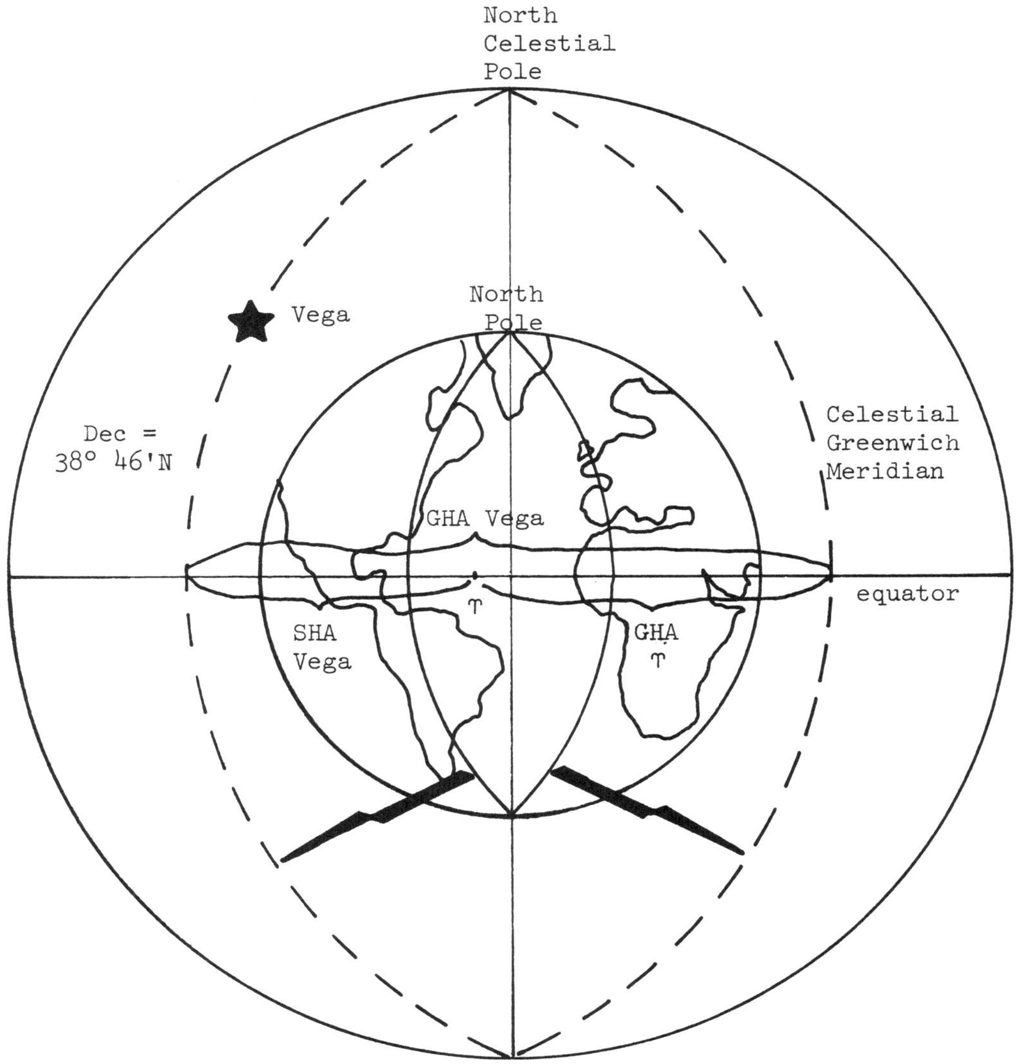

In the case where SHA star and GHA Aries add up to more than 360°, a whole circle or 360° is subtracted from the total to obtain the most reduced form of GHA star.

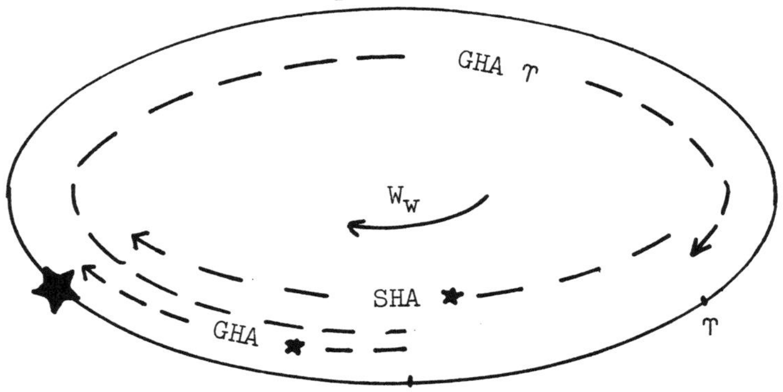


As a summary of the three celestial coordinates we will be using, let us refer to the table below.

| Coordinate | Measured From | Measured To | Direction Measured | Limits of Measurement |
|---|---|---|---|---|
| Declination | equator | body | north or south | 0° to 90° |
| Greenwich Hour Angle | Greenwich Meridian | body | westward | 0° to 360° |
| Sidereal Hour Angle | Vernal equinox | body | westward | 0° to 360° |

It may be easier to get a feel for the celestial coordinates if we could establish the position of the celestial equator in the sky. Above the horizon, it will run from the east point towards your meridian, crossing your meridian at an altitude of 90° minus your latitude. In other words, if your latitude is 42° N, the celestial equator will cross your meridian at 48° altitude. From this point, it runs on to the west point of the horizon.

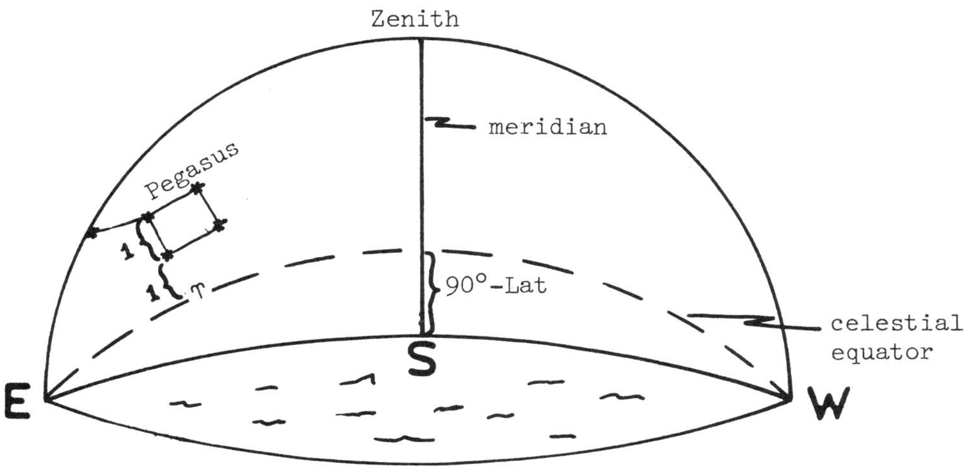


In southern latitudes, the celestial equator will cross the northern section of the meridian.

The vernal equinox can be roughly positioned on the equator by finding the constellation of Pegasus (if it is visible at the time you observe), taking the left side of the square as one unit of length and proceeding down from the lower left star in the square one more unit. The vernal equinox will be slightly to the right of where you arrived.

Our sight reduction forms are fairly self explanatory as to where to enter GHA, Dec, and SHA. We go into the Nautical Almanac with Greenwich time and date and pick out the value for the hour of GMT. In the case of a star, GHA is chosen out of the Aries column. At the bottom of the planets and Sun column and in separate columns of their own in the Moon section we find a small-type number designated "v" or "d" (the Sun has no "v" and the stars have no "v" or "d"). The "v" is an extra correction for additional longitude movement of the celestial body and the "d" is an extra correction for additional declination movement of the body. Planets, Sun and Moon move on their own in orbits around the Sun and earth and this change of position in the sky is accounted for in the "v" and "d" corrections. The "v" correction will always be positive except in the case of Venus where it may be negative. In this case, the "v" will be marked with a negative sign. The "d" correction can be either positive or negative depending on the trend of the declination. Look at the declination column of the body in question at the time in question and see if it is increasing or decreasing. This will establish the sign, increasing being positive, decreasing being negative. Note the examples on the following page from 18 August 1976 at 1300. The arrow indicates direction of decreasing declination.

1976 AUGUST 16, 17, 18 (MON., TUES., WED.)

| G.M.T. | ARIES | VENUS −3.3 | | MARS +1.9 | | JUPITER −2.0 | | SATURN +0.5 | | SUN | | MOON | | | | |
|---|---|---|---|---|---|---|---|---|---|---|---|---|---|---|---|---|
| | G.H.A. | G.H.A. | Dec. | G.H.A. | Dec. | G.H.A. | Dec. | G.H.A. | Dec. | G.H.A. | Dec. | G.H.A. | v | Dec. | d | H.P. |
| d h | ° ′ | ° ′ | ° ′ | ° ′ | ° ′ | ° ′ | ° ′ | ° ′ | ° ′ | ° ′ | ° ′ | ° ′ | ′ | ° ′ | ′ | ′ |
| 18 00 | 326 29.1 | 162 39.8 | N 8 25.4 | 149 51.3 | N 2 14.2 | 268 57.5 | N19 01.6 | 194 52.0 | N18 30.9 | 179 02.2 | N13 07.9 | 273 20.5 | 12.6 | N17 26.8 | 4.6 | 54.5 |
| 01 | 341 31.5 | 177 39.4 | 24.2 | 164 52.3 | 13.5 | 283 59.7 | 01.7 | 209 54.2 | 30.8 | 194 02.3 | 07.1 | 287 52.1 | 12.5 | 17 31.4 | 4.6 | 54.5 |
| 02 | 356 34.0 | 192 39.0 | 23.0 | 179 53.3 | 12.9 | 299 01.9 | 01.7 | 224 56.3 | 30.8 | 209 02.5 | 06.3 | 302 23.6 | 12.4 | 17 36.0 | 4.5 | 54.5 |
| 03 | 11 36.5 | 207 38.6 | ·· 21.8 | 194 54.3 | ·· 12.2 | 314 04.1 | ·· 01.8 | 239 58.5 | ·· 30.7 | 224 02.6 | ·· 05.5 | 316 55.0 | 12.4 | 17 40.5 | 4.4 | 54.5 |
| 04 | 26 38.9 | 222 38.2 | 20.6 | 209 55.3 | 11.6 | 329 06.3 | 01.8 | 255 00.6 | 30.6 | 239 02.7 | 04.6 | 331 26.4 | 12.4 | 17 44.9 | 4.3 | 54.5 |
| 05 | 41 41.4 | 237 37.8 | 19.3 | 224 56.4 | 10.9 | 344 08.5 | 01.9 | 270 02.7 | 30.5 | 254 02.9 | 03.8 | 345 57.8 | 12.4 | 17 49.2 | 4.2 | 54.5 |
| 06 | 56 43.9 | 252 37.4 | N 8 18.1 | 239 57.4 | N 2 10.3 | 359 10.8 | N19 01.9 | 285 04.9 | N18 30.5 | 269 03.0 | N13 03.0 | 0 29.2 | 12.2 | N17 53.4 | 4.2 | 54.6 |
| 07 | 71 46.3 | 267 37.0 | 16.9 | 254 58.4 | 09.6 | 14 13.0 | 02.0 | 300 07.0 | 30.4 | 284 03.2 | 02.2 | 15 00.4 | 12.3 | 17 57.6 | 4.0 | 54.6 |
| W 08 | 86 48.8 | 282 36.6 | 15.7 | 269 59.4 | 09.0 | 29 15.2 | 02.0 | 315 09.2 | 30.3 | 299 03.3 | 01.4 | 29 31.7 | 12.2 | 18 01.6 | 4.0 | 54.6 |
| E 09 | 101 51.3 | 297 36.2 | ·· 14.5 | 285 00.4 | ·· 08.3 | 44 17.4 | ·· 02.1 | 330 11.3 | ·· 30.2 | 314 03.4 | 13 00.6 | 44 02.9 | 12.2 | 18 05.6 | 3.9 | 54.6 |
| D 10 | 116 53.7 | 312 35.8 | 13.3 | 300 01.4 | 07.6 | 59 19.6 | 02.1 | 345 13.5 | 30.1 | 329 03.6 | 12 59.8 | 58 34.1 | 12.1 | 18 09.5 | 3.9 | 54.6 |
| N 11 | 131 56.2 | 327 35.4 | 12.1 | 315 02.5 | 07.0 | 74 21.8 | 02.2 | 0 15.6 | 30.1 | 344 03.7 | 59.0 | 73 05.2 | 12.1 | 18 13.4 | 3.7 | 54.6 |
| E 12 | 146 58.6 | 342 35.0 | N 8 10.9 | 330 03.5 | N 2 06.3 | 89 24.0 | N19 02.2 | 15 17.8 | N18 30.0 | 359 03.9 | N12 58.2 | 87 36.3 | 12.0 | N18 17.1 | 3.7 | 54.7 |
| S 13 | 162 01.1 | 357 34.6 | 09.7 | 345 04.5 | 05.7 | 104 26.2 | 02.3 | 30 19.9 | 29.9 | 14 04.0 | 57.4 | 102 07.3 | 12.0 | 18 20.8 | 3.6 | 54.7 |
| D 14 | 177 03.6 | 12 34.2 | 08.5 | 0 05.5 | 05.0 | 119 28.4 | 02.3 | 45 22.0 | 29.8 | 29 04.1 | 56.6 | 116 38.3 | 12.0 | 18 24.4 | 3.5 | 54.7 |
| A 15 | 192 06.0 | 27 33.8 | ·· 07.3 | 15 06.5 | ·· 04.4 | 134 30.6 | ·· 02.4 | 60 24.2 | ·· 29.7 | 44 04.3 | ·· 55.7 | 131 09.3 | 11.9 | 18 27.9 | 3.4 | 54.7 |
| Y 16 | 207 08.5 | 42 33.4 | 06.1 | 30 07.5 | 03.7 | 149 32.8 | 02.4 | 75 26.3 | 29.7 | 59 04.4 | 54.9 | 145 40.2 | 11.9 | 18 31.3 | 3.3 | 54.7 |
| 17 | 222 11.0 | 57 33.0 | 04.9 | 45 08.6 | 03.1 | 164 35.0 | 02.4 | 90 28.5 | 29.6 | 74 04.6 | 54.1 | 160 11.1 | 11.9 | 18 34.6 | 3.2 | 54.7 |
| 18 | 237 13.4 | 72 32.7 | N 8 03.7 | 60 09.6 | N 2 02.4 | 179 37.2 | N19 02.5 | 105 30.6 | N18 29.5 | 89 04.7 | N12 53.3 | 174 42.0 | 11.8 | N18 37.8 | 3.2 | 54.8 |
| 19 | 252 15.9 | 87 32.3 | 02.5 | 75 10.6 | 01.8 | 194 39.4 | 02.5 | 120 32.8 | 29.4 | 104 04.9 | 52.5 | 189 12.8 | 11.7 | 18 41.0 | 3.1 | 54.8 |
| 20 | 267 18.4 | 102 31.9 | 01.3 | 90 11.6 | 01.1 | 209 41.6 | 02.6 | 135 34.9 | 29.3 | 119 05.0 | 51.7 | 203 43.5 | 11.7 | 18 44.1 | 2.9 | 54.8 |
| 21 | 282 20.8 | 117 31.5 | 8 00.1 | 105 12.6 | 2 00.5 | 224 43.8 | ·· 02.6 | 150 37.0 | ·· 29.3 | 134 05.1 | ·· 50.9 | 218 14.2 | 11.7 | 18 47.0 | 2.9 | 54.8 |
| 22 | 297 23.3 | 132 31.1 | 7 58.9 | 120 13.6 | 1 59.8 | 239 46.0 | 02.7 | 165 39.2 | 29.2 | 149 05.3 | 50.0 | 232 44.9 | 11.6 | 18 49.9 | 2.9 | 54.8 |
| 23 | 312 25.8 | 147 30.7 | 57.6 | 135 14.6 | 59.2 | 254 48.3 | 02.7 | 180 41.3 | 29.1 | 164 05.4 | 49.2 | 247 15.5 | 11.6 | 18 52.8 | 2.7 | 54.8 |
| Mer. Pass. | h m 2 17.6 | v −0.4 | d 1.2 | v 1.0 | d 0.7 | v 2.2 | d 0.0 | v 2.1 | d 0.1 | S.D. 15.8 | d 0.8 | S.D. 14.8 | | 14.8 | | 14.9 |

These "v" and "d" numbers are only reference numbers for the celestial body's movement in one hour. If we took a sextant sight at thirty minutes after the hour, the actual correction would be 30/60 or ½ of the reference numbers. To save our doing the arithmetic, we enter the yellow pages in the back of the Nautical Almanac with the minute and second of our sight, pull out a value for the earth's movement in columns entitled Sun-Planets, Aries and Moon, and then go the the right hand side of the minute box and find the "v" or "d" values. The corresponding number to these values is the correction factor, to be added or subtracted as the sign of the "v" or "d". If we took our sight at $31^m\ 15^s$ after the hour, the corrections for the "v" and "d" values above and the increment for the earth's rotation during that time would be as follows.

| Body | "v" | "v" corr$^n$ | "d" | "d" corr$^n$ | increment |
|---|---|---|---|---|---|
| Venus | − 0.4 | −0.2 | −1.2 | −0.6 | 7° 48!8 |
| Mars | + 1.0 | +0.5 | −0.7 | −0.4 | 7° 48!8 |
| Jupiter | + 2.2 | +1.2 | 0.0 | 0.0 | 7° 48!8 |
| Saturn | + 2.1 | +1.1 | −0.1 | −0.1 | 7° 48!8 |
| Sun | none | none | −0.8 | −0.4 | 7° 48!8 |
| Moon | +12.0 | +6.3 | +3.6 | +1.9 | 7° 27!4 |
| Star | none | none | none | none | 7° 50!0 |

| 30m | SUN PLANETS | ARIES | MOON | v or d | Corrn | v or d | Corrn | v or d | Corrn |
|---|---|---|---|---|---|---|---|---|---|
| s | ° ′ | ° ′ | ° ′ | ′ | ′ | ′ | ′ | ′ | ′ |
| 00 | 7 30·0 | 7 31·2 | 7 09·5 | 0·0 | 0·0 | 6·0 | 3·1 | 12·0 | 6·1 |
| 01 | 7 30·3 | 7 31·5 | 7 09·7 | 0·1 | 0·1 | 6·1 | 3·1 | 12·1 | 6·2 |
| 02 | 7 30·5 | 7 31·7 | 7 10·0 | 0·2 | 0·1 | 6·2 | 3·2 | 12·2 | 6·2 |
| 03 | 7 30·8 | 7 32·0 | 7 10·2 | 0·3 | 0·2 | 6·3 | 3·2 | 12·3 | 6·3 |
| 04 | 7 31·0 | 7 32·2 | 7 10·5 | 0·4 | 0·2 | 6·4 | 3·3 | 12·4 | 6·3 |
| 05 | 7 31·3 | 7 32·5 | 7 10·7 | 0·5 | 0·3 | 6·5 | 3·3 | 12·5 | 6·4 |
| 06 | 7 31·5 | 7 32·7 | 7 10·9 | 0·6 | 0·3 | 6·6 | 3·4 | 12·6 | 6·4 |
| 07 | 7 31·8 | 7 33·0 | 7 11·2 | 0·7 | 0·4 | 6·7 | 3·4 | 12·7 | 6·5 |
| 08 | 7 32·0 | 7 33·2 | 7 11·4 | 0·8 | 0·4 | 6·8 | 3·5 | 12·8 | 6·5 |
| 09 | 7 32·3 | 7 33·5 | 7 11·6 | 0·9 | 0·5 | 6·9 | 3·5 | 12·9 | 6·6 |
| 10 | 7 32·5 | 7 33·7 | 7 11·9 | 1·0 | 0·5 | 7·0 | 3·6 | 13·0 | 6·6 |
| 11 | 7 32·8 | 7 34·0 | 7 12·1 | 1·1 | 0·6 | 7·1 | 3·6 | 13·1 | 6·7 |
| 12 | 7 33·0 | 7 34·2 | 7 12·4 | 1·2 | 0·6 | 7·2 | 3·7 | 13·2 | 6·7 |
| 13 | 7 33·3 | 7 34·5 | 7 12·6 | 1·3 | 0·7 | 7·3 | 3·7 | 13·3 | 6·8 |
| 14 | 7 33·5 | 7 34·7 | 7 12·8 | 1·4 | 0·7 | 7·4 | 3·8 | 13·4 | 6·8 |
| 15 | 7 33·8 | 7 35·0 | 7 13·1 | 1·5 | 0·8 | 7·5 | 3·8 | 13·5 | 6·9 |
| 16 | 7 34·0 | 7 35·2 | 7 13·3 | 1·6 | 0·8 | 7·6 | 3·9 | 13·6 | 6·9 |
| 17 | 7 34·3 | 7 35·5 | 7 13·6 | 1·7 | 0·9 | 7·7 | 3·9 | 13·7 | 7·0 |
| 18 | 7 34·5 | 7 35·7 | 7 13·8 | 1·8 | 0·9 | 7·8 | 4·0 | 13·8 | 7·0 |
| 19 | 7 34·8 | 7 36·0 | 7 14·0 | 1·9 | 1·0 | 7·9 | 4·0 | 13·9 | 7·1 |
| 20 | 7 35·0 | 7 36·2 | 7 14·3 | 2·0 | 1·0 | 8·0 | 4·1 | 14·0 | 7·1 |
| 21 | 7 35·3 | 7 36·5 | 7 14·5 | 2·1 | 1·1 | 8·1 | 4·1 | 14·1 | 7·2 |
| 22 | 7 35·5 | 7 36·7 | 7 14·7 | 2·2 | 1·1 | 8·2 | 4·2 | 14·2 | 7·2 |
| 23 | 7 35·8 | 7 37·0 | 7 15·0 | 2·3 | 1·2 | 8·3 | 4·2 | 14·3 | 7·3 |
| 24 | 7 36·0 | 7 37·2 | 7 15·2 | 2·4 | 1·2 | 8·4 | 4·3 | 14·4 | 7·3 |
| 25 | 7 36·3 | 7 37·5 | 7 15·5 | 2·5 | 1·3 | 8·5 | 4·3 | 14·5 | 7·4 |
| 26 | 7 36·5 | 7 37·7 | 7 15·7 | 2·6 | 1·3 | 8·6 | 4·4 | 14·6 | 7·4 |
| 27 | 7 36·8 | 7 38·0 | 7 15·9 | 2·7 | 1·4 | 8·7 | 4·4 | 14·7 | 7·5 |
| 28 | 7 37·0 | 7 38·3 | 7 16·2 | 2·8 | 1·4 | 8·8 | 4·5 | 14·8 | 7·5 |
| 29 | 7 37·3 | 7 38·5 | 7 16·4 | 2·9 | 1·5 | 8·9 | 4·5 | 14·9 | 7·6 |
| 30 | 7 37·5 | 7 38·8 | 7 16·7 | 3·0 | 1·5 | 9·0 | 4·6 | 15·0 | 7·6 |
| 31 | 7 37·8 | 7 39·0 | 7 16·9 | 3·1 | 1·6 | 9·1 | 4·6 | 15·1 | 7·7 |
| 32 | 7 38·0 | 7 39·3 | 7 17·1 | 3·2 | 1·6 | 9·2 | 4·7 | 15·2 | 7·7 |
| 33 | 7 38·3 | 7 39·5 | 7 17·4 | 3·3 | 1·7 | 9·3 | 4·7 | 15·3 | 7·8 |
| 34 | 7 38·5 | 7 39·8 | 7 17·6 | 3·4 | 1·7 | 9·4 | 4·8 | 15·4 | 7·8 |
| 35 | 7 38·8 | 7 40·0 | 7 17·9 | 3·5 | 1·8 | 9·5 | 4·8 | 15·5 | 7·9 |
| 36 | 7 39·0 | 7 40·3 | 7 18·1 | 3·6 | 1·8 | 9·6 | 4·9 | 15·6 | 7·9 |
| 37 | 7 39·3 | 7 40·5 | 7 18·3 | 3·7 | 1·9 | 9·7 | 4·9 | 15·7 | 8·0 |

| 31m | SUN PLANETS | ARIES | MOON | v or d | Corrn | v or d | Corrn | v or d | Corrn |
|---|---|---|---|---|---|---|---|---|---|
| s | ° ′ | ° ′ | ° ′ | ′ | ′ | ′ | ′ | ′ | ′ |
| 00 | 7 45·0 | 7 46·3 | 7 23·8 | 0·0 | 0·0 | 6·0 | 3·2 | 12·0 | 6·3 |
| 01 | 7 45·3 | 7 46·5 | 7 24·1 | 0·1 | 0·1 | 6·1 | 3·2 | 12·1 | 6·4 |
| 02 | 7 45·5 | 7 46·8 | 7 24·3 | 0·2 | 0·1 | 6·2 | 3·3 | 12·2 | 6·4 |
| 03 | 7 45·8 | 7 47·0 | 7 24·5 | 0·3 | 0·2 | 6·3 | 3·3 | 12·3 | 6·5 |
| 04 | 7 46·0 | 7 47·3 | 7 24·8 | 0·4 | 0·2 | 6·4 | 3·4 | 12·4 | 6·5 |
| 05 | 7 46·3 | 7 47·5 | 7 25·0 | 0·5 | 0·3 | 6·5 | 3·4 | 12·5 | 6·6 |
| 06 | 7 46·5 | 7 47·8 | 7 25·2 | 0·6 | 0·3 | 6·6 | 3·5 | 12·6 | 6·6 |
| 07 | 7 46·8 | 7 48·0 | 7 25·5 | 0·7 | 0·4 | 6·7 | 3·5 | 12·7 | 6·7 |
| 08 | 7 47·0 | 7 48·3 | 7 25·7 | 0·8 | 0·4 | 6·8 | 3·6 | 12·8 | 6·7 |
| 09 | 7 47·3 | 7 48·5 | 7 26·0 | 0·9 | 0·5 | 6·9 | 3·6 | 12·9 | 6·8 |
| 10 | 7 47·5 | 7 48·8 | 7 26·2 | 1·0 | 0·5 | 7·0 | 3·7 | 13·0 | 6·8 |
| 11 | 7 47·8 | 7 49·0 | 7 26·4 | 1·1 | 0·6 | 7·1 | 3·7 | 13·1 | 6·9 |
| 12 | 7 48·0 | 7 49·3 | 7 26·7 | 1·2 | 0·6 | 7·2 | 3·8 | 13·2 | 6·9 |
| 13 | 7 48·3 | 7 49·5 | 7 26·9 | 1·3 | 0·7 | 7·3 | 3·8 | 13·3 | 7·0 |
| 14 | 7 48·5 | 7 49·8 | 7 27·2 | 1·4 | 0·7 | 7·4 | 3·9 | 13·4 | 7·0 |
| 15 | 7 48·8 | 7 50·0 | 7 27·4 | 1·5 | 0·8 | 7·5 | 3·9 | 13·5 | 7·1 |
| 16 | 7 49·0 | 7 50·3 | 7 27·6 | 1·6 | 0·8 | 7·6 | 4·0 | 13·6 | 7·1 |
| 17 | 7 49·3 | 7 50·5 | 7 27·9 | 1·7 | 0·9 | 7·7 | 4·0 | 13·7 | 7·2 |
| 18 | 7 49·5 | 7 50·8 | 7 28·1 | 1·8 | 0·9 | 7·8 | 4·1 | 13·8 | 7·2 |
| 19 | 7 49·8 | 7 51·0 | 7 28·4 | 1·9 | 1·0 | 7·9 | 4·1 | 13·9 | 7·3 |
| 20 | 7 50·0 | 7 51·3 | 7 28·6 | 2·0 | 1·1 | 8·0 | 4·2 | 14·0 | 7·4 |
| 21 | 7 50·3 | 7 51·5 | 7 28·8 | 2·1 | 1·1 | 8·1 | 4·3 | 14·1 | 7·4 |
| 22 | 7 50·5 | 7 51·8 | 7 29·1 | 2·2 | 1·2 | 8·2 | 4·3 | 14·2 | 7·5 |
| 23 | 7 50·8 | 7 52·0 | 7 29·3 | 2·3 | 1·2 | 8·3 | 4·4 | 14·3 | 7·5 |
| 24 | 7 51·0 | 7 52·3 | 7 29·5 | 2·4 | 1·3 | 8·4 | 4·4 | 14·4 | 7·6 |
| 25 | 7 51·3 | 7 52·5 | 7 29·8 | 2·5 | 1·3 | 8·5 | 4·5 | 14·5 | 7·6 |
| 26 | 7 51·5 | 7 52·8 | 7 30·0 | 2·6 | 1·4 | 8·6 | 4·5 | 14·6 | 7·7 |
| 27 | 7 51·8 | 7 53·0 | 7 30·3 | 2·7 | 1·4 | 8·7 | 4·6 | 14·7 | 7·7 |
| 28 | 7 52·0 | 7 53·3 | 7 30·5 | 2·8 | 1·5 | 8·8 | 4·6 | 14·8 | 7·8 |
| 29 | 7 52·3 | 7 53·5 | 7 30·7 | 2·9 | 1·5 | 8·9 | 4·7 | 14·9 | 7·8 |
| 30 | 7 52·5 | 7 53·8 | 7 31·0 | 3·0 | 1·6 | 9·0 | 4·7 | 15·0 | 7·9 |
| 31 | 7 52·8 | 7 54·0 | 7 31·2 | 3·1 | 1·6 | 9·1 | 4·8 | 15·1 | 7·9 |
| 32 | 7 53·0 | 7 54·3 | 7 31·5 | 3·2 | 1·7 | 9·2 | 4·8 | 15·2 | 8·0 |
| 33 | 7 53·3 | 7 54·5 | 7 31·7 | 3·3 | 1·7 | 9·3 | 4·9 | 15·3 | 8·0 |
| 34 | 7 53·5 | 7 54·8 | 7 31·9 | 3·4 | 1·8 | 9·4 | 4·9 | 15·4 | 8·1 |
| 35 | 7 53·8 | 7 55·0 | 7 32·2 | 3·5 | 1·8 | 9·5 | 5·0 | 15·5 | 8·1 |
| 36 | 7 54·0 | 7 55·3 | 7 32·4 | 3·6 | 1·9 | 9·6 | 5·0 | 15·6 | 8·2 |
| 37 | 7 54·3 | 7 55·5 | 7 32·6 | 3·7 | 1·9 | 9·7 | 5·1 | 15·7 | 8·2 |

The following examples of finding GHA and Dec of Sun, Moon, planets and stars given GMT and Greenwich date will illustrate the use of the Nautical Almanac.

Given: GMT 14h 16m 20s — Grnch Date 13 May 1976 — Venus

From Nautical Almanac

| | | | |
|---|---|---|---|
| ~~SHA star only~~ | ° ' | | |
| GHA 14h | 40° 15.'1 | Dec (N) 14° 50.'3 | |
| 16m 20s | 4° 05.'0 | d (+) 1.0 corr | + 0.'3 |
| v (−) 0.5 corr | − 0.'1 | Dec Body | 14° 50.'6 (N) |
| TOTAL | ° ' | | |
| ±360° | | | |
| GHA Body | 44° 20.'0 | | |

Given: GMT 20h 09m 13s — Grnch Date 12 August 1976 — Jupiter

From Nautical Almanac

| | | | |
|---|---|---|---|
| ~~SHA star only~~ | ° ' | | |
| GHA 20h | 204° 26.'6 | Dec (N) 18° 55.'0 | |
| 09m 13s | 2° 18.'3 | d (+) 0.1 corr | + 0.'0 |
| v ± 2.2 corr | + 0.'3 | Dec Body | 18° 55.'0 (N) |
| TOTAL | ° ' | | |
| ±360° | | | |
| GHA Body | 206° 45.'2 | | |

Given: GMT 01h 33m 47s — Grnch Date 20 March 1976 — Sun

From Nautical Almanac

| | | | |
|---|---|---|---|
| ~~SHA star only~~ | ° ' | | |
| GHA 01h | 193° 06.'3 | Dec (S) 0° 10.'7 | |
| 33m 47s | 8° 26.'8 | d (−) 1.0 corr | − 0.'6 |
| v ± ___ corr | ' | Dec Body | 0° 10.'1 (S) |
| TOTAL | ° ' | | |
| ±360° | | | |
| GHA Body | 201° 33.'1 | | |

Given: GMT 15h 18m 11s — Grnch Date 27 February 1976 — Moon

From Nautical Almanac

| | ° | ' | | |
|---|---|---|---|---|
| ~~SHA star only~~ | | | | |
| GHA 15h | 68° | 55.8 | Dec (N/S circled S) | 12° 27.8 |
| 18m 11s | 4° | 20.3 | d ± 8.6 corr | − 2.7 |
| v ± 12.9 corr | + | 4.0 | Dec Body | 12° 25.1 (N/S circled S) |
| TOTAL | | | | |
| ± 360° | | | | |
| GHA Body | 73° | 20.1 | | |

Given: GMT 09h 36m 30s — Grnch Date 19 November 1976 — Betelgeuse

From Nautical Almanac

| | ° | ' | | |
|---|---|---|---|---|
| SHA star only | 271° | 30.8 | | |
| GHA 09h | 193° | 31.1 | Dec (N/S circled N) | 7° 24.2 |
| 36m 30s | 9° | 09.0 | d ± ___ corr | |
| v ± ___ corr | | | Dec Body | ° ' N/S |
| TOTAL | 474° | 10.9 | | |
| ± 360° | | | | |
| GHA Body | 114° | 10.9 | | |

Given: GMT 23h 25m 06s — Grnch Date 5 July 1976 — Polaris

(SHA & Dec. of Polaris are found on Page 236. Interpolation is not required.)

From Nautical Almanac

| | ° | ' | | |
|---|---|---|---|---|
| SHA star only | 327° | 42.3 | | |
| GHA 23h | 269° | 03.6 | Dec (N/S circled N) | 89° 09.1 |
| 25m 06s | 6° | 17.5 | d ± ___ corr | |
| v ± ___ corr | | | Dec Body | ° ' N/S |
| TOTAL | 603° | 03.4 | | |
| ± 360° | | | | |
| GHA Body | 243° | 03.4 | | |

## EXERCISE 3

Find GHA and Dec of each of the following bodies, year is 1976.

| | Body | W.T. | W.E. | Local Date | DR Lat | DR Long |
|---|---|---|---|---|---|---|
| 1. | Sun LL | 10-16-30 | $16^s$ fast | 27 Feb. | 42° 20!0 N | 68° 16!7 W |
| 2. | Mars | 18-32-07 | $22^s$ fast | 13 April | 30° 18!6 N | 175° 10!1 E |
| 3. | Moon UL | 07-18-04 | $10^s$ slow | 20 March | 35° 07!4 S | 79° 46!1 W |
| 4. | Sun UL | 12-00-00 | 0 | 25 Dec. | 31° 00!0 S | 123° 54!6 W |
| 5. | Venus | 16-54-00 | $1^m$ slow | 25 Dec. | 34° 14!7 N | 56° 21!8 W |
| 6. | Moon LL | 05-25-00 | $35^s$ slow | 21 March | 40° 20!0 N | 71° 28!3 W |
| 7. | Jupiter | 16-57-10 | $5^s$ slow | 8 Jan. | 39° 29!0 N | 140° 26!1 E |

## EXERCISE 4

Find GHA and Dec of each of the following stars, year is 1976.

| | | | | | | |
|---|---|---|---|---|---|---|
| 8. | Vega | 20-10-00 | $10^s$ fast | 4 July | 45° 21!6 N | 97° 12!3 W |
| 9. | Denebola | 19-37-23 | $28^s$ fast | 18 June | 40° 34!2 N | 24° 34!2 W |
| 10. | Achernar | 19-30-20 | $6^s$ slow | 19 Nov. | 43° 44!0 S | 12° 00!0 W |
| 11. | Spica | 19-20-13 | $1^m$ fast | 12 May | 41° 15!4 N | 71° 26!3 W |
| 12. | Regulus | 04-09-25 | $13^s$ fast | 18 Dec. | 32° 52!0 N | 37° 47!0 E |
| 13. | Rasalhague | 19-52-00 | $1^m54^s$ fast | 12 Aug. | 43° 17!5 N | 65° 12!0 W |
| 14. | Polaris | 04-35-00 | $1^m57^s$ fast | 13 Aug. | 42° 59!0 N | 66° 24!8 W |

(for Polaris GHA & Dec see page 236)

# Chapter 7

# H.O. 229

H.O. Publication No. 229 is one of many types of sight reduction tables, the value of which is to relate the position of the sighted celestial body to our ship's real position by means of an intermediate position, an assumed position or AP. This AP is close enough to our DR so that it can be plotted on small position plotting sheets in the vicinity of our DR. From the AP we will plot our lines of position to establish our fix.

H.O. 229 is printed for bands of 15° of latitude. Volume 1 covers 0° through 15° (north or south), Volume 2 covers 15° through 30° etc. We shall only be dealing with Volume 3 in this book, latitudes 30° through 45°. The first half of the Volume includes latitudes 30° through 37°, the second half 38° through 45°. Numbers used to enter the volume are local hour angle (LHA) found in the four corners of the book opening, latitude heading each column, and declination on the left and right columns of each page, used to establish the line in the column we wish. To find out which page of the opening we need (since LHA for both pages can be the same), we have to note whether our latitude is the same name or contrary name to the declination. If latitude and declination were both north or both south, name would be SAME. If one value were north and the other south, the names would be CONTRARY. LHA in three of the four corners is the same, in the lower right corner is different than in the other three. The horizontal stepped line on the right page divides the page in half, the lower half belonging to the lower right LHA, the upper half belonging to the upper right LHA. Notice that all the entry values to H.O. 229 are whole degrees, with no additional minutes.

To obtain the entry values, we first have to get GHA and Dec of the celestial body and know a rough dead reckoning position near the time of our sight. Assume the position of our DR and of the celestial body are given as in Example 1 on the following page. The AP latitude would be the closest whole degree to our DR latitude, in this case 32° S. Since declination is north, latitude and declination would be of contrary name. The AP longitude needs to be close to our DR longitude, say within 30', such that when subtracted from GHA (if west longitude) or added to GHA (if east longitude), the resulting number is a whole degree with no additional minutes. In Example 1, since our longitude is west, the minutes of our AP Lo have to be 26.8 so that when subtracted from GHA, the result is 00.0 minutes. With minutes already dictated, we now have to find a degree of AP Lo such that AP Lo and DR Lo are within 30 minutes of each other. Choosing 70° 26!8 we satisfy this criterion since 70° 47!0 minus 70° 26!8 gives us 20!2. We subtract AP Lo from GHA Body and find a LHA of 29°. Notice that we have now fudged an assumed position so that the resulting numbers used to enter H.O. 229 are whole degrees.

Example 1.

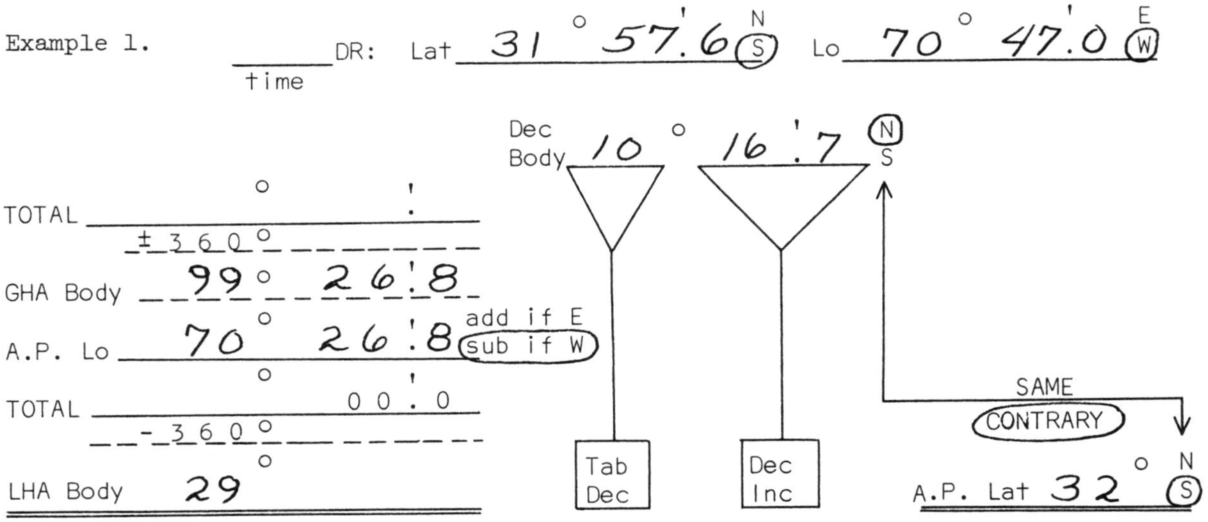


In Example 2, we are given a DR position near the time of sight and the GHA of the body at the time of sight. The closest whole degree of latitude to our DR latitude is 41° N, entered in the space after AP Lat. Since this has the same name as our declination (both north), we circle SAME. For an assumed position longitude, we need minutes such that when added to our GHA minutes (east longitude requires adding GHA and AP Lo) there is a result of zero minutes. To do this, we find minutes to make the result 60 minutes, therefore converting these minutes to one degree and leaving zero minutes in their place. In this case, 10!0 when added to GHA minutes of 50.0 gives the required 60!0. If we choose 172° 10!0 for our AP Lo, this places our DR longitude only 9!2 from the AP Lo, within 30!0. Adding GHA and AP Lo, we get 393° 60!0 or 394°. Reducing this by subtracting a whole circle or 360° from it, we obtain 34° for a LHA.

Example 2.

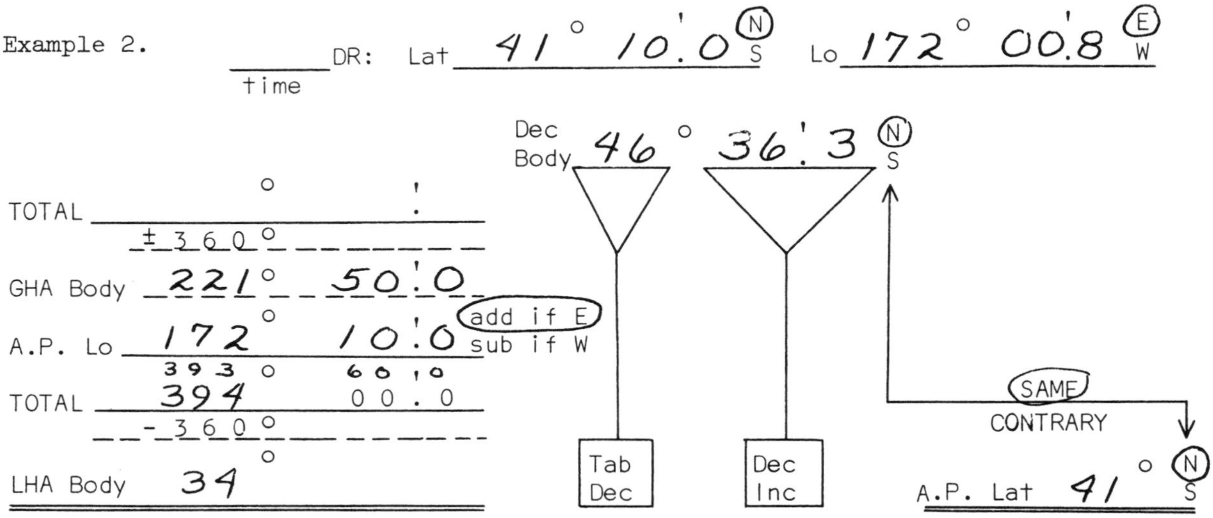

In Example 3, the closest whole degree to 45° 25' N would be 45° N which we will use for our AP Lat. It is the SAME name as our declination, both being north. In east longitude, we need minutes of 59.4 to ADD to GHA minutes of 00.6 to give us 60 minutes, convertible to one degree. Our AP Lo should therefore be 165° 59'.4, only 11'.9 from our DR Lo. When adding GHA and AP Lo, we get 214° 60' or 215°.

Example 3.

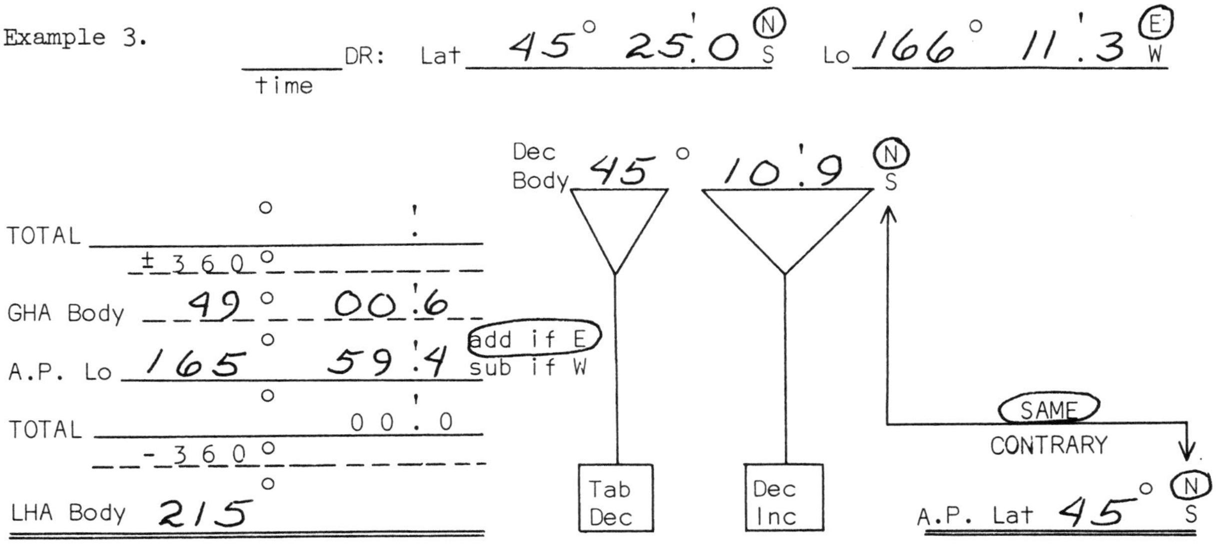


To hold continuity, let us work a complete example down to this point. In Example 4, rather than reducing our GHA to 14° 13'.4, we leave it as 374° 13'.4 so that we can subtract our AP Lo of 68° 13'.4 from it. In some cases, we may need to add 360° to our GHA to make it possible to subtract AP Lo.

Example 4: Given: 0530 DR, 37° 22'.0 N, 67° 52'.0 W, Height of eye 8 feet,
W.T. 05-32-17, W.E. $1^m$ $31^s$ fast, September 29, 1976
$H_s$ of Regulus 35° 29'.5, I.C. +2.0

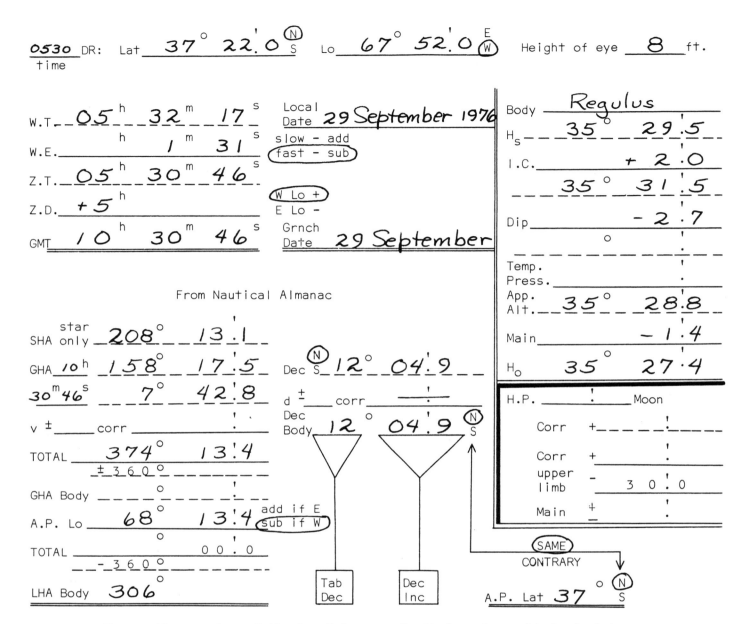

0530 DR: Lat 37° 22.0' (N) S   Lo 67° 52.0' E (W)   Height of eye 8 ft.
time

| | | |
|---|---|---|
| W.T. 05h 32m 17s | Local Date 29 September 1976 | Body Regulus |
| W.E. 1m 31s | slow - add / (fast - sub) | $H_s$ 35° 29.5' |
| Z.T. 05h 30m 46s | | I.C. + 2.0' |
| Z.D. +5h | (W Lo +) / E Lo - | 35° 31.5' |
| GMT 10h 30m 46s | Grnch Date 29 September | Dip - 2.7' |
| | | ° ' |
| | | Temp. / Press. ' |
| | | App. Alt. 35° 28.8' |
| | | Main - 1.4' |
| | | $H_o$ 35° 27.4' |

From Nautical Almanac

| | | |
|---|---|---|
| SHA star only 208° 13.1' | | H.P. ' Moon |
| GHA 10h 158° 17.5' | Dec (N) S 12° 04.9' | Corr + ' |
| 30m 46s 7° 42.8' | d ± corr ' | Corr + ' |
| v ± corr ' | Dec Body 12° 04.9' (N) S | upper limb - 30.0' |
| TOTAL 374° 13.4' | | Main ± ' |
| ±360° | | |
| GHA Body ° ' | Tab Dec / Dec Inc | (SAME) / CONTRARY |
| A.P. Lo 68° 13.4' add if E / (sub if W) | | |
| TOTAL 00.0' | | |
| -360° | | |
| LHA Body 306° | | A.P. Lat 37° (N) S |

To see the meaning of the local hour angle that we have obtained, let us look at the circular diagram in the lower left hand corner of our sight reduction sheets. The circle is the earth's equator, the center of the circle is the south pole and the vertical line labeled "G" is the lower part of the Greenwich meridian. Looking at the earth from the south pole, westward would be counterclockwise.

Local hour angle is defined as the angle measured westward from our meridian to the hour circle (a sky meridian) going through the celestial body. The limits of LHA are 0° to 360°. First we place our meridian on the diagram, designated by the letter "M": In previous Example 1, our AP longitude is about 70° W. Starting at the Greenwich meridian, we measure westward an angle of 70° and mark it as our longitude. The GHA of the body is about 99° and since this is always measured westward, we measure a counterclockwise angle of 99° from the Greenwich meridian and mark this on our diagram. The LHA is the angle measured from our meridian to the body's "meridian", a rather small angle of 29°, always a westward measurement.

In Example 2, longitude is measured eastward from the Greenwich meridian, GHA always westward. LHA is as noted.

In Example 4, note that the GHA of 374° or 14° puts us in the same spot on the diagram.

1. GHA = 99°, AP Lo = 70°W
LHA = 29°

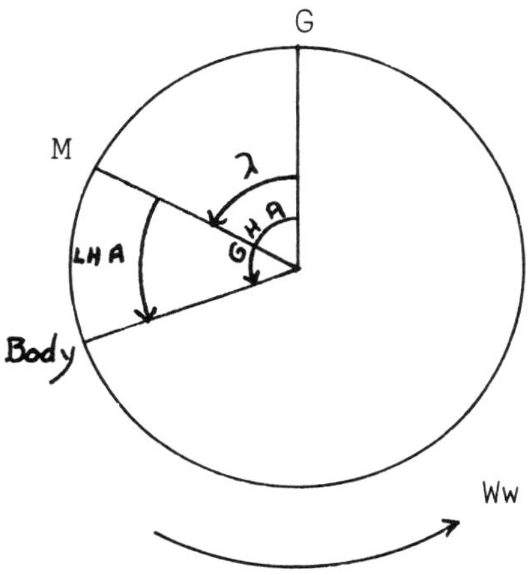


2. GHA = 222°, AP Lo = 172°E
LHA = 34°

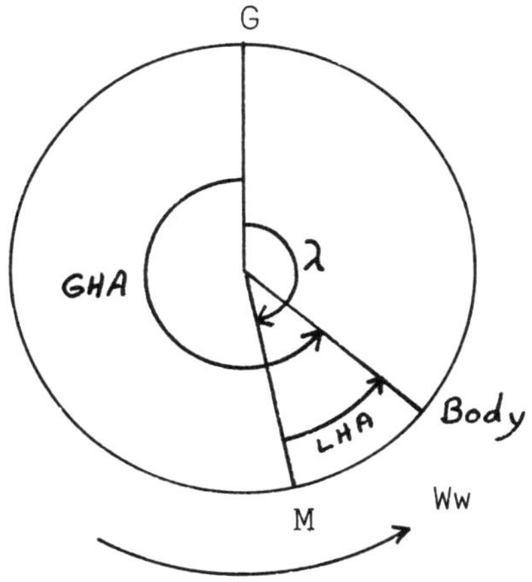


4. GHA = 14°, AP Lo = 68°W
LHA = 306°

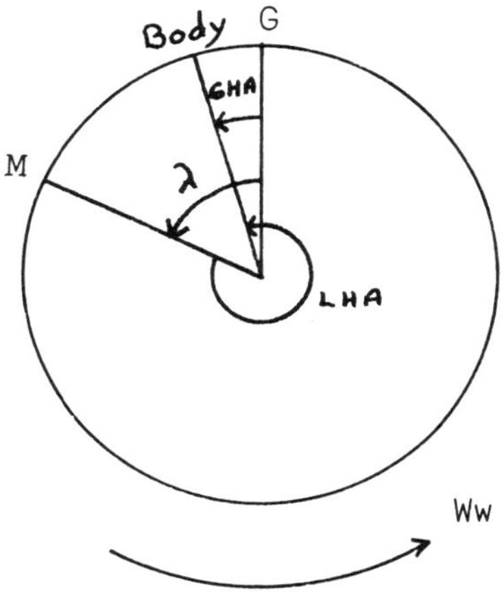


We see then that local hour angle relates the celestial body to our meridian. If LHA = 0°, the body would be on our meridian such as in a noon Sun sight. If LHA is a small angle, the body would be to the west of our meridian, say in the southwestern sky. If LHA is on the order of 300° or more, the body would be in the eastern or southeastern sky.

To obtain values from H.O. 229, we need five pieces of information - LHA, AP Lat, tabular declination (the whole degree of declination), declination increment (the additional minutes of declination), and SAME vs. CONTRARY.

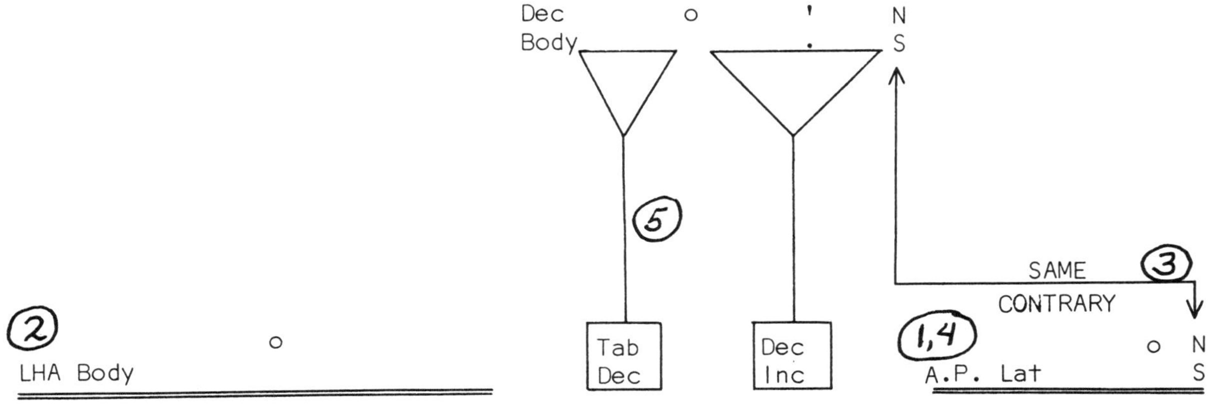

The order of entry is as follows (see diagram on previous page).

| | Value | Use |
|---|---|---|
| 1) | AP Lat | Designates which half of the book you should be in. For Volume III of H.O. 229: 30°-37° front half, 38°-45° back half. |
| 2) | LHA | Places you in the correct book opening, found in the page corners. |
| 3) | SAME/CONT. | Decides the correct page of the book opening, found at page top. |
| 4) | AP Lat | Heads the column you need on the page. |
| 5) | Tab Dec | Found in the left and right columns of page, points out the correct line of the latitude column. |

The results of your entry are.

| | Value | Definition |
|---|---|---|
| 1) | $H_c$ | Altitude of the celestial body computed for the assumed position, using a whole degree of declination. |
| 2) | d | The change in $H_c$ for one degree of declination. Its sign is given. |
| 3) | Z | The azimuth (bearing) of the celestial body and its GP, measured from north or south in an eastward or westward direction, depending upon latitude and LHA. This will be converted to $Z_n$, an azimuth measured from north eastward. |

These values are placed horizontally in the line on our sight reduction form entitled Tabular Values.

| | $H_c$ | d | DSD | Z eye interp. |
|---|---|---|---|---|
| Tabular Values | ° ' . | + − ' . | + ' . | ° . |

Remember that these numbers are obtained assuming a whole degree of declination. The $H_c$ will be corrected for the additional minutes of declination in a few moments. The Z we interpolate by eye in the tables. If our declination increment (Dec Inc) is 20.'0, 1/3 of a degree, we interpolate 1/3 of the way between Z in our line of Tabular Values and the Z in the next line down (the line for the declination one degree greater than ours.) Note the interpolation in the next example where LHA = 28°, CONTRARY, AP Lat = 30° N, Dec = 10° 36.'0 S.

| | | | | | |
|---|---|---|---|---|---|
| Tab Dec | 10° | | Z = 141°.7 | | 3/5 x °.7 = .42 or °.4 |
| Our Dec | 10° 36′.0 | $\frac{36}{60} = \frac{3}{5}$ | ↓ incr. | diff. of +°.7 | 141°.7 + °.4 = 142°.1 |
| Tab Dec | 11° | | Z = 142°.4 | | Our Z = 142°.1 |

Note that since the Z is increasing as we increase declination, we <u>add</u> the °.4 to the Z of 141°.7. In some cases, the increase or decrease in Z is negligible. In other cases, the change can amount to two degrees or more. It is wise to always check and evaluate the interpolation factor. In cases where interpolation changes Z by one or two tenths of a degree, consider the inability to accurately plot this difference on your compass rose and you may disregard the difference in Z. This interpolated Z will fill the space provided on the sight reduction form.

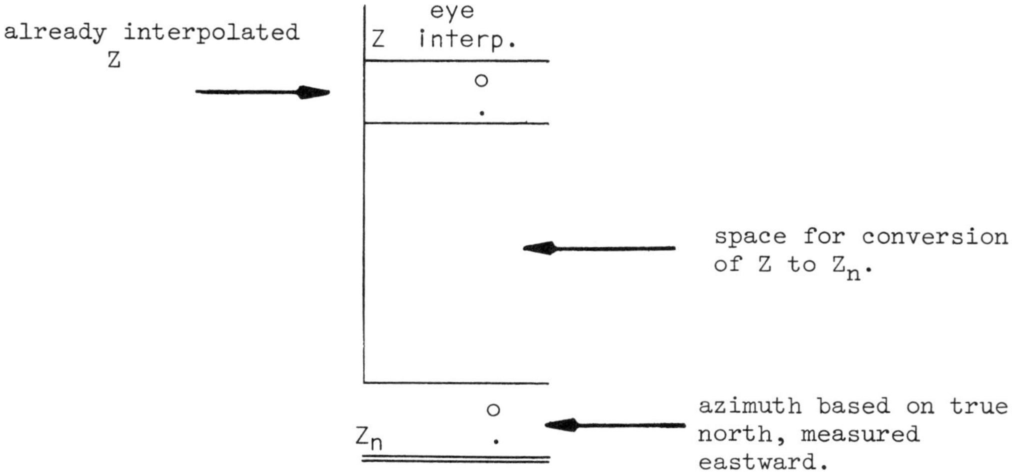


Conversion of Z to $Z_n$ depends on our latitude and the magnitude of LHA. These azimuths are always based on true north. For north latitude, if

LHA greater than 180°, $Z_n = Z$
LHA less than 180°, $Z_n = 360° - Z$

This information is found in the upper right corner of every left hand page of H.O. 229.

For south latitude, if LHA greater than 180°, $Z_n = 180° - Z$
LHA less than 180°, $Z_n = 180° + Z$

This information is found in the lower left corner of every right hand page of H.O. 229.

We have interpolated Z for declination increment and then converted it to a bearing based on true north, measured eastward 0° to 360°. Now we must interpolate $H_c$ for the additional minutes of declination, Dec Inc. The value "d" tells us the change in $H_c$ for one degree of declination change and also the direction in which $H_c$ is changing, increasing (+) or decreasing (-). We could solve this correctional factor for Dec Inc by a simple formula,

$$\frac{\text{Dec Inc}}{60'} \times d = \text{Net Correction.}$$

With a calculator, this is the simplest way of obtaining the correction of $H_c$. Remember the sign of "d" will also be the sign of the Net Corr. However, there are interpolation tables inside the front and back covers which accomplish the same result. To use them, we must separate "d" into several parts, noted as tens, units and decimals. Tens is the first digit of "d" with a zero added, units is the second digit, decimals is the third digit of "d" after the decimal point. For instance,

| d | tens | units | decimals |
|---|---|---|---|
| 54!6 | 50 | 4 | .6 |
| 23!7 | 20 | 3 | .7 |
| 18!9 | 10 | 8 | .9 |

Enter the interpolation table with Dec Inc. The inside of the front cover opening includes Dec Inc of 0!0 through 31!9. The back interpolation table covers 28!0 through 59!9. Opposite Dec Inc, take the value in the correct column of tens designated by "d". Enter this in the Interpolation Table section of the sight reduction sheets as tens. In the decimals column, notice that .0 to .9 is repeated eight times down the page. Choose the box of .0 to .9 that is to the right of your Dec Inc and enter it with units of "d" and decimals of "d". This value is recorded in the units and decimals part of the interpolation table on your sight reduction sheet. The two parts are then added together, given the sign of "d" and entered in the Net Correction box. Combined with the tabular value of $H_c$, this will give you $H_c$ for the full declination of the body.

Let us look at some examples of interpolation.

Dec Inc = 44!7 "d" = +32!6 (30 for tens, 2 for units, .6 for decimals)

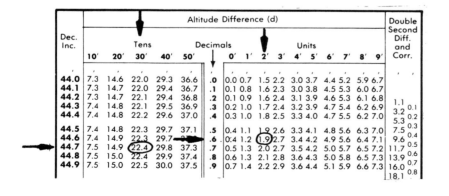

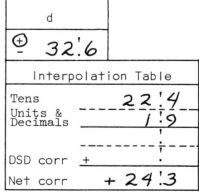

| Dec. Inc. | Altitude Difference (d) Tens 10′ | 20′ | 30′ | 40′ | 50′ | Decimals | Units 0′ | 1′ | 2′ | 3′ | 4′ | 5′ | 6′ | 7′ | 8′ | 9′ |
|---|---|---|---|---|---|---|---|---|---|---|---|---|---|---|---|---|
| 44.0 | 7.3 | 14.6 | 22.0 | 29.3 | 36.6 | .0 | 0.0 | 0.7 | 1.5 | 2.2 | 3.0 | 3.7 | 4.4 | 5.2 | 5.9 | 6.7 |
| 44.1 | 7.3 | 14.7 | 22.0 | 29.4 | 36.7 | .1 | 0.1 | 0.8 | 1.6 | 2.3 | 3.0 | 3.8 | 4.5 | 5.3 | 6.0 | 6.7 |
| 44.2 | 7.3 | 14.7 | 22.1 | 29.4 | 36.8 | .2 | 0.1 | 0.9 | 1.6 | 2.4 | 3.1 | 3.9 | 4.6 | 5.3 | 6.1 | 6.8 |
| 44.3 | 7.4 | 14.8 | 22.1 | 29.5 | 36.9 | .3 | 0.2 | 1.0 | 1.7 | 2.4 | 3.2 | 3.9 | 4.7 | 5.4 | 6.2 | 6.9 |
| 44.4 | 7.4 | 14.8 | 22.2 | 29.6 | 37.0 | .4 | 0.3 | 1.0 | 1.8 | 2.5 | 3.3 | 4.0 | 4.7 | 5.5 | 6.2 | 7.0 |
| 44.5 | 7.4 | 14.8 | 22.3 | 29.7 | 37.1 | .5 | 0.4 | 1.1 | 1.9 | 2.6 | 3.3 | 4.1 | 4.8 | 5.6 | 6.3 | 7.0 |
| 44.6 | 7.4 | 14.9 | 22.3 | 29.7 | [illegible] | .6 | 0.4 | 1.2 | 1.9 | 2.7 | 3.4 | 4.2 | 4.9 | 5.6 | 6.4 | 7.1 |
| 44.7 | 7.5 | 14.9 | 22.4 | 29.8 | 37.3 | .7 | 0.5 | 1.3 | 2.0 | 2.7 | 3.5 | 4.2 | 5.0 | 5.7 | 6.5 | 7.2 |
| 44.8 | 7.5 | 15.0 | 22.4 | 29.9 | 37.4 | .8 | 0.6 | 1.3 | 2.1 | 2.8 | 3.6 | 4.3 | 5.0 | 5.8 | 6.5 | 7.3 |
| 44.9 | 7.5 | 15.0 | 22.5 | 30.0 | 37.5 | .9 | 0.7 | 1.4 | 2.2 | 2.9 | 3.6 | 4.4 | 5.1 | 5.9 | 6.6 | 7.3 |

| Double Second Diff. and Corr. | |
|---|---|
| 1.1 | |
| | 0.1 |
| 3.2 | |
| | 0.2 |
| 5.3 | |
| | 0.3 |
| 7.5 | |
| | 0.4 |
| 9.6 | |
| | 0.5 |
| 11.7 | |
| | 0.6 |
| 13.9 | |
| | 0.7 |
| 16.0 | |
| | 0.8 |
| 18.1 | |

| d | |
|---|---|
| ± | 32!6 (+ circled) |

| Interpolation Table | |
|---|---|
| Tens | 22!4 |
| Units & Decimals | 1!9 |
| | |
| DSD corr | + |
| Net corr | + 24!3 |

Dec Inc = 25!9 "d" = -53!4 (50 for tens, 3 for units, .4 for decimals)

| Dec. Inc. | Tens 10′ | 20′ | 30′ | 40′ | 50′ | Decimals | Units 0′ | 1′ | 2′ | 3′ | 4′ | 5′ | 6′ | 7′ | 8′ | 9′ | Double Second Diff. and Corr. | |
|---|---|---|---|---|---|---|---|---|---|---|---|---|---|---|---|---|---|---|
| ′ | ′ | ′ | ′ | ′ | ′ | ′ | ′ | ′ | ′ | ′ | ′ | ′ | ′ | ′ | ′ | ′ | ′ | ′ |
| **24.0** | 4.0 | 8.0 | 12.0 | 16.0 | 20.0 | **.0** | 0.0 | 0.4 | 0.8 | 1.2 | 1.6 | 2.0 | 2.4 | 2.9 | 3.3 | 3.7 | 0.8 | |
| **24.1** | 4.0 | 8.0 | 12.0 | 16.0 | 20.1 | **.1** | 0.0 | 0.4 | 0.9 | 1.3 | 1.7 | 2.1 | 2.5 | 2.9 | 3.3 | 3.7 | 2.5 | 0.1 |
| **24.2** | 4.0 | 8.0 | 12.1 | 16.1 | 20.1 | **.2** | 0.1 | 0.5 | 0.9 | 1.3 | 1.7 | 2.1 | 2.5 | 2.9 | 3.3 | 3.8 | 4.1 | 0.2 |
| **24.3** | 4.0 | 8.1 | 12.1 | 16.2 | 20.2 | **.3** | 0.1 | 0.5 | 0.9 | 1.3 | 1.8 | 2.2 | 2.6 | 3.0 | 3.4 | 3.8 | 5.8 | 0.3 |
| **24.4** | 4.1 | 8.1 | 12.2 | 16.3 | 20.3 | **.4** | 0.2 | 0.6 | 1.0 | 1.4 | 1.8 | 2.2 | 2.6 | 3.0 | 3.4 | 3.8 | 7.4 | 0.4 |
| **24.5** | 4.1 | 8.2 | 12.3 | 16.3 | 20.4 | **.5** | 0.2 | 0.6 | 1.0 | 1.4 | 1.8 | 2.2 | 2.7 | 3.1 | 3.5 | 3.9 | 9.1 | 0.5 |
| **24.6** | 4.1 | 8.2 | 12.3 | 16.4 | 20.5 | **.6** | 0.2 | 0.7 | 1.1 | 1.5 | 1.9 | 2.3 | 2.7 | 3.1 | 3.5 | 3.9 | 10.7 | 0.6 |
| **24.7** | 4.1 | 8.3 | 12.4 | 16.5 | 20.6 | **.7** | 0.3 | 0.7 | 1.1 | 1.5 | 1.9 | 2.3 | 2.7 | 3.1 | 3.6 | 4.0 | 12.3 | 0.7 |
| **24.8** | 4.2 | 8.3 | 12.4 | 16.6 | 20.7 | **.8** | 0.3 | 0.7 | 1.1 | 1.6 | 2.0 | 2.4 | 2.8 | 3.2 | 3.6 | 4.0 | 14.0 | 0.8 |
| **24.9** | 4.2 | 8.3 | 12.5 | 16.6 | 20.8 | **.9** | 0.4 | 0.8 | 1.2 | 1.6 | 2.0 | 2.4 | 2.8 | 3.2 | 3.6 | 4.0 | 15.6 | 0.9 |
| | | | | | | | | | | | | | | | | | 17.3 | 1.0 |
| **25.0** | 4.1 | 8.3 | 12.5 | 16.6 | 20.8 | **.0** | 0.0 | 0.4 | 0.8 | 1.3 | 1.7 | 2.1 | 2.5 | 3.0 | 3.4 | 3.8 | 18.9 | 1.1 |
| **25.1** | 4.2 | 8.3 | 12.5 | 16.7 | 20.9 | **.1** | 0.0 | 0.5 | 0.9 | 1.3 | 1.7 | 2.2 | 2.6 | 3.0 | 3.4 | 3.9 | 20.6 | 1.2 |
| **25.2** | 4.2 | 8.4 | 12.6 | 16.8 | 21.0 | **.2** | 0.1 | 0.5 | 0.9 | 1.4 | 1.8 | 2.2 | 2.6 | 3.1 | 3.5 | 3.9 | 22.2 | 1.3 |
| **25.3** | 4.2 | 8.4 | 12.6 | 16.9 | 21.1 | **.3** | 0.1 | 0.6 | 1.0 | 1.4 | 1.8 | 2.3 | 2.7 | 3.1 | 3.5 | 4.0 | 23.9 | 1.4 |
| **25.4** | 4.2 | 8.5 | 12.7 | 16.9 | [illegible] | **.4** | 0.2 | 0.6 | 1.0 | 1.4 | 1.9 | 2.3 | 2.7 | 3.1 | 3.6 | 4.0 | 25.5 | 1.5 |
| | | | | | | | | | | | | | | | | | 27.2 | 1.6 |
| **25.5** | 4.3 | 8.5 | 12.8 | 17.0 | 21.3 | **.5** | 0.2 | 0.6 | 1.1 | 1.5 | 1.9 | 2.3 | 2.8 | 3.2 | 3.6 | 4.0 | 28.8 | 1.7 |
| **25.6** | 4.3 | 8.5 | 12.8 | 17.1 | 21.3 | **.6** | 0.3 | 0.7 | 1.1 | 1.5 | 2.0 | 2.4 | 2.8 | 3.2 | 3.7 | 4.1 | 30.4 | 1.8 |
| **25.7** | 4.3 | 8.6 | 12.9 | 17.2 | 21.4 | **.7** | 0.3 | 0.7 | 1.1 | 1.6 | 2.0 | 2.4 | 2.8 | 3.3 | 3.7 | 4.1 | 32.1 | 1.9 |
| **25.8** | 4.3 | 8.6 | 12.9 | 17.2 | 21.5 | **.8** | 0.3 | 0.8 | 1.2 | 1.6 | 2.0 | 2.5 | 2.9 | 3.3 | 3.7 | 4.2 | 33.7 | 2.0 |
| **25.9** | 4.4 | 8.7 | 13.0 | 17.3 | 21.6 | **.9** | 0.4 | 0.8 | 1.2 | 1.7 | 2.1 | 2.5 | 2.9 | 3.4 | 3.8 | 4.2 | 35.4 | 2.1 |

| d | |
|---|---|
| + ⊖ 53'.4 | + '. |

| Interpolation Table | |
|---|---|
| Tens | 21'.6 |
| Units & Decimals | 1'.4 |
| | '. |
| DSD corr | + . |
| Net corr | − 23'.0 |

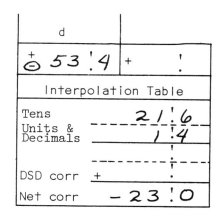

Doing these examples by direct calculation, we obtain the following figures.

$$\frac{44!7}{60'} \times +32!6 = 24!3 \qquad \frac{25!9}{60'} \times -53!4 = -23!1$$

The values of Net Corr will always agree with the interpolation table to within one tenth of a minute.

In the case of "d" being 60!0, found when the body is on your meridian (LHA = 0°), by direct calculation we see that 60/60 x Dec Inc = Dec Inc. In other words, the Net Corr is the same as the declination increment. If you wish to use the interpolation tables, divide the "d" of 60 into 50 for tens and 10 for tens (no units or decimals) or 50 for tens, 9 for units and .9 for decimals (approximating 60 with 59.9). Either way, the values should compare to within a tenth of a minute except when DSD correction is indicated (see below).

Occasionally for very high altitude bodies, there is an additional correction needed for more accuracy in interpolation. This correction is referred to as the double-second difference (DSD) correction and the need for its use is indicated by observing "d". If it is printed in italics and followed by a small dot, the DSD correction is in order. For example, assume a LHA of 15°, AP Lat of 31° N, latitude SAME name as declination, declination of 25° 46!8 N. This places us on page 32 of H.O. 229 with values as follows.

| | $H_c$ | d | DSD |
|---|---|---|---|
| Tabular Values | 75° 28'.7 | ⊕ − 26'.3 | + 6'.6 |

DSD is obtained by taking the difference between the "d" above ours and the "d" below ours, in this case 29!5 minus 22!9 = 6!6. Its sign is always positive, the correction therefore being also positive. To obtain the correction value, enter the interpolation table per usual with Dec Inc of 46!8. In the table to the far right, we find that 6!6 lies between 5!8 and 8!1, giving a correction value of +0!3. Enter this in the interpolation table, combine with the two parts and record the net correction.

## 15°, 345° L.H.A. LATITUDE

| Dec. | 30° Hc | 30° d | 30° Z | 31° Hc | 31° d | 31° Z | 32° Hc | 32° d | 32° Z |
|---|---|---|---|---|---|---|---|---|---|
| ° | ° ' | ' | ° | ° ' | ' | ° | ° ' | ' | ° |
| 0 | 56 46.4 | +54.7 | 151.8 | 55 53.4 | +55.0 | 152.5 | 55 00.0 | +55.3 | 153.2 |
| 1 | 57 41.1 | 54.3 | 151.0 | 56 48.4 | 54.7 | 151.8 | 55 55.3 | 55.1 | 152.5 |
| 2 | 58 35.4 | 54.0 | 150.2 | 57 43.1 | 54.4 | 151.0 | 56 50.4 | 54.8 | 151.8 |
| 3 | 59 29.4 | 53.6 | 149.4 | 58 37.5 | 54.1 | 150.2 | 57 45.2 | 54.6 | 151.0 |
| 4 | 60 23.0 | 53.3 | 148.5 | 59 31.6 | 53.8 | 149.4 | 58 39.8 | 54.2 | 150.2 |
| 5 | 61 16.3 | +52.9 | 147.6 | 60 25.4 | +53.4 | 148.5 | 59 34.0 | +53.9 | 149.4 |
| 6 | 62 09.2 | 52.4 | 146.6 | 61 18.8 | 53.0 | 147.6 | 60 27.9 | 53.5 | 148.5 |
| 7 | 63 01.6 | 51.9 | 145.5 | 62 11.8 | 52.6 | 146.6 | 61 21.4 | 53.2 | 147.6 |
| 8 | 63 53.5 | 51.3 | 144.4 | 63 04.4 | 52.0 | 145.5 | 62 14.6 | 52.7 | 146.6 |
| 9 | 64 44.8 | 50.8 | 143.2 | 63 56.4 | 51.5 | 144.4 | 63 07.3 | 52.2 | 145.6 |
| 10 | 65 35.6 | +50.0 | 141.9 | 64 47.9 | +50.9 | 143.2 | 63 59.5 | +51.6 | 144.5 |
| 11 | 66 25.6 | 49.3 | 140.6 | 65 38.8 | 50.2 | 142.0 | 64 51.1 | 51.1 | 143.3 |
| 12 | 67 14.9 | 48.5 | 139.1 | 66 29.0 | 49.5 | 140.6 | 65 42.2 | 50.4 | 142.0 |
| 13 | 68 03.4 | 47.5 | 137.6 | 67 18.5 | 48.7 | 139.2 | 66 32.6 | 49.7 | 140.7 |
| 14 | 68 50.9 | 46.5 | 135.9 | 68 07.2 | 47.7 | 137.6 | 67 22.3 | 48.8 | 139.3 |
| 15 | 69 37.4 | +45.3 | 134.1 | 68 54.9 | +46.7 | 136.0 | 68 11.1 | +48.0 | 137.7 |
| 16 | 70 22.7 | 44.0 | 132.2 | 69 41.6 | 45.6 | 134.2 | 68 59.1 | 46.9 | 136.1 |
| 17 | 71 06.7 | 42.5 | 130.1 | 70 27.2 | 44.2 | 132.3 | 69 46.0 | 45.8 | 134.3 |
| 18 | 71 49.2 | 40.9 | 127.9 | 71 11.4 | 42.8 | 130.2 | 70 31.8 | 44.5 | 132.4 |
| 19 | 72 30.1 | 39.0 | 125.5 | 71 54.2 | 41.1 | 128.0 | 71 16.3 | 43.0 | 130.3 |
| 20 | 73 09.1 | +37.0• | 122.9 | 72 35.3 | +39.3 | 125.6 | 71 59.3 | +41.4 | 128.1 |
| 21 | 73 46.1 | 34.6• | 120.2 | 73 14.6 | 37.3• | 123.1 | 72 40.7 | 39.6 | 125.8 |
| 22 | 74 20.7 | 32.1• | 117.2 | 73 51.9 | 34.9• | 120.3 | 73 20.3 | 37.5• | 123.2 |
| 23 | 74 52.8 | 29.2• | 114.0 | 74 26.8 | 32.4• | 117.3 | 73 57.8 | 35.3• | 120.4 |
| 24 | 75 22.0 | 26.1• | 110.6 | 74 59.2 | 29.5• | 114.1 | 74 33.1 | 32.6• | 117.4 |
| 25 | 75 48.1 | +22.6• | 107.0 | 75 28.7 | +26.3• | 110.7 | 75 05.7 | +29.8• | 114.2 |
| 26 | 76 10.7 | 18.8• | 103.2 | 75 55.0 | 22.9• | 107.1 | 75 35.5 | 26.7• | 110.8 |
| 27 | 76 29.5 | 14.8• | 99.2 | 76 17.9 | 19.1• | 103.2 | 76 02.2 | 23.1• | 107.1 |
| 28 | 76 44.3 | 10.6• | 95.0 | 76 37.0 | 15.0• | 99.2 | 76 25.3 | 19.4• | 103.3 |
| 29 | 76 54.9 | 6.2• | 90.6 | 76 52.0 | 10.8• | 94.9 | 76 44.7 | 15.2• | 99.2 |
| 30 | 77 01.1 | + 1.7• | 86.2 | 77 02.8 | + 6.3• | 90.6 | 76 59.9 | +11.0• | 94.9 |
| 31 | 77 02.8 | − 2.9• | 81.8 | 77 09.1 | + 1.8• | 86.1 | 77 10.9 | 6.5• | 90.5 |
| 32 | 76 59.9 | 7.3• | 77.3 | 77 10.9 | − 2.8• | 81.6 | 77 17.4 | + 1.8• | 86.0 |
| 33 | 76 52.6 | 11.8• | 72.9 | 77 08.1 | 7.4• | 77.1 | 77 19.2 | − 2.8• | 81.5 |
| 34 | 76 40.8 | 15.9• | 68.6 | 77 00.7 | 11.8• | 72.7 | 77 16.4 | 7.4• | 76.9 |

Altitude Difference (d)

| Dec. Inc. | Tens 10' | 20' | 30' | 40' | 50' | Decimals | Units 0' | 1' | 2' | 3' | 4' | 5' | 6' | 7' | 8' | 9' |
|---|---|---|---|---|---|---|---|---|---|---|---|---|---|---|---|---|
| ' | ' | ' | ' | ' | ' | ' | ' | ' | ' | ' | ' | ' | ' | ' | ' | ' |
| 46.0 | 7.6 | 15.3 | 23.0 | 30.6 | 38.3 | .0 | 0.0 | 0.8 | 1.5 | 2.3 | 3.1 | 3.9 | 4.6 | 5.4 | 6.2 | 7.0 |
| 46.1 | 7.7 | 15.3 | 23.0 | 30.7 | 38.4 | .1 | 0.1 | 0.9 | 1.6 | 2.4 | 3.2 | 4.0 | 4.7 | 5.5 | 6.3 | 7.1 |
| 46.2 | 7.7 | 15.4 | 23.1 | 30.8 | 38.5 | .2 | 0.2 | 0.9 | 1.7 | 2.5 | 3.3 | 4.0 | 4.8 | 5.6 | 6.4 | 7.1 |
| 46.3 | 7.7 | 15.4 | 23.1 | 30.9 | [illegible] | .3 | 0.2 | 1.0 | 1.8 | 2.6 | 3.3 | 4.1 | 4.9 | 5.7 | 6.4 | 7.2 |
| 46.4 | 7.7 | 15.5 | 23.2 | 30.9 | 38.7 | .4 | 0.3 | 1.1 | 1.9 | 2.6 | 3.4 | 4.2 | 5.0 | 5.7 | 6.5 | 7.3 |
| 46.5 | 7.8 | 15.5 | 23.3 | 31.0 | 38.8 | .5 | 0.4 | 1.2 | 1.9 | 2.7 | 3.5 | 4.3 | 5.0 | 5.8 | 6.6 | 7.4 |
| 46.6 | 7.8 | 15.5 | 23.3 | 31.1 | 38.8 | .6 | 0.5 | 1.2 | 2.0 | 2.8 | 3.6 | 4.3 | 5.1 | 5.9 | 6.7 | 7.4 |
| 46.7 | 7.8 | 15.6 | 23.4 | 31.2 | 38.9 | .7 | 0.5 | 1.3 | 2.1 | 2.9 | 3.6 | 4.4 | 5.2 | 6.0 | 6.7 | 7.5 |
| 46.8 | 7.8 | 15.6 | 23.4 | 31.2 | 39.0 | .8 | 0.6 | 1.4 | 2.2 | 2.9 | 3.7 | 4.5 | 5.3 | 6.0 | 6.8 | 7.6 |
| 46.9 | 7.9 | 15.7 | 23.5 | 31.3 | 39.1 | .9 | 0.7 | 1.5 | 2.2 | 3.0 | 3.8 | 4.6 | 5.3 | 6.1 | 6.9 | 7.7 |
| 47.0 | 7.8 | 15.6 | 23.5 | 31.3 | 39.1 | .0 | 0.0 | 0.8 | 1.6 | 2.4 | 3.2 | 4.0 | 4.7 | 5.5 | 6.3 | 7.1 |
| 47.1 | 7.8 | 15.7 | 23.5 | 31.4 | 39.2 | .1 | 0.1 | 0.9 | 1.7 | 2.5 | 3.2 | 4.0 | 4.8 | 5.6 | 6.4 | 7.2 |
| 47.2 | 7.8 | 15.7 | 23.6 | 31.4 | 39.3 | .2 | 0.2 | 0.9 | 1.7 | 2.5 | 3.3 | 4.1 | 4.9 | 5.7 | 6.5 | 7.3 |
| 47.3 | 7.9 | 15.8 | 23.6 | 31.5 | 39.4 | .3 | 0.2 | 1.0 | 1.8 | 2.6 | 3.4 | 4.2 | 5.0 | 5.8 | 6.6 | 7.4 |
| 47.4 | 7.9 | 15.8 | 23.7 | 31.6 | 39.5 | .4 | 0.3 | 1.1 | 1.9 | 2.7 | 3.5 | 4.3 | 5.1 | 5.9 | 6.6 | 7.4 |

| Double Second Diff. | and Corr. |
|---|---|
| 1.2 | |
| | 0.1 |
| 3.5 | |
| | 0.2 |
| 5.8 | |
| | 0.3 |
| 8.1 | |
| | 0.4 |
| 10.5 | |
| | 0.5 |
| 12.8 | |
| | 0.6 |
| 15.1 | |
| | 0.7 |
| 17.4 | |
| | 0.8 |
| 19.8 | |
| | 0.9 |
| 22.1 | |
| | 1.0 |
| 24.4 | |
| | 1.1 |
| 26.7 | |
| | 1.2 |
| 29.1 | |
| | 1.3 |
| 31.4 | |
| | 1.4 |
| 33.7 | |
| | 1.5 |
| 36.0 | |

| Interpolation Table | |
|---|---|
| Tens | 15!6 |
| Units & Decimals | 4!9 |
| | + 20!5 |
| DSD corr | + 0!3 |
| Net corr | + 20!8 |

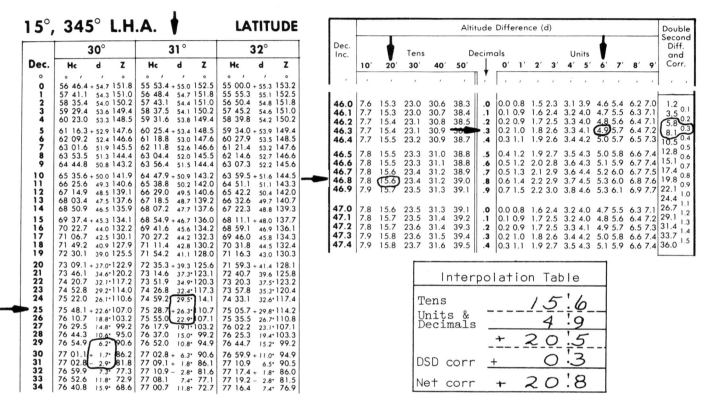

Note that farther down in the columns above, the "d" changes sign, from positive to negative. In this case, when declination puts us at the point of change, look at a number line to see that we should add the two d's on either side of ours to get the difference between them. Take the example of Lat 30°, Dec 30°.

DSD

| d values | −2.9 | 0 | +1.7 | +6.2 |
|---|---|---|---|---|
| | at dec 31° | | at dec 30° | at dec 29° |

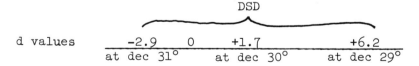

The difference between the two **d**'s on either side of ours (+1.7) is

$$+6.2 - (-2.9) = +6.2 + 2.9 = +9.1$$

In summary then, when the values of "d" on either side of ours have opposite sign, add them to get the difference. When the values of "d" on either side of ours have the same sign, subtract them to get the difference.

After getting $H_c$, we then enter $H_o$ from the altitude correction section and subtract the smaller of the two altitudes from the larger. This gives us the intercept, labelled "a". Assuming our DR and sextant sight are fairly accurate and we have reduced the sight properly, the intercept is usually less than 30!0. When we enter H.O. 229, a quick check to see if we have made a gross error up to that point is to compare the tabular $H_c$ with our $H_o$. They should be within a degree or so. Our net correction will reduce this difference.

After obtaining our intercept, we then check to see which value, $H_c$ or $H_o$, is greater. If $H_o$ is more we circle T which stands for towards, remembered by Ho Mo To. If $H_c$ is greater than $H_o$, we circle A which stands for away. To understand the meaning of towards and away, let us remember Chapter 2 where we established circles of position around three celestial bodies. Since these circles were so huge that they couldn't be plotted on our charts or plotting sheets, we now have established an assumed position (AP) that we use as a middleman. This AP may be between us and the geographical position (GP) of the body or on the other side of us from the GP. Let us take the first case where the AP is between us and the GP. $H_c$ is the altitude of the celestial body from the AP, $H_o$ is the altitude of the celestial body from our real position (RP).

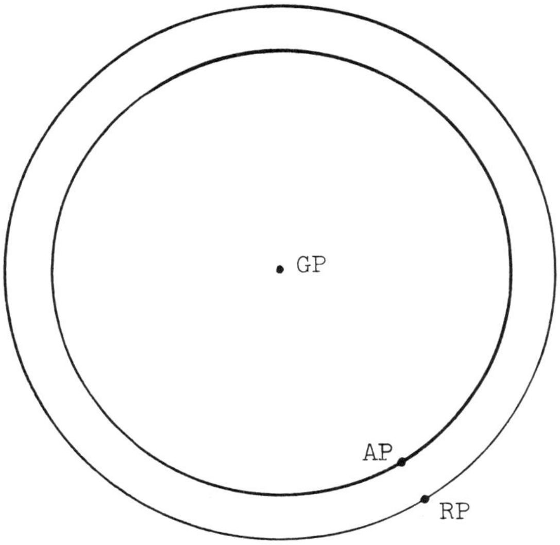


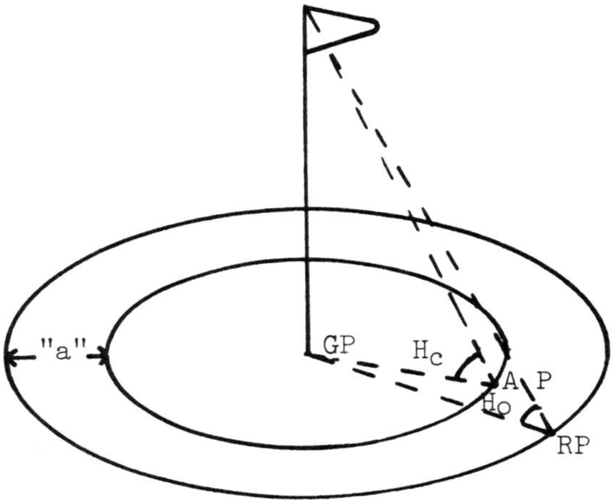


Notice that in the diagram to the right, the flagpole (an analogy to the celestial body) appears higher the closer you are to it. Therefore, in this case, $H_c$ is greater than $H_o$. Our plotting will be done from the assumed position. The $Z_n$ establishes the azimuth of the GP from the AP or RP, assuming they are reasonably close to each other. Our question now is whether we should plot on the bearing of $Z_n$ toward the GP from our AP or away from the GP from our AP to reach the RP. In this case, we need to plot from the AP away from GP to get to RP. Therefore, if $H_c$ is greater than $H_o$, we plot away from the GP, in the opposite direction of $Z_n$. The intercept is the distance between the two circles of position. With an intercept of 10', we would plot 10 nautical miles away from our AP to reach the circle of position on which lies our RP. By interchanging AP and RP, $H_c$ and $H_o$, we can see the reasoning behind the other case where if $H_o$ is more, we plot towards the GP (in a direction of $Z_n$) from the AP to reach the circle of position on which lies our RP. Plotting will be discussed in more detail in the next chapter.

Let us now work through the four examples mentioned earlier to obtain the "a" and $Z_n$ values.

Example 1. LHA = 29°, Tab Dec = 10°, Dec Inc = 16!7 N, AP Lat = 32° S, CONTRARY. These values place us in the top half of page 61 in H.O. 229.

**LATITUDE CONTRARY**

| Dec. | 30° Hc | 30° d | 30° Z | 31° Hc | 31° d | 31° Z | 32° Hc | 32° d | 32° Z | 33° Hc | 33° d | 33° Z |
|---|---|---|---|---|---|---|---|---|---|---|---|---|
| ° | ° ′ | ′ | ° | ° ′ | ′ | ° | ° ′ | ′ | ° | ° ′ | ′ | ° |
| 0 | 49 14.4 | −46.2 | 132.1 | 48 33.8 | −46.9 | 132.9 | 47 52.7 | −47.6 | 133.7 | 47 10.9 | −48.3 | 134.5 |
| 1 | 48 28.2 | 46.7 | 133.0 | 47 46.9 | 47.4 | 133.8 | 47 05.1 | 48.1 | 134.6 | 46 22.6 | 48.6 | 135.4 |
| 2 | 47 41.5 | 47.1 | 134.0 | 46 59.5 | 47.7 | 134.7 | 46 17.0 | 48.4 | 135.5 | 45 34.0 | 49.0 | 136.2 |
| 3 | 46 54.4 | 47.6 | 134.9 | 46 11.8 | 48.2 | 135.6 | 45 28.6 | 48.8 | 136.3 | 44 45.0 | 49.4 | 137.0 |
| 4 | 46 06.8 | 47.9 | 135.8 | 45 23.6 | 48.6 | 136.5 | 44 39.8 | 49.1 | 137.2 | 43 55.6 | 49.7 | 137.8 |
| 5 | 45 18.9 | −48.3 | 136.6 | 44 35.0 | −48.9 | 137.3 | 43 50.7 | −49.4 | 138.0 | 43 05.9 | −50.0 | 138.6 |
| 6 | 44 30.6 | 48.7 | 137.5 | 43 46.1 | 49.2 | 138.1 | 43 01.3 | 49.8 | 138.7 | 42 15.9 | 50.2 | 139.3 |
| 7 | 43 41.9 | 49.0 | 138.3 | 42 56.9 | 49.5 | 138.9 | 42 11.5 | 50.1 | 139.5 | 41 25.7 | 50.6 | 140.1 |
| 8 | 42 52.9 | 49.3 | 139.1 | 42 07.4 | 49.9 | 139.7 | 41 21.4 | 50.3 | 140.2 | 40 35.1 | 50.8 | 140.8 |
| 9 | 42 03.6 | 49.7 | 139.8 | 41 17.5 | 50.1 | 140.4 | 40 31.1 | 50.6 | 141.0 | 39 44.3 | 51.0 | 141.5 |
| 10 | 41 13.9 | −49.9 | 140.6 | 40 27.4 | −50.4 | 141.1 | 39 40.5 | −50.8 | 141.7 | 38 53.3 | −51.3 | 142.2 |
| 11 | 40 24.0 | 50.2 | 141.3 | 39 37.0 | 50.6 | 141.8 | 38 49.7 | 51.1 | 142.3 | 38 02.0 | 51.5 | 142.8 |
| 12 | 39 33.8 | 50.4 | 142.0 | 38 46.4 | 50.9 | 142.5 | 37 58.6 | 51.3 | 143.0 | 37 10.5 | 51.7 | 143.5 |
| 13 | 38 43.4 | 50.7 | 142.7 | 37 55.5 | 51.1 | 143.2 | 37 07.3 | 51.5 | 143.7 | 36 18.8 | 51.9 | 144.1 |
| 14 | 37 52.7 | 50.9 | 143.4 | 37 04.4 | 51.4 | 143.9 | 36 15.8 | 51.8 | 144.3 | 35 26.9 | 52.1 | 144.7 |

Altitude Difference (d)

| Dec. Inc. | Tens 10′ | 20′ | 30′ | 40′ | 50′ | Decimals | Units 0′ | 1′ | 2′ | 3′ | 4′ | 5′ | 6′ | 7′ |
|---|---|---|---|---|---|---|---|---|---|---|---|---|---|---|
| ′ | ′ | ′ | ′ | ′ | ′ | ′ | ′ | ′ | ′ | ′ | ′ | ′ | ′ | ′ |
| 16.0 | 2.6 | 5.3 | 8.0 | 10.6 | 13.3 | .0 | 0.0 | 0.3 | 0.5 | 0.8 | 1.1 | 1.4 | 1.6 | 1.9 |
| 16.1 | 2.7 | 5.3 | 8.0 | 10.7 | 13.4 | .1 | 0.0 | 0.3 | 0.6 | 0.9 | 1.1 | 1.4 | 1.7 | 2.0 |
| 16.2 | 2.7 | 5.4 | 8.1 | 10.8 | 13.5 | .2 | 0.1 | 0.3 | 0.6 | 0.9 | 1.2 | 1.4 | 1.7 | 2.0 |
| 16.3 | 2.7 | 5.4 | 8.1 | 10.9 | 13.6 | .3 | 0.1 | 0.4 | 0.6 | 0.9 | 1.2 | 1.5 | 1.7 | 2.0 |
| 16.4 | 2.7 | 5.5 | 8.2 | 10.9 | 13.7 | .4 | 0.1 | 0.4 | 0.7 | 0.9 | 1.2 | 1.5 | 1.8 | 2.0 |
| 16.5 | 2.8 | 5.5 | 8.3 | 11.0 | 13.8 | .5 | 0.1 | 0.4 | 0.7 | 1.0 | 1.2 | 1.5 | 1.8 | 2.1 |
| 16.6 | 2.8 | 5.5 | 8.3 | 11.1 | 13.8 | .6 | 0.2 | 0.4 | 0.7 | 1.0 | 1.3 | 1.5 | 1.8 | 2.1 |
| 16.7 | 2.8 | 5.6 | 8.4 | 11.2 | 13.9 | .7 | 0.2 | 0.5 | 0.7 | 1.0 | 1.3 | 1.6 | 1.8 | 2.1 |
| 16.8 | 2.8 | 5.6 | 8.4 | 11.2 | [illegible] | .8 | 0.2 | 0.5 | 0.8 | 1.0 | 1.3 | 1.6 | 1.9 | 2.1 |
| 16.9 | 2.9 | 5.7 | 8.5 | 11.3 | 14.1 | .9 | 0.2 | 0.5 | 0.8 | 1.1 | 1.3 | 1.6 | 1.9 | 2.2 |

Since our declination is <u>roughly</u> ¼ of the way between declinations of 10° and 11°, we interpolate Z as ¼ of the way between 141°7 and 142°3, giving a value of 141°9. Since latitude is south and LHA is less than 180°, $Z_n$ = 180° + Z or 321°9. Interpolation values are marked above. Net correction is negative since "d" is negative. Assume an $H_o$ of 39° 36!4 and we find that this is greater than $H_c$ by 10!0. Intercept is therefore 10 minutes (or nautical miles) towards $Z_n$ from the AP.

| | $H_c$ | d | DSD | Z eye interp. |
|---|---|---|---|---|
| Tabular Values | 39° 40!5 | + (−) 50!8 | + ! | 141°9 |
| Net corr | ° −14!1 | Interpolation Table | | 180.0 + 141.9 |
| $H_c$ | 39° 26!4 | Tens 13!9; Units & Decimals 0!2 | | |
| $H_o$ | 39° 36!4 | DSD corr + ; Net corr 14!1 | | |
| a | 10!0 | (T) Ho>Hc; A Ho<Hc | | $Z_n$ 321°9 |

Example 2. LHA = 34°, Tab Dec = 46°, Dec Inc = 36!3 N, AP Lat = 41° N, SAME
This places us in the middle of page 252 of H.O. 229.

**34°, 326° L.H.A. LATITUDE SAME NA**

| Dec. | 38° Hc | 38° d | 38° Z | 40° Hc | 40° d | 40° Z | 41° Hc | 41° d | 41° Z |
|---|---|---|---|---|---|---|---|---|---|
| ° | ° ′ | ′ | ° | ° ′ | ′ | ° | ° ′ | ′ | ° |
| 0 | 40 47.4 | + 48.6 | 132.4 | 39 25.6 | + 49.7 | 133.6 | 38 43.9 | + 50.4 | 134.2 |
| 1 | 41 36.0 | 48.4 | 131.6 | 40 15.3 | 49.6 | 132.9 | 39 34.3 | 50.1 | 133.5 |
| 2 | 42 24.4 | 47.9 | 130.8 | 41 04.9 | 49.2 | 132.1 | 40 24.4 | 49.8 | 132.8 |
| 3 | 43 12.3 | 47.6 | 130.0 | 41 54.1 | 48.9 | 131.4 | 41 14.2 | 49.5 | 132.0 |
| 4 | 43 59.9 | 47.3 | 129.2 | 42 43.0 | 48.6 | 130.6 | 42 03.7 | 49.2 | 131.3 |
| 40 | 63 39.7 | + 5.9• | 74.9 | 64 06.9 | + 10.5• | 78.9 | 64 17.4 | + 12.9• | 80.9 |
| 41 | 63 45.6 | 3.9• | 72.7 | 64 17.4 | 8.5• | 76.6 | 64 30.3 | 10.7• | 78.7 |
| 42 | 63 49.5 | + 1.7• | 70.4 | 64 25.9 | 6.2• | 74.3 | 64 41.0 | 8.6• | 76.4 |
| 43 | 63 51.2 | − 0.4• | 68.1 | 64 32.1 | 4.1• | 72.0 | 64 49.6 | 6.4• | 74.0 |
| 44 | 63 50.8 | 2.6• | 65.9 | 64 36.2 | + 1.8• | 69.7 | 64 56.0 | 4.2• | 71.7 |
| 45 | 63 48.2 | − 4.7• | 63.6 | 64 38.0 | − 0.3• | 67.4 | 65 00.2 | + 1.9• | 69.3 |
| 46 | 63 43.5 | 6.7• | 61.3 | 64 37.7 | 2.6• | 65.0 | 65 02.1 | − 0.3• | 67.0 |
| 47 | 63 36.8 | 8.9• | 59.1 | 64 35.1 | 4.7• | 62.7 | 65 01.8 | 2.6• | 64.6 |
| 48 | 63 27.9 | 10.9• | 56.9 | 64 30.4 | 6.9• | 60.4 | 64 59.2 | 4.8• | 62.2 |
| 49 | 63 17.0 | 12.9 | 54.7 | 64 23.5 | 9.1• | 58.1 | 64 54.4 | 7.0• | 59.9 |
| 50 | 63 04.1 | − 14.8 | 52.5 | 64 14.4 | − 11.1• | 55.8 | 64 47.4 | − 9.2• | 57.6 |
| 51 | 62 49.3 | 16.7 | 50.4 | 64 03.3 | 13.3• | 53.5 | 64 38.2 | 11.4• | 55.2 |
| 52 | 62 32.6 | 18.6 | 48.3 | 63 50.0 | 15.2 | 51.3 | 64 26.8 | 13.4• | 53.0 |
| 53 | 62 14.0 | 20.4 | 46.2 | 63 34.8 | 17.2 | 49.1 | 64 13.4 | 15.5• | 50.7 |
| 54 | 61 53.6 | 22.0 | 44.2 | 63 17.6 | 19.1 | 47.0 | 63 57.9 | 17.4 | 48.5 |

| Dec. Inc. | Tens 10′ | 20′ | 30′ | 40′ | 50′ | Decimals | Units 0′ | 1′ | 2′ | 3′ | 4′ | 5′ | 6′ | 7′ | 8′ | 9′ |
|---|---|---|---|---|---|---|---|---|---|---|---|---|---|---|---|---|
| ′ | ′ | ′ | ′ | ′ | ′ | ′ | ′ | ′ | ′ | ′ | ′ | ′ | ′ | ′ | ′ | ′ |
| 36.0 | 6.0 | 12.0 | 18.0 | 24.0 | 30.0 | .0 | 0.0 | 0.6 | 1.2 | 1.8 | 2.4 | 3.0 | 3.6 | 4.3 | 4.9 | 5.5 |
| 36.1 | 6.0 | 12.0 | 18.0 | 24.0 | 30.1 | .1 | 0.1 | 0.7 | 1.3 | 1.9 | 2.5 | 3.1 | 3.7 | 4.3 | 4.9 | 5.5 |
| 36.2 | 6.0 | 12.0 | 18.1 | 24.1 | 30.1 | .2 | 0.1 | 0.7 | 1.3 | 1.9 | 2.6 | 3.2 | 3.8 | 4.4 | 5.0 | 5.6 |
| 36.3 | 6.0 | 12.1 | 18.1 | 24.2 | [illegible] | .3 | 0.2 | 0.8 | 1.4 | 2.0 | 2.6 | 3.2 | 3.8 | 4.4 | 5.0 | 5.7 |
| 36.4 | 6.1 | 12.1 | 18.2 | 24.3 | 30.3 | .4 | 0.2 | 0.9 | 1.5 | 2.1 | 2.7 | 3.3 | 3.9 | 4.5 | 5.1 | 5.7 |
| 36.5 | 6.1 | 12.2 | 18.3 | 24.3 | 30.4 | .5 | 0.3 | 0.9 | 1.5 | 2.1 | 2.7 | 3.3 | 4.0 | 4.6 | 5.2 | 5.8 |
| 36.6 | 6.1 | 12.2 | 18.3 | 24.4 | 30.5 | .6 | 0.4 | 1.0 | 1.6 | 2.2 | 2.8 | 3.4 | 4.0 | 4.6 | 5.2 | 5.8 |
| 36.7 | 6.1 | 12.3 | 18.4 | 24.5 | 30.6 | .7 | 0.4 | 1.0 | 1.6 | 2.3 | 2.9 | 3.5 | 4.1 | 4.7 | 5.3 | 5.9 |
| 36.8 | 6.2 | 12.3 | 18.4 | 24.6 | 30.7 | .8 | 0.5 | 1.1 | 1.7 | 2.3 | 2.9 | 3.5 | 4.1 | 4.7 | 5.4 | 6.0 |
| 36.9 | 6.2 | 12.3 | 18.5 | 24.6 | 30.8 | .9 | 0.5 | 1.2 | 1.8 | 2.4 | 3.0 | 3.6 | 4.2 | 4.8 | 5.4 | 6.0 |
| 37.0 | 6.1 | 12.3 | 18.5 | 24.6 | 30.8 | .0 | 0.0 | 0.6 | 1.2 | 1.9 | 2.5 | 3.1 | 3.7 | 4.4 | 5.0 | 5.6 |
| 37.1 | 6.2 | 12.3 | 18.5 | 24.7 | 30.9 | .1 | 0.1 | 0.7 | 1.3 | 1.9 | 2.6 | 3.2 | 3.8 | 4.4 | 5.1 | 5.7 |
| 37.2 | 6.2 | 12.4 | 18.6 | 24.8 | 31.0 | .2 | 0.1 | 0.7 | 1.4 | 2.0 | 2.6 | 3.2 | 3.9 | 4.5 | 5.1 | 5.7 |
| 37.3 | 6.2 | 12.4 | 18.6 | 24.9 | 31.1 | .3 | 0.2 | 0.8 | 1.4 | 2.1 | 2.7 | 3.3 | 3.9 | 4.6 | 5.2 | 5.8 |
| 37.4 | 6.2 | 12.5 | 18.7 | 24.9 | 31.2 | .4 | 0.2 | 0.9 | 1.5 | 2.1 | 2.7 | 3.4 | 4.0 | 4.6 | 5.2 | 5.9 |
| 37.5 | 6.3 | 12.5 | 18.8 | 25.0 | 31.3 | .5 | 0.3 | 0.9 | 1.6 | 2.2 | 2.8 | 3.4 | 4.1 | 4.7 | 5.3 | 5.9 |
| 37.6 | 6.3 | 12.5 | 18.8 | 25.1 | 31.3 | .6 | 0.4 | 1.0 | 1.6 | 2.2 | 2.9 | 3.5 | 4.1 | 4.7 | 5.4 | 6.0 |
| 37.7 | 6.3 | 12.6 | 18.9 | 25.2 | 31.4 | .7 | 0.4 | 1.1 | 1.7 | 2.3 | 2.9 | 3.6 | 4.2 | 4.8 | 5.4 | 6.1 |
| 37.8 | 6.3 | 12.6 | 18.9 | 25.2 | 31.5 | .8 | 0.5 | 1.1 | 1.7 | 2.4 | 3.0 | 3.6 | 4.2 | 4.9 | 5.5 | 6.1 |
| 37.9 | 6.4 | 12.7 | 19.0 | 25.3 | 31.6 | .9 | 0.6 | 1.2 | 1.8 | 2.4 | 3.1 | 3.7 | 4.3 | 4.9 | 5.6 | 6.2 |

| Double Second Diff. | and Corr. |
|---|---|
| ′ | ′ |
| 0.8 | |
| | 0.1 |
| 2.5 | |
| | 0.2 |
| 4.2 | |
| | 0.3 |
| 5.9 | |
| | 0.4 |
| 7.6 | |
| | 0.5 |
| 9.3 | |
| | 0.6 |
| 11.0 | |
| | 0.7 |
| 12.7 | |
| | 0.8 |
| 14.4 | |
| | 0.9 |
| 16.1 | |
| | 1.0 |
| 17.8 | |
| | 1.1 |
| 19.5 | |
| | 1.2 |
| 21.2 | |
| | 1.3 |
| 22.8 | |
| | 1.4 |
| 24.5 | |
| | 1.5 |
| 26.2 | |
| | 1.6 |
| 27.9 | |
| | 1.7 |
| 29.6 | |
| | 1.8 |
| 31.3 | |
| | 1.9 |
| 33.0 | |
| | 2.0 |
| 34.7 | |

We have a DSD correction here. Our "d" of -0!3 is bracketed by +1!9 and -2!6, the difference between these two numbers being 4!5. In interpolation, there are no tens, therefore, the first part is zero. No units and .3 decimals leaves us with just 0!2, negative since "d" is negative. Going farther to the right into the DSD correction column, we find that the Dec Inc 36!3 puts us in the correction column starting with 0!8, ending with 34!7. Our DSD of 4.5 lies between 4.2 and 5.9, giving a correction of 0!3, always positive. Net correction is +0!1. Interpolation of Z is done by seeing that 36!3 (Dec Inc) is roughly 6/10 of the way through the degree. Therefore, interpolate 6/10 of the way between 67.0 (Z at 46° Dec) and 64.6 (Z at 47° Dec). Six tenths of the difference between the two Z's is 6/10 x 2.4 = 1.4. Z is decreasing as declination increases so <u>subtract</u> 1.4 from 67.0, leaving an interpolated Z of 65°6. By conversion rules, north latitude with LHA less than 180° gives a $Z_n$ = 360° - Z. $Z_n$ then equals 294°4. Assuming an $H_o$ of 65° 00!0, we find that $H_c$ is greater by 2!2, therefore, this intercept is plotted from the AP AWAY from the azimuth of 294°4.

| | $H_c$ | d | DSD | Z eye interp. |
|---|---|---|---|---|
| Tabular Values | 65° 02!1 | ± (−) 0!3 | + 4!5 | 65°6 |
| Net corr | + 0!1 | Interpolation Table | | |
| | | Tens | 0!0 | 360.0 |
| $H_c$ | 65° 02!2 | Units & Decimals | 0!2 | −65.6 |
| | | | − 0!2 | |
| $H_o$ | 65° 00!0 | DSD corr | + 0!3 | |
| | | Net corr | + 0!1 | |
| a | 2!2 | T $H_o$>$H_c$ / (A) $H_o$<$H_c$ | | $Z_n$ 294°4 |

Example 3. LHA = 215°, Tab Dec = 45°, Dec Inc = 10°.9 N, AP Lat = 45° N, SAME
This places us below the stepped line on page 255 of H.O. 229.

Note that in this case, the lower right hand corner of the right hand page has a different LHA than the other three corners. Also, the bottom of the page is for SAME (associated with LHA 145°, 215°) and the upper half is CONTRARY (associated with LHA 35°, 325°). Interpolation for $H_c$ and Z is per normal. Since latitude is north and LHA is greater than 180°, $Z_n$ = Z. Assuming $H_o$ = 5° 23'.2, greater than $H_c$, the intercept is towards.

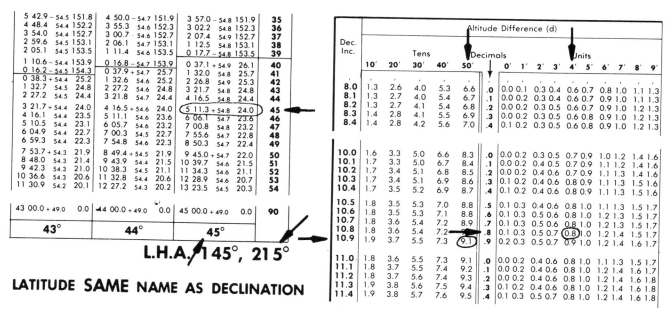

| 43° | | | 44° | | | 45° | | | Dec. |
|---|---|---|---|---|---|---|---|---|---|
| 5 42.9 | −54.5 | 151.8 | 4 50.0 | −54.7 | 151.9 | 3 57.0 | −54.8 | 151.9 | 35 |
| 4 48.4 | 54.4 | 152.2 | 3 55.3 | 54.6 | 152.3 | 3 02.2 | 54.8 | 152.3 | 36 |
| 3 54.0 | 54.4 | 152.7 | 3 00.7 | 54.6 | 152.7 | 2 07.4 | 54.9 | 152.7 | 37 |
| 2 59.6 | 54.5 | 153.1 | 2 06.1 | 54.7 | 153.1 | 1 12.5 | 54.8 | 153.1 | 38 |
| 2 05.1 | 54.5 | 153.5 | 1 11.4 | 54.6 | 153.5 | 0 17.7 | −54.8 | 153.5 | 39 |
| 1 10.6 | −54.4 | 153.9 | 0 16.8 | −54.7 | 153.9 | 0 37.1 | +54.9 | 26.1 | 40 |
| 0 16.2 | −54.5 | 154.3 | 0 37.9 | +54.7 | 25.7 | 1 32.0 | 54.8 | 25.7 | 41 |
| 0 38.3 | +54.4 | 25.2 | 1 32.6 | 54.6 | 25.2 | 2 26.8 | 54.9 | 25.3 | 42 |
| 1 32.7 | 54.5 | 24.8 | 2 27.2 | 54.6 | 24.8 | 3 21.7 | 54.8 | 24.8 | 43 |
| 2 27.2 | 54.5 | 24.4 | 3 21.8 | 54.7 | 24.4 | 4 16.5 | 54.8 | 24.4 | 44 |
| 3 21.7 | +54.4 | 24.0 | 4 16.5 | +54.6 | 24.0 | 5 11.3 | +54.8 | 24.0 | 45 |
| 4 16.1 | 54.4 | 23.5 | 5 11.1 | 54.6 | 23.6 | 6 06.1 | 54.7 | 23.6 | 46 |
| 5 10.5 | 54.4 | 23.1 | 6 05.7 | 54.6 | 23.2 | 7 00.8 | 54.8 | 23.2 | 47 |
| 6 04.9 | 54.4 | 22.7 | 7 00.3 | 54.5 | 22.7 | 7 55.6 | 54.7 | 22.8 | 48 |
| 6 59.3 | 54.4 | 22.3 | 7 54.8 | 54.6 | 22.3 | 8 50.3 | 54.7 | 22.4 | 49 |
| 7 53.7 | +54.3 | 21.9 | 8 49.4 | +54.5 | 21.9 | 9 45.0 | +54.7 | 22.0 | 50 |
| 8 48.0 | 54.3 | 21.4 | 9 43.9 | 54.4 | 21.5 | 10 39.7 | 54.6 | 21.5 | 51 |
| 9 42.3 | 54.3 | 21.0 | 10 38.3 | 54.5 | 21.1 | 11 34.3 | 54.6 | 21.1 | 52 |
| 10 36.6 | 54.3 | 20.6 | 11 32.8 | 54.4 | 20.6 | 12 28.9 | 54.6 | 20.7 | 53 |
| 11 30.9 | 54.2 | 20.1 | 12 27.2 | 54.3 | 20.2 | 13 23.5 | 54.5 | 20.3 | 54 |
| 43 00.0 | +49.0 | 0.0 | 44 00.0 | +49.0 | 0.0 | 45 00.0 | +49.0 | 0.0 | 90 |
| 43° | | | 44° | | | 45° | | | |

**L.H.A. 145°, 215°**

**LATITUDE SAME NAME AS DECLINATION**

| Dec. Inc. | Altitude Difference (d) Tens 10' | 20' | 30' | 40' | 50' | Decimals | Units 0' | 1' | 2' | 3' | 4' | 5' | 6' | 7' | 8' | 9' |
|---|---|---|---|---|---|---|---|---|---|---|---|---|---|---|---|---|
| 8.0 | 1.3 | 2.6 | 4.0 | 5.3 | 6.6 | .0 | 0.0 | 0.1 | 0.3 | 0.4 | 0.6 | 0.7 | 0.8 | 1.0 | 1.1 | 1.3 |
| 8.1 | 1.3 | 2.7 | 4.0 | 5.4 | 6.7 | .1 | 0.0 | 0.2 | 0.3 | 0.4 | 0.6 | 0.7 | 0.9 | 1.0 | 1.1 | 1.3 |
| 8.2 | 1.3 | 2.7 | 4.1 | 5.4 | 6.8 | .2 | 0.0 | 0.2 | 0.3 | 0.5 | 0.6 | 0.7 | 0.9 | 1.0 | 1.2 | 1.3 |
| 8.3 | 1.4 | 2.8 | 4.1 | 5.5 | 6.9 | .3 | 0.0 | 0.2 | 0.3 | 0.5 | 0.6 | 0.8 | 0.9 | 1.0 | 1.2 | 1.3 |
| 8.4 | 1.4 | 2.8 | 4.2 | 5.6 | 7.0 | .4 | 0.1 | 0.2 | 0.3 | 0.5 | 0.6 | 0.8 | 0.9 | 1.0 | 1.2 | 1.3 |
| 10.0 | 1.6 | 3.3 | 5.0 | 6.6 | 8.3 | .0 | 0.0 | 0.2 | 0.3 | 0.5 | 0.7 | 0.9 | 1.0 | 1.2 | 1.4 | 1.6 |
| 10.1 | 1.7 | 3.3 | 5.0 | 6.7 | 8.4 | .1 | 0.0 | 0.2 | 0.4 | 0.5 | 0.7 | 0.9 | 1.1 | 1.2 | 1.4 | 1.6 |
| 10.2 | 1.7 | 3.4 | 5.1 | 6.8 | 8.5 | .2 | 0.0 | 0.2 | 0.4 | 0.6 | 0.7 | 0.9 | 1.1 | 1.3 | 1.4 | 1.6 |
| 10.3 | 1.7 | 3.4 | 5.1 | 6.9 | 8.6 | .3 | 0.1 | 0.2 | 0.4 | 0.6 | 0.8 | 0.9 | 1.1 | 1.3 | 1.5 | 1.6 |
| 10.4 | 1.7 | 3.5 | 5.2 | 6.9 | 8.7 | .4 | 0.1 | 0.2 | 0.4 | 0.6 | 0.8 | 0.9 | 1.1 | 1.3 | 1.5 | 1.6 |
| 10.5 | 1.8 | 3.5 | 5.3 | 7.0 | 8.8 | .5 | 0.1 | 0.3 | 0.4 | 0.6 | 0.8 | 1.0 | 1.1 | 1.3 | 1.5 | 1.7 |
| 10.6 | 1.8 | 3.5 | 5.3 | 7.1 | 8.8 | .6 | 0.1 | 0.3 | 0.5 | 0.6 | 0.8 | 1.0 | 1.2 | 1.3 | 1.5 | 1.7 |
| 10.7 | 1.8 | 3.6 | 5.4 | 7.2 | 8.9 | .7 | 0.1 | 0.3 | 0.5 | 0.6 | 0.8 | 1.0 | 1.2 | 1.3 | 1.5 | 1.7 |
| 10.8 | 1.8 | 3.6 | 5.4 | 7.2 | [illegible] | .8 | 0.1 | 0.3 | 0.5 | 0.7 | 0.8 | 1.0 | 1.2 | 1.4 | 1.5 | 1.7 |
| 10.9 | 1.9 | 3.7 | 5.5 | 7.3 | 9.1 | .9 | 0.2 | 0.3 | 0.5 | 0.7 | 0.9 | 1.0 | 1.2 | 1.4 | 1.6 | 1.7 |
| 11.0 | 1.8 | 3.6 | 5.5 | 7.3 | 9.1 | .0 | 0.0 | 0.2 | 0.4 | 0.6 | 0.8 | 1.0 | 1.1 | 1.3 | 1.5 | 1.7 |
| 11.1 | 1.8 | 3.7 | 5.5 | 7.4 | 9.2 | .1 | 0.0 | 0.2 | 0.4 | 0.6 | 0.8 | 1.0 | 1.2 | 1.4 | 1.6 | 1.7 |
| 11.2 | 1.8 | 3.7 | 5.6 | 7.4 | 9.3 | .2 | 0.0 | 0.2 | 0.4 | 0.6 | 0.8 | 1.0 | 1.2 | 1.4 | 1.6 | 1.8 |
| 11.3 | 1.9 | 3.8 | 5.6 | 7.5 | 9.4 | .3 | 0.1 | 0.2 | 0.4 | 0.6 | 0.8 | 1.0 | 1.2 | 1.4 | 1.6 | 1.8 |
| 11.4 | 1.9 | 3.8 | 5.7 | 7.6 | 9.5 | .4 | 0.1 | 0.3 | 0.5 | 0.7 | 0.8 | 1.0 | 1.2 | 1.4 | 1.6 | 1.8 |

| | $H_c$ | d | DSD | Z eye interp. |
|---|---|---|---|---|
| Tabular Values | 5° 11'.3 | (+) 54'.8 | + ' . | 23°.9 |
| Net corr | ° + 9'.9 | Interpolation Table | | |
| | | Tens | 9'.1 | |
| $H_c$ | 5° 21'.2 | Units & Decimals | 0'.8 | $Z_n$ = Z |
| $H_o$ | 5° 23'.2 | DSD corr | + ' . | |
| | | Net corr | 9'.9 | |
| a | 2'.0 | (T) $H_o > H_c$ / A $H_o < H_c$ | | $Z_n$ 023°.9 |

Example 4. LHA = 306°, Tab Dec = 12°, Dec Inc = 04'.9 N, AP Lat = 37° N, SAME
This places us on page 110 in the upper right corner of H.O. 229.
Interpolation is per normal, $Z_n$ = Z.

N. Lat. { L.H.A. greater than 180° .....Zn=Z ; L.H.A. less than 180° .....Zn=360°−Z }

| 36° Hc | 36° d | 36° Z | 37° Hc | 37° d | 37° Z | Dec. |
|---|---|---|---|---|---|---|
| ° ′ | ′ | ° | ° ′ | ′ | ° | ° |
| 28 23.6 | +40.0 | 113.1 | 27 59.8 | +40.8 | 113.6 | 0 |
| 29 03.6 | 39.6 | 112.3 | 28 40.6 | 40.4 | 112.8 | 1 |
| 29 43.2 | 39.2 | 111.4 | 29 21.0 | 40.1 | 111.9 | 2 |
| 30 22.4 | 38.9 | 110.5 | 30 01.1 | 39.8 | 111.1 | 3 |
| 31 01.3 | 38.6 | 109.7 | 30 40.9 | 39.4 | 110.2 | 4 |
| 31 39.9 | +38.1 | 108.8 | 31 20.3 | +39.1 | 109.3 | 5 |
| 32 18.0 | 37.8 | 107.8 | 31 59.4 | 38.6 | 108.4 | 6 |
| 32 55.8 | 37.4 | 106.9 | 32 38.0 | 38.3 | 107.5 | 7 |
| 33 33.2 | 36.9 | 106.0 | 33 16.3 | 37.9 | 106.6 | 8 |
| 34 10.1 | 36.5 | 105.0 | 33 54.2 | 37.4 | 105.7 | 9 |
| 34 46.6 | +36.0 | 104.1 | 34 31.6 | +37.0 | 104.7 | 10 |
| 35 22.6 | 35.5 | 103.1 | 35 08.6 | 36.6 | 103.8 | 11 |
| 35 58.1 | 35.1 | 102.1 | 35 45.2 | 36.0 | 102.8 | 12 |
| 36 33.2 | 34.5 | 101.1 | 36 21.2 | 35.6 | 101.8 | 13 |
| 37 07.7 | 34.0 | 100.1 | 36 56.8 | 35.1 | 100.8 | 14 |
| 37 41.7 | +33.4 | 99.0 | 37 31.9 | +34.5 | 99.8 | 15 |
| 38 15.1 | 32.9 | 98.0 | 38 06.4 | 34.0 | 98.8 | 16 |
| 38 48.0 | 32.3 | 96.9 | 38 40.4 | 33.3 | 97.7 | 17 |
| 39 20.3 | 31.6 | 95.8 | 39 13.7 | 32.8 | 96.6 | 18 |
| 39 51.9 | 31.0 | 94.7 | 39 46.5 | 32.2 | 95.6 | 19 |
| 40 22.9 | +30.4 | 93.6 | 40 18.7 | +31.6 | 94.5 | 20 |
| 40 53.3 | 29.7 | 92.5 | 40 50.3 | 30.8 | 93.3 | 21 |
| 41 23.0 | 29.0 | 91.3 | 41 21.1 | 30.2 | 92.2 | 22 |
| 41 52.0 | 28.2 | 90.1 | 41 51.3 | 29.5 | 91.0 | 23 |
| 42 20.2 | 27.5 | 89.0 | 42 20.8 | 28.8 | 89.9 | 24 |

| | $H_c$ | d | DSD | Z eye interp. |
|---|---|---|---|---|
| Tabular Values | 35° 45'.2 | ⊕ − 36'.0 | + ' . | 102°.7 |
| Net corr | ° + 2'.9 | Interpolation Table | | |
| | | Tens | 2'.5 | |
| $H_c$ | 35° 48'.1 | Units & Decimals | 0'.4 | |
| | | | ' . | |
| $H_o$ | 35° 27'.4 | DSD corr | + . | |
| | | Net corr | 2'.9 | |
| a | 20'.7 | T $H_o>H_c$ / Ⓐ $H_o<H_c$ | | $Z_n$ 102°.7 |

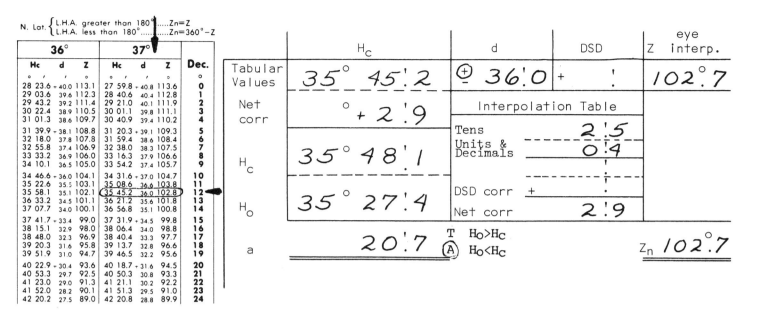

In preparation for plotting, we need three pieces of information from our sight reduction sheets. The rest of the figures were merely means of obtaining the necessary plotting information. In addition, some information for labeling may be extracted.

For Plotting: A.P. Lat ______ ° N/S

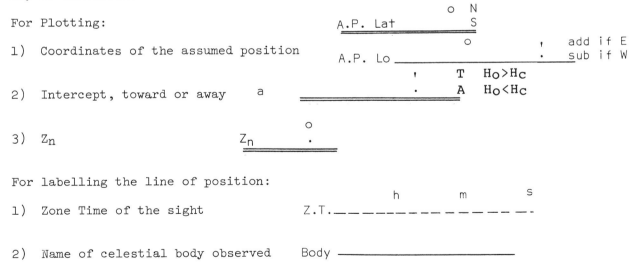

1) Coordinates of the assumed position A.P. Lo ______ ° ______ ' . (add if E, sub if W)

2) Intercept, toward or away a ______ ' . T $H_o>H_c$ / A $H_o<H_c$

3) $Z_n$ $Z_n$ ______ ° .

For labelling the line of position:

1) Zone Time of the sight Z.T. ______ h ______ m ______ s

2) Name of celestial body observed Body ______

## EXERCISE 5

Find $H_o$ and complete the solution to get "a" and $Z_n$ using the data already obtained from Exercises 3 and 4.

| | Body | Ht. of Eye | $H_s$ | I.C. | Pressure and Temp. |
|---|---|---|---|---|---|
| 1. | Sun LL | 10.5 feet | 35°43!0 | - 3!0 | standard |
| 2. | Mars | 15 feet | 78°44!6 | + 1!0 | standard |
| 3. | Moon UL | 24 feet | 47°53!4 | + 0!7 | standard |
| 4. | Sun UL | 6 feet | 81°48!0 | - 1!7 | standard |
| 5. | Venus | 6 feet | 31°38!3 | - 2!0 | standard |
| 6. | Moon LL | 8.5 feet | 28°08!9 | + 2!5 | standard |
| 7. | Jupiter | 5 feet | 55°10!5 | + 6!2 | standard |
| 8. | Vega | 0 | 45°13!8 | + 1!8 | standard |
| 9. | Denebola | 17.4 feet | 53°20!3 | - 1!0 | standard |
| 10. | Achernar | 27.3 feet | 67°02!1 | + 3!4 | standard |
| 11. | Spica | 12.5 feet | 28°02!5 | - 2!5 | standard |
| 12. | Regulus | 10 feet | 67°25!8 | - 1!0 | standard |
| 13. | Rasalhague | 8 feet | 58°37!6 | -22!1 | standard |
| 14. | Polaris | 8 feet | 44°20!9 | -21!9 | standard |

(SHA & Dec. of Polaris are found on Page 236. Interpolation is not required.)

# *Chapter 8*

# *Plotting Celestial Lines of Position*

Using small position plotting sheets, we can plot a fix from celestial observations, then transfer the fix to our chart. Therefore, our plotting sheets are worksheets to minimize the amount of writing on our charts.

To plot a line of position, we first locate the assumed position for the sight on the plotting sheet. This assumed position will give us clues as to the correct central meridian and central parallel to use. Since the AP Lat is always a whole degree, we can choose this value for the central parallel. The central meridian can be the nearest whole or half degree of longitude to the AP Long. Remember on the scale of longitudes at the bottom of the sheet to mark the horizontal line that corresponds to your latitude. On this scale you will measure only longitude. Latitude and distance are measured on the central meridian.

In Example 1, let us assume two sights are taken with results as follows:

| | Body | AP | "a" | $Z_n$ | Z.T. |
|---|---|---|---|---|---|
| 1) | Moon | 30° N<br>49° 40' W | 10!0 T | 200° | 1700 |
| 2) | Sun | 30° N<br>49° 47' W | 8!3 A | 301° | 1700 |

Mark the central meridian of your plotting sheet 50° W, central parallel 30° N. With this information, we see that at 1700, the Moon has a true azimuth of 200°. Plot the AP, put a circle around the point. From the AP, we will draw this bearing line (a dashed line) TOWARD 200° (since the intercept is labelled toward) for a distance of 10 nautical miles, measured on the central meridian. After making a mark on our dashed line 10 n.m. away from the AP, we then draw a line perpendicular to the azimuth line such that the perpendicular line goes through this mark. This last line is our line of position, our LOP. To figure the perpendicularity of the LOP, the navigator can use a right angle triangle against the parallel rulers or another triangle or he can add or subtract 90° from the $Z_n$ to get the bearing of the LOP and plot this line independently from the plotting of the bearing line. In this case, the LOP has an azimuth of 200° ± 90° = 290° or 110°.

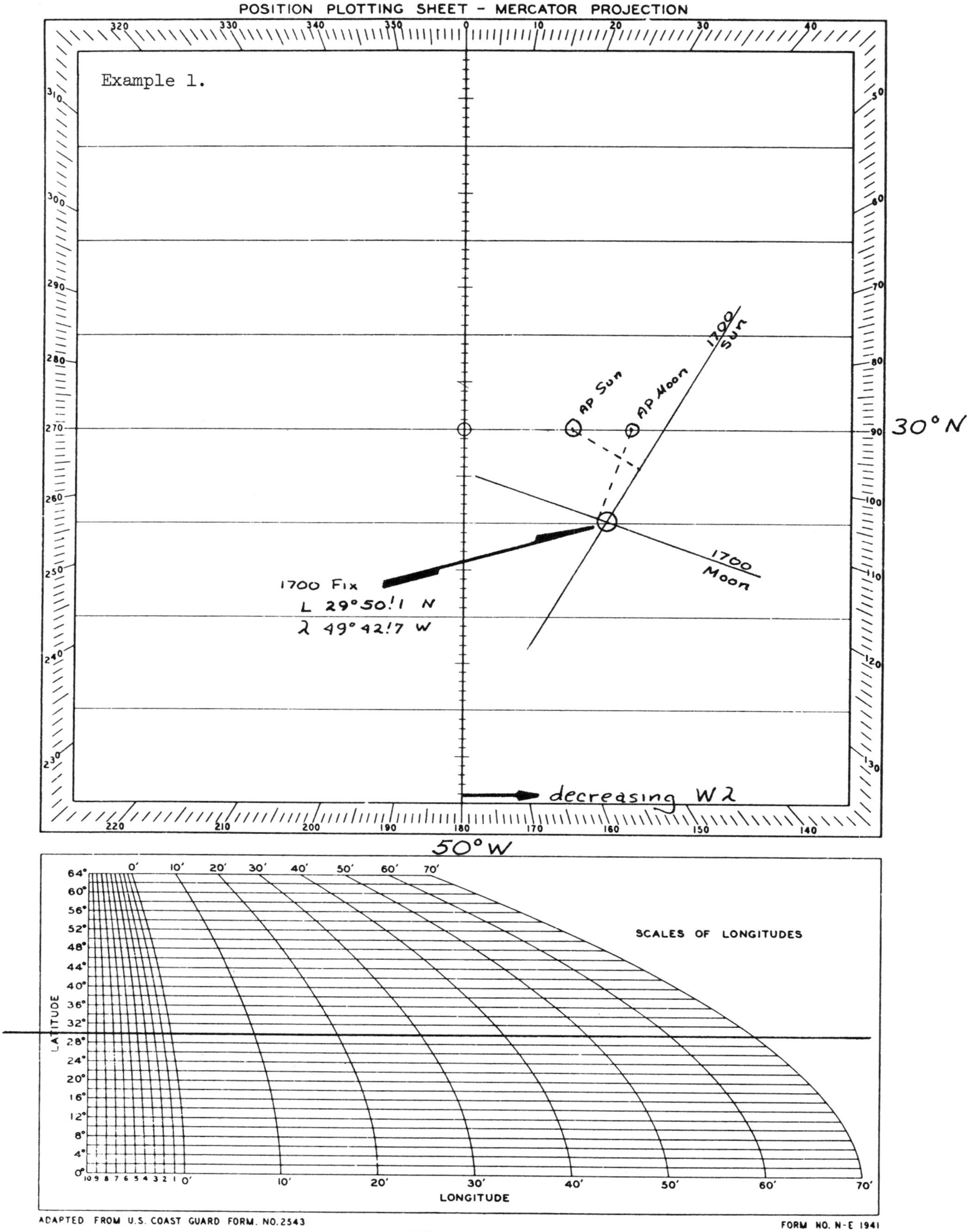
POSITION PLOTTING SHEET - MERCATOR PROJECTION
Example 1.
1700 Sun
AP Sun
AP Moon
30° N
1700 Moon
1700 Fix
L 29°50!1 N
λ 49°42!7 W
decreasing Wλ
50° W
SCALES OF LONGITUDES
LATITUDE
LONGITUDE
ADAPTED FROM U.S. COAST GUARD FORM. NO. 2543
FORM NO. N-E 1941

For the 1700 sun sight, again plot the AP for the Sun, from this point plot AWAY from 301° by 8.3 nautical miles, make a mark here and draw a perpendicular line to the azimuth line through this mark. At the junction of this LOP and the LOP of the Moon, draw a circle. This is the position of the ship or the FIX. Label it 1700 FIX and record its latitude and longitude.

The lines of position are labelled with the ship's time (Zone Time or Daylight Saving Time) of sight in four digits above the line, the body observed below the line.

1700
Moon

The assumed positions are labelled AP 1 or AP 2, in the order with which the sights are taken. Some navigators prefer to label them AP Sun, AP Moon.

It is advantageous to do as little writing on the plotting sheet as possible so symbology is sometimes helpful. In the case of more than one star being used, star names can be abbreviated such as Reg for Regulus, Bet for Betelgeuse, V for Vega, etc. The following symbols can be used for other bodies.

| | | | |
|---|---|---|---|
| Sun | ☉ | Mars | ♂ |
| Moon | ☽ | Saturn | ♄ |
| Venus | ♀ | Star | ★ |
| Jupiter | ♃ | | |

For a fix, you need at least two lines of position, preferably three. If possible, for a two body fix, the bearings of the bodies should be close to 90° apart, making the LOP's cross also at near 90°. With this situation, there is a minimum of error of the fix even if there is a small error in the sextant reading or sight reduction. For instance, if two LOPs crossed at an angle of only 20°, and the bearing of one of the lines was off by one degree, the resulting error in the fix would be greater than if the bodies were 90° apart.

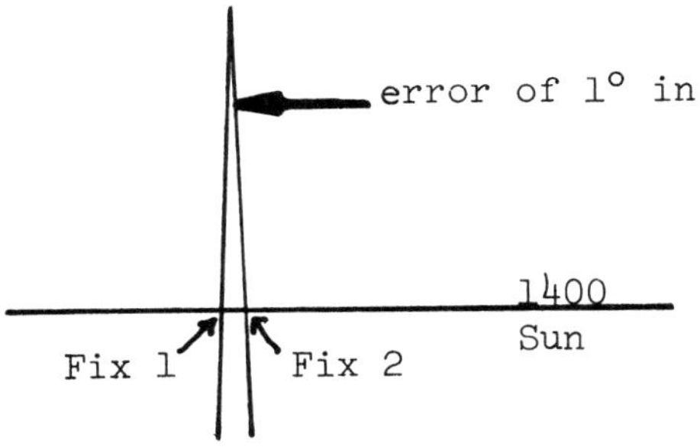


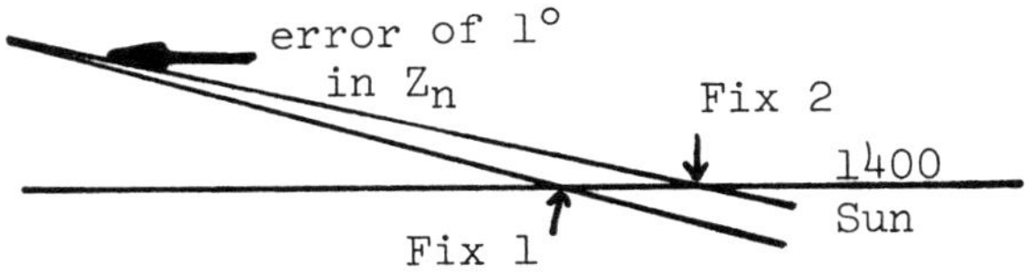

For a three body fix, the bodies should be close to 60° apart or 120° apart, these numbers obtained by dividing 180° or 360° by the number of bodies observed. This will make a point fix if your sights are perfect, a small equilateral triangle otherwise.

One line of position will never give you a fix. Some navigators use one LOP to give an estimated position although this EP is most probably NOT where you are. A course should always be plotted from your DR, not the EP. To get an EP, let us assume the following sight.

| Body | AP | "a" | $Z_n$ | Z.T. |
|---|---|---|---|---|
| Sun | 45° N<br>160° 25' E | 8!0 T | 145° | 1030 |

Also assume the 1030 DR of 44° 40' N, 160° 20' E. From 1030, the ship will proceed on course 040° at a speed of 10 knots.

After plotting the 1030 Sun LOP and the 1030 DR, the 1030 EP is obtained by drawing a dashed perpendicular line to the LOP through the 1030 DR. Where the perpendicular line crosses the LOP, make a point with a square around it and label it 1030 EP. This is the best estimate you can make with the information at hand of your position. However, you should proceed from your DR and not from your EP. See Example 2.

Two special cases of the use of one line of position follow:

1) Observing a body dead ahead or dead astern (its LOP will be perpendicular to your course line)

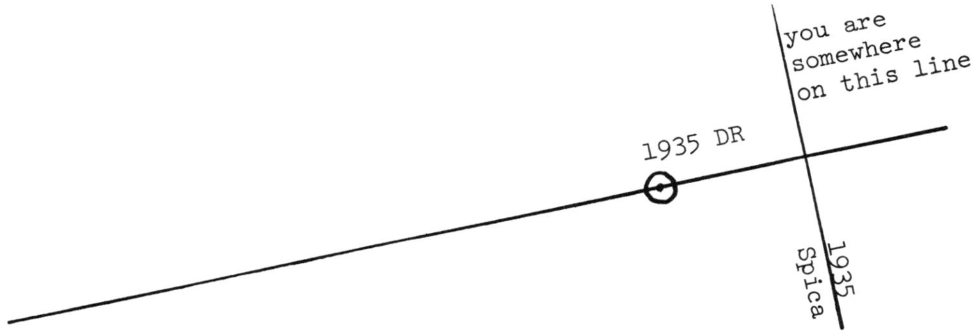


In this case, the line of position checks on your speed. If the LOP lies ahead of your DR of the same time, then your ship is going faster than you estimated (see above). If the LOP lies behind your DR of the same time, your ship is going slower than you estimated. In the latter example, every position on that LOP would be behind your DR.

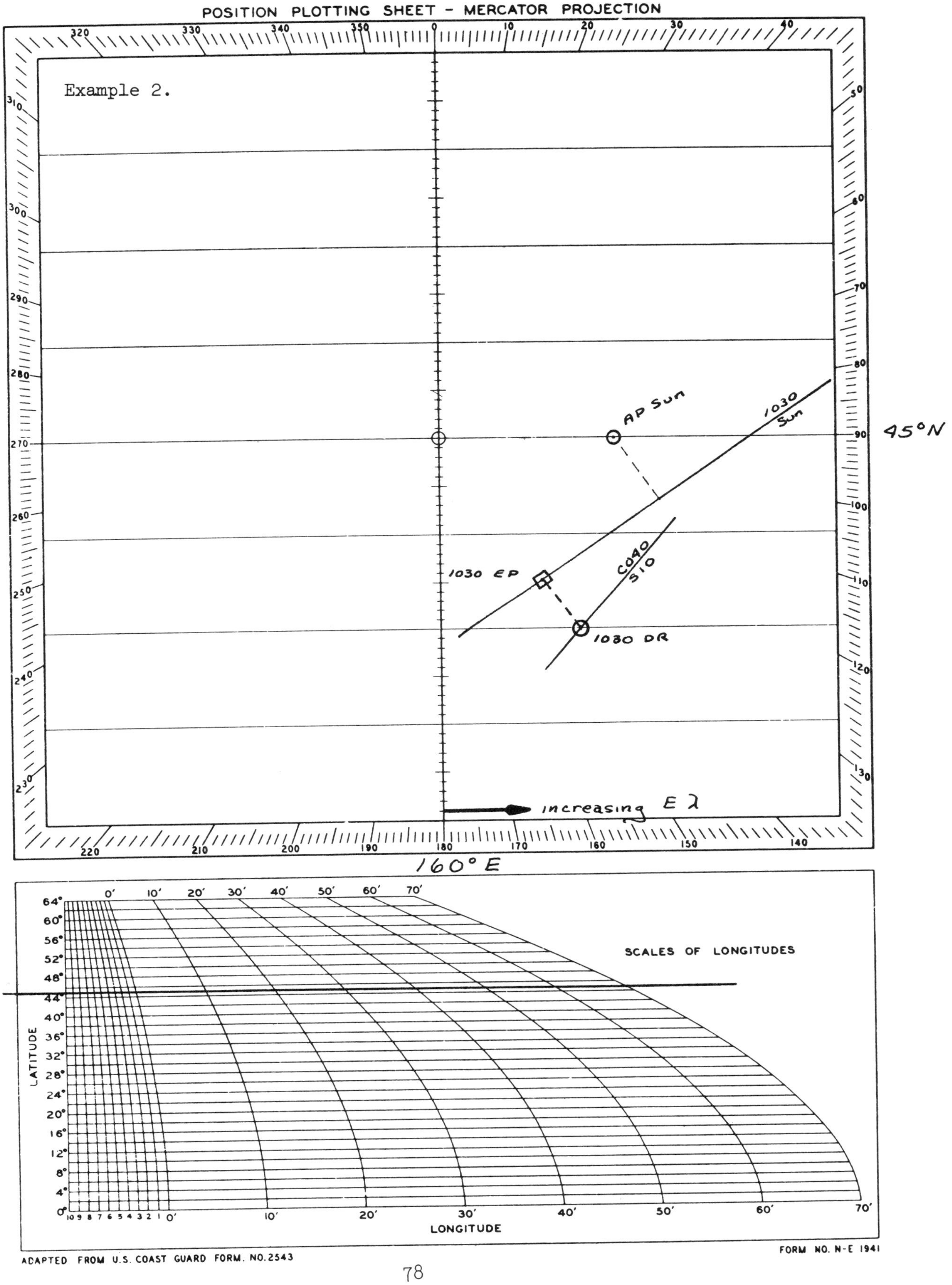
POSITION PLOTTING SHEET - MERCATOR PROJECTION
Example 2.
AP Sun
1030 Sun
45°N
1030 EP
C040
310
1030 DR
increasing E λ
160° E
SCALES OF LONGITUDES
LATITUDE
LONGITUDE
ADAPTED FROM U.S. COAST GUARD FORM. NO.2543
FORM NO. N-E 1941

2) Observing a body abeam (its LOP will be parallel to your course line)

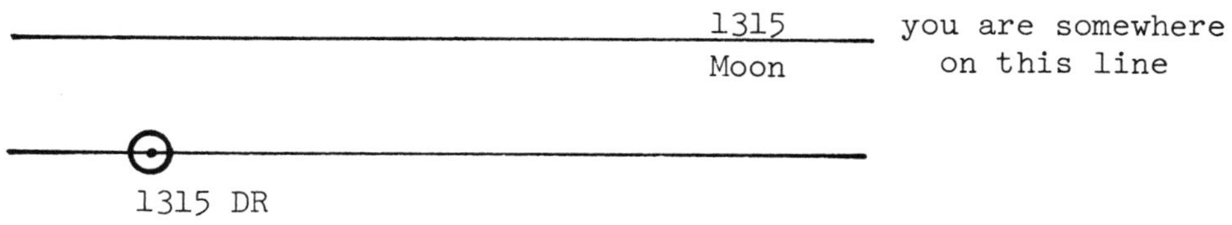


In this case, the line of position checks on your course. If the LOP lies to the north of your course line, this shows that your ship is being set to the northward (see above diagram). If the LOP lies to the south of the course line, this shows that your ship is being set southward.

It will be seen later that single lines of position can be used to check latitude. Methods are also available for longitude checks by a single LOP.

Lines of position from piloting procedures, radionavigation, and celestial navigation may be crossed with each other to give a fix. We can treat the celestial lines of position as straight lines even though they are actually parts of circles. The radii of these circles are so great, however, that the segments of the circles will be equivalent to straight lines for all practical purposes.

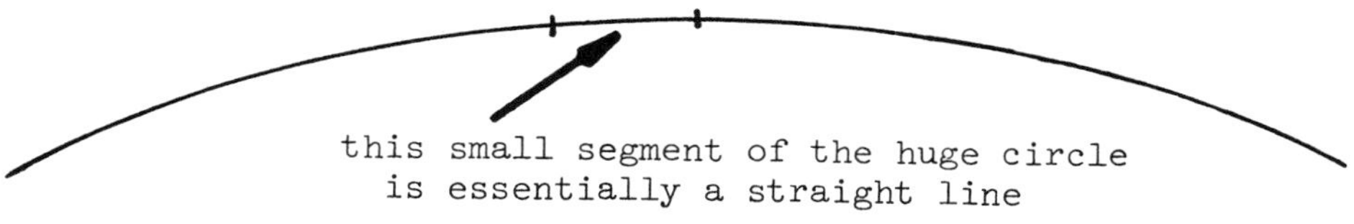


In Example 1, we assumed that both the Sun and Moon sight were taken at the same time. However, most times this is not the case. If two bodies were observed twenty minutes apart and the ship was proceeding on course during these twenty minutes, we have to advance the earlier sight to the later time. Generally the advancing is made to the time of the last sight although in some cases the navigator may wish to retard a line to obtain a fix for an earlier time.

To advance a LOP, we need to know the course and speed of the ship. Assume in Example 3 that our 1600 DR is 19° 40' N, 60° 00' W. Course is 080°, speed 10 knots. The Moon is observed at 1600 and we wish to advance it to 1630 when

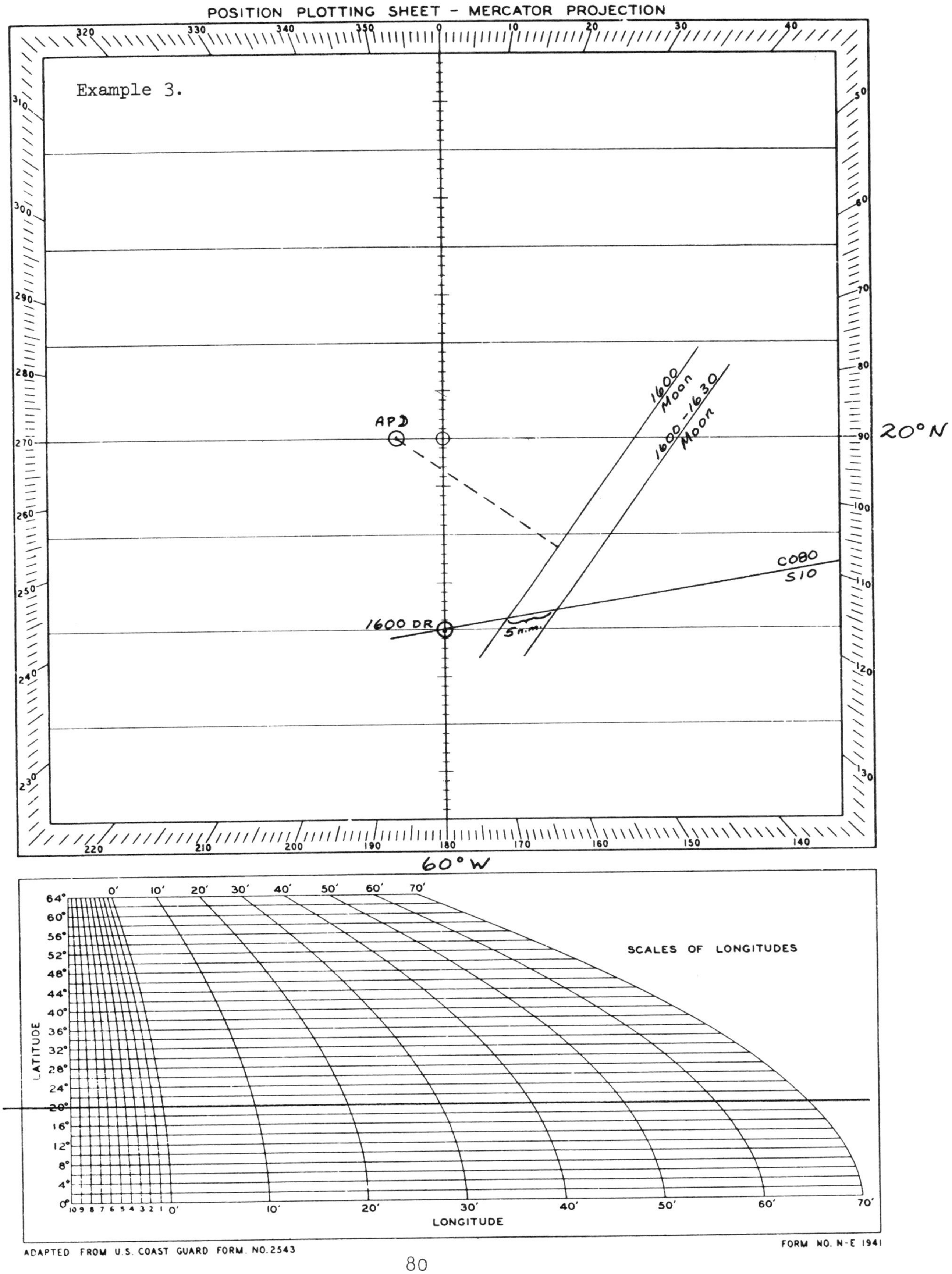
POSITION PLOTTING SHEET - MERCATOR PROJECTION
Example 3.
AP☽
1600 Moon
1600-1630 Moon
C080
S10
1600 DR
5 n.mi.
20°N
60°W
SCALES OF LONGITUDES
LATITUDE
LONGITUDE
ADAPTED FROM U.S. COAST GUARD FORM. NO. 2543
FORM NO. N-E 1941

we will observe the Sun. The AP is 20° N, 60° 05' W. $Z_n$ = 125°, the intercept is 20' T. We can plot our 1600 Moon LOP as usual, using a plotting sheet with central parallel 20° N, central meridian 60° W. To advance the 1600 Moon to 1630, we mark where the 1600 Moon crosses our course line. From this point we measure off how far the ship has traveled in the 30 minutes in the direction of the course. In this case, the ship will travel 10 nautical miles in one hour, therefore 5 nautical miles in 30 minutes. Through the point on the course line 5 nautical miles from the crossing of the 1600 Moon, draw a new line of position parallel to the old one. This is labeled with sight time dash advanced time on the top of the line, the body on the bottom.

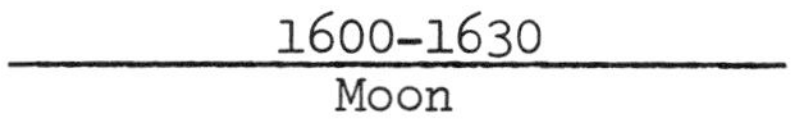


Remember to always measure the advance along the course line in the direction of travel. To retard the same line, the procedure would be the same except that the line would be retarded in the direction opposite that of travel.

Remember to measure this 5 nautical mile distance from the distance scale on the central meridian.

If the LOP is perpendicular to your course line, an advance of a certain distance (x) will reflect maximum movement in your LOP. If the LOP intersects your course line at a small angle, the same advance will move the LOP very little.

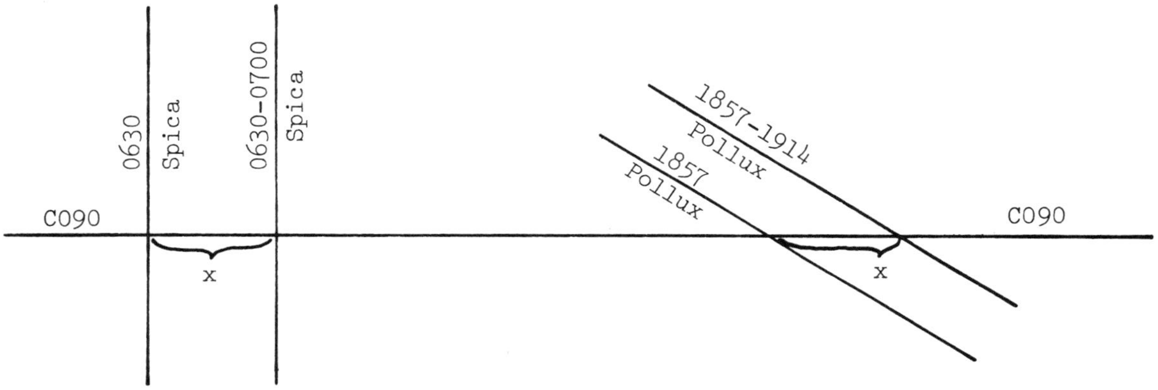


In some cases, the LOP will not cross with the course line as you have plotted it on your plotting sheet. To eliminate the necessity of extending your plotting sheet with more pieces of paper until the two lines will cross, just plot a new course line (same direction) at a different spot on your plotting sheet where it will cross with the LOP. Then advance your line per usual. See Example 4.

It will sometimes be the case that a line of position will have to be advanced over a time period when a course and/or speed change are involved. There are two methods by which this may be done as illustrated on page 83. Assume we have the situation where from the 1000 DR the vessel proceeds on course 045° at speed of 20 knots. At 1100, course is changed to 355°, speed to 23 knots. A sight of the Sun is taken at 1015 and must be advanced to 1200 when another sight is taken.

POSITION PLOTTING SHEET - MERCATOR PROJECTION

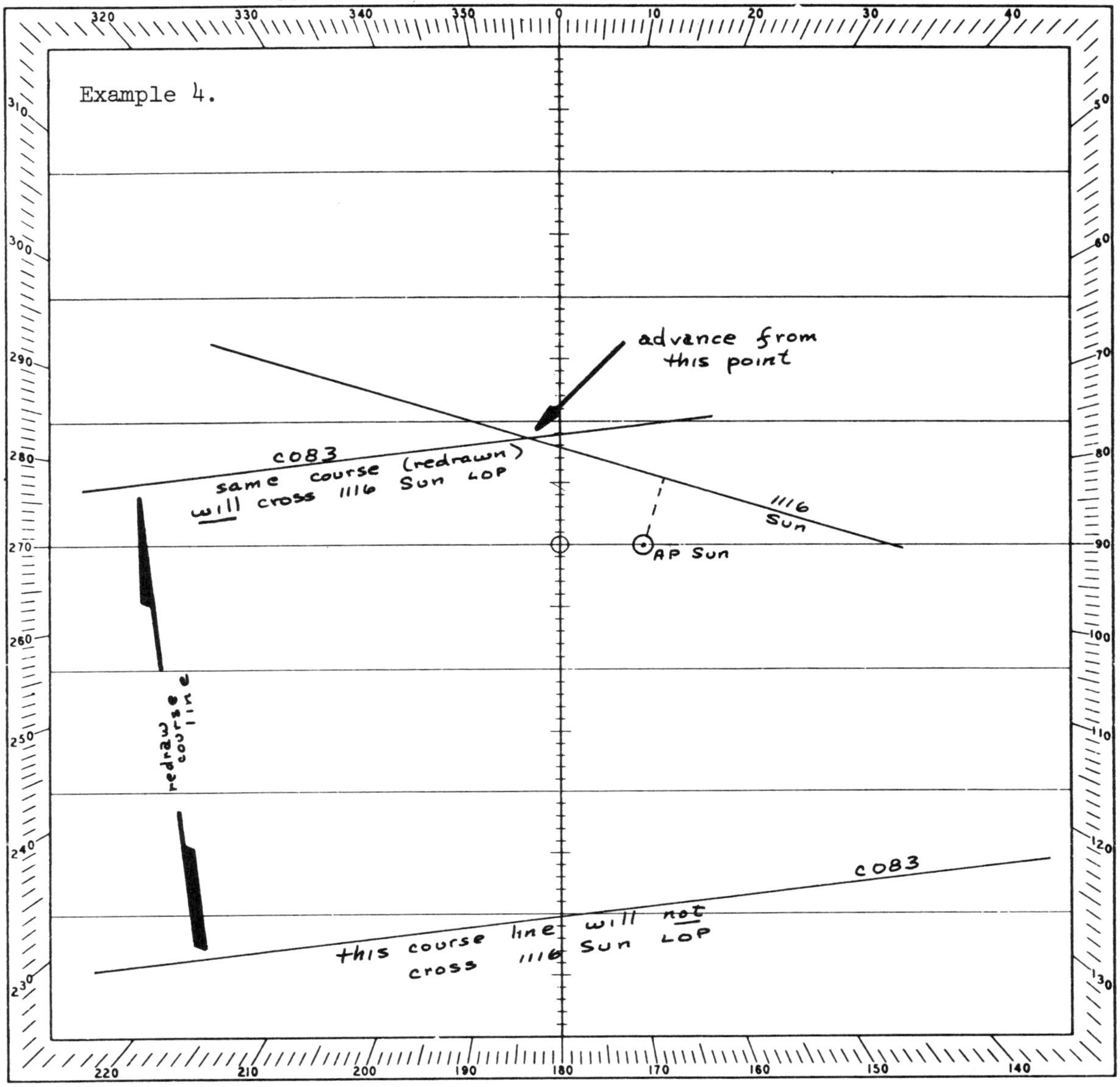


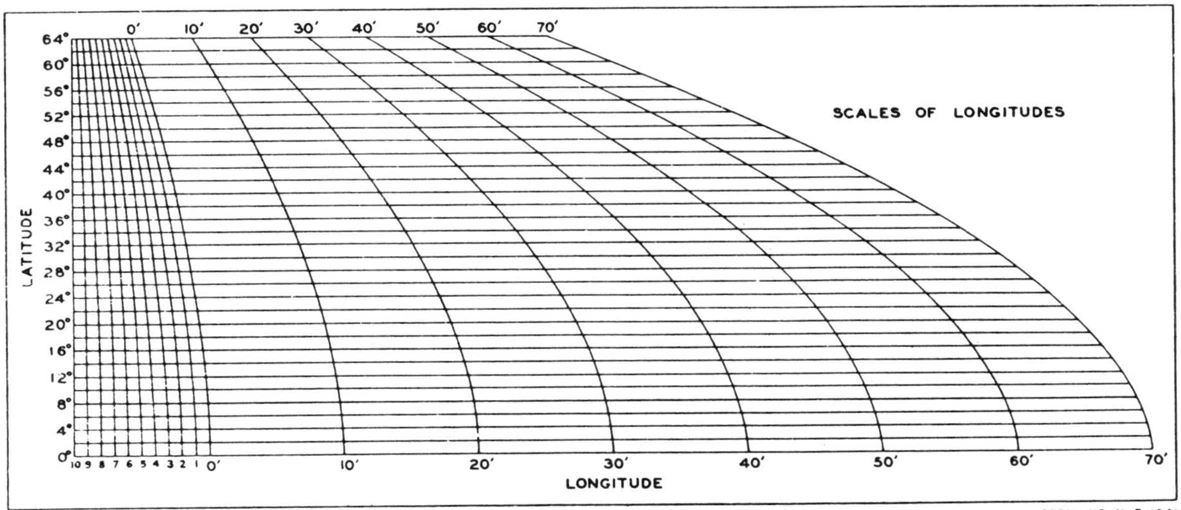


ADAPTED FROM U.S. COAST GUARD FORM. NO. 2543

FORM NO. N-E 1941

Method 1 involves figuring a course made good (CMG) and distance made good (DMG) of the vessel between the two sight times. The DR is plotted for these two times (1015 and 1200) and a line drawn between the two points. The distance between the DR s is the distance made good, the bearing of the constructed line the course made good. This line may need to be extended to cross with the 1015 LOP. The LOP is then advanced along this constructed line by the amount designated by DMG. The advanced LOP is labeled per usual.

Method 2 is a two or more stepped method. First the 1015 LOP is advanced to the time of course and/or speed change (in this case 1100). The 1015-1100 LOP is plotted. Where this LOP crosses the <u>new</u> course line is the starting point for the second step. The LOP is advanced along the new course and/or speed until the next sight time or until course or speed are changed again. This method can be rather tedious when many course and speed changes are involved. However, it does save the CMG line construction and figuring of distance made good. I prefer Method 1 for most cases.

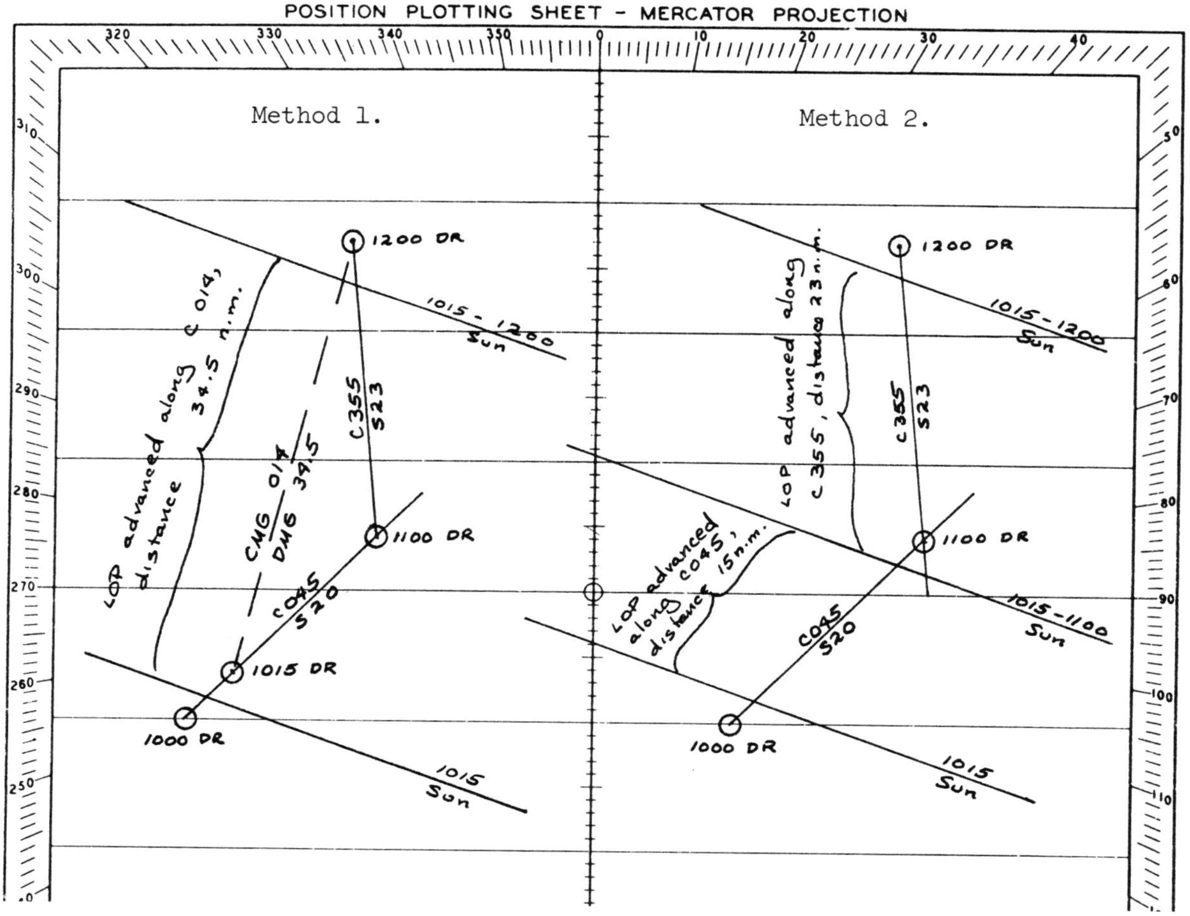

When a fix is obtained by advancing a line of position more than 30 minutes, the fix is called a running fix, labeled R. FIX. This type of fix is not as accurate as a fix obtained by sighting bodies almost simultaneously because the R. FIX is subject to the ship's errors in course and speed. However, often during the day you have no other choice than observing the Sun at intervals of an hour or more and advancing the earlier sight to the later one to obtain a position. Just remember that your ship probably is not at the position labeled R. FIX although this point is as good an estimation as you can make until evening comes and you can observe three bodies during the twilight.

Example 5 shows the plotting of a running fix with the following information:

| Body | AP | "a" | $Z_n$ | Z.T. |
|---|---|---|---|---|
| Regulus | 50° N<br>149° 30' W | 5'.3 A | 100°.6 | 18-00-20 |
| Betelgeuse | 50° N<br>149°48' W | 11'.4 T | 161°.5 | 18-14-53 |
| Venus | 50° N<br>150° 11' W | 14'.8 A | 224°.9 | 18-39-47 |

1800 DR has Lat 49° 40' N, Long 150° W. Course is 075°, speed 16 knots.

In this example, the Regulus LOP needs to be advanced from 1800 to 1840 (round zone time off to the nearest minute). At a speed of 16 knots, 40/60 x 16 = 10.6 nautical miles. Advance the 1800 LOP along the course line by this amount.

The Betelgeuse LOP is almost parallel to the course line. The advance of 25/60 x 16 = 6.7 n.m. would make essentially no change in the Betelgeuse LOP.

The Venus LOP is plotted with no advance since it was sighted at the time we wish for our fix. The three lines cross in a tiny cocked hat, an equilateral triangle, and we shall choose as our position the center of the triangle. It is labeled 1840 R. FIX and recorded.

Remember that the assumed position depends on the dead reckoning position near the time of sight. If sights are spaced several hours apart or if the ship's speed is great, you may have the AP Lat of the two sights a degree different. In this case, choose your central parallel as the half degree between the AP latitudes. For instance, if the AP Lat of one sight is 27° N, of the other sight 28° N, choose the central parallel as 27° 30' N. This way, both assumed positions will fit on one plotting sheet. Survey the range of the AP longitudes in the same way to choose the value of the central meridian.

With more plotting practice, you will find that you can eliminate some of the drawing. You may wish to not even draw the dashed azimuth lines. In place of the long solid line of the LOP at the time of sight (if it is to be advanced), you can make only a mark on the course line where this sight time LOP would cross, then draw in only the advanced LOP. These omissions are suggested only after the navigator fully understands and feels confident with the plotting procedures.

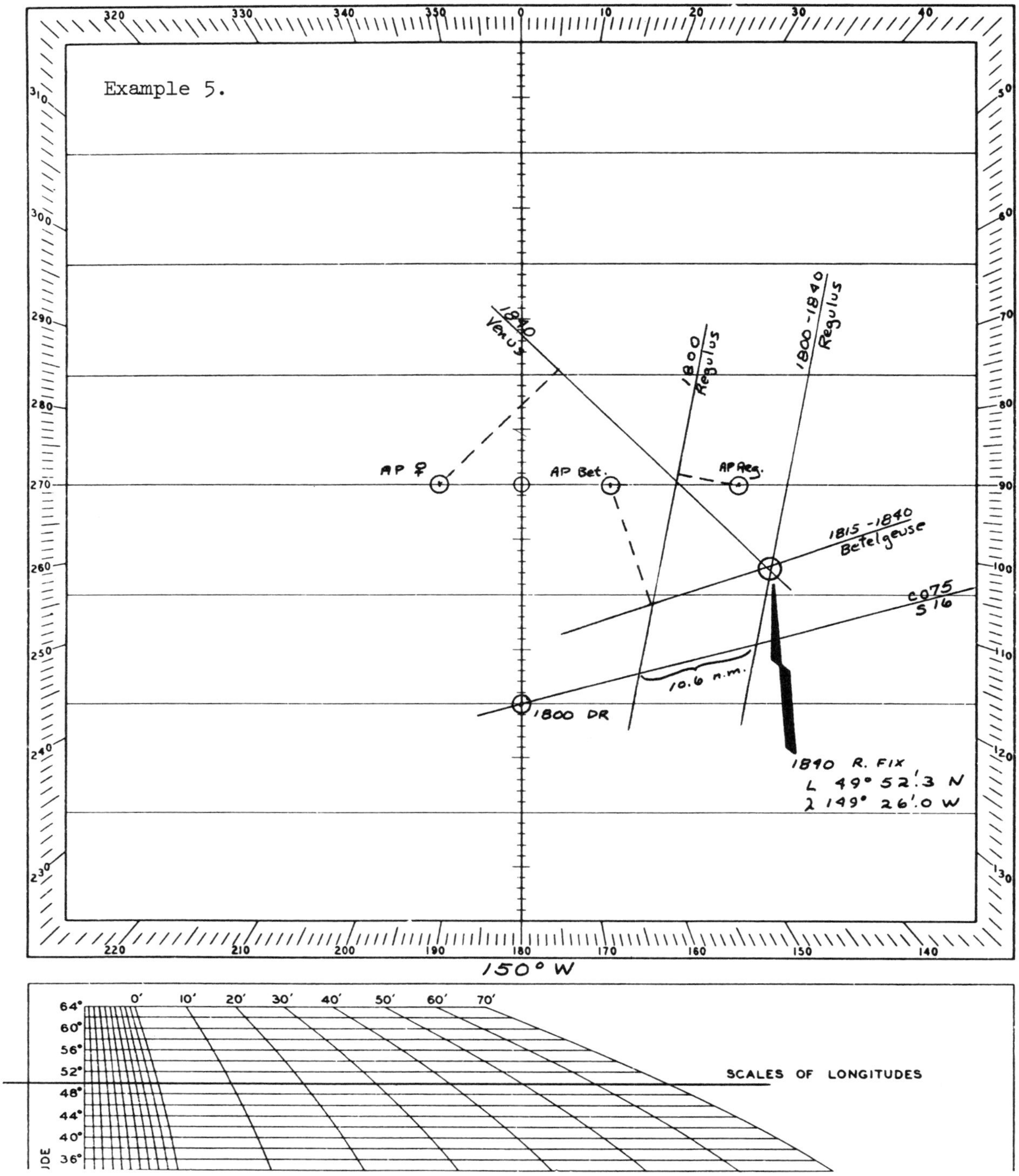

# EXERCISE 6

<u>Fix I</u> -- Label the central meridian 156° W, central parallel 34° N.

| Time of Sight | Body | AP Lat | AP Long | "a" | $Z_n$ |
|---|---|---|---|---|---|
| 0530 | Venus | 34° N | 155° 34'.6 W | 10'.3 A | 092°.1 |
| 0530 | Saturn | 34° N | 155° 43'.2 W | 7'.0 A | 145°.2 |
| 0530 | Polaris | 34° N | 155° 39'.4 W | 7'.5 T | 359°.3 |

Plot and record the 0530 Fix.

---

<u>Fix II</u> -- Label the central meridian 68° 30' W, central parallel 37° N.

0400 DR L - 37° 30' N
λ - 68° 40' W

course 145° - speed 5k

| Time of Sight | Body | AP Lat | AP Long | "a" | $Z_n$ |
|---|---|---|---|---|---|
| 0410 | Hamal | 37° N | 68° 55'.9 W | 6'.7 T | 083°.6 |
| 0420 | Fomalhaut | 37° N | 68° 43'.4 W | 23'.0 A | 160°.6 |
| 0430 | Vega | 37° N | 68° 11'.6 W | 35'.7 T | 287°.5 |

Plot and record the 0430 Fix.

---

<u>Fix III</u> -- Label the central meridian 64° 30' W, central parallel 39° 30' N.

1910 DR L - 39° 28'.4 N
λ - 64° 43'.6 W

course 160° - speed 10k

| Time of Sight | Body | AP Lat | AP Long | "a" | $Z_n$ |
|---|---|---|---|---|---|
| 1910 | Venus | 39° N | 64° 38'.6 W | 4'.4 A | 270°.8 |
| 1920 | Regulus | 39° N | 64° 41'.2 W | 9'.8 A | 125°.9 |
| 1930 | Polaris | 39° N | 64° 30'.0 W | 23'.0 T | 000° |

Plot and record the 1920 Fix. This requires retarding the 1930 LOP.

Fix IV -- Label the central meridian 155° E, central parallel 42° S.

0330 DR L - 41° 31!0 S
λ - 155° 00!0 E

course 110° - speed 10k

| Time of Sight | Body | AP Lat | AP Long | "a" | $Z_n$ |
|---|---|---|---|---|---|
| 0315 | Canopus | 42° S | 155° 20!2 E | 8!0 A | 230°8 |
| 0330 | Rigil Kent | 42° S | 155° 07!4 E | 5!8 A | 143°3 |
| 0345 | Alphard | 42° S | 154° 36!2 E | 24!5 T | 019°3 |

Plot and record the 0345 Fix.

---

Fix V -- Label the central meridian 129° W, central parallel 35° 20' N.

0630 DR L - 35° 30!0 N
λ - 128° 30!0 W

course 230° - speed 12k

| Time of Sight | Body | AP Lat | AP Long | "a" | $Z_n$ |
|---|---|---|---|---|---|
| 0630 | Moon | 36° N | 128° 11!2 W | 29!3 T | 233°2 |
| 1138 | Sun | 35° N | 128° 24!6 W | 14!5 T | 180°0 |

Plot the 0630 DR and the 1130 DR. Then plot the 0630 Moon LOP, advance it to 1138 and cross it with the 1138 Sun LOP, a noon sight of the Sun. Notice that the 1138 Sun is a horizontal line, giving by itself the ship's latitude.

Plot and record the 1138 Running Fix.

# Chapter 9

# From Observation to Fix

We have come to the point now where the knowledge gained in the last eight chapters can be assembled. From information gathered from the sextant, timepiece and DR track, we can plot our ship's position on the chart or plotting sheet.

The following two body and three body fixes are made on 7 April 1976. Constants throughout are:

| | |
|---|---|
| Height of eye | 9.5 feet |
| Index correction | -2!7 |
| Watch error | $1^m$ $03^s$ fast |
| All time standard zone time. | |

The first fix uses a small plotting sheet with central meridian 61° W, central parallel 40° N. The 1030 DR is 39° 40' N, 60° 36' W. Course from this point is 342°, speed 12 knots. The "observation" yields these values.

| Body | W.T. | $H_s$ |
|---|---|---|
| Sun UL | 12-06-46 | 57° 25!2 |
| Moon UL | 13-30-07 | 25° 17!4 |

For the sun sight observed at 1206 ZT, we need to update our DR position. For convenience we'll choose the 1200 DR since it is on the hour and is reasonably close to the time of sight. With these new coordinates, we reduce the sun sight with values as found on the work sheet that follows. Notice that this sight was taken near local apparent noon, i.e. when the Sun was in the south. The "d" value from H.O. 229 will be 60!0 which gives a net correction equal to the declination increment.

The Moon is observed at 1329 ZT, once again necessitating an updated DR. Course and speed are as before. The 1330 DR is plotted from the 1200 DR since we have not yet obtained a fix to correct a previous DR. The Moon LOP is plotted and the Sun LOP is advanced along the course line for 16.6 nautical miles ($1^h$ $23^m$ at 12 knots). Since the Sun line was advanced more than an hour, the resulting

1329 fix is called a running fix or R. FIX. This fix shows an ideal situation for a two body fix since the lines of position are almost perpendicular to each other.

The second fix is observed during evening twilight. The 1930 DR is 41° N, 63° W, the center of our plotting sheet. Course to this point and beyond is 289°, speed 15 knots. Sights are as follows.

| Body | W.T. | $H_s$ |
|---|---|---|
| Capella | 18-54-21 | 62° 03.'2 |
| Mars | 19-07-11 | 67° 32.'9 |
| Polaris | 19-31-41 | 40° 49.'8 |

The plot shows the Capella and Mars LOPs advanced along the course line to intersect the Polaris LOP at a point fix.

SIGHT REDUCTION BY H.O. 229

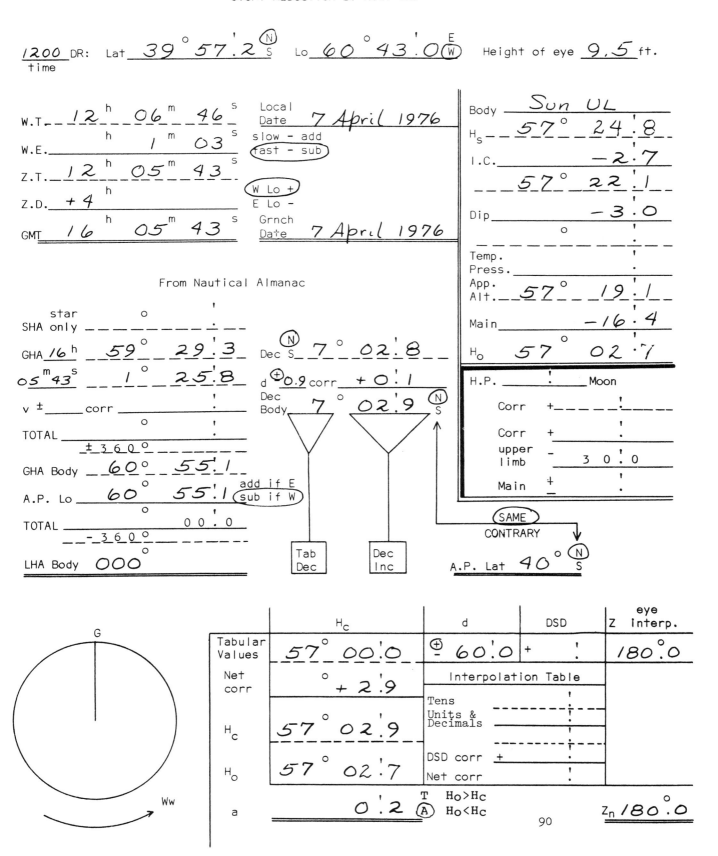

1200 DR: Lat 39° 57'.2 (N) S    Lo 60° 43'.0 E (W)    Height of eye 9.5 ft.
time

| | | | | |
|---|---|---|---|---|
| W.T. | 12h 06m 46s | | Local Date | 7 April 1976 |
| W.E. | 1m 03s | | slow - add / (fast - sub) | |
| Z.T. | 12h 05m 43s | | | |
| Z.D. | +4h | | (W Lo +) / E Lo - | |
| GMT | 16h 05m 43s | | Grnch Date | 7 April 1976 |

| | |
|---|---|
| Body | Sun UL |
| $H_s$ | 57° 24'.8 |
| I.C. | -2'.7 |
| | 57° 22'.1 |
| Dip | -3'.0 |
| | |
| Temp. Press. | |
| App. Alt. | 57° 19'.1 |
| Main | -16'.4 |
| $H_o$ | 57° 02'.7 |

| Moon | |
|---|---|
| H.P. | |
| Corr | + |
| Corr | + |
| upper limb | - 30'.0 |
| Main | ± |

From Nautical Almanac

| | |
|---|---|
| star SHA only | |
| GHA 16h | 59° 29'.3 |
| 05m 43s | 1° 25'.8 |
| v ± corr | |
| TOTAL | |
| ±360° | |
| GHA Body | 60° 55'.1 |
| A.P. Lo | 60° 55'.1 (add if E / (sub if W)) |
| TOTAL | 00'.0 |
| -360° | |
| LHA Body | 000° |

| | |
|---|---|
| Dec (N) S | 7° 02'.8 |
| d (+)0.9 corr | +0'.1 |
| Dec Body | 7° 02'.9 (N) S |

Tab Dec    Dec Inc

(SAME) CONTRARY

A.P. Lat 40° (N) S

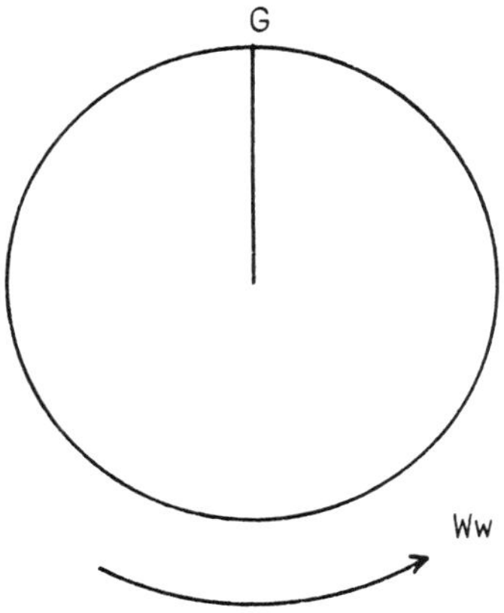


| | $H_c$ | d | DSD | Z eye interp. |
|---|---|---|---|---|
| Tabular Values | 57° 00'.0 | (+) - 60'.0 | + | 180°.0 |
| Net corr | +2'.9 | Interpolation Table | | |
| | | Tens | | |
| | | Units & Decimals | | |
| $H_c$ | 57° 02'.9 | | | |
| $H_o$ | 57° 02'.7 | DSD corr + | | |
| | | Net corr | | |
| a | 0'.2 | T Ho>Hc / (A) Ho<Hc | | $Z_n$ 180°.0 |

# SIGHT REDUCTION BY H.O. 229

1330 DR: Lat 40° 14'.2 (N) S  Lo 60° 50'.5 E (W)  Height of eye 9.5 ft.
time

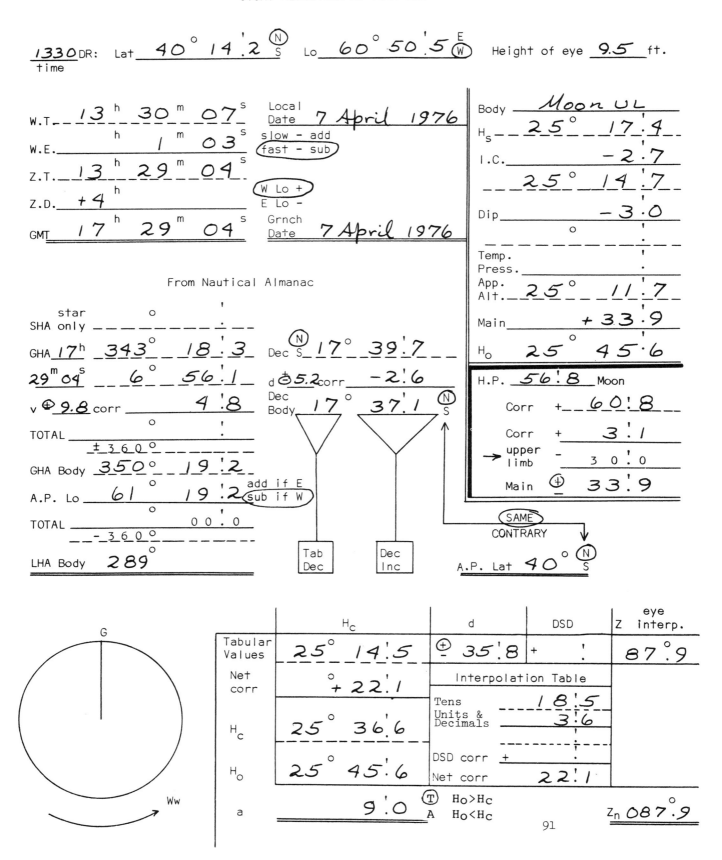

W.T. 13h 30m 07s  Local Date 7 April 1976
W.E. 1m 03s  slow - add / (fast - sub)
Z.T. 13h 29m 04s
Z.D. +4h  (W Lo +) / E Lo -
GMT 17h 29m 04s  Grnch Date 7 April 1976

Body Moon UL
$H_s$ 25° 17'.4
I.C. -2'.7
25° 14'.7
Dip -3'.0
Temp. Press.
App. Alt. 25° 11'.7
Main +33'.9
$H_o$ 25° 45'.6

H.P. 56'.8 Moon
Corr + 60'.8
Corr + 3'.1
→ upper limb - 30'.0
Main (+) 33'.9

From Nautical Almanac

star SHA only
GHA 17h 343° 18'.3  Dec (N) S 17° 39'.7
29m 04s 6° 56'.1  d (-) 5.2 corr -2'.6
v (+) 9.8 corr 4'.8  Dec Body 17° 37'.1 (N) S
TOTAL
±360°
GHA Body 350° 19'.2
A.P. Lo 61° 19'.2  add if E / (sub if W)
TOTAL 00'.0
-360°
LHA Body 289°

Tab Dec | Dec Inc

(SAME) / CONTRARY

A.P. Lat 40° (N) S

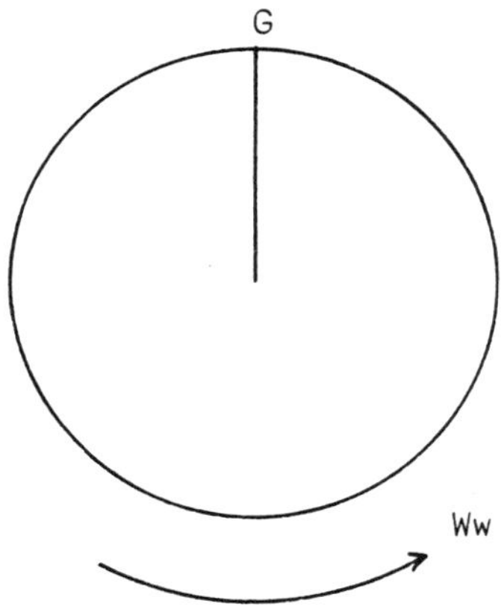


| | $H_c$ | d | DSD | Z eye interp. |
|---|---|---|---|---|
| Tabular Values | 25° 14'.5 | (+) 35'.8 | + | 87°.9 |
| Net corr | +22'.1 | Interpolation Table | | |
| | | Tens | 18'.5 | |
| | | Units & Decimals | 3'.6 | |
| $H_c$ | 25° 36'.6 | | | |
| $H_o$ | 25° 45'.6 | DSD corr | + | |
| | | Net corr | 22'.1 | |
| a | 9'.0 | (T) $H_o > H_c$ / A $H_o < H_c$ | | $Z_n$ 087°.9 |

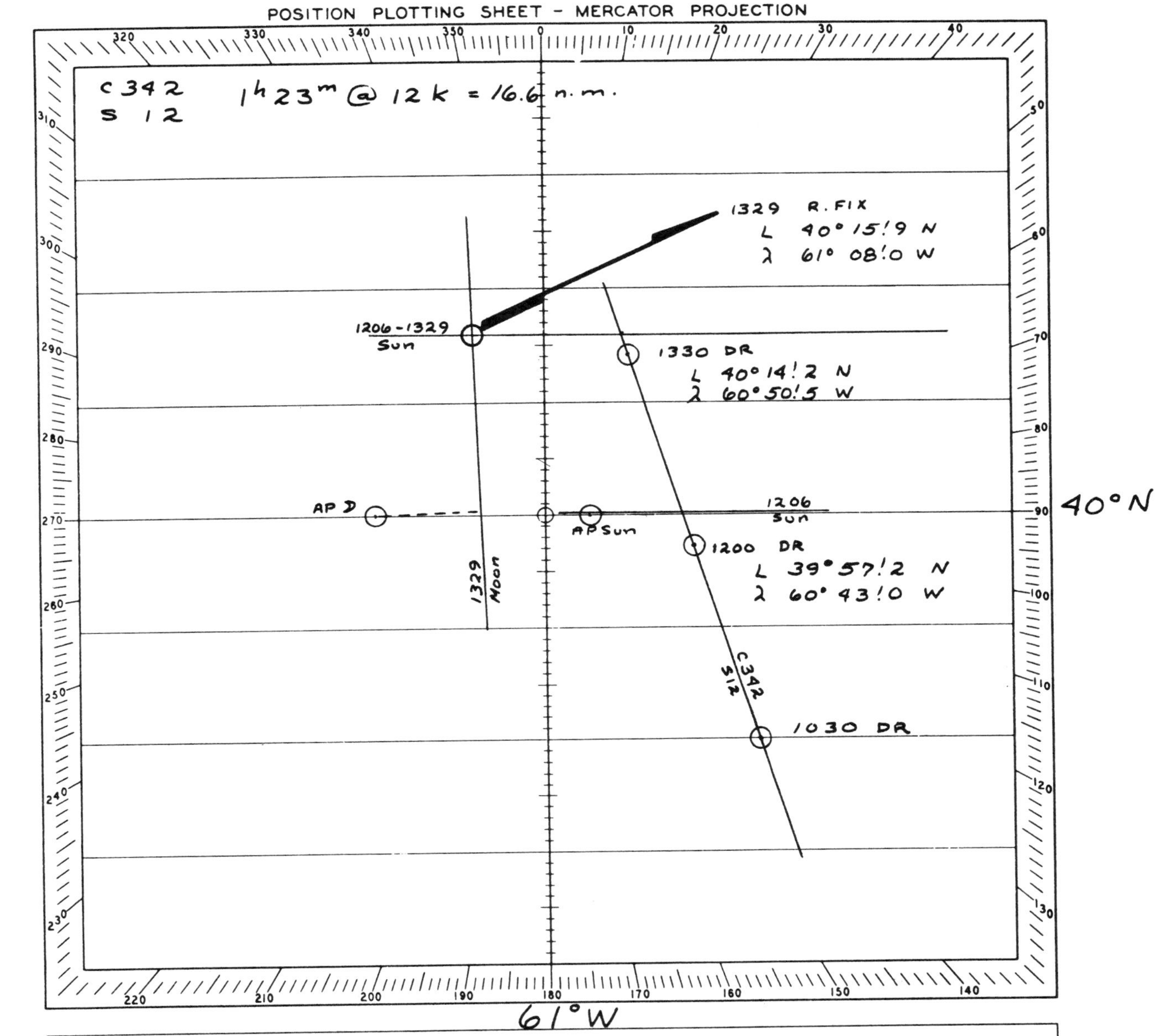


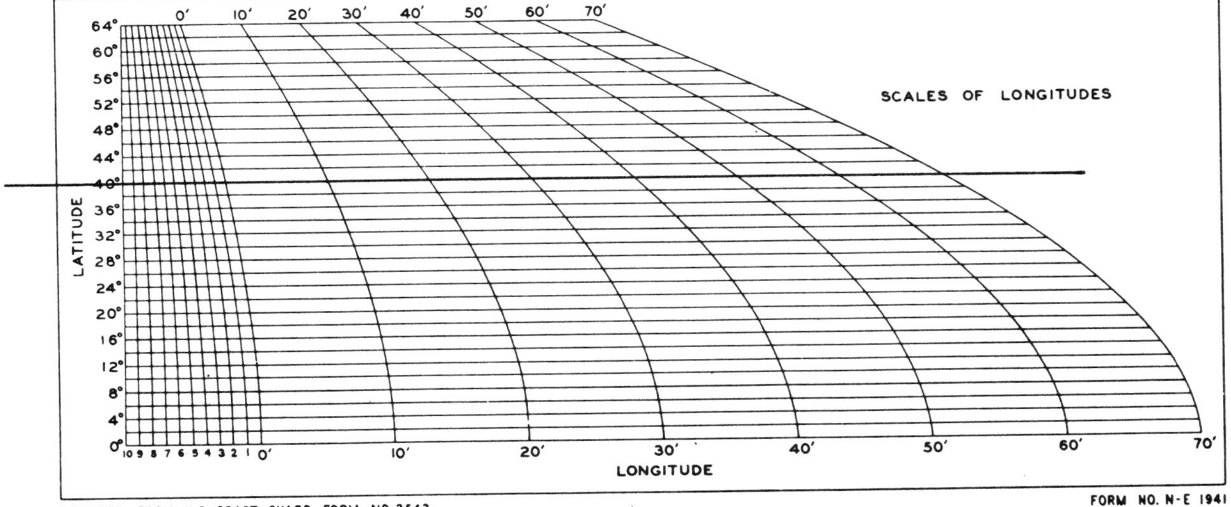


ADAPTED FROM U.S. COAST GUARD FORM. NO. 2543

FORM NO. N-E 1941

# SIGHT REDUCTION BY H.O. 229

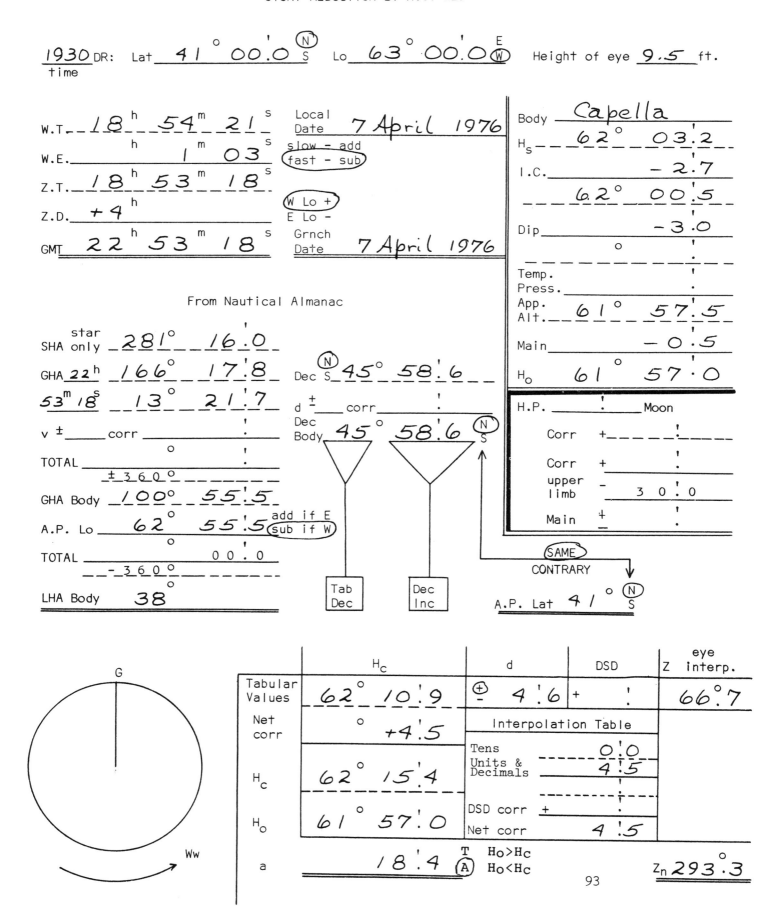

1930 DR: Lat 41° 00.'0 (N)/S  Lo 63° 00.'0 E/(W)  Height of eye 9.5 ft.
time

| | |
|---|---|
| W.T. | 18h 54m 21s |
| W.E. | 1m 03s |
| Z.T. | 18h 53m 18s |
| Z.D. | +4h |
| GMT | 22h 53m 18s |

Local Date: 7 April 1976
slow - add
(fast - sub)
(W Lo +)
E Lo -
Grnch Date: 7 April 1976

| | |
|---|---|
| Body | Capella |
| $H_s$ | 62° 03.'2 |
| I.C. | -2.'7 |
| | 62° 00.'5 |
| Dip | -3.'0 |
| | ° ' |
| Temp. Press. | |
| App. Alt. | 61° 57.'5 |
| Main | -0.'5 |
| $H_o$ | 61° 57.'0 |

| | |
|---|---|
| H.P. | Moon |
| Corr + | |
| Corr + | |
| upper limb - | 30.'0 |
| Main ± | |

From Nautical Almanac

| | |
|---|---|
| SHA (star only) | 281° 16.'0 |
| GHA 22h | 166° 17.'8 |
| 53m 18s | 13° 21.'7 |
| v ± corr | |
| TOTAL | |
| ±360° | |
| GHA Body | 100° 55.'5 |
| A.P. Lo | 62° 55.'5 add if E / (sub if W) |
| TOTAL | 00.'0 |
| -360° | |
| LHA Body | 38° |

Dec (N)/S 45° 58.'6
d ± corr
Dec Body 45° 58.'6 (N)/S

Tab Dec | Dec Inc

(SAME) / CONTRARY

A.P. Lat 41° (N)/S

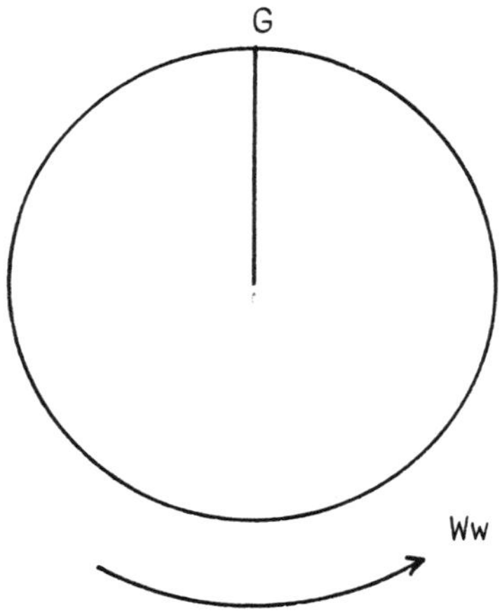


| | $H_c$ | d | DSD | Z (eye interp.) |
|---|---|---|---|---|
| Tabular Values | 62° 10.'9 | (+)/- 4.'6 | + ' | 66.°7 |
| Net corr | +4.'5 | Interpolation Table | | |
| $H_c$ | 62° 15.'4 | Tens | 0.'0 | |
| | | Units & Decimals | 4.'5 | |
| $H_o$ | 61° 57.'0 | DSD corr | + | |
| | | Net corr | 4.'5 | |
| a | 18.'4 T/(A) $H_o>H_c$ / $H_o<H_c$ | | | $Z_n$ 293.°3 |

SIGHT REDUCTION BY H.O. 229

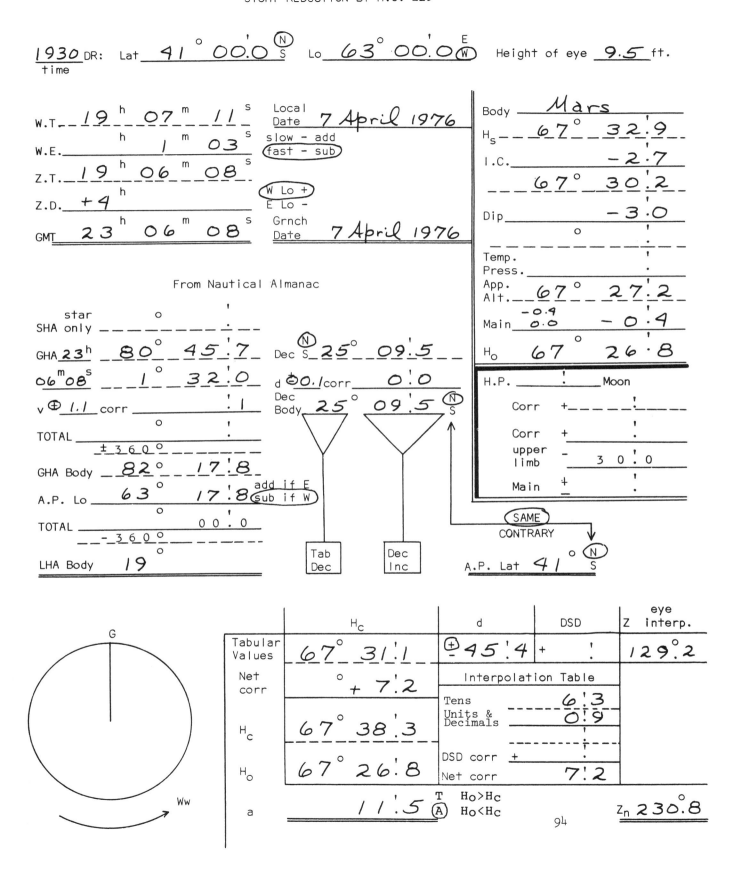

1930 DR: Lat 41° 00.0' (N)/S Lo 63° 00.0' E/(W) Height of eye 9.5 ft.
time

| | |
|---|---|
| W.T. | 19h 07m 11s |
| W.E. | 1m 03s |
| Z.T. | 19h 06m 08s |
| Z.D. | +4h |
| GMT | 23h 06m 08s |

Local Date 7 April 1976
slow - add
(fast - sub)

(W Lo +)
E Lo -

Grnch Date 7 April 1976

| | |
|---|---|
| Body | Mars |
| $H_s$ | 67° 32.9' |
| I.C. | -2.7' |
| | 67° 30.2' |
| Dip | -3.0' |
| | ° ' |
| Temp. / Press. | |
| App. Alt. | 67° 27.2' |
| Main (-0.4 / 0.0) | -0.4' |
| $H_o$ | 67° 26.8' |

| | |
|---|---|
| H.P. | Moon |
| Corr | + |
| Corr | + |
| upper limb | - 30.0' |
| Main | ± |

From Nautical Almanac

| | | | |
|---|---|---|---|
| star SHA only | ° ' | | |
| GHA 23h | 80° 45.7' | Dec (N)/S | 25° 09.5' |
| 06m 08s | 1° 32.0' | d (±)0.1 corr | 0.0' |
| v (+) 1.1 corr | .1' | Dec Body | 25° 09.5' (N)/S |
| TOTAL | ° ' | | |
| ±360° | | | |
| GHA Body | 82° 17.8' | | |
| A.P. Lo | 63° 17.8' add if E / (sub if W) | | |
| TOTAL | 00.0' | | |
| -360° | | | |
| LHA Body | 19° | | |

Tab Dec — Dec Inc

(SAME) / CONTRARY

A.P. Lat 41° (N)/S

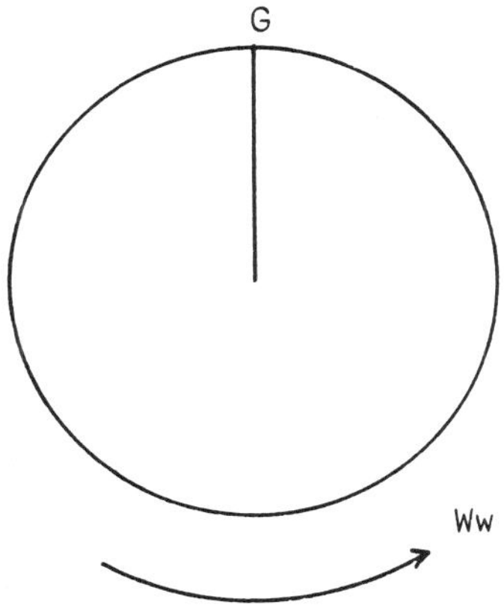


| | $H_c$ | d | DSD | Z eye interp. |
|---|---|---|---|---|
| Tabular Values | 67° 31.1' | (±)45.4' | + ' | 129.2° |
| Net corr | + 7.2' | Interpolation Table | | |
| $H_c$ | 67° 38.3' | Tens | 6.3' | |
| | | Units & Decimals | 0.9' | |
| $H_o$ | 67° 26.8' | DSD corr | + | |
| | | Net corr | 7.2' | |
| a | 11.5' T/(A) | $H_o>H_c$ / $H_o<H_c$ | | $Z_n$ 230.8° |

# SIGHT REDUCTION BY H.O. 229

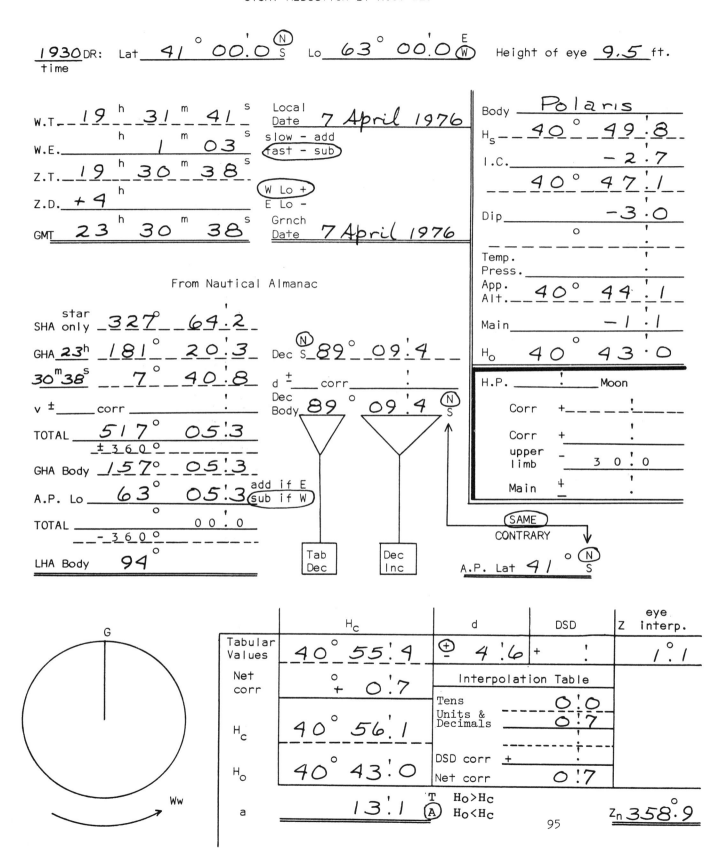

1930 DR: Lat 41° 00.0' (N) S  Lo 63° 00.0' E (W)  Height of eye 9.5 ft.
time

| | | | |
|---|---|---|---|
| W.T. | 19h 31m 41s | Local Date | 7 April 1976 |
| W.E. | 1m 03s | slow - add / (fast - sub) | |
| Z.T. | 19h 30m 38s | | |
| Z.D. | +4h | (W Lo +) / E Lo - | |
| GMT | 23h 30m 38s | Grnch Date | 7 April 1976 |

| | |
|---|---|
| Body | Polaris |
| $H_s$ | 40° 49.'8 |
| I.C. | -2.'7 |
| | 40° 47.'1 |
| Dip | -3.'0 |
| | ° . |
| Temp. / Press. | . |
| App. Alt. | 40° 44.'1 |
| Main | -1.'1 |
| $H_o$ | 40° 43.'0 |

| | |
|---|---|
| H.P. | : Moon |
| Corr | + : |
| Corr | + : |
| upper limb | - 30:0 |
| Main | ± : |

From Nautical Almanac

| | | | |
|---|---|---|---|
| SHA star only | 327° 64.'2 | | |
| GHA 23h | 181° 20.'3 | Dec (N) S | 89° 09.'4 |
| 30m38s | 7° 40.'8 | d ± corr | : |
| v ± corr | : | Dec Body | 89° 09.'4 (N) S |
| TOTAL | 517° 05.'3 | | |
| | ±360° | | |
| GHA Body | 157° 05.'3 | | |
| A.P. Lo | 63° 05.'3 | add if E / (sub if W) | |
| TOTAL | 00.'0 | | |
| | -360° | | |
| LHA Body | 94° | | |

Tab Dec  Dec Inc

(SAME) / CONTRARY

A.P. Lat 41° (N) S

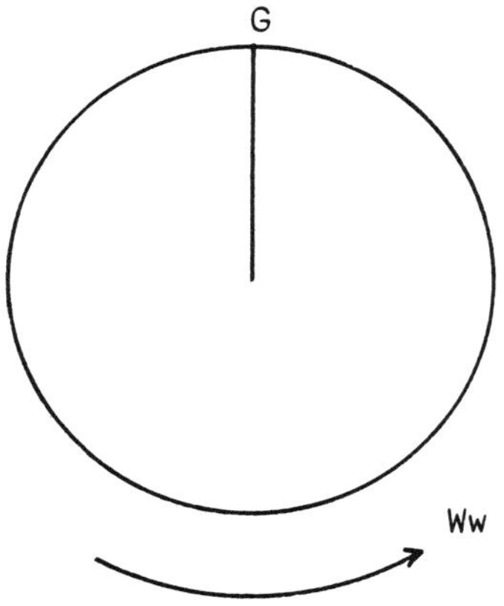


| | $H_c$ | d | DSD | Z / eye interp. |
|---|---|---|---|---|
| Tabular Values | 40° 55.'4 | (+) / − 4.'6 | + : | 1.°1 |
| Net corr | + 0.'7 | Interpolation Table | | |
| | | Tens | 0.'0 | |
| $H_c$ | 40° 56.'1 | Units & Decimals | 0.'7 | |
| $H_o$ | 40° 43.'0 | DSD corr | + : | |
| | | Net corr | 0.'7 | |
| a | 13.'1 | T $H_o > H_c$ / (A) $H_o < H_c$ | | $Z_n$ 358.°9 |

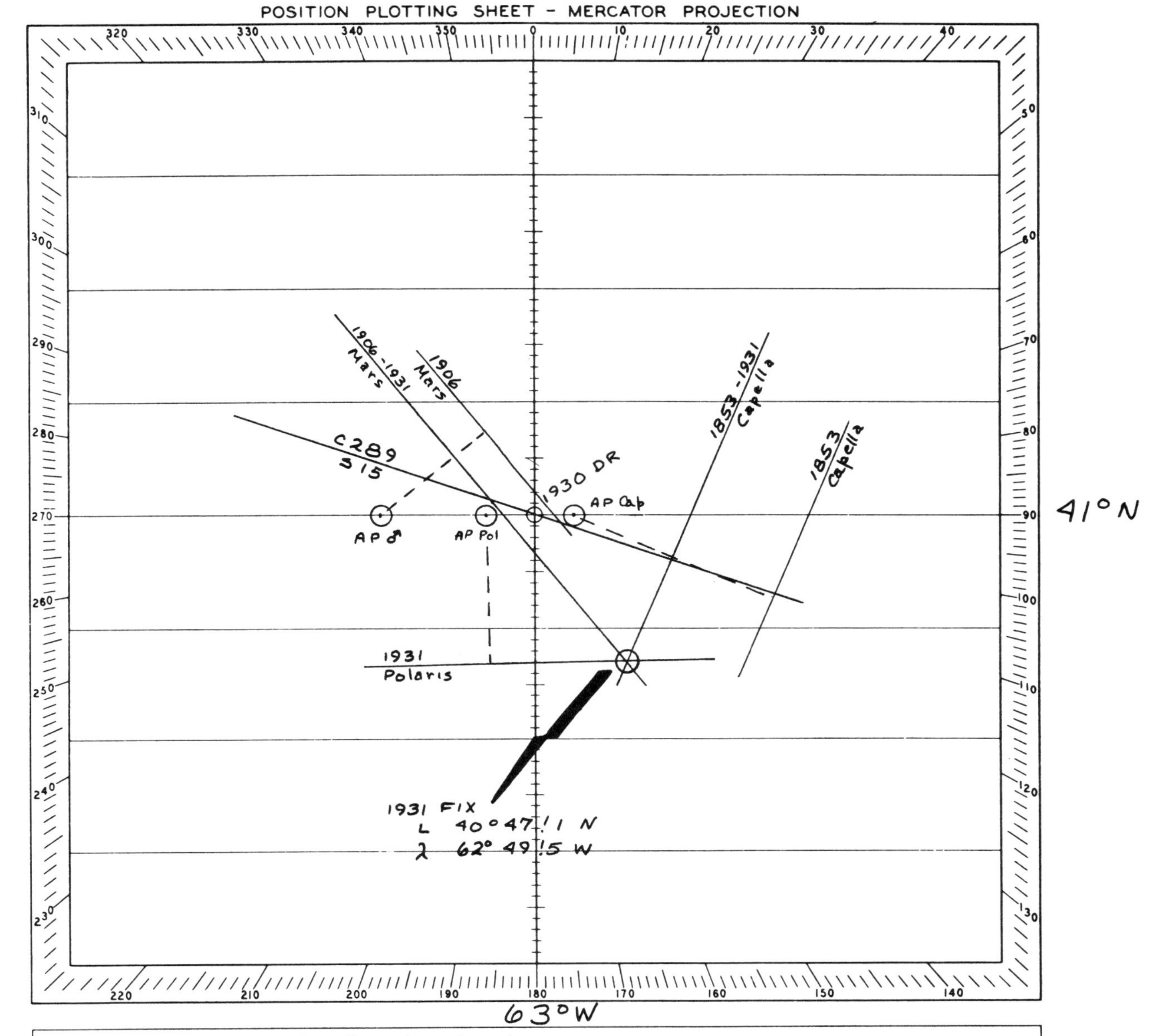


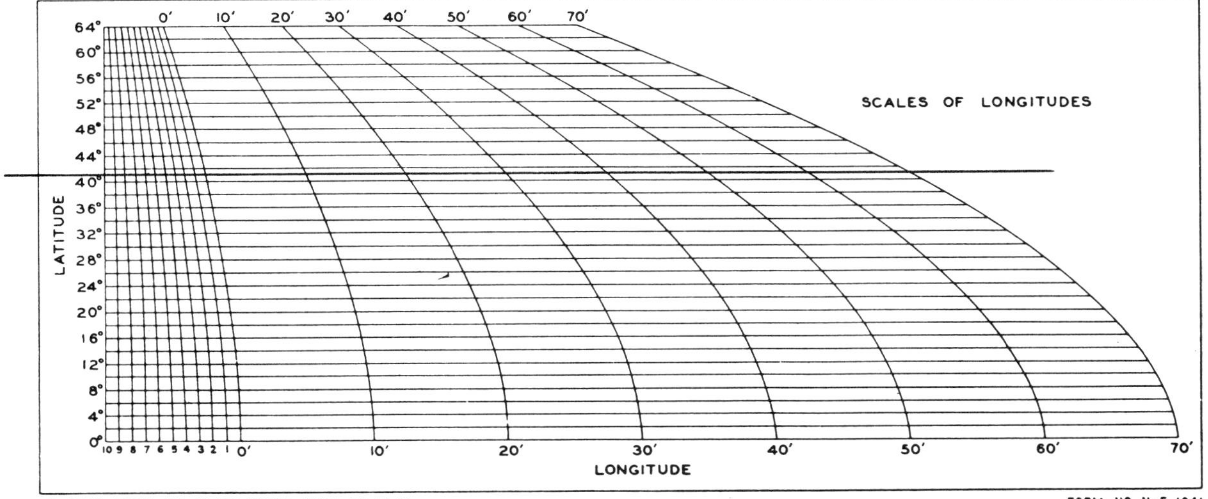


ADAPTED FROM U.S. COAST GUARD FORM. NO. 2543

FORM NO. N-E 1941

## EXERCISE 7

Reduce the following sights by H.O. 229 to obtain a fix.

1. Plot and record the 2010 fix, local date of 5 July 1976.

   a) 2010 DR  L  36° 42' N
      λ  179° 13' E

   Course 105°, speed 24 knots

   b) W.E. on Z.T., $1^m\ 03^s$ slow; Height of eye, 27 feet;
   I.C. +2!5; plotting sheet centrals, 37° N, 179° E

   c) The following stars were observed in the evening twilight.

| Star | W.T. | $H_s$ |
|---|---|---|
| Spica | 19-39-58 | 39° 44!5 |
| Dubhe | 19-49-58 | 48° 20!0 |
| Vega | 20-09-13 | 48° 03!9 |

2. Plot and record the 1900 fix, local date 22 March 1976.

   a) 1900 DR  L  36° 27' N
      λ  136° 54' W

   Course 054°, speed 36 knots

   b) W.E. on Z.T., $1^m\ 23^s$ fast; Height of eye, 12.6 feet;
   I.C. -1!0; plotting sheet centrals, 36° N, 137° W

   c) The following stars were observed at about 6:45 p.m.

| Star | W.T. | $H_s$ |
|---|---|---|
| Alphard | 18-42-00 | 30° 00!4 |
| Menkar | 18-51-45 | 29° 21!8 |
| Kochab | 19-01-15 | 27° 48!5 |

3. Plot and record the 0450 fix, local date 18 February 1976.

a) 0450 DR    L    36° 53' S
              λ    53° 05' W

Course 072°, speed 24 knots

b) W.E. on Z.T., $25^s$ fast;    Height of eye, 30 feet;
I.C. -2!0;    plotting sheet centrals, 37° S, 53° W;
temperature 5° C, pressure 1032 mb

c) The following stars were observed before sunrise.

| Star | W.T. | $H_s$ |
|---|---|---|
| Arcturus | 04-30-28 | 33° 22!6 |
| Altair | 04-41-33 | 8° 20!1 |
| Canopus | 04-50-32 | 9° 21!5 |

4. Plot and record the 1101 fix, local date of 22 April 1976.

a) 1100 DR    L    30° N
              λ    25° W

Course 280°, speed 7 knots

b) W.E. on Z.T., $31^s$ slow;    Height of eye, 11 feet;
I.C. -3!6;    plotting sheet centrals, 30° N, 25° W

c) The following bodies were observed before noon.

| Body | W.T. | $H_s$ |
|---|---|---|
| Sun LL | 10-58-16 | 70° 00!2 |
| Moon UL | 11-00-10 | 16° 36!8 |

5. Plot and record the 1500 Running Fix, local date of 6 July 1976.

a) 1500 DR L 36° 20' N
λ 156° 16' E

Course 220°, speed 8 knots

b) W.E. on Z.T., $47^s$ fast; Height of eye, 6 feet;
I.C. 0!0; plotting sheet centrals, 36° 30' N, 156° E

c) The sun was observed twice on the same day.

| Body | W.T. | $H_s$ |
|---|---|---|
| Sun LL | 12-16-13 | 73° 39!7 |
| Sun UL | 15-00-47 | 45° 11!5 |

Note: Remember to plot the 1200 DR to get nearer latitude and longitude for the time of the first sight.

6. Plot and record the 2000 fix, local date of 7 July 1976.

a) 2000 DR L 43° 29!0 N
λ 67° 38!0 W

Course 045°, speed 5 knots

b) W.E. on Z.T., $35^s$ slow; Height of eye, 10.5 feet;
I.C. -1!8; plotting sheet centrals, 43° 30' N, 68° W

c) The Moon and Mars were observed in the evening.

| Body | W.T. | $H_s$ |
|---|---|---|
| Moon LL | 19-20-07 | 25° 37!3 |
| Mars | 19-59-26 | 15° 29!8 |

# Chapter 10

# Sunrise, Sunset, Twilights, Local Apparent Noon

For an observer to plan his time of sextant observation during twilights or at meridian passage, it is necessary that he be able to prefigure times of these phenomena. The Nautical Almanac, on the right hand side of each daily page opening, lists the times of sunrise, sunset, nautical twilight and civil twilight for every two, five or ten degrees of latitude. Interpolation is necessary for intermediate latitudes. The times listed are zone times for the center of every time zone so must be adjusted for your specific longitude (or longitude variance from the center of the zone).

Sunrise and sunset occur at the time that the Sun's upper limb touches the horizon. Civil twilight is established as when the Sun's center is 6° below the horizon, nautical twilight when the Sun's center is 12° below the horizon. At civil twilight, we would consider it "getting dark" (or "getting light" in the morning). Nautical twilight marks the point where the horizon is of no more practical use for sextant observation. In the morning, it marks the time when sights can be begun.

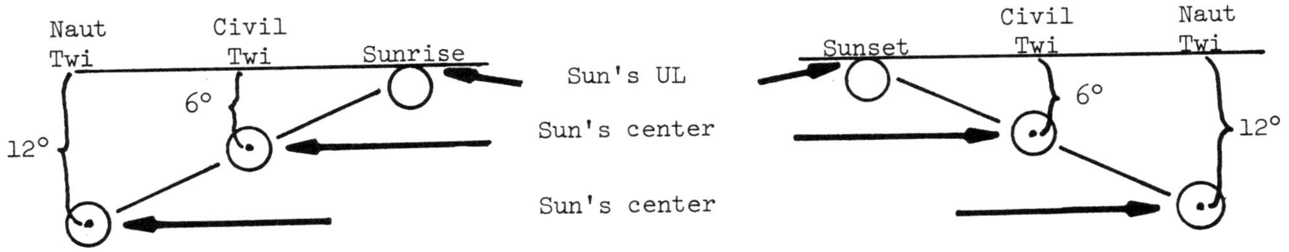


The length of twilight varies depending on your latitude and the time of year. At times, you may have only twenty minutes of twilight whereas in another situation twilight may last almost two hours. Of course, within the arctic circle, twilight can last all night.

For high latitudes, some of the phenomena do not occur. The symbols indicating this are:

□ Sun or Moon remains continuously above the horizon;
■ Sun or Moon remains continuously below the horizon;
//// twilight lasts all night.

To interpolate for latitude, let us take the example of 8 January, latitude 42° N. For the center of each time zone, the times of morning nautical twilight and sunrise are as follows.

| Lat. | Twilight Naut. | Twilight Civil | Sunrise |
|---|---|---|---|
| ° | h m | h m | h m |
| N 72 | 08 16 | 10 22 | ■ |
| N 70 | 07 59 | 09 38 | ■ |
| 68 | 07 45 | 09 09 | 11 15 |
| 66 | 07 33 | 08 47 | 10 15 |
| 64 | 07 23 | 08 29 | 09 41 |
| 62 | 07 15 | 08 15 | 09 17 |
| 60 | 07 07 | 08 02 | 08 58 |
| N 58 | 07 00 | 07 52 | 08 42 |
| 56 | 06 54 | 07 42 | 08 28 |
| 54 | 06 48 | 07 34 | 08 17 |
| 52 | 06 43 | 07 26 | 08 06 |
| 50 | 06 39 | 07 19 | 07 57 |
| 45 | 06 28 | 07 04 | 07 38 |
| N 40 | 06 18 | 06 52 | 07 22 |
| 35 | 06 09 | 06 41 | 07 08 |
| 30 | 06 01 | 06 31 | 06 57 |
| 20 | 05 46 | 06 13 | 06 37 |
| N 10 | 05 30 | 05 56 | 06 19 |
| 0 | 05 14 | 05 40 | 06 03 |

| | Naut Twi | | Sunrise | |
|---|---|---|---|---|
| N 45° | 0628 | $10^m \times 2/5 = 4^m$ | 0738 | $16^m \times 2/5 = 6^m$ |
| N 42° | 0622 | 0618 + 4 = 0622 | 0728 | 0722 + 6 = 0728 |
| N 40° | 0618 | | 0722 | |

Since 42° is 2/5 of the interval between 40° and 45°, we interpolate the difference between bracketing latitudes, rounding to the nearest minute. In each case, we added the difference in time to the time value for the lower latitude. The resulting time is standard zone time for the center of every zone. To get daylight time, add one hour.

In addition to interpolation for latitude, we must apply a correction for longitude, a correction which will apply the same way to all Sun and Moon phenomena. If we take the angular difference between our DR longitude and the center of our time zone, then convert this difference to time, we have found the correction. If we are to the east or right of the center of our zone, the correction is negative (since the Sun seems to move from east to west due to the earth's rotation). If we are to the west or left of the center of our zone, the correction is positive, the phenomena occurs for us after it occurred at the center of the zone.

Let us take the example of a DR longitude of 55° W. The center of our zone (the nearest whole number divisible by 15) is 60° W. We are 5° to the east or right of the zone center.

$$1^\circ \text{ of arc} = 4^m \text{ of time}$$

Therefore, 5° of arc converts to $20^m$ of time, a negative correction since we are to the east of the center of the zone. The longitude correction would be $-20^m$, applicable to sunrise, sunset, twilights, meridian passages and Moon phenomena. For the Moon, correction must also be made for orbital motion.

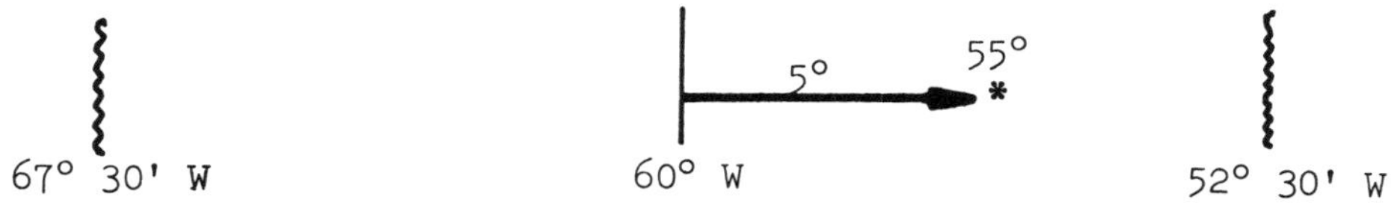

If our longitude were 146° 45' E, the center of our zone would be 150° E. We are 3° 15' to the left or west of the center of the zone. This converts to $3\frac{1}{4} \times 4 = 13$ minutes, a positive correction. The longitude correction would be $+13^m$, applied to the interpolated time of the phenomena.

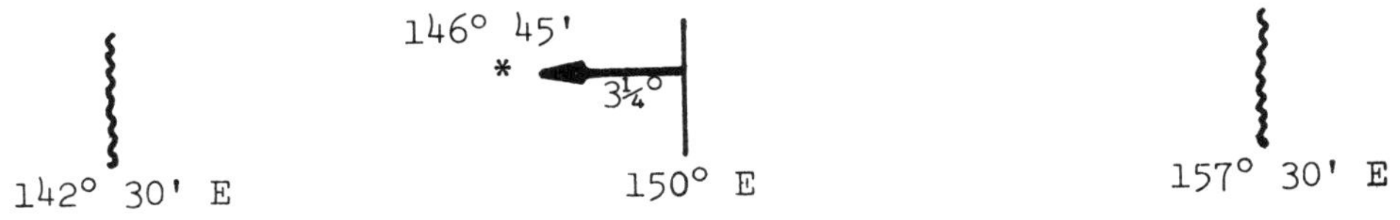


Let us now take two full examples.

Example 1. What is the standard zone time for observation of evening stars on 14 April 1976? Our DR position is Lat 18° 40' S, Long 109° 20' W.

| Lat. | Sunset | Twilight Civil | Twilight Naut. |
|---|---|---|---|
| ° | h m | h m | h m |
| N 72 | 20 14 | 21 52 | //// |
| N 70 | 19 58 | 21 18 | //// |
| 68 | 19 46 | 20 54 | 23 03 |
| 66 | 19 36 | 20 36 | 22 10 |
| 64 | 19 27 | 20 21 | 21 40 |
| 62 | 19 20 | 20 09 | 21 17 |
| 60 | 19 13 | 19 59 | 21 00 |
| N 10 | 18 10 | 18 32 | 18 57 |
| 0 | 18 04 | 18 25 | 18 49 |
| S 10 | 17 57 | 18 19 | 18 43 |
| 20 | 17 51 | 18 13 | 18 38 |
| 30 | 17 43 | 18 07 | 18 35 |
| 35 | 17 38 | 18 04 | 18 33 |
| 40 | 17 33 | 18 01 | 18 32 |
| 45 | 17 28 | 17 57 | 18 31 |

| | Sunset | Naut Twi |
|---|---|---|
| S 10° | 1757 | 1843 |
| S 19° | 1752 | 1839 |
| S 20° | 1751 | 1838 |

Sunset: $.9 \times 6^m = 5^m$

Naut Twi: $.9 \times 5^m = 4^m$ or $5^m$

Since we are 4° 20' to the west of the center of our zone (105° W), our longitude correction is $4\ 1/3 \times 4^m = 17^m$, a positive correction.

Sunset: 1752 + 17 = 1809
Nautical Twilight: 1839 + 17 = 1856

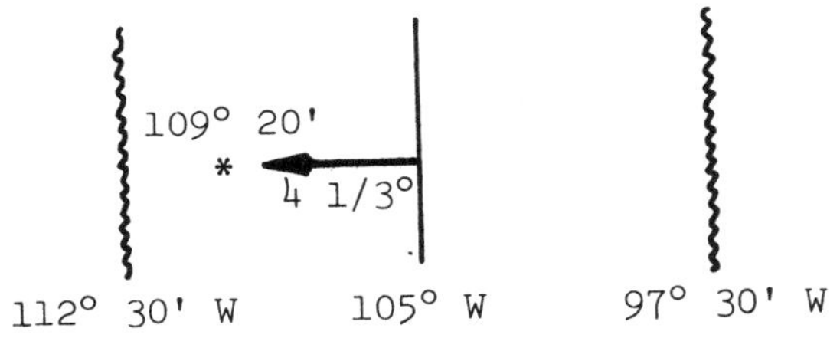

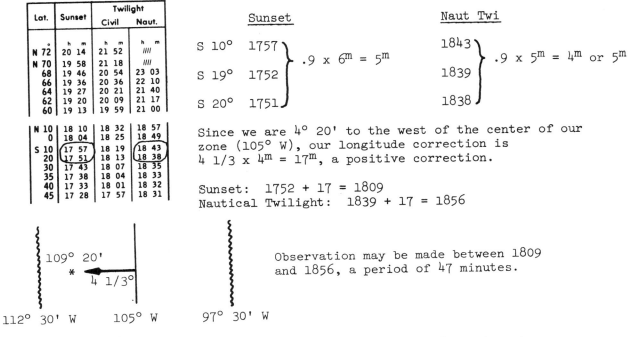

Observation may be made between 1809 and 1856, a period of 47 minutes.

Example 2. What is the <u>daylight</u> time for observation of morning stars on 6 July 1976? Our DR position is Lat 51° 37' N, Long 51° 37' E.

| Lat. | Twilight Naut. | Twilight Civil | Sunrise |
|---|---|---|---|
| ° | h m | h m | h m |
| N 72 | ▭ | ▭ | ▭ |
| N 70 | ▭ | ▭ | ▭ |
| 68 | ▭ | ▭ | ▭ |
| 66 | //// | //// | 00 52 |
| 64 | //// | //// | 01 51 |
| 62 | //// | //// | 02 24 |
| 60 | //// | 01 16 | 02 48 |
| N 58 | //// | 01 56 | 03 07 |
| 56 | //// | 02 23 | 03 23 |
| 54 | 01 10 | 02 44 | 03 36 |
| 52 | 01 47 | 03 01 | 03 48 |
| 50 | 02 12 | 03 15 | 03 58 |
| 45 | 02 55 | 03 43 | 04 20 |

| | Naut Twi | Sunrise |
|---|---|---|
| N 52° | 0147 | 0348 |
| N 51°37' | 0152 | 0350 |
| N 50° | 0212 | 0358 |

Naut Twi: $\frac{97}{120} \times 25^m = 20^m$

Sunrise: $\frac{97}{120} \times 10^m = 8^m$

Since we are 6° 37' to the east of the center of our zone (45° E), our longitude correction is 6.6 x $4^m$ = $26^m$, a negative correction.

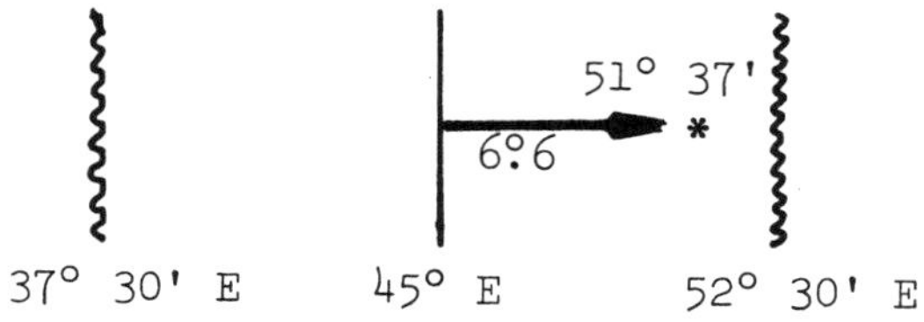


Nautical Twilight: 0152 - 26 = 0126 + $1^h$ = 0226 (daylight)

Sunrise: 0350 - 26 = 0324 + $1^h$ = 0424 (daylight)

Observation may be made between 0226 and 0424, a period of $1^h$ $58^m$.

Of course, the observation periods mentioned above are not fully used in practice. Stars are not visible the minute after sunset nor are atmospheric conditions always good enough to allow the horizon to be visible until the end of nautical twilight (assuming evening observation). However, it is best to be prepared earlier than need be and have a rough idea as to how long your observation period will be.

The times of sunrise, sunset and twilights are stated for a three day period and are rounded off to the nearest minute. By perusing the daily pages, you will notice that the change in time each day is roughly one minute for mid latitudes.

The procedure for finding the rough time of local apparent noon (LAN) is identical to the above except that no interpolation for latitude is necessary, only a longitude correction. Time of meridian passage of the Sun is noted at the bottom of the twilight etc. column for each day of the page. Often the time of Sun meridian passage will be the same for all three days listed on the page. The time of meridian passage will be when the Sun is exactly in the south or north (on the meridian) for every latitude at the center of a time zone. This time will vary from 1200 by the equation of time listed to the left of the meridian passage column.

Using the two examples above, we find that meridian passage of the Sun for 14 April is 1200. Applying the longitude correction in Example 1 of +$17^m$, we find the time of LAN for our DR position to be 1217. The Sun will be at its highest altitude of the day for that position at 1217.

In Example 2, meridian passage for 6 July is 1205. Applying the longitude correction of -$26^m$, the DR position has LAN at 1205 - 26 = 1139, 1239 daylight time.

April

| Day | SUN Eqn. of Time 00h | 12h | Mer. Pass. |
|---|---|---|---|
| | m s | m s | h m |
| 12 | 00 52 | 00 45 | 12 01 |
| 13 | 00 37 | 00 29 | 12 00 |
| 14 | 00 22 | 00 14 | 12 00 |

July

| Day | SUN Eqn. of Time 00h | 12h | Mer. Pass. |
|---|---|---|---|
| | m s | m s | h m |
| 5 | 04 28 | 04 33 | 12 05 |
| 6 | 04 38 | 04 43 | 12 05 |
| 7 | 04 48 | 04 53 | 12 05 |

A more exact way of establishing the time of LAN is to find the hour, minute and second when the Sun has its GHA equal to your longitude. Unless you know your longitude exactly, the extra effort in the GHA procedure is not warranted. However, assuming your position is known, let us work through Example 1. Our longitude is 109° 20' W. Looking in the GHA column of the Sun for 14 April, we find that the GHA brackets this number at $19^h$ and $20^h$. To find how far through the 19th hour we should interpolate, subtract the GHA at the smaller hour (19) from our longitude.

| | | | | | | | | |
|---|---|---|---|---|---|---|---|---|
| 14 | 00 | 179 54.7 | N 9 22.5 | 7 21.6 | 6.6 | S 8 49.7 | 11.7 | 61.4 |
| | 01 | 194 54.8 | 23.4 | 21 47.2 | 6.6 | 9 01.4 | 11.7 | 61.4 |
| | 02 | 209 55.0 | 24.3 | 36 12.8 | 6.6 | 9 13.1 | 11.5 | 61.4 |
| | 03 | 224 55.2 | ·· 25.2 | 50 38.4 | 6.5 | 9 24.6 | 11.5 | 61.4 |
| | 04 | 239 55.3 | 26.1 | 65 03.9 | 6.4 | 9 36.1 | 11.5 | 61.4 |
| | 05 | 254 55.5 | 27.0 | 79 29.3 | 6.4 | 9 47.6 | 11.4 | 61.4 |
| | 06 | 269 55.6 | N 9 27.9 | 93 54.7 | 6.4 | S 9 59.0 | 11.3 | 61.4 |
| WEDNESDAY | 07 | 284 55.8 | 28.8 | 108 20.1 | 6.3 | 10 10.3 | 11.2 | 61.4 |
| | 08 | 299 55.9 | 29.7 | 122 45.4 | 6.3 | 10 21.5 | 11.2 | 61.4 |
| | 09 | 314 56.1 | ·· 30.6 | 137 10.7 | 6.2 | 10 32.7 | 11.1 | 61.4 |
| | 10 | 329 56.2 | 31.5 | 151 35.9 | 6.2 | 10 43.8 | 11.0 | 61.4 |
| | 11 | 344 56.4 | 32.4 | 166 01.1 | 6.2 | 10 54.8 | 11.0 | 61.4 |
| | 12 | 359 56.6 | N 9 33.3 | 180 26.3 | 6.1 | S11 05.8 | 10.8 | 61.4 |
| | 13 | 14 56.7 | 34.2 | 194 51.4 | 6.1 | 11 16.6 | 10.8 | 61.4 |
| | 14 | 29 56.9 | 35.1 | 209 16.5 | 6.0 | 11 27.4 | 10.7 | 61.4 |
| | 15 | 44 57.0 | ·· 36.0 | 223 41.5 | 6.0 | 11 38.1 | 10.6 | 61.4 |
| | 16 | 59 57.2 | 36.9 | 238 06.5 | 5.9 | 11 48.7 | 10.6 | 61.4 |
| | 17 | 74 57.3 | 37.8 | 252 31.4 | 5.9 | 11 59.3 | 10.4 | 61.4 |
| | 18 | 89 57.5 | N 9 38.7 | 266 56.3 | 5.9 | S12 09.7 | 10.4 | 61.4 |
| | 19 | 104 57.6 | 39.6 | 281 21.2 | 5.8 | 12 20.1 | 10.3 | 61.4 |
| | 20 | 119 57.8 | 40.5 | 295 46.0 | 5.8 | 12 30.4 | 10.2 | 61.4 |

109° 20!0 λ
104° 57!6 $19^h$
4° 22!4 of arc = $17^m$ $30^s$ of time

Add this time to $19^h$ giving the time of LAN at your position as 19-17-30. This is Greenwich Mean Time and since your zone description is $7^h$, subtract the ZD in west longitudes to convert GMT to ZT.

ZT of LAN is 12-17-30.

A conversion of arc to time table is the first yellow page in the back of the Nautical Almanac. It is reproduced in the appendix on page 236.

In Example 2, our longitude of 51° 37' E must be converted to a western longitude (0° to 360°) to compare to GHA. West longitude = 360° - east longitude. Therefore, our longitude would be 360° - 51° 37' = 308° 23' W. This figure on 6 July would be found in the GHA Sun column between $08^h$ and $09^h$.

| | | | | | | | | |
|---|---|---|---|---|---|---|---|---|
| 6 | 00 | 178 50.4 | N22 41.9 | 75 40.7 | 8.3 | S12 34.3 | 9.5 | 59.5 |
| | 01 | 193 50.3 | 41.7 | 90 08.0 | 8.2 | 12 43.8 | 9.4 | 59.5 |
| | 02 | 208 50.2 | 41.4 | 104 35.2 | 8.1 | 12 53.2 | 9.3 | 59.5 |
| | 03 | 223 50.1 | ·· 41.2 | 119 02.3 | 8.1 | 13 02.5 | 9.2 | 59.5 |
| | 04 | 238 50.0 | 40.9 | 133 29.4 | 8.0 | 13 11.7 | 9.2 | 59.5 |
| | 05 | 253 49.9 | 40.7 | 147 56.4 | 8.0 | 13 20.9 | 9.1 | 59.5 |
| | 06 | 268 49.8 | N22 40.4 | 162 23.4 | 7.9 | S13 30.0 | 9.0 | 59.5 |
| | 07 | 283 49.7 | 40.2 | 176 50.3 | 7.9 | 13 39.0 | 8.9 | 59.5 |
| | 08 | 298 49.6 | 39.9 | 191 17.2 | 7.8 | 13 47.9 | 8.8 | 59.5 |
| TUESDAY | 09 | 313 49.5 | ·· 39.7 | 205 44.0 | 7.7 | 13 56.7 | 8.7 | 59.5 |
| | 10 | 328 49.4 | 39.4 | 220 10.7 | 7.8 | 14 05.4 | 8.7 | 59.5 |
| | 11 | 343 49.3 | 39.1 | 234 37.5 | 7.6 | 14 14.1 | 8.6 | 59.5 |
| | 12 | 358 49.2 | N22 38.9 | 249 04.1 | 7.7 | S14 22.7 | 8.4 | 59.5 |
| | 13 | 13 49.1 | 38.6 | 263 30.8 | 7.5 | 14 31.1 | 8.4 | 59.5 |
| | 14 | 28 49.0 | 38.4 | 277 57.3 | 7.5 | 14 39.5 | 8.3 | 59.5 |
| | 15 | 43 48.9 | ·· 38.1 | 292 23.8 | 7.5 | 14 47.8 | 8.2 | 59.5 |
| | 16 | 58 48.8 | 37.8 | 306 50.3 | 7.4 | 14 56.0 | 8.2 | 59.5 |
| | 17 | 73 48.7 | 37.6 | 321 16.7 | 7.4 | 15 04.2 | 8.0 | 59.5 |

308° 23!0 λ
298° 49!6 $08^h$
9° 33!4 of arc = $38^m$ $14^s$ of time

Add this time of $08^h$, giving the time of LAN at your position as 08-17-30, Greenwich Mean Time. Your zone description is $3^h$ and in east longitudes you must add this to GMT to get ZT.

ZT of LAN is 11-38-14, 12-38-14 daylight time.

## CONVERSION OF ARC TO TIME

| 0°–59° ° | h m | 60°–119° ° | h m | 120°–179° ° | h m |
|---|---|---|---|---|---|
| **0** | 0 00 | **60** | 4 00 | **120** | 8 00 |
| **1** | 0 04 | **61** | 4 04 | **121** | 8 04 |
| **2** | 0 08 | **62** | 4 08 | **122** | 8 08 |
| **3** | 0 12 | **63** | 4 12 | **123** | 8 12 |
| **4** | 0 16 | **64** | 4 16 | **124** | 8 16 |
| **5** | 0 20 | **65** | 4 20 | **125** | 8 20 |
| **6** | 0 24 | **66** | 4 24 | **126** | 8 24 |
| **7** | 0 28 | **67** | 4 28 | **127** | 8 28 |
| **8** | 0 32 | **68** | 4 32 | **128** | 8 32 |
| **9** | 0 36 | **69** | 4 36 | **129** | 8 36 |

$$4^{\circ} + 22'.4 = 17^{m}\ 30^{s}$$

$$9^{\circ} + 33'.4 = 38^{m}\ 14^{s}$$

| | 0′·00 | 0′·25 | 0′·50 | 0′·75 |
|---|---|---|---|---|
| **20** | 1 20 | 1 21 | 1 22 | 1 23 |
| **21** | 1 24 | 1 25 | 1 26 | 1 27 |
| **22** | 1 28 | 1 29 | 1 30 | 1 31 |
| **23** | 1 32 | 1 33 | 1 34 | 1 35 |
| **24** | 1 36 | 1 37 | 1 38 | 1 39 |
| **25** | 1 40 | 1 41 | 1 42 | 1 43 |
| **26** | 1 44 | 1 45 | 1 46 | 1 47 |
| **27** | 1 48 | 1 49 | 1 50 | 1 51 |
| **28** | 1 52 | 1 53 | 1 54 | 1 55 |
| **29** | 1 56 | 1 57 | 1 58 | 1 59 |
| **30** | 2 00 | 2 01 | 2 02 | 2 03 |
| **31** | 2 04 | 2 05 | 2 06 | 2 07 |
| **32** | 2 08 | 2 09 | 2 10 | 2 11 |
| **33** | 2 12 | 2 13 | 2 14 | 2 15 |
| **34** | 2 16 | 2 17 | 2 18 | 2 19 |

## EXERCISE 8

1. To the nearest minute, what are the times of sunrise, sunset, beginning of morning twilight and end of evening twilight for the following dates and places?

   a) Lat 41° 20' N, Long 71° 58' W; 25 December 1976

   b) Lat 54° N, Long 75° W; 7 May 1976

   c) Lat 33° S, Long 1° W; 25 November 1976

   d) Lat 26° N, Long 17° E; 20 March 1976

   e) Lat 10° S, Long 164° E; 19 October 1976

2. Predict the zone time of LAN for the following locations using Almanac figures for meridian passage of the Sun.

| | Latitude | Longitude | Local Date (1976) |
|---|---|---|---|
| a) | 16° 27'.6 S | 70° 16'.8 W | 6 June |
| b) | 27° 00'.8 N | 153° 27'.3 W | 23 January |
| c) | 41° 19'.7 N | 172° 54'.4 W | 18 April |
| d) | 32° 42'.1 S | 143° 18'.6 E | 18 October |
| e) | 54° 37'.6 N | 94° 43'.2 E | 30 August |
| f) | 73° 18'.5 S | 11° 06'.8 E | 5 May |

3. Predict the exact Z.T. of LAN for the following two DR Positions, using the methods of GHA of the Sun.

| | a | b |
|---|---|---|
| DR Lat | 41° 19'.7 N | 32° 42'.1 S |
| DR Long | 71° 54'.4 W | 143° 18'.6 E |
| Local Date | 18 April 1976 | 18 October 1976 |

# Chapter 11

# Star Finder H.O. 2102–D, Star Identification

Once the times of twilights are established, a star finder can be used to prefigure the altitudes and azimuths of the Moon, planets and brightest stars. This eliminates the need for memorization of the stars and constellations of different seasons and also enables the navigator to have an idea in which section of the sky to expect to see the first bright celestial body. He can also prefigure what three bodies would give the best fix as far as azimuth spread.

Star finder 2102-D has an opaque plastic base plate on which are printed the navigational stars for both hemispheres, northern stars on one side with the north celestial pole at the pin in the middle and southern stars on the other side. If you are in north latitudes, use the side of the base plate with the north celestial pole up. Nine templates are of clear plastic with varying shaped grids printed on them in blue. These templates are for every ten degrees of latitude, starting with 5°, 15° and going through 85°. One side of the template is used for south latitude, the other for north. The outside of the grid is the horizon of the observer of the particular latitude designated on the template and around the horizon azimuths are marked every five degrees and numbered every ten degrees. The elliptical lines parallel to the horizon mark altitude with 90° being at the cross in the middle of the grid.

Choose the template with latitude closest to yours and place it on the pin of the base plate, being sure that both template and base plate are oriented with either north or south upward, depending on your latitude. When the arrow on the template is "dialed" to the correct number on the outside edge of the base plate, the stars within the grid will be those above your horizon. By using the altitude and azimuth markings, the navigator can make a list of the altitudes and azimuths of those celestial bodies that will be above his horizon. There will be a slight error in numbers due to the approximation of latitude but since bright stars are not very near to each other in the sky, this will cause no confusion when the computed altitudes and azimuths are used to identify objects. Sometimes planets pass near stars but remembering that planets don't twinkle (unless very close to the horizon) and stars do twinkle will eliminate any confusion between them.

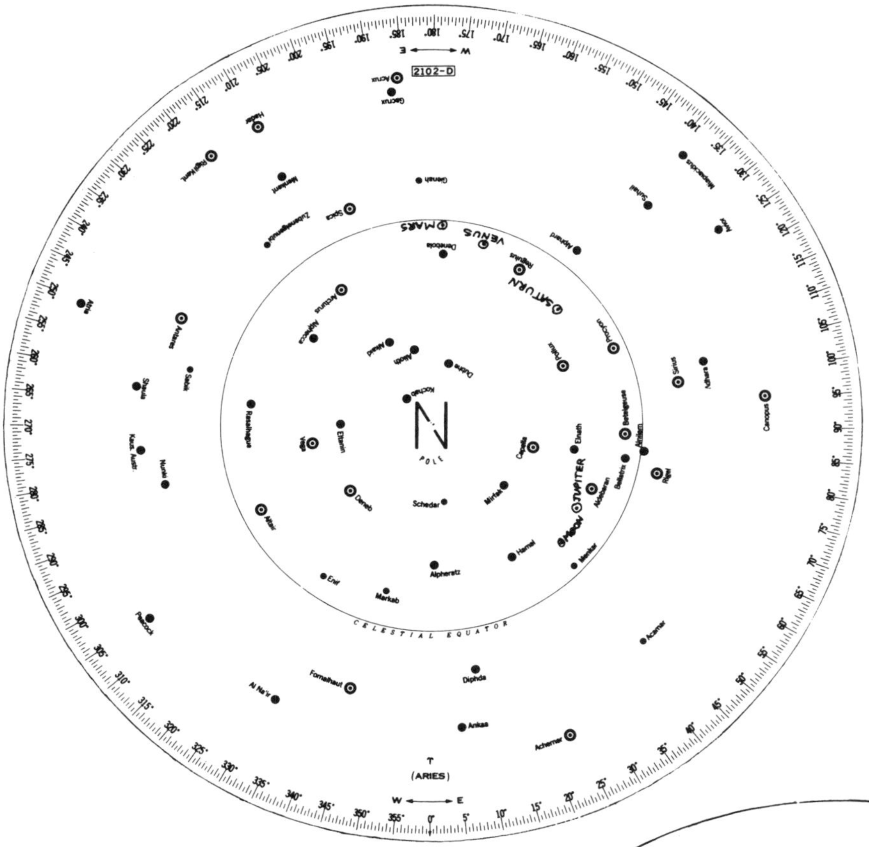

Star finder north base plate

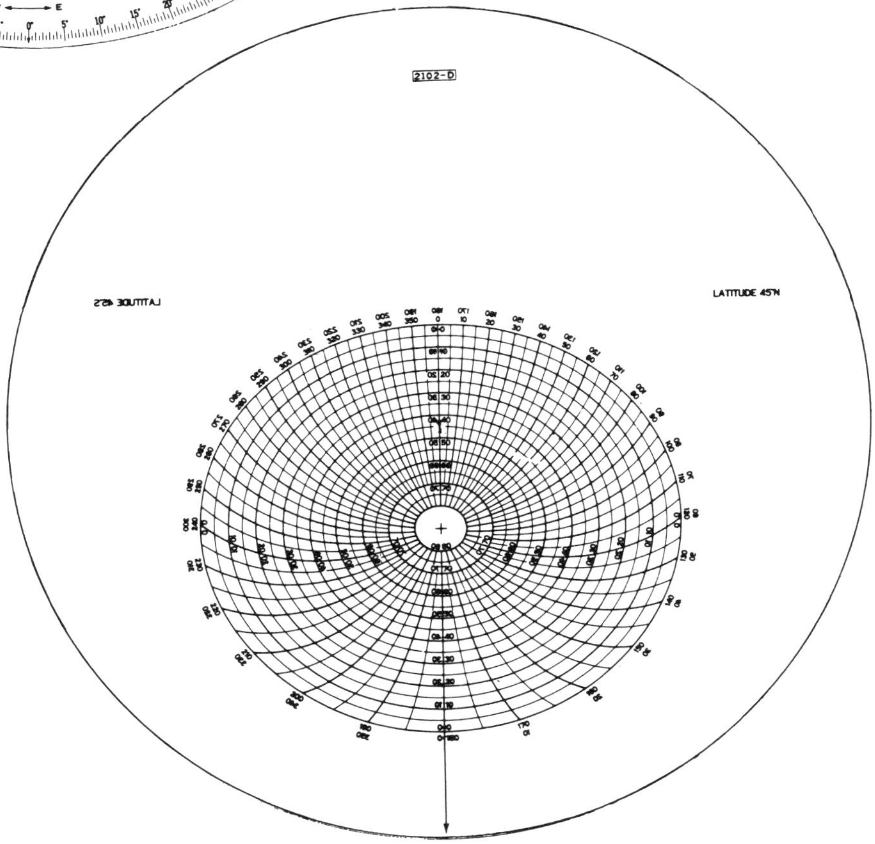

Template for latitudes near 45° N

Let us assume that we wish to set the star finder for morning twilight on 17 August 1976. With a DR position of Lat 43° N and Long 65° W, we first need to figure the time of nautical twilight and sunrise. Latitude interpolation and longitude correction of +20 minutes gives us a twilight range between 0420 and 0528 standard zone time. Choosing a convenient midpoint of 0500, we need to find the local hour angle of Aries at this time. This will be our dialing number.

Local hour angle of Aries = GHA Aries - west longitude
= GHA Aries + east longitude

First convert zone time to GMT. The zone description for 65° W is $4^h$. Therefore, GMT will be 0500 + $4^h$ = 0900.

| | | |
|---|---|---|
| 17 | 00 | 325 29.9 |
| | 01 | 340 32.4 |
| | 02 | 355 34.9 |
| | 03 | 10 37.3 |
| | 04 | 25 39.8 |
| | 05 | 40 42.3 |
| | 06 | 55 44.7 |
| | 07 | 70 47.2 |
| | 08 | 85 49.6 |
| T | 09 | 100 52.1 |
| U | 10 | 115 54.6 |
| E | 11 | 130 57.0 |

| | | |
|---|---|---|
| GHA Aries | $09^h$ | 100° 52!1 |
| West Longitude | | -65° 00!0 |
| LHA Aries | | 35° 52!1 or 36° |

Round this off to the nearest whole or half degree.

Place the 45° N template on the base plate with north side up, put the arrow of the template over the 36° mark on the base plate and secure the two with a paper clip. The stars that will be above your horizon at 0500 ZT will now be inside your grid.

The best stars to choose are those marked with the largest circles (these are the brightest stars) and those between 15° and 75° altitude. With still a large choice, try to find three stars whose azimuths are roughly 60° apart or 120° apart. Then make a list as follows.

| | | Azimuth | Altitude |
|---|---|---|---|
| 60° apart $Z_n$ | Pollux | 075° | 25° |
| | Rigel | 132° | 23° |
| | Diphda | 205° | 24° |
| 120° apart $Z_n$ | Rigel | 132° | 23° |
| | Polaris | 000° | 45° |
| | Alpheratz | 245° | 60° |

By writing azimuth in three digits and altitude in two digits, you can more easily catch an error of entering a number in the wrong column.

You now have a choice of two sets of three stars that will give a nice fix and you know which areas to search in the twilight to find the stars you have chosen. By making a more extensive list, you may sight as many stars as you

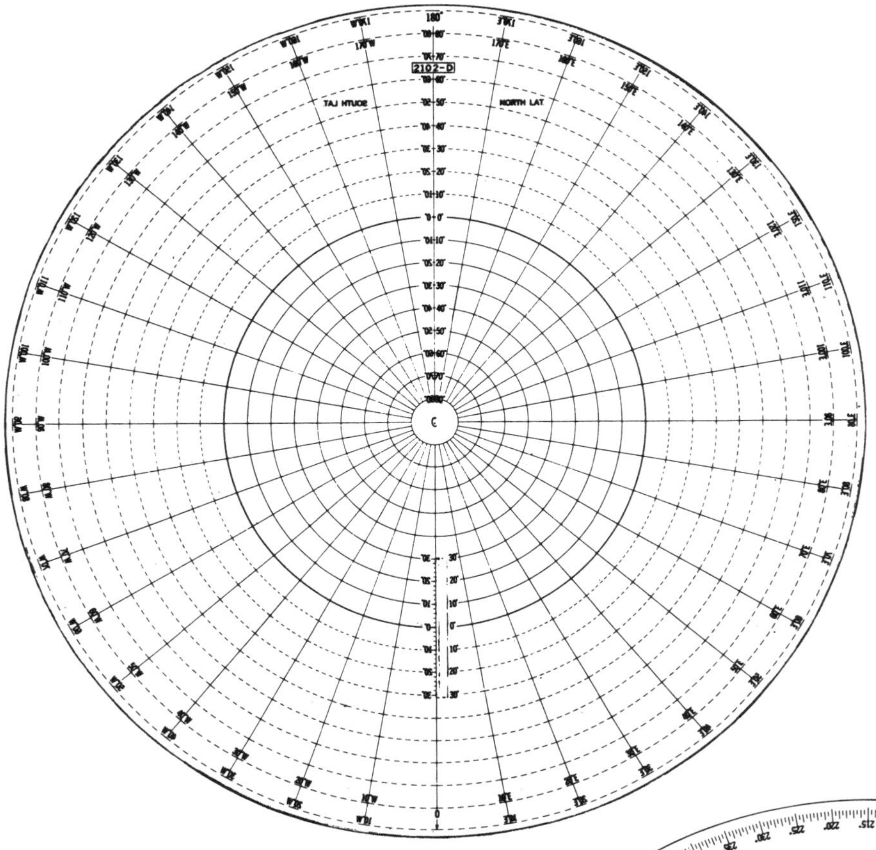


Planet locator for star finder

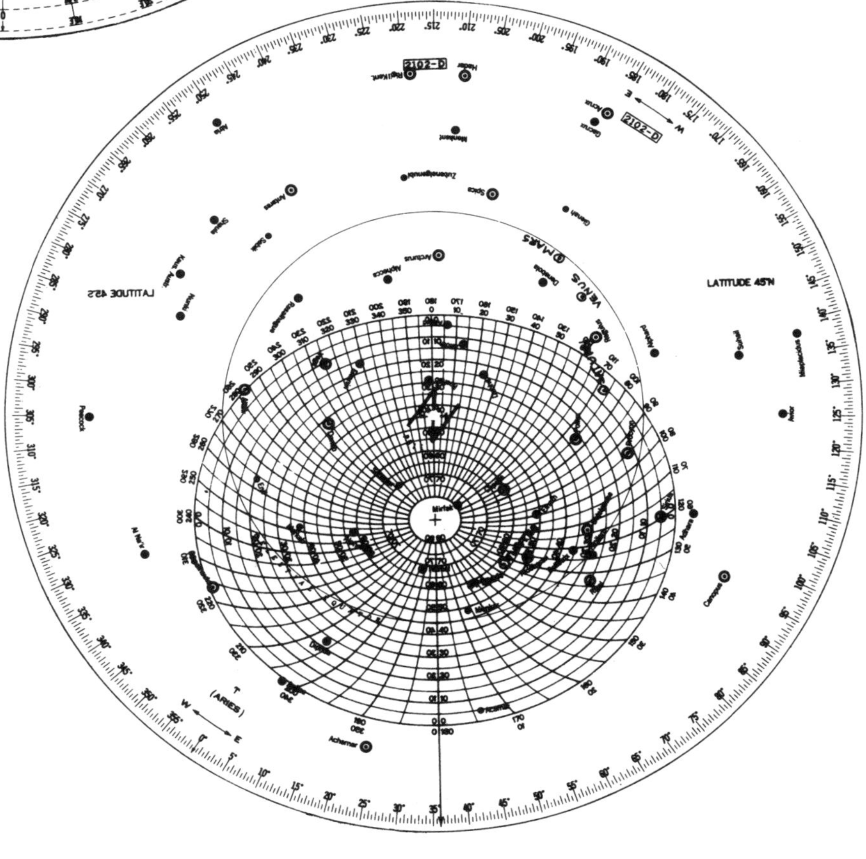


Base plate and 45°N template set for LHA of 36° (text example)

wish. When marking down their sextant altitudes, also make a note of their rough bearing. By referring to your star list, you can later identify which star you observed.

The surface of the base plate is such that you can mark on it with pencil and later erase your marks. Therefore, plotting positions of the Moon and planets will increase your choice of celestial objects. To do this plotting, declination and right ascension of the bodies are needed for the time of observation. Declination is easily found by entering the almanac at 0900 GMT on 17 August and choosing the column of the desired body.

$$\text{Right ascension (RA)} = \text{GHA Aries} - \text{GHA body (for Moon and Sun)}$$
$$= 360^\circ - \text{SHA body (for planets)}$$

SHA of planets is found just below the star column in the daily pages. GHA of the Sun and Moon is found per usual, using GMT as entering time. Round off all values to the nearest whole or half degree for convenience. When the RA and Dec have been found, place the template with red lines and numbers on it on top of the base plate, remembering to put NORTH LAT. or SOUTH LAT. up as the case may be. Dial the arrow to the number on the base plate corresponding to the body's RA. In the slot on the template, count the declination from the 0° circle, going TOWARD the center if the declination and your latitude are the SAME name, going AWAY from the center if the declination and your latitude are CONTRARY name. Make a pencil mark on the base plate at the correct spot and label it with symbols or words. Then proceed as usual with the blue grid template to ascertain altitude and azimuth of the bodies. Of course, some of the bodies will not be above the horizon.

Below are the figures for RA and Dec at 0900 GMT on 17 August 1976. Also listed are the azimuths and altitudes.

| Body | RA | Dec (N Lat) | Azimuth | Altitude |
|---|---|---|---|---|
| Moon | 101° - 55½° = 45½° | N 16°, SAME | 159° | 58° |
| Jupiter | 360° - 302½° = 57½° | N 19°, SAME | 136° | 57° |
| Saturn | 360° - 228½° = 131½° | N 18½°, SAME | 073° | 8° |
| Mars | 360° - 184° = 176° | N 2½°, SAME | below horizon | |
| Venus | 360° - 197° = 163° | N 8½°, SAME | below horizon | |

All of these bodies are plotted toward the center from the 0° circle since declination and latitude are of SAME name. Jupiter could replace Rigel in our star list since their azimuths are close.

If a time were chosen for setting the star finder that was not an even hour, remember to get the minute and second correction to GHA Aries from the yellow pages and add it to the value for the whole hour. Then apply longitude to get LHA Aries.

| | | |
|---|---|---|
| Vega | 80 57.4 | N38 46.0 |
| Zuben'ubi | 137 36.1 | S15 56.7 |

| | S.H.A. ° ′ | Mer. Pass. h m |
|---|---|---|
| Venus | 197 19.5 | 13 09 |
| Mars | 183 56.9 | 14 01 |
| Jupiter | 302 34.8 | 6 07 |
| Saturn | 228 30.7 | 11 02 |

| G.M.T. | | SUN | | MOON | | | | |
|---|---|---|---|---|---|---|---|---|
| d | h | G.H.A. ° ′ | Dec. ° ′ | G.H.A. ° ′ | v ′ | Dec. ° ′ | d ′ | H.P. ′ |
| 17 | 00 | 178 59.0 | N13 27.1 | 284 31.9 | 13.4 | N15 13.6 | 6.4 | 54.3 |
| | 01 | 193 59.1 | 26.3 | 299 04.3 | 13.5 | 15 20.0 | 6.3 | 54.3 |
| | 02 | 208 59.2 | 25.5 | 313 36.8 | 13.3 | 15 26.3 | 6.2 | 54.3 |
| | 03 | 223 59.4 | ·· 24.7 | 328 09.1 | 13.4 | 15 32.5 | 6.1 | 54.3 |
| | 04 | 238 59.5 | 23.9 | 342 41.5 | 13.3 | 15 38.6 | 6.1 | 54.3 |
| | 05 | 253 59.6 | 23.1 | 357 13.8 | 13.3 | 15 44.7 | 6.0 | 54.3 |
| | 06 | 268 59.8 | N13 22.3 | 11 46.1 | 13.2 | N15 50.7 | 6.0 | 54.3 |
| | 07 | 283 59.9 | 21.5 | 26 18.3 | 13.2 | 15 56.7 | 5.8 | 54.3 |
| | 08 | 299 00.0 | 20.7 | 40 50.5 | 13.2 | 16 02.5 | 5.8 | 54.3 |
| T | 09 | 314 00.2 | ·· 19.9 | 55 22.7 | 13.1 | 16 08.3 | 5.8 | 54.3 |
| U | 10 | 329 00.3 | 19.1 | 69 54.8 | 13.1 | 16 14.1 | 5.7 | 54.3 |
| E | 11 | 344 00.4 | 18.3 | 84 26.9 | 13.1 | 16 19.8 | 5.6 | 54.3 |
| S | 12 | 359 00.6 | N13 17.5 | 98 59.0 | 13.0 | N16 25.4 | 5.5 | 54.4 |
| D | 13 | 14 00.7 | 16.7 | 113 31.0 | 13.0 | 16 30.9 | 5.4 | 54.4 |
| A | 14 | 29 00.8 | 15.9 | 128 03.0 | 12.9 | 16 36.3 | 5.4 | 54.4 |
| Y | 15 | 44 01.0 | ·· 15.1 | 142 34.9 | 12.9 | 16 41.7 | 5.3 | 54.4 |
| | 16 | 59 01.1 | 14.3 | 157 06.8 | 12.8 | 16 47.0 | 5.3 | 54.4 |
| | 17 | 74 01.2 | 13.5 | 171 38.6 | 12.9 | 16 52.3 | 5.1 | 54.4 |
| | 18 | 89 01.4 | N13 12.7 | 186 10.5 | 12.7 | N16 57.4 | 5.1 | 54.4 |
| | 19 | 104 01.5 | 11.9 | 200 42.2 | 12.8 | 17 02.5 | 5.0 | 54.4 |
| | 20 | 119 01.6 | 11.1 | 215 14.0 | 12.7 | 17 07.5 | 5.0 | 54.4 |
| | 21 | 134 01.8 | ·· 10.3 | 229 45.7 | 12.6 | 17 12.5 | 4.8 | 54.4 |
| | 22 | 149 01.9 | 09.5 | 244 17.3 | 12.7 | 17 17.3 | 4.8 | 54.5 |
| | 23 | 164 02.1 | 08.7 | 258 49.0 | 12.5 | 17 22.1 | 4.7 | 54.5 |

Using the star finder is probably the quickest, surest and most useful way of finding stars and planets in the twilights. However, there are other options available to the navigator. The paper star map printed for each month and often found in newspapers or astronomical magazines provides a way of locating constellations and the most popular bright stars. A rough idea can be obtained of the directions of the objects but certainly not to the degree of accuracy of H.O. 2102-D. These paper maps are usually drawn for a specific time such as 8 pm which does not always coincide with twilight. Other paper varieties can be "dialed" to the needed date and time though still don't have altitude and azimuth lines on them. Star charts are available which cover the complete sky. The observer locates the meridian which corresponds to his month and time and estimates the breadth of the chart necessary on each side of the meridian.

All of the above methods are aids to refresh the navigator's memory of the constantly changing stellar display. A particular star will rise four minutes earlier each day, accumulating to two hours a month, twenty four hours a year. Therefore, the sky a year from now will be the same as tonight's but the seasons in between will host a variety of constellations at a given time of evening or morning. An excellent way of studying the sky is to visit a planetarium. The machinery can be set for any time and date and can simulate twilight when only the brightest stars are visible. Latitude can be changed as well as longitude within a zone. Many planetariums have an altitude and azimuth grid for making up star lists. The Moon and planets can be included for a particular date though their positions will change with respect to the stars from night to night.

Unfortunately, only single stars are visible in the early twilight, not whole constellations. An advantage of observing in the morning twilight is that the constellations are visible before the sky brightens and the bright stars can be pre-located for observation when the horizon allows. The evening twilight observer has to rely on his memory of a recent night's sky or else sight his stars during twilight and then identify them later as the twilight fades. Once a set of stars is found, the same stars can be used for several weeks as long as partial cloudiness doesn't obscure them. Eventually they will get too low (below 15°) where refraction becomes a big factor or too high (above 75°) where sighting is difficult and azimuth change is great for a small time period.

In locating navigational stars within constellations, there are three key patterns which act as excellent guides. The Big Dipper (the brightest stars in the constellation of Ursa Major) is visible all year around from latitudes above 40° N. Orion is an evening constellation in the winter, morning pattern in the summer. The Summer Triangle is visible in the evening during the summer, in the morning during the winter. Each of these patterns will be diagramed and discussed separately.

In both celestial hemispheres, there is a total of 88 constellations. Many of them are obscure and for the most part the star patterns don't resemble their constellation names. Often, then, nicknames are applied which better describe the grouping of stars. The brightest stars have proper names, many of them Arabic as evidenced by the multitude of names beginning with A. An alternative way of identifying the bright stars is by their Greek letter designation. The first Greek letter, $\alpha$, is given to the brightest star in the constellation. Therefore, Arcturus is alternatively known as $\alpha$ Bootis. The second brightest star is labeled $\beta$ , the third $\gamma$ . In a few cases the magnitudes of stars were misestimated or, as in the case of the Big Dipper, the stars were labeled in order of their position in the constellation. All the bright stars are listed in the back of the Nautical Almanac by both popular name and Greek letter designation. This list is more extensive than the daily page list in the event that the navigator is able to sight a fainter star than usual. The first eight letters only of the Greek alphabet will be shown here since fainter stars than the Theta star in a constellation are very seldom sighted.

| | | | |
|---|---|---|---|
| $\alpha$ | Alpha | $\varepsilon$ | Epsilon |
| $\beta$ | Beta | $\zeta$ | Zeta |
| $\gamma$ | Gamma | $\eta$ | Eta |
| $\delta$ | Delta | $\theta$ | Theta |

Our first guide to finding bright stars will be the Big Dipper, part of Ursa Major, the Big Bear. The seven stars are easily found in the northern sky and as mentioned before are always above the horizon for observers in latitudes above 40° N. During winter evenings it is close to the horizon and in summer it is high in the sky, positioned upside down. Dubhe is located at the end of the Dipper's bowl. The two end stars in the bowl are approximately 5° apart and serve as a good yardstick in the sky. These stars are often referred to as Pointer Stars since they point to Polaris, the North Star. This Pole star is at the end of the handle of the Little Dipper which seems to pour water back into the Big Dipper. Kochab is the bright star at the end of the bowl of the Little Dipper.

Continuing on by Polaris, the Pointers direct us to Schedar in Queen Cassiopeia. This navigational star is at the long point of the W or M. At the short point is Ruchbah, of interest mainly because it is in line with

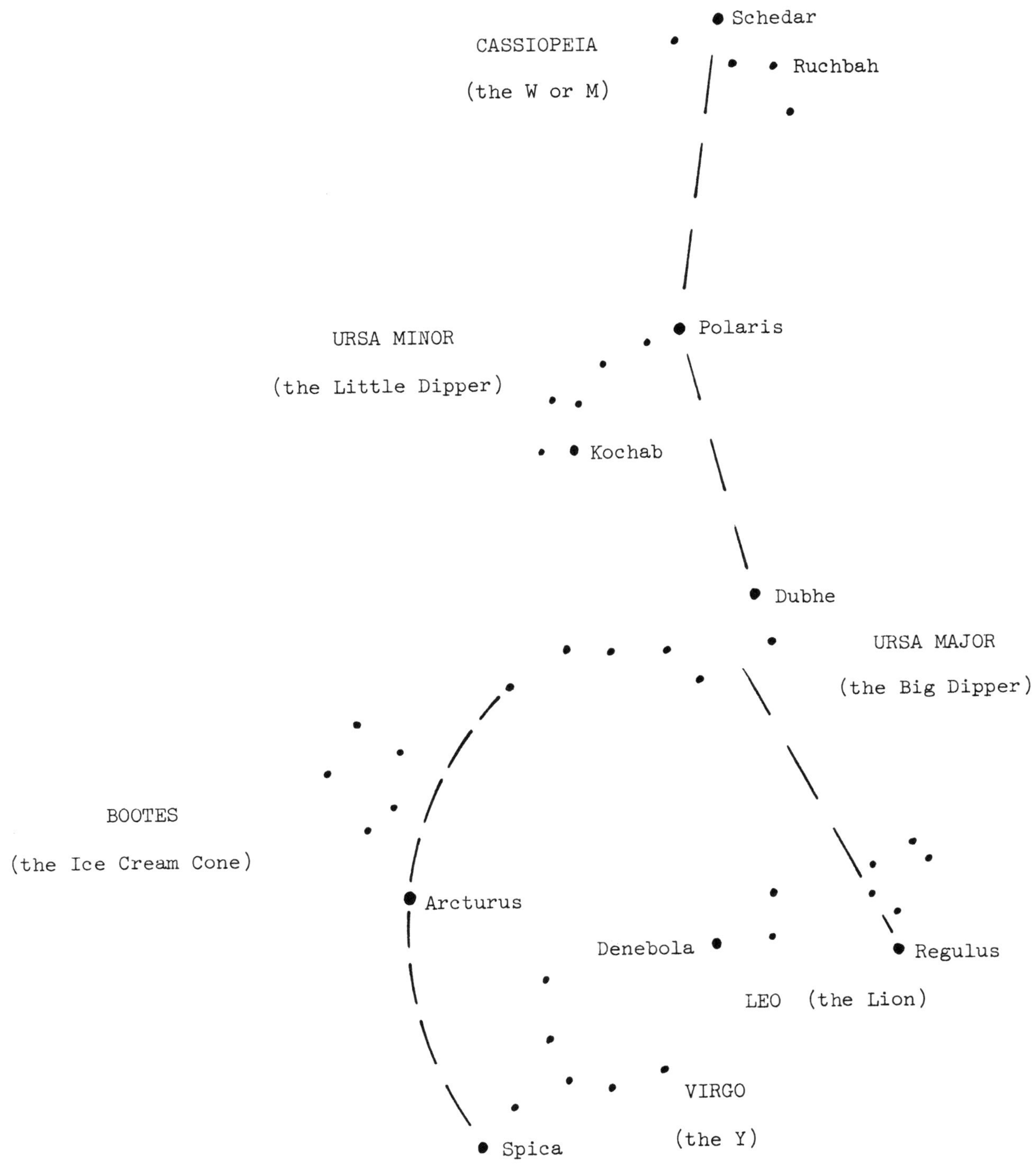


Using the Big Dipper as a Guide

Polaris and the true north celestial pole. As will be seen in the next chapter, the altitude of the north celestial pole equals the observer's latitude in the northern hemisphere. The minor corrections that need to be made can be estimated (assuming a lifeboat situation with no Polaris tables) by using Ruchbah. Polaris is about 50' from the true pole and Ruchbah is on the opposite side of Polaris from the pole. Therefore, if Ruchbah is above Polaris, Polaris is 50' higher than the pole. If Ruchbah is below Polaris, 50' must be added to the altitude of Polaris to equal the altitude of the pole. If Ruchbah is the same altitude as Polaris, no correction to the pole height is necessary. In intermediate situations,a good estimate of the needed correction must suffice.

Using the Big Dipper again, the arc of its handle points to Arcturus, one of the two brightest summer stars. Continuing along this arc we find the blue-white star Spica. Colors of stars indicate temperature, blue-white being hot and red being comparatively cooler.

A line drawn straight down the middle of the bowl of the Big Dipper points to Regulus in the foot of Leo. Above Regulus is the head of Leo looking like a backwards question mark or a sickle. At the tip of the tail of Leo is Denebola. The appearance of Leo in the evening sky heralds springtime and boat launching!

The winter sky is dominated by Orion, easily found by locating the three belt stars Alnitak, Alnilam and Mintaka going from lower left to upper right. Mintaka is almost on the celestial equator. The bright stars outlining the body of Orion make a rectangular shape enclosing the belt. Saiph is the only one of the four not listed in the daily page star list in the Nautical Almanac. Rigel is one of the stars in the Winter Hexagon, a pattern involving several constellations. The belt of Orion points to two more stars in the hexagon. Downward from the belt is Sirius, the brightest star in the nighttime sky. It is in one of Orion's hunting dogs, Canis Major. Procyon, above and to the left of Sirius, is in the small hunting dog. Upward from the belt of Orion is Aldebaran, the red eye of Taurus the Bull. The "V" shaped head and tiny dipper shaped heart (the Pleiades) of Taurus are open clusters of stars and a delight to peruse with binoculars. Yellow Capella is at the top of the hexagon with a small triangle of stars nearby. In mythology Capella was a goat, the three stars her kids. In play one day, the god Jupiter broke off one of Capella's horns. To make amends, Jupiter turned the horn into a special one - the Horn of Plenty or Cornucopia - which had the power of being filled with whatever its owner might desire. The stars on the left side of the hexagon, going from Capella to Sirius, are often referred to as the Arc of Capella.

The remaining two stars in the hexagon are Castor and Pollux, the heads of the Gemini twins. To keep their order straight, remember that the "C" stars are next to each other (Capella and Castor) as are the "P" stars (Pollux and Procyon). Inside the Winter Hexagon is the giant red star, Betelgeuse. Its diameter varies from 360 times that of our Sun to 530 times!

Our last major guide is the large Summer Triangle, a pattern which encompasses the brightest stars of three constellations along the Milky Way. Vega is the brightest of the three, rivaling Arcturus in the summer sky. Altair is flanked by two dimmer stars, somewhat the same configuration as Orion's

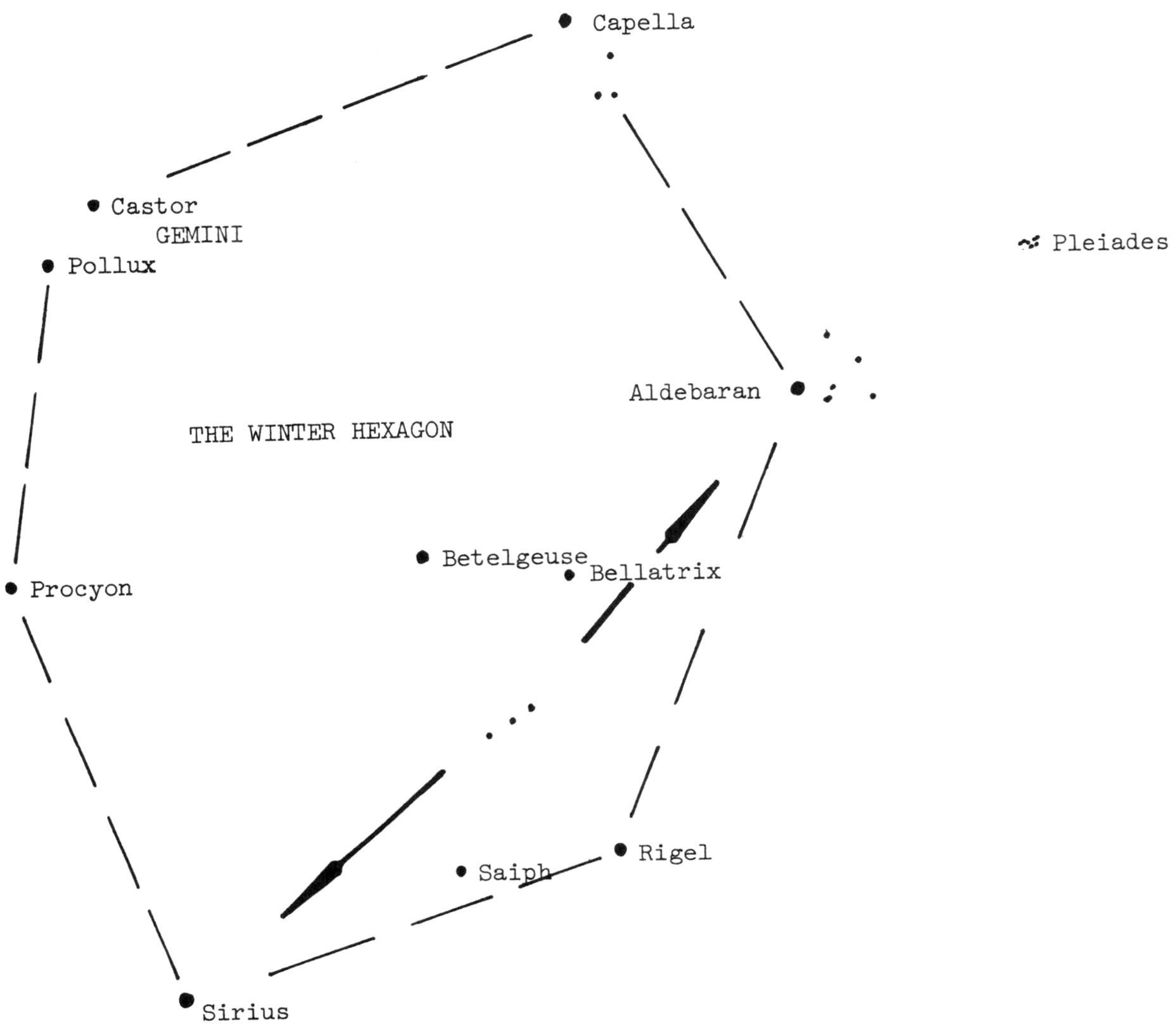


Using Orion as a Guide

belt. Deneb is at the head of the Northern Cross, the long axis of which is inside the triangle. The Summer Triangle is visible in the east in the summer evening twilight and in the west in the summer morning twilight - double duty.

To the east of the Summer Triangle is another geometrical figure, the square of Pegasus, the flying horse. Alpheratz and Markab are at opposite corners of the square while Diphda and Fomalhaut are found by extending below the left and right side of the square. Alpheratz is actually α Andromedae but is more easily located when thought of as part of the square. Pegasus heralds autumn and boat hauling when it appears in the evening sky. Viewing the heavens during a night passage can be so much more rewarding when the myriad of stars is organized into patterns interrelated by mythology and a common origin.

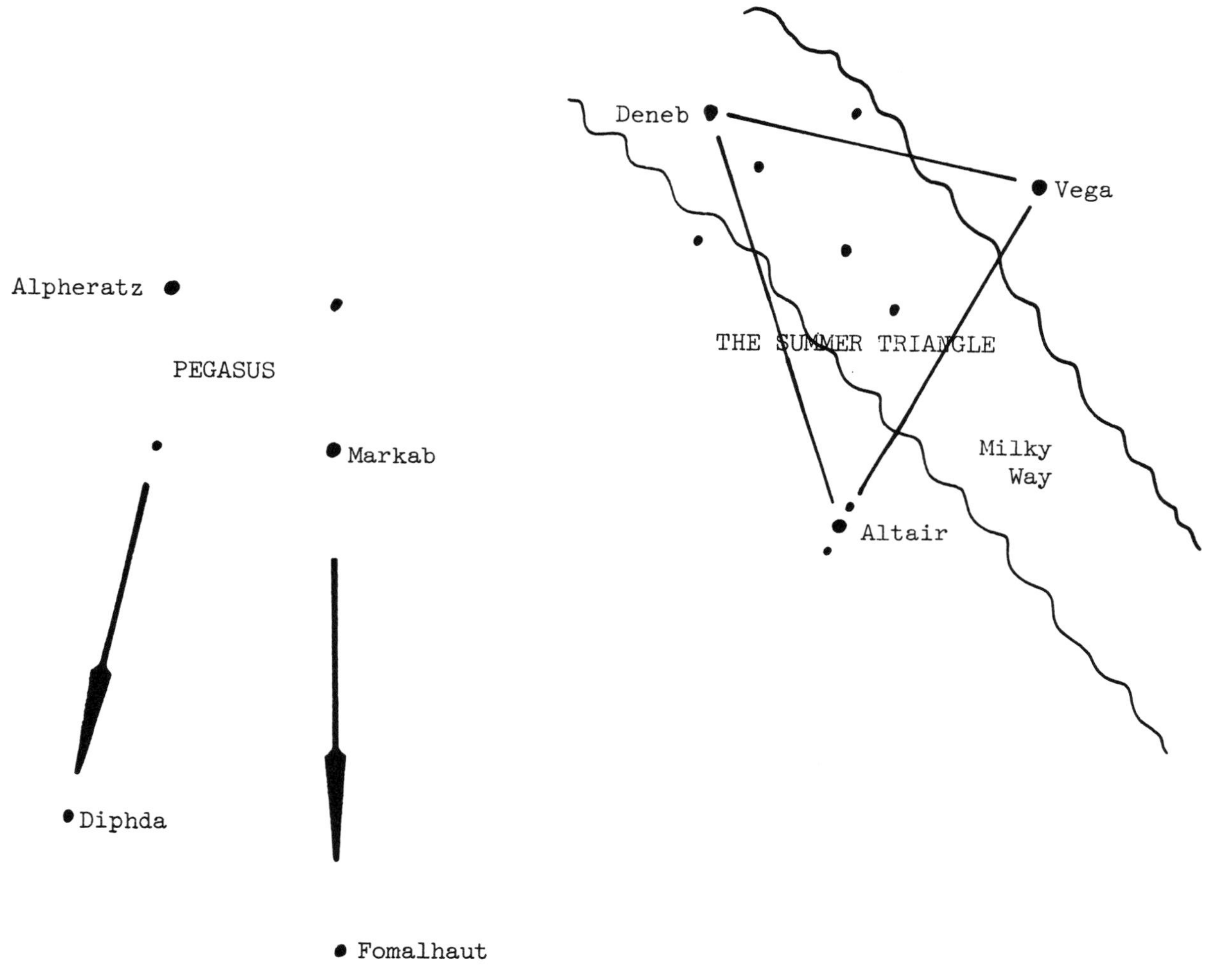


Pegasus and the Summer Triangle

On pages 235 and 236 are copies of the star charts and part of the master star list appearing at the back of the Nautical Almanac just before the Polaris table and "yellow pages" showing increments and corrections.

The round chart at the left shows the northern stars with Polaris (α Ursae Minoris), more familiarly known as the North Star, near the center of the chart and the Big Dipper in Ursa Major to the right of the center. The round chart at the right shows the stars around the south pole of the heavens. Conspicuous in its absence is a south polar star. To the left of the chart's center is Crux, the famous Southern Cross containing the star Gacrux (γ Crucis). The rectangular charts show stars and patterns between 30°N and 30°S declination; among them is Orion containing Rigel (β Orionis). As previously mentioned, the major stars within a constellation are given a Greek letter beginning with α, the brightest star, and continuing down the alphabet with progressively fainter stars. The Greek letter is followed by the Latin genitive case of the constellation name. So β Orionis translates into β of Orion.

To locate a star such as Rigel (β Orionis) in the master star list, first locate the star on the star chart. Orion is on the right-hand rectangular chart. Rigel's SHA, read from the chart, appears to be about 282°. With the proper name of Rigel and the SHA of 282° before us, we turn to the right-hand star list (July - December) and search the bold-faced degree column of SHA for 282° or a number close to that. Then look in the name list beside that SHA for Rigel. For August SHA = 281° 38!8, Dec. S 8° 13!6. For March follow the horizontal line to the left of the name, Rigel, onto the left-hand page (notice particularly that the left-hand list of names shows ONLY Greek letter names) SHA = 281° 39!0, Dec. S 8° 13!9. This technique and master list of 173 stars would be used principally for stars that are not listed on the daily pages. No interpolation of tabulated data is required.

To learn the relative brightness of stars, we look in the column headed Mag. (magnitude). Sirius, the brightest star of the night sky has a magnitude of -1.6 . The faintest star visible to the well dark adapted naked eye, under ideal conditions, is about magnitude +6.0 . LARGER POSITIVE NUMBERS INDICATE FAINTER STARS.

On the daily pages of the Nautical Almanac, at the tops of the columns showing GHA & Dec. of planets, there appears a number beside the planet's name which is its magnitude for that date. For example, at the top of the daily page of the Nautical Almanac for June 14, 15, 16, we find the magnitude of Jupiter to be -1.6, thus it has the same brightness on that date as Sirius (mentioned above). Venus on this date is -3.5, so it is brighter than Jupiter or Sirius. A difference of 5 magnitudes would indicate that the brighter star is brighter by a factor of 100 times! The magnitude scale is logarithmic. Due to the changing distance between earth and the other planets and their changing distance from the sun, their magnitudes are continually varying.

# EXERCISE 9

1. Using your star finder, make a list of six bright navigational stars with their approximate altitudes and azimuths for each of the following times and DR positions. Which ones would make a good threesome for a fix? (There usually is more than one grouping that would be satisfactory.)

   a) fifteen minutes after sunset, 20 March 1976
   Lat 45° N Long 50° W

   b) twenty minutes before sunrise, 21 June 1976
   Lat 31° S Long 153° E

   c) sunset, 23 September 1976
   Lat 21° N Long 131° E

   d) sunrise, 22 December 1976
   Lat 55° S Long 146° W

2. Of the four brightest planets and the Moon, which will be visible at the above times and places, and what will be their altitudes and azimuths?

# Chapter 12

# Meridian and Ex-meridian Sights

Meridian sights, or sights taken when the celestial body is on one's meridian bearing due north or due south, are advantageous in several ways. If there was a large error in longitude, the resulting error in latitude would be negligible. These sights give latitude so are valuable even though they may be the only sight taken at the time. Lastly, there are short-cut methods of solving for latitude without involving sight reduction tables.

One such type of sight is the Polaris sight. Polaris, the Pole Star or the North Star is not one of the 57 bright navigational stars but it can be observed near the end of evening twilight or beginning of morning twilight. Its value lies in the fact that it is so close to the north celestial pole that to the naked eye it does not seem to move all night long. Therefore, it always points out the northern direction, is visible to everyone in the northern hemisphere, and its altitude is equal to the observer's latitude with a few minor corrections. The equality of the altitude of the north celestial pole (NCP) and the latitude of the observer is shown in the following diagram.

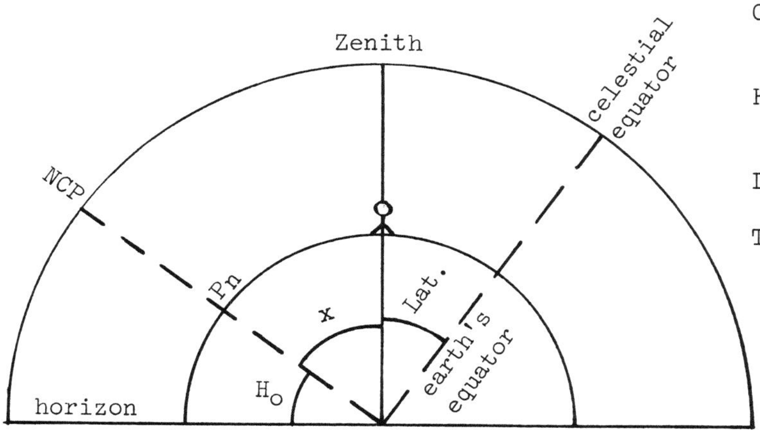


Cel. eq. to NCP = 90°
Lat = 90° - x

Horizon to zenith = 90°
$H_o$ = 90° - x

Lat = 90° - x = $H_o$

Therefore Lat = $H_o$

A sight is taken and sextant altitude corrected as with any other star sight. At the GMT of the sight, LHA Aries is found just as it was for star finder use.

LHA Aries = GHA Aries - west longitude
= GHA Aries + east longitude

Then the Polaris tables are entered to get three corrections.

$a_0$ is a function only of the LHA Aries and is equal to the distance of the pole star from the north celestial pole multiplied by cos t where t is a local hour angle measured from 0° to 180°, east or west.

$a_1$ is the tilt of Polaris' diurnal circle with respect to the vertical and depends only on the observer's latitude.

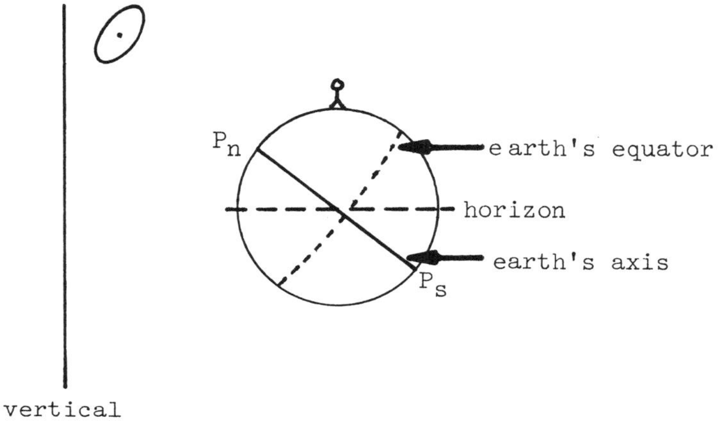


$a_2$ accounts for the change in celestial coordinates (SHA and Dec) due to the wobbling of the earth's axis and aberration, a shift in direction of starlight due to the revolution of the earth. In 1976, Polaris' declination is about 89° 09!4 N, meaning that Polaris is 50!6 away from the true celestial pole. In the year 2101, Polaris will be the closest to the true pole with declination of 89° 32!5, less than a half degree from the pole.

The Polaris tables are the last white pages in the <u>Nautical Almanac</u>. In Example 1 (see complete examples following the excerpts), LHA Aries is 120° 07!8. The column headed with 120° - 129° is entered, noticing that each line of the top part of the column is for one of the degrees at the head (i.e. 120°, 121°, ..., 130°). Since LHA Aries is 7.8/60 of the way between 120° and 121°, we interpolate between the $a_0$ values of 57!2 and 58!1, giving a correction of 57!3 entered in the $a_0$ box. Continuing down the same column, enter the next section with the closest latitude to your DR latitude. Since our DR latitude is 42° N, we would enter with 40°, giving an $a_1$ correction of !5, entered in the Polaris table corrections box under $a_1$. Lastly, in the same column, enter with the month when the sight was taken, in this case April, giving 1!0 as an $a_2$ correction. Add these three corrections together and then add this sum to ($H_o$ - 1°). This gives latitude directly.

Example 2 is done in the same manner with the difference found when obtaining LHA Aries. East longitude is added to GHA Aries to get LHA Aries.

| L.H.A. ARIES | 120°–129° | 130°–139° | 140°–149° | 150°–159° | 160°–169° |
|---|---|---|---|---|---|
| | $a_0$ | $a_0$ | $a_0$ | $a_0$ | $a_0$ |
| ° | ° ′ | ° ′ | ° ′ | ° ′ | ° ′ |
| 0 | 0 57·2 | 1 06·0 | 1 14·5 | 1 22·6 | 1 29·9 |
| 1 | 58·1 | 06·8 | 15·3 | 23·4 | 30·6 |
| 2 | 58·9 | 07·7 | 16·2 | 24·1 | 31·3 |
| 3 | 0 59·8 | 08·6 | 17·0 | 24·9 | 32·0 |
| 4 | 1 00·7 | 09·4 | 17·8 | 25·6 | 32·6 |
| 5 | 1 01·6 | 1 10·3 | 1 18·6 | 1 26·4 | 1 33·3 |
| 6 | 02·5 | 11·1 | 19·4 | 27·1 | 33·9 |
| 7 | 03·3 | 12·0 | 20·2 | 27·8 | 34·5 |
| 8 | 04·2 | 12·8 | 21·0 | 28·5 | 35·1 |
| 9 | 05·1 | 13·7 | 21·8 | 29·2 | 35·7 |
| 10 | 1 06·0 | 1 14·5 | 1 22·6 | 1 29·9 | 1 36·3 |
| Lat. | $a_1$ | $a_1$ | $a_1$ | $a_1$ | $a_1$ |
| ° | ′ | ′ | ′ | ′ | ′ |
| 0 | 0·2 | 0·2 | 0·2 | 0·3 | 0·4 |
| 10 | ·2 | ·2 | ·3 | ·3 | ·4 |
| 20 | ·3 | ·3 | ·3 | ·4 | ·4 |
| 30 | ·4 | ·4 | ·4 | ·4 | ·5 |
| 40 | 0·5 | 0·5 | 0·5 | 0·5 | 0·5 |
| 45 | ·5 | ·5 | ·5 | ·5 | ·6 |
| 50 | ·6 | ·6 | ·6 | ·6 | ·6 |
| 55 | ·7 | ·7 | ·7 | ·7 | ·6 |
| 60 | ·8 | ·8 | ·8 | ·7 | ·7 |
| 62 | 0·9 | 0·8 | 0·8 | 0·8 | 0·7 |
| 64 | 0·9 | 0·9 | ·9 | ·8 | ·8 |
| 66 | 1·0 | 1·0 | 0·9 | ·9 | ·8 |
| 68 | 1·1 | 1·1 | 1·0 | 0·9 | 0·9 |
| Month | $a_2$ | $a_2$ | $a_2$ | $a_2$ | $a_2$ |
| | ′ | ′ | ′ | ′ | ′ |
| Jan. | 0·6 | 0·6 | 0·6 | 0·6 | 0·5 |
| Feb. | ·8 | ·8 | ·7 | ·7 | ·7 |
| Mar. | 0·9 | 0·9 | 0·9 | 0·8 | ·8 |
| Apr. | 1·0 | 1·0 | 1·0 | 1·0 | 0·9 |
| May | 0·9 | 1·0 | 1·0 | 1·0 | 1·0 |
| June | ·8 | 0·9 | 0·9 | 1·0 | 1·0 |
| July | 0·7 | 0·7 | 0·8 | 0·8 | 0·9 |
| Aug. | ·5 | ·6 | ·6 | ·7 | ·7 |
| Sept. | ·3 | ·4 | ·4 | ·5 | ·6 |
| Oct. | 0·3 | 0·3 | 0·3 | 0·3 | 0·4 |
| Nov. | ·2 | ·2 | ·2 | ·2 | ·2 |
| Dec. | 0·3 | 0·3 | 0·2 | 0·2 | 0·2 |

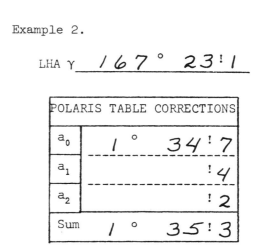

Example 1.

LHA ♈ 120° 07!8

| POLARIS TABLE CORRECTIONS | |
|---|---|
| $a_0$ | ° 57!3 |
| $a_1$ | 0!5 |
| $a_2$ | 1!0 |
| Sum | ° 58!8 |

Example 2.

LHA ♈ 167° 23!1

| POLARIS TABLE CORRECTIONS | |
|---|---|
| $a_0$ | 1° 34!7 |
| $a_1$ | !4 |
| $a_2$ | !2 |
| Sum | 1° 35!3 |

Example 1.

LATITUDE BY POLARIS 1840 DR Lat 42° 00!0 N DR Lo 75° 10!6 E / (W) Ht of eye 12 ft.

| | | | | |
|---|---|---|---|---|
| W.T. | 18h 40m 00s | | Body | POLARIS |
| W.E. | m — s | slow - add / fast - sub | $H_s$ | 42° 33!2 |
| Z.T. | h m s | Local Date 11 April 1976 | I.C. | 0!0 |
| Z.D. | +5h | (W Lo +) / E Lo - | | 42° 33!2 |
| GMT | 23h 40m 00s | Grnch Date 11 April 1976 | Dip | - 3!4 |
| | | | App. Alt. | 42° 29!8 |
| GHA γ 23h | 185° 16!8 | | Main | - 1!1 |
| 40m 00s | 10° 01!6 | | $H_o$ | 42° 28!7 |
| TOTAL | ° ! | | - | 1° 00!0 |
| ±360° GHA γ | 195° 18!4 | | | 41° 28!7 |
| DR Lo | 75° 10!6 | add if E / (sub if W) | + | ° 58!8 |
| LHA γ | 120° 07!8 | | Lat | 42° 27!5 N |

| POLARIS TABLE CORRECTIONS | |
|---|---|
| $a_0$ | ° 57!3 |
| $a_1$ | 0!5 |
| $a_2$ | 1!0 |
| Sum | ° 58!8 → |

Example 2.

LATITUDE BY POLARIS 0546 DR Lat 16° 43!6 N DR Lo 167° 18!1 (E) / W Ht of eye 8 ft.

| | | | | |
|---|---|---|---|---|
| W.T. | 05h 46m 17s | | Body | POLARIS |
| W.E. | - m 29s | slow - add / (fast - sub) | $H_s$ | 16° 27!7 |
| Z.T. | 05h 45m 48s | Local Date 10 December 1976 | I.C. | - 11!5 |
| Z.D. | -11h | W Lo + / E Lo - | | 16° 16!2 |
| GMT | 18h 45m 48s | Grnch Date 9 Dec. 1976 | Dip | - -2!7 |
| | | | App. Alt. | 16° 13!5 |
| GHA γ 18h | 348° 36!1 | | Main | - 3!3 |
| 45m 48s | 11° 28!9 | | $H_o$ | 16° 10!2 |
| TOTAL | 360° 05!0 | | - | 1° 00!0 |
| ±360° GHA γ | 000° 05!0 | | | 15° 10!2 |
| DR Lo | 167° 18!1 | add if E / sub if W | + | 1° 35!3 |
| LHA γ | 167° 23!1 | | Lat | 16° 45!5 N |

| POLARIS TABLE CORRECTIONS | |
|---|---|
| $a_0$ | 1° 34!7 |
| $a_1$ | !4 |
| $a_2$ | !2 |
| Sum | 1° 35!3 → |

Another type of meridian sight is the noon sun sight, long popular because of ease of identification and observation of the body and because of lack of need of exact time. The Sun is sighted at its highest altitude of the day, found by prefiguring the time of local apparent noon or, more simply, by watching the Sun until it ceases to climb and hangs at the same altitude for several seconds before beginning to drop. Most often a combination of the two techniques is used since knowing exact time of LAN is dependent on knowing your longitude precisely.

If time allows, a safer method of getting the peak altitude of the Sun is to draw a noon curve. This entails observing the Sun at two minute intervals for about fifteen minutes before and after estimated noon. It is helpful to have a stopwatch to mark the intervals or else another person to call off the time to you. At each interval, the sextant altitude is noted, and later a graph is drawn plotting altitude (vertical axis) against time (horizontal axis). A smooth curve is drawn through the points plotted and the peak of the curve is taken as the altitude on the meridian. This method aids in eliminating bad sights and gives more confidence in a correct altitude. Also, if some sights are not taken due to clouds or unforseen circumstances aboard ship, the curve can still be plotted and meridian altitude figured.

The following graph shows an example of a noon curve. Note that the curve is symmetrical on either side of LAN. Noon was estimated as 1210 ZT but was found to occur roughly two minutes later, the error in estimation due to an inaccurate knowledge of the longitude of the ship.

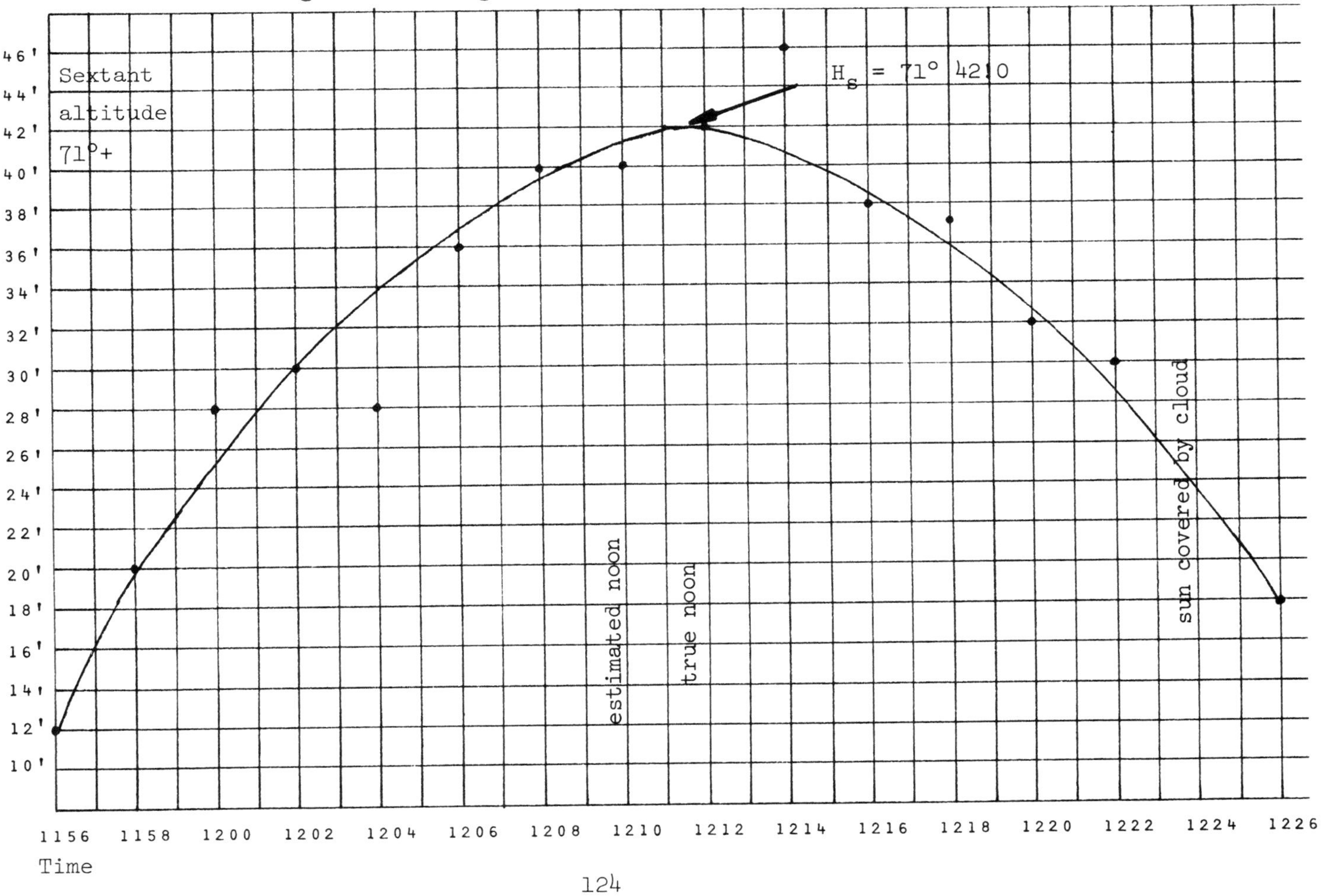

Once the sextant altitude of the body is found, it is then corrected for index error, height of eye, refraction, semidiameter etc. The corrected sextant altitude ($H_o$) is then combined with the Sun's declination and 90° to obtain latitude directly. The manner in which this combination occurs depends on the observer's latitude (roughly known) and the Sun's declination - which is greater and whether the names are the same or contrary. Declination is found in the normal way in the Nautical Almanac, remembering to enter with Greenwich Mean Time and to interpolate for the number of minutes through the hour that you observed.

In Case 1, declination and latitude are the same name. In the diagram, the semicircle is the observer's meridian with points marked on it as follows: S for south, E for celestial equator, ⊙ for Sun's position on the meridian, Z for zenith and N for north. The horizon is the ellipse with north, east, south and west marked on it. Declination (d) is the angle between the celestial equator and the Sun (remember to note whether the Sun is north or south of the equator), $H_o$ is the altitude of the Sun above the horizon, and latitude (L) is the angle between the equator and the zenith (the declination of the zenith or the angle between the earth's equator and the observer's position on earth).

Case 1a, declination north, latitude north, $Z_n$ = 180°.

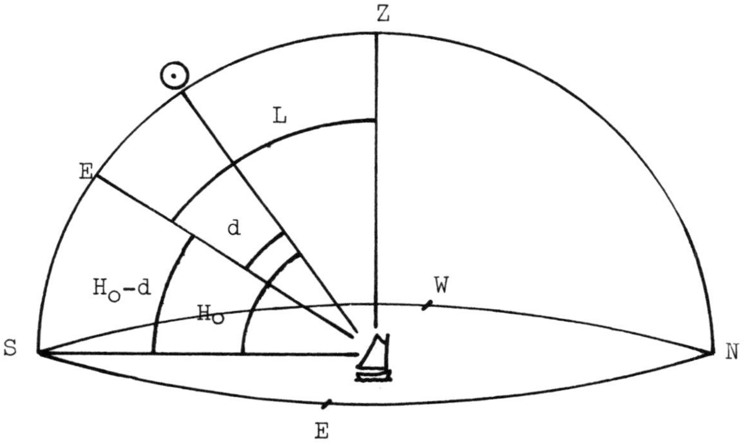


Example 1a.

Ho = 55° 10!7
d = 21° 16!9 N
L = 56° N (DR estimate)

Solution:

 89° 60!0
-55° 10!7
 34° 49!3
+21° 16!9
 56° 06!2 N = your latitude

$L = 90° - (H_o - d)$
$= 90° - H_o + d$

Case 1b, declination south, latitude south, $Z_n$ = 000°.

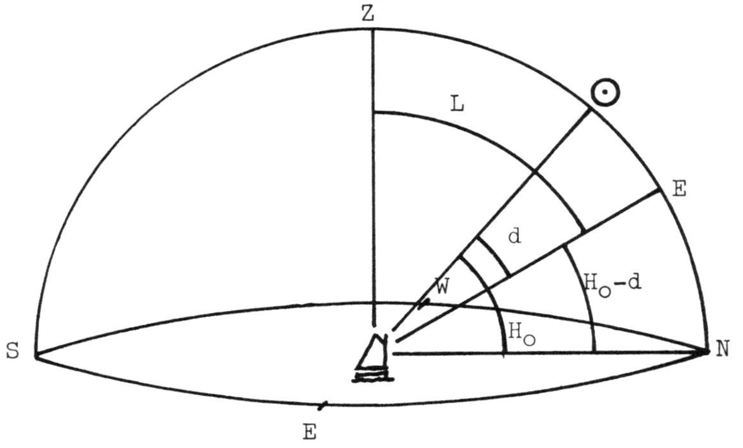


Example 1b.

$H_o$ = 48° 20!0
d = 18° 02!0 S
L = 60° S (DR estimate)

Solution:

  89° 60!0
 -48° 20!0
  41° 40!0
 +18° 02!0
  59° 42!0 S = your latitude

$L = 90° - (H_o - d)$
$= 90° - H_o + d$

Case 2a, declination south, latitude north, $Z_n$ = 180°.

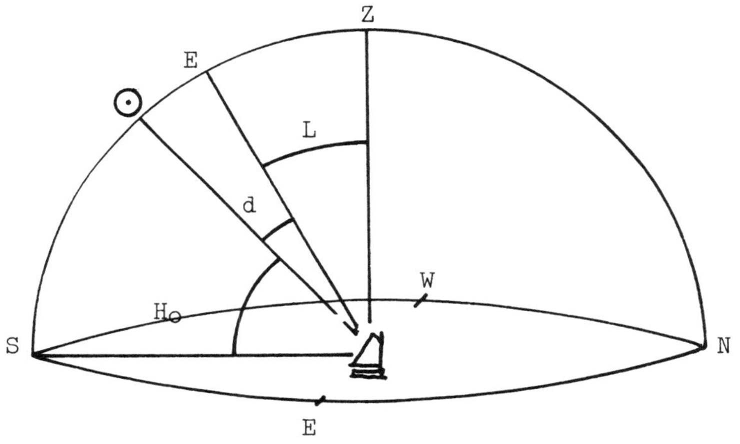


Example 2a.

$H_o$ = 47° 23!1
d = 14° 19!7 S
L = 28° N (DR estimate)

Solution:

  89° 60!0
 -47° 23!1
  42° 36!9
 -14° 19!7
  28° 17!2 N = your latitude

$L = 90° - H_o - d$

Case 2b, declination north, latitude south, $Z_n$ = 000°.

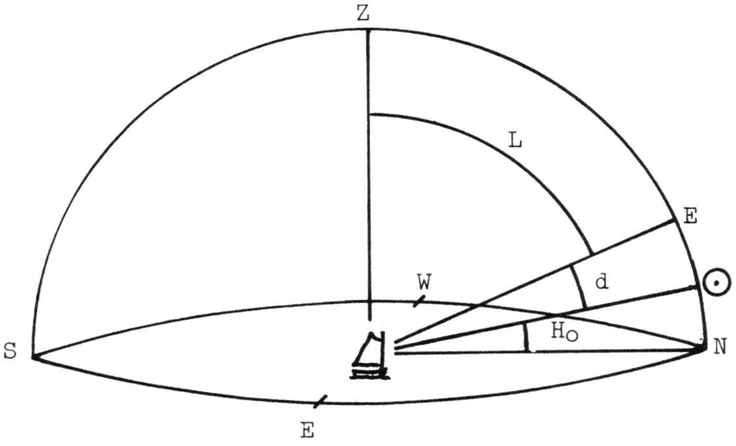


Example 2b.

$H_o$ = 11° 15!2
d = 12° 42!6
L = 66° S (DR estimate)

Solution:

  89° 60!0
 -11° 15!2
  78° 44!8
 -12° 42!6
  66° 02!2 S = your latitude

$L = 90° - H_o - d$

Case 3, declination north, latitude north, Sun over the zenith.

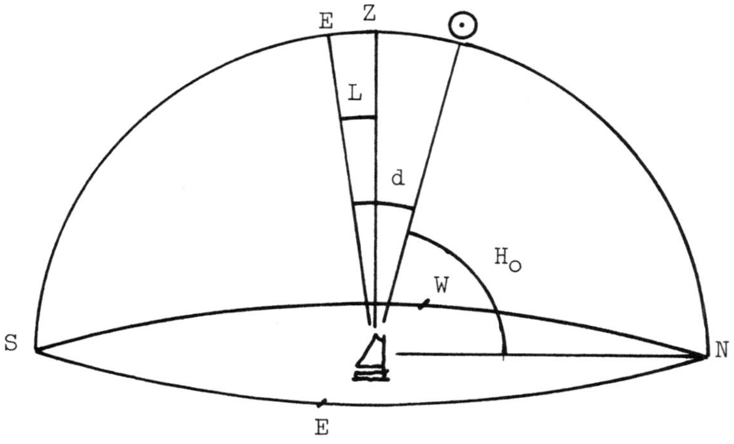


Example 3.

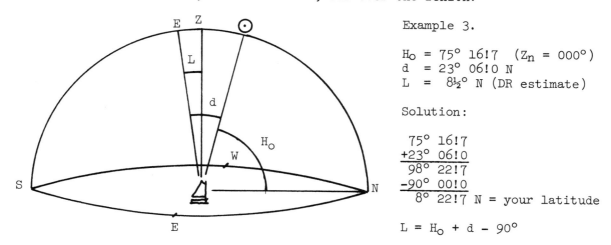

$H_o$ = 75° 16!7 ($Z_n$ = 000°)
d = 23° 06!0 N
L = 8½° N (DR estimate)

Solution:

| |
|---|
| 75° 16!7 |
| +23° 06!0 |
| 98° 22!7 |
| -90° 00!0 |
| 8° 22!7 N = your latitude |

L = $H_o$ + d - 90°

The counterpart to Case 3 (declination south, latitude south, Sun over the zenith) is left to the student to diagram. The solution is identical to Case 3.

Let us take a full example using the previously graphed noon curve. $H_s$ was found to be 71° 42!0, time of noon about 1212 zone time. Assume index correction of -4!3, height of eye of 12 feet, date of 12 April 1976, adjusted DR position of 27° N, 132° 15' E, Sun observed in the south.

Zone description will be -9$^h$ so GMT of LAN will be 0312. The declination of the Sun at that time will be

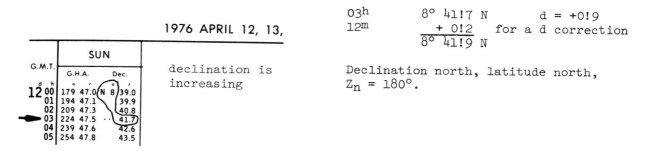

1976 APRIL 12, 13,

| G.M.T. d h | SUN G.H.A. ° ′ | SUN Dec. ° ′ |
|---|---|---|
| 12 00 | 179 47.0 | N 8 39.0 |
| 01 | 194 47.1 | 39.9 |
| 02 | 209 47.3 | 40.8 |
| → 03 | 224 47.5 | 41.7 |
| 04 | 239 47.6 | 42.6 |
| 05 | 254 47.8 | 43.5 |

declination is increasing

| | | |
|---|---|---|
| 03$^h$ | 8° 41!7 N | d = +0!9 |
| 12$^m$ | + 0!2 | for a d correction |
| | 8° 41!9 N | |

Declination north, latitude north, $Z_n$ = 180°.

This is like Case 1a. Latitude = 90° - $H_o$ + d. Sextant altitude is corrected as follows with a resulting latitude.

Local Date 12 April 1976

Height of eye 12 ft.

| | |
|---|---|
| Body | Sun LL |
| $H_s$ | 71° 42'.0 |
| I.C. | −4.3 |
| | 71° 37'.7 |
| Dip | −3.4 |
| App. Alt. | 71° 34'.3 |
| Main | +15.6 |
| $H_o$ | 71° 49'.9 |

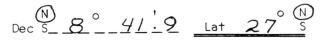

Dec (N) 8° 41'.9   Lat 27° (N)

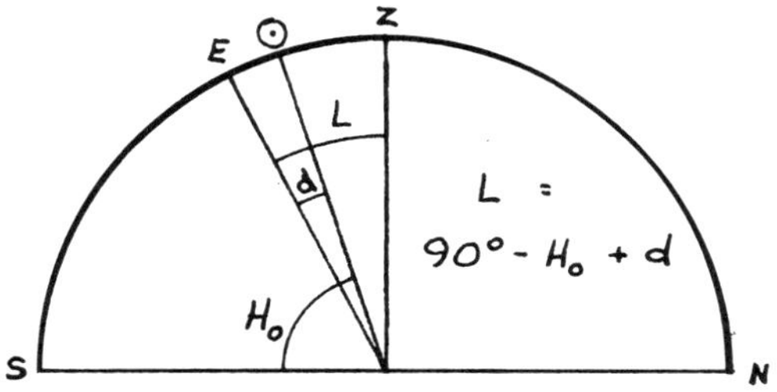


Latitude may be plotted as a horizontal line through the appropriate figure, serving as one line of position. In the days before longitude could be determined, a ship's master would sail to the parallel of latitude of his destination (latitude being found by Polaris or noon Sun sights) and then sail east or west along that parallel until he arrived at his destination.

Sun declination tables are available for noon Sun computations so the purchase of a nautical almanac is not necessary.

Latitude may be computed in a similar manner using any other celestial body as it crosses the meridian.

DR λ = 132° 15' E
ZD = -9

| |
|---|
| 89° 60!0 |
| −71° 49!9 |
| 18° 10!1 |
| + 8° 41!9 |
| 26° 52!0 |

GMT 0312
ZT 1212
time

Lat 26° 52'.0 (N)

In the event that cloudiness or personal circumstances do not allow a noon curve or a single sight at LAN, a process called "reduction to the meridian" is available. An ex-meridian observation is made a few minutes before or after LAN and by means of Table 29 and 30 in Bowditch, the difference in altitude between this sight and the sight that would have been observed at LAN is figured. The difference is added to the ex-meridian altitude. The latitude at the time of observation is figured in the same manner as a noon sight. Years ago, navigators depended on their noon sight for a latitude check so the method described above was a help when situations warranted. However, the modern navigator has tabular means to convert a sight at any time of day into a line of position so the noon latitude is not as necessary.

Assume a navigator on 12 May 1976 has a DR of 38° 10' N, 69° 15' W. He observes the Sun at zone time (standard) of $11^h$ $35^m$ $58^s$. What correction is needed to reduce this sight to one observed on the meridian?

By means we have already discussed, the time of LAN can be figured as $11^h\ 33^m\ 18^s$ ZT, a time difference from the ex-meridian observation of $2^m\ 40^s$. Declination is extracted from the <u>Nautical Almanac</u> using GMT of the observation.

Enter Table 29 with Lat (38° 10' N) and Declination (18° 17' N). Both of these values are labeled the SAME name. Note the headings on each page referring to declination same name as or contrary name to latitude. Choosing the correct page heading, go down the column of declination and across the line of latitude. Extract the value 4".3. This is the change of altitude in one minute from the meridian transit and is labelled "a". Use this value to enter Table 30. Choose the page with a column headed by the time difference between LAN and your sight, in our case $2^m\ 40^s$. Go down this column until you reach the line designated by "a". This gives a value of 0'.5, a number to be added to the ex-meridian observation to give the altitude of the Sun on upper meridian transit.

Interpolation was not necessary in this case although in some situations, determined by examining the differences in tabular values, interpolation will increase accuracy. This method should not be used beyond the limits of Table 30.

**TABLE 29**

Altitude Factor

*a*, the change of altitude in one minute from ... used for entering table 30

| Latitude | Declination same name as latitude, upper transit: add correct | | | | | | | | |
|---|---|---|---|---|---|---|---|---|---|
| | 12° | 13° | 14° | 15° | 16° | 17° | 18° | 19° | 20° |
| ° | " | " | " | " | " | " | " | " | " |
| 0 | 9.2 | 8.5 | 7.9 | 7.3 | 6.8 | 6.4 | 6.0 | 5.7 | 5.4 |
| 1 | 10.1 | 9.2 | 8.5 | 7.8 | 7.3 | 6.8 | 6.4 | 6.0 | 5.7 |
| 2 | 11.1 | 10.0 | 9.2 | 8.4 | 7.8 | 7.2 | 6.8 | 6.3 | 6.0 |
| 3 | 12.3 | 11.0 | 10.0 | 9.1 | 8.4 | 7.8 | 7.2 | 6.7 | 6.3 |
| 4 | 13.8 | 12.2 | 10.9 | 9.9 | 9.1 | 8.3 | 7.7 | 7.2 | 6.7 |
| 30 | 5.4 | 5.7 | 6.0 | 6.4 | 6.8 | 7.2 | 7.8 | 8.4 | 9.2 |
| 31 | 5.1 | 5.3 | 5.6 | 5.9 | 6.3 | 6.7 | 7.1 | 7.7 | 8.3 |
| 32 | 4.8 | 5.0 | 5.2 | 5.5 | 5.8 | 6.2 | 6.5 | 7.0 | 7.5 |
| 33 | 4.5 | 4.7 | 4.9 | 5.1 | 5.4 | 5.7 | 6.1 | 6.4 | 6.9 |
| 34 | 4.3 | 4.4 | 4.6 | 4.8 | 5.1 | 5.3 | 5.6 | 5.9 | 6.3 |
| 35 | 4.0 | 4.2 | 4.4 | 4.5 | 4.7 | 5.0 | 5.2 | 5.5 | 5.8 |
| 36 | 3.8 | 4.0 | 4.1 | 4.3 | 4.5 | 4.7 | 4.9 | 5.1 | 5.4 |
| 37 | 3.6 | 3.8 | 3.9 | 4.0 | 4.2 | 4.4 | 4.6 | 4.8 | 5.0 |
| 38 | 3.4 | 3.6 | 3.7 | 3.8 | 4.0 | 4.1 | 4.3 | 4.5 | 4.7 |
| 39 | 3.3 | 3.4 | 3.5 | 3.6 | 3.8 | 3.9 | 4.0 | 4.2 | 4.4 |

**TABLE 30**

Change of Altitude in Given Time from

| *a* (table 29) | t, meridian angle | | | | | | | | |
|---|---|---|---|---|---|---|---|---|---|
| | 5' | 10' | 15' | 20' | 25' | 30' | 35' | 40' | 45' |
| | $0^m\ 20^s$ | $0^m\ 40^s$ | $1^m\ 00^s$ | $1^m\ 20^s$ | $1^m\ 40^s$ | $2^m\ 00^s$ | $2^m\ 20^s$ | $2^m\ 40^s$ | $3^m\ 00^s$ |
| " | ' | ' | ' | ' | ' | ' | ' | ' | ' |
| 0.1 | 0.0 | 0.0 | 0.0 | 0.0 | 0.0 | 0.0 | 0.0 | 0.0 | 0.0 |
| 0.2 | 0.0 | 0.0 | 0.0 | 0.0 | 0.0 | 0.0 | 0.0 | 0.0 | 0.0 |
| 0.3 | 0.0 | 0.0 | 0.0 | 0.0 | 0.0 | 0.0 | 0.0 | 0.0 | 0.0 |
| 0.4 | 0.0 | 0.0 | 0.0 | 0.0 | 0.0 | 0.0 | 0.0 | 0.0 | 0.1 |
| 0.5 | 0.0 | 0.0 | 0.0 | 0.0 | 0.0 | 0.0 | 0.0 | 0.1 | 0.1 |
| 0.6 | 0.0 | 0.0 | 0.0 | 0.0 | 0.0 | 0.0 | 0.1 | 0.1 | 0.1 |
| 0.7 | 0.0 | 0.0 | 0.0 | 0.0 | 0.0 | 0.0 | 0.1 | 0.1 | 0.1 |
| 0.8 | 0.0 | 0.0 | 0.0 | 0.0 | 0.0 | 0.1 | 0.1 | 0.1 | 0.1 |
| 0.9 | 0.0 | 0.0 | 0.0 | 0.0 | 0.0 | 0.1 | 0.1 | 0.1 | 0.1 |
| 1.0 | 0.0 | 0.0 | 0.0 | 0.0 | 0.0 | 0.1 | 0.1 | 0.1 | 0.2 |
| 2.0 | 0.0 | 0.0 | 0.0 | 0.1 | 0.1 | 0.1 | 0.2 | 0.2 | 0.3 |
| 3.0 | 0.0 | 0.0 | 0.0 | 0.1 | 0.1 | 0.2 | 0.3 | 0.4 | 0.4 |
| 4.0 | 0.0 | 0.0 | 0.1 | 0.1 | 0.2 | 0.3 | 0.4 | 0.5 | 0.6 |
| 5.0 | 0.0 | 0.0 | 0.1 | 0.1 | 0.2 | 0.3 | 0.5 | 0.6 | 0.8 |
| 6.0 | 0.0 | 0.0 | 0.1 | 0.2 | 0.3 | 0.4 | 0.5 | 0.7 | 0.9 |

Once the ex-meridian observation is corrected, the sight can be worked as a normal noon Sun sight to give latitude <u>at the time of the ex-meridian observation</u>. This latitude can be plotted as a horizontal (a) line of position. However, if there is reasonable doubt as to the DR longitude or if the ex-meridian observation is made well before or after LAN, the azimuth of the Sun at the time of observation should be figured. The line of position (b) would run perpendicular to this azimuth, going through the point established by the calculated latitude and the assumed longitude (c).

This process can be used with other celestial bodies also.

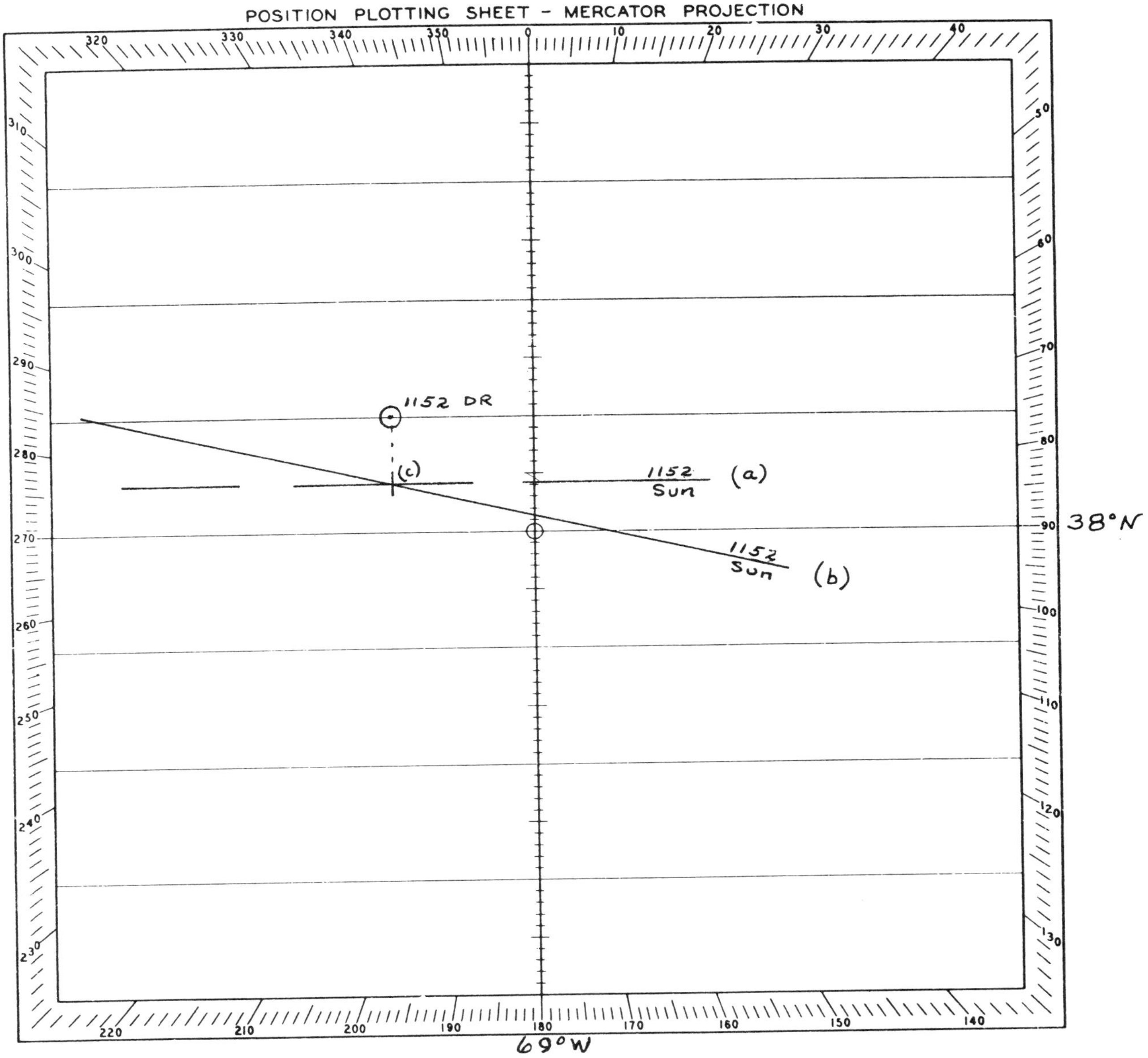

EXERCISE 10

1. Find the ship's latitude in each of the following situations. Use the Polaris tables reproduced in Appendix 2.

| | a | b | c | d |
|---|---|---|---|---|
| Local Date | 26 August 1976 | 4 July 1976 | 31 March 1976 | 23 November 1976 |
| DR Lat | 60° 00!0 N | 15° 21!6 N | 39° 47!3 N | 41° N |
| DR Long | 165° 17!2 E | 16° 21!6 E | 69° 03!1 W | 72° W |
| W.T. | 20-02-06 | 05-00-00 | 19-00-21 | 06-20-01 |
| W.E. on W.T. | 2$^m$ 16$^s$ slow | 10$^s$ fast | 21$^s$ slow | 1$^m$ 05$^s$ fast |
| Ht of eye | 6 feet | 23 feet | 11.9 feet | 20 feet |
| $H_s$ Polaris | 59° 27!6 | 16° 21!6 | 39° 49!6 | 40° 28!4 |
| I.C. | +1!0 | -4!7 | -2!6 | +3!0 |

2. Check 1 d. using H.O. 229. Plot the line of position and record the latitude.

3. Determine ship's latitude from the following data for noon sights of the Sun. All observations are of the Sun's lower limb.

| | a | b | c |
|---|---|---|---|
| Local Date | 12 April 1976 | 22 December 1976 | 23 June 1976 |
| DR Lat | 46° 25!5 N | 41° 04!0 N | 39° 47!0 S |
| DR Long | 152° 28!6 W | 55° 40!0 W | 102° 31!0 E |
| W.T. | 12-10-20 | 11-42-48 | 12-09-49 |
| W.E. on Z.T. | 12$^s$ slow | 1$^m$ 24$^s$ fast | 2$^m$ 13$^s$ slow |
| $H_s$ Sun | 52° 17!2 | 25° 09!5 | 26° 09!3 |
| I.C. | -2!0 | +3!5 | +1!5 |
| Ht of eye | 20 feet | 17 feet | 8 feet |
| $Z_n$ | 180° | 180° | 000° |

4. Determine ship's latitude from the following data for noon sights of the Sun. All observations are of the Sun's upper limb.

| | a | b | c |
|---|---|---|---|
| Local Date | 17 August 1976 | 26 August 1976 | 1 October 1976 |
| DR Lat | 43° 58!8 N | 36° 46!6 N | 31° 12!5 N |
| DR Long | 68° 02!1 W | 123° 35!8 W | 31° 08!8 W |
| Z.T. (standard) | 11-36-04 | 12-16-00 | 11-54-10 |
| $H_s$ | 59° 48!8 | 63° 50!1 | 56° 25!4 |
| I.C. | -2!2 | +2!8 | -10!0 |
| Ht of eye | 7 feet | 8.3 feet | 10 feet |
| $Z_n$ | 180° | 180° | 180° |

5. Determine the ship's latitude from meridian sights of the following bodies.

| | a | b |
|---|---|---|
| Local Date | 31 March 1976 | 1 December 1976 |
| DR Lat | 44° 00!0 N | 44° 30!0 S |
| DR Long | 136° 43!7 E | 157° 25!1 E |
| W.T. | 19-10-00 | 19-32-22 |
| W.E. on Z.T. | $0^s$ | $12^s$ slow |
| Body | Saturn | Diphda |
| $H_s$ | 67° 08!5 | 63° 37!5 |
| I.C. | 0!0 | -2!6 |
| Ht of eye | 70 feet | 3.2 feet |
| $Z_n$ | 180° | 000° |

6. Draw a noon curve for the following sights of the Sun's lower limb and establish ship's latitude.

May 7, 1976; DR Lat 32° N; Ht. of eye 10'; I.C. = -7!9; Z.D. = +4

| Z.T. | $H_s$ |
|---|---|
| 12-40 | 75° 14!5 |
| 12-41 | 75° 17!3 |
| 12-42 | 75° 20!9 |
| 12-44 | 75° 21!3 |
| 12-48 | 75° 23!2 |
| 12-49 | 75° 24!1 |
| 12-51 | 75° 22!0 |
| 12-53 | 75° 21!0 |
| 12-54 | 75° 19!7 |
| 12-55 | 75° 17!1 |
| 12-56 | 75° 16!1 |
| 12-57 | 75° 13!5 |
| 12-58 | 75° 13!1 |

7. Figure the correction to the ex-meridian altitude of the Sun observed on 24 October 1976 at 11-39-48 zone time.
DR Lat 10° N, DR Long 164° E.

8. Find the ship's latitude from the following ex-meridian observation made on 8 January 1976 at 12-00-00 zone time.
Sun LL, $H_s$ = 59° 21!7, I.C. = +2!1, Ht. of eye = 12 feet,
DR Lat 52° 47' S, DR Long 39° 30' W.

# Chapter 13

# The Navigator's Day's Work

At this point in the study, all the basic procedures of celestial navigation have been discussed. It is now time to "put it all together" in a day's work problem where a sample situation of a celestial navigator is posed. A typical order of events for each day would be to ascertain times for sighting (morning and evening twilights, LAN, times when two Sun sights or a Sun and Moon sight would give a good crossing of LOPs), sighting and working the morning fix, plotting courses and speeds until a mid-day fix or running fix, sighting and working this fix, plotting the DR track until evening sights, and sighting and working the evening fix. On rare occasions the Moon will light the horizon under it sufficiently to allow sights past evening twilight.

The following day's work problem is a possible situation in the day of a celestial navigator (at least numerically if not narratively). It is worked in full to allow checking of procedures and figures. There are six day's work problems following in the exercises to enable the reader to prove true the slogan "Practice makes perfect". Practice at least speeds up the process.

Day's Work Example:

1. On 15 June 1976, Pranklin Franklin (navigator and owner of the racing sloop Lightning) was still maneuvering a wet run of the rhumb line for the Newport - Bermuda race. He was madly striving to make Newport for the start of the race but his reputation of playing pranks on others had spread and recently nature and his companions had turned the tables on him. Such incidents as gin in the water tanks, three waterspouts in one day, a case of jackknives in the binnacle and an altered chronometer had greatly messed up Pranklin's time schedule.

2. The morning was reasonably clear and on course 306° True at speed of 5 knots, Pranklin figured his 1200 DR to be 36° 35' N, 68° W. Label the central meridian of a small position plotting sheet 68° W, central parallel 37° N. All times are eastern daylight, W.E. is $13^s$ slow, I.C. is -0!8, height of eye is 13 feet. Pranklin was able to get a nice point 1233 running fix from the following set of sights.

| Body | W.T. | $H_s$ |
|---|---|---|
| Moon UL | 07-13-27 | 16° 32'.7 |
| Sun UL | 10-50-10 | 64° 44'.9 |
| Sun LL | 12-32-32 (LAN) | 76° 30'.6 |

3. He was thrilled to be not too far to the west of the rhumb line with Caryn Seamount abeam (starboard side). Heading on the rhumb line course of 329° T, speed 6 knots, Pranklin found himself in the middle of a horrendous thundershower. Lightning was flashing constantly and suddenly Pranklin's mind lit up with the remembrance that 224 years ago today, his great-great-great-great-great- grandfather had discovered that lightning was electricity. This in addition to the earlier point fix built Pranklin's ego to great heights and the storm passed quickly.

4. Pranklin meanwhile devised several pranks to play on his fellow sailors during the forthcoming race and was so engrossed with these thoughts that sunset almost caught him unaware. The sky had cleared beautifully and Pranklin quickly shot three bright objects but, since he had not prepared his star list in advance, was not entirely sure of correct identification. He could feel a celestial prank in the air but had learned not to get riled. Besides, an old navigator buddy of his, Pierre, had offered some bit of wisdom that always seemed to pull him out of a lousy fix smelling like pine tar - "If the LOP doesn't fit, force it." This is just what Pranklin did, shamefully. Can you find the error such that the 2033 fix will still be on the course line?

| Body | W.T. | $H_s$ |
|---|---|---|
| Vega | 20-17-03 | 30° 00'.6 |
| Spica | 20-20-50 (meridian transit) | 41° 39'.0 |
| Pollux | 20-32-48 | 19° 38'.5 |

5. With about 270 miles to go to Newport and only 30 miles before the *Lightning* crossed the approximate position of the axis of the Gulf Stream, Pranklin pressed onward with somewhat modified thoughts of prank playing in the future.

SIGHT REDUCTION BY H.O. 229

1200 DR: Lat 36° 35.0' (N) S Lo 68° 00.0' E (W) Height of eye 13 ft.
time

| | | | |
|---|---|---|---|
| Daylight W.T. 07h 13m 27s | Local Date 15 June 1976 | Body | Moon UL |
| W.E. 13s | (slow - add) fast - sub | $H_s$ | 16° 32.'7 |
| Z.T. 07h 13m 40s | | I.C. | − 0.'8 |
| | | | 16° 31.'9 |
| Z.D. +4h | (W Lo +) E Lo − | Dip | −3.'5 |
| GMT 11h 13m 40s | Grnch Date 15 June 1976 | | ° ' |
| | | Temp. Press. | |
| | | App. Alt. | 16° 28.'4 |
| | | Main | + 35.'9 |
| | | $H_o$ | 17° 04.'3 |

From Nautical Almanac

| | | | |
|---|---|---|---|
| star SHA only | ° ' | | |
| GHA 11h | 120° 49.'4 | Dec N (S) | 13° 32.'9 |
| 13m 40s | 3° 15.'7 | d ±(−)8.4 corr | − 1.'9 |
| v ± 10.6 corr | 2.'4 | Dec Body | 13° 31.'0 N (S) |
| TOTAL | ° ' | | |
| ±360° | | | |
| GHA Body | 124° 07.'5 | | |
| A.P. Lo | 68° 07.'5 add if E (sub if W) | | |
| TOTAL | 00.'0 | | |
| −360° | | | |
| LHA Body | 056° | | |

| | |
|---|---|
| H.P. | 57.'2 Moon |
| Corr | + 62.'7 |
| Corr | + 3.'2 |
| upper limb | − 30.'0 |
| Main | (+) − 35.'9 |

Tab Dec — Dec Inc

SAME (CONTRARY)

A.P. Lat 37° (N) S

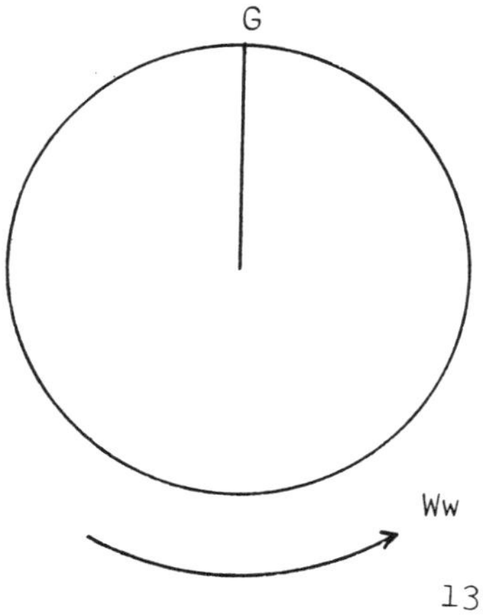


| | $H_c$ | d | DSD | Z eye interp. |
|---|---|---|---|---|
| Tabular Values | 17° 26.'6 | + (−) 43.'3 | + ' | 122.°5 |
| Net corr | ° − 22.'3 | Interpolation Table | | |
| $H_c$ | 17° 04.'3 | Tens 20.'6; Units & Decimals 1.'7 | | $Z_n$ = 360 − Z |
| $H_o$ | 17° 04.'3 | DSD corr +; Net corr 22.'3 | | |
| a | 0.'0 T $H_o > H_c$ A $H_o < H_c$ | | | $Z_n$ 237.°5 |

advance 26.6 n.m.

SIGHT REDUCTION BY H.O. 229

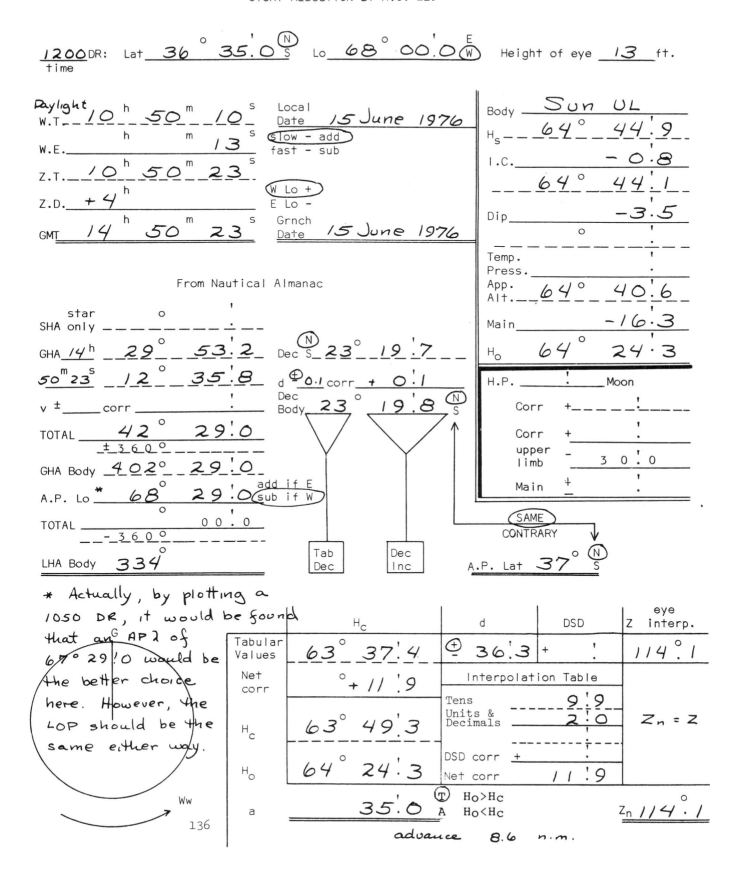

1200 DR: Lat 36° 35.0' (N) S   Lo 68° 00.0' E (W)   Height of eye 13 ft.
time

| | | | |
|---|---|---|---|
| Daylight W.T. | 10h 50m 10s | Local Date | 15 June 1976 |
| W.E. | 13s | (slow - add) fast - sub | |
| Z.T. | 10h 50m 23s | | |
| Z.D. | +4h | (W Lo +) E Lo - | |
| GMT | 14h 50m 23s | Grnch Date | 15 June 1976 |

| | |
|---|---|
| Body | Sun UL |
| $H_s$ | 64° 44.'9 |
| I.C. | -0.'8 |
| | 64° 44.'1 |
| Dip | -3.'5 |
| | °  ' |
| Temp. Press. | |
| App. Alt. | 64° 40.'6 |
| Main | -16.'3 |
| $H_o$ | 64° 24.'3 |

| Moon | |
|---|---|
| H.P. | ' |
| Corr | + ' |
| Corr | + ' |
| upper limb | - 30.'0 |
| Main | ± ' |

From Nautical Almanac

| | | | |
|---|---|---|---|
| star SHA only | ° ' | | |
| GHA 14h | 29° 53.'2 | Dec (N) S | 23° 19.'7 |
| 50m 23s | 12° 35.'8 | d (+)0.1 corr | +0.'1 |
| v ± corr | ' | Dec Body | 23° 19.'8 (N) S |
| TOTAL | 42° 29.'0 | | |
| | ±360° | | |
| GHA Body | 402° 29.'0 | | |
| A.P. Lo* | 68° 29.'0 | add if E (sub if W) | |
| TOTAL | ° 00.'0 | | |
| | -360° | | |
| LHA Body | 334° | | |

Tab Dec | Dec Inc

(SAME) CONTRARY

A.P. Lat 37° (N) S

* Actually, by plotting a 1050 DR, it would be found that an AP λ of 67° 29.'0 would be the better choice here. However, the LOP should be the same either way.

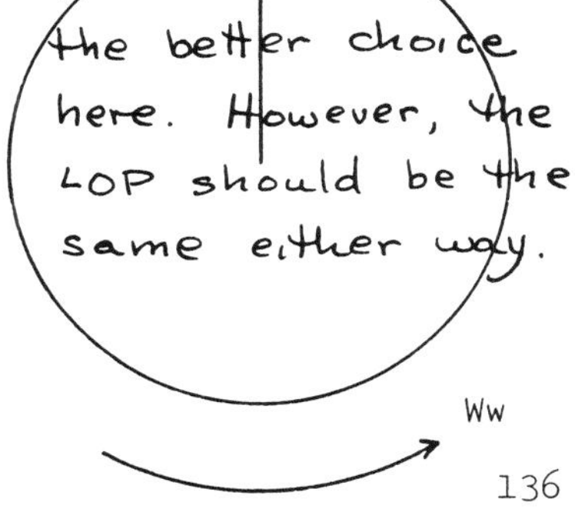


| | $H_c$ | d | DSD | Z eye interp. |
|---|---|---|---|---|
| Tabular Values | 63° 37.'4 | (+) 36.'3 | + ' | 114.°1 |
| Net corr | + 11.'9 | Interpolation Table | | |
| | | Tens | 9.'9 | |
| $H_c$ | 63° 49.'3 | Units & Decimals | 2.'0 | $Z_n = Z$ |
| | | | ' | |
| | | DSD corr | + ' | |
| $H_o$ | 64° 24.'3 | Net corr | 11.'9 | |

a 35.'0 (T) A   Ho>Hc / Ho<Hc   $Z_n$ 114.°1

advance 8.6 n.m.

SIGHT REDUCTION BY H.O. 229

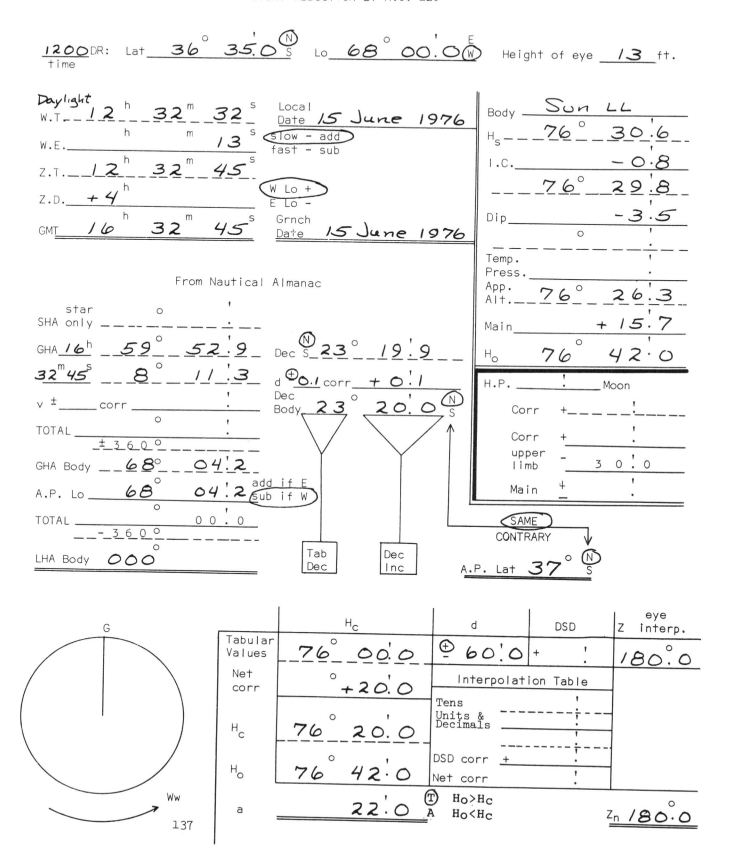

1200 DR: Lat 36° 35.0' (N)/S   Lo 68° 00.0' E/(W)   Height of eye 13 ft.
time

| | | | | |
|---|---|---|---|---|
| Daylight W.T. | 12h | 32m | 32s | Local Date 15 June 1976 |
| W.E. | h | m | 13s | (slow - add) / fast - sub |
| Z.T. | 12h | 32m | 45s | |
| Z.D. | +4h | | | (W Lo +) / E Lo - |
| GMT | 16h | 32m | 45s | Grnch Date 15 June 1976 |

| | |
|---|---|
| Body | Sun LL |
| $H_s$ | 76° 30.6' |
| I.C. | -0.8' |
| | 76° 29.8' |
| Dip | -3.5' |
| | ° ' |
| Temp. Press. | ' |
| App. Alt. | 76° 26.3' |
| Main | +15.7' |
| $H_o$ | 76° 42.0' |

| H.P. | ' | Moon |
|---|---|---|
| Corr | + | ' |
| Corr | + | ' |
| upper limb | - | 30.0' |
| Main | ± | ' |

From Nautical Almanac

| | | |
|---|---|---|
| star SHA only | ° | ' |
| GHA 16h | 59° | 52.9' |
| 32m 45s | 8° | 11.3' |
| v ± ___ corr | | ' |
| TOTAL | ° | ' |
| ±360° | | |
| GHA Body | 68° | 04.2' |
| A.P. Lo | 68° | 04.2' (add if E / sub if W) |
| TOTAL | ° | 00.0' |
| -360° | | |
| LHA Body | 000° | |

Dec (N)/S 23° 19.9'
d (+)0.1 corr +0.1'
Dec Body 23° 20.0' (N)/S

Tab Dec   Dec Inc

(SAME) / CONTRARY

A.P. Lat 37° (N)/S

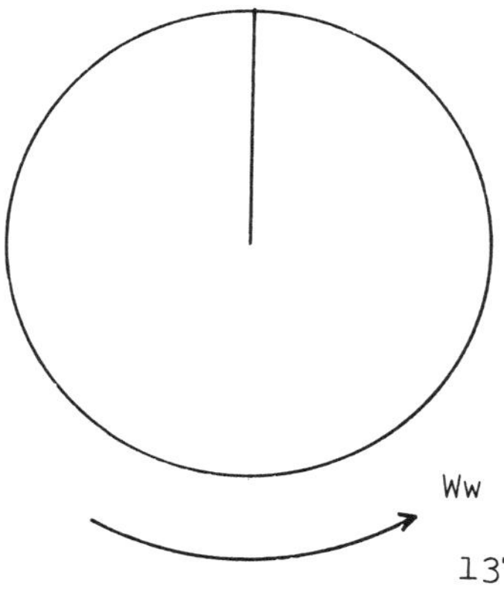


| | $H_c$ | d | DSD | Z eye interp. |
|---|---|---|---|---|
| Tabular Values | 76° 00.0' | (+)/- 60.0' | + ' | 180.0° |
| Net corr | +20.0' | Interpolation Table | | |
| | | Tens | ' | |
| $H_c$ | 76° 20.0' | Units & Decimals | ' | |
| | | | ' | |
| $H_o$ | 76° 42.0' | DSD corr | + ' | |
| | | Net corr | ' | |
| a | 22.0' (T)/A | Ho>Hc / Ho<Hc | | $Z_n$ 180.0° |

SIGHT REDUCTION BY H.O. 229

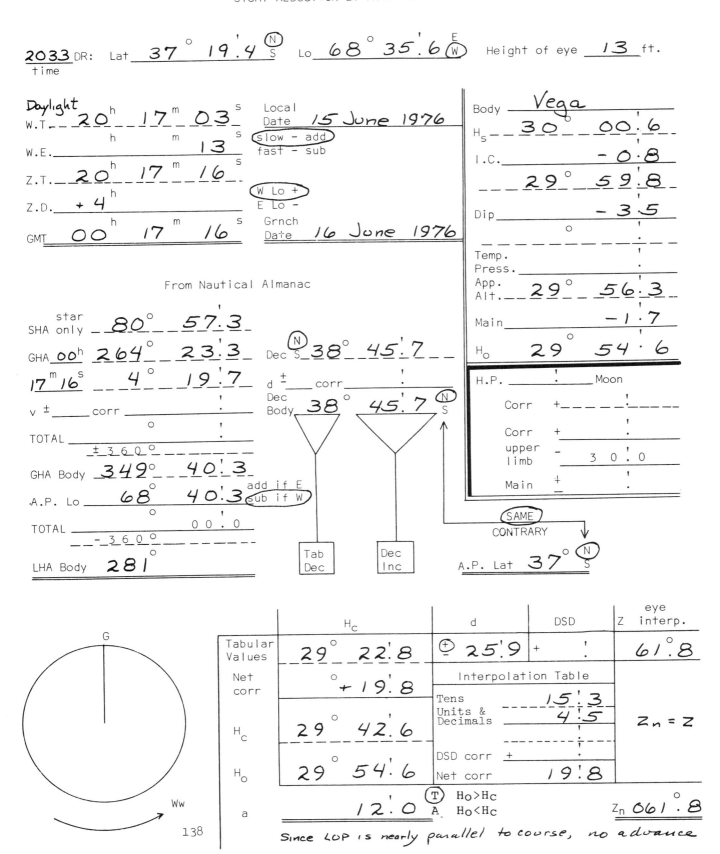

2033 DR: Lat 37° 19.4' (N) S  Lo 68° 35.6' E (W)  Height of eye 13 ft.
time

| | | | |
|---|---|---|---|
| Daylight W.T. | 20h 17m 03s | Local Date | 15 June 1976 |
| W.E. | 13s | (slow - add) fast - sub | |
| Z.T. | 20h 17m 16s | | |
| Z.D. | + 4h | (W Lo +) E Lo - | |
| GMT | 00h 17m 16s | Grnch Date | 16 June 1976 |

| | |
|---|---|
| Body | Vega |
| $H_s$ | 30° 00.6' |
| I.C. | -0.8 |
| | 29° 59.8' |
| Dip | -3.5 |
| | |
| Temp. Press. | |
| App. Alt. | 29° 56.3' |
| Main | -1.7 |
| $H_o$ | 29° 54.6' |

| | |
|---|---|
| H.P. | Moon |
| Corr + | |
| Corr + | |
| upper limb - | 30.0 |
| Main ± | |

From Nautical Almanac

| | | | |
|---|---|---|---|
| SHA star only | 80° 57.3' | | |
| GHA 00h | 264° 23.3' | Dec (N) S | 38° 45.7' |
| 17m 16s | 4° 19.7' | d ± corr | |
| v ± corr | | Dec Body | 38° 45.7' (N) S |
| TOTAL | | | |
| ±360° | | | |
| GHA Body | 349° 40.3' | | |
| A.P. Lo | 68° 40.3' | add if E (sub if W) | |
| TOTAL | 00° 00.0' | | |
| -360° | | | |
| LHA Body | 281° | | |

Tab Dec — Dec Inc

(SAME) CONTRARY

A.P. Lat 37° (N) S

| | $H_c$ | d | DSD | Z eye interp. |
|---|---|---|---|---|
| Tabular Values | 29° 22.8' | (+) - 25.9' | + | 61.8° |
| Net corr | +19.8' | Interpolation Table | | Zn = Z |
| | | Tens | 15.3' | |
| | | Units & Decimals | 4.5' | |
| $H_c$ | 29° 42.6' | | | |
| | | DSD corr + | | |
| $H_o$ | 29° 54.6' | Net corr | 19.8' | |
| a | 12.0' | (T) Ho>Hc / A Ho<Hc | | $Z_n$ 061.8° |

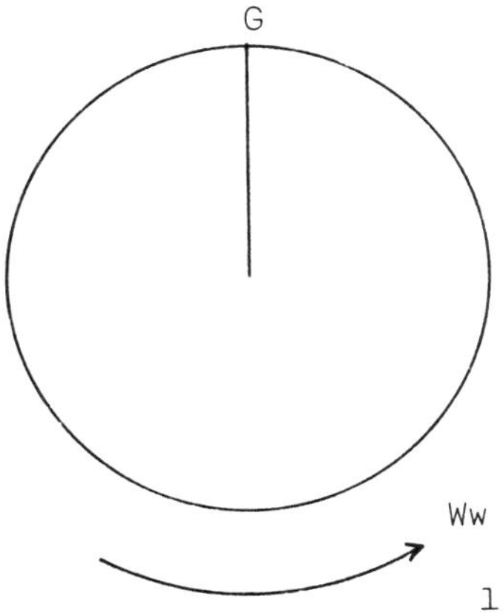


Since LOP is nearly parallel to course, no advance

SIGHT REDUCTION BY H.O. 229

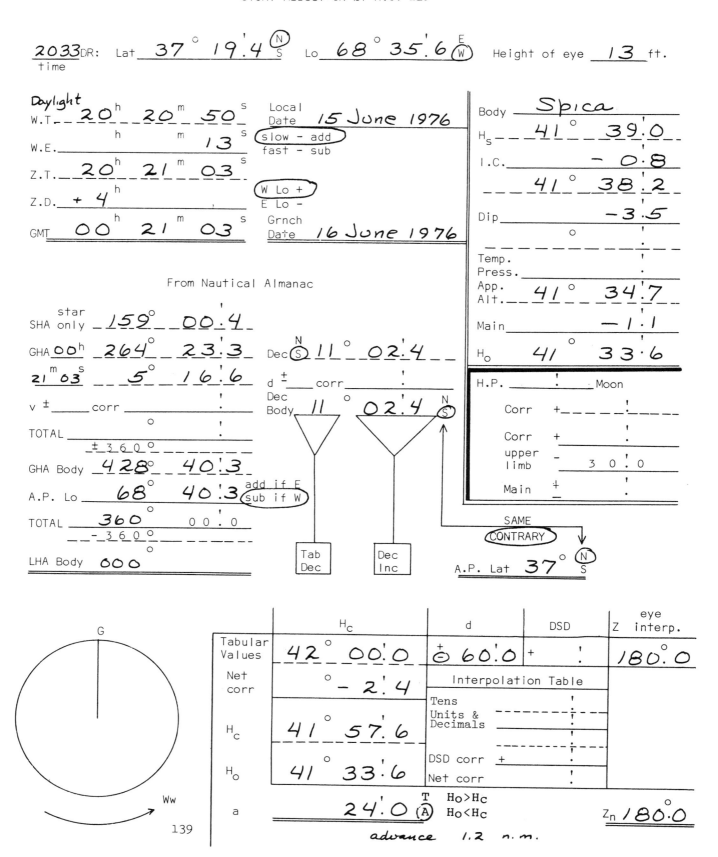

2033 DR: Lat 37° 19.4' (N) S  Lo 68° 35.6' E (W)  Height of eye 13 ft.
time

| | | |
|---|---|---|
| Daylight W.T. | 20h 20m 50s | Local Date 15 June 1976 |
| W.E. | 13s | (slow - add) fast - sub |
| Z.T. | 20h 21m 03s | |
| Z.D. | + 4h | (W Lo +) E Lo - |
| GMT | 00h 21m 03s | Grnch Date 16 June 1976 |

| | |
|---|---|
| Body | Spica |
| Hs | 41° 39.0' |
| I.C. | - 0.8 |
| | 41° 38.2' |
| Dip | -3.5 |
| | ° ' |
| Temp. Press. | |
| App. Alt. | 41° 34.7' |
| Main | -1.1 |
| Ho | 41° 33.6 |

| | |
|---|---|
| H.P. | ' Moon |
| Corr | + ' |
| Corr | + ' |
| upper limb | - 30.0 |
| Main | ± ' |

From Nautical Almanac

| | | |
|---|---|---|
| SHA star only | 159° 00.4 | |
| GHA 00h | 264° 23.3 | Dec N (S) 11° 02.4' |
| 21m 03s | 5° 16.6 | d ± corr ' |
| v ± corr | ' | Dec Body 11° 02.4' N (S) |
| TOTAL | ° ' | |
| | ± 360° | |
| GHA Body | 428° 40.3 | |
| A.P. Lo | 68° 40.3 | add if E (sub if W) |
| TOTAL | 360° 00.0 | |
| | - 360° | |
| LHA Body | 000 | |

Tab Dec | Dec Inc

SAME / (CONTRARY)

A.P. Lat 37° (N) S

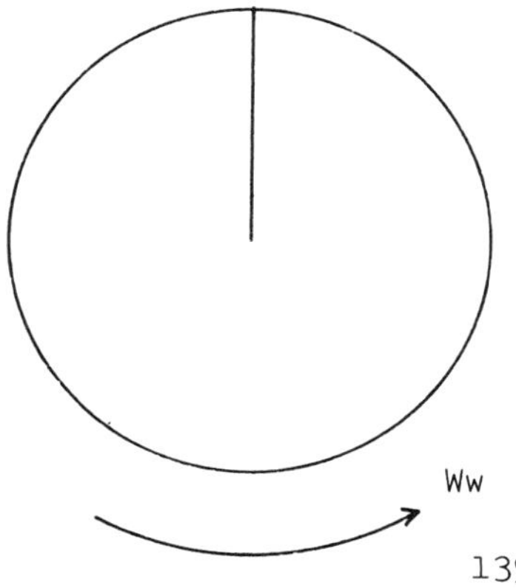


| | Hc | d | DSD | Z eye interp. |
|---|---|---|---|---|
| Tabular Values | 42° 00.0' | + (-) 60.0' | + ' | 180.0° |
| Net corr | ° - 2.4' | Interpolation Table | | |
| | | Tens | ' | |
| Hc | 41° 57.6 | Units & Decimals | ' | |
| | | | ' | |
| | | DSD corr | + ' | |
| Ho | 41° 33.6 | Net corr | ' | |
| a | 24.0' T (A) Ho>Hc Ho<Hc | | | Zn 180.0° |

advance 1.2 n.m.

SIGHT REDUCTION BY H.O. 229

*Pollux is mistaken identity.*

2033 time DR: Lat 37° 19.'4 (N) Lo 68° 35.'6 (W) Height of eye 13 ft.

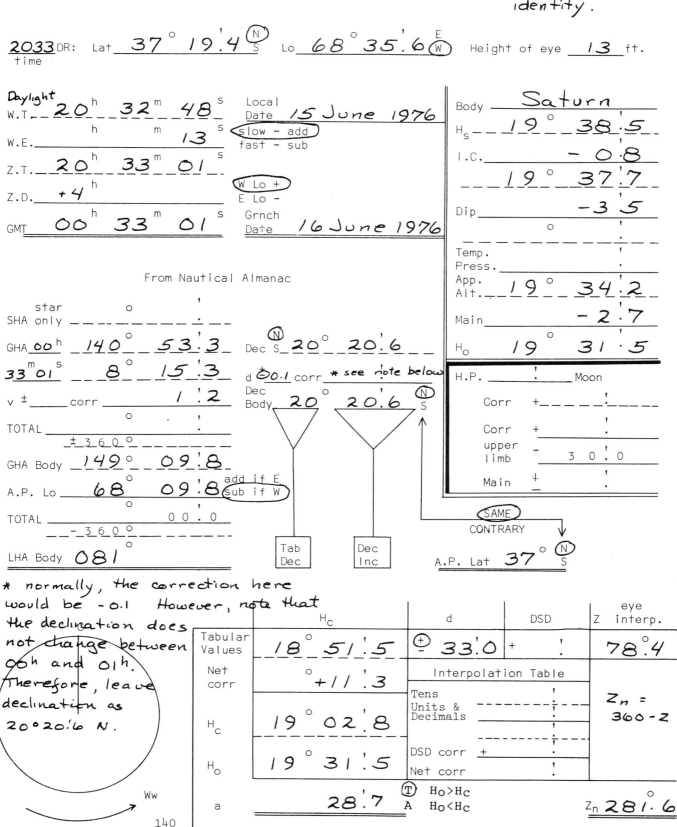

| | | | |
|---|---|---|---|
| Daylight W.T. | 20h 32m 48s | Local Date | 15 June 1976 |
| W.E. | 13s | (slow - add) fast - sub | |
| Z.T. | 20h 33m 01s | | |
| Z.D. | +4h | (W Lo +) E Lo - | |
| GMT | 00h 33m 01s | Grnch Date | 16 June 1976 |

| | |
|---|---|
| Body | Saturn |
| $H_s$ | 19° 38.'5 |
| I.C. | - 0.'8 |
| | 19° 37.'7 |
| Dip | -3.'5 |
| Temp. Press. | |
| App. Alt. | 19° 34.'2 |
| Main | -2.'7 |
| $H_o$ | 19° 31.'5 |
| H.P. Moon | |
| Corr | + |
| Corr | + |
| upper limb | - 30.'0 |
| Main | ± |

From Nautical Almanac

| | | | |
|---|---|---|---|
| star SHA only | | Dec (N) S | 20° 20.'6 |
| GHA 00h | 140° 53.'3 | d ±0.1 corr | * see note below |
| 33m 01s | 8° 15.'3 | Dec Body | 20° 20.'6 (N) S |
| v ± corr | 1.'2 | | |
| TOTAL ±360° | | | |
| GHA Body | 149° 09.'8 | | |
| A.P. Lo | 68° 09.'8 | add if E (sub if W) | |
| TOTAL -360° | 00.'0 | | |
| LHA Body | 081° | Tab Dec | Dec Inc |

(SAME) CONTRARY

A.P. Lat 37° (N) S

* normally, the correction here would be -0.1 However, note that the declination does not change between 00h and 01h. Therefore, leave declination as 20°20.'6 N.

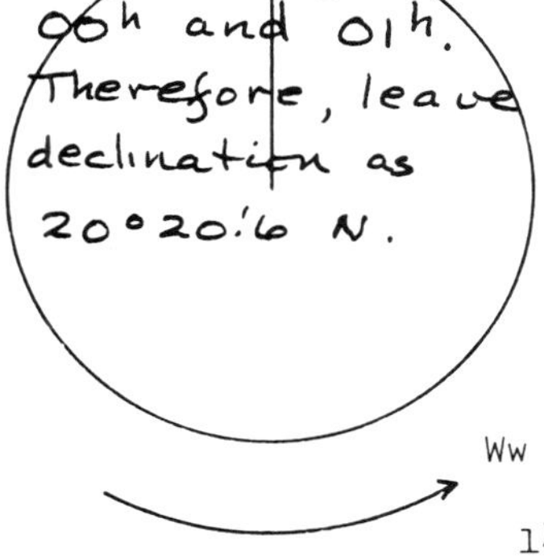

| | $H_c$ | d | DSD | Z eye interp. |
|---|---|---|---|---|
| Tabular Values | 18° 51.'5 | (+) 33.'0 | + | 78.°4 |
| Net corr | +11.'3 | Interpolation Table | | $Z_n$ = 360 - Z |
| | | Tens | | |
| | | Units & Decimals | | |
| $H_c$ | 19° 02.'8 | | | |
| $H_o$ | 19° 31.'5 | DSD corr + | | |
| | | Net corr | | |
| a | 28.'7 | (T) Ho>Hc A Ho<Hc | | $Z_n$ 281.°6 |

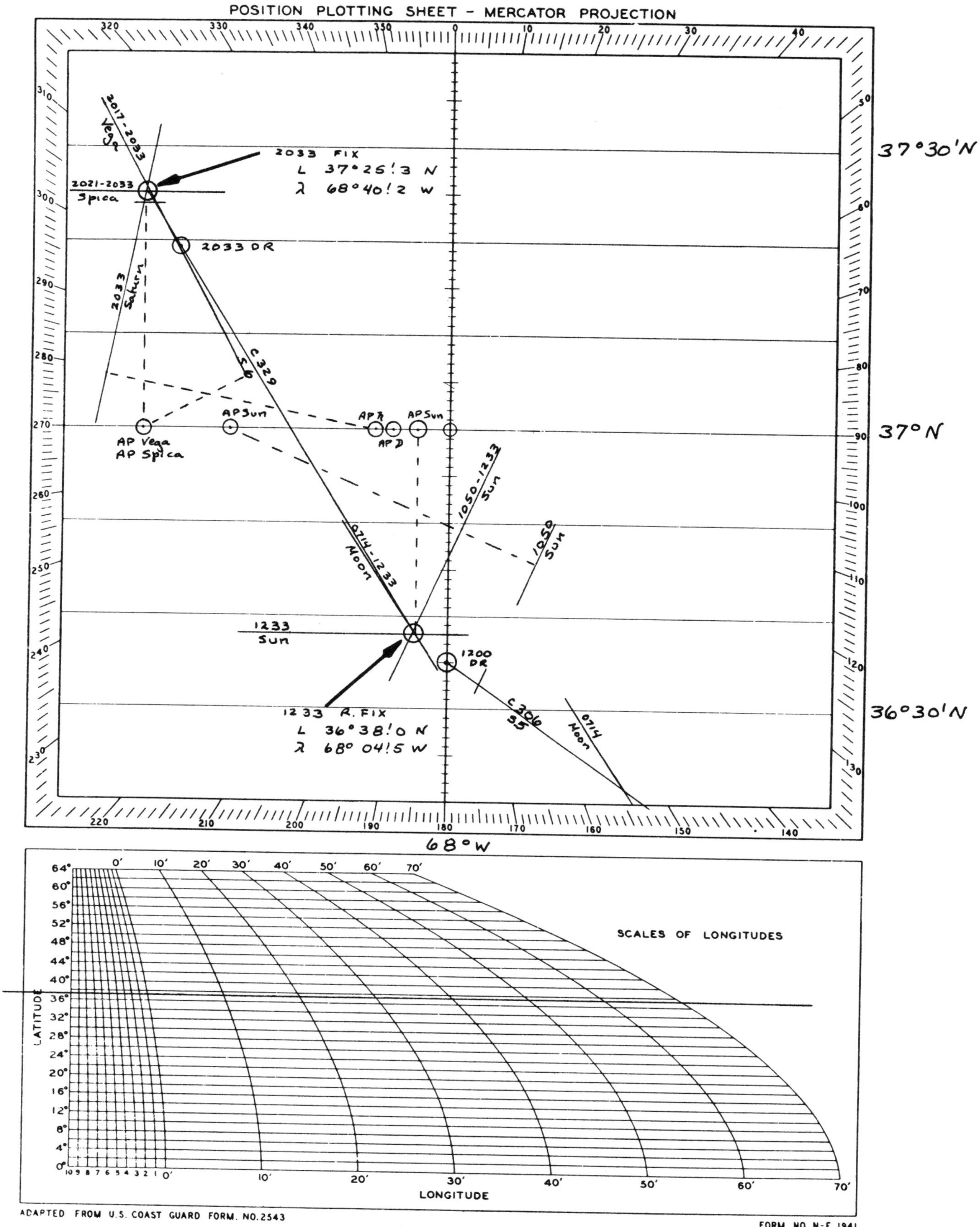
POSITION PLOTTING SHEET - MERCATOR PROJECTION
2033 FIX
L 37°25!3 N
λ 68°40!2 W
2033 DR
2017-2033 Vega
2021-2033 Spica
2033 Saturn
C 329
S 6
AP Vega
AP Spica
AP Sun
AP ♄
AP ☽
AP Sun
1050-1233 Sun
1050 Sun
0714-1233 Moon
1233 Sun
1200 DR
1233 R. FIX
L 36°38!0 N
λ 68° 04!5 W
C 306
S 5
0714 Moon
37°30'N
37°N
36°30'N
68°W
SCALES OF LONGITUDES
LATITUDE
LONGITUDE
ADAPTED FROM U.S. COAST GUARD FORM. NO. 2543
FORM NO. N-E 1941

## EXERCISE 11

Day's Work Problem I.

1. On 29 February 1976, the two lady crew of the crafty ketch Sadie Hawkins awoke to another day of man hunting. The absence of a Moon that day detracted from the romanticism of the venture but Big Bertha and Sextant Sally had a feeling that this would be their lucky day. Traditionally, no man could refuse their marriage proposals on this extra day in the leap year. Their destination was Inaccessible Island (near Tristan Island, L 37° 03' S, λ 12° 18' W) where they had heard two handsome young men were marooned.

2. At 0430 on 29 February, Big Bertha (in charge of piloting and dead reckoning aspects of navigation) alerted Sextant Sally that the Hawkins' DR was L 41° 12' S, λ 14° 05' W, her course 040° and speed 10 knots. Sky conditions looked good for celestial observations, Sextant Sally's domain. Index correction was -1!6, height of eye 4.6 meters and watch error 20 seconds slow. Plot the 0518 fix.

| Body | W.T.(standard) | $H_s$ |
|---|---|---|
| Spica | 04-52-41 | 49° 30!9 |
| Acrux | 05-03-35 | 54° 15!5 |
| Venus | 05-17-50 | 22° 11!3 |

3. Big Bertha was truly grateful to Sextant Sally for her sights of Spica and Acrux for they gave her excellent checks on her course and speed respectively, and from the 0518 fix it did appear that both factors were in considerable error. Proceeding from the 0518 fix on a new course 050° and increased speed of 15 knots (they wanted to make Inaccessible Island before their day ran out), the Sadie Hawkins lumbered through the Atlantic with a determined crew. No Moon was available but Sextant Sally sighted the Sun saucily, searingly and smashingly.

| Body | W.T. | $H_s$ |
|---|---|---|
| Sun LL | 11-10-21 | 55° 44!4 |

At 1145 course was changed to 340°, speed remained at 15 knots.

| | | |
|---|---|---|
| Sun UL | 14-42-00 | 43° 00!3 |

Plot the 1111, 1145 and 1442 DR positions and the 1442 running fix.

Note: Remember to use the 1442 DR position for figuring AP of 1442 sight. Note course change in advancing 1111 sight.

4. With the rest of the afternoon and evening left to sail and a good breeze and determination to drive them, the two gals thought their mission

destination within easy range. However, jealousy set in as is so often the case and Big Bertha read in the initials of the sights that day.

S A V e          Sextant Sally

Since Sally had a way with stars and messages, Bertha thought she was sending a biased message ahead to the marooned men. However, Sally suggested that Bertha shoot her BB gun in a NNE direction and that would even the message score as long as she didn't maim one of the soon to be discovered men.

Later that evening, with minutes to spare they entered the harbor to be greeted by a sea of masts. Switching on their searchlight they were horrified to see the Ada & Helen, the Mary & Jane, the Elizabeth & Maud, and even the Sally & Bertha all at anchor. Across the waters echoed the shrieks of the Maenads as they pursued their prey.

Day's Work Problem II.

1. On 14 April 1976, Peter Rabbit, aboard his ship Cottontail, was in the middle of his yearly pilgrimage to Easter Island. Seas were calm, the morning twilight had just begun and Peter was eager to establish his exact position. Use the following values throughout.

| | |
|---|---|
| I.C. | +2!1 |
| Ht. of PR's eye | 4.0 feet |
| W.E. | $26^s$ fast |

Label central meridians and central parallels of 3 small plotting sheets 107° W, 41° S; 108° W, 40° S; and 109° W, 39° S.

2. From the stationary 0600 DR position of latitude 41° 20' S, longitude 106° 40' W, Peter took a round of morning sights, easily viewing Venus due to the clarity of the air.

| Body | W.T. | $H_s$ |
|---|---|---|
| Venus | 05-45-13 | 6° 19!7 |
| Altair | 06-00-26 | 39° 37!3 |
| Achernar | 06-10-42 | 33° 29!5 |

Plot and record the 0610 fix.
Temperature is 60° F, pressure is 30.00 inches. (Ship stationary until 0610).

3. From the 0610 fix, Peter proceeded on course 310°, speed 20 knots. Seeing that no Moon would be visible most of the day, Peter hastened to get a sight of the Sun to advance to a later Sun sight.

| | | |
|---|---|---|
| Sun UL | 10-10-10 | 32° 55!5 |

Continuing on course 310° for a half hour, Peter then (at 1040) changed course to due north, speed to 15 knots.

4. With sufficient time to munch a few carrots and niblets of lettuce, Peter's newly sharpened eyes caught the lower limb of the Sun at 12-09-59 with altitude of 40° 17!0. He advanced the 1010 Sun LOP for a 1210 R. Fix. (Note the change in course and speed when you advance the Sun LOP.)

5. Trimming Cottontail's sails, Peter increased speed to 22 knots and changed course from the 1210 R. Fix to 295°. At 1410, due to change of wind direction and speed, Peter altered course to 333°, speed to 10 knots. Anticipating a relaxing afternoon, Peter hippity-hopped to his liquor shop below and mixed up an invigorating Cottontail special cocktail. By 1730, he figured he had better check his position. Therefore, Mr. Peter Rabbit sighted Miaplacidus, Procyon and Rigel as follows.

| | | |
|---|---|---|
| M | 17-41-17 | 54° 14!5 |
| P | 17-58-27 | 45° 40!9 |
| R | 18-10-00 | 47° 36!1 |

Seeing that his 1810 fix longitude was nearly that of Easter Island, Peter headed due north to hopefully sight Easter Island before the 4th of July.

## Day's Work Problem III.

1. The Lone Roly Poli on board the hydrofoil Quicksilver was taking his one week vacation in the Mediterranean. He had caught the travelling bug after reading in his World Almanac about the August anniversaries of transportation:

| | | |
|---|---|---|
| 1 August | First auto trip across U.S. ended, San Francisco to New York | (1903) |
| 10 August | First electric street railway in U.S. (Baltimore) | (1885) |
| 15 August | First ship passed through Panama Canal | (1914) |
| 17 August | First trip on steamboat Clermont by Robert Fulton, New York to Albany | (1807) |

He thought he'd endeavor to be the first hydrofoil operator to gallop across the Gulf of Tonto (I mean Taranto) from Gallipoli to Crotone, Italy, navigating with celestial sights alone.

2. Label the central meridian of a small plotting sheet 17° 30' E, central parallel 40° N. Height of Roly's eye is 21 feet, I.C. is +4!4, W.E. is 18 seconds fast on standard zone time. Roly departed from Capo Gallo Light (L 40° 41' N, λ 17° 56' E) on course 210°, speed 40 knots. Departure time on 26 August 1976 was 0405. At 0450, Roly changed course to 140°, speed 15 knots.

3. Shortly after 0450 Roly saw Jupiter gleaming in the south-southeast. Sighting it at 04-54-18 with altitude of 67° 58!6, Roly plotted this LOP before chugging his breakfast of rolls and oats. At 0550, he changed course

to 115° but only drifted with the breeze at estimated speed of 3 knots. Running-fixing his position at 0645 with a Sun sight, he found himself on the B-line run between Gallipoli and Crotone.

| | | |
|---|---|---|
| Sun LL | 06-45-22 = W.T. | 16° 55!1 = $H_s$ |

4. From the 0645 R. Fix, Roly changed course to 213° and revved Quicksilver up to 70 knots. In less than an hour the passage to Crotone had been completed!

| | | |
|---|---|---|
| Gallipoli | L 40° 04' N | λ 17° 59' E |
| Crotone | L 39° 05' N | λ 17° 08' E |

This was quite disturbing since Roly wished to make a day of it. The solution seemed to be to zip back and forth on the B-line. This he did. Around noon, the air service cook, Georgie Porgie, flew in some pudding and pie and Gallo wine which sustained Roly until evening sights. By this time, Roly was a bit confused as to his actual position. He guessed his 1900 DR to be 39° 30' N, 17° 30' E. Speed was 20 knots, course 213°. The following sights were taken.

| Body | W.T. | $H_s$ |
|---|---|---|
| Vega | 18-45-16 | 74° 23!0 |
| Antares | 19-01-43 | 22° 24!2 |
| Alioth | 19-13-30 | 41° 05!9 |

Having satisfied (with a point fix no less) his desire for a celestial passage, Roly zipped back to Capo Gallo Light for a snooze.

Day's Work Problem IV.

1. It was November, it was cold and Tom Turkey aboard Gobbledygook Express was pressing onward toward the Cranberry Isles off the coast of Maine (rough Lat 44° 15' N, Long 68° 15' W). His family had celebrated Thanksgiving there for decades and Tom wanted to join them this year in the worst way. He had been eating slack salted pollack and soggy saltines for weeks so was especially looking forward to a full spread on the table. Things were not going well however. His 1700 DR on the evening of 24 November was 38° 40' N and 65° 35' W, a long way from his destination. Course was 345°, speed 12 knots.

2. To better establish his chances of timely arrival, Tom sought the skies for help. Working on standard zone time with I.C. = +0!8 and height of eye 17 feet, Tom obtained the following sights. He set his stopwatch to the WWV time signal (Universal Coordinated Time) at $21^h\ 10^m\ 00^s$. Plot and record the 1747 fix.

| Body | Stopwatch reading | $H_s$ |
|---|---|---|
| Venus | $05^m\ 16^s$ | 19° 15!8 |

| | | |
|---|---|---|
| Vega | $19^m\ 23^s$ | 57° 55!7 |
| Polaris | $36^m\ 49^s$ | 39° 06!2 |

3. Note that Venus is in conjunction with a navigational star. By comparing SHA and Dec of Venus to those in the Nautical Almanac star list (or another method if your prefer), which star would this be? Since magnitude of the star is +2.1 and magnitude of Venus is -3.6 (meaning that Venus is about 190 times brighter than the star), there is no problem in confusing one for the other. Also, planets don't twinkle, stars do.

4. Confirming that indeed time was growing short and distance to travel was considerable, Tom's tastebuds urged him to maintain speed at 12 knots, wind direction made him alter course to 300°. He watched the Moon set, prefigured stars for a morning fix and caught a bit of shut-eye. Awaking at 0600, he figured his DR at that time and then realized he had crossed the border into the eastern time zone. Resetting his watch, he relabelled his DR (to what time?) and started his stopwatch at 1025 UTC. Plot and record the 0611 fix.

| Body | Stopwatch reading | $H_s$ |
|---|---|---|
| Denebola | $20^m\ 06^s$ | 59° 38!0 |
| Capella | $29^m\ 54^s$ | 32° 59!1 |
| Saturn | $45^m\ 31^s$ | 58° 31!7 |

Note: Capella was a special choice for this day because in Greek mythology, it represents the She Goat who brought up the infant Jupiter. One day in play, Jupiter broke off one of the Goat's horns and thereafter gave it the power of being filled with whatever the possessor would like. We call it now "Horn of plenty" or "Cornucopia." As you can imagine, Tom wished for his turkey dinner as he sighted the star.

5. By now, Tom realized that he would not be able to make his destination before midnight. He renamed his vessel Gobbledygook Turtle and decided to enjoy his day despite the menu. Plodding northward on course 005°, speed still 12 knots, Tom convinced his seasick wife Squashblossom to come on deck. They turned on the radio and danced the "mashed potato" through lunchtime. As the Sun was nearing the horizon, Tom noticed that the Moon was about to cross the meridian so planned simultaneous sights at meridian passage. Squashblossom sighted the Sun while Tom took the Moon. Stopwatch was started at 2015 UTC, results were as follows. Plot the 1511 DR and 1522 fix.

| Body | Stopwatch reading | $H_s$ |
|---|---|---|
| Sun UL | $06^m\ 52^s$ | 6° 27!9 |
| Moon LL | $06^m\ 52^s$ | 32° 13!2 |

6. Finding their fix to be the same latitude as Plymouth and same rough longitude as the Cranberry Isles, Tom and Squashblossom felt more in the Thanksgiving spirit as they stuffed themselves on more slack salted pollack and a pumpkin leftover from Halloween.

## Day's Work Problem V.

1. We three ships of Santaland are
Bearing gifts we traverse afar
Fending typhoons, reading cartoons,
Following yonder star.

Chorus: To be sung after each verse as per traditional John Hopkins' carol.

O-, Star of wonder, Star of night,
Star of royal beauty bright
Westward leading, still proceeding,
Guide us to thy perfect light.

2. Destination: Three Kings Islands.
Santa came, his sextant in hand-
Lovely clear nights, only star sights
Facts follow; point fix planned.

Local Date: 25 December 1976
Ht. of eye: 4 meters
I.C.: -4!7
W.E.: 7 seconds fast

Keep in mind the central parallel on your plotting sheet when chosing AP Lat for H.O. 229

Plotting sheet centrals:
34° S, 172° E
0300 DR: L 33° 27!0 S
λ 172° 16!0 E

Course: due westward
Speed: 6 knots

| Star | W.T. | $H_s$ |
|---|---|---|
| AVior | 03-29-06 | 58° 37!3 |
| Adhara | 03-47-58 | 45° 06!8 |
| RIgel Kent | 04-03-46 | 44° 17!6 |

Plot and record the 0400 DR and 0404 fix.
Proceed on course 230°, speed 6 knots.

3. Santa sailed on into the morn
Tending sheets and blowing his horn.
He was hurried and was worried
Without him, kids would mourn.

4. "Noon" arrived, a latitude check -
Watch and sextant out on deck
Arithmetic, copacetic,
Santa would never wreck!

| Star (our nearest) | W.T. | $H_s$ |
|---|---|---|
| Sun LL | 11-34-36 | 79° 17!5 |

Plot the latitude line, proceed from the 1130 DR on course 108°, speed 4 knots.

5. Sunset came and no time to spoon
Lots of stars and even a Moon.
Sighted thricely, plotted nicely -
Islands would appear soon.

| Star | W.T. | $H_s$ |
|---|---|---|
| Menkar | 19-10-34 | 48° 49!1 |
| Enif | 19-21-21 | 14° 18!6 |
| RIgel | 19-35-53 | 42° 32!5 |

Plot and record the 1930 DR and 1936 fix.

6. Santa chose his stars carefully,
Message in them, caps as you see.
Awful spelling but worth yelling how
All Christmas days should be.

Day's Work Problem VI.

1. Quadruplets, born of good navigation-minded stock, set sail from the Panama Canal in the spring of 1976. The Bowditch, navigated by Eeny and Meeny sailed southwest, the Lecky navigated by Miney and Mo sailed north-east. Their progress was slow since the Lecky was leaky and the Bowditch was bluffbowed. However, the morning of their birthday, 3 September, found them still in one piece sailing merrily under sunshine, starshine and moonshine. They each were especially interested in finding their position accurately that day so that they could record it in the navigation annals they planned to write upon circumnavigation completion. Reduce the sights and plot and record the positions as indicated in the following situations.

2. Since Eeny and Meeny liked to eat or sleep during twilight, they chose to get a two body fix with the Sun and gibbous Moon. The Bowditch's 1300 DR was Latitude 38° 16!7 S, Longitude 126° 43!6 E, course was 295°, speed 7 knots. Plot the 1500 DR and then plot and record the 1510 running fix. Index correction was +3!7, watch error was 19 seconds slow and height of eye was 26 feet.

| Body | W.T. (standard) | $H_s$ |
|---|---|---|
| Sun LL | 13-27-10 | 36° 41!7 |
| Moon UL | 15-09-52 | 32° 49!7 |

3. That same evening, the Lecky and her crew, operating on daylight time, observed a nice round of celestial objects. Their 1800 DR had been established as Latitude 33° 47!0 N, Longitude 38° 10!0 W. Plot and record their 1930 DR and 1930 fix. Index correction was -2!3, height of eye was 7.5 feet and watch error was 1 minute fast. Course throughout was 025°, speed 10 knots. Temperature was 80° F, pressure was 30.75 inches.

| Body | W.T. (daylight) | $H_s$ |
|---|---|---|
| Venus | 18-55-29 | 11° 44!6 |
| Vega | 19-07-47 | 75° 30!7 |
| Polaris | 19-30-04 | 33° 42!1 |

4. After completing these sight reductions which encompassed about every possible quirk that a basic navigator should be able to handle, the quadruplets soaked up the moonshine and continued on their cruise, hoping to take a more advanced navigation course when they returned to Panama.

# Chapter 14

# H.O. 211

Thus far, we have been reducing our sextant sights by using numerical tables entitled H.O. 229. These tables solve trigonometric formulae to enable us to plot from a location reasonably close to our DR rather than from the geographical position of the celestial body which could be thousands of miles away from our DR. H.O. 229, however, is only one of several methods available to the navigator to solve these formulae. Other publications such as H.O. 214 and H.O. 211 achieve this end by tabular means. Trigonometric tables or a calculator solve the formulae directly. This chapter will explain the use of H.O. 211 while calculator methods will be discussed in a later chapter.

H.O. 211 was devised by Lt. Arthur Ageton (who later became Admiral) and is often referred to as Ageton's Method. The government no longer prints it as a separate volume although they have included it as Table 35 in Volume II of Bowditch's American Practical Navigator. Some private concerns still publish the single booklet and some navigation texts include the tables in their appendices.

There are several advantages of H.O. 211 over other sight reduction tables such as H.O. 229. First of all, the one small booklet covers sight reduction in any location in the world. It takes six reasonably bulky volumes of H.O. 229 to supply the same coverage. The method of entry into the tables and of obtaining the tabular values follows a straightforward set of rules and no knowledge of mathematics is necessary except that of addition and subtraction. Thirdly, the intercept will always be small unless your DR is in great error, your sextant sight is bad or your sight reduction has a mistake in it. Assuming the first two situations are reasonably accurate, it is therefore easy to locate a sight reduction mistake without having to plot the results first. Lastly, all plotting is done from one position, usually a recent DR. This eliminates the need (and clutter!) for plotting a separate AP for each sight. An alternative to using the DR is to pick a convenient spot on your plotting sheet such as the center. This will make your intercepts slightly larger but the advantageous simplicity of locating the plotting point is obvious.

For those wishing to improve their skill with the sextant, H.O. 211 provides a convenient way to numerically check your accuracy without plotting. If the coordinates of the sight location are known exactly and the sight reduction is done without error, the amount of the intercept will be the error in your sextant sight (assuming index correction, dip and main correction are evaluated correctly). The sight reduction can even be worked ahead of time for an almost "instant" check on sextant sight accuracy.

The disadvantages of H.O. 211 stem mainly around human tendencies to make simple addition and subtraction mistakes and to miscopy numbers. There are several entries into the tables and four instances where numbers from one to six digits are combined. Use of a four function calculator is of help but this adds further the possibility of human mispunching. Sight reduction by H.O. 211 takes longer than by H.O. 229 also, unless the navigator has practiced on a few hundred sights - recently.

The most frustrating disadvantage of H.O. 211 is the difficulty in spotting an error in sight reduction until $H_c$ is obtained, the next to the last step of the procedure. The one to six digit tabular values are log secants and log cosecants multiplied by 100,000. They bear no obvious relationship to the entry values as far as discovering an entry mistake is concerned. The best way to overcome this disadvantage is to double check every entry and numerical combination as it is made.

No effort will be made here to derive the formulae used in Ageton's Method. Suffice it to say that H.O. 211 solves the spherical triangle by dividing it into two right triangles. The designations, R, K and K ~ L refer to constructed parts of these triangles.

Each of the 36 pages of H.O. 211 is divided into five major columns headed and footed by boldface whole and whole-plus-half degree numbers. Additional minutes and half minutes are in narrow columns at the extreme left and right sides of the page. The major columns are further halved into subcolumns entitled A and B. Numbers in the B column are also in boldface type. Two simple rules we will discuss later are at the top of the pages of each book opening.

The procedure involved in sight reduction by H.O. 211 can be divided into twenty steps. They will be listed below with elaborations as needed. References will be made to the two worked fixes that follow: Jupiter and Venus in Fix 1 and Miaplacidus, Regulus and Sirius in Fix 2.

1. Obtain GHA and Dec of body, $H_o$ and DR position just as done for H.O. 229.

2. Get LHA Body (0° to 360°) by subtracting a west DR longitude from GHA body or adding an east DR longitude to GHA body.

   The DR chosen here should be for a time reasonably close to the time period during which sights are taken. For ease of plotting, this point may be a convenient crossing of a parallel and meridian on your plotting sheet or chart. Just remember that the end results of your sight reduction will be plotted from the point that you choose now.

3. Convert LHA to "t" (0° to 180°, E or W). If LHA is less than 180°, t = LHA. If LHA is greater than 180°, t = 360° - LHA.

   A diagram is provided on the sight reduction forms to do this conversion visually. The meridian angle "t" is measured from the observer's meridian east or west to the hour circle through the celestial body, whichever way gives the smallest angle.

Example: Venus, Fix 1. GHA = 321° 19!6, DR Lo = 57° 06!0 W.

In this case, the shortest angle between the DR longitude and Venus' hour circle is measured eastward and is equal to 360° - LHA. Label "t" E.

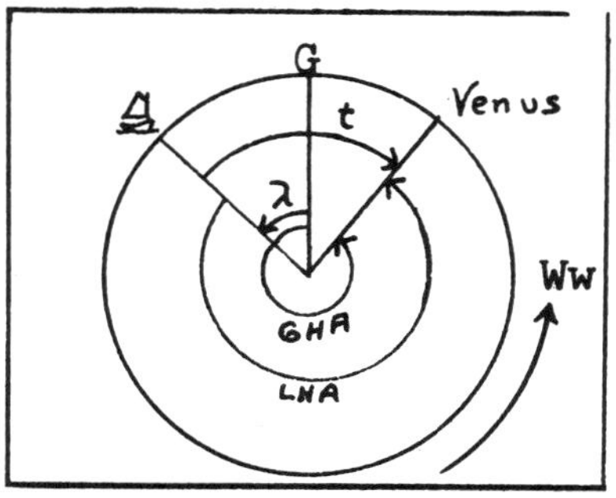


| | | | |
|---|---|---|---|
| GHA Body | 321° | 19!6 | |
| D R Lo | 57° | 06!0 | W |
| 360° | ° | ! | |
| LHA Body | 264° | 13!6 | |
| t (H.A.) | 95° | 46!4 | (E) W |

Example: Miaplacidus, Fix 2. GHA = 264° 43!7, DR Lo = 126° 25!7 E

Longitude is measured east or clockwise on this diagram. LHA is measured westward from the meridian of the ship and happens to be the quickest way to the star's hour circle. Therefore, LHA = t.

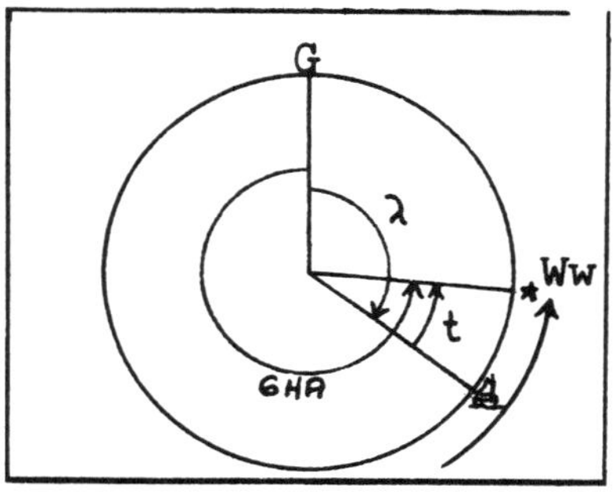


| | | | |
|---|---|---|---|
| GHA Body | 264° | 43!7 | |
| D R Lo | 126° | 25!7 | E |
| 360° | 391° | 09!4 | |
| LHA Body | 31° | 09!4 | |
| t (H.A.) | 31° | 09!4 | E (W) |

4. Bring down Dec, DR Lat and $H_o$ from the top part of the form and enter in corresponding spaces in the lower left hand part of the form.

5. Enter H.O. 211 with "t", extract the A digits and enter them in the first ADD column on the form (hereafter called column 1).

The value "t" may be found at the head or foot of the columns in H.O. 211. Choose the whole or half degree value closest to but less than "t". The difference between this heading and the actual "t" should be found (to the nearest half minute) at the far left if the headings are used or at the far right of the page if the footings are used. Going down or up the column and across this difference will yield an A and B.

Only the A is needed and it should be entered on the first line of column 1 on the form.

6. Enter H.O. 211 with Dec. Body (in the same manner as with "t"), write the B digits on the second line of column 1, the A digits on the first line of the first SUBTRACT column (hereafter called column 2).

7. Add A and B in column 1, obtaining an A for the line designated at the far left as "R".
"R" is of no interest to us so its value will be left blank.

8. Look up the "R" A, get the corresponding B, enter this B in column 2, and repeat the B and A on the same line in the next two columns (hereafter called column 3 and column 4).

9. Subtract B from A in column 2, obtaining a result which we will call "sum A".

10. Get "K" by looking up the second column "sum A", taking "K" from the top of the table if "t" is less than 90°, taking "K" from the bottom of the table if "t" is greater than 90°. Give "K" the same name (N or S) as the Dec. Body.
When taking degrees from the bottom of the table, be sure to use minutes in the column to the far right of the page in H.O. 211.

11. Obtain K~L by adding "K" to "L" ("L" is latitude) if they have different names or subtracting the smaller from the larger if they have the same name.

12. Enter H.O. 211 with K~L, obtaining just the B. Put this value in column 3.

13. Add the two Bs in column 3, obtaining A of column 3.

14. Look up this A of column 3, getting $H_c$ and the corresponding B for column 4.
$H_c$ is always taken from the top of the page since it will never exceed 90°. The proximity of $H_c$ to $H_o$ is your first check on possible sight reduction errors so far.

15. Get "a" by combining $H_c$ and $H_o$, subtracting the smaller from the larger. Label "a" A (away) if $H_c$ is greater than $H_o$. Vice versa for toward (T).

16. Subtract the B in column 4 from the A in column 4, obtaining column 4 "result A".

17. Look up column 4 "result A" to get Z, taking Z from the bottom of the table unless "K" is the same name and greater than "L", in which case take Z from the top of the table.

18. Give Z the label of N or S to correspond to latitude, E or W to correspond to "t".

19. Convert Z to $Z_n$ by using the diagram at the bottom of the form or by the following table.

| Z | $Z_n$ |
|---|---|
| N and E | Z |
| N and W | 360 - Z |
| S and E | 180 - Z |
| S and W | 180 + Z |

Remember that $Z_n$ is always measured from the north eastward. Change the degrees and minutes of Z to degrees and tenths of degrees before converting to $Z_n$.

Example: Jupiter, Fix 1. Latitude N, "t" W.

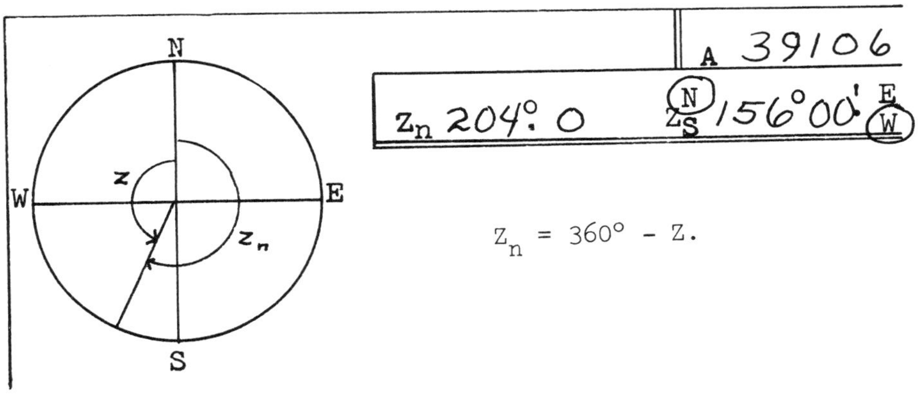


$Z_n$ = 360° - Z.

Example: Venus, Fix 1. Latitude N, "t" E.

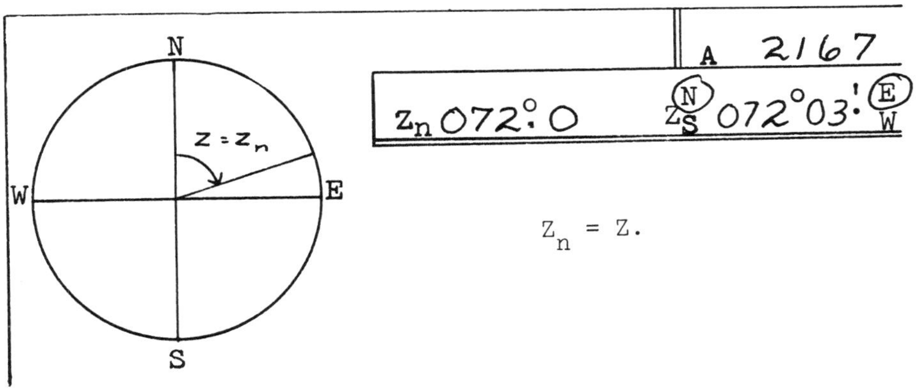


$Z_n$ = Z.

Example: Regulus, Fix 2. Latitude S, "t" W.

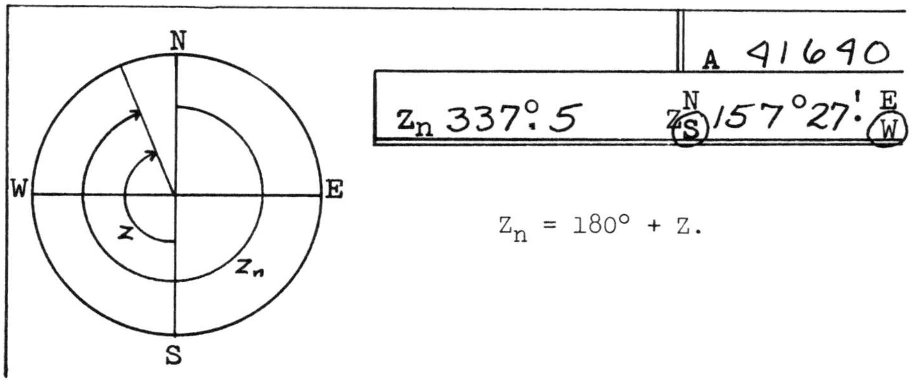


20. Plot the lines of position from your DR (or previously chosen point) using the "a" and $Z_n$. Advance the LOPs when necessary, using the same procedure as with H.O. 229.

The important point to remember here is to plot from the position used in the sight reduction, generally the DR. If two different DRs are used, such as in the case with two Sun lines with quite a time spread where an updated DR is used with the second sight, remember to plot the later sight from the later DR. The line of position of the earlier sight should be advanced along the course line for the amount of run between the two sights.

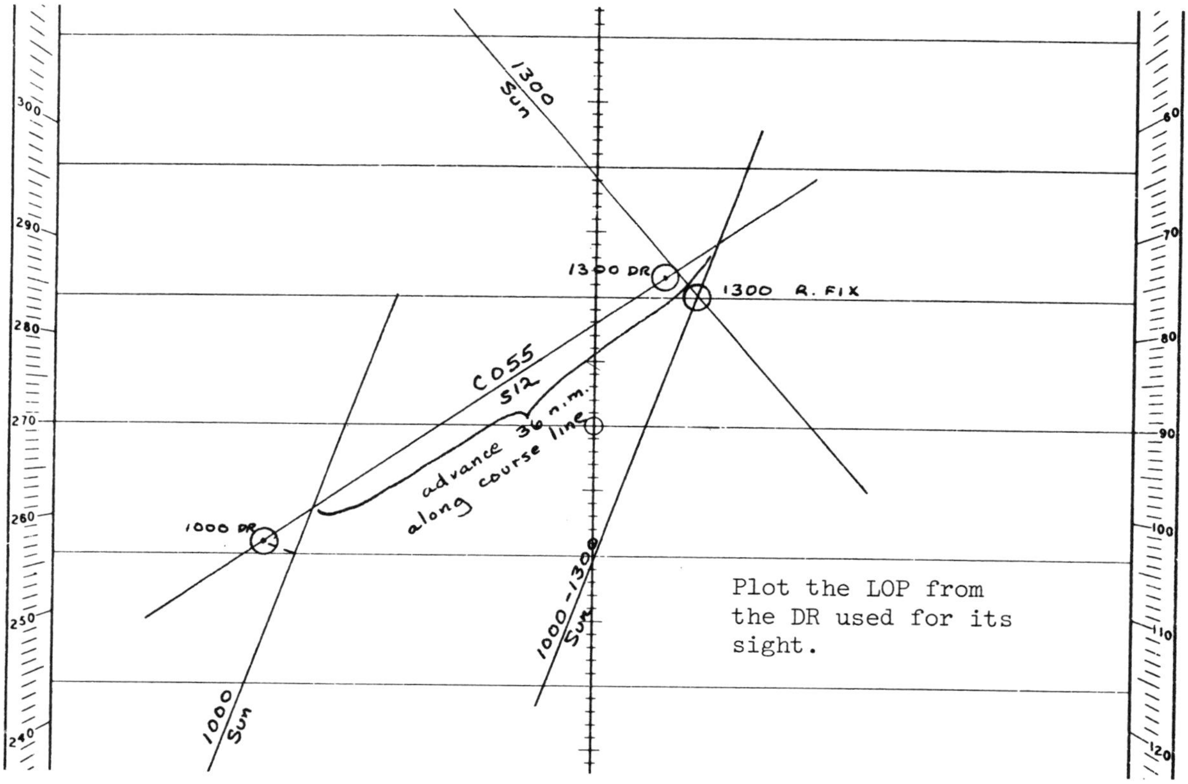

H.O. 211 gives an accuracy of solution to within five-tenths of a minute in altitude and an average error of two-tenths of a minute. Greater accuracy than this can be obtained by interpolating each entry and extraction although the time spent in this endeavor seems hardly worth the negligible difference. Would that the navigator's sextant sight had this guaranteed accuracy!

Two full fixes will follow with notes at different points during the sight reduction. The Venus sight in Fix 1 has references to the sections of H.O. 211 that are used.

A hint: In writing down the tabular values in the four columns on the form, take care to place the decimals, units, tens, hundreds etc. under each other. This helps to eliminate some addition or subtraction errors.

0350 (TIME) Course 040° Speed 15 k

## SIGHT REDUCTION BY H.O. 211

Fix 1

DR: Lat 54° 29′ N Lo 57° 06′ W Ht. of Eye ________ ft.

W.T. 03 h 45 m 17 s

Body Venus

| A | B | ′ |
|---|---|---|
| 222.9 | 99544 | 18 |
| 222.3 | 99606 | |
| 221.6 | 99668 | 17 |
| 221.0 | 99731 | |
| 220.3 | 99793 | 16 |
| 219.7 | 99856 | |
| 219.1 | 99918 | 15 |
| 218.4 | 99981 | |
| 217.8 | 100044 | 14 |
| 217.2 | 100107 | |
| 216.5 | 100170 | 13 |
| 215.9 | 100233 | |
| 205.3 | 101321 | 4 |
| 204.7 | 101386 | |
| 204.1 | 101451 | 3 |
| 203.5 | 101516 | |
| 202.8 | 101581 | 2 |
| 202.2 | 101646 | |
| 201.6 | 101712 | 1 |
| 201.0 | 101777 | |
| 200.4 | 101843 | 0 |
| 95° 30′ | | |

| ′ | 22° 00′ A | B |
|---|---|---|
| 0 | 42642 | 3283 |
| | 42627 | 3286 |
| 1 | 42611 | 3288 |
| | 42596 | 3291 |
| 24 | 41899 | 3407 |
| | 41884 | 3410 |
| 25 | 41869 | 3412 |
| | 41853 | 3415 |
| 26 | 41838 | 3418 |
| | 41823 | 3420 |
| 27 | 41808 | 3423 |
| | 41792 | 3425 |
| 28 | 41777 | 3428 |
| | 41762 | 3431 |
| 29 | 41746 | 3433 |
| | 41731 | 3436 |
| 30 | 41716 | 3438 |
| ′ | A | B |
| | 157° 30′ | |

| A | B | ′ |
|---|---|---|
| 3662 | 40457 | 12 |
| 3659 | 40471 | |
| 3657 | 40486 | 11 |
| 3654 | 40501 | |
| 3651 | 40516 | 10 |
| 3648 | 40530 | |
| 3646 | 40545 | 9 |
| 3643 | 40560 | |
| 3640 | 40575 | 8 |
| 3638 | 40590 | |
| 3635 | 40604 | 7 |
| 3632 | 40619 | |
| 3608 | 40753 | 2 |
| 3605 | 40768 | |
| 3603 | 40782 | 1 |
| 3600 | 40797 | |
| 3597 | 40812 | 0 |
| 113° 00′ | | |

| A | B | ′ |
|---|---|---|
| 1247 | 62659 | 10 |
| 1246 | 62685 | |
| 1244 | 62711 | 9 |
| 1243 | 62737 | |
| 1241 | 62763 | 8 |
| 1240 | 62789 | |
| 1238 | 62815 | 7 |
| 1237 | 62841 | |
| 1235 | 62867 | 6 |
| 1234 | 62893 | |
| 1232 | 62919 | 5 |
| 1230 | 62945 | |
| 1229 | 62971 | 4 |
| 1227 | 62998 | |
| 1226 | 63024 | 3 |
| 1224 | 63050 | |
| 1223 | 63076 | 2 |
| 1221 | 63103 | |
| 1220 | 63129 | 1 |
| 1218 | 63155 | |
| 1217 | 63181 | 0 |
| 103° 30′ | | |

| ′ | 49° 00′ A | B |
|---|---|---|
| 0 | 12222 | 18306 |
| | 12216 | 18313 |
| 1 | 12211 | 18320 |
| | 12205 | 18327 |
| 2 | 12200 | 18335 |
| | 12195 | 18342 |
| 3 | 12189 | 18349 |
| | 12184 | 18357 |
| 4 | 12178 | 18364 |
| | 12173 | 18371 |
| 5 | 12167 | 18378 |
| | 12162 | 18386 |
| 6 | 12156 | 18393 |
| | 12151 | 18400 |
| 7 | 12145 | 18408 |
| | 12140 | 18415 |
| 8 | 12134 | 18422 |
| | 12129 | 18429 |
| 9 | 12123 | 18437 |
| | 12118 | 18444 |
| 10 | 12112 | 18451 |
| | 12107 | 18459 |
| 11 | 12102 | 18466 |
| | 12096 | 18473 |
| 12 | 12091 | 18481 |
| | 12085 | 18488 |
| 13 | 12080 | 18495 |
| | 12074 | 18503 |

| ′ | 14° 30′ A | B |
|---|---|---|
| 0 | 60140 | 1406 |
| | 60116 | 1407 |
| 1 | 60091 | 1409 |
| | 60067 | 1411 |
| 24 | 58984 | 1485 |
| | 58960 | 1487 |
| 25 | 58937 | 1489 |
| | 58913 | 1490 |
| 26 | 58889 | 1492 |
| | 58866 | 1494 |
| 27 | 58842 | 1495 |
| | 58818 | 1497 |
| 28 | 58795 | 1499 |
| | 58771 | 1500 |
| 29 | 58748 | 1502 |
| | 58724 | 1504 |
| 30 | 58700 | 1506 |
| ′ | A | B |
| | 165° 00′ | |

| ′ | 72° 00′ A | B |
|---|---|---|
| 0 | 2179 | 51002 |
| | 2177 | 51021 |
| 1 | 2175 | 51041 |
| | 2173 | 51060 |
| 2 | 2171 | 51080 |
| | 2169 | 51099 |
| 3 | 2167 | 51119 |
| | 2165 | 51138 |

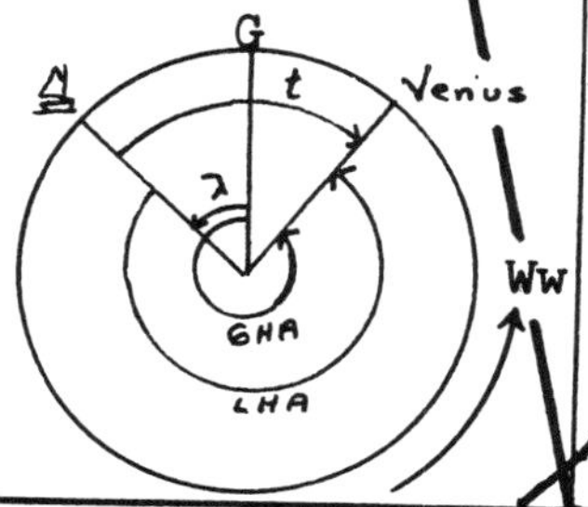


GHA Body 321° 19.6′

D R Lo 57° 06.0′ W

——360°

LHA Body 264° 13.6′

t (H.A.) 95° 46.4′ E/W

Dec. Body 22° 28.9′ N/S

R

K 103° 39.0′ N/S

DR Lat 54° 29.0′ N/S

(K~L) 49° 10.0′

$H_c$ 14° 54.5′

$H_o$ 14° 56.5′

a T/A 2.0 mi

$H_o > H_c$ so Towards

| ADD COLUMN 1 | SUBTRACT COLUMN 2 | ADD COLUMN 3 | SUBTRACT AZIMUTH COLUMN 4 |
|---|---|---|---|
| A 221.0 | | | |
| B 3433 | A 41746 | | |
| A 3654.0 | B 40501 | B 40501 | A 3654 |
| | A 1245 | | |
| | | B 18451 | |
| | | A 58952 | B 1487 |
| | | | A 2167 |

"t" is greater than 90°, take K from bottom of table

K and L same name so K ~ L = K − L

$Z_n$ 072.0°  Z N/S 072° 03′ E/W

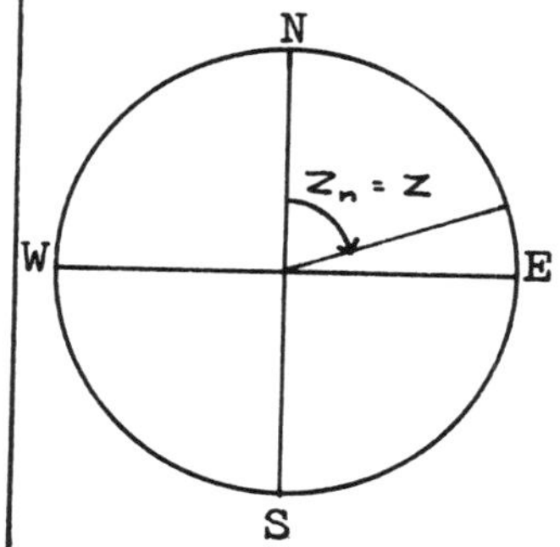


K is same name and greater than latitude so take Z from top of table

Fix 1

0350
(TIME)

SIGHT REDUCTION BY H.O. 211

DR: Lat 54° 29' N    Lo 57° 06' W    Ht. of Eye ______ ft.

| | | | |
|---|---|---|---|
| W.T. 03 h 50 m 00 s | Date ______ slow - add, fast - sub | Body | Jupiter |
| W.E. h m s | | $H_s$ | ° ' |
| Z.T. h m s | | I.C. | ' |
| Z.D. h | | | ° ' |
| G.M.T. h m s | Date (Grnch) ______ | Dip | ' |
| | | | ° ' |
| | | Temp. Press. | ' |
| | | App. Alt. | ° ' |
| | | Main | ' |
| | | $H_o$ | 26° 31'.2 |

FROM NAUTICAL ALMANAC

| | ° | ' |
|---|---|---|
| SHA ✲ | | |
| GHA h | | |
| m s | | |
| v ____ corr | | |
| ____ 360° | | |
| GHA Body | 78° | 34'.2 |
| D R Lo | 57° | 06'.0 |
| ____ 360° | | |
| LHA Body | 21° | 28'.2 |
| t (H.A.) | 21° | 28'.2 E (W) |
| Dec. Body | 6° | 25'.2 N (S) |
| R | | |
| K | 6° | 53'.5 N (S) |
| DR Lat | 54° | 29'.0 (N) S |
| (K~L) | 61° | 22'.5 |
| $H_c$ | 26° | 30'.5 |
| $H_o$ | 26° | 31'.2 |
| a (T) A | | 0.7 mi |

$H_o > H_c$ so Towards

| | |
|---|---|
| Dec | ° ' |
| d ____ corr | ' |
| Dec. Body | S 6° 25'.2 |

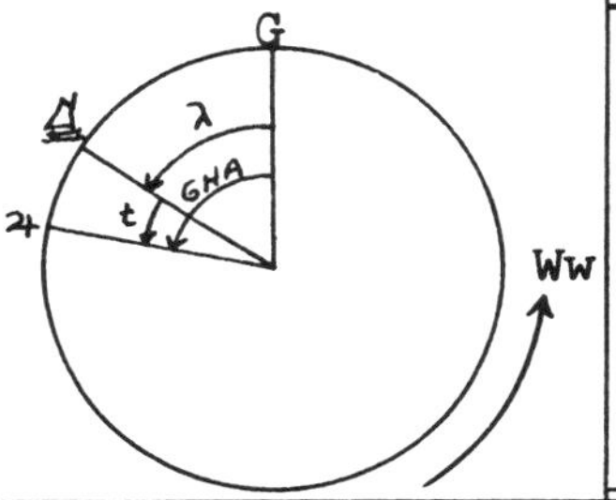


| H.P. | ' | MOON |
|---|---|---|
| Corr | + | ' |
| Corr | + | ' |
| Upper Limb | -30' - | |
| Main | ± | ' |

| ADD COLUMN 1 | SUBTRACT COLUMN 2 | ADD COLUMN 3 | SUBTRACT AZIMUTH COLUMN 4 |
|---|---|---|---|
| A 43657 | | | |
| B 273 | A 95172 | | |
| A 43930 | B 3080 | B 3080 | A 43930 |
| | A 92092 | | |
| | | B 31960 | |
| | | A 35040 | B 4824 |
| | | | A 39106 |

K takes same name as declination

K and L are different names so K~L = K+L

$Z_n$ 204°.0    (N) Z S 156° 00' E (W)

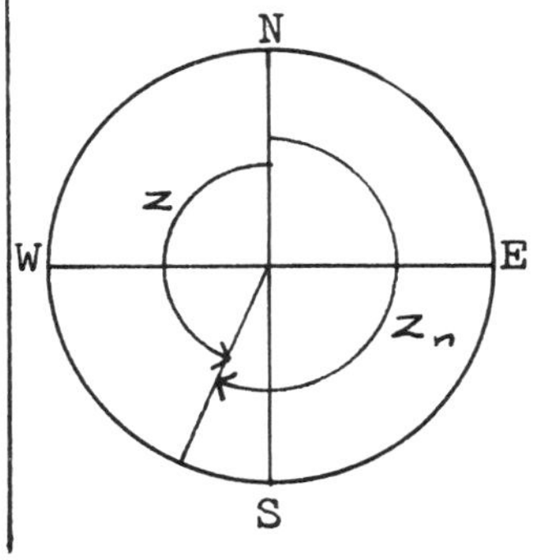


$Z_n = 360 - Z$

Fix 1

Both the 0345 Venus and the 0350 Jupiter LOPs are plotted from the 0350 DR. The 0345 Venus is advanced 1.3 n.m. along the course line.

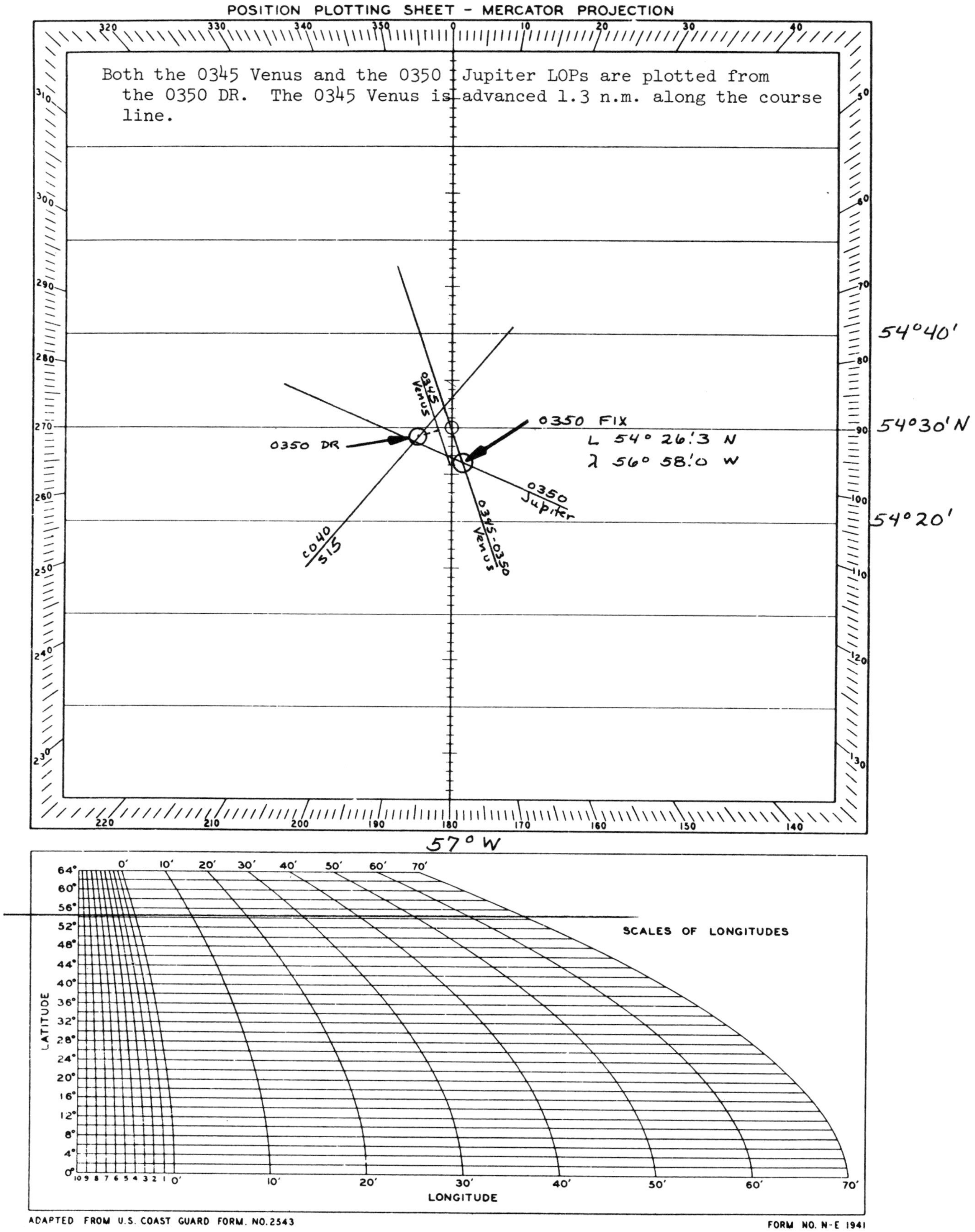

Course 180°

1708 Speed 30 k SIGHT REDUCTION BY H.O. 211 Fix 2

(TIME)

DR: Lat 41° 14!6 S Lo 126° 25!7 E Ht. of Eye ______ ft.

W.T. 16h 59m 02s Date ______ Body Miaplacidus

W.E. h m s slow - add fast - sub $H_s$ ° '

Z.T. h m s I.C. '

Z.D. h ° '

G.M.T. h m s Date (Grnch) ______ Dip '

FROM NAUTICAL ALMANAC

° ' Temp. Press. '

App. Alt. ° '

SHA ✲ ° ' Dec ° '

GHA h ° ' d ___ corr ' Main '

m s ° ' Dec. Body 69° 37!1 S $H_o$ 57° 13!4

v ___ corr '

H.P. ___ ' ___ MOON

360° ° ' Corr + '

GHA Body 264° 43!7 Corr + '

D R Lo 126° 25!7 E Upper Limb -30' -

360° 391° 09!4 Main ± '

LHA Body 31° 09!4

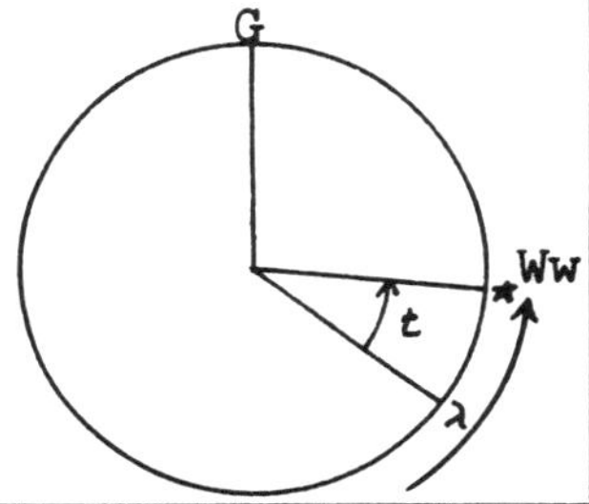


| | | | |
|---|---|---|---|
| t (H.A.) 31° 09!4 (E/W: W) | | | |

| | ADD | SUBTRACT | ADD | SUBTRACT AZIMUTH |
|---|---|---|---|---|
| t (H.A.) 31° 09!4 W | A 28617 | | | |
| Dec. Body 69° 37!1 S | B 45805 | A 2808 | | |
| R | A 74422 | B 717 | B 717 | A 74422 |
| K 72° 22!0 S | | A 2091 | | |
| DR Lat 41° 14!6 S | | | | |
| (K~L) 31° 07!4 | | | B 6750 | |
| $H_c$ 57° 21!5 | | | A 7467 | B 26810 |
| $H_o$ 57° 13!4 | | | | A 47612 |
| a (T/A: A) 8.1 mi | | | | |

$Z_n$ 199°.5 Z (N/S: S) 19° 31!.  (E/W: W)

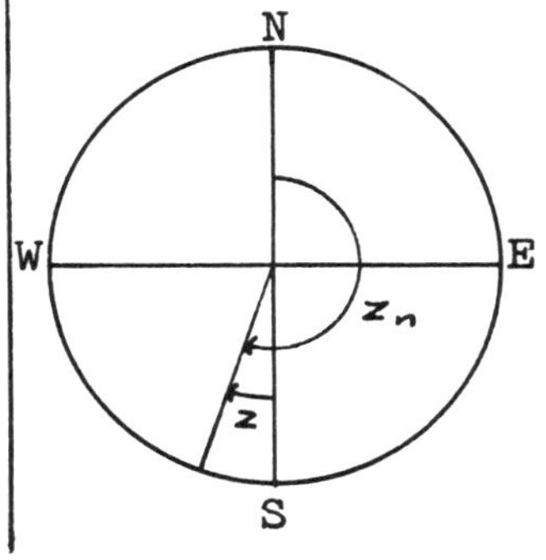

1708
(TIME)

Fix 2

# SIGHT REDUCTION BY H.O. 211

DR: Lat 41° 14'.6 S Lo 126° 25'.7 E Ht. of Eye ______ ft.

W.T. 17h 04m 30s
W.E. h m s
Z.T. h m s
Z.D. h
G.M.T. h m s

Date ______
slow - add
fast - sub

Date ______
(Grnch)

Body Regulus
$H_s$ ° '
I.C.
° '
Dip
° '
Temp.
Press.
App. Alt. ° '
Main
$H_o$ 33° 58'.1

H.P. ' MOON
Corr +
Corr +
Upper Limb -30' -
Main ±

## FROM NAUTICAL ALMANAC

SHA * ° '
GHA h ° '
m s ° '
v ___ corr ___
—360° ° '
GHA Body 252° 34'.1
D R Lo 126° 25'.7 E
—360° 378° 59'.8
LHA Body 18° 59'.8
t (H.A.) 18° 59'.8 E (W)

Dec ° '
d ___ corr ___
Dec. Body 12° 05'.5 N

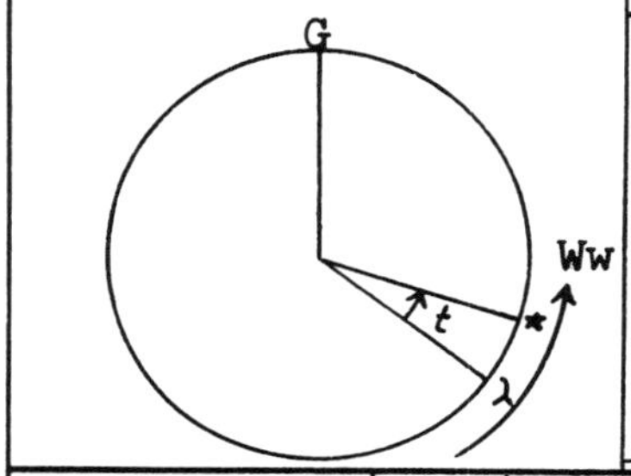


Dec. Body 12° 05'.5 (N) S
R
K 12° 46'.0 (N) S
DR Lat 41° 14'.6 N (S)
(K~L) 54° 00'.6
$H_c$ 33° 51'.5
$H_o$ 33° 58'.1
a (T) A 6.6 mi

| ADD | SUBTRACT | ADD | SUBTRACT AZIMUTH |
|---|---|---|---|
| A 48736 | | | |
| B 974 | A 67886 | | |
| A 49710 | B 2321 | B 2321 | A 49710 |
| | A 65565 | | |
| | | B 23087 | |
| | | A 25408 | B 8070 |
| | | | A 41640 |

$Z_n$ 337°.5  Z N (S) 157° 27' E (W)

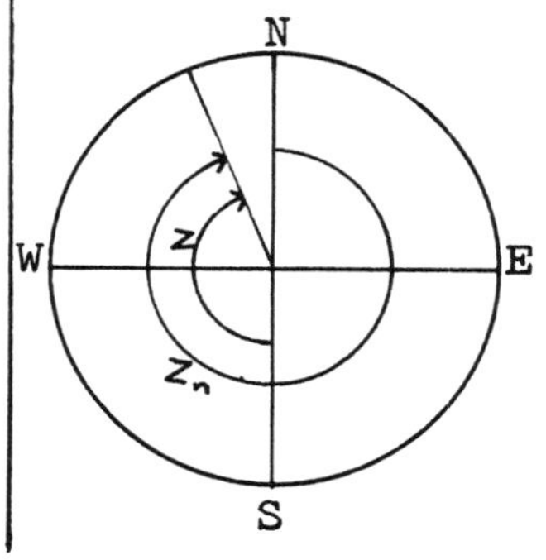

Fix 2

1708
(TIME)

SIGHT REDUCTION BY H.O. 211

DR: Lat 41° 14'.6 S    Lo 126° 25'.7 E    Ht. of Eye ______ ft.

| | | | |
|---|---|---|---|
| W.T. | 17 h 10 m 10 s | Date | |
| W.E. | h m s | slow - add / fast - sub | |
| Z.T. | h m s | | |
| Z.D. | h | | |
| G.M.T. | h m s | Date (Grnch) | |

| | |
|---|---|
| Body | Sirius |
| $H_s$ | ° ' |
| I.C. | ' |
| | ° ' |
| Dip | ' |
| | ° ' |
| Temp. Press. | ' |
| App. Alt. | ° ' |
| Main | ' |
| $H_o$ | 24° 57'.6 |

| | |
|---|---|
| H.P. | ' MOON |
| Corr | + ' |
| Corr | + ' |
| Upper Limb | -30' - |
| Main | ± ' |

FROM NAUTICAL ALMANAC

| | |
|---|---|
| SHA * | ° ' |
| GHA h | ° ' |
| m s | ° ' |
| v corr | ' |
| —360° | ° ' |
| GHA Body | 304° 44'.4 |
| D R Lo | 126° 25'.7 E |
| —360° | 431° 10'.1 |
| LHA Body | 71° 10'.1 |
| t (H.A.) | 71° 10'.1 E (W) |
| Dec. Body | 16° 40'.9 N (S) |
| R | |
| K | 42° 52'.5 N (S) |
| DR Lat | 41° 14'.6 N (S) |
| (K~L) | 1° 37'.9 |
| $H_c$ | 24° 57'.0 |
| $H_o$ | 24° 57'.6 |
| a | (T) A 0.6 mi |

| | |
|---|---|
| Dec | ° ' |
| d corr | ' |
| Dec. Body | 16° 40'.9 S |

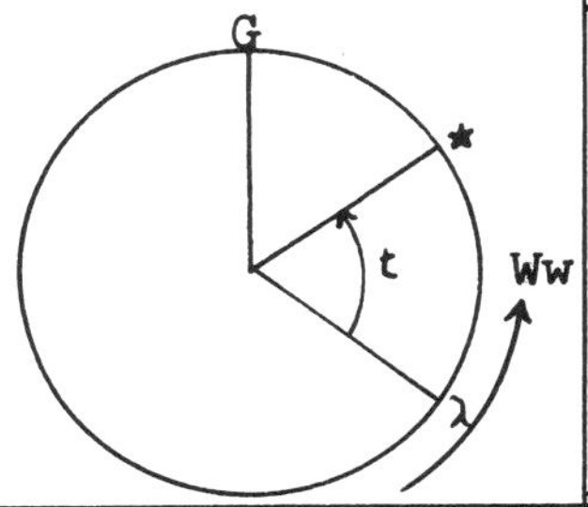


| ADD | SUBTRACT | ADD | SUBTRACT AZIMUTH |
|---|---|---|---|
| A 2390 | | | |
| B 1868 | A 54199 | | |
| A 4258 | B 37473 | B 37473 | A 4258 |
| | A 16726 | | |
| | | B 17.6 | |
| | | A 37490.6 | B 4255 |
| | | | A 0003 |

$Z_n$ 269°.3    Z N (S) 89° 19'. E (W)

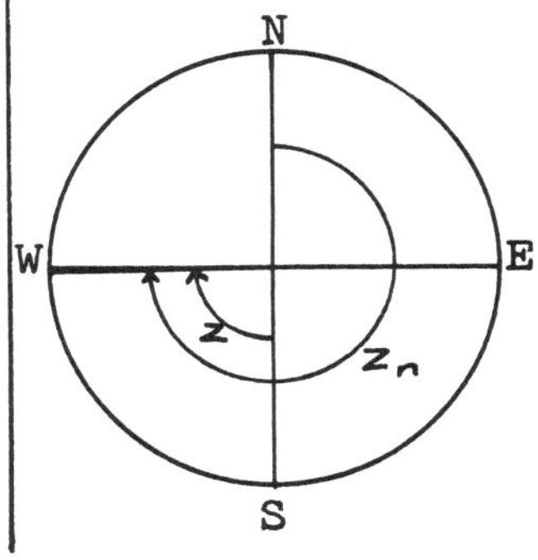

Fix 2

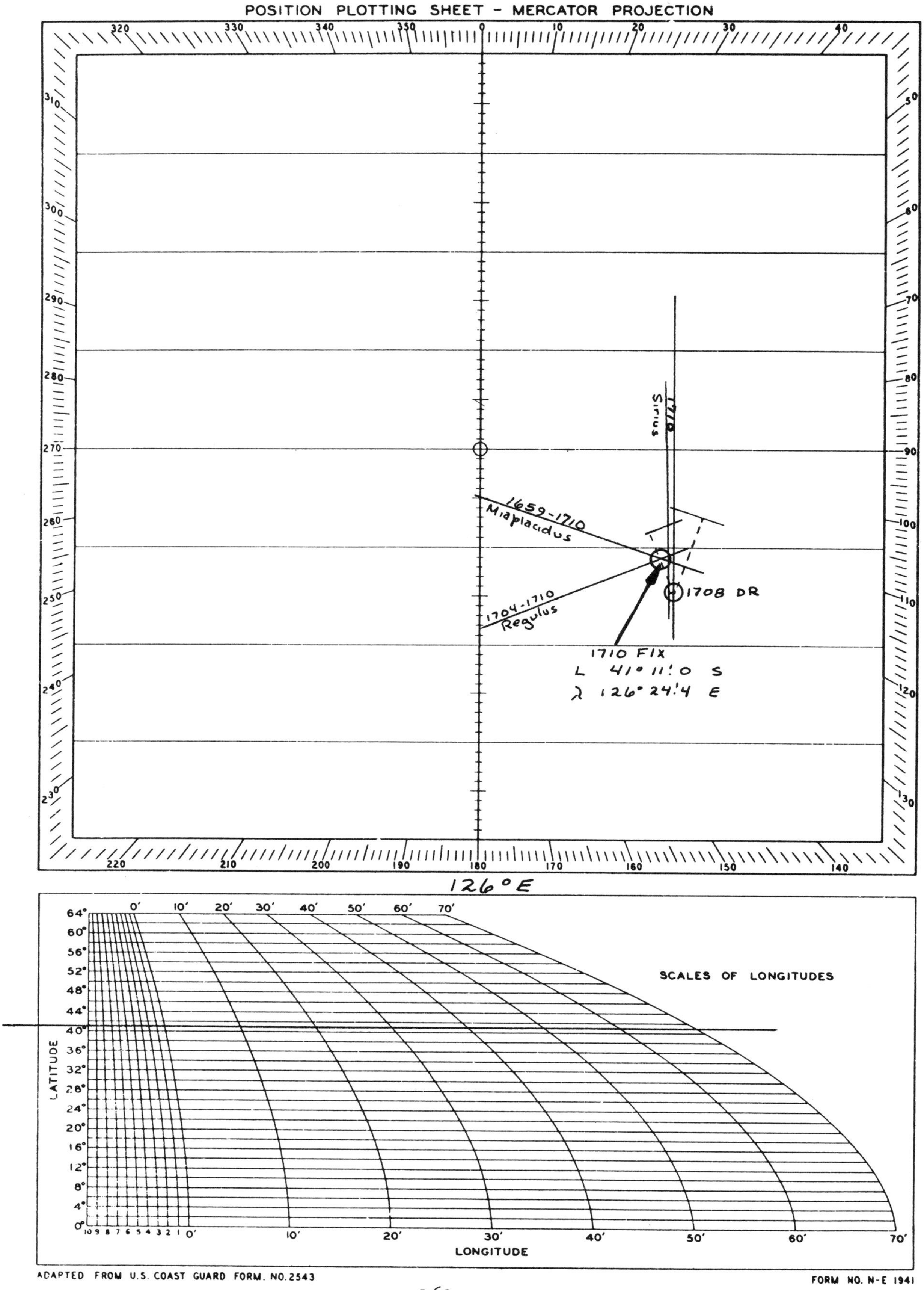
POSITION PLOTTING SHEET - MERCATOR PROJECTION
40°50'
41°S
41°10'
1710 Sirius
1659-1710 Miaplacidus
1704-1710 Regulus
1708 DR
1710 FIX
L 41° 11!0 S
λ 126° 24!4 E
126°E
SCALES OF LONGITUDES
LATITUDE
LONGITUDE
ADAPTED FROM U.S. COAST GUARD FORM. NO. 2543
FORM NO. N-E 1941

# EXERCISE 12

1. Reduce the sights of the voyages on the Lecky and Bowditch in Exercise 11 by H.O. 211. Plot each line of position and each fix, comparing the results with those obtained by H.O. 229.

2. Plot the following fixes using H.O. 211 to reduce the sights.

   a) 0521 Fix (0520 DR is given)

| Body | Rasalhague | Mars | Moon |
|---|---|---|---|
| Z.T. | 04-39-59 | 05-00-01 | 05-20-41 |
| $H_o$ | 63° 51!3 | 21° 39!4 | 14° 40!0 |
| DR Lat | 38° 41!2 N | same | same |
| DR Long | 70° 00!8 W | | |
| Course | 250° | same | same |
| Speed | 6 knots | | |
| GHA | 71° 15!9 | 393° 12!0 | 360° 39!3 |
| Dec | 12° 34!5 N | 20° 16!9 S | 1° 54!4 S |

   b) 0519 Fix (0500 DR is given)

| Body | Diphda | Acrux | Saturn |
|---|---|---|---|
| Z.T. | 04-48-06 | 05-07-10 | 05-18-54 |
| $H_o$ | 21° 47!8 | 31° 53!4 | 27° 52!3 |
| DR Lat | 38° 40!0 S | same | same |
| DR Long | 141° 10!0 W | | |
| Course | 152° | same | same |
| Speed | 15 knots | | |
| GHA | 217° 15!1 | 46° 19!9 | 125° 31!4 |
| Dec | 18° 07!3 S | 62° 57!5 S | 21° 40!2 N |

# Chapter 15

# The Navigational Triangle

In Chapter 2, the basic theory of celestial lighthouses was discussed and brief mention was made of using sight reduction tables to enable plotting to be done on small charts rather than huge globes. In following chapters two specific means, H.O. 229 and H.O. 211, were employed to achieve these ends, plotting from an intermediate position near the ship's real position. These sight reduction tables are methods of solving a spherical triangle to find the altitude and azimuth of a celestial body from that intermediate position (AP or DR). If we are sufficiently close to the intermediate position, the azimuth of the body there will be the same as for our real position. The difference in altitudes is the plotted intercept, "a".

The purpose of this chapter is to set up the navigational triangle for the intermediate position. This will be a spherical triangle so will operate under laws of spherical trigonometry. Formulae can be derived to solve for $H_c$ and $Z_n$, parts of the triangle.

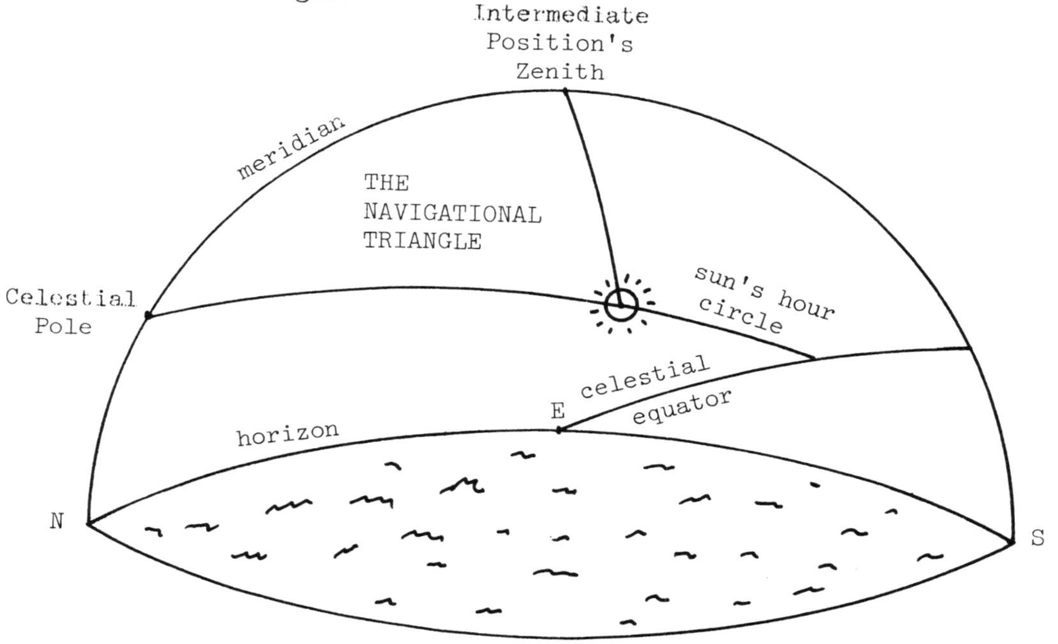

We will first look at the triangle from the earth's surface. In the diagram on the previous page, the horizon, the zenith and meridian of the intermediate position, the celestial pole, the celestial equator and the celestial body (the Sun in this case) and its hour circle are placed. The navigational triangle's sides will run through the elevated pole (north pole in this case), the zenith and the Sun. The next task is to ascertain the parts of the triangle.

We know that the altitude of the pole is equal to the intermediate position's latitude. The angle from the horizon to the zenith is 90°. Therefore, one side of the triangle is equal to 90° minus latitude or colatitude.

We know that the angle between the Sun and the equator is the Sun's declination. Between the equator and the pole is 90°. Therefore, a second side of the triangle is 90° minus declination or codeclination.

The angle at the pole is the angle between the intermediate position's meridian and the hour circle through the Sun. We have referred to this as LHA or "t" and have obtained it by combining longitude with GHA of the Sun. We have thus found two sides of the triangle and an included angle. With this information, the rest of the parts of the triangle can be found.

Inputs thus far are:

1. Latitude, either that of the AP or the DR
2. Declination of the Sun, found from the <u>Nautical Almanac</u>
3. LHA or "t", found by combining GHA Sun and AP or DR longitude

These are exactly the same inputs used for entering H.O. 229 or H.O. 211.

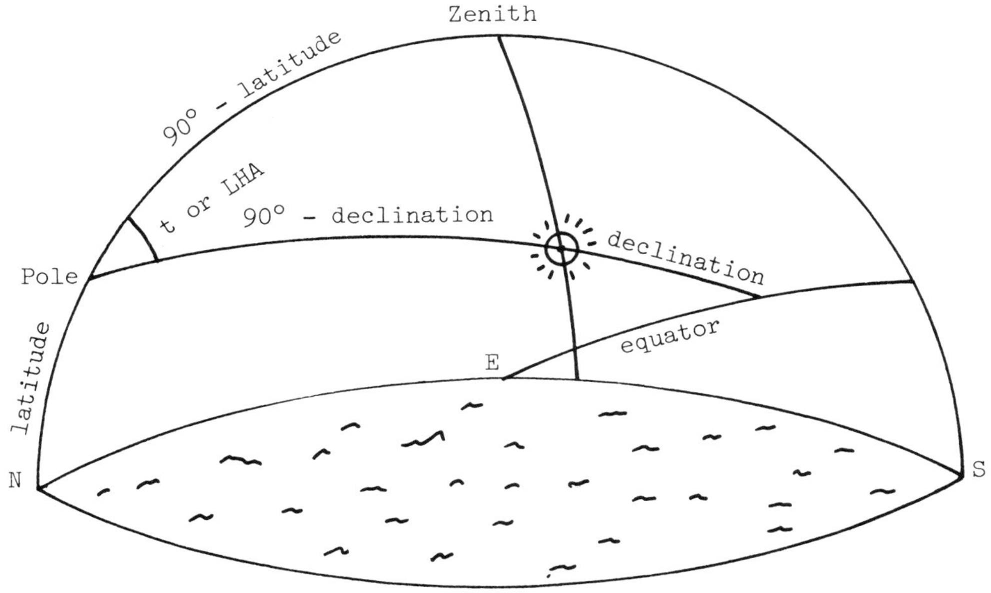

Parts of the triangle we wish to solve for are the third side and one other angle. The altitude of the Sun at the intermediate position is known as $H_c$. This is measured from the horizon to the Sun. From the horizon to the zenith is 90°. Therefore, the angle between the zenith and the Sun must be 90° - $H_c$. Actually, we only wish $H_c$ so the sight reduction tables convert for us.

The angle we wish is the azimuth or bearing of the Sun. This is designated as Z and is later converted to $Z_n$. Z is the angle between the meridian of the intermediate position and the vertical circle through the Sun.

Sight reduction tables provide results as follows:

1. $H_c$ for the intermediate position, compared with $H_o$ to get "a"
2. Z which is then converted to $Z_n$

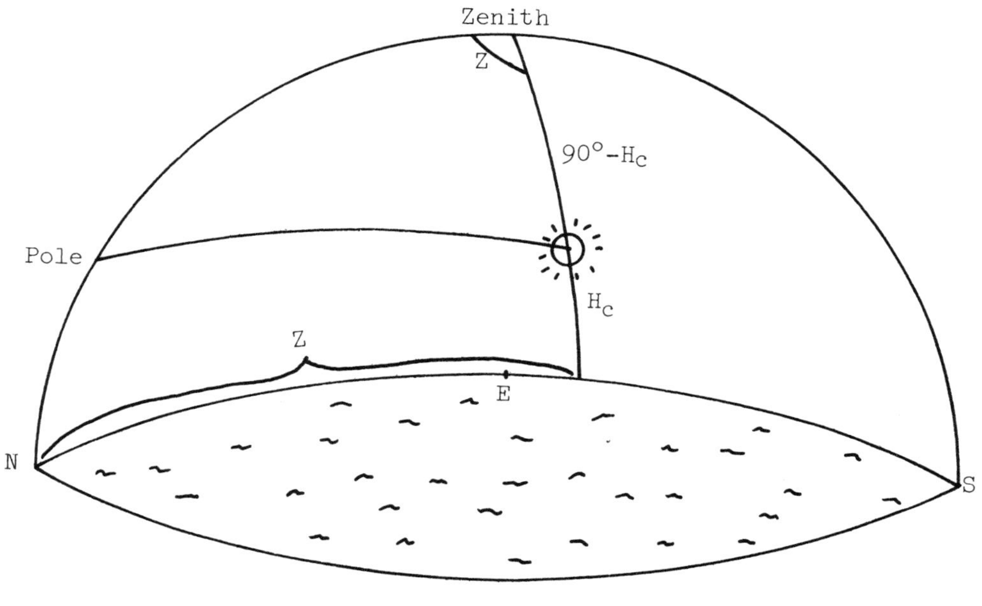

We can project this triangle to the surface of the earth and be a space traveler looking in. By placing the intermediate position's horizon on the diagram also, $H_c$ and $Z_n$ can be shown. The parts of the triangle are the same as discussed on the previous page.

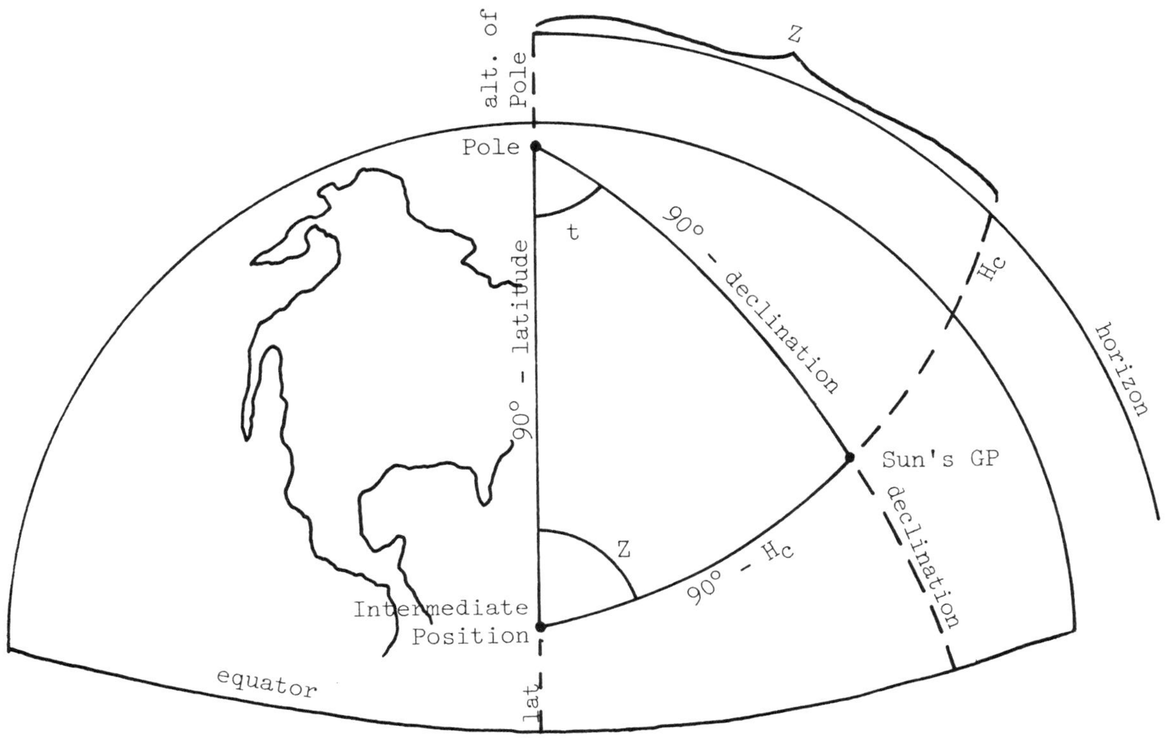


There are many ways, trigonometrically, to solve such a triangle with the information at hand. Some formulae will be explored in Chapter 19 when calculator methods are discussed. Trigonometric tables may be used, of course, in place of calculators. Derivation of these formulae will be left to the mathematics buff. However, one further note is in order.

When Lt. Ageton devised H.O. 211, he based it on the premise that a right triangle was simpler to solve than other types. Therefore, he divided the navigational triangle into two right triangles with construction line "R" through the Sun's GP and perpendicular to the observer's meridian. "K" was the arc between the equator and the point where "R" intersected the meridian. In the case drawn, K ~ L is equal to K - L. The tabular values in H.O. 211 are log cosecants and log secants (multiplied by 100,000) of the various angles in the two triangles.

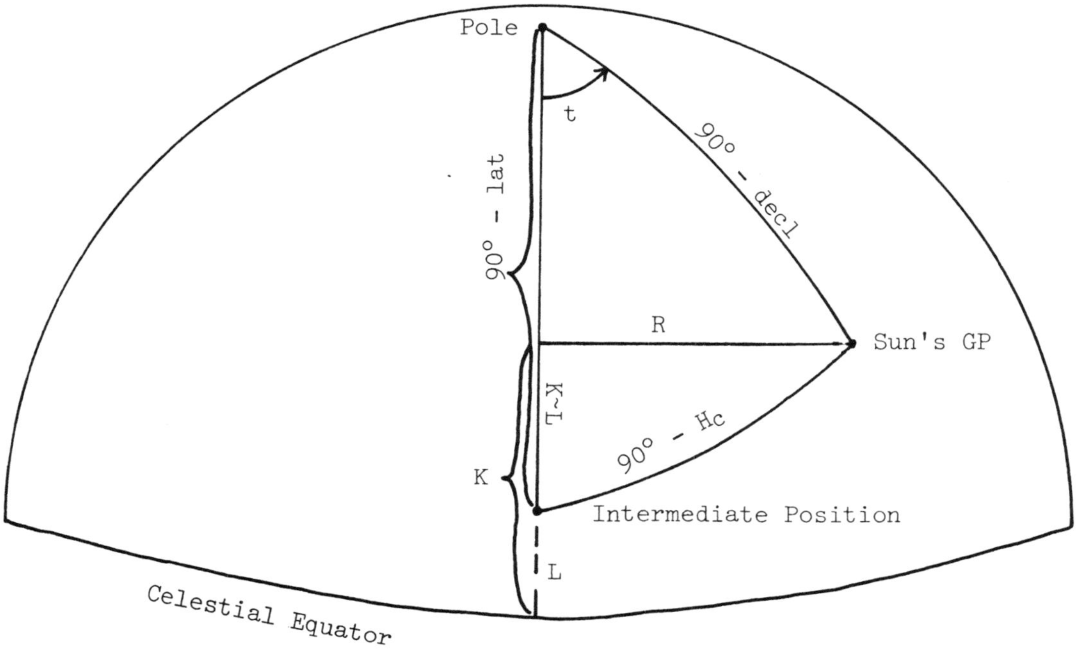

Pole
t
90° - decl
90° - lat
R
Sun's GP
K~L
90° - Hc
K
Intermediate Position
L
Celestial Equator

# Chapter 16

# Construction of Mercator Projection Plotting Sheets

There are many and varied types of plotting sheets on the market now, most of the commonly used kinds employing the Mercator projection. However, it is a fairly simple task to construct one of your own to conform to your cruise parameters or your chart table size. Table 5 from Bowditch, a ruler (metric or not), and a piece of blank paper of the size desired are all that is necessary. The cost is minimal compared to purchasing printed sheets.

The advantage of constructing a Mercator projection grid is that all parallels and meridians are straight lines intersecting at 90° angles. On the earth of course, these lines are circles but for a small area, the straight line approximation is adequate. Courses or rhumblines are straight lines, crossing each meridian at the same angle. Great circle tracks are curved lines. We will discuss this more later. For short distances, rhumblines give sufficient accuracy.

The primary task in constructing a Mercator grid is to figure the ratio between one degree of latitude and one degree of longitude at that particular latitude. Table 5 will do this for us.

Assume that we wish to construct a Mercator projection grid with latitude limits of 45° N to 50° N spread over ten inches. We will keep the longitude units constant and vary the latitude scale as most charts do. Entering Table 5 with our latitude limits (45° to 50°) we find the corresponding meridional parts.

**TABLE 5**

Meridional Parts

| 44° | 45° | 46° | 47° | 48° | 49° | Lat. |
|---|---|---|---|---|---|---|
| | | | | | | ′ |
| 2929. 6 | 3013. 5 | 3098. 8 | 3185. 7 | 3274. 2 | 3364. 5 | 0 |
| 31. 0 | 14. 9 | 3100. 2 | 87. 1 | 75. 7 | 66. 0 | 1 |
| 32. 4 | 16. 3 | 01. 7 | 88. 6 | 77. 2 | 67. 5 | 2 |

50° yields 3456.6
45° yields 3013.5

diff. 443.1

$10 \div 443.1 = 0.02257$

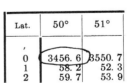

| Lat. | 50° | 51° |
|---|---|---|
| ′ | | |
| 0 | 3456. 6 | 3550. 7 |
| 1 | 58. 2 | 52. 3 |
| 2 | 59. 7 | 53. 9 |

Divide this difference (443.1) into the number of inches you are alloting for latitude coverage (10"). This division will yield .02257 which will be the length of one minute of longitude.

$$1^\circ \text{ of longitude} = 0.02257 \times 60 = 1.354 \text{ inches}$$

Each degree of longitude therefore will be about 1.4 inches wide. Meridians can be drawn this distance apart to the extent that the width of your paper will allow. For better accuracy, space all meridians from an origin, using multiples of 1.354 (2.708, 4.062, 5.416, 6.770, 8.124 etc.)

To find the varying distances between parallels, extract from Table 5 the meridional parts for each degree of latitude and subtract from these figures the meridional parts corresponding to the base latitude of 45°. Multiply these differences by 0.02257 to get the distance in inches between the 45° parallel and the parallels above it.

| | | | |
|---|---|---|---|
| 46° yields 3098.8 | 47° yields 3185.7 | 48° yields 3274.2 | 49° yields 3364.5 |
| 45° 3013.5 | 3013.5 | 3013.5 | 3013.5 |
| 85.3 | 172.2 | 260.7 | 351.0 |
| x .02257 = 1.93" | x .02257 = 3.89" | x .02257 = 5.88" | x .02257 = 7.92" |

The 50° parallel will of course be 10" from the 45° parallel. The degrees can be subdivided into 60 minutes and a compass rose can either be drawn in or cut from a chart or old plotting sheet and pasted on, aligning true north and south with the meridians.

In our second example, we will work with south latitude but the procedure is the same. Remember to increase latitude by going down on the paper.

Construct a Mercator projection grid with latitude limits 20° S to 26° S fit into twenty inches. Make the sheet sixteen inches wide, fitting as much longitude coverage as possible.

26° yields 1606.3
20° yields 1217.2

diff. 389.1 divided into 20" = 0.0514 = 1' of longitude
1° of longitude = 60 x .0514 = 3.084"

From the origin, meridians will be drawn at 3.084", 6.168", 9.252", 12.336" and 15.42"

Parallels will be spaced as follows, working down from 20° S. Remember that 26° to 20° will be 20" apart.

25° yields 1540.2 Difference = 323.0 x .0514 = 16.60"
20° 1217.2

24° yields 1474.6 Difference = 257.4 x .0514 = 13.23"
20° 1217.2

23° yields 1409.5 Difference = 192.3 x .0514 = 9.88"
20° 1217.2

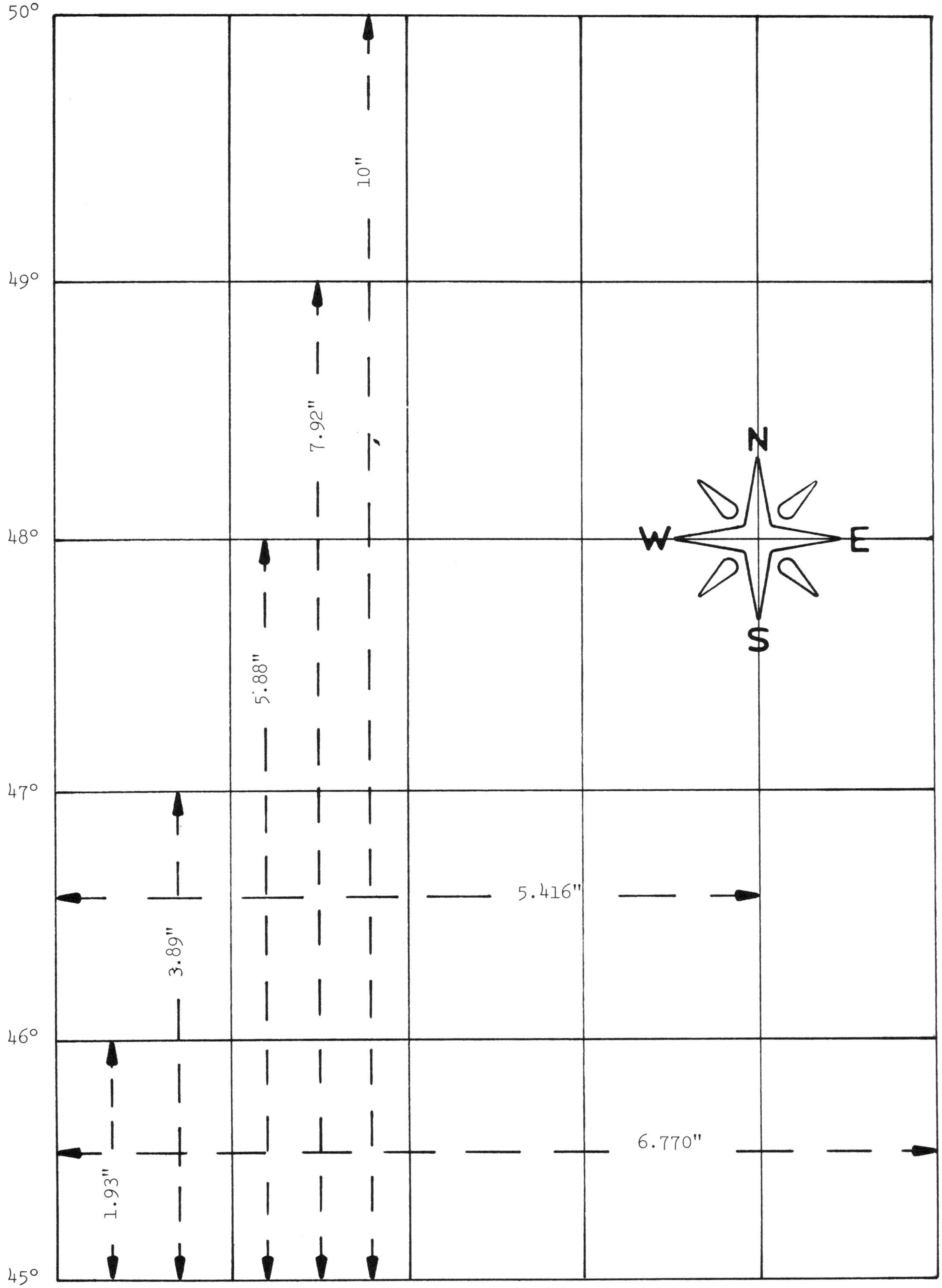
50°
49°
48°
47°
46°
45°
10"
7.92"
5.88"
3.89"
1.93"
5.416"
6.770"
N
W
E
S

22° yields 1345.0    Difference = 127.8 x .0514 = 6.57"
20°    1217.2

21° yields 1280.9    Difference = 63.7 x .0514 = 3.27"
20°    1217.2

Notice that the distance between each parallel does not change a great amount. The largest distance is 3.4" between 26° and 25°. Between 21° and 20° is 3.27", only a tenth of an inch different from the largest span. For latitudes near the equator the change will be minimal whereas near the poles, the difference between parallels five degrees apart will have a considerable variation. Near the poles a Mercator projection is not practical and other methods are used.

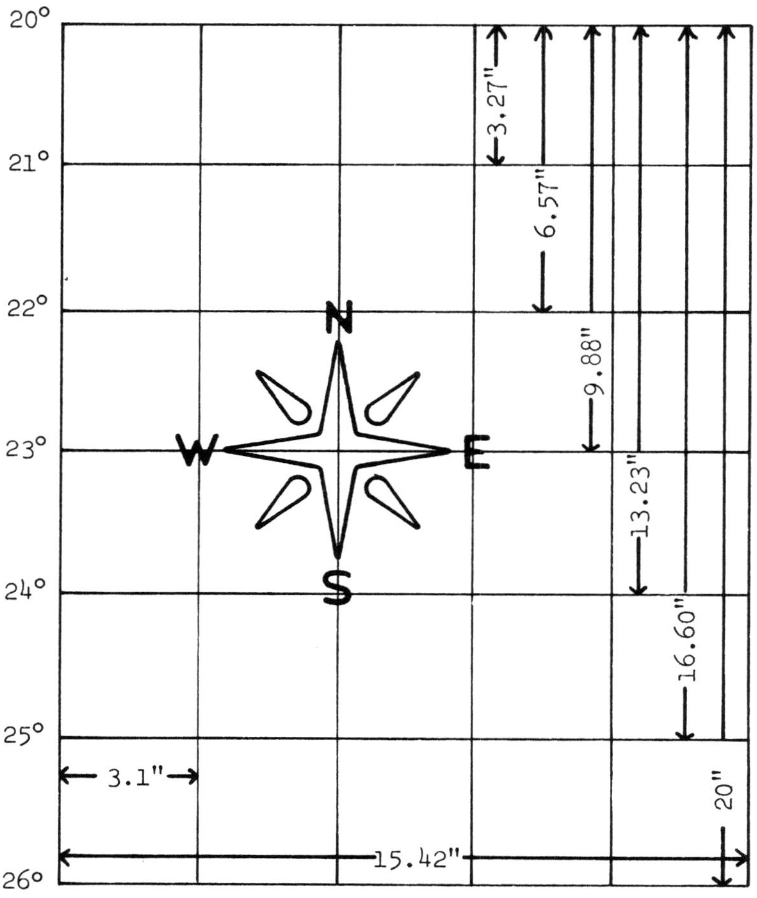

## EXERCISE 13

1. Construct a Mercator Projection grid, latitude limits 30° N to 33° N in 10 inches. Use an 8 1/2" x 11" sheet of paper, fitting in as much longitude coverage as feasible.

2. Construct a Mercator Projection grid, latitude limits 55° S to 60° S in 20 inches. Use a 19" x 25" sheet of paper, fitting in as much longitude coverage as feasible.

# Chapter 17

# Mercator Sailing

Thus far, we have been plotting courses and distances from a DR or fix to get positions of future DRs. However, there is a mathematical solution to this procedure which gives, especially over long distances, much more accurate coordinates. The method is referred to as Mercator sailing and can be employed in two different ways:

1) To find true course and distance in nautical miles between point 1 and point 2.

2) To find coordinates of point 2 given the coordinates of point 1 and course and speed.

It should be remembered that the courses and distances obtained are those that would otherwise be solved graphically on a Mercator chart and are <u>not</u> the quickest routes as plotted on a sphere. We will work with this latter topic when we discuss great circle sailing in the next chapter.

We shall approach Mercator sailing by three different methods which range from complete formula (A) to complete tabular (C). The in-between method (B) uses simpler trigonometric formulae in conjunction with Table 5 in Bowditch (Meridional Parts). The results of the three methods vary little as will be seen.

Our first example will involve finding true course ($C_n$) and distance (D) in nautical miles between two points as follows.

Thatcher Island Light off Cape Ann to Cape Sable Light on Nova Scotia

$L_1 = 42^\circ\ 38'$ N $\qquad L_2 = 43^\circ\ 23'$ N

$\lambda_1 = 70^\circ\ 34'$ W $\qquad \lambda_2 = 65^\circ\ 37'$ W

Method A.

$$C = \tan^{-1}\left(\frac{\pi\ (\lambda_1 - \lambda_2)}{180\ [\ln \tan\ (45^\circ + \tfrac{1}{2}L_2) - \ln \tan\ (45^\circ + \tfrac{1}{2}L_1)]}\right)$$

$$D = \frac{60\ (L_2 - L_1)}{\cos C} \qquad \text{OR} \qquad D = 60\ (\lambda_2 - \lambda_1) \cos L \qquad \text{if } \cos C = 0$$

A calculator with simple trig functions is of obvious help here although the formulae may be solved with trig tables. The natural log (ln) may be solved either way also. Solution is straightforward. Coordinates must be converted to decimal degrees before combining in the calculator.

$$\pi\ (\lambda_1 - \lambda_2) = +15.5509$$

$$180\ [\ldots\ldots.] = 180\ (.8420 - .8241) = +3.2222$$

$$C = \tan^{-1}\ (4.8262) = 078.^{\circ}3$$

We must inspect the direction between our two points to be sure that this C is figured eastward from north. We label C north or south depending on the direction between $L_1$ and $L_2$. In this case the direction is north. We label C east or west depending on the direction between $\lambda_1$ and $\lambda_2$. In this case the direction is east. Therefore, $_N C_E$ is equivalent to $C_n$ and needs no further conversion. The other three cases follow, similar to Z and $Z_n$ conversion.

$C_n = 360° - {}_N C_W.$ $\qquad$ $C_n = 180° - {}_S C_E.$ $\qquad$ $C_n = 180° + {}_S C_W.$

$$D = \frac{60\ (0.^{\circ}75)}{.2028} = 221.9 \text{ n.m.}$$

Method B.

$$C = \tan^{-1}\left(\frac{DLo}{m}\right)$$

$$D = \frac{DLat}{\cos C}$$

DLo = difference of longitudes, in minutes E or W

DLat = difference of latitudes, in minutes N or S

m = difference of meridional parts between $L_1$ and $L_2$ found in Table 5

DLo = 4° 57' = 297' E
DLat = 45' N
m = 2878.6 - 2817.3 = 61.3

$$C = \tan^{-1} \frac{297}{61.3} = \text{N}78.^{\circ}3\text{E}$$

$$C_n = 078.^{\circ}3$$

$$D = \frac{45}{.20} = 222.6 \text{ n.m.}$$

| Lat. | 40° | 41° | 42° | 43° |
|---|---|---|---|---|
| 20 | 2633.8 | 2712.8 | 2793.0 | 2874.5 |
| 21 | 35.1 | 14.1 | 94.4 | 75.9 |
| 22 | 36.4 | 15.4 | 95.7 | 77.3 |
| 23 | 37.7 | 16.8 | 97.1 | 2878.6 |
| 24 | 39.0 | 18.1 | 98.4 | 80.0 |
| 25 | 2640.3 | 2719.4 | 2799.8 | 2881.4 |
| 26 | 41.6 | 20.7 | 2801.1 | 82.8 |
| 27 | 42.9 | 22.1 | 02.5 | 84.1 |
| 28 | 44.3 | 23.4 | 03.8 | 85.5 |
| 29 | 45.6 | 24.7 | 05.2 | 86.9 |
| 30 | 2646.9 | 2726.1 | 2806.5 | 2888.2 |
| 31 | 48.2 | 27.4 | 07.9 | 89.6 |
| 32 | 49.5 | 28.7 | 09.2 | 91.0 |
| 33 | 50.8 | 30.1 | 10.6 | 92.4 |
| 34 | 52.1 | 31.4 | 11.9 | 93.7 |
| 35 | 2653.4 | 2732.7 | 2813.3 | 2895.1 |
| 36 | 54.7 | 34.1 | 14.6 | 96.5 |
| 37 | 56.0 | 35.4 | 16.0 | 97.9 |
| 38 | 57.4 | 36.7 | 2817.3 | 2899.3 |
| 39 | 58.7 | 38.1 | 18.7 | 2900.6 |

Method C.

Inspection of Table 3, the Traverse Table, in Bowditch.

Substitute "m" as the heading (or footing) of the DLat column.

Substitute DLo as the heading (or footing) of the Dep. column.

Peruse Table 3 until these two numbers (61.3 and 297) are found side by side in their relabeled columns. The closest correspondence of these numbers is found on the page with "C" of 78° (we used the relabeled footings rather than the relabeled headings in this case so the course at the foot of the page is chosen).

Convert "C" to $C_n$ as before. $C_n = 078°$

In that same book opening, enter the column printed as DLat with DLat of 45' (enter from the bottom if your course was chosen from the bottom) to get the corresponding distance of 216 or 217 n.m.

| | | | | | | | | |
|---|---|---|---|---|---|---|---|---|
| 171 | 167.3 | 35.6 | 231 | 226.0 | 48.0 | 291 | 284.6 | 60.5 |
| 72 | 168.2 | 35.8 | 32 | 226.9 | 48.2 | 92 | 285.6 | 60.7 |
| 73 | 169.2 | 36.0 | 33 | 227.9 | 48.4 | 93 | 286.6 | 60.9 |
| 74 | 170.2 | 36.2 | 34 | 228.9 | 48.7 | 94 | 287.6 | 61.1 |
| 75 | 171.2 | 36.4 | 35 | 229.9 | 48.9 | 95 | 288.6 | 61.3 |
| 76 | 172.2 | 36.6 | 36 | 230.8 | 49.1 | 96 | 289.5 | 61.5 |
| 77 | 173.1 | 36.8 | 37 | 231.8 | 49.3 | 97 | 290.5 | 61.7 |
| 78 | 174.1 | 37.0 | 38 | 232.8 | 49.5 | 98 | 291.5 | 62.0 |
| 79 | 175.1 | 37.2 | 39 | 233.8 | 49.7 | 99 | 292.5 | 62.2 |
| 80 | 176.1 | 37.4 | 40 | 234.8 | 49.9 | 300 | 293.4 | 62.4 |
| Dist. | Dep. | D. Lat. | Dist. | Dep. | D. Lat. | Dist. | Dep. | D. Lat. |
| | | | | | | | DLo | m |

78°

| Dist. | D. Lat. | Dep. |
|---|---|---|
| N. | N×Cos. | N×Sin. |
| Hypotenuse | Side Adj. | Side Opp. |

| | | | | | | | | |
|---|---|---|---|---|---|---|---|---|
| 151 | 147.7 | 31.4 | 211 | 206.4 | 43.9 | 271 | 265.1 | 56.3 |
| 52 | 148.7 | 31.6 | 12 | 207.4 | 44.1 | 72 | 266.1 | 56.6 |
| 53 | 149.7 | 31.8 | 13 | 208.3 | 44.3 | 73 | 267.0 | 56.8 |
| 54 | 150.6 | 32.0 | 14 | 209.3 | 44.5 | 74 | 268.0 | 57.0 |
| 55 | 151.6 | 32.2 | 15 | 210.3 | 44.7 | 75 | 269.0 | 57.2 |
| 56 | 152.6 | 32.4 | 216 | 211.3 | 44.9 | 76 | 270.0 | 57.4 |
| 57 | 153.6 | 32.6 | 17 | 212.3 | 45.1 | 77 | 270.9 | 57.6 |
| 58 | 154.5 | 32.9 | 18 | 213.2 | 45.3 | 78 | 271.9 | 57.8 |
| 59 | 155.5 | 33.1 | 19 | 214.2 | 45.5 | 79 | 272.9 | 58.0 |
| 60 | 156.5 | 33.3 | 20 | 215.2 | 45.7 | 80 | 273.9 | 58.2 |
| Dist. | Dep. | D. Lat. | Dist. | Dep. | D. Lat. | Dist. | Dep. | D. Lat. |

78°

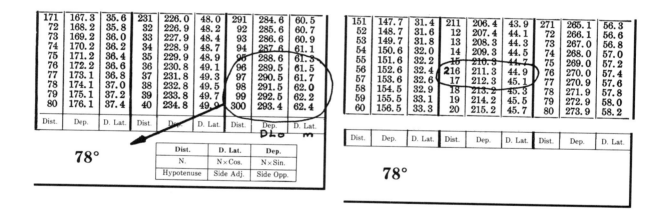

If "m" and DLo are too large to be tabulated in the required columns, divide each of them by 10 and search again. The rest of the procedure continues as before.

This method is lengthier than Method B because of the time spent perusing the tables. Some accuracy is also lost in using Table 3. However, in the absence of trig tables or a calculator, Method C is useful to know.

The other aspect of Mercator sailing involves finding the coordinates of a future DR (point 2) if point 1 and course and distance are known.

Assume we are leaving Pitcairn Island in the Pacific ($L_1 = 25^\circ\ 04'$ S, $\lambda_1 = 130^\circ\ 05'$ W) on course 038° and travel for a distance of 450 nautical miles. What will be the coordinates of the point reached?

Method A.

$$\lambda_2 = \lambda_1 - \tan C \left\{ \frac{180\ [\ln \tan (45 + \tfrac{1}{2}L_2) - \ln \tan (45 + \tfrac{1}{2}L_1)]}{\pi} \right\}$$

$$L_2 = \frac{D \cos C}{60} + L_1$$

All coordinates are in decimal degrees. Solve for $L_2$ first. E and S are neg.

$$L_2 = \frac{450\ (\cos 38^\circ)}{60} + (-25^\circ.0667) = 5^\circ.9101 - 25^\circ.0667 = -19^\circ.1566 = 19^\circ\ 09'.4 \text{ S}$$

$$\lambda_2 = 130^\circ.0833 - \tan 38^\circ \left[ \frac{180\ (-0.3408 - (-0.4522))}{\pi} \right]$$

$$= 130^\circ.0833 - 0.7813\ (6.3830) = 125^\circ.0963 = 125^\circ\ 05'.8 \text{ W}$$

Method B.

$DLat = D \cos C$ — DLat and DLo are differences in latitudes and longitudes in minutes of arc.

$DLo = m \tan C$ — m = meridional difference between $L_2$ and $L_1$ found in Table 5.

E and S are negative.

$DLat = 450\ (\cos 38^\circ) = 354'.6 = 5^\circ\ 54'.6$

$L_2 = L_1 + DLat = -25^\circ\ 04' + 5^\circ\ 54'.6 = 19^\circ\ 09'.4$ S

$m = 1544.5 - 1163.8 = 380.7$
(this will be negative, $-25^\circ - (-19^\circ)$)

$DLo = -380.7\ (\tan 38^\circ) = -297'.4 = -4^\circ\ 57'.4$

$\lambda_2 = \lambda_1 + DLo = 130^\circ\ 05' + (-4^\circ\ 57'.4) = 125^\circ\ 07'.6$ W

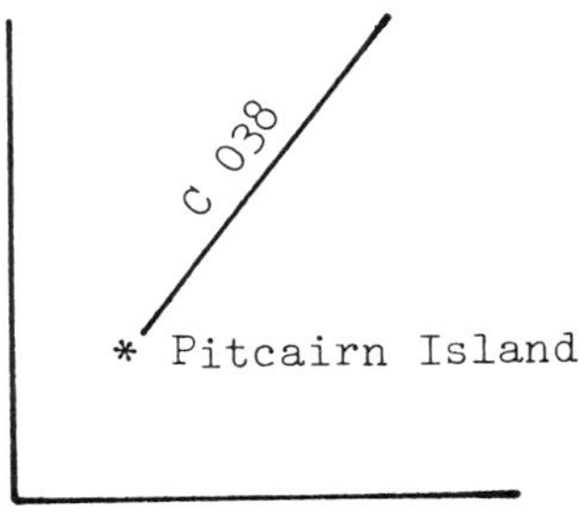


By drawing a rough diagram of the situation, it can be easily reasoned as to how to apply DLat to $L_1$ and DLo to $\lambda_2$ to obtain the correct figure.

Method C.

Inspection of Table 3, the Traverse Table, in Bowditch.

Enter Table 3 with the course (038°) and distance (450). Since 38° is a page heading, go down the distance column.

Extract the corresponding DLat (354!6) and apply to $L_1$ as in Method B to get $L_2$.

Get "m" as in Method B (380.7).

Substitute "m" as the heading (or footing) of the DLat column.

Substitute DLo as the heading (or footing) of the Dep. column.

Locate "m" of 380.7 (use heading of DLat since 38° heads the page) and extract the corresponding DLo of 297!4.

Apply DLo to $\lambda_1$ to get $\lambda_2$ as done in Method B.

322° | 038° — 218° | 142°

**TABLE 3**

Traverse **38°** Table

322° | 038° — 218° | 142°

m DLo

| Dist. | D. Lat. | Dep. | Dist. | D. Lat. | Dep. | Dist. | D. Lat. | Dep. | Dist. | D. Lat. | Dep. | Dist. | D. Lat. | Dep. |
|---|---|---|---|---|---|---|---|---|---|---|---|---|---|---|
| 301 | 237.2 | 185.3 | 361 | 284.5 | 222.3 | 421 | 331.8 | 259.2 | 481 | 37[illegible].0 | 296.1 | 541 | 426.3 | 333.1 |
| 02 | 238.0 | 185.9 | 62 | 285.3 | 222.9 | 22 | 332.5 | 259.8 | 82 | 379.8 | 296.7 | 42 | 427.1 | 333.7 |
| 03 | 238.8 | 186.6 | 63 | 286.0 | 223.5 | 23 | 333.3 | 260.4 | 83 | 380.6 | 297.4 | 43 | 427.9 | 334.3 |
| 04 | 239.6 | 187.2 | 64 | 286.8 | 224.1 | 24 | 334.1 | 261.0 | 84 | 381.4 | 298.0 | 44 | 428.7 | 334.9 |
| 05 | 240.3 | 187.8 | 65 | 287.6 | 224.7 | 25 | 334.9 | 261.7 | 85 | 382.2 | 298.6 | 45 | 429.5 | 335.5 |
| 06 | 241.1 | 188.4 | 66 | 288.4 | 225.3 | 26 | 335.7 | 262.3 | 86 | 383.0 | 299.2 | 46 | 430.3 | 336.2 |
| 07 | 241.9 | 189.0 | 67 | 289.2 | 225.9 | 27 | 336.5 | 262.9 | 87 | 383.8 | 299.8 | 47 | 431.0 | 336.8 |
| 08 | 242.7 | 189.6 | 68 | 290.0 | 226.6 | 28 | 337.3 | 263.5 | 88 | 384.5 | 300.4 | 48 | 431.8 | 337.4 |
| 09 | 243.5 | 190.2 | 69 | 290.8 | 227.2 | 29 | 338.1 | 264.1 | 89 | 385.3 | 301.1 | 49 | 432.6 | 338.0 |
| 10 | 244.3 | 190.9 | 70 | 291.6 | 227.8 | 30 | 338.8 | 264.7 | 90 | 386.1 | 301.7 | 50 | 433.4 | 338.6 |
| 311 | 245.1 | 191.5 | 371 | 292.4 | 228.4 | 431 | 339.6 | 265.4 | 491 | 386.9 | 302.3 | 551 | 434.2 | 339.2 |
| 12 | 245.9 | 192.1 | 72 | 293.1 | 229.0 | 32 | 340.4 | 266.0 | 92 | 387.7 | 302.9 | 52 | 435.0 | 339.8 |
| 13 | 246.6 | 192.7 | 73 | 293.9 | 229.6 | 33 | 341.2 | 266.6 | 93 | 388.5 | 303.5 | 53 | 435.8 | 340.5 |
| 14 | 247.4 | 193.3 | 74 | 294.7 | 230.3 | 34 | 342.0 | 267.2 | 94 | 389.3 | 304.1 | 54 | 436.6 | 341.1 |
| 15 | 248.2 | 193.9 | 75 | 295.5 | 230.9 | 35 | 342.8 | 267.8 | 95 | 390.1 | 304.8 | 55 | 437.3 | 341.7 |
| 16 | 249.0 | 194.5 | 76 | 296.3 | 231.5 | 36 | 343.6 | 268.4 | 96 | 390.9 | 305.4 | 56 | 438.1 | 342.3 |
| 17 | 249.8 | 195.2 | 77 | 297.1 | 232.1 | 37 | 344.4 | 269.0 | 97 | 391.6 | 306.0 | 57 | 438.9 | 342.9 |
| 18 | 250.6 | 195.8 | 78 | 297.9 | 232.7 | 38 | 345.1 | 269.7 | 98 | 392.4 | 306.6 | 58 | 439.7 | 343.5 |
| 19 | 251.4 | 196.4 | 79 | 298.7 | 233.3 | 39 | 345.9 | 270.3 | 99 | 393.2 | 307.2 | 59 | 440.5 | 344.2 |
| 20 | 252.2 | 197.0 | 80 | 299.4 | 234.0 | 40 | 346.7 | 270.9 | 500 | 394.0 | 307.8 | 60 | 441.3 | 344.8 |
| 321 | 253.0 | 197.6 | 381 | 300.2 | 234.6 | 441 | 347.5 | 271.5 | 501 | 394.8 | 308.4 | 561 | 442.1 | 345.4 |
| 22 | 253.7 | 198.2 | 82 | 301.0 | 235.2 | 42 | 348.3 | 272.1 | 02 | 395.6 | 309.1 | 62 | 442.9 | 346.0 |
| 23 | 254.5 | 198.9 | 83 | 301.8 | 235.8 | 43 | 349.1 | 272.7 | 03 | 396.4 | 309.7 | 63 | 443.7 | 346.6 |
| 24 | 255.3 | 199.5 | 84 | 302.6 | 236.4 | 44 | 349.9 | 273.4 | 04 | 397.2 | 310.3 | 64 | 444.4 | 347.2 |
| 25 | 256.1 | 200.1 | 85 | 303.4 | 237.0 | 45 | 350.7 | 274.0 | 05 | 397.9 | 310.9 | 65 | 445.2 | 347.8 |
| 26 | 256.9 | 200.7 | 86 | 304.2 | 237.6 | 46 | 351.5 | 274.6 | 06 | 398.7 | 311.5 | 66 | 446.0 | 348.5 |
| 27 | 257.7 | 201.3 | 87 | 305.0 | 238.3 | 47 | 352.2 | 275.2 | 07 | 399.5 | 312.1 | 67 | 446.8 | 349.1 |
| 28 | 258.5 | 201.9 | 88 | 305.7 | 238.9 | 48 | 353.0 | 275.8 | 08 | 400.3 | 312.8 | 68 | 447.6 | 349.7 |
| 29 | 259.3 | 202.6 | 89 | 306.5 | 239.5 | 49 | 353.8 | 276.4 | 09 | 401.1 | 313.4 | 69 | 448.4 | 350.3 |
| 30 | 260.0 | 203.2 | 90 | 307.3 | 240.1 | 450 | 354.6 | 277.0 | 10 | 401.9 | 314.0 | 70 | 449.2 | 350.9 |
| 331 | 260.8 | 203.8 | 391 | 308.1 | 240.7 | 451 | 355.4 | 277.7 | 511 | 402.7 | 314.6 | 571 | 450.0 | 351.5 |
| 32 | 261.6 | 204.4 | 92 | 308.9 | 241.3 | 52 | 356.2 | 278.3 | 12 | 403.5 | 315.2 | 72 | 450.7 | 352.2 |
| 33 | 262.4 | 205.0 | 93 | 309.7 | 242.0 | 53 | 357.0 | 278.9 | 13 | 404.2 | 315.8 | 73 | 451.5 | 352.8 |
| 34 | 263.2 | 205.6 | 94 | 310.5 | 242.6 | 54 | 357.8 | 279.5 | 14 | 405.0 | 316.5 | 74 | 452.3 | 353.4 |
| 35 | 264.0 | 206.2 | 95 | 311.3 | 243.2 | 55 | 358.5 | 280.1 | 15 | 405.8 | 317.1 | 75 | 453.1 | 354.0 |
| 36 | 264.8 | 206.9 | 96 | 312.1 | 243.8 | 56 | 359.3 | 280.7 | 16 | 406.6 | 317.7 | 76 | 453.9 | 354.6 |
| 37 | 265.6 | 207.5 | 97 | 312.8 | 244.4 | 57 | 360.1 | 281.4 | 17 | 407.4 | 318.3 | 77 | 454.7 | 355.2 |
| 38 | 266.3 | 208.1 | 98 | 313.6 | 245.0 | 58 | 360.9 | 282.0 | 18 | 408.2 | 318.9 | 78 | 455.5 | 355.7 |
| 39 | 267.1 | 208.7 | 99 | 314.4 | 245.6 | 59 | 361.7 | 282.6 | 19 | 409.0 | 319.5 | 79 | 456.3 | 356.5 |
| 40 | 267.9 | 209.3 | 400 | 315.2 | 246.3 | 60 | 362.5 | 283.2 | 20 | 409.8 | 320.1 | 80 | 457.0 | 357.1 |

Sometimes "m" needs to be divided by 10 so that it will fit within the range of the DLat on the page. If this is necessary, multiply the corresponding DLo by 10 also.

## EXERCISE 14

1. Calculate the true course and nautical mile distance from

| Tristan da Cunha | to | Gough Island |
|---|---|---|
| $L_1$ 37° 03' S | | $L_2$ 40° 20' S |
| $\lambda_1$ 12° 18' W | | $\lambda_2$ 10° 00' W |

2. Calculate the true course and nautical mile distance from

| Cape Maria van Diemen Light, New Zealand | to | Eddystone Point Light, Tasmania |
|---|---|---|
| $L_1$ 34° 29' S | | $L_2$ 41° 00' S |
| $\lambda_1$ 172° 38' E | | $\lambda_2$ 148° 21' E |

3. Calculate the true course and nautical mile distance from

| Block Island Southeast Point Light | to | North Rock Light, Bermuda |
|---|---|---|
| $L_1$ 41° 09' N | | $L_2$ 32° 28' N |
| $\lambda_1$ 71° 33' W | | $\lambda_2$ 64° 46' W |

4. A vessel leaves Dondra Head Light (L 5° 55' N, $\lambda$ 80° 36' E) and sails on course 160° true for 350 nautical miles. What is the latitude and the longitude of the point of arrival?

5. A raft is pushed off from Port Hedland (L 20° 18' S, $\lambda$ 118° 35' E) on the northwest coast of Australia. It drifts on course 310° for 110 nautical miles. What is the latitude and the longitude of the raft after this leg of its voyage?

6. A mermaid starts swimming from Loop Head Light (L 52° 34' N, $\lambda$ 9° 56' W) in Ireland and crawls on course 252° for 240 nautical miles. What is the latitude and longitude of this resting point?

# Chapter 18

# Great Circle Sailing

When we have been speaking of courses to steer, we have been referring to rhumbline courses, a course that always maintains constant true direction. On a Mercator chart, this course would be a straight line and therefore would be very easy to plot. However, our earth is not a flat surface and the shortest distance between two points is not a rhumbline but a great circle. We spoke of great circles in Chapter 1, using the equator as an example. If we passed a plane through the center of the earth and marked where this plane intersected the surface of the earth, this intersection would be a great circle. For short distances, a rhumbline is an adequate approximation but for ocean crossings the great circle route saves considerable distance. In some cases, the great circle route is not desirable since it may cross land or bring the vessel into excessively high latitudes or into dangerous waters. Theoretically a great circle route will constantly change true direction but we will divide the circle into several short rhumblines which will closely approximate the circle and will reduce course changes.

A great circle route is one side of a spherical triangle such as we discussed in Chapter 15. The corners of the triangle are the (1) point of departure, (2) point of destination and (3) elevated pole. We are interested in finding information regarding the arc between $P_1$ and $P_2$.

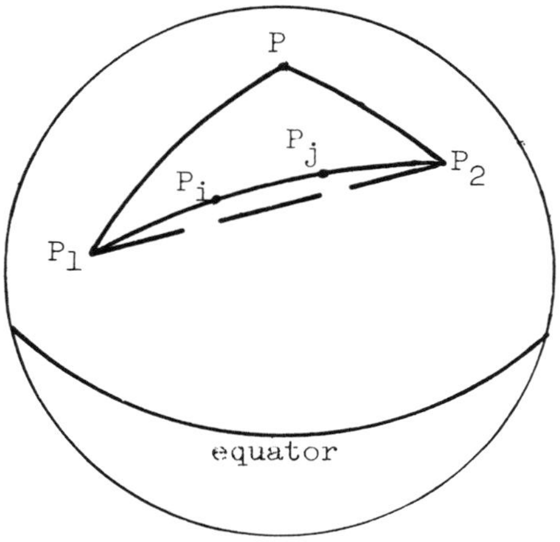


$P$ = elevated pole
$P_1$ = point of departure
$P_2$ = point of destination
$P_i$, $P_j$ = intermediate points along great circle route
$P_1$ to $P_2$ = great circle route

Dashed line is the rhumbline, always equatorward from the great circle route.

The great circle route can be solved most easily by using gnomonic projection charts. These are published by the U.S. Navy Hydrographic Office to cover the principal navigable waters of the world. With this projection, a great circle is a straight line. The great circle is plotted and intermediate points such as $P_i$ and $P_j$ are taken from this line and replotted on a Mercator projection chart. Courses and distances are taken off the Mercator chart between these intermediate points by the normal rhumbline methods. The more intermediate points there are, the more accurate the correspondence between the series of rhumblines and the great circle. A longitude difference of 5° between these points is considered adequate.

The great circle route can also be figured by spherical trigonometry. By a series of rather involved trigonometric formulae, the initial great circle course, the great circle distance, and latitudes and longitudes of points along the great circle course can be figured. This involves more mathematics than many navigators are willing to undertake. Sight reduction tables can also be used to solve the triangle when substitutions are made as follows:

| Sight reduction term | Great circle term |
|---|---|
| AP of observer | Point of departure |
| GP of body | Point of destination |
| Meridian angle (LHA or t) | Difference of longitude |
| Azimuth angle ($Z_n$) | Initial course angle |
| Zenith distance (90° - altitude) | Great circle distance |

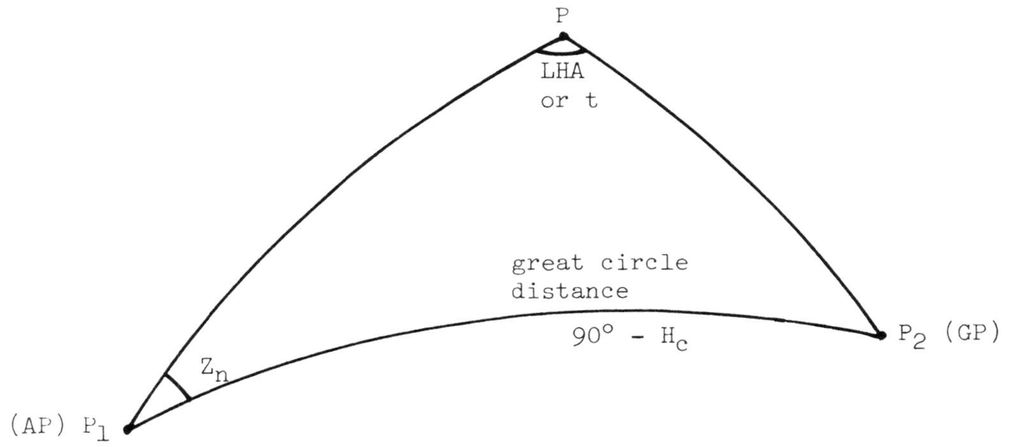


I offer in this chapter a third method assuming a calculator is available which only involves one formula to find the latitude of intermediate points when longitude is specified. For example, if the navigator wishes to go from Bermuda to the Azores, choose intermediate points of longitude, say every five or ten degrees, and then solve for the latitudes where these longitudes cross the great circle course. Once these points are known, the formulae we used for rhumbline sailing can be used to find the courses and distances between these points.

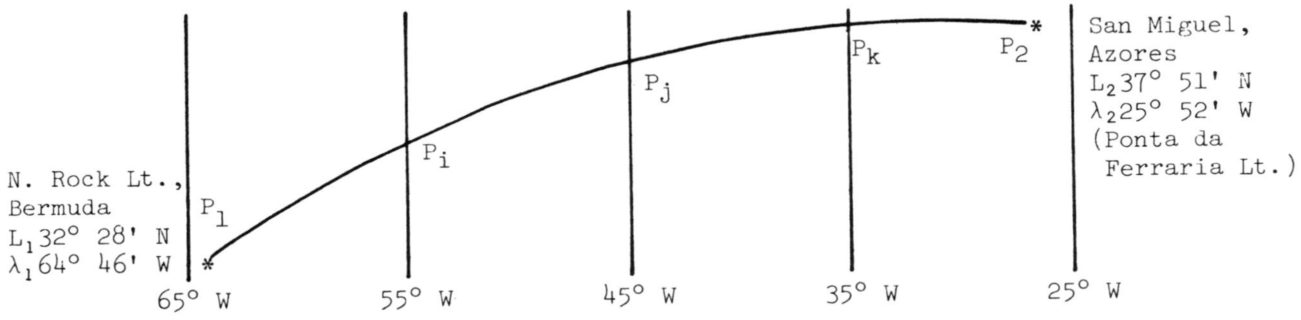


The formula to solve for the intermediate latitudes when longitudes are specified is as follows.

$$L_i = \tan^{-1}\left(\frac{\tan L_2 \sin(\lambda_i - \lambda_1) - \tan L_1 \sin(\lambda_i - \lambda_2)}{\sin(\lambda_2 - \lambda_1)}\right)$$

East longitudes and south latitudes are specified as negative numbers. This formula cannot be used when $\lambda_2 = \lambda_1$. Coordinates must be converted to decimal degrees.

We should first start by solving for $L_i$ for the point $P_i$ when $\lambda_i$ is specified to be 55° W.

$$L_i = \tan^{-1} \frac{\tan 37.85 \sin(55 - 64.7667) - \tan 32.4667 \sin(55 - 25.8667)}{\sin(25.8667 - 64.7667)}$$

$$= \tan^{-1} \frac{(-0.1318 - 0.3098)}{-0.6280}$$

$$= \tan^{-1} (0.7032)$$

$$= 35\overset{\circ}{.}1144 = 35^\circ\ 06\overset{'}{.}9 \text{ N.}$$

$L_j$ can be similarly found by substituting $\lambda_j$ for $\lambda_i$, yielding a latitude for point $P_j$ of $36\overset{\circ}{.}8916$ or $36^\circ\ 53\overset{'}{.}5$ N. After doing the formula once, storing the coordinates for $P_1$ and $P_2$, the only new input for this second time was $\lambda_j$ of 45°.

Lastly, $L_k$ can be found by substituting 35° W for $\lambda_k$. This yields a latitude of $37^\circ\ 46\overset{'}{.}9$.

We now have the following points along the great circle route.

| Point | Latitude | Longitude | |
|---|---|---|---|
| $P_1$ | $32^\circ\ 28\overset{'}{.}0$ N | 64° 46' W | Bermuda |
| $P_i$ | $35^\circ\ 06\overset{'}{.}9$ | 55° | |
| $P_j$ | $36^\circ\ 53\overset{'}{.}5$ | 45° | |
| $P_k$ | $37^\circ\ 46\overset{'}{.}9$ | 35° | |
| $P_2$ | $37^\circ\ 51\overset{'}{.}0$ | 25° 52' | Azores |

The next step is to find the rhumbline courses and distances between each point by Mercator sailing such as we did in Chapter 17. I will do it by Method B (formula and Table 5) although Methods A or C may be done equally well.

$P_1$ to $P_i$:

$$DLo = 64^\circ\ 46' - 55^\circ = 9^\circ\ 46' = 586'\ E$$
$$DLat = 35^\circ\ 06'.9 - 32^\circ\ 28'.0 = 2^\circ\ 38'.9 = 158'.9\ N$$
$$m = 2239.3 - 2049.0 = 190.3$$

$$C = \tan^{-1}\left(\frac{DLo}{m}\right) = N72^\circ.0091\ E \qquad C_n = 072^\circ$$

$$D = \frac{DLat}{\cos C} = 514.46 \text{ nautical miles.}$$

$P_i$ to $P_j$:

$$DLo = 55^\circ - 45^\circ = 10^\circ = 600'\ E$$
$$DLat = 36^\circ\ 53'.5 - 35^\circ\ 06'.9 = 1^\circ\ 46'.6 = 106'.6\ N$$
$$m = 2370.5 - 2239.3 = 131.2$$

$$C = \tan^{-1} \frac{600}{131.2} = N77^\circ.6655\ E \qquad C_n = 077^\circ.7$$

$$D = \frac{106.6}{.2136} = 499.02 \text{ nautical miles.}$$

$P_j$ to $P_k$:

$$DLo = 45^\circ - 35^\circ = 10^\circ = 600'\ E$$
$$DLat = 37^\circ\ 46'.9 - 36^\circ\ 53'.5 = 53'.4\ N$$
$$m = 2437.4 - 2370.5 = 66.9$$

$$C = \tan^{-1} \frac{600}{66.9} = N83^\circ.6378\ E \qquad C_n = 083^\circ.6$$

$$D = \frac{53.4}{.1108} = 481.89 \text{ nautical miles.}$$

$P_k$ to $P_2$:

$$DLo = 35^\circ - 25^\circ\ 52' = 9^\circ\ 08' = 548'\ E$$
$$DLat = 37^\circ\ 51'.0 - 37^\circ\ 46'.9 = 4'.1\ N$$
$$m = 2442.6 - 2437.4 = 5.2$$

$$C = \tan^{-1} \frac{548}{5.2} = N89^\circ.4563\ E \qquad C_n = 089^\circ.5$$

$$D = \frac{4.1}{.0095} = 432.1 \text{ nautical miles.}$$

In summary, the courses to follow between the points would be 072°, 077°.7, 083°.6, and 089°.5. The combined distances yield 1927.47 nautical miles.

## EXERCISE 15

1. A ship leaves Cape Town headed for New York City. Starting from lat. 33° 53!3 S, long. 18° 23!1 E (near Green Point Light) and ending near Ambrose Light at lat. 40° 27!1 N, long. 73° 49!4 W, calculate:

    a) latitudes on the great circle course at longitudes 15° W and 45° W.

    b) the rhumbline courses and distances on each of the three legs using the points found in question "a".

2. A ship is sailing from Manila to Los Angeles. The captain wishes to use great circle plotting and rhumbline navigation from lat. 12° 45!2 N, long. 124° 20!1 E off the entrance to San Bernadino Straight to lat. 33° 48!8 N, long. 120° 07!1 W, five miles south of Santa Rosa Island.

    a) Calculate the latitudes on the great circle course at longitudes 150° E, 180° and 150° W.

    b) Calculate the rhumbline courses and distances on each of the four legs.

# Chapter 19

# Calculator Methods of Sight Reduction

In chapter 15 we discussed the spherical triangle set up when a sextant sight is reduced to numbers that can sensibly be plotted on a chart or small area plotting sheet. In previous chapters we learned how to employ sight reduction tables to solve this triangle, specifically H.O. 229 and H.O. 211. Now we shall turn to calculators to do this sight reduction for us.

There can be no doubt that calculators make our work easier, quicker, and diminish the bane of all navigators - inaccuracy. They fall naturally into three groups, depending on price and how much of the task you want them to do. As you can guess, there is a direct relationship between the two. The first group, the most expensive, are the dedicated or prompting kind. You switch them on and they ask the questions. There are several programs, including one that calculates backwards to the heavenly body's altitude and azimuth from a DR, so you can adjust the sextant and be likely to have the body in the mirror waiting for you! These can also do your three-body-fix plotting for you in their little heads and read out latitude and longitude. Usually, though, they begin with index correction and end with intercept and $Z_n$. Incidentally, these contain their own almanac. The second group are the programmable calculators which will solve the celestial triangle, given LHA, Dec. Body and AP or DR latitude. They give intercept and $Z_n$. Of course you have to be able to program them yourself but for many this can be fun and a challenge. Conversion to and from decimal degrees can also be included in the program. The third group of calculators are the less expensive scientific calculators that have trigonometric functions (sine, cosine and tangent), one memory, and exchange function between memory and display. They require about 30 keystroke entries in the correct order and with no mistakes but - you want H.O. 229 back? Angles must be converted to decimal degrees.

Before discussing the formulae, the following points should be remembered.

1) All angles must be entered as decimal degrees.
2) Southern latitudes and southern declinations must be entered as negative numbers. (Eliminate this step for Modified 602 formulae.)
3) The meridian angle used is LHA, the 0° - 360° angle measured from the local meridian westward. If "t" (0° - 180°, E or W) is used, the eastern "t"s must be entered as negative numbers.

4) The $H_c$ and $Z_n$ obtained will be in decimal degrees. $H_c$ must then be converted to degrees-minutes-tenths of minutes.

The input for the formulae is the same as it was for entering the sight reduction tables: LHA, declination, Latitude (DR or AP). These numbers must be obtained by using the Nautical Almanac as previously done. I shall offer two sets of formulae, the first one the quicker but requiring four or five storage memories (unless the user wishes to write down the intermediate answers or re-enter one of the three inputs.) The second set may be done with just one memory providing the calculator has provisions for exchanging the number in memory for the displayed number. Each set of formulae requires a conversion from Z to $Z_n$.

Now the formulae.

$$H_c = \sin^{-1} (\sin d \sin L + \cos d \cos L \cos LHA)$$

$$Z = \cos^{-1} \left( \frac{\sin d - \sin L \sin H_c}{\cos L \cos H_c} \right)$$

if $\sin LHA < 0$, $Z_n = Z$

if $\sin LHA \geq 0$, $Z_n = 360 - Z$

The formula for $H_c$ should be solved first since $\sin H_c$ is needed for the second formula. In fact, the sum ($\sin d \sin L + \cos d \cos L \cos LHA$) equals $\sin H_c$ so this sum should be stored for use in the second formula before the arc sin is taken to get $H_c$.

The second set of formulae is a modification of Japanese H.O. Publication Number 602, Brief Celestial Navigation, and involves dropping a perpendicular from the celestial body in the celestial triangle so that now two right triangles may be solved instead of one non-right triangle. This method is similar to that employed by H.O. 211 where the co-latitude side of the triangle is divided into two parts, ($90° - K$) and ($K \sim L$). The "k" we shall use in this formula will refer to the ($90° - K$) side of one of the right triangles. This Modified 602 was supplied to me by one of my past students, George Hall, a Chemistry professor at my Alma Mater.

$$k = \tan^{-1} \left( \frac{\cos LHA}{\tan d} \right)$$

$$Z = \tan^{-1} \left( \frac{\tan LHA \sin k}{\cos (k + L)} \right)$$

$$H_c = \tan^{-1} \{\tan (k + L) \cos Z\}$$

LHA is always positive.

d is + if d and L SAME name.
d is - if d and L CONTRARY name.

L is always entered as a positive number.

In this case, Z is solved for first since cos Z is used in the $H_c$ formula. $H_c$ may be positive or negative, the sign of which is ignored except in the conversion from Z to $Z_n$. Z may also be positive or negative so remember to use its sign also in the Z to $Z_n$ conversion.

| If: | | $Z_n$ = |
|---|---|---|
| | $H_c$ positive, L north | $360 - Z$ |
| | $H_c$ positive, L south | $180 + Z$ |
| | $H_c$ negative, L north | $180 - Z$ |
| | $H_c$ negative, L south | $360 + Z$ |

## SIGHT REDUCTION BY SCIENTIFIC CALCULATOR

Calculator must use algebraic notation, needs one memory, exchange button and trig. functions. Use either the DR or AP, but for all angles convert minutes to decimal degree by dividing by 60. Write these down beforehand.

LHA - always positive.
Dec Body - same name as L, Positive; contrary name, Negative, symbol D.
DR or AP Lat - always Positive, symbol L.

| MEMORY | ACTION | DISPLAY | WRITE DOWN |
|---|---|---|---|
| | enter LHA | LHA | |
| LHA | store | LHA | |
| | cos | cosLHA | |
| | ÷D(sign?) tan = | tanK | |
| | inv tan | K | |
| | sin | sinK | |
| sinK | exchange | LHA | |
| | tan | tanLHA | |
| | x recall = | tanLHA x sinK | |
| tanLHA x sinK | exchange | sinK | |
| | inv sin | K | |
| | + L = | (K + L) | |
| K + L | exchange | tanLHA x sinK | |
| | ÷recall cos = | tan{tanLHA x sinK/cos(K + L)} | |
| | inv tan | Z | WRITE DOWN WITH SIGN |
| | cos | cosZ | |
| cosZ | exchange | (K + L) | |
| | tan | tan(K + L) | |
| | x recall = | $\tan H_c$ | |
| | inv tan | $H_c$ | WRITE DOWN WITH SIGN |

Rules for $Z_n$

$H_c>0$, L north, $Z_n = 360 - Z$
$H_c>0$, L south, $Z_n = 180 + Z$
$H_c<0$, L north, $Z_n = 180 - Z$
$H_c<0$, L south, $Z_n = 360 + Z$

As convenient as a calculator may seem for sight reduction, it is not advised as the sole method of solution. It is always nice to override calculator malfunction and power loss with knowledge of a tabular method.

Two further words of advice. On board a vessel, the calculator inside a clear plastic bag with a packet of silica gel enclosed helps to keep moisture out. The keys can still be punched through the plastic. Also, some displays do not show up clearly in bright sunshine. If your queasy stomach prompts you to reduce your noon sight on deck, a makeshift hood over the display will shield some of the sunlight and allow the numbers to be better viewed.

# Chapter 20

# Two Other Uses of Calculators

For those navigators wishing to pursue the use of calculators in celestial navigation, this chapter offers two additional sets of formulae that may be of interest. Both bypass sight reduction tables, the first supplying plottable information and the second giving the fix coordinates directly.

The first formula allows the navigator to specify a particular latitude and obtain a corresponding longitude, this point being one of many through which the line of position would pass. Once two such points are found for each sight, they can be plotted and a line drawn between them. This is the sight's line of position. A reasonable estimate of the observer's latitude is helpful in reducing the number of times the formula is applied such that the points are in the scope of the plotting sheet. This formula was taken from the United States Naval Observatory Circular #155, Almanac for Computers, 1977, 1 October 1976.

$$\text{Longitude} = \text{GHA Body} \pm \cos^{-1}\left(\frac{\sin H_o - \sin L \sin d}{\cos L \cos d}\right)$$

GHA = Greenwich Hour Angle found at the time of sight
$H_o$ = corrected sextant altitude
L = specified latitude
d = declination at the time of sight
Longitude = corresponding longitude to L specified

North and west coordinates are positive, south and east are negative. The ± operation is + for bodies east of the meridian and - for bodies west of the meridian.

Assume a pair of Sun sights yielding the following data.

| Body | Z.T. | GHA | Dec | $H_o$ |
|---|---|---|---|---|
| Sun LL | 11-05-04 | 61° 16!9 | 23° 24!7 S | 23° 29!6 |
| Sun UL | 13-41-14 | 100° 18!8 | 23° 24!5 S | 26° 54!9 |

The ship's 1340 DR is: L 38° 20' N, λ 86° 43' W (land based!). Course to this point has been 206°, speed 10 knots. Let us specify the following latitudes for each sight and find the corresponding longitudes.

1105 Sun: 38° 30' N and 38° 40' N (obtain $P_1$ and $P_2$)
1341 Sun: 38° 15' N and 38° 20' N (obtain $P_3$ and $P_4$)

Since the 1105 Sun is east of the meridian the ± operation will be +. By the same token the operation will be - for the 1341 Sun which will be west of the meridian.

The formula for $P_1$ sets up as follows.

$$\text{Longitude}_1 = 61° \ 16!9 + \cos^{-1}\left(\frac{\sin 23° \ 29!6 - \sin 38° \ 30' \sin -23° \ 24!7}{\cos 38° \ 30' \cos -23° \ 24!7}\right)$$

The angles must be converted to decimal degrees before getting the trigonometric values.

$$\text{Longitude}_1 = 61°\!.2817 + \cos^{-1}\left(\frac{.3986 - (.6225)(-.3973)}{(.7826)(.9177)}\right)$$

If the decimal numbers are held in the calculator to the extended number of places, the resulting longitude is 87° 11!5 W (slightly different if only the four digit decimals are combined). Therefore,

$P_1$ = Latitude 38° 30!0 N
Longitude 87° 11!5 W.

The point is plotted (see plot that follows) and is one of the points along the 1105 Sun line of position. Correspondingly, $P_2$ can be solved.

$P_2$ = Latitude 38° 40!0 N
Longitude 86° 44!9 W

With these two points, the 1105 Sun LOP can be drawn. It will then need to be advanced to 1341 for a distance of 26 nautical miles along course 206°.

The 1341 LOP is drawn between solved points $P_3$ and $P_4$.

$P_3$ = Latitude 38° 15!0 N
Longitude 86° 06!0 W

$P_4$ = Latitude 38° 20!0 N
Longitude 86° 30!8 W

The crossing of this 1341 LOP with the advanced 1105 Sun LOP gives the 1341 running fix.

The most uncertain part of this procedure is choosing satisfactory latitudes such that the points will lie within plotting range. For a sight of a body on the prime vertical (resulting in a vertical line of position) any latitude will work. For a sight of a body on the meridian (resulting in a horizontal line of position) only one latitude will work. It is advantageous to steer clear of situations where the body is even close to the meridian for this reason.

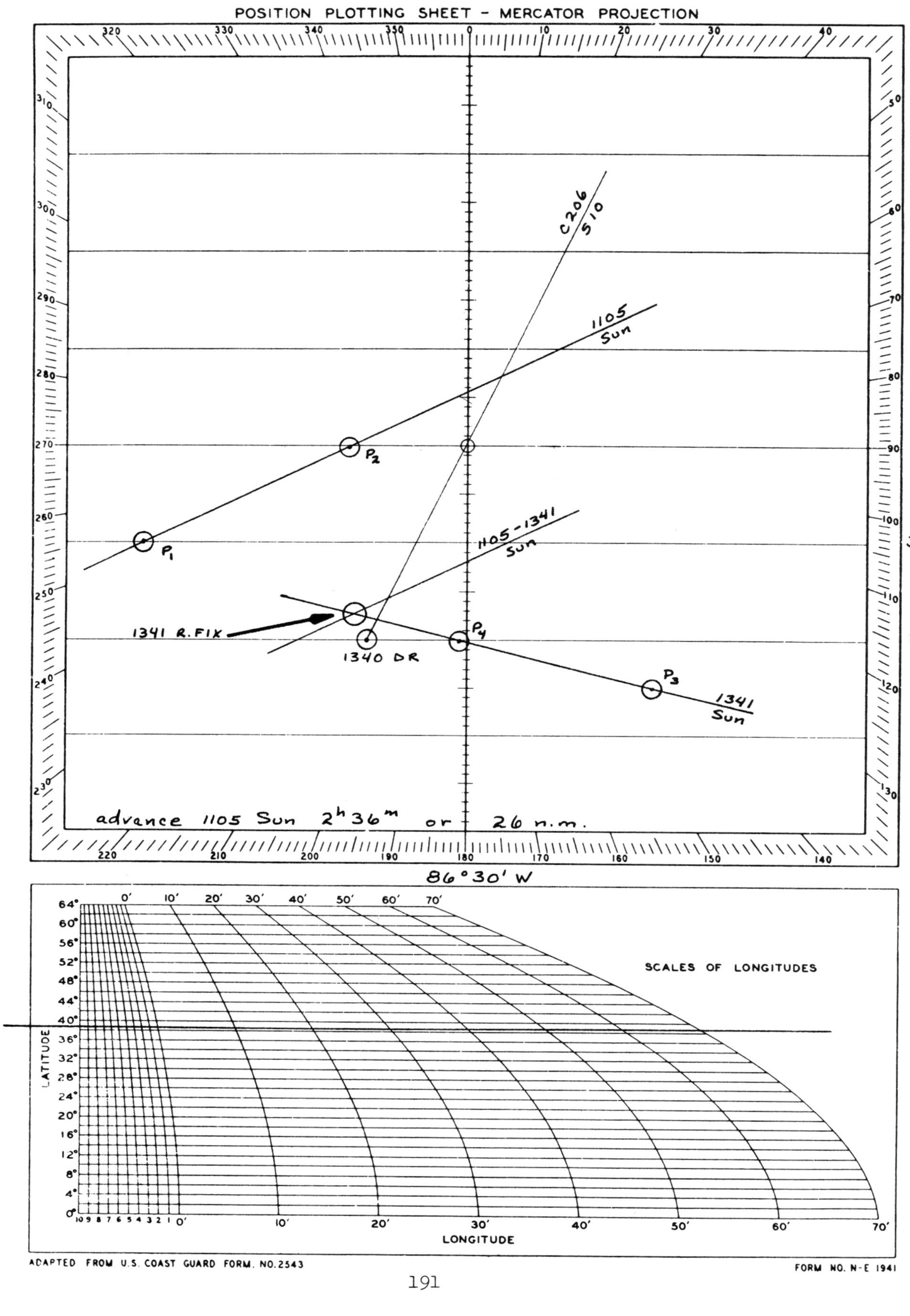
POSITION PLOTTING SHEET - MERCATOR PROJECTION
C206
S10
39°
1105
Sun
38°40' N
P2
P1
1105-1341
Sun
38°30'
1341 R. FIX
P4
1340 DR
38°20'
P3
1341
Sun
advance 1105 Sun 2h 36m or 26 n.m.
38°
86°30' W
SCALES OF LONGITUDES
LATITUDE
LONGITUDE
ADAPTED FROM U.S. COAST GUARD FORM. NO.2543
FORM NO. N-E 1941

A programmable calculator and use of storage memories greatly shorten the solution time as can be imagined.

The second formula which follows yields latitude and longitude directly from two simultaneous sights. No sight reduction tables or plotting are necessary. There are further formulae for non-simultaneous sights but they will not be dealt with here. The following equations are summarized from an article by M.F. A'Hearn and G.S. Rossano in Navigation, Journal of the Institute of Navigation, Spring 1977, Volume 24.

North and west are positive angles, south and east are negative angles. Needed input is sidereal hour angle (SHA), declination (d) and corrected sextant altitude (h) of the two bodies, GHA Body 1.

1. $\cos D = \sin d_1 \sin d_2 + \cos d_1 \cos d_2 \cos \Delta t$

   D = great circle distance between stars
   d = declination
   $\Delta t = SHA_1 - SHA_2$

2. $$\cos \alpha = \frac{\sin d_2 - \sin d_1 \cos D}{\cos d_1 \sin D}$$

   $\alpha$ = the angle formed at star 1 between the hour circle through star 1 and the great circle arc from star 1 to star 2

3. $$\cos \beta = \frac{\sin h_2 - \sin h_1 \cos D}{\cos h_1 \sin D}$$

   h = corrected sextant altitude
   $\beta$ = the angle at star 1 between the vertical circle through star 1 and the great circle arc from star 1 to star 2

4. $\pi = \pm (\alpha \pm \beta)$

   $\pi$ = parallactic angle, angle at star 1 between vertical circle through star 1 and the hour circle through star 1

   $\alpha$, $\beta$, $\pi$ are all less than or equal to 180°
   + if measured northeastward
   - if measured northwestward

   ± outside parenthesis is + if star 1 is west of star 2
   - if star 1 is east of star 2

   ± inside parenthesis is + if great circle arc from star 1 to star 2 crosses navigator's meridian between the elevated pole and the zenith
   - if it does not cross as above
   (determine this by observation at time of taking sights; otherwise by trial and error to see which condition places the fix near the DR)

5. $\sin L = \sin h_1 \sin d_1 + \cos h_1 \cos d_1 \cos \pi$

THIS YIELDS LATITUDE

6. $\cos LHA_1 = \dfrac{\sin h_1 - \sin d_1 \sin L}{\cos d_1 \cos L}$ sign of LHA (or t) = sign of $\pi$

7. $\lambda = GHA_1 - LHA_1$

THIS YIELDS LONGITUDE

For our example we shall choose two stars, Gacrux and Al Na'ir, both observed at 17-37-16 zone time. Necessary information is as follows:

| Body | SHA | GHA | Declination | Corrected Sextant Altitude |
|---|---|---|---|---|
| Gacrux (Star 1) | $172^\circ\ 31'.3$ | $383^\circ\ 50'.2$ | $56^\circ\ 59'.5$ S | $53^\circ\ 25'.3$ |
| Al Na'ir (Star 2) | $28^\circ\ 17'.1$ | not needed | $47^\circ\ 04'.0$ S | $18^\circ\ 38'.8$ |

Intermediate numbers and results are below. Angles are changed to decimal degrees.

1. $\cos D = (-.8386)(-.7321) + (.5448)(.6811)(-.8114)$
$= .6140 + (-.3011)$
$= .3129$

2. $\cos \alpha = \dfrac{(-.7321) - (-.8386)(.3129)}{(.5448)(.9498)} = \dfrac{-.4698}{.5174} = -.9079$

$\alpha = 155^\circ.2163$ or $155^\circ\ 13'.0$

3. $\cos \beta = \dfrac{.3197 - (.8030)(.3129)}{(.5959)(.9498)} = \dfrac{.0685}{.5660} = .1210$

$\beta = 83^\circ.0529$ or $83^\circ\ 03'.2$

4. $\pi = \pm(\alpha \pm \beta)$. In this case, $\pi = \alpha - \beta$ (see diagram)

$= 155^\circ.2163 - 83^\circ.0529 = 72^\circ.1634$

5. $\sin L = (.8030)(-.8386) + (.5959)(.5448)(.3063) = -.5740$

$L = 35^\circ.0288$ S or $35^\circ\ 01'.7$ S

6. $\cos LHA_1 = \dfrac{.8030 - (-.8386)(-.5740)}{(.5448)(.8189)} = .7212$

$LHA_1 = 43^\circ.8491$ or $43^\circ\ 50'.9$ (positive sign)

7. $\lambda = 383^\circ.8367 - 43^\circ.8491 = 339^\circ.9875$ W or $20^\circ.0125$ E or $20^\circ\ 00'.8$ E.

Resulting fix: L 35° 01!7 S
λ 20° 00!8 E

The following diagrams depict the above situation.

The two sets of formulae discussed in this chapter are only a beginning of what the calculator can explore in celestial navigation. Further examples of calculator application can be found in manuals sold with programmable instruments.

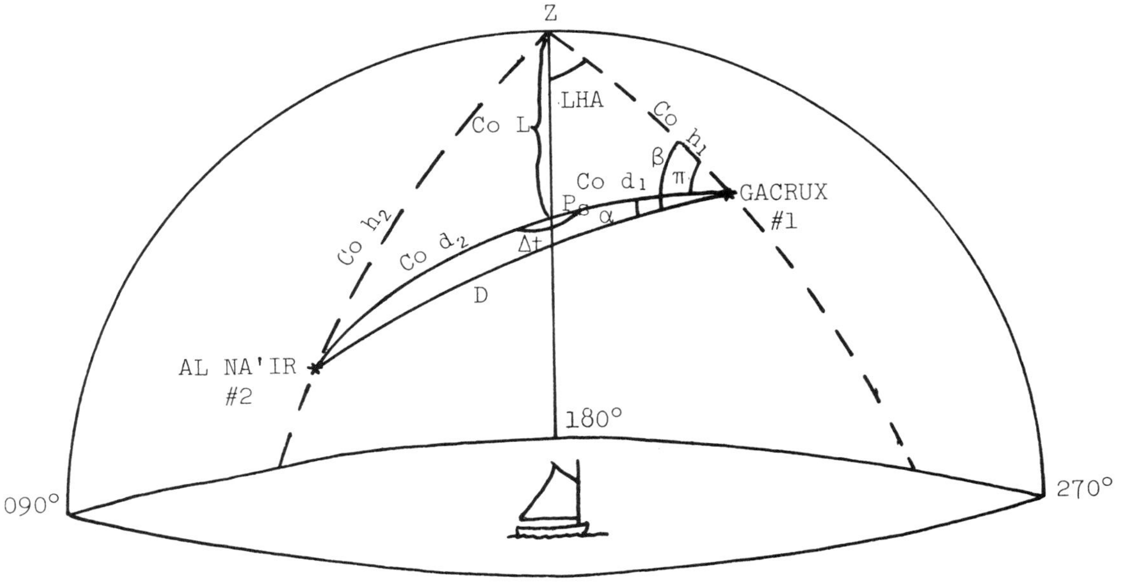


Solve for latitude

$$\sin L = \sin h_1 \sin d_1 + \cos h_1 \cos d_1 \cos \pi$$

Solve for longitude

$$\lambda = GHA_1 - LHA_1$$

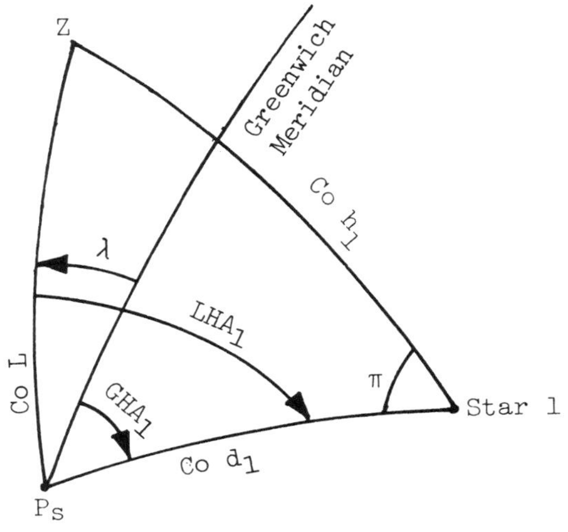

# Appendix 1

## Answers to Exercises

EXERCISE 1

| | | | | |
|---|---|---|---|---|
| 1. | 1900 DR | 35° 57!5 N, | 70° 08!0 W | 6.2 nautical miles apart |
| | 1900 Fix | 36° 03!5 N, | 70° 08!1 W | |
| | 0100 DR | 36° 13!3 N, | 69° 25!2 W | |
| 2. | 2045 DR | 43° 37!0 N, | 69° 29!0 W | |
| | 2045 Fix | 43° 38!6 N, | 69° 26!4 W | |
| | 2257 DR | 43° 48!5 N, | 69° 33!0 W | |
| 3. | 2200 Fix | 15° 17!1 S, | 155° 19!7 E | |
| | 2400 DR | 15° 29!0 S, | 155° 00!5 E | |

EXERCISE 2

| | |
|---|---|
| 1. | 48° 39!4 |
| 2. | 30° 57!8 |
| 3. | 53° 59!7 |
| 4. | 27° 10!6 |
| 5. | 42° 22!4 |
| 6. | 37° 56!0 |
| 7. | 18° 04!0 |
| 8. | 60° 54!1 |
| 9. | 34° 53!0 |
| 10. | 8° 07!9 |
| 11. | 63° 31!9 |
| 12. | 42° 42!9 |
| 13. | 9° 02!8 |
| 14. | 71° 50!1 |
| 15. | 8° 10!3 |
| 16. | 46° 58!7 |
| 17. | 12° 13!8 |
| 18. | 27° 21!5 |

EXERCISE 3

| | GHA | Dec |
|---|---|---|
| 1. | 45° 50!4 | 8° 30!6 S |
| 2. | 196° 00!7 | 24° 52!4 N |
| 3. | 123° 28!7 | 18° 49!4 S |
| 4. | 119° 53!9 | 23° 22!4 S |
| 5. | 86° 09!7 | 16° 54!6 S |
| 6. | 82° 32!7 | 19° 51!2 S |
| 7. | 210° 57!6 | 5° 10!9 N |

EXERCISE 4

| | | |
|---|---|---|
| 8. | 36° 37!1 | 38° 45!8 N |
| 9. | 54° 30!7 | 14° 42!2 N |
| 10. | 342° 22!7 | 57° 21!4 S |
| 11. | 34° 42!0 | 11° 02!4 S |
| 12. | 312° 17!4 | 12° 04!6 N |
| 13. | 55° 36!4 | 12° 34!8 N |
| 14. | 57° 41!0 | 89° 09!2 N |

EXERCISE 5

| | A.P. Lo | "a" | $Z_n$ |
|---|---|---|---|
| 1. | 67° 50'.4 W | 14'.5 T | 152°.9 |
| 2. | 174° 59'.3 E | 17'.3 A | 244°.9 |
| 3. | 79° 28'.7 W | 13'.9 T | 280°.8 |
| 4. | 123° 53'.9 W | 7'.5 A | 025°.9 |
| 5. | 56° 09'.7 W | 4'.6 A | 214°.1 |
| 6. | 71° 32'.7 W | 1'.9 A | 191°.8 |
| 7. | 140° 02'.4 E | 1'.2 T | 164°.1 |
| 8. | 97° 37'.1 W | 0'.5 T | 075°.6 |
| 9. | 24° 30'.7 W | 14'.2 T | 233°.5 |
| 10. | 12° 22'.7 W | 4'.1 A | 136°.1 |
| 11. | 71° 42'.0 W | 8'.5 T | 138°.1 |
| 12. | 37° 42'.6 E | 11'.7 T | 154°.0 |
| 13. | 65° 36'.4 W | 10'.2 A | 161°.1 |
| 14. | 66° 41'.0 W | 5'.2 T | 000°.2 |

EXERCISE 6

| | | Latitude | Longitude |
|---|---|---|---|
| I | 0530 Fix | 34° 07'.1 N | 155° 46'.1 W |
| II | 0430 Fix | 37° 22'.0 N | 68° 49'.0 W |
| III | 1920 Fix | 39° 25'.5 N | 64° 32'.0 W |
| IV | 0345 Fix | 41° 46'.8 S | 155° 24'.3 E |
| V | 1138 R. Fix | 34° 45'.5 N | 129° 22'.2 W |

EXERCISE 7

| | Body | A.P. Lo | "a" | $Z_n$ | Fix |
|---|---|---|---|---|---|
| 1. | Spica | 179° 18'.4 E | 18'.5 T | 201°.8 | 2010 Fix: |
| | Dubhe | 179° 22'.5 E | 1'.5 A | 324°.5 | 36° 44'.0 N |
| | Vega | 179° 01'.6 E | 2'.2 T | 070°.4 | 179° 11'.5 E |
| 2. | Alphard | 137° 18'.1 W | 3'.8 T | 129°.0 | 1900 Fix: |
| | Menkar | 137° 06'.0 W | 13'.6 A | 251°.8 | 36° 19'.2 N |
| | Kochab | 137° 02'.4 W | 22'.0 T | 015°.5 | 136° 48'.0 W |
| 3. | Arcturus | 53° 18'.7 W | 2'.1 T | 350°.9 | 0450 Fix: |
| | Altair | 53° 20'.1 W | 8'.0 T | 072°.6 | 36° 53'.7 S |
| | Canopus | 53° 07'.6 W | 8'.0 A | 207°.6 | 53° 05'.1 W |
| 4. | Sun LL | 25° 05'.1 W | 5'.3 T | 150°.2 | 1101 Fix: |
| | Moon UL | 25° 05'.1 W | 1'.5 T | 246°.3 | 29° 54'.1 N |
| | | | | | 25° 04'.0 W |

EXERCISE 7 (continued)

| | Body | A.P. Lo | "a" | $Z_n$ | Fix |
|---|---|---|---|---|---|
| 5. | Sun LL | 156° 18!3 E | 10!0 T | 211°1 | 1500 R. Fix: |
| | Sun UL | 156° 10!1 E | 4!4 A | 267°0 | 36° 24!9 N |
| | | | | | 156° 13!0 E |
| 6. | Moon LL | 67° 31!6 W | 33!9 A | 165°0 | 2000 Fix: |
| | Mars | 68° 00!9 W | 15!2 A | 272°4 | 43° 35!5 N |
| | | | | | 67° 37!7 W |

EXERCISE 8

| | Sunrise | Sunset | Morn Twilight | Eve Twilight |
|---|---|---|---|---|
| 1a. | 0712 | 1624 | 0606 | 1729 |
| b. | 0412 | 1943 | 0230 | 2126 |
| c. | 0449 | 1852 | 0348 | 1954 |
| d. | 0556 | 1803 | 0506 | 1853 |
| e. | 0538 | 1800 | 0452 | 1846 |

2a. 1140
b. 1226
c. 1131
d. 1212
e. 1142
f. 1213

3a. $11^h\ 46^m\ 52^s$
b. $12^h\ 11^m\ 57^s$

EXERCISE 9

| | | Some Stars | Alt. | Az. | Possible Good Threesome |
|---|---|---|---|---|---|
| 1a. | GMT = 2147 | Regulus | 33° | 110° | * |
| | LHA Aries = 95° 17!8 | Procyon | 48° | 152° | |
| | Template = 45° N | Sirius | 29° | 174° | * |
| | | Betelgeuse | 52° | 192° | |
| | | Rigel | 35° | 202° | |
| | | Aldebaran | 53° | 227° | * |
| b. | GMT = 2026 (20 June) | Rigel | 22° | 085° | |
| | LHA Aries = 8° 40!3 | Canopus | 29° | 137° | * |
| | Template = 35° S | Achernar | 65° | 160° | |
| | | Peacock | 43° | 222° | |
| | | Al Na'ir | 60° | 235° | |

EXERCISE 9 (continued)

| | Some Stars | Alt. | Az. | Possible Good Threesome |
|---|---|---|---|---|
| b. (continued) | Nunki | 18° | 251° | * |
| | Alpheratz | 26° | 353° | |
| | Hamal | 28° | 024° | * |
| c. GMT = 0912<br>LHA Aries = 271° 20!7<br>Template = 25° N | Deneb | 53° | 047° | * |
| | Altair | 60° | 120° | |
| | Nunki | 37° | 166° | |
| | Shaula | 27° | 188° | |
| | Antares | 34° | 206° | |
| | Arcturus | 37° | 276° | |
| | Alphecca | 56° | 281° | * |
| | Kochab | 35° | 345° | * |
| d. GMT = 1301<br>LHA Aries = 140° 27!6<br>Template = 55° S | Regulus | 22° | 012° | * |
| | Spica | 26° | 072° | * |
| | Rigel Kent | 50° | 132° | * |
| | Achernar | 33° | 216° | |
| | Canopus | 64° | 257° | |
| | Rigel | 22° | 289° | |
| | Sirius | 41° | 306° | |
| | Procyon | 26° | 331° | |

| | Body | RA | Plot | Alt. | Az. |
|---|---|---|---|---|---|
| 2a. | Mars | 91° | 26° Towards | 70° | 185° |
| | Jupiter | 27° | 10° Towards | 24° | 265° |
| | Saturn | 118° | 21° Towards | 57° | 130° |
| | Moon and Venus not visible. | | | | |
| b. | Moon | 11° | 8° Away | 46° | 005° |
| | Jupiter | 48° | 17° Away | 25° | 043° |
| | Venus, Mars and Saturn not visible. | | | | |
| c. | Venus | 203° | 10° Away | 16° | 250° |
| | Mars | 197° | 7° Away | 12° | 255° |
| | Moon, Jupiter and Saturn not visible. | | | | |
| d. | Mars | 261° | 24° Towards | 2° | 130° |
| | Saturn | 139° | 17° Away | 17° | 000° |
| | Moon, Venus and Jupiter not visible. | | | | |

EXERCISE 10

1a. 59° 48!8 N
b. 15° 26!6 N
c. 39° 41!7 N
d. 40° 56!8 N

## EXERCISE 10 (continued)

2. A.P. Lo = 71° 32'.0, "a" = 2'.7 A, $Z_n$ = 359°.1, L = 40° 57'.0 N

3a. 46° 33'.1 N
 b. 41° 10'.6 N
 c. 40° 12'.2 S

4a. 43° 46'.2 N
 b. 36° 35'.4 N
 c. 30° 41'.9 N

5a. 44° 19'.4 N
 b. 44° 34'.1 S

6. $H_s$ = 75° 24'.2 L = 31° 30'.0 N (will vary slightly depending on fitting of curve)

7. correction = +6'.0

8. correction = +8'.4, L = 52° 33'.5 S

## EXERCISE 11

| | | Latitude | Longitude |
|---|---|---|---|
| I | 0518 Fix | 40° 54'.8 S | 14° 10'.5 W |
| | 1442 DR | 39° 09'.5 S | 12° 53'.0 W |
| | 1442 R. Fix | 39° 02'.5 S | 12° 47'.4 W |
| II | 0610 Fix | 41° 15'.4 S | 106° 43'.7 W |
| | 1210 R. Fix | 39° 48'.0 S | 108° 08'.0 W |
| | 1810 Fix | 38° 39'.8 S | 109° 29'.0 W |
| III | 0645 R. Fix | 39° 59'.2 N | 17° 55'.0 E |
| | 1913 Fix | 39° 32'.5 N | 17° 24'.5 E |
| IV | 1747 Fix | 38° 42'.8 N | 65° 44'.8 W |
| | Venus is in conjunction with NUNKI, 0600 DR relabelled 0500 DR, zone +5 | | |
| | 0611 Fix | 40° 00'.2 N | 68° 19'.5 W |
| | 1522 Fix | 41° 57'.2 N | 68° 15'.3 W |
| V | 0400 DR | 33° 27'.0 S | 172° 08'.9 E |
| | 0404 Fix | 33° 30'.0 S | 172° 04'.2 E |
| | 1135 Sun LOP | 33° 58'.5 S (same as 1130 DR) | |
| | 1930 DR | 34° 08'.5 S | 171° 59'.7 E |
| | 1936 Fix | 34° 11'.0 S | 171° 55'.0 E |

EXERCISE 11 (continued)

| | | Latitude | Longitude |
|---|---|---|---|
| VI | 1500 DR | 38° 10'.8 S | 126° 27'.4 E |
| | 1510 R. Fix | 38° 04'.0 S | 126° 48'.9 E |
| | 1930 DR | 34° 00'.5 N | 38° 02'.2 W |
| | 1930 Fix | 34° 05'.5 N | 37° 54'.8 W |

EXERCISE 12

1. Fixes given above in Exercise 11 - VI.

| | Body | "a" | $Z_n$ | Fix |
|---|---|---|---|---|
| 2a. | Rasalhague | 0'.7 A | 182°.8 | 0521 Fix |
| | Mars | 1'.6 A | 142°.8 | L 38° 40'.8 N |
| | Moon | 3'.5 A | 104°.8 | λ 70° 06'.0 W |
| b. | Diphda | 5'.7 A | 263°.8 | 0519 Fix |
| | Acrux | 4'.9 T | 147°.8 | L 38° 44'.5 S |
| | Saturn | 2'.7 A | 016°.5 | λ 140° 59'.5 W |

EXERCISE 13

1. Meridians spaced 2.86 inches apart.
   Parallels spaced at intervals - 0, 3.3, 6.63 and 10 inches.

2. Meridians spaced 2.15 inches apart.
   Parallels spaced at intervals - 0, 3.78, 7.67, 11.66, 15.76 and 20 inches.

EXERCISE 14

Answers are averaged between Methods A and B.

1. Course = 151°.3, distance = 224.6 nautical miles.

2. Course = 251°.3, distance = 1217.8 nautical miles.

3. Course = 148°.0, distance = 614.9 nautical miles.

Answers are as found by Method B.

4. L = 00° 26'.1 N    λ = 82° 35'.1 E

5. L = 19° 07'.3 S    λ = 117° 06'.1 E

6. L = 51° 19'.8 N    λ = 16° 05'.6 W

EXERCISE 15

1a. 6° 01'.6 S and 23° 41'.4 N.
 b. 311°.8, 2508.27 nautical miles; 315°.2, 2511.76 nautical miles; 304°.5, 1775.46 nautical miles.

2a. 29° 47'.2 N, 39° 41'.6 N and 40° 52'.0 N.
 b. 054°.6, 1763.03 nautical miles; 068°.15, 1596.8 nautical miles; 087°.1, 1380.69 nautical miles; 106°.5, 1491.04 nautical miles.

1a and 1b are done by Method B.

# Appendix 2

## Nautical Almanac Excerpts

All pages from the 1976 Nautical Almanac needed for the text examples and exercises are included in this appendix.

Index to Appendix 2

# ALTITUDE CORRECTION TABLES 10°-90°—SUN, STARS, PLANETS

## SUN

| OCT.—MAR. App. Alt. | Lower Limb | Upper Limb | APR.—SEPT. App. Alt. | Lower Limb | Upper Limb |
|---|---|---|---|---|---|
| ° ′ | ′ | ′ | ° ′ | ′ | ′ |
| 9 34 | +10·8 | −21·5 | 9 39 | +10·6 | −21·2 |
| 9 45 | +10·9 | −21·4 | 9 51 | +10·7 | −21·1 |
| 9 56 | +11·0 | −21·3 | 10 03 | +10·8 | −21·0 |
| 10 08 | +11·1 | −21·2 | 10 15 | +10·9 | −20·9 |
| 10 21 | +11·2 | −21·1 | 10 27 | +11·0 | −20·8 |
| 10 34 | +11·3 | −21·0 | 10 40 | +11·1 | −20·7 |
| 10 47 | +11·4 | −20·9 | 10 54 | +11·2 | −20·6 |
| 11 01 | +11·5 | −20·8 | 11 08 | +11·3 | −20·5 |
| 11 15 | +11·6 | −20·7 | 11 23 | +11·4 | −20·4 |
| 11 30 | +11·7 | −20·6 | 11 38 | +11·5 | −20·3 |
| 11 46 | +11·8 | −20·5 | 11 54 | +11·6 | −20·2 |
| 12 02 | +11·9 | −20·4 | 12 10 | +11·7 | −20·1 |
| 12 19 | +12·0 | −20·3 | 12 28 | +11·8 | −20·0 |
| 12 37 | +12·1 | −20·2 | 12 46 | +11·9 | −19·9 |
| 12 55 | +12·2 | −20·1 | 13 05 | +12·0 | −19·8 |
| 13 14 | +12·3 | −20·0 | 13 24 | +12·1 | −19·7 |
| 13 35 | +12·4 | −19·9 | 13 45 | +12·2 | −19·6 |
| 13 56 | +12·5 | −19·8 | 14 07 | +12·3 | −19·5 |
| 14 18 | +12·6 | −19·7 | 14 30 | +12·4 | −19·4 |
| 14 42 | +12·7 | −19·6 | 14 54 | +12·5 | −19·3 |
| 15 06 | +12·8 | −19·5 | 15 19 | +12·6 | −19·2 |
| 15 32 | +12·9 | −19·4 | 15 46 | +12·7 | −19·1 |
| 15 59 | +13·0 | −19·3 | 16 14 | +12·8 | −19·0 |
| 16 28 | +13·1 | −19·2 | 16 44 | +12·9 | −18·9 |
| 16 59 | +13·2 | −19·1 | 17 15 | +13·0 | −18·8 |
| 17 32 | +13·3 | −19·0 | 17 48 | +13·1 | −18·7 |
| 18 06 | +13·4 | −18·9 | 18 24 | +13·2 | −18·6 |
| 18 42 | +13·5 | −18·8 | 19 01 | +13·3 | −18·5 |
| 19 21 | +13·6 | −18·7 | 19 42 | +13·4 | −18·4 |
| 20 03 | +13·7 | −18·6 | 20 25 | +13·5 | −18·3 |
| 20 48 | +13·8 | −18·5 | 21 11 | +13·6 | −18·2 |
| 21 35 | +13·9 | −18·4 | 22 00 | +13·7 | −18·1 |
| 22 26 | +14·0 | −18·3 | 22 54 | +13·8 | −18·0 |
| 23 22 | +14·1 | −18·2 | 23 51 | +13·9 | −17·9 |
| 24 21 | +14·2 | −18·1 | 24 53 | +14·0 | −17·8 |
| 25 26 | +14·3 | −18·0 | 26 00 | +14·1 | −17·7 |
| 26 36 | +14·4 | −17·9 | 27 13 | +14·2 | −17·6 |
| 27 52 | +14·5 | −17·8 | 28 33 | +14·3 | −17·5 |
| 29 15 | +14·6 | −17·7 | 30 00 | +14·4 | −17·4 |
| 30 46 | +14·7 | −17·6 | 31 35 | +14·5 | −17·3 |
| 32 26 | +14·8 | −17·5 | 33 20 | +14·6 | −17·2 |
| 34 17 | +14·9 | −17·4 | 35 17 | +14·7 | −17·1 |
| 36 20 | +15·0 | −17·3 | 37 26 | +14·8 | −17·0 |
| 38 36 | +15·1 | −17·2 | 39 50 | +14·9 | −16·9 |
| 41 08 | +15·2 | −17·1 | 42 31 | +15·0 | −16·8 |
| 43 59 | +15·3 | −17·0 | 45 31 | +15·1 | −16·7 |
| 47 10 | +15·4 | −16·9 | 48 55 | +15·2 | −16·6 |
| 50 46 | +15·5 | −16·8 | 52 44 | +15·3 | −16·5 |
| 54 49 | +15·6 | −16·7 | 57 02 | +15·4 | −16·4 |
| 59 23 | +15·7 | −16·6 | 61 51 | +15·5 | −16·3 |
| 64 30 | +15·8 | −16·5 | 67 17 | +15·6 | −16·2 |
| 70 12 | +15·9 | −16·4 | 73 16 | +15·7 | −16·1 |
| 76 26 | +16·0 | −16·3 | 79 43 | +15·8 | −16·0 |
| 83 05 | +16·1 | −16·2 | 86 32 | +15·9 | −15·9 |
| 90 00 | | | 90 00 | | |

## STARS AND PLANETS

| App. Alt. | Corrⁿ |
|---|---|
| ° ′ | ′ |
| 9 56 | −5·3 |
| 10 08 | −5·2 |
| 10 20 | −5·1 |
| 10 33 | −5·0 |
| 10 46 | −4·9 |
| 11 00 | −4·8 |
| 11 14 | −4·7 |
| 11 29 | −4·6 |
| 11 45 | −4·5 |
| 12 01 | −4·4 |
| 12 18 | −4·3 |
| 12 35 | −4·2 |
| 12 54 | −4·1 |
| 13 13 | −4·0 |
| 13 33 | −3·9 |
| 13 54 | −3·8 |
| 14 16 | −3·7 |
| 14 40 | −3·6 |
| 15 04 | −3·5 |
| 15 30 | −3·4 |
| 15 57 | −3·3 |
| 16 26 | −3·2 |
| 16 56 | −3·1 |
| 17 28 | −3·0 |
| 18 02 | −2·9 |
| 18 38 | −2·8 |
| 19 17 | −2·7 |
| 19 58 | −2·6 |
| 20 42 | −2·5 |
| 21 28 | −2·4 |
| 22 19 | −2·3 |
| 23 13 | −2·2 |
| 24 11 | −2·1 |
| 25 14 | −2·0 |
| 26 22 | −1·9 |
| 27 36 | −1·8 |
| 28 56 | −1·7 |
| 30 24 | −1·6 |
| 32 00 | −1·5 |
| 33 45 | −1·4 |
| 35 40 | −1·3 |
| 37 48 | −1·2 |
| 40 08 | −1·1 |
| 42 44 | −1·0 |
| 45 36 | −0·9 |
| 48 47 | −0·8 |
| 52 18 | −0·7 |
| 56 11 | −0·6 |
| 60 28 | −0·5 |
| 65 08 | −0·4 |
| 70 11 | −0·3 |
| 75 34 | −0·2 |
| 81 13 | −0·1 |
| 87 03 | 0·0 |
| 90 00 | |

| App. Alt. | Additional Corrⁿ |
|---|---|
| **1976** | |
| **VENUS** | |
| Jan. 1—Dec. 12 | |
| 0° | +0′·1 |
| 42 | |
| Dec. 13—Dec. 31 | |
| 0° | +0′·2 |
| 47 | |
| **MARS** | |
| Jan. 1—Feb. 19 | |
| 0° | +0′·2 |
| 41 | +0·1 |
| 75 | |
| Feb. 20—Dec. 31 | |
| 0° | +0′·1 |
| 60 | |

## DIP

| Ht. of Eye (m) | Corrⁿ | Ht. of Eye (ft.) |
|---|---|---|
| m | ′ | ft. |
| 2·4 | −2·8 | 8·0 |
| 2·6 | −2·9 | 8·6 |
| 2·8 | −3·0 | 9·2 |
| 3·0 | −3·1 | 9·8 |
| 3·2 | −3·2 | 10·5 |
| 3·4 | −3·3 | 11·2 |
| 3·6 | −3·4 | 11·9 |
| 3·8 | −3·5 | 12·6 |
| 4·0 | −3·6 | 13·3 |
| 4·3 | −3·7 | 14·1 |
| 4·5 | −3·8 | 14·9 |
| 4·7 | −3·9 | 15·7 |
| 5·0 | −4·0 | 16·5 |
| 5·2 | −4·1 | 17·4 |
| 5·5 | −4·2 | 18·3 |
| 5·8 | −4·3 | 19·1 |
| 6·1 | −4·4 | 20·1 |
| 6·3 | −4·5 | 21·0 |
| 6·6 | −4·6 | 22·0 |
| 6·9 | −4·7 | 22·9 |
| 7·2 | −4·8 | 23·9 |
| 7·5 | −4·9 | 24·9 |
| 7·9 | −5·0 | 26·0 |
| 8·2 | −5·1 | 27·1 |
| 8·5 | −5·2 | 28·1 |
| 8·8 | −5·3 | 29·2 |
| 9·2 | −5·4 | 30·4 |
| 9·5 | −5·5 | 31·5 |
| 9·9 | −5·6 | 32·7 |
| 10·3 | −5·7 | 33·9 |
| 10·6 | −5·8 | 35·1 |
| 11·0 | −5·9 | 36·3 |
| 11·4 | −6·0 | 37·6 |
| 11·8 | −6·1 | 38·9 |
| 12·2 | −6·2 | 40·1 |
| 12·6 | −6·3 | 41·5 |
| 13·0 | −6·4 | 42·8 |
| 13·4 | −6·5 | 44·2 |
| 13·8 | −6·6 | 45·5 |
| 14·2 | −6·7 | 46·9 |
| 14·7 | −6·8 | 48·4 |
| 15·1 | −6·9 | 49·8 |
| 15·5 | −7·0 | 51·3 |
| 16·0 | −7·1 | 52·8 |
| 16·5 | −7·2 | 54·3 |
| 16·9 | −7·3 | 55·8 |
| 17·4 | −7·4 | 57·4 |
| 17·9 | −7·5 | 58·9 |
| 18·4 | −7·6 | 60·5 |
| 18·8 | −7·7 | 62·1 |
| 19·3 | −7·8 | 63·8 |
| 19·8 | −7·9 | 65·4 |
| 20·4 | −8·0 | 67·1 |
| 20·9 | −8·1 | 68·8 |
| 21·4 | | 70·5 |

| Ht. of Eye | Corrⁿ |
|---|---|
| m | ′ |
| 1·0 | −1·8 |
| 1·5 | −2·2 |
| 2·0 | −2·5 |
| 2·5 | −2·8 |
| 3·0 | −3·0 |
| See table ← | |
| m | |
| 20 | −7·9 |
| 22 | −8·3 |
| 24 | −8·6 |
| 26 | −9·0 |
| 28 | −9·3 |
| 30 | −9·6 |
| 32 | −10·0 |
| 34 | −10·3 |
| 36 | −10·6 |
| 38 | −10·8 |
| 40 | −11·1 |
| 42 | −11·4 |
| 44 | −11·7 |
| 46 | −11·9 |
| 48 | −12·2 |
| ft. | |
| 2 | −1·4 |
| 4 | −1·9 |
| 6 | −2·4 |
| 8 | −2·7 |
| 10 | −3·1 |
| See table ← | |
| ft. | |
| 70 | −8·1 |
| 75 | −8·4 |
| 80 | −8·7 |
| 85 | −8·9 |
| 90 | −9·2 |
| 95 | −9·5 |
| 100 | −9·7 |
| 105 | −9·9 |
| 110 | −10·2 |
| 115 | −10·4 |
| 120 | −10·6 |
| 125 | −10·8 |
| 130 | −11·1 |
| 135 | −11·3 |
| 140 | −11·5 |
| 145 | −11·7 |
| 150 | −11·9 |
| 155 | −12·1 |

# ALTITUDE CORRECTION TABLES 0°-10°—SUN, STARS, PLANETS A3

| App. Alt. | SUN OCT.—MAR. Lower Limb | Upper Limb | SUN APR.—SEPT. Lower Limb | Upper Limb | STARS PLANETS |
|---|---|---|---|---|---|
| ° ′ | ′ | ′ | ′ | ′ | ′ |
| 0 00 | −18·2 | −50·5 | −18·4 | −50·2 | −34·5 |
| 03 | 17·5 | 49·8 | 17·8 | 49·6 | 33·8 |
| 06 | 16·9 | 49·2 | 17·1 | 48·9 | 33·2 |
| 09 | 16·3 | 48·6 | 16·5 | 48·3 | 32·6 |
| 12 | 15·7 | 48·0 | 15·9 | 47·7 | 32·0 |
| 15 | 15·1 | 47·4 | 15·3 | 47·1 | 31·4 |
| 0 18 | −14·5 | −46·8 | −14·8 | −46·6 | −30·8 |
| 21 | 14·0 | 46·3 | 14·2 | 46·0 | 30·3 |
| 24 | 13·5 | 45·8 | 13·7 | 45·5 | 29·8 |
| 27 | 12·9 | 45·2 | 13·2 | 45·0 | 29·2 |
| 30 | 12·4 | 44·7 | 12·7 | 44·5 | 28·7 |
| 33 | 11·9 | 44·2 | 12·2 | 44·0 | 28·2 |
| 0 36 | −11·5 | −43·8 | −11·7 | −43·5 | −27·8 |
| 39 | 11·0 | 43·3 | 11·2 | 43·0 | 27·3 |
| 42 | 10·5 | 42·8 | 10·8 | 42·6 | 26·8 |
| 45 | 10·1 | 42·4 | 10·3 | 42·1 | 26·4 |
| 48 | 9·6 | 41·9 | 9·9 | 41·7 | 25·9 |
| 51 | 9·2 | 41·5 | 9·5 | 41·3 | 25·5 |
| 0 54 | −8·8 | −41·1 | −9·1 | −40·9 | −25·1 |
| 0 57 | 8·4 | 40·7 | 8·7 | 40·5 | 24·7 |
| 1 00 | 8·0 | 40·3 | 8·3 | 40·1 | 24·3 |
| 03 | 7·7 | 40·0 | 7·9 | 39·7 | 24·0 |
| 06 | 7·3 | 39·6 | 7·5 | 39·3 | 23·6 |
| 09 | 6·9 | 39·2 | 7·2 | 39·0 | 23·2 |
| 1 12 | −6·6 | −38·9 | −6·8 | −38·6 | −22·9 |
| 15 | 6·2 | 38·5 | 6·5 | 38·3 | 22·5 |
| 18 | 5·9 | 38·2 | 6·2 | 38·0 | 22·2 |
| 21 | 5·6 | 37·9 | 5·8 | 37·6 | 21·9 |
| 24 | 5·3 | 37·6 | 5·5 | 37·3 | 21·6 |
| 27 | 4·9 | 37·2 | 5·2 | 37·0 | 21·2 |
| 1 30 | −4·6 | −36·9 | −4·9 | −36·7 | −20·9 |
| 35 | 4·2 | 36·5 | 4·4 | 36·2 | 20·5 |
| 40 | 3·7 | 36·0 | 4·0 | 35·8 | 20·0 |
| 45 | 3·2 | 35·5 | 3·5 | 35·3 | 19·5 |
| 50 | 2·8 | 35·1 | 3·1 | 34·9 | 19·1 |
| 1 55 | 2·4 | 34·7 | 2·6 | 34·4 | 18·7 |
| 2 00 | −2·0 | −34·3 | −2·2 | −34·0 | −18·3 |
| 05 | 1·6 | 33·9 | 1·8 | 33·6 | 17·9 |
| 10 | 1·2 | 33·5 | 1·5 | 33·3 | 17·5 |
| 15 | 0·9 | 33·2 | 1·1 | 32·9 | 17·2 |
| 20 | 0·5 | 32·8 | 0·8 | 32·6 | 16·8 |
| 25 | −0·2 | 32·5 | 0·4 | 32·2 | 16·5 |
| 2 30 | +0·2 | −32·1 | −0·1 | −31·9 | −16·1 |
| 35 | 0·5 | 31·8 | +0·2 | 31·6 | 15·8 |
| 40 | 0·8 | 31·5 | 0·5 | 31·3 | 15·5 |
| 45 | 1·1 | 31·2 | 0·8 | 31·0 | 15·2 |
| 50 | 1·4 | 30·9 | 1·1 | 30·7 | 14·9 |
| 2 55 | 1·6 | 30·7 | 1·4 | 30·4 | 14·7 |
| 3 00 | +1·9 | −30·4 | +1·7 | −30·1 | −14·4 |
| 05 | 2·2 | 30·1 | 1·9 | 29·9 | 14·1 |
| 10 | 2·4 | 29·9 | 2·1 | 29·7 | 13·9 |
| 15 | 2·6 | 29·7 | 2·4 | 29·4 | 13·7 |
| 20 | 2·9 | 29·4 | 2·6 | 29·2 | 13·4 |
| 25 | 3·1 | 29·2 | 2·9 | 28·9 | 13·2 |
| 3 30 | +3·3 | −29·0 | +3·1 | −28·7 | −13·0 |

| App. Alt. | SUN OCT.—MAR. Lower Limb | Upper Limb | SUN APR.—SEPT. Lower Limb | Upper Limb | STARS PLANETS |
|---|---|---|---|---|---|
| ° ′ | ′ | ′ | ′ | ′ | ′ |
| 3 30 | +3·3 | −29·0 | +3·1 | −28·7 | −13·0 |
| 35 | 3·6 | 28·7 | 3·3 | 28·5 | 12·7 |
| 40 | 3·8 | 28·5 | 3·5 | 28·3 | 12·5 |
| 45 | 4·0 | 28·3 | 3·7 | 28·1 | 12·3 |
| 50 | 4·2 | 28·1 | 3·9 | 27·9 | 12·1 |
| 3 55 | 4·4 | 27·9 | 4·1 | 27·7 | 11·9 |
| 4 00 | +4·5 | −27·8 | +4·3 | −27·5 | −11·8 |
| 05 | 4·7 | 27·6 | 4·5 | 27·3 | 11·6 |
| 10 | 4·9 | 27·4 | 4·6 | 27·2 | 11·4 |
| 15 | 5·1 | 27·2 | 4·8 | 27·0 | 11·2 |
| 20 | 5·2 | 27·1 | 5·0 | 26·8 | 11·1 |
| 25 | 5·4 | 26·9 | 5·1 | 26·7 | 10·9 |
| 4 30 | +5·6 | −26·7 | +5·3 | −26·5 | −10·7 |
| 35 | 5·7 | 26·6 | 5·5 | 26·3 | 10·6 |
| 40 | 5·9 | 26·4 | 5·6 | 26·2 | 10·4 |
| 45 | 6·0 | 26·3 | 5·8 | 26·0 | 10·3 |
| 50 | 6·2 | 26·1 | 5·9 | 25·9 | 10·1 |
| 4 55 | 6·3 | 26·0 | 6·0 | 25·8 | 10·0 |
| 5 00 | +6·4 | −25·9 | +6·2 | −25·6 | −9·9 |
| 05 | 6·6 | 25·7 | 6·3 | 25·5 | 9·7 |
| 10 | 6·7 | 25·6 | 6·4 | 25·4 | 9·6 |
| 15 | 6·8 | 25·5 | 6·6 | 25·2 | 9·5 |
| 20 | 6·9 | 25·4 | 6·7 | 25·1 | 9·4 |
| 25 | 7·1 | 25·2 | 6·8 | 25·0 | 9·2 |
| 5 30 | +7·2 | −25·1 | +6·9 | −24·9 | −9·1 |
| 35 | 7·3 | 25·0 | 7·0 | 24·8 | 9·0 |
| 40 | 7·4 | 24·9 | 7·2 | 24·6 | 8·9 |
| 45 | 7·5 | 24·8 | 7·3 | 24·5 | 8·8 |
| 50 | 7·6 | 24·7 | 7·4 | 24·4 | 8·7 |
| 5 55 | 7·7 | 24·6 | 7·5 | 24·3 | 8·6 |
| 6 00 | +7·8 | −24·5 | +7·6 | −24·2 | −8·5 |
| 10 | 8·0 | 24·3 | 7·8 | 24·0 | 8·3 |
| 20 | 8·2 | 24·1 | 8·0 | 23·8 | 8·1 |
| 30 | 8·4 | 23·9 | 8·1 | 23·7 | 7·9 |
| 40 | 8·6 | 23·7 | 8·3 | 23·5 | 7·7 |
| 6 50 | 8·7 | 23·6 | 8·5 | 23·3 | 7·6 |
| 7 00 | +8·9 | −23·4 | +8·6 | −23·2 | −7·4 |
| 10 | 9·1 | 23·2 | 8·8 | 23·0 | 7·2 |
| 20 | 9·2 | 23·1 | 9·0 | 22·8 | 7·1 |
| 30 | 9·3 | 23·0 | 9·1 | 22·7 | 7·0 |
| 40 | 9·5 | 22·8 | 9·2 | 22·6 | 6·8 |
| 7 50 | 9·6 | 22·7 | 9·4 | 22·4 | 6·7 |
| 8 00 | +9·7 | −22·6 | +9·5 | −22·3 | −6·6 |
| 10 | 9·9 | 22·4 | 9·6 | 22·2 | 6·4 |
| 20 | 10·0 | 22·3 | 9·7 | 22·1 | 6·3 |
| 30 | 10·1 | 22·2 | 9·8 | 22·0 | 6·2 |
| 40 | 10·2 | 22·1 | 10·0 | 21·8 | 6·1 |
| 8 50 | 10·3 | 22·0 | 10·1 | 21·7 | 6·0 |
| 9 00 | +10·4 | −21·9 | +10·2 | −21·6 | −5·9 |
| 10 | 10·5 | 21·8 | 10·3 | 21·5 | 5·8 |
| 20 | 10·6 | 21·7 | 10·4 | 21·4 | 5·7 |
| 30 | 10·7 | 21·6 | 10·5 | 21·3 | 5·6 |
| 40 | 10·8 | 21·5 | 10·6 | 21·2 | 5·5 |
| 9 50 | 10·9 | 21·4 | 10·6 | 21·2 | 5·4 |
| 10 00 | +11·0 | −21·3 | +10·7 | −21·1 | −5·3 |

# ALTITUDE CORRECTION TABLES 0°–35°—MOON

| App. Alt. | 0°–4° Corr$^{n}$ | 5°–9° Corr$^{n}$ | 10°–14° Corr$^{n}$ | 15°–19° Corr$^{n}$ | 20°–24° Corr$^{n}$ | 25°–29° Corr$^{n}$ | 30°–34° Corr$^{n}$ | App. Alt. |
|---|---|---|---|---|---|---|---|---|
| 00 | 0° 33·8 | 5° 58·2 | 10° 62·1 | 15° 62·8 | 20° 62·2 | 25° 60·8 | 30° 58·9 | 00 |
| 10 | 35·9 | 58·5 | 62·2 | 62·8 | 62·1 | 60·8 | 58·8 | 10 |
| 20 | 37·8 | 58·7 | 62·2 | 62·8 | 62·1 | 60·7 | 58·8 | 20 |
| 30 | 39·6 | 58·9 | 62·3 | 62·8 | 62·1 | 60·7 | 58·7 | 30 |
| 40 | 41·2 | 59·1 | 62·3 | 62·8 | 62·0 | 60·6 | 58·6 | 40 |
| 50 | 42·6 | 59·3 | 62·4 | 62·7 | 62·0 | 60·6 | 58·5 | 50 |
| 00 | 1 44·0 | 6 59·5 | 11 62·4 | 16 62·7 | 21 62·0 | 26 60·5 | 31 58·5 | 00 |
| 10 | 45·2 | 59·7 | 62·4 | 62·7 | 61·9 | 60·4 | 58·4 | 10 |
| 20 | 46·3 | 59·9 | 62·5 | 62·7 | 61·9 | 60·4 | 58·3 | 20 |
| 30 | 47·3 | 60·0 | 62·5 | 62·7 | 61·9 | 60·3 | 58·2 | 30 |
| 40 | 48·3 | 60·2 | 62·5 | 62·7 | 61·8 | 60·3 | 58·2 | 40 |
| 50 | 49·2 | 60·3 | 62·6 | 62·7 | 61·8 | 60·2 | 58·1 | 50 |
| 00 | 2 50·0 | 7 60·5 | 12 62·6 | 17 62·7 | 22 61·7 | 27 60·1 | 32 58·0 | 00 |
| 10 | 50·8 | 60·6 | 62·6 | 62·6 | 61·7 | 60·1 | 57·9 | 10 |
| 20 | 51·4 | 60·7 | 62·6 | 62·6 | 61·6 | 60·0 | 57·8 | 20 |
| 30 | 52·1 | 60·9 | 62·7 | 62·6 | 61·6 | 59·9 | 57·8 | 30 |
| 40 | 52·7 | 61·0 | 62·7 | 62·6 | 61·5 | 59·9 | 57·7 | 40 |
| 50 | 53·3 | 61·1 | 62·7 | 62·6 | 61·5 | 59·8 | 57·6 | 50 |
| 00 | 3 53·8 | 8 61·2 | 13 62·7 | 18 62·5 | 23 61·5 | 28 59·7 | 33 57·5 | 00 |
| 10 | 54·3 | 61·3 | 62·7 | 62·5 | 61·4 | 59·7 | 57·4 | 10 |
| 20 | 54·8 | 61·4 | 62·7 | 62·5 | 61·4 | 59·6 | 57·4 | 20 |
| 30 | 55·2 | 61·5 | 62·8 | 62·5 | 61·3 | 59·6 | 57·3 | 30 |
| 40 | 55·6 | 61·6 | 62·8 | 62·4 | 61·3 | 59·5 | 57·2 | 40 |
| 50 | 56·0 | 61·6 | 62·8 | 62·4 | 61·2 | 59·4 | 57·1 | 50 |
| 00 | 4 56·4 | 9 61·7 | 14 62·8 | 19 62·4 | 24 61·2 | 29 59·3 | 34 57·0 | 00 |
| 10 | 56·7 | 61·8 | 62·8 | 62·3 | 61·1 | 59·3 | 56·9 | 10 |
| 20 | 57·1 | 61·9 | 62·8 | 62·3 | 61·1 | 59·2 | 56·9 | 20 |
| 30 | 57·4 | 61·9 | 62·8 | 62·3 | 61·0 | 59·1 | 56·8 | 30 |
| 40 | 57·7 | 62·0 | 62·8 | 62·2 | 60·9 | 59·1 | 56·7 | 40 |
| 50 | 57·9 | 62·1 | 62·8 | 62·2 | 60·9 | 59·0 | 56·6 | 50 |
| H.P. | L U | L U | L U | L U | L U | L U | L U | H.P. |
| 54·0 | 0·3 0·9 | 0·3 0·9 | 0·4 1·0 | 0·5 1·1 | 0·6 1·2 | 0·7 1·3 | 0·9 1·5 | 54·0 |
| 54·3 | 0·7 1·1 | 0·7 1·2 | 0·7 1·2 | 0·8 1·3 | 0·9 1·4 | 1·1 1·5 | 1·2 1·7 | 54·3 |
| 54·6 | 1·1 1·4 | 1·1 1·4 | 1·1 1·4 | 1·2 1·5 | 1·3 1·6 | 1·4 1·7 | 1·5 1·8 | 54·6 |
| 54·9 | 1·4 1·6 | 1·5 1·6 | 1·5 1·6 | 1·6 1·7 | 1·6 1·8 | 1·8 1·9 | 1·9 2·0 | 54·9 |
| 55·2 | 1·8 1·8 | 1·8 1·8 | 1·9 1·9 | 1·9 1·9 | 2·0 2·0 | 2·1 2·1 | 2·2 2·2 | 55·2 |
| 55·5 | 2·2 2·0 | 2·2 2·0 | 2·3 2·1 | 2·3 2·1 | 2·4 2·2 | 2·4 2·3 | 2·5 2·4 | 55·5 |
| 55·8 | 2·6 2·2 | 2·6 2·2 | 2·6 2·3 | 2·7 2·3 | 2·7 2·4 | 2·8 2·4 | 2·9 2·5 | 55·8 |
| 56·1 | 3·0 2·4 | 3·0 2·5 | 3·0 2·5 | 3·0 2·5 | 3·1 2·6 | 3·1 2·6 | 3·2 2·7 | 56·1 |
| 56·4 | 3·4 2·7 | 3·4 2·7 | 3·4 2·7 | 3·4 2·7 | 3·4 2·8 | 3·5 2·8 | 3·5 2·9 | 56·4 |
| 56·7 | 3·7 2·9 | 3·7 2·9 | 3·8 2·9 | 3·8 2·9 | 3·8 3·0 | 3·8 3·0 | 3·9 3·0 | 56·7 |
| 57·0 | 4·1 3·1 | 4·1 3·1 | 4·1 3·1 | 4·1 3·1 | 4·2 3·1 | 4·2 3·2 | 4·2 3·2 | 57·0 |
| 57·3 | 4·5 3·3 | 4·5 3·3 | 4·5 3·3 | 4·5 3·3 | 4·5 3·3 | 4·5 3·4 | 4·6 3·4 | 57·3 |
| 57·6 | 4·9 3·5 | 4·9 3·5 | 4·9 3·5 | 4·9 3·5 | 4·9 3·5 | 4·9 3·5 | 4·9 3·6 | 57·6 |
| 57·9 | 5·3 3·8 | 5·3 3·8 | 5·2 3·8 | 5·2 3·7 | 5·2 3·7 | 5·2 3·7 | 5·2 3·7 | 57·9 |
| 58·2 | 5·6 4·0 | 5·6 4·0 | 5·6 4·0 | 5·6 4·0 | 5·6 3·9 | 5·6 3·9 | 5·6 3·9 | 58·2 |
| 58·5 | 6·0 4·2 | 6·0 4·2 | 6·0 4·2 | 6·0 4·2 | 6·0 4·1 | 5·9 4·1 | 5·9 4·1 | 58·5 |
| 58·8 | 6·4 4·4 | 6·4 4·4 | 6·4 4·4 | 6·3 4·4 | 6·3 4·3 | 6·3 4·3 | 6·2 4·2 | 58·8 |
| 59·1 | 6·8 4·6 | 6·8 4·6 | 6·7 4·6 | 6·7 4·6 | 6·7 4·5 | 6·6 4·5 | 6·6 4·4 | 59·1 |
| 59·4 | 7·2 4·8 | 7·1 4·8 | 7·1 4·8 | 7·1 4·8 | 7·0 4·7 | 7·0 4·7 | 6·9 4·6 | 59·4 |
| 59·7 | 7·5 5·1 | 7·5 5·0 | 7·5 5·0 | 7·5 5·0 | 7·4 4·9 | 7·3 4·8 | 7·2 4·7 | 59·7 |
| 60·0 | 7·9 5·3 | 7·9 5·3 | 7·9 5·2 | 7·8 5·2 | 7·8 5·1 | 7·7 5·0 | 7·6 4·9 | 60·0 |
| 60·3 | 8·3 5·5 | 8·3 5·5 | 8·2 5·4 | 8·2 5·4 | 8·1 5·3 | 8·0 5·2 | 7·9 5·1 | 60·3 |
| 60·6 | 8·7 5·7 | 8·7 5·7 | 8·6 5·7 | 8·6 5·6 | 8·5 5·5 | 8·4 5·4 | 8·2 5·3 | 60·6 |
| 60·9 | 9·1 5·9 | 9·0 5·9 | 9·0 5·9 | 8·9 5·8 | 8·8 5·7 | 8·7 5·6 | 8·6 5·4 | 60·9 |
| 61·2 | 9·5 6·2 | 9·4 6·1 | 9·4 6·1 | 9·3 6·0 | 9·2 5·9 | 9·1 5·8 | 8·9 5·6 | 61·2 |
| 61·5 | 9·8 6·4 | 9·8 6·3 | 9·7 6·3 | 9·7 6·2 | 9·5 6·1 | 9·4 5·9 | 9·2 5·8 | 61·5 |

## DIP

| Ht. of Eye (m) | Corr$^{n}$ | Ht. of Eye (ft.) | Ht. of Eye (m) | Corr$^{n}$ | Ht. of Eye (ft.) |
|---|---|---|---|---|---|
| 2·4 | | 8·0 | 9·5 | | 31·5 |
| | −2·8 | | | −5·5 | |
| 2·6 | | 8·6 | 9·9 | | 32·7 |
| | −2·9 | | | −5·6 | |
| 2·8 | | 9·2 | 10·3 | | 33·9 |
| | −3·0 | | | −5·7 | |
| 3·0 | | 9·8 | 10·6 | | 35·1 |
| | −3·1 | | | −5·8 | |
| 3·2 | | 10·5 | 11·0 | | 36·3 |
| | −3·2 | | | −5·9 | |
| 3·4 | | 11·2 | 11·4 | | 37·6 |
| | −3·3 | | | −6·0 | |
| 3·6 | | 11·9 | 11·8 | | 38·9 |
| | −3·4 | | | −6·1 | |
| 3·8 | | 12·6 | 12·2 | | 40·1 |
| | −3·5 | | | −6·2 | |
| 4·0 | | 13·3 | 12·6 | | 41·5 |
| | −3·6 | | | −6·3 | |
| 4·3 | | 14·1 | 13·0 | | 42·8 |
| | −3·7 | | | −6·4 | |
| 4·5 | | 14·9 | 13·4 | | 44·2 |
| | −3·8 | | | −6·5 | |
| 4·7 | | 15·7 | 13·8 | | 45·5 |
| | −3·9 | | | −6·6 | |
| 5·0 | | 16·5 | 14·2 | | 46·9 |
| | −4·0 | | | −6·7 | |
| 5·2 | | 17·4 | 14·7 | | 48·4 |
| | −4·1 | | | −6·8 | |
| 5·5 | | 18·3 | 15·1 | | 49·8 |
| | −4·2 | | | −6·9 | |
| 5·8 | | 19·1 | 15·5 | | 51·3 |
| | −4·3 | | | −7·0 | |
| 6·1 | | 20·1 | 16·0 | | 52·8 |
| | −4·4 | | | −7·1 | |
| 6·3 | | 21·0 | 16·5 | | 54·3 |
| | −4·5 | | | −7·2 | |
| 6·6 | | 22·0 | 16·9 | | 55·8 |
| | −4·6 | | | −7·3 | |
| 6·9 | | 22·9 | 17·4 | | 57·4 |
| | −4·7 | | | −7·4 | |
| 7·2 | | 23·9 | 17·9 | | 58·9 |
| | −4·8 | | | −7·5 | |
| 7·5 | | 24·9 | 18·4 | | 60·5 |
| | −4·9 | | | −7·6 | |
| 7·9 | | 26·0 | 18·8 | | 62·1 |
| | −5·0 | | | −7·7 | |
| 8·2 | | 27·1 | 19·3 | | 63·8 |
| | −5·1 | | | −7·8 | |
| 8·5 | | 28·1 | 19·8 | | 65·4 |
| | −5·2 | | | −7·9 | |
| 8·8 | | 29·2 | 20·4 | | 67·1 |
| | −5·3 | | | −8·0 | |
| 9·2 | | 30·4 | 20·9 | | 68·8 |
| | −5·4 | | | −8·1 | |
| 9·5 | | 31·5 | 21·4 | | 70·5 |

## MOON CORRECTION TABLE

The correction is in two parts; the first correction is taken from the upper part of the table with argument apparent altitude, and the second from the lower part, with argument H.P., in the same column as that from which the first correction was taken. Separate corrections are given in the lower part for lower (L) and upper (U) limbs. All corrections are to be **added** to apparent altitude, *but 30′ is to be subtracted from the altitude of the upper limb.*

For corrections for pressure and temperature see page A4.

For bubble sextant observations ignore dip, take the mean of upper and lower limb corrections and subtract 15′ from the altitude.

App. Alt. = Apparent altitude = Sextant altitude corrected for index error and dip.

# ALTITUDE CORRECTION TABLES 35°–90°—MOON

| App. Alt. | 35°–39° Corr$^{n}$ | 40°–44° Corr$^{n}$ | 45°–49° Corr$^{n}$ | 50°–54° Corr$^{n}$ | 55°–59° Corr$^{n}$ | 60°–64° Corr$^{n}$ | 65°–69° Corr$^{n}$ | 70°–74° Corr$^{n}$ | 75°–79° Corr$^{n}$ | 80°–84° Corr$^{n}$ | 85°–89° Corr$^{n}$ | App. Alt. |
|---|---|---|---|---|---|---|---|---|---|---|---|---|
| 00 | 35° 56·5 | 40° 53·7 | 45° 50·5 | 50° 46·9 | 55° 43·1 | 60° 38·9 | 65° 34·6 | 70° 30·1 | 75° 25·3 | 80° 20·5 | 85° 15·6 | 00 |
| 10 | 56·4 | 53·6 | 50·4 | 46·8 | 42·9 | 38·8 | 34·4 | 29·9 | 25·2 | 20·4 | 15·5 | 10 |
| 20 | 56·3 | 53·5 | 50·2 | 46·7 | 42·8 | 38·7 | 34·3 | 29·7 | 25·0 | 20·2 | 15·3 | 20 |
| 30 | 56·2 | 53·4 | 50·1 | 46·5 | 42·7 | 38·5 | 34·1 | 29·6 | 24·9 | 20·0 | 15·1 | 30 |
| 40 | 56·2 | 53·3 | 50·0 | 46·4 | 42·5 | 38·4 | 34·0 | 29·4 | 24·7 | 19·9 | 15·0 | 40 |
| 50 | 56·1 | 53·2 | 49·9 | 46·3 | 42·4 | 38·2 | 33·8 | 29·3 | 24·5 | 19·7 | 14·8 | 50 |
| 00 | 36 56·0 | 41 53·1 | 46 49·8 | 51 46·2 | 56 42·3 | 61 38·1 | 66 33·7 | 71 29·1 | 76 24·4 | 81 19·6 | 86 14·6 | 00 |
| 10 | 55·9 | 53·0 | 49·7 | 46·0 | 42·1 | 37·9 | 33·5 | 29·0 | 24·2 | 19·4 | 14·5 | 10 |
| 20 | 55·8 | 52·8 | 49·5 | 45·9 | 42·0 | 37·8 | 33·4 | 28·8 | 24·1 | 19·2 | 14·3 | 20 |
| 30 | 55·7 | 52·7 | 49·4 | 45·8 | 41·8 | 37·7 | 33·2 | 28·7 | 23·9 | 19·1 | 14·1 | 30 |
| 40 | 55·6 | 52·6 | 49·3 | 45·7 | 41·7 | 37·5 | 33·1 | 28·5 | 23·8 | 18·9 | 14·0 | 40 |
| 50 | 55·5 | 52·5 | 49·2 | 45·5 | 41·6 | 37·4 | 32·9 | 28·3 | 23·6 | 18·7 | 13·8 | 50 |
| 00 | 37 55·4 | 42 52·4 | 47 49·1 | 52 45·4 | 57 41·4 | 62 37·2 | 67 32·8 | 72 28·2 | 77 23·4 | 82 18·6 | 87 13·7 | 00 |
| 10 | 55·3 | 52·3 | 49·0 | 45·3 | 41·3 | 37·1 | 32·6 | 28·0 | 23·3 | 18·4 | 13·5 | 10 |
| 20 | 55·2 | 52·2 | 48·8 | 45·2 | 41·2 | 36·9 | 32·5 | 27·9 | 23·1 | 18·2 | 13·3 | 20 |
| 30 | 55·1 | 52·1 | 48·7 | 45·0 | 41·0 | 36·8 | 32·3 | 27·7 | 22·9 | 18·1 | 13·2 | 30 |
| 40 | 55·0 | 52·0 | 48·6 | 44·9 | 40·9 | 36·6 | 32·2 | 27·6 | 22·8 | 17·9 | 13·0 | 40 |
| 50 | 55·0 | 51·9 | 48·5 | 44·8 | 40·8 | 36·5 | 32·0 | 27·4 | 22·6 | 17·8 | 12·8 | 50 |
| 00 | 38 54·9 | 43 51·8 | 48 48·4 | 53 44·6 | 58 40·6 | 63 36·4 | 68 31·9 | 73 27·2 | 78 22·5 | 83 17·6 | 88 12·7 | 00 |
| 10 | 54·8 | 51·7 | 48·2 | 44·5 | 40·5 | 36·2 | 31·7 | 27·1 | 22·3 | 17·4 | 12·5 | 10 |
| 20 | 54·7 | 51·6 | 48·1 | 44·4 | 40·3 | 36·1 | 31·6 | 26·9 | 22·1 | 17·3 | 12·3 | 20 |
| 30 | 54·6 | 51·5 | 48·0 | 44·2 | 40·2 | 35·9 | 31·4 | 26·8 | 22·0 | 17·1 | 12·2 | 30 |
| 40 | 54·5 | 51·4 | 47·9 | 44·1 | 40·1 | 35·8 | 31·3 | 26·6 | 21·8 | 16·9 | 12·0 | 40 |
| 50 | 54·4 | 51·2 | 47·8 | 44·0 | 39·9 | 35·6 | 31·1 | 26·5 | 21·7 | 16·8 | 11·8 | 50 |
| 00 | 39 54·3 | 44 51·1 | 49 47·6 | 54 43·9 | 59 39·8 | 64 35·5 | 69 31·0 | 74 26·3 | 79 21·5 | 84 16·6 | 89 11·7 | 00 |
| 10 | 54·2 | 51·0 | 47·5 | 43·7 | 39·6 | 35·3 | 30·8 | 26·1 | 21·3 | 16·5 | 11·5 | 10 |
| 20 | 54·1 | 50·9 | 47·4 | 43·6 | 39·5 | 35·2 | 30·7 | 26·0 | 21·2 | 16·3 | 11·4 | 20 |
| 30 | 54·0 | 50·8 | 47·3 | 43·5 | 39·4 | 35·0 | 30·5 | 25·8 | 21·0 | 16·1 | 11·2 | 30 |
| 40 | 53·9 | 50·7 | 47·2 | 43·3 | 39·2 | 34·9 | 30·4 | 25·7 | 20·9 | 16·0 | 11·0 | 40 |
| 50 | 53·8 | 50·6 | 47·0 | 43·2 | 39·1 | 34·7 | 30·2 | 25·5 | 20·7 | 15·8 | 10·9 | 50 |
| H.P. | L U | L U | L U | L U | L U | L U | L U | L U | L U | L U | L U | H.P. |
| 54·0 | 1·1 1·7 | 1·3 1·9 | 1·5 2·1 | 1·7 2·4 | 2·0 2·6 | 2·3 2·9 | 2·6 3·2 | 2·9 3·5 | 3·2 3·8 | 3·5 4·1 | 3·8 4·5 | 54·0 |
| 54·3 | 1·4 1·8 | 1·6 2·0 | 1·8 2·2 | 2·0 2·5 | 2·3 2·7 | 2·5 3·0 | 2·8 3·2 | 3·0 3·5 | 3·3 3·8 | 3·6 4·1 | 3·9 4·4 | 54·3 |
| 54·6 | 1·7 2·0 | 1·9 2·2 | 2·1 2·4 | 2·3 2·6 | 2·5 2·8 | 2·7 3·0 | 3·0 3·3 | 3·2 3·5 | 3·5 3·8 | 3·7 4·1 | 4·0 4·3 | 54·6 |
| 54·9 | 2·0 2·2 | 2·2 2·3 | 2·3 2·5 | 2·5 2·7 | 2·7 2·9 | 2·9 3·1 | 3·2 3·3 | 3·4 3·5 | 3·6 3·8 | 3·9 4·0 | 4·1 4·3 | 54·9 |
| 55·2 | 2·3 2·3 | 2·5 2·4 | 2·6 2·6 | 2·8 2·8 | 3·0 2·9 | 3·2 3·1 | 3·4 3·3 | 3·6 3·5 | 3·8 3·7 | 4·0 4·0 | 4·2 4·2 | 55·2 |
| 55·5 | 2·7 2·5 | 2·8 2·6 | 2·9 2·7 | 3·1 2·9 | 3·2 3·0 | 3·4 3·2 | 3·6 3·4 | 3·7 3·5 | 3·9 3·7 | 4·1 3·9 | 4·3 4·1 | 55·5 |
| 55·8 | 3·0 2·6 | 3·1 2·7 | 3·2 2·8 | 3·3 3·0 | 3·5 3·1 | 3·6 3·3 | 3·8 3·4 | 3·9 3·6 | 4·1 3·7 | 4·2 3·9 | 4·4 4·0 | 55·8 |
| 56·1 | 3·3 2·8 | 3·4 2·9 | 3·5 3·0 | 3·6 3·1 | 3·7 3·2 | 3·8 3·3 | 4·0 3·4 | 4·1 3·6 | 4·2 3·7 | 4·4 3·8 | 4·5 4·0 | 56·1 |
| 56·4 | 3·6 2·9 | 3·7 3·0 | 3·8 3·1 | 3·9 3·2 | 3·9 3·3 | 4·0 3·4 | 4·1 3·5 | 4·3 3·6 | 4·4 3·7 | 4·5 3·8 | 4·6 3·9 | 56·4 |
| 56·7 | 3·9 3·1 | 4·0 3·1 | 4·1 3·2 | 4·1 3·3 | 4·2 3·3 | 4·3 3·4 | 4·3 3·5 | 4·4 3·6 | 4·5 3·7 | 4·6 3·8 | 4·7 3·8 | 56·7 |
| 57·0 | 4·3 3·2 | 4·3 3·3 | 4·3 3·3 | 4·4 3·4 | 4·4 3·4 | 4·5 3·5 | 4·5 3·5 | 4·6 3·6 | 4·7 3·6 | 4·7 3·7 | 4·8 3·8 | 57·0 |
| 57·3 | 4·6 3·4 | 4·6 3·4 | 4·6 3·4 | 4·6 3·5 | 4·7 3·5 | 4·7 3·5 | 4·7 3·6 | 4·8 3·6 | 4·8 3·6 | 4·8 3·7 | 4·9 3·7 | 57·3 |
| 57·6 | 4·9 3·6 | 4·9 3·6 | 4·9 3·6 | 4·9 3·6 | 4·9 3·6 | 4·9 3·6 | 4·9 3·6 | 4·9 3·6 | 5·0 3·6 | 5·0 3·6 | 5·0 3·6 | 57·6 |
| 57·9 | 5·2 3·7 | 5·2 3·7 | 5·2 3·7 | 5·2 3·7 | 5·2 3·7 | 5·1 3·6 | 5·1 3·6 | 5·1 3·6 | 5·1 3·6 | 5·1 3·6 | 5·1 3·6 | 57·9 |
| 58·2 | 5·5 3·9 | 5·5 3·8 | 5·5 3·8 | 5·4 3·8 | 5·4 3·7 | 5·4 3·7 | 5·3 3·7 | 5·3 3·6 | 5·2 3·6 | 5·2 3·5 | 5·2 3·5 | 58·2 |
| 58·5 | 5·9 4·0 | 5·8 4·0 | 5·8 3·9 | 5·7 3·9 | 5·6 3·8 | 5·6 3·8 | 5·5 3·7 | 5·5 3·6 | 5·4 3·6 | 5·3 3·5 | 5·3 3·4 | 58·5 |
| 58·8 | 6·2 4·2 | 6·1 4·1 | 6·0 4·1 | 6·0 4·0 | 5·9 3·9 | 5·8 3·8 | 5·7 3·7 | 5·6 3·6 | 5·5 3·5 | 5·4 3·5 | 5·3 3·4 | 58·8 |
| 59·1 | 6·5 4·3 | 6·4 4·3 | 6·3 4·2 | 6·2 4·1 | 6·1 4·0 | 6·0 3·9 | 5·9 3·8 | 5·8 3·6 | 5·7 3·5 | 5·6 3·4 | 5·4 3·3 | 59·1 |
| 59·4 | 6·8 4·5 | 6·7 4·4 | 6·6 4·3 | 6·5 4·2 | 6·4 4·1 | 6·2 3·9 | 6·1 3·8 | 6·0 3·7 | 5·8 3·5 | 5·7 3·4 | 5·5 3·2 | 59·4 |
| 59·7 | 7·1 4·6 | 7·0 4·5 | 6·9 4·4 | 6·8 4·3 | 6·6 4·1 | 6·5 4·0 | 6·3 3·8 | 6·2 3·7 | 6·0 3·5 | 5·8 3·3 | 5·6 3·2 | 59·7 |
| 60·0 | 7·5 4·8 | 7·3 4·7 | 7·2 4·5 | 7·0 4·4 | 6·9 4·2 | 6·7 4·0 | 6·5 3·9 | 6·3 3·7 | 6·1 3·5 | 5·9 3·3 | 5·7 3·1 | 60·0 |
| 60·3 | 7·8 5·0 | 7·6 4·8 | 7·5 4·7 | 7·3 4·5 | 7·1 4·3 | 6·9 4·1 | 6·7 3·9 | 6·5 3·7 | 6·3 3·5 | 6·0 3·2 | 5·8 3·0 | 60·3 |
| 60·6 | 8·1 5·1 | 7·9 5·0 | 7·7 4·8 | 7·6 4·6 | 7·3 4·4 | 7·1 4·2 | 6·9 3·9 | 6·7 3·7 | 6·4 3·4 | 6·2 3·2 | 5·9 2·9 | 60·6 |
| 60·9 | 8·4 5·3 | 8·2 5·1 | 8·0 4·9 | 7·8 4·7 | 7·6 4·5 | 7·3 4·2 | 7·1 4·0 | 6·8 3·7 | 6·6 3·4 | 6·3 3·2 | 6·0 2·9 | 60·9 |
| 61·2 | 8·7 5·4 | 8·5 5·2 | 8·3 5·0 | 8·1 4·8 | 7·8 4·5 | 7·6 4·3 | 7·3 4·0 | 7·0 3·7 | 6·7 3·4 | 6·4 3·1 | 6·1 2·8 | 61·2 |
| 61·5 | 9·1 5·6 | 8·8 5·4 | 8·6 5·1 | 8·3 4·9 | 8·1 4·6 | 7·8 4·3 | 7·5 4·0 | 7·2 3·7 | 6·9 3·4 | 6·5 3·1 | 6·2 2·7 | 61·5 |

# A4 ALTITUDE CORRECTION TABLES—ADDITIONAL CORRECTIONS

## ADDITIONAL REFRACTION CORRECTIONS FOR NON-STANDARD CONDITIONS

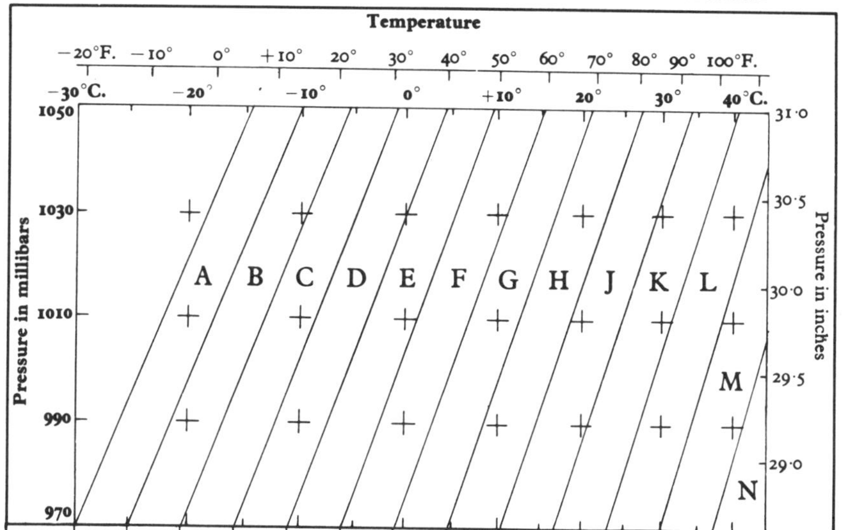


| App. Alt. | A | B | C | D | E | F | G | H | J | K | L | M | N | App. Alt. |
|---|---|---|---|---|---|---|---|---|---|---|---|---|---|---|
| ° ′ | ′ | ′ | ′ | ′ | ′ | ′ | ′ | ′ | ′ | ′ | ′ | ′ | ′ | ° ′ |
| 0 00 | −6·9 | −5·7 | −4·6 | −3·4 | −2·3 | −1·1 | 0·0 | +1·1 | +2·3 | +3·4 | +4·6 | +5·7 | +6·9 | 0 00 |
| 0 30 | 5·2 | 4·4 | 3·5 | 2·6 | 1·7 | 0·9 | 0·0 | 0·9 | 1·7 | 2·6 | 3·5 | 4·4 | 5·2 | 0 30 |
| 1 00 | 4·3 | 3·5 | 2·8 | 2·1 | 1·4 | 0·7 | 0·0 | 0·7 | 1·4 | 2·1 | 2·8 | 3·5 | 4·3 | 1 00 |
| 1 30 | 3·5 | 2·9 | 2·4 | 1·8 | 1·2 | 0·6 | 0·0 | 0·6 | 1·2 | 1·8 | 2·4 | 2·9 | 3·5 | 1 30 |
| 2 00 | 3·0 | 2·5 | 2·0 | 1·5 | 1·0 | 0·5 | 0·0 | 0·5 | 1·0 | 1·5 | 2·0 | 2·5 | 3·0 | 2 00 |
| 2 30 | −2·5 | −2·1 | −1·6 | −1·2 | −0·8 | −0·4 | 0·0 | +0·4 | +0·8 | +1·2 | +1·6 | +2·1 | +2·5 | 2 30 |
| 3 00 | 2·2 | 1·8 | 1·5 | 1·1 | 0·7 | 0·4 | 0·0 | 0·4 | 0·7 | 1·1 | 1·5 | 1·8 | 2·2 | 3 00 |
| 3 30 | 2·0 | 1·6 | 1·3 | 1·0 | 0·7 | 0·3 | 0·0 | 0·3 | 0·7 | 1·0 | 1·3 | 1·6 | 2·0 | 3 30 |
| 4 00 | 1·8 | 1·5 | 1·2 | 0·9 | 0·6 | 0·3 | 0·0 | 0·3 | 0·6 | 0·9 | 1·2 | 1·5 | 1·8 | 4 00 |
| 4 30 | 1·6 | 1·4 | 1·1 | 0·8 | 0·5 | 0·3 | 0·0 | 0·3 | 0·5 | 0·8 | 1·1 | 1·4 | 1·6 | 4 30 |
| 5 00 | −1·5 | −1·3 | −1·0 | −0·8 | −0·5 | −0·2 | 0·0 | +0·2 | +0·5 | +0·8 | +1·0 | +1·3 | +1·5 | 5 00 |
| 6 | 1·3 | 1·1 | 0·9 | 0·6 | 0·4 | 0·2 | 0·0 | 0·2 | 0·4 | 0·6 | 0·9 | 1·1 | 1·3 | 6 |
| 7 | 1·1 | 0·9 | 0·7 | 0·6 | 0·4 | 0·2 | 0·0 | 0·2 | 0·4 | 0·6 | 0·7 | 0·9 | 1·1 | 7 |
| 8 | 1·0 | 0·8 | 0·7 | 0·5 | 0·3 | 0·2 | 0·0 | 0·2 | 0·3 | 0·5 | 0·7 | 0·8 | 1·0 | 8 |
| 9 | 0·9 | 0·7 | 0·6 | 0·4 | 0·3 | 0·1 | 0·0 | 0·1 | 0·3 | 0·4 | 0·6 | 0·7 | 0·9 | 9 |
| 10 00 | −0·8 | −0·7 | −0·5 | −0·4 | −0·3 | −0·1 | 0·0 | +0·1 | +0·3 | +0·4 | +0·5 | +0·7 | +0·8 | 10 00 |
| 12 | 0·7 | 0·6 | 0·5 | 0·3 | 0·2 | 0·1 | 0·0 | 0·1 | 0·2 | 0·3 | 0·5 | 0·6 | 0·7 | 12 |
| 14 | 0·6 | 0·5 | 0·4 | 0·3 | 0·2 | 0·1 | 0·0 | 0·1 | 0·2 | 0·3 | 0·4 | 0·5 | 0·6 | 14 |
| 16 | 0·5 | 0·4 | 0·3 | 0·3 | 0·2 | 0·1 | 0·0 | 0·1 | 0·2 | 0·3 | 0·3 | 0·4 | 0·5 | 16 |
| 18 | 0·4 | 0·4 | 0·3 | 0·2 | 0·2 | 0·1 | 0·0 | 0·1 | 0·2 | 0·2 | 0·3 | 0·4 | 0·4 | 18 |
| 20 00 | −0·4 | −0·3 | −0·3 | −0·2 | −0·1 | −0·1 | 0·0 | +0·1 | +0·1 | +0·2 | +0·3 | +0·3 | +0·4 | 20 00 |
| 25 | 0·3 | 0·3 | 0·2 | 0·2 | 0·1 | −0·1 | 0·0 | +0·1 | 0·1 | 0·2 | 0·2 | 0·3 | 0·3 | 25 |
| 30 | 0·3 | 0·2 | 0·2 | 0·1 | 0·1 | 0·0 | 0·0 | 0·0 | 0·1 | 0·1 | 0·2 | 0·2 | 0·3 | 30 |
| 35 | 0·2 | 0·2 | 0·1 | 0·1 | 0·1 | 0·0 | 0·0 | 0·0 | 0·1 | 0·1 | 0·1 | 0·2 | 0·2 | 35 |
| 40 | 0·2 | 0·1 | 0·1 | 0·1 | −0·1 | 0·0 | 0·0 | 0·0 | +0·1 | 0·1 | 0·1 | 0·1 | 0·2 | 40 |
| 50 00 | −0·1 | −0·1 | −0·1 | −0·1 | 0·0 | 0·0 | 0·0 | 0·0 | 0·0 | +0·1 | +0·1 | +0·1 | +0·1 | 50 00 |

The graph is entered with arguments temperature and pressure to find a zone letter; using as arguments this zone letter and apparent altitude (sextant altitude corrected for dip), a correction is taken from the table. This correction is to be applied to the sextant altitude in addition to the corrections for standard conditions.



# 1976 JANUARY 7, 8, 9 (WED., THURS., FRI.)

| | G.M.T. | ARIES | VENUS −3.6 | | MARS −0.9 | | JUPITER −2.0 | | SATURN −0.1 | |
|---|---|---|---|---|---|---|---|---|---|---|
| | | G.H.A. | G.H.A. | Dec. | G.H.A. | Dec. | G.H.A. | Dec. | G.H.A. | Dec. |
| | d h | ° ′ | ° ′ | ° ′ | ° ′ | ° ′ | ° ′ | ° ′ | ° ′ | ° ′ |
| | 7 00 | 105 42.0 | 220 34.8 | S19 24.3 | 31 15.3 | N25 51.0 | 90 26.8 | N 5 07.7 | 342 49.7 | N20 17.1 |
| | 01 | 120 44.5 | 235 34.1 | 24.9 | 46 18.3 | 50.9 | 105 29.1 | 07.8 | 357 52.4 | 17.1 |
| | 02 | 135 46.9 | 250 33.4 | 25.5 | 61 21.3 | 50.9 | 120 31.3 | 07.9 | 12 55.1 | 17.2 |
| | 03 | 150 49.4 | 265 32.8 | ·· 26.0 | 76 24.3 | ·· 50.8 | 135 33.6 | ·· 08.0 | 27 57.7 | ·· 17.2 |
| | 04 | 165 51.9 | 280 32.1 | 26.6 | 91 27.2 | 50.8 | 150 35.9 | 08.1 | 43 00.4 | 17.3 |
| | 05 | 180 54.3 | 295 31.4 | 27.2 | 106 30.2 | 50.8 | 165 38.1 | 08.2 | 58 03.1 | 17.3 |
| | 06 | 195 56.8 | 310 30.8 | S19 27.8 | 121 33.2 | N25 50.7 | 180 40.4 | N 5 08.3 | 73 05.7 | N20 17.3 |
| W | 07 | 210 59.3 | 325 30.1 | 28.4 | 136 36.1 | 50.7 | 195 42.6 | 08.4 | 88 08.4 | 17.4 |
| E | 08 | 226 01.7 | 340 29.4 | 28.9 | 151 39.1 | 50.6 | 210 44.9 | 08.5 | 103 11.1 | 17.4 |
| D | 09 | 241 04.2 | 355 28.7 | ·· 29.5 | 166 42.1 | ·· 50.6 | 225 47.1 | ·· 08.6 | 118 13.7 | ·· 17.5 |
| N | 10 | 256 06.7 | 10 28.1 | 30.1 | 181 45.0 | 50.5 | 240 49.4 | 08.7 | 133 16.4 | 17.5 |
| E | 11 | 271 09.1 | 25 27.4 | 30.7 | 196 48.0 | 50.5 | 255 51.7 | 08.8 | 148 19.1 | 17.6 |
| S | 12 | 286 11.6 | 40 26.7 | S19 31.3 | 211 51.0 | N25 50.4 | 270 53.9 | N 5 08.9 | 163 21.7 | N20 17.6 |
| D | 13 | 301 14.0 | 55 26.0 | 31.8 | 226 53.9 | 50.4 | 285 56.2 | 09.0 | 178 24.4 | 17.7 |
| A | 14 | 316 16.5 | 70 25.3 | 32.4 | 241 56.9 | 50.4 | 300 58.4 | 09.1 | 193 27.1 | 17.7 |
| Y | 15 | 331 19.0 | 85 24.7 | ·· 33.0 | 256 59.8 | ·· 50.3 | 316 00.7 | ·· 09.2 | 208 29.7 | ·· 17.8 |
| | 16 | 346 21.4 | 100 24.0 | 33.6 | 272 02.8 | 50.3 | 331 02.9 | 09.3 | 223 32.4 | 17.8 |
| | 17 | 1 23.9 | 115 23.3 | 34.1 | 287 05.7 | 50.2 | 346 05.2 | 09.4 | 238 35.1 | 17.9 |
| | 18 | 16 26.4 | 130 22.6 | S19 34.7 | 302 08.7 | N25 50.2 | 1 07.4 | N 5 09.5 | 253 37.7 | N20 17.9 |
| | 19 | 31 28.8 | 145 21.9 | 35.3 | 317 11.7 | 50.1 | 16 09.7 | 09.6 | 268 40.4 | 18.0 |
| | 20 | 46 31.3 | 160 21.3 | 35.8 | 332 14.6 | 50.1 | 31 11.9 | 09.7 | 283 43.1 | 18.0 |
| | 21 | 61 33.8 | 175 20.6 | ·· 36.4 | 347 17.5 | ·· 50.0 | 46 14.2 | ·· 09.8 | 298 45.7 | ·· 18.1 |
| | 22 | 76 36.2 | 190 19.9 | 37.0 | 2 20.5 | 50.0 | 61 16.5 | 09.9 | 313 48.4 | 18.1 |
| | 23 | 91 38.7 | 205 19.2 | 37.5 | 17 23.4 | 50.0 | 76 18.7 | 10.0 | 328 51.1 | 18.1 |
| | 8 00 | 106 41.2 | 220 18.5 | S19 38.1 | 32 26.4 | N25 49.9 | 91 21.0 | N 5 10.1 | 343 53.7 | N20 18.2 |
| | 01 | 121 43.6 | 235 17.9 | 38.7 | 47 29.3 | 49.9 | 106 23.2 | 10.2 | 358 56.4 | 18.2 |
| | 02 | 136 46.1 | 250 17.2 | 39.2 | 62 32.3 | 49.8 | 121 25.5 | 10.3 | 13 59.1 | 18.3 |
| | 03 | 151 48.5 | 265 16.5 | ·· 39.8 | 77 35.2 | ·· 49.8 | 136 27.7 | ·· 10.4 | 29 01.7 | ·· 18.3 |
| | 04 | 166 51.0 | 280 15.8 | 40.4 | 92 38.1 | 49.7 | 151 30.0 | 10.5 | 44 04.4 | 18.4 |
| | 05 | 181 53.5 | 295 15.1 | 40.9 | 107 41.1 | 49.7 | 166 32.2 | 10.6 | 59 07.1 | 18.4 |
| | 06 | 196 55.9 | 310 14.4 | S19 41.5 | 122 44.0 | N25 49.6 | 181 34.5 | N 5 10.7 | 74 09.7 | N20 18.5 |
| | 07 | 211 58.4 | 325 13.7 | 42.0 | 137 46.9 | 49.6 | 196 36.7 | 10.8 | 89 12.4 | 18.5 |
| T | 08 | 227 00.9 | 340 13.1 | 42.6 | 152 49.9 | 49.6 | 211 39.0 | 10.9 | 104 15.1 | 18.6 |
| H | 09 | 242 03.3 | 355 12.4 | ·· 43.2 | 167 52.8 | ·· 49.5 | 226 41.2 | ·· 11.0 | 119 17.7 | ·· 18.6 |
| U | 10 | 257 05.8 | 10 11.7 | 43.7 | 182 55.7 | 49.5 | 241 43.5 | 11.1 | 134 20.4 | 18.7 |
| R | 11 | 272 08.3 | 25 11.0 | 44.3 | 197 58.6 | 49.4 | 256 45.7 | 11.2 | 149 23.1 | 18.7 |
| S | 12 | 287 10.7 | 40 10.3 | S19 44.8 | 213 01.6 | N25 49.4 | 271 48.0 | N 5 11.3 | 164 25.8 | N20 18.8 |
| D | 13 | 302 13.2 | 55 09.6 | 45.4 | 228 04.5 | 49.3 | 286 50.2 | 11.4 | 179 28.4 | 18.8 |
| A | 14 | 317 15.6 | 70 08.9 | 45.9 | 243 07.4 | 49.3 | 301 52.4 | 11.5 | 194 31.1 | 18.9 |
| Y | 15 | 332 18.1 | 85 08.2 | ·· 46.5 | 258 10.3 | ·· 49.2 | 316 54.7 | ·· 11.6 | 209 33.8 | ·· 18.9 |
| | 16 | 347 20.6 | 100 07.5 | 47.0 | 273 13.2 | 49.2 | 331 56.9 | 11.7 | 224 36.4 | 18.9 |
| | 17 | 2 23.0 | 115 06.9 | 47.6 | 288 16.2 | 49.2 | 346 59.2 | 11.8 | 239 39.1 | 19.0 |
| | 18 | 17 25.5 | 130 06.2 | S19 48.1 | 303 19.1 | N25 49.1 | 2 01.4 | N 5 11.9 | 254 41.8 | N20 19.0 |
| | 19 | 32 28.0 | 145 05.5 | 48.7 | 318 22.0 | 49.1 | 17 03.7 | 12.0 | 269 44.4 | 19.1 |
| | 20 | 47 30.4 | 160 04.8 | 49.2 | 333 24.9 | 49.0 | 32 05.9 | 12.2 | 284 47.1 | 19.1 |
| | 21 | 62 32.9 | 175 04.1 | ·· 49.8 | 348 27.8 | ·· 49.0 | 47 08.2 | ·· 12.3 | 299 49.8 | ·· 19.2 |
| | 22 | 77 35.4 | 190 03.4 | 50.3 | 3 30.7 | 48.9 | 62 10.4 | 12.4 | 314 52.4 | 19.2 |
| | 23 | 92 37.8 | 205 02.7 | 50.9 | 18 33.6 | 48.9 | 77 12.7 | 12.5 | 329 55.1 | 19.3 |
| | 9 00 | 107 40.3 | 220 02.0 | S19 51.4 | 33 36.5 | N25 48.8 | 92 14.9 | N 5 12.6 | 344 57.8 | N20 19.3 |
| | 01 | 122 42.8 | 235 01.3 | 52.0 | 48 39.4 | 48.8 | 107 17.2 | 12.7 | 0 00.4 | 19.4 |
| | 02 | 137 45.2 | 250 00.6 | 52.5 | 63 42.3 | 48.8 | 122 19.4 | 12.8 | 15 03.1 | 19.4 |
| | 03 | 152 47.7 | 264 59.9 | ·· 53.0 | 78 45.2 | ·· 48.7 | 137 21.6 | ·· 12.9 | 30 05.8 | ·· 19.5 |
| | 04 | 167 50.1 | 279 59.2 | 53.6 | 93 48.1 | 48.7 | 152 23.9 | 13.0 | 45 08.5 | 19.5 |
| | 05 | 182 52.6 | 294 58.5 | 54.1 | 108 51.0 | 48.6 | 167 26.1 | 13.1 | 60 11.1 | 19.6 |
| | 06 | 197 55.1 | 309 57.8 | S19 54.7 | 123 53.9 | N25 48.6 | 182 28.4 | N 5 13.2 | 75 13.8 | N20 19.6 |
| | 07 | 212 57.5 | 324 57.1 | 55.2 | 138 56.8 | 48.5 | 197 30.6 | 13.3 | 90 16.5 | 19.7 |
| | 08 | 228 00.0 | 339 56.4 | 55.7 | 153 59.7 | 48.5 | 212 32.9 | 13.4 | 105 19.1 | 19.7 |
| F | 09 | 243 02.5 | 354 55.7 | ·· 56.3 | 169 02.6 | ·· 48.5 | 227 35.1 | ·· 13.5 | 120 21.8 | ·· 19.7 |
| R | 10 | 258 04.9 | 9 55.0 | 56.8 | 184 05.5 | 48.4 | 242 37.3 | 13.6 | 135 24.5 | 19.8 |
| I | 11 | 273 07.4 | 24 54.3 | 57.3 | 199 08.4 | 48.4 | 257 39.6 | 13.7 | 150 27.1 | 19.8 |
| D | 12 | 288 09.9 | 39 53.6 | S19 57.9 | 214 11.3 | N25 48.3 | 272 41.8 | N 5 13.8 | 165 29.8 | N20 19.9 |
| A | 13 | 303 12.3 | 54 52.9 | 58.4 | 229 14.1 | 48.3 | 287 44.1 | 13.9 | 180 32.5 | 19.9 |
| Y | 14 | 318 14.8 | 69 52.2 | 58.9 | 244 17.0 | 48.2 | 302 46.3 | 14.0 | 195 35.2 | 20.0 |
| | 15 | 333 17.3 | 84 51.5 | 19 59.5 | 259 19.9 | ·· 48.2 | 317 48.5 | ·· 14.1 | 210 37.8 | ·· 20.0 |
| | 16 | 348 19.7 | 99 50.8 | 20 00.0 | 274 22.8 | 48.1 | 332 50.8 | 14.2 | 225 40.5 | 20.1 |
| | 17 | 3 22.2 | 114 50.1 | 00.5 | 289 25.7 | 48.1 | 347 53.0 | 14.3 | 240 43.2 | 20.1 |
| | 18 | 18 24.6 | 129 49.4 | S20 01.1 | 304 28.5 | N25 48.1 | 2 55.3 | N 5 14.4 | 255 45.8 | N20 20.2 |
| | 19 | 33 27.1 | 144 48.7 | 01.6 | 319 31.4 | 48.0 | 17 57.5 | 14.6 | 270 48.5 | 20.2 |
| | 20 | 48 29.6 | 159 48.0 | 02.1 | 334 34.3 | 48.0 | 32 59.7 | 14.7 | 285 51.2 | 20.3 |
| | 21 | 63 32.0 | 174 47.3 | ·· 02.6 | 349 37.2 | ·· 47.9 | 48 02.0 | ·· 14.8 | 300 53.8 | ·· 20.3 |
| | 22 | 78 34.5 | 189 46.6 | 03.2 | 4 40.0 | 47.9 | 63 04.2 | 14.9 | 315 56.5 | 20.4 |
| | 23 | 93 37.0 | 204 45.9 | 03.7 | 19 42.9 | 47.8 | 78 06.5 | 15.0 | 330 59.2 | 20.4 |
| | Mer. Pass. | h m 16 50.5 | v −0.7 | d 0.6 | v 2.9 | d 0.0 | v 2.2 | d 0.1 | v 2.7 | d 0.0 |

| STARS Name | S.H.A. | Dec. |
|---|---|---|
| | ° ′ | ° ′ |
| Acamar | 315 39.4 | S40 24.2 |
| Achernar | 335 47.6 | S57 21.8 |
| Acrux | 173 40.6 | S62 57.8 |
| Adhara | 255 34.2 | S28 56.5 |
| Aldebaran | 291 21.3 | N16 27.7 |
| Alioth | 166 45.3 | N56 05.0 |
| Alkaid | 153 21.1 | N49 25.6 |
| Al Na'ir | 28 19.3 | S47 04.7 |
| Alnilam | 276 14.6 | S 1 13.1 |
| Alphard | 218 23.4 | S 8 33.4 |
| Alphecca | 126 35.0 | N26 47.6 |
| Alpheratz | 358 12.7 | N28 57.7 |
| Altair | 62 35.9 | N 8 48.3 |
| Ankaa | 353 43.4 | S42 26.3 |
| Antares | 113 01.0 | S26 22.7 |
| Arcturus | 146 21.5 | N19 18.2 |
| Atria | 108 28.6 | S68 58.9 |
| Avior | 234 28.8 | S59 26.0 |
| Bellatrix | 279 01.8 | N 6 19.6 |
| Betelgeuse | 271 31.4 | N 7 24.1 |
| Canopus | 264 08.0 | S52 41.1 |
| Capella | 281 15.5 | N45 58.5 |
| Deneb | 49 51.0 | N45 11.9 |
| Denebola | 183 02.2 | N14 42.1 |
| Diphda | 349 24.1 | S18 07.2 |
| Dubhe | 194 25.7 | N61 52.4 |
| Elnath | 278 47.8 | N28 35.3 |
| Eltanin | 90 59.7 | N51 29.5 |
| Enif | 34 14.9 | N 9 46.0 |
| Fomalhaut | 15 55.1 | S29 45.0 |
| Gacrux | 172 32.1 | S56 58.6 |
| Gienah | 176 21.1 | S17 24.6 |
| Hadar | 149 28.0 | S60 15.2 |
| Hamal | 328 32.4 | N23 21.1 |
| Kaus Aust. | 84 21.4 | S34 23.7 |
| Kochab | 137 19.5 | N74 14.9 |
| Markab | 14 06.5 | N15 04.7 |
| Menkar | 314 44.3 | N 3 59.8 |
| Menkent | 148 40.8 | S36 15.0 |
| Miaplacidus | 221 44.7 | S69 37.1 |
| Mirfak | 309 20.3 | N49 46.8 |
| Nunki | 76 33.5 | S26 19.6 |
| Peacock | 54 04.0 | S56 48.8 |
| Pollux | 244 01.6 | N28 04.9 |
| Procyon | 245 28.7 | N 5 17.1 |
| Rasalhague | 96 32.8 | N12 34.6 |
| Regulus | 208 13.1 | N12 04.9 |
| Rigel | 281 38.7 | S 8 13.8 |
| Rigil Kent. | 140 30.3 | S60 43.9 |
| Sabik | 102 45.1 | S15 41.7 |
| Schedar | 350 12.6 | N56 24.7 |
| Shaula | 97 00.4 | S37 05.1 |
| Sirius | 258 58.1 | S16 41.1 |
| Spica | 159 00.9 | S11 02.2 |
| Suhail | 223 12.7 | S43 20.2 |
| Vega | 80 58.4 | N38 45.7 |
| Zuben'ubi | 137 36.7 | S15 56.5 |

| | S.H.A. | Mer. Pass. |
|---|---|---|
| | ° ′ | h m |
| Venus | 113 37.4 | 9 19 |
| Mars | 285 45.2 | 21 46 |
| Jupiter | 344 39.8 | 17 52 |
| Saturn | 237 12.6 | 1 04 |

# 1976 JANUARY 7, 8, 9 (WED., THURS., FRI.)

| Day | G.M.T. h | SUN G.H.A. ° ′ | SUN Dec. ° ′ | MOON G.H.A. ° ′ | v ′ | MOON Dec. ° ′ | d ′ | H.P. ′ |
|---|---|---|---|---|---|---|---|---|
| 7 (Wednesday) | 00 | 178 32.9 | S22 30.2 | 118 06.7 | 15.5 | S 0 26.8 | 10.4 | 54.5 |
| | 01 | 193 32.6 | 29.9 | 132 41.2 | 15.5 | 0 16.4 | 10.5 | 54.5 |
| | 02 | 208 32.3 | 29.6 | 147 15.7 | 15.5 | S 0 05.9 | 10.5 | 54.4 |
| | 03 | 223 32.0 | ·· 29.3 | 161 50.2 | 15.5 | N 0 04.6 | 10.4 | 54.4 |
| | 04 | 238 31.8 | 29.0 | 176 24.7 | 15.5 | 0 15.0 | 10.5 | 54.4 |
| | 05 | 253 31.5 | 28.7 | 190 59.2 | 15.6 | 0 25.5 | 10.4 | 54.4 |
| | 06 | 268 31.2 | S22 28.4 | 205 33.8 | 15.5 | N 0 35.9 | 10.5 | 54.4 |
| | 07 | 283 30.9 | 28.1 | 220 08.3 | 15.6 | 0 46.4 | 10.4 | 54.4 |
| | 08 | 298 30.7 | 27.8 | 234 42.9 | 15.6 | 0 56.8 | 10.4 | 54.4 |
| | 09 | 313 30.4 | ·· 27.5 | 249 17.5 | 15.5 | 1 07.2 | 10.4 | 54.4 |
| | 10 | 328 30.1 | 27.2 | 263 52.0 | 15.6 | 1 17.6 | 10.4 | 54.4 |
| | 11 | 343 29.8 | 26.9 | 278 26.6 | 15.6 | 1 28.0 | 10.4 | 54.4 |
| | 12 | 358 29.6 | S22 26.6 | 293 01.2 | 15.6 | N 1 38.4 | 10.4 | 54.3 |
| | 13 | 13 29.3 | 26.3 | 307 35.8 | 15.6 | 1 48.8 | 10.4 | 54.3 |
| | 14 | 28 29.0 | 26.0 | 322 10.4 | 15.6 | 1 59.2 | 10.3 | 54.3 |
| | 15 | 43 28.7 | ·· 25.7 | 336 45.0 | 15.6 | 2 09.5 | 10.4 | 54.3 |
| | 16 | 58 28.5 | 25.4 | 351 19.6 | 15.6 | 2 19.9 | 10.3 | 54.3 |
| | 17 | 73 28.2 | 25.1 | 5 54.2 | 15.6 | 2 30.2 | 10.3 | 54.3 |
| | 18 | 88 27.9 | S22 24.7 | 20 28.8 | 15.6 | N 2 40.5 | 10.3 | 54.3 |
| | 19 | 103 27.7 | 24.4 | 35 03.4 | 15.6 | 2 50.8 | 10.3 | 54.3 |
| | 20 | 118 27.4 | 24.1 | 49 38.0 | 15.7 | 3 01.1 | 10.3 | 54.3 |
| | 21 | 133 27.1 | ·· 23.8 | 64 12.7 | 15.6 | 3 11.4 | 10.3 | 54.3 |
| | 22 | 148 26.8 | 23.5 | 78 47.3 | 15.6 | 3 21.7 | 10.2 | 54.3 |
| | 23 | 163 26.6 | 23.2 | 93 21.9 | 15.6 | 3 31.9 | 10.3 | 54.3 |
| 8 (Thursday) | 00 | 178 26.3 | S22 22.9 | 107 56.5 | 15.6 | N 3 42.2 | 10.2 | 54.3 |
| | 01 | 193 26.0 | 22.5 | 122 31.1 | 15.6 | 3 52.4 | 10.2 | 54.3 |
| | 02 | 208 25.8 | 22.2 | 137 05.7 | 15.5 | 4 02.6 | 10.1 | 54.3 |
| | 03 | 223 25.5 | ·· 21.9 | 151 40.2 | 15.6 | 4 12.7 | 10.2 | 54.2 |
| | 04 | 238 25.2 | 21.6 | 166 14.8 | 15.6 | 4 22.9 | 10.1 | 54.2 |
| | 05 | 253 25.0 | 21.3 | 180 49.4 | 15.6 | 4 33.0 | 10.2 | 54.2 |
| | 06 | 268 24.7 | S22 20.9 | 195 24.0 | 15.5 | N 4 43.2 | 10.1 | 54.2 |
| | 07 | 283 24.4 | 20.6 | 209 58.5 | 15.6 | 4 53.3 | 10.0 | 54.2 |
| | 08 | 298 24.2 | 20.3 | 224 33.1 | 15.5 | 5 03.3 | 10.1 | 54.2 |
| | 09 | 313 23.9 | ·· 20.0 | 239 07.6 | 15.5 | 5 13.4 | 10.0 | 54.2 |
| | 10 | 328 23.6 | 19.6 | 253 42.1 | 15.5 | 5 23.4 | 10.0 | 54.2 |
| | 11 | 343 23.4 | 19.3 | 268 16.6 | 15.5 | 5 33.4 | 10.0 | 54.2 |
| | 12 | 358 23.1 | S22 19.0 | 282 51.1 | 15.5 | N 5 43.4 | 10.0 | 54.2 |
| | 13 | 13 22.8 | 18.7 | 297 25.6 | 15.5 | 5 53.4 | 9.9 | 54.2 |
| | 14 | 28 22.5 | 18.3 | 312 00.1 | 15.5 | 6 03.3 | 10.0 | 54.2 |
| | 15 | 43 22.3 | ·· 18.0 | 326 34.6 | 15.4 | 6 13.3 | 9.9 | 54.2 |
| | 16 | 58 22.0 | 17.7 | 341 09.0 | 15.4 | 6 23.2 | 9.8 | 54.2 |
| | 17 | 73 21.7 | 17.3 | 355 43.4 | 15.4 | 6 33.0 | 9.9 | 54.2 |
| | 18 | 88 21.5 | S22 17.0 | 10 17.8 | 15.4 | N 6 42.9 | 9.8 | 54.2 |
| | 19 | 103 21.2 | 16.7 | 24 52.2 | 15.4 | 6 52.7 | 9.8 | 54.2 |
| | 20 | 118 21.0 | 16.4 | 39 26.6 | 15.3 | 7 02.5 | 9.7 | 54.2 |
| | 21 | 133 20.7 | ·· 16.0 | 54 00.9 | 15.3 | 7 12.2 | 9.7 | 54.2 |
| | 22 | 148 20.4 | 15.7 | 68 35.2 | 15.3 | 7 21.9 | 9.7 | 54.2 |
| | 23 | 163 20.2 | 15.4 | 83 09.5 | 15.3 | 7 31.6 | 9.7 | 54.2 |
| 9 (Friday) | 00 | 178 19.9 | S22 15.0 | 97 43.8 | 15.3 | N 7 41.3 | 9.7 | 54.2 |
| | 01 | 193 19.6 | 14.7 | 112 18.1 | 15.2 | 7 51.0 | 9.6 | 54.2 |
| | 02 | 208 19.4 | 14.3 | 126 52.3 | 15.2 | 8 00.6 | 9.5 | 54.2 |
| | 03 | 223 19.1 | ·· 14.0 | 141 26.5 | 15.2 | 8 10.1 | 9.6 | 54.2 |
| | 04 | 238 18.8 | 13.7 | 156 00.7 | 15.2 | 8 19.7 | 9.5 | 54.2 |
| | 05 | 253 18.6 | 13.3 | 170 34.9 | 15.1 | 8 29.2 | 9.5 | 54.2 |
| | 06 | 268 18.3 | S22 13.0 | 185 09.0 | 15.1 | N 8 38.7 | 9.4 | 54.2 |
| | 07 | 283 18.0 | 12.6 | 199 43.1 | 15.1 | 8 48.1 | 9.5 | 54.3 |
| | 08 | 298 17.8 | 12.3 | 214 17.2 | 15.0 | 8 57.6 | 9.3 | 54.3 |
| | 09 | 313 17.5 | ·· 12.0 | 228 51.2 | 15.0 | 9 06.9 | 9.4 | 54.3 |
| | 10 | 328 17.3 | 11.6 | 243 25.2 | 15.0 | 9 16.3 | 9.3 | 54.3 |
| | 11 | 343 17.0 | 11.3 | 257 59.2 | 15.0 | 9 25.6 | 9.3 | 54.3 |
| | 12 | 358 16.7 | S22 10.9 | 272 33.2 | 14.9 | N 9 34.9 | 9.2 | 54.3 |
| | 13 | 13 16.5 | 10.6 | 287 07.1 | 14.9 | 9 44.1 | 9.2 | 54.3 |
| | 14 | 28 16.2 | 10.2 | 301 41.0 | 14.8 | 9 53.3 | 9.2 | 54.3 |
| | 15 | 43 15.9 | ·· 09.9 | 316 14.8 | 14.9 | 10 02.5 | 9.1 | 54.3 |
| | 16 | 58 15.7 | 09.6 | 330 48.7 | 14.7 | 10 11.6 | 9.1 | 54.3 |
| | 17 | 73 15.4 | 09.2 | 345 22.4 | 14.8 | 10 20.7 | 9.0 | 54.3 |
| | 18 | 88 15.2 | S22 08.9 | 359 56.2 | 14.7 | N10 29.7 | 9.0 | 54.3 |
| | 19 | 103 14.9 | 08.5 | 14 29.9 | 14.7 | 10 38.7 | 9.0 | 54.3 |
| | 20 | 118 14.6 | 08.2 | 29 03.6 | 14.6 | 10 47.7 | 8.9 | 54.3 |
| | 21 | 133 14.4 | ·· 07.8 | 43 37.2 | 14.6 | 10 56.6 | 8.9 | 54.3 |
| | 22 | 148 14.1 | 07.5 | 58 10.8 | 14.6 | 11 05.5 | 8.8 | 54.4 |
| | 23 | 163 13.9 | 07.1 | 72 44.4 | 14.5 | 11 14.3 | 8.8 | 54.4 |
| | | S.D. 16.3 | d 0.3 | S.D. 14.8 | | 14.8 | | 14.8 |

| Lat. | Twilight Naut. h m | Twilight Civil h m | Sunrise h m | Moonrise 7 h m | Moonrise 8 h m | Moonrise 9 h m | Moonrise 10 h m |
|---|---|---|---|---|---|---|---|
| N 72 | 08 16 | 10 22 | ■ | 10 10 | 09 59 | 09 47 | 09 33 |
| N 70 | 07 59 | 09 38 | ■ | 10 11 | 10 06 | 10 01 | 09 55 |
| 68 | 07 45 | 09 09 | 11 15 | 10 13 | 10 12 | 10 12 | 10 13 |
| 66 | 07 33 | 08 47 | 10 15 | 10 14 | 10 17 | 10 21 | 10 27 |
| 64 | 07 23 | 08 29 | 09 41 | 10 15 | 10 22 | 10 29 | 10 39 |
| 62 | 07 15 | 08 15 | 09 17 | 10 16 | 10 25 | 10 36 | 10 49 |
| 60 | 07 07 | 08 02 | 08 58 | 10 16 | 10 29 | 10 42 | 10 57 |
| N 58 | 07 00 | 07 52 | 08 42 | 10 17 | 10 31 | 10 47 | 11 05 |
| 56 | 06 54 | 07 42 | 08 28 | 10 18 | 10 34 | 10 52 | 11 12 |
| 54 | 06 48 | 07 34 | 08 17 | 10 18 | 10 36 | 10 56 | 11 18 |
| 52 | 06 43 | 07 26 | 08 06 | 10 19 | 10 39 | 11 00 | 11 23 |
| 50 | 06 39 | 07 19 | 07 57 | 10 19 | 10 41 | 11 03 | 11 28 |
| 45 | 06 28 | 07 04 | 07 38 | 10 20 | 10 45 | 11 11 | 11 39 |
| N 40 | 06 18 | 06 52 | 07 22 | 10 21 | 10 48 | 11 17 | 11 47 |
| 35 | 06 09 | 06 41 | 07 08 | 10 22 | 10 52 | 11 22 | 11 55 |
| 30 | 06 01 | 06 31 | 06 57 | 10 22 | 10 54 | 11 27 | 12 02 |
| 20 | 05 46 | 06 13 | 06 37 | 10 24 | 10 59 | 11 35 | 12 14 |
| N 10 | 05 30 | 05 56 | 06 19 | 10 25 | 11 03 | 11 43 | 12 24 |
| 0 | 05 14 | 05 40 | 06 03 | 10 26 | 11 07 | 11 50 | 12 34 |
| S 10 | 04 56 | 05 23 | 05 46 | 10 27 | 11 12 | 11 57 | 12 43 |
| 20 | 04 35 | 05 04 | 05 28 | 10 28 | 11 16 | 12 04 | 12 54 |
| 30 | 04 07 | 04 40 | 05 07 | 10 29 | 11 21 | 12 13 | 13 06 |
| 35 | 03 49 | 04 25 | 04 55 | 10 30 | 11 24 | 12 18 | 13 13 |
| 40 | 03 27 | 04 08 | 04 40 | 10 30 | 11 27 | 12 24 | 13 21 |
| 45 | 02 59 | 03 47 | 04 23 | 10 31 | 11 31 | 12 30 | 13 30 |
| S 50 | 02 17 | 03 19 | 04 02 | 10 33 | 11 36 | 12 38 | 13 41 |
| 52 | 01 53 | 03 05 | 03 52 | 10 33 | 11 38 | 12 42 | 13 47 |
| 54 | 01 19 | 02 49 | 03 41 | 10 34 | 11 40 | 12 46 | 13 52 |
| 56 | //// | 02 29 | 03 28 | 10 34 | 11 43 | 12 51 | 13 59 |
| 58 | //// | 02 03 | 03 12 | 10 35 | 11 46 | 12 56 | 14 06 |
| S 60 | //// | 01 26 | 02 54 | 10 36 | 11 49 | 13 01 | 14 14 |

| Lat. | Sunset h m | Twilight Civil h m | Twilight Naut. h m | Moonset 7 h m | Moonset 8 h m | Moonset 9 h m | Moonset 10 h m |
|---|---|---|---|---|---|---|---|
| N 72 | ■ | 13 51 | 15 57 | 23 31 | 25 11 | 01 11 | 02 54 |
| N 70 | ■ | 14 35 | 16 14 | 23 26 | 24 59 | 00 59 | 02 33 |
| 68 | 12 59 | 15 04 | 16 28 | 23 22 | 24 49 | 00 49 | 02 17 |
| 66 | 13 58 | 15 26 | 16 40 | 23 18 | 24 41 | 00 41 | 02 04 |
| 64 | 14 32 | 15 44 | 16 50 | 23 16 | 24 34 | 00 34 | 01 53 |
| 62 | 14 56 | 15 58 | 16 58 | 23 13 | 24 29 | 00 29 | 01 44 |
| 60 | 15 15 | 16 11 | 17 06 | 23 11 | 24 24 | 00 24 | 01 36 |
| N 58 | 15 31 | 16 21 | 17 13 | 23 09 | 24 19 | 00 19 | 01 29 |
| 56 | 15 45 | 16 31 | 17 19 | 23 07 | 24 15 | 00 15 | 01 23 |
| 54 | 15 56 | 16 39 | 17 24 | 23 06 | 24 12 | 00 12 | 01 18 |
| 52 | 16 07 | 16 47 | 17 30 | 23 04 | 24 09 | 00 09 | 01 13 |
| 50 | 16 16 | 16 53 | 17 34 | 23 03 | 24 06 | 00 06 | 01 09 |
| 45 | 16 35 | 17 08 | 17 45 | 23 00 | 24 00 | 00 00 | 00 59 |
| N 40 | 16 51 | 17 21 | 17 55 | 22 58 | 23 54 | 24 51 | 00 51 |
| 35 | 17 04 | 17 32 | 18 04 | 22 56 | 23 50 | 24 44 | 00 44 |
| 30 | 17 16 | 17 42 | 18 12 | 22 54 | 23 46 | 24 38 | 00 38 |
| 20 | 17 36 | 18 00 | 18 27 | 22 51 | 23 39 | 24 28 | 00 28 |
| N 10 | 17 53 | 18 16 | 18 42 | 22 48 | 23 33 | 24 19 | 00 19 |
| 0 | 18 10 | 18 33 | 18 58 | 22 46 | 23 28 | 24 11 | 00 11 |
| S 10 | 18 27 | 18 50 | 19 16 | 22 43 | 23 22 | 24 02 | 00 02 |
| 20 | 18 45 | 19 09 | 19 38 | 22 41 | 23 16 | 23 53 | 24 33 |
| 30 | 19 06 | 19 33 | 20 05 | 22 37 | 23 10 | 23 43 | 24 19 |
| 35 | 19 18 | 19 47 | 20 23 | 22 36 | 23 06 | 23 37 | 24 12 |
| 40 | 19 32 | 20 04 | 20 45 | 22 34 | 23 01 | 23 31 | 24 03 |
| 45 | 19 49 | 20 25 | 21 13 | 22 31 | 22 56 | 23 23 | 23 53 |
| S 50 | 20 10 | 20 53 | 21 54 | 22 29 | 22 50 | 23 14 | 23 40 |
| 52 | 20 20 | 21 07 | 22 18 | 22 27 | 22 48 | 23 10 | 23 35 |
| 54 | 20 31 | 21 23 | 22 51 | 22 26 | 22 45 | 23 05 | 23 28 |
| 56 | 20 44 | 21 43 | //// | 22 24 | 22 41 | 23 00 | 23 21 |
| 58 | 21 00 | 22 08 | //// | 22 23 | 22 38 | 22 54 | 23 14 |
| S 60 | 21 18 | 22 44 | //// | 22 21 | 22 33 | 22 48 | 23 05 |

| Day | SUN Eqn. of Time 00ʰ m s | SUN Eqn. of Time 12ʰ m s | SUN Mer. Pass. h m | MOON Mer. Pass. Upper h m | MOON Mer. Pass. Lower h m | MOON Age d | Phase |
|---|---|---|---|---|---|---|---|
| 7 | 05 48 | 06 01 | 12 06 | 16 36 | 04 15 | 06 | ◐ |
| 8 | 06 14 | 06 27 | 12 06 | 17 18 | 04 57 | 07 | |
| 9 | 06 40 | 06 53 | 12 07 | 18 00 | 05 39 | 08 | |

# 1976 JANUARY 22, 23, 24 (THURS., FRI., SAT.)

| Day | G.M.T. h | SUN G.H.A. ° ′ | SUN Dec. ° ′ | MOON G.H.A. ° ′ | v ′ | MOON Dec. ° ′ | d ′ | H.P. ′ |
|---|---|---|---|---|---|---|---|---|
| 22 (Thursday) | 00 | 177 10.5 | S19 55.1 | 297 01.2 | 9.6 | S 5 17.5 | 12.1 | 59.6 |
| | 01 | 192 10.3 | 54.5 | 311 29.8 | 9.6 | 5 29.6 | 12.1 | 59.6 |
| | 02 | 207 10.1 | 54.0 | 325 58.4 | 9.5 | 5 41.7 | 12.0 | 59.6 |
| | 03 | 222 10.0 | ·· 53.4 | 340 26.9 | 9.5 | 5 53.7 | 12.0 | 59.6 |
| | 04 | 237 09.8 | 52.9 | 354 55.4 | 9.6 | 6 05.7 | 12.0 | 59.6 |
| | 05 | 252 09.6 | 52.3 | 9 24.0 | 9.5 | 6 17.7 | 11.9 | 59.6 |
| | 06 | 267 09.4 | S19 51.8 | 23 52.5 | 9.5 | S 6 29.6 | 11.9 | 59.6 |
| | 07 | 282 09.3 | 51.2 | 38 21.0 | 9.5 | 6 41.5 | 11.8 | 59.5 |
| | 08 | 297 09.1 | 50.6 | 52 49.5 | 9.4 | 6 53.3 | 11.8 | 59.5 |
| | 09 | 312 08.9 | ·· 50.1 | 67 17.9 | 9.5 | 7 05.1 | 11.8 | 59.5 |
| | 10 | 327 08.8 | 49.5 | 81 46.4 | 9.4 | 7 16.9 | 11.7 | 59.5 |
| | 11 | 342 08.6 | 48.9 | 96 14.8 | 9.5 | 7 28.6 | 11.6 | 59.5 |
| | 12 | 357 08.4 | S19 48.4 | 110 43.3 | 9.4 | S 7 40.2 | 11.6 | 59.5 |
| | 13 | 12 08.2 | 47.8 | 125 11.7 | 9.4 | 7 51.8 | 11.6 | 59.5 |
| | 14 | 27 08.1 | 47.3 | 139 40.1 | 9.3 | 8 03.4 | 11.5 | 59.5 |
| | 15 | 42 07.9 | ·· 46.7 | 154 08.4 | 9.4 | 8 14.9 | 11.4 | 59.5 |
| | 16 | 57 07.7 | 46.1 | 168 36.8 | 9.3 | 8 26.3 | 11.4 | 59.5 |
| | 17 | 72 07.6 | 45.6 | 183 05.1 | 9.3 | 8 37.7 | 11.3 | 59.4 |
| | 18 | 87 07.4 | S19 45.0 | 197 33.4 | 9.3 | S 8 49.0 | 11.3 | 59.4 |
| | 19 | 102 07.2 | 44.4 | 212 01.7 | 9.3 | 9 00.3 | 11.2 | 59.4 |
| | 20 | 117 07.0 | 43.9 | 226 30.0 | 9.3 | 9 11.5 | 11.2 | 59.4 |
| | 21 | 132 06.9 | ·· 43.3 | 240 58.3 | 9.2 | 9 22.7 | 11.1 | 59.4 |
| | 22 | 147 06.7 | 42.7 | 255 26.5 | 9.2 | 9 33.8 | 11.0 | 59.4 |
| | 23 | 162 06.5 | 42.1 | 269 54.7 | 9.2 | 9 44.8 | 11.0 | 59.4 |
| 23 (Friday) | 00 | 177 06.4 | S19 41.6 | 284 22.9 | 9.2 | S 9 55.8 | 10.9 | 59.4 |
| | 01 | 192 06.2 | 41.0 | 298 51.1 | 9.1 | 10 06.7 | 10.9 | 59.3 |
| | 02 | 207 06.0 | 40.4 | 313 19.2 | 9.1 | 10 17.6 | 10.7 | 59.3 |
| | 03 | 222 05.9 | ·· 39.9 | 327 47.3 | 9.1 | 10 28.3 | 10.8 | 59.3 |
| | 04 | 237 05.7 | 39.3 | 342 15.4 | 9.1 | 10 39.1 | 10.6 | 59.3 |
| | 05 | 252 05.5 | 38.7 | 356 43.5 | 9.0 | 10 49.7 | 10.6 | 59.3 |
| | 06 | 267 05.4 | S19 38.1 | 11 11.5 | 9.1 | S11 00.3 | 10.5 | 59.3 |
| | 07 | 282 05.2 | 37.6 | 25 39.6 | 9.0 | 11 10.8 | 10.4 | 59.3 |
| | 08 | 297 05.0 | 37.0 | 40 07.6 | 8.9 | 11 21.2 | 10.4 | 59.2 |
| | 09 | 312 04.9 | ·· 36.4 | 54 35.5 | 9.0 | 11 31.6 | 10.3 | 59.2 |
| | 10 | 327 04.7 | 35.8 | 69 03.5 | 8.9 | 11 41.9 | 10.2 | 59.2 |
| | 11 | 342 04.5 | 35.3 | 83 31.4 | 8.9 | 11 52.1 | 10.2 | 59.2 |
| | 12 | 357 04.4 | S19 34.7 | 97 59.3 | 8.9 | S12 02.3 | 10.0 | 59.2 |
| | 13 | 12 04.2 | 34.1 | 112 27.2 | 8.8 | 12 12.3 | 10.0 | 59.2 |
| | 14 | 27 04.1 | 33.5 | 126 55.0 | 8.8 | 12 22.3 | 10.0 | 59.2 |
| | 15 | 42 03.9 | ·· 32.9 | 141 22.8 | 8.8 | 12 32.3 | 9.8 | 59.1 |
| | 16 | 57 03.7 | 32.4 | 155 50.6 | 8.8 | 12 42.1 | 9.7 | 59.1 |
| | 17 | 72 03.6 | 31.8 | 170 18.4 | 8.7 | 12 51.8 | 9.7 | 59.1 |
| | 18 | 87 03.4 | S19 31.2 | 184 46.1 | 8.7 | S13 01.5 | 9.6 | 59.1 |
| | 19 | 102 03.2 | 30.6 | 199 13.8 | 8.7 | 13 11.1 | 9.5 | 59.1 |
| | 20 | 117 03.1 | 30.0 | 213 41.5 | 8.7 | 13 20.6 | 9.5 | 59.1 |
| | 21 | 132 02.9 | ·· 29.4 | 228 09.2 | 8.6 | 13 30.1 | 9.3 | 59.1 |
| | 22 | 147 02.8 | 28.9 | 242 36.8 | 8.6 | 13 39.4 | 9.2 | 59.0 |
| | 23 | 162 02.6 | 28.3 | 257 04.4 | 8.6 | 13 48.6 | 9.2 | 59.0 |
| 24 (Saturday) | 00 | 177 02.4 | S19 27.7 | 271 32.0 | 8.5 | S13 57.8 | 9.1 | 59.0 |
| | 01 | 192 02.3 | 27.1 | 285 59.5 | 8.5 | 14 06.9 | 9.0 | 59.0 |
| | 02 | 207 02.1 | 26.5 | 300 27.0 | 8.5 | 14 15.9 | 8.9 | 59.0 |
| | 03 | 222 02.0 | ·· 25.9 | 314 54.5 | 8.5 | 14 24.8 | 8.8 | 59.0 |
| | 04 | 237 01.8 | 25.3 | 329 22.0 | 8.4 | 14 33.6 | 8.7 | 58.9 |
| | 05 | 252 01.6 | 24.7 | 343 49.4 | 8.4 | 14 42.3 | 8.7 | 58.9 |
| | 06 | 267 01.5 | S19 24.2 | 358 16.8 | 8.4 | S14 51.0 | 8.5 | 58.9 |
| | 07 | 282 01.3 | 23.6 | 12 44.2 | 8.3 | 14 59.5 | 8.4 | 58.9 |
| | 08 | 297 01.2 | 23.0 | 27 11.5 | 8.4 | 15 07.9 | 8.4 | 58.9 |
| | 09 | 312 01.0 | ·· 22.4 | 41 38.9 | 8.3 | 15 16.3 | 8.2 | 58.9 |
| | 10 | 327 00.9 | 21.8 | 56 06.2 | 8.2 | 15 24.5 | 8.2 | 58.9 |
| | 11 | 342 00.7 | 21.2 | 70 33.4 | 8.3 | 15 32.7 | 8.0 | 58.8 |
| | 12 | 357 00.5 | S19 20.6 | 85 00.7 | 8.2 | S15 40.7 | 8.0 | 58.8 |
| | 13 | 12 00.4 | 20.0 | 99 27.9 | 8.2 | 15 48.7 | 7.9 | 58.8 |
| | 14 | 27 00.2 | 19.4 | 113 55.1 | 8.1 | 15 56.6 | 7.7 | 58.8 |
| | 15 | 42 00.1 | ·· 18.8 | 128 22.2 | 8.2 | 16 04.3 | 7.7 | 58.8 |
| | 16 | 56 59.9 | 18.2 | 142 49.4 | 8.1 | 16 12.0 | 7.5 | 58.8 |
| | 17 | 71 59.8 | 17.6 | 157 16.5 | 8.0 | 16 19.5 | 7.5 | 58.7 |
| | 18 | 86 59.6 | S19 17.0 | 171 43.5 | 8.1 | S16 27.0 | 7.3 | 58.7 |
| | 19 | 101 59.5 | 16.4 | 186 10.6 | 8.0 | 16 34.3 | 7.3 | 58.7 |
| | 20 | 116 59.3 | 15.8 | 200 37.6 | 8.0 | 16 41.6 | 7.1 | 58.7 |
| | 21 | 131 59.1 | ·· 15.2 | 215 04.6 | 8.0 | 16 48.7 | 7.1 | 58.7 |
| | 22 | 146 59.0 | 14.6 | 229 31.6 | 8.0 | 16 55.8 | 6.9 | 58.7 |
| | 23 | 161 58.8 | 14.0 | 243 58.6 | 7.9 | 17 02.7 | 6.8 | 58.6 |
| | | S.D. 16.3 | d 0.6 | S.D. 16.2 | | 16.1 | | 16.0 |

| Lat. | Twilight Naut. h m | Twilight Civil h m | Sunrise h m | Moonrise 22 h m | Moonrise 23 h m | Moonrise 24 h m | Moonrise 25 h m |
|---|---|---|---|---|---|---|---|
| N 72 | 07 42 | 09 22 | ■ | 25 22 | 01 22 | 03 36 | ■ |
| N 70 | 07 30 | 08 55 | 10 48 | 25 04 | 01 04 | 03 03 | 05 07 |
| 68 | 07 20 | 08 35 | 10 01 | 24 51 | 00 51 | 02 39 | 04 26 |
| 66 | 07 12 | 08 19 | 09 30 | 24 39 | 00 39 | 02 21 | 03 59 |
| 64 | 07 04 | 08 06 | 09 08 | 24 30 | 00 30 | 02 06 | 03 38 |
| 62 | 06 58 | 07 55 | 08 50 | 24 22 | 00 22 | 01 54 | 03 21 |
| 60 | 06 52 | 07 45 | 08 35 | 24 15 | 00 15 | 01 43 | 03 07 |
| N 58 | 06 47 | 07 36 | 08 23 | 24 09 | 00 09 | 01 34 | 02 55 |
| 56 | 06 42 | 07 29 | 08 12 | 24 04 | 00 04 | 01 26 | 02 45 |
| 54 | 06 38 | 07 22 | 08 02 | 23 59 | 25 19 | 01 19 | 02 36 |
| 52 | 06 34 | 07 16 | 07 54 | 23 55 | 25 13 | 01 13 | 02 28 |
| 50 | 06 30 | 07 10 | 07 46 | 23 51 | 25 07 | 01 07 | 02 20 |
| 45 | 06 22 | 06 58 | 07 30 | 23 43 | 24 55 | 00 55 | 02 05 |
| N 40 | 06 14 | 06 47 | 07 16 | 23 36 | 24 45 | 00 45 | 01 52 |
| 35 | 06 07 | 06 38 | 07 05 | 23 30 | 24 36 | 00 36 | 01 41 |
| 30 | 06 00 | 06 29 | 06 55 | 23 25 | 24 29 | 00 29 | 01 32 |
| 20 | 05 47 | 06 14 | 06 38 | 23 16 | 24 16 | 00 16 | 01 16 |
| N 10 | 05 35 | 06 00 | 06 22 | 23 08 | 24 05 | 00 05 | 01 02 |
| 0 | 05 21 | 05 46 | 06 08 | 23 01 | 23 54 | 24 49 | 00 49 |
| S 10 | 05 05 | 05 31 | 05 54 | 22 54 | 23 44 | 24 36 | 00 36 |
| 20 | 04 46 | 05 14 | 05 38 | 22 46 | 23 33 | 24 22 | 00 22 |
| 30 | 04 22 | 04 53 | 05 20 | 22 38 | 23 20 | 24 06 | 00 06 |
| 35 | 04 06 | 04 41 | 05 09 | 22 33 | 23 13 | 23 57 | 24 45 |
| 40 | 03 47 | 04 26 | 04 57 | 22 27 | 23 05 | 23 47 | 24 33 |
| 45 | 03 23 | 04 08 | 04 42 | 22 21 | 22 56 | 23 35 | 24 19 |
| S 50 | 02 50 | 03 44 | 04 25 | 22 13 | 22 44 | 23 20 | 24 02 |
| 52 | 02 32 | 03 33 | 04 16 | 22 10 | 22 39 | 23 13 | 23 54 |
| 54 | 02 10 | 03 20 | 04 07 | 22 06 | 22 33 | 23 06 | 23 45 |
| 56 | 01 40 | 03 04 | 03 56 | 22 02 | 22 27 | 22 57 | 23 35 |
| 58 | 00 44 | 02 46 | 03 44 | 21 57 | 22 20 | 22 48 | 23 23 |
| S 60 | //// | 02 22 | 03 29 | 21 52 | 22 12 | 22 37 | 23 10 |

| Lat. | Sunset h m | Twilight Civil h m | Twilight Naut. h m | Moonset 22 h m | Moonset 23 h m | Moonset 24 h m | Moonset 25 h m |
|---|---|---|---|---|---|---|---|
| N 72 | ■ | 15 03 | 16 43 | 08 59 | 08 44 | 08 22 | ■ |
| N 70 | 13 37 | 15 29 | 16 54 | 09 09 | 09 03 | 08 56 | 08 47 |
| 68 | 14 24 | 15 49 | 17 04 | 09 17 | 09 18 | 09 21 | 09 28 |
| 66 | 14 54 | 16 05 | 17 13 | 09 24 | 09 31 | 09 41 | 09 56 |
| 64 | 15 16 | 16 18 | 17 20 | 09 30 | 09 42 | 09 56 | 10 17 |
| 62 | 15 34 | 16 29 | 17 26 | 09 36 | 09 51 | 10 09 | 10 35 |
| 60 | 15 49 | 16 39 | 17 32 | 09 40 | 09 58 | 10 20 | 10 49 |
| N 58 | 16 01 | 16 48 | 17 37 | 09 44 | 10 05 | 10 30 | 11 02 |
| 56 | 16 12 | 16 55 | 17 41 | 09 48 | 10 11 | 10 39 | 11 12 |
| 54 | 16 22 | 17 02 | 17 46 | 09 51 | 10 17 | 10 46 | 11 22 |
| 52 | 16 30 | 17 08 | 17 50 | 09 54 | 10 22 | 10 53 | 11 30 |
| 50 | 16 38 | 17 14 | 17 53 | 09 57 | 10 26 | 10 59 | 11 38 |
| 45 | 16 54 | 17 26 | 18 02 | 10 03 | 10 36 | 11 13 | 11 54 |
| N 40 | 17 07 | 17 36 | 18 09 | 10 08 | 10 44 | 11 24 | 12 08 |
| 35 | 17 19 | 17 46 | 18 16 | 10 12 | 10 51 | 11 33 | 12 19 |
| 30 | 17 29 | 17 54 | 18 23 | 10 16 | 10 57 | 11 41 | 12 29 |
| 20 | 17 46 | 18 09 | 18 36 | 10 22 | 11 08 | 11 56 | 12 46 |
| N 10 | 18 01 | 18 23 | 18 49 | 10 28 | 11 17 | 12 08 | 13 01 |
| 0 | 18 15 | 18 37 | 19 03 | 10 33 | 11 26 | 12 20 | 13 15 |
| S 10 | 18 30 | 18 52 | 19 18 | 10 39 | 11 35 | 12 32 | 13 29 |
| 20 | 18 45 | 19 09 | 19 37 | 10 45 | 11 45 | 12 45 | 13 44 |
| 30 | 19 03 | 19 29 | 20 01 | 10 51 | 11 55 | 12 59 | 14 01 |
| 35 | 19 14 | 19 42 | 20 16 | 10 55 | 12 02 | 13 07 | 14 11 |
| 40 | 19 26 | 19 57 | 20 35 | 10 59 | 12 09 | 13 17 | 14 23 |
| 45 | 19 40 | 20 15 | 20 59 | 11 04 | 12 17 | 13 28 | 14 36 |
| S 50 | 19 58 | 20 38 | 21 32 | 11 11 | 12 27 | 13 42 | 14 53 |
| 52 | 20 06 | 20 49 | 21 49 | 11 13 | 12 32 | 13 48 | 15 01 |
| 54 | 20 15 | 21 02 | 22 10 | 11 16 | 12 37 | 13 56 | 15 10 |
| 56 | 20 26 | 21 17 | 22 39 | 11 20 | 12 43 | 14 04 | 15 19 |
| 58 | 20 38 | 21 35 | 23 29 | 11 24 | 12 49 | 14 12 | 15 30 |
| S 60 | 20 52 | 21 59 | //// | 11 28 | 12 57 | 14 23 | 15 43 |

| Day | SUN Eqn. of Time 00ʰ m s | SUN Eqn. of Time 12ʰ m s | SUN Mer. Pass. h m | MOON Mer. Pass. Upper h m | MOON Mer. Pass. Lower h m | MOON Age d | Phase |
|---|---|---|---|---|---|---|---|
| 22 | 11 18 | 11 26 | 12 11 | 04 21 | 16 47 | 21 | ◑ |
| 23 | 11 34 | 11 42 | 12 12 | 05 14 | 17 40 | 22 | |
| 24 | 11 50 | 11 58 | 12 12 | 06 07 | 18 34 | 23 | |

## 1976 FEBRUARY 18, 19, 20 (WED., THURS., FRI.)

| G.M.T. | ARIES G.H.A. | VENUS −3.4 G.H.A. | VENUS Dec. | MARS +0.3 G.H.A. | MARS Dec. | JUPITER −1.7 G.H.A. | JUPITER Dec. | SATURN +0.1 G.H.A. | SATURN Dec. |
|---|---|---|---|---|---|---|---|---|---|
| d h | ° ′ | ° ′ | ° ′ | ° ′ | ° ′ | ° ′ | ° ′ | ° ′ | ° ′ |
| 18 00 | 147 05.8 | 207 07.1 | S20 30.6 | 69 13.0 | N25 43.8 | 126 16.7 | N 7 34.4 | 27 37.2 | N21 01.5 |
| 01 | 162 08.3 | 222 06.3 | 30.1 | 84 14.7 | 43.8 | 141 18.7 | 34.6 | 42 39.8 | 01.6 |
| 02 | 177 10.8 | 237 05.5 | 29.6 | 99 16.4 | 43.9 | 156 20.7 | 34.8 | 57 42.5 | 01.6 |
| 03 | 192 13.2 | 252 04.7 | 29.1 | 114 18.1 | 43.9 | 171 22.7 | 34.9 | 72 45.1 | 01.6 |
| 04 | 207 15.7 | 267 03.9 | 28.6 | 129 19.7 | 43.9 | 186 24.8 | 35.1 | 87 47.7 | 01.7 |
| 05 | 222 18.2 | 282 03.2 | 28.1 | 144 21.4 | 43.9 | 201 26.8 | 35.3 | 102 50.4 | 01.7 |
| 06 | 237 20.6 | 297 02.4 | S20 27.6 | 159 23.1 | N25 43.9 | 216 28.8 | N 7 35.5 | 117 53.0 | N21 01.7 |
| W 07 | 252 23.1 | 312 01.6 | 27.1 | 174 24.8 | 44.0 | 231 30.9 | 35.7 | 132 55.6 | 01.8 |
| E 08 | 267 25.6 | 327 00.8 | 26.6 | 189 26.4 | 44.0 | 246 32.9 | 35.9 | 147 58.2 | 01.8 |
| D 09 | 282 28.0 | 342 00.0 | 26.1 | 204 28.1 | 44.0 | 261 34.9 | 36.0 | 163 00.9 | 01.8 |
| N 10 | 297 30.5 | 356 59.3 | 25.6 | 219 29.8 | 44.0 | 276 36.9 | 36.2 | 178 03.5 | 01.9 |
| E 11 | 312 32.9 | 11 58.5 | 25.1 | 234 31.4 | 44.1 | 291 39.0 | 36.4 | 193 06.1 | 01.9 |
| S 12 | 327 35.4 | 26 57.7 | S20 24.6 | 249 33.1 | N25 44.1 | 306 41.0 | N 7 36.6 | 208 08.8 | N21 01.9 |
| D 13 | 342 37.9 | 41 56.9 | 24.1 | 264 34.8 | 44.1 | 321 43.0 | 36.8 | 223 11.4 | 02.0 |
| A 14 | 357 40.3 | 56 56.2 | 23.6 | 279 36.4 | 44.1 | 336 45.0 | 37.0 | 238 14.0 | 02.0 |
| Y 15 | 12 42.8 | 71 55.4 | 23.1 | 294 38.1 | 44.2 | 351 47.1 | 37.1 | 253 16.7 | 02.0 |
| 16 | 27 45.3 | 86 54.6 | 22.6 | 309 39.8 | 44.2 | 6 49.1 | 37.3 | 268 19.3 | 02.1 |
| 17 | 42 47.7 | 101 53.8 | 22.1 | 324 41.4 | 44.2 | 21 51.1 | 37.5 | 283 21.9 | 02.1 |
| 18 | 57 50.2 | 116 53.0 | S20 21.6 | 339 43.1 | N25 44.2 | 36 53.1 | N 7 37.7 | 298 24.5 | N21 02.1 |
| 19 | 72 52.7 | 131 52.3 | 21.1 | 354 44.8 | 44.2 | 51 55.2 | 37.9 | 313 27.2 | 02.2 |
| 20 | 87 55.1 | 146 51.5 | 20.6 | 9 46.4 | 44.3 | 66 57.2 | 38.1 | 328 29.8 | 02.2 |
| 21 | 102 57.6 | 161 50.7 | 20.1 | 24 48.1 | 44.3 | 81 59.2 | 38.2 | 343 32.4 | 02.2 |
| 22 | 118 00.1 | 176 50.0 | 19.6 | 39 49.8 | 44.3 | 97 01.2 | 38.4 | 358 35.1 | 02.3 |
| 23 | 133 02.5 | 191 49.2 | 19.1 | 54 51.4 | 44.3 | 112 03.3 | 38.6 | 13 37.7 | 02.3 |
| 19 00 | 148 05.0 | 206 48.4 | S20 18.6 | 69 53.1 | N25 44.4 | 127 05.3 | N 7 38.8 | 28 40.3 | N21 02.3 |
| 01 | 163 07.4 | 221 47.6 | 18.0 | 84 54.7 | 44.4 | 142 07.3 | 39.0 | 43 42.9 | 02.4 |
| 02 | 178 09.9 | 236 46.9 | 17.5 | 99 56.4 | 44.4 | 157 09.3 | 39.2 | 58 45.6 | 02.4 |
| 03 | 193 12.4 | 251 46.1 | 17.0 | 114 58.1 | 44.4 | 172 11.4 | 39.3 | 73 48.2 | 02.4 |
| 04 | 208 14.8 | 266 45.3 | 16.5 | 129 59.7 | 44.5 | 187 13.4 | 39.5 | 88 50.8 | 02.5 |
| 05 | 223 17.3 | 281 44.5 | 16.0 | 145 01.4 | 44.5 | 202 15.4 | 39.7 | 103 53.5 | 02.5 |
| 06 | 238 19.8 | 296 43.8 | S20 15.4 | 160 03.0 | N25 44.5 | 217 17.4 | N 7 39.9 | 118 56.1 | N21 02.5 |
| 07 | 253 22.2 | 311 43.0 | 14.9 | 175 04.7 | 44.5 | 232 19.4 | 40.1 | 133 58.7 | 02.6 |
| T 08 | 268 24.7 | 326 42.2 | 14.4 | 190 06.3 | 44.5 | 247 21.5 | 40.3 | 149 01.3 | 02.6 |
| H 09 | 283 27.2 | 341 41.5 | 13.9 | 205 08.0 | 44.6 | 262 23.5 | 40.4 | 164 04.0 | 02.6 |
| U 10 | 298 29.6 | 356 40.7 | 13.4 | 220 09.6 | 44.6 | 277 25.5 | 40.6 | 179 06.6 | 02.7 |
| R 11 | 313 32.1 | 11 39.9 | 12.8 | 235 11.3 | 44.6 | 292 27.5 | 40.8 | 194 09.2 | 02.7 |
| S 12 | 328 34.6 | 26 39.1 | S20 12.3 | 250 12.9 | N25 44.6 | 307 29.6 | N 7 41.0 | 209 11.8 | N21 02.7 |
| D 13 | 343 37.0 | 41 38.4 | 11.8 | 265 14.6 | 44.7 | 322 31.6 | 41.2 | 224 14.5 | 02.8 |
| A 14 | 358 39.5 | 56 37.6 | 11.3 | 280 16.2 | 44.7 | 337 33.6 | 41.4 | 239 17.1 | 02.8 |
| Y 15 | 13 41.9 | 71 36.8 | 10.7 | 295 17.9 | 44.7 | 352 35.6 | 41.5 | 254 19.7 | 02.8 |
| 16 | 28 44.4 | 86 36.1 | 10.2 | 310 19.5 | 44.7 | 7 37.6 | 41.7 | 269 22.3 | 02.9 |
| 17 | 43 46.9 | 101 35.3 | 09.7 | 325 21.2 | 44.8 | 22 39.7 | 41.9 | 284 25.0 | 02.9 |
| 18 | 58 49.3 | 116 34.5 | S20 09.1 | 340 22.8 | N25 44.8 | 37 41.7 | N 7 42.1 | 299 27.6 | N21 02.9 |
| 19 | 73 51.8 | 131 33.8 | 08.6 | 355 24.5 | 44.8 | 52 43.7 | 42.3 | 314 30.2 | 03.0 |
| 20 | 88 54.3 | 146 33.0 | 08.1 | 10 26.1 | 44.8 | 67 45.7 | 42.5 | 329 32.8 | 03.0 |
| 21 | 103 56.7 | 161 32.2 | 07.5 | 25 27.7 | 44.8 | 82 47.7 | 42.6 | 344 35.5 | 03.0 |
| 22 | 118 59.2 | 176 31.5 | 07.0 | 40 29.4 | 44.9 | 97 49.8 | 42.8 | 359 38.1 | 03.1 |
| 23 | 134 01.7 | 191 30.7 | 06.5 | 55 31.0 | 44.9 | 112 51.8 | 43.0 | 14 40.7 | 03.1 |
| 20 00 | 149 04.1 | 206 29.9 | S20 05.9 | 70 32.7 | N25 44.9 | 127 53.8 | N 7 43.2 | 29 43.3 | N21 03.1 |
| 01 | 164 06.6 | 221 29.2 | 05.4 | 85 34.3 | 44.9 | 142 55.8 | 43.4 | 44 46.0 | 03.2 |
| 02 | 179 09.0 | 236 28.4 | 04.8 | 100 35.9 | 45.0 | 157 57.8 | 43.6 | 59 48.6 | 03.2 |
| 03 | 194 11.5 | 251 27.6 | 04.3 | 115 37.6 | 45.0 | 172 59.9 | 43.8 | 74 51.2 | 03.2 |
| 04 | 209 14.0 | 266 26.9 | 03.8 | 130 39.2 | 45.0 | 188 01.9 | 43.9 | 89 53.8 | 03.3 |
| 05 | 224 16.4 | 281 26.1 | 03.2 | 145 40.9 | 45.0 | 203 03.9 | 44.1 | 104 56.5 | 03.3 |
| 06 | 239 18.9 | 296 25.4 | S20 02.7 | 160 42.5 | N25 45.0 | 218 05.9 | N 7 44.3 | 119 59.1 | N21 03.3 |
| 07 | 254 21.4 | 311 24.6 | 02.1 | 175 44.1 | 45.1 | 233 07.9 | 44.5 | 135 01.7 | 03.4 |
| 08 | 269 23.8 | 326 23.8 | 01.6 | 190 45.8 | 45.1 | 248 10.0 | 44.7 | 150 04.3 | 03.4 |
| F 09 | 284 26.3 | 341 23.1 | 01.0 | 205 47.4 | 45.1 | 263 12.0 | 44.9 | 165 07.0 | 03.4 |
| R 10 | 299 28.8 | 356 22.3 | 20 00.5 | 220 49.0 | 45.1 | 278 14.0 | 45.0 | 180 09.6 | 03.5 |
| I 11 | 314 31.2 | 11 21.5 | 19 59.9 | 235 50.7 | 45.2 | 293 16.0 | 45.2 | 195 12.2 | 03.5 |
| D 12 | 329 33.7 | 26 20.8 | S19 59.4 | 250 52.3 | N25 45.2 | 308 18.0 | N 7 45.4 | 210 14.8 | N21 03.5 |
| A 13 | 344 36.2 | 41 20.0 | 58.8 | 265 53.9 | 45.2 | 323 20.0 | 45.6 | 225 17.5 | 03.6 |
| Y 14 | 359 38.6 | 56 19.3 | 58.3 | 280 55.5 | 45.2 | 338 22.1 | 45.8 | 240 20.1 | 03.6 |
| 15 | 14 41.1 | 71 18.5 | 57.7 | 295 57.2 | 45.3 | 353 24.1 | 46.0 | 255 22.7 | 03.6 |
| 16 | 29 43.5 | 86 17.7 | 57.2 | 310 58.8 | 45.3 | 8 26.1 | 46.2 | 270 25.3 | 03.7 |
| 17 | 44 46.0 | 101 17.0 | 56.6 | 326 00.4 | 45.3 | 23 28.1 | 46.3 | 285 27.9 | 03.7 |
| 18 | 59 48.5 | 116 16.2 | S19 56.0 | 341 02.1 | N25 45.3 | 38 30.1 | N 7 46.5 | 300 30.6 | N21 03.7 |
| 19 | 74 50.9 | 131 15.5 | 55.5 | 356 03.7 | 45.3 | 53 32.2 | 46.7 | 315 33.2 | 03.8 |
| 20 | 89 53.4 | 146 14.7 | 54.9 | 11 05.3 | 45.4 | 68 34.2 | 46.9 | 330 35.8 | 03.8 |
| 21 | 104 55.9 | 161 14.0 | 54.4 | 26 06.9 | 45.4 | 83 36.2 | 47.1 | 345 38.4 | 03.8 |
| 22 | 119 58.3 | 176 13.2 | 53.8 | 41 08.6 | 45.4 | 98 38.2 | 47.3 | 0 41.1 | 03.9 |
| 23 | 135 00.8 | 191 12.4 | 53.3 | 56 10.2 | 45.4 | 113 40.2 | 47.5 | 15 43.7 | 03.9 |
| Mer. Pass. | h m 14 05.4 | v −0.8 | d 0.5 | v 1.6 | d 0.0 | v 2.0 | d 0.2 | v 2.6 | d 0.0 |

| STARS Name | S.H.A. | Dec. |
|---|---|---|
| | ° ′ | ° ′ |
| Acamar | 315 39.7 | S40 24.3 |
| Achernar | 335 47.9 | S57 21.7 |
| Acrux | 173 40.1 | S62 58.0 |
| Adhara | 255 34.3 | S28 56.7 |
| Aldebaran | 291 21.5 | N16 27.7 |
| Alioth | 166 44.8 | N56 05.0 |
| Alkaid | 153 20.7 | N49 25.6 |
| Al Na'ir | 28 19.3 | S47 04.6 |
| Alnilam | 276 14.6 | S 1 13.2 |
| Alphard | 218 23.3 | S 8 33.5 |
| Alphecca | 126 34.7 | N26 47.4 |
| Alpheratz | 358 12.8 | N28 57.6 |
| Altair | 62 35.8 | N 8 48.3 |
| Ankaa | 353 43.6 | S42 26.3 |
| Antares | 113 00.7 | S26 22.7 |
| Arcturus | 146 21.1 | N19 18.1 |
| Atria | 108 27.8 | S68 58.8 |
| Avior | 234 28.8 | S59 26.2 |
| Bellatrix | 279 01.9 | N 6 19.6 |
| Betelgeuse | 271 31.4 | N 7 24.1 |
| Canopus | 264 08.2 | S52 41.3 |
| Capella | 281 15.7 | N45 58.6 |
| Deneb | 49 51.0 | N45 11.7 |
| Denebola | 183 01.9 | N14 42.1 |
| Diphda | 349 24.2 | S18 07.2 |
| Dubhe | 194 25.3 | N61 52.5 |
| Elnath | 278 47.9 | N28 35.3 |
| Eltanin | 90 59.4 | N51 29.3 |
| Enif | 34 14.9 | N 9 45.9 |
| Fomalhaut | 15 55.2 | S29 45.0 |
| Gacrux | 172 31.7 | S56 58.8 |
| Gienah | 176 20.9 | S17 24.7 |
| Hadar | 149 27.4 | S60 15.4 |
| Hamal | 328 32.5 | N23 21.0 |
| Kaus Aust. | 84 21.2 | S34 23.7 |
| Kochab | 137 18.6 | N74 14.9 |
| Markab | 14 06.5 | N15 04.6 |
| Menkar | 314 44.4 | N 3 59.7 |
| Menkent | 148 40.4 | S36 15.1 |
| Miaplacidus | 221 44.7 | S69 37.3 |
| Mirfak | 309 20.5 | N49 46.8 |
| Nunki | 76 33.2 | S26 19.5 |
| Peacock | 54 03.8 | S56 48.6 |
| Pollux | 244 01.6 | N28 04.9 |
| Procyon | 245 28.7 | N 5 17.0 |
| Rasalhague | 96 32.6 | N12 34.5 |
| Regulus | 208 12.9 | N12 04.8 |
| Rigel | 281 38.9 | S 8 13.9 |
| Rigil Kent. | 140 29.7 | S60 44.0 |
| Sabik | 102 44.8 | S15 41.7 |
| Schedar | 350 12.9 | N56 24.6 |
| Shaula | 97 00.1 | S37 05.1 |
| Sirius | 258 58.2 | S16 41.3 |
| Spica | 159 00.6 | S11 02.3 |
| Suhail | 223 12.6 | S43 20.4 |
| Vega | 80 58.2 | N38 45.5 |
| Zuben'ubi | 137 36.3 | S15 56.6 |

| | S.H.A. | Mer. Pass. |
|---|---|---|
| | ° ′ | h m |
| Venus | 58 43.4 | 10 13 |
| Mars | 281 48.1 | 19 18 |
| Jupiter | 339 00.3 | 15 30 |
| Saturn | 240 35.3 | 22 01 |

## 1976 FEBRUARY 27, 28, 29 (FRI., SAT., SUN.)

| G.M.T. | ARIES G.H.A. | VENUS −3.4 G.H.A. | VENUS Dec. | MARS +0.5 G.H.A. | MARS Dec. | JUPITER −1.7 G.H.A. | JUPITER Dec. | SATURN +0.1 G.H.A. | SATURN Dec. |
|---|---|---|---|---|---|---|---|---|---|
| d h | ° ′ | ° ′ | ° ′ | ° ′ | ° ′ | ° ′ | ° ′ | ° ′ | ° ′ |
| 27 00 | 155 58.1 | 204 26.8 | S18 21.4 | 74 57.4 | N25 48.4 | 133 30.9 | N 8 14.8 | 37 02.2 | N21 08.3 |
| 01 | 171 00.6 | 219 26.1 | 20.7 | 89 58.9 | 48.4 | 148 32.9 | 15.0 | 52 04.8 | 08.3 |
| 02 | 186 03.0 | 234 25.4 | 20.0 | 105 00.4 | 48.4 | 163 34.9 | 15.2 | 67 07.4 | 08.4 |
| 03 | 201 05.5 | 249 24.7 | 19.3 | 120 01.9 | 48.4 | 178 36.9 | 15.4 | 82 10.0 | 08.4 |
| 04 | 216 07.9 | 264 24.0 | 18.6 | 135 03.5 | 48.4 | 193 38.9 | 15.6 | 97 12.6 | 08.4 |
| 05 | 231 10.4 | 279 23.3 | 17.9 | 150 05.0 | 48.4 | 208 40.9 | 15.8 | 112 15.2 | 08.4 |
| 06 | 246 12.9 | 294 22.6 | S18 17.2 | 165 06.5 | N25 48.5 | 223 42.9 | N 8 16.0 | 127 17.8 | N21 08.5 |
| 07 | 261 15.3 | 309 21.9 | 16.5 | 180 08.0 | 48.5 | 238 44.9 | 16.2 | 142 20.4 | 08.5 |
| 08 | 276 17.8 | 324 21.2 | 15.8 | 195 09.5 | 48.5 | 253 46.9 | 16.4 | 157 23.0 | 08.5 |
| F 09 | 291 20.3 | 339 20.5 | 15.1 | 210 11.0 | 48.5 | 268 48.9 | 16.6 | 172 25.6 | 08.6 |
| R 10 | 306 22.7 | 354 19.8 | 14.3 | 225 12.5 | 48.5 | 283 50.9 | 16.7 | 187 28.2 | 08.6 |
| I 11 | 321 25.2 | 9 19.1 | 13.6 | 240 14.0 | 48.5 | 298 52.9 | 16.9 | 202 30.8 | 08.6 |
| D 12 | 336 27.7 | 24 18.4 | S18 12.9 | 255 15.5 | N25 48.6 | 313 54.8 | N 8 17.1 | 217 33.4 | N21 08.6 |
| A 13 | 351 30.1 | 39 17.7 | 12.2 | 270 17.0 | 48.6 | 328 56.8 | 17.3 | 232 36.0 | 08.7 |
| Y 14 | 6 32.6 | 54 17.0 | 11.5 | 285 18.5 | 48.6 | 343 58.8 | 17.5 | 247 38.6 | 08.7 |
| 15 | 21 35.1 | 69 16.4 | 10.8 | 300 20.0 | 48.6 | 359 00.8 | 17.7 | 262 41.2 | 08.7 |
| 16 | 36 37.5 | 84 15.7 | 10.1 | 315 21.6 | 48.6 | 14 02.8 | 17.9 | 277 43.8 | 08.8 |
| 17 | 51 40.0 | 99 15.0 | 09.3 | 330 23.1 | 48.6 | 29 04.8 | 18.1 | 292 46.4 | 08.8 |
| 18 | 66 42.4 | 114 14.3 | S18 08.6 | 345 24.6 | N25 48.7 | 44 06.8 | N 8 18.3 | 307 49.0 | N21 08.8 |
| 19 | 81 44.9 | 129 13.6 | 07.9 | 0 26.1 | 48.7 | 59 08.8 | 18.5 | 322 51.6 | 08.8 |
| 20 | 96 47.4 | 144 12.9 | 07.2 | 15 27.6 | 48.7 | 74 10.8 | 18.7 | 337 54.2 | 08.9 |
| 21 | 111 49.8 | 159 12.2 | 06.5 | 30 29.1 | 48.7 | 89 12.8 | 18.9 | 352 56.8 | 08.9 |
| 22 | 126 52.3 | 174 11.5 | 05.7 | 45 30.6 | 48.7 | 104 14.8 | 19.1 | 7 59.4 | 08.9 |
| 23 | 141 54.8 | 189 10.8 | 05.0 | 60 32.1 | 48.7 | 119 16.7 | 19.3 | 23 02.0 | 08.9 |
| 28 00 | 156 57.2 | 204 10.1 | S18 04.3 | 75 33.6 | N25 48.8 | 134 18.7 | N 8 19.4 | 38 04.6 | N21 09.0 |
| 01 | 171 59.7 | 219 09.4 | 03.6 | 90 35.1 | 48.8 | 149 20.7 | 19.6 | 53 07.2 | 09.0 |
| 02 | 187 02.2 | 234 08.8 | 02.8 | 105 36.6 | 48.8 | 164 22.7 | 19.8 | 68 09.8 | 09.0 |
| 03 | 202 04.6 | 249 08.1 | 02.1 | 120 38.1 | 48.8 | 179 24.7 | 20.0 | 83 12.4 | 09.1 |
| 04 | 217 07.1 | 264 07.4 | 01.4 | 135 39.5 | 48.8 | 194 26.7 | 20.2 | 98 14.9 | 09.1 |
| 05 | 232 09.6 | 279 06.7 | 18 00.7 | 150 41.0 | 48.8 | 209 28.7 | 20.4 | 113 17.5 | 09.1 |
| 06 | 247 12.0 | 294 06.0 | S17 59.9 | 165 42.5 | N25 48.8 | 224 30.7 | N 8 20.6 | 128 20.1 | N21 09.1 |
| 07 | 262 14.5 | 309 05.3 | 59.2 | 180 44.0 | 48.9 | 239 32.7 | 20.8 | 143 22.7 | 09.2 |
| S 08 | 277 16.9 | 324 04.6 | 58.5 | 195 45.5 | 48.9 | 254 34.7 | 21.0 | 158 25.3 | 09.2 |
| A 09 | 292 19.4 | 339 04.0 | 57.7 | 210 47.0 | 48.9 | 269 36.6 | 21.2 | 173 27.9 | 09.2 |
| T 10 | 307 21.9 | 354 03.3 | 57.0 | 225 48.5 | 48.9 | 284 38.6 | 21.4 | 188 30.5 | 09.2 |
| U 11 | 322 24.3 | 9 02.6 | 56.3 | 240 50.0 | 48.9 | 299 40.6 | 21.6 | 203 33.1 | 09.3 |
| R 12 | 337 26.8 | 24 01.9 | S17 55.5 | 255 51.5 | N25 48.9 | 314 42.6 | N 8 21.8 | 218 35.7 | N21 09.3 |
| D 13 | 352 29.3 | 39 01.2 | 54.8 | 270 53.0 | 49.0 | 329 44.6 | 22.0 | 233 38.3 | 09.3 |
| A 14 | 7 31.7 | 54 00.5 | 54.1 | 285 54.5 | 49.0 | 344 46.6 | 22.1 | 248 40.9 | 09.4 |
| Y 15 | 22 34.2 | 68 59.9 | 53.3 | 300 56.0 | 49.0 | 359 48.6 | 22.3 | 263 43.5 | 09.4 |
| 16 | 37 36.7 | 83 59.2 | 52.6 | 315 57.4 | 49.0 | 14 50.6 | 22.5 | 278 46.1 | 09.4 |
| 17 | 52 39.1 | 98 58.5 | 51.9 | 330 58.9 | 49.0 | 29 52.6 | 22.7 | 293 48.7 | 09.4 |
| 18 | 67 41.6 | 113 57.8 | S17 51.1 | 346 00.4 | N25 49.0 | 44 54.5 | N 8 22.9 | 308 51.3 | N21 09.5 |
| 19 | 82 44.0 | 128 57.1 | 50.4 | 1 01.9 | 49.0 | 59 56.5 | 23.1 | 323 53.9 | 09.5 |
| 20 | 97 46.5 | 143 56.5 | 49.6 | 16 03.4 | 49.1 | 74 58.5 | 23.3 | 338 56.4 | 09.5 |
| 21 | 112 49.0 | 158 55.8 | 48.9 | 31 04.9 | 49.1 | 90 00.5 | 23.5 | 353 59.0 | 09.5 |
| 22 | 127 51.4 | 173 55.1 | 48.2 | 46 06.4 | 49.1 | 105 02.5 | 23.7 | 9 01.6 | 09.6 |
| 23 | 142 53.9 | 188 54.4 | 47.4 | 61 07.8 | 49.1 | 120 04.5 | 23.9 | 24 04.2 | 09.6 |
| 29 00 | 157 56.4 | 203 53.7 | S17 46.7 | 76 09.3 | N25 49.1 | 135 06.5 | N 8 24.1 | 39 06.8 | N21 09.6 |
| 01 | 172 58.8 | 218 53.1 | 45.9 | 91 10.8 | 49.1 | 150 08.5 | 24.3 | 54 09.4 | 09.6 |
| 02 | 188 01.3 | 233 52.4 | 45.2 | 106 12.3 | 49.1 | 165 10.4 | 24.5 | 69 12.0 | 09.7 |
| 03 | 203 03.8 | 248 51.7 | 44.4 | 121 13.8 | 49.2 | 180 12.4 | 24.7 | 84 14.6 | 09.7 |
| 04 | 218 06.2 | 263 51.0 | 43.7 | 136 15.3 | 49.2 | 195 14.4 | 24.9 | 99 17.2 | 09.7 |
| 05 | 233 08.7 | 278 50.4 | 42.9 | 151 16.7 | 49.2 | 210 16.4 | 25.0 | 114 19.8 | 09.7 |
| 06 | 248 11.2 | 293 49.7 | S17 42.2 | 166 18.2 | N25 49.2 | 225 18.4 | N 8 25.2 | 129 22.4 | N21 09.8 |
| 07 | 263 13.6 | 308 49.0 | 41.4 | 181 19.7 | 49.2 | 240 20.4 | 25.4 | 144 24.9 | 09.8 |
| 08 | 278 16.1 | 323 48.3 | 40.7 | 196 21.2 | 49.2 | 255 22.4 | 25.6 | 159 27.5 | 09.8 |
| S 09 | 293 18.5 | 338 47.7 | 39.9 | 211 22.6 | 49.2 | 270 24.3 | 25.8 | 174 30.1 | 09.9 |
| U 10 | 308 21.0 | 353 47.0 | 39.2 | 226 24.1 | 49.3 | 285 26.3 | 26.0 | 189 32.7 | 09.9 |
| N 11 | 323 23.5 | 8 46.3 | 38.4 | 241 25.6 | 49.3 | 300 28.3 | 26.2 | 204 35.3 | 09.9 |
| D 12 | 338 25.9 | 23 45.6 | S17 37.7 | 256 27.1 | N25 49.3 | 315 30.3 | N 8 26.4 | 219 37.9 | N21 09.9 |
| A 13 | 353 28.4 | 38 45.0 | 36.9 | 271 28.5 | 49.3 | 330 32.3 | 26.6 | 234 40.5 | 10.0 |
| Y 14 | 8 30.9 | 53 44.3 | 36.1 | 286 30.0 | 49.3 | 345 34.3 | 26.8 | 249 43.1 | 10.0 |
| 15 | 23 33.3 | 68 43.6 | 35.4 | 301 31.5 | 49.3 | 0 36.3 | 27.0 | 264 45.7 | 10.0 |
| 16 | 38 35.8 | 83 42.9 | 34.6 | 316 33.0 | 49.3 | 15 38.2 | 27.2 | 279 48.3 | 10.0 |
| 17 | 53 38.3 | 98 42.3 | 33.9 | 331 34.4 | 49.4 | 30 40.2 | 27.4 | 294 50.8 | 10.1 |
| 18 | 68 40.7 | 113 41.6 | S17 33.1 | 346 35.9 | N25 49.4 | 45 42.2 | N 8 27.6 | 309 53.4 | N21 10.1 |
| 19 | 83 43.2 | 128 40.9 | 32.3 | 1 37.4 | 49.4 | 60 44.2 | 27.8 | 324 56.0 | 10.1 |
| 20 | 98 45.7 | 143 40.3 | 31.6 | 16 38.8 | 49.4 | 75 46.2 | 28.0 | 339 58.6 | 10.1 |
| 21 | 113 48.1 | 158 39.6 | 30.8 | 31 40.3 | 49.4 | 90 48.2 | 28.2 | 355 01.2 | 10.2 |
| 22 | 128 50.6 | 173 38.9 | 30.1 | 46 41.8 | 49.4 | 105 50.2 | 28.3 | 10 03.8 | 10.2 |
| 23 | 143 53.0 | 188 38.3 | 29.3 | 61 43.3 | 49.4 | 120 52.1 | 28.5 | 25 06.4 | 10.2 |
| Mer. Pass. | h m 13 30.0 | v −0.7 | d 0.7 | v 1.5 | d 0.0 | v 2.0 | d 0.2 | v 2.6 | d 0.0 |

| STARS Name | S.H.A. | Dec. |
|---|---|---|
| | ° ′ | ° ′ |
| Acamar | 315 39.7 | S40 24.3 |
| Achernar | 335 48.0 | S57 21.7 |
| Acrux | 173 40.0 | S62 58.0 |
| Adhara | 255 34.3 | S28 56.7 |
| Aldebaran | 291 21.5 | N16 27.7 |
| Alioth | 166 44.7 | N56 05.0 |
| Alkaid | 153 20.6 | N49 25.6 |
| Al Na'ir | 28 19.2 | S47 04.6 |
| Alnilam | 276 14.7 | S 1 13.2 |
| Alphard | 218 23.3 | S 8 33.6 |
| Alphecca | 126 34.6 | N26 47.4 |
| Alpheratz | 358 12.8 | N28 57.6 |
| Altair | 62 35.8 | N 8 48.2 |
| Ankaa | 353 43.6 | S42 26.2 |
| Antares | 113 00.6 | S26 22.7 |
| Arcturus | 146 21.1 | N19 18.1 |
| Atria | 108 27.6 | S68 58.8 |
| Avior | 234 28.9 | S59 26.3 |
| Bellatrix | 279 01.9 | N 6 19.6 |
| Betelgeuse | 271 31.5 | N 7 24.0 |
| Canopus | 264 08.3 | S52 41.3 |
| Capella | 281 15.7 | N45 58.6 |
| Deneb | 49 50.9 | N45 11.6 |
| Denebola | 183 01.8 | N14 42.1 |
| Diphda | 349 24.2 | S18 07.1 |
| Dubhe | 194 25.2 | N61 52.6 |
| Elnath | 278 47.9 | N28 35.3 |
| Eltanin | 90 59.3 | N51 29.3 |
| Enif | 34 14.9 | N 9 45.9 |
| Fomalhaut | 15 55.2 | S29 45.0 |
| Gacrux | 172 31.6 | S56 58.8 |
| Gienah | 176 20.8 | S17 24.7 |
| Hadar | 149 27.3 | S60 15.4 |
| Hamal | 328 32.6 | N23 21.0 |
| Kaus Aust. | 84 21.1 | S34 23.7 |
| Kochab | 137 18.4 | N74 14.9 |
| Markab | 14 06.5 | N15 04.6 |
| Menkar | 314 44.4 | N 3 59.7 |
| Menkent | 148 40.4 | S36 15.2 |
| Miaplacidus | 221 44.7 | S69 37.4 |
| Mirfak | 309 20.6 | N49 46.8 |
| Nunki | 76 33.2 | S26 19.5 |
| Peacock | 54 03.7 | S56 48.6 |
| Pollux | 244 01.6 | N28 05.0 |
| Procyon | 245 28.7 | N 5 17.0 |
| Rasalhague | 96 32.5 | N12 34.5 |
| Regulus | 208 12.9 | N12 04.8 |
| Rigel | 281 38.9 | S 8 13.9 |
| Rigil Kent. | 140 29.6 | S60 44.0 |
| Sabik | 102 44.7 | S15 41.8 |
| Schedar | 350 12.9 | N56 24.6 |
| Shaula | 97 00.0 | S37 05.1 |
| Sirius | 258 58.2 | S16 41.3 |
| Spica | 159 00.5 | S11 02.4 |
| Suhail | 223 12.6 | S43 20.4 |
| Vega | 80 58.1 | N38 45.5 |
| Zuben'ubi | 137 36.3 | S15 56.7 |

| | S.H.A. | Mer. Pass. |
|---|---|---|
| | ° ′ | h m |
| Venus | 47 12.9 | 10 24 |
| Mars | 278 36.3 | 18 56 |
| Jupiter | 337 21.5 | 15 01 |
| Saturn | 241 07.3 | 21 24 |

## 1976 FEBRUARY 27, 28, 29 (FRI., SAT., SUN.)

| G.M.T. | SUN G.H.A. | SUN Dec. | MOON G.H.A. | v | MOON Dec. | d | H.P. |
|---|---|---|---|---|---|---|---|
| d h | ° ′ | ° ′ | ° ′ | ′ | ° ′ | ′ | ′ |
| 27 00 | 176 45.3 | S 8 44.8 | 211 03.9 | 12.1 | S14 30.0 | 7.7 | 55.6 |
| 01 | 191 45.4 | 43.9 | 225 35.0 | 12.1 | 14 22.3 | 7.8 | 55.6 |
| 02 | 206 45.5 | 43.0 | 240 06.1 | 12.2 | 14 14.5 | 7.8 | 55.6 |
| 03 | 221 45.6 | ·· 42.0 | 254 37.3 | 12.2 | 14 06.7 | 8.0 | 55.6 |
| 04 | 236 45.7 | 41.1 | 269 08.5 | 12.3 | 13 58.7 | 7.9 | 55.6 |
| 05 | 251 45.8 | 40.2 | 283 39.8 | 12.4 | 13 50.8 | 8.1 | 55.5 |
| 06 | 266 46.0 | S 8 39.2 | 298 11.2 | 12.4 | S13 42.7 | 8.1 | 55.5 |
| 07 | 281 46.1 | 38.3 | 312 42.6 | 12.5 | 13 34.6 | 8.1 | 55.5 |
| 08 | 296 46.2 | 37.4 | 327 14.1 | 12.5 | 13 26.5 | 8.2 | 55.5 |
| F 09 | 311 46.3 | ·· 36.4 | 341 45.6 | 12.6 | 13 18.3 | 8.3 | 55.5 |
| R 10 | 326 46.4 | 35.5 | 356 17.2 | 12.6 | 13 10.0 | 8.4 | 55.4 |
| I 11 | 341 46.5 | 34.6 | 10 48.8 | 12.7 | 13 01.6 | 8.3 | 55.4 |
| D 12 | 356 46.6 | S 8 33.6 | 25 20.5 | 12.7 | S12 53.3 | 8.5 | 55.4 |
| A 13 | 11 46.7 | 32.7 | 39 52.2 | 12.8 | 12 44.8 | 8.5 | 55.4 |
| Y 14 | 26 46.8 | 31.7 | 54 24.0 | 12.8 | 12 36.3 | 8.5 | 55.4 |
| 15 | 41 46.9 | ·· 30.8 | 68 55.8 | 12.9 | 12 27.8 | 8.6 | 55.4 |
| 16 | 56 47.0 | 29.9 | 83 27.7 | 12.9 | 12 19.2 | 8.7 | 55.3 |
| 17 | 71 47.1 | 28.9 | 97 59.6 | 13.0 | 12 10.5 | 8.7 | 55.3 |
| 18 | 86 47.2 | S 8 28.0 | 112 31.6 | 13.1 | S12 01.8 | 8.7 | 55.3 |
| 19 | 101 47.3 | 27.0 | 127 03.7 | 13.1 | 11 53.1 | 8.8 | 55.3 |
| 20 | 116 47.4 | 26.1 | 141 35.8 | 13.1 | 11 44.3 | 8.9 | 55.3 |
| 21 | 131 47.6 | ·· 25.2 | 156 07.9 | 13.2 | 11 35.4 | 8.8 | 55.2 |
| 22 | 146 47.7 | 24.2 | 170 40.1 | 13.2 | 11 26.6 | 9.0 | 55.2 |
| 23 | 161 47.8 | 23.3 | 185 12.3 | 13.3 | 11 17.6 | 9.0 | 55.2 |
| 28 00 | 176 47.9 | S 8 22.3 | 199 44.6 | 13.3 | S11 08.6 | 9.0 | 55.2 |
| 01 | 191 48.0 | 21.4 | 214 16.9 | 13.4 | 10 59.6 | 9.1 | 55.2 |
| 02 | 206 48.1 | 20.5 | 228 49.3 | 13.4 | 10 50.5 | 9.1 | 55.2 |
| 03 | 221 48.2 | ·· 19.5 | 243 21.7 | 13.5 | 10 41.4 | 9.1 | 55.1 |
| 04 | 236 48.3 | 18.6 | 257 54.2 | 13.5 | 10 32.3 | 9.3 | 55.1 |
| 05 | 251 48.4 | 17.6 | 272 26.7 | 13.6 | 10 23.0 | 9.2 | 55.1 |
| 06 | 266 48.5 | S 8 16.7 | 286 59.3 | 13.6 | S10 13.8 | 9.3 | 55.1 |
| 07 | 281 48.7 | 15.8 | 301 31.9 | 13.6 | 10 04.5 | 9.3 | 55.1 |
| S 08 | 296 48.8 | 14.8 | 316 04.5 | 13.7 | 9 55.2 | 9.4 | 55.1 |
| A 09 | 311 48.9 | ·· 13.9 | 330 37.2 | 13.8 | 9 45.8 | 9.4 | 55.0 |
| T 10 | 326 49.0 | 12.9 | 345 10.0 | 13.7 | 9 36.4 | 9.4 | 55.0 |
| U 11 | 341 49.1 | 12.0 | 359 42.7 | 13.9 | 9 27.0 | 9.5 | 55.0 |
| R 12 | 356 49.2 | S 8 11.1 | 14 15.6 | 13.8 | S 9 17.5 | 9.5 | 55.0 |
| D 13 | 11 49.3 | 10.1 | 28 48.4 | 13.9 | 9 08.0 | 9.5 | 55.0 |
| A 14 | 26 49.4 | 09.2 | 43 21.3 | 14.0 | 8 58.5 | 9.6 | 55.0 |
| Y 15 | 41 49.5 | ·· 08.2 | 57 54.3 | 14.0 | 8 48.9 | 9.6 | 55.0 |
| 16 | 56 49.7 | 07.3 | 72 27.3 | 14.0 | 8 39.3 | 9.6 | 54.9 |
| 17 | 71 49.8 | 06.3 | 87 00.3 | 14.1 | 8 29.7 | 9.7 | 54.9 |
| 18 | 86 49.9 | S 8 05.4 | 101 33.4 | 14.1 | S 8 20.0 | 9.7 | 54.9 |
| 19 | 101 50.0 | 04.5 | 116 06.5 | 14.1 | 8 10.3 | 9.7 | 54.9 |
| 20 | 116 50.1 | 03.5 | 130 39.6 | 14.2 | 8 00.6 | 9.8 | 54.9 |
| 21 | 131 50.2 | ·· 02.6 | 145 12.8 | 14.2 | 7 50.8 | 9.8 | 54.9 |
| 22 | 146 50.3 | 01.6 | 159 46.0 | 14.3 | 7 41.0 | 9.8 | 54.8 |
| 23 | 161 50.5 | 8 00.7 | 174 19.3 | 14.3 | 7 31.2 | 9.8 | 54.8 |
| 29 00 | 176 50.6 | S 7 59.7 | 188 52.6 | 14.3 | S 7 21.4 | 9.9 | 54.8 |
| 01 | 191 50.7 | 58.8 | 203 25.9 | 14.4 | 7 11.5 | 9.9 | 54.8 |
| 02 | 206 50.8 | 57.8 | 217 59.3 | 14.4 | 7 01.6 | 9.9 | 54.8 |
| 03 | 221 50.9 | ·· 56.9 | 232 32.7 | 14.4 | 6 51.7 | 10.0 | 54.8 |
| 04 | 236 51.0 | 55.9 | 247 06.1 | 14.5 | 6 41.7 | 9.9 | 54.8 |
| 05 | 251 51.2 | 55.0 | 261 39.6 | 14.5 | 6 31.8 | 10.0 | 54.7 |
| 06 | 266 51.3 | S 7 54.1 | 276 13.1 | 14.6 | S 6 21.8 | 10.0 | 54.7 |
| 07 | 281 51.4 | 53.1 | 290 46.7 | 14.5 | 6 11.8 | 10.0 | 54.7 |
| 08 | 296 51.5 | 52.2 | 305 20.2 | 14.6 | 6 01.8 | 10.1 | 54.7 |
| S 09 | 311 51.6 | ·· 51.2 | 319 53.8 | 14.7 | 5 51.7 | 10.1 | 54.7 |
| U 10 | 326 51.7 | 50.3 | 334 27.5 | 14.6 | 5 41.6 | 10.1 | 54.7 |
| N 11 | 341 51.9 | 49.3 | 349 01.1 | 14.7 | 5 31.5 | 10.1 | 54.7 |
| D 12 | 356 52.0 | S 7 48.4 | 3 34.8 | 14.7 | S 5 21.4 | 10.1 | 54.7 |
| A 13 | 11 52.1 | 47.4 | 18 08.5 | 14.8 | 5 11.3 | 10.1 | 54.6 |
| Y 14 | 26 52.2 | 46.5 | 32 42.3 | 14.8 | 5 01.2 | 10.2 | 54.6 |
| 15 | 41 52.3 | ·· 45.5 | 47 16.1 | 14.8 | 4 51.0 | 10.2 | 54.6 |
| 16 | 56 52.4 | 44.6 | 61 49.9 | 14.8 | 4 40.8 | 10.1 | 54.6 |
| 17 | 71 52.6 | 43.6 | 76 23.7 | 14.9 | 4 30.7 | 10.2 | 54.6 |
| 18 | 86 52.7 | S 7 42.7 | 90 57.6 | 14.8 | S 4 20.5 | 10.2 | 54.6 |
| 19 | 101 52.8 | 41.7 | 105 31.4 | 14.9 | 4 10.3 | 10.3 | 54.6 |
| 20 | 116 52.9 | 40.8 | 120 05.3 | 15.0 | 4 00.0 | 10.2 | 54.6 |
| 21 | 131 53.0 | ·· 39.8 | 134 39.3 | 14.9 | 3 49.8 | 10.3 | 54.5 |
| 22 | 146 53.2 | 38.9 | 149 13.2 | 15.0 | 3 39.5 | 10.2 | 54.5 |
| 23 | 161 53.3 | 37.9 | 163 47.2 | 15.0 | 3 29.3 | 10.3 | 54.5 |
| | S.D. 16.2 | d 0.9 | S.D. 15.1 | | 15.0 | | 14.9 |

| Lat. | Twilight Naut. | Twilight Civil | Sunrise | Moonrise 27 | Moonrise 28 | Moonrise 29 | Moonrise 1 |
|---|---|---|---|---|---|---|---|
| ° | h m | h m | h m | h m | h m | h m | h m |
| N 72 | 05 20 | 06 37 | 07 47 | 07 23 | 07 08 | 06 56 | 06 46 |
| N 70 | 05 24 | 06 34 | 07 37 | 06 57 | 06 52 | 06 48 | 06 43 |
| 68 | 05 27 | 06 31 | 07 28 | 06 37 | 06 39 | 06 40 | 06 41 |
| 66 | 05 29 | 06 28 | 07 21 | 06 22 | 06 29 | 06 34 | 06 39 |
| 64 | 05 32 | 06 26 | 07 14 | 06 09 | 06 20 | 06 29 | 06 37 |
| 62 | 05 33 | 06 24 | 07 09 | 05 58 | 06 12 | 06 25 | 06 35 |
| 60 | 05 34 | 06 22 | 07 04 | 05 48 | 06 06 | 06 21 | 06 34 |
| N 58 | 05 35 | 06 21 | 07 00 | 05 40 | 06 00 | 06 17 | 06 33 |
| 56 | 05 36 | 06 19 | 06 57 | 05 32 | 05 55 | 06 14 | 06 32 |
| 54 | 05 37 | 06 18 | 06 53 | 05 26 | 05 50 | 06 11 | 06 31 |
| 52 | 05 37 | 06 16 | 06 50 | 05 20 | 05 46 | 06 09 | 06 30 |
| 50 | 05 38 | 06 15 | 06 48 | 05 15 | 05 42 | 06 06 | 06 29 |
| 45 | 05 38 | 06 12 | 06 41 | 05 03 | 05 34 | 06 01 | 06 27 |
| N 40 | 05 38 | 06 09 | 06 36 | 04 54 | 05 27 | 05 57 | 06 26 |
| 35 | 05 37 | 06 07 | 06 32 | 04 45 | 05 21 | 05 53 | 06 24 |
| 30 | 05 36 | 06 04 | 06 28 | 04 38 | 05 15 | 05 50 | 06 23 |
| 20 | 05 34 | 05 59 | 06 21 | 04 25 | 05 06 | 05 44 | 06 21 |
| N 10 | 05 30 | 05 54 | 06 15 | 04 14 | 04 58 | 05 39 | 06 19 |
| 0 | 05 24 | 05 49 | 06 09 | 04 04 | 04 50 | 05 35 | 06 18 |
| S 10 | 05 17 | 05 42 | 06 03 | 03 54 | 04 43 | 05 30 | 06 16 |
| 20 | 05 08 | 05 35 | 05 57 | 03 42 | 04 34 | 05 25 | 06 14 |
| 30 | 04 56 | 05 25 | 05 49 | 03 30 | 04 25 | 05 19 | 06 13 |
| 35 | 04 49 | 05 19 | 05 45 | 03 22 | 04 20 | 05 16 | 06 11 |
| 40 | 04 39 | 05 12 | 05 40 | 03 14 | 04 14 | 05 12 | 06 10 |
| 45 | 04 27 | 05 04 | 05 34 | 03 04 | 04 06 | 05 08 | 06 09 |
| S 50 | 04 12 | 04 54 | 05 27 | 02 52 | 03 58 | 05 03 | 06 07 |
| 52 | 04 05 | 04 49 | 05 24 | 02 47 | 03 54 | 05 00 | 06 06 |
| 54 | 03 57 | 04 43 | 05 20 | 02 40 | 03 49 | 04 58 | 06 05 |
| 56 | 03 47 | 04 37 | 05 16 | 02 34 | 03 44 | 04 55 | 06 04 |
| 58 | 03 36 | 04 30 | 05 12 | 02 26 | 03 39 | 04 51 | 06 03 |
| S 60 | 03 23 | 04 22 | 05 07 | 02 17 | 03 33 | 04 48 | 06 02 |

| Lat. | Sunset | Twilight Civil | Twilight Naut. | Moonset 27 | Moonset 28 | Moonset 29 | Moonset 1 |
|---|---|---|---|---|---|---|---|
| ° | h m | h m | h m | h m | h m | h m | h m |
| N 72 | 16 40 | 17 50 | 19 09 | 13 24 | 15 14 | 16 57 | 18 36 |
| N 70 | 16 51 | 17 54 | 19 04 | 13 48 | 15 28 | 17 03 | 18 36 |
| 68 | 16 59 | 17 56 | 19 01 | 14 07 | 15 39 | 17 09 | 18 36 |
| 66 | 17 06 | 17 59 | 18 58 | 14 22 | 15 48 | 17 13 | 18 37 |
| 64 | 17 12 | 18 01 | 18 56 | 14 34 | 15 56 | 17 17 | 18 37 |
| 62 | 17 18 | 18 03 | 18 54 | 14 44 | 16 03 | 17 20 | 18 37 |
| 60 | 17 22 | 18 05 | 18 53 | 14 53 | 16 09 | 17 23 | 18 37 |
| N 58 | 17 26 | 18 06 | 18 51 | 15 01 | 16 14 | 17 26 | 18 37 |
| 56 | 17 30 | 18 08 | 18 51 | 15 07 | 16 18 | 17 28 | 18 37 |
| 54 | 17 33 | 18 09 | 18 50 | 15 13 | 16 22 | 17 30 | 18 37 |
| 52 | 17 36 | 18 10 | 18 49 | 15 19 | 16 26 | 17 32 | 18 37 |
| 50 | 17 39 | 18 11 | 18 49 | 15 24 | 16 29 | 17 34 | 18 38 |
| 45 | 17 45 | 18 14 | 18 48 | 15 34 | 16 36 | 17 37 | 18 38 |
| N 40 | 17 50 | 18 17 | 18 48 | 15 43 | 16 42 | 17 40 | 18 38 |
| 35 | 17 54 | 18 19 | 18 49 | 15 50 | 16 47 | 17 43 | 18 38 |
| 30 | 17 58 | 18 22 | 18 50 | 15 57 | 16 51 | 17 45 | 18 38 |
| 20 | 18 04 | 18 27 | 18 52 | 16 08 | 16 59 | 17 49 | 18 38 |
| N 10 | 18 10 | 18 32 | 18 56 | 16 17 | 17 06 | 17 52 | 18 38 |
| 0 | 18 16 | 18 37 | 19 01 | 16 27 | 17 12 | 17 56 | 18 38 |
| S 10 | 18 22 | 18 43 | 19 08 | 16 36 | 17 18 | 17 59 | 18 38 |
| 20 | 18 28 | 18 51 | 19 17 | 16 45 | 17 25 | 18 02 | 18 38 |
| 30 | 18 36 | 19 00 | 19 29 | 16 56 | 17 32 | 18 06 | 18 39 |
| 35 | 18 40 | 19 06 | 19 36 | 17 02 | 17 36 | 18 08 | 18 39 |
| 40 | 18 45 | 19 12 | 19 45 | 17 09 | 17 41 | 18 10 | 18 39 |
| 45 | 18 50 | 19 21 | 19 57 | 17 18 | 17 47 | 18 13 | 18 39 |
| S 50 | 18 57 | 19 31 | 20 12 | 17 27 | 17 53 | 18 17 | 18 39 |
| 52 | 19 00 | 19 36 | 20 19 | 17 32 | 17 56 | 18 18 | 18 39 |
| 54 | 19 04 | 19 41 | 20 27 | 17 37 | 18 00 | 18 20 | 18 39 |
| 56 | 19 08 | 19 47 | 20 36 | 17 43 | 18 03 | 18 22 | 18 39 |
| 58 | 19 12 | 19 54 | 20 47 | 17 49 | 18 07 | 18 24 | 18 39 |
| S 60 | 19 17 | 20 02 | 21 00 | 17 56 | 18 12 | 18 26 | 18 39 |

| Day | SUN Eqn. of Time 00h | SUN Eqn. of Time 12h | SUN Mer. Pass. | MOON Mer. Pass. Upper | MOON Mer. Pass. Lower | Age | Phase |
|---|---|---|---|---|---|---|---|
| | m s | m s | h m | h m | h m | d | |
| 27 | 12 59 | 12 54 | 12 13 | 10 15 | 22 39 | 27 | ● |
| 28 | 12 49 | 12 43 | 12 13 | 11 01 | 23 23 | 28 | |
| 29 | 12 38 | 12 32 | 12 13 | 11 45 | 24 07 | 29 | |



## 1976 MARCH 19, 20, 21 (FRI., SAT., SUN.)

| G.M.T. | ARIES G.H.A. | VENUS −3.3 G.H.A. | VENUS Dec. | MARS +0.9 G.H.A. | MARS Dec. | JUPITER −1.6 G.H.A. | JUPITER Dec. | SATURN +0.2 G.H.A. | SATURN Dec. |
|---|---|---|---|---|---|---|---|---|---|
| d h | ° ′ | ° ′ | ° ′ | ° ′ | ° ′ | ° ′ | ° ′ | ° ′ | ° ′ |
| 19 00 | 176 40.0 | 199 30.7 | S10 47.7 | 86 26.9 | N25 45.9 | 149 59.7 | N 9 55.2 | 58 29.6 | N21 18.0 |
| 01 | 191 42.5 | 214 30.2 | 46.6 | 101 28.2 | 45.9 | 165 01.7 | 55.4 | 73 32.1 | 18.0 |
| 02 | 206 44.9 | 229 29.8 | 45.5 | 116 29.4 | 45.8 | 180 03.6 | 55.6 | 88 34.6 | 18.0 |
| 03 | 221 47.4 | 244 29.3 | ·· 44.5 | 131 30.6 | ·· 45.8 | 195 05.5 | ·· 55.8 | 103 37.1 | ·· 18.0 |
| 04 | 236 49.8 | 259 28.8 | 43.4 | 146 31.9 | 45.7 | 210 07.5 | 56.0 | 118 39.6 | 18.0 |
| 05 | 251 52.3 | 274 28.3 | 42.3 | 161 33.1 | 45.7 | 225 09.4 | 56.2 | 133 42.1 | 18.0 |
| 06 | 266 54.8 | 289 27.8 | S10 41.3 | 176 34.4 | N25 45.7 | 240 11.3 | N 9 56.4 | 148 44.6 | N21 18.1 |
| 07 | 281 57.2 | 304 27.4 | 40.2 | 191 35.6 | 45.6 | 255 13.3 | 56.6 | 163 47.1 | 18.1 |
| 08 | 296 59.7 | 319 26.9 | 39.1 | 206 36.9 | 45.6 | 270 15.2 | 56.8 | 178 49.6 | 18.1 |
| F 09 | 312 02.2 | 334 26.4 | ·· 38.1 | 221 38.1 | ·· 45.6 | 285 17.1 | ·· 57.0 | 193 52.1 | ·· 18.1 |
| R 10 | 327 04.6 | 349 25.9 | 37.0 | 236 39.4 | 45.5 | 300 19.1 | 57.3 | 208 54.6 | 18.1 |
| I 11 | 342 07.1 | 4 25.4 | 35.9 | 251 40.6 | 45.5 | 315 21.0 | 57.5 | 223 57.1 | 18.1 |
| D 12 | 357 09.6 | 19 25.0 | S10 34.8 | 266 41.8 | N25 45.5 | 330 22.9 | N 9 57.7 | 238 59.7 | N21 18.1 |
| A 13 | 12 12.0 | 34 24.5 | 33.8 | 281 43.1 | 45.4 | 345 24.9 | 57.9 | 254 02.2 | 18.1 |
| Y 14 | 27 14.5 | 49 24.0 | 32.7 | 296 44.3 | 45.4 | 0 26.8 | 58.1 | 269 04.7 | 18.1 |
| 15 | 42 16.9 | 64 23.5 | ·· 31.6 | 311 45.6 | ·· 45.3 | 15 28.7 | ·· 58.3 | 284 07.2 | ·· 18.1 |
| 16 | 57 19.4 | 79 23.1 | 30.6 | 326 46.8 | 45.3 | 30 30.7 | 58.5 | 299 09.7 | 18.2 |
| 17 | 72 21.9 | 94 22.6 | 29.5 | 341 48.0 | 45.3 | 45 32.6 | 58.7 | 314 12.2 | 18.2 |
| 18 | 87 24.3 | 109 22.1 | S10 28.4 | 356 49.3 | N25 45.2 | 60 34.5 | N 9 58.9 | 329 14.7 | N21 18.2 |
| 19 | 102 26.8 | 124 21.6 | 27.3 | 11 50.5 | 45.2 | 75 36.5 | 59.1 | 344 17.2 | 18.2 |
| 20 | 117 29.3 | 139 21.2 | 26.3 | 26 51.8 | 45.2 | 90 38.4 | 59.3 | 359 19.7 | 18.2 |
| 21 | 132 31.7 | 154 20.7 | ·· 25.2 | 41 53.0 | ·· 45.1 | 105 40.3 | ·· 59.5 | 14 22.2 | ·· 18.2 |
| 22 | 147 34.2 | 169 20.2 | 24.1 | 56 54.2 | 45.1 | 120 42.3 | 59.7 | 29 24.7 | 18.2 |
| 23 | 162 36.7 | 184 19.7 | 23.0 | 71 55.5 | 45.0 | 135 44.2 | 9 59.9 | 44 27.2 | 18.2 |
| 20 00 | 177 39.1 | 199 19.3 | S10 22.0 | 86 56.7 | N25 45.0 | 150 46.1 | N10 00.1 | 59 29.7 | N21 18.2 |
| 01 | 192 41.6 | 214 18.8 | 20.9 | 101 58.0 | 45.0 | 165 48.1 | 00.3 | 74 32.2 | 18.2 |
| 02 | 207 44.1 | 229 18.3 | 19.8 | 116 59.2 | 44.9 | 180 50.0 | 00.5 | 89 34.7 | 18.3 |
| 03 | 222 46.5 | 244 17.9 | ·· 18.7 | 132 00.4 | ·· 44.9 | 195 51.9 | ·· 00.7 | 104 37.2 | ·· 18.3 |
| 04 | 237 49.0 | 259 17.4 | 17.7 | 147 01.7 | 44.9 | 210 53.9 | 00.9 | 119 39.7 | 18.3 |
| 05 | 252 51.4 | 274 16.9 | 16.6 | 162 02.9 | 44.8 | 225 55.8 | 01.1 | 134 42.2 | 18.3 |
| 06 | 267 53.9 | 289 16.4 | S10 15.5 | 177 04.1 | N25 44.8 | 240 57.7 | N10 01.3 | 149 44.7 | N21 18.3 |
| 07 | 282 56.4 | 304 16.0 | 14.4 | 192 05.4 | 44.7 | 255 59.6 | 01.5 | 164 47.2 | 18.3 |
| S 08 | 297 58.8 | 319 15.5 | 13.3 | 207 06.6 | 44.7 | 271 01.6 | 01.7 | 179 49.7 | 18.3 |
| A 09 | 313 01.3 | 334 15.0 | ·· 12.3 | 222 07.8 | ·· 44.7 | 286 03.5 | ·· 02.0 | 194 52.2 | ·· 18.3 |
| T 10 | 328 03.8 | 349 14.6 | 11.2 | 237 09.1 | 44.6 | 301 05.4 | 02.2 | 209 54.7 | 18.3 |
| U 11 | 343 06.2 | 4 14.1 | 10.1 | 252 10.3 | 44.6 | 316 07.4 | 02.4 | 224 57.2 | 18.3 |
| R 12 | 358 08.7 | 19 13.6 | S10 09.0 | 267 11.5 | N25 44.5 | 331 09.3 | N10 02.6 | 239 59.7 | N21 18.3 |
| D 13 | 13 11.2 | 34 13.2 | 07.9 | 282 12.8 | 44.5 | 346 11.2 | 02.8 | 255 02.2 | 18.3 |
| A 14 | 28 13.6 | 49 12.7 | 06.8 | 297 14.0 | 44.4 | 1 13.2 | 03.0 | 270 04.7 | 18.4 |
| Y 15 | 43 16.1 | 64 12.2 | ·· 05.8 | 312 15.2 | ·· 44.4 | 16 15.1 | ·· 03.2 | 285 07.2 | ·· 18.4 |
| 16 | 58 18.6 | 79 11.7 | 04.7 | 327 16.5 | 44.4 | 31 17.0 | 03.4 | 300 09.7 | 18.4 |
| 17 | 73 21.0 | 94 11.3 | 03.6 | 342 17.7 | 44.3 | 46 19.0 | 03.6 | 315 12.2 | 18.4 |
| 18 | 88 23.5 | 109 10.8 | S10 02.5 | 357 18.9 | N25 44.3 | 61 20.9 | N10 03.8 | 330 14.7 | N21 18.4 |
| 19 | 103 25.9 | 124 10.3 | 01.4 | 12 20.2 | 44.2 | 76 22.8 | 04.0 | 345 17.2 | 18.4 |
| 20 | 118 28.4 | 139 09.9 | 10 00.3 | 27 21.4 | 44.2 | 91 24.7 | 04.2 | 0 19.7 | 18.4 |
| 21 | 133 30.9 | 154 09.4 | 9 59.3 | 42 22.6 | ·· 44.2 | 106 26.7 | ·· 04.4 | 15 22.2 | ·· 18.4 |
| 22 | 148 33.3 | 169 08.9 | 58.2 | 57 23.9 | 44.1 | 121 28.6 | 04.6 | 30 24.7 | 18.4 |
| 23 | 163 35.8 | 184 08.5 | 57.1 | 72 25.1 | 44.1 | 136 30.5 | 04.8 | 45 27.2 | 18.4 |
| 21 00 | 178 38.3 | 199 08.0 | S 9 56.0 | 87 26.3 | N25 44.0 | 151 32.5 | N10 05.0 | 60 29.7 | N21 18.4 |
| 01 | 193 40.7 | 214 07.6 | 54.9 | 102 27.5 | 44.0 | 166 34.4 | 05.2 | 75 32.2 | 18.5 |
| 02 | 208 43.2 | 229 07.1 | 53.8 | 117 28.8 | 43.9 | 181 36.3 | 05.4 | 90 34.7 | 18.5 |
| 03 | 223 45.7 | 244 06.6 | ·· 52.7 | 132 30.0 | ·· 43.9 | 196 38.3 | ·· 05.6 | 105 37.2 | ·· 18.5 |
| 04 | 238 48.1 | 259 06.2 | 51.6 | 147 31.2 | 43.9 | 211 40.2 | 05.8 | 120 39.6 | 18.5 |
| 05 | 253 50.6 | 274 05.7 | 50.5 | 162 32.5 | 43.8 | 226 42.1 | 06.0 | 135 42.1 | 18.5 |
| 06 | 268 53.0 | 289 05.2 | S 9 49.5 | 177 33.7 | N25 43.8 | 241 44.0 | N10 06.3 | 150 44.6 | N21 18.5 |
| 07 | 283 55.5 | 304 04.8 | 48.4 | 192 34.9 | 43.7 | 256 46.0 | 06.5 | 165 47.1 | 18.5 |
| 08 | 298 58.0 | 319 04.3 | 47.3 | 207 36.1 | 43.7 | 271 47.9 | 06.7 | 180 49.6 | 18.5 |
| S 09 | 314 00.4 | 334 03.9 | ·· 46.2 | 222 37.4 | ·· 43.6 | 286 49.8 | ·· 06.9 | 195 52.1 | ·· 18.5 |
| U 10 | 329 02.9 | 349 03.4 | 45.1 | 237 38.6 | 43.6 | 301 51.8 | 07.1 | 210 54.6 | 18.5 |
| N 11 | 344 05.4 | 4 02.9 | 44.0 | 252 39.8 | 43.6 | 316 53.7 | 07.3 | 225 57.1 | 18.5 |
| D 12 | 359 07.8 | 19 02.5 | S 9 42.9 | 267 41.0 | N25 43.5 | 331 55.6 | N10 07.5 | 240 59.6 | N21 18.5 |
| A 13 | 14 10.3 | 34 02.0 | 41.8 | 282 42.3 | 43.5 | 346 57.6 | 07.7 | 256 02.1 | 18.5 |
| Y 14 | 29 12.8 | 49 01.5 | 40.7 | 297 43.5 | 43.4 | 1 59.5 | 07.9 | 271 04.6 | 18.6 |
| 15 | 44 15.2 | 64 01.1 | ·· 39.6 | 312 44.7 | ·· 43.4 | 17 01.4 | ·· 08.1 | 286 07.1 | ·· 18.6 |
| 16 | 59 17.7 | 79 00.6 | 38.5 | 327 45.9 | 43.3 | 32 03.3 | 08.3 | 301 09.6 | 18.6 |
| 17 | 74 20.2 | 94 00.2 | 37.4 | 342 47.1 | 43.3 | 47 05.3 | 08.5 | 316 12.1 | 18.6 |
| 18 | 89 22.6 | 108 59.7 | S 9 36.3 | 357 48.4 | N25 43.2 | 62 07.2 | N10 08.7 | 331 14.6 | N21 18.6 |
| 19 | 104 25.1 | 123 59.3 | 35.2 | 12 49.6 | 43.2 | 77 09.1 | 08.9 | 346 17.1 | 18.6 |
| 20 | 119 27.5 | 138 58.8 | 34.1 | 27 50.8 | 43.2 | 92 11.0 | 09.1 | 1 19.6 | 18.6 |
| 21 | 134 30.0 | 153 58.3 | ·· 33.0 | 42 52.0 | ·· 43.1 | 107 13.0 | ·· 09.3 | 16 22.0 | ·· 18.6 |
| 22 | 149 32.5 | 168 57.9 | 31.9 | 57 53.3 | 43.1 | 122 14.9 | 09.5 | 31 24.5 | 18.6 |
| 23 | 164 34.9 | 183 57.4 | 30.8 | 72 54.5 | 43.0 | 137 16.8 | 09.7 | 46 27.0 | 18.6 |
| Mer. Pass. | h m 12 07.4 | v −0.5 | d 1.1 | v 1.2 | d 0.0 | v 1.9 | d 0.2 | v 2.5 | d 0.0 |

### STARS

| Name | S.H.A. | Dec. |
|---|---|---|
| | ° ′ | ° ′ |
| Acamar | 315 39.8 | S40 24.2 |
| Achernar | 335 48.1 | S57 21.6 |
| Acrux | 173 39.9 | S62 58.2 |
| Adhara | 255 34.4 | S28 56.7 |
| Aldebaran | 291 21.6 | N16 27.6 |
| Alioth | 166 44.6 | N56 05.1 |
| Alkaid | 153 20.5 | N49 25.7 |
| Al Na'ir | 28 19.2 | S47 04.5 |
| Alnilam | 276 14.8 | S 1 13.2 |
| Alphard | 218 23.3 | S 8 33.6 |
| Alphecca | 126 34.5 | N26 47.4 |
| Alpheratz | 358 12.8 | N28 57.5 |
| Altair | 62 35.6 | N 8 48.2 |
| Ankaa | 353 43.7 | S42 26.2 |
| Antares | 113 00.4 | S26 22.8 |
| Arcturus | 146 21.0 | N19 18.1 |
| Atria | 108 27.3 | S68 58.9 |
| Avior | 234 29.1 | S59 26.4 |
| Bellatrix | 279 02.0 | N 6 19.6 |
| Betelgeuse | 271 31.6 | N 7 24.0 |
| Canopus | 264 08.5 | S52 41.4 |
| Capella | 281 15.9 | N45 58.6 |
| Deneb | 49 50.8 | N45 11.6 |
| Denebola | 183 01.8 | N14 42.1 |
| Diphda | 349 24.2 | S18 07.1 |
| Dubhe | 194 25.2 | N61 52.7 |
| Elnath | 278 48.0 | N28 35.3 |
| Eltanin | 90 59.1 | N51 29.2 |
| Enif | 34 14.8 | N 9 45.9 |
| Fomalhaut | 15 55.1 | S29 44.9 |
| Gacrux | 172 31.5 | S56 58.9 |
| Gienah | 176 20.8 | S17 24.8 |
| Hadar | 149 27.1 | S60 15.5 |
| Hamal | 328 32.6 | N23 21.0 |
| Kaus Aust. | 84 20.9 | S34 23.7 |
| Kochab | 137 18.1 | N74 14.9 |
| Markab | 14 06.5 | N15 04.6 |
| Menkar | 314 44.5 | N 3 59.7 |
| Menkent | 148 40.2 | S36 15.3 |
| Miaplacidus | 221 44.9 | S69 37.5 |
| Mirfak | 309 20.7 | N49 46.7 |
| Nunki | 76 33.0 | S26 19.5 |
| Peacock | 54 03.5 | S56 48.5 |
| Pollux | 244 01.7 | N28 05.0 |
| Procyon | 245 28.8 | N 5 17.0 |
| Rasalhague | 96 32.4 | N12 34.5 |
| Regulus | 208 12.9 | N12 04.8 |
| Rigel | 281 39.0 | S 8 13.9 |
| Rigil Kent. | 140 29.4 | S60 44.1 |
| Sabik | 102 44.5 | S15 41.8 |
| Schedar | 350 13.0 | N56 24.5 |
| Shaula | 96 59.8 | S37 05.1 |
| Sirius | 258 58.3 | S16 41.3 |
| Spica | 159 00.4 | S11 02.4 |
| Suhail | 223 12.7 | S43 20.5 |
| Vega | 80 57.9 | N38 45.5 |
| Zuben'ubi | 137 36.1 | S15 56.7 |

| | S.H.A. | Mer. Pass. |
|---|---|---|
| | ° ′ | h m |
| Venus | 21 40.1 | 10 43 |
| Mars | 269 17.6 | 18 11 |
| Jupiter | 333 07.0 | 13 55 |
| Saturn | 241 50.6 | 19 59 |

# 1976 MARCH 19, 20, 21 (FRI., SAT., SUN.)

| G.M.T. | SUN G.H.A. | SUN Dec. | MOON G.H.A. | v | MOON Dec. | d | H.P. |
|---|---|---|---|---|---|---|---|
| 19 00 | 178 01.7 | S 0 35.4 | 320 04.3 | 6.1 | S14 53.6 | 8.6 | 60.6 |
| 01 | 193 01.9 | 34.4 | 334 29.4 | 6.2 | 15 02.2 | 8.5 | 60.6 |
| 02 | 208 02.1 | 33.4 | 348 54.6 | 6.1 | 15 10.7 | 8.4 | 60.5 |
| 03 | 223 02.3 | ·· 32.4 | 3 19.7 | 6.1 | 15 19.1 | 8.2 | 60.5 |
| 04 | 238 02.5 | 31.4 | 17 44.8 | 6.1 | 15 27.3 | 8.2 | 60.5 |
| 05 | 253 02.6 | 30.5 | 32 09.9 | 6.1 | 15 35.5 | 8.0 | 60.4 |
| 06 | 268 02.8 | S 0 29.5 | 46 35.0 | 6.0 | S15 43.5 | 7.9 | 60.4 |
| 07 | 283 03.0 | 28.5 | 61 00.0 | 6.1 | 15 51.4 | 7.8 | 60.4 |
| 08 | 298 03.2 | 27.5 | 75 25.1 | 6.1 | 15 59.2 | 7.7 | 60.4 |
| 09 | 313 03.4 | ·· 26.5 | 89 50.2 | 6.0 | 16 06.9 | 7.6 | 60.3 |
| 10 | 328 03.6 | 25.5 | 104 15.2 | 6.0 | 16 14.5 | 7.4 | 60.3 |
| 11 | 343 03.7 | 24.5 | 118 40.2 | 6.1 | 16 21.9 | 7.3 | 60.3 |
| 12 | 358 03.9 | S 0 23.5 | 133 05.3 | 6.0 | S16 29.2 | 7.2 | 60.2 |
| 13 | 13 04.1 | 22.6 | 147 30.3 | 6.0 | 16 36.4 | 7.1 | 60.2 |
| 14 | 28 04.3 | 21.6 | 161 55.3 | 6.0 | 16 43.5 | 7.0 | 60.2 |
| 15 | 43 04.5 | ·· 20.6 | 176 20.3 | 6.0 | 16 50.5 | 6.9 | 60.1 |
| 16 | 58 04.7 | 19.6 | 190 45.3 | 6.0 | 16 57.4 | 6.7 | 60.1 |
| 17 | 73 04.9 | 18.6 | 205 10.3 | 6.0 | 17 04.1 | 6.6 | 60.1 |
| 18 | 88 05.0 | S 0 17.6 | 219 35.3 | 6.0 | S17 10.7 | 6.5 | 60.1 |
| 19 | 103 05.2 | 16.6 | 234 00.3 | 6.0 | 17 17.2 | 6.3 | 60.0 |
| 20 | 118 05.4 | 15.6 | 248 25.3 | 6.0 | 17 23.5 | 6.3 | 60.0 |
| 21 | 133 05.6 | ·· 14.6 | 262 50.3 | 6.0 | 17 29.8 | 6.1 | 60.0 |
| 22 | 148 05.8 | 13.7 | 277 15.3 | 6.0 | 17 35.9 | 6.0 | 59.9 |
| 23 | 163 06.0 | 12.7 | 291 40.3 | 6.0 | 17 41.9 | 5.8 | 59.9 |
| 20 00 | 178 06.2 | S 0 11.7 | 306 05.3 | 6.0 | S17 47.7 | 5.8 | 59.9 |
| 01 | 193 06.3 | 10.7 | 320 30.3 | 6.0 | 17 53.5 | 5.6 | 59.8 |
| 02 | 208 06.5 | 09.7 | 334 55.3 | 6.0 | 17 59.1 | 5.5 | 59.8 |
| 03 | 223 06.7 | ·· 08.7 | 349 20.3 | 6.0 | 18 04.6 | 5.3 | 59.8 |
| 04 | 238 06.9 | 07.7 | 3 45.3 | 6.0 | 18 09.9 | 5.2 | 59.7 |
| 05 | 253 07.1 | 06.7 | 18 10.3 | 6.1 | 18 15.1 | 5.1 | 59.7 |
| 06 | 268 07.3 | S 0 05.8 | 32 35.4 | 6.0 | S18 20.2 | 5.0 | 59.7 |
| 07 | 283 07.5 | 04.8 | 47 00.4 | 6.1 | 18 25.2 | 4.9 | 59.6 |
| 08 | 298 07.6 | 03.8 | 61 25.5 | 6.0 | 18 30.1 | 4.7 | 59.6 |
| 09 | 313 07.8 | ·· 02.8 | 75 50.5 | 6.1 | 18 34.8 | 4.6 | 59.6 |
| 10 | 328 08.0 | 01.8 | 90 15.6 | 6.1 | 18 39.4 | 4.4 | 59.5 |
| 11 | 343 08.2 | S 0 00.8 | 104 40.7 | 6.1 | 18 43.8 | 4.3 | 59.5 |
| 12 | 358 08.4 | N 0 00.2 | 119 05.8 | 6.1 | S18 48.1 | 4.2 | 59.4 |
| 13 | 13 08.6 | 01.2 | 133 30.9 | 6.1 | 18 52.3 | 4.1 | 59.4 |
| 14 | 28 08.8 | 02.1 | 147 56.0 | 6.2 | 18 56.4 | 4.0 | 59.4 |
| 15 | 43 09.0 | ·· 03.1 | 162 21.2 | 6.2 | 19 00.4 | 3.8 | 59.3 |
| 16 | 58 09.1 | 04.1 | 176 46.4 | 6.1 | 19 04.2 | 3.6 | 59.3 |
| 17 | 73 09.3 | 05.1 | 191 11.5 | 6.3 | 19 07.8 | 3.6 | 59.3 |
| 18 | 88 09.5 | N 0 06.1 | 205 36.8 | 6.2 | S19 11.4 | 3.4 | 59.2 |
| 19 | 103 09.7 | 07.1 | 220 02.0 | 6.2 | 19 14.8 | 3.3 | 59.2 |
| 20 | 118 09.9 | 08.1 | 234 27.2 | 6.3 | 19 18.1 | 3.2 | 59.2 |
| 21 | 133 10.1 | ·· 09.1 | 248 52.5 | 6.3 | 19 21.3 | 3.0 | 59.1 |
| 22 | 148 10.3 | 10.0 | 263 17.8 | 6.3 | 19 24.3 | 2.9 | 59.1 |
| 23 | 163 10.4 | 11.0 | 277 43.1 | 6.4 | 19 27.2 | 2.8 | 59.1 |
| 21 00 | 178 10.6 | N 0 12.0 | 292 08.5 | 6.4 | S19 30.0 | 2.6 | 59.0 |
| 01 | 193 10.8 | 13.0 | 306 33.9 | 6.4 | 19 32.6 | 2.5 | 59.0 |
| 02 | 208 11.0 | 14.0 | 320 59.3 | 6.4 | 19 35.1 | 2.4 | 58.9 |
| 03 | 223 11.2 | ·· 15.0 | 335 24.7 | 6.5 | 19 37.5 | 2.3 | 58.9 |
| 04 | 238 11.4 | 16.0 | 349 50.2 | 6.5 | 19 39.8 | 2.1 | 58.9 |
| 05 | 253 11.6 | 17.0 | 4 15.7 | 6.5 | 19 41.9 | 2.0 | 58.8 |
| 06 | 268 11.8 | N 0 17.9 | 18 41.2 | 6.5 | S19 43.9 | 1.9 | 58.8 |
| 07 | 283 11.9 | 18.9 | 33 06.7 | 6.6 | 19 45.8 | 1.7 | 58.8 |
| 08 | 298 12.1 | 19.9 | 47 32.3 | 6.7 | 19 47.5 | 1.6 | 58.7 |
| 09 | 313 12.3 | ·· 20.9 | 61 58.0 | 6.6 | 19 49.1 | 1.5 | 58.7 |
| 10 | 328 12.5 | 21.9 | 76 23.6 | 6.7 | 19 50.6 | 1.4 | 58.7 |
| 11 | 343 12.7 | 22.9 | 90 49.3 | 6.8 | 19 52.0 | 1.2 | 58.6 |
| 12 | 358 12.9 | N 0 23.9 | 105 15.1 | 6.7 | S19 53.2 | 1.1 | 58.6 |
| 13 | 13 13.1 | 24.9 | 119 40.8 | 6.9 | 19 54.3 | 1.0 | 58.5 |
| 14 | 28 13.3 | 25.8 | 134 06.7 | 6.8 | 19 55.3 | 0.8 | 58.5 |
| 15 | 43 13.4 | ·· 26.8 | 148 32.5 | 6.9 | 19 56.1 | 0.7 | 58.5 |
| 16 | 58 13.6 | 27.8 | 162 58.4 | 7.0 | 19 56.8 | 0.6 | 58.4 |
| 17 | 73 13.8 | 28.8 | 177 24.4 | 6.9 | 19 57.4 | 0.5 | 58.4 |
| 18 | 88 14.0 | N 0 29.8 | 191 50.3 | 7.1 | S19 57.9 | 0.3 | 58.4 |
| 19 | 103 14.2 | 30.8 | 206 16.4 | 7.0 | 19 58.2 | 0.3 | 58.3 |
| 20 | 118 14.4 | 31.8 | 220 42.4 | 7.2 | 19 58.5 | 0.1 | 58.3 |
| 21 | 133 14.6 | ·· 32.7 | 235 08.6 | 7.1 | 19 58.6 | 0.1 | 58.2 |
| 22 | 148 14.8 | 33.7 | 249 34.7 | 7.2 | 19 58.5 | 0.1 | 58.2 |
| 23 | 163 14.9 | 34.7 | 264 00.9 | 7.3 | 19 58.4 | 0.3 | 58.2 |
| | S.D. 16.1 | d 1.0 | S.D. 16.4 | | 16.2 | | 16.0 |

| Lat. | Twilight Naut. | Twilight Civil | Sunrise | Moonrise 19 | 20 | 21 | 22 |
|---|---|---|---|---|---|---|---|
| N 72 | 03 21 | 04 50 | 05 58 | 00 26 | ■ | ■ | ■ |
| N 70 | 03 40 | 04 58 | 05 59 | 25 57 | 01 57 | 04 08 | ■ |
| 68 | 03 55 | 05 04 | 06 00 | 25 14 | 01 14 | 02 49 | 03 54 |
| 66 | 04 06 | 05 09 | 06 01 | 24 45 | 00 45 | 02 11 | 03 14 |
| 64 | 04 16 | 05 14 | 06 01 | 24 24 | 00 24 | 01 45 | 02 47 |
| 62 | 04 24 | 05 17 | 06 02 | 24 06 | 00 06 | 01 24 | 02 26 |
| 60 | 04 31 | 05 20 | 06 02 | 23 52 | 25 07 | 01 07 | 02 08 |
| N 58 | 04 36 | 05 23 | 06 02 | 23 40 | 24 53 | 00 53 | 01 54 |
| 56 | 04 41 | 05 25 | 06 02 | 23 29 | 24 41 | 00 41 | 01 41 |
| 54 | 04 46 | 05 27 | 06 03 | 23 20 | 24 31 | 00 31 | 01 31 |
| 52 | 04 49 | 05 29 | 06 03 | 23 11 | 24 21 | 00 21 | 01 21 |
| 50 | 04 53 | 05 31 | 06 03 | 23 04 | 24 13 | 00 13 | 01 12 |
| 45 | 05 00 | 05 34 | 06 03 | 22 48 | 23 55 | 24 54 | 00 54 |
| N 40 | 05 05 | 05 37 | 06 04 | 22 35 | 23 41 | 24 39 | 00 39 |
| 35 | 05 09 | 05 39 | 06 04 | 22 24 | 23 28 | 24 27 | 00 27 |
| 30 | 05 12 | 05 40 | 06 04 | 22 15 | 23 18 | 24 16 | 00 16 |
| 20 | 05 17 | 05 42 | 06 04 | 21 58 | 22 59 | 23 57 | 24 51 |
| N 10 | 05 19 | 05 43 | 06 04 | 21 44 | 22 43 | 23 41 | 24 35 |
| 0 | 05 20 | 05 43 | 06 04 | 21 30 | 22 29 | 23 25 | 24 20 |
| S 10 | 05 19 | 05 43 | 06 04 | 21 17 | 22 14 | 23 10 | 24 06 |
| 20 | 05 16 | 05 42 | 06 04 | 21 03 | 21 58 | 22 54 | 23 50 |
| 30 | 05 12 | 05 40 | 06 03 | 20 47 | 21 40 | 22 35 | 23 32 |
| 35 | 05 08 | 05 38 | 06 03 | 20 38 | 21 29 | 22 24 | 23 22 |
| 40 | 05 04 | 05 36 | 06 03 | 20 27 | 21 17 | 22 12 | 23 10 |
| 45 | 04 59 | 05 33 | 06 02 | 20 15 | 21 03 | 21 57 | 22 55 |
| S 50 | 04 51 | 05 29 | 06 02 | 20 00 | 20 46 | 21 39 | 22 38 |
| 52 | 04 48 | 05 28 | 06 02 | 19 53 | 20 38 | 21 31 | 22 30 |
| 54 | 04 44 | 05 26 | 06 01 | 19 45 | 20 29 | 21 21 | 22 21 |
| 56 | 04 39 | 05 24 | 06 01 | 19 36 | 20 19 | 21 11 | 22 11 |
| 58 | 04 34 | 05 21 | 06 00 | 19 27 | 20 08 | 20 58 | 21 59 |
| S 60 | 04 28 | 05 18 | 06 00 | 19 15 | 19 54 | 20 44 | 21 45 |

| Lat. | Sunset | Twilight Civil | Twilight Naut. | Moonset 19 | 20 | 21 | 22 |
|---|---|---|---|---|---|---|---|
| N 72 | 18 19 | 19 28 | 20 59 | 04 50 | ■ | ■ | ■ |
| N 70 | 18 18 | 19 20 | 20 39 | 05 28 | 05 23 | 05 13 | ■ |
| 68 | 18 17 | 19 13 | 20 24 | 05 54 | 06 06 | 06 32 | 07 25 |
| 66 | 18 16 | 19 08 | 20 12 | 06 15 | 06 35 | 07 10 | 08 05 |
| 64 | 18 16 | 19 03 | 20 02 | 06 31 | 06 58 | 07 37 | 08 32 |
| 62 | 18 15 | 19 00 | 19 53 | 06 45 | 07 15 | 07 58 | 08 53 |
| 60 | 18 15 | 18 56 | 19 47 | 06 56 | 07 30 | 08 15 | 09 11 |
| N 58 | 18 14 | 18 54 | 19 41 | 07 07 | 07 43 | 08 29 | 09 25 |
| 56 | 18 14 | 18 51 | 19 35 | 07 15 | 07 54 | 08 41 | 09 37 |
| 54 | 18 14 | 18 49 | 19 31 | 07 23 | 08 03 | 08 52 | 09 48 |
| 52 | 18 13 | 18 47 | 19 27 | 07 30 | 08 12 | 09 01 | 09 57 |
| 50 | 18 13 | 18 45 | 19 23 | 07 37 | 08 20 | 09 10 | 10 06 |
| 45 | 18 12 | 18 42 | 19 16 | 07 50 | 08 36 | 09 28 | 10 24 |
| N 40 | 18 12 | 18 39 | 19 11 | 08 02 | 08 50 | 09 42 | 10 39 |
| 35 | 18 12 | 18 37 | 19 07 | 08 12 | 09 01 | 09 55 | 10 51 |
| 30 | 18 11 | 18 35 | 19 03 | 08 20 | 09 12 | 10 06 | 11 02 |
| 20 | 18 11 | 18 33 | 18 59 | 08 35 | 09 29 | 10 24 | 11 21 |
| N 10 | 18 11 | 18 32 | 18 56 | 08 48 | 09 44 | 10 41 | 11 37 |
| 0 | 18 11 | 18 31 | 18 55 | 09 00 | 09 58 | 10 56 | 11 52 |
| S 10 | 18 11 | 18 32 | 18 56 | 09 12 | 10 12 | 11 11 | 12 07 |
| 20 | 18 11 | 18 33 | 18 58 | 09 25 | 10 28 | 11 27 | 12 23 |
| 30 | 18 11 | 18 35 | 19 03 | 09 40 | 10 45 | 11 46 | 12 42 |
| 35 | 18 11 | 18 37 | 19 06 | 09 49 | 10 55 | 11 57 | 12 52 |
| 40 | 18 12 | 18 39 | 19 10 | 09 59 | 11 07 | 12 09 | 13 05 |
| 45 | 18 12 | 18 41 | 19 15 | 10 10 | 11 20 | 12 24 | 13 19 |
| S 50 | 18 12 | 18 44 | 19 22 | 10 24 | 11 37 | 12 42 | 13 37 |
| 52 | 18 12 | 18 46 | 19 26 | 10 31 | 11 45 | 12 50 | 13 45 |
| 54 | 18 13 | 18 48 | 19 30 | 10 38 | 11 54 | 13 00 | 13 54 |
| 56 | 18 13 | 18 50 | 19 34 | 10 46 | 12 04 | 13 10 | 14 04 |
| 58 | 18 13 | 18 52 | 19 39 | 10 56 | 12 15 | 13 22 | 14 16 |
| S 60 | 18 14 | 18 55 | 19 45 | 11 06 | 12 28 | 13 37 | 14 30 |

| Day | SUN Eqn. of Time 00h | 12h | Mer. Pass. | MOON Mer. Pass. Upper | Lower | Age | Phase |
|---|---|---|---|---|---|---|---|
| 19 | 07 54 | 07 45 | 12 08 | 02 46 | 15 15 | 19 | ◑ |
| 20 | 07 36 | 07 27 | 12 07 | 03 44 | 16 13 | 20 | |
| 21 | 07 18 | 07 09 | 12 07 | 04 42 | 17 11 | 21 | |

# 1976 MARCH 22, 23, 24 (MON., TUES., WED.)

| G.M.T. | ARIES G.H.A. | VENUS −3.3 G.H.A. | Dec. | MARS +0.9 G.H.A. | Dec. | JUPITER −1.6 G.H.A. | Dec. | SATURN +0.2 G.H.A. | Dec. |
|---|---|---|---|---|---|---|---|---|---|
| 22 00 | 179 37.4 | 198 57.0 | S 9 29.7 | 87 55.7 | N25 43.0 | 152 18.8 | N10 09.9 | 61 29.5 | N21 18.6 |
| 01 | 194 39.9 | 213 56.5 | 28.7 | 102 56.9 | 42.9 | 167 20.7 | 10.1 | 76 32.0 | 18.6 |
| 02 | 209 42.3 | 228 56.1 | 27.6 | 117 58.1 | 42.9 | 182 22.6 | 10.3 | 91 34.5 | 18.6 |
| 03 | 224 44.8 | 243 55.6 | ·· 26.5 | 132 59.3 | ·· 42.8 | 197 24.5 | ·· 10.6 | 106 37.0 | ·· 18.7 |
| 04 | 239 47.3 | 258 55.1 | 25.3 | 148 00.6 | 42.8 | 212 26.5 | 10.8 | 121 39.5 | 18.7 |
| 05 | 254 49.7 | 273 54.7 | 24.2 | 163 01.8 | 42.7 | 227 28.4 | 11.0 | 136 42.0 | 18.7 |
| 06 | 269 52.2 | 288 54.2 | S 9 23.1 | 178 03.0 | N25 42.7 | 242 30.3 | N10 11.2 | 151 44.5 | N21 18.7 |
| 07 | 284 54.7 | 303 53.8 | 22.0 | 193 04.2 | 42.6 | 257 32.3 | 11.4 | 166 47.0 | 18.7 |
| 08 | 299 57.1 | 318 53.3 | 20.9 | 208 05.4 | 42.6 | 272 34.2 | 11.6 | 181 49.5 | 18.7 |
| 09 | 314 59.6 | 333 52.9 | ·· 19.8 | 223 06.7 | ·· 42.5 | 287 36.1 | ·· 11.8 | 196 51.9 | ·· 18.7 |
| 10 | 330 02.0 | 348 52.4 | 18.7 | 238 07.9 | 42.5 | 302 38.0 | 12.0 | 211 54.4 | 18.7 |
| 11 | 345 04.5 | 3 52.0 | 17.6 | 253 09.1 | 42.5 | 317 40.0 | 12.2 | 226 56.9 | 18.7 |
| 12 | 0 07.0 | 18 51.5 | S 9 16.5 | 268 10.3 | N25 42.4 | 332 41.9 | N10 12.4 | 241 59.4 | N21 18.7 |
| 13 | 15 09.4 | 33 51.1 | 15.4 | 283 11.5 | 42.4 | 347 43.8 | 12.6 | 257 01.9 | 18.7 |
| 14 | 30 11.9 | 48 50.6 | 14.3 | 298 12.7 | 42.3 | 2 45.7 | 12.8 | 272 04.4 | 18.7 |
| 15 | 45 14.4 | 63 50.2 | ·· 13.2 | 313 13.9 | ·· 42.3 | 17 47.7 | ·· 13.0 | 287 06.9 | ·· 18.7 |
| 16 | 60 16.8 | 78 49.7 | 12.1 | 328 15.2 | 42.2 | 32 49.6 | 13.2 | 302 09.4 | 18.7 |
| 17 | 75 19.3 | 93 49.3 | 11.0 | 343 16.4 | 42.2 | 47 51.5 | 13.4 | 317 11.9 | 18.8 |
| 18 | 90 21.8 | 108 48.8 | S 9 09.9 | 358 17.6 | N25 42.1 | 62 53.4 | N10 13.6 | 332 14.3 | N21 18.8 |
| 19 | 105 24.2 | 123 48.4 | 08.8 | 13 18.8 | 42.1 | 77 55.4 | 13.8 | 347 16.8 | 18.8 |
| 20 | 120 26.7 | 138 47.9 | 07.7 | 28 20.0 | 42.0 | 92 57.3 | 14.0 | 2 19.3 | 18.8 |
| 21 | 135 29.2 | 153 47.5 | ·· 06.6 | 43 21.2 | ·· 42.0 | 107 59.2 | ·· 14.2 | 17 21.8 | ·· 18.8 |
| 22 | 150 31.6 | 168 47.0 | 05.5 | 58 22.4 | 41.9 | 123 01.1 | 14.5 | 32 24.3 | 18.8 |
| 23 | 165 34.1 | 183 46.6 | 04.4 | 73 23.6 | 41.9 | 138 03.1 | 14.7 | 47 26.8 | 18.8 |
| 23 00 | 180 36.5 | 198 46.1 | S 9 03.2 | 88 24.9 | N25 41.8 | 153 05.0 | N10 14.9 | 62 29.3 | N21 18.8 |
| 01 | 195 39.0 | 213 45.7 | 02.1 | 103 26.1 | 41.8 | 168 06.9 | 15.1 | 77 31.8 | 18.8 |
| 02 | 210 41.5 | 228 45.2 | 9 01.0 | 118 27.3 | 41.7 | 183 08.9 | 15.3 | 92 34.2 | 18.8 |
| 03 | 225 43.9 | 243 44.8 | 8 59.9 | 133 28.5 | ·· 41.7 | 198 10.8 | ·· 15.5 | 107 36.7 | ·· 18.8 |
| 04 | 240 46.4 | 258 44.3 | 58.8 | 148 29.7 | 41.6 | 213 12.7 | 15.7 | 122 39.2 | 18.8 |
| 05 | 255 48.9 | 273 43.9 | 57.7 | 163 30.9 | 41.6 | 228 14.6 | 15.9 | 137 41.7 | 18.8 |
| 06 | 270 51.3 | 288 43.4 | S 8 56.6 | 178 32.1 | N25 41.5 | 243 16.6 | N10 16.1 | 152 44.2 | N21 18.8 |
| 07 | 285 53.8 | 303 43.0 | 55.5 | 193 33.3 | 41.5 | 258 18.5 | 16.3 | 167 46.7 | 18.8 |
| 08 | 300 56.3 | 318 42.5 | 54.4 | 208 34.5 | 41.4 | 273 20.4 | 16.5 | 182 49.2 | 18.9 |
| 09 | 315 58.7 | 333 42.1 | ·· 53.2 | 223 35.7 | ·· 41.4 | 288 22.3 | ·· 16.7 | 197 51.6 | ·· 18.9 |
| 10 | 331 01.2 | 348 41.6 | 52.1 | 238 36.9 | 41.3 | 303 24.3 | 16.9 | 212 54.1 | 18.9 |
| 11 | 346 03.6 | 3 41.2 | 51.0 | 253 38.2 | 41.3 | 318 26.2 | 17.1 | 227 56.6 | 18.9 |
| 12 | 1 06.1 | 18 40.7 | S 8 49.9 | 268 39.4 | N25 41.2 | 333 28.1 | N10 17.3 | 242 59.1 | N21 18.9 |
| 13 | 16 08.6 | 33 40.3 | 48.8 | 283 40.6 | 41.2 | 348 30.0 | 17.5 | 258 01.6 | 18.9 |
| 14 | 31 11.0 | 48 39.9 | 47.7 | 298 41.8 | 41.1 | 3 32.0 | 17.7 | 273 04.1 | 18.9 |
| 15 | 46 13.5 | 63 39.4 | ·· 46.6 | 313 43.0 | ·· 41.0 | 18 33.9 | ·· 17.9 | 288 06.6 | ·· 18.9 |
| 16 | 61 16.0 | 78 39.0 | 45.4 | 328 44.2 | 41.0 | 33 35.8 | 18.1 | 303 09.0 | 18.9 |
| 17 | 76 18.4 | 93 38.5 | 44.3 | 343 45.4 | 40.9 | 48 37.7 | 18.3 | 318 11.5 | 18.9 |
| 18 | 91 20.9 | 108 38.1 | S 8 43.2 | 358 46.6 | N25 40.9 | 63 39.6 | N10 18.6 | 333 14.0 | N21 18.9 |
| 19 | 106 23.4 | 123 37.6 | 42.1 | 13 47.8 | 40.8 | 78 41.6 | 18.8 | 348 16.5 | 18.9 |
| 20 | 121 25.8 | 138 37.2 | 41.0 | 28 49.0 | 40.8 | 93 43.5 | 19.0 | 3 19.0 | 18.9 |
| 21 | 136 28.3 | 153 36.7 | ·· 39.8 | 43 50.2 | ·· 40.7 | 108 45.4 | ·· 19.2 | 18 21.5 | ·· 18.9 |
| 22 | 151 30.8 | 168 36.3 | 38.7 | 58 51.4 | 40.7 | 123 47.3 | 19.4 | 33 23.9 | 18.9 |
| 23 | 166 33.2 | 183 35.9 | 37.6 | 73 52.6 | 40.6 | 138 49.3 | 19.6 | 48 26.4 | 18.9 |
| 24 00 | 181 35.7 | 198 35.4 | S 8 36.5 | 88 53.8 | N25 40.6 | 153 51.2 | N10 19.8 | 63 28.9 | N21 19.0 |
| 01 | 196 38.1 | 213 35.0 | 35.4 | 103 55.0 | 40.5 | 168 53.1 | 20.0 | 78 31.4 | 19.0 |
| 02 | 211 40.6 | 228 34.5 | 34.3 | 118 56.2 | 40.5 | 183 55.0 | 20.2 | 93 33.9 | 19.0 |
| 03 | 226 43.1 | 243 34.1 | ·· 33.1 | 133 57.4 | ·· 40.4 | 198 57.0 | ·· 20.4 | 108 36.3 | ·· 19.0 |
| 04 | 241 45.5 | 258 33.7 | 32.0 | 148 58.6 | 40.4 | 213 58.9 | 20.6 | 123 38.8 | 19.0 |
| 05 | 256 48.0 | 273 33.2 | 30.9 | 163 59.8 | 40.3 | 229 00.8 | 20.8 | 138 41.3 | 19.0 |
| 06 | 271 50.5 | 288 32.8 | S 8 29.8 | 179 01.0 | N25 40.2 | 244 02.7 | N10 21.0 | 153 43.8 | N21 19.0 |
| 07 | 286 52.9 | 303 32.3 | 28.6 | 194 02.2 | 40.2 | 259 04.7 | 21.2 | 168 46.3 | 19.0 |
| 08 | 301 55.4 | 318 31.9 | 27.5 | 209 03.4 | 40.1 | 274 06.6 | 21.4 | 183 48.8 | 19.0 |
| 09 | 316 57.9 | 333 31.5 | ·· 26.4 | 224 04.6 | ·· 40.1 | 289 08.5 | ·· 21.6 | 198 51.2 | ·· 19.0 |
| 10 | 332 00.3 | 348 31.0 | 25.3 | 239 05.8 | 40.0 | 304 10.4 | 21.8 | 213 53.7 | 19.0 |
| 11 | 347 02.8 | 3 30.6 | 24.2 | 254 07.0 | 40.0 | 319 12.3 | 22.0 | 228 56.2 | 19.0 |
| 12 | 2 05.3 | 18 30.2 | S 8 23.0 | 269 08.2 | N25 39.9 | 334 14.3 | N10 22.3 | 243 58.7 | N21 19.0 |
| 13 | 17 07.7 | 33 29.7 | 21.9 | 284 09.4 | 39.9 | 349 16.2 | 22.5 | 259 01.2 | 19.0 |
| 14 | 32 10.2 | 48 29.3 | 20.8 | 299 10.6 | 39.8 | 4 18.1 | 22.7 | 274 03.6 | 19.0 |
| 15 | 47 12.6 | 63 28.8 | ·· 19.7 | 314 11.8 | ·· 39.7 | 19 20.0 | ·· 22.9 | 289 06.1 | ·· 19.0 |
| 16 | 62 15.1 | 78 28.4 | 18.5 | 329 13.0 | 39.7 | 34 22.0 | 23.1 | 304 08.6 | 19.0 |
| 17 | 77 17.6 | 93 28.0 | 17.4 | 344 14.2 | 39.6 | 49 23.9 | 23.3 | 319 11.1 | 19.0 |
| 18 | 92 20.0 | 108 27.5 | S 8 16.3 | 359 15.4 | N25 39.6 | 64 25.8 | N10 23.5 | 334 13.5 | N21 19.1 |
| 19 | 107 22.5 | 123 27.1 | 15.1 | 14 16.6 | 39.5 | 79 27.7 | 23.7 | 349 16.0 | 19.1 |
| 20 | 122 25.0 | 138 26.7 | 14.0 | 29 17.8 | 39.5 | 94 29.6 | 23.9 | 4 18.5 | 19.1 |
| 21 | 137 27.4 | 153 26.2 | ·· 12.9 | 44 19.0 | ·· 39.4 | 109 31.6 | ·· 24.1 | 19 21.0 | ·· 19.1 |
| 22 | 152 29.9 | 168 25.8 | 11.8 | 59 20.2 | 39.3 | 124 33.5 | 24.3 | 34 23.5 | 19.1 |
| 23 | 167 32.4 | 183 25.4 | 10.6 | 74 21.4 | 39.3 | 139 35.4 | 24.5 | 49 25.9 | 19.1 |
| Mer. Pass. | 11 55.6 | v −0.4 | d 1.1 | v 1.2 | d 0.1 | v 1.9 | d 0.2 | v 2.5 | d 0.0 |

| STARS Name | S.H.A. | Dec. |
|---|---|---|
| Acamar | 315 39.8 | S40 24.2 |
| Achernar | 335 48.1 | S57 21.6 |
| Acrux | 173 39.9 | S62 58.2 |
| Adhara | 255 34.4 | S28 56.7 |
| Aldebaran | 291 21.6 | N16 27.6 |
| Alioth | 166 44.6 | N56 05.1 |
| Alkaid | 153 20.5 | N49 25.7 |
| Al Na'ir | 28 19.1 | S47 04.5 |
| Alnilam | 276 14.8 | S 1 13.2 |
| Alphard | 218 23.3 | S 8 33.6 |
| Alphecca | 126 34.5 | N26 47.4 |
| Alpheratz | 358 12.8 | N28 57.5 |
| Altair | 62 35.6 | N 8 48.2 |
| Ankaa | 353 43.7 | S42 26.1 |
| Antares | 113 00.4 | S26 22.8 |
| Arcturus | 146 20.9 | N19 18.1 |
| Atria | 108 27.2 | S68 58.9 |
| Avior | 234 29.1 | S59 26.4 |
| Bellatrix | 279 02.1 | N 6 19.6 |
| Betelgeuse | 271 31.6 | N 7 24.0 |
| Canopus | 264 08.5 | S52 41.4 |
| Capella | 281 15.9 | N45 58.6 |
| Deneb | 49 50.8 | N45 11.5 |
| Denebola | 183 01.8 | N14 42.1 |
| Diphda | 349 24.2 | S18 07.1 |
| Dubhe | 194 25.2 | N61 52.7 |
| Elnath | 278 48.0 | N28 35.3 |
| Eltanin | 90 59.1 | N51 29.2 |
| Enif | 34 14.8 | N 9 45.9 |
| Fomalhaut | 15 55.1 | S29 44.9 |
| Gacrux | 172 31.5 | S56 58.9 |
| Gienah | 176 20.7 | S17 24.8 |
| Hadar | 149 27.0 | S60 15.5 |
| Hamal | 328 32.6 | N23 21.0 |
| Kaus Aust. | 84 20.9 | S34 23.7 |
| Kochab | 137 18.0 | N74 14.9 |
| Markab | 14 06.5 | N15 04.6 |
| Menkar | 314 44.5 | N 3 59.7 |
| Menkent | 148 40.2 | S36 15.3 |
| Miaplacidus | 221 44.9 | S69 37.5 |
| Mirfak | 309 20.7 | N49 46.7 |
| Nunki | 76 33.0 | S26 19.5 |
| Peacock | 54 03.5 | S56 48.5 |
| Pollux | 244 01.7 | N28 05.0 |
| Procyon | 245 28.8 | N 5 17.0 |
| Rasalhague | 96 32.3 | N12 34.5 |
| Regulus | 208 12.9 | N12 04.8 |
| Rigel | 281 39.0 | S 8 13.9 |
| Rigil Kent. | 140 29.4 | S60 44.1 |
| Sabik | 102 44.5 | S15 41.8 |
| Schedar | 350 13.0 | N56 24.5 |
| Shaula | 96 59.8 | S37 05.1 |
| Sirius | 258 58.3 | S16 41.3 |
| Spica | 159 00.4 | S11 02.4 |
| Suhail | 223 12.7 | S43 20.5 |
| Vega | 80 57.9 | N38 45.5 |
| Zuben'ubi | 137 36.1 | S15 56.7 |

| | S.H.A. | Mer. Pass. |
|---|---|---|
| Venus | 18 09.6 | 10 45 |
| Mars | 267 48.3 | 18 05 |
| Jupiter | 332 28.5 | 13 46 |
| Saturn | 241 52.7 | 19 47 |

## 1976 MAR. 31, APRIL 1, 2 (WED., THURS., FRI.)

| G.M.T. d | h | ARIES G.H.A. | VENUS −3.3 G.H.A. | VENUS Dec. | MARS +1.1 G.H.A. | MARS Dec. | JUPITER −1.6 G.H.A. | JUPITER Dec. | SATURN +0.3 G.H.A. | SATURN Dec. |
|---|---|---|---|---|---|---|---|---|---|---|
| | | ° ′ | ° ′ | ° ′ | ° ′ | ° ′ | ° ′ | ° ′ | ° ′ | ° ′ |
| 31 (WEDNESDAY) | 00 | 188 29.6 | 197 25.2 | S 5 23.3 | 92 11.2 | N25 29.0 | 159 13.2 | N10 54.3 | 70 23.0 | N21 19.4 |
| | 01 | 203 32.1 | 212 24.8 | 22.1 | 107 12.3 | 29.0 | 174 15.1 | 54.5 | 85 25.5 | 19.4 |
| | 02 | 218 34.6 | 227 24.4 | 21.0 | 122 13.5 | 28.9 | 189 17.0 | 54.7 | 100 27.9 | 19.4 |
| | 03 | 233 37.0 | 242 24.0 | ·· 19.8 | 137 14.6 | ·· 28.8 | 204 19.0 | ·· 54.9 | 115 30.4 | ·· 19.4 |
| | 04 | 248 39.5 | 257 23.6 | 18.6 | 152 15.7 | 28.7 | 219 20.9 | 55.1 | 130 32.8 | 19.4 |
| | 05 | 263 42.0 | 272 23.2 | 17.4 | 167 16.9 | 28.6 | 234 22.8 | 55.4 | 145 35.3 | 19.4 |
| | 06 | 278 44.4 | 287 22.8 | S 5 16.3 | 182 18.0 | N25 28.5 | 249 24.7 | N10 55.6 | 160 37.7 | N21 19.4 |
| | 07 | 293 46.9 | 302 22.4 | 15.1 | 197 19.2 | 28.5 | 264 26.6 | 55.8 | 175 40.2 | 19.4 |
| | 08 | 308 49.4 | 317 22.0 | 13.9 | 212 20.3 | 28.4 | 279 28.5 | 56.0 | 190 42.6 | 19.4 |
| | 09 | 323 51.8 | 332 21.7 | ·· 12.7 | 227 21.5 | ·· 28.3 | 294 30.4 | ·· 56.2 | 205 45.1 | ·· 19.4 |
| | 10 | 338 54.3 | 347 21.3 | 11.5 | 242 22.6 | 28.2 | 309 32.3 | 56.4 | 220 47.5 | 19.4 |
| | 11 | 353 56.7 | 2 20.9 | 10.4 | 257 23.8 | 28.1 | 324 34.2 | 56.6 | 235 50.0 | 19.4 |
| | 12 | 8 59.2 | 17 20.5 | S 5 09.2 | 272 24.9 | N25 28.0 | 339 36.1 | N10 56.8 | 250 52.4 | N21 19.4 |
| | 13 | 24 01.7 | 32 20.1 | 08.0 | 287 26.1 | 27.9 | 354 38.1 | 57.0 | 265 54.9 | 19.4 |
| | 14 | 39 04.1 | 47 19.7 | 06.8 | 302 27.2 | 27.9 | 9 40.0 | 57.2 | 280 57.3 | 19.4 |
| | 15 | 54 06.6 | 62 19.3 | ·· 05.6 | 317 28.4 | ·· 27.8 | 24 41.9 | ·· 57.4 | 295 59.7 | ·· 19.4 |
| | 16 | 69 09.1 | 77 18.9 | 04.5 | 332 29.5 | 27.7 | 39 43.8 | 57.6 | 311 02.2 | 19.4 |
| | 17 | 84 11.5 | 92 18.5 | 03.3 | 347 30.6 | 27.6 | 54 45.7 | 57.8 | 326 04.6 | 19.4 |
| | 18 | 99 14.0 | 107 18.1 | S 5 02.1 | 2 31.8 | N25 27.5 | 69 47.6 | N10 58.0 | 341 07.1 | N21 19.4 |
| | 19 | 114 16.5 | 122 17.7 | 5 00.9 | 17 32.9 | 27.4 | 84 49.5 | 58.2 | 356 09.5 | 19.4 |
| | 20 | 129 18.9 | 137 17.3 | 4 59.7 | 32 34.1 | 27.3 | 99 51.4 | 58.4 | 11 12.0 | 19.4 |
| | 21 | 144 21.4 | 152 16.9 | ·· 58.6 | 47 35.2 | ·· 27.2 | 114 53.3 | ·· 58.6 | 26 14.4 | ·· 19.4 |
| | 22 | 159 23.9 | 167 16.5 | 57.4 | 62 36.4 | 27.2 | 129 55.2 | 58.9 | 41 16.9 | 19.4 |
| | 23 | 174 26.3 | 182 16.1 | 56.2 | 77 37.5 | 27.1 | 144 57.1 | 59.1 | 56 19.3 | 19.4 |
| 1 (THURSDAY) | 00 | 189 28.8 | 197 15.7 | S 4 55.0 | 92 38.6 | N25 27.0 | 159 59.1 | N10 59.3 | 71 21.7 | N21 19.4 |
| | 01 | 204 31.2 | 212 15.4 | 53.8 | 107 39.8 | 26.9 | 175 01.0 | 59.5 | 86 24.2 | 19.4 |
| | 02 | 219 33.7 | 227 15.0 | 52.7 | 122 40.9 | 26.8 | 190 02.9 | 59.7 | 101 26.6 | 19.4 |
| | 03 | 234 36.2 | 242 14.6 | ·· 51.5 | 137 42.1 | ·· 26.7 | 205 04.8 | 10 59.9 | 116 29.1 | ·· 19.4 |
| | 04 | 249 38.6 | 257 14.2 | 50.3 | 152 43.2 | 26.6 | 220 06.7 | 11 00.1 | 131 31.5 | 19.4 |
| | 05 | 264 41.1 | 272 13.8 | 49.1 | 167 44.3 | 26.5 | 235 08.6 | 00.3 | 146 34.0 | 19.4 |
| | 06 | 279 43.6 | 287 13.4 | S 4 47.9 | 182 45.5 | N25 26.4 | 250 10.5 | N11 00.5 | 161 36.4 | N21 19.4 |
| | 07 | 294 46.0 | 302 13.0 | 46.7 | 197 46.6 | 26.4 | 265 12.4 | 00.7 | 176 38.8 | 19.4 |
| | 08 | 309 48.5 | 317 12.6 | 45.6 | 212 47.8 | 26.3 | 280 14.3 | 00.9 | 191 41.3 | 19.4 |
| | 09 | 324 51.0 | 332 12.2 | ·· 44.4 | 227 48.9 | ·· 26.2 | 295 16.2 | ·· 01.1 | 206 43.7 | ·· 19.4 |
| | 10 | 339 53.4 | 347 11.8 | 43.2 | 242 50.0 | 26.1 | 310 18.1 | 01.3 | 221 46.2 | 19.4 |
| | 11 | 354 55.9 | 2 11.4 | 42.0 | 257 51.2 | 26.0 | 325 20.1 | 01.5 | 236 48.6 | 19.4 |
| | 12 | 9 58.4 | 17 11.1 | S 4 40.8 | 272 52.3 | N25 25.9 | 340 22.0 | N11 01.7 | 251 51.0 | N21 19.4 |
| | 13 | 25 00.8 | 32 10.7 | 39.6 | 287 53.5 | 25.8 | 355 23.9 | 01.9 | 266 53.5 | 19.4 |
| | 14 | 40 03.3 | 47 10.3 | 38.4 | 302 54.6 | 25.7 | 10 25.8 | 02.1 | 281 55.9 | 19.4 |
| | 15 | 55 05.7 | 62 09.9 | ·· 37.3 | 317 55.7 | ·· 25.6 | 25 27.7 | ·· 02.3 | 296 58.4 | ·· 19.4 |
| | 16 | 70 08.2 | 77 09.5 | 36.1 | 332 56.9 | 25.5 | 40 29.6 | 02.6 | 312 00.8 | 19.3 |
| | 17 | 85 10.7 | 92 09.1 | 34.9 | 347 58.0 | 25.4 | 55 31.5 | 02.8 | 327 03.3 | 19.3 |
| | 18 | 100 13.1 | 107 08.7 | S 4 33.7 | 2 59.1 | N25 25.4 | 70 33.4 | N11 03.0 | 342 05.7 | N21 19.3 |
| | 19 | 115 15.6 | 122 08.3 | 32.5 | 18 00.3 | 25.3 | 85 35.3 | 03.2 | 357 08.1 | 19.3 |
| | 20 | 130 18.1 | 137 07.9 | 31.3 | 33 01.4 | 25.2 | 100 37.2 | 03.4 | 12 10.6 | 19.3 |
| | 21 | 145 20.5 | 152 07.6 | ·· 30.1 | 48 02.6 | ·· 25.1 | 115 39.1 | ·· 03.6 | 27 13.0 | ·· 19.3 |
| | 22 | 160 23.0 | 167 07.2 | 29.0 | 63 03.7 | 25.0 | 130 41.0 | 03.8 | 42 15.4 | 19.3 |
| | 23 | 175 25.5 | 182 06.8 | 27.8 | 78 04.8 | 24.9 | 145 42.9 | 04.0 | 57 17.9 | 19.3 |
| 2 (FRIDAY) | 00 | 190 27.9 | 197 06.4 | S 4 26.6 | 93 06.0 | N25 24.8 | 160 44.9 | N11 04.2 | 72 20.3 | N21 19.3 |
| | 01 | 205 30.4 | 212 06.0 | 25.4 | 108 07.1 | 24.7 | 175 46.8 | 04.4 | 87 22.8 | 19.3 |
| | 02 | 220 32.8 | 227 05.6 | 24.2 | 123 08.2 | 24.6 | 190 48.7 | 04.6 | 102 25.2 | 19.3 |
| | 03 | 235 35.3 | 242 05.2 | ·· 23.0 | 138 09.4 | ·· 24.5 | 205 50.6 | ·· 04.8 | 117 27.6 | ·· 19.3 |
| | 04 | 250 37.8 | 257 04.8 | 21.8 | 153 10.5 | 24.4 | 220 52.5 | 05.0 | 132 30.1 | 19.3 |
| | 05 | 265 40.2 | 272 04.5 | 20.6 | 168 11.6 | 24.3 | 235 54.4 | 05.2 | 147 32.5 | 19.3 |
| | 06 | 280 42.7 | 287 04.1 | S 4 19.4 | 183 12.8 | N25 24.2 | 250 56.3 | N11 05.4 | 162 34.9 | N21 19.3 |
| | 07 | 295 45.2 | 302 03.7 | 18.3 | 198 13.9 | 24.1 | 265 58.2 | 05.6 | 177 37.4 | 19.3 |
| | 08 | 310 47.6 | 317 03.3 | 17.1 | 213 15.0 | 24.1 | 281 00.1 | 05.8 | 192 39.8 | 19.3 |
| | 09 | 325 50.1 | 332 02.9 | ·· 15.9 | 228 16.2 | ·· 24.0 | 296 02.0 | ·· 06.0 | 207 42.3 | ·· 19.3 |
| | 10 | 340 52.6 | 347 02.5 | 14.7 | 243 17.3 | 23.9 | 311 03.9 | 06.2 | 222 44.7 | 19.3 |
| | 11 | 355 55.0 | 2 02.1 | 13.5 | 258 18.4 | 23.8 | 326 05.8 | 06.5 | 237 47.1 | 19.3 |
| | 12 | 10 57.5 | 17 01.7 | S 4 12.3 | 273 19.6 | N25 23.7 | 341 07.7 | N11 06.7 | 252 49.6 | N21 19.3 |
| | 13 | 26 00.0 | 32 01.4 | 11.1 | 288 20.7 | 23.6 | 356 09.6 | 06.9 | 267 52.0 | 19.3 |
| | 14 | 41 02.4 | 47 01.0 | 09.9 | 303 21.8 | 23.5 | 11 11.5 | 07.1 | 282 54.4 | 19.3 |
| | 15 | 56 04.9 | 62 00.6 | ·· 08.7 | 318 23.0 | ·· 23.4 | 26 13.5 | ·· 07.3 | 297 56.9 | ·· 19.3 |
| | 16 | 71 07.3 | 77 00.2 | 07.5 | 333 24.1 | 23.3 | 41 15.4 | 07.5 | 312 59.3 | 19.3 |
| | 17 | 86 09.8 | 91 59.8 | 06.4 | 348 25.2 | 23.2 | 56 17.3 | 07.7 | 328 01.7 | 19.3 |
| | 18 | 101 12.3 | 106 59.4 | S 4 05.2 | 3 26.4 | N25 23.1 | 71 19.2 | N11 07.9 | 343 04.2 | N21 19.3 |
| | 19 | 116 14.7 | 121 59.1 | 04.0 | 18 27.5 | 23.0 | 86 21.1 | 08.1 | 358 06.6 | 19.3 |
| | 20 | 131 17.2 | 136 58.7 | 02.8 | 33 28.6 | 22.9 | 101 23.0 | 08.3 | 13 09.1 | 19.3 |
| | 21 | 146 19.7 | 151 58.3 | ·· 01.6 | 48 29.7 | ·· 22.8 | 116 24.9 | ·· 08.5 | 28 11.5 | ·· 19.3 |
| | 22 | 161 22.1 | 166 57.9 | 4 00.4 | 63 30.9 | 22.7 | 131 26.8 | 08.7 | 43 13.9 | 19.3 |
| | 23 | 176 24.6 | 181 57.5 | 3 59.2 | 78 32.0 | 22.6 | 146 28.7 | 08.9 | 58 16.4 | 19.3 |
| Mer. Pass. | | 11h 20.2m | v −0.4 | d 1.2 | v 1.1 | d 0.1 | v 1.9 | d 0.2 | v 2.4 | d 0.0 |

**STARS**

| Name | S.H.A. | Dec. |
|---|---|---|
| | ° ′ | ° ′ |
| Acamar | 315 39.9 | S40 24.2 |
| Achernar | 335 48.1 | S57 21.5 |
| Acrux | 173 39.9 | S62 58.2 |
| Adhara | 255 34.5 | S28 56.7 |
| Aldebaran | 291 21.6 | N16 27.6 |
| Alioth | 166 44.6 | N56 05.2 |
| Alkaid | 153 20.4 | N49 25.7 |
| Al Na'ir | 28 19.1 | S47 04.4 |
| Alnilam | 276 14.8 | S 1 13.2 |
| Alphard | 218 23.3 | S 8 33.6 |
| Alphecca | 126 34.4 | N26 47.5 |
| Alpheratz | 358 12.8 | N28 57.5 |
| Altair | 62 35.6 | N 8 48.2 |
| Ankaa | 353 43.6 | S42 26.1 |
| Antares | 113 00.3 | S26 22.8 |
| Arcturus | 146 20.9 | N19 18.2 |
| Atria | 108 27.0 | S68 58.9 |
| Avior | 234 29.2 | S59 26.4 |
| Bellatrix | 279 02.1 | N 6 19.6 |
| Betelgeuse | 271 31.6 | N 7 24.0 |
| Canopus | 264 08.6 | S52 41.4 |
| Capella | 281 15.9 | N45 58.6 |
| Deneb | 49 50.7 | N45 11.5 |
| Denebola | 183 01.8 | N14 42.1 |
| Diphda | 349 24.2 | S18 07.1 |
| Dubhe | 194 25.3 | N61 52.7 |
| Elnath | 278 48.1 | N28 35.3 |
| Eltanin | 90 59.0 | N51 29.2 |
| Enif | 34 14.8 | N 9 45.9 |
| Fomalhaut | 15 55.1 | S29 44.8 |
| Gacrux | 172 31.5 | S56 59.0 |
| Gienah | 176 20.7 | S17 24.8 |
| Hadar | 149 27.0 | S60 15.5 |
| Hamal | 328 32.6 | N23 21.0 |
| Kaus Aust. | 84 20.8 | S34 23.7 |
| Kochab | 137 17.9 | N74 15.0 |
| Markab | 14 06.5 | N15 04.6 |
| Menkar | 314 44.5 | N 3 59.7 |
| Menkent | 148 40.2 | S36 15.3 |
| Miaplacidus | 221 45.0 | S69 37.6 |
| Mirfak | 309 20.8 | N49 46.7 |
| Nunki | 76 32.9 | S26 19.5 |
| Peacock | 54 03.4 | S56 48.5 |
| Pollux | 244 01.8 | N28 05.0 |
| Procyon | 245 28.9 | N 5 17.0 |
| Rasalhague | 96 32.3 | N12 34.5 |
| Regulus | 208 13.0 | N12 04.8 |
| Rigel | 281 39.0 | S 8 13.9 |
| Rigil Kent. | 140 29.3 | S60 44.2 |
| Sabik | 102 44.5 | S15 41.8 |
| Schedar | 350 13.0 | N56 24.4 |
| Shaula | 96 59.7 | S37 05.1 |
| Sirius | 258 58.4 | S16 41.3 |
| Spica | 159 00.4 | S11 02.4 |
| Suhail | 223 12.7 | S43 20.6 |
| Vega | 80 57.8 | N38 45.5 |
| Zuben'ubi | 137 36.1 | S15 56.7 |

| | S.H.A. ° ′ | Mer. Pass. h m |
|---|---|---|
| Venus | 7 47.0 | 10 51 |
| Mars | 263 09.9 | 17 48 |
| Jupiter | 330 30.3 | 13 18 |
| Saturn | 241 53.0 | 19 11 |

## 1976 APRIL 6, 7, 8 (TUES., WED., THURS.)

| G.M.T. d | h | ARIES G.H.A. | VENUS −3.3 G.H.A. | VENUS Dec. | MARS +1.2 G.H.A. | MARS Dec. | JUPITER −1.6 G.H.A. | JUPITER Dec. | SATURN +0.3 G.H.A. | SATURN Dec. |
|---|---|---|---|---|---|---|---|---|---|---|
| | | ° ′ | ° ′ | ° ′ | ° ′ | ° ′ | ° ′ | ° ′ | ° ′ | ° ′ |
| 6 (TUESDAY) | 00 | 194 24.5 | 196 29.9 | S 2 31.7 | 94 53.7 | N25 15.0 | 163 47.7 | N11 23.9 | 76 13.5 | N21 18.9 |
| | 01 | 209 26.9 | 211 29.5 | 30.5 | 109 54.9 | 14.9 | 178 49.6 | 24.1 | 91 15.9 | 18.9 |
| | 02 | 224 29.4 | 226 29.2 | 29.2 | 124 56.0 | 14.8 | 193 51.5 | 24.3 | 106 18.3 | 18.9 |
| | 03 | 239 31.9 | 241 28.8 | ·· 28.0 | 139 57.1 | ·· 14.7 | 208 53.4 | ·· 24.5 | 121 20.7 | ·· 18.9 |
| | 04 | 254 34.3 | 256 28.4 | 26.8 | 154 58.2 | 14.5 | 223 55.3 | 24.7 | 136 23.1 | 18.9 |
| | 05 | 269 36.8 | 271 28.1 | 25.6 | 169 59.3 | 14.4 | 238 57.2 | 24.9 | 151 25.6 | 18.9 |
| | 06 | 284 39.3 | 286 27.7 | S 2 24.4 | 185 00.4 | N25 14.3 | 253 59.1 | N11 25.1 | 166 28.0 | N21 18.9 |
| | 07 | 299 41.7 | 301 27.3 | 23.2 | 200 01.5 | 14.2 | 269 01.0 | 25.3 | 181 30.4 | 18.9 |
| | 08 | 314 44.2 | 316 26.9 | 22.0 | 215 02.6 | 14.1 | 284 02.9 | 25.5 | 196 32.8 | 18.9 |
| | 09 | 329 46.6 | 331 26.6 | ·· 20.8 | 230 03.7 | ·· 14.0 | 299 04.8 | ·· 25.7 | 211 35.2 | ·· 18.9 |
| | 10 | 344 49.1 | 346 26.2 | 19.6 | 245 04.8 | 13.9 | 314 06.7 | 26.0 | 226 37.7 | 18.9 |
| | 11 | 359 51.6 | 1 25.8 | 18.4 | 260 06.0 | 13.8 | 329 08.6 | 26.2 | 241 40.1 | 18.9 |
| | 12 | 14 54.0 | 16 25.4 | S 2 17.2 | 275 07.1 | N25 13.6 | 344 10.5 | N11 26.4 | 256 42.5 | N21 18.9 |
| | 13 | 29 56.5 | 31 25.1 | 16.0 | 290 08.2 | 13.5 | 359 12.4 | 26.6 | 271 44.9 | 18.9 |
| | 14 | 44 59.0 | 46 24.7 | 14.8 | 305 09.3 | 13.4 | 14 14.3 | 26.8 | 286 47.3 | 18.9 |
| | 15 | 60 01.4 | 61 24.3 | ·· 13.6 | 320 10.4 | ·· 13.3 | 29 16.2 | ·· 27.0 | 301 49.7 | ·· 18.9 |
| | 16 | 75 03.9 | 76 24.0 | 12.4 | 335 11.5 | 13.2 | 44 18.1 | 27.2 | 316 52.2 | 18.8 |
| | 17 | 90 06.4 | 91 23.6 | 11.1 | 350 12.6 | 13.1 | 59 20.0 | 27.4 | 331 54.6 | 18.8 |
| | 18 | 105 08.8 | 106 23.2 | S 2 09.9 | 5 13.7 | N25 13.0 | 74 21.9 | N11 27.6 | 346 57.0 | N21 18.8 |
| | 19 | 120 11.3 | 121 22.8 | 08.7 | 20 14.8 | 12.8 | 89 23.8 | 27.8 | 1 59.4 | 18.8 |
| | 20 | 135 13.8 | 136 22.5 | 07.5 | 35 15.9 | 12.7 | 104 25.7 | 28.0 | 17 01.8 | 18.8 |
| | 21 | 150 16.2 | 151 22.1 | ·· 06.3 | 50 17.0 | ·· 12.6 | 119 27.6 | ·· 28.2 | 32 04.2 | ·· 18.8 |
| | 22 | 165 18.7 | 166 21.7 | 05.1 | 65 18.1 | 12.5 | 134 29.5 | 28.4 | 47 06.6 | 18.8 |
| | 23 | 180 21.1 | 181 21.4 | 03.9 | 80 19.2 | 12.4 | 149 31.4 | 28.6 | 62 09.1 | 18.8 |
| 7 (WEDNESDAY) | 00 | 195 23.6 | 196 21.0 | S 2 02.7 | 95 20.3 | N25 12.3 | 164 33.3 | N11 28.8 | 77 11.5 | N21 18.8 |
| | 01 | 210 26.1 | 211 20.6 | 01.5 | 110 21.4 | 12.1 | 179 35.2 | 29.0 | 92 13.9 | 18.8 |
| | 02 | 225 28.5 | 226 20.3 | 2 00.3 | 125 22.6 | 12.0 | 194 37.1 | 29.2 | 107 16.3 | 18.8 |
| | 03 | 240 31.0 | 241 19.9 | 1 59.1 | 140 23.7 | ·· 11.9 | 209 39.0 | ·· 29.4 | 122 18.7 | ·· 18.8 |
| | 04 | 255 33.5 | 256 19.5 | 57.9 | 155 24.8 | 11.8 | 224 40.9 | 29.6 | 137 21.1 | 18.8 |
| | 05 | 270 35.9 | 271 19.1 | 56.6 | 170 25.9 | 11.7 | 239 42.8 | 29.8 | 152 23.5 | 18.8 |
| | 06 | 285 38.4 | 286 18.8 | S 1 55.4 | 185 27.0 | N25 11.6 | 254 44.7 | N11 30.0 | 167 26.0 | N21 18.8 |
| | 07 | 300 40.9 | 301 18.4 | 54.2 | 200 28.1 | 11.4 | 269 46.6 | 30.3 | 182 28.4 | 18.8 |
| | 08 | 315 43.3 | 316 18.0 | 53.0 | 215 29.2 | 11.3 | 284 48.5 | 30.5 | 197 30.8 | 18.7 |
| | 09 | 330 45.8 | 331 17.7 | ·· 51.8 | 230 30.3 | ·· 11.2 | 299 50.4 | ·· 30.7 | 212 33.2 | ·· 18.7 |
| | 10 | 345 48.3 | 346 17.3 | 50.6 | 245 31.4 | 11.1 | 314 52.3 | 30.9 | 227 35.6 | 18.7 |
| | 11 | 0 50.7 | 1 16.9 | 49.4 | 260 32.5 | 11.0 | 329 54.2 | 31.1 | 242 38.0 | 18.7 |
| | 12 | 15 53.2 | 16 16.6 | S 1 48.2 | 275 33.6 | N25 10.8 | 344 56.1 | N11 31.3 | 257 40.4 | N21 18.7 |
| | 13 | 30 55.6 | 31 16.2 | 47.0 | 290 34.7 | 10.7 | 359 58.0 | 31.5 | 272 42.8 | 18.7 |
| | 14 | 45 58.1 | 46 15.8 | 45.8 | 305 35.8 | 10.6 | 14 59.9 | 31.7 | 287 45.3 | 18.7 |
| | 15 | 61 00.6 | 61 15.4 | ·· 44.6 | 320 36.9 | ·· 10.5 | 30 01.8 | ·· 31.9 | 302 47.7 | ·· 18.7 |
| | 16 | 76 03.0 | 76 15.1 | 43.3 | 335 38.0 | 10.4 | 45 03.7 | 32.1 | 317 50.1 | 18.7 |
| | 17 | 91 05.5 | 91 14.7 | 42.1 | 350 39.1 | 10.2 | 60 05.6 | 32.3 | 332 52.5 | 18.7 |
| | 18 | 106 08.0 | 106 14.3 | S 1 40.9 | 5 40.2 | N25 10.1 | 75 07.5 | N11 32.5 | 347 54.9 | N21 18.7 |
| | 19 | 121 10.4 | 121 14.0 | 39.7 | 20 41.3 | 10.0 | 90 09.4 | 32.7 | 2 57.3 | 18.7 |
| | 20 | 136 12.9 | 136 13.6 | 38.5 | 35 42.4 | 09.9 | 105 11.3 | 32.9 | 17 59.7 | 18.7 |
| | 21 | 151 15.4 | 151 13.2 | ·· 37.3 | 50 43.5 | ·· 09.8 | 120 13.2 | ·· 33.1 | 33 02.1 | ·· 18.7 |
| | 22 | 166 17.8 | 166 12.9 | 36.1 | 65 44.6 | 09.6 | 135 15.1 | 33.3 | 48 04.5 | 18.6 |
| | 23 | 181 20.3 | 181 12.5 | 34.9 | 80 45.7 | 09.5 | 150 17.0 | 33.5 | 63 06.9 | 18.6 |
| 8 (THURSDAY) | 00 | 196 22.8 | 196 12.1 | S 1 33.7 | 95 46.8 | N25 09.4 | 165 18.9 | N11 33.7 | 78 09.4 | N21 18.6 |
| | 01 | 211 25.2 | 211 11.8 | 32.4 | 110 47.9 | 09.3 | 180 20.8 | 33.9 | 93 11.8 | 18.6 |
| | 02 | 226 27.7 | 226 11.4 | 31.2 | 125 49.0 | 09.2 | 195 22.7 | 34.1 | 108 14.2 | 18.6 |
| | 03 | 241 30.1 | 241 11.0 | ·· 30.0 | 140 50.1 | ·· 09.0 | 210 24.6 | ·· 34.3 | 123 16.6 | ·· 18.6 |
| | 04 | 256 32.6 | 256 10.7 | 28.8 | 155 51.2 | 08.9 | 225 26.5 | 34.5 | 138 19.0 | 18.6 |
| | 05 | 271 35.1 | 271 10.3 | 27.6 | 170 52.3 | 08.8 | 240 28.4 | 34.8 | 153 21.4 | 18.6 |
| | 06 | 286 37.5 | 286 09.9 | S 1 26.4 | 185 53.4 | N25 08.7 | 255 30.3 | N11 35.0 | 168 23.8 | N21 18.6 |
| | 07 | 301 40.0 | 301 09.6 | 25.2 | 200 54.5 | 08.5 | 270 32.2 | 35.2 | 183 26.2 | 18.6 |
| | 08 | 316 42.5 | 316 09.2 | 24.0 | 215 55.6 | 08.4 | 285 34.1 | 35.4 | 198 28.6 | 18.6 |
| | 09 | 331 44.9 | 331 08.8 | ·· 22.8 | 230 56.7 | ·· 08.3 | 300 36.0 | ·· 35.6 | 213 31.0 | ·· 18.6 |
| | 10 | 346 47.4 | 346 08.5 | 21.5 | 245 57.8 | 08.2 | 315 37.9 | 35.8 | 228 33.4 | 18.6 |
| | 11 | 1 49.9 | 1 08.1 | 20.3 | 260 58.9 | 08.1 | 330 39.8 | 36.0 | 243 35.8 | 18.5 |
| | 12 | 16 52.3 | 16 07.7 | S 1 19.1 | 276 00.0 | N25 07.9 | 345 41.7 | N11 36.2 | 258 38.3 | N21 18.5 |
| | 13 | 31 54.8 | 31 07.4 | 17.9 | 291 01.1 | 07.8 | 0 43.6 | 36.4 | 273 40.7 | 18.5 |
| | 14 | 46 57.2 | 46 07.0 | 16.7 | 306 02.2 | 07.7 | 15 45.5 | 36.6 | 288 43.1 | 18.5 |
| | 15 | 61 59.7 | 61 06.6 | ·· 15.5 | 321 03.3 | ·· 07.6 | 30 47.4 | ·· 36.8 | 303 45.5 | ·· 18.5 |
| | 16 | 77 02.2 | 76 06.3 | 14.3 | 336 04.4 | 07.4 | 45 49.3 | 37.0 | 318 47.9 | 18.5 |
| | 17 | 92 04.6 | 91 05.9 | 13.1 | 351 05.5 | 07.3 | 60 51.2 | 37.2 | 333 50.3 | 18.5 |
| | 18 | 107 07.1 | 106 05.5 | S 1 11.8 | 6 06.6 | N25 07.2 | 75 53.1 | N11 37.4 | 348 52.7 | N21 18.5 |
| | 19 | 122 09.6 | 121 05.2 | 10.6 | 21 07.7 | 07.1 | 90 55.0 | 37.6 | 3 55.1 | 18.5 |
| | 20 | 137 12.0 | 136 04.8 | 09.4 | 36 08.8 | 06.9 | 105 56.9 | 37.8 | 18 57.5 | 18.5 |
| | 21 | 152 14.5 | 151 04.4 | ·· 08.2 | 51 09.9 | ·· 06.8 | 120 58.8 | ·· 38.0 | 33 59.9 | ·· 18.5 |
| | 22 | 167 17.0 | 166 04.1 | 07.0 | 66 11.0 | 06.7 | 136 00.7 | 38.2 | 49 02.3 | 18.5 |
| | 23 | 182 19.4 | 181 03.7 | 05.8 | 81 12.1 | 06.6 | 151 02.6 | 38.4 | 64 04.7 | 18.4 |
| Mer. Pass. | | 10h 56.6m | v −0.4 | d 1.2 | v 1.1 | d 0.1 | v 1.9 | d 0.2 | v 2.4 | d 0.0 |

**STARS**

| Name | S.H.A. | Dec. |
|---|---|---|
| | ° ′ | ° ′ |
| Acamar | 315 39.9 | S40 24.2 |
| Achernar | 335 48.1 | S57 21.5 |
| Acrux | 173 39.9 | S62 58.3 |
| Adhara | 255 34.5 | S28 56.7 |
| Aldebaran | 291 21.7 | N16 27.6 |
| Alioth | 166 44.6 | N56 05.2 |
| Alkaid | 153 20.4 | N49 25.7 |
| Al Na'ir | 28 19.0 | S47 04.4 |
| Alnilam | 276 14.8 | S 1 13.2 |
| Alphard | 218 23.3 | S 8 33.6 |
| Alphecca | 126 34.4 | N26 47.5 |
| Alpheratz | 358 12.8 | N28 57.5 |
| Altair | 62 35.5 | N 8 48.2 |
| Ankaa | 353 43.6 | S42 26.1 |
| Antares | 113 00.3 | S26 22.8 |
| Arcturus | 146 20.9 | N19 18.2 |
| Atria | 108 26.9 | S68 58.9 |
| Avior | 234 29.2 | S59 26.4 |
| Bellatrix | 279 02.1 | N 6 19.6 |
| Betelgeuse | 271 31.6 | N 7 24.0 |
| Canopus | 264 08.7 | S52 41.4 |
| Capella | 281 16.0 | N45 58.6 |
| Deneb | 49 50.7 | N45 11.5 |
| Denebola | 183 01.8 | N14 42.1 |
| Diphda | 349 24.2 | S18 07.1 |
| Dubhe | 194 25.3 | N61 52.8 |
| Elnath | 278 48.1 | N28 35.3 |
| Eltanin | 90 59.0 | N51 29.3 |
| Enif | 34 14.7 | N 9 45.9 |
| Fomalhaut | 15 55.0 | S29 44.8 |
| Gacrux | 172 31.5 | S56 59.0 |
| Gienah | 176 20.7 | S17 24.8 |
| Hadar | 149 27.0 | S60 15.6 |
| Hamal | 328 32.6 | N23 21.0 |
| Kaus Aust. | 84 20.7 | S34 23.7 |
| Kochab | 137 17.8 | N74 15.0 |
| Markab | 14 06.4 | N15 04.6 |
| Menkar | 314 44.6 | N 3 59.7 |
| Menkent | 148 40.2 | S36 15.3 |
| Miaplacidus | 221 45.1 | S69 37.6 |
| Mirfak | 309 20.8 | N49 46.7 |
| Nunki | 76 32.9 | S26 19.5 |
| Peacock | 54 03.3 | S56 48.4 |
| Pollux | 244 01.8 | N28 05.0 |
| Procyon | 245 28.9 | N 5 17.0 |
| Rasalhague | 96 32.2 | N12 34.5 |
| Regulus | 208 13.0 | N12 04.8 |
| Rigel | 281 39.1 | S 8 13.9 |
| Rigil Kent. | 140 29.2 | S60 44.2 |
| Sabik | 102 44.4 | S15 41.8 |
| Schedar | 350 13.0 | N56 24.4 |
| Shaula | 96 59.7 | S37 05.1 |
| Sirius | 258 58.4 | S16 41.3 |
| Spica | 159 00.4 | S11 02.4 |
| Suhail | 223 12.8 | S43 20.6 |
| Vega | 80 57.8 | N38 45.5 |
| Zuben'ubi | 137 36.1 | S15 56.7 |

| | S.H.A. ° ′ | Mer. Pass. h m |
|---|---|---|
| Venus | 0 57.4 | 10 55 |
| Mars | 259 56.7 | 17 37 |
| Jupiter | 329 09.7 | 13 00 |
| Saturn | 241 47.9 | 18 48 |

## 1976 APRIL 6, 7, 8 (TUES., WED., THURS.)

| G.M.T. d h | SUN G.H.A. ° ′ | SUN Dec. ° ′ | MOON G.H.A. ° ′ | v ′ | MOON Dec. ° ′ | d ′ | H.P. ′ |
|---|---|---|---|---|---|---|---|
| 6 00 | 179 22.3 | N 6 25.1 | 109 26.2 | 10.4 | N19 48.1 | 1.1 | 55.6 |
| 01 | 194 22.4 | 26.1 | 123 55.6 | 10.4 | 19 47.0 | 1.2 | 55.6 |
| 02 | 209 22.6 | 27.0 | 138 25.0 | 10.4 | 19 45.8 | 1.2 | 55.6 |
| 03 | 224 22.8 | · · 27.9 | 152 54.4 | 10.4 | 19 44.6 | 1.4 | 55.7 |
| 04 | 239 23.0 | 28.9 | 167 23.8 | 10.3 | 19 43.2 | 1.5 | 55.7 |
| 05 | 254 23.1 | 29.8 | 181 53.1 | 10.3 | 19 41.7 | 1.6 | 55.7 |
| 06 | 269 23.3 | N 6 30.8 | 196 22.4 | 10.3 | N19 40.1 | 1.6 | 55.7 |
| 07 | 284 23.5 | 31.7 | 210 51.7 | 10.3 | 19 38.5 | 1.8 | 55.8 |
| 08 | 299 23.7 | 32.7 | 225 21.0 | 10.2 | 19 36.7 | 1.9 | 55.8 |
| 09 | 314 23.9 | · · 33.6 | 239 50.2 | 10.2 | 19 34.8 | 2.0 | 55.8 |
| 10 | 329 24.0 | 34.6 | 254 19.4 | 10.3 | 19 32.8 | 2.1 | 55.9 |
| 11 | 344 24.2 | 35.5 | 268 48.7 | 10.2 | 19 30.7 | 2.2 | 55.9 |
| 12 | 359 24.4 | N 6 36.4 | 283 17.9 | 10.1 | N19 28.5 | 2.3 | 55.9 |
| 13 | 14 24.6 | 37.4 | 297 47.0 | 10.2 | 19 26.2 | 2.4 | 55.9 |
| 14 | 29 24.7 | 38.3 | 312 16.2 | 10.1 | 19 23.8 | 2.5 | 56.0 |
| 15 | 44 24.9 | · · 39.3 | 326 45.3 | 10.2 | 19 21.3 | 2.6 | 56.0 |
| 16 | 59 25.1 | 40.2 | 341 14.5 | 10.1 | 19 18.7 | 2.7 | 56.0 |
| 17 | 74 25.3 | 41.2 | 355 43.6 | 10.1 | 19 16.0 | 2.8 | 56.1 |
| 18 | 89 25.5 | N 6 42.1 | 10 12.7 | 10.0 | N19 13.2 | 3.0 | 56.1 |
| 19 | 104 25.6 | 43.0 | 24 41.7 | 10.1 | 19 10.2 | 3.0 | 56.1 |
| 20 | 119 25.8 | 44.0 | 39 10.8 | 10.1 | 19 07.2 | 3.1 | 56.1 |
| 21 | 134 26.0 | · · 44.9 | 53 39.9 | 10.0 | 19 04.1 | 3.3 | 56.2 |
| 22 | 149 26.2 | 45.9 | 68 08.9 | 10.0 | 19 00.8 | 3.3 | 56.2 |
| 23 | 164 26.3 | 46.8 | 82 37.9 | 10.0 | 18 57.5 | 3.4 | 56.2 |
| 7 00 | 179 26.5 | N 6 47.7 | 97 06.9 | 10.0 | N18 54.1 | 3.6 | 56.3 |
| 01 | 194 26.7 | 48.7 | 111 35.9 | 10.0 | 18 50.5 | 3.6 | 56.3 |
| 02 | 209 26.9 | 49.6 | 126 04.9 | 10.0 | 18 46.9 | 3.8 | 56.3 |
| 03 | 224 27.0 | · · 50.6 | 140 33.9 | 9.9 | 18 43.1 | 3.8 | 56.4 |
| 04 | 239 27.2 | 51.5 | 155 02.8 | 10.0 | 18 39.3 | 4.0 | 56.4 |
| 05 | 254 27.4 | 52.4 | 169 31.8 | 9.9 | 18 35.3 | 4.1 | 56.4 |
| 06 | 269 27.6 | N 6 53.4 | 184 00.7 | 9.9 | N18 31.2 | 4.1 | 56.5 |
| 07 | 284 27.7 | 54.3 | 198 29.6 | 9.9 | 18 27.1 | 4.3 | 56.5 |
| 08 | 299 27.9 | 55.3 | 212 58.5 | 9.9 | 18 22.8 | 4.4 | 56.5 |
| 09 | 314 28.1 | · · 56.2 | 227 27.4 | 9.9 | 18 18.4 | 4.5 | 56.6 |
| 10 | 329 28.3 | 57.1 | 241 56.3 | 9.9 | 18 13.9 | 4.5 | 56.6 |
| 11 | 344 28.4 | 58.1 | 256 25.2 | 9.9 | 18 09.4 | 4.7 | 56.6 |
| 12 | 359 28.6 | N 6 59.0 | 270 54.1 | 9.8 | N18 04.7 | 4.8 | 56.7 |
| 13 | 14 28.8 | 6 59.9 | 285 22.9 | 9.9 | 17 59.9 | 4.9 | 56.7 |
| 14 | 29 29.0 | 7 00.9 | 299 51.8 | 9.8 | 17 55.0 | 5.0 | 56.7 |
| 15 | 44 29.2 | · · 01.8 | 314 20.6 | 9.9 | 17 50.0 | 5.1 | 56.8 |
| 16 | 59 29.3 | 02.8 | 328 49.5 | 9.8 | 17 44.9 | 5.2 | 56.8 |
| 17 | 74 29.5 | 03.7 | 343 18.3 | 9.8 | 17 39.7 | 5.2 | 56.8 |
| 18 | 89 29.7 | N 7 04.6 | 357 47.1 | 9.8 | N17 34.5 | 5.4 | 56.9 |
| 19 | 104 29.9 | 05.6 | 12 15.9 | 9.8 | 17 29.1 | 5.5 | 56.9 |
| 20 | 119 30.0 | 06.5 | 26 44.7 | 9.8 | 17 23.6 | 5.6 | 56.9 |
| 21 | 134 30.2 | · · 07.4 | 41 13.5 | 9.8 | 17 18.0 | 5.7 | 57.0 |
| 22 | 149 30.4 | 08.4 | 55 42.3 | 9.7 | 17 12.3 | 5.8 | 57.0 |
| 23 | 164 30.5 | 09.3 | 70 11.0 | 9.8 | 17 06.5 | 5.9 | 57.0 |
| 8 00 | 179 30.7 | N 7 10.2 | 84 39.8 | 9.8 | N17 00.6 | 6.0 | 57.1 |
| 01 | 194 30.9 | 11.2 | 99 08.6 | 9.7 | 16 54.6 | 6.1 | 57.1 |
| 02 | 209 31.1 | 12.1 | 113 37.3 | 9.8 | 16 48.5 | 6.2 | 57.2 |
| 03 | 224 31.2 | · · 13.1 | 128 06.1 | 9.7 | 16 42.3 | 6.3 | 57.2 |
| 04 | 239 31.4 | 14.0 | 142 34.8 | 9.8 | 16 36.0 | 6.4 | 57.2 |
| 05 | 254 31.6 | 14.9 | 157 03.6 | 9.7 | 16 29.6 | 6.5 | 57.3 |
| 06 | 269 31.8 | N 7 15.9 | 171 32.3 | 9.7 | N16 23.1 | 6.6 | 57.3 |
| 07 | 284 31.9 | 16.8 | 186 01.0 | 9.7 | 16 16.5 | 6.7 | 57.3 |
| 08 | 299 32.1 | 17.7 | 200 29.7 | 9.7 | 16 09.8 | 6.8 | 57.4 |
| 09 | 314 32.3 | · · 18.7 | 214 58.4 | 9.7 | 16 03.0 | 6.9 | 57.4 |
| 10 | 329 32.5 | 19.6 | 229 27.1 | 9.7 | 15 56.1 | 6.9 | 57.4 |
| 11 | 344 32.6 | 20.5 | 243 55.8 | 9.7 | 15 49.2 | 7.1 | 57.5 |
| 12 | 359 32.8 | N 7 21.5 | 258 24.5 | 9.7 | N15 42.1 | 7.2 | 57.5 |
| 13 | 14 33.0 | 22.4 | 272 53.2 | 9.7 | 15 34.9 | 7.3 | 57.6 |
| 14 | 29 33.2 | 23.3 | 287 21.9 | 9.7 | 15 27.6 | 7.3 | 57.6 |
| 15 | 44 33.3 | · · 24.2 | 301 50.6 | 9.7 | 15 20.3 | 7.5 | 57.6 |
| 16 | 59 33.5 | 25.2 | 316 19.3 | 9.6 | 15 12.8 | 7.5 | 57.7 |
| 17 | 74 33.7 | 26.1 | 330 47.9 | 9.7 | 15 05.3 | 7.7 | 57.7 |
| 18 | 89 33.8 | N 7 27.0 | 345 16.6 | 9.6 | N14 57.6 | 7.7 | 57.8 |
| 19 | 104 34.0 | 28.0 | 359 45.2 | 9.7 | 14 49.9 | 7.8 | 57.8 |
| 20 | 119 34.2 | 28.9 | 14 13.9 | 9.6 | 14 42.1 | 8.0 | 57.8 |
| 21 | 134 34.4 | · · 29.8 | 28 42.5 | 9.7 | 14 34.1 | 8.0 | 57.9 |
| 22 | 149 34.5 | 30.8 | 43 11.2 | 9.6 | 14 26.1 | 8.1 | 57.9 |
| 23 | 164 34.7 | 31.7 | 57 39.8 | 9.6 | 14 18.0 | 8.2 | 57.9 |
| | S.D. 16.0 | d 0.9 | S.D. 15.2 | | 15.4 | | 15.7 |

| Lat. ° | Twilight Naut. h m | Twilight Civil h m | Sunrise h m | Moonrise 6 h m | Moonrise 7 h m | Moonrise 8 h m | Moonrise 9 h m |
|---|---|---|---|---|---|---|---|
| N 72 | //// | 03 02 | 04 24 | □ | □ | 08 32 | 10 42 |
| N 70 | 01 23 | 03 24 | 04 35 | 05 44 | 07 26 | 09 15 | 11 06 |
| 68 | 02 08 | 03 41 | 04 44 | 06 51 | 08 10 | 09 43 | 11 24 |
| 66 | 02 36 | 03 55 | 04 51 | 07 26 | 08 39 | 10 05 | 11 38 |
| 64 | 02 57 | 04 06 | 04 57 | 07 52 | 09 01 | 10 22 | 11 50 |
| 62 | 03 14 | 04 15 | 05 03 | 08 12 | 09 18 | 10 35 | 12 00 |
| 60 | 03 27 | 04 23 | 05 07 | 08 28 | 09 33 | 10 47 | 12 09 |
| N 58 | 03 39 | 04 30 | 05 11 | 08 42 | 09 45 | 10 57 | 12 16 |
| 56 | 03 48 | 04 36 | 05 15 | 08 54 | 09 56 | 11 06 | 12 23 |
| 54 | 03 57 | 04 42 | 05 18 | 09 04 | 10 06 | 11 14 | 12 29 |
| 52 | 04 04 | 04 46 | 05 21 | 09 14 | 10 14 | 11 21 | 12 34 |
| 50 | 04 10 | 04 51 | 05 24 | 09 22 | 10 22 | 11 27 | 12 39 |
| 45 | 04 24 | 05 00 | 05 30 | 09 39 | 10 38 | 11 41 | 12 49 |
| N 40 | 04 34 | 05 07 | 05 35 | 09 54 | 10 51 | 11 52 | 12 57 |
| 35 | 04 43 | 05 13 | 05 39 | 10 06 | 11 02 | 12 02 | 13 05 |
| 30 | 04 50 | 05 18 | 05 42 | 10 17 | 11 12 | 12 10 | 13 11 |
| 20 | 05 00 | 05 26 | 05 49 | 10 35 | 11 28 | 12 24 | 13 22 |
| N 10 | 05 08 | 05 33 | 05 54 | 10 51 | 11 43 | 12 37 | 13 32 |
| 0 | 05 14 | 05 38 | 05 59 | 11 05 | 11 57 | 12 49 | 13 41 |
| S 10 | 05 18 | 05 43 | 06 04 | 11 20 | 12 10 | 13 00 | 13 50 |
| 20 | 05 21 | 05 47 | 06 08 | 11 36 | 12 25 | 13 13 | 13 59 |
| 30 | 05 22 | 05 50 | 06 14 | 11 54 | 12 42 | 13 27 | 14 10 |
| 35 | 05 23 | 05 52 | 06 17 | 12 05 | 12 51 | 13 35 | 14 16 |
| 40 | 05 22 | 05 54 | 06 21 | 12 17 | 13 03 | 13 45 | 14 24 |
| 45 | 05 22 | 05 56 | 06 25 | 12 31 | 13 15 | 13 55 | 14 32 |
| S 50 | 05 20 | 05 57 | 06 30 | 12 49 | 13 31 | 14 09 | 14 42 |
| 52 | 05 19 | 05 58 | 06 32 | 12 57 | 13 39 | 14 15 | 14 46 |
| 54 | 05 18 | 05 59 | 06 35 | 13 06 | 13 47 | 14 22 | 14 51 |
| 56 | 05 17 | 06 00 | 06 37 | 13 17 | 13 56 | 14 29 | 14 57 |
| 58 | 05 15 | 06 01 | 06 40 | 13 28 | 14 06 | 14 37 | 15 03 |
| S 60 | 05 14 | 06 02 | 06 43 | 13 42 | 14 18 | 14 47 | 15 10 |

| Lat. ° | Sunset h m | Twilight Civil h m | Twilight Naut. h m | Moonset 6 h m | Moonset 7 h m | Moonset 8 h m | Moonset 9 h m |
|---|---|---|---|---|---|---|---|
| N 72 | 19 44 | 21 08 | //// | □ | □ | 04 51 | 04 29 |
| N 70 | 19 32 | 20 44 | 22 54 | 04 03 | 04 08 | 04 07 | 04 04 |
| 68 | 19 23 | 20 26 | 22 03 | 02 56 | 03 24 | 03 38 | 03 45 |
| 66 | 19 15 | 20 12 | 21 33 | 02 20 | 02 54 | 03 16 | 03 30 |
| 64 | 19 09 | 20 01 | 21 11 | 01 54 | 02 32 | 02 58 | 03 17 |
| 62 | 19 03 | 19 51 | 20 54 | 01 34 | 02 14 | 02 43 | 03 06 |
| 60 | 18 58 | 19 43 | 20 40 | 01 18 | 01 59 | 02 31 | 02 57 |
| N 58 | 18 54 | 19 36 | 20 28 | 01 04 | 01 46 | 02 20 | 02 49 |
| 56 | 18 50 | 19 29 | 20 18 | 00 52 | 01 35 | 02 11 | 02 41 |
| 54 | 18 47 | 19 24 | 20 09 | 00 42 | 01 25 | 02 03 | 02 35 |
| 52 | 18 44 | 19 19 | 20 02 | 00 32 | 01 17 | 01 55 | 02 29 |
| 50 | 18 41 | 19 15 | 19 55 | 00 24 | 01 09 | 01 49 | 02 24 |
| 45 | 18 35 | 19 05 | 19 41 | 00 06 | 00 52 | 01 34 | 02 12 |
| N 40 | 18 30 | 18 58 | 19 31 | 24 39 | 00 39 | 01 22 | 02 03 |
| 35 | 18 26 | 18 52 | 19 22 | 24 27 | 00 27 | 01 12 | 01 55 |
| 30 | 18 22 | 18 47 | 19 15 | 24 17 | 00 17 | 01 03 | 01 47 |
| 20 | 18 16 | 18 38 | 19 04 | 24 00 | 00 00 | 00 48 | 01 35 |
| N 10 | 18 10 | 18 32 | 18 56 | 23 44 | 24 34 | 00 34 | 01 24 |
| 0 | 18 05 | 18 26 | 18 50 | 23 30 | 24 22 | 00 22 | 01 13 |
| S 10 | 18 00 | 18 22 | 18 46 | 23 16 | 24 09 | 00 09 | 01 03 |
| 20 | 17 56 | 18 17 | 18 43 | 23 00 | 23 55 | 24 52 | 00 52 |
| 30 | 17 50 | 18 14 | 18 41 | 22 42 | 23 39 | 24 39 | 00 39 |
| 35 | 17 46 | 18 12 | 18 41 | 22 32 | 23 30 | 24 31 | 00 31 |
| 40 | 17 43 | 18 10 | 18 41 | 22 20 | 23 19 | 24 23 | 00 23 |
| 45 | 17 38 | 18 08 | 18 42 | 22 06 | 23 07 | 24 13 | 00 13 |
| S 50 | 17 33 | 18 06 | 18 43 | 21 49 | 22 52 | 24 01 | 00 01 |
| 52 | 17 31 | 18 05 | 18 44 | 21 41 | 22 45 | 23 55 | 25 10 |
| 54 | 17 29 | 18 04 | 18 45 | 21 32 | 22 37 | 23 49 | 25 05 |
| 56 | 17 26 | 18 03 | 18 46 | 21 22 | 22 28 | 23 42 | 25 00 |
| 58 | 17 23 | 18 02 | 18 48 | 21 10 | 22 18 | 23 34 | 24 55 |
| S 60 | 17 20 | 18 01 | 18 49 | 20 57 | 22 07 | 23 25 | 24 49 |

| Day | SUN Eqn. of Time 00ʰ m s | SUN Eqn. of Time 12ʰ m s | SUN Mer. Pass. h m | MOON Mer. Pass. Upper h m | MOON Mer. Pass. Lower h m | MOON Age d | Phase |
|---|---|---|---|---|---|---|---|
| 6 | 02 31 | 02 23 | 12 02 | 17 18 | 04 52 | 07 | ◐ |
| 7 | 02 14 | 02 06 | 12 02 | 18 09 | 05 43 | 08 | |
| 8 | 01 57 | 01 49 | 12 02 | 19 01 | 06 35 | 09 | |

## 1976 APRIL 9, 10, 11 (FRI., SAT., SUN.)

| G.M.T. d h | ARIES G.H.A. ° ′ | VENUS −3.3 G.H.A. ° ′ | VENUS Dec. ° ′ | MARS +1.2 G.H.A. ° ′ | MARS Dec. ° ′ | JUPITER −1.6 G.H.A. ° ′ | JUPITER Dec. ° ′ | SATURN +0.3 G.H.A. ° ′ | SATURN Dec. ° ′ |
|---|---|---|---|---|---|---|---|---|---|
| 9 00 | 197 21.9 | 196 03.3 | S 1 04.6 | 96 13.1 | N25 06.4 | 166 04.5 | N11 38.6 | 79 07.1 | N21 18.4 |
| 01 | 212 24.4 | 211 03.0 | 03.4 | 111 14.2 | 06.3 | 181 06.4 | 38.8 | 94 09.5 | 18.4 |
| 02 | 227 26.8 | 226 02.6 | 02.1 | 126 15.3 | 06.2 | 196 08.3 | 39.0 | 109 11.9 | 18.4 |
| 03 | 242 29.3 | 241 02.2 | 1 00.9 | 141 16.4 | · · 06.1 | 211 10.2 | · · 39.2 | 124 14.3 | · · 18.4 |
| 04 | 257 31.7 | 256 01.9 | 0 59.7 | 156 17.5 | 05.9 | 226 12.0 | 39.5 | 139 16.7 | 18.4 |
| 05 | 272 34.2 | 271 01.5 | 58.5 | 171 18.6 | 05.8 | 241 13.9 | 39.7 | 154 19.1 | 18.4 |
| 06 | 287 36.7 | 286 01.1 | S 0 57.3 | 186 19.7 | N25 05.7 | 256 15.8 | N11 39.9 | 169 21.5 | N21 18.4 |
| 07 | 302 39.1 | 301 00.8 | 56.1 | 201 20.8 | 05.5 | 271 17.7 | 40.1 | 184 24.0 | 18.4 |
| 08 | 317 41.6 | 316 00.4 | 54.9 | 216 21.9 | 05.4 | 286 19.6 | 40.3 | 199 26.4 | 18.4 |
| 09 | 332 44.1 | 331 00.0 | · · 53.6 | 231 23.0 | · · 05.3 | 301 21.5 | · · 40.5 | 214 28.8 | · · 18.4 |
| 10 | 347 46.5 | 345 59.7 | 52.4 | 246 24.1 | 05.2 | 316 23.4 | 40.7 | 229 31.2 | 18.4 |
| 11 | 2 49.0 | 0 59.3 | 51.2 | 261 25.2 | 05.0 | 331 25.3 | 40.9 | 244 33.6 | 18.3 |
| 12 | 17 51.5 | 15 58.9 | S 0 50.0 | 276 26.3 | N25 04.9 | 346 27.2 | N11 41.1 | 259 36.0 | N21 18.3 |
| 13 | 32 53.9 | 30 58.6 | 48.8 | 291 27.4 | 04.8 | 1 29.1 | 41.3 | 274 38.4 | 18.3 |
| 14 | 47 56.4 | 45 58.2 | 47.6 | 306 28.5 | 04.6 | 16 31.0 | 41.5 | 289 40.8 | 18.3 |
| 15 | 62 58.9 | 60 57.8 | · · 46.4 | 321 29.6 | · · 04.5 | 31 32.9 | · · 41.7 | 304 43.2 | · · 18.3 |
| 16 | 78 01.3 | 75 57.5 | 45.1 | 336 30.6 | 04.4 | 46 34.8 | 41.9 | 319 45.6 | 18.3 |
| 17 | 93 03.8 | 90 57.1 | 43.9 | 351 31.7 | 04.3 | 61 36.7 | 42.1 | 334 48.0 | 18.3 |
| 18 | 108 06.2 | 105 56.7 | S 0 42.7 | 6 32.8 | N25 04.1 | 76 38.6 | N11 42.3 | 349 50.4 | N21 18.3 |
| 19 | 123 08.7 | 120 56.4 | 41.5 | 21 33.9 | 04.0 | 91 40.5 | 42.5 | 4 52.8 | 18.3 |
| 20 | 138 11.2 | 135 56.0 | 40.3 | 36 35.0 | 03.9 | 106 42.4 | 42.7 | 19 55.2 | 18.3 |
| 21 | 153 13.6 | 150 55.6 | · · 39.1 | 51 36.1 | · · 03.7 | 121 44.3 | · · 42.9 | 34 57.6 | · · 18.3 |
| 22 | 168 16.1 | 165 55.3 | 37.9 | 66 37.2 | 03.6 | 136 46.2 | 43.1 | 50 00.0 | 18.2 |
| 23 | 183 18.6 | 180 54.9 | 36.6 | 81 38.3 | 03.5 | 151 48.1 | 43.3 | 65 02.4 | 18.2 |
| 10 00 | 198 21.0 | 195 54.5 | S 0 35.4 | 96 39.4 | N25 03.3 | 166 50.0 | N11 43.5 | 80 04.8 | N21 18.2 |
| 01 | 213 23.5 | 210 54.2 | 34.2 | 111 40.5 | 03.2 | 181 51.9 | 43.7 | 95 07.2 | 18.2 |
| 02 | 228 26.0 | 225 53.8 | 33.0 | 126 41.5 | 03.1 | 196 53.8 | 43.9 | 110 09.6 | 18.2 |
| 03 | 243 28.4 | 240 53.5 | · · 31.8 | 141 42.6 | · · 03.0 | 211 55.7 | · · 44.1 | 125 12.0 | · · 18.2 |
| 04 | 258 30.9 | 255 53.1 | 30.6 | 156 43.7 | 02.8 | 226 57.6 | 44.3 | 140 14.4 | 18.2 |
| 05 | 273 33.3 | 270 52.7 | 29.4 | 171 44.8 | 02.7 | 241 59.5 | 44.6 | 155 16.8 | 18.2 |
| 06 | 288 35.8 | 285 52.4 | S 0 28.1 | 186 45.9 | N25 02.6 | 257 01.4 | N11 44.8 | 170 19.2 | N21 18.2 |
| 07 | 303 38.3 | 300 52.0 | 26.9 | 201 47.0 | 02.4 | 272 03.3 | 45.0 | 185 21.6 | 18.2 |
| 08 | 318 40.7 | 315 51.6 | 25.7 | 216 48.1 | 02.3 | 287 05.2 | 45.2 | 200 24.0 | 18.2 |
| 09 | 333 43.2 | 330 51.3 | · · 24.5 | 231 49.2 | · · 02.2 | 302 07.1 | · · 45.4 | 215 26.4 | · · 18.1 |
| 10 | 348 45.7 | 345 50.9 | 23.3 | 246 50.3 | 02.0 | 317 09.0 | 45.6 | 230 28.8 | 18.1 |
| 11 | 3 48.1 | 0 50.5 | 22.1 | 261 51.4 | 01.9 | 332 10.9 | 45.8 | 245 31.2 | 18.1 |
| 12 | 18 50.6 | 15 50.2 | S 0 20.8 | 276 52.4 | N25 01.8 | 347 12.8 | N11 46.0 | 260 33.6 | N21 18.1 |
| 13 | 33 53.1 | 30 49.8 | 19.6 | 291 53.5 | 01.6 | 2 14.6 | 46.2 | 275 36.0 | 18.1 |
| 14 | 48 55.5 | 45 49.4 | 18.4 | 306 54.6 | 01.5 | 17 16.5 | 46.4 | 290 38.4 | 18.1 |
| 15 | 63 58.0 | 60 49.1 | · · 17.2 | 321 55.7 | · · 01.4 | 32 18.4 | · · 46.6 | 305 40.8 | · · 18.1 |
| 16 | 79 00.5 | 75 48.7 | 16.0 | 336 56.8 | 01.2 | 47 20.3 | 46.8 | 320 43.2 | 18.1 |
| 17 | 94 02.9 | 90 48.4 | 14.8 | 351 57.9 | 01.1 | 62 22.2 | 47.0 | 335 45.6 | 18.1 |
| 18 | 109 05.4 | 105 48.0 | S 0 13.6 | 6 59.0 | N25 01.0 | 77 24.1 | N11 47.2 | 350 47.9 | N21 18.1 |
| 19 | 124 07.8 | 120 47.6 | 12.3 | 22 00.0 | 00.8 | 92 26.0 | 47.4 | 5 50.3 | 18.0 |
| 20 | 139 10.3 | 135 47.3 | 11.1 | 37 01.1 | 00.7 | 107 27.9 | 47.6 | 20 52.7 | 18.0 |
| 21 | 154 12.8 | 150 46.9 | · · 09.9 | 52 02.2 | · · 00.6 | 122 29.8 | · · 47.8 | 35 55.1 | · · 18.0 |
| 22 | 169 15.2 | 165 46.5 | 08.7 | 67 03.3 | 00.4 | 137 31.7 | 48.0 | 50 57.5 | 18.0 |
| 23 | 184 17.7 | 180 46.2 | 07.5 | 82 04.4 | 00.3 | 152 33.6 | 48.2 | 65 59.9 | 18.0 |
| 11 00 | 199 20.2 | 195 45.8 | S 0 06.3 | 97 05.5 | N25 00.1 | 167 35.5 | N11 48.4 | 81 02.3 | N21 18.0 |
| 01 | 214 22.6 | 210 45.4 | 05.0 | 112 06.6 | 25 00.0 | 182 37.4 | 48.6 | 96 04.7 | 18.0 |
| 02 | 229 25.1 | 225 45.1 | 03.8 | 127 07.6 | 24 59.9 | 197 39.3 | 48.8 | 111 07.1 | 18.0 |
| 03 | 244 27.6 | 240 44.7 | · · 02.6 | 142 08.7 | · · 59.7 | 212 41.2 | · · 49.0 | 126 09.5 | · · 18.0 |
| 04 | 259 30.0 | 255 44.4 | 01.4 | 157 09.8 | 59.6 | 227 43.1 | 49.2 | 141 11.9 | 18.0 |
| 05 | 274 32.5 | 270 44.0 | S 0 00.2 | 172 10.9 | 59.5 | 242 45.0 | 49.4 | 156 14.3 | 17.9 |
| 06 | 289 34.9 | 285 43.6 | N 0 01.0 | 187 12.0 | N24 59.3 | 257 46.9 | N11 49.6 | 171 16.7 | N21 17.9 |
| 07 | 304 37.4 | 300 43.3 | 02.3 | 202 13.1 | 59.2 | 272 48.8 | 49.8 | 186 19.1 | 17.9 |
| 08 | 319 39.9 | 315 42.9 | 03.5 | 217 14.2 | 59.0 | 287 50.7 | 50.1 | 201 21.5 | 17.9 |
| 09 | 334 42.3 | 330 42.5 | · · 04.7 | 232 15.2 | · · 58.9 | 302 52.6 | · · 50.3 | 216 23.9 | · · 17.9 |
| 10 | 349 44.8 | 345 42.2 | 05.9 | 247 16.3 | 58.8 | 317 54.5 | 50.5 | 231 26.3 | 17.9 |
| 11 | 4 47.3 | 0 41.8 | 07.1 | 262 17.4 | 58.6 | 332 56.4 | 50.7 | 246 28.7 | 17.9 |
| 12 | 19 49.7 | 15 41.4 | N 0 08.3 | 277 18.5 | N24 58.5 | 347 58.2 | N11 50.9 | 261 31.1 | N21 17.9 |
| 13 | 34 52.2 | 30 41.1 | 09.6 | 292 19.6 | 58.4 | 3 00.1 | 51.1 | 276 33.4 | 17.9 |
| 14 | 49 54.7 | 45 40.7 | 10.8 | 307 20.7 | 58.2 | 18 02.0 | 51.3 | 291 35.8 | 17.9 |
| 15 | 64 57.1 | 60 40.4 | · · 12.0 | 322 21.7 | · · 58.1 | 33 03.9 | · · 51.5 | 306 38.2 | · · 17.8 |
| 16 | 79 59.6 | 75 40.0 | 13.2 | 337 22.8 | 57.9 | 48 05.8 | 51.7 | 321 40.6 | 17.8 |
| 17 | 95 02.1 | 90 39.6 | 14.4 | 352 23.9 | 57.8 | 63 07.7 | 51.9 | 336 43.0 | 17.8 |
| 18 | 110 04.5 | 105 39.3 | N 0 15.6 | 7 25.0 | N24 57.7 | 78 09.6 | N11 52.1 | 351 45.4 | N21 17.8 |
| 19 | 125 07.0 | 120 38.9 | 16.9 | 22 26.1 | 57.5 | 93 11.5 | 52.3 | 6 47.8 | 17.8 |
| 20 | 140 09.4 | 135 38.5 | 18.1 | 37 27.2 | 57.4 | 108 13.4 | 52.5 | 21 50.2 | 17.8 |
| 21 | 155 11.9 | 150 38.2 | · · 19.3 | 52 28.2 | · · 57.2 | 123 15.3 | · · 52.7 | 36 52.6 | · · 17.8 |
| 22 | 170 14.4 | 165 37.8 | 20.5 | 67 29.3 | 57.1 | 138 17.2 | 52.9 | 51 55.0 | 17.8 |
| 23 | 185 16.8 | 180 37.4 | 21.7 | 82 30.4 | 57.0 | 153 19.1 | 53.1 | 66 57.4 | 17.8 |
| Mer. Pass. | h m 10 44.8 | v −0.4 | d 1.2 | v 1.1 | d 0.1 | v 1.9 | d 0.2 | v 2.4 | d 0.0 |

| STARS Name | S.H.A. ° ′ | Dec. ° ′ |
|---|---|---|
| Acamar | 315 39.9 | S40 24.1 |
| Achernar | 335 48.1 | S57 21.5 |
| Acrux | 173 39.9 | S62 58.3 |
| Adhara | 255 34.5 | S28 56.7 |
| Aldebaran | 291 21.7 | N16 27.6 |
| Alioth | 166 44.6 | N56 05.2 |
| Alkaid | 153 20.4 | N49 25.8 |
| Al Na'ir | 28 19.0 | S47 04.4 |
| Alnilam | 276 14.9 | S 1 13.2 |
| Alphard | 218 23.4 | S 8 33.6 |
| Alphecca | 126 34.4 | N26 47.5 |
| Alpheratz | 358 12.7 | N28 57.5 |
| Altair | 62 35.5 | N 8 48.2 |
| Ankaa | 353 43.6 | S42 26.1 |
| Antares | 113 00.3 | S26 22.8 |
| Arcturus | 146 20.9 | N19 18.2 |
| Atria | 108 26.9 | S68 58.9 |
| Avior | 234 29.3 | S59 26.4 |
| Bellatrix | 279 02.1 | N 6 19.6 |
| Betelgeuse | 271 31.7 | N 7 24.0 |
| Canopus | 264 08.7 | S52 41.4 |
| Capella | 281 16.0 | N45 58.5 |
| Deneb | 49 50.6 | N45 11.5 |
| Denebola | 183 01.8 | N14 42.1 |
| Diphda | 349 24.2 | S18 07.0 |
| Dubhe | 194 25.3 | N61 52.8 |
| Elnath | 278 48.1 | N28 35.3 |
| Eltanin | 90 58.9 | N51 29.3 |
| Enif | 34 14.7 | N 9 45.9 |
| Fomalhaut | 15 55.0 | S29 44.8 |
| Gacrux | 172 31.5 | S56 59.0 |
| Gienah | 176 20.7 | S17 24.8 |
| Hadar | 149 26.9 | S60 15.6 |
| Hamal | 328 32.6 | N23 21.0 |
| Kaus Aust. | 84 20.7 | S34 23.7 |
| Kochab | 137 17.8 | N74 15.0 |
| Markab | 14 06.4 | N15 04.6 |
| Menkar | 314 44.6 | N 3 59.7 |
| Menkent | 148 40.1 | S36 15.3 |
| Miaplacidus | 221 45.1 | S69 37.6 |
| Mirfak | 309 20.8 | N49 46.7 |
| Nunki | 76 32.8 | S26 19.5 |
| Peacock | 54 03.3 | S56 48.4 |
| Pollux | 244 01.8 | N28 05.0 |
| Procyon | 245 28.9 | N 5 17.0 |
| Rasalhague | 96 32.2 | N12 34.5 |
| Regulus | 208 13.0 | N12 04.8 |
| Rigel | 281 39.1 | S 8 13.9 |
| Rigil Kent. | 140 29.2 | S60 44.2 |
| Sabik | 102 44.4 | S15 41.8 |
| Schedar | 350 13.0 | N56 24.4 |
| Shaula | 96 59.6 | S37 05.1 |
| Sirius | 258 58.4 | S16 41.3 |
| Spica | 159 00.4 | S11 02.4 |
| Suhail | 223 12.8 | S43 20.6 |
| Vega | 80 57.8 | N38 45.5 |
| Zuben'ubi | 137 36.0 | S15 56.7 |

| | S.H.A. ° ′ | Mer. Pass. h m |
|---|---|---|
| Venus | 357 33.5 | 10 57 |
| Mars | 258 18.3 | 17 32 |
| Jupiter | 328 29.0 | 12 51 |
| Saturn | 241 43.8 | 18 37 |

| G.M.T. | ARIES G.H.A. | VENUS −3.3 G.H.A. | VENUS Dec. | MARS +1.2 G.H.A. | MARS Dec. | JUPITER −1.6 G.H.A. | JUPITER Dec. | SATURN +0.3 G.H.A. | SATURN Dec. |
|---|---|---|---|---|---|---|---|---|---|
| d h | ° ′ | ° ′ | ° ′ | ° ′ | ° ′ | ° ′ | ° ′ | ° ′ | ° ′ |
| 12 00 | 200 19.3 | 195 37.1 | N 0 22.9 | 97 31.5 | N24 56.8 | 168 21.0 | N11 53.3 | 81 59.8 | N21 17.7 |
| 01 | 215 21.8 | 210 36.7 | 24.2 | 112 32.6 | 56.7 | 183 22.9 | 53.5 | 97 02.1 | 17.7 |
| 02 | 230 24.2 | 225 36.4 | 25.4 | 127 33.6 | 56.5 | 198 24.8 | 53.7 | 112 04.5 | 17.7 |
| 03 | 245 26.7 | 240 36.0 | ·· 26.6 | 142 34.7 | ·· 56.4 | 213 26.7 | ·· 53.9 | 127 06.9 | ·· 17.7 |
| 04 | 260 29.2 | 255 35.6 | 27.8 | 157 35.8 | 56.3 | 228 28.6 | 54.1 | 142 09.3 | 17.7 |
| 05 | 275 31.6 | 270 35.3 | 29.0 | 172 36.9 | 56.1 | 243 30.5 | 54.3 | 157 11.7 | 17.7 |
| 06 | 290 34.1 | 285 34.9 | N 0 30.2 | 187 38.0 | N24 56.0 | 258 32.4 | N11 54.5 | 172 14.1 | N21 17.7 |
| 07 | 305 36.6 | 300 34.5 | 31.5 | 202 39.0 | 55.8 | 273 34.2 | 54.7 | 187 16.5 | 17.7 |
| 08 | 320 39.0 | 315 34.2 | 32.7 | 217 40.1 | 55.7 | 288 36.1 | 54.9 | 202 18.9 | 17.7 |
| M 09 | 335 41.5 | 330 33.8 | ·· 33.9 | 232 41.2 | ·· 55.5 | 303 38.0 | ·· 55.1 | 217 21.3 | ·· 17.6 |
| O 10 | 350 43.9 | 345 33.5 | 35.1 | 247 42.3 | 55.4 | 318 39.9 | 55.3 | 232 23.7 | 17.6 |
| N 11 | 5 46.4 | 0 33.1 | 36.3 | 262 43.4 | 55.3 | 333 41.8 | 55.5 | 247 26.0 | 17.6 |
| D 12 | 20 48.9 | 15 32.7 | N 0 37.5 | 277 44.4 | N24 55.1 | 348 43.7 | N11 55.7 | 262 28.4 | N21 17.6 |
| A 13 | 35 51.3 | 30 32.4 | 38.8 | 292 45.5 | 55.0 | 3 45.6 | 55.9 | 277 30.8 | 17.6 |
| Y 14 | 50 53.8 | 45 32.0 | 40.0 | 307 46.6 | 54.8 | 18 47.5 | 56.2 | 292 33.2 | 17.6 |
| 15 | 65 56.3 | 60 31.6 | ·· 41.2 | 322 47.7 | ·· 54.7 | 33 49.4 | ·· 56.4 | 307 35.6 | ·· 17.6 |
| 16 | 80 58.7 | 75 31.3 | 42.4 | 337 48.7 | 54.5 | 48 51.3 | 56.6 | 322 38.0 | 17.6 |
| 17 | 96 01.2 | 90 30.9 | 43.6 | 352 49.8 | 54.4 | 63 53.2 | 56.8 | 337 40.4 | 17.6 |
| 18 | 111 03.7 | 105 30.5 | N 0 44.8 | 7 50.9 | N24 54.2 | 78 55.1 | N11 57.0 | 352 42.8 | N21 17.5 |
| 19 | 126 06.1 | 120 30.2 | 46.1 | 22 52.0 | 54.1 | 93 57.0 | 57.2 | 7 45.1 | 17.5 |
| 20 | 141 08.6 | 135 29.8 | 47.3 | 37 53.1 | 54.0 | 108 58.9 | 57.4 | 22 47.5 | 17.5 |
| 21 | 156 11.0 | 150 29.5 | ·· 48.5 | 52 54.1 | ·· 53.8 | 124 00.8 | ·· 57.6 | 37 49.9 | ·· 17.5 |
| 22 | 171 13.5 | 165 29.1 | 49.7 | 67 55.2 | 53.7 | 139 02.7 | 57.8 | 52 52.3 | 17.5 |
| 23 | 186 16.0 | 180 28.7 | 50.9 | 82 56.3 | 53.5 | 154 04.6 | 58.0 | 67 54.7 | 17.5 |
| 13 00 | 201 18.4 | 195 28.4 | N 0 52.2 | 97 57.4 | N24 53.4 | 169 06.4 | N11 58.2 | 82 57.1 | N21 17.5 |
| 01 | 216 20.9 | 210 28.0 | 53.4 | 112 58.4 | 53.2 | 184 08.3 | 58.4 | 97 59.5 | 17.5 |
| 02 | 231 23.4 | 225 27.6 | 54.6 | 127 59.5 | 53.1 | 199 10.2 | 58.6 | 113 01.8 | 17.4 |
| 03 | 246 25.8 | 240 27.3 | ·· 55.8 | 143 00.6 | ·· 52.9 | 214 12.1 | ·· 58.8 | 128 04.2 | ·· 17.4 |
| 04 | 261 28.3 | 255 26.9 | 57.0 | 158 01.7 | 52.8 | 229 14.0 | 59.0 | 143 06.6 | 17.4 |
| 05 | 276 30.8 | 270 26.6 | 58.2 | 173 02.7 | 52.6 | 244 15.9 | 59.2 | 158 09.0 | 17.4 |
| 06 | 291 33.2 | 285 26.2 | N 0 59.5 | 188 03.8 | N24 52.5 | 259 17.8 | N11 59.4 | 173 11.4 | N21 17.4 |
| 07 | 306 35.7 | 300 25.8 | 1 00.7 | 203 04.9 | 52.3 | 274 19.7 | 59.6 | 188 13.8 | 17.4 |
| T 08 | 321 38.2 | 315 25.5 | 01.9 | 218 06.0 | 52.2 | 289 21.6 | 11 59.8 | 203 16.2 | 17.4 |
| U 09 | 336 40.6 | 330 25.1 | ·· 03.1 | 233 07.1 | ·· 52.0 | 304 23.5 | 12 00.0 | 218 18.5 | ·· 17.4 |
| E 10 | 351 43.1 | 345 24.7 | 04.3 | 248 08.1 | 51.9 | 319 25.4 | 00.2 | 233 20.9 | 17.4 |
| S 11 | 6 45.5 | 0 24.4 | 05.5 | 263 09.2 | 51.8 | 334 27.3 | 00.4 | 248 23.3 | 17.3 |
| D 12 | 21 48.0 | 15 24.0 | N 1 06.8 | 278 10.3 | N24 51.6 | 349 29.2 | N12 00.6 | 263 25.7 | N21 17.3 |
| A 13 | 36 50.5 | 30 23.6 | 08.0 | 293 11.4 | 51.5 | 4 31.1 | 00.8 | 278 28.1 | 17.3 |
| Y 14 | 51 52.9 | 45 23.3 | 09.2 | 308 12.4 | 51.3 | 19 32.9 | 01.0 | 293 30.5 | 17.3 |
| 15 | 66 55.4 | 60 22.9 | ·· 10.4 | 323 13.5 | ·· 51.2 | 34 34.8 | ·· 01.2 | 308 32.8 | ·· 17.3 |
| 16 | 81 57.9 | 75 22.6 | 11.6 | 338 14.6 | 51.0 | 49 36.7 | 01.4 | 323 35.2 | 17.3 |
| 17 | 97 00.3 | 90 22.2 | 12.8 | 353 15.6 | 50.9 | 64 38.6 | 01.6 | 338 37.6 | 17.3 |
| 18 | 112 02.8 | 105 21.8 | N 1 14.1 | 8 16.7 | N24 50.7 | 79 40.5 | N12 01.8 | 353 40.0 | N21 17.3 |
| 19 | 127 05.3 | 120 21.5 | 15.3 | 23 17.8 | 50.6 | 94 42.4 | 02.0 | 8 42.4 | 17.2 |
| 20 | 142 07.7 | 135 21.1 | 16.5 | 38 18.9 | 50.4 | 109 44.3 | 02.2 | 23 44.8 | 17.2 |
| 21 | 157 10.2 | 150 20.7 | ·· 17.7 | 53 19.9 | ·· 50.3 | 124 46.2 | ·· 02.4 | 38 47.1 | ·· 17.2 |
| 22 | 172 12.6 | 165 20.4 | 18.9 | 68 21.0 | 50.1 | 139 48.1 | 02.6 | 53 49.5 | 17.2 |
| 23 | 187 15.1 | 180 20.0 | 20.1 | 83 22.1 | 50.0 | 154 50.0 | 02.8 | 68 51.9 | 17.2 |
| 14 00 | 202 17.6 | 195 19.7 | N 1 21.4 | 98 23.2 | N24 49.8 | 169 51.9 | N12 03.0 | 83 54.3 | N21 17.2 |
| 01 | 217 20.0 | 210 19.3 | 22.6 | 113 24.2 | 49.7 | 184 53.8 | 03.3 | 98 56.7 | 17.2 |
| 02 | 232 22.5 | 225 18.9 | 23.8 | 128 25.3 | 49.5 | 199 55.7 | 03.5 | 113 59.0 | 17.2 |
| 03 | 247 25.0 | 240 18.6 | ·· 25.0 | 143 26.4 | ·· 49.3 | 214 57.6 | ·· 03.7 | 129 01.4 | ·· 17.1 |
| 04 | 262 27.4 | 255 18.2 | 26.2 | 158 27.4 | 49.2 | 229 59.4 | 03.9 | 144 03.8 | 17.1 |
| 05 | 277 29.9 | 270 17.8 | 27.4 | 173 28.5 | 49.0 | 245 01.3 | 04.1 | 159 06.2 | 17.1 |
| 06 | 292 32.4 | 285 17.5 | N 1 28.7 | 188 29.6 | N24 48.9 | 260 03.2 | N12 04.3 | 174 08.6 | N21 17.1 |
| W 07 | 307 34.8 | 300 17.1 | 29.9 | 203 30.7 | 48.7 | 275 05.1 | 04.5 | 189 10.9 | 17.1 |
| E 08 | 322 37.3 | 315 16.7 | 31.1 | 218 31.7 | 48.6 | 290 07.0 | 04.7 | 204 13.3 | 17.1 |
| D 09 | 337 39.8 | 330 16.4 | ·· 32.3 | 233 32.8 | ·· 48.4 | 305 08.9 | ·· 04.9 | 219 15.7 | ·· 17.1 |
| N 10 | 352 42.2 | 345 16.0 | 33.5 | 248 33.9 | 48.3 | 320 10.8 | 05.1 | 234 18.1 | 17.1 |
| E 11 | 7 44.7 | 0 15.7 | 34.7 | 263 34.9 | 48.1 | 335 12.7 | 05.3 | 249 20.5 | 17.0 |
| S 12 | 22 47.1 | 15 15.3 | N 1 36.0 | 278 36.0 | N24 48.0 | 350 14.6 | N12 05.5 | 264 22.8 | N21 17.0 |
| D 13 | 37 49.6 | 30 14.9 | 37.2 | 293 37.1 | 47.8 | 5 16.5 | 05.7 | 279 25.2 | 17.0 |
| A 14 | 52 52.1 | 45 14.6 | 38.4 | 308 38.2 | 47.7 | 20 18.4 | 05.9 | 294 27.6 | 17.0 |
| Y 15 | 67 54.5 | 60 14.2 | ·· 39.6 | 323 39.2 | ·· 47.5 | 35 20.3 | ·· 06.1 | 309 30.0 | ·· 17.0 |
| 16 | 82 57.0 | 75 13.8 | 40.8 | 338 40.3 | 47.4 | 50 22.2 | 06.3 | 324 32.4 | 17.0 |
| 17 | 97 59.5 | 90 13.5 | 42.0 | 353 41.4 | 47.2 | 65 24.0 | 06.5 | 339 34.7 | 17.0 |
| 18 | 113 01.9 | 105 13.1 | N 1 43.3 | 8 42.4 | N24 47.0 | 80 25.9 | N12 06.7 | 354 37.1 | N21 16.9 |
| 19 | 128 04.4 | 120 12.7 | 44.5 | 23 43.5 | 46.9 | 95 27.8 | 06.9 | 9 39.5 | 16.9 |
| 20 | 143 06.9 | 135 12.4 | 45.7 | 38 44.6 | 46.7 | 110 29.7 | 07.1 | 24 41.9 | 16.9 |
| 21 | 158 09.3 | 150 12.0 | ·· 46.9 | 53 45.6 | ·· 46.6 | 125 31.6 | ·· 07.3 | 39 44.3 | ·· 16.9 |
| 22 | 173 11.8 | 165 11.7 | 48.1 | 68 46.7 | 46.4 | 140 33.5 | 07.5 | 54 46.6 | 16.9 |
| 23 | 188 14.3 | 180 11.3 | 49.3 | 83 47.8 | 46.3 | 155 35.4 | 07.7 | 69 49.0 | 16.9 |
| Mer. Pass. | h m 10 33.0 | v −0.4 | d 1.2 | v 1.1 | d 0.1 | v 1.9 | d 0.2 | v 2.4 | d 0.0 |

| STARS Name | S.H.A. | Dec. |
|---|---|---|
| | ° ′ | ° ′ |
| Acamar | 315 39.9 | S40 24.1 |
| Achernar | 335 48.1 | S57 21.4 |
| Acrux | 173 39.9 | S62 58.3 |
| Adhara | 255 34.5 | S28 56.7 |
| Aldebaran | 291 21.7 | N16 27.6 |
| Alioth | 166 44.6 | N56 05.2 |
| Alkaid | 153 20.4 | N49 25.8 |
| Al Na'ir | 28 19.0 | S47 04.4 |
| Alnilam | 276 14.9 | S 1 13.2 |
| Alphard | 218 23.4 | S 8 33.6 |
| Alphecca | 126 34.3 | N26 47.5 |
| Alpheratz | 358 12.7 | N28 57.5 |
| Altair | 62 35.5 | N 8 48.2 |
| Ankaa | 353 43.6 | S42 26.0 |
| Antares | 113 00.3 | S26 22.8 |
| Arcturus | 146 20.9 | N19 18.2 |
| Atria | 108 26.8 | S68 58.9 |
| Avior | 234 29.3 | S59 26.4 |
| Bellatrix | 279 02.1 | N 6 19.6 |
| Betelgeuse | 271 31.7 | N 7 24.0 |
| Canopus | 264 08.7 | S52 41.4 |
| Capella | 281 16.0 | N45 58.5 |
| Deneb | 49 50.6 | N45 11.5 |
| Denebola | 183 01.8 | N14 42.1 |
| Diphda | 349 24.2 | S18 07.0 |
| Dubhe | 194 25.3 | N61 52.8 |
| Elnath | 278 48.1 | N28 35.3 |
| Eltanin | 90 58.9 | N51 29.3 |
| Enif | 34 14.7 | N 9 45.9 |
| Fomalhaut | 15 55.0 | S29 44.8 |
| Gacrux | 172 31.5 | S56 59.0 |
| Gienah | 176 20.7 | S17 24.8 |
| Hadar | 149 26.9 | S60 15.6 |
| Hamal | 328 32.6 | N23 21.0 |
| Kaus Aust. | 84 20.7 | S34 23.7 |
| Kochab | 137 17.8 | N74 15.0 |
| Markab | 14 06.4 | N15 04.6 |
| Menkar | 314 44.6 | N 3 59.7 |
| Menkent | 148 40.1 | S36 15.3 |
| Miaplacidus | 221 45.2 | S69 37.6 |
| Mirfak | 309 20.8 | N49 46.7 |
| Nunki | 76 32.8 | S26 19.5 |
| Peacock | 54 03.2 | S56 48.4 |
| Pollux | 244 01.8 | N28 05.0 |
| Procyon | 245 28.9 | N 5 17.0 |
| Rasalhague | 96 32.2 | N12 34.5 |
| Regulus | 208 13.0 | N12 04.8 |
| Rigel | 281 39.1 | S 8 13.9 |
| Rigil Kent. | 140 29.2 | S60 44.2 |
| Sabik | 102 44.4 | S15 41.8 |
| Schedar | 350 12.9 | N56 24.4 |
| Shaula | 96 59.6 | S37 05.1 |
| Sirius | 258 58.4 | S16 41.3 |
| Spica | 159 00.4 | S11 02.4 |
| Suhail | 223 12.8 | S43 20.6 |
| Vega | 80 57.7 | N38 45.5 |
| Zuben'ubi | 137 36.0 | S15 56.7 |

| | S.H.A. | Mer. Pass. |
|---|---|---|
| | ° ′ | h m |
| Venus | 354 09.9 | 10 58 |
| Mars | 256 38.9 | 17 27 |
| Jupiter | 327 48.0 | 12 42 |
| Saturn | 241 38.6 | 18 25 |

1976 APRIL 12, 13, 14 (MON., TUES., WED.)

| G.M.T. | SUN G.H.A. | SUN Dec. | MOON G.H.A. | v | Dec. | d | H.P. |
|---|---|---|---|---|---|---|---|
| d h | ° ′ | ° ′ | ° ′ | ′ | ° ′ | ′ | ′ |
| 12 00 | 179 47.0 | N 8 39.0 | 34 01.7 | 8.6 | N 1 09.0 | 12.6 | 60.6 |
| 01 | 194 47.1 | 39.9 | 48 29.3 | 8.5 | 0 56.4 | 12.6 | 60.6 |
| 02 | 209 47.3 | 40.8 | 62 56.8 | 8.4 | 0 43.8 | 12.6 | 60.7 |
| 03 | 224 47.5 | ·· 41.7 | 77 24.2 | 8.5 | 0 31.2 | 12.7 | 60.7 |
| 04 | 239 47.6 | 42.6 | 91 51.7 | 8.4 | 0 18.5 | 12.7 | 60.7 |
| 05 | 254 47.8 | 43.5 | 106 19.1 | 8.3 | N 0 05.8 | 12.6 | 60.7 |
| 06 | 269 48.0 | N 8 44.5 | 120 46.4 | 8.4 | S 0 06.8 | 12.7 | 60.8 |
| 07 | 284 48.1 | 45.4 | 135 13.8 | 8.3 | 0 19.5 | 12.7 | 60.8 |
| 08 | 299 48.3 | 46.3 | 149 41.1 | 8.3 | 0 32.2 | 12.8 | 60.8 |
| M 09 | 314 48.4 | ·· 47.2 | 164 08.4 | 8.2 | 0 45.0 | 12.7 | 60.8 |
| O 10 | 329 48.6 | 48.1 | 178 35.6 | 8.2 | 0 57.7 | 12.7 | 60.9 |
| N 11 | 344 48.8 | 49.0 | 193 02.8 | 8.2 | 1 10.4 | 12.7 | 60.9 |
| D 12 | 359 48.9 | N 8 49.9 | 207 30.0 | 8.1 | S 1 23.1 | 12.8 | 60.9 |
| A 13 | 14 49.1 | 50.8 | 221 57.1 | 8.1 | 1 35.9 | 12.7 | 60.9 |
| Y 14 | 29 49.3 | 51.7 | 236 24.2 | 8.1 | 1 48.6 | 12.7 | 61.0 |
| 15 | 44 49.4 | ·· 52.7 | 250 51.3 | 8.0 | 2 01.3 | 12.7 | 61.0 |
| 16 | 59 49.6 | 53.6 | 265 18.3 | 8.0 | 2 14.0 | 12.7 | 61.0 |
| 17 | 74 49.7 | 54.5 | 279 45.3 | 7.9 | 2 26.7 | 12.8 | 61.0 |
| 18 | 89 49.9 | N 8 55.4 | 294 12.2 | 8.0 | S 2 39.5 | 12.7 | 61.0 |
| 19 | 104 50.1 | 56.3 | 308 39.2 | 7.8 | 2 52.2 | 12.7 | 61.1 |
| 20 | 119 50.2 | 57.2 | 323 06.0 | 7.9 | 3 04.9 | 12.6 | 61.1 |
| 21 | 134 50.4 | ·· 58.1 | 337 32.9 | 7.8 | 3 17.5 | 12.7 | 61.1 |
| 22 | 149 50.5 | 59.0 | 351 59.7 | 7.7 | 3 30.2 | 12.7 | 61.1 |
| 23 | 164 50.7 | 8 59.9 | 6 26.4 | 7.7 | 3 42.9 | 12.6 | 61.1 |
| 13 00 | 179 50.9 | N 9 00.8 | 20 53.1 | 7.7 | S 3 55.5 | 12.6 | 61.2 |
| 01 | 194 51.0 | 01.7 | 35 19.8 | 7.6 | 4 08.1 | 12.6 | 61.2 |
| 02 | 209 51.2 | 02.6 | 49 46.4 | 7.6 | 4 20.7 | 12.6 | 61.2 |
| 03 | 224 51.3 | ·· 03.5 | 64 13.0 | 7.6 | 4 33.3 | 12.6 | 61.2 |
| 04 | 239 51.5 | 04.4 | 78 39.6 | 7.5 | 4 45.9 | 12.5 | 61.2 |
| 05 | 254 51.7 | 05.4 | 93 06.1 | 7.5 | 4 58.4 | 12.5 | 61.2 |
| 06 | 269 51.8 | N 9 06.3 | 107 32.6 | 7.4 | S 5 10.9 | 12.5 | 61.3 |
| 07 | 284 52.0 | 07.2 | 121 59.0 | 7.4 | 5 23.4 | 12.5 | 61.3 |
| T 08 | 299 52.1 | 08.1 | 136 25.4 | 7.3 | 5 35.9 | 12.4 | 61.3 |
| U 09 | 314 52.3 | ·· 09.0 | 150 51.7 | 7.3 | 5 48.3 | 12.4 | 61.3 |
| E 10 | 329 52.5 | 09.9 | 165 18.0 | 7.3 | 6 00.7 | 12.3 | 61.3 |
| S 11 | 344 52.6 | 10.8 | 179 44.3 | 7.2 | 6 13.0 | 12.3 | 61.3 |
| D 12 | 359 52.8 | N 9 11.7 | 194 10.5 | 7.1 | S 6 25.3 | 12.3 | 61.3 |
| A 13 | 14 52.9 | 12.6 | 208 36.6 | 7.2 | 6 37.6 | 12.3 | 61.3 |
| Y 14 | 29 53.1 | 13.5 | 223 02.8 | 7.0 | 6 49.9 | 12.2 | 61.3 |
| 15 | 44 53.3 | ·· 14.4 | 237 28.8 | 7.1 | 7 02.1 | 12.1 | 61.4 |
| 16 | 59 53.4 | 15.3 | 251 54.9 | 7.0 | 7 14.2 | 12.1 | 61.4 |
| 17 | 74 53.6 | 16.2 | 266 20.9 | 6.9 | 7 26.3 | 12.1 | 61.4 |
| 18 | 89 53.7 | N 9 17.1 | 280 46.8 | 6.9 | S 7 38.4 | 12.0 | 61.4 |
| 19 | 104 53.9 | 18.0 | 295 12.7 | 6.9 | 7 50.4 | 12.0 | 61.4 |
| 20 | 119 54.1 | 18.9 | 309 38.6 | 6.8 | 8 02.4 | 11.9 | 61.4 |
| 21 | 134 54.2 | ·· 19.8 | 324 04.4 | 6.8 | 8 14.3 | 11.9 | 61.4 |
| 22 | 149 54.4 | 20.7 | 338 30.2 | 6.7 | 8 26.2 | 11.8 | 61.4 |
| 23 | 164 54.5 | 21.6 | 352 55.9 | 6.7 | 8 38.0 | 11.7 | 61.4 |
| 14 00 | 179 54.7 | N 9 22.5 | 7 21.6 | 6.6 | S 8 49.7 | 11.7 | 61.4 |
| 01 | 194 54.8 | 23.4 | 21 47.2 | 6.6 | 9 01.4 | 11.7 | 61.4 |
| 02 | 209 55.0 | 24.3 | 36 12.8 | 6.6 | 9 13.1 | 11.5 | 61.4 |
| 03 | 224 55.2 | ·· 25.2 | 50 38.4 | 6.5 | 9 24.6 | 11.5 | 61.4 |
| 04 | 239 55.3 | 26.1 | 65 03.9 | 6.4 | 9 36.1 | 11.5 | 61.4 |
| 05 | 254 55.5 | 27.0 | 79 29.3 | 6.4 | 9 47.6 | 11.4 | 61.4 |
| 06 | 269 55.6 | N 9 27.9 | 93 54.7 | 6.4 | S 9 59.0 | 11.3 | 61.4 |
| W 07 | 284 55.8 | 28.8 | 108 20.1 | 6.3 | 10 10.3 | 11.2 | 61.4 |
| E 08 | 299 55.9 | 29.7 | 122 45.4 | 6.3 | 10 21.5 | 11.2 | 61.4 |
| D 09 | 314 56.1 | ·· 30.6 | 137 10.7 | 6.2 | 10 32.7 | 11.1 | 61.4 |
| N 10 | 329 56.2 | 31.5 | 151 35.9 | 6.2 | 10 43.8 | 11.0 | 61.4 |
| E 11 | 344 56.4 | 32.4 | 166 01.1 | 6.2 | 10 54.8 | 11.0 | 61.4 |
| S 12 | 359 56.6 | N 9 33.3 | 180 26.3 | 6.1 | S11 05.8 | 10.8 | 61.4 |
| D 13 | 14 56.7 | 34.2 | 194 51.4 | 6.1 | 11 16.6 | 10.8 | 61.4 |
| A 14 | 29 56.9 | 35.1 | 209 16.5 | 6.0 | 11 27.4 | 10.7 | 61.4 |
| Y 15 | 44 57.0 | ·· 36.0 | 223 41.5 | 6.0 | 11 38.1 | 10.6 | 61.4 |
| 16 | 59 57.2 | 36.9 | 238 06.5 | 5.9 | 11 48.7 | 10.6 | 61.4 |
| 17 | 74 57.3 | 37.8 | 252 31.4 | 5.9 | 11 59.3 | 10.4 | 61.4 |
| 18 | 89 57.5 | N 9 38.7 | 266 56.3 | 5.9 | S12 09.7 | 10.4 | 61.4 |
| 19 | 104 57.6 | 39.6 | 281 21.2 | 5.8 | 12 20.1 | 10.3 | 61.4 |
| 20 | 119 57.8 | 40.5 | 295 46.0 | 5.8 | 12 30.4 | 10.2 | 61.4 |
| 21 | 134 58.0 | ·· 41.4 | 310 10.8 | 5.7 | 12 40.6 | 10.1 | 61.4 |
| 22 | 149 58.1 | 42.2 | 324 35.5 | 5.7 | 12 50.7 | 10.0 | 61.4 |
| 23 | 164 58.3 | 43.1 | 339 00.2 | 5.7 | 13 00.7 | 9.9 | 61.4 |
| | S.D. 16.0 | d 0.9 | S.D. 16.6 | | 16.7 | | 16.7 |

| Lat. | Twilight Naut. | Twilight Civil | Sunrise | Moonrise 12 | Moonrise 13 | Moonrise 14 | Moonrise 15 |
|---|---|---|---|---|---|---|---|
| ° | h m | h m | h m | h m | h m | h m | h m |
| N 72 | //// | 02 16 | 03 51 | 16 53 | 19 02 | 21 20 | 23 56 |
| N 70 | //// | 02 48 | 04 06 | 16 49 | 18 49 | 20 54 | 23 03 |
| 68 | 01 11 | 03 11 | 04 18 | 16 46 | 18 39 | 20 35 | 22 30 |
| 66 | 01 57 | 03 28 | 04 28 | 16 44 | 18 31 | 20 20 | 22 07 |
| 64 | 02 26 | 03 42 | 04 36 | 16 41 | 18 24 | 20 07 | 21 48 |
| 62 | 02 47 | 03 54 | 04 43 | 16 40 | 18 18 | 19 57 | 21 33 |
| 60 | 03 04 | 04 04 | 04 49 | 16 38 | 18 13 | 19 48 | 21 20 |
| N 58 | 03 18 | 04 12 | 04 55 | 16 37 | 18 08 | 19 40 | 21 10 |
| 56 | 03 30 | 04 20 | 05 00 | 16 35 | 18 04 | 19 34 | 21 00 |
| 54 | 03 40 | 04 26 | 05 04 | 16 34 | 18 01 | 19 27 | 20 52 |
| 52 | 03 48 | 04 32 | 05 08 | 16 33 | 17 57 | 19 22 | 20 44 |
| 50 | 03 56 | 04 38 | 05 11 | 16 32 | 17 54 | 19 17 | 20 38 |
| 45 | 04 12 | 04 49 | 05 19 | 16 30 | 17 48 | 19 06 | 20 23 |
| N 40 | 04 24 | 04 57 | 05 25 | 16 29 | 17 43 | 18 58 | 20 12 |
| 35 | 04 34 | 05 05 | 05 31 | 16 27 | 17 38 | 18 50 | 20 02 |
| 30 | 04 42 | 05 11 | 05 35 | 16 26 | 17 34 | 18 44 | 19 53 |
| 20 | 04 55 | 05 21 | 05 44 | 16 24 | 17 27 | 18 32 | 19 38 |
| N 10 | 05 05 | 05 29 | 05 51 | 16 22 | 17 21 | 18 23 | 19 25 |
| 0 | 05 12 | 05 36 | 05 57 | 16 20 | 17 16 | 18 13 | 19 13 |
| S 10 | 05 18 | 05 42 | 06 04 | 16 19 | 17 10 | 18 04 | 19 01 |
| 20 | 05 22 | 05 48 | 06 10 | 16 17 | 17 05 | 17 55 | 18 48 |
| 30 | 05 26 | 05 54 | 06 18 | 16 15 | 16 58 | 17 44 | 18 33 |
| 35 | 05 27 | 05 57 | 06 22 | 16 14 | 16 54 | 17 38 | 18 25 |
| 40 | 05 28 | 06 00 | 06 27 | 16 12 | 16 50 | 17 31 | 18 15 |
| 45 | 05 29 | 06 03 | 06 33 | 16 11 | 16 45 | 17 23 | 18 04 |
| S 50 | 05 29 | 06 06 | 06 39 | 16 09 | 16 39 | 17 13 | 17 51 |
| 52 | 05 29 | 06 08 | 06 42 | 16 09 | 16 37 | 17 08 | 17 45 |
| 54 | 05 29 | 06 10 | 06 46 | 16 08 | 16 34 | 17 03 | 17 38 |
| 56 | 05 28 | 06 12 | 06 49 | 16 07 | 16 31 | 16 58 | 17 30 |
| 58 | 05 28 | 06 13 | 06 53 | 16 06 | 16 27 | 16 52 | 17 22 |
| S 60 | 05 27 | 06 15 | 06 58 | 16 05 | 16 23 | 16 45 | 17 12 |

| Lat. | Sunset | Twilight Civil | Twilight Naut. | Moonset 12 | Moonset 13 | Moonset 14 | Moonset 15 |
|---|---|---|---|---|---|---|---|
| ° | h m | h m | h m | h m | h m | h m | h m |
| N 72 | 20 14 | 21 52 | //// | 03 54 | 03 44 | 03 32 | 03 16 |
| N 70 | 19 58 | 21 18 | //// | 03 54 | 03 50 | 03 47 | 03 43 |
| 68 | 19 46 | 20 54 | 23 03 | 03 54 | 03 56 | 03 59 | 04 03 |
| 66 | 19 36 | 20 36 | 22 10 | 03 54 | 04 00 | 04 09 | 04 20 |
| 64 | 19 27 | 20 21 | 21 40 | 03 54 | 04 04 | 04 17 | 04 33 |
| 62 | 19 20 | 20 09 | 21 17 | 03 53 | 04 08 | 04 24 | 04 44 |
| 60 | 19 13 | 19 59 | 21 00 | 03 53 | 04 11 | 04 31 | 04 54 |
| N 58 | 19 08 | 19 50 | 20 46 | 03 53 | 04 14 | 04 36 | 05 03 |
| 56 | 19 03 | 19 43 | 20 34 | 03 53 | 04 16 | 04 41 | 05 10 |
| 54 | 18 58 | 19 36 | 20 23 | 03 53 | 04 18 | 04 46 | 05 17 |
| 52 | 18 54 | 19 30 | 20 14 | 03 53 | 04 20 | 04 50 | 05 23 |
| 50 | 18 51 | 19 25 | 20 06 | 03 53 | 04 22 | 04 53 | 05 29 |
| 45 | 18 43 | 19 13 | 19 50 | 03 53 | 04 26 | 05 01 | 05 41 |
| N 40 | 18 36 | 19 05 | 19 38 | 03 53 | 04 29 | 05 08 | 05 50 |
| 35 | 18 31 | 18 57 | 19 28 | 03 52 | 04 32 | 05 14 | 05 59 |
| 30 | 18 26 | 18 50 | 19 19 | 03 52 | 04 35 | 05 19 | 06 06 |
| 20 | 18 18 | 18 40 | 19 06 | 03 52 | 04 39 | 05 28 | 06 19 |
| N 10 | 18 10 | 18 32 | 18 57 | 03 52 | 04 43 | 05 36 | 06 31 |
| 0 | 18 04 | 18 25 | 18 49 | 03 52 | 04 46 | 05 43 | 06 41 |
| S 10 | 17 57 | 18 19 | 18 43 | 03 51 | 04 50 | 05 50 | 06 52 |
| 20 | 17 51 | 18 13 | 18 38 | 03 51 | 04 54 | 05 58 | 07 04 |
| 30 | 17 43 | 18 07 | 18 35 | 03 51 | 04 58 | 06 07 | 07 17 |
| 35 | 17 38 | 18 04 | 18 33 | 03 50 | 05 01 | 06 12 | 07 24 |
| 40 | 17 33 | 18 01 | 18 32 | 03 50 | 05 04 | 06 18 | 07 33 |
| 45 | 17 28 | 17 57 | 18 31 | 03 50 | 05 07 | 06 25 | 07 43 |
| S 50 | 17 21 | 17 54 | 18 31 | 03 49 | 05 11 | 06 33 | 07 55 |
| 52 | 17 18 | 17 52 | 18 31 | 03 49 | 05 13 | 06 37 | 08 01 |
| 54 | 17 14 | 17 50 | 18 31 | 03 49 | 05 15 | 06 41 | 08 07 |
| 56 | 17 11 | 17 48 | 18 32 | 03 49 | 05 17 | 06 46 | 08 14 |
| 58 | 17 07 | 17 47 | 18 32 | 03 49 | 05 19 | 06 51 | 08 22 |
| S 60 | 17 02 | 17 44 | 18 32 | 03 48 | 05 22 | 06 57 | 08 31 |

| Day | SUN Eqn. of Time 00h | SUN Eqn. of Time 12h | SUN Mer. Pass. | MOON Mer. Pass. Upper | MOON Mer. Pass. Lower | MOON Age | MOON Phase |
|---|---|---|---|---|---|---|---|
| | m s | m s | h m | h m | h m | d | |
| 12 | 00 52 | 00 45 | 12 01 | 22 33 | 10 06 | 13 | ○ |
| 13 | 00 37 | 00 29 | 12 00 | 23 29 | 11 01 | 14 | |
| 14 | 00 22 | 00 14 | 12 00 | 24 27 | 11 58 | 15 | |

| G.M.T. | ARIES G.H.A. | VENUS −3.3 G.H.A. | VENUS Dec. | MARS +1.3 G.H.A. | MARS Dec. | JUPITER −1.6 G.H.A. | JUPITER Dec. | SATURN +0.3 G.H.A. | SATURN Dec. |
|---|---|---|---|---|---|---|---|---|---|
| d h | ° ′ | ° ′ | ° ′ | ° ′ | ° ′ | ° ′ | ° ′ | ° ′ | ° ′ |
| 15 00 | 203 16.7 | 195 10.9 | N 1 50.6 | 98 48.9 | N24 46.1 | 170 37.3 | N12 07.9 | 84 51.4 | N21 16.9 |
| 01 | 218 19.2 | 210 10.6 | 51.8 | 113 49.9 | 46.0 | 185 39.2 | 08.1 | 99 53.8 | 16.9 |
| 02 | 233 21.6 | 225 10.2 | 53.0 | 128 51.0 | 45.8 | 200 41.1 | 08.3 | 114 56.1 | 16.8 |
| 03 | 248 24.1 | 240 09.8 | ·· 54.2 | 143 52.1 | ·· 45.6 | 215 43.0 | ·· 08.5 | 129 58.5 | ·· 16.8 |
| 04 | 263 26.6 | 255 09.5 | 55.4 | 158 53.1 | 45.5 | 230 44.9 | 08.7 | 145 00.9 | 16.8 |
| 05 | 278 29.0 | 270 09.1 | 56.6 | 173 54.2 | 45.3 | 245 46.7 | 08.9 | 160 03.3 | 16.8 |
| 06 | 293 31.5 | 285 08.7 | N 1 57.9 | 188 55.3 | N24 45.2 | 260 48.6 | N12 09.1 | 175 05.6 | N21 16.8 |
| T 07 | 308 34.0 | 300 08.4 | 1 59.1 | 203 56.3 | 45.0 | 275 50.5 | 09.3 | 190 08.0 | 16.8 |
| H 08 | 323 36.4 | 315 08.0 | 2 00.3 | 218 57.4 | 44.9 | 290 52.4 | 09.5 | 205 10.4 | 16.8 |
| U 09 | 338 38.9 | 330 07.6 | ·· 01.5 | 233 58.5 | ·· 44.7 | 305 54.3 | ·· 09.7 | 220 12.8 | ·· 16.7 |
| R 10 | 353 41.4 | 345 07.3 | 02.7 | 248 59.5 | 44.5 | 320 56.2 | 09.9 | 235 15.1 | 16.7 |
| S 11 | 8 43.8 | 0 06.9 | 03.9 | 264 00.6 | 44.4 | 335 58.1 | 10.1 | 250 17.5 | 16.7 |
| D 12 | 23 46.3 | 15 06.5 | N 2 05.2 | 279 01.7 | N24 44.2 | 351 00.0 | N12 10.3 | 265 19.9 | N21 16.7 |
| A 13 | 38 48.7 | 30 06.2 | 06.4 | 294 02.7 | 44.1 | 6 01.9 | 10.5 | 280 22.3 | 16.7 |
| Y 14 | 53 51.2 | 45 05.8 | 07.6 | 309 03.8 | 43.9 | 21 03.8 | 10.7 | 295 24.6 | 16.7 |
| 15 | 68 53.7 | 60 05.5 | ·· 08.8 | 324 04.9 | ·· 43.7 | 36 05.7 | ·· 10.9 | 310 27.0 | ·· 16.7 |
| 16 | 83 56.1 | 75 05.1 | 10.0 | 339 05.9 | 43.6 | 51 07.5 | 11.1 | 325 29.4 | 16.6 |
| 17 | 98 58.6 | 90 04.7 | 11.2 | 354 07.0 | 43.4 | 66 09.4 | 11.3 | 340 31.8 | 16.6 |
| 18 | 114 01.1 | 105 04.4 | N 2 12.4 | 9 08.1 | N24 43.3 | 81 11.3 | N12 11.5 | 355 34.1 | N21 16.6 |
| 19 | 129 03.5 | 120 04.0 | 13.7 | 24 09.1 | 43.1 | 96 13.2 | 11.7 | 10 36.5 | 16.6 |
| 20 | 144 06.0 | 135 03.6 | 14.9 | 39 10.2 | 42.9 | 111 15.1 | 11.9 | 25 38.9 | 16.6 |
| 21 | 159 08.5 | 150 03.3 | ·· 16.1 | 54 11.3 | ·· 42.8 | 126 17.0 | ·· 12.1 | 40 41.3 | ·· 16.6 |
| 22 | 174 10.9 | 165 02.9 | 17.3 | 69 12.3 | 42.6 | 141 18.9 | 12.4 | 55 43.6 | 16.6 |
| 23 | 189 13.4 | 180 02.5 | 18.5 | 84 13.4 | 42.5 | 156 20.8 | 12.6 | 70 46.0 | 16.5 |
| 16 00 | 204 15.9 | 195 02.2 | N 2 19.7 | 99 14.5 | N24 42.3 | 171 22.7 | N12 12.8 | 85 48.4 | N21 16.5 |
| 01 | 219 18.3 | 210 01.8 | 21.0 | 114 15.5 | 42.1 | 186 24.6 | 13.0 | 100 50.7 | 16.5 |
| 02 | 234 20.8 | 225 01.4 | 22.2 | 129 16.6 | 42.0 | 201 26.5 | 13.2 | 115 53.1 | 16.5 |
| 03 | 249 23.2 | 240 01.1 | ·· 23.4 | 144 17.6 | ·· 41.8 | 216 28.3 | ·· 13.4 | 130 55.5 | ·· 16.5 |
| 04 | 264 25.7 | 255 00.7 | 24.6 | 159 18.7 | 41.7 | 231 30.2 | 13.6 | 145 57.9 | 16.5 |
| 05 | 279 28.2 | 270 00.3 | 25.8 | 174 19.8 | 41.5 | 246 32.1 | 13.8 | 161 00.2 | 16.5 |
| 06 | 294 30.6 | 285 00.0 | N 2 27.0 | 189 20.8 | N24 41.3 | 261 34.0 | N12 14.0 | 176 02.6 | N21 16.4 |
| 07 | 309 33.1 | 299 59.6 | 28.2 | 204 21.9 | 41.2 | 276 35.9 | 14.2 | 191 05.0 | 16.4 |
| 08 | 324 35.6 | 314 59.2 | 29.5 | 219 23.0 | 41.0 | 291 37.8 | 14.4 | 206 07.3 | 16.4 |
| F 09 | 339 38.0 | 329 58.9 | ·· 30.7 | 234 24.0 | ·· 40.8 | 306 39.7 | ·· 14.6 | 221 09.7 | ·· 16.4 |
| R 10 | 354 40.5 | 344 58.5 | 31.9 | 249 25.1 | 40.7 | 321 41.6 | 14.8 | 236 12.1 | 16.4 |
| I 11 | 9 43.0 | 359 58.1 | 33.1 | 264 26.2 | 40.5 | 336 43.5 | 15.0 | 251 14.5 | 16.4 |
| D 12 | 24 45.4 | 14 57.8 | N 2 34.3 | 279 27.2 | N24 40.3 | 351 45.4 | N12 15.2 | 266 16.8 | N21 16.3 |
| A 13 | 39 47.9 | 29 57.4 | 35.5 | 294 28.3 | 40.2 | 6 47.3 | 15.4 | 281 19.2 | 16.3 |
| Y 14 | 54 50.4 | 44 57.0 | 36.7 | 309 29.3 | 40.0 | 21 49.1 | 15.6 | 296 21.6 | 16.3 |
| 15 | 69 52.8 | 59 56.7 | ·· 38.0 | 324 30.4 | ·· 39.9 | 36 51.0 | ·· 15.8 | 311 23.9 | ·· 16.3 |
| 16 | 84 55.3 | 74 56.3 | 39.2 | 339 31.5 | 39.7 | 51 52.9 | 16.0 | 326 26.3 | 16.3 |
| 17 | 99 57.7 | 89 55.9 | 40.4 | 354 32.5 | 39.5 | 66 54.8 | 16.2 | 341 28.7 | 16.3 |
| 18 | 115 00.2 | 104 55.6 | N 2 41.6 | 9 33.6 | N24 39.4 | 81 56.7 | N12 16.4 | 356 31.0 | N21 16.3 |
| 19 | 130 02.7 | 119 55.2 | 42.8 | 24 34.7 | 39.2 | 96 58.6 | 16.6 | 11 33.4 | 16.3 |
| 20 | 145 05.1 | 134 54.8 | 44.0 | 39 35.7 | 39.0 | 112 00.5 | 16.8 | 26 35.8 | 16.2 |
| 21 | 160 07.6 | 149 54.5 | ·· 45.2 | 54 36.8 | ·· 38.9 | 127 02.4 | ·· 17.0 | 41 38.1 | ·· 16.2 |
| 22 | 175 10.1 | 164 54.1 | 46.5 | 69 37.8 | 38.7 | 142 04.3 | 17.2 | 56 40.5 | 16.2 |
| 23 | 190 12.5 | 179 53.7 | 47.7 | 84 38.9 | 38.5 | 157 06.2 | 17.4 | 71 42.9 | 16.2 |
| 17 00 | 205 15.0 | 194 53.4 | N 2 48.9 | 99 40.0 | N24 38.4 | 172 08.0 | N12 17.6 | 86 45.3 | N21 16.2 |
| 01 | 220 17.5 | 209 53.0 | 50.1 | 114 41.0 | 38.2 | 187 09.9 | 17.8 | 101 47.6 | 16.2 |
| 02 | 235 19.9 | 224 52.6 | 51.3 | 129 42.1 | 38.0 | 202 11.8 | 18.0 | 116 50.0 | 16.1 |
| 03 | 250 22.4 | 239 52.3 | ·· 52.5 | 144 43.1 | ·· 37.9 | 217 13.7 | ·· 18.2 | 131 52.4 | ·· 16.1 |
| 04 | 265 24.8 | 254 51.9 | 53.7 | 159 44.2 | 37.7 | 232 15.6 | 18.4 | 146 54.7 | 16.1 |
| 05 | 280 27.3 | 269 51.5 | 55.0 | 174 45.3 | 37.5 | 247 17.5 | 18.6 | 161 57.1 | 16.1 |
| 06 | 295 29.8 | 284 51.2 | N 2 56.2 | 189 46.3 | N24 37.4 | 262 19.4 | N12 18.8 | 176 59.5 | N21 16.1 |
| S 07 | 310 32.2 | 299 50.8 | 57.4 | 204 47.4 | 37.2 | 277 21.3 | 19.0 | 192 01.8 | 16.1 |
| A 08 | 325 34.7 | 314 50.4 | 58.6 | 219 48.4 | 37.0 | 292 23.2 | 19.2 | 207 04.2 | 16.1 |
| T 09 | 340 37.2 | 329 50.1 | 2 59.8 | 234 49.5 | ·· 36.9 | 307 25.0 | ·· 19.4 | 222 06.6 | ·· 16.0 |
| U 10 | 355 39.6 | 344 49.7 | 3 01.0 | 249 50.6 | 36.7 | 322 26.9 | 19.6 | 237 08.9 | 16.0 |
| R 11 | 10 42.1 | 359 49.3 | 02.2 | 264 51.6 | 36.5 | 337 28.8 | 19.8 | 252 11.3 | 16.0 |
| D 12 | 25 44.6 | 14 49.0 | N 3 03.4 | 279 52.7 | N24 36.3 | 352 30.7 | N12 20.0 | 267 13.7 | N21 16.0 |
| A 13 | 40 47.0 | 29 48.6 | 04.7 | 294 53.7 | 36.2 | 7 32.6 | 20.2 | 282 16.0 | 16.0 |
| Y 14 | 55 49.5 | 44 48.2 | 05.9 | 309 54.8 | 36.0 | 22 34.5 | 20.4 | 297 18.4 | 16.0 |
| 15 | 70 52.0 | 59 47.9 | ·· 07.1 | 324 55.9 | ·· 35.8 | 37 36.4 | ·· 20.6 | 312 20.7 | ·· 15.9 |
| 16 | 85 54.4 | 74 47.5 | 08.3 | 339 56.9 | 35.7 | 52 38.3 | 20.8 | 327 23.1 | 15.9 |
| 17 | 100 56.9 | 89 47.1 | 09.5 | 354 58.0 | 35.5 | 67 40.2 | 21.0 | 342 25.5 | 15.9 |
| 18 | 115 59.3 | 104 46.8 | N 3 10.7 | 9 59.0 | N24 35.3 | 82 42.1 | N12 21.2 | 357 27.8 | N21 15.9 |
| 19 | 131 01.8 | 119 46.4 | 11.9 | 25 00.1 | 35.2 | 97 43.9 | 21.4 | 12 30.2 | 15.9 |
| 20 | 146 04.3 | 134 46.0 | 13.1 | 40 01.2 | 35.0 | 112 45.8 | 21.6 | 27 32.6 | 15.9 |
| 21 | 161 06.7 | 149 45.7 | ·· 14.4 | 55 02.2 | ·· 34.8 | 127 47.7 | ·· 21.8 | 42 34.9 | ·· 15.8 |
| 22 | 176 09.2 | 164 45.3 | 15.6 | 70 03.3 | 34.6 | 142 49.6 | 22.0 | 57 37.3 | 15.8 |
| 23 | 191 11.7 | 179 44.9 | 16.8 | 85 04.3 | 34.5 | 157 51.5 | 22.2 | 72 39.7 | 15.8 |
| Mer. Pass. | h m 10 21.2 | v −0.4 | d 1.2 | v 1.1 | d 0.2 | v 1.9 | d 0.2 | v 2.4 | d 0.0 |

STARS

| Name | S.H.A. | Dec. |
|---|---|---|
| | ° ′ | ° ′ |
| Acamar | 315 39.9 | S40 24.1 |
| Achernar | 335 48.1 | S57 21.4 |
| Acrux | 173 39.9 | S62 58.3 |
| Adhara | 255 34.5 | S28 56.7 |
| Aldebaran | 291 21.7 | N16 27.6 |
| Alioth | 166 44.6 | N56 05.3 |
| Alkaid | 153 20.4 | N49 25.8 |
| Al Na'ir | 28 19.0 | S47 04.4 |
| Alnilam | 276 14.9 | S 1 13.2 |
| Alphard | 218 23.4 | S 8 33.6 |
| Alphecca | 126 34.3 | N26 47.5 |
| Alpheratz | 358 12.7 | N28 57.5 |
| Altair | 62 35.4 | N 8 48.2 |
| Ankaa | 353 43.6 | S42 26.0 |
| Antares | 113 00.2 | S26 22.8 |
| Arcturus | 146 20.9 | N19 18.2 |
| Atria | 108 26.8 | S68 58.9 |
| Avior | 234 29.3 | S59 26.4 |
| Bellatrix | 279 02.2 | N 6 19.6 |
| Betelgeuse | 271 31.7 | N 7 24.0 |
| Canopus | 264 08.7 | S52 41.4 |
| Capella | 281 16.0 | N45 58.5 |
| Deneb | 49 50.6 | N45 11.5 |
| Denebola | 183 01.8 | N14 42.1 |
| Diphda | 349 24.2 | S18 07.0 |
| Dubhe | 194 25.3 | N61 52.8 |
| Elnath | 278 48.1 | N28 35.2 |
| Eltanin | 90 58.9 | N51 29.3 |
| Enif | 34 14.7 | N 9 45.9 |
| Fomalhaut | 15 55.0 | S29 44.8 |
| Gacrux | 172 31.5 | S56 59.1 |
| Gienah | 176 20.7 | S17 24.8 |
| Hadar | 149 26.9 | S60 15.6 |
| Hamal | 328 32.6 | N23 21.0 |
| Kaus Aust. | 84 20.7 | S34 23.7 |
| Kochab | 137 17.8 | N74 15.1 |
| Markab | 14 06.4 | N15 04.6 |
| Menkar | 314 44.6 | N 3 59.7 |
| Menkent | 148 40.1 | S36 15.3 |
| Miaplacidus | 221 45.2 | S69 37.6 |
| Mirfak | 309 20.8 | N49 46.7 |
| Nunki | 76 32.8 | S26 19.5 |
| Peacock | 54 03.2 | S56 48.4 |
| Pollux | 244 01.8 | N28 05.0 |
| Procyon | 245 28.9 | N 5 17.0 |
| Rasalhague | 96 32.2 | N12 34.5 |
| Regulus | 208 13.0 | N12 04.8 |
| Rigel | 281 39.1 | S 8 13.9 |
| Rigil Kent. | 140 29.2 | S60 44.2 |
| Sabik | 102 44.3 | S15 41.8 |
| Schedar | 350 12.9 | N56 24.4 |
| Shaula | 96 55.6 | S37 05.1 |
| Sirius | 258 58.4 | S16 41.3 |
| Spica | 159 00.4 | S11 02.4 |
| Suhail | 223 12.8 | S43 20.6 |
| Vega | 80 57.7 | N38 45.5 |
| Zuben'ubi | 137 36.0 | S15 56.7 |

| | S.H.A. | Mer. Pass. |
|---|---|---|
| | ° ′ | h m |
| Venus | 350 46.3 | 11 00 |
| Mars | 254 58.6 | 17 22 |
| Jupiter | 327 06.8 | 12 33 |
| Saturn | 241 32.5 | 18 14 |



| G.M.T. | SUN G.H.A. | SUN Dec. | MOON G.H.A. | v | Dec. | d | H.P. |
|---|---|---|---|---|---|---|---|
| d h | ° ′ | ° ′ | ° ′ | ′ | ° ′ | ′ | ′ |
| 18 00 | 180 09.1 | N10 47.6 | 310 20.2 | 5.6 | S19 49.2 | 0.7 | 59.4 |
| 01 | 195 09.2 | 48.5 | 324 44.8 | 5.7 | 19 49.9 | 0.5 | 59.4 |
| 02 | 210 09.3 | 49.4 | 339 09.5 | 5.7 | 19 50.4 | 0.4 | 59.3 |
| 03 | 225 09.5 | ·· 50.3 | 353 34.2 | 5.8 | 19 50.8 | 0.3 | 59.3 |
| 04 | 240 09.6 | 51.1 | 7 59.0 | 5.8 | 19 51.1 | 0.2 | 59.3 |
| 05 | 255 09.8 | 52.0 | 22 23.8 | 5.9 | 19 51.3 | 0.0 | 59.2 |
| 06 | 270 09.9 | N10 52.9 | 36 48.7 | 5.9 | S19 51.3 | 0.1 | 59.2 |
| 07 | 285 10.0 | 53.7 | 51 13.6 | 6.0 | 19 51.2 | 0.3 | 59.1 |
| 08 | 300 10.2 | 54.6 | 65 38.6 | 6.1 | 19 50.9 | 0.4 | 59.1 |
| S 09 | 315 10.3 | ·· 55.5 | 80 03.7 | 6.1 | 19 50.5 | 0.5 | 59.1 |
| U 10 | 330 10.5 | 56.4 | 94 28.8 | 6.1 | 19 50.0 | 0.6 | 59.0 |
| N 11 | 345 10.6 | 57.2 | 108 53.9 | 6.2 | 19 49.4 | 0.8 | 59.0 |
| D 12 | 0 10.7 | N10 58.1 | 123 19.1 | 6.3 | S19 48.6 | 0.8 | 58.9 |
| A 13 | 15 10.9 | 59.0 | 137 44.4 | 6.3 | 19 47.8 | 1.1 | 58.9 |
| Y 14 | 30 11.0 | 10 59.8 | 152 09.7 | 6.4 | 19 46.7 | 1.1 | 58.9 |
| 15 | 45 11.2 | 11 00.7 | 166 35.1 | 6.5 | 19 45.6 | 1.3 | 58.8 |
| 16 | 60 11.3 | 01.6 | 181 00.6 | 6.5 | 19 44.3 | 1.4 | 58.8 |
| 17 | 75 11.4 | 02.4 | 195 26.1 | 6.6 | 19 42.9 | 1.5 | 58.7 |
| 18 | 90 11.6 | N11 03.3 | 209 51.7 | 6.7 | S19 41.4 | 1.6 | 58.7 |
| 19 | 105 11.7 | 04.2 | 224 17.4 | 6.7 | 19 39.8 | 1.8 | 58.7 |
| 20 | 120 11.9 | 05.0 | 238 43.1 | 6.7 | 19 38.0 | 1.9 | 58.6 |
| 21 | 135 12.0 | ·· 05.9 | 253 08.8 | 6.9 | 19 36.1 | 2.0 | 58.6 |
| 22 | 150 12.1 | 06.8 | 267 34.7 | 6.9 | 19 34.1 | 2.1 | 58.5 |
| 23 | 165 12.3 | 07.6 | 282 00.6 | 7.0 | 19 32.0 | 2.2 | 58.5 |
| 19 00 | 180 12.4 | N11 08.5 | 296 26.6 | 7.1 | S19 29.8 | 2.4 | 58.5 |
| 01 | 195 12.5 | 09.4 | 310 52.7 | 7.1 | 19 27.4 | 2.5 | 58.4 |
| 02 | 210 12.7 | 10.2 | 325 18.8 | 7.2 | 19 24.9 | 2.6 | 58.4 |
| 03 | 225 12.8 | ·· 11.1 | 339 45.0 | 7.3 | 19 22.3 | 2.7 | 58.3 |
| 04 | 240 13.0 | 12.0 | 354 11.3 | 7.3 | 19 19.6 | 2.8 | 58.3 |
| 05 | 255 13.1 | 12.8 | 8 37.6 | 7.4 | 19 16.8 | 3.0 | 58.3 |
| 06 | 270 13.2 | N11 13.7 | 23 04.0 | 7.5 | S19 13.8 | 3.0 | 58.2 |
| 07 | 285 13.4 | 14.5 | 37 30.5 | 7.6 | 19 10.8 | 3.2 | 58.2 |
| 08 | 300 13.5 | 15.4 | 51 57.1 | 7.6 | 19 07.6 | 3.2 | 58.1 |
| M 09 | 315 13.6 | ·· 16.3 | 66 23.7 | 7.7 | 19 04.4 | 3.4 | 58.1 |
| O 10 | 330 13.8 | 17.1 | 80 50.4 | 7.8 | 19 01.0 | 3.5 | 58.1 |
| N 11 | 345 13.9 | 18.0 | 95 17.2 | 7.9 | 18 57.5 | 3.6 | 58.0 |
| D 12 | 0 14.0 | N11 18.9 | 109 44.1 | 7.9 | S18 53.9 | 3.7 | 58.0 |
| A 13 | 15 14.2 | 19.7 | 124 11.0 | 8.0 | 18 50.2 | 3.9 | 57.9 |
| Y 14 | 30 14.3 | 20.6 | 138 38.0 | 8.1 | 18 46.3 | 3.9 | 57.9 |
| 15 | 45 14.4 | ·· 21.4 | 153 05.1 | 8.2 | 18 42.4 | 4.0 | 57.9 |
| 16 | 60 14.6 | 22.3 | 167 32.3 | 8.3 | 18 38.4 | 4.1 | 57.8 |
| 17 | 75 14.7 | 23.2 | 181 59.6 | 8.3 | 18 34.3 | 4.3 | 57.8 |
| 18 | 90 14.8 | N11 24.0 | 196 26.9 | 8.4 | S18 30.0 | 4.3 | 57.7 |
| 19 | 105 15.0 | 24.9 | 210 54.3 | 8.5 | 18 25.7 | 4.5 | 57.7 |
| 20 | 120 15.1 | 25.7 | 225 21.8 | 8.6 | 18 21.2 | 4.5 | 57.7 |
| 21 | 135 15.2 | ·· 26.6 | 239 49.4 | 8.6 | 18 16.7 | 4.6 | 57.6 |
| 22 | 150 15.4 | 27.5 | 254 17.0 | 8.8 | 18 12.1 | 4.8 | 57.6 |
| 23 | 165 15.5 | 28.3 | 268 44.8 | 8.8 | 18 07.3 | 4.8 | 57.5 |
| 20 00 | 180 15.6 | N11 29.2 | 283 12.6 | 8.9 | S18 02.5 | 4.9 | 57.5 |
| 01 | 195 15.8 | 30.0 | 297 40.5 | 9.0 | 17 57.6 | 5.0 | 57.5 |
| 02 | 210 15.9 | 30.9 | 312 08.5 | 9.0 | 17 52.6 | 5.2 | 57.4 |
| 03 | 225 16.0 | ·· 31.7 | 326 36.5 | 9.1 | 17 47.4 | 5.2 | 57.4 |
| 04 | 240 16.2 | 32.6 | 341 04.6 | 9.3 | 17 42.2 | 5.3 | 57.3 |
| 05 | 255 16.3 | 33.5 | 355 32.9 | 9.3 | 17 36.9 | 5.4 | 57.3 |
| 06 | 270 16.4 | N11 34.3 | 10 01.2 | 9.3 | S17 31.5 | 5.4 | 57.3 |
| 07 | 285 16.6 | 35.2 | 24 29.5 | 9.5 | 17 26.1 | 5.6 | 57.2 |
| 08 | 300 16.7 | 36.0 | 38 58.0 | 9.5 | 17 20.5 | 5.7 | 57.2 |
| T 09 | 315 16.8 | ·· 36.9 | 53 26.5 | 9.6 | 17 14.8 | 5.7 | 57.2 |
| U 10 | 330 17.0 | 37.7 | 67 55.1 | 9.7 | 17 09.1 | 5.8 | 57.1 |
| E 11 | 345 17.1 | 38.6 | 82 23.8 | 9.8 | 17 03.3 | 6.0 | 57.1 |
| S 12 | 0 17.2 | N11 39.4 | 96 52.6 | 9.9 | S16 57.3 | 6.0 | 57.0 |
| D 13 | 15 17.4 | 40.3 | 111 21.5 | 9.9 | 16 51.3 | 6.0 | 57.0 |
| A 14 | 30 17.5 | 41.1 | 125 50.4 | 10.0 | 16 45.3 | 6.2 | 57.0 |
| Y 15 | 45 17.6 | ·· 42.0 | 140 19.4 | 10.1 | 16 39.1 | 6.2 | 56.9 |
| 16 | 60 17.7 | 42.9 | 154 48.5 | 10.2 | 16 32.9 | 6.4 | 56.9 |
| 17 | 75 17.9 | 43.7 | 169 17.7 | 10.3 | 16 26.5 | 6.4 | 56.9 |
| 18 | 90 18.0 | N11 44.6 | 183 47.0 | 10.3 | S16 20.1 | 6.5 | 56.8 |
| 19 | 105 18.1 | 45.4 | 198 16.3 | 10.4 | 16 13.6 | 6.5 | 56.8 |
| 20 | 120 18.3 | 46.3 | 212 45.7 | 10.5 | 16 07.1 | 6.6 | 56.8 |
| 21 | 135 18.4 | ·· 47.1 | 227 15.2 | 10.6 | 16 00.5 | 6.8 | 56.7 |
| 22 | 150 18.5 | 48.0 | 241 44.8 | 10.7 | 15 53.7 | 6.7 | 56.7 |
| 23 | 165 18.6 | 48.8 | 256 14.5 | 10.7 | 15 47.0 | 6.9 | 56.6 |
| | S.D. 15.9 | d 0.9 | S.D. 16.1 | | 15.8 | | 15.5 |

| Lat. | Twilight Naut. | Twilight Civil | Sunrise | Moonrise 18 | Moonrise 19 | Moonrise 20 | Moonrise 21 |
|---|---|---|---|---|---|---|---|
| ° | h m | h m | h m | h m | h m | h m | h m |
| N 72 | //// | 01 12 | 03 15 | ■ | ■ | 04 40 | 03 55 |
| N 70 | //// | 02 05 | 03 36 | ■ | 03 28 | 03 24 | 03 20 |
| 68 | //// | 02 37 | 03 52 | 01 39 | 02 26 | 02 46 | 02 56 |
| 66 | 01 02 | 03 00 | 04 05 | 01 00 | 01 50 | 02 19 | 02 36 |
| 64 | 01 49 | 03 18 | 04 15 | 00 33 | 01 25 | 01 59 | 02 21 |
| 62 | 02 18 | 03 32 | 04 24 | 00 12 | 01 05 | 01 42 | 02 08 |
| 60 | 02 39 | 03 44 | 04 32 | 24 49 | 00 49 | 01 28 | 01 56 |
| N 58 | 02 57 | 03 55 | 04 39 | 24 35 | 00 35 | 01 16 | 01 47 |
| 56 | 03 11 | 04 04 | 04 45 | 24 23 | 00 23 | 01 05 | 01 38 |
| 54 | 03 22 | 04 11 | 04 50 | 24 12 | 00 12 | 00 56 | 01 31 |
| 52 | 03 33 | 04 18 | 04 55 | 24 03 | 00 03 | 00 48 | 01 24 |
| 50 | 03 42 | 04 25 | 04 59 | 23 55 | 24 41 | 00 41 | 01 18 |
| 45 | 04 00 | 04 38 | 05 09 | 23 37 | 24 25 | 00 25 | 01 05 |
| N 40 | 04 14 | 04 48 | 05 16 | 23 23 | 24 12 | 00 12 | 00 54 |
| 35 | 04 26 | 04 57 | 05 23 | 23 11 | 24 01 | 00 01 | 00 44 |
| 30 | 04 35 | 05 04 | 05 29 | 23 00 | 23 51 | 24 36 | 00 36 |
| 20 | 04 50 | 05 16 | 05 39 | 22 42 | 23 34 | 24 22 | 00 22 |
| N 10 | 05 01 | 05 26 | 05 48 | 22 26 | 23 19 | 24 09 | 00 09 |
| 0 | 05 10 | 05 35 | 05 56 | 22 11 | 23 06 | 23 57 | 24 46 |
| S 10 | 05 18 | 05 42 | 06 04 | 21 56 | 22 52 | 23 46 | 24 37 |
| 20 | 05 24 | 05 50 | 06 12 | 21 40 | 22 37 | 23 33 | 24 27 |
| 30 | 05 29 | 05 57 | 06 21 | 21 21 | 22 21 | 23 19 | 24 15 |
| 35 | 05 31 | 06 01 | 06 27 | 21 11 | 22 11 | 23 10 | 24 09 |
| 40 | 05 34 | 06 05 | 06 33 | 20 59 | 22 00 | 23 01 | 24 01 |
| 45 | 05 36 | 06 10 | 06 40 | 20 44 | 21 46 | 22 50 | 23 53 |
| S 50 | 05 38 | 06 15 | 06 48 | 20 27 | 21 30 | 22 36 | 23 42 |
| 52 | 05 38 | 06 18 | 06 52 | 20 18 | 21 23 | 22 30 | 23 37 |
| 54 | 05 39 | 06 20 | 06 57 | 20 09 | 21 14 | 22 23 | 23 32 |
| 56 | 05 40 | 06 23 | 07 01 | 19 59 | 21 05 | 22 15 | 23 26 |
| 58 | 05 40 | 06 26 | 07 06 | 19 47 | 20 54 | 22 06 | 23 19 |
| S 60 | 05 41 | 06 29 | 07 12 | 19 33 | 20 42 | 21 56 | 23 11 |

| Lat. | Sunset | Twilight Civil | Twilight Naut. | Moonset 18 | Moonset 19 | Moonset 20 | Moonset 21 |
|---|---|---|---|---|---|---|---|
| ° | h m | h m | h m | h m | h m | h m | h m |
| N 72 | 20 47 | 23 01 | //// | ■ | ■ | 06 07 | 08 38 |
| N 70 | 20 26 | 22 00 | //// | ■ | 05 25 | 07 22 | 09 11 |
| 68 | 20 10 | 21 26 | //// | 05 14 | 06 27 | 07 59 | 09 35 |
| 66 | 19 56 | 21 02 | 23 09 | 05 53 | 07 02 | 08 26 | 09 53 |
| 64 | 19 45 | 20 43 | 22 15 | 06 20 | 07 27 | 08 46 | 10 08 |
| 62 | 19 36 | 20 28 | 21 44 | 06 41 | 07 47 | 09 02 | 10 21 |
| 60 | 19 28 | 20 16 | 21 22 | 06 59 | 08 03 | 09 16 | 10 31 |
| N 58 | 19 21 | 20 06 | 21 04 | 07 13 | 08 17 | 09 27 | 10 40 |
| 56 | 19 15 | 19 56 | 20 50 | 07 25 | 08 28 | 09 37 | 10 48 |
| 54 | 19 09 | 19 48 | 20 38 | 07 36 | 08 39 | 09 46 | 10 55 |
| 52 | 19 05 | 19 41 | 20 27 | 07 46 | 08 48 | 09 54 | 11 02 |
| 50 | 19 00 | 19 35 | 20 18 | 07 54 | 08 56 | 10 01 | 11 08 |
| 45 | 18 50 | 19 22 | 20 00 | 08 12 | 09 13 | 10 16 | 11 20 |
| N 40 | 18 42 | 19 11 | 19 45 | 08 27 | 09 27 | 10 29 | 11 30 |
| 35 | 18 36 | 19 02 | 19 33 | 08 40 | 09 39 | 10 39 | 11 39 |
| 30 | 18 30 | 18 54 | 19 24 | 08 51 | 09 50 | 10 49 | 11 46 |
| 20 | 18 20 | 18 42 | 19 09 | 09 09 | 10 07 | 11 04 | 11 59 |
| N 10 | 18 11 | 18 32 | 18 57 | 09 26 | 10 23 | 11 18 | 12 10 |
| 0 | 18 02 | 18 24 | 18 48 | 09 41 | 10 37 | 11 31 | 12 21 |
| S 10 | 17 54 | 18 16 | 18 40 | 09 56 | 10 52 | 11 44 | 12 32 |
| 20 | 17 46 | 18 08 | 18 34 | 10 12 | 11 07 | 11 57 | 12 43 |
| 30 | 17 36 | 18 01 | 18 29 | 10 31 | 11 25 | 12 13 | 12 55 |
| 35 | 17 31 | 17 57 | 18 26 | 10 41 | 11 35 | 12 22 | 13 03 |
| 40 | 17 25 | 17 52 | 18 24 | 10 54 | 11 47 | 12 32 | 13 11 |
| 45 | 17 18 | 17 47 | 18 22 | 11 08 | 12 00 | 12 44 | 13 21 |
| S 50 | 17 09 | 17 42 | 18 20 | 11 26 | 12 17 | 12 58 | 13 32 |
| 52 | 17 05 | 17 40 | 18 19 | 11 34 | 12 25 | 13 05 | 13 38 |
| 54 | 17 01 | 17 37 | 18 18 | 11 44 | 12 33 | 13 12 | 13 44 |
| 56 | 16 56 | 17 34 | 18 18 | 11 54 | 12 43 | 13 21 | 13 50 |
| 58 | 16 51 | 17 31 | 18 17 | 12 06 | 12 54 | 13 30 | 13 57 |
| S 60 | 16 45 | 17 28 | 18 16 | 12 20 | 13 07 | 13 41 | 14 06 |

| Day | SUN Eqn. of Time 00ʰ | SUN Eqn. of Time 12ʰ | SUN Mer. Pass. | MOON Mer. Pass. Upper | MOON Mer. Pass. Lower | MOON Age | MOON Phase |
|---|---|---|---|---|---|---|---|
| | m s | m s | h m | h m | h m | d | |
| 18 | 00 36 | 00 43 | 11 59 | 03 27 | 15 56 | 19 | |
| 19 | 00 49 | 00 56 | 11 59 | 04 24 | 16 52 | 20 | |
| 20 | 01 02 | 01 09 | 11 59 | 05 18 | 17 44 | 21 | |

# 1976 APRIL 21, 22, 23 (WED., THURS., FRI.)

| | G.M.T. | SUN G.H.A. | SUN Dec. | MOON G.H.A. | v | MOON Dec. | d | H.P. |
|---|---|---|---|---|---|---|---|---|
| | d h | ° ′ | ° ′ | ° ′ | ′ | ° ′ | ′ | ′ |
| | 21 00 | 180 18.8 | N11 49.7 | 270 44.2 | 10.8 | S15 40.1 | 6.9 | 56.6 |
| | 01 | 195 18.9 | 50.5 | 285 14.0 | 10.9 | 15 33.2 | 7.0 | 56.6 |
| | 02 | 210 19.0 | 51.4 | 299 43.9 | 11.0 | 15 26.2 | 7.1 | 56.5 |
| | 03 | 225 19.2 | · · 52.2 | 314 13.9 | 11.0 | 15 19.1 | 7.1 | 56.5 |
| | 04 | 240 19.3 | 53.1 | 328 43.9 | 11.1 | 15 12.0 | 7.3 | 56.5 |
| | 05 | 255 19.4 | 53.9 | 343 14.0 | 11.2 | 15 04.7 | 7.2 | 56.4 |
| | 06 | 270 19.5 | N11 54.8 | 357 44.2 | 11.3 | S14 57.5 | 7.4 | 56.4 |
| | 07 | 285 19.7 | 55.6 | 12 14.5 | 11.3 | 14 50.1 | 7.4 | 56.4 |
| W | 08 | 300 19.8 | 56.4 | 26 44.8 | 11.4 | 14 42.7 | 7.5 | 56.3 |
| E | 09 | 315 19.9 | · · 57.3 | 41 15.2 | 11.5 | 14 35.2 | 7.5 | 56.3 |
| D | 10 | 330 20.0 | 58.1 | 55 45.7 | 11.6 | 14 27.7 | 7.6 | 56.3 |
| N | 11 | 345 20.2 | 59.0 | 70 16.3 | 11.7 | 14 20.1 | 7.7 | 56.2 |
| E | 12 | 0 20.3 | N11 59.8 | 84 47.0 | 11.7 | S14 12.4 | 7.7 | 56.2 |
| S | 13 | 15 20.4 | 12 00.7 | 99 17.7 | 11.8 | 14 04.7 | 7.8 | 56.2 |
| D | 14 | 30 20.5 | 01.5 | 113 48.5 | 11.8 | 13 56.9 | 7.8 | 56.1 |
| A | 15 | 45 20.7 | · · 02.4 | 128 19.3 | 11.9 | 13 49.1 | 7.9 | 56.1 |
| Y | 16 | 60 20.8 | 03.2 | 142 50.2 | 12.0 | 13 41.2 | 8.0 | 56.1 |
| | 17 | 75 20.9 | 04.1 | 157 21.2 | 12.1 | 13 33.2 | 8.0 | 56.0 |
| | 18 | 90 21.0 | N12 04.9 | 171 52.3 | 12.1 | S13 25.2 | 8.0 | 56.0 |
| | 19 | 105 21.2 | 05.7 | 186 23.4 | 12.3 | 13 17.2 | 8.2 | 56.0 |
| | 20 | 120 21.3 | 06.6 | 200 54.7 | 12.2 | 13 09.0 | 8.1 | 55.9 |
| | 21 | 135 21.4 | · · 07.4 | 215 25.9 | 12.4 | 13 00.9 | 8.3 | 55.9 |
| | 22 | 150 21.5 | 08.3 | 229 57.3 | 12.4 | 12 52.6 | 8.3 | 55.9 |
| | 23 | 165 21.7 | 09.1 | 244 28.7 | 12.5 | 12 44.3 | 8.3 | 55.9 |
| | 22 00 | 180 21.8 | N12 10.0 | 259 00.2 | 12.5 | S12 36.0 | 8.4 | 55.8 |
| | 01 | 195 21.9 | 10.8 | 273 31.7 | 12.6 | 12 27.6 | 8.4 | 55.8 |
| | 02 | 210 22.0 | 11.6 | 288 03.3 | 12.7 | 12 19.2 | 8.5 | 55.8 |
| | 03 | 225 22.2 | · · 12.5 | 302 35.0 | 12.7 | 12 10.7 | 8.5 | 55.7 |
| | 04 | 240 22.3 | 13.3 | 317 06.7 | 12.8 | 12 02.2 | 8.6 | 55.7 |
| | 05 | 255 22.4 | 14.2 | 331 38.5 | 12.9 | 11 53.6 | 8.6 | 55.7 |
| | 06 | 270 22.5 | N12 15.0 | 346 10.4 | 12.9 | S11 45.0 | 8.7 | 55.7 |
| | 07 | 285 22.7 | 15.8 | 0 42.3 | 13.0 | 11 36.3 | 8.7 | 55.6 |
| T | 08 | 300 22.8 | 16.7 | 15 14.3 | 13.1 | 11 27.6 | 8.8 | 55.6 |
| H | 09 | 315 22.9 | · · 17.5 | 29 46.4 | 13.1 | 11 18.8 | 8.8 | 55.6 |
| U | 10 | 330 23.0 | 18.3 | 44 18.5 | 13.2 | 11 10.0 | 8.8 | 55.5 |
| R | 11 | 345 23.1 | 19.2 | 58 50.7 | 13.2 | 11 01.2 | 8.9 | 55.5 |
| S | 12 | 0 23.3 | N12 20.0 | 73 22.9 | 13.3 | S10 52.3 | 9.0 | 55.5 |
| D | 13 | 15 23.4 | 20.9 | 87 55.2 | 13.3 | 10 43.3 | 8.9 | 55.5 |
| A | 14 | 30 23.5 | 21.7 | 102 27.5 | 13.4 | 10 34.4 | 9.0 | 55.4 |
| Y | 15 | 45 23.6 | · · 22.5 | 116 59.9 | 13.5 | 10 25.4 | 9.1 | 55.4 |
| | 16 | 60 23.7 | 23.4 | 131 32.4 | 13.5 | 10 16.3 | 9.1 | 55.4 |
| | 17 | 75 23.9 | 24.2 | 146 04.9 | 13.6 | 10 07.2 | 9.1 | 55.4 |
| | 18 | 90 24.0 | N12 25.0 | 160 37.5 | 13.6 | S 9 58.1 | 9.1 | 55.3 |
| | 19 | 105 24.1 | 25.9 | 175 10.1 | 13.7 | 9 49.0 | 9.2 | 55.3 |
| | 20 | 120 24.2 | 26.7 | 189 42.8 | 13.7 | 9 39.8 | 9.3 | 55.3 |
| | 21 | 135 24.3 | · · 27.5 | 204 15.5 | 13.8 | 9 30.5 | 9.2 | 55.2 |
| | 22 | 150 24.5 | 28.4 | 218 48.3 | 13.9 | 9 21.3 | 9.3 | 55.2 |
| | 23 | 165 24.6 | 29.2 | 233 21.2 | 13.8 | 9 12.0 | 9.3 | 55.2 |
| | 23 00 | 180 24.7 | N12 30.0 | 247 54.0 | 14.0 | S 9 02.7 | 9.4 | 55.2 |
| | 01 | 195 24.8 | 30.9 | 262 27.0 | 14.0 | 8 53.3 | 9.4 | 55.2 |
| | 02 | 210 24.9 | 31.7 | 277 00.0 | 14.0 | 8 43.9 | 9.4 | 55.1 |
| | 03 | 225 25.0 | · · 32.5 | 291 33.0 | 14.1 | 8 34.5 | 9.5 | 55.1 |
| | 04 | 240 25.2 | 33.4 | 306 06.1 | 14.1 | 8 25.0 | 9.4 | 55.1 |
| | 05 | 255 25.3 | 34.2 | 320 39.2 | 14.2 | 8 15.6 | 9.5 | 55.1 |
| | 06 | 270 25.4 | N12 35.0 | 335 12.4 | 14.2 | S 8 06.1 | 9.6 | 55.0 |
| | 07 | 285 25.5 | 35.9 | 349 45.6 | 14.3 | 7 56.5 | 9.5 | 55.0 |
| | 08 | 300 25.6 | 36.7 | 4 18.9 | 14.3 | 7 47.0 | 9.6 | 55.0 |
| F | 09 | 315 25.8 | · · 37.5 | 18 52.2 | 14.3 | 7 37.4 | 9.6 | 55.0 |
| R | 10 | 330 25.9 | 38.4 | 33 25.5 | 14.4 | 7 27.8 | 9.7 | 54.9 |
| I | 11 | 345 26.0 | 39.2 | 47 58.9 | 14.4 | 7 18.1 | 9.6 | 54.9 |
| D | 12 | 0 26.1 | N12 40.0 | 62 32.3 | 14.5 | S 7 08.5 | 9.7 | 54.9 |
| A | 13 | 15 26.2 | 40.8 | 77 05.8 | 14.5 | 6 58.8 | 9.7 | 54.9 |
| Y | 14 | 30 26.3 | 41.7 | 91 39.3 | 14.6 | 6 49.1 | 9.8 | 54.9 |
| | 15 | 45 26.4 | · · 42.5 | 106 12.9 | 14.6 | 6 39.3 | 9.7 | 54.8 |
| | 16 | 60 26.6 | 43.3 | 120 46.5 | 14.6 | 6 29.6 | 9.8 | 54.8 |
| | 17 | 75 26.7 | 44.2 | 135 20.1 | 14.7 | 6 19.8 | 9.8 | 54.8 |
| | 18 | 90 26.8 | N12 45.0 | 149 53.8 | 14.7 | S 6 10.0 | 9.8 | 54.8 |
| | 19 | 105 26.9 | 45.8 | 164 27.5 | 14.7 | 6 00.2 | 9.8 | 54.8 |
| | 20 | 120 27.0 | 46.6 | 179 01.2 | 14.8 | 5 50.4 | 9.9 | 54.7 |
| | 21 | 135 27.1 | · · 47.5 | 193 35.0 | 14.8 | 5 40.5 | 9.8 | 54.7 |
| | 22 | 150 27.2 | 48.3 | 208 08.8 | 14.8 | 5 30.7 | 9.9 | 54.7 |
| | 23 | 165 27.4 | 49.1 | 222 42.6 | 14.9 | 5 20.8 | 9.9 | 54.7 |
| | | S.D. 15.9 | d 0.8 | S.D. 15.3 | | 15.1 | | 15.0 |

| Lat. | Twilight Naut. | Twilight Civil | Sunrise | Moonrise 21 | Moonrise 22 | Moonrise 23 | Moonrise 24 |
|---|---|---|---|---|---|---|---|
| ° | h m | h m | h m | h m | h m | h m | h m |
| N 72 | //// | //// | 02 57 | 03 55 | 03 38 | 03 26 | 03 16 |
| N 70 | //// | 01 39 | 03 20 | 03 20 | 03 17 | 03 13 | 03 09 |
| 68 | //// | 02 19 | 03 38 | 02 56 | 03 00 | 03 03 | 03 04 |
| 66 | //// | 02 45 | 03 53 | 02 36 | 02 47 | 02 54 | 03 00 |
| 64 | 01 27 | 03 05 | 04 05 | 02 21 | 02 36 | 02 47 | 02 56 |
| 62 | 02 02 | 03 21 | 04 15 | 02 08 | 02 26 | 02 40 | 02 52 |
| 60 | 02 26 | 03 35 | 04 23 | 01 56 | 02 18 | 02 35 | 02 49 |
| N 58 | 02 45 | 03 46 | 04 31 | 01 47 | 02 11 | 02 30 | 02 47 |
| 56 | 03 01 | 03 55 | 04 37 | 01 38 | 02 04 | 02 26 | 02 45 |
| 54 | 03 14 | 04 04 | 04 43 | 01 31 | 01 59 | 02 22 | 02 42 |
| 52 | 03 25 | 04 11 | 04 48 | 01 24 | 01 53 | 02 18 | 02 41 |
| 50 | 03 34 | 04 18 | 04 53 | 01 18 | 01 49 | 02 15 | 02 39 |
| 45 | 03 54 | 04 32 | 05 04 | 01 05 | 01 38 | 02 08 | 02 35 |
| N 40 | 04 09 | 04 44 | 05 12 | 00 54 | 01 30 | 02 02 | 02 32 |
| 35 | 04 21 | 04 53 | 05 19 | 00 44 | 01 23 | 01 57 | 02 29 |
| 30 | 04 32 | 05 01 | 05 26 | 00 36 | 01 16 | 01 53 | 02 27 |
| 20 | 04 48 | 05 14 | 05 37 | 00 22 | 01 05 | 01 45 | 02 22 |
| N 10 | 05 00 | 05 25 | 05 46 | 00 09 | 00 55 | 01 38 | 02 19 |
| 0 | 05 09 | 05 34 | 05 55 | 24 46 | 00 46 | 01 32 | 02 15 |
| S 10 | 05 18 | 05 42 | 06 04 | 24 37 | 00 37 | 01 25 | 02 12 |
| 20 | 05 25 | 05 50 | 06 13 | 24 27 | 00 27 | 01 18 | 02 08 |
| 30 | 05 31 | 05 59 | 06 23 | 24 15 | 00 15 | 01 10 | 02 04 |
| 35 | 05 34 | 06 03 | 06 29 | 24 09 | 00 09 | 01 06 | 02 01 |
| 40 | 05 36 | 06 08 | 06 36 | 24 01 | 00 01 | 01 01 | 01 58 |
| 45 | 05 39 | 06 14 | 06 44 | 23 53 | 24 55 | 00 55 | 01 55 |
| S 50 | 05 42 | 06 20 | 06 53 | 23 42 | 24 47 | 00 47 | 01 51 |
| 52 | 05 43 | 06 22 | 06 57 | 23 37 | 24 44 | 00 44 | 01 50 |
| 54 | 05 44 | 06 25 | 07 02 | 23 32 | 24 40 | 00 40 | 01 48 |
| 56 | 05 45 | 06 28 | 07 07 | 23 26 | 24 36 | 00 36 | 01 45 |
| 58 | 05 46 | 06 32 | 07 13 | 23 19 | 24 32 | 00 32 | 01 43 |
| S 60 | 05 47 | 06 36 | 07 19 | 23 11 | 24 27 | 00 27 | 01 40 |

| Lat. | Sunset | Twilight Civil | Twilight Naut. | Moonset 21 | Moonset 22 | Moonset 23 | Moonset 24 |
|---|---|---|---|---|---|---|---|
| ° | h m | h m | h m | h m | h m | h m | h m |
| N 72 | 21 05 | //// | //// | 08 38 | 10 34 | 12 19 | 13 58 |
| N 70 | 20 40 | 22 26 | //// | 09 11 | 10 53 | 12 30 | 14 03 |
| 68 | 20 22 | 21 44 | //// | 09 35 | 11 09 | 12 39 | 14 06 |
| 66 | 20 07 | 21 16 | //// | 09 53 | 11 21 | 12 46 | 14 09 |
| 64 | 19 55 | 20 55 | 22 38 | 10 08 | 11 31 | 12 52 | 14 11 |
| 62 | 19 44 | 20 38 | 22 00 | 10 21 | 11 40 | 12 57 | 14 13 |
| 60 | 19 35 | 20 25 | 21 34 | 10 31 | 11 47 | 13 02 | 14 15 |
| N 58 | 19 28 | 20 13 | 21 14 | 10 40 | 11 54 | 13 06 | 14 17 |
| 56 | 19 21 | 20 03 | 20 59 | 10 48 | 11 59 | 13 09 | 14 18 |
| 54 | 19 15 | 19 54 | 20 45 | 10 55 | 12 05 | 13 13 | 14 20 |
| 52 | 19 10 | 19 47 | 20 34 | 11 02 | 12 09 | 13 16 | 14 21 |
| 50 | 19 05 | 19 40 | 20 24 | 11 08 | 12 13 | 13 18 | 14 22 |
| 45 | 18 54 | 19 26 | 20 04 | 11 20 | 12 22 | 13 24 | 14 24 |
| N 40 | 18 45 | 19 14 | 19 49 | 11 30 | 12 30 | 13 29 | 14 26 |
| 35 | 18 38 | 19 05 | 19 36 | 11 39 | 12 36 | 13 33 | 14 28 |
| 30 | 18 32 | 18 56 | 19 26 | 11 46 | 12 42 | 13 36 | 14 29 |
| 20 | 18 21 | 18 43 | 19 10 | 11 59 | 12 52 | 13 42 | 14 32 |
| N 10 | 18 11 | 18 32 | 18 57 | 12 10 | 13 00 | 13 48 | 14 34 |
| 0 | 18 02 | 18 23 | 18 48 | 12 21 | 13 08 | 13 53 | 14 36 |
| S 10 | 17 53 | 18 15 | 18 39 | 12 32 | 13 16 | 13 58 | 14 38 |
| 20 | 17 44 | 18 06 | 18 32 | 12 43 | 13 24 | 14 03 | 14 40 |
| 30 | 17 33 | 17 58 | 18 26 | 12 55 | 13 34 | 14 09 | 14 42 |
| 35 | 17 27 | 17 53 | 18 23 | 13 03 | 13 39 | 14 12 | 14 44 |
| 40 | 17 21 | 17 48 | 18 20 | 13 11 | 13 45 | 14 16 | 14 45 |
| 45 | 17 13 | 17 43 | 18 17 | 13 21 | 13 52 | 14 21 | 14 47 |
| S 50 | 17 03 | 17 37 | 18 14 | 13 32 | 14 01 | 14 26 | 14 49 |
| 52 | 16 59 | 17 34 | 18 13 | 13 38 | 14 05 | 14 28 | 14 50 |
| 54 | 16 54 | 17 31 | 18 12 | 13 44 | 14 09 | 14 31 | 14 51 |
| 56 | 16 49 | 17 28 | 18 11 | 13 50 | 14 14 | 14 34 | 14 52 |
| 58 | 16 43 | 17 24 | 18 10 | 13 57 | 14 19 | 14 37 | 14 53 |
| S 60 | 16 36 | 17 20 | 18 09 | 14 06 | 14 25 | 14 41 | 14 55 |

| Day | SUN Eqn. of Time 00ʰ | SUN Eqn. of Time 12ʰ | SUN Mer. Pass. | MOON Mer. Pass. Upper | MOON Mer. Pass. Lower | Age | Phase |
|---|---|---|---|---|---|---|---|
| | m s | m s | h m | h m | h m | d | |
| 21 | 01 15 | 01 21 | 11 59 | 06 09 | 18 34 | 22 | ◑ |
| 22 | 01 27 | 01 33 | 11 58 | 06 57 | 19 20 | 23 | |
| 23 | 01 39 | 01 44 | 11 58 | 07 42 | 20 04 | 24 | |

# 1976 MAY 3, 4, 5 (MON., TUES., WED.)

| | G.M.T. | SUN G.H.A. | SUN Dec. | MOON G.H.A. | v | MOON Dec. | d | H.P. |
|---|---|---|---|---|---|---|---|---|
| | d h | ° ′ | ° ′ | ° ′ | ′ | ° ′ | ′ | ′ |
| | 3 00 | 180 46.8 | N15 38.8 | 139 11.8 | 10.6 | N19 49.6 | 0.5 | 55.3 |
| | 01 | 195 46.9 | 39.5 | 153 41.4 | 10.6 | 19 49.1 | 0.6 | 55.3 |
| | 02 | 210 46.9 | 40.3 | 168 11.0 | 10.6 | 19 48.5 | 0.6 | 55.3 |
| | 03 | 225 47.0 | · · 41.0 | 182 40.6 | 10.6 | 19 47.9 | 0.8 | 55.3 |
| | 04 | 240 47.1 | 41.7 | 197 10.2 | 10.5 | 19 47.1 | 0.9 | 55.3 |
| | 05 | 255 47.1 | 42.5 | 211 39.7 | 10.5 | 19 46.2 | 1.0 | 55.4 |
| | 06 | 270 47.2 | N15 43.2 | 226 09.2 | 10.6 | N19 45.2 | 1.1 | 55.4 |
| | 07 | 285 47.3 | 44.0 | 240 38.8 | 10.5 | 19 44.1 | 1.2 | 55.4 |
| | 08 | 300 47.3 | 44.7 | 255 08.3 | 10.5 | 19 42.9 | 1.3 | 55.4 |
| M | 09 | 315 47.4 | · · 45.4 | 269 37.8 | 10.4 | 19 41.6 | 1.4 | 55.4 |
| O | 10 | 330 47.5 | 46.1 | 284 07.2 | 10.5 | 19 40.2 | 1.5 | 55.5 |
| N | 11 | 345 47.5 | 46.9 | 298 36.7 | 10.5 | 19 38.7 | 1.6 | 55.5 |
| D | 12 | 0 47.6 | N15 47.6 | 313 06.2 | 10.4 | N19 37.1 | 1.7 | 55.5 |
| A | 13 | 15 47.6 | 48.3 | 327 35.6 | 10.4 | 19 35.4 | 1.8 | 55.5 |
| Y | 14 | 30 47.7 | 49.1 | 342 05.0 | 10.5 | 19 33.6 | 2.0 | 55.5 |
| | 15 | 45 47.8 | · · 49.8 | 356 34.5 | 10.4 | 19 31.6 | 2.0 | 55.6 |
| | 16 | 60 47.8 | 50.5 | 11 03.9 | 10.4 | 19 29.6 | 2.1 | 55.6 |
| | 17 | 75 47.9 | 51.3 | 25 33.3 | 10.4 | 19 27.5 | 2.2 | 55.6 |
| | 18 | 90 47.9 | N15 52.0 | 40 02.7 | 10.4 | N19 25.3 | 2.3 | 55.6 |
| | 19 | 105 48.0 | 52.7 | 54 32.1 | 10.4 | 19 23.0 | 2.4 | 55.6 |
| | 20 | 120 48.1 | 53.4 | 69 01.5 | 10.3 | 19 20.6 | 2.5 | 55.7 |
| | 21 | 135 48.1 | · · 54.2 | 83 30.8 | 10.4 | 19 18.1 | 2.6 | 55.7 |
| | 22 | 150 48.2 | 54.9 | 98 00.2 | 10.4 | 19 15.5 | 2.8 | 55.7 |
| | 23 | 165 48.2 | 55.6 | 112 29.6 | 10.3 | 19 12.7 | 2.8 | 55.7 |
| | 4 00 | 180 48.3 | N15 56.3 | 126 58.9 | 10.4 | N19 09.9 | 2.9 | 55.8 |
| | 01 | 195 48.4 | 57.1 | 141 28.3 | 10.3 | 19 07.0 | 3.0 | 55.8 |
| | 02 | 210 48.4 | 57.8 | 155 57.6 | 10.3 | 19 04.0 | 3.1 | 55.8 |
| | 03 | 225 48.5 | · · 58.5 | 170 26.9 | 10.4 | 19 00.9 | 3.3 | 55.8 |
| | 04 | 240 48.5 | 15 59.2 | 184 56.3 | 10.3 | 18 57.6 | 3.3 | 55.9 |
| | 05 | 255 48.6 | 16 00.0 | 199 25.6 | 10.3 | 18 54.3 | 3.4 | 55.9 |
| | 06 | 270 48.7 | N16 00.7 | 213 54.9 | 10.4 | N18 50.9 | 3.5 | 55.9 |
| | 07 | 285 48.7 | 01.4 | 228 24.3 | 10.3 | 18 47.4 | 3.7 | 55.9 |
| T | 08 | 300 48.8 | 02.1 | 242 53.6 | 10.3 | 18 43.7 | 3.7 | 56.0 |
| U | 09 | 315 48.8 | · · 02.9 | 257 22.9 | 10.3 | 18 40.0 | 3.8 | 56.0 |
| E | 10 | 330 48.9 | 03.6 | 271 52.2 | 10.3 | 18 36.2 | 3.9 | 56.0 |
| S | 11 | 345 48.9 | 04.3 | 286 21.5 | 10.4 | 18 32.3 | 4.1 | 56.0 |
| D | 12 | 0 49.0 | N16 05.0 | 300 50.9 | 10.3 | N18 28.2 | 4.1 | 56.0 |
| A | 13 | 15 49.1 | 05.7 | 315 20.2 | 10.3 | 18 24.1 | 4.2 | 56.1 |
| Y | 14 | 30 49.1 | 06.5 | 329 49.5 | 10.3 | 18 19.9 | 4.3 | 56.1 |
| | 15 | 45 49.2 | · · 07.2 | 344 18.8 | 10.3 | 18 15.6 | 4.5 | 56.1 |
| | 16 | 60 49.2 | 07.9 | 358 48.1 | 10.3 | 18 11.1 | 4.5 | 56.2 |
| | 17 | 75 49.3 | 08.6 | 13 17.4 | 10.3 | 18 06.6 | 4.6 | 56.2 |
| | 18 | 90 49.3 | N16 09.3 | 27 46.7 | 10.4 | N18 02.0 | 4.7 | 56.2 |
| | 19 | 105 49.4 | 10.0 | 42 16.1 | 10.3 | 17 57.3 | 4.8 | 56.2 |
| | 20 | 120 49.4 | 10.8 | 56 45.4 | 10.3 | 17 52.5 | 4.9 | 56.3 |
| | 21 | 135 49.5 | · · 11.5 | 71 14.7 | 10.3 | 17 47.6 | 5.0 | 56.3 |
| | 22 | 150 49.5 | 12.2 | 85 44.0 | 10.4 | 17 42.6 | 5.1 | 56.3 |
| | 23 | 165 49.6 | 12.9 | 100 13.4 | 10.3 | 17 37.5 | 5.2 | 56.3 |
| | 5 00 | 180 49.7 | N16 13.6 | 114 42.7 | 10.3 | N17 32.3 | 5.3 | 56.4 |
| | 01 | 195 49.7 | 14.3 | 129 12.0 | 10.3 | 17 27.0 | 5.4 | 56.4 |
| | 02 | 210 49.8 | 15.0 | 143 41.3 | 10.4 | 17 21.6 | 5.5 | 56.4 |
| | 03 | 225 49.8 | · · 15.8 | 158 10.7 | 10.3 | 17 16.1 | 5.6 | 56.4 |
| | 04 | 240 49.9 | 16.5 | 172 40.0 | 10.4 | 17 10.5 | 5.7 | 56.5 |
| | 05 | 255 49.9 | 17.2 | 187 09.4 | 10.3 | 17 04.8 | 5.8 | 56.5 |
| | 06 | 270 50.0 | N16 17.9 | 201 38.7 | 10.4 | N16 59.0 | 5.8 | 56.5 |
| W | 07 | 285 50.0 | 18.6 | 216 08.1 | 10.3 | 16 53.2 | 6.0 | 56.5 |
| E | 08 | 300 50.1 | 19.3 | 230 37.4 | 10.4 | 16 47.2 | 6.1 | 56.6 |
| D | 09 | 315 50.1 | · · 20.0 | 245 06.8 | 10.3 | 16 41.1 | 6.1 | 56.6 |
| N | 10 | 330 50.2 | 20.7 | 259 36.1 | 10.4 | 16 35.0 | 6.2 | 56.6 |
| E | 11 | 345 50.2 | 21.4 | 274 05.5 | 10.4 | 16 28.8 | 6.4 | 56.7 |
| S | 12 | 0 50.3 | N16 22.2 | 288 34.9 | 10.4 | N16 22.4 | 6.4 | 56.7 |
| D | 13 | 15 50.3 | 22.9 | 303 04.3 | 10.3 | 16 16.0 | 6.5 | 56.7 |
| A | 14 | 30 50.4 | 23.6 | 317 33.6 | 10.4 | 16 09.5 | 6.6 | 56.7 |
| Y | 15 | 45 50.4 | · · 24.3 | 332 03.0 | 10.4 | 16 02.9 | 6.7 | 56.8 |
| | 16 | 60 50.5 | 25.0 | 346 32.4 | 10.4 | 15 56.2 | 6.8 | 56.8 |
| | 17 | 75 50.5 | 25.7 | 1 01.8 | 10.4 | 15 49.4 | 6.9 | 56.8 |
| | 18 | 90 50.6 | N16 26.4 | 15 31.2 | 10.4 | N15 42.5 | 7.0 | 56.9 |
| | 19 | 105 50.6 | 27.1 | 30 00.6 | 10.4 | 15 35.5 | 7.1 | 56.9 |
| | 20 | 120 50.7 | 27.8 | 44 30.0 | 10.5 | 15 28.4 | 7.1 | 56.9 |
| | 21 | 135 50.7 | · · 28.5 | 58 59.5 | 10.4 | 15 21.3 | 7.2 | 57.0 |
| | 22 | 150 50.8 | 29.2 | 73 28.9 | 10.4 | 15 14.1 | 7.4 | 57.0 |
| | 23 | 165 50.8 | 29.9 | 87 58.3 | 10.4 | 15 06.7 | 7.4 | 57.0 |
| | | S.D. 15.9 | d 0.7 | S.D. 15.1 | | 15.3 | | 15.4 |

| Lat. | Twilight Naut. | Twilight Civil | Sunrise | Moonrise 3 | Moonrise 4 | Moonrise 5 | Moonrise 6 |
|---|---|---|---|---|---|---|---|
| ° | h m | h m | h m | h m | h m | h m | h m |
| N 72 | //// | //// | 01 24 | ▭ | ▭ | 05 58 | 08 10 |
| N 70 | //// | //// | 02 13 | 03 33 | 05 06 | 06 51 | 08 39 |
| 68 | //// | 00 17 | 02 43 | 04 44 | 05 56 | 07 24 | 09 00 |
| 66 | //// | 01 36 | 03 06 | 05 21 | 06 27 | 07 48 | 09 17 |
| 64 | //// | 02 11 | 03 23 | 05 47 | 06 50 | 08 06 | 09 30 |
| 62 | 00 14 | 02 36 | 03 38 | 06 07 | 07 09 | 08 22 | 09 42 |
| 60 | 01 25 | 02 55 | 03 50 | 06 24 | 07 24 | 08 34 | 09 51 |
| N 58 | 01 57 | 03 11 | 04 00 | 06 37 | 07 37 | 08 45 | 10 00 |
| 56 | 02 20 | 03 24 | 04 09 | 06 49 | 07 48 | 08 55 | 10 07 |
| 54 | 02 39 | 03 35 | 04 18 | 07 00 | 07 58 | 09 03 | 10 14 |
| 52 | 02 54 | 03 45 | 04 25 | 07 09 | 08 07 | 09 11 | 10 20 |
| 50 | 03 06 | 03 54 | 04 31 | 07 18 | 08 14 | 09 17 | 10 25 |
| 45 | 03 32 | 04 12 | 04 45 | 07 35 | 08 31 | 09 32 | 10 37 |
| N 40 | 03 51 | 04 27 | 04 56 | 07 50 | 08 45 | 09 44 | 10 46 |
| 35 | 04 06 | 04 39 | 05 06 | 08 02 | 08 56 | 09 54 | 10 54 |
| 30 | 04 19 | 04 49 | 05 15 | 08 13 | 09 06 | 10 03 | 11 01 |
| 20 | 04 39 | 05 06 | 05 29 | 08 31 | 09 24 | 10 18 | 11 13 |
| N 10 | 04 54 | 05 20 | 05 42 | 08 47 | 09 39 | 10 31 | 11 24 |
| 0 | 05 07 | 05 32 | 05 53 | 09 02 | 09 53 | 10 44 | 11 34 |
| S 10 | 05 18 | 05 43 | 06 05 | 09 17 | 10 07 | 10 56 | 11 44 |
| 20 | 05 28 | 05 54 | 06 17 | 09 33 | 10 22 | 11 09 | 11 55 |
| 30 | 05 37 | 06 06 | 06 31 | 09 51 | 10 39 | 11 24 | 12 07 |
| 35 | 05 42 | 06 12 | 06 39 | 10 02 | 10 49 | 11 33 | 12 14 |
| 40 | 05 47 | 06 19 | 06 48 | 10 14 | 11 01 | 11 43 | 12 22 |
| 45 | 05 52 | 06 27 | 06 58 | 10 29 | 11 14 | 11 55 | 12 31 |
| S 50 | 05 58 | 06 36 | 07 11 | 10 47 | 11 30 | 12 09 | 12 42 |
| 52 | 06 00 | 06 41 | 07 17 | 10 55 | 11 38 | 12 15 | 12 47 |
| 54 | 06 03 | 06 45 | 07 23 | 11 04 | 11 47 | 12 23 | 12 53 |
| 56 | 06 06 | 06 50 | 07 31 | 11 15 | 11 56 | 12 31 | 12 59 |
| 58 | 06 08 | 06 55 | 07 39 | 11 27 | 12 07 | 12 40 | 13 06 |
| S 60 | 06 11 | 07 02 | 07 48 | 11 41 | 12 20 | 12 50 | 13 14 |

| Lat. | Sunset | Twilight Civil | Twilight Naut. | Moonset 3 | Moonset 4 | Moonset 5 | Moonset 6 |
|---|---|---|---|---|---|---|---|
| ° | h m | h m | h m | h m | h m | h m | h m |
| N 72 | 22 38 | //// | //// | ▭ | ▭ | 03 14 | 02 47 |
| N 70 | 21 46 | //// | //// | 02 06 | 02 19 | 02 19 | 02 17 |
| 68 | 21 14 | //// | //// | 00 55 | 01 29 | 01 46 | 01 55 |
| 66 | 20 51 | 22 24 | //// | 00 18 | 00 57 | 01 21 | 01 37 |
| 64 | 20 33 | 21 47 | //// | 24 33 | 00 33 | 01 02 | 01 23 |
| 62 | 20 18 | 21 21 | //// | 24 14 | 00 14 | 00 47 | 01 11 |
| 60 | 20 05 | 21 01 | 22 34 | 23 59 | 24 33 | 00 33 | 01 00 |
| N 58 | 19 55 | 20 45 | 22 00 | 23 46 | 24 22 | 00 22 | 00 51 |
| 56 | 19 45 | 20 31 | 21 36 | 23 34 | 24 12 | 00 12 | 00 44 |
| 54 | 19 37 | 20 20 | 21 17 | 23 24 | 24 03 | 00 03 | 00 36 |
| 52 | 19 30 | 20 09 | 21 02 | 23 16 | 23 56 | 24 30 | 00 30 |
| 50 | 19 23 | 20 01 | 20 49 | 23 08 | 23 49 | 24 24 | 00 24 |
| 45 | 19 09 | 19 42 | 20 23 | 22 51 | 23 33 | 24 12 | 00 12 |
| N 40 | 18 58 | 19 27 | 20 04 | 22 37 | 23 21 | 24 01 | 00 01 |
| 35 | 18 48 | 19 15 | 19 48 | 22 25 | 23 10 | 23 52 | 24 32 |
| 30 | 18 39 | 19 05 | 19 35 | 22 14 | 23 01 | 23 45 | 24 26 |
| 20 | 18 25 | 18 48 | 19 15 | 21 57 | 22 45 | 23 31 | 24 16 |
| N 10 | 18 12 | 18 34 | 19 00 | 21 41 | 22 30 | 23 19 | 24 07 |
| 0 | 18 00 | 18 22 | 18 47 | 21 26 | 22 17 | 23 08 | 23 58 |
| S 10 | 17 49 | 18 10 | 18 36 | 21 12 | 22 04 | 22 57 | 23 50 |
| 20 | 17 36 | 17 59 | 18 25 | 20 56 | 21 49 | 22 44 | 23 40 |
| 30 | 17 22 | 17 47 | 18 16 | 20 38 | 21 33 | 22 30 | 23 30 |
| 35 | 17 14 | 17 41 | 18 11 | 20 27 | 21 23 | 22 22 | 23 24 |
| 40 | 17 05 | 17 34 | 18 06 | 20 15 | 21 12 | 22 13 | 23 17 |
| 45 | 16 55 | 17 26 | 18 01 | 20 01 | 20 59 | 22 02 | 23 08 |
| S 50 | 16 42 | 17 16 | 17 55 | 19 44 | 20 44 | 21 49 | 22 58 |
| 52 | 16 36 | 17 12 | 17 52 | 19 35 | 20 36 | 21 43 | 22 54 |
| 54 | 16 29 | 17 08 | 17 50 | 19 26 | 20 28 | 21 36 | 22 49 |
| 56 | 16 22 | 17 03 | 17 47 | 19 16 | 20 19 | 21 28 | 22 43 |
| 58 | 16 14 | 16 57 | 17 44 | 19 04 | 20 08 | 21 20 | 22 37 |
| S 60 | 16 04 | 16 51 | 17 41 | 18 50 | 19 56 | 21 10 | 22 30 |

| Day | SUN Eqn. of Time 00ʰ | SUN Eqn. of Time 12ʰ | SUN Mer. Pass. | MOON Mer. Pass. Upper | MOON Mer. Pass. Lower | Age | Phase |
|---|---|---|---|---|---|---|---|
| | m s | m s | h m | h m | h m | d | |
| 3 | 03 07 | 03 10 | 11 57 | 15 14 | 02 49 | 04 | ◐ |
| 4 | 03 13 | 03 16 | 11 57 | 16 05 | 03 40 | 05 | |
| 5 | 03 19 | 03 21 | 11 57 | 16 56 | 04 30 | 06 | |

## 1976 MAY 6, 7, 8 (THURS., FRI., SAT.)

| G.M.T. | | SUN G.H.A. | SUN Dec. | MOON G.H.A. | MOON v | MOON Dec. | MOON d | MOON H.P. |
|---|---|---|---|---|---|---|---|---|
| d h | | ° ′ | ° ′ | ° ′ | ′ | ° ′ | ′ | ′ |
| 6 00 | | 180 50.9 | N16 30.6 | 102 27.7 | 10.5 | N14 59.3 | 7.5 | 57.0 |
| 01 | | 195 50.9 | 31.3 | 116 57.2 | 10.4 | 14 51.8 | 7.6 | 57.1 |
| 02 | | 210 51.0 | 32.0 | 131 26.6 | 10.5 | 14 44.2 | 7.6 | 57.1 |
| 03 | | 225 51.0 | .. 32.7 | 145 56.1 | 10.4 | 14 36.6 | 7.8 | 57.1 |
| 04 | | 240 51.1 | 33.4 | 160 25.5 | 10.5 | 14 28.8 | 7.8 | 57.2 |
| 05 | | 255 51.1 | 34.1 | 174 55.0 | 10.4 | 14 21.0 | 8.0 | 57.2 |
| 06 | | 270 51.2 | N16 34.8 | 189 24.4 | 10.5 | N14 13.0 | 8.0 | 57.2 |
| 07 | | 285 51.2 | 35.5 | 203 53.9 | 10.5 | 14 05.0 | 8.1 | 57.3 |
| 08 | T | 300 51.3 | 36.2 | 218 23.4 | 10.4 | 13 56.9 | 8.2 | 57.3 |
| 09 | H | 315 51.3 | .. 36.9 | 232 52.8 | 10.5 | 13 48.7 | 8.2 | 57.3 |
| 10 | U | 330 51.3 | 37.6 | 247 22.3 | 10.5 | 13 40.5 | 8.4 | 57.3 |
| 11 | R | 345 51.4 | 38.3 | 261 51.8 | 10.5 | 13 32.1 | 8.4 | 57.4 |
| 12 | S | 0 51.4 | N16 39.0 | 276 21.3 | 10.5 | N13 23.7 | 8.5 | 57.4 |
| 13 | D | 15 51.5 | 39.7 | 290 50.8 | 10.5 | 13 15.2 | 8.6 | 57.4 |
| 14 | A | 30 51.5 | 40.4 | 305 20.3 | 10.5 | 13 06.6 | 8.6 | 57.5 |
| 15 | Y | 45 51.6 | .. 41.1 | 319 49.8 | 10.5 | 12 58.0 | 8.8 | 57.5 |
| 16 | | 60 51.6 | 41.8 | 334 19.3 | 10.5 | 12 49.2 | 8.8 | 57.5 |
| 17 | | 75 51.7 | 42.5 | 348 48.8 | 10.5 | 12 40.4 | 8.9 | 57.6 |
| 18 | | 90 51.7 | N16 43.2 | 3 18.3 | 10.5 | N12 31.5 | 8.9 | 57.6 |
| 19 | | 105 51.7 | 43.9 | 17 47.8 | 10.5 | 12 22.6 | 9.1 | 57.6 |
| 20 | | 120 51.8 | 44.6 | 32 17.3 | 10.5 | 12 13.5 | 9.1 | 57.7 |
| 21 | | 135 51.8 | .. 45.3 | 46 46.8 | 10.5 | 12 04.4 | 9.2 | 57.7 |
| 22 | | 150 51.9 | 46.0 | 61 16.3 | 10.5 | 11 55.2 | 9.3 | 57.7 |
| 23 | | 165 51.9 | 46.7 | 75 45.8 | 10.5 | 11 45.9 | 9.3 | 57.8 |
| 7 00 | | 180 52.0 | N16 47.3 | 90 15.3 | 10.5 | N11 36.6 | 9.4 | 57.8 |
| 01 | | 195 52.0 | 48.0 | 104 44.8 | 10.5 | 11 27.2 | 9.5 | 57.8 |
| 02 | | 210 52.0 | 48.7 | 119 14.3 | 10.5 | 11 17.7 | 9.6 | 57.9 |
| 03 | | 225 52.1 | .. 49.4 | 133 43.8 | 10.5 | 11 08.1 | 9.6 | 57.9 |
| 04 | | 240 52.1 | 50.1 | 148 13.3 | 10.5 | 10 58.5 | 9.7 | 57.9 |
| 05 | | 255 52.2 | 50.8 | 162 42.8 | 10.5 | 10 48.8 | 9.8 | 58.0 |
| 06 | | 270 52.2 | N16 51.5 | 177 12.3 | 10.5 | N10 39.0 | 9.8 | 58.0 |
| 07 | | 285 52.3 | 52.2 | 191 41.8 | 10.5 | 10 29.2 | 9.9 | 58.0 |
| 08 | | 300 52.3 | 52.9 | 206 11.3 | 10.5 | 10 19.3 | 10.0 | 58.1 |
| 09 | F | 315 52.3 | .. 53.5 | 220 40.8 | 10.5 | 10 09.3 | 10.1 | 58.1 |
| 10 | R | 330 52.4 | 54.2 | 235 10.3 | 10.5 | 9 59.2 | 10.1 | 58.1 |
| 11 | I | 345 52.4 | 54.9 | 249 39.8 | 10.5 | 9 49.1 | 10.1 | 58.2 |
| 12 | D | 0 52.5 | N16 55.6 | 264 09.3 | 10.5 | N 9 39.0 | 10.3 | 58.2 |
| 13 | A | 15 52.5 | 56.3 | 278 38.8 | 10.5 | 9 28.7 | 10.3 | 58.2 |
| 14 | Y | 30 52.5 | 57.0 | 293 08.3 | 10.5 | 9 18.4 | 10.3 | 58.3 |
| 15 | | 45 52.6 | .. 57.7 | 307 37.8 | 10.4 | 9 08.1 | 10.4 | 58.3 |
| 16 | | 60 52.6 | 58.3 | 322 07.2 | 10.5 | 8 57.7 | 10.5 | 58.3 |
| 17 | | 75 52.6 | 59.0 | 336 36.7 | 10.4 | 8 47.2 | 10.6 | 58.4 |
| 18 | | 90 52.7 | N16 59.7 | 351 06.1 | 10.5 | N 8 36.6 | 10.6 | 58.4 |
| 19 | | 105 52.7 | 17 00.4 | 5 35.6 | 10.4 | 8 26.0 | 10.6 | 58.4 |
| 20 | | 120 52.8 | 01.1 | 20 05.0 | 10.4 | 8 15.4 | 10.7 | 58.5 |
| 21 | | 135 52.8 | .. 01.8 | 34 34.4 | 10.5 | 8 04.7 | 10.8 | 58.5 |
| 22 | | 150 52.8 | 02.4 | 49 03.9 | 10.4 | 7 53.9 | 10.9 | 58.5 |
| 23 | | 165 52.9 | 03.1 | 63 33.3 | 10.4 | 7 43.0 | 10.8 | 58.6 |
| 8 00 | | 180 52.9 | N17 03.8 | 78 02.7 | 10.4 | N 7 32.2 | 11.0 | 58.6 |
| 01 | | 195 52.9 | 04.5 | 92 32.1 | 10.3 | 7 21.2 | 11.0 | 58.6 |
| 02 | | 210 53.0 | 05.2 | 107 01.4 | 10.4 | 7 10.2 | 11.0 | 58.7 |
| 03 | | 225 53.0 | .. 05.8 | 121 30.8 | 10.4 | 6 59.2 | 11.1 | 58.7 |
| 04 | | 240 53.1 | 06.5 | 136 00.2 | 10.3 | 6 48.1 | 11.2 | 58.7 |
| 05 | | 255 53.1 | 07.2 | 150 29.5 | 10.3 | 6 36.9 | 11.1 | 58.8 |
| 06 | | 270 53.1 | N17 07.9 | 164 58.8 | 10.4 | N 6 25.8 | 11.3 | 58.8 |
| 07 | | 285 53.2 | 08.5 | 179 28.2 | 10.3 | 6 14.5 | 11.3 | 58.8 |
| 08 | S | 300 53.2 | 09.2 | 193 57.5 | 10.2 | 6 03.2 | 11.3 | 58.9 |
| 09 | A | 315 53.2 | .. 09.9 | 208 26.7 | 10.3 | 5 51.9 | 11.4 | 58.9 |
| 10 | T | 330 53.3 | 10.6 | 222 56.0 | 10.3 | 5 40.5 | 11.4 | 58.9 |
| 11 | U | 345 53.3 | 11.2 | 237 25.3 | 10.2 | 5 29.1 | 11.5 | 58.9 |
| 12 | R | 0 53.3 | N17 11.9 | 251 54.5 | 10.2 | N 5 17.6 | 11.5 | 59.0 |
| 13 | D | 15 53.4 | 12.6 | 266 23.7 | 10.2 | 5 06.1 | 11.6 | 59.0 |
| 14 | A | 30 53.4 | 13.3 | 280 52.9 | 10.2 | 4 54.5 | 11.6 | 59.0 |
| 15 | Y | 45 53.4 | .. 13.9 | 295 22.1 | 10.2 | 4 42.9 | 11.6 | 59.1 |
| 16 | | 60 53.5 | 14.6 | 309 51.3 | 10.1 | 4 31.3 | 11.7 | 59.1 |
| 17 | | 75 53.5 | 15.3 | 324 20.4 | 10.1 | 4 19.6 | 11.7 | 59.1 |
| 18 | | 90 53.5 | N17 15.9 | 338 49.5 | 10.1 | N 4 07.9 | 11.8 | 59.2 |
| 19 | | 105 53.6 | 16.6 | 353 18.6 | 10.1 | 3 56.1 | 11.7 | 59.2 |
| 20 | | 120 53.6 | 17.3 | 7 47.7 | 10.0 | 3 44.4 | 11.9 | 59.2 |
| 21 | | 135 53.6 | .. 18.0 | 22 16.7 | 10.1 | 3 32.5 | 11.8 | 59.3 |
| 22 | | 150 53.7 | 18.6 | 36 45.8 | 10.0 | 3 20.7 | 11.9 | 59.3 |
| 23 | | 165 53.7 | 19.3 | 51 14.8 | 10.0 | 3 08.8 | 11.9 | 59.3 |
| | | S.D. 15.9 | d 0.7 | S.D. 15.6 | | 15.9 | | 16.1 |

| Lat. | Twilight Naut. | Twilight Civil | Sunrise | Moonrise 6 | Moonrise 7 | Moonrise 8 | Moonrise 9 |
|---|---|---|---|---|---|---|---|
| ° | h m | h m | h m | h m | h m | h m | h m |
| N 72 | //// | //// | 00 46 | 08 10 | 10 11 | 12 09 | 14 07 |
| N 70 | //// | //// | 01 53 | 08 39 | 10 27 | 12 16 | 14 07 |
| 68 | //// | //// | 02 29 | 09 00 | 10 40 | 12 22 | 14 07 |
| 66 | //// | 01 12 | 02 54 | 09 17 | 10 51 | 12 28 | 14 07 |
| 64 | //// | 01 56 | 03 13 | 09 30 | 11 00 | 12 32 | 14 07 |
| 62 | //// | 02 24 | 03 29 | 09 42 | 11 07 | 12 36 | 14 07 |
| 60 | 01 04 | 02 45 | 03 42 | 09 51 | 11 13 | 12 39 | 14 07 |
| N 58 | 01 44 | 03 02 | 03 53 | 10 00 | 11 19 | 12 42 | 14 07 |
| 56 | 02 10 | 03 16 | 04 03 | 10 07 | 11 24 | 12 44 | 14 07 |
| 54 | 02 30 | 03 29 | 04 12 | 10 14 | 11 29 | 12 46 | 14 07 |
| 52 | 02 46 | 03 39 | 04 19 | 10 20 | 11 33 | 12 49 | 14 07 |
| 50 | 03 00 | 03 49 | 04 26 | 10 25 | 11 36 | 12 50 | 14 07 |
| 45 | 03 26 | 04 08 | 04 41 | 10 37 | 11 44 | 12 54 | 14 07 |
| N 40 | 03 47 | 04 23 | 04 53 | 10 46 | 11 51 | 12 58 | 14 07 |
| 35 | 04 03 | 04 36 | 05 03 | 10 54 | 11 57 | 13 01 | 14 07 |
| 30 | 04 16 | 04 47 | 05 12 | 11 01 | 12 02 | 13 03 | 14 07 |
| 20 | 04 37 | 05 04 | 05 28 | 11 13 | 12 10 | 13 08 | 14 07 |
| N 10 | 04 53 | 05 19 | 05 41 | 11 24 | 12 18 | 13 12 | 14 07 |
| 0 | 05 06 | 05 31 | 05 53 | 11 34 | 12 25 | 13 16 | 14 07 |
| S 10 | 05 18 | 05 43 | 06 05 | 11 44 | 12 32 | 13 19 | 14 07 |
| 20 | 05 29 | 05 55 | 06 18 | 11 55 | 12 39 | 13 23 | 14 07 |
| 30 | 05 39 | 06 08 | 06 33 | 12 07 | 12 48 | 13 28 | 14 07 |
| 35 | 05 44 | 06 14 | 06 41 | 12 14 | 12 53 | 13 30 | 14 08 |
| 40 | 05 50 | 06 22 | 06 51 | 12 22 | 12 58 | 13 33 | 14 08 |
| 45 | 05 55 | 06 31 | 07 02 | 12 31 | 13 05 | 13 37 | 14 08 |
| S 50 | 06 02 | 06 40 | 07 15 | 12 42 | 13 12 | 13 41 | 14 08 |
| 52 | 06 04 | 06 45 | 07 22 | 12 47 | 13 16 | 13 42 | 14 08 |
| 54 | 06 07 | 06 50 | 07 29 | 12 53 | 13 20 | 13 44 | 14 08 |
| 56 | 06 10 | 06 55 | 07 36 | 12 59 | 13 24 | 13 47 | 14 08 |
| 58 | 06 14 | 07 01 | 07 45 | 13 06 | 13 29 | 13 49 | 14 08 |
| S 60 | 06 17 | 07 08 | 07 55 | 13 14 | 13 34 | 13 52 | 14 08 |

| Lat. | Sunset | Twilight Civil | Twilight Naut. | Moonset 6 | Moonset 7 | Moonset 8 | Moonset 9 |
|---|---|---|---|---|---|---|---|
| ° | h m | h m | h m | h m | h m | h m | h m |
| N 72 | 23 27 | //// | //// | 02 47 | 02 32 | 02 21 | 02 11 |
| N 70 | 22 06 | //// | //// | 02 17 | 02 14 | 02 11 | 02 08 |
| 68 | 21 28 | //// | //// | 01 55 | 02 00 | 02 03 | 02 05 |
| 66 | 21 02 | 22 49 | //// | 01 37 | 01 48 | 01 56 | 02 03 |
| 64 | 20 42 | 22 02 | //// | 01 23 | 01 38 | 01 50 | 02 01 |
| 62 | 20 26 | 21 32 | //// | 01 11 | 01 30 | 01 45 | 01 59 |
| 60 | 20 13 | 21 10 | 22 56 | 01 00 | 01 22 | 01 41 | 01 58 |
| N 58 | 20 01 | 20 53 | 22 13 | 00 51 | 01 16 | 01 37 | 01 56 |
| 56 | 19 51 | 20 38 | 21 46 | 00 44 | 01 10 | 01 33 | 01 55 |
| 54 | 19 43 | 20 26 | 21 26 | 00 36 | 01 05 | 01 30 | 01 54 |
| 52 | 19 35 | 20 15 | 21 09 | 00 30 | 01 00 | 01 27 | 01 53 |
| 50 | 19 28 | 20 06 | 20 55 | 00 24 | 00 56 | 01 25 | 01 52 |
| 45 | 19 13 | 19 46 | 20 28 | 00 12 | 00 47 | 01 19 | 01 50 |
| N 40 | 19 01 | 19 31 | 20 07 | 00 01 | 00 39 | 01 14 | 01 49 |
| 35 | 18 50 | 19 18 | 19 51 | 24 32 | 00 32 | 01 10 | 01 47 |
| 30 | 18 41 | 19 07 | 19 38 | 24 26 | 00 26 | 01 06 | 01 46 |
| 20 | 18 26 | 18 49 | 19 17 | 24 16 | 00 16 | 01 00 | 01 44 |
| N 10 | 18 13 | 18 34 | 19 00 | 24 07 | 00 07 | 00 54 | 01 42 |
| 0 | 18 00 | 18 22 | 18 47 | 23 58 | 24 49 | 00 49 | 01 40 |
| S 10 | 17 48 | 18 10 | 18 35 | 23 50 | 24 43 | 00 43 | 01 38 |
| 20 | 17 35 | 17 58 | 18 24 | 23 40 | 24 38 | 00 38 | 01 36 |
| 30 | 17 20 | 17 45 | 18 14 | 23 30 | 24 31 | 00 31 | 01 33 |
| 35 | 17 12 | 17 38 | 18 08 | 23 24 | 24 27 | 00 27 | 01 32 |
| 40 | 17 02 | 17 31 | 18 03 | 23 17 | 24 23 | 00 23 | 01 30 |
| 45 | 16 51 | 17 22 | 17 57 | 23 08 | 24 17 | 00 17 | 01 29 |
| S 50 | 16 37 | 17 12 | 17 51 | 22 58 | 24 11 | 00 11 | 01 26 |
| 52 | 16 31 | 17 07 | 17 48 | 22 54 | 24 08 | 00 08 | 01 25 |
| 54 | 16 24 | 17 02 | 17 45 | 22 49 | 24 05 | 00 05 | 01 24 |
| 56 | 16 16 | 16 57 | 17 42 | 22 43 | 24 02 | 00 02 | 01 23 |
| 58 | 16 07 | 16 51 | 17 39 | 22 37 | 23 58 | 25 22 | 01 22 |
| S 60 | 15 57 | 16 44 | 17 35 | 22 30 | 23 53 | 25 20 | 01 20 |

| Day | SUN Eqn. of Time 00ʰ | SUN Eqn. of Time 12ʰ | SUN Mer. Pass. | MOON Mer. Pass. Upper | MOON Mer. Pass. Lower | MOON Age | MOON Phase |
|---|---|---|---|---|---|---|---|
| | m s | m s | h m | h m | h m | d | |
| 6 | 03 23 | 03 26 | 11 57 | 17 46 | 05 21 | 07 | ◐ |
| 7 | 03 28 | 03 30 | 11 57 | 18 37 | 06 12 | 08 | |
| 8 | 03 32 | 03 33 | 11 56 | 19 28 | 07 02 | 09 | |

## 1976 MAY 12, 13, 14 (WED., THURS., FRI.)

| G.M.T. | | ARIES G.H.A. | VENUS −3.4 G.H.A. | VENUS Dec. | MARS +1.6 G.H.A. | MARS Dec. | JUPITER −1.6 G.H.A. | JUPITER Dec. | SATURN +0.4 G.H.A. | SATURN Dec. |
|---|---|---|---|---|---|---|---|---|---|---|
| d h | | ° ′ | ° ′ | ° ′ | ° ′ | ° ′ | ° ′ | ° ′ | ° ′ | ° ′ |
| 12 00 | | 229 53.5 | 190 35.5 | N14 12.2 | 109 56.5 | N22 18.3 | 190 58.5 | N14 13.9 | 109 54.1 | N21 00.9 |
| 01 | | 244 55.9 | 205 35.0 | 13.2 | 124 57.5 | 18.0 | 206 00.4 | 14.1 | 124 56.4 | 00.8 |
| 02 | | 259 58.4 | 220 34.4 | 14.3 | 139 58.6 | 17.7 | 221 02.3 | 14.3 | 139 58.6 | 00.8 |
| 03 | | 275 00.8 | 235 33.9 | .. 15.3 | 154 59.6 | .. 17.4 | 236 04.1 | .. 14.5 | 155 00.9 | .. 00.8 |
| 04 | | 290 03.3 | 250 33.4 | 16.3 | 170 00.6 | 17.1 | 251 06.0 | 14.6 | 170 03.1 | 00.7 |
| 05 | | 305 05.8 | 265 32.9 | 17.3 | 185 01.6 | 16.8 | 266 07.9 | 14.8 | 185 05.4 | 00.7 |
| 06 | | 320 08.2 | 280 32.3 | N14 18.3 | 200 02.6 | N22 16.5 | 281 09.8 | N14 15.0 | 200 07.7 | N21 00.7 |
| 07 | W | 335 10.7 | 295 31.8 | 19.3 | 215 03.6 | 16.2 | 296 11.7 | 15.2 | 215 09.9 | 00.6 |
| 08 | E | 350 13.2 | 310 31.3 | 20.3 | 230 04.6 | 15.9 | 311 13.6 | 15.4 | 230 12.2 | 00.6 |
| 09 | D | 5 15.6 | 325 30.7 | .. 21.3 | 245 05.6 | .. 15.6 | 326 15.4 | .. 15.6 | 245 14.5 | .. 00.6 |
| 10 | N | 20 18.1 | 340 30.2 | 22.3 | 260 06.6 | 15.3 | 341 17.3 | 15.7 | 260 16.7 | 00.5 |
| 11 | E | 35 20.6 | 355 29.7 | 23.3 | 275 07.6 | 15.0 | 356 19.2 | 15.9 | 275 19.0 | 00.5 |
| 12 | S | 50 23.0 | 10 29.1 | N14 24.3 | 290 08.6 | N22 14.7 | 11 21.1 | N14 16.1 | 290 21.3 | N21 00.5 |
| 13 | D | 65 25.5 | 25 28.6 | 25.3 | 305 09.6 | 14.4 | 26 23.0 | 16.3 | 305 23.5 | 00.4 |
| 14 | A | 80 28.0 | 40 28.1 | 26.3 | 320 10.6 | 14.1 | 41 24.9 | 16.5 | 320 25.8 | 00.4 |
| 15 | Y | 95 30.4 | 55 27.5 | .. 27.3 | 335 11.6 | .. 13.8 | 56 26.7 | .. 16.7 | 335 28.1 | .. 00.3 |
| 16 | | 110 32.9 | 70 27.0 | 28.3 | 350 12.6 | 13.5 | 71 28.6 | 16.9 | 350 30.3 | 00.3 |
| 17 | | 125 35.3 | 85 26.5 | 29.3 | 5 13.7 | 13.2 | 86 30.5 | 17.0 | 5 32.6 | 00.3 |
| 18 | | 140 37.8 | 100 25.9 | N14 30.4 | 20 14.7 | N22 12.8 | 101 32.4 | N14 17.2 | 20 34.8 | N21 00.2 |
| 19 | | 155 40.3 | 115 25.4 | 31.4 | 35 15.7 | 12.5 | 116 34.3 | 17.4 | 35 37.1 | 00.2 |
| 20 | | 170 42.7 | 130 24.9 | 32.4 | 50 16.7 | 12.2 | 131 36.2 | 17.6 | 50 39.4 | 00.2 |
| 21 | | 185 45.2 | 145 24.3 | .. 33.4 | 65 17.7 | .. 11.9 | 146 38.1 | .. 17.8 | 65 41.6 | .. 00.1 |
| 22 | | 200 47.7 | 160 23.8 | 34.3 | 80 18.7 | 11.6 | 161 39.9 | 18.0 | 80 43.9 | 00.1 |
| 23 | | 215 50.1 | 175 23.2 | 35.3 | 95 19.7 | 11.3 | 176 41.8 | 18.1 | 95 46.2 | 00.1 |
| 13 00 | | 230 52.6 | 190 22.7 | N14 36.3 | 110 20.7 | N22 11.0 | 191 43.7 | N14 18.3 | 110 48.4 | N21 00.0 |
| 01 | | 245 55.1 | 205 22.2 | 37.3 | 125 21.7 | 10.7 | 206 45.6 | 18.5 | 125 50.7 | 00.0 |
| 02 | | 260 57.5 | 220 21.6 | 38.3 | 140 22.7 | 10.4 | 221 47.5 | 18.7 | 140 52.9 | 21 00.0 |
| 03 | | 276 00.0 | 235 21.1 | .. 39.3 | 155 23.7 | .. 10.1 | 236 49.4 | .. 18.9 | 155 55.2 | 20 59.9 |
| 04 | | 291 02.4 | 250 20.5 | 40.3 | 170 24.7 | 09.8 | 251 51.2 | 19.1 | 170 57.5 | 59.9 |
| 05 | | 306 04.9 | 265 20.0 | 41.3 | 185 25.7 | 09.5 | 266 53.1 | 19.2 | 185 59.7 | 59.8 |
| 06 | | 321 07.4 | 280 19.5 | N14 42.3 | 200 26.7 | N22 09.2 | 281 55.0 | N14 19.4 | 201 02.0 | N20 59.8 |
| 07 | | 336 09.8 | 295 18.9 | 43.3 | 215 27.7 | 08.9 | 296 56.9 | 19.6 | 216 04.3 | 59.8 |
| 08 | T | 351 12.3 | 310 18.4 | 44.3 | 230 28.7 | 08.6 | 311 58.8 | 19.8 | 231 06.5 | 59.7 |
| 09 | H | 6 14.8 | 325 17.8 | .. 45.3 | 245 29.8 | .. 08.3 | 327 00.7 | .. 20.0 | 246 08.8 | .. 59.7 |
| 10 | U | 21 17.2 | 340 17.3 | 46.3 | 260 30.8 | 07.9 | 342 02.5 | 20.2 | 261 11.0 | 59.7 |
| 11 | R | 36 19.7 | 355 16.8 | 47.3 | 275 31.8 | 07.6 | 357 04.4 | 20.3 | 276 13.3 | 59.6 |
| 12 | S | 51 22.2 | 10 16.2 | N14 48.3 | 290 32.8 | N22 07.3 | 12 06.3 | N14 20.5 | 291 15.6 | N20 59.6 |
| 13 | D | 66 24.6 | 25 15.7 | 49.3 | 305 33.8 | 07.0 | 27 08.2 | 20.7 | 306 17.8 | 59.6 |
| 14 | A | 81 27.1 | 40 15.1 | 50.3 | 320 34.8 | 06.7 | 42 10.1 | 20.9 | 321 20.1 | 59.5 |
| 15 | Y | 96 29.6 | 55 14.6 | .. 51.2 | 335 35.8 | .. 06.4 | 57 12.0 | .. 21.1 | 336 22.3 | .. 59.5 |
| 16 | | 111 32.0 | 70 14.0 | 52.2 | 350 36.8 | 06.1 | 72 13.8 | 21.2 | 351 24.6 | 59.4 |
| 17 | | 126 34.5 | 85 13.5 | 53.2 | 5 37.8 | 05.8 | 87 15.7 | 21.4 | 6 26.9 | 59.4 |
| 18 | | 141 36.9 | 100 12.9 | N14 54.2 | 20 38.8 | N22 05.5 | 102 17.6 | N14 21.6 | 21 29.1 | N20 59.4 |
| 19 | | 156 39.4 | 115 12.4 | 55.2 | 35 39.8 | 05.2 | 117 19.5 | 21.8 | 36 31.4 | 59.3 |
| 20 | | 171 41.9 | 130 11.8 | 56.2 | 50 40.8 | 04.9 | 132 21.4 | 22.0 | 51 33.6 | 59.3 |
| 21 | | 186 44.3 | 145 11.3 | .. 57.2 | 65 41.8 | .. 04.5 | 147 23.3 | .. 22.2 | 66 35.9 | .. 59.3 |
| 22 | | 201 46.8 | 160 10.7 | 58.1 | 80 42.8 | 04.2 | 162 25.2 | 22.3 | 81 38.2 | 59.2 |
| 23 | | 216 49.3 | 175 10.2 | 14 59.1 | 95 43.8 | 03.9 | 177 27.0 | 22.5 | 96 40.4 | 59.2 |
| 14 00 | | 231 51.7 | 190 09.6 | N15 00.1 | 110 44.8 | N22 03.6 | 192 28.9 | N14 22.7 | 111 42.7 | N20 59.1 |
| 01 | | 246 54.2 | 205 09.1 | 01.1 | 125 45.8 | 03.3 | 207 30.8 | 22.9 | 126 44.9 | 59.1 |
| 02 | | 261 56.7 | 220 08.5 | 02.1 | 140 46.9 | 03.0 | 222 32.7 | 23.1 | 141 47.2 | 59.1 |
| 03 | | 276 59.1 | 235 08.0 | .. 03.1 | 155 47.9 | .. 02.7 | 237 34.6 | .. 23.3 | 156 49.5 | .. 59.0 |
| 04 | | 292 01.6 | 250 07.4 | 04.0 | 170 48.9 | 02.4 | 252 36.5 | 23.4 | 171 51.7 | 59.0 |
| 05 | | 307 04.1 | 265 06.9 | 05.0 | 185 49.9 | 02.0 | 267 38.3 | 23.6 | 186 54.0 | 59.0 |
| 06 | | 322 06.5 | 280 06.3 | N15 06.0 | 200 50.9 | N22 01.7 | 282 40.2 | N14 23.8 | 201 56.2 | N20 58.9 |
| 07 | | 337 09.0 | 295 05.8 | 07.0 | 215 51.9 | 01.4 | 297 42.1 | 24.0 | 216 58.5 | 58.9 |
| 08 | | 352 11.4 | 310 05.2 | 07.9 | 230 52.9 | 01.1 | 312 44.0 | 24.2 | 232 00.7 | 58.8 |
| 09 | F | 7 13.9 | 325 04.7 | .. 08.9 | 245 53.9 | .. 00.8 | 327 45.9 | .. 24.4 | 247 03.0 | .. 58.8 |
| 10 | R | 22 16.4 | 340 04.1 | 09.9 | 260 54.9 | 00.5 | 342 47.8 | 24.5 | 262 05.3 | 58.8 |
| 11 | I | 37 18.8 | 355 03.6 | 10.9 | 275 55.9 | 22 00.2 | 357 49.6 | 24.7 | 277 07.5 | 58.7 |
| 12 | D | 52 21.3 | 10 03.0 | N15 11.9 | 290 56.9 | N21 59.9 | 12 51.5 | N14 24.9 | 292 09.8 | N20 58.7 |
| 13 | A | 67 23.8 | 25 02.5 | 12.8 | 305 57.9 | 59.5 | 27 53.4 | 25.1 | 307 12.0 | 58.7 |
| 14 | Y | 82 26.2 | 40 01.9 | 13.8 | 320 58.9 | 59.2 | 42 55.3 | 25.3 | 322 14.3 | 58.6 |
| 15 | | 97 28.7 | 55 01.4 | .. 14.8 | 335 59.9 | .. 58.9 | 57 57.2 | .. 25.4 | 337 16.5 | .. 58.6 |
| 16 | | 112 31.2 | 70 00.8 | 15.7 | 351 00.9 | 58.6 | 72 59.1 | 25.6 | 352 18.8 | 58.6 |
| 17 | | 127 33.6 | 85 00.2 | 16.7 | 6 01.9 | 58.3 | 88 01.0 | 25.8 | 7 21.1 | 58.5 |
| 18 | | 142 36.1 | 99 59.7 | N15 17.7 | 21 02.9 | N21 58.0 | 103 02.8 | N14 26.0 | 22 23.3 | N20 58.5 |
| 19 | | 157 38.5 | 114 59.1 | 18.7 | 36 03.9 | 57.7 | 118 04.7 | 26.2 | 37 25.6 | 58.4 |
| 20 | | 172 41.0 | 129 58.6 | 19.6 | 51 04.9 | 57.3 | 133 06.6 | 26.4 | 52 27.8 | 58.4 |
| 21 | | 187 43.5 | 144 58.0 | .. 20.6 | 66 06.0 | .. 57.0 | 148 08.5 | .. 26.5 | 67 30.1 | .. 58.4 |
| 22 | | 202 45.9 | 159 57.5 | 21.6 | 81 07.0 | 56.7 | 163 10.4 | 26.7 | 82 32.3 | 58.3 |
| 23 | | 217 48.4 | 174 56.9 | 22.5 | 96 08.0 | 56.4 | 178 12.3 | 26.9 | 97 34.6 | 58.3 |
| Mer. Pass. | | h m 8 35.1 | v −0.5 | d 1.0 | v 1.0 | d 0.3 | v 1.9 | d 0.2 | v 2.3 | d 0.0 |

**STARS**

| Name | S.H.A. | Dec. |
|---|---|---|
| | ° ′ | ° ′ |
| Acamar | 315 39.9 | S40 24.0 |
| Achernar | 335 48.0 | S57 21.3 |
| Acrux | 173 40.0 | S62 58.4 |
| Adhara | 255 34.7 | S28 56.7 |
| Aldebaran | 291 21.7 | N16 27.6 |
| Alioth | 166 44.7 | N56 05.4 |
| Alkaid | 153 20.4 | N49 25.9 |
| Al Na'ir | 28 18.7 | S47 04.3 |
| Alnilam | 276 14.9 | S 1 13.1 |
| Alphard | 218 23.5 | S 8 33.6 |
| Alphecca | 126 34.2 | N26 47.6 |
| Alpheratz | 358 12.6 | N28 57.5 |
| Altair | 62 35.2 | N 8 48.3 |
| Ankaa | 353 43.5 | S42 25.9 |
| Antares | 113 00.1 | S26 22.8 |
| Arcturus | 146 20.8 | N19 18.3 |
| Atria | 108 26.5 | S68 59.0 |
| Avior | 234 29.6 | S59 26.4 |
| Bellatrix | 279 02.2 | N 6 19.6 |
| Betelgeuse | 271 31.7 | N 7 24.1 |
| Canopus | 264 08.9 | S52 41.3 |
| Capella | 281 16.1 | N45 58.5 |
| Deneb | 49 50.3 | N45 11.6 |
| Denebola | 183 01.9 | N14 42.2 |
| Diphda | 349 24.1 | S18 06.9 |
| Dubhe | 194 25.6 | N61 52.9 |
| Elnath | 278 48.2 | N28 35.2 |
| Eltanin | 90 58.7 | N51 29.4 |
| Enif | 34 14.5 | N 9 45.9 |
| Fomalhaut | 15 54.8 | S29 44.7 |
| Gacrux | 172 31.6 | S56 59.2 |
| Gienah | 176 20.8 | S17 24.9 |
| Hadar | 149 26.9 | S60 15.7 |
| Hamal | 328 32.6 | N23 21.0 |
| Kaus Aust. | 84 20.5 | S34 23.7 |
| Kochab | 137 17.8 | N74 15.2 |
| Markab | 14 06.2 | N15 04.6 |
| Menkar | 314 44.5 | N 3 59.8 |
| Menkent | 148 40.1 | S36 15.4 |
| Miaplacidus | 221 45.6 | S69 37.6 |
| Mirfak | 309 20.8 | N49 46.6 |
| Nunki | 76 32.6 | S26 19.5 |
| Peacock | 54 02.9 | S56 48.4 |
| Pollux | 244 02.0 | N28 05.0 |
| Procyon | 245 29.0 | N 5 17.0 |
| Rasalhague | 96 32.0 | N12 34.6 |
| Regulus | 208 13.1 | N12 04.9 |
| Rigel | 281 39.2 | S 8 13.9 |
| Rigil Kent. | 140 29.1 | S60 44.3 |
| Sabik | 102 44.2 | S15 41.8 |
| Schedar | 350 12.7 | N56 24.3 |
| Shaula | 96 59.4 | S37 05.1 |
| Sirius | 258 58.5 | S16 41.3 |
| Spica | 159 00.4 | S11 02.4 |
| Suhail | 223 13.0 | S43 20.6 |
| Vega | 80 57.5 | N38 45.6 |
| Zuben'ubi | 137 36.0 | S15 56.7 |

| | S.H.A. | Mer. Pass. |
|---|---|---|
| | ° ′ | h m |
| Venus | 319 30.1 | 11 19 |
| Mars | 239 28.1 | 16 38 |
| Jupiter | 320 51.1 | 11 12 |
| Saturn | 239 55.8 | 16 34 |

# 1976 MAY 12, 13, 14 (WED., THURS., FRI.)

| G.M.T. | SUN G.H.A. | SUN Dec. | MOON G.H.A. | v | MOON Dec. | d | H.P. |
|---|---|---|---|---|---|---|---|
| d h | ° ′ | ° ′ | ° ′ | ′ | ° ′ | ′ | ′ |
| 12 00 | 180 55.3 | N18 06.7 | 26 44.6 | 6.6 | S11 20.1 | 10.6 | 61.0 |
| 01 | 195 55.3 | 07.3 | 41 10.2 | 6.5 | 11 30.7 | 10.5 | 61.0 |
| 02 | 210 55.3 | 07.9 | 55 35.7 | 6.5 | 11 41.2 | 10.5 | 61.0 |
| 03 | 225 55.4 | ·· 08.6 | 70 01.2 | 6.5 | 11 51.7 | 10.3 | 61.0 |
| 04 | 240 55.4 | 09.2 | 84 26.7 | 6.3 | 12 02.0 | 10.3 | 61.0 |
| 05 | 255 55.4 | 09.8 | 98 52.0 | 6.4 | 12 12.3 | 10.2 | 61.0 |
| 06 | 270 55.4 | N18 10.4 | 113 17.4 | 6.2 | S12 22.5 | 10.2 | 61.0 |
| 07 | 285 55.4 | 11.1 | 127 42.6 | 6.2 | 12 32.7 | 10.0 | 61.0 |
| W 08 | 300 55.4 | 11.7 | 142 07.8 | 6.2 | 12 42.7 | 10.0 | 61.0 |
| E 09 | 315 55.4 | ·· 12.3 | 156 33.0 | 6.1 | 12 52.7 | 9.8 | 61.0 |
| D 10 | 330 55.4 | 13.0 | 170 58.1 | 6.0 | 13 02.5 | 9.8 | 61.0 |
| N 11 | 345 55.5 | 13.6 | 185 23.1 | 6.0 | 13 12.3 | 9.7 | 61.0 |
| E S 12 | 0 55.5 | N18 14.2 | 199 48.1 | 5.9 | S13 22.0 | 9.6 | 61.0 |
| D 13 | 15 55.5 | 14.8 | 214 13.0 | 5.9 | 13 31.6 | 9.5 | 61.0 |
| A 14 | 30 55.5 | 15.4 | 228 37.9 | 5.8 | 13 41.1 | 9.4 | 61.0 |
| Y 15 | 45 55.5 | ·· 16.1 | 243 02.7 | 5.8 | 13 50.5 | 9.4 | 61.0 |
| 16 | 60 55.5 | 16.7 | 257 27.5 | 5.7 | 13 59.9 | 9.2 | 61.0 |
| 17 | 75 55.5 | 17.3 | 271 52.2 | 5.7 | 14 09.1 | 9.1 | 61.0 |
| 18 | 90 55.5 | N18 17.9 | 286 16.9 | 5.6 | S14 18.2 | 9.0 | 61.0 |
| 19 | 105 55.5 | 18.6 | 300 41.5 | 5.6 | 14 27.2 | 9.0 | 61.0 |
| 20 | 120 55.5 | 19.2 | 315 06.1 | 5.5 | 14 36.2 | 8.8 | 61.0 |
| 21 | 135 55.5 | ·· 19.8 | 329 30.6 | 5.5 | 14 45.0 | 8.7 | 61.0 |
| 22 | 150 55.6 | 20.4 | 343 55.1 | 5.4 | 14 53.7 | 8.6 | 61.0 |
| 23 | 165 55.6 | 21.0 | 358 19.5 | 5.3 | 15 02.3 | 8.5 | 61.0 |
| 13 00 | 180 55.6 | N18 21.6 | 12 43.8 | 5.4 | S15 10.8 | 8.4 | 61.0 |
| 01 | 195 55.6 | 22.3 | 27 08.2 | 5.2 | 15 19.2 | 8.3 | 61.0 |
| 02 | 210 55.6 | 22.9 | 41 32.4 | 5.3 | 15 27.5 | 8.2 | 61.0 |
| 03 | 225 55.6 | ·· 23.5 | 55 56.7 | 5.2 | 15 35.7 | 8.1 | 61.0 |
| 04 | 240 55.6 | 24.1 | 70 20.9 | 5.1 | 15 43.8 | 7.9 | 61.0 |
| 05 | 255 55.6 | 24.7 | 84 45.0 | 5.1 | 15 51.7 | 7.9 | 61.0 |
| 06 | 270 55.6 | N18 25.3 | 99 09.1 | 5.1 | S15 59.6 | 7.7 | 61.0 |
| 07 | 285 55.6 | 26.0 | 113 33.2 | 5.0 | 16 07.3 | 7.6 | 61.0 |
| T 08 | 300 55.6 | 26.6 | 127 57.2 | 5.0 | 16 14.9 | 7.5 | 61.0 |
| H 09 | 315 55.6 | ·· 27.2 | 142 21.2 | 4.9 | 16 22.4 | 7.4 | 61.0 |
| U 10 | 330 55.6 | 27.8 | 156 45.1 | 4.9 | 16 29.8 | 7.2 | 61.0 |
| R 11 | 345 55.6 | 28.4 | 171 09.0 | 4.9 | 16 37.0 | 7.2 | 61.0 |
| S 12 | 0 55.6 | N18 29.0 | 185 32.9 | 4.8 | S16 44.2 | 7.0 | 60.9 |
| D 13 | 15 55.6 | 29.6 | 199 56.7 | 4.8 | 16 51.2 | 6.9 | 60.9 |
| A 14 | 30 55.6 | 30.2 | 214 20.5 | 4.8 | 16 58.1 | 6.7 | 60.9 |
| Y 15 | 45 55.7 | ·· 30.8 | 228 44.3 | 4.7 | 17 04.8 | 6.7 | 60.9 |
| 16 | 60 55.7 | 31.5 | 243 08.0 | 4.7 | 17 11.5 | 6.5 | 60.9 |
| 17 | 75 55.7 | 32.1 | 257 31.7 | 4.7 | 17 18.0 | 6.4 | 60.9 |
| 18 | 90 55.7 | N18 32.7 | 271 55.4 | 4.6 | S17 24.4 | 6.3 | 60.9 |
| 19 | 105 55.7 | 33.3 | 286 19.0 | 4.7 | 17 30.7 | 6.1 | 60.9 |
| 20 | 120 55.7 | 33.9 | 300 42.7 | 4.5 | 17 36.8 | 6.0 | 60.9 |
| 21 | 135 55.7 | ·· 34.5 | 315 06.2 | 4.6 | 17 42.8 | 5.9 | 60.8 |
| 22 | 150 55.7 | 35.1 | 329 29.8 | 4.6 | 17 48.7 | 5.7 | 60.8 |
| 23 | 165 55.7 | 35.7 | 343 53.4 | 4.5 | 17 54.4 | 5.6 | 60.8 |
| 14 00 | 180 55.7 | N18 36.3 | 358 16.9 | 4.5 | S18 00.0 | 5.5 | 60.8 |
| 01 | 195 55.7 | 36.9 | 12 40.4 | 4.5 | 18 05.5 | 5.3 | 60.8 |
| 02 | 210 55.7 | 37.5 | 27 03.9 | 4.5 | 18 10.8 | 5.2 | 60.8 |
| 03 | 225 55.7 | ·· 38.1 | 41 27.4 | 4.4 | 18 16.0 | 5.1 | 60.7 |
| 04 | 240 55.7 | 38.7 | 55 50.8 | 4.5 | 18 21.1 | 5.0 | 60.7 |
| 05 | 255 55.7 | 39.3 | 70 14.3 | 4.4 | 18 26.1 | 4.8 | 60.7 |
| 06 | 270 55.7 | N18 39.9 | 84 37.7 | 4.4 | S18 30.9 | 4.6 | 60.7 |
| 07 | 285 55.7 | 40.5 | 99 01.1 | 4.4 | 18 35.5 | 4.6 | 60.7 |
| 08 | 300 55.7 | 41.1 | 113 24.5 | 4.5 | 18 40.1 | 4.4 | 60.6 |
| F 09 | 315 55.7 | ·· 41.7 | 127 48.0 | 4.4 | 18 44.5 | 4.2 | 60.6 |
| R 10 | 330 55.7 | 42.3 | 142 11.4 | 4.3 | 18 48.7 | 4.1 | 60.6 |
| I 11 | 345 55.7 | 42.9 | 156 34.7 | 4.4 | 18 52.8 | 4.0 | 60.6 |
| D 12 | 0 55.7 | N18 43.5 | 170 58.1 | 4.4 | S18 56.8 | 3.9 | 60.6 |
| A 13 | 15 55.7 | 44.1 | 185 21.5 | 4.4 | 19 00.7 | 3.7 | 60.5 |
| Y 14 | 30 55.7 | 44.7 | 199 44.9 | 4.4 | 19 04.4 | 3.5 | 60.5 |
| 15 | 45 55.7 | ·· 45.3 | 214 08.3 | 4.4 | 19 07.9 | 3.4 | 60.5 |
| 16 | 60 55.7 | 45.9 | 228 31.7 | 4.4 | 19 11.3 | 3.3 | 60.5 |
| 17 | 75 55.7 | 46.5 | 242 55.1 | 4.4 | 19 14.6 | 3.2 | 60.4 |
| 18 | 90 55.7 | N18 47.1 | 257 18.5 | 4.5 | S19 17.8 | 2.9 | 60.4 |
| 19 | 105 55.7 | 47.7 | 271 42.0 | 4.4 | 19 20.7 | 2.9 | 60.4 |
| 20 | 120 55.7 | 48.3 | 286 05.4 | 4.4 | 19 23.6 | 2.7 | 60.4 |
| 21 | 135 55.7 | ·· 48.9 | 300 28.8 | 4.5 | 19 26.3 | 2.6 | 60.3 |
| 22 | 150 55.7 | 49.5 | 314 52.3 | 4.4 | 19 28.9 | 2.4 | 60.3 |
| 23 | 165 55.7 | 50.1 | 329 15.7 | 4.5 | 19 31.3 | 2.3 | 60.3 |
| | S.D. 15.9 | d 0.6 | S.D. 16.6 | | 16.6 | | 16.5 |

| Lat. | Twilight Naut. | Twilight Civil | Sunrise | Moonrise 12 | Moonrise 13 | Moonrise 14 | Moonrise 15 |
|---|---|---|---|---|---|---|---|
| ° | h m | h m | h m | h m | h m | h m | h m |
| N 72 | □ | □ | □ | 20 41 | ■ | ■ | ■ |
| N 70 | //// | //// | 01 04 | 20 06 | 22 16 | 24 28 | 00 28 |
| 68 | //// | //// | 01 58 | 19 41 | 21 34 | 23 13 | 24 19 |
| 66 | //// | //// | 02 30 | 19 22 | 21 06 | 22 36 | 23 41 |
| 64 | //// | 01 22 | 02 53 | 19 07 | 20 44 | 22 09 | 23 14 |
| 62 | //// | 02 00 | 03 12 | 18 55 | 20 27 | 21 49 | 22 53 |
| 60 | //// | 02 26 | 03 27 | 18 44 | 20 13 | 21 32 | 22 36 |
| N 58 | 01 13 | 02 46 | 03 40 | 18 35 | 20 01 | 21 18 | 22 22 |
| 56 | 01 48 | 03 02 | 03 51 | 18 27 | 19 50 | 21 06 | 22 09 |
| 54 | 02 12 | 03 16 | 04 01 | 18 19 | 19 41 | 20 55 | 21 59 |
| 52 | 02 31 | 03 28 | 04 09 | 18 13 | 19 33 | 20 46 | 21 49 |
| 50 | 02 47 | 03 38 | 04 17 | 18 07 | 19 26 | 20 38 | 21 40 |
| 45 | 03 17 | 03 59 | 04 33 | 17 55 | 19 10 | 20 20 | 21 22 |
| N 40 | 03 39 | 04 16 | 04 47 | 17 44 | 18 57 | 20 06 | 21 08 |
| 35 | 03 56 | 04 30 | 04 58 | 17 36 | 18 46 | 19 53 | 20 55 |
| 30 | 04 11 | 04 42 | 05 08 | 17 28 | 18 36 | 19 43 | 20 44 |
| 20 | 04 33 | 05 01 | 05 25 | 17 15 | 18 20 | 19 24 | 20 26 |
| N 10 | 04 51 | 05 17 | 05 39 | 17 04 | 18 06 | 19 08 | 20 09 |
| 0 | 05 06 | 05 31 | 05 53 | 16 53 | 17 53 | 18 54 | 19 54 |
| S 10 | 05 19 | 05 44 | 06 06 | 16 42 | 17 40 | 18 39 | 19 39 |
| 20 | 05 31 | 05 57 | 06 20 | 16 31 | 17 26 | 18 23 | 19 23 |
| 30 | 05 42 | 06 11 | 06 36 | 16 18 | 17 10 | 18 05 | 19 04 |
| 35 | 05 48 | 06 19 | 06 46 | 16 11 | 17 00 | 17 55 | 18 53 |
| 40 | 05 55 | 06 27 | 06 56 | 16 03 | 16 50 | 17 43 | 18 41 |
| 45 | 06 02 | 06 37 | 07 09 | 15 53 | 16 38 | 17 29 | 18 26 |
| S 50 | 06 09 | 06 48 | 07 24 | 15 42 | 16 23 | 17 12 | 18 08 |
| 52 | 06 12 | 06 53 | 07 31 | 15 36 | 16 16 | 17 04 | 18 00 |
| 54 | 06 16 | 06 59 | 07 39 | 15 31 | 16 08 | 16 55 | 17 51 |
| 56 | 06 20 | 07 05 | 07 47 | 15 24 | 16 00 | 16 45 | 17 40 |
| 58 | 06 24 | 07 12 | 07 57 | 15 17 | 15 50 | 16 33 | 17 28 |
| S 60 | 06 28 | 07 20 | 08 09 | 15 08 | 15 39 | 16 20 | 17 14 |

| Lat. | Sunset | Twilight Civil | Twilight Naut. | Moonset 12 | Moonset 13 | Moonset 14 | Moonset 15 |
|---|---|---|---|---|---|---|---|
| ° | h m | h m | h m | h m | h m | h m | h m |
| N 72 | □ | □ | □ | 01 37 | 01 17 | ■ | ■ |
| N 70 | 22 58 | //// | //// | 01 57 | 01 53 | 01 49 | 01 45 |
| 68 | 21 59 | //// | //// | 02 12 | 02 19 | 02 31 | 03 00 |
| 66 | 21 26 | //// | //// | 02 25 | 02 38 | 03 00 | 03 38 |
| 64 | 21 02 | 22 37 | //// | 02 36 | 02 55 | 03 22 | 04 04 |
| 62 | 20 43 | 21 57 | //// | 02 45 | 03 08 | 03 40 | 04 25 |
| 60 | 20 27 | 21 30 | //// | 02 53 | 03 19 | 03 54 | 04 42 |
| N 58 | 20 14 | 21 09 | 22 45 | 03 00 | 03 29 | 04 07 | 04 56 |
| 56 | 20 03 | 20 52 | 22 08 | 03 06 | 03 38 | 04 18 | 05 08 |
| 54 | 19 53 | 20 38 | 21 43 | 03 12 | 03 46 | 04 27 | 05 19 |
| 52 | 19 44 | 20 26 | 21 24 | 03 17 | 03 53 | 04 36 | 05 28 |
| 50 | 19 36 | 20 16 | 21 08 | 03 21 | 03 59 | 04 44 | 05 37 |
| 45 | 19 20 | 19 54 | 20 37 | 03 31 | 04 12 | 05 00 | 05 55 |
| N 40 | 19 06 | 19 37 | 20 15 | 03 39 | 04 24 | 05 14 | 06 09 |
| 35 | 18 55 | 19 23 | 19 57 | 03 47 | 04 33 | 05 25 | 06 22 |
| 30 | 18 45 | 19 11 | 19 42 | 03 53 | 04 42 | 05 35 | 06 33 |
| 20 | 18 28 | 18 52 | 19 20 | 04 04 | 04 56 | 05 52 | 06 51 |
| N 10 | 18 14 | 18 36 | 19 02 | 04 13 | 05 09 | 06 08 | 07 07 |
| 0 | 18 00 | 18 22 | 18 47 | 04 22 | 05 21 | 06 22 | 07 23 |
| S 10 | 17 46 | 18 08 | 18 34 | 04 31 | 05 33 | 06 36 | 07 38 |
| 20 | 17 32 | 17 55 | 18 22 | 04 41 | 05 46 | 06 51 | 07 54 |
| 30 | 17 16 | 17 41 | 18 10 | 04 52 | 06 01 | 07 08 | 08 12 |
| 35 | 17 06 | 17 33 | 18 04 | 04 58 | 06 09 | 07 18 | 08 23 |
| 40 | 16 56 | 17 25 | 17 57 | 05 06 | 06 19 | 07 30 | 08 36 |
| 45 | 16 43 | 17 15 | 17 51 | 05 14 | 06 30 | 07 43 | 08 50 |
| S 50 | 16 28 | 17 04 | 17 43 | 05 24 | 06 44 | 08 00 | 09 08 |
| 52 | 16 21 | 16 59 | 17 40 | 05 29 | 06 51 | 08 08 | 09 16 |
| 54 | 16 13 | 16 53 | 17 36 | 05 34 | 06 58 | 08 17 | 09 26 |
| 56 | 16 04 | 16 47 | 17 32 | 05 40 | 07 06 | 08 26 | 09 36 |
| 58 | 15 55 | 16 40 | 17 28 | 05 47 | 07 15 | 08 38 | 09 48 |
| S 60 | 15 43 | 16 32 | 17 24 | 05 54 | 07 26 | 08 50 | 10 02 |

| Day | SUN Eqn. of Time 00ʰ | SUN Eqn. of Time 12ʰ | SUN Mer. Pass. | MOON Mer. Pass. Upper | MOON Mer. Pass. Lower | MOON Age | Phase |
|---|---|---|---|---|---|---|---|
| | m s | m s | h m | h m | h m | d | |
| 12 | 03 41 | 03 42 | 11 56 | 23 07 | 10 38 | 13 | ○ |
| 13 | 03 42 | 03 43 | 11 56 | 24 07 | 11 37 | 14 | |
| 14 | 03 43 | 03 43 | 11 56 | 00 07 | 12 38 | 15 | |

# 1976 JUNE 5, 6, 7 (SAT., SUN., MON.)

| G.M.T. | SUN G.H.A. | SUN Dec. | MOON G.H.A. | v | MOON Dec. | d | H.P. |
|---|---|---|---|---|---|---|---|
| d h | ° ′ | ° ′ | ° ′ | ′ | ° ′ | ′ | ′ |
| 5 00 | 180 24.4 | N22 32.1 | 95 48.6 | 10.8 | N 4 16.2 | 11.5 | 58.5 |
| 01 | 195 24.3 | 32.4 | 110 18.4 | 10.9 | 4 04.7 | 11.5 | 58.5 |
| 02 | 210 24.2 | 32.7 | 124 48.3 | 10.8 | 3 53.2 | 11.5 | 58.5 |
| 03 | 225 24.0 | ·· 32.9 | 139 18.1 | 10.9 | 3 41.7 | 11.6 | 58.6 |
| 04 | 240 23.9 | 33.2 | 153 48.0 | 10.8 | 3 30.1 | 11.6 | 58.6 |
| 05 | 255 23.8 | 33.5 | 168 17.8 | 10.8 | 3 18.5 | 11.6 | 58.6 |
| 06 | 270 23.7 | N22 33.8 | 182 47.6 | 10.8 | N 3 06.9 | 11.6 | 58.6 |
| 07 | 285 23.6 | 34.0 | 197 17.4 | 10.8 | 2 55.3 | 11.7 | 58.6 |
| S 08 | 300 23.5 | 34.3 | 211 47.2 | 10.8 | 2 43.6 | 11.7 | 58.7 |
| A 09 | 315 23.4 | ·· 34.6 | 226 17.0 | 10.7 | 2 31.9 | 11.7 | 58.7 |
| T 10 | 330 23.3 | 34.8 | 240 46.7 | 10.8 | 2 20.2 | 11.7 | 58.7 |
| U 11 | 345 23.2 | 35.1 | 255 16.5 | 10.7 | 2 08.5 | 11.8 | 58.7 |
| R 12 | 0 23.1 | N22 35.4 | 269 46.2 | 10.7 | N 1 56.7 | 11.8 | 58.8 |
| D 13 | 15 22.9 | 35.6 | 284 15.9 | 10.6 | 1 44.9 | 11.8 | 58.8 |
| A 14 | 30 22.8 | 35.9 | 298 45.5 | 10.7 | 1 33.1 | 11.8 | 58.8 |
| Y 15 | 45 22.7 | ·· 36.2 | 313 15.2 | 10.6 | 1 21.3 | 11.8 | 58.8 |
| 16 | 60 22.6 | 36.4 | 327 44.8 | 10.6 | 1 09.5 | 11.8 | 58.9 |
| 17 | 75 22.5 | 36.7 | 342 14.4 | 10.6 | 0 57.7 | 11.9 | 58.9 |
| 18 | 90 22.4 | N22 37.0 | 356 44.0 | 10.6 | N 0 45.8 | 11.9 | 58.9 |
| 19 | 105 22.3 | 37.2 | 11 13.6 | 10.5 | 0 33.9 | 11.9 | 58.9 |
| 20 | 120 22.2 | 37.5 | 25 43.1 | 10.6 | 0 22.0 | 11.9 | 59.0 |
| 21 | 135 22.0 | ·· 37.8 | 40 12.7 | 10.4 | N 0 10.1 | 11.9 | 59.0 |
| 22 | 150 21.9 | 38.0 | 54 42.1 | 10.5 | S 0 01.8 | 11.9 | 59.0 |
| 23 | 165 21.8 | 38.3 | 69 11.6 | 10.5 | 0 13.7 | 11.9 | 59.0 |
| 6 00 | 180 21.7 | N22 38.5 | 83 41.1 | 10.4 | S 0 25.6 | 12.0 | 59.0 |
| 01 | 195 21.6 | 38.8 | 98 10.5 | 10.3 | 0 37.6 | 11.9 | 59.1 |
| 02 | 210 21.5 | 39.1 | 112 39.8 | 10.4 | 0 49.5 | 11.9 | 59.1 |
| 03 | 225 21.4 | ·· 39.3 | 127 09.2 | 10.3 | 1 01.4 | 12.0 | 59.1 |
| 04 | 240 21.3 | 39.6 | 141 38.5 | 10.3 | 1 13.4 | 11.9 | 59.1 |
| 05 | 255 21.1 | 39.8 | 156 07.8 | 10.3 | 1 25.3 | 12.0 | 59.2 |
| 06 | 270 21.0 | N22 40.1 | 170 37.1 | 10.2 | S 1 37.3 | 12.0 | 59.2 |
| 07 | 285 20.9 | 40.3 | 185 06.3 | 10.2 | 1 49.3 | 11.9 | 59.2 |
| 08 | 300 20.8 | 40.6 | 199 35.5 | 10.2 | 2 01.2 | 12.0 | 59.2 |
| S 09 | 315 20.7 | ·· 40.8 | 214 04.7 | 10.1 | 2 13.2 | 11.9 | 59.3 |
| U 10 | 330 20.6 | 41.1 | 228 33.8 | 10.1 | 2 25.1 | 11.9 | 59.3 |
| N 11 | 345 20.5 | 41.4 | 243 02.9 | 10.0 | 2 37.0 | 12.0 | 59.3 |
| D 12 | 0 20.3 | N22 41.6 | 257 31.9 | 10.1 | S 2 49.0 | 11.9 | 59.3 |
| A 13 | 15 20.2 | 41.9 | 272 01.0 | 9.9 | 3 00.9 | 11.9 | 59.3 |
| Y 14 | 30 20.1 | 42.1 | 286 29.9 | 10.0 | 3 12.8 | 11.9 | 59.4 |
| 15 | 45 20.0 | ·· 42.4 | 300 58.9 | 9.9 | 3 24.7 | 11.9 | 59.4 |
| 16 | 60 19.9 | 42.6 | 315 27.8 | 9.8 | 3 36.6 | 11.9 | 59.4 |
| 17 | 75 19.8 | 42.9 | 329 56.6 | 9.9 | 3 48.5 | 11.9 | 59.4 |
| 18 | 90 19.7 | N22 43.1 | 344 25.5 | 9.8 | S 4 00.4 | 11.9 | 59.4 |
| 19 | 105 19.5 | 43.3 | 358 54.3 | 9.7 | 4 12.3 | 11.8 | 59.5 |
| 20 | 120 19.4 | 43.6 | 13 23.0 | 9.7 | 4 24.1 | 11.9 | 59.5 |
| 21 | 135 19.3 | ·· 43.8 | 27 51.7 | 9.6 | 4 36.0 | 11.8 | 59.5 |
| 22 | 150 19.2 | 44.1 | 42 20.3 | 9.7 | 4 47.8 | 11.8 | 59.5 |
| 23 | 165 19.1 | 44.3 | 56 49.0 | 9.5 | 4 59.6 | 11.7 | 59.5 |
| 7 00 | 180 19.0 | N22 44.6 | 71 17.5 | 9.5 | S 5 11.3 | 11.8 | 59.6 |
| 01 | 195 18.9 | 44.8 | 85 46.0 | 9.5 | 5 23.1 | 11.7 | 59.6 |
| 02 | 210 18.7 | 45.1 | 100 14.5 | 9.5 | 5 34.8 | 11.7 | 59.6 |
| 03 | 225 18.6 | ·· 45.3 | 114 43.0 | 9.3 | 5 46.5 | 11.7 | 59.6 |
| 04 | 240 18.5 | 45.5 | 129 11.3 | 9.4 | 5 58.2 | 11.7 | 59.6 |
| 05 | 255 18.4 | 45.8 | 143 39.7 | 9.3 | 6 09.9 | 11.6 | 59.7 |
| 06 | 270 18.3 | N22 46.0 | 158 08.0 | 9.2 | S 6 21.5 | 11.6 | 59.7 |
| 07 | 285 18.2 | 46.3 | 172 36.2 | 9.2 | 6 33.1 | 11.5 | 59.7 |
| 08 | 300 18.0 | 46.5 | 187 04.4 | 9.1 | 6 44.6 | 11.6 | 59.7 |
| M 09 | 315 17.9 | ·· 46.7 | 201 32.5 | 9.1 | 6 56.2 | 11.5 | 59.7 |
| O 10 | 330 17.8 | 47.0 | 216 00.6 | 9.1 | 7 07.7 | 11.4 | 59.8 |
| N 11 | 345 17.7 | 47.2 | 230 28.7 | 8.9 | 7 19.1 | 11.5 | 59.8 |
| D 12 | 0 17.6 | N22 47.4 | 244 56.6 | 9.0 | S 7 30.6 | 11.3 | 59.8 |
| A 13 | 15 17.5 | 47.7 | 259 24.6 | 8.9 | 7 41.9 | 11.4 | 59.8 |
| Y 14 | 30 17.3 | 47.9 | 273 52.5 | 8.8 | 7 53.3 | 11.3 | 59.8 |
| 15 | 45 17.2 | ·· 48.1 | 288 20.3 | 8.8 | 8 04.6 | 11.3 | 59.8 |
| 16 | 60 17.1 | 48.4 | 302 48.1 | 8.7 | 8 15.9 | 11.2 | 59.9 |
| 17 | 75 17.0 | 48.6 | 317 15.8 | 8.6 | 8 27.1 | 11.2 | 59.9 |
| 18 | 90 16.9 | N22 48.8 | 331 43.4 | 8.7 | S 8 38.3 | 11.1 | 59.9 |
| 19 | 105 16.8 | 49.1 | 346 11.1 | 8.5 | 8 49.4 | 11.1 | 59.9 |
| 20 | 120 16.6 | 49.3 | 0 38.6 | 8.5 | 9 00.5 | 11.0 | 59.9 |
| 21 | 135 16.5 | ·· 49.5 | 15 06.1 | 8.5 | 9 11.5 | 11.0 | 59.9 |
| 22 | 150 16.4 | 49.7 | 29 33.6 | 8.3 | 9 22.5 | 11.0 | 60.0 |
| 23 | 165 16.3 | 50.0 | 44 00.9 | 8.4 | 9 33.5 | 10.9 | 60.0 |
| | S.D. 15.8 | d 0.3 | S.D. 16.0 | | 16.2 | | 16.3 |

| Lat. | Twilight Naut. | Twilight Civil | Sunrise | Moonrise 5 | Moonrise 6 | Moonrise 7 | Moonrise 8 |
|---|---|---|---|---|---|---|---|
| ° | h m | h m | h m | h m | h m | h m | h m |
| N 72 | □ | □ | □ | 11 37 | 13 34 | 15 35 | 17 46 |
| N 70 | □ | □ | □ | 11 40 | 13 29 | 15 22 | 17 20 |
| 68 | □ | □ | □ | 11 42 | 13 25 | 15 12 | 17 01 |
| 66 | //// | //// | 00 50 | 11 44 | 13 22 | 15 03 | 16 46 |
| 64 | //// | //// | 01 46 | 11 45 | 13 19 | 14 56 | 16 33 |
| 62 | //// | //// | 02 19 | 11 47 | 13 17 | 14 49 | 16 23 |
| 60 | //// | 01 12 | 02 43 | 11 48 | 13 15 | 14 44 | 16 14 |
| N 58 | //// | 01 51 | 03 02 | 11 49 | 13 13 | 14 39 | 16 06 |
| 56 | //// | 02 18 | 03 17 | 11 50 | 13 12 | 14 35 | 15 59 |
| 54 | 01 06 | 02 38 | 03 31 | 11 51 | 13 10 | 14 31 | 15 53 |
| 52 | 01 42 | 02 55 | 03 42 | 11 51 | 13 09 | 14 28 | 15 48 |
| 50 | 02 07 | 03 09 | 03 53 | 11 52 | 13 08 | 14 25 | 15 43 |
| 45 | 02 49 | 03 37 | 04 14 | 11 54 | 13 05 | 14 18 | 15 32 |
| N 40 | 03 18 | 03 59 | 04 31 | 11 55 | 13 03 | 14 13 | 15 24 |
| 35 | 03 40 | 04 17 | 04 46 | 11 56 | 13 01 | 14 08 | 15 16 |
| 30 | 03 58 | 04 31 | 04 58 | 11 57 | 13 00 | 14 04 | 15 09 |
| 20 | 04 26 | 04 55 | 05 20 | 11 59 | 12 57 | 13 57 | 14 58 |
| N 10 | 04 48 | 05 15 | 05 38 | 12 00 | 12 54 | 13 50 | 14 48 |
| 0 | 05 07 | 05 32 | 05 55 | 12 02 | 12 52 | 13 45 | 14 39 |
| S 10 | 05 23 | 05 49 | 06 12 | 12 03 | 12 50 | 13 39 | 14 30 |
| 20 | 05 38 | 06 06 | 06 30 | 12 04 | 12 48 | 13 33 | 14 20 |
| 30 | 05 54 | 06 24 | 06 50 | 12 06 | 12 45 | 13 26 | 14 09 |
| 35 | 06 03 | 06 34 | 07 02 | 12 07 | 12 44 | 13 22 | 14 03 |
| 40 | 06 11 | 06 45 | 07 16 | 12 08 | 12 42 | 13 18 | 13 56 |
| 45 | 06 21 | 06 58 | 07 32 | 12 10 | 12 40 | 13 12 | 13 48 |
| S 50 | 06 32 | 07 13 | 07 52 | 12 11 | 12 38 | 13 06 | 13 38 |
| 52 | 06 37 | 07 21 | 08 01 | 12 12 | 12 37 | 13 04 | 13 33 |
| 54 | 06 43 | 07 28 | 08 12 | 12 13 | 12 36 | 13 01 | 13 28 |
| 56 | 06 48 | 07 37 | 08 23 | 12 14 | 12 35 | 12 57 | 13 23 |
| 58 | 06 55 | 07 47 | 08 37 | 12 15 | 12 33 | 12 54 | 13 17 |
| S 60 | 07 02 | 07 58 | 08 54 | 12 16 | 12 32 | 12 49 | 13 10 |

| Lat. | Sunset | Twilight Civil | Twilight Naut. | Moonset 5 | Moonset 6 | Moonset 7 | Moonset 8 |
|---|---|---|---|---|---|---|---|
| ° | h m | h m | h m | h m | h m | h m | h m |
| N 72 | □ | □ | □ | 00 28 | 00 18 | {00 08 / 23 56} | 23 41 |
| N 70 | □ | □ | □ | 00 22 | 00 19 | 00 15 | 00 11 |
| 68 | □ | □ | □ | 00 18 | 00 19 | 00 21 | 00 24 |
| 66 | 23 12 | //// | //// | 00 14 | 00 20 | 00 26 | 00 34 |
| 64 | 22 13 | //// | //// | 00 11 | 00 21 | 00 31 | 00 42 |
| 62 | 21 39 | //// | //// | 00 08 | 00 21 | 00 34 | 00 50 |
| 60 | 21 15 | 22 47 | //// | 00 05 | 00 21 | 00 38 | 00 56 |
| N 58 | 20 56 | 22 07 | //// | 00 03 | 00 22 | 00 41 | 01 02 |
| 56 | 20 40 | 21 40 | //// | 00 01 | 00 22 | 00 43 | 01 07 |
| 54 | 20 27 | 21 20 | 22 54 | 24 22 | 00 22 | 00 46 | 01 12 |
| 52 | 20 15 | 21 03 | 22 17 | 24 22 | 00 22 | 00 48 | 01 16 |
| 50 | 20 05 | 20 49 | 21 51 | 24 23 | 00 23 | 00 50 | 01 20 |
| 45 | 19 43 | 20 20 | 21 09 | 24 23 | 00 23 | 00 54 | 01 28 |
| N 40 | 19 26 | 19 58 | 20 39 | 24 24 | 00 24 | 00 58 | 01 35 |
| 35 | 19 11 | 19 41 | 20 17 | 24 24 | 00 24 | 01 01 | 01 40 |
| 30 | 18 59 | 19 26 | 19 59 | 24 24 | 00 24 | 01 04 | 01 46 |
| 20 | 18 38 | 19 02 | 19 31 | 24 25 | 00 25 | 01 09 | 01 55 |
| N 10 | 18 19 | 18 42 | 19 09 | 24 25 | 00 25 | 01 13 | 02 03 |
| 0 | 18 02 | 18 25 | 18 51 | 24 26 | 00 26 | 01 17 | 02 10 |
| S 10 | 17 45 | 18 08 | 18 34 | 24 26 | 00 26 | 01 21 | 02 18 |
| 20 | 17 28 | 17 51 | 18 19 | 24 26 | 00 26 | 01 25 | 02 26 |
| 30 | 17 07 | 17 33 | 18 03 | 24 27 | 00 27 | 01 30 | 02 35 |
| 35 | 16 55 | 17 23 | 17 55 | 24 27 | 00 27 | 01 33 | 02 40 |
| 40 | 16 41 | 17 12 | 17 46 | 24 27 | 00 27 | 01 36 | 02 46 |
| 45 | 16 26 | 16 59 | 17 36 | 24 27 | 00 27 | 01 40 | 02 53 |
| S 50 | 16 06 | 16 44 | 17 25 | 24 28 | 00 28 | 01 44 | 03 02 |
| 52 | 15 56 | 16 36 | 17 20 | 24 28 | 00 28 | 01 46 | 03 06 |
| 54 | 15 45 | 16 28 | 17 14 | 24 28 | 00 28 | 01 48 | 03 10 |
| 56 | 15 33 | 16 20 | 17 08 | 24 28 | 00 28 | 01 51 | 03 15 |
| 58 | 15 20 | 16 10 | 17 02 | 24 28 | 00 28 | 01 53 | 03 20 |
| S 60 | 15 03 | 15 59 | 16 55 | 24 29 | 00 29 | 01 56 | 03 26 |

| Day | SUN Eqn. of Time 00ʰ | SUN Eqn. of Time 12ʰ | SUN Mer. Pass. | MOON Mer. Pass. Upper | MOON Mer. Pass. Lower | MOON Age | Phase |
|---|---|---|---|---|---|---|---|
| | m s | m s | h m | h m | h m | d | |
| 5 | 01 38 | 01 32 | 11 58 | 18 14 | 05 48 | 07 | ◐ |
| 6 | 01 27 | 01 22 | 11 59 | 19 05 | 06 39 | 08 | |
| 7 | 01 16 | 01 11 | 11 59 | 19 57 | 07 31 | 09 | |

| G.M.T. | ARIES G.H.A. | VENUS −3.5 G.H.A. | VENUS Dec. | MARS +1.8 G.H.A. | MARS Dec. | JUPITER −1.6 G.H.A. | JUPITER Dec. | SATURN +0.5 G.H.A. | SATURN Dec. |
|---|---|---|---|---|---|---|---|---|---|
| d h | ° ′ | ° ′ | ° ′ | ° ′ | ° ′ | ° ′ | ° ′ | ° ′ | ° ′ |
| 14 00 | 262 25.0 | 181 13.4 | N23 17.3 | 123 12.4 | N17 13.2 | 216 01.6 | N16 26.1 | 139 09.0 | N20 23.5 |
| 01 | 277 27.5 | 196 12.5 | 17.6 | 138 13.4 | 12.8 | 231 03.6 | 26.2 | 154 11.2 | 23.4 |
| 02 | 292 30.0 | 211 11.7 | 17.8 | 153 14.4 | 12.3 | 246 05.5 | 26.4 | 169 13.4 | 23.3 |
| 03 | 307 32.4 | 226 10.8 | ·· 18.1 | 168 15.4 | ·· 11.8 | 261 07.4 | ·· 26.5 | 184 15.5 | ·· 23.3 |
| 04 | 322 34.9 | 241 09.9 | 18.4 | 183 16.4 | 11.4 | 276 09.3 | 26.7 | 199 17.7 | 23.2 |
| 05 | 337 37.4 | 256 09.1 | 18.7 | 198 17.4 | 10.9 | 291 11.3 | 26.8 | 214 19.9 | 23.2 |
| 06 | 352 39.8 | 271 08.2 | N23 19.0 | 213 18.4 | N17 10.4 | 306 13.2 | N16 26.9 | 229 22.1 | N20 23.1 |
| 07 | 7 42.3 | 286 07.3 | 19.2 | 228 19.4 | 10.0 | 321 15.1 | 27.1 | 244 24.2 | 23.0 |
| M 08 | 22 44.8 | 301 06.5 | 19.5 | 243 20.5 | 09.5 | 336 17.0 | 27.2 | 259 26.4 | 23.0 |
| O 09 | 37 47.2 | 316 05.6 | ·· 19.8 | 258 21.5 | ·· 09.1 | 351 18.9 | ·· 27.4 | 274 28.6 | ·· 22.9 |
| N 10 | 52 49.7 | 331 04.7 | 20.1 | 273 22.5 | 08.6 | 6 20.9 | 27.5 | 289 30.8 | 22.9 |
| D 11 | 67 52.2 | 346 03.8 | 20.3 | 288 23.5 | 08.1 | 21 22.8 | 27.7 | 304 32.9 | 22.8 |
| A 12 | 82 54.6 | 1 03.0 | N23 20.6 | 303 24.5 | N17 07.7 | 36 24.7 | N16 27.8 | 319 35.1 | N20 22.8 |
| Y 13 | 97 57.1 | 16 02.1 | 20.9 | 318 25.5 | 07.2 | 51 26.6 | 28.0 | 334 37.3 | 22.7 |
| 14 | 112 59.5 | 31 01.2 | 21.2 | 333 26.5 | 06.7 | 66 28.6 | 28.1 | 349 39.5 | 22.6 |
| 15 | 128 02.0 | 46 00.4 | ·· 21.4 | 348 27.5 | ·· 06.3 | 81 30.5 | ·· 28.3 | 4 41.6 | ·· 22.6 |
| 16 | 143 04.5 | 60 59.5 | 21.7 | 3 28.6 | 05.8 | 96 32.4 | 28.4 | 19 43.8 | 22.5 |
| 17 | 158 06.9 | 75 58.6 | 22.0 | 18 29.6 | 05.3 | 111 34.3 | 28.6 | 34 46.0 | 22.5 |
| 18 | 173 09.4 | 90 57.8 | N23 22.2 | 33 30.6 | N17 04.8 | 126 36.3 | N16 28.7 | 49 48.2 | N20 22.4 |
| 19 | 188 11.9 | 105 56.9 | 22.5 | 48 31.6 | 04.4 | 141 38.2 | 28.9 | 64 50.3 | 22.3 |
| 20 | 203 14.3 | 120 56.0 | 22.8 | 63 32.6 | 03.9 | 156 40.1 | 29.0 | 79 52.5 | 22.3 |
| 21 | 218 16.8 | 135 55.2 | ·· 23.0 | 78 33.6 | ·· 03.4 | 171 42.0 | ·· 29.1 | 94 54.7 | ·· 22.2 |
| 22 | 233 19.3 | 150 54.3 | 23.3 | 93 34.6 | 03.0 | 186 43.9 | 29.3 | 109 56.8 | 22.2 |
| 23 | 248 21.7 | 165 53.4 | 23.5 | 108 35.6 | 02.5 | 201 45.9 | 29.4 | 124 59.0 | 22.1 |
| 15 00 | 263 24.2 | 180 52.5 | N23 23.8 | 123 36.7 | N17 02.0 | 216 47.8 | N16 29.6 | 140 01.2 | N20 22.0 |
| 01 | 278 26.7 | 195 51.7 | 24.0 | 138 37.7 | 01.6 | 231 49.7 | 29.7 | 155 03.4 | 22.0 |
| 02 | 293 29.1 | 210 50.8 | 24.3 | 153 38.7 | 01.1 | 246 51.6 | 29.9 | 170 05.5 | 21.9 |
| 03 | 308 31.6 | 225 49.9 | ·· 24.6 | 168 39.7 | ·· 00.6 | 261 53.6 | ·· 30.0 | 185 07.7 | ·· 21.9 |
| 04 | 323 34.0 | 240 49.1 | 24.8 | 183 40.7 | 17 00.2 | 276 55.5 | 30.2 | 200 09.9 | 21.8 |
| 05 | 338 36.5 | 255 48.2 | 25.1 | 198 41.7 | 16 59.7 | 291 57.4 | 30.3 | 215 12.1 | 21.8 |
| 06 | 353 39.0 | 270 47.3 | N23 25.3 | 213 42.7 | N16 59.2 | 306 59.3 | N16 30.5 | 230 14.2 | N20 21.7 |
| 07 | 8 41.4 | 285 46.4 | 25.6 | 228 43.7 | 58.8 | 322 01.3 | 30.6 | 245 16.4 | 21.6 |
| T 08 | 23 43.9 | 300 45.6 | 25.8 | 243 44.8 | 58.3 | 337 03.2 | 30.7 | 260 18.6 | 21.6 |
| U 09 | 38 46.4 | 315 44.7 | ·· 26.1 | 258 45.8 | ·· 57.8 | 352 05.1 | ·· 30.9 | 275 20.7 | ·· 21.5 |
| E 10 | 53 48.8 | 330 43.8 | 26.3 | 273 46.8 | 57.3 | 7 07.0 | 31.0 | 290 22.9 | 21.5 |
| S 11 | 68 51.3 | 345 42.9 | 26.6 | 288 47.8 | 56.9 | 22 09.0 | 31.2 | 305 25.1 | 21.4 |
| D 12 | 83 53.8 | 0 42.1 | N23 26.8 | 303 48.8 | N16 56.4 | 37 10.9 | N16 31.3 | 320 27.3 | N20 21.3 |
| A 13 | 98 56.2 | 15 41.2 | 27.0 | 318 49.8 | 55.9 | 52 12.8 | 31.5 | 335 29.4 | 21.3 |
| Y 14 | 113 58.7 | 30 40.3 | 27.3 | 333 50.8 | 55.5 | 67 14.7 | 31.6 | 350 31.6 | 21.2 |
| 15 | 129 01.1 | 45 39.4 | ·· 27.5 | 348 51.8 | ·· 55.0 | 82 16.7 | ·· 31.8 | 5 33.8 | ·· 21.2 |
| 16 | 144 03.6 | 60 38.6 | 27.8 | 3 52.9 | 54.5 | 97 18.6 | 31.9 | 20 35.9 | 21.1 |
| 17 | 159 06.1 | 75 37.7 | 28.0 | 18 53.9 | 54.0 | 112 20.5 | 32.1 | 35 38.1 | 21.0 |
| 18 | 174 08.5 | 90 36.8 | N23 28.2 | 33 54.9 | N16 53.6 | 127 22.4 | N16 32.2 | 50 40.3 | N20 21.0 |
| 19 | 189 11.0 | 105 35.9 | 28.5 | 48 55.9 | 53.1 | 142 24.4 | 32.3 | 65 42.5 | 20.9 |
| 20 | 204 13.5 | 120 35.1 | 28.7 | 63 56.9 | 52.6 | 157 26.3 | 32.5 | 80 44.6 | 20.9 |
| 21 | 219 15.9 | 135 34.2 | ·· 28.9 | 78 57.9 | ·· 52.2 | 172 28.2 | ·· 32.6 | 95 46.8 | ·· 20.8 |
| 22 | 234 18.4 | 150 33.3 | 29.2 | 93 58.9 | 51.7 | 187 30.1 | 32.8 | 110 49.0 | 20.8 |
| 23 | 249 20.9 | 165 32.4 | 29.4 | 108 59.9 | 51.2 | 202 32.1 | 32.9 | 125 51.1 | 20.7 |
| 16 00 | 264 23.3 | 180 31.6 | N23 29.6 | 124 01.0 | N16 50.7 | 217 34.0 | N16 33.1 | 140 53.3 | N20 20.6 |
| 01 | 279 25.8 | 195 30.7 | 29.9 | 139 02.0 | 50.3 | 232 35.9 | 33.2 | 155 55.5 | 20.6 |
| 02 | 294 28.3 | 210 29.8 | 30.1 | 154 03.0 | 49.8 | 247 37.8 | 33.4 | 170 57.7 | 20.5 |
| 03 | 309 30.7 | 225 28.9 | ·· 30.3 | 169 04.0 | ·· 49.3 | 262 39.8 | ·· 33.5 | 185 59.8 | ·· 20.5 |
| 04 | 324 33.2 | 240 28.1 | 30.5 | 184 05.0 | 48.8 | 277 41.7 | 33.6 | 201 02.0 | 20.4 |
| 05 | 339 35.6 | 255 27.2 | 30.8 | 199 06.0 | 48.4 | 292 43.6 | 33.8 | 216 04.2 | 20.3 |
| 06 | 354 38.1 | 270 26.3 | N23 31.0 | 214 07.0 | N16 47.9 | 307 45.6 | N16 33.9 | 231 06.3 | N20 20.3 |
| W 07 | 9 40.6 | 285 25.4 | 31.2 | 229 08.0 | 47.4 | 322 47.5 | 34.1 | 246 08.5 | 20.2 |
| E 08 | 24 43.0 | 300 24.5 | 31.4 | 244 09.1 | 46.9 | 337 49.4 | 34.2 | 261 10.7 | 20.2 |
| D 09 | 39 45.5 | 315 23.7 | ·· 31.6 | 259 10.1 | ·· 46.5 | 352 51.3 | ·· 34.4 | 276 12.8 | ·· 20.1 |
| N 10 | 54 48.0 | 330 22.8 | 31.9 | 274 11.1 | 46.0 | 7 53.3 | 34.5 | 291 15.0 | 20.0 |
| E 11 | 69 50.4 | 345 21.9 | 32.1 | 289 12.1 | 45.5 | 22 55.2 | 34.7 | 306 17.2 | 20.0 |
| S 12 | 84 52.9 | 0 21.0 | N23 32.3 | 304 13.1 | N16 45.0 | 37 57.1 | N16 34.8 | 321 19.4 | N20 19.9 |
| D 13 | 99 55.4 | 15 20.2 | 32.5 | 319 14.1 | 44.6 | 52 59.0 | 34.9 | 336 21.5 | 19.9 |
| A 14 | 114 57.8 | 30 19.3 | 32.7 | 334 15.1 | 44.1 | 68 01.0 | 35.1 | 351 23.7 | 19.8 |
| Y 15 | 130 00.3 | 45 18.4 | ·· 32.9 | 349 16.2 | ·· 43.6 | 83 02.9 | ·· 35.2 | 6 25.9 | ·· 19.7 |
| 16 | 145 02.8 | 60 17.5 | 33.1 | 4 17.2 | 43.1 | 98 04.8 | 35.4 | 21 28.0 | 19.7 |
| 17 | 160 05.2 | 75 16.6 | 33.3 | 19 18.2 | 42.7 | 113 06.8 | 35.5 | 36 30.2 | 19.6 |
| 18 | 175 07.7 | 90 15.8 | N23 33.6 | 34 19.2 | N16 42.2 | 128 08.7 | N16 35.7 | 51 32.4 | N20 19.6 |
| 19 | 190 10.1 | 105 14.9 | 33.8 | 49 20.2 | 41.7 | 143 10.6 | 35.8 | 66 34.5 | 19.5 |
| 20 | 205 12.6 | 120 14.0 | 34.0 | 64 21.2 | 41.2 | 158 12.5 | 35.9 | 81 36.7 | 19.4 |
| 21 | 220 15.1 | 135 13.1 | ·· 34.2 | 79 22.2 | ·· 40.8 | 173 14.5 | ·· 36.1 | 96 38.9 | ·· 19.4 |
| 22 | 235 17.5 | 150 12.2 | 34.4 | 94 23.2 | 40.3 | 188 16.4 | 36.2 | 111 41.0 | 19.3 |
| 23 | 250 20.0 | 165 11.4 | 34.6 | 109 24.3 | 39.8 | 203 18.3 | 36.4 | 126 43.2 | 19.3 |
| Mer. Pass. | h m 6 25.3 | $v$ −0.9 | $d$ 0.2 | $v$ 1.0 | $d$ 0.5 | $v$ 1.9 | $d$ 0.1 | $v$ 2.2 | $d$ 0.1 |

STARS

| Name | S.H.A. | Dec. |
|---|---|---|
| | ° ′ | ° ′ |
| Acamar | 315 39.8 | S40 23.8 |
| Achernar | 335 47.8 | S57 21.1 |
| Acrux | 173 40.2 | S62 58.5 |
| Adhara | 255 34.7 | S28 56.6 |
| Aldebaran | 291 21.6 | N16 27.7 |
| Alioth | 166 44.9 | N56 05.5 |
| Alkaid | 153 20.5 | N49 26.0 |
| Al Na'ir | 28 18.4 | S47 04.2 |
| Alnilam | 276 14.9 | S 1 13.1 |
| Alphard | 218 23.6 | S 8 33.5 |
| Alphecca | 126 34.2 | N26 47.7 |
| Alpheratz | 358 12.3 | N28 57.5 |
| Altair | 62 35.0 | N 8 48.4 |
| Ankaa | 353 43.2 | S42 25.8 |
| Antares | 113 00.0 | S26 22.8 |
| Arcturus | 146 20.9 | N19 18.3 |
| Atria | 108 26.2 | S68 59.2 |
| Avior | 234 29.8 | S59 26.3 |
| Bellatrix | 279 02.2 | N 6 19.6 |
| Betelgeuse | 271 31.7 | N 7 24.1 |
| Canopus | 264 09.0 | S52 41.1 |
| Capella | 281 16.0 | N45 58.4 |
| Deneb | 49 50.0 | N45 11.7 |
| Denebola | 183 02.0 | N14 42.2 |
| Diphda | 349 23.9 | S18 06.8 |
| Dubhe | 194 25.8 | N61 52.9 |
| Elnath | 278 48.1 | N28 35.2 |
| Eltanin | 90 58.5 | N51 29.6 |
| Enif | 34 14.2 | N 9 46.1 |
| Fomalhaut | 15 54.5 | S29 44.6 |
| Gacrux | 172 31.7 | S56 59.2 |
| Gienah | 176 20.9 | S17 24.9 |
| Hadar | 149 26.9 | S60 15.9 |
| Hamal | 328 32.4 | N23 21.0 |
| Kaus Aust. | 84 20.2 | S34 23.7 |
| Kochab | 137 18.1 | N74 15.3 |
| Markab | 14 06.0 | N15 04.7 |
| Menkar | 314 44.4 | N 3 59.8 |
| Menkent | 148 40.1 | S36 15.5 |
| Miaplacidus | 221 46.0 | S69 37.6 |
| Mirfak | 309 20.6 | N49 46.5 |
| Nunki | 76 32.4 | S26 19.5 |
| Peacock | 54 02.5 | S56 48.4 |
| Pollux | 244 02.0 | N28 05.0 |
| Procyon | 245 29.1 | N 5 17.0 |
| Rasalhague | 96 31.9 | N12 34.7 |
| Regulus | 208 13.2 | N12 04.9 |
| Rigel | 281 39.1 | S 8 13.8 |
| Rigil Kent. | 140 29.1 | S60 44.5 |
| Sabik | 102 44.1 | S15 41.7 |
| Schedar | 350 12.4 | N56 24.3 |
| Shaula | 96 59.2 | S37 05.2 |
| Sirius | 258 58.6 | S16 41.2 |
| Spica | 159 00.4 | S11 02.4 |
| Suhail | 223 13.1 | S43 20.5 |
| Vega | 80 57.3 | N38 45.7 |
| Zuben'ubi | 137 35.9 | S15 56.7 |

| | S.H.A. | Mer. Pass. |
|---|---|---|
| | ° ′ | h m |
| Venus | 277 28.4 | 11 57 |
| Mars | 220 12.5 | 15 44 |
| Jupiter | 313 23.6 | 9 32 |
| Saturn | 236 37.0 | 14 38 |



1976 JUNE 14, 15, 16 (MON., TUES., WED.)

| G.M.T. | SUN G.H.A. | SUN Dec. | MOON G.H.A. | $v$ | MOON Dec. | $d$ | H.P. |
|---|---|---|---|---|---|---|---|
| d h | ° ′ | ° ′ | ° ′ | ′ | ° ′ | ′ | ′ |
| 14 00 | 179 58.2 | N23 15.5 | 334 26.5 | 7.7 | S17 40.8 | 5.6 | 58.4 |
| 01 | 194 58.0 | 15.6 | 348 53.2 | 7.7 | 17 35.2 | 5.7 | 58.4 |
| 02 | 209 57.9 | 15.8 | 3 19.9 | 7.9 | 17 29.5 | 5.8 | 58.4 |
| 03 | 224 57.8 | ·· 15.9 | 17 46.8 | 7.9 | 17 23.7 | 5.9 | 58.3 |
| 04 | 239 57.6 | 16.0 | 32 13.7 | 8.0 | 17 17.8 | 5.9 | 58.3 |
| 05 | 254 57.5 | 16.1 | 46 40.7 | 8.1 | 17 11.9 | 6.1 | 58.3 |
| 06 | 269 57.4 | N23 16.3 | 61 07.8 | 8.2 | S17 05.8 | 6.2 | 58.2 |
| 07 | 284 57.3 | 16.4 | 75 35.0 | 8.2 | 16 59.6 | 6.3 | 58.2 |
| 08 | 299 57.1 | 16.5 | 90 02.2 | 8.3 | 16 53.3 | 6.4 | 58.2 |
| M 09 | 314 57.0 | ·· 16.6 | 104 29.5 | 8.4 | 16 46.9 | 6.4 | 58.1 |
| O 10 | 329 56.9 | 16.7 | 118 56.9 | 8.5 | 16 40.5 | 6.6 | 58.1 |
| N 11 | 344 56.7 | 16.8 | 133 24.4 | 8.6 | 16 33.9 | 6.6 | 58.1 |
| D 12 | 359 56.6 | N23 17.0 | 147 52.0 | 8.7 | S16 27.3 | 6.7 | 58.0 |
| A 13 | 14 56.5 | 17.1 | 162 19.7 | 8.7 | 16 20.6 | 6.8 | 58.0 |
| Y 14 | 29 56.3 | 17.2 | 176 47.4 | 8.9 | 16 13.8 | 6.9 | 57.9 |
| 15 | 44 56.2 | ·· 17.3 | 191 15.3 | 8.9 | 16 06.9 | 7.0 | 57.9 |
| 16 | 59 56.1 | 17.4 | 205 43.2 | 9.0 | 15 59.9 | 7.1 | 57.9 |
| 17 | 74 55.9 | 17.5 | 220 11.2 | 9.0 | 15 52.8 | 7.1 | 57.8 |
| 18 | 89 55.8 | N23 17.7 | 234 39.2 | 9.2 | S15 45.7 | 7.2 | 57.8 |
| 19 | 104 55.7 | 17.8 | 249 07.4 | 9.3 | 15 38.5 | 7.3 | 57.8 |
| 20 | 119 55.5 | 17.9 | 263 35.7 | 9.3 | 15 31.2 | 7.4 | 57.7 |
| 21 | 134 55.4 | ·· 18.0 | 278 04.0 | 9.4 | 15 23.8 | 7.5 | 57.7 |
| 22 | 149 55.3 | 18.1 | 292 32.4 | 9.5 | 15 16.3 | 7.5 | 57.7 |
| 23 | 164 55.1 | 18.2 | 307 00.9 | 9.6 | 15 08.8 | 7.6 | 57.6 |
| 15 00 | 179 55.0 | N23 18.3 | 321 29.5 | 9.7 | S15 01.2 | 7.7 | 57.6 |
| 01 | 194 54.9 | 18.4 | 335 58.2 | 9.7 | 14 53.5 | 7.7 | 57.6 |
| 02 | 209 54.8 | 18.5 | 350 26.9 | 9.8 | 14 45.8 | 7.9 | 57.5 |
| 03 | 224 54.6 | ·· 18.6 | 4 55.7 | 10.0 | 14 37.9 | 7.9 | 57.5 |
| 04 | 239 54.5 | 18.7 | 19 24.7 | 10.0 | 14 30.0 | 7.9 | 57.5 |
| 05 | 254 54.4 | 18.8 | 33 53.7 | 10.1 | 14 22.1 | 8.0 | 57.4 |
| 06 | 269 54.2 | N23 18.9 | 48 22.8 | 10.1 | S14 14.1 | 8.1 | 57.4 |
| 07 | 284 54.1 | 19.0 | 62 51.9 | 10.3 | 14 06.0 | 8.2 | 57.4 |
| T 08 | 299 54.0 | 19.1 | 77 21.2 | 10.3 | 13 57.8 | 8.2 | 57.3 |
| U 09 | 314 53.8 | ·· 19.3 | 91 50.5 | 10.4 | 13 49.6 | 8.3 | 57.3 |
| E 10 | 329 53.7 | 19.4 | 106 19.9 | 10.5 | 13 41.3 | 8.4 | 57.3 |
| S 11 | 344 53.6 | 19.5 | 120 49.4 | 10.6 | 13 32.9 | 8.4 | 57.2 |
| D 12 | 359 53.4 | N23 19.6 | 135 19.0 | 10.6 | S13 24.5 | 8.5 | 57.2 |
| A 13 | 14 53.3 | 19.7 | 149 48.6 | 10.8 | 13 16.0 | 8.5 | 57.2 |
| Y 14 | 29 53.2 | 19.7 | 164 18.4 | 10.8 | 13 07.5 | 8.6 | 57.1 |
| 15 | 44 53.0 | ·· 19.8 | 178 48.2 | 10.9 | 12 58.9 | 8.6 | 57.1 |
| 16 | 59 52.9 | 19.9 | 193 18.1 | 10.9 | 12 50.3 | 8.7 | 57.0 |
| 17 | 74 52.8 | 20.0 | 207 48.0 | 11.1 | 12 41.6 | 8.8 | 57.0 |
| 18 | 89 52.6 | N23 20.1 | 222 18.1 | 11.1 | S12 32.8 | 8.8 | 57.0 |
| 19 | 104 52.5 | 20.2 | 236 48.2 | 11.2 | 12 24.0 | 8.8 | 56.9 |
| 20 | 119 52.4 | 20.3 | 251 18.4 | 11.3 | 12 15.2 | 8.9 | 56.9 |
| 21 | 134 52.2 | ·· 20.4 | 265 48.7 | 11.4 | 12 06.3 | 9.0 | 56.9 |
| 22 | 149 52.1 | 20.5 | 280 19.1 | 11.4 | 11 57.3 | 9.0 | 56.8 |
| 23 | 164 52.0 | 20.6 | 294 49.5 | 11.5 | 11 48.3 | 9.1 | 56.8 |
| 16 00 | 179 51.8 | N23 20.7 | 309 20.0 | 11.6 | S11 39.2 | 9.1 | 56.8 |
| 01 | 194 51.7 | 20.8 | 323 50.6 | 11.7 | 11 30.1 | 9.1 | 56.7 |
| 02 | 209 51.6 | 20.9 | 338 21.3 | 11.7 | 11 21.0 | 9.2 | 56.7 |
| 03 | 224 51.4 | ·· 21.0 | 352 52.0 | 11.8 | 11 11.8 | 9.2 | 56.7 |
| 04 | 239 51.3 | 21.0 | 7 22.8 | 11.9 | 11 02.6 | 9.3 | 56.6 |
| 05 | 254 51.2 | 21.1 | 21 53.7 | 12.0 | 10 53.3 | 9.4 | 56.6 |
| 06 | 269 51.0 | N23 21.2 | 36 24.7 | 12.0 | S10 43.9 | 9.3 | 56.6 |
| W 07 | 284 50.9 | 21.3 | 50 55.7 | 12.1 | 10 34.6 | 9.4 | 56.5 |
| E 08 | 299 50.8 | 21.4 | 65 26.8 | 12.2 | 10 25.2 | 9.5 | 56.5 |
| D 09 | 314 50.6 | ·· 21.5 | 79 58.0 | 12.2 | 10 15.7 | 9.4 | 56.5 |
| N 10 | 329 50.5 | 21.6 | 94 29.2 | 12.3 | 10 06.3 | 9.6 | 56.4 |
| E 11 | 344 50.4 | 21.6 | 109 00.5 | 12.4 | 9 56.7 | 9.5 | 56.4 |
| S 12 | 359 50.2 | N23 21.7 | 123 31.9 | 12.4 | S 9 47.2 | 9.6 | 56.4 |
| D 13 | 14 50.1 | 21.8 | 138 03.3 | 12.6 | 9 37.6 | 9.6 | 56.3 |
| A 14 | 29 50.0 | 21.9 | 152 34.9 | 12.5 | 9 28.0 | 9.7 | 56.3 |
| Y 15 | 44 49.8 | ·· 22.0 | 167 06.4 | 12.7 | 9 18.3 | 9.7 | 56.3 |
| 16 | 59 49.7 | 22.0 | 181 38.1 | 12.7 | 9 08.6 | 9.7 | 56.2 |
| 17 | 74 49.6 | 22.1 | 196 09.8 | 12.8 | 8 58.9 | 9.7 | 56.2 |
| 18 | 89 49.4 | N23 22.2 | 210 41.6 | 12.8 | S 8 49.2 | 9.8 | 56.2 |
| 19 | 104 49.3 | 22.3 | 225 13.4 | 12.9 | 8 39.4 | 9.8 | 56.2 |
| 20 | 119 49.2 | 22.4 | 239 45.3 | 12.9 | 8 29.6 | 9.9 | 56.1 |
| 21 | 134 49.0 | ·· 22.4 | 254 17.2 | 13.1 | 8 19.7 | 9.8 | 56.1 |
| 22 | 149 48.9 | 22.5 | 268 49.3 | 13.1 | 8 09.9 | 9.9 | 56.1 |
| 23 | 164 48.8 | 22.6 | 283 21.4 | 13.1 | 8 00.0 | 9.9 | 56.0 |
| | S.D. 15.8 | $d$ 0.1 | S.D. 15.8 | | 15.6 | | 15.4 |

| Lat. | Twilight Naut. | Twilight Civil | Sunrise | Moonrise 14 | Moonrise 15 | Moonrise 16 | Moonrise 17 |
|---|---|---|---|---|---|---|---|
| ° | h m | h m | h m | h m | h m | h m | h m |
| N 72 | □ | □ | □ | 01 03 | 00 20 | {00 02 / 23 50} | 23 40 |
| N 70 | □ | □ | □ | 23 46 | 23 43 | 23 39 | 23 35 |
| 68 | □ | □ | □ | 23 22 | 23 27 | 23 29 | 23 31 |
| 66 | □ | □ | □ | 23 03 | 23 14 | 23 21 | 23 27 |
| 64 | //// | //// | 01 33 | 22 48 | 23 03 | 23 15 | 23 24 |
| 62 | //// | //// | 02 10 | 22 35 | 22 54 | 23 09 | 23 21 |
| 60 | //// | 00 53 | 02 36 | 22 24 | 22 46 | 23 04 | 23 19 |
| N 58 | //// | 01 41 | 02 56 | 22 15 | 22 40 | 22 59 | 23 17 |
| 56 | //// | 02 11 | 03 13 | 22 07 | 22 33 | 22 55 | 23 15 |
| 54 | 00 49 | 02 33 | 03 27 | 21 59 | 22 28 | 22 52 | 23 13 |
| 52 | 01 33 | 02 51 | 03 39 | 21 52 | 22 23 | 22 49 | 23 11 |
| 50 | 02 01 | 03 06 | 03 50 | 21 46 | 22 18 | 22 46 | 23 10 |
| 45 | 02 46 | 03 35 | 04 13 | 21 33 | 22 09 | 22 39 | 23 07 |
| N 40 | 03 16 | 03 58 | 04 30 | 21 23 | 22 00 | 22 34 | 23 04 |
| 35 | 03 39 | 04 16 | 04 45 | 21 13 | 21 53 | 22 29 | 23 02 |
| 30 | 03 58 | 04 31 | 04 58 | 21 05 | 21 47 | 22 25 | 23 00 |
| 20 | 04 27 | 04 56 | 05 20 | 20 51 | 21 36 | 22 18 | 22 56 |
| N 10 | 04 49 | 05 16 | 05 39 | 20 39 | 21 27 | 22 11 | 22 53 |
| 0 | 05 08 | 05 34 | 05 57 | 20 27 | 21 18 | 22 05 | 22 50 |
| S 10 | 05 25 | 05 51 | 06 14 | 20 16 | 21 09 | 21 59 | 22 47 |
| 20 | 05 41 | 06 08 | 06 32 | 20 03 | 20 59 | 21 53 | 22 44 |
| 30 | 05 57 | 06 27 | 06 54 | 19 49 | 20 48 | 21 46 | 22 41 |
| 35 | 06 06 | 06 38 | 07 06 | 19 41 | 20 42 | 21 41 | 22 39 |
| 40 | 06 16 | 06 49 | 07 20 | 19 31 | 20 35 | 21 37 | 22 37 |
| 45 | 06 26 | 07 03 | 07 37 | 19 20 | 20 26 | 21 31 | 22 34 |
| S 50 | 06 38 | 07 19 | 07 57 | 19 07 | 20 16 | 21 24 | 22 31 |
| 52 | 06 43 | 07 26 | 08 07 | 19 00 | 20 12 | 21 21 | 22 29 |
| 54 | 06 48 | 07 35 | 08 18 | 18 54 | 20 06 | 21 18 | 22 28 |
| 56 | 06 54 | 07 44 | 08 31 | 18 46 | 20 01 | 21 14 | 22 26 |
| 58 | 07 01 | 07 54 | 08 45 | 18 37 | 19 54 | 21 10 | 22 24 |
| S 60 | 07 09 | 08 05 | 09 03 | 18 27 | 19 47 | 21 05 | 22 22 |

| Lat. | Sunset | Twilight Civil | Twilight Naut. | Moonset 14 | Moonset 15 | Moonset 16 | Moonset 17 |
|---|---|---|---|---|---|---|---|
| ° | h m | h m | h m | h m | h m | h m | h m |
| N 72 | □ | □ | □ | 02 40 | 05 15 | 07 15 | 09 04 |
| N 70 | □ | □ | □ | 03 52 | 05 47 | 07 33 | 09 13 |
| 68 | □ | □ | □ | 04 29 | 06 10 | 07 48 | 09 21 |
| 66 | □ | □ | □ | 04 55 | 06 28 | 07 59 | 09 28 |
| 64 | 22 29 | //// | //// | 05 15 | 06 42 | 08 09 | 09 33 |
| 62 | 21 51 | //// | //// | 05 31 | 06 54 | 08 17 | 09 38 |
| 60 | 21 25 | 23 09 | //// | 05 45 | 07 04 | 08 24 | 09 42 |
| N 58 | 21 05 | 22 20 | //// | 05 56 | 07 13 | 08 30 | 09 45 |
| 56 | 20 48 | 21 50 | //// | 06 06 | 07 21 | 08 36 | 09 49 |
| 54 | 20 34 | 21 28 | 23 14 | 06 15 | 07 28 | 08 41 | 09 51 |
| 52 | 20 22 | 21 10 | 22 28 | 06 23 | 07 34 | 08 45 | 09 54 |
| 50 | 20 11 | 20 55 | 22 01 | 06 30 | 07 40 | 08 49 | 09 56 |
| 45 | 19 48 | 20 26 | 21 15 | 06 45 | 07 52 | 08 58 | 10 01 |
| N 40 | 19 30 | 20 03 | 20 45 | 06 57 | 08 02 | 09 05 | 10 06 |
| 35 | 19 15 | 19 45 | 20 22 | 07 08 | 08 10 | 09 11 | 10 09 |
| 30 | 19 02 | 19 30 | 20 03 | 07 17 | 08 18 | 09 16 | 10 12 |
| 20 | 18 40 | 19 05 | 19 34 | 07 33 | 08 30 | 09 25 | 10 18 |
| N 10 | 18 22 | 18 45 | 19 12 | 07 46 | 08 41 | 09 33 | 10 23 |
| 0 | 18 04 | 18 27 | 18 53 | 07 59 | 08 52 | 09 41 | 10 27 |
| S 10 | 17 47 | 18 09 | 18 36 | 08 12 | 09 02 | 09 48 | 10 32 |
| 20 | 17 28 | 17 52 | 18 20 | 08 25 | 09 13 | 09 56 | 10 36 |
| 30 | 17 07 | 17 33 | 18 03 | 08 41 | 09 25 | 10 05 | 10 42 |
| 35 | 16 55 | 17 23 | 17 55 | 08 50 | 09 33 | 10 10 | 10 45 |
| 40 | 16 41 | 17 11 | 17 45 | 09 00 | 09 41 | 10 16 | 10 48 |
| 45 | 16 24 | 16 58 | 17 35 | 09 12 | 09 50 | 10 23 | 10 52 |
| S 50 | 16 03 | 16 42 | 17 23 | 09 26 | 10 01 | 10 31 | 10 57 |
| 52 | 15 53 | 16 34 | 17 18 | 09 33 | 10 07 | 10 35 | 10 59 |
| 54 | 15 42 | 16 26 | 17 12 | 09 40 | 10 12 | 10 39 | 11 01 |
| 56 | 15 30 | 16 17 | 17 06 | 09 48 | 10 19 | 10 43 | 11 04 |
| 58 | 15 15 | 16 07 | 16 59 | 09 57 | 10 26 | 10 48 | 11 07 |
| S 60 | 14 58 | 15 55 | 16 52 | 10 08 | 10 34 | 10 54 | 11 10 |

| Day | SUN Eqn. of Time 00ʰ | SUN Eqn. of Time 12ʰ | SUN Mer. Pass. | MOON Mer. Pass. Upper | MOON Mer. Pass. Lower | Age | Phase |
|---|---|---|---|---|---|---|---|
| | m s | m s | h m | h m | h m | d | |
| 14 | 00 07 | 00 13 | 12 00 | 01 46 | 14 13 | 16 | |
| 15 | 00 20 | 00 26 | 12 00 | 02 40 | 15 05 | 17 | |
| 16 | 00 32 | 00 39 | 12 01 | 03 29 | 15 53 | 18 | |

## 1976 JUNE 17, 18, 19 (THURS., FRI., SAT.)

| G.M.T. | ARIES G.H.A. | VENUS −3.5 G.H.A. | VENUS Dec. | MARS +1.8 G.H.A. | MARS Dec. | JUPITER −1.7 G.H.A. | JUPITER Dec. | SATURN +0.5 G.H.A. | SATURN Dec. |
|---|---|---|---|---|---|---|---|---|---|
| d h | ° ′ | ° ′ | ° ′ | ° ′ | ° ′ | ° ′ | ° ′ | ° ′ | ° ′ |
| 17 00 | 265 22.5 | 180 10.5 | N23 34.8 | 124 25.3 | N16 39.3 | 218 20.2 | N16 36.5 | 141 45.4 | N20 19.2 |
| 01 | 280 24.9 | 195 09.6 | 35.0 | 139 26.3 | 38.8 | 233 22.2 | 36.7 | 156 47.6 | 19.1 |
| 02 | 295 27.4 | 210 08.7 | 35.2 | 154 27.3 | 38.4 | 248 24.1 | 36.8 | 171 49.7 | 19.1 |
| 03 | 310 29.9 | 225 07.8 | ·· 35.4 | 169 28.3 | ·· 37.9 | 263 26.0 | ·· 36.9 | 186 51.9 | ·· 19.0 |
| 04 | 325 32.3 | 240 07.0 | 35.6 | 184 29.3 | 37.4 | 278 28.0 | 37.1 | 201 54.1 | 19.0 |
| 05 | 340 34.8 | 255 06.1 | 35.8 | 199 30.3 | 36.9 | 293 29.9 | 37.2 | 216 56.2 | 18.9 |
| 06 | 355 37.3 | 270 05.2 | N23 36.0 | 214 31.4 | N16 36.5 | 308 31.8 | N16 37.4 | 231 58.4 | N20 18.8 |
| 07 | 10 39.7 | 285 04.3 | 36.2 | 229 32.4 | 36.0 | 323 33.8 | 37.5 | 247 00.6 | 18.8 |
| T 08 | 25 42.2 | 300 03.4 | 36.3 | 244 33.4 | 35.5 | 338 35.7 | 37.7 | 262 02.7 | 18.7 |
| H 09 | 40 44.6 | 315 02.5 | ·· 36.5 | 259 34.4 | ·· 35.0 | 353 37.6 | ·· 37.8 | 277 04.9 | ·· 18.7 |
| U 10 | 55 47.1 | 330 01.7 | 36.7 | 274 35.4 | 34.5 | 8 39.5 | 37.9 | 292 07.1 | 18.6 |
| R 11 | 70 49.6 | 345 00.8 | 36.9 | 289 36.4 | 34.1 | 23 41.5 | 38.1 | 307 09.2 | 18.5 |
| S 12 | 85 52.0 | 359 59.9 | N23 37.1 | 304 37.4 | N16 33.6 | 38 43.4 | N16 38.2 | 322 11.4 | N20 18.5 |
| D 13 | 100 54.5 | 14 59.0 | 37.3 | 319 38.5 | 33.1 | 53 45.3 | 38.4 | 337 13.6 | 18.4 |
| A 14 | 115 57.0 | 29 58.1 | 37.5 | 334 39.5 | 32.6 | 68 47.3 | 38.5 | 352 15.7 | 18.4 |
| Y 15 | 130 59.4 | 44 57.2 | ·· 37.6 | 349 40.5 | ·· 32.1 | 83 49.2 | ·· 38.7 | 7 17.9 | ·· 18.3 |
| 16 | 146 01.9 | 59 56.4 | 37.8 | 4 41.5 | 31.7 | 98 51.1 | 38.8 | 22 20.1 | 18.2 |
| 17 | 161 04.4 | 74 55.5 | 38.0 | 19 42.5 | 31.2 | 113 53.0 | 38.9 | 37 22.2 | 18.2 |
| 18 | 176 06.8 | 89 54.6 | N23 38.2 | 34 43.5 | N16 30.7 | 128 55.0 | N16 39.1 | 52 24.4 | N20 18.1 |
| 19 | 191 09.3 | 104 53.7 | 38.4 | 49 44.5 | 30.2 | 143 56.9 | 39.2 | 67 26.6 | 18.1 |
| 20 | 206 11.7 | 119 52.8 | 38.5 | 64 45.6 | 29.7 | 158 58.8 | 39.4 | 82 28.7 | 18.0 |
| 21 | 221 14.2 | 134 51.9 | ·· 38.7 | 79 46.6 | ·· 29.3 | 174 00.8 | ·· 39.5 | 97 30.9 | ·· 17.9 |
| 22 | 236 16.7 | 149 51.1 | 38.9 | 94 47.6 | 28.8 | 189 02.7 | 39.7 | 112 33.1 | 17.9 |
| 23 | 251 19.1 | 164 50.2 | 39.1 | 109 48.6 | 28.3 | 204 04.6 | 39.8 | 127 35.2 | 17.8 |
| 18 00 | 266 21.6 | 179 49.3 | N23 39.2 | 124 49.6 | N16 27.8 | 219 06.6 | N16 39.9 | 142 37.4 | N20 17.8 |
| 01 | 281 24.1 | 194 48.4 | 39.4 | 139 50.6 | 27.3 | 234 08.5 | 40.1 | 157 39.6 | 17.7 |
| 02 | 296 26.5 | 209 47.5 | 39.6 | 154 51.6 | 26.8 | 249 10.4 | 40.2 | 172 41.7 | 17.6 |
| 03 | 311 29.0 | 224 46.6 | ·· 39.7 | 169 52.7 | ·· 26.4 | 264 12.3 | ·· 40.4 | 187 43.9 | ·· 17.6 |
| 04 | 326 31.5 | 239 45.7 | 39.9 | 184 53.7 | 25.9 | 279 14.3 | 40.5 | 202 46.1 | 17.5 |
| 05 | 341 33.9 | 254 44.9 | 40.1 | 199 54.7 | 25.4 | 294 16.2 | 40.6 | 217 48.3 | 17.5 |
| 06 | 356 36.4 | 269 44.0 | N23 40.2 | 214 55.7 | N16 24.9 | 309 18.1 | N16 40.8 | 232 50.4 | N20 17.4 |
| 07 | 11 38.9 | 284 43.1 | 40.4 | 229 56.7 | 24.4 | 324 20.1 | 40.9 | 247 52.6 | 17.3 |
| 08 | 26 41.3 | 299 42.2 | 40.6 | 244 57.7 | 24.0 | 339 22.0 | 41.1 | 262 54.8 | 17.3 |
| F 09 | 41 43.8 | 314 41.3 | ·· 40.7 | 259 58.7 | ·· 23.5 | 354 23.9 | ·· 41.2 | 277 56.9 | ·· 17.2 |
| R 10 | 56 46.2 | 329 40.4 | 40.9 | 274 59.8 | 23.0 | 9 25.9 | 41.4 | 292 59.1 | 17.1 |
| I 11 | 71 48.7 | 344 39.5 | 41.0 | 290 00.8 | 22.5 | 24 27.8 | 41.5 | 308 01.2 | 17.1 |
| D 12 | 86 51.2 | 359 38.7 | N23 41.2 | 305 01.8 | N16 22.0 | 39 29.7 | N16 41.6 | 323 03.4 | N20 17.0 |
| A 13 | 101 53.6 | 14 37.8 | 41.4 | 320 02.8 | 21.5 | 54 31.7 | 41.8 | 338 05.6 | 17.0 |
| Y 14 | 116 56.1 | 29 36.9 | 41.5 | 335 03.8 | 21.0 | 69 33.6 | 41.9 | 353 07.7 | 16.9 |
| 15 | 131 58.6 | 44 36.0 | ·· 41.7 | 350 04.8 | ·· 20.6 | 84 35.5 | ·· 42.1 | 8 09.9 | ·· 16.8 |
| 16 | 147 01.0 | 59 35.1 | 41.8 | 5 05.8 | 20.1 | 99 37.5 | 42.2 | 23 12.1 | 16.8 |
| 17 | 162 03.5 | 74 34.2 | 42.0 | 20 06.9 | 19.6 | 114 39.4 | 42.3 | 38 14.2 | 16.7 |
| 18 | 177 06.0 | 89 33.3 | N23 42.1 | 35 07.9 | N16 19.1 | 129 41.3 | N16 42.5 | 53 16.4 | N20 16.7 |
| 19 | 192 08.4 | 104 32.4 | 42.3 | 50 08.9 | 18.6 | 144 43.3 | 42.6 | 68 18.6 | 16.6 |
| 20 | 207 10.9 | 119 31.6 | 42.4 | 65 09.9 | 18.1 | 159 45.2 | 42.8 | 83 20.7 | 16.5 |
| 21 | 222 13.4 | 134 30.7 | ·· 42.6 | 80 10.9 | ·· 17.7 | 174 47.1 | ·· 42.9 | 98 22.9 | ·· 16.5 |
| 22 | 237 15.8 | 149 29.8 | 42.7 | 95 11.9 | 17.2 | 189 49.1 | 43.0 | 113 25.1 | 16.4 |
| 23 | 252 18.3 | 164 28.9 | 42.9 | 110 12.9 | 16.7 | 204 51.0 | 43.2 | 128 27.2 | 16.4 |
| 19 00 | 267 20.7 | 179 28.0 | N23 43.0 | 125 14.0 | N16 16.2 | 219 52.9 | N16 43.3 | 143 29.4 | N20 16.3 |
| 01 | 282 23.2 | 194 27.1 | 43.1 | 140 15.0 | 15.7 | 234 54.9 | 43.5 | 158 31.6 | 16.2 |
| 02 | 297 25.7 | 209 26.2 | 43.3 | 155 16.0 | 15.2 | 249 56.8 | 43.6 | 173 33.7 | 16.2 |
| 03 | 312 28.1 | 224 25.3 | ·· 43.4 | 170 17.0 | ·· 14.7 | 264 58.7 | ·· 43.7 | 188 35.9 | ·· 16.1 |
| 04 | 327 30.6 | 239 24.5 | 43.6 | 185 18.0 | 14.3 | 280 00.6 | 43.9 | 203 38.1 | 16.1 |
| 05 | 342 33.1 | 254 23.6 | 43.7 | 200 19.0 | 13.8 | 295 02.6 | 44.0 | 218 40.2 | 16.0 |
| 06 | 357 35.5 | 269 22.7 | N23 43.8 | 215 20.1 | N16 13.3 | 310 04.5 | N16 44.2 | 233 42.4 | N20 15.9 |
| 07 | 12 38.0 | 284 21.8 | 44.0 | 230 21.1 | 12.8 | 325 06.4 | 44.3 | 248 44.6 | 15.9 |
| S 08 | 27 40.5 | 299 20.9 | 44.1 | 245 22.1 | 12.3 | 340 08.4 | 44.4 | 263 46.7 | 15.8 |
| A 09 | 42 42.9 | 314 20.0 | ·· 44.2 | 260 23.1 | ·· 11.8 | 355 10.3 | ·· 44.6 | 278 48.9 | ·· 15.7 |
| T 10 | 57 45.4 | 329 19.1 | 44.4 | 275 24.1 | 11.3 | 10 12.3 | 44.7 | 293 51.1 | 15.7 |
| U 11 | 72 47.8 | 344 18.2 | 44.5 | 290 25.1 | 10.8 | 25 14.2 | 44.9 | 308 53.2 | 15.6 |
| R 12 | 87 50.3 | 359 17.3 | N23 44.6 | 305 26.1 | N16 10.4 | 40 16.1 | N16 45.0 | 323 55.4 | N20 15.6 |
| D 13 | 102 52.8 | 14 16.4 | 44.7 | 320 27.2 | 09.9 | 55 18.1 | 45.1 | 338 57.5 | 15.5 |
| A 14 | 117 55.2 | 29 15.6 | 44.9 | 335 28.2 | 09.4 | 70 20.0 | 45.3 | 353 59.7 | 15.4 |
| Y 15 | 132 57.7 | 44 14.7 | ·· 45.0 | 350 29.2 | ·· 08.9 | 85 21.9 | ·· 45.4 | 9 01.9 | ·· 15.4 |
| 16 | 148 00.2 | 59 13.8 | 45.1 | 5 30.2 | 08.4 | 100 23.9 | 45.6 | 24 04.0 | 15.3 |
| 17 | 163 02.6 | 74 12.9 | 45.2 | 20 31.2 | 07.9 | 115 25.8 | 45.7 | 39 06.2 | 15.3 |
| 18 | 178 05.1 | 89 12.0 | N23 45.4 | 35 32.2 | N16 07.4 | 130 27.7 | N16 45.8 | 54 08.4 | N20 15.2 |
| 19 | 193 07.6 | 104 11.1 | 45.5 | 50 33.3 | 06.9 | 145 29.7 | 46.0 | 69 10.5 | 15.1 |
| 20 | 208 10.0 | 119 10.2 | 45.6 | 65 34.3 | 06.4 | 160 31.6 | 46.1 | 84 12.7 | 15.1 |
| 21 | 223 12.5 | 134 09.3 | ·· 45.7 | 80 35.3 | ·· 06.0 | 175 33.5 | ·· 46.3 | 99 14.9 | ·· 15.0 |
| 22 | 238 15.0 | 149 08.4 | 45.8 | 95 36.3 | 05.5 | 190 35.5 | 46.4 | 114 17.0 | 14.9 |
| 23 | 253 17.4 | 164 07.5 | 46.0 | 110 37.3 | 05.0 | 205 37.4 | 46.5 | 129 19.2 | 14.9 |
| Mer. Pass. | h m 6 13.5 | v −0.9 | d 0.2 | v 1.0 | d 0.5 | v 1.9 | d 0.1 | v 2.2 | d 0.1 |

**STARS**

| Name | S.H.A. | Dec. |
|---|---|---|
| | ° ′ | ° ′ |
| Acamar | 315 39.8 | S40 23.8 |
| Achernar | 335 47.7 | S57 21.1 |
| Acrux | 173 40.2 | S62 58.5 |
| Adhara | 255 34.7 | S28 56.5 |
| Aldebaran | 291 21.6 | N16 27.7 |
| Alioth | 166 44.9 | N56 05.5 |
| Alkaid | 153 20.5 | N49 26.0 |
| Al Na'ir | 28 18.3 | S47 04.2 |
| Alnilam | 276 14.9 | S 1 13.1 |
| Alphard | 218 23.6 | S 8 33.5 |
| Alphecca | 126 34.2 | N26 47.7 |
| Alpheratz | 358 12.3 | N28 57.5 |
| Altair | 62 35.0 | N 8 48.4 |
| Ankaa | 353 43.2 | S42 25.7 |
| Antares | 113 00.0 | S26 22.8 |
| Arcturus | 146 20.9 | N19 18.4 |
| Atria | 108 26.2 | S68 59.2 |
| Avior | 234 29.9 | S59 26.3 |
| Bellatrix | 279 02.2 | N 6 19.6 |
| Betelgeuse | 271 31.7 | N 7 24.1 |
| Canopus | 264 09.0 | S52 41.1 |
| Capella | 281 16.0 | N45 58.4 |
| Deneb | 49 50.0 | N45 11.7 |
| Denebola | 183 02.0 | N14 42.2 |
| Diphda | 349 23.8 | S18 06.8 |
| Dubhe | 194 25.9 | N61 52.9 |
| Elnath | 278 48.1 | N28 35.2 |
| Eltanin | 90 58.5 | N51 29.6 |
| Enif | 34 14.2 | N 9 46.1 |
| Fomalhaut | 15 54.5 | S29 44.6 |
| Gacrux | 172 31.8 | S56 59.2 |
| Gienah | 176 20.9 | S17 24.9 |
| Hadar | 149 27.0 | S60 15.9 |
| Hamal | 328 32.3 | N23 21.0 |
| Kaus Aust. | 84 20.2 | S34 23.7 |
| Kochab | 137 18.1 | N74 15.4 |
| Markab | 14 05.9 | N15 04.7 |
| Menkar | 314 44.4 | N 3 59.8 |
| Menkent | 148 40.1 | S36 15.5 |
| Miaplacidus | 221 46.1 | S69 37.6 |
| Mirfak | 309 20.6 | N49 46.5 |
| Nunki | 76 32.4 | S26 19.5 |
| Peacock | 54 02.4 | S56 48.4 |
| Pollux | 244 02.0 | N28 05.0 |
| Procyon | 245 29.1 | N 5 17.0 |
| Rasalhague | 96 31.9 | N12 34.7 |
| Regulus | 208 13.2 | N12 04.9 |
| Rigel | 281 39.1 | S 8 13.8 |
| Rigil Kent. | 140 29.2 | S60 44.5 |
| Sabik | 102 44.1 | S15 41.7 |
| Schedar | 350 12.3 | N56 24.3 |
| Shaula | 96 59.2 | S37 05.2 |
| Sirius | 258 58.6 | S16 41.2 |
| Spica | 159 00.4 | S11 02.4 |
| Suhail | 223 13.2 | S43 20.5 |
| Vega | 80 57.3 | N38 45.7 |
| Zuben'ubi | 137 35.9 | S15 56.7 |

| | S.H.A. | Mer. Pass. |
|---|---|---|
| | ° ′ | h m |
| Venus | 273 27.7 | 12 01 |
| Mars | 218 28.0 | 15 40 |
| Jupiter | 312 45.0 | 9 22 |
| Saturn | 236 15.8 | 14 27 |

## 1976 JUNE 20, 21, 22 (SUN., MON., TUES.)

| G.M.T. | ARIES G.H.A. | VENUS −3.5 G.H.A. | VENUS Dec. | MARS +1.8 G.H.A. | MARS Dec. | JUPITER −1.7 G.H.A. | JUPITER Dec. | SATURN +0.5 G.H.A. | SATURN Dec. |
|---|---|---|---|---|---|---|---|---|---|
| d h | ° ′ | ° ′ | ° ′ | ° ′ | ° ′ | ° ′ | ° ′ | ° ′ | ° ′ |
| 20 00 | 268 19.9 | 179 06.6 | N23 46.1 | 125 38.3 | N16 04.5 | 220 39.3 | N16 46.7 | 144 21.3 | N20 14.8 |
| 01 | 283 22.3 | 194 05.8 | 46.2 | 140 39.3 | 04.0 | 235 41.3 | 46.8 | 159 23.5 | 14.8 |
| 02 | 298 24.8 | 209 04.9 | 46.3 | 155 40.4 | 03.5 | 250 43.2 | 47.0 | 174 25.7 | 14.7 |
| 03 | 313 27.3 | 224 04.0 | ·· 46.4 | 170 41.4 | ·· 03.0 | 265 45.1 | ·· 47.1 | 189 27.8 | ·· 14.6 |
| 04 | 328 29.7 | 239 03.1 | 46.5 | 185 42.4 | 02.5 | 280 47.1 | 47.2 | 204 30.0 | 14.6 |
| 05 | 343 32.2 | 254 02.2 | 46.6 | 200 43.4 | 02.0 | 295 49.0 | 47.4 | 219 32.2 | 14.5 |
| 06 | 358 34.7 | 269 01.3 | N23 46.7 | 215 44.4 | N16 01.5 | 310 50.9 | N16 47.5 | 234 34.3 | N20 14.5 |
| 07 | 13 37.1 | 284 00.4 | 46.8 | 230 45.4 | 01.0 | 325 52.9 | 47.7 | 249 36.5 | 14.4 |
| 08 | 28 39.6 | 298 59.5 | 46.9 | 245 46.5 | 00.6 | 340 54.8 | 47.8 | 264 38.7 | 14.3 |
| S 09 | 43 42.1 | 313 58.6 | ·· 47.0 | 260 47.5 | 16 00.1 | 355 56.8 | ·· 47.9 | 279 40.8 | ·· 14.3 |
| U 10 | 58 44.5 | 328 57.7 | 47.1 | 275 48.5 | 15 59.6 | 10 58.7 | 48.1 | 294 43.0 | 14.2 |
| N 11 | 73 47.0 | 343 56.8 | 47.2 | 290 49.5 | 59.1 | 26 00.6 | 48.2 | 309 45.1 | 14.1 |
| D 12 | 88 49.4 | 358 55.9 | N23 47.3 | 305 50.5 | N15 58.6 | 41 02.6 | N16 48.3 | 324 47.3 | N20 14.1 |
| A 13 | 103 51.9 | 13 55.1 | 47.4 | 320 51.5 | 58.1 | 56 04.5 | 48.5 | 339 49.5 | 14.0 |
| Y 14 | 118 54.4 | 28 54.2 | 47.5 | 335 52.6 | 57.6 | 71 06.4 | 48.6 | 354 51.6 | 14.0 |
| 15 | 133 56.8 | 43 53.3 | ·· 47.6 | 350 53.6 | ·· 57.1 | 86 08.4 | ·· 48.8 | 9 53.8 | ·· 13.9 |
| 16 | 148 59.3 | 58 52.4 | 47.7 | 5 54.6 | 56.6 | 101 10.3 | 48.9 | 24 56.0 | 13.8 |
| 17 | 164 01.8 | 73 51.5 | 47.8 | 20 55.6 | 56.1 | 116 12.2 | 49.0 | 39 58.1 | 13.8 |
| 18 | 179 04.2 | 88 50.6 | N23 47.9 | 35 56.6 | N15 55.6 | 131 14.2 | N16 49.2 | 55 00.3 | N20 13.7 |
| 19 | 194 06.7 | 103 49.7 | 48.0 | 50 57.6 | 55.1 | 146 16.1 | 49.3 | 70 02.4 | 13.6 |
| 20 | 209 09.2 | 118 48.8 | 48.1 | 65 58.6 | 54.6 | 161 18.1 | 49.5 | 85 04.6 | 13.6 |
| 21 | 224 11.6 | 133 47.9 | ·· 48.2 | 80 59.7 | ·· 54.1 | 176 20.0 | ·· 49.6 | 100 06.8 | ·· 13.5 |
| 22 | 239 14.1 | 148 47.0 | 48.3 | 96 00.7 | 53.7 | 191 21.9 | 49.7 | 115 08.9 | 13.5 |
| 23 | 254 16.6 | 163 46.1 | 48.3 | 111 01.7 | 53.2 | 206 23.9 | 49.9 | 130 11.1 | 13.4 |
| 21 00 | 269 19.0 | 178 45.2 | N23 48.4 | 126 02.7 | N15 52.7 | 221 25.8 | N16 50.0 | 145 13.3 | N20 13.3 |
| 01 | 284 21.5 | 193 44.3 | 48.5 | 141 03.7 | 52.2 | 236 27.7 | 50.1 | 160 15.4 | 13.3 |
| 02 | 299 23.9 | 208 43.4 | 48.6 | 156 04.7 | 51.7 | 251 29.7 | 50.3 | 175 17.6 | 13.2 |
| 03 | 314 26.4 | 223 42.5 | ·· 48.7 | 171 05.8 | ·· 51.2 | 266 31.6 | ·· 50.4 | 190 19.7 | ·· 13.1 |
| 04 | 329 28.9 | 238 41.7 | 48.8 | 186 06.8 | 50.7 | 281 33.6 | 50.6 | 205 21.9 | 13.1 |
| 05 | 344 31.3 | 253 40.8 | 48.8 | 201 07.8 | 50.2 | 296 35.5 | 50.7 | 220 24.1 | 13.0 |
| 06 | 359 33.8 | 268 39.9 | N23 48.9 | 216 08.8 | N15 49.7 | 311 37.4 | N16 50.8 | 235 26.2 | N20 13.0 |
| 07 | 14 36.3 | 283 39.0 | 49.0 | 231 09.8 | 49.2 | 326 39.4 | 51.0 | 250 28.4 | 12.9 |
| 08 | 29 38.7 | 298 38.1 | 49.1 | 246 10.8 | 48.7 | 341 41.3 | 51.1 | 265 30.5 | 12.8 |
| M 09 | 44 41.2 | 313 37.2 | ·· 49.1 | 261 11.9 | ·· 48.2 | 356 43.3 | ·· 51.2 | 280 32.7 | ·· 12.8 |
| O 10 | 59 43.7 | 328 36.3 | 49.2 | 276 12.9 | 47.7 | 11 45.2 | 51.4 | 295 34.9 | 12.7 |
| N 11 | 74 46.1 | 343 35.4 | 49.3 | 291 13.9 | 47.2 | 26 47.1 | 51.5 | 310 37.0 | 12.6 |
| D 12 | 89 48.6 | 358 34.5 | N23 49.3 | 306 14.9 | N15 46.7 | 41 49.1 | N16 51.7 | 325 39.2 | N20 12.6 |
| A 13 | 104 51.1 | 13 33.6 | 49.4 | 321 15.9 | 46.2 | 56 51.0 | 51.8 | 340 41.4 | 12.5 |
| Y 14 | 119 53.5 | 28 32.7 | 49.5 | 336 16.9 | 45.7 | 71 52.9 | 51.9 | 355 43.5 | 12.5 |
| 15 | 134 56.0 | 43 31.8 | ·· 49.5 | 351 18.0 | ·· 45.2 | 86 54.9 | ·· 52.1 | 10 45.7 | ·· 12.4 |
| 16 | 149 58.4 | 58 30.9 | 49.6 | 6 19.0 | 44.7 | 101 56.8 | 52.2 | 25 47.8 | 12.3 |
| 17 | 165 00.9 | 73 30.0 | 49.7 | 21 20.0 | 44.2 | 116 58.8 | 52.3 | 40 50.0 | 12.3 |
| 18 | 180 03.4 | 88 29.1 | N23 49.7 | 36 21.0 | N15 43.7 | 132 00.7 | N16 52.5 | 55 52.2 | N20 12.2 |
| 19 | 195 05.8 | 103 28.2 | 49.8 | 51 22.0 | 43.2 | 147 02.6 | 52.6 | 70 54.3 | 12.1 |
| 20 | 210 08.3 | 118 27.3 | 49.9 | 66 23.0 | 42.7 | 162 04.6 | 52.7 | 85 56.5 | 12.1 |
| 21 | 225 10.8 | 133 26.5 | ·· 49.9 | 81 24.1 | ·· 42.2 | 177 06.5 | ·· 52.9 | 100 58.6 | ·· 12.0 |
| 22 | 240 13.2 | 148 25.6 | 50.0 | 96 25.1 | 41.7 | 192 08.5 | 53.0 | 116 00.8 | 12.0 |
| 23 | 255 15.7 | 163 24.7 | 50.0 | 111 26.1 | 41.2 | 207 10.4 | 53.2 | 131 03.0 | 11.9 |
| 22 00 | 270 18.2 | 178 23.8 | N23 50.1 | 126 27.1 | N15 40.7 | 222 12.3 | N16 53.3 | 146 05.1 | N20 11.8 |
| 01 | 285 20.6 | 193 22.9 | 50.1 | 141 28.1 | 40.2 | 237 14.3 | 53.4 | 161 07.3 | 11.8 |
| 02 | 300 23.1 | 208 22.0 | 50.2 | 156 29.1 | 39.7 | 252 16.2 | 53.6 | 176 09.4 | 11.7 |
| 03 | 315 25.5 | 223 21.1 | ·· 50.2 | 171 30.2 | ·· 39.2 | 267 18.2 | ·· 53.7 | 191 11.6 | ·· 11.6 |
| 04 | 330 28.0 | 238 20.2 | 50.3 | 186 31.2 | 38.7 | 282 20.1 | 53.8 | 206 13.8 | 11.6 |
| 05 | 345 30.5 | 253 19.3 | 50.3 | 201 32.2 | 38.2 | 297 22.0 | 54.0 | 221 15.9 | 11.5 |
| 06 | 0 32.9 | 268 18.4 | N23 50.4 | 216 33.2 | N15 37.7 | 312 24.0 | N16 54.1 | 236 18.1 | N20 11.5 |
| 07 | 15 35.4 | 283 17.5 | 50.4 | 231 34.2 | 37.2 | 327 25.9 | 54.2 | 251 20.2 | 11.4 |
| T 08 | 30 37.9 | 298 16.6 | 50.5 | 246 35.3 | 36.7 | 342 27.9 | 54.4 | 266 22.4 | 11.3 |
| U 09 | 45 40.3 | 313 15.7 | ·· 50.5 | 261 36.3 | ·· 36.2 | 357 29.8 | ·· 54.5 | 281 24.6 | ·· 11.3 |
| E 10 | 60 42.8 | 328 14.8 | 50.6 | 276 37.3 | 35.7 | 12 31.7 | 54.7 | 296 26.7 | 11.2 |
| S 11 | 75 45.3 | 343 13.9 | 50.6 | 291 38.3 | 35.2 | 27 33.7 | 54.8 | 311 28.9 | 11.1 |
| D 12 | 90 47.7 | 358 13.0 | N23 50.7 | 306 39.3 | N15 34.7 | 42 35.6 | N16 54.9 | 326 31.0 | N20 11.1 |
| A 13 | 105 50.2 | 13 12.1 | 50.7 | 321 40.3 | 34.2 | 57 37.6 | 55.1 | 341 33.2 | 11.0 |
| Y 14 | 120 52.7 | 28 11.2 | 50.7 | 336 41.4 | 33.7 | 72 39.5 | 55.2 | 356 35.4 | 11.0 |
| 15 | 135 55.1 | 43 10.3 | ·· 50.8 | 351 42.4 | ·· 33.2 | 87 41.5 | ·· 55.3 | 11 37.5 | ·· 10.9 |
| 16 | 150 57.6 | 58 09.4 | 50.8 | 6 43.4 | 32.7 | 102 43.4 | 55.5 | 26 39.7 | 10.8 |
| 17 | 166 00.0 | 73 08.5 | 50.8 | 21 44.4 | 32.2 | 117 45.3 | 55.6 | 41 41.8 | 10.8 |
| 18 | 181 02.5 | 88 07.6 | N23 50.9 | 36 45.4 | N15 31.7 | 132 47.3 | N16 55.7 | 56 44.0 | N20 10.7 |
| 19 | 196 05.0 | 103 06.7 | 50.9 | 51 46.4 | 31.2 | 147 49.2 | 55.9 | 71 46.1 | 10.6 |
| 20 | 211 07.4 | 118 05.9 | 50.9 | 66 47.5 | 30.7 | 162 51.2 | 56.0 | 86 48.3 | 10.6 |
| 21 | 226 09.9 | 133 05.0 | ·· 51.0 | 81 48.5 | ·· 30.2 | 177 53.1 | ·· 56.1 | 101 50.5 | ·· 10.5 |
| 22 | 241 12.4 | 148 04.1 | 51.0 | 96 49.5 | 29.7 | 192 55.0 | 56.3 | 116 52.6 | 10.4 |
| 23 | 256 14.8 | 163 03.2 | 51.0 | 111 50.5 | 29.2 | 207 57.0 | 56.4 | 131 54.8 | 10.4 |
| Mer. Pass. | h m 6 01.7 | v −0.9 | d 0.1 | v 1.0 | d 0.5 | v 1.9 | d 0.1 | v 2.2 | d 0.1 |

**STARS**

| Name | S.H.A. | Dec. |
|---|---|---|
| | ° ′ | ° ′ |
| Acamar | 315 39.7 | S40 23.8 |
| Achernar | 335 47.7 | S57 21.1 |
| Acrux | 173 40.3 | S62 58.5 |
| Adhara | 255 34.7 | S28 56.5 |
| Aldebaran | 291 21.6 | N16 27.7 |
| Alioth | 166 44.9 | N56 05.5 |
| Alkaid | 153 20.6 | N49 26.0 |
| Al Na'ir | 28 18.3 | S47 04.2 |
| Alnilam | 276 14.9 | S 1 13.1 |
| Alphard | 218 23.6 | S 8 33.5 |
| Alphecca | 126 34.2 | N26 47.7 |
| Alpheratz | 358 12.3 | N28 57.5 |
| Altair | 62 35.0 | N 8 48.4 |
| Ankaa | 353 43.1 | S42 25.7 |
| Antares | 113 00.0 | S26 22.8 |
| Arcturus | 146 20.9 | N19 18.4 |
| Atria | 108 26.2 | S68 59.2 |
| Avior | 234 29.9 | S59 26.3 |
| Bellatrix | 279 02.1 | N 6 19.7 |
| Betelgeuse | 271 31.7 | N 7 24.1 |
| Canopus | 264 09.0 | S52 41.1 |
| Capella | 281 16.0 | N45 58.4 |
| Deneb | 49 50.0 | N45 11.7 |
| Denebola | 183 02.0 | N14 42.2 |
| Diphda | 349 23.8 | S18 06.8 |
| Dubhe | 194 25.9 | N61 52.9 |
| Elnath | 278 48.1 | N28 35.2 |
| Eltanin | 90 58.5 | N51 29.6 |
| Enif | 34 14.2 | N 9 46.1 |
| Fomalhaut | 15 54.5 | S29 44.6 |
| Gacrux | 172 31.8 | S56 59.2 |
| Gienah | 176 20.9 | S17 24.8 |
| Hadar | 149 27.0 | S60 15.9 |
| Hamal | 328 32.3 | N23 21.0 |
| Kaus Aust. | 84 20.2 | S34 23.7 |
| Kochab | 137 18.1 | N74 15.4 |
| Markab | 14 05.9 | N15 04.7 |
| Menkar | 314 44.4 | N 3 59.8 |
| Menkent | 148 40.1 | S36 15.5 |
| Miaplacidus | 221 46.1 | S69 37.6 |
| Mirfak | 309 20.6 | N49 46.5 |
| Nunki | 76 32.3 | S26 19.5 |
| Peacock | 54 02.4 | S56 48.4 |
| Pollux | 244 02.0 | N28 05.0 |
| Procyon | 245 29.1 | N 5 17.0 |
| Rasalhague | 96 31.9 | N12 34.7 |
| Regulus | 208 13.2 | N12 04.9 |
| Rigel | 281 39.1 | S 8 13.8 |
| Rigil Kent. | 140 29.2 | S60 44.5 |
| Sabik | 102 44.1 | S15 41.7 |
| Schedar | 350 12.3 | N56 24.3 |
| Shaula | 96 59.2 | S37 05.2 |
| Sirius | 258 58.6 | S16 41.2 |
| Spica | 159 00.4 | S11 02.4 |
| Suhail | 223 13.2 | S43 20.5 |
| Vega | 80 57.3 | N38 45.8 |
| Zuben'ubi | 137 36.0 | S15 56.7 |

| | S.H.A. | Mer. Pass. |
|---|---|---|
| | ° ′ | h m |
| Venus | 269 26.2 | 12 06 |
| Mars | 216 43.7 | 15 35 |
| Jupiter | 312 06.8 | 9 13 |
| Saturn | 235 54.2 | 14 17 |

## 1976 JUNE 20, 21, 22 (SUN., MON., TUES.)

| G.M.T. | SUN G.H.A. | SUN Dec. | MOON G.H.A. | v | MOON Dec. | d | H.P. |
|---|---|---|---|---|---|---|---|
| 20 00 | 179 38.9 | N23 26.1 | 266 11.3 | 15.3 | N 4 23.0 | 9.9 | 54.4 |
| 01 | 194 38.7 | 26.1 | 280 45.6 | 15.2 | 4 32.9 | 9.9 | 54.4 |
| 02 | 209 38.6 | 26.1 | 295 19.8 | 15.3 | 4 42.8 | 9.8 | 54.4 |
| 03 | 224 38.5 | ·· 26.1 | 309 54.1 | 15.2 | 4 52.6 | 9.8 | 54.4 |
| 04 | 239 38.3 | 26.2 | 324 28.3 | 15.3 | 5 02.4 | 9.8 | 54.4 |
| 05 | 254 38.2 | 26.2 | 339 02.6 | 15.3 | 5 12.2 | 9.8 | 54.4 |
| 06 | 269 38.1 | N23 26.2 | 353 36.9 | 15.2 | N 5 22.0 | 9.7 | 54.4 |
| 07 | 284 37.9 | 26.2 | 8 11.1 | 15.2 | 5 31.7 | 9.7 | 54.4 |
| 08 | 299 37.8 | 26.2 | 22 45.3 | 15.3 | 5 41.4 | 9.7 | 54.3 |
| S 09 | 314 37.6 | ·· 26.3 | 37 19.6 | 15.2 | 5 51.1 | 9.7 | 54.3 |
| U 10 | 329 37.5 | 26.3 | 51 53.8 | 15.2 | 6 00.8 | 9.6 | 54.3 |
| N 11 | 344 37.4 | 26.3 | 66 28.0 | 15.2 | 6 10.4 | 9.6 | 54.3 |
| D 12 | 359 37.2 | N23 26.3 | 81 02.2 | 15.2 | N 6 20.0 | 9.6 | 54.3 |
| A 13 | 14 37.1 | 26.3 | 95 36.4 | 15.2 | 6 29.6 | 9.5 | 54.3 |
| Y 14 | 29 37.0 | 26.3 | 110 10.6 | 15.2 | 6 39.1 | 9.5 | 54.3 |
| 15 | 44 36.8 | ·· 26.3 | 124 44.8 | 15.2 | 6 48.6 | 9.5 | 54.3 |
| 16 | 59 36.7 | 26.3 | 139 19.0 | 15.1 | 6 58.1 | 9.5 | 54.3 |
| 17 | 74 36.6 | 26.4 | 153 53.1 | 15.2 | 7 07.6 | 9.4 | 54.3 |
| 18 | 89 36.4 | N23 26.4 | 168 27.3 | 15.1 | N 7 17.0 | 9.4 | 54.3 |
| 19 | 104 36.3 | 26.4 | 183 01.4 | 15.1 | 7 26.4 | 9.4 | 54.3 |
| 20 | 119 36.1 | 26.4 | 197 35.5 | 15.1 | 7 35.8 | 9.3 | 54.3 |
| 21 | 134 36.0 | ·· 26.4 | 212 09.6 | 15.1 | 7 45.1 | 9.3 | 54.3 |
| 22 | 149 35.9 | 26.4 | 226 43.7 | 15.0 | 7 54.4 | 9.3 | 54.2 |
| 23 | 164 35.7 | 26.4 | 241 17.7 | 15.1 | 8 03.7 | 9.2 | 54.2 |
| 21 00 | 179 35.6 | N23 26.4 | 255 51.8 | 15.0 | N 8 12.9 | 9.2 | 54.2 |
| 01 | 194 35.5 | 26.4 | 270 25.8 | 15.0 | 8 22.1 | 9.2 | 54.2 |
| 02 | 209 35.3 | 26.4 | 284 59.8 | 15.0 | 8 31.3 | 9.1 | 54.2 |
| 03 | 224 35.2 | ·· 26.4 | 299 33.8 | 15.0 | 8 40.4 | 9.1 | 54.2 |
| 04 | 239 35.1 | 26.4 | 314 07.8 | 14.9 | 8 49.5 | 9.0 | 54.2 |
| 05 | 254 34.9 | 26.4 | 328 41.7 | 15.0 | 8 58.5 | 9.0 | 54.2 |
| 06 | 269 34.8 | N23 26.4 | 343 15.7 | 14.9 | N 9 07.5 | 9.0 | 54.2 |
| 07 | 284 34.7 | 26.4 | 357 49.6 | 14.8 | 9 16.5 | 9.0 | 54.2 |
| 08 | 299 34.5 | 26.4 | 12 23.4 | 14.9 | 9 25.5 | 8.9 | 54.2 |
| M 09 | 314 34.4 | ·· 26.4 | 26 57.3 | 14.8 | 9 34.4 | 8.8 | 54.2 |
| O 10 | 329 34.2 | 26.4 | 41 31.1 | 14.8 | 9 43.2 | 8.9 | 54.2 |
| N 11 | 344 34.1 | 26.4 | 56 04.9 | 14.8 | 9 52.1 | 8.8 | 54.2 |
| D 12 | 359 34.0 | N23 26.4 | 70 38.7 | 14.8 | N10 00.9 | 8.7 | 54.2 |
| A 13 | 14 33.8 | 26.4 | 85 12.5 | 14.7 | 10 09.6 | 8.7 | 54.2 |
| Y 14 | 29 33.7 | 26.4 | 99 46.2 | 14.7 | 10 18.3 | 8.7 | 54.2 |
| 15 | 44 33.6 | ·· 26.4 | 114 19.9 | 14.7 | 10 27.0 | 8.6 | 54.2 |
| 16 | 59 33.4 | 26.4 | 128 53.6 | 14.6 | 10 35.6 | 8.6 | 54.2 |
| 17 | 74 33.3 | 26.4 | 143 27.2 | 14.7 | 10 44.2 | 8.5 | 54.2 |
| 18 | 89 33.2 | N23 26.4 | 158 00.9 | 14.5 | N10 52.7 | 8.5 | 54.2 |
| 19 | 104 33.0 | 26.4 | 172 34.4 | 14.6 | 11 01.2 | 8.4 | 54.2 |
| 20 | 119 32.9 | 26.3 | 187 08.0 | 14.5 | 11 09.6 | 8.4 | 54.2 |
| 21 | 134 32.7 | ·· 26.3 | 201 41.5 | 14.5 | 11 18.0 | 8.4 | 54.2 |
| 22 | 149 32.6 | 26.3 | 216 15.0 | 14.5 | 11 26.4 | 8.3 | 54.2 |
| 23 | 164 32.5 | 26.3 | 230 48.5 | 14.4 | 11 34.7 | 8.2 | 54.2 |
| 22 00 | 179 32.3 | N23 26.3 | 245 21.9 | 14.4 | N11 42.9 | 8.2 | 54.2 |
| 01 | 194 32.2 | 26.3 | 259 55.3 | 14.4 | 11 51.1 | 8.2 | 54.2 |
| 02 | 209 32.1 | 26.3 | 274 28.7 | 14.3 | 11 59.3 | 8.1 | 54.2 |
| 03 | 224 31.9 | ·· 26.3 | 289 02.0 | 14.3 | 12 07.4 | 8.1 | 54.2 |
| 04 | 239 31.8 | 26.2 | 303 35.3 | 14.3 | 12 15.5 | 8.0 | 54.2 |
| 05 | 254 31.7 | 26.2 | 318 08.6 | 14.2 | 12 23.5 | 8.0 | 54.2 |
| 06 | 269 31.5 | N23 26.2 | 332 41.8 | 14.2 | N12 31.5 | 7.9 | 54.2 |
| 07 | 284 31.4 | 26.2 | 347 15.0 | 14.1 | 12 39.4 | 7.8 | 54.2 |
| 08 | 299 31.3 | 26.2 | 1 48.1 | 14.2 | 12 47.2 | 7.9 | 54.2 |
| T 09 | 314 31.1 | ·· 26.2 | 16 21.3 | 14.0 | 12 55.1 | 7.7 | 54.2 |
| U 10 | 329 31.0 | 26.1 | 30 54.3 | 14.1 | 13 02.8 | 7.7 | 54.2 |
| E 11 | 344 30.8 | 26.1 | 45 27.4 | 14.0 | 13 10.5 | 7.7 | 54.2 |
| S 12 | 359 30.7 | N23 26.1 | 60 00.4 | 13.9 | N13 18.2 | 7.6 | 54.2 |
| D 13 | 14 30.6 | 26.1 | 74 33.3 | 14.0 | 13 25.8 | 7.5 | 54.3 |
| A 14 | 29 30.4 | 26.1 | 89 06.3 | 13.9 | 13 33.3 | 7.5 | 54.3 |
| Y 15 | 44 30.3 | ·· 26.0 | 103 39.2 | 13.8 | 13 40.8 | 7.4 | 54.3 |
| 16 | 59 30.2 | 26.0 | 118 12.0 | 13.8 | 13 48.2 | 7.4 | 54.3 |
| 17 | 74 30.0 | 26.0 | 132 44.8 | 13.8 | 13 55.6 | 7.3 | 54.3 |
| 18 | 89 29.9 | N23 26.0 | 147 17.6 | 13.7 | N14 02.9 | 7.3 | 54.3 |
| 19 | 104 29.8 | 25.9 | 161 50.3 | 13.7 | 14 10.2 | 7.2 | 54.3 |
| 20 | 119 29.6 | 25.9 | 176 23.0 | 13.6 | 14 17.4 | 7.1 | 54.3 |
| 21 | 134 29.5 | ·· 25.9 | 190 55.6 | 13.6 | 14 24.5 | 7.1 | 54.3 |
| 22 | 149 29.4 | 25.8 | 205 28.2 | 13.6 | 14 31.6 | 7.0 | 54.3 |
| 23 | 164 29.2 | 25.8 | 220 00.8 | 13.5 | 14 38.6 | 7.0 | 54.3 |
| | S.D. 15.8 | d 0.0 | S.D. 14.8 | | 14.8 | | 14.8 |

| Lat. | Twilight Naut. | Twilight Civil | Sunrise | Moonrise 20 | Moonrise 21 | Moonrise 22 | Moonrise 23 |
|---|---|---|---|---|---|---|---|
| N 72 | □ | □ | □ | 23 13 | 23 02 | 22 48 | 22 24 |
| N 70 | □ | □ | □ | 23 24 | 23 21 | 23 18 | 23 16 |
| 68 | □ | □ | □ | 23 34 | 23 36 | 23 40 | 23 48 |
| 66 | □ | □ | □ | 23 42 | 23 48 | 23 58 | 24 12 |
| 64 | //// | //// | 01 31 | 23 48 | 23 59 | 24 12 | 00 12 |
| 62 | //// | //// | 02 09 | 23 54 | 24 08 | 00 08 | 00 24 |
| 60 | //// | 00 49 | 02 36 | 23 59 | 24 15 | 00 15 | 00 35 |
| N 58 | //// | 01 40 | 02 56 | 24 04 | 00 04 | 00 22 | 00 44 |
| 56 | //// | 02 10 | 03 13 | 24 08 | 00 08 | 00 28 | 00 51 |
| 54 | 00 45 | 02 33 | 03 27 | 24 12 | 00 12 | 00 33 | 00 59 |
| 52 | 01 32 | 02 51 | 03 40 | 24 15 | 00 15 | 00 38 | 01 05 |
| 50 | 02 00 | 03 06 | 03 50 | 24 18 | 00 18 | 00 43 | 01 11 |
| 45 | 02 46 | 03 36 | 04 13 | 24 24 | 00 24 | 00 52 | 01 23 |
| N 40 | 03 17 | 03 58 | 04 31 | 00 01 | 00 30 | 01 00 | 01 33 |
| 35 | 03 40 | 04 17 | 04 46 | 00 03 | 00 35 | 01 07 | 01 42 |
| 30 | 03 58 | 04 32 | 04 59 | 00 06 | 00 39 | 01 13 | 01 50 |
| 20 | 04 28 | 04 57 | 05 21 | 00 09 | 00 46 | 01 24 | 02 04 |
| N 10 | 04 50 | 05 17 | 05 40 | 00 13 | 00 53 | 01 33 | 02 15 |
| 0 | 05 09 | 05 36 | 05 58 | 00 16 | 00 59 | 01 42 | 02 27 |
| S 10 | 05 26 | 05 53 | 06 16 | 00 19 | 01 05 | 01 51 | 02 38 |
| 20 | 05 43 | 06 10 | 06 34 | 00 23 | 01 11 | 02 00 | 02 50 |
| 30 | 05 59 | 06 29 | 06 55 | 00 27 | 01 19 | 02 11 | 03 04 |
| 35 | 06 08 | 06 40 | 07 08 | 00 29 | 01 23 | 02 17 | 03 12 |
| 40 | 06 17 | 06 51 | 07 22 | 00 32 | 01 28 | 02 25 | 03 21 |
| 45 | 06 28 | 07 05 | 07 39 | 00 35 | 01 34 | 02 33 | 03 32 |
| S 50 | 06 40 | 07 21 | 07 59 | 00 38 | 01 41 | 02 43 | 03 45 |
| 52 | 06 45 | 07 29 | 08 10 | 00 40 | 01 44 | 02 48 | 03 51 |
| 54 | 06 50 | 07 37 | 08 21 | 00 42 | 01 48 | 02 53 | 03 58 |
| 56 | 06 57 | 07 46 | 08 33 | 00 44 | 01 52 | 02 59 | 04 05 |
| 58 | 07 03 | 07 56 | 08 48 | 00 46 | 01 56 | 03 05 | 04 14 |
| S 60 | 07 11 | 08 08 | 09 06 | 00 49 | 02 01 | 03 13 | 04 23 |

| Lat. | Sunset | Twilight Civil | Twilight Naut. | Moonset 20 | Moonset 21 | Moonset 22 | Moonset 23 |
|---|---|---|---|---|---|---|---|
| N 72 | □ | □ | □ | 14 02 | 15 42 | 17 28 | 19 28 |
| N 70 | □ | □ | □ | 13 52 | 15 25 | 16 59 | 18 37 |
| 68 | □ | □ | □ | 13 44 | 15 11 | 16 38 | 18 05 |
| 66 | □ | □ | □ | 13 38 | 15 00 | 16 21 | 17 42 |
| 64 | 22 32 | //// | //// | 13 32 | 14 50 | 16 08 | 17 24 |
| 62 | 21 54 | //// | //// | 13 28 | 14 42 | 15 56 | 17 09 |
| 60 | 21 28 | 23 14 | //// | 13 23 | 14 35 | 15 46 | 16 56 |
| N 58 | 21 07 | 22 23 | //// | 13 20 | 14 29 | 15 38 | 16 46 |
| 56 | 20 50 | 21 53 | //// | 13 16 | 14 24 | 15 31 | 16 36 |
| 54 | 20 36 | 21 31 | 23 18 | 13 14 | 14 19 | 15 24 | 16 28 |
| 52 | 20 24 | 21 13 | 22 31 | 13 11 | 14 15 | 15 18 | 16 21 |
| 50 | 20 13 | 20 57 | 22 03 | 13 09 | 14 11 | 15 13 | 16 14 |
| 45 | 19 50 | 20 28 | 21 18 | 13 03 | 14 02 | 15 01 | 16 00 |
| N 40 | 19 32 | 20 05 | 20 47 | 12 59 | 13 55 | 14 52 | 15 48 |
| 35 | 19 17 | 19 47 | 20 24 | 12 55 | 13 49 | 14 44 | 15 38 |
| 30 | 19 04 | 19 32 | 20 05 | 12 52 | 13 44 | 14 36 | 15 29 |
| 20 | 18 42 | 19 07 | 19 36 | 12 46 | 13 35 | 14 24 | 15 14 |
| N 10 | 18 23 | 18 46 | 19 13 | 12 41 | 13 27 | 14 13 | 15 01 |
| 0 | 18 05 | 18 28 | 18 54 | 12 37 | 13 19 | 14 03 | 14 49 |
| S 10 | 17 48 | 18 11 | 18 37 | 12 32 | 13 12 | 13 53 | 14 37 |
| 20 | 17 29 | 17 53 | 18 21 | 12 27 | 13 04 | 13 43 | 14 24 |
| 30 | 17 08 | 17 35 | 18 04 | 12 21 | 12 55 | 13 30 | 14 09 |
| 35 | 16 56 | 17 24 | 17 56 | 12 18 | 12 50 | 13 23 | 14 00 |
| 40 | 16 41 | 17 12 | 17 46 | 12 14 | 12 44 | 13 15 | 13 50 |
| 45 | 16 25 | 16 59 | 17 36 | 12 10 | 12 37 | 13 06 | 13 39 |
| S 50 | 16 04 | 16 43 | 17 24 | 12 05 | 12 29 | 12 55 | 13 25 |
| 52 | 15 54 | 16 35 | 17 19 | 12 03 | 12 25 | 12 50 | 13 18 |
| 54 | 15 43 | 16 27 | 17 13 | 12 00 | 12 21 | 12 44 | 13 11 |
| 56 | 15 30 | 16 18 | 17 07 | 11 57 | 12 16 | 12 38 | 13 03 |
| 58 | 15 15 | 16 07 | 17 00 | 11 54 | 12 11 | 12 31 | 12 54 |
| S 60 | 14 58 | 15 56 | 16 52 | 11 51 | 12 05 | 12 23 | 12 44 |

| Day | SUN Eqn. of Time 00h | SUN Eqn. of Time 12h | SUN Mer. Pass. | MOON Mer. Pass. Upper | MOON Mer. Pass. Lower | Age | Phase |
|---|---|---|---|---|---|---|---|
| 20 | 01 24 | 01 31 | 12 02 | 06 26 | 18 48 | 22 | |
| 21 | 01 37 | 01 44 | 12 02 | 07 09 | 19 31 | 23 | |
| 22 | 01 50 | 01 57 | 12 02 | 07 53 | 20 15 | 24 | |

## 1976 JUNE 23, 24, 25 (WED., THURS., FRI.)

| G.M.T. | SUN G.H.A. | SUN Dec. | MOON G.H.A. | v | MOON Dec. | d | H.P. |
|---|---|---|---|---|---|---|---|
| 23 00 | 179 29.1 | N23 25.8 | 234 33.3 | 13.4 | N14 45.6 | 6.9 | 54.3 |
| 01 | 194 28.9 | 25.8 | 249 05.7 | 13.5 | 14 52.5 | 6.8 | 54.3 |
| 02 | 209 28.8 | 25.7 | 263 38.2 | 13.3 | 14 59.3 | 6.8 | 54.3 |
| 03 | 224 28.7 | ·· 25.7 | 278 10.5 | 13.4 | 15 06.1 | 6.7 | 54.4 |
| 04 | 239 28.5 | 25.7 | 292 42.9 | 13.3 | 15 12.8 | 6.6 | 54.4 |
| 05 | 254 28.4 | 25.6 | 307 15.2 | 13.2 | 15 19.4 | 6.6 | 54.4 |
| 06 | 269 28.3 | N23 25.6 | 321 47.4 | 13.2 | N15 26.0 | 6.5 | 54.4 |
| W 07 | 284 28.1 | 25.6 | 336 19.6 | 13.2 | 15 32.5 | 6.5 | 54.4 |
| E 08 | 299 28.0 | 25.5 | 350 51.8 | 13.1 | 15 39.0 | 6.4 | 54.4 |
| D 09 | 314 27.9 | ·· 25.5 | 5 23.9 | 13.1 | 15 45.4 | 6.3 | 54.4 |
| N 10 | 329 27.7 | 25.5 | 19 56.0 | 13.0 | 15 51.7 | 6.2 | 54.4 |
| E 11 | 344 27.6 | 25.4 | 34 28.0 | 13.0 | 15 57.9 | 6.2 | 54.4 |
| S 12 | 359 27.5 | N23 25.4 | 49 00.0 | 12.9 | N16 04.1 | 6.1 | 54.4 |
| D 13 | 14 27.3 | 25.3 | 63 31.9 | 12.9 | 16 10.2 | 6.1 | 54.5 |
| A 14 | 29 27.2 | 25.3 | 78 03.8 | 12.8 | 16 16.3 | 5.9 | 54.5 |
| Y 15 | 44 27.1 | ·· 25.3 | 92 35.6 | 12.8 | 16 22.2 | 5.9 | 54.5 |
| 16 | 59 26.9 | 25.2 | 107 07.4 | 12.7 | 16 28.1 | 5.9 | 54.5 |
| 17 | 74 26.8 | 25.2 | 121 39.1 | 12.7 | 16 34.0 | 5.7 | 54.5 |
| 18 | 89 26.6 | N23 25.1 | 136 10.8 | 12.7 | N16 39.7 | 5.7 | 54.5 |
| 19 | 104 26.5 | 25.1 | 150 42.5 | 12.6 | 16 45.4 | 5.6 | 54.5 |
| 20 | 119 26.4 | 25.0 | 165 14.1 | 12.5 | 16 51.0 | 5.6 | 54.5 |
| 21 | 134 26.2 | ·· 25.0 | 179 45.6 | 12.5 | 16 56.6 | 5.4 | 54.5 |
| 22 | 149 26.1 | 25.0 | 194 17.1 | 12.5 | 17 02.0 | 5.4 | 54.6 |
| 23 | 164 26.0 | 24.9 | 208 48.6 | 12.4 | 17 07.4 | 5.3 | 54.6 |
| 24 00 | 179 25.8 | N23 24.9 | 223 20.0 | 12.4 | N17 12.7 | 5.3 | 54.6 |
| 01 | 194 25.7 | 24.8 | 237 51.4 | 12.3 | 17 18.0 | 5.2 | 54.6 |
| 02 | 209 25.6 | 24.8 | 252 22.7 | 12.3 | 17 23.2 | 5.0 | 54.6 |
| 03 | 224 25.4 | ·· 24.7 | 266 54.0 | 12.2 | 17 28.2 | 5.0 | 54.6 |
| 04 | 239 25.3 | 24.7 | 281 25.2 | 12.2 | 17 33.2 | 5.0 | 54.6 |
| 05 | 254 25.2 | 24.6 | 295 56.4 | 12.1 | 17 38.2 | 4.8 | 54.7 |
| 06 | 269 25.0 | N23 24.6 | 310 27.5 | 12.1 | N17 43.0 | 4.8 | 54.7 |
| T 07 | 284 24.9 | 24.5 | 324 58.6 | 12.0 | 17 47.8 | 4.7 | 54.7 |
| H 08 | 299 24.8 | 24.5 | 339 29.6 | 12.0 | 17 52.5 | 4.6 | 54.7 |
| U 09 | 314 24.6 | ·· 24.4 | 354 00.6 | 11.9 | 17 57.1 | 4.5 | 54.7 |
| R 10 | 329 24.5 | 24.4 | 8 31.5 | 11.9 | 18 01.6 | 4.5 | 54.7 |
| S 11 | 344 24.4 | 24.3 | 23 02.4 | 11.9 | 18 06.1 | 4.3 | 54.7 |
| D 12 | 359 24.2 | N23 24.2 | 37 33.3 | 11.8 | N18 10.4 | 4.3 | 54.8 |
| A 13 | 14 24.1 | 24.2 | 52 04.1 | 11.7 | 18 14.7 | 4.2 | 54.8 |
| Y 14 | 29 24.0 | 24.1 | 66 34.8 | 11.7 | 18 18.9 | 4.1 | 54.8 |
| 15 | 44 23.8 | ·· 24.1 | 81 05.5 | 11.7 | 18 23.0 | 4.0 | 54.8 |
| 16 | 59 23.7 | 24.0 | 95 36.2 | 11.6 | 18 27.0 | 4.0 | 54.8 |
| 17 | 74 23.6 | 24.0 | 110 06.8 | 11.6 | 18 31.0 | 3.8 | 54.8 |
| 18 | 89 23.4 | N23 23.9 | 124 37.4 | 11.5 | N18 34.8 | 3.8 | 54.9 |
| 19 | 104 23.3 | 23.8 | 139 07.9 | 11.5 | 18 38.6 | 3.7 | 54.9 |
| 20 | 119 23.2 | 23.8 | 153 38.4 | 11.4 | 18 42.3 | 3.6 | 54.9 |
| 21 | 134 23.0 | ·· 23.7 | 168 08.8 | 11.4 | 18 45.9 | 3.5 | 54.9 |
| 22 | 149 22.9 | 23.7 | 182 39.2 | 11.4 | 18 49.4 | 3.4 | 54.9 |
| 23 | 164 22.8 | 23.6 | 197 09.6 | 11.3 | 18 52.8 | 3.3 | 54.9 |
| 25 00 | 179 22.6 | N23 23.5 | 211 39.9 | 11.2 | N18 56.1 | 3.3 | 55.0 |
| 01 | 194 22.5 | 23.5 | 226 10.1 | 11.3 | 18 59.4 | 3.1 | 55.0 |
| 02 | 209 22.3 | 23.4 | 240 40.4 | 11.1 | 19 02.5 | 3.1 | 55.0 |
| 03 | 224 22.2 | ·· 23.3 | 255 10.5 | 11.2 | 19 05.6 | 2.9 | 55.0 |
| 04 | 239 22.1 | 23.3 | 269 40.7 | 11.0 | 19 08.5 | 2.9 | 55.0 |
| 05 | 254 21.9 | 23.2 | 284 10.7 | 11.1 | 19 11.4 | 2.8 | 55.1 |
| 06 | 269 21.8 | N23 23.1 | 298 40.8 | 11.0 | N19 14.2 | 2.7 | 55.1 |
| 07 | 284 21.7 | 23.1 | 313 10.8 | 11.0 | 19 16.9 | 2.6 | 55.1 |
| 08 | 299 21.5 | 23.0 | 327 40.8 | 10.9 | 19 19.5 | 2.5 | 55.1 |
| F 09 | 314 21.4 | ·· 22.9 | 342 10.7 | 10.9 | 19 22.0 | 2.4 | 55.1 |
| R 10 | 329 21.3 | 22.8 | 356 40.6 | 10.8 | 19 24.4 | 2.3 | 55.1 |
| I 11 | 344 21.1 | 22.8 | 11 10.4 | 10.8 | 19 26.7 | 2.2 | 55.2 |
| D 12 | 359 21.0 | N23 22.7 | 25 40.2 | 10.8 | N19 28.9 | 2.1 | 55.2 |
| A 13 | 14 20.9 | 22.6 | 40 10.0 | 10.7 | 19 31.0 | 2.0 | 55.2 |
| Y 14 | 29 20.7 | 22.6 | 54 39.7 | 10.7 | 19 33.0 | 2.0 | 55.2 |
| 15 | 44 20.6 | ·· 22.5 | 69 09.4 | 10.6 | 19 35.0 | 1.8 | 55.2 |
| 16 | 59 20.5 | 22.4 | 83 39.0 | 10.6 | 19 36.8 | 1.7 | 55.3 |
| 17 | 74 20.4 | 22.3 | 98 08.6 | 10.6 | 19 38.5 | 1.6 | 55.3 |
| 18 | 89 20.2 | N23 22.3 | 112 38.2 | 10.5 | N19 40.1 | 1.6 | 55.3 |
| 19 | 104 20.1 | 22.2 | 127 07.7 | 10.5 | 19 41.7 | 1.4 | 55.3 |
| 20 | 119 20.0 | 22.1 | 141 37.2 | 10.5 | 19 43.1 | 1.4 | 55.3 |
| 21 | 134 19.8 | ·· 22.0 | 156 06.7 | 10.4 | 19 44.5 | 1.2 | 55.4 |
| 22 | 149 19.7 | 21.9 | 170 36.1 | 10.4 | 19 45.7 | 1.1 | 55.4 |
| 23 | 164 19.6 | 21.9 | 185 05.5 | 10.4 | 19 46.8 | 1.1 | 55.4 |
| | S.D. 15.8 | d 0.1 | S.D. 14.8 | | 14.9 | | 15.0 |

| Lat. | Twilight Naut. | Twilight Civil | Sunrise | Moonrise 23 | Moonrise 24 | Moonrise 25 | Moonrise 26 |
|---|---|---|---|---|---|---|---|
| N 72 | □ | □ | □ | 22 24 | □ | □ | □ |
| N 70 | □ | □ | □ | 23 16 | 23 15 | 23 23 | 24 21 |
| 68 | □ | □ | □ | 23 48 | 24 03 | 00 03 | 00 33 |
| 66 | □ | □ | □ | 24 12 | 00 12 | 00 34 | 01 10 |
| 64 | //// | //// | 01 32 | 00 12 | 00 31 | 00 57 | 01 36 |
| 62 | //// | //// | 02 10 | 00 24 | 00 46 | 01 16 | 01 56 |
| 60 | //// | 00 50 | 02 37 | 00 35 | 00 59 | 01 31 | 02 13 |
| N 58 | //// | 01 41 | 02 57 | 00 44 | 01 10 | 01 44 | 02 27 |
| 56 | //// | 02 11 | 03 14 | 00 51 | 01 20 | 01 55 | 02 39 |
| 54 | 00 46 | 02 34 | 03 28 | 00 59 | 01 28 | 02 05 | 02 49 |
| 52 | 01 33 | 02 52 | 03 40 | 01 05 | 01 36 | 02 14 | 02 59 |
| 50 | 02 01 | 03 07 | 03 51 | 01 11 | 01 43 | 02 21 | 03 07 |
| 45 | 02 47 | 03 36 | 04 14 | 01 23 | 01 58 | 02 38 | 03 25 |
| N 40 | 03 17 | 03 59 | 04 32 | 01 33 | 02 10 | 02 52 | 03 39 |
| 35 | 03 40 | 04 17 | 04 47 | 01 42 | 02 21 | 03 04 | 03 52 |
| 30 | 03 59 | 04 33 | 05 00 | 01 50 | 02 30 | 03 14 | 04 02 |
| 20 | 04 28 | 04 58 | 05 22 | 02 04 | 02 46 | 03 32 | 04 21 |
| N 10 | 04 51 | 05 18 | 05 41 | 02 15 | 03 00 | 03 47 | 04 37 |
| 0 | 05 10 | 05 36 | 05 59 | 02 27 | 03 13 | 04 02 | 04 52 |
| S 10 | 05 27 | 05 53 | 06 16 | 02 38 | 03 26 | 04 16 | 05 07 |
| 20 | 05 43 | 06 11 | 06 35 | 02 50 | 03 41 | 04 32 | 05 23 |
| 30 | 06 00 | 06 30 | 06 56 | 03 04 | 03 57 | 04 50 | 05 42 |
| 35 | 06 08 | 06 40 | 07 08 | 03 12 | 04 06 | 05 00 | 05 53 |
| 40 | 06 18 | 06 52 | 07 22 | 03 21 | 04 17 | 05 12 | 06 05 |
| 45 | 06 28 | 07 05 | 07 39 | 03 32 | 04 30 | 05 26 | 06 20 |
| S 50 | 06 40 | 07 21 | 08 00 | 03 45 | 04 45 | 05 44 | 06 38 |
| 52 | 06 45 | 07 29 | 08 10 | 03 51 | 04 53 | 05 52 | 06 47 |
| 54 | 06 51 | 07 37 | 08 21 | 03 58 | 05 01 | 06 01 | 06 56 |
| 56 | 06 57 | 07 46 | 08 34 | 04 05 | 05 10 | 06 11 | 07 07 |
| 58 | 07 04 | 07 57 | 08 48 | 04 14 | 05 20 | 06 23 | 07 19 |
| S 60 | 07 11 | 08 08 | 09 06 | 04 23 | 05 32 | 06 37 | 07 33 |

| Lat. | Sunset | Twilight Civil | Twilight Naut. | Moonset 23 | Moonset 24 | Moonset 25 | Moonset 26 |
|---|---|---|---|---|---|---|---|
| N 72 | □ | □ | □ | 19 28 | □ | □ | □ |
| N 70 | □ | □ | □ | 18 37 | 20 17 | 21 53 | 22 42 |
| 68 | □ | □ | □ | 18 05 | 19 29 | 20 43 | 21 34 |
| 66 | □ | □ | □ | 17 42 | 18 59 | 20 06 | 20 58 |
| 64 | 22 32 | //// | //// | 17 24 | 18 36 | 19 40 | 20 32 |
| 62 | 21 54 | //// | //// | 17 09 | 18 18 | 19 20 | 20 12 |
| 60 | 21 28 | 23 13 | //// | 16 56 | 18 03 | 19 04 | 19 56 |
| N 58 | 21 07 | 22 23 | //// | 16 46 | 17 50 | 18 50 | 19 42 |
| 56 | 20 51 | 21 53 | //// | 16 36 | 17 39 | 18 38 | 19 30 |
| 54 | 20 36 | 21 31 | 23 18 | 16 28 | 17 30 | 18 27 | 19 19 |
| 52 | 20 24 | 21 13 | 22 31 | 16 21 | 17 21 | 18 18 | 19 10 |
| 50 | 20 13 | 20 58 | 22 03 | 16 14 | 17 13 | 18 10 | 19 02 |
| 45 | 19 51 | 20 28 | 21 18 | 16 00 | 16 57 | 17 52 | 18 44 |
| N 40 | 19 33 | 20 06 | 20 47 | 15 48 | 16 44 | 17 38 | 18 30 |
| 35 | 19 18 | 19 47 | 20 24 | 15 38 | 16 32 | 17 26 | 18 17 |
| 30 | 19 05 | 19 32 | 20 05 | 15 29 | 16 22 | 17 15 | 18 06 |
| 20 | 18 43 | 19 07 | 19 36 | 15 14 | 16 05 | 16 57 | 17 48 |
| N 10 | 18 24 | 18 47 | 19 14 | 15 01 | 15 50 | 16 41 | 17 32 |
| 0 | 18 06 | 18 29 | 18 55 | 14 49 | 15 36 | 16 26 | 17 17 |
| S 10 | 17 49 | 18 11 | 18 38 | 14 37 | 15 22 | 16 11 | 17 02 |
| 20 | 17 30 | 17 54 | 18 22 | 14 24 | 15 08 | 15 55 | 16 45 |
| 30 | 17 09 | 17 35 | 18 05 | 14 09 | 14 51 | 15 37 | 16 27 |
| 35 | 16 56 | 17 25 | 17 56 | 14 00 | 14 41 | 15 26 | 16 16 |
| 40 | 16 42 | 17 13 | 17 47 | 13 50 | 14 29 | 15 14 | 16 04 |
| 45 | 16 25 | 16 59 | 17 37 | 13 39 | 14 16 | 14 59 | 15 49 |
| S 50 | 16 05 | 16 43 | 17 25 | 13 25 | 14 00 | 14 42 | 15 31 |
| 52 | 15 55 | 16 36 | 17 19 | 13 18 | 13 52 | 14 33 | 15 22 |
| 54 | 15 44 | 16 28 | 17 14 | 13 11 | 13 44 | 14 24 | 15 13 |
| 56 | 15 31 | 16 18 | 17 08 | 13 03 | 13 35 | 14 14 | 15 02 |
| 58 | 15 16 | 16 08 | 17 01 | 12 54 | 13 24 | 14 02 | 14 50 |
| S 60 | 14 59 | 15 57 | 16 53 | 12 44 | 13 12 | 13 48 | 14 36 |

| Day | SUN Eqn. of Time 00h | SUN Eqn. of Time 12h | SUN Mer. Pass. | MOON Mer. Pass. Upper | MOON Mer. Pass. Lower | Age | Phase |
|---|---|---|---|---|---|---|---|
| 23 | 02 03 | 02 10 | 12 02 | 08 38 | 21 01 | 25 | |
| 24 | 02 16 | 02 23 | 12 02 | 09 25 | 21 49 | 26 | |
| 25 | 02 29 | 02 36 | 12 03 | 10 14 | 22 39 | 27 | |

## 1976 JULY 2, 3, 4 (FRI., SAT., SUN.)

| G.M.T. d | h | ARIES G.H.A. | VENUS −3.5 G.H.A. | VENUS Dec. | MARS +1.9 G.H.A. | MARS Dec. | JUPITER −1.7 G.H.A. | JUPITER Dec. | SATURN +0.5 G.H.A. | SATURN Dec. | STARS Name | S.H.A. | Dec. |
|---|---|---|---|---|---|---|---|---|---|---|---|---|---|
| 2 | 00 | 280 09.6 | 174 49.8 | N23 27.8 | 130 32.0 | N13 36.3 | 230 01.3 | N17 24.3 | 154 41.8 | N19 56.1 | Acamar | 315 39.6 | S40 23.7 |
| | 01 | 295 12.0 | 189 48.9 | 27.6 | 145 33.0 | 35.7 | 245 03.3 | 24.5 | 169 44.0 | 56.1 | Achernar | 335 47.6 | S57 21.0 |
| | 02 | 310 14.5 | 204 48.1 | 27.4 | 160 34.0 | 35.2 | 260 05.2 | 24.6 | 184 46.1 | 56.0 | Acrux | 173 40.4 | S62 58.5 |
| | 03 | 325 16.9 | 219 47.2 | ·· 27.1 | 175 35.0 | ·· 34.7 | 275 07.2 | ·· 24.7 | 199 48.3 | ·· 55.9 | Adhara | 255 34.7 | S28 56.5 |
| | 04 | 340 19.4 | 234 46.3 | 26.9 | 190 36.1 | 34.1 | 290 09.2 | 24.8 | 214 50.4 | 55.9 | Aldebaran | 291 21.5 | N16 27.7 |
| | 05 | 355 21.9 | 249 45.4 | 26.6 | 205 37.1 | 33.6 | 305 11.1 | 24.9 | 229 52.5 | 55.8 | | | |
| | 06 | 10 24.3 | 264 44.6 | N23 26.4 | 220 38.1 | N13 33.1 | 320 13.1 | N17 25.1 | 244 54.7 | N19 55.7 | Alioth | 166 45.0 | N56 05.5 |
| | 07 | 25 26.8 | 279 43.7 | 26.1 | 235 39.1 | 32.5 | 335 15.1 | 25.2 | 259 56.8 | 55.6 | Alkaid | 153 20.6 | N49 26.1 |
| | 08 | 40 29.3 | 294 42.8 | 25.9 | 250 40.1 | 32.0 | 350 17.0 | 25.3 | 274 59.0 | 55.6 | Al Na'ir | 28 18.2 | S47 04.2 |
| F | 09 | 55 31.7 | 309 41.9 | ·· 25.6 | 265 41.2 | ·· 31.4 | 5 19.0 | ·· 25.4 | 290 01.1 | ·· 55.5 | Alnilam | 276 14.9 | S 1 13.0 |
| R | 10 | 70 34.2 | 324 41.1 | 25.4 | 280 42.2 | 30.9 | 20 21.0 | 25.5 | 305 03.3 | 55.4 | Alphard | 218 23.6 | S 8 33.5 |
| I | 11 | 85 36.7 | 339 40.2 | 25.1 | 295 43.2 | 30.4 | 35 23.0 | 25.7 | 320 05.4 | 55.4 | | | |
| D | 12 | 100 39.1 | 354 39.3 | N23 24.9 | 310 44.2 | N13 29.8 | 50 24.9 | N17 25.8 | 335 07.6 | N19 55.3 | Alphecca | 126 34.3 | N26 47.8 |
| A | 13 | 115 41.6 | 9 38.4 | 24.6 | 325 45.3 | 29.3 | 65 26.9 | 25.9 | 350 09.7 | 55.2 | Alpheratz | 358 12.2 | N28 57.6 |
| Y | 14 | 130 44.1 | 24 37.6 | 24.4 | 340 46.3 | 28.7 | 80 28.9 | 26.0 | 5 11.9 | 55.2 | Altair | 62 35.0 | N 8 48.5 |
| | 15 | 145 46.5 | 39 36.7 | ·· 24.1 | 355 47.3 | ·· 28.2 | 95 30.8 | ·· 26.2 | 20 14.0 | ·· 55.1 | Ankaa | 353 43.0 | S42 25.7 |
| | 16 | 160 49.0 | 54 35.8 | 23.9 | 10 48.3 | 27.7 | 110 32.8 | 26.3 | 35 16.2 | 55.0 | Antares | 113 00.0 | S26 22.8 |
| | 17 | 175 51.4 | 69 34.9 | 23.6 | 25 49.4 | 27.1 | 125 34.8 | 26.4 | 50 18.3 | 55.0 | | | |
| | 18 | 190 53.9 | 84 34.1 | N23 23.3 | 40 50.4 | N13 26.6 | 140 36.8 | N17 26.5 | 65 20.4 | N19 54.9 | Arcturus | 146 20.9 | N19 18.4 |
| | 19 | 205 56.4 | 99 33.2 | 23.1 | 55 51.4 | 26.0 | 155 38.7 | 26.6 | 80 22.6 | 54.8 | Atria | 108 26.2 | S68 59.3 |
| | 20 | 220 58.8 | 114 32.3 | 22.8 | 70 52.4 | 25.5 | 170 40.7 | 26.8 | 95 24.7 | 54.8 | Avior | 234 29.9 | S59 26.3 |
| | 21 | 236 01.3 | 129 31.5 | ·· 22.5 | 85 53.5 | ·· 25.0 | 185 42.7 | ·· 26.9 | 110 26.9 | ·· 54.7 | Bellatrix | 279 02.1 | N 6 19.7 |
| | 22 | 251 03.8 | 144 30.6 | 22.3 | 100 54.5 | 24.4 | 200 44.6 | 27.0 | 125 29.0 | 54.6 | Betelgeuse | 271 31.7 | N 7 24.1 |
| | 23 | 266 06.2 | 159 29.7 | 22.0 | 115 55.5 | 23.9 | 215 46.6 | 27.1 | 140 31.2 | 54.6 | | | |
| 3 | 00 | 281 08.7 | 174 28.8 | N23 21.7 | 130 56.5 | N13 23.3 | 230 48.6 | N17 27.2 | 155 33.3 | N19 54.5 | Canopus | 264 09.0 | S52 41.0 |
| | 01 | 296 11.2 | 189 28.0 | 21.5 | 145 57.6 | 22.8 | 245 50.6 | 27.4 | 170 35.5 | 54.4 | Capella | 281 15.9 | N45 58.4 |
| | 02 | 311 13.6 | 204 27.1 | 21.2 | 160 58.6 | 22.3 | 260 52.5 | 27.5 | 185 37.6 | 54.3 | Deneb | 49 49.9 | N45 11.8 |
| | 03 | 326 16.1 | 219 26.2 | ·· 20.9 | 175 59.6 | ·· 21.7 | 275 54.5 | ·· 27.6 | 200 39.8 | ·· 54.3 | Denebola | 183 02.0 | N14 42.2 |
| | 04 | 341 18.5 | 234 25.3 | 20.7 | 191 00.6 | 21.2 | 290 56.5 | 27.7 | 215 41.9 | 54.2 | Diphda | 349 23.7 | S18 06.7 |
| | 05 | 356 21.0 | 249 24.5 | 20.4 | 206 01.7 | 20.6 | 305 58.4 | 27.8 | 230 44.0 | 54.1 | | | |
| | 06 | 11 23.5 | 264 23.6 | N23 20.1 | 221 02.7 | N13 20.1 | 321 00.4 | N17 28.0 | 245 46.2 | N19 54.1 | Dubhe | 194 26.0 | N61 52.9 |
| | 07 | 26 25.9 | 279 22.7 | 19.8 | 236 03.7 | 19.5 | 336 02.4 | 28.1 | 260 48.3 | 54.0 | Elnath | 278 48.1 | N28 35.2 |
| S | 08 | 41 28.4 | 294 21.9 | 19.6 | 251 04.7 | 19.0 | 351 04.4 | 28.2 | 275 50.5 | 53.9 | Eltanin | 90 58.5 | N51 29.7 |
| A | 09 | 56 30.9 | 309 21.0 | ·· 19.3 | 266 05.7 | ·· 18.5 | 6 06.3 | ·· 28.3 | 290 52.6 | ·· 53.9 | Enif | 34 14.1 | N 9 46.1 |
| T | 10 | 71 33.3 | 324 20.1 | 19.0 | 281 06.8 | 17.9 | 21 08.3 | 28.4 | 305 54.8 | 53.8 | Fomalhaut | 15 54.4 | S29 44.5 |
| U | 11 | 86 35.8 | 339 19.3 | 18.7 | 296 07.8 | 17.4 | 36 10.3 | 28.6 | 320 56.9 | 53.7 | | | |
| R | 12 | 101 38.3 | 354 18.4 | N23 18.4 | 311 08.8 | N13 16.8 | 51 12.3 | N17 28.7 | 335 59.1 | N19 53.7 | Gacrux | 172 31.9 | S56 59.2 |
| D | 13 | 116 40.7 | 9 17.5 | 18.2 | 326 09.8 | 16.3 | 66 14.2 | 28.8 | 351 01.2 | 53.6 | Gienah | 176 20.9 | S17 24.8 |
| A | 14 | 131 43.2 | 24 16.6 | 17.9 | 341 10.9 | 15.7 | 81 16.2 | 28.9 | 6 03.3 | 53.5 | Hadar | 149 27.1 | S60 15.9 |
| Y | 15 | 146 45.7 | 39 15.8 | ·· 17.6 | 356 11.9 | ·· 15.2 | 96 18.2 | ·· 29.0 | 21 05.5 | ·· 53.5 | Hamal | 328 32.2 | N23 21.0 |
| | 16 | 161 48.1 | 54 14.9 | 17.3 | 11 12.9 | 14.7 | 111 20.2 | 29.2 | 36 07.6 | 53.4 | Kaus Aust. | 84 20.2 | S34 23.7 |
| | 17 | 176 50.6 | 69 14.0 | 17.0 | 26 13.9 | 14.1 | 126 22.1 | 29.3 | 51 09.8 | 53.3 | | | |
| | 18 | 191 53.0 | 84 13.2 | N23 16.7 | 41 15.0 | N13 13.6 | 141 24.1 | N17 29.4 | 66 11.9 | N19 53.3 | Kochab | 137 18.3 | N74 15.4 |
| | 19 | 206 55.5 | 99 12.3 | 16.4 | 56 16.0 | 13.0 | 156 26.1 | 29.5 | 81 14.1 | 53.2 | Markab | 14 05.8 | N15 04.8 |
| | 20 | 221 58.0 | 114 11.4 | 16.1 | 71 17.0 | 12.5 | 171 28.1 | 29.6 | 96 16.2 | 53.1 | Menkar | 314 44.3 | N 3 59.9 |
| | 21 | 237 00.4 | 129 10.6 | ·· 15.9 | 86 18.0 | ·· 11.9 | 186 30.0 | ·· 29.8 | 111 18.4 | ·· 53.0 | Menkent | 148 40.2 | S36 15.5 |
| | 22 | 252 02.9 | 144 09.7 | 15.6 | 101 19.1 | 11.4 | 201 32.0 | 29.9 | 126 20.5 | 53.0 | Miaplacidus | 221 46.2 | S69 37.5 |
| | 23 | 267 05.4 | 159 08.8 | 15.3 | 116 20.1 | 10.9 | 216 34.0 | 30.0 | 141 22.7 | 52.9 | | | |
| 4 | 00 | 282 07.8 | 174 08.0 | N23 15.0 | 131 21.1 | N13 10.3 | 231 36.0 | N17 30.1 | 156 24.8 | N19 52.8 | Mirfak | 309 20.4 | N49 46.5 |
| | 01 | 297 10.3 | 189 07.1 | 14.7 | 146 22.1 | 09.8 | 246 37.9 | 30.2 | 171 26.9 | 52.8 | Nunki | 76 32.3 | S26 19.5 |
| | 02 | 312 12.8 | 204 06.2 | 14.4 | 161 23.2 | 09.2 | 261 39.9 | 30.4 | 186 29.1 | 52.7 | Peacock | 54 02.3 | S56 48.4 |
| | 03 | 327 15.2 | 219 05.4 | ·· 14.1 | 176 24.2 | ·· 08.7 | 276 41.9 | ·· 30.5 | 201 31.2 | ·· 52.6 | Pollux | 244 02.0 | N28 05.0 |
| | 04 | 342 17.7 | 234 04.5 | 13.8 | 191 25.2 | 08.1 | 291 43.9 | 30.6 | 216 33.4 | 52.6 | Procyon | 245 29.1 | N 5 17.1 |
| | 05 | 357 20.1 | 249 03.6 | 13.5 | 206 26.2 | 07.6 | 306 45.8 | 30.7 | 231 35.5 | 52.5 | | | |
| | 06 | 12 22.6 | 264 02.8 | N23 13.2 | 221 27.3 | N13 07.0 | 321 47.8 | N17 30.8 | 246 37.7 | N19 52.4 | Rasalhague | 96 31.9 | N12 34.7 |
| | 07 | 27 25.1 | 279 01.9 | 12.9 | 236 28.3 | 06.5 | 336 49.8 | 31.0 | 261 39.8 | 52.4 | Regulus | 208 13.2 | N12 04.9 |
| | 08 | 42 27.5 | 294 01.0 | 12.6 | 251 29.3 | 05.9 | 351 51.8 | 31.1 | 276 41.9 | 52.3 | Rigel | 281 39.0 | S 8 13.7 |
| S | 09 | 57 30.0 | 309 00.2 | ·· 12.3 | 266 30.3 | ·· 05.4 | 6 53.7 | ·· 31.2 | 291 44.1 | ·· 52.2 | Rigil Kent. | 140 29.2 | S60 44.5 |
| U | 10 | 72 32.5 | 323 59.3 | 11.9 | 281 31.4 | 04.9 | 21 55.7 | 31.3 | 306 46.2 | 52.1 | Sabik | 102 44.0 | S15 41.7 |
| N | 11 | 87 34.9 | 338 58.5 | 11.6 | 296 32.4 | 04.3 | 36 57.7 | 31.4 | 321 48.4 | 52.1 | | | |
| D | 12 | 102 37.4 | 353 57.6 | N23 11.3 | 311 33.4 | N13 03.8 | 51 59.7 | N17 31.5 | 336 50.5 | N19 52.0 | Schedar | 350 12.2 | N56 24.3 |
| A | 13 | 117 39.9 | 8 56.7 | 11.0 | 326 34.4 | 03.2 | 67 01.7 | 31.7 | 351 52.7 | 51.9 | Shaula | 96 59.2 | S37 05.2 |
| Y | 14 | 132 42.3 | 23 55.9 | 10.7 | 341 35.5 | 02.7 | 82 03.6 | 31.8 | 6 54.8 | 51.9 | Sirius | 258 58.5 | S16 41.1 |
| | 15 | 147 44.8 | 38 55.0 | ·· 10.4 | 356 36.5 | ·· 02.1 | 97 05.6 | ·· 31.9 | 21 57.0 | ·· 51.8 | Spica | 159 00.5 | S11 02.4 |
| | 16 | 162 47.3 | 53 54.1 | 10.1 | 11 37.5 | 01.6 | 112 07.6 | 32.0 | 36 59.1 | 51.7 | Suhail | 223 13.2 | S43 20.5 |
| | 17 | 177 49.7 | 68 53.3 | 09.8 | 26 38.5 | 01.0 | 127 09.6 | 32.1 | 52 01.2 | 51.7 | | | |
| | 18 | 192 52.2 | 83 52.4 | N23 09.4 | 41 39.6 | N13 00.5 | 142 11.5 | N17 32.3 | 67 03.4 | N19 51.6 | Vega | 80 57.3 | N38 45.8 |
| | 19 | 207 54.6 | 98 51.6 | 09.1 | 56 40.6 | 12 59.9 | 157 13.5 | 32.4 | 82 05.5 | 51.5 | Zuben'ubi | 137 36.0 | S15 56.7 |
| | 20 | 222 57.1 | 113 50.7 | 08.8 | 71 41.6 | 59.4 | 172 15.5 | 32.5 | 97 07.7 | 51.5 | | | |
| | 21 | 237 59.6 | 128 49.8 | ·· 08.5 | 86 42.6 | ·· 58.8 | 187 17.5 | ·· 32.6 | 112 09.8 | ·· 51.4 | | | |
| | 22 | 253 02.0 | 143 49.0 | 08.2 | 101 43.7 | 58.3 | 202 19.5 | 32.7 | 127 12.0 | 51.3 | | | |
| | 23 | 268 04.5 | 158 48.1 | 07.8 | 116 44.7 | 57.7 | 217 21.4 | 32.8 | 142 14.1 | 51.2 | | | |
| Mer. Pass. | | 5 14.6 (h m) | v −0.9 | d 0.3 | v 1.0 | d 0.5 | v 2.0 | d 0.1 | v 2.1 | d 0.1 | | | |

| | S.H.A. (° ′) | Mer. Pass. (h m) |
|---|---|---|
| Venus | 253 20.1 | 12 23 |
| Mars | 209 47.8 | 15 15 |
| Jupiter | 309 39.9 | 8 36 |
| Saturn | 234 24.6 | 13 36 |

## 1976 JULY 5, 6, 7 (MON., TUES., WED.)

| G.M.T. d | h | ARIES G.H.A. | VENUS −3.4 G.H.A. | VENUS Dec. | MARS +1.9 G.H.A. | MARS Dec. | JUPITER −1.8 G.H.A. | JUPITER Dec. | SATURN +0.5 G.H.A. | SATURN Dec. | STARS Name | S.H.A. | Dec. |
|---|---|---|---|---|---|---|---|---|---|---|---|---|---|
| 5 | 00 | 283 07.0 | 173 47.2 | N23 07.5 | 131 45.7 | N12 57.2 | 232 23.4 | N17 33.0 | 157 16.2 | N19 51.2 | Acamar | 315 39.6 | S40 23.7 |
| | 01 | 298 09.4 | 188 46.4 | 07.2 | 146 46.7 | 56.6 | 247 25.4 | 33.1 | 172 18.4 | 51.1 | Achernar | 335 47.5 | S57 21.0 |
| | 02 | 313 11.9 | 203 45.5 | 06.9 | 161 47.8 | 56.1 | 262 27.4 | 33.2 | 187 20.5 | 51.0 | Acrux | 173 40.4 | S62 58.5 |
| | 03 | 328 14.4 | 218 44.7 | ·· 06.5 | 176 48.8 | ·· 55.5 | 277 29.3 | ·· 33.3 | 202 22.7 | ·· 51.0 | Adhara | 255 34.7 | S28 56.5 |
| | 04 | 343 16.8 | 233 43.8 | 06.2 | 191 49.8 | 55.0 | 292 31.3 | 33.4 | 217 24.8 | 50.9 | Aldebaran | 291 21.5 | N16 27.7 |
| | 05 | 358 19.3 | 248 43.0 | 05.9 | 206 50.8 | 54.4 | 307 33.3 | 33.6 | 232 27.0 | 50.8 | | | |
| | 06 | 13 21.8 | 263 42.1 | N23 05.5 | 221 51.9 | N12 53.9 | 322 35.3 | N17 33.7 | 247 29.1 | N19 50.8 | Alioth | 166 45.0 | N56 05.5 |
| | 07 | 28 24.2 | 278 41.2 | 05.2 | 236 52.9 | 53.3 | 337 37.3 | 33.8 | 262 31.2 | 50.7 | Alkaid | 153 20.6 | N49 26.1 |
| | 08 | 43 26.7 | 293 40.4 | 04.9 | 251 53.9 | 52.8 | 352 39.2 | 33.9 | 277 33.4 | 50.6 | Al Na'ir | 28 18.2 | S47 04.2 |
| M | 09 | 58 29.1 | 308 39.5 | ·· 04.5 | 266 54.9 | ·· 52.3 | 7 41.2 | ·· 34.0 | 292 35.5 | ·· 50.6 | Alnilam | 276 14.8 | S 1 13.0 |
| O | 10 | 73 31.6 | 323 38.7 | 04.2 | 281 56.0 | 51.7 | 22 43.2 | 34.1 | 307 37.7 | 50.5 | Alphard | 218 23.6 | S 8 33.5 |
| N | 11 | 88 34.1 | 338 37.8 | 03.9 | 296 57.0 | 51.2 | 37 45.2 | 34.3 | 322 39.8 | 50.4 | | | |
| D | 12 | 103 36.5 | 353 36.9 | N23 03.5 | 311 58.0 | N12 50.6 | 52 47.2 | N17 34.4 | 337 42.0 | N19 50.3 | Alphecca | 126 34.3 | N26 47.8 |
| A | 13 | 118 39.0 | 8 36.1 | 03.2 | 326 59.0 | 50.1 | 67 49.1 | 34.5 | 352 44.1 | 50.3 | Alpheratz | 358 12.1 | N28 57.6 |
| Y | 14 | 133 41.5 | 23 35.2 | 02.8 | 342 00.1 | 49.5 | 82 51.1 | 34.6 | 7 46.3 | 50.2 | Altair | 62 34.9 | N 8 48.5 |
| | 15 | 148 43.9 | 38 34.4 | ·· 02.5 | 357 01.1 | ·· 49.0 | 97 53.1 | ·· 34.7 | 22 48.4 | ·· 50.1 | Ankaa | 353 43.0 | S42 25.7 |
| | 16 | 163 46.4 | 53 33.5 | 02.2 | 12 02.1 | 48.4 | 112 55.1 | 34.8 | 37 50.5 | 50.1 | Antares | 113 00.0 | S26 22.8 |
| | 17 | 178 48.9 | 68 32.7 | 01.8 | 27 03.2 | 47.8 | 127 57.1 | 35.0 | 52 52.7 | 50.0 | | | |
| | 18 | 193 51.3 | 83 31.8 | N23 01.5 | 42 04.2 | N12 47.3 | 142 59.1 | N17 35.1 | 67 54.8 | N19 49.9 | Arcturus | 146 20.9 | N19 18.4 |
| | 19 | 208 53.8 | 98 31.0 | 01.1 | 57 05.2 | 46.7 | 158 01.0 | 35.2 | 82 57.0 | 49.9 | Atria | 108 26.3 | S68 59.3 |
| | 20 | 223 56.2 | 113 30.1 | 00.8 | 72 06.2 | 46.2 | 173 03.0 | 35.3 | 97 59.1 | 49.8 | Avior | 234 29.9 | S59 26.3 |
| | 21 | 238 58.7 | 128 29.2 | ·· 00.4 | 87 07.3 | ·· 45.6 | 188 05.0 | ·· 35.4 | 113 01.2 | ·· 49.7 | Bellatrix | 279 02.1 | N 6 19.7 |
| | 22 | 254 01.2 | 143 28.4 | 23 00.1 | 102 08.3 | 45.1 | 203 07.0 | 35.5 | 128 03.4 | 49.7 | Betelgeuse | 271 31.7 | N 7 24.1 |
| | 23 | 269 03.6 | 158 27.5 | 22 59.7 | 117 09.3 | 44.5 | 218 09.0 | 35.7 | 143 05.5 | 49.6 | | | |
| 6 | 00 | 284 06.1 | 173 26.7 | N22 59.4 | 132 10.3 | N12 44.0 | 233 10.9 | N17 35.8 | 158 07.7 | N19 49.5 | Canopus | 264 09.0 | S52 41.0 |
| | 01 | 299 08.6 | 188 25.8 | 59.0 | 147 11.4 | 43.4 | 248 12.9 | 35.9 | 173 09.8 | 49.4 | Capella | 281 15.9 | N45 58.4 |
| | 02 | 314 11.0 | 203 25.0 | 58.7 | 162 12.4 | 42.9 | 263 14.9 | 36.0 | 188 12.0 | 49.4 | Deneb | 49 49.9 | N45 11.8 |
| | 03 | 329 13.5 | 218 24.1 | ·· 58.3 | 177 13.4 | ·· 42.3 | 278 16.9 | ·· 36.1 | 203 14.1 | ·· 49.3 | Denebola | 183 02.0 | N14 42.2 |
| | 04 | 344 16.0 | 233 23.3 | 57.9 | 192 14.4 | 41.8 | 293 18.9 | 36.2 | 218 16.2 | 49.2 | Diphda | 349 23.7 | S18 06.7 |
| | 05 | 359 18.4 | 248 22.4 | 57.6 | 207 15.5 | 41.2 | 308 20.9 | 36.3 | 233 18.4 | 49.2 | | | |
| | 06 | 14 20.9 | 263 21.6 | N22 57.2 | 222 16.5 | N12 40.7 | 323 22.8 | N17 36.5 | 248 20.5 | N19 49.1 | Dubhe | 194 26.0 | N61 52.9 |
| | 07 | 29 23.4 | 278 20.7 | 56.9 | 237 17.5 | 40.1 | 338 24.8 | 36.6 | 263 22.7 | 49.0 | Elnath | 278 48.1 | N28 35.2 |
| | 08 | 44 25.8 | 293 19.9 | 56.5 | 252 18.5 | 39.6 | 353 26.8 | 36.7 | 278 24.8 | 49.0 | Eltanin | 90 58.5 | N51 29.7 |
| T | 09 | 59 28.3 | 308 19.0 | ·· 56.1 | 267 19.6 | ·· 39.0 | 8 28.8 | ·· 36.8 | 293 27.0 | ·· 48.9 | Enif | 34 14.1 | N 9 46.1 |
| U | 10 | 74 30.7 | 323 18.2 | 55.8 | 282 20.6 | 38.5 | 23 30.8 | 36.9 | 308 29.1 | 48.8 | Fomalhaut | 15 54.4 | S29 44.5 |
| E | 11 | 89 33.2 | 338 17.3 | 55.4 | 297 21.6 | 37.9 | 38 32.8 | 37.0 | 323 31.2 | 48.7 | | | |
| S | 12 | 104 35.7 | 353 16.5 | N22 55.0 | 312 22.6 | N12 37.4 | 53 34.7 | N17 37.2 | 338 33.4 | N19 48.7 | Gacrux | 172 31.9 | S56 59.2 |
| D | 13 | 119 38.1 | 8 15.6 | 54.7 | 327 23.7 | 36.8 | 68 36.7 | 37.3 | 353 35.5 | 48.6 | Gienah | 176 20.9 | S17 24.8 |
| A | 14 | 134 40.6 | 23 14.8 | 54.3 | 342 24.7 | 36.3 | 83 38.7 | 37.4 | 8 37.7 | 48.5 | Hadar | 149 27.1 | S60 15.9 |
| Y | 15 | 149 43.1 | 38 13.9 | ·· 53.9 | 357 25.7 | ·· 35.7 | 98 40.7 | ·· 37.5 | 23 39.8 | ·· 48.5 | Hamal | 328 32.2 | N23 21.0 |
| | 16 | 164 45.5 | 53 13.1 | 53.6 | 12 26.8 | 35.1 | 113 42.7 | 37.6 | 38 42.0 | 48.4 | Kaus Aust. | 84 20.2 | S34 23.7 |
| | 17 | 179 48.0 | 68 12.2 | 53.2 | 27 27.8 | 34.6 | 128 44.7 | 37.7 | 53 44.1 | 48.3 | | | |
| | 18 | 194 50.5 | 83 11.4 | N22 52.8 | 42 28.8 | N12 34.0 | 143 46.7 | N17 37.9 | 68 46.2 | N19 48.3 | Kochab | 137 18.4 | N74 15.4 |
| | 19 | 209 52.9 | 98 10.5 | 52.4 | 57 29.8 | 33.5 | 158 48.6 | 38.0 | 83 48.4 | 48.2 | Markab | 14 05.8 | N15 04.8 |
| | 20 | 224 55.4 | 113 09.7 | 52.1 | 72 30.9 | 32.9 | 173 50.6 | 38.1 | 98 50.5 | 48.1 | Menkar | 314 44.3 | N 3 59.9 |
| | 21 | 239 57.9 | 128 08.8 | ·· 51.7 | 87 31.9 | ·· 32.4 | 188 52.6 | ·· 38.2 | 113 52.7 | ·· 48.0 | Menkent | 148 40.2 | S36 15.5 |
| | 22 | 255 00.3 | 143 08.0 | 51.3 | 102 32.9 | 31.8 | 203 54.6 | 38.3 | 128 54.8 | 48.0 | Miaplacidus | 221 46.3 | S69 37.5 |
| | 23 | 270 02.8 | 158 07.1 | 50.9 | 117 33.9 | 31.3 | 218 56.6 | 38.4 | 143 56.9 | 47.9 | | | |
| 7 | 00 | 285 05.2 | 173 06.3 | N22 50.5 | 132 35.0 | N12 30.7 | 233 58.6 | N17 38.5 | 158 59.1 | N19 47.8 | Mirfak | 309 20.4 | N49 46.5 |
| | 01 | 300 07.7 | 188 05.4 | 50.2 | 147 36.0 | 30.2 | 249 00.6 | 38.7 | 174 01.2 | 47.8 | Nunki | 76 32.3 | S26 19.5 |
| | 02 | 315 10.2 | 203 04.6 | 49.8 | 162 37.0 | 29.6 | 264 02.5 | 38.8 | 189 03.4 | 47.7 | Peacock | 54 02.3 | S56 48.4 |
| | 03 | 330 12.6 | 218 03.8 | ·· 49.4 | 177 38.0 | ·· 29.0 | 279 04.5 | ·· 38.9 | 204 05.5 | ·· 47.6 | Pollux | 244 02.0 | N28 05.0 |
| | 04 | 345 15.1 | 233 02.9 | 49.0 | 192 39.1 | 28.5 | 294 06.5 | 39.0 | 219 07.6 | 47.6 | Procyon | 245 29.1 | N 5 17.1 |
| | 05 | 0 17.6 | 248 02.1 | 48.6 | 207 40.1 | 27.9 | 309 08.5 | 39.1 | 234 09.8 | 47.5 | | | |
| | 06 | 15 20.0 | 263 01.2 | N22 48.2 | 222 41.1 | N12 27.4 | 324 10.5 | N17 39.2 | 249 11.9 | N19 47.4 | Rasalhague | 96 31.9 | N12 34.7 |
| | 07 | 30 22.5 | 278 00.4 | 47.8 | 237 42.2 | 26.8 | 339 12.5 | 39.3 | 264 14.1 | 47.3 | Regulus | 208 13.2 | N12 04.9 |
| W | 08 | 45 25.0 | 292 59.5 | 47.4 | 252 43.2 | 26.3 | 354 14.5 | 39.5 | 279 16.2 | 47.3 | Rigel | 281 39.0 | S 8 13.7 |
| E | 09 | 60 27.4 | 307 58.7 | ·· 47.1 | 267 44.2 | ·· 25.7 | 9 16.4 | ·· 39.6 | 294 18.4 | ·· 47.2 | Rigil Kent. | 140 29.3 | S60 44.5 |
| D | 10 | 75 29.9 | 322 57.8 | 46.7 | 282 45.2 | 25.2 | 24 18.4 | 39.7 | 309 20.5 | 47.1 | Sabik | 102 44.1 | S15 41.7 |
| N | 11 | 90 32.4 | 337 57.0 | 46.3 | 297 46.3 | 24.6 | 39 20.4 | 39.8 | 324 22.6 | 47.1 | | | |
| E | 12 | 105 34.8 | 352 56.2 | N22 45.9 | 312 47.3 | N12 24.0 | 54 22.4 | N17 39.9 | 339 24.8 | N19 47.0 | Schedar | 350 12.1 | N56 24.3 |
| S | 13 | 120 37.3 | 7 55.3 | 45.5 | 327 48.3 | 23.5 | 69 24.4 | 40.0 | 354 26.9 | 46.9 | Shaula | 96 59.2 | S37 05.2 |
| D | 14 | 135 39.7 | 22 54.5 | 45.1 | 342 49.3 | 22.9 | 84 26.4 | 40.1 | 9 29.1 | 46.8 | Sirius | 258 58.5 | S16 41.1 |
| A | 15 | 150 42.2 | 37 53.6 | ·· 44.7 | 357 50.4 | ·· 22.4 | 99 28.4 | ·· 40.3 | 24 31.2 | ·· 46.8 | Spica | 159 00.5 | S11 02.4 |
| Y | 16 | 165 44.7 | 52 52.8 | 44.3 | 12 51.4 | 21.8 | 114 30.4 | 40.4 | 39 33.3 | 46.7 | Suhail | 223 13.2 | S43 20.5 |
| | 17 | 180 47.1 | 67 52.0 | 43.9 | 27 52.4 | 21.3 | 129 32.3 | 40.5 | 54 35.5 | 46.6 | | | |
| | 18 | 195 49.6 | 82 51.1 | N22 43.5 | 42 53.4 | N12 20.7 | 144 34.3 | N17 40.6 | 69 37.6 | N19 46.6 | Vega | 80 57.3 | N38 45.8 |
| | 19 | 210 52.1 | 97 50.3 | 43.1 | 57 54.5 | 20.1 | 159 36.3 | 40.7 | 84 39.8 | 46.5 | Zuben'ubi | 137 36.0 | S15 56.7 |
| | 20 | 225 54.5 | 112 49.4 | 42.7 | 72 55.5 | 19.6 | 174 38.3 | 40.8 | 99 41.9 | 46.4 | | | |
| | 21 | 240 57.0 | 127 48.6 | ·· 42.3 | 87 56.5 | ·· 19.0 | 189 40.3 | ·· 40.9 | 114 44.0 | ·· 46.4 | | | |
| | 22 | 255 59.5 | 142 47.8 | 41.9 | 102 57.6 | 18.5 | 204 42.3 | 41.1 | 129 46.2 | 46.3 | | | |
| | 23 | 271 01.9 | 157 46.9 | 41.5 | 117 58.6 | 17.9 | 219 44.3 | 41.2 | 144 48.3 | 46.2 | | | |
| Mer. Pass. | | 5 02.8 (h m) | v −0.8 | d 0.4 | v 1.0 | d 0.6 | v 2.0 | d 0.1 | v 2.1 | d 0.1 | | | |

| | S.H.A. (° ′) | Mer. Pass. (h m) |
|---|---|---|
| Venus | 249 20.6 | 12 27 |
| Mars | 208 04.2 | 15 10 |
| Jupiter | 309 04.8 | 8 26 |
| Saturn | 234 01.6 | 13 26 |

# 1976 JULY 5, 6, 7 (MON., TUES., WED.)

| | G.M.T. | SUN G.H.A. | SUN Dec. | MOON G.H.A. | v | MOON Dec. | d | H.P. |
|---|---|---|---|---|---|---|---|---|
| | d h | ° ′ | ° ′ | ° ′ | ′ | ° ′ | ′ | ′ |
| | 5 00 | 178 53.0 | N22 47.7 | 88 32.6 | 9.4 | S 8 27.5 | 10.9 | 59.3 |
| | 01 | 193 52.9 | 47.5 | 103 01.0 | 9.3 | 8 38.4 | 10.9 | 59.3 |
| | 02 | 208 52.8 | 47.2 | 117 29.3 | 9.3 | 8 49.3 | 10.9 | 59.3 |
| | 03 | 223 52.7 | · · 47.0 | 131 57.6 | 9.2 | 9 00.2 | 10.7 | 59.3 |
| | 04 | 238 52.6 | 46.8 | 146 25.8 | 9.2 | 9 10.9 | 10.8 | 59.3 |
| | 05 | 253 52.5 | 46.5 | 160 54.0 | 9.2 | 9 21.7 | 10.6 | 59.3 |
| | 06 | 268 52.4 | N22 46.3 | 175 22.2 | 9.1 | S 9 32.3 | 10.7 | 59.3 |
| | 07 | 283 52.3 | 46.1 | 189 50.3 | 9.0 | 9 43.0 | 10.5 | 59.3 |
| | 08 | 298 52.1 | 45.8 | 204 18.3 | 9.0 | 9 53.5 | 10.5 | 59.4 |
| M | 09 | 313 52.0 | · · 45.6 | 218 46.3 | 9.0 | 10 04.0 | 10.5 | 59.4 |
| O | 10 | 328 51.9 | 45.4 | 233 14.3 | 8.9 | 10 14.5 | 10.4 | 59.4 |
| N | 11 | 343 51.8 | 45.1 | 247 42.2 | 8.9 | 10 24.9 | 10.4 | 59.4 |
| D | 12 | 358 51.7 | N22 44.9 | 262 10.1 | 8.8 | S10 35.3 | 10.2 | 59.4 |
| A | 13 | 13 51.6 | 44.6 | 276 37.9 | 8.8 | 10 45.5 | 10.3 | 59.4 |
| Y | 14 | 28 51.5 | 44.4 | 291 05.7 | 8.7 | 10 55.8 | 10.1 | 59.4 |
| | 15 | 43 51.4 | · · 44.1 | 305 33.4 | 8.7 | 11 05.9 | 10.1 | 59.4 |
| | 16 | 58 51.3 | 43.9 | 320 01.1 | 8.6 | 11 16.0 | 10.0 | 59.4 |
| | 17 | 73 51.2 | 43.7 | 334 28.7 | 8.6 | 11 26.0 | 10.0 | 59.4 |
| | 18 | 88 51.1 | N22 43.4 | 348 56.3 | 8.5 | S11 36.0 | 9.9 | 59.4 |
| | 19 | 103 51.0 | 43.2 | 3 23.8 | 8.5 | 11 45.9 | 9.8 | 59.4 |
| | 20 | 118 50.9 | 42.9 | 17 51.3 | 8.5 | 11 55.7 | 9.8 | 59.4 |
| | 21 | 133 50.8 | · · 42.7 | 32 18.8 | 8.3 | 12 05.5 | 9.7 | 59.4 |
| | 22 | 148 50.7 | 42.4 | 46 46.1 | 8.4 | 12 15.2 | 9.6 | 59.4 |
| | 23 | 163 50.6 | 42.2 | 61 13.5 | 8.2 | 12 24.8 | 9.5 | 59.5 |
| | 6 00 | 178 50.4 | N22 41.9 | 75 40.7 | 8.3 | S12 34.3 | 9.5 | 59.5 |
| | 01 | 193 50.3 | 41.7 | 90 08.0 | 8.2 | 12 43.8 | 9.4 | 59.5 |
| | 02 | 208 50.2 | 41.4 | 104 35.2 | 8.1 | 12 53.2 | 9.3 | 59.5 |
| | 03 | 223 50.1 | · · 41.2 | 119 02.3 | 8.1 | 13 02.5 | 9.2 | 59.5 |
| | 04 | 238 50.0 | 40.9 | 133 29.4 | 8.0 | 13 11.7 | 9.2 | 59.5 |
| | 05 | 253 49.9 | 40.7 | 147 56.4 | 8.0 | 13 20.9 | 9.1 | 59.5 |
| | 06 | 268 49.8 | N22 40.4 | 162 23.4 | 7.9 | S13 30.0 | 9.0 | 59.5 |
| | 07 | 283 49.7 | 40.2 | 176 50.3 | 7.9 | 13 39.0 | 8.9 | 59.5 |
| | 08 | 298 49.6 | 39.9 | 191 17.2 | 7.8 | 13 47.9 | 8.8 | 59.5 |
| T | 09 | 313 49.5 | · · 39.7 | 205 44.0 | 7.7 | 13 56.7 | 8.7 | 59.5 |
| U | 10 | 328 49.4 | 39.4 | 220 10.7 | 7.8 | 14 05.4 | 8.7 | 59.5 |
| E | 11 | 343 49.3 | 39.1 | 234 37.5 | 7.6 | 14 14.1 | 8.6 | 59.5 |
| S D | 12 | 358 49.2 | N22 38.9 | 249 04.1 | 7.7 | S14 22.7 | 8.4 | 59.5 |
| A | 13 | 13 49.1 | 38.6 | 263 30.8 | 7.5 | 14 31.1 | 8.4 | 59.5 |
| Y | 14 | 28 49.0 | 38.4 | 277 57.3 | 7.5 | 14 39.5 | 8.3 | 59.5 |
| | 15 | 43 48.9 | · · 38.1 | 292 23.8 | 7.5 | 14 47.8 | 8.2 | 59.5 |
| | 16 | 58 48.8 | 37.8 | 306 50.3 | 7.4 | 14 56.0 | 8.2 | 59.5 |
| | 17 | 73 48.7 | 37.6 | 321 16.7 | 7.4 | 15 04.2 | 8.0 | 59.5 |
| | 18 | 88 48.6 | N22 37.3 | 335 43.1 | 7.3 | S15 12.2 | 7.9 | 59.5 |
| | 19 | 103 48.5 | 37.1 | 350 09.4 | 7.3 | 15 20.1 | 7.8 | 59.5 |
| | 20 | 118 48.4 | 36.8 | 4 35.7 | 7.2 | 15 27.9 | 7.8 | 59.5 |
| | 21 | 133 48.3 | · · 36.5 | 19 01.9 | 7.2 | 15 35.7 | 7.6 | 59.5 |
| | 22 | 148 48.2 | 36.3 | 33 28.1 | 7.1 | 15 43.3 | 7.5 | 59.5 |
| | 23 | 163 48.1 | 36.0 | 47 54.2 | 7.1 | 15 50.8 | 7.5 | 59.5 |
| | 7 00 | 178 48.0 | N22 35.7 | 62 20.3 | 7.0 | S15 58.3 | 7.3 | 59.5 |
| | 01 | 193 47.9 | 35.5 | 76 46.3 | 7.0 | 16 05.6 | 7.3 | 59.5 |
| | 02 | 208 47.8 | 35.2 | 91 12.3 | 6.9 | 16 12.9 | 7.1 | 59.5 |
| | 03 | 223 47.7 | · · 34.9 | 105 38.2 | 6.9 | 16 20.0 | 7.0 | 59.5 |
| | 04 | 238 47.6 | 34.7 | 120 04.1 | 6.8 | 16 27.0 | 6.9 | 59.5 |
| | 05 | 253 47.5 | 34.4 | 134 29.9 | 6.8 | 16 33.9 | 6.8 | 59.5 |
| | 06 | 268 47.4 | N22 34.1 | 148 55.7 | 6.8 | S16 40.7 | 6.7 | 59.5 |
| W | 07 | 283 47.3 | 33.9 | 163 21.5 | 6.7 | 16 47.4 | 6.6 | 59.5 |
| E | 08 | 298 47.2 | 33.6 | 177 47.2 | 6.6 | 16 54.0 | 6.5 | 59.5 |
| D | 09 | 313 47.1 | · · 33.3 | 192 12.8 | 6.7 | 17 00.5 | 6.4 | 59.5 |
| N | 10 | 328 47.0 | 33.1 | 206 38.5 | 6.5 | 17 06.9 | 6.3 | 59.5 |
| E | 11 | 343 46.9 | 32.8 | 221 04.0 | 6.6 | 17 13.2 | 6.1 | 59.5 |
| S | 12 | 358 46.8 | N22 32.5 | 235 29.6 | 6.5 | S17 19.3 | 6.1 | 59.5 |
| D | 13 | 13 46.7 | 32.2 | 249 55.1 | 6.4 | 17 25.4 | 5.9 | 59.5 |
| A | 14 | 28 46.6 | 32.0 | 264 20.5 | 6.5 | 17 31.3 | 5.8 | 59.5 |
| Y | 15 | 43 46.5 | · · 31.7 | 278 46.0 | 6.4 | 17 37.1 | 5.7 | 59.5 |
| | 16 | 58 46.4 | 31.4 | 293 11.4 | 6.3 | 17 42.8 | 5.6 | 59.5 |
| | 17 | 73 46.3 | 31.1 | 307 36.7 | 6.3 | 17 48.4 | 5.5 | 59.5 |
| | 18 | 88 46.2 | N22 30.8 | 322 02.0 | 6.3 | S17 53.9 | 5.3 | 59.5 |
| | 19 | 103 46.1 | 30.6 | 336 27.3 | 6.2 | 17 59.2 | 5.3 | 59.5 |
| | 20 | 118 46.0 | 30.3 | 350 52.5 | 6.2 | 18 04.5 | 5.1 | 59.5 |
| | 21 | 133 45.9 | · · 30.0 | 5 17.7 | 6.2 | 18 09.6 | 5.0 | 59.5 |
| | 22 | 148 45.8 | 29.7 | 19 42.9 | 6.1 | 18 14.6 | 4.8 | 59.5 |
| | 23 | 163 45.7 | 29.5 | 34 08.0 | 6.1 | 18 19.4 | 4.8 | 59.5 |
| | | S.D. 15.8 | d 0.3 | S.D. 16.2 | | 16.2 | | 16.2 |

| Lat. | Twilight Naut. | Twilight Civil | Sunrise | Moonrise 5 | 6 | 7 | 8 |
|---|---|---|---|---|---|---|---|
| ° | h m | h m | h m | h m | h m | h m | h m |
| N 72 | ▭ | ▭ | ▭ | 15 10 | 17 25 | ■ | ■ |
| N 70 | ▭ | ▭ | ▭ | 14 50 | 16 48 | 18 50 | 20 56 |
| 68 | ▭ | ▭ | ▭ | 14 34 | 16 22 | 18 08 | 19 41 |
| 66 | //// | //// | 00 52 | 14 22 | 16 02 | 17 39 | 19 04 |
| 64 | //// | //// | 01 51 | 14 11 | 15 46 | 17 17 | 18 38 |
| 62 | //// | //// | 02 24 | 14 02 | 15 33 | 17 00 | 18 17 |
| 60 | //// | 01 16 | 02 48 | 13 55 | 15 22 | 16 46 | 18 01 |
| N 58 | //// | 01 56 | 03 07 | 13 48 | 15 12 | 16 33 | 17 47 |
| 56 | //// | 02 23 | 03 23 | 13 42 | 15 04 | 16 23 | 17 35 |
| 54 | 01 10 | 02 44 | 03 36 | 13 37 | 14 57 | 16 13 | 17 24 |
| 52 | 01 47 | 03 01 | 03 48 | 13 32 | 14 50 | 16 05 | 17 15 |
| 50 | 02 12 | 03 15 | 03 58 | 13 28 | 14 44 | 15 58 | 17 06 |
| 45 | 02 55 | 03 43 | 04 20 | 13 19 | 14 31 | 15 42 | 16 49 |
| N 40 | 03 24 | 04 05 | 04 37 | 13 12 | 14 21 | 15 29 | 16 34 |
| 35 | 03 46 | 04 22 | 04 52 | 13 05 | 14 12 | 15 18 | 16 22 |
| 30 | 04 04 | 04 37 | 05 04 | 12 59 | 14 04 | 15 08 | 16 11 |
| 20 | 04 32 | 05 01 | 05 26 | 12 50 | 13 50 | 14 52 | 15 53 |
| N 10 | 04 54 | 05 21 | 05 44 | 12 41 | 13 39 | 14 38 | 15 37 |
| 0 | 05 13 | 05 39 | 06 01 | 12 33 | 13 28 | 14 24 | 15 22 |
| S 10 | 05 29 | 05 55 | 06 18 | 12 25 | 13 17 | 14 11 | 15 08 |
| 20 | 05 44 | 06 12 | 06 36 | 12 17 | 13 05 | 13 57 | 14 52 |
| 30 | 06 00 | 06 30 | 06 56 | 12 07 | 12 52 | 13 41 | 14 34 |
| 35 | 06 09 | 06 40 | 07 08 | 12 02 | 12 44 | 13 31 | 14 23 |
| 40 | 06 18 | 06 51 | 07 22 | 11 56 | 12 36 | 13 21 | 14 11 |
| 45 | 06 27 | 07 04 | 07 38 | 11 49 | 12 26 | 13 08 | 13 57 |
| S 50 | 06 39 | 07 20 | 07 58 | 11 40 | 12 14 | 12 53 | 13 40 |
| 52 | 06 43 | 07 27 | 08 07 | 11 37 | 12 08 | 12 46 | 13 32 |
| 54 | 06 49 | 07 35 | 08 18 | 11 32 | 12 02 | 12 39 | 13 23 |
| 56 | 06 55 | 07 43 | 08 30 | 11 28 | 11 56 | 12 30 | 13 13 |
| 58 | 07 01 | 07 53 | 08 44 | 11 22 | 11 48 | 12 20 | 13 02 |
| S 60 | 07 08 | 08 04 | 09 00 | 11 16 | 11 39 | 12 09 | 12 49 |

| Lat. | Sunset | Twilight Civil | Twilight Naut. | Moonset 5 | 6 | 7 | 8 |
|---|---|---|---|---|---|---|---|
| ° | h m | h m | h m | h m | h m | h m | h m |
| N 72 | ▭ | ▭ | ▭ | 22 02 | 21 42 | ■ | ■ |
| N 70 | ▭ | ▭ | ▭ | 22 24 | 22 20 | 22 17 | 22 14 |
| 68 | ▭ | ▭ | ▭ | 22 41 | 22 47 | 23 00 | 23 28 |
| 66 | 23 12 | //// | //// | 22 55 | 23 08 | 23 29 | 24 06 |
| 64 | 22 16 | //// | //// | 23 06 | 23 25 | 23 52 | 24 32 |
| 62 | 21 44 | //// | //// | 23 16 | 23 38 | 24 09 | 00 09 |
| 60 | 21 20 | 22 50 | //// | 23 24 | 23 50 | 24 24 | 00 24 |
| N 58 | 21 01 | 22 11 | //// | 23 32 | 24 00 | 00 00 | 00 37 |
| 56 | 20 46 | 21 45 | //// | 23 38 | 24 09 | 00 09 | 00 48 |
| 54 | 20 32 | 21 25 | 22 57 | 23 44 | 24 17 | 00 17 | 00 57 |
| 52 | 20 21 | 21 08 | 22 21 | 23 50 | 24 24 | 00 24 | 01 06 |
| 50 | 20 10 | 20 54 | 21 56 | 23 54 | 24 31 | 00 31 | 01 14 |
| 45 | 19 49 | 20 26 | 21 14 | 24 05 | 00 05 | 00 44 | 01 30 |
| N 40 | 19 32 | 20 04 | 20 45 | 24 14 | 00 14 | 00 56 | 01 44 |
| 35 | 19 17 | 19 47 | 20 23 | 24 21 | 00 21 | 01 06 | 01 55 |
| 30 | 19 05 | 19 32 | 20 05 | 24 28 | 00 28 | 01 14 | 02 05 |
| 20 | 18 44 | 19 08 | 19 37 | 24 39 | 00 39 | 01 29 | 02 23 |
| N 10 | 18 25 | 18 48 | 19 15 | 24 49 | 00 49 | 01 42 | 02 38 |
| 0 | 18 08 | 18 31 | 18 57 | 00 05 | 00 59 | 01 54 | 02 52 |
| S 10 | 17 52 | 18 14 | 18 40 | 00 12 | 01 08 | 02 07 | 03 06 |
| 20 | 17 34 | 17 58 | 18 25 | 00 18 | 01 18 | 02 20 | 03 21 |
| 30 | 17 13 | 17 39 | 18 09 | 00 26 | 01 30 | 02 35 | 03 39 |
| 35 | 17 01 | 17 29 | 18 01 | 00 30 | 01 37 | 02 43 | 03 49 |
| 40 | 16 48 | 17 18 | 17 52 | 00 35 | 01 44 | 02 53 | 04 00 |
| 45 | 16 32 | 17 05 | 17 42 | 00 41 | 01 53 | 03 05 | 04 14 |
| S 50 | 16 12 | 16 50 | 17 31 | 00 48 | 02 04 | 03 19 | 04 31 |
| 52 | 16 03 | 16 43 | 17 26 | 00 51 | 02 09 | 03 26 | 04 38 |
| 54 | 15 52 | 16 35 | 17 21 | 00 55 | 02 15 | 03 33 | 04 47 |
| 56 | 15 40 | 16 26 | 17 15 | 00 59 | 02 21 | 03 41 | 04 57 |
| 58 | 15 26 | 16 17 | 17 09 | 01 03 | 02 28 | 03 51 | 05 08 |
| S 60 | 15 10 | 16 06 | 17 02 | 01 08 | 02 36 | 04 01 | 05 21 |

| Day | SUN Eqn. of Time 00h | SUN Eqn. of Time 12h | SUN Mer. Pass. | MOON Mer. Pass. Upper | MOON Mer. Pass. Lower | Age | Phase |
|---|---|---|---|---|---|---|---|
| | m s | m s | h m | h m | h m | d | |
| 5 | 04 28 | 04 33 | 12 05 | 18 46 | 06 19 | 08 | |
| 6 | 04 38 | 04 43 | 12 05 | 19 41 | 07 13 | 09 | |
| 7 | 04 48 | 04 53 | 12 05 | 20 38 | 08 09 | 10 | |

# 1976 JULY 8, 9, 10 (THURS., FRI., SAT.)

| | G.M.T. | ARIES G.H.A. | VENUS −3.4 G.H.A. | Dec. | MARS +1.9 G.H.A. | Dec. | JUPITER −1.8 G.H.A. | Dec. | SATURN +0.5 G.H.A. | Dec. |
|---|---|---|---|---|---|---|---|---|---|---|
| | d h | ° ′ | ° ′ | ° ′ | ° ′ | ° ′ | ° ′ | ° ′ | ° ′ | ° ′ |
| | 8 00 | 286 04.4 | 172 46.1 | N22 41.0 | 132 59.6 | N12 17.3 | 234 46.3 | N17 41.3 | 159 50.5 | N19 46.1 |
| | 01 | 301 06.8 | 187 45.2 | 40.6 | 148 00.6 | 16.8 | 249 48.3 | 41.4 | 174 52.6 | 46.1 |
| | 02 | 316 09.3 | 202 44.4 | 40.2 | 163 01.7 | 16.2 | 264 50.3 | 41.5 | 189 54.8 | 46.0 |
| | 03 | 331 11.8 | 217 43.6 | · · 39.8 | 178 02.7 | · · 15.7 | 279 52.2 | · · 41.6 | 204 56.9 | · · 45.9 |
| | 04 | 346 14.2 | 232 42.7 | 39.4 | 193 03.7 | 15.1 | 294 54.2 | 41.7 | 219 59.0 | 45.9 |
| | 05 | 1 16.7 | 247 41.9 | 39.0 | 208 04.8 | 14.6 | 309 56.2 | 41.8 | 235 01.2 | 45.8 |
| | 06 | 16 19.2 | 262 41.1 | N22 38.6 | 223 05.8 | N12 14.0 | 324 58.2 | N17 42.0 | 250 03.3 | N19 45.7 |
| | 07 | 31 21.6 | 277 40.2 | 38.1 | 238 06.8 | 13.4 | 340 00.2 | 42.1 | 265 05.5 | 45.6 |
| T | 08 | 46 24.1 | 292 39.4 | 37.7 | 253 07.8 | 12.9 | 355 02.2 | 42.2 | 280 07.6 | 45.6 |
| H | 09 | 61 26.6 | 307 38.5 | · · 37.3 | 268 08.9 | · · 12.3 | 10 04.2 | · · 42.3 | 295 09.7 | · · 45.5 |
| U | 10 | 76 29.0 | 322 37.7 | 36.9 | 283 09.9 | 11.8 | 25 06.2 | 42.4 | 310 11.9 | 45.4 |
| R | 11 | 91 31.5 | 337 36.9 | 36.5 | 298 10.9 | 11.2 | 40 08.2 | 42.5 | 325 14.0 | 45.4 |
| S | 12 | 106 34.0 | 352 36.0 | N22 36.0 | 313 11.9 | N12 10.6 | 55 10.2 | N17 42.6 | 340 16.2 | N19 45.3 |
| D | 13 | 121 36.4 | 7 35.2 | 35.6 | 328 13.0 | 10.1 | 70 12.1 | 42.7 | 355 18.3 | 45.2 |
| A | 14 | 136 38.9 | 22 34.4 | 35.2 | 343 14.0 | 09.5 | 85 14.1 | 42.9 | 10 20.4 | 45.2 |
| Y | 15 | 151 41.3 | 37 33.5 | · · 34.8 | 358 15.0 | · · 09.0 | 100 16.1 | · · 43.0 | 25 22.6 | · · 45.1 |
| | 16 | 166 43.8 | 52 32.7 | 34.3 | 13 16.1 | 08.4 | 115 18.1 | 43.1 | 40 24.7 | 45.0 |
| | 17 | 181 46.3 | 67 31.9 | 33.9 | 28 17.1 | 07.8 | 130 20.1 | 43.2 | 55 26.9 | 44.9 |
| | 18 | 196 48.7 | 82 31.0 | N22 33.5 | 43 18.1 | N12 07.3 | 145 22.1 | N17 43.3 | 70 29.0 | N19 44.9 |
| | 19 | 211 51.2 | 97 30.2 | 33.1 | 58 19.1 | 06.7 | 160 24.1 | 43.4 | 85 31.1 | 44.8 |
| | 20 | 226 53.7 | 112 29.4 | 32.6 | 73 20.2 | 06.1 | 175 26.1 | 43.5 | 100 33.3 | 44.7 |
| | 21 | 241 56.1 | 127 28.5 | · · 32.2 | 88 21.2 | · · 05.6 | 190 28.1 | · · 43.6 | 115 35.4 | · · 44.7 |
| | 22 | 256 58.6 | 142 27.7 | 31.8 | 103 22.2 | 05.0 | 205 30.1 | 43.8 | 130 37.6 | 44.6 |
| | 23 | 272 01.1 | 157 26.9 | 31.3 | 118 23.2 | 04.5 | 220 32.1 | 43.9 | 145 39.7 | 44.5 |
| | 9 00 | 287 03.5 | 172 26.1 | N22 30.9 | 133 24.3 | N12 03.9 | 235 34.1 | N17 44.0 | 160 41.8 | N19 44.4 |
| | 01 | 302 06.0 | 187 25.2 | 30.4 | 148 25.3 | 03.3 | 250 36.1 | 44.1 | 175 44.0 | 44.4 |
| | 02 | 317 08.5 | 202 24.4 | 30.0 | 163 26.3 | 02.8 | 265 38.1 | 44.2 | 190 46.1 | 44.3 |
| | 03 | 332 10.9 | 217 23.6 | · · 29.6 | 178 27.4 | · · 02.2 | 280 40.0 | · · 44.3 | 205 48.3 | · · 44.2 |
| | 04 | 347 13.4 | 232 22.7 | 29.1 | 193 28.4 | 01.7 | 295 42.0 | 44.4 | 220 50.4 | 44.2 |
| | 05 | 2 15.8 | 247 21.9 | 28.7 | 208 29.4 | 01.1 | 310 44.0 | 44.5 | 235 52.5 | 44.1 |
| | 06 | 17 18.3 | 262 21.1 | N22 28.2 | 223 30.4 | N12 00.5 | 325 46.0 | N17 44.6 | 250 54.7 | N19 44.0 |
| | 07 | 32 20.8 | 277 20.3 | 27.8 | 238 31.5 | 12 00.0 | 340 48.0 | 44.8 | 265 56.8 | 43.9 |
| | 08 | 47 23.2 | 292 19.4 | 27.3 | 253 32.5 | 11 59.4 | 355 50.0 | 44.9 | 280 59.0 | 43.9 |
| F | 09 | 62 25.7 | 307 18.6 | · · 26.9 | 268 33.5 | · · 58.8 | 10 52.0 | · · 45.0 | 296 01.1 | · · 43.8 |
| R | 10 | 77 28.2 | 322 17.8 | 26.5 | 283 34.6 | 58.3 | 25 54.0 | 45.1 | 311 03.2 | 43.7 |
| I | 11 | 92 30.6 | 337 16.9 | 26.0 | 298 35.6 | 57.7 | 40 56.0 | 45.2 | 326 05.4 | 43.7 |
| D | 12 | 107 33.1 | 352 16.1 | N22 25.6 | 313 36.6 | N11 57.2 | 55 58.0 | N17 45.3 | 341 07.5 | N19 43.6 |
| A | 13 | 122 35.6 | 7 15.3 | 25.1 | 328 37.6 | 56.6 | 71 00.0 | 45.4 | 356 09.6 | 43.5 |
| Y | 14 | 137 38.0 | 22 14.5 | 24.7 | 343 38.7 | 56.0 | 86 02.0 | 45.5 | 11 11.8 | 43.4 |
| | 15 | 152 40.5 | 37 13.6 | · · 24.2 | 358 39.7 | · · 55.5 | 101 04.0 | · · 45.6 | 26 13.9 | · · 43.4 |
| | 16 | 167 43.0 | 52 12.8 | 23.7 | 13 40.7 | 54.9 | 116 06.0 | 45.8 | 41 16.1 | 43.3 |
| | 17 | 182 45.4 | 67 12.0 | 23.3 | 28 41.8 | 54.3 | 131 08.0 | 45.9 | 56 18.2 | 43.2 |
| | 18 | 197 47.9 | 82 11.2 | N22 22.8 | 43 42.8 | N11 53.8 | 146 10.0 | N17 46.0 | 71 20.3 | N19 43.2 |
| | 19 | 212 50.3 | 97 10.3 | 22.4 | 58 43.8 | 53.2 | 161 12.0 | 46.1 | 86 22.5 | 43.1 |
| | 20 | 227 52.8 | 112 09.5 | 21.9 | 73 44.8 | 52.6 | 176 14.0 | 46.2 | 101 24.6 | 43.0 |
| | 21 | 242 55.3 | 127 08.7 | · · 21.5 | 88 45.9 | · · 52.1 | 191 16.0 | · · 46.3 | 116 26.8 | · · 42.9 |
| | 22 | 257 57.7 | 142 07.9 | 21.0 | 103 46.9 | 51.5 | 206 17.9 | 46.4 | 131 28.9 | 42.9 |
| | 23 | 273 00.2 | 157 07.1 | 20.5 | 118 47.9 | 50.9 | 221 19.9 | 46.5 | 146 31.0 | 42.8 |
| | 10 00 | 288 02.7 | 172 06.2 | N22 20.1 | 133 49.0 | N11 50.4 | 236 21.9 | N17 46.6 | 161 33.2 | N19 42.7 |
| | 01 | 303 05.1 | 187 05.4 | 19.6 | 148 50.0 | 49.8 | 251 23.9 | 46.8 | 176 35.3 | 42.7 |
| | 02 | 318 07.6 | 202 04.6 | 19.1 | 163 51.0 | 49.2 | 266 25.9 | 46.9 | 191 37.5 | 42.6 |
| | 03 | 333 10.1 | 217 03.8 | · · 18.7 | 178 52.0 | · · 48.7 | 281 27.9 | · · 47.0 | 206 39.6 | · · 42.5 |
| | 04 | 348 12.5 | 232 03.0 | 18.2 | 193 53.1 | 48.1 | 296 29.9 | 47.1 | 221 41.7 | 42.4 |
| | 05 | 3 15.0 | 247 02.1 | 17.7 | 208 54.1 | 47.6 | 311 31.9 | 47.2 | 236 43.9 | 42.4 |
| | 06 | 18 17.5 | 262 01.3 | N22 17.3 | 223 55.1 | N11 47.0 | 326 33.9 | N17 47.3 | 251 46.0 | N19 42.3 |
| | 07 | 33 19.9 | 277 00.5 | 16.8 | 238 56.2 | 46.4 | 341 35.9 | 47.4 | 266 48.2 | 42.2 |
| S | 08 | 48 22.4 | 291 59.7 | 16.3 | 253 57.2 | 45.9 | 356 37.9 | 47.5 | 281 50.3 | 42.2 |
| A | 09 | 63 24.8 | 306 58.9 | · · 15.8 | 268 58.2 | · · 45.3 | 11 39.9 | · · 47.6 | 296 52.4 | · · 42.1 |
| T | 10 | 78 27.3 | 321 58.0 | 15.4 | 283 59.2 | 44.7 | 26 41.9 | 47.7 | 311 54.6 | 42.0 |
| U | 11 | 93 29.8 | 336 57.2 | 14.9 | 299 00.3 | 44.2 | 41 43.9 | 47.9 | 326 56.7 | 41.9 |
| R | 12 | 108 32.2 | 351 56.4 | N22 14.4 | 314 01.3 | N11 43.6 | 56 45.9 | N17 48.0 | 341 58.8 | N19 41.9 |
| D | 13 | 123 34.7 | 6 55.6 | 13.9 | 329 02.3 | 43.0 | 71 47.9 | 48.1 | 357 01.0 | 41.8 |
| A | 14 | 138 37.2 | 21 54.8 | 13.5 | 344 03.4 | 42.5 | 86 49.9 | 48.2 | 12 03.1 | 41.7 |
| Y | 15 | 153 39.6 | 36 54.0 | · · 13.0 | 359 04.4 | · · 41.9 | 101 51.9 | · · 48.3 | 27 05.3 | · · 41.7 |
| | 16 | 168 42.1 | 51 53.1 | 12.5 | 14 05.4 | 41.3 | 116 53.9 | 48.4 | 42 07.4 | 41.6 |
| | 17 | 183 44.6 | 66 52.3 | 12.0 | 29 06.4 | 40.8 | 131 55.9 | 48.5 | 57 09.5 | 41.5 |
| | 18 | 198 47.0 | 81 51.5 | N22 11.5 | 44 07.5 | N11 40.2 | 146 57.9 | N17 48.6 | 72 11.7 | N19 41.4 |
| | 19 | 213 49.5 | 96 50.7 | 11.0 | 59 08.5 | 39.6 | 161 59.9 | 48.7 | 87 13.8 | 41.4 |
| | 20 | 228 51.9 | 111 49.9 | 10.6 | 74 09.5 | 39.1 | 177 01.9 | 48.8 | 102 16.0 | 41.3 |
| | 21 | 243 54.4 | 126 49.1 | · · 10.1 | 89 10.6 | · · 38.5 | 192 03.9 | · · 48.9 | 117 18.1 | · · 41.2 |
| | 22 | 258 56.9 | 141 48.3 | 09.6 | 104 11.6 | 37.9 | 207 05.9 | 49.1 | 132 20.2 | 41.2 |
| | 23 | 273 59.3 | 156 47.4 | 09.1 | 119 12.6 | 37.3 | 222 07.9 | 49.2 | 147 22.4 | 41.1 |
| | Mer. Pass. | h m 4 51.0 | v −0.8 | d 0.5 | v 1.0 | d 0.6 | v 2.0 | d 0.1 | v 2.1 | d 0.1 |

| STARS Name | S.H.A. | Dec. |
|---|---|---|
| | ° ′ | ° ′ |
| Acamar | 315 39.6 | S40 23.7 |
| Achernar | 335 47.5 | S57 21.0 |
| Acrux | 173 40.4 | S62 58.5 |
| Adhara | 255 34.7 | S28 56.5 |
| Aldebaran | 291 21.5 | N16 27.7 |
| Alioth | 166 45.1 | N56 05.5 |
| Alkaid | 153 20.7 | N49 26.1 |
| Al Na'ir | 28 18.2 | S47 04.2 |
| Alnilam | 276 14.8 | S 1 13.0 |
| Alphard | 218 23.6 | S 8 33.5 |
| Alphecca | 126 34.3 | N26 47.8 |
| Alpheratz | 358 12.1 | N28 57.6 |
| Altair | 62 34.9 | N 8 48.5 |
| Ankaa | 353 43.0 | S42 25.7 |
| Antares | 113 00.0 | S26 22.8 |
| Arcturus | 146 20.9 | N19 18.4 |
| Atria | 108 26.3 | S68 59.3 |
| Avior | 234 29.9 | S59 26.2 |
| Bellatrix | 279 02.1 | N 6 19.7 |
| Betelgeuse | 271 31.6 | N 7 24.1 |
| Canopus | 264 09.0 | S52 41.0 |
| Capella | 281 15.9 | N45 58.4 |
| Deneb | 49 49.9 | N45 11.8 |
| Denebola | 183 02.0 | N14 42.2 |
| Diphda | 349 23.7 | S18 06.7 |
| Dubhe | 194 26.0 | N61 52.8 |
| Elnath | 278 48.0 | N28 35.2 |
| Eltanin | 90 58.5 | N51 29.7 |
| Enif | 34 14.1 | N 9 46.1 |
| Fomalhaut | 15 54.3 | S29 44.5 |
| Gacrux | 172 31.9 | S56 59.2 |
| Gienah | 176 20.9 | S17 24.8 |
| Hadar | 149 27.1 | S60 15.9 |
| Hamal | 328 32.2 | N23 21.0 |
| Kaus Aust. | 84 20.2 | S34 23.7 |
| Kochab | 137 18.4 | N74 15.4 |
| Markab | 14 05.8 | N15 04.8 |
| Menkar | 314 44.2 | N 3 59.9 |
| Menkent | 148 40.2 | S36 15.5 |
| Miaplacidus | 221 46.3 | S69 37.5 |
| Mirfak | 309 20.4 | N49 46.5 |
| Nunki | 76 32.3 | S26 19.5 |
| Peacock | 54 02.3 | S56 48.4 |
| Pollux | 244 02.0 | N28 05.0 |
| Procyon | 245 29.1 | N 5 17.1 |
| Rasalhague | 96 31.9 | N12 34.8 |
| Regulus | 208 13.2 | N12 04.9 |
| Rigel | 281 39.0 | S 8 13.7 |
| Rigil Kent. | 140 29.3 | S60 44.5 |
| Sabik | 102 44.0 | S15 41.7 |
| Schedar | 350 12.1 | N56 24.3 |
| Shaula | 96 59.2 | S37 05.2 |
| Sirius | 258 58.5 | S16 41.1 |
| Spica | 159 00.5 | S11 02.4 |
| Suhail | 223 13.2 | S43 20.5 |
| Vega | 80 57.3 | N38 45.9 |
| Zuben'ubi | 137 36.0 | S15 56.7 |

| | S.H.A. | Mer. Pass. |
|---|---|---|
| | ° ′ | h m |
| Venus | 245 22.5 | 12 31 |
| Mars | 206 20.8 | 15 05 |
| Jupiter | 308 30.5 | 8 17 |
| Saturn | 233 38.3 | 13 15 |

# 1976 JULY 8, 9, 10 (THURS., FRI., SAT.)

| G.M.T. (d h) | SUN G.H.A. | SUN Dec. | MOON G.H.A. | v | Dec. | d | H.P. |
|---|---|---|---|---|---|---|---|
| 8 00 | 178 45.6 | N22 29.2 | 48 33.1 | 6.1 | S18 24.2 | 4.6 | 59.5 |
| 01 | 193 45.5 | 28.9 | 62 58.2 | 6.1 | 18 28.8 | 4.5 | 59.5 |
| 02 | 208 45.4 | 28.6 | 77 23.3 | 6.0 | 18 33.3 | 4.4 | 59.5 |
| 03 | 223 45.3 | ·· 28.3 | 91 48.3 | 6.0 | 18 37.7 | 4.3 | 59.5 |
| 04 | 238 45.2 | 28.0 | 106 13.3 | 6.0 | 18 42.0 | 4.1 | 59.4 |
| 05 | 253 45.1 | 27.8 | 120 38.3 | 5.9 | 18 46.1 | 4.0 | 59.4 |
| 06 | 268 45.0 | N22 27.5 | 135 03.2 | 5.9 | S18 50.1 | 3.9 | 59.4 |
| 07 | 283 44.9 | 27.2 | 149 28.1 | 5.9 | 18 54.0 | 3.8 | 59.4 |
| T 08 | 298 44.8 | 26.9 | 163 53.0 | 5.9 | 18 57.8 | 3.6 | 59.4 |
| H 09 | 313 44.7 | ·· 26.6 | 178 17.9 | 5.8 | 19 01.4 | 3.5 | 59.4 |
| U 10 | 328 44.7 | 26.3 | 192 42.7 | 5.9 | 19 04.9 | 3.4 | 59.4 |
| R 11 | 343 44.6 | 26.0 | 207 07.6 | 5.8 | 19 08.3 | 3.2 | 59.4 |
| S 12 | 358 44.5 | N22 25.7 | 221 32.4 | 5.8 | S19 11.5 | 3.2 | 59.4 |
| D 13 | 13 44.4 | 25.4 | 235 57.2 | 5.8 | 19 14.7 | 3.0 | 59.4 |
| A 14 | 28 44.3 | 25.2 | 250 22.0 | 5.8 | 19 17.7 | 2.8 | 59.4 |
| Y 15 | 43 44.2 | ·· 24.9 | 264 46.8 | 5.7 | 19 20.5 | 2.7 | 59.4 |
| 16 | 58 44.1 | 24.6 | 279 11.5 | 5.8 | 19 23.2 | 2.7 | 59.4 |
| 17 | 73 44.0 | 24.3 | 293 36.3 | 5.7 | 19 25.9 | 2.4 | 59.3 |
| 18 | 88 43.9 | N22 24.0 | 308 01.0 | 5.8 | S19 28.3 | 2.4 | 59.3 |
| 19 | 103 43.8 | 23.7 | 322 25.8 | 5.7 | 19 30.7 | 2.2 | 59.3 |
| 20 | 118 43.7 | 23.4 | 336 50.5 | 5.7 | 19 32.9 | 2.1 | 59.3 |
| 21 | 133 43.6 | ·· 23.1 | 351 15.2 | 5.7 | 19 35.0 | 1.9 | 59.3 |
| 22 | 148 43.5 | 22.8 | 5 39.9 | 5.7 | 19 36.9 | 1.8 | 59.3 |
| 23 | 163 43.4 | 22.5 | 20 04.6 | 5.7 | 19 38.7 | 1.7 | 59.3 |
| 9 00 | 178 43.3 | N22 22.2 | 34 29.3 | 5.7 | S19 40.4 | 1.6 | 59.3 |
| 01 | 193 43.3 | 21.9 | 48 54.0 | 5.7 | 19 42.0 | 1.4 | 59.3 |
| 02 | 208 43.2 | 21.6 | 63 18.7 | 5.7 | 19 43.4 | 1.3 | 59.2 |
| 03 | 223 43.1 | ·· 21.3 | 77 43.4 | 5.8 | 19 44.7 | 1.2 | 59.2 |
| 04 | 238 43.0 | 21.0 | 92 08.2 | 5.7 | 19 45.9 | 1.0 | 59.2 |
| 05 | 253 42.9 | 20.7 | 106 32.9 | 5.7 | 19 46.9 | 0.9 | 59.2 |
| 06 | 268 42.8 | N22 20.4 | 120 57.6 | 5.7 | S19 47.8 | 0.7 | 59.2 |
| 07 | 283 42.7 | 20.1 | 135 22.3 | 5.8 | 19 48.5 | 0.7 | 59.2 |
| 08 | 298 42.6 | 19.8 | 149 47.1 | 5.7 | 19 49.2 | 0.5 | 59.2 |
| F 09 | 313 42.5 | ·· 19.5 | 164 11.8 | 5.8 | 19 49.7 | 0.4 | 59.2 |
| R 10 | 328 42.4 | 19.2 | 178 36.6 | 5.8 | 19 50.1 | 0.2 | 59.1 |
| I 11 | 343 42.3 | 18.9 | 193 01.4 | 5.7 | 19 50.3 | 0.1 | 59.1 |
| D 12 | 358 42.2 | N22 18.6 | 207 26.1 | 5.8 | S19 50.4 | 0.0 | 59.1 |
| A 13 | 13 42.2 | 18.3 | 221 50.9 | 5.9 | 19 50.4 | 0.2 | 59.1 |
| Y 14 | 28 42.1 | 18.0 | 236 15.8 | 5.8 | 19 50.2 | 0.3 | 59.1 |
| 15 | 43 42.0 | ·· 17.7 | 250 40.6 | 5.9 | 19 49.9 | 0.4 | 59.1 |
| 16 | 58 41.9 | 17.4 | 265 05.5 | 5.9 | 19 49.5 | 0.5 | 59.1 |
| 17 | 73 41.8 | 17.0 | 279 30.4 | 5.9 | 19 49.0 | 0.7 | 59.0 |
| 18 | 88 41.7 | N22 16.7 | 293 55.3 | 5.9 | S19 48.3 | 0.8 | 59.0 |
| 19 | 103 41.6 | 16.4 | 308 20.2 | 5.9 | 19 47.5 | 1.0 | 59.0 |
| 20 | 118 41.5 | 16.1 | 322 45.1 | 6.0 | 19 46.5 | 1.0 | 59.0 |
| 21 | 133 41.4 | ·· 15.8 | 337 10.1 | 6.0 | 19 45.5 | 1.2 | 59.0 |
| 22 | 148 41.4 | 15.5 | 351 35.1 | 6.1 | 19 44.3 | 1.4 | 59.0 |
| 23 | 163 41.3 | 15.2 | 6 00.2 | 6.0 | 19 42.9 | 1.4 | 58.9 |
| 10 00 | 178 41.2 | N22 14.9 | 20 25.2 | 6.1 | S19 41.5 | 1.6 | 58.9 |
| 01 | 193 41.1 | 14.5 | 34 50.3 | 6.2 | 19 39.9 | 1.7 | 58.9 |
| 02 | 208 41.0 | 14.2 | 49 15.5 | 6.1 | 19 38.2 | 1.8 | 58.9 |
| 03 | 223 40.9 | ·· 13.9 | 63 40.6 | 6.3 | 19 36.4 | 2.0 | 58.9 |
| 04 | 238 40.8 | 13.6 | 78 05.9 | 6.2 | 19 34.4 | 2.1 | 58.9 |
| 05 | 253 40.7 | 13.3 | 92 31.1 | 6.3 | 19 32.3 | 2.2 | 58.8 |
| 06 | 268 40.7 | N22 13.0 | 106 56.4 | 6.3 | S19 30.1 | 2.3 | 58.8 |
| 07 | 283 40.6 | 12.6 | 121 21.7 | 6.4 | 19 27.8 | 2.5 | 58.8 |
| S 08 | 298 40.5 | 12.3 | 135 47.1 | 6.4 | 19 25.3 | 2.6 | 58.8 |
| A 09 | 313 40.4 | ·· 12.0 | 150 12.5 | 6.4 | 19 22.7 | 2.7 | 58.8 |
| T 10 | 328 40.3 | 11.7 | 164 37.9 | 6.5 | 19 20.0 | 2.8 | 58.7 |
| U 11 | 343 40.2 | 11.4 | 179 03.4 | 6.5 | 19 17.2 | 3.0 | 58.7 |
| R 12 | 358 40.1 | N22 11.0 | 193 28.9 | 6.6 | S19 14.2 | 3.0 | 58.7 |
| D 13 | 13 40.1 | 10.7 | 207 54.5 | 6.7 | 19 11.2 | 3.2 | 58.7 |
| A 14 | 28 40.0 | 10.4 | 222 20.2 | 6.6 | 19 08.0 | 3.4 | 58.7 |
| Y 15 | 43 39.9 | ·· 10.1 | 236 45.8 | 6.8 | 19 04.6 | 3.4 | 58.6 |
| 16 | 58 39.8 | 09.8 | 251 11.6 | 6.7 | 19 01.2 | 3.5 | 58.6 |
| 17 | 73 39.7 | 09.4 | 265 37.3 | 6.9 | 18 57.7 | 3.7 | 58.6 |
| 18 | 88 39.6 | N22 09.1 | 280 03.2 | 6.9 | S18 54.0 | 3.8 | 58.6 |
| 19 | 103 39.5 | 08.8 | 294 29.1 | 6.9 | 18 50.2 | 3.9 | 58.6 |
| 20 | 118 39.5 | 08.4 | 308 55.0 | 7.0 | 18 46.3 | 4.0 | 58.5 |
| 21 | 133 39.4 | ·· 08.1 | 323 21.0 | 7.0 | 18 42.3 | 4.1 | 58.5 |
| 22 | 148 39.3 | 07.8 | 337 47.0 | 7.2 | 18 38.2 | 4.3 | 58.5 |
| 23 | 163 39.2 | 07.5 | 352 13.2 | 7.1 | 18 33.9 | 4.3 | 58.5 |
| | S.D. 15.8 | d 0.3 | S.D. 16.2 | | 16.1 | | 16.0 |

| Lat. | Twilight Naut. | Twilight Civil | Sunrise | Moonrise 8 | Moonrise 9 | Moonrise 10 | Moonrise 11 |
|---|---|---|---|---|---|---|---|
| ° | h m | h m | h m | h m | h m | h m | h m |
| N 72 | □ | □ | □ | ■ | ■ | ■ | 22 47 |
| N 70 | □ | □ | □ | 20 56 | 22 08 | 22 05 | 22 02 |
| 68 | □ | □ | □ | 19 41 | 20 46 | 21 18 | 21 32 |
| 66 | //// | //// | 01 07 | 19 04 | 20 07 | 20 47 | 21 09 |
| 64 | //// | //// | 01 59 | 18 38 | 19 40 | 20 24 | 20 52 |
| 62 | //// | //// | 02 30 | 18 17 | 19 20 | 20 05 | 20 37 |
| 60 | //// | 01 26 | 02 53 | 18 01 | 19 03 | 19 50 | 20 24 |
| N 58 | //// | 02 02 | 03 11 | 17 47 | 18 48 | 19 37 | 20 14 |
| 56 | //// | 02 28 | 03 26 | 17 35 | 18 36 | 19 26 | 20 04 |
| 54 | 01 19 | 02 48 | 03 40 | 17 24 | 18 25 | 19 16 | 19 56 |
| 52 | 01 53 | 03 04 | 03 51 | 17 15 | 18 16 | 19 07 | 19 48 |
| 50 | 02 16 | 03 18 | 04 01 | 17 06 | 18 07 | 18 59 | 19 42 |
| 45 | 02 58 | 03 46 | 04 22 | 16 49 | 17 49 | 18 42 | 19 27 |
| N 40 | 03 26 | 04 07 | 04 39 | 16 34 | 17 35 | 18 28 | 19 15 |
| 35 | 03 48 | 04 24 | 04 54 | 16 22 | 17 22 | 18 17 | 19 05 |
| 30 | 04 06 | 04 39 | 05 06 | 16 11 | 17 11 | 18 06 | 18 56 |
| 20 | 04 33 | 05 02 | 05 27 | 15 53 | 16 52 | 17 49 | 18 41 |
| N 10 | 04 55 | 05 22 | 05 45 | 15 37 | 16 36 | 17 33 | 18 27 |
| 0 | 05 13 | 05 39 | 06 02 | 15 22 | 16 21 | 17 19 | 18 14 |
| S 10 | 05 29 | 05 55 | 06 18 | 15 08 | 16 06 | 17 04 | 18 02 |
| 20 | 05 45 | 06 12 | 06 36 | 14 52 | 15 50 | 16 49 | 17 48 |
| 30 | 06 00 | 06 30 | 06 56 | 14 34 | 15 31 | 16 31 | 17 32 |
| 35 | 06 08 | 06 40 | 07 07 | 14 23 | 15 20 | 16 21 | 17 23 |
| 40 | 06 17 | 06 51 | 07 21 | 14 11 | 15 08 | 16 09 | 17 13 |
| 45 | 06 27 | 07 03 | 07 37 | 13 57 | 14 53 | 15 55 | 17 01 |
| S 50 | 06 37 | 07 18 | 07 56 | 13 40 | 14 36 | 15 38 | 16 46 |
| 52 | 06 42 | 07 25 | 08 05 | 13 32 | 14 27 | 15 30 | 16 39 |
| 54 | 06 47 | 07 33 | 08 16 | 13 23 | 14 18 | 15 21 | 16 31 |
| 56 | 06 53 | 07 41 | 08 27 | 13 13 | 14 07 | 15 11 | 16 23 |
| 58 | 06 59 | 07 51 | 08 41 | 13 02 | 13 55 | 15 00 | 16 13 |
| S 60 | 07 06 | 08 01 | 08 57 | 12 49 | 13 41 | 14 47 | 16 02 |

| Lat. | Sunset | Twilight Civil | Twilight Naut. | Moonset 8 | Moonset 9 | Moonset 10 | Moonset 11 |
|---|---|---|---|---|---|---|---|
| ° | h m | h m | h m | h m | h m | h m | h m |
| N 72 | □ | □ | □ | ■ | ■ | ■ | ■ |
| N 70 | □ | □ | □ | 22 14 | 23 04 | 25 07 | 01 07 |
| 68 | □ | □ | □ | 23 28 | 24 27 | 00 27 | 01 54 |
| 66 | 22 59 | //// | //// | 24 06 | 00 06 | 01 05 | 02 25 |
| 64 | 22 10 | //// | //// | 24 32 | 00 32 | 01 31 | 02 47 |
| 62 | 21 39 | //// | //// | 00 09 | 00 53 | 01 52 | 03 05 |
| 60 | 21 16 | 22 42 | //// | 00 24 | 01 10 | 02 09 | 03 20 |
| N 58 | 20 58 | 22 06 | //// | 00 37 | 01 24 | 02 23 | 03 33 |
| 56 | 20 43 | 21 41 | //// | 00 48 | 01 36 | 02 35 | 03 44 |
| 54 | 20 30 | 21 22 | 22 49 | 00 57 | 01 47 | 02 46 | 03 53 |
| 52 | 20 19 | 21 05 | 22 16 | 01 06 | 01 56 | 02 55 | 04 02 |
| 50 | 20 09 | 20 52 | 21 53 | 01 14 | 02 05 | 03 04 | 04 10 |
| 45 | 19 48 | 20 24 | 21 12 | 01 30 | 02 23 | 03 22 | 04 26 |
| N 40 | 19 31 | 20 03 | 20 43 | 01 44 | 02 37 | 03 36 | 04 39 |
| 35 | 19 17 | 19 46 | 20 22 | 01 55 | 02 50 | 03 49 | 04 51 |
| 30 | 19 04 | 19 31 | 20 04 | 02 05 | 03 01 | 03 59 | 05 00 |
| 20 | 18 43 | 19 08 | 19 37 | 02 23 | 03 19 | 04 18 | 05 17 |
| N 10 | 18 26 | 18 48 | 19 15 | 02 38 | 03 35 | 04 34 | 05 32 |
| 0 | 18 09 | 18 31 | 18 57 | 02 52 | 03 50 | 04 49 | 05 46 |
| S 10 | 17 52 | 18 15 | 18 41 | 03 06 | 04 06 | 05 04 | 05 59 |
| 20 | 17 35 | 17 59 | 18 26 | 03 21 | 04 22 | 05 20 | 06 14 |
| 30 | 17 15 | 17 41 | 18 10 | 03 39 | 04 40 | 05 38 | 06 30 |
| 35 | 17 03 | 17 31 | 18 02 | 03 49 | 04 51 | 05 48 | 06 40 |
| 40 | 16 50 | 17 20 | 17 54 | 04 00 | 05 03 | 06 01 | 06 51 |
| 45 | 16 34 | 17 07 | 17 44 | 04 14 | 05 18 | 06 15 | 07 04 |
| S 50 | 16 15 | 16 52 | 17 33 | 04 31 | 05 36 | 06 32 | 07 19 |
| 52 | 16 05 | 16 45 | 17 28 | 04 38 | 05 44 | 06 40 | 07 27 |
| 54 | 15 55 | 16 38 | 17 23 | 04 47 | 05 53 | 06 49 | 07 35 |
| 56 | 15 43 | 16 29 | 17 18 | 04 57 | 06 04 | 07 00 | 07 44 |
| 58 | 15 30 | 16 20 | 17 12 | 05 08 | 06 16 | 07 11 | 07 54 |
| S 60 | 15 14 | 16 09 | 17 05 | 05 21 | 06 30 | 07 25 | 08 06 |

| Day | SUN Eqn. of Time 00h | SUN Eqn. of Time 12h | SUN Mer. Pass. | MOON Mer. Pass. Upper | MOON Mer. Pass. Lower | Age | Phase |
|---|---|---|---|---|---|---|---|
| | m s | m s | h m | h m | h m | d | |
| 8 | 04 57 | 05 02 | 12 05 | 21 36 | 09 07 | 11 | ○ |
| 9 | 05 06 | 05 11 | 12 05 | 22 35 | 10 06 | 12 | |
| 10 | 05 15 | 05 19 | 12 05 | 23 32 | 11 04 | 13 | |

# 1976 AUGUST 10, 11, 12 (TUES., WED., THURS.)

| G.M.T. (d h) | ARIES G.H.A. | VENUS −3.4 G.H.A. | VENUS Dec. | MARS +1.9 G.H.A. | MARS Dec. | JUPITER −1.9 G.H.A. | JUPITER Dec. | SATURN +0.5 G.H.A. | SATURN Dec. |
|---|---|---|---|---|---|---|---|---|---|
| 10 00 | 318 36.0 | 164 02.9 | N12 07.6 | 146 35.3 | N 4 18.4 | 261 59.8 | N18 51.0 | 188 01.2 | N18 46.1 |
| 01 | 333 38.4 | 179 02.4 | 06.5 | 161 36.3 | 17.8 | 277 02.0 | 51.0 | 203 03.3 | 46.0 |
| 02 | 348 40.9 | 194 01.9 | 05.4 | 176 37.3 | 17.1 | 292 04.1 | 51.1 | 218 05.4 | 46.0 |
| 03 | 3 43.4 | 209 01.4 | ·· 04.2 | 191 38.3 | ·· 16.5 | 307 06.3 | ·· 51.1 | 233 07.6 | ·· 45.9 |
| 04 | 18 45.8 | 224 01.0 | 03.1 | 206 39.4 | 15.8 | 322 08.4 | 51.2 | 248 09.7 | 45.8 |
| 05 | 33 48.3 | 239 00.5 | 02.0 | 221 40.4 | 15.2 | 337 10.6 | 51.3 | 263 11.9 | 45.7 |
| 06 | 48 50.8 | 254 00.0 | N12 00.9 | 236 41.4 | N 4 14.6 | 352 12.7 | N18 51.3 | 278 14.0 | N18 45.6 |
| 07 | 63 53.2 | 268 59.6 | 11 59.8 | 251 42.4 | 13.9 | 7 14.9 | 51.4 | 293 16.1 | 45.6 |
| T 08 | 78 55.7 | 283 59.1 | 58.7 | 266 43.5 | 13.3 | 22 17.0 | 51.4 | 308 18.3 | 45.5 |
| U 09 | 93 58.2 | 298 58.6 | ·· 57.6 | 281 44.5 | ·· 12.6 | 37 19.2 | ·· 51.5 | 323 20.4 | ·· 45.4 |
| E 10 | 109 00.6 | 313 58.2 | 56.5 | 296 45.5 | 12.0 | 52 21.3 | 51.6 | 338 22.5 | 45.3 |
| S 11 | 124 03.1 | 328 57.7 | 55.3 | 311 46.5 | 11.3 | 67 23.5 | 51.6 | 353 24.7 | 45.2 |
| D 12 | 139 05.5 | 343 57.2 | N11 54.2 | 326 47.6 | N 4 10.7 | 82 25.6 | N18 51.7 | 8 26.8 | N18 45.2 |
| A 13 | 154 08.0 | 358 56.8 | 53.1 | 341 48.6 | 10.1 | 97 27.8 | 51.8 | 23 29.0 | 45.1 |
| Y 14 | 169 10.5 | 13 56.3 | 52.0 | 356 49.6 | 09.4 | 112 29.9 | 51.8 | 38 31.1 | 45.0 |
| 15 | 184 12.9 | 28 55.9 | ·· 50.9 | 11 50.6 | ·· 08.8 | 127 32.1 | ·· 51.9 | 53 33.2 | ·· 44.9 |
| 16 | 199 15.4 | 43 55.4 | 49.8 | 26 51.7 | 08.1 | 142 34.3 | 51.9 | 68 35.4 | 44.8 |
| 17 | 214 17.9 | 58 54.9 | 48.6 | 41 52.7 | 07.5 | 157 36.4 | 52.0 | 83 37.5 | 44.8 |
| 18 | 229 20.3 | 73 54.5 | N11 47.5 | 56 53.7 | N 4 06.8 | 172 38.6 | N18 52.1 | 98 39.6 | N18 44.7 |
| 19 | 244 22.8 | 88 54.0 | 46.4 | 71 54.7 | 06.2 | 187 40.7 | 52.1 | 113 41.8 | 44.6 |
| 20 | 259 25.3 | 103 53.5 | 45.3 | 86 55.7 | 05.6 | 202 42.9 | 52.2 | 128 43.9 | 44.5 |
| 21 | 274 27.7 | 118 53.1 | ·· 44.2 | 101 56.8 | ·· 04.9 | 217 45.0 | ·· 52.2 | 143 46.1 | ·· 44.4 |
| 22 | 289 30.2 | 133 52.6 | 43.0 | 116 57.8 | 04.3 | 232 47.2 | 52.3 | 158 48.2 | 44.4 |
| 23 | 304 32.6 | 148 52.2 | 41.9 | 131 58.8 | 03.6 | 247 49.3 | 52.4 | 173 50.3 | 44.3 |
| 11 00 | 319 35.1 | 163 51.7 | N11 40.8 | 146 59.8 | N 4 03.0 | 262 51.5 | N18 52.4 | 188 52.5 | N18 44.2 |
| 01 | 334 37.6 | 178 51.2 | 39.7 | 162 00.9 | 02.3 | 277 53.7 | 52.5 | 203 54.6 | 44.1 |
| 02 | 349 40.0 | 193 50.8 | 38.5 | 177 01.9 | 01.7 | 292 55.8 | 52.5 | 218 56.7 | 44.1 |
| 03 | 4 42.5 | 208 50.3 | ·· 37.4 | 192 02.9 | ·· 01.1 | 307 58.0 | ·· 52.6 | 233 58.9 | ·· 44.0 |
| 04 | 19 45.0 | 223 49.9 | 36.3 | 207 03.9 | 4 00.4 | 323 00.1 | 52.7 | 249 01.0 | 43.9 |
| 05 | 34 47.4 | 238 49.4 | 35.2 | 222 05.0 | 3 59.8 | 338 02.3 | 52.7 | 264 03.2 | 43.8 |
| 06 | 49 49.9 | 253 48.9 | N11 34.1 | 237 06.0 | N 3 59.1 | 353 04.4 | N18 52.8 | 279 05.3 | N18 43.7 |
| W 07 | 64 52.4 | 268 48.5 | 32.9 | 252 07.0 | 58.5 | 8 06.6 | 52.8 | 294 07.4 | 43.7 |
| E 08 | 79 54.8 | 283 48.0 | 31.8 | 267 08.0 | 57.8 | 23 08.8 | 52.9 | 309 09.6 | 43.6 |
| D 09 | 94 57.3 | 298 47.6 | ·· 30.7 | 282 09.1 | ·· 57.2 | 38 10.9 | ·· 53.0 | 324 11.7 | ·· 43.5 |
| N 10 | 109 59.8 | 313 47.1 | 29.5 | 297 10.1 | 56.6 | 53 13.1 | 53.0 | 339 13.8 | 43.4 |
| E 11 | 125 02.2 | 328 46.7 | 28.4 | 312 11.1 | 55.9 | 68 15.2 | 53.1 | 354 16.0 | 43.3 |
| S 12 | 140 04.7 | 343 46.2 | N11 27.3 | 327 12.1 | N 3 55.3 | 83 17.4 | N18 53.1 | 9 18.1 | N18 43.3 |
| D 13 | 155 07.1 | 358 45.7 | 26.2 | 342 13.2 | 54.6 | 98 19.5 | 53.2 | 24 20.3 | 43.2 |
| A 14 | 170 09.6 | 13 45.3 | 25.0 | 357 14.2 | 54.0 | 113 21.7 | 53.3 | 39 22.4 | 43.1 |
| Y 15 | 185 12.1 | 28 44.8 | ·· 23.9 | 12 15.2 | ·· 53.3 | 128 23.9 | ·· 53.3 | 54 24.5 | ·· 43.0 |
| 16 | 200 14.5 | 43 44.4 | 22.8 | 27 16.2 | 52.7 | 143 26.0 | 53.4 | 69 26.7 | 42.9 |
| 17 | 215 17.0 | 58 43.9 | 21.6 | 42 17.3 | 52.1 | 158 28.2 | 53.4 | 84 28.8 | 42.9 |
| 18 | 230 19.5 | 73 43.5 | N11 20.5 | 57 18.3 | N 3 51.4 | 173 30.4 | N18 53.5 | 99 30.9 | N18 42.8 |
| 19 | 245 21.9 | 88 43.0 | 19.4 | 72 19.3 | 50.8 | 188 32.5 | 53.6 | 114 33.1 | 42.7 |
| 20 | 260 24.4 | 103 42.6 | 18.2 | 87 20.3 | 50.1 | 203 34.7 | 53.6 | 129 35.2 | 42.6 |
| 21 | 275 26.9 | 118 42.1 | ·· 17.1 | 102 21.3 | ·· 49.5 | 218 36.8 | ·· 53.7 | 144 37.4 | ·· 42.6 |
| 22 | 290 29.3 | 133 41.7 | 16.0 | 117 22.4 | 48.8 | 233 39.0 | 53.7 | 159 39.5 | 42.5 |
| 23 | 305 31.8 | 148 41.2 | 14.8 | 132 23.4 | 48.2 | 248 41.2 | 53.8 | 174 41.6 | 42.4 |
| 12 00 | 320 34.2 | 163 40.8 | N11 13.7 | 147 24.4 | N 3 47.5 | 263 43.3 | N18 53.9 | 189 43.8 | N18 42.3 |
| 01 | 335 36.7 | 178 40.3 | 12.6 | 162 25.4 | 46.9 | 278 45.5 | 53.9 | 204 45.9 | 42.2 |
| 02 | 350 39.2 | 193 39.9 | 11.4 | 177 26.5 | 46.3 | 293 47.6 | 54.0 | 219 48.1 | 42.2 |
| 03 | 5 41.6 | 208 39.4 | ·· 10.3 | 192 27.5 | ·· 45.6 | 308 49.8 | ·· 54.0 | 234 50.2 | ·· 42.1 |
| 04 | 20 44.1 | 223 39.0 | 09.2 | 207 28.5 | 45.0 | 323 52.0 | 54.1 | 249 52.3 | 42.0 |
| 05 | 35 46.6 | 238 38.5 | 08.0 | 222 29.5 | 44.3 | 338 54.1 | 54.1 | 264 54.5 | 41.9 |
| 06 | 50 49.0 | 253 38.1 | N11 06.9 | 237 30.6 | N 3 43.7 | 353 56.3 | N18 54.2 | 279 56.6 | N18 41.8 |
| 07 | 65 51.5 | 268 37.6 | 05.7 | 252 31.6 | 43.0 | 8 58.5 | 54.3 | 294 58.7 | 41.8 |
| T 08 | 80 54.0 | 283 37.2 | 04.6 | 267 32.6 | 42.4 | 24 00.6 | 54.3 | 310 00.9 | 41.7 |
| H 09 | 95 56.4 | 298 36.7 | ·· 03.5 | 282 33.6 | ·· 41.7 | 39 02.8 | ·· 54.4 | 325 03.0 | ·· 41.6 |
| U 10 | 110 58.9 | 313 36.3 | 02.3 | 297 34.6 | 41.1 | 54 05.0 | 54.4 | 340 05.2 | 41.5 |
| R 11 | 126 01.4 | 328 35.8 | 01.2 | 312 35.7 | 40.5 | 69 07.1 | 54.5 | 355 07.3 | 41.4 |
| S 12 | 141 03.8 | 343 35.4 | N11 00.1 | 327 36.7 | N 3 39.8 | 84 09.3 | N18 54.6 | 10 09.4 | N18 41.4 |
| D 13 | 156 06.3 | 358 34.9 | 10 58.9 | 342 37.7 | 39.2 | 99 11.5 | 54.6 | 25 11.6 | 41.3 |
| A 14 | 171 08.7 | 13 34.5 | 57.8 | 357 38.7 | 38.5 | 114 13.6 | 54.7 | 40 13.7 | 41.2 |
| Y 15 | 186 11.2 | 28 34.1 | ·· 56.6 | 12 39.8 | ·· 37.9 | 129 15.8 | ·· 54.7 | 55 15.9 | ·· 41.1 |
| 16 | 201 13.7 | 43 33.6 | 55.5 | 27 40.8 | 37.2 | 144 18.0 | 54.8 | 70 18.0 | 41.1 |
| 17 | 216 16.1 | 58 33.2 | 54.3 | 42 41.8 | 36.6 | 159 20.1 | 54.8 | 85 20.1 | 41.0 |
| 18 | 231 18.6 | 73 32.7 | N10 53.2 | 57 42.8 | N 3 35.9 | 174 22.3 | N18 54.9 | 100 22.3 | N18 40.9 |
| 19 | 246 21.1 | 88 32.3 | 52.1 | 72 43.8 | 35.3 | 189 24.5 | 55.0 | 115 24.4 | 40.8 |
| 20 | 261 23.5 | 103 31.8 | 50.9 | 87 44.9 | 34.7 | 204 26.6 | 55.0 | 130 26.5 | 40.7 |
| 21 | 276 26.0 | 118 31.4 | ·· 49.8 | 102 45.9 | ·· 34.0 | 219 28.8 | ·· 55.1 | 145 28.7 | ·· 40.7 |
| 22 | 291 28.5 | 133 31.0 | 48.6 | 117 46.9 | 33.4 | 234 31.0 | 55.1 | 160 30.8 | 40.6 |
| 23 | 306 30.9 | 148 30.5 | 47.5 | 132 47.9 | 32.7 | 249 33.1 | 55.2 | 175 33.0 | 40.5 |
| Mer. Pass. | 2 41.2 | v −0.5 | d 1.1 | v 1.0 | d 0.6 | v 2.2 | d 0.1 | v 2.1 | d 0.1 |

| STARS Name | S.H.A. | Dec. |
|---|---|---|
| Acamar | 315 39.3 | S40 23.6 |
| Achernar | 335 47.1 | S57 21.0 |
| Acrux | 173 40.7 | S62 58.4 |
| Adhara | 255 34.6 | S28 56.3 |
| Aldebaran | 291 21.3 | N16 27.7 |
| Alioth | 166 45.3 | N56 05.4 |
| Alkaid | 153 20.9 | N49 26.1 |
| Al Na'ir | 28 18.0 | S47 04.2 |
| Alnilam | 276 14.6 | S 1 12.9 |
| Alphard | 218 23.6 | S 8 33.4 |
| Alphecca | 126 34.4 | N26 47.8 |
| Alpheratz | 358 11.9 | N28 57.7 |
| Altair | 62 34.9 | N 8 48.6 |
| Ankaa | 353 42.7 | S42 25.7 |
| Antares | 113 00.1 | S26 22.8 |
| Arcturus | 146 21.0 | N19 18.4 |
| Atria | 108 26.5 | S68 59.4 |
| Avior | 234 29.9 | S59 26.1 |
| Bellatrix | 279 01.9 | N 6 19.7 |
| Betelgeuse | 271 31.5 | N 7 24.2 |
| Canopus | 264 08.8 | S52 40.8 |
| Capella | 281 15.6 | N45 58.3 |
| Deneb | 49 49.8 | N45 12.0 |
| Denebola | 183 02.1 | N14 42.2 |
| Diphda | 349 23.4 | S18 06.7 |
| Dubhe | 194 26.2 | N61 52.7 |
| Elnath | 278 47.8 | N28 35.2 |
| Eltanin | 90 58.7 | N51 29.8 |
| Enif | 34 13.9 | N 9 46.3 |
| Fomalhaut | 15 54.1 | S29 44.5 |
| Gacrux | 172 32.1 | S56 59.2 |
| Gienah | 176 21.0 | S17 24.8 |
| Hadar | 149 27.4 | S60 15.9 |
| Hamal | 328 31.9 | N23 21.1 |
| Kaus Aust. | 84 20.2 | S34 23.7 |
| Kochab | 137 19.1 | N74 15.4 |
| Markab | 14 05.6 | N15 04.9 |
| Menkar | 314 44.0 | N 4 00.0 |
| Menkent | 148 40.3 | S36 15.4 |
| Miaplacidus | 221 46.4 | S69 37.4 |
| Mirfak | 309 20.0 | N49 46.5 |
| Nunki | 76 32.3 | S26 19.5 |
| Peacock | 54 02.2 | S56 48.5 |
| Pollux | 244 01.9 | N28 04.9 |
| Procyon | 245 29.0 | N 5 17.1 |
| Rasalhague | 96 31.9 | N12 34.8 |
| Regulus | 208 13.2 | N12 04.9 |
| Rigel | 281 38.8 | S 8 13.6 |
| Rigil Kent. | 140 29.6 | S60 44.5 |
| Sabik | 102 44.1 | S15 41.7 |
| Schedar | 350 11.7 | N56 24.5 |
| Shaula | 96 59.2 | S37 05.3 |
| Sirius | 258 58.4 | S16 41.0 |
| Spica | 159 00.6 | S11 02.4 |
| Suhail | 223 13.2 | S43 20.3 |
| Vega | 80 57.4 | N38 46.0 |
| Zuben'ubi | 137 36.1 | S15 56.7 |

| | S.H.A. | Mer. Pass. |
|---|---|---|
| | ° ′ | h m |
| Venus | 204 16.6 | 13 05 |
| Mars | 187 24.7 | 14 11 |
| Jupiter | 303 16.4 | 6 28 |
| Saturn | 229 17.4 | 11 23 |

## 1976 AUGUST 13, 14, 15 (FRI., SAT., SUN.)

| G.M.T. | ARIES | VENUS −3.3 | | MARS +1.9 | | JUPITER −1.9 | | SATURN +0.5 | | STARS | | |
|---|---|---|---|---|---|---|---|---|---|---|---|---|
| | G.H.A. | G.H.A. | Dec. | G.H.A. | Dec. | G.H.A. | Dec. | G.H.A. | Dec. | Name | S.H.A. | Dec. |
| d h | ° ′ | ° ′ | ° ′ | ° ′ | ° ′ | ° ′ | ° ′ | ° ′ | ° ′ | | ° ′ | ° ′ |
| 13 00 | 321 33.4 | 163 30.1 | N10 46.3 | 147 49.0 | N 3 32.1 | 264 35.3 | N18 55.2 | 190 35.1 | N18 40.4 | Acamar | 315 39.3 | S40 23.6 |
| 01 | 336 35.9 | 178 29.6 | 45.2 | 162 50.0 | 31.4 | 279 37.5 | 55.3 | 205 37.2 | 40.3 | Achernar | 335 47.1 | S57 21.0 |
| 02 | 351 38.3 | 193 29.2 | 44.0 | 177 51.0 | 30.8 | 294 39.6 | 55.4 | 220 39.4 | 40.3 | Acrux | 173 40.7 | S62 58.4 |
| 03 | 6 40.8 | 208 28.8 | ·· 42.9 | 192 52.0 | ·· 30.1 | 309 41.8 | ·· 55.4 | 235 41.5 | ·· 40.2 | Adhara | 255 34.6 | S28 56.3 |
| 04 | 21 43.2 | 223 28.3 | 41.7 | 207 53.0 | 29.5 | 324 44.0 | 55.5 | 250 43.7 | 40.1 | Aldebaran | 291 21.3 | N16 27.7 |
| 05 | 36 45.7 | 238 27.9 | 40.6 | 222 54.1 | 28.8 | 339 46.1 | 55.5 | 265 45.8 | 40.0 | | | |
| 06 | 51 48.2 | 253 27.4 | N10 39.4 | 237 55.1 | N 3 28.2 | 354 48.3 | N18 55.6 | 280 47.9 | N18 39.9 | Alioth | 166 45.3 | N56 05.4 |
| 07 | 66 50.6 | 268 27.0 | 38.3 | 252 56.1 | 27.5 | 9 50.5 | 55.6 | 295 50.1 | 39.9 | Alkaid | 153 20.9 | N49 26.1 |
| 08 | 81 53.1 | 283 26.6 | 37.1 | 267 57.1 | 26.9 | 24 52.7 | 55.7 | 310 52.2 | 39.8 | Al Na'ir | 28 17.9 | S47 04.2 |
| F 09 | 96 55.6 | 298 26.1 | ·· 36.0 | 282 58.2 | ·· 26.3 | 39 54.8 | ·· 55.8 | 325 54.4 | ·· 39.7 | Alnilam | 276 14.6 | S 1 12.9 |
| R 10 | 111 58.0 | 313 25.7 | 34.8 | 297 59.2 | 25.6 | 54 57.0 | 55.8 | 340 56.5 | 39.6 | Alphard | 218 23.6 | S 8 33.4 |
| I 11 | 127 00.5 | 328 25.2 | 33.7 | 313 00.2 | 25.0 | 69 59.2 | 55.9 | 355 58.6 | 39.5 | | | |
| D 12 | 142 03.0 | 343 24.8 | N10 32.5 | 328 01.2 | N 3 24.3 | 85 01.3 | N18 55.9 | 11 00.8 | N18 39.5 | Alphecca | 126 34.4 | N26 47.8 |
| A 13 | 157 05.4 | 358 24.4 | 31.4 | 343 02.2 | 23.7 | 100 03.5 | 56.0 | 26 02.9 | 39.4 | Alpheratz | 358 11.9 | N28 57.7 |
| Y 14 | 172 07.9 | 13 23.9 | 30.2 | 358 03.3 | 23.0 | 115 05.7 | 56.0 | 41 05.1 | 39.3 | Altair | 62 34.9 | N 8 48.6 |
| 15 | 187 10.3 | 28 23.5 | ·· 29.1 | 13 04.3 | ·· 22.4 | 130 07.9 | ·· 56.1 | 56 07.2 | ·· 39.2 | Ankaa | 353 42.7 | S42 25.7 |
| 16 | 202 12.8 | 43 23.1 | 27.9 | 28 05.3 | 21.7 | 145 10.0 | 56.2 | 71 09.3 | 39.2 | Antares | 113 00.1 | S26 22.8 |
| 17 | 217 15.3 | 58 22.6 | 26.8 | 43 06.3 | 21.1 | 160 12.2 | 56.2 | 86 11.5 | 39.1 | | | |
| 18 | 232 17.7 | 73 22.2 | N10 25.6 | 58 07.4 | N 3 20.4 | 175 14.4 | N18 56.3 | 101 13.6 | N18 39.0 | Arcturus | 146 21.1 | N19 18.4 |
| 19 | 247 20.2 | 88 21.8 | 24.4 | 73 08.4 | 19.8 | 190 16.6 | 56.3 | 116 15.8 | 38.9 | Atria | 108 26.6 | S68 59.4 |
| 20 | 262 22.7 | 103 21.3 | 23.3 | 88 09.4 | 19.1 | 205 18.7 | 56.4 | 131 17.9 | 38.8 | Avior | 234 29.9 | S59 26.1 |
| 21 | 277 25.1 | 118 20.9 | ·· 22.1 | 103 10.4 | ·· 18.5 | 220 20.9 | ·· 56.4 | 146 20.0 | ·· 38.8 | Bellatrix | 279 01.9 | N 6 19.7 |
| 22 | 292 27.6 | 133 20.5 | 21.0 | 118 11.4 | 17.8 | 235 23.1 | 56.5 | 161 22.2 | 38.7 | Betelgeuse | 271 31.4 | N 7 24.2 |
| 23 | 307 30.1 | 148 20.0 | 19.8 | 133 12.5 | 17.2 | 250 25.3 | 56.5 | 176 24.3 | 38.6 | | | |
| 14 00 | 322 32.5 | 163 19.6 | N10 18.7 | 148 13.5 | N 3 16.6 | 265 27.4 | N18 56.6 | 191 26.4 | N18 38.5 | Canopus | 264 08.8 | S52 40.8 |
| 01 | 337 35.0 | 178 19.2 | 17.5 | 163 14.5 | 15.9 | 280 29.6 | 56.7 | 206 28.6 | 38.4 | Capella | 281 15.6 | N45 58.3 |
| 02 | 352 37.5 | 193 18.7 | 16.3 | 178 15.5 | 15.3 | 295 31.8 | 56.7 | 221 30.7 | 38.4 | Deneb | 49 49.9 | N45 12.0 |
| 03 | 7 39.9 | 208 18.3 | ·· 15.2 | 193 16.5 | ·· 14.6 | 310 34.0 | ·· 56.8 | 236 32.9 | ·· 38.3 | Denebola | 183 02.1 | N14 42.2 |
| 04 | 22 42.4 | 223 17.9 | 14.0 | 208 17.6 | 14.0 | 325 36.1 | 56.8 | 251 35.0 | 38.2 | Diphda | 349 23.4 | S18 06.7 |
| 05 | 37 44.8 | 238 17.4 | 12.9 | 223 18.6 | 13.3 | 340 38.3 | 56.9 | 266 37.1 | 38.1 | | | |
| 06 | 52 47.3 | 253 17.0 | N10 11.7 | 238 19.6 | N 3 12.7 | 355 40.5 | N18 56.9 | 281 39.3 | N18 38.0 | Dubhe | 194 26.2 | N61 52.7 |
| 07 | 67 49.8 | 268 16.6 | 10.5 | 253 20.6 | 12.0 | 10 42.7 | 57.0 | 296 41.4 | 38.0 | Elnath | 278 47.8 | N28 35.2 |
| S 08 | 82 52.2 | 283 16.2 | 09.4 | 268 21.6 | 11.4 | 25 44.8 | 57.0 | 311 43.6 | 37.9 | Eltanin | 90 58.7 | N51 29.8 |
| A 09 | 97 54.7 | 298 15.7 | ·· 08.2 | 283 22.7 | ·· 10.7 | 40 47.0 | ·· 57.1 | 326 45.7 | ·· 37.8 | Enif | 34 13.9 | N 9 46.3 |
| T 10 | 112 57.2 | 313 15.3 | 07.0 | 298 23.7 | 10.1 | 55 49.2 | 57.1 | 341 47.8 | 37.7 | Fomalhaut | 15 54.1 | S29 44.5 |
| U 11 | 127 59.6 | 328 14.9 | 05.9 | 313 24.7 | 09.4 | 70 51.4 | 57.2 | 356 50.0 | 37.6 | | | |
| R 12 | 143 02.1 | 343 14.4 | N10 04.7 | 328 25.7 | N 3 08.8 | 85 53.6 | N18 57.3 | 11 52.1 | N18 37.6 | Gacrux | 172 32.1 | S56 59.1 |
| D 13 | 158 04.6 | 358 14.0 | 03.5 | 343 26.8 | 08.1 | 100 55.7 | 57.3 | 26 54.3 | 37.5 | Gienah | 176 21.0 | S17 24.8 |
| A 14 | 173 07.0 | 13 13.6 | 02.4 | 358 27.8 | 07.5 | 115 57.9 | 57.4 | 41 56.4 | 37.4 | Hadar | 149 27.4 | S60 15.9 |
| Y 15 | 188 09.5 | 28 13.2 | ·· 01.2 | 13 28.8 | ·· 06.8 | 131 00.1 | ·· 57.4 | 56 58.6 | ·· 37.3 | Hamal | 328 31.9 | N23 21.1 |
| 16 | 203 11.9 | 43 12.7 | 10 00.1 | 28 29.8 | 06.2 | 146 02.3 | 57.5 | 72 00.7 | 37.3 | Kaus Aust. | 84 20.2 | S34 23.7 |
| 17 | 218 14.4 | 58 12.3 | 9 58.9 | 43 30.8 | 05.5 | 161 04.5 | 57.5 | 87 02.8 | 37.2 | | | |
| 18 | 233 16.9 | 73 11.9 | N 9 57.7 | 58 31.9 | N 3 04.9 | 176 06.6 | N18 57.6 | 102 05.0 | N18 37.1 | Kochab | 137 19.1 | N74 15.4 |
| 19 | 248 19.3 | 88 11.5 | 56.6 | 73 32.9 | 04.2 | 191 08.8 | 57.6 | 117 07.1 | 37.0 | Markab | 14 05.6 | N15 04.9 |
| 20 | 263 21.8 | 103 11.0 | 55.4 | 88 33.9 | 03.6 | 206 11.0 | 57.7 | 132 09.3 | 36.9 | Menkar | 314 44.0 | N 4 00.0 |
| 21 | 278 24.3 | 118 10.6 | ·· 54.2 | 103 34.9 | ·· 03.0 | 221 13.2 | ·· 57.7 | 147 11.4 | ·· 36.9 | Menkent | 148 40.3 | S36 15.4 |
| 22 | 293 26.7 | 133 10.2 | 53.0 | 118 35.9 | 02.3 | 236 15.4 | 57.8 | 162 13.5 | 36.8 | Miaplacidus | 221 46.4 | S69 37.3 |
| 23 | 308 29.2 | 148 09.8 | 51.9 | 133 37.0 | 01.7 | 251 17.5 | 57.9 | 177 15.7 | 36.7 | | | |
| 15 00 | 323 31.7 | 163 09.3 | N 9 50.7 | 148 38.0 | N 3 01.0 | 266 19.7 | N18 57.9 | 192 17.8 | N18 36.6 | Mirfak | 309 20.0 | N49 46.5 |
| 01 | 338 34.1 | 178 08.9 | 49.5 | 163 39.0 | 3 00.4 | 281 21.9 | 58.0 | 207 20.0 | 36.5 | Nunki | 76 32.3 | S26 19.5 |
| 02 | 353 36.6 | 193 08.5 | 48.4 | 178 40.0 | 2 59.7 | 296 24.1 | 58.0 | 222 22.1 | 36.5 | Peacock | 54 02.2 | S56 48.5 |
| 03 | 8 39.1 | 208 08.1 | ·· 47.2 | 193 41.0 | ·· 59.1 | 311 26.3 | ·· 58.1 | 237 24.2 | ·· 36.4 | Pollux | 244 01.9 | N28 04.9 |
| 04 | 23 41.5 | 223 07.7 | 46.0 | 208 42.1 | 58.4 | 326 28.4 | 58.1 | 252 26.4 | 36.3 | Procyon | 245 28.9 | N 5 17.1 |
| 05 | 38 44.0 | 238 07.2 | 44.9 | 223 43.1 | 57.8 | 341 30.6 | 58.2 | 267 28.5 | 36.2 | | | |
| 06 | 53 46.4 | 253 06.8 | N 9 43.7 | 238 44.1 | N 2 57.1 | 356 32.8 | N18 58.2 | 282 30.7 | N18 36.1 | Rasalhague | 96 31.9 | N12 34.8 |
| 07 | 68 48.9 | 268 06.4 | 42.5 | 253 45.1 | 56.5 | 11 35.0 | 58.3 | 297 32.8 | 36.1 | Regulus | 208 13.2 | N12 04.9 |
| 08 | 83 51.4 | 283 06.0 | 41.3 | 268 46.1 | 55.8 | 26 37.2 | 58.3 | 312 34.9 | 36.0 | Rigel | 281 38.8 | S 8 13.6 |
| S 09 | 98 53.8 | 298 05.5 | ·· 40.2 | 283 47.2 | ·· 55.2 | 41 39.4 | ·· 58.4 | 327 37.1 | ·· 35.9 | Rigil Kent. | 140 29.6 | S60 44.5 |
| U 10 | 113 56.3 | 313 05.1 | 39.0 | 298 48.2 | 54.5 | 56 41.6 | 58.4 | 342 39.2 | 35.8 | Sabik | 102 44.1 | S15 41.7 |
| N 11 | 128 58.8 | 328 04.7 | 37.8 | 313 49.2 | 53.9 | 71 43.7 | 58.5 | 357 41.4 | 35.8 | | | |
| D 12 | 144 01.2 | 343 04.3 | N 9 36.6 | 328 50.2 | N 2 53.2 | 86 45.9 | N18 58.6 | 12 43.5 | N18 35.7 | Schedar | 350 11.7 | N56 24.5 |
| A 13 | 159 03.7 | 358 03.9 | 35.5 | 343 51.2 | 52.6 | 101 48.1 | 58.6 | 27 45.6 | 35.6 | Shaula | 96 59.2 | S37 05.3 |
| Y 14 | 174 06.2 | 13 03.5 | 34.3 | 358 52.3 | 51.9 | 116 50.3 | 58.7 | 42 47.8 | 35.5 | Sirius | 258 58.4 | S16 41.0 |
| 15 | 189 08.6 | 28 03.0 | ·· 33.1 | 13 53.3 | ·· 51.3 | 131 52.5 | ·· 58.7 | 57 49.9 | ·· 35.4 | Spica | 159 00.6 | S11 02.4 |
| 16 | 204 11.1 | 43 02.6 | 31.9 | 28 54.3 | 50.6 | 146 54.7 | 58.8 | 72 52.1 | 35.4 | Suhail | 223 13.2 | S43 20.3 |
| 17 | 219 13.6 | 58 02.2 | 30.8 | 43 55.3 | 50.0 | 161 56.8 | 58.8 | 87 54.2 | 35.3 | | | |
| 18 | 234 16.0 | 73 01.8 | N 9 29.6 | 58 56.3 | N 2 49.3 | 176 59.0 | N18 58.9 | 102 56.4 | N18 35.2 | Vega | 80 57.4 | N38 46.0 |
| 19 | 249 18.5 | 88 01.4 | 28.4 | 73 57.3 | 48.7 | 192 01.2 | 58.9 | 117 58.5 | 35.1 | Zuben'ubi | 137 36.1 | S15 56.7 |
| 20 | 264 20.9 | 103 01.0 | 27.2 | 88 58.4 | 48.0 | 207 03.4 | 59.0 | 133 00.6 | 35.0 | | S.H.A. | Mer. Pass. |
| 21 | 279 23.4 | 118 00.5 | ·· 26.0 | 103 59.4 | ·· 47.4 | 222 05.6 | ·· 59.0 | 148 02.8 | ·· 35.0 | | ° ′ | h m |
| 22 | 294 25.9 | 133 00.1 | 24.9 | 119 00.4 | 46.7 | 237 07.8 | 59.1 | 163 04.9 | 34.9 | Venus | 200 47.1 | 13 07 |
| 23 | 309 28.3 | 147 59.7 | 23.7 | 134 01.4 | 46.1 | 252 10.0 | 59.1 | 178 07.1 | 34.8 | Mars | 185 41.0 | 14 06 |
| Mer. Pass. | h m 2 29.4 | v −0.4 | d 1.2 | v 1.0 | d 0.6 | v 2.2 | d 0.1 | v 2.1 | d 0.1 | Jupiter | 302 54.9 | 6 17 |
| | | | | | | | | | | Saturn | 228 53.9 | 11 13 |

## 1976 AUGUST 16, 17, 18 (MON., TUES., WED.)

| G.M.T. | ARIES | VENUS −3.3 | | MARS +1.9 | | JUPITER −2.0 | | SATURN +0.5 | | STARS | | |
|---|---|---|---|---|---|---|---|---|---|---|---|---|
| | G.H.A. | G.H.A. | Dec. | G.H.A. | Dec. | G.H.A. | Dec. | G.H.A. | Dec. | Name | S.H.A. | Dec. |
| d h | ° ′ | ° ′ | ° ′ | ° ′ | ° ′ | ° ′ | ° ′ | ° ′ | ° ′ | | ° ′ | ° ′ |
| 16 00 | 324 30.8 | 162 59.3 | N 9 22.5 | 149 02.4 | N 2 45.4 | 267 12.2 | N18 59.2 | 193 09.2 | N18 34.7 | Acamar | 315 39.3 | S40 23.6 |
| 01 | 339 33.3 | 177 58.9 | 21.3 | 164 03.5 | 44.8 | 282 14.4 | 59.2 | 208 11.3 | 34.6 | Achernar | 335 47.1 | S57 21.0 |
| 02 | 354 35.7 | 192 58.5 | 20.1 | 179 04.5 | 44.1 | 297 16.5 | 59.3 | 223 13.5 | 34.6 | Acrux | 173 40.7 | S62 58.4 |
| 03 | 9 38.2 | 207 58.1 | ·· 19.0 | 194 05.5 | ·· 43.5 | 312 18.7 | ·· 59.3 | 238 15.6 | ·· 34.5 | Adhara | 255 34.5 | S28 56.3 |
| 04 | 24 40.7 | 222 57.6 | 17.8 | 209 06.5 | 42.8 | 327 20.9 | 59.4 | 253 17.8 | 34.4 | Aldebaran | 291 21.2 | N16 27.7 |
| 05 | 39 43.1 | 237 57.2 | 16.6 | 224 07.5 | 42.2 | 342 23.1 | 59.4 | 268 19.9 | 34.3 | | | |
| 06 | 54 45.6 | 252 56.8 | N 9 15.4 | 239 08.6 | N 2 41.5 | 357 25.3 | N18 59.5 | 283 22.0 | N18 34.2 | Alioth | 166 45.3 | N56 05.4 |
| 07 | 69 48.0 | 267 56.4 | 14.2 | 254 09.6 | 40.9 | 12 27.5 | 59.6 | 298 24.2 | 34.2 | Alkaid | 153 20.9 | N49 26.0 |
| 08 | 84 50.5 | 282 56.0 | 13.0 | 269 10.6 | 40.2 | 27 29.7 | 59.6 | 313 26.3 | 34.1 | Al Na'ir | 28 17.9 | S47 04.3 |
| M 09 | 99 53.0 | 297 55.6 | ·· 11.9 | 284 11.6 | ·· 39.6 | 42 31.9 | ·· 59.7 | 328 28.5 | ·· 34.0 | Alnilam | 276 14.6 | S 1 12.9 |
| O 10 | 114 55.4 | 312 55.2 | 10.7 | 299 12.6 | 38.9 | 57 34.1 | 59.7 | 343 30.6 | 33.9 | Alphard | 218 23.6 | S 8 33.4 |
| N 11 | 129 57.9 | 327 54.8 | 09.5 | 314 13.6 | 38.3 | 72 36.3 | 59.8 | 358 32.8 | 33.9 | | | |
| D 12 | 145 00.4 | 342 54.3 | N 9 08.3 | 329 14.7 | N 2 37.6 | 87 38.4 | N18 59.8 | 13 34.9 | N18 33.8 | Alphecca | 126 34.4 | N26 47.8 |
| A 13 | 160 02.8 | 357 53.9 | 07.1 | 344 15.7 | 37.0 | 102 40.6 | 59.9 | 28 37.0 | 33.7 | Alpheratz | 358 11.8 | N28 57.8 |
| Y 14 | 175 05.3 | 12 53.5 | 05.9 | 359 16.7 | 36.3 | 117 42.8 | 18 59.9 | 43 39.2 | 33.6 | Altair | 62 34.9 | N 8 48.6 |
| 15 | 190 07.8 | 27 53.1 | ·· 04.7 | 14 17.7 | ·· 35.7 | 132 45.0 | 19 00.0 | 58 41.3 | ·· 33.5 | Ankaa | 353 42.7 | S42 25.7 |
| 16 | 205 10.2 | 42 52.7 | 03.6 | 29 18.7 | 35.0 | 147 47.2 | 00.0 | 73 43.5 | 33.5 | Antares | 113 00.1 | S26 22.8 |
| 17 | 220 12.7 | 57 52.3 | 02.4 | 44 19.8 | 34.4 | 162 49.4 | 00.1 | 88 45.6 | 33.4 | | | |
| 18 | 235 15.2 | 72 51.9 | N 9 01.2 | 59 20.8 | N 2 33.7 | 177 51.6 | N19 00.1 | 103 47.8 | N18 33.3 | Arcturus | 146 21.1 | N19 18.4 |
| 19 | 250 17.6 | 87 51.5 | 9 00.0 | 74 21.8 | 33.1 | 192 53.8 | 00.2 | 118 49.9 | 33.2 | Atria | 108 26.6 | S68 59.4 |
| 20 | 265 20.1 | 102 51.1 | 8 58.8 | 89 22.8 | 32.4 | 207 56.0 | 00.2 | 133 52.0 | 33.1 | Avior | 234 29.9 | S59 26.0 |
| 21 | 280 22.5 | 117 50.7 | ·· 57.6 | 104 23.8 | ·· 31.8 | 222 58.2 | ·· 00.3 | 148 54.2 | ·· 33.1 | Bellatrix | 279 01.8 | N 6 19.8 |
| 22 | 295 25.0 | 132 50.3 | 56.4 | 119 24.8 | 31.1 | 238 00.4 | 00.3 | 163 56.3 | 33.0 | Betelgeuse | 271 31.4 | N 7 24.2 |
| 23 | 310 27.5 | 147 49.8 | 55.2 | 134 25.9 | 30.5 | 253 02.6 | 00.4 | 178 58.5 | 32.9 | | | |
| 17 00 | 325 29.9 | 162 49.4 | N 8 54.0 | 149 26.9 | N 2 29.8 | 268 04.8 | N19 00.4 | 194 00.6 | N18 32.8 | Canopus | 264 08.8 | S52 40.8 |
| 01 | 340 32.4 | 177 49.0 | 52.9 | 164 27.9 | 29.2 | 283 07.0 | 00.5 | 209 02.7 | 32.7 | Capella | 281 15.5 | N45 58.3 |
| 02 | 355 34.9 | 192 48.6 | 51.7 | 179 28.9 | 28.5 | 298 09.2 | 00.5 | 224 04.9 | 32.7 | Deneb | 49 49.9 | N45 12.0 |
| 03 | 10 37.3 | 207 48.2 | ·· 50.5 | 194 29.9 | ·· 27.9 | 313 11.4 | ·· 00.6 | 239 07.0 | ·· 32.6 | Denebola | 183 02.1 | N14 42.2 |
| 04 | 25 39.8 | 222 47.8 | 49.3 | 209 30.9 | 27.2 | 328 13.6 | 00.6 | 254 09.2 | 32.5 | Diphda | 349 23.4 | S18 06.6 |
| 05 | 40 42.3 | 237 47.4 | 48.1 | 224 32.0 | 26.6 | 343 15.7 | 00.7 | 269 11.3 | 32.4 | | | |
| 06 | 55 44.7 | 252 47.0 | N 8 46.9 | 239 33.0 | N 2 25.9 | 358 17.9 | N19 00.7 | 284 13.5 | N18 32.3 | Dubhe | 194 26.2 | N61 52.7 |
| 07 | 70 47.2 | 267 46.6 | 45.7 | 254 34.0 | 25.3 | 13 20.1 | 00.8 | 299 15.6 | 32.3 | Elnath | 278 47.8 | N28 35.2 |
| T 08 | 85 49.6 | 282 46.2 | 44.5 | 269 35.0 | 24.6 | 28 22.3 | 00.8 | 314 17.7 | 32.2 | Eltanin | 90 58.7 | N51 29.9 |
| U 09 | 100 52.1 | 297 45.8 | ·· 43.3 | 284 36.0 | ·· 24.0 | 43 24.5 | ·· 00.9 | 329 19.9 | ·· 32.1 | Enif | 34 13.9 | N 9 46.3 |
| E 10 | 115 54.6 | 312 45.4 | 42.1 | 299 37.1 | 23.3 | 58 26.7 | 00.9 | 344 22.0 | 32.0 | Fomalhaut | 15 54.1 | S29 44.5 |
| S 11 | 130 57.0 | 327 45.0 | 40.9 | 314 38.1 | 22.6 | 73 28.9 | 01.0 | 359 24.2 | 32.0 | | | |
| D 12 | 145 59.5 | 342 44.6 | N 8 39.7 | 329 39.1 | N 2 22.0 | 88 31.1 | N19 01.0 | 14 26.3 | N18 31.9 | Gacrux | 172 32.1 | S56 59.1 |
| A 13 | 161 02.0 | 357 44.2 | 38.5 | 344 40.1 | 21.3 | 103 33.3 | 01.1 | 29 28.5 | 31.8 | Gienah | 176 21.0 | S17 24.8 |
| Y 14 | 176 04.4 | 12 43.8 | 37.3 | 359 41.1 | 20.7 | 118 35.5 | 01.1 | 44 30.6 | 31.7 | Hadar | 149 27.4 | S60 15.9 |
| 15 | 191 06.9 | 27 43.4 | ·· 36.1 | 14 42.1 | ·· 20.0 | 133 37.7 | ·· 01.2 | 59 32.7 | ·· 31.6 | Hamal | 328 31.9 | N23 21.1 |
| 16 | 206 09.4 | 42 43.0 | 34.9 | 29 43.2 | 19.4 | 148 39.9 | 01.2 | 74 34.9 | 31.6 | Kaus Aust. | 84 20.2 | S34 23.7 |
| 17 | 221 11.8 | 57 42.6 | 33.7 | 44 44.2 | 18.7 | 163 42.1 | 01.3 | 89 37.0 | 31.5 | | | |
| 18 | 236 14.3 | 72 42.2 | N 8 32.5 | 59 45.2 | N 2 18.1 | 178 44.3 | N19 01.3 | 104 39.2 | N18 31.4 | Kochab | 137 19.2 | N74 15.4 |
| 19 | 251 16.8 | 87 41.8 | 31.4 | 74 46.2 | 17.4 | 193 46.5 | 01.4 | 119 41.3 | 31.3 | Markab | 14 05.6 | N15 04.9 |
| 20 | 266 19.2 | 102 41.4 | 30.2 | 89 47.2 | 16.8 | 208 48.7 | 01.4 | 134 43.5 | 31.2 | Menkar | 314 43.9 | N 4 00.0 |
| 21 | 281 21.7 | 117 41.0 | ·· 29.0 | 104 48.2 | ·· 16.1 | 223 50.9 | ·· 01.5 | 149 45.6 | ·· 31.2 | Menkent | 148 40.4 | S36 15.4 |
| 22 | 296 24.1 | 132 40.6 | 27.8 | 119 49.3 | 15.5 | 238 53.1 | 01.5 | 164 47.7 | 31.1 | Miaplacidus | 221 46.4 | S69 37.3 |
| 23 | 311 26.6 | 147 40.2 | 26.6 | 134 50.3 | 14.8 | 253 55.3 | 01.6 | 179 49.9 | 31.0 | | | |
| 18 00 | 326 29.1 | 162 39.8 | N 8 25.4 | 149 51.3 | N 2 14.2 | 268 57.5 | N19 01.6 | 194 52.0 | N18 30.9 | Mirfak | 309 20.0 | N49 46.5 |
| 01 | 341 31.5 | 177 39.4 | 24.2 | 164 52.3 | 13.5 | 283 59.7 | 01.7 | 209 54.2 | 30.8 | Nunki | 76 32.3 | S26 19.5 |
| 02 | 356 34.0 | 192 39.0 | 23.0 | 179 53.3 | 12.9 | 299 01.9 | 01.7 | 224 56.3 | 30.8 | Peacock | 54 02.2 | S56 48.6 |
| 03 | 11 36.5 | 207 38.6 | ·· 21.8 | 194 54.3 | ·· 12.2 | 314 04.1 | ·· 01.8 | 239 58.5 | ·· 30.7 | Pollux | 244 01.8 | N28 04.9 |
| 04 | 26 38.9 | 222 38.2 | 20.6 | 209 55.3 | 11.6 | 329 06.3 | 01.8 | 255 00.6 | 30.6 | Procyon | 245 28.9 | N 5 17.1 |
| 05 | 41 41.4 | 237 37.8 | 19.3 | 224 56.4 | 10.9 | 344 08.5 | 01.9 | 270 02.7 | 30.5 | | | |
| 06 | 56 43.9 | 252 37.4 | N 8 18.1 | 239 57.4 | N 2 10.3 | 359 10.8 | N19 01.9 | 285 04.9 | N18 30.5 | Rasalhague | 96 32.0 | N12 34.8 |
| W 07 | 71 46.3 | 267 37.0 | 16.9 | 254 58.4 | 09.6 | 14 13.0 | 02.0 | 300 07.0 | 30.4 | Regulus | 208 13.2 | N12 04.9 |
| E 08 | 86 48.8 | 282 36.6 | 15.7 | 269 59.4 | 09.0 | 29 15.2 | 02.0 | 315 09.2 | 30.3 | Rigel | 281 38.8 | S 8 13.6 |
| D 09 | 101 51.3 | 297 36.2 | ·· 14.5 | 285 00.4 | ·· 08.3 | 44 17.4 | ·· 02.1 | 330 11.3 | ·· 30.2 | Rigil Kent. | 140 29.6 | S60 44.5 |
| N 10 | 116 53.7 | 312 35.8 | 13.3 | 300 01.4 | 07.6 | 59 19.6 | 02.1 | 345 13.5 | 30.1 | Sabik | 102 44.1 | S15 41.7 |
| E 11 | 131 56.2 | 327 35.4 | 12.1 | 315 02.5 | 07.0 | 74 21.8 | 02.2 | 0 15.6 | 30.1 | | | |
| S 12 | 146 58.6 | 342 35.0 | N 8 10.9 | 330 03.5 | N 2 06.3 | 89 24.0 | N19 02.2 | 15 17.8 | N18 30.0 | Schedar | 350 11.7 | N56 24.5 |
| D 13 | 162 01.1 | 357 34.6 | 09.7 | 345 04.5 | 05.7 | 104 26.2 | 02.3 | 30 19.9 | 29.9 | Shaula | 96 59.3 | S37 05.3 |
| A 14 | 177 03.6 | 12 34.2 | 08.5 | 0 05.5 | 05.0 | 119 28.4 | 02.3 | 45 22.0 | 29.8 | Sirius | 258 58.4 | S16 41.0 |
| Y 15 | 192 06.0 | 27 33.8 | ·· 07.3 | 15 06.5 | ·· 04.4 | 134 30.6 | ·· 02.4 | 60 24.2 | ·· 29.7 | Spica | 159 00.6 | S11 02.4 |
| 16 | 207 08.5 | 42 33.4 | 06.1 | 30 07.5 | 03.7 | 149 32.8 | 02.4 | 75 26.3 | 29.7 | Suhail | 223 13.2 | S43 20.3 |
| 17 | 222 11.0 | 57 33.0 | 04.9 | 45 08.6 | 03.1 | 164 35.0 | 02.4 | 90 28.5 | 29.6 | | | |
| 18 | 237 13.4 | 72 32.7 | N 8 03.7 | 60 09.6 | N 2 02.4 | 179 37.2 | N19 02.5 | 105 30.6 | N18 29.5 | Vega | 80 57.4 | N38 46.0 |
| 19 | 252 15.9 | 87 32.3 | 02.5 | 75 10.6 | 01.8 | 194 39.4 | 02.5 | 120 32.8 | 29.4 | Zuben'ubi | 137 36.1 | S15 56.7 |
| 20 | 267 18.4 | 102 31.9 | 01.3 | 90 11.6 | 01.1 | 209 41.6 | 02.6 | 135 34.9 | 29.3 | | S.H.A. | Mer. Pass. |
| 21 | 282 20.8 | 117 31.5 | 8 00.1 | 105 12.6 | 2 00.5 | 224 43.8 | ·· 02.6 | 150 37.0 | ·· 29.3 | | ° ′ | h m |
| 22 | 297 23.3 | 132 31.1 | 7 58.9 | 120 13.6 | 1 59.8 | 239 46.0 | 02.7 | 165 39.2 | 29.2 | Venus | 197 19.5 | 13 09 |
| 23 | 312 25.8 | 147 30.7 | 57.6 | 135 14.6 | 59.2 | 254 48.3 | 02.7 | 180 41.3 | 29.1 | Mars | 183 56.9 | 14 01 |
| Mer. Pass. | h m 2 17.6 | v −0.4 | d 1.2 | v 1.0 | d 0.7 | v 2.2 | d 0.0 | v 2.1 | d 0.1 | Jupiter | 302 34.8 | 6 07 |
| | | | | | | | | | | Saturn | 228 30.7 | 11 02 |

# 1976 AUGUST 16, 17, 18 (MON., TUES., WED.)

| G.M.T. d h | SUN G.H.A. | SUN Dec. | MOON G.H.A. | v | MOON Dec. | d | H.P. |
|---|---|---|---|---|---|---|---|
| 16 00 | 178 55.8 | N13 46.2 | 295 23.1 | 14.2 | N12 22.8 | 7.8 | 54.2 |
| 01 | 193 56.0 | 45.4 | 309 56.3 | 14.2 | 12 30.6 | 7.7 | 54.2 |
| 02 | 208 56.1 | 44.6 | 324 29.5 | 14.2 | 12 38.3 | 7.7 | 54.2 |
| 03 | 223 56.2 | · · 43.8 | 339 02.7 | 14.1 | 12 46.0 | 7.6 | 54.2 |
| 04 | 238 56.3 | 43.0 | 353 35.8 | 14.1 | 12 53.6 | 7.6 | 54.2 |
| 05 | 253 56.5 | 42.2 | 8 08.9 | 14.0 | 13 01.2 | 7.5 | 54.2 |
| 06 | 268 56.6 | N13 41.4 | 22 41.9 | 14.1 | N13 08.7 | 7.4 | 54.2 |
| 07 | 283 56.7 | 40.6 | 37 15.0 | 14.0 | 13 16.1 | 7.4 | 54.2 |
| 08 | 298 56.9 | 39.8 | 51 48.0 | 14.0 | 13 23.5 | 7.3 | 54.2 |
| M 09 | 313 57.0 | · · 39.0 | 66 21.0 | 13.9 | 13 30.8 | 7.3 | 54.2 |
| O 10 | 328 57.1 | 38.3 | 80 53.9 | 13.9 | 13 38.1 | 7.2 | 54.2 |
| N 11 | 343 57.2 | 37.5 | 95 26.8 | 13.9 | 13 45.3 | 7.2 | 54.2 |
| D 12 | 358 57.4 | N13 36.7 | 109 59.7 | 13.9 | N13 52.5 | 7.1 | 54.2 |
| A 13 | 13 57.5 | 35.9 | 124 32.6 | 13.8 | 13 59.6 | 7.0 | 54.2 |
| Y 14 | 28 57.6 | 35.1 | 139 05.4 | 13.8 | 14 06.6 | 7.0 | 54.2 |
| 15 | 43 57.8 | · · 34.3 | 153 38.2 | 13.8 | 14 13.6 | 6.9 | 54.2 |
| 16 | 58 57.9 | 33.5 | 168 11.0 | 13.7 | 14 20.5 | 6.9 | 54.2 |
| 17 | 73 58.0 | 32.7 | 182 43.7 | 13.7 | 14 27.4 | 6.8 | 54.2 |
| 18 | 88 58.2 | N13 31.9 | 197 16.4 | 13.7 | N14 34.2 | 6.7 | 54.2 |
| 19 | 103 58.3 | 31.1 | 211 49.1 | 13.6 | 14 40.9 | 6.7 | 54.2 |
| 20 | 118 58.4 | 30.3 | 226 21.7 | 13.6 | 14 47.6 | 6.6 | 54.3 |
| 21 | 133 58.6 | · · 29.5 | 240 54.3 | 13.6 | 14 54.2 | 6.5 | 54.3 |
| 22 | 148 58.7 | 28.7 | 255 26.9 | 13.5 | 15 00.7 | 6.5 | 54.3 |
| 23 | 163 58.8 | 27.9 | 269 59.4 | 13.5 | 15 07.2 | 6.4 | 54.3 |
| 17 00 | 178 59.0 | N13 27.1 | 284 31.9 | 13.4 | N15 13.6 | 6.4 | 54.3 |
| 01 | 193 59.1 | 26.3 | 299 04.3 | 13.5 | 15 20.0 | 6.3 | 54.3 |
| 02 | 208 59.2 | 25.5 | 313 36.8 | 13.3 | 15 26.3 | 6.2 | 54.3 |
| 03 | 223 59.4 | · · 24.7 | 328 09.1 | 13.4 | 15 32.5 | 6.1 | 54.3 |
| 04 | 238 59.5 | 23.9 | 342 41.5 | 13.3 | 15 38.6 | 6.1 | 54.3 |
| 05 | 253 59.6 | 23.1 | 357 13.8 | 13.3 | 15 44.7 | 6.0 | 54.3 |
| 06 | 268 59.8 | N13 22.3 | 11 46.1 | 13.2 | N15 50.7 | 6.0 | 54.3 |
| 07 | 283 59.9 | 21.5 | 26 18.3 | 13.2 | 15 56.7 | 5.8 | 54.3 |
| 08 | 299 00.0 | 20.7 | 40 50.5 | 13.2 | 16 02.5 | 5.8 | 54.3 |
| T 09 | 314 00.2 | · · 19.9 | 55 22.7 | 13.1 | 16 08.3 | 5.8 | 54.3 |
| U 10 | 329 00.3 | 19.1 | 69 54.8 | 13.1 | 16 14.1 | 5.7 | 54.3 |
| E 11 | 344 00.4 | 18.3 | 84 26.9 | 13.1 | 16 19.8 | 5.6 | 54.3 |
| S 12 | 359 00.6 | N13 17.5 | 98 59.0 | 13.0 | N16 25.4 | 5.5 | 54.4 |
| D 13 | 14 00.7 | 16.7 | 113 31.0 | 13.0 | 16 30.9 | 5.4 | 54.4 |
| A 14 | 29 00.8 | 15.9 | 128 03.0 | 12.9 | 16 36.3 | 5.4 | 54.4 |
| Y 15 | 44 01.0 | · · 15.1 | 142 34.9 | 12.9 | 16 41.7 | 5.3 | 54.4 |
| 16 | 59 01.1 | 14.3 | 157 06.8 | 12.8 | 16 47.0 | 5.3 | 54.4 |
| 17 | 74 01.2 | 13.5 | 171 38.6 | 12.9 | 16 52.3 | 5.1 | 54.4 |
| 18 | 89 01.4 | N13 12.7 | 186 10.5 | 12.7 | N16 57.4 | 5.1 | 54.4 |
| 19 | 104 01.5 | 11.9 | 200 42.2 | 12.8 | 17 02.5 | 5.0 | 54.4 |
| 20 | 119 01.6 | 11.1 | 215 14.0 | 12.7 | 17 07.5 | 5.0 | 54.4 |
| 21 | 134 01.8 | · · 10.3 | 229 45.7 | 12.6 | 17 12.5 | 4.8 | 54.4 |
| 22 | 149 01.9 | 09.5 | 244 17.3 | 12.7 | 17 17.3 | 4.8 | 54.5 |
| 23 | 164 02.1 | 08.7 | 258 49.0 | 12.5 | 17 22.1 | 4.7 | 54.5 |
| 18 00 | 179 02.2 | N13 07.9 | 273 20.5 | 12.6 | N17 26.8 | 4.6 | 54.5 |
| 01 | 194 02.3 | 07.1 | 287 52.1 | 12.5 | 17 31.4 | 4.6 | 54.5 |
| 02 | 209 02.5 | 06.3 | 302 23.6 | 12.4 | 17 36.0 | 4.5 | 54.5 |
| 03 | 224 02.6 | · · 05.5 | 316 55.0 | 12.4 | 17 40.5 | 4.4 | 54.5 |
| 04 | 239 02.7 | 04.6 | 331 26.4 | 12.4 | 17 44.9 | 4.3 | 54.5 |
| 05 | 254 02.9 | 03.8 | 345 57.8 | 12.4 | 17 49.2 | 4.2 | 54.5 |
| 06 | 269 03.0 | N13 03.0 | 0 29.2 | 12.2 | N17 53.4 | 4.2 | 54.6 |
| 07 | 284 03.2 | 02.2 | 15 00.4 | 12.3 | 17 57.6 | 4.0 | 54.6 |
| W 08 | 299 03.3 | 01.4 | 29 31.7 | 12.2 | 18 01.6 | 4.0 | 54.6 |
| E 09 | 314 03.4 | 13 00.6 | 44 02.9 | 12.2 | 18 05.6 | 3.9 | 54.6 |
| D 10 | 329 03.6 | 12 59.8 | 58 34.1 | 12.1 | 18 09.5 | 3.9 | 54.6 |
| N 11 | 344 03.7 | 59.0 | 73 05.2 | 12.1 | 18 13.4 | 3.7 | 54.6 |
| E 12 | 359 03.9 | N12 58.2 | 87 36.3 | 12.0 | N18 17.1 | 3.7 | 54.7 |
| S 13 | 14 04.0 | 57.4 | 102 07.3 | 12.0 | 18 20.8 | 3.6 | 54.7 |
| D 14 | 29 04.1 | 56.6 | 116 38.3 | 12.0 | 18 24.4 | 3.5 | 54.7 |
| A 15 | 44 04.3 | · · 55.7 | 131 09.3 | 11.9 | 18 27.9 | 3.4 | 54.7 |
| Y 16 | 59 04.4 | 54.9 | 145 40.2 | 11.9 | 18 31.3 | 3.3 | 54.7 |
| 17 | 74 04.6 | 54.1 | 160 11.1 | 11.9 | 18 34.6 | 3.2 | 54.7 |
| 18 | 89 04.7 | N12 53.3 | 174 42.0 | 11.8 | N18 37.8 | 3.2 | 54.8 |
| 19 | 104 04.9 | 52.5 | 189 12.8 | 11.7 | 18 41.0 | 3.1 | 54.8 |
| 20 | 119 05.0 | 51.7 | 203 43.5 | 11.7 | 18 44.1 | 2.9 | 54.8 |
| 21 | 134 05.1 | · · 50.9 | 218 14.2 | 11.7 | 18 47.0 | 2.9 | 54.8 |
| 22 | 149 05.3 | 50.0 | 232 44.9 | 11.6 | 18 49.9 | 2.9 | 54.8 |
| 23 | 164 05.4 | 49.2 | 247 15.5 | 11.6 | 18 52.8 | 2.7 | 54.8 |
| | S.D. 15.8 | d 0.8 | S.D. 14.8 | | 14.8 | | 14.9 |

| Lat. | Twilight Naut. | Twilight Civil | Sunrise | Moonrise 16 | Moonrise 17 | Moonrise 18 | Moonrise 19 |
|---|---|---|---|---|---|---|---|
| N 72 | //// | //// | 02 38 | 19 20 | 18 58 | □ | □ |
| N 70 | //// | 00 58 | 03 06 | 19 50 | 19 50 | 19 53 | 20 11 |
| 68 | //// | 01 58 | 03 28 | 20 13 | 20 22 | 20 39 | 21 12 |
| 66 | //// | 02 31 | 03 44 | 20 30 | 20 46 | 21 10 | 21 47 |
| 64 | 00 51 | 02 55 | 03 58 | 20 45 | 21 05 | 21 32 | 22 12 |
| 62 | 01 45 | 03 13 | 04 09 | 20 57 | 21 20 | 21 50 | 22 32 |
| 60 | 02 15 | 03 28 | 04 19 | 21 08 | 21 33 | 22 05 | 22 48 |
| N 58 | 02 37 | 03 41 | 04 27 | 21 17 | 21 44 | 22 18 | 23 01 |
| 56 | 02 54 | 03 52 | 04 35 | 21 25 | 21 54 | 22 29 | 23 13 |
| 54 | 03 09 | 04 01 | 04 41 | 21 32 | 22 02 | 22 39 | 23 23 |
| 52 | 03 21 | 04 09 | 04 47 | 21 38 | 22 10 | 22 48 | 23 32 |
| 50 | 03 32 | 04 17 | 04 52 | 21 44 | 22 17 | 22 55 | 23 41 |
| 45 | 03 53 | 04 32 | 05 04 | 21 56 | 22 32 | 23 12 | 23 58 |
| N 40 | 04 10 | 04 44 | 05 13 | 22 07 | 22 44 | 23 26 | 24 12 |
| 35 | 04 23 | 04 55 | 05 21 | 22 16 | 22 54 | 23 37 | 24 25 |
| 30 | 04 34 | 05 03 | 05 28 | 22 24 | 23 04 | 23 47 | 24 35 |
| 20 | 04 51 | 05 18 | 05 40 | 22 37 | 23 20 | 24 05 | 00 05 |
| N 10 | 05 04 | 05 29 | 05 51 | 22 49 | 23 34 | 24 20 | 00 20 |
| 0 | 05 15 | 05 39 | 06 01 | 23 00 | 23 47 | 24 34 | 00 34 |
| S 10 | 05 24 | 05 49 | 06 10 | 23 12 | 24 00 | 00 00 | 00 49 |
| 20 | 05 32 | 05 58 | 06 20 | 23 24 | 24 14 | 00 14 | 01 04 |
| 30 | 05 39 | 06 07 | 06 32 | 23 38 | 24 30 | 00 30 | 01 22 |
| 35 | 05 42 | 06 12 | 06 38 | 23 46 | 24 39 | 00 39 | 01 32 |
| 40 | 05 46 | 06 18 | 06 45 | 23 55 | 24 50 | 00 50 | 01 44 |
| 45 | 05 49 | 06 24 | 06 54 | 24 06 | 00 06 | 01 03 | 01 58 |
| S 50 | 05 53 | 06 31 | 07 04 | 24 19 | 00 19 | 01 18 | 02 15 |
| 52 | 05 54 | 06 34 | 07 09 | 24 25 | 00 25 | 01 26 | 02 23 |
| 54 | 05 56 | 06 37 | 07 14 | 24 32 | 00 32 | 01 34 | 02 32 |
| 56 | 05 58 | 06 41 | 07 20 | 24 40 | 00 40 | 01 43 | 02 42 |
| 58 | 05 59 | 06 45 | 07 27 | 24 48 | 00 48 | 01 53 | 02 54 |
| S 60 | 06 01 | 06 50 | 07 34 | 24 58 | 00 58 | 02 05 | 03 07 |

| Lat. | Sunset | Twilight Civil | Twilight Naut. | Moonset 16 | Moonset 17 | Moonset 18 | Moonset 19 |
|---|---|---|---|---|---|---|---|
| N 72 | 21 26 | //// | //// | 14 05 | 16 01 | □ | □ |
| N 70 | 20 58 | 22 57 | //// | 13 35 | 15 10 | 16 45 | 18 09 |
| 68 | 20 38 | 22 04 | //// | 13 14 | 14 39 | 15 59 | 17 09 |
| 66 | 20 21 | 21 33 | //// | 12 57 | 14 15 | 15 30 | 16 34 |
| 64 | 20 08 | 21 10 | 23 05 | 12 43 | 13 57 | 15 07 | 16 09 |
| 62 | 19 57 | 20 52 | 22 18 | 12 31 | 13 42 | 14 49 | 15 49 |
| 60 | 19 48 | 20 38 | 21 50 | 12 21 | 13 30 | 14 35 | 15 33 |
| N 58 | 19 39 | 20 25 | 21 28 | 12 13 | 13 19 | 14 22 | 15 20 |
| 56 | 19 32 | 20 15 | 21 11 | 12 05 | 13 10 | 14 11 | 15 08 |
| 54 | 19 26 | 20 05 | 20 57 | 11 59 | 13 02 | 14 02 | 14 58 |
| 52 | 19 20 | 19 57 | 20 45 | 11 53 | 12 54 | 13 53 | 14 49 |
| 50 | 19 15 | 19 50 | 20 35 | 11 47 | 12 48 | 13 46 | 14 41 |
| 45 | 19 03 | 19 35 | 20 14 | 11 36 | 12 33 | 13 29 | 14 23 |
| N 40 | 18 54 | 19 23 | 19 58 | 11 26 | 12 22 | 13 16 | 14 09 |
| 35 | 18 46 | 19 13 | 19 45 | 11 18 | 12 12 | 13 05 | 13 57 |
| 30 | 18 39 | 19 04 | 19 34 | 11 11 | 12 03 | 12 55 | 13 47 |
| 20 | 18 27 | 18 50 | 19 17 | 10 58 | 11 48 | 12 38 | 13 29 |
| N 10 | 18 17 | 18 39 | 19 04 | 10 47 | 11 35 | 12 23 | 13 13 |
| 0 | 18 07 | 18 29 | 18 53 | 10 37 | 11 22 | 12 09 | 12 58 |
| S 10 | 17 58 | 18 19 | 18 44 | 10 27 | 11 10 | 11 56 | 12 43 |
| 20 | 17 48 | 18 10 | 18 37 | 10 16 | 10 57 | 11 41 | 12 28 |
| 30 | 17 37 | 18 01 | 18 29 | 10 04 | 10 42 | 11 24 | 12 10 |
| 35 | 17 30 | 17 56 | 18 26 | 09 57 | 10 34 | 11 14 | 11 59 |
| 40 | 17 23 | 17 51 | 18 23 | 09 49 | 10 24 | 11 03 | 11 47 |
| 45 | 17 15 | 17 45 | 18 19 | 09 39 | 10 12 | 10 50 | 11 33 |
| S 50 | 17 04 | 17 38 | 18 16 | 09 28 | 09 58 | 10 34 | 11 16 |
| 52 | 17 00 | 17 35 | 18 14 | 09 23 | 09 52 | 10 26 | 11 07 |
| 54 | 16 54 | 17 31 | 18 13 | 09 17 | 09 45 | 10 18 | 10 58 |
| 56 | 16 49 | 17 28 | 18 12 | 09 11 | 09 37 | 10 09 | 10 48 |
| 58 | 16 42 | 17 24 | 18 10 | 09 03 | 09 28 | 09 58 | 10 36 |
| S 60 | 16 35 | 17 19 | 18 08 | 08 55 | 09 18 | 09 46 | 10 23 |

| Day | SUN Eqn. of Time 00h | SUN Eqn. of Time 12h | SUN Mer. Pass. | MOON Mer. Pass. Upper | MOON Mer. Pass. Lower | Age | Phase |
|---|---|---|---|---|---|---|---|
| | m s | m s | h m | h m | h m | d | |
| 16 | 04 17 | 04 11 | 12 04 | 04 26 | 16 49 | 20 | ◑ |
| 17 | 04 04 | 03 58 | 12 04 | 05 11 | 17 35 | 21 | |
| 18 | 03 51 | 03 45 | 12 04 | 05 58 | 18 22 | 22 | |

# 1976 AUGUST 25, 26, 27 (WED., THURS., FRI.)

| G.M.T. d h | ARIES G.H.A. | VENUS −3.3 G.H.A. | VENUS Dec. | MARS +1.9 G.H.A. | MARS Dec. | JUPITER −2.1 G.H.A. | JUPITER Dec. | SATURN +0.6 G.H.A. | SATURN Dec. |
|---|---|---|---|---|---|---|---|---|---|
| 25 00 | 333 23.0 | 161 36.7 | N 4 58.9 | 152 41.1 | N 0 24.0 | 275 11.6 | N19 08.9 | 200 52.7 | N18 17.7 |
| 01 | 348 25.5 | 176 36.4 | 57.6 | 167 42.1 | 23.3 | 290 13.9 | 09.0 | 215 54.9 | 17.6 |
| 02 | 3 28.0 | 191 36.0 | 56.4 | 182 43.1 | 22.7 | 305 16.1 | 09.0 | 230 57.0 | 17.5 |
| 03 | 18 30.4 | 206 35.7 | · · 55.1 | 197 44.1 | · · 22.0 | 320 18.4 | · · 09.0 | 245 59.2 | · · 17.5 |
| 04 | 33 32.9 | 221 35.3 | 53.9 | 212 45.1 | 21.4 | 335 20.6 | 09.1 | 261 01.3 | 17.4 |
| 05 | 48 35.4 | 236 34.9 | 52.6 | 227 46.1 | 20.7 | 350 22.9 | 09.1 | 276 03.5 | 17.3 |
| 06 | 63 37.8 | 251 34.6 | N 4 51.4 | 242 47.1 | N 0 20.0 | 5 25.1 | N19 09.2 | 291 05.6 | N18 17.2 |
| 07 | 78 40.3 | 266 34.2 | 50.1 | 257 48.1 | 19.4 | 20 27.4 | 09.2 | 306 07.8 | 17.1 |
| W 08 | 93 42.8 | 281 33.9 | 48.8 | 272 49.1 | 18.7 | 35 29.7 | 09.2 | 321 09.9 | 17.1 |
| E 09 | 108 45.2 | 296 33.5 | · · 47.6 | 287 50.1 | · · 18.1 | 50 31.9 | · · 09.3 | 336 12.1 | · · 17.0 |
| D 10 | 123 47.7 | 311 33.2 | 46.3 | 302 51.1 | 17.4 | 65 34.2 | 09.3 | 351 14.2 | 16.9 |
| N 11 | 138 50.2 | 326 32.8 | 45.1 | 317 52.2 | 16.7 | 80 36.4 | 09.3 | 6 16.4 | 16.8 |
| E 12 | 153 52.6 | 341 32.5 | N 4 43.8 | 332 53.2 | N 0 16.1 | 95 38.7 | N19 09.4 | 21 18.5 | N18 16.7 |
| S 13 | 168 55.1 | 356 32.1 | 42.6 | 347 54.2 | 15.4 | 110 40.9 | 09.4 | 36 20.7 | 16.7 |
| D 14 | 183 57.5 | 11 31.8 | 41.3 | 2 55.2 | 14.8 | 125 43.2 | 09.4 | 51 22.8 | 16.6 |
| A 15 | 199 00.0 | 26 31.4 | · · 40.1 | 17 56.2 | · · 14.1 | 140 45.4 | · · 09.5 | 66 25.0 | · · 16.5 |
| Y 16 | 214 02.5 | 41 31.1 | 38.8 | 32 57.2 | 13.4 | 155 47.7 | 09.5 | 81 27.1 | 16.4 |
| 17 | 229 04.9 | 56 30.7 | 37.5 | 47 58.2 | 12.8 | 170 50.0 | 09.6 | 96 29.3 | 16.4 |
| 18 | 244 07.4 | 71 30.4 | N 4 36.3 | 62 59.2 | N 0 12.1 | 185 52.2 | N19 09.6 | 111 31.5 | N18 16.3 |
| 19 | 259 09.9 | 86 30.0 | 35.0 | 78 00.2 | 11.5 | 200 54.5 | 09.6 | 126 33.6 | 16.2 |
| 20 | 274 12.3 | 101 29.7 | 33.8 | 93 01.2 | 10.8 | 215 56.7 | 09.7 | 141 35.8 | 16.1 |
| 21 | 289 14.8 | 116 29.3 | · · 32.5 | 108 02.2 | · · 10.1 | 230 59.0 | · · 09.7 | 156 37.9 | · · 16.0 |
| 22 | 304 17.3 | 131 29.0 | 31.2 | 123 03.2 | 09.5 | 246 01.2 | 09.7 | 171 40.1 | 16.0 |
| 23 | 319 19.7 | 146 28.6 | 30.0 | 138 04.2 | 08.8 | 261 03.5 | 09.8 | 186 42.2 | 15.9 |
| 26 00 | 334 22.2 | 161 28.3 | N 4 28.7 | 153 05.2 | N 0 08.2 | 276 05.8 | N19 09.8 | 201 44.4 | N18 15.8 |
| 01 | 349 24.6 | 176 27.9 | 27.5 | 168 06.2 | 07.5 | 291 08.0 | 09.9 | 216 46.5 | 15.7 |
| 02 | 4 27.1 | 191 27.6 | 26.2 | 183 07.2 | 06.9 | 306 10.3 | 09.9 | 231 48.7 | 15.7 |
| 03 | 19 29.6 | 206 27.2 | · · 24.9 | 198 08.2 | · · 06.2 | 321 12.5 | · · 09.9 | 246 50.8 | · · 15.6 |
| 04 | 34 32.0 | 221 26.9 | 23.7 | 213 09.2 | 05.5 | 336 14.8 | 10.0 | 261 53.0 | 15.5 |
| 05 | 49 34.5 | 236 26.5 | 22.4 | 228 10.2 | 04.9 | 351 17.1 | 10.0 | 276 55.1 | 15.4 |
| 06 | 64 37.0 | 251 26.2 | N 4 21.2 | 243 11.2 | N 0 04.2 | 6 19.3 | N19 10.0 | 291 57.3 | N18 15.3 |
| 07 | 79 39.4 | 266 25.8 | 19.9 | 258 12.2 | 03.6 | 21 21.6 | 10.1 | 306 59.4 | 15.3 |
| T 08 | 94 41.9 | 281 25.5 | 18.6 | 273 13.2 | 02.9 | 36 23.9 | 10.1 | 322 01.6 | 15.2 |
| H 09 | 109 44.4 | 296 25.1 | · · 17.4 | 288 14.2 | · · 02.2 | 51 26.1 | · · 10.1 | 337 03.7 | · · 15.1 |
| U 10 | 124 46.8 | 311 24.8 | 16.1 | 303 15.2 | 01.6 | 66 28.4 | 10.2 | 352 05.9 | 15.0 |
| R 11 | 139 49.3 | 326 24.4 | 14.9 | 318 16.2 | 00.9 | 81 30.6 | 10.2 | 7 08.0 | 14.9 |
| S 12 | 154 51.8 | 341 24.1 | N 4 13.6 | 333 17.2 | N 0 00.3 | 96 32.9 | N19 10.2 | 22 10.2 | N18 14.9 |
| D 13 | 169 54.2 | 356 23.7 | 12.3 | 348 18.2 | S 0 00.4 | 111 35.2 | 10.3 | 37 12.4 | 14.8 |
| A 14 | 184 56.7 | 11 23.4 | 11.1 | 3 19.2 | 01.1 | 126 37.4 | 10.3 | 52 14.5 | 14.7 |
| Y 15 | 199 59.1 | 26 23.0 | · · 09.8 | 18 20.2 | · · 01.7 | 141 39.7 | · · 10.3 | 67 16.7 | · · 14.6 |
| 16 | 215 01.6 | 41 22.7 | 08.6 | 33 21.2 | 02.4 | 156 42.0 | 10.4 | 82 18.8 | 14.6 |
| 17 | 230 04.1 | 56 22.3 | 07.3 | 48 22.2 | 03.0 | 171 44.2 | 10.4 | 97 21.0 | 14.5 |
| 18 | 245 06.5 | 71 22.0 | N 4 06.0 | 63 23.2 | S 0 03.7 | 186 46.5 | N19 10.5 | 112 23.1 | N18 14.4 |
| 19 | 260 09.0 | 86 21.6 | 04.8 | 78 24.2 | 04.4 | 201 48.8 | 10.5 | 127 25.3 | 14.3 |
| 20 | 275 11.5 | 101 21.3 | 03.5 | 93 25.2 | 05.0 | 216 51.0 | 10.5 | 142 27.4 | 14.2 |
| 21 | 290 13.9 | 116 20.9 | · · 02.2 | 108 26.2 | · · 05.7 | 231 53.3 | · · 10.6 | 157 29.6 | · · 14.2 |
| 22 | 305 16.4 | 131 20.6 | 4 01.0 | 123 27.3 | 06.3 | 246 55.6 | 10.6 | 172 31.7 | 14.1 |
| 23 | 320 18.9 | 146 20.2 | 3 59.7 | 138 28.3 | 07.0 | 261 57.8 | 10.6 | 187 33.9 | 14.0 |
| 27 00 | 335 21.3 | 161 19.9 | N 3 58.4 | 153 29.3 | S 0 07.7 | 277 00.1 | N19 10.7 | 202 36.0 | N18 13.9 |
| 01 | 350 23.8 | 176 19.5 | 57.2 | 168 30.3 | 08.3 | 292 02.4 | 10.7 | 217 38.2 | 13.9 |
| 02 | 5 26.3 | 191 19.2 | 55.9 | 183 31.3 | 09.0 | 307 04.6 | 10.7 | 232 40.3 | 13.8 |
| 03 | 20 28.7 | 206 18.9 | · · 54.7 | 198 32.3 | · · 09.6 | 322 06.9 | · · 10.8 | 247 42.5 | · · 13.7 |
| 04 | 35 31.2 | 221 18.5 | 53.4 | 213 33.3 | 10.3 | 337 09.2 | 10.8 | 262 44.7 | 13.6 |
| 05 | 50 33.6 | 236 18.2 | 52.1 | 228 34.3 | 11.0 | 352 11.4 | 10.8 | 277 46.8 | 13.5 |
| 06 | 65 36.1 | 251 17.8 | N 3 50.9 | 243 35.3 | S 0 11.6 | 7 13.7 | N19 10.9 | 292 49.0 | N18 13.5 |
| 07 | 80 38.6 | 266 17.5 | 49.6 | 258 36.3 | 12.3 | 22 16.0 | 10.9 | 307 51.1 | 13.4 |
| 08 | 95 41.0 | 281 17.1 | 48.3 | 273 37.3 | 12.9 | 37 18.2 | 10.9 | 322 53.3 | 13.3 |
| F 09 | 110 43.5 | 296 16.8 | · · 47.1 | 288 38.3 | · · 13.6 | 52 20.5 | · · 11.0 | 337 55.4 | · · 13.2 |
| R 10 | 125 46.0 | 311 16.4 | 45.8 | 303 39.3 | 14.3 | 67 22.8 | 11.0 | 352 57.6 | 13.2 |
| I 11 | 140 48.4 | 326 16.1 | 44.5 | 318 40.3 | 14.9 | 82 25.0 | 11.0 | 7 59.7 | 13.1 |
| D 12 | 155 50.9 | 341 15.8 | N 3 43.3 | 333 41.3 | S 0 15.6 | 97 27.3 | N19 11.1 | 23 01.9 | N18 13.0 |
| A 13 | 170 53.4 | 356 15.4 | 42.0 | 348 42.3 | 16.2 | 112 29.6 | 11.1 | 38 04.0 | 12.9 |
| Y 14 | 185 55.8 | 11 15.1 | 40.7 | 3 43.3 | 16.9 | 127 31.9 | 11.1 | 53 06.2 | 12.8 |
| 15 | 200 58.3 | 26 14.7 | · · 39.5 | 18 44.3 | · · 17.6 | 142 34.1 | · · 11.2 | 68 08.4 | · · 12.8 |
| 16 | 216 00.7 | 41 14.4 | 38.2 | 33 45.3 | 18.2 | 157 36.4 | 11.2 | 83 10.5 | 12.7 |
| 17 | 231 03.2 | 56 14.0 | 36.9 | 48 46.3 | 18.9 | 172 38.7 | 11.2 | 98 12.7 | 12.6 |
| 18 | 246 05.7 | 71 13.7 | N 3 35.7 | 63 47.3 | S 0 19.5 | 187 40.9 | N19 11.3 | 113 14.8 | N18 12.5 |
| 19 | 261 08.1 | 86 13.3 | 34.4 | 78 48.3 | 20.2 | 202 43.2 | 11.3 | 128 17.0 | 12.5 |
| 20 | 276 10.6 | 101 13.0 | 33.1 | 93 49.3 | 20.9 | 217 45.5 | 11.3 | 143 19.1 | 12.4 |
| 21 | 291 13.1 | 116 12.7 | · · 31.9 | 108 50.3 | · · 21.5 | 232 47.8 | · · 11.4 | 158 21.3 | · · 12.3 |
| 22 | 306 15.5 | 131 12.3 | 30.6 | 123 51.3 | 22.2 | 247 50.0 | 11.4 | 173 23.4 | 12.2 |
| 23 | 321 18.0 | 146 12.0 | 29.3 | 138 52.3 | 22.9 | 262 52.3 | 11.4 | 188 25.6 | 12.1 |
| Mer. Pass. | 1h 42.2m | v −0.3 | d 1.3 | v 1.0 | d 0.7 | v 2.3 | d 0.0 | v 2.2 | d 0.1 |

## STARS

| Name | S.H.A. | Dec. |
|---|---|---|
| Acamar | 315 39.2 | S40 23.6 |
| Achernar | 335 47.0 | S57 21.0 |
| Acrux | 173 40.8 | S62 58.4 |
| Adhara | 255 34.5 | S28 56.3 |
| Aldebaran | 291 21.2 | N16 27.8 |
| Alioth | 166 45.4 | N56 05.4 |
| Alkaid | 153 21.0 | N49 26.0 |
| Al Na'ir | 28 17.9 | S47 04.3 |
| Alnilam | 276 14.5 | S 1 12.9 |
| Alphard | 218 23.5 | S 8 33.4 |
| Alphecca | 126 34.5 | N26 47.8 |
| Alpheratz | 358 11.8 | N28 57.8 |
| Altair | 62 34.9 | N 8 48.6 |
| Ankaa | 353 42.6 | S42 25.7 |
| Antares | 113 00.2 | S26 22.8 |
| Arcturus | 146 21.1 | N19 18.4 |
| Atria | 108 26.7 | S68 59.4 |
| Avior | 234 29.8 | S59 26.0 |
| Bellatrix | 279 01.8 | N 6 19.8 |
| Betelgeuse | 271 31.4 | N 7 24.2 |
| Canopus | 264 08.7 | S52 40.8 |
| Capella | 281 15.4 | N45 58.3 |
| Deneb | 49 49.9 | N45 12.1 |
| Denebola | 183 02.1 | N14 42.2 |
| Diphda | 349 23.3 | S18 06.6 |
| Dubhe | 194 26.2 | N61 52.7 |
| Elnath | 278 47.7 | N28 35.2 |
| Eltanin | 90 58.8 | N51 29.9 |
| Enif | 34 13.9 | N 9 46.3 |
| Fomalhaut | 15 54.1 | S29 44.5 |
| Gacrux | 172 32.2 | S56 59.1 |
| Gienah | 176 21.0 | S17 24.7 |
| Hadar | 149 27.5 | S60 15.8 |
| Hamal | 328 31.8 | N23 21.2 |
| Kaus Aust. | 84 20.2 | S34 23.8 |
| Kochab | 137 19.3 | N74 15.4 |
| Markab | 14 05.5 | N15 05.0 |
| Menkar | 314 43.9 | N 4 00.0 |
| Menkent | 148 40.4 | S36 15.4 |
| Miaplacidus | 221 46.3 | S69 37.3 |
| Mirfak | 309 19.9 | N49 46.6 |
| Nunki | 76 32.3 | S26 19.5 |
| Peacock | 54 02.2 | S56 48.6 |
| Pollux | 244 01.8 | N28 04.9 |
| Procyon | 245 28.9 | N 5 17.1 |
| Rasalhague | 96 32.0 | N12 34.9 |
| Regulus | 208 13.2 | N12 04.9 |
| Rigel | 281 38.7 | S 8 13.6 |
| Rigil Kent. | 140 29.7 | S60 44.5 |
| Sabik | 102 44.2 | S15 41.7 |
| Schedar | 350 11.6 | N56 24.5 |
| Shaula | 96 59.3 | S37 05.3 |
| Sirius | 258 58.3 | S16 41.0 |
| Spica | 159 00.6 | S11 02.3 |
| Suhail | 223 13.2 | S43 20.3 |
| Vega | 80 57.4 | N38 46.0 |
| Zuben'ubi | 137 36.1 | S15 56.7 |

| | S.H.A. | Mer. Pass. |
|---|---|---|
| Venus | 187 06.1 | 13 14 |
| Mars | 178 43.0 | 13 47 |
| Jupiter | 301 43.6 | 5 35 |
| Saturn | 227 22.2 | 10 32 |

# 1976 AUGUST 25, 26, 27 (WED., THURS., FRI.)

| G.M.T. d | h | SUN G.H.A. ° ′ | SUN Dec. ° ′ | MOON G.H.A. ° ′ | $v$ ′ | MOON Dec. ° ′ | $d$ ′ | H.P. ′ |
|---|---|---|---|---|---|---|---|---|
| 25 | 00 | 179 28.1 | N10 47.6 | 186 56.9 | 9.3 | N 8 26.3 | 10.8 | 59.1 |
| | 01 | 194 28.3 | 46.7 | 201 25.2 | 9.2 | 8 15.5 | 10.8 | 59.2 |
| | 02 | 209 28.5 | 45.9 | 215 53.4 | 9.3 | 8 04.7 | 11.0 | 59.2 |
| | 03 | 224 28.7 | ·· 45.0 | 230 21.7 | 9.3 | 7 53.7 | 10.9 | 59.2 |
| | 04 | 239 28.8 | 44.1 | 244 50.0 | 9.3 | 7 42.8 | 11.1 | 59.2 |
| | 05 | 254 29.0 | 43.3 | 259 18.3 | 9.3 | 7 31.7 | 11.0 | 59.3 |
| | 06 | 269 29.2 | N10 42.4 | 273 46.6 | 9.3 | N 7 20.7 | 11.2 | 59.3 |
| W | 07 | 284 29.3 | 41.5 | 288 14.9 | 9.3 | 7 09.5 | 11.2 | 59.3 |
| E | 08 | 299 29.5 | 40.7 | 302 43.2 | 9.3 | 6 58.3 | 11.2 | 59.3 |
| D | 09 | 314 29.7 | ·· 39.8 | 317 11.5 | 9.3 | 6 47.1 | 11.3 | 59.4 |
| N | 10 | 329 29.9 | 38.9 | 331 39.8 | 9.3 | 6 35.8 | 11.3 | 59.4 |
| E | 11 | 344 30.0 | 38.1 | 346 08.1 | 9.3 | 6 24.5 | 11.4 | 59.4 |
| S | 12 | 359 30.2 | N10 37.2 | 0 36.4 | 9.3 | N 6 13.1 | 11.4 | 59.4 |
| D | 13 | 14 30.4 | 36.3 | 15 04.7 | 9.3 | 6 01.7 | 11.5 | 59.4 |
| A | 14 | 29 30.5 | 35.5 | 29 33.0 | 9.3 | 5 50.2 | 11.5 | 59.5 |
| Y | 15 | 44 30.7 | ·· 34.6 | 44 01.3 | 9.3 | 5 38.7 | 11.5 | 59.5 |
| | 16 | 59 30.9 | 33.7 | 58 29.6 | 9.2 | 5 27.2 | 11.6 | 59.5 |
| | 17 | 74 31.1 | 32.9 | 72 57.8 | 9.3 | 5 15.6 | 11.6 | 59.5 |
| | 18 | 89 31.2 | N10 32.0 | 87 26.1 | 9.3 | N 5 04.0 | 11.7 | 59.6 |
| | 19 | 104 31.4 | 31.1 | 101 54.4 | 9.3 | 4 52.3 | 11.7 | 59.6 |
| | 20 | 119 31.6 | 30.3 | 116 22.7 | 9.2 | 4 40.6 | 11.7 | 59.6 |
| | 21 | 134 31.8 | ·· 29.4 | 130 50.9 | 9.3 | 4 28.9 | 11.8 | 59.6 |
| | 22 | 149 31.9 | 28.5 | 145 19.2 | 9.3 | 4 17.1 | 11.8 | 59.6 |
| | 23 | 164 32.1 | 27.7 | 159 47.5 | 9.2 | 4 05.3 | 11.8 | 59.7 |
| 26 | 00 | 179 32.3 | N10 26.8 | 174 15.7 | 9.3 | N 3 53.5 | 11.9 | 59.7 |
| | 01 | 194 32.5 | 25.9 | 188 44.0 | 9.2 | 3 41.6 | 11.9 | 59.7 |
| | 02 | 209 32.6 | 25.1 | 203 12.2 | 9.2 | 3 29.7 | 11.9 | 59.7 |
| | 03 | 224 32.8 | ·· 24.2 | 217 40.4 | 9.3 | 3 17.8 | 11.9 | 59.7 |
| | 04 | 239 33.0 | 23.3 | 232 08.7 | 9.2 | 3 05.9 | 12.0 | 59.7 |
| | 05 | 254 33.2 | 22.5 | 246 36.9 | 9.2 | 2 53.9 | 12.0 | 59.8 |
| | 06 | 269 33.3 | N10 21.6 | 261 05.1 | 9.2 | N 2 41.9 | 12.0 | 59.8 |
| | 07 | 284 33.5 | 20.7 | 275 33.3 | 9.2 | 2 29.9 | 12.0 | 59.8 |
| T | 08 | 299 33.7 | 19.8 | 290 01.5 | 9.2 | 2 17.9 | 12.1 | 59.8 |
| H | 09 | 314 33.9 | ·· 19.0 | 304 29.7 | 9.2 | 2 05.8 | 12.1 | 59.8 |
| U | 10 | 329 34.0 | 18.1 | 318 57.9 | 9.2 | 1 53.7 | 12.1 | 59.8 |
| R | 11 | 344 34.2 | 17.2 | 333 26.1 | 9.2 | 1 41.6 | 12.1 | 59.9 |
| S | 12 | 359 34.4 | N10 16.4 | 347 54.3 | 9.1 | N 1 29.5 | 12.1 | 59.9 |
| D | 13 | 14 34.6 | 15.5 | 2 22.4 | 9.2 | 1 17.4 | 12.1 | 59.9 |
| A | 14 | 29 34.7 | 14.6 | 16 50.6 | 9.1 | 1 05.3 | 12.2 | 59.9 |
| Y | 15 | 44 34.9 | ·· 13.7 | 31 18.7 | 9.2 | 0 53.1 | 12.1 | 59.9 |
| | 16 | 59 35.1 | 12.9 | 45 46.9 | 9.1 | 0 41.0 | 12.2 | 59.9 |
| | 17 | 74 35.3 | 12.0 | 60 15.0 | 9.1 | 0 28.8 | 12.1 | 59.9 |
| | 18 | 89 35.5 | N10 11.1 | 74 43.1 | 9.1 | N 0 16.7 | 12.2 | 60.0 |
| | 19 | 104 35.6 | 10.2 | 89 11.2 | 9.1 | N 0 04.5 | 12.2 | 60.0 |
| | 20 | 119 35.8 | 09.4 | 103 39.3 | 9.1 | S 0 07.7 | 12.2 | 60.0 |
| | 21 | 134 36.0 | ·· 08.5 | 118 07.4 | 9.0 | 0 19.9 | 12.2 | 60.0 |
| | 22 | 149 36.2 | 07.6 | 132 35.4 | 9.1 | 0 32.1 | 12.1 | 60.0 |
| | 23 | 164 36.3 | 06.7 | 147 03.5 | 9.0 | 0 44.2 | 12.2 | 60.0 |
| 27 | 00 | 179 36.5 | N10 05.9 | 161 31.5 | 9.0 | S 0 56.4 | 12.2 | 60.0 |
| | 01 | 194 36.7 | 05.0 | 175 59.5 | 9.1 | 1 08.6 | 12.2 | 60.0 |
| | 02 | 209 36.9 | 04.1 | 190 27.6 | 8.9 | 1 20.8 | 12.1 | 60.0 |
| | 03 | 224 37.1 | ·· 03.2 | 204 55.5 | 9.0 | 1 32.9 | 12.2 | 60.0 |
| | 04 | 239 37.2 | 02.4 | 219 23.5 | 9.0 | 1 45.1 | 12.2 | 60.1 |
| | 05 | 254 37.4 | 01.5 | 233 51.5 | 8.9 | 1 57.3 | 12.1 | 60.1 |
| | 06 | 269 37.6 | N10 00.6 | 248 19.4 | 9.0 | S 2 09.4 | 12.1 | 60.1 |
| | 07 | 284 37.8 | 9 59.7 | 262 47.4 | 8.9 | 2 21.5 | 12.2 | 60.1 |
| | 08 | 299 38.0 | 58.9 | 277 15.3 | 8.9 | 2 33.7 | 12.1 | 60.1 |
| F | 09 | 314 38.1 | ·· 58.0 | 291 43.2 | 8.9 | 2 45.8 | 12.1 | 60.1 |
| R | 10 | 329 38.3 | 57.1 | 306 11.1 | 8.8 | 2 57.9 | 12.0 | 60.1 |
| I | 11 | 344 38.5 | 56.2 | 320 38.9 | 8.9 | 3 09.9 | 12.1 | 60.1 |
| D | 12 | 359 38.7 | N 9 55.3 | 335 06.8 | 8.8 | S 3 22.0 | 12.0 | 60.1 |
| A | 13 | 14 38.9 | 54.5 | 349 34.6 | 8.8 | 3 34.0 | 12.1 | 60.1 |
| Y | 14 | 29 39.0 | 53.6 | 4 02.4 | 8.8 | 3 46.1 | 12.0 | 60.1 |
| | 15 | 44 39.2 | ·· 52.7 | 18 30.2 | 8.7 | 3 58.1 | 11.9 | 60.1 |
| | 16 | 59 39.4 | 51.8 | 32 57.9 | 8.8 | 4 10.0 | 12.0 | 60.1 |
| | 17 | 74 39.6 | 50.9 | 47 25.7 | 8.7 | 4 22.0 | 11.9 | 60.1 |
| | 18 | 89 39.8 | N 9 50.1 | 61 53.4 | 8.7 | S 4 33.9 | 11.9 | 60.1 |
| | 19 | 104 39.9 | 49.2 | 76 21.1 | 8.7 | 4 45.8 | 11.9 | 60.1 |
| | 20 | 119 40.1 | 48.3 | 90 48.8 | 8.7 | 4 57.7 | 11.8 | 60.1 |
| | 21 | 134 40.3 | ·· 47.4 | 105 16.5 | 8.6 | 5 09.5 | 11.8 | 60.1 |
| | 22 | 149 40.5 | 46.5 | 119 44.1 | 8.6 | 5 21.3 | 11.8 | 60.1 |
| | 23 | 164 40.7 | 45.7 | 134 11.7 | 8.6 | 5 33.1 | 11.7 | 60.1 |
| | | S.D. 15.9 | $d$ 0.9 | S.D. 16.2 | | 16.3 | | 16.4 |

| Lat. | Twilight Naut. | Twilight Civil | Sunrise | Moonrise 25 | 26 | 27 | 28 |
|---|---|---|---|---|---|---|---|
| ° | h m | h m | h m | h m | h m | h m | h m |
| N 72 | //// | 01 39 | 03 30 | 04 05 | 06 05 | 08 05 | 10 08 |
| N 70 | //// | 02 23 | 03 49 | 04 16 | 06 08 | 08 01 | 09 56 |
| 68 | //// | 02 51 | 04 03 | 04 26 | 06 11 | 07 58 | 09 46 |
| 66 | 01 25 | 03 12 | 04 15 | 04 34 | 06 14 | 07 55 | 09 38 |
| 64 | 02 04 | 03 29 | 04 25 | 04 40 | 06 16 | 07 53 | 09 31 |
| 62 | 02 31 | 03 42 | 04 33 | 04 46 | 06 18 | 07 51 | 09 25 |
| 60 | 02 50 | 03 54 | 04 40 | 04 51 | 06 19 | 07 49 | 09 20 |
| N 58 | 03 06 | 04 03 | 04 47 | 04 55 | 06 21 | 07 48 | 09 15 |
| 56 | 03 19 | 04 12 | 04 52 | 04 59 | 06 22 | 07 47 | 09 12 |
| 54 | 03 31 | 04 19 | 04 57 | 05 02 | 06 23 | 07 45 | 09 08 |
| 52 | 03 40 | 04 26 | 05 02 | 05 05 | 06 24 | 07 44 | 09 05 |
| 50 | 03 49 | 04 31 | 05 06 | 05 08 | 06 25 | 07 43 | 09 02 |
| 45 | 04 06 | 04 44 | 05 15 | 05 14 | 06 27 | 07 41 | 08 56 |
| N 40 | 04 20 | 04 54 | 05 22 | 05 19 | 06 29 | 07 39 | 08 51 |
| 35 | 04 31 | 05 02 | 05 28 | 05 23 | 06 30 | 07 38 | 08 46 |
| 30 | 04 40 | 05 09 | 05 34 | 05 27 | 06 31 | 07 37 | 08 42 |
| 20 | 04 54 | 05 20 | 05 43 | 05 34 | 06 34 | 07 34 | 08 36 |
| N 10 | 05 05 | 05 30 | 05 51 | 05 40 | 06 36 | 07 32 | 08 30 |
| 0 | 05 13 | 05 37 | 05 58 | 05 45 | 06 38 | 07 31 | 08 24 |
| S 10 | 05 20 | 05 45 | 06 06 | 05 50 | 06 39 | 07 29 | 08 19 |
| 20 | 05 25 | 05 51 | 06 13 | 05 56 | 06 42 | 07 27 | 08 13 |
| 30 | 05 30 | 05 58 | 06 22 | 06 03 | 06 44 | 07 25 | 08 07 |
| 35 | 05 32 | 06 02 | 06 27 | 06 07 | 06 45 | 07 24 | 08 03 |
| 40 | 05 34 | 06 05 | 06 33 | 06 11 | 06 47 | 07 22 | 07 59 |
| 45 | 05 35 | 06 09 | 06 39 | 06 16 | 06 48 | 07 21 | 07 54 |
| S 50 | 05 37 | 06 14 | 06 47 | 06 22 | 06 50 | 07 19 | 07 48 |
| 52 | 05 37 | 06 16 | 06 50 | 06 24 | 06 51 | 07 18 | 07 46 |
| 54 | 05 37 | 06 18 | 06 54 | 06 27 | 06 52 | 07 17 | 07 43 |
| 56 | 05 38 | 06 21 | 06 59 | 06 31 | 06 54 | 07 16 | 07 40 |
| 58 | 05 38 | 06 23 | 07 03 | 06 34 | 06 55 | 07 15 | 07 36 |
| S 60 | 05 38 | 06 26 | 07 09 | 06 38 | 06 56 | 07 14 | 07 32 |

| Lat. | Sunset | Twilight Civil | Twilight Naut. | Moonset 25 | 26 | 27 | 28 |
|---|---|---|---|---|---|---|---|
| ° | h m | h m | h m | h m | h m | h m | h m |
| N 72 | 20 29 | 22 16 | //// | 19 11 | 19 02 | 18 53 | 18 43 |
| N 70 | 20 12 | 21 36 | //// | 19 05 | 19 02 | 19 00 | 18 57 |
| 68 | 19 57 | 21 08 | //// | 18 59 | 19 02 | 19 05 | 19 09 |
| 66 | 19 46 | 20 48 | 22 30 | 18 55 | 19 02 | 19 10 | 19 19 |
| 64 | 19 37 | 20 32 | 21 54 | 18 51 | 19 02 | 19 14 | 19 27 |
| 62 | 19 29 | 20 19 | 21 29 | 18 48 | 19 02 | 19 17 | 19 34 |
| 60 | 19 21 | 20 08 | 21 10 | 18 45 | 19 03 | 19 20 | 19 40 |
| N 58 | 19 15 | 19 59 | 20 55 | 18 42 | 19 03 | 19 23 | 19 45 |
| 56 | 19 10 | 19 50 | 20 42 | 18 40 | 19 03 | 19 25 | 19 50 |
| 54 | 19 05 | 19 43 | 20 31 | 18 38 | 19 03 | 19 28 | 19 54 |
| 52 | 19 01 | 19 37 | 20 22 | 18 36 | 19 03 | 19 30 | 19 58 |
| 50 | 18 57 | 19 31 | 20 13 | 18 34 | 19 03 | 19 31 | 20 02 |
| 45 | 18 48 | 19 19 | 19 56 | 18 30 | 19 03 | 19 35 | 20 10 |
| N 40 | 18 41 | 19 09 | 19 43 | 18 27 | 19 03 | 19 39 | 20 16 |
| 35 | 18 35 | 19 01 | 19 32 | 18 24 | 19 03 | 19 42 | 20 22 |
| 30 | 18 29 | 18 54 | 19 23 | 18 22 | 19 03 | 19 44 | 20 27 |
| 20 | 18 20 | 18 43 | 19 09 | 18 18 | 19 03 | 19 48 | 20 35 |
| N 10 | 18 12 | 18 34 | 18 59 | 18 14 | 19 03 | 19 52 | 20 43 |
| 0 | 18 05 | 18 26 | 18 50 | 18 10 | 19 03 | 19 56 | 20 50 |
| S 10 | 17 58 | 18 19 | 18 44 | 18 06 | 19 03 | 20 00 | 20 57 |
| 20 | 17 50 | 18 13 | 18 38 | 18 02 | 19 03 | 20 03 | 21 05 |
| 30 | 17 42 | 18 06 | 18 34 | 17 58 | 19 02 | 20 08 | 21 14 |
| 35 | 17 37 | 18 02 | 18 32 | 17 55 | 19 02 | 20 10 | 21 19 |
| 40 | 17 31 | 17 59 | 18 30 | 17 52 | 19 02 | 20 13 | 21 24 |
| 45 | 17 25 | 17 55 | 18 29 | 17 48 | 19 02 | 20 17 | 21 31 |
| S 50 | 17 17 | 17 50 | 18 28 | 17 44 | 19 02 | 20 21 | 21 39 |
| 52 | 17 14 | 17 48 | 18 28 | 17 42 | 19 02 | 20 22 | 21 43 |
| 54 | 17 10 | 17 46 | 18 27 | 17 40 | 19 02 | 20 24 | 21 47 |
| 56 | 17 06 | 17 44 | 18 27 | 17 38 | 19 02 | 20 27 | 21 51 |
| 58 | 17 01 | 17 41 | 18 27 | 17 35 | 19 02 | 20 29 | 21 56 |
| S 60 | 16 56 | 17 39 | 18 27 | 17 32 | 19 02 | 20 32 | 22 02 |

| Day | SUN Eqn. of Time 00ʰ | SUN Eqn. of Time 12ʰ | SUN Mer. Pass. | MOON Mer. Pass. Upper | MOON Mer. Pass. Lower | Age | Phase |
|---|---|---|---|---|---|---|---|
| | m s | m s | h m | h m | h m | d | |
| 25 | 02 08 | 02 00 | 12 02 | 11 57 | 24 24 | 00 | ● |
| 26 | 01 51 | 01 43 | 12 02 | 12 50 | 00 24 | 01 | |
| 27 | 01 34 | 01 26 | 12 01 | 13 43 | 01 17 | 02 | |

# 1976 AUGUST 28, 29, 30 (SAT., SUN., MON.)

| G.M.T. d | h | SUN G.H.A. ° ′ | SUN Dec. ° ′ | MOON G.H.A. ° ′ | $v$ ′ | MOON Dec. ° ′ | $d$ ′ | H.P. ′ |
|---|---|---|---|---|---|---|---|---|
| 28 | 00 | 179 40.8 | N 9 44.8 | 148 39.3 | 8.6 | S 5 44.8 | 11.7 | 60.1 |
| | 01 | 194 41.0 | 43.9 | 163 06.9 | 8.6 | 5 56.5 | 11.7 | 60.2 |
| | 02 | 209 41.2 | 43.0 | 177 34.5 | 8.5 | 6 08.2 | 11.6 | 60.2 |
| | 03 | 224 41.4 | ·· 42.1 | 192 02.0 | 8.5 | 6 19.8 | 11.6 | 60.2 |
| | 04 | 239 41.6 | 41.2 | 206 29.5 | 8.5 | 6 31.4 | 11.5 | 60.2 |
| | 05 | 254 41.8 | 40.4 | 220 57.0 | 8.4 | 6 42.9 | 11.5 | 60.1 |
| | 06 | 269 41.9 | N 9 39.5 | 235 24.4 | 8.5 | S 6 54.4 | 11.5 | 60.1 |
| | 07 | 284 42.1 | 38.6 | 249 51.9 | 8.4 | 7 05.9 | 11.4 | 60.1 |
| S | 08 | 299 42.3 | 37.7 | 264 19.3 | 8.3 | 7 17.3 | 11.3 | 60.1 |
| A | 09 | 314 42.5 | ·· 36.8 | 278 46.6 | 8.4 | 7 28.6 | 11.3 | 60.1 |
| T | 10 | 329 42.7 | 35.9 | 293 14.0 | 8.3 | 7 39.9 | 11.3 | 60.1 |
| U | 11 | 344 42.9 | 35.1 | 307 41.3 | 8.3 | 7 51.2 | 11.2 | 60.1 |
| R | 12 | 359 43.1 | N 9 34.2 | 322 08.6 | 8.3 | S 8 02.4 | 11.2 | 60.1 |
| D | 13 | 14 43.2 | 33.3 | 336 35.9 | 8.3 | 8 13.6 | 11.1 | 60.1 |
| A | 14 | 29 43.4 | 32.4 | 351 03.2 | 8.2 | 8 24.7 | 11.0 | 60.1 |
| Y | 15 | 44 43.6 | ·· 31.5 | 5 30.4 | 8.2 | 8 35.7 | 11.0 | 60.1 |
| | 16 | 59 43.8 | 30.6 | 19 57.6 | 8.2 | 8 46.7 | 11.0 | 60.1 |
| | 17 | 74 44.0 | 29.7 | 34 24.8 | 8.1 | 8 57.7 | 10.9 | 60.1 |
| | 18 | 89 44.2 | N 9 28.9 | 48 51.9 | 8.1 | S 9 08.6 | 10.8 | 60.1 |
| | 19 | 104 44.3 | 28.0 | 63 19.0 | 8.1 | 9 19.4 | 10.7 | 60.1 |
| | 20 | 119 44.5 | 27.1 | 77 46.1 | 8.1 | 9 30.1 | 10.7 | 60.1 |
| | 21 | 134 44.7 | ·· 26.2 | 92 13.2 | 8.0 | 9 40.8 | 10.7 | 60.1 |
| | 22 | 149 44.9 | 25.3 | 106 40.2 | 8.0 | 9 51.5 | 10.5 | 60.1 |
| | 23 | 164 45.1 | 24.4 | 121 07.2 | 8.0 | 10 02.0 | 10.5 | 60.1 |
| 29 | 00 | 179 45.3 | N 9 23.5 | 135 34.2 | 8.0 | S10 12.5 | 10.5 | 60.1 |
| | 01 | 194 45.5 | 22.6 | 150 01.2 | 7.9 | 10 23.0 | 10.3 | 60.1 |
| | 02 | 209 45.6 | 21.7 | 164 28.1 | 7.9 | 10 33.3 | 10.3 | 60.1 |
| | 03 | 224 45.8 | ·· 20.9 | 178 55.0 | 7.9 | 10 43.6 | 10.3 | 60.0 |
| | 04 | 239 46.0 | 20.0 | 193 21.9 | 7.8 | 10 53.9 | 10.1 | 60.0 |
| | 05 | 254 46.2 | 19.1 | 207 48.7 | 7.8 | 11 04.0 | 10.1 | 60.0 |
| | 06 | 269 46.4 | N 9 18.2 | 222 15.5 | 7.8 | S11 14.1 | 10.0 | 60.0 |
| | 07 | 284 46.6 | 17.3 | 236 42.3 | 7.8 | 11 24.1 | 9.9 | 60.0 |
| | 08 | 299 46.8 | 16.4 | 251 09.1 | 7.7 | 11 34.0 | 9.9 | 60.0 |
| S | 09 | 314 47.0 | ·· 15.5 | 265 35.8 | 7.7 | 11 43.9 | 9.7 | 60.0 |
| U | 10 | 329 47.1 | 14.6 | 280 02.5 | 7.7 | 11 53.6 | 9.7 | 60.0 |
| N | 11 | 344 47.3 | 13.7 | 294 29.2 | 7.6 | 12 03.3 | 9.7 | 60.0 |
| D | 12 | 359 47.5 | N 9 12.8 | 308 55.8 | 7.6 | S12 13.0 | 9.5 | 60.0 |
| A | 13 | 14 47.7 | 12.0 | 323 22.4 | 7.6 | 12 22.5 | 9.4 | 59.9 |
| Y | 14 | 29 47.9 | 11.1 | 337 49.0 | 7.6 | 12 31.9 | 9.4 | 59.9 |
| | 15 | 44 48.1 | ·· 10.2 | 352 15.6 | 7.5 | 12 41.3 | 9.3 | 59.9 |
| | 16 | 59 48.3 | 09.3 | 6 42.1 | 7.5 | 12 50.6 | 9.2 | 59.9 |
| | 17 | 74 48.5 | 08.4 | 21 08.6 | 7.5 | 12 59.8 | 9.1 | 59.9 |
| | 18 | 89 48.7 | N 9 07.5 | 35 35.1 | 7.5 | S13 08.9 | 9.0 | 59.9 |
| | 19 | 104 48.8 | 06.6 | 50 01.6 | 7.4 | 13 17.9 | 8.9 | 59.9 |
| | 20 | 119 49.0 | 05.7 | 64 28.0 | 7.4 | 13 26.8 | 8.9 | 59.9 |
| | 21 | 134 49.2 | ·· 04.8 | 78 54.4 | 7.4 | 13 35.7 | 8.7 | 59.9 |
| | 22 | 149 49.4 | 03.9 | 93 20.8 | 7.3 | 13 44.4 | 8.7 | 59.8 |
| | 23 | 164 49.6 | 03.0 | 107 47.1 | 7.3 | 13 53.1 | 8.5 | 59.8 |
| 30 | 00 | 179 49.8 | N 9 02.1 | 122 13.4 | 7.3 | S14 01.6 | 8.5 | 59.8 |
| | 01 | 194 50.0 | 01.2 | 136 39.7 | 7.3 | 14 10.1 | 8.4 | 59.8 |
| | 02 | 209 50.2 | 9 00.3 | 151 06.0 | 7.2 | 14 18.5 | 8.3 | 59.8 |
| | 03 | 224 50.4 | 8 59.4 | 165 32.2 | 7.2 | 14 26.8 | 8.1 | 59.8 |
| | 04 | 239 50.5 | 58.5 | 179 58.4 | 7.2 | 14 34.9 | 8.1 | 59.8 |
| | 05 | 254 50.7 | 57.7 | 194 24.6 | 7.2 | 14 43.0 | 8.0 | 59.7 |
| | 06 | 269 50.9 | N 8 56.8 | 208 50.8 | 7.2 | S14 51.0 | 7.9 | 59.7 |
| | 07 | 284 51.1 | 55.9 | 223 17.0 | 7.1 | 14 58.9 | 7.8 | 59.7 |
| | 08 | 299 51.3 | 55.0 | 237 43.1 | 7.1 | 15 06.7 | 7.7 | 59.7 |
| M | 09 | 314 51.5 | ·· 54.1 | 252 09.2 | 7.0 | 15 14.4 | 7.6 | 59.7 |
| O | 10 | 329 51.7 | 53.2 | 266 35.2 | 7.1 | 15 22.0 | 7.4 | 59.7 |
| N | 11 | 344 51.9 | 52.3 | 281 01.3 | 7.0 | 15 29.4 | 7.4 | 59.6 |
| D | 12 | 359 52.1 | N 8 51.4 | 295 27.3 | 7.0 | S15 36.8 | 7.3 | 59.6 |
| A | 13 | 14 52.3 | 50.5 | 309 53.3 | 7.0 | 15 44.1 | 7.1 | 59.6 |
| Y | 14 | 29 52.5 | 49.6 | 324 19.3 | 7.0 | 15 51.2 | 7.1 | 59.6 |
| | 15 | 44 52.7 | ·· 48.7 | 338 45.3 | 6.9 | 15 58.3 | 7.0 | 59.6 |
| | 16 | 59 52.8 | 47.8 | 353 11.2 | 7.0 | 16 05.3 | 6.8 | 59.6 |
| | 17 | 74 53.0 | 46.9 | 7 37.2 | 6.9 | 16 12.1 | 6.7 | 59.5 |
| | 18 | 89 53.2 | N 8 46.0 | 22 03.1 | 6.9 | S16 18.8 | 6.7 | 59.5 |
| | 19 | 104 53.4 | 45.1 | 36 29.0 | 6.8 | 16 25.5 | 6.5 | 59.5 |
| | 20 | 119 53.6 | 44.2 | 50 54.8 | 6.9 | 16 32.0 | 6.4 | 59.5 |
| | 21 | 134 53.8 | ·· 43.3 | 65 20.7 | 6.8 | 16 38.4 | 6.3 | 59.5 |
| | 22 | 149 54.0 | 42.4 | 79 46.5 | 6.9 | 16 44.7 | 6.2 | 59.5 |
| | 23 | 164 54.2 | 41.5 | 94 12.4 | 6.8 | 16 50.9 | 6.0 | 59.4 |
| | | S.D. 15.9 | $d$ 0.9 | S.D. 16.4 | | 16.3 | | 16.2 |

| Lat. | Twilight Naut. | Twilight Civil | Sunrise | Moonrise 28 | 29 | 30 | 31 |
|---|---|---|---|---|---|---|---|
| ° | h m | h m | h m | h m | h m | h m | h m |
| N 72 | //// | 02 07 | 03 46 | 10 08 | 12 16 | 14 34 | ■ |
| N 70 | //// | 02 42 | 04 02 | 09 56 | 11 52 | 13 50 | 15 47 |
| 68 | 00 55 | 03 06 | 04 15 | 09 46 | 11 34 | 13 21 | 15 01 |
| 66 | 01 50 | 03 24 | 04 25 | 09 38 | 11 20 | 12 59 | 14 31 |
| 64 | 02 21 | 03 39 | 04 34 | 09 31 | 11 08 | 12 42 | 14 09 |
| 62 | 02 43 | 03 51 | 04 41 | 09 25 | 10 58 | 12 28 | 13 51 |
| 60 | 03 01 | 04 02 | 04 48 | 09 20 | 10 50 | 12 16 | 13 36 |
| N 58 | 03 15 | 04 11 | 04 53 | 09 15 | 10 42 | 12 06 | 13 24 |
| 56 | 03 27 | 04 18 | 04 58 | 09 12 | 10 36 | 11 57 | 13 13 |
| 54 | 03 38 | 04 25 | 05 03 | 09 08 | 10 30 | 11 49 | 13 03 |
| 52 | 03 47 | 04 31 | 05 07 | 09 05 | 10 25 | 11 42 | 12 55 |
| 50 | 03 54 | 04 36 | 05 10 | 09 02 | 10 20 | 11 36 | 12 47 |
| 45 | 04 11 | 04 48 | 05 18 | 08 56 | 10 10 | 11 22 | 12 31 |
| N 40 | 04 23 | 04 57 | 05 25 | 08 51 | 10 01 | 11 11 | 12 18 |
| 35 | 04 33 | 05 04 | 05 30 | 08 46 | 09 54 | 11 02 | 12 07 |
| 30 | 04 42 | 05 11 | 05 35 | 08 42 | 09 48 | 10 53 | 11 57 |
| 20 | 04 55 | 05 21 | 05 44 | 08 36 | 09 37 | 10 39 | 11 40 |
| N 10 | 05 05 | 05 30 | 05 51 | 08 30 | 09 28 | 10 26 | 11 25 |
| 0 | 05 12 | 05 37 | 05 58 | 08 24 | 09 19 | 10 15 | 11 12 |
| S 10 | 05 18 | 05 43 | 06 04 | 08 19 | 09 10 | 10 03 | 10 58 |
| 20 | 05 23 | 05 49 | 06 11 | 08 13 | 09 01 | 09 51 | 10 44 |
| 30 | 05 27 | 05 55 | 06 19 | 08 07 | 08 51 | 09 37 | 10 27 |
| 35 | 05 28 | 05 58 | 06 23 | 08 03 | 08 45 | 09 29 | 10 18 |
| 40 | 05 29 | 06 01 | 06 28 | 07 59 | 08 38 | 09 20 | 10 07 |
| 45 | 05 30 | 06 04 | 06 34 | 07 54 | 08 30 | 09 09 | 09 54 |
| S 50 | 05 31 | 06 08 | 06 41 | 07 48 | 08 20 | 08 57 | 09 38 |
| 52 | 05 31 | 06 10 | 06 44 | 07 46 | 08 16 | 08 51 | 09 31 |
| 54 | 05 31 | 06 12 | 06 47 | 07 43 | 08 11 | 08 44 | 09 23 |
| 56 | 05 30 | 06 13 | 06 51 | 07 40 | 08 06 | 08 37 | 09 14 |
| 58 | 05 30 | 06 15 | 06 55 | 07 36 | 08 00 | 08 29 | 09 04 |
| S 60 | 05 30 | 06 18 | 07 00 | 07 32 | 07 54 | 08 19 | 08 52 |

| Lat. | Sunset | Twilight Civil | Twilight Naut. | Moonset 28 | 29 | 30 | 31 |
|---|---|---|---|---|---|---|---|
| ° | h m | h m | h m | h m | h m | h m | h m |
| N 72 | 20 12 | 21 48 | //// | 18 43 | 18 30 | 18 10 | ■ |
| N 70 | 19 57 | 21 15 | //// | 18 57 | 18 55 | 18 54 | 18 57 |
| 68 | 19 45 | 20 52 | 22 54 | 19 09 | 19 15 | 19 24 | 19 43 |
| 66 | 19 35 | 20 34 | 22 06 | 19 19 | 19 30 | 19 47 | 20 13 |
| 64 | 19 26 | 20 20 | 21 37 | 19 27 | 19 43 | 20 05 | 20 36 |
| 62 | 19 19 | 20 08 | 21 15 | 19 34 | 19 54 | 20 19 | 20 54 |
| 60 | 19 13 | 19 58 | 20 58 | 19 40 | 20 03 | 20 32 | 21 09 |
| N 58 | 19 07 | 19 50 | 20 44 | 19 45 | 20 11 | 20 43 | 21 22 |
| 56 | 19 02 | 19 42 | 20 33 | 19 50 | 20 18 | 20 52 | 21 33 |
| 54 | 18 58 | 19 35 | 20 22 | 19 54 | 20 25 | 21 00 | 21 43 |
| 52 | 18 54 | 19 30 | 20 14 | 19 58 | 20 30 | 21 08 | 21 52 |
| 50 | 18 50 | 19 24 | 20 06 | 20 02 | 20 36 | 21 14 | 22 00 |
| 45 | 18 43 | 19 13 | 19 50 | 20 10 | 20 47 | 21 29 | 22 16 |
| N 40 | 18 36 | 19 04 | 19 37 | 20 16 | 20 57 | 21 41 | 22 30 |
| 35 | 18 31 | 18 57 | 19 27 | 20 22 | 21 05 | 21 51 | 22 42 |
| 30 | 18 26 | 18 50 | 19 19 | 20 27 | 21 12 | 22 00 | 22 52 |
| 20 | 18 18 | 18 40 | 19 06 | 20 35 | 21 24 | 22 16 | 23 09 |
| N 10 | 18 11 | 18 32 | 18 57 | 20 43 | 21 35 | 22 29 | 23 25 |
| 0 | 18 04 | 18 25 | 18 49 | 20 50 | 21 45 | 22 42 | 23 39 |
| S 10 | 17 58 | 18 19 | 18 43 | 20 57 | 21 56 | 22 55 | 23 53 |
| 20 | 17 51 | 18 13 | 18 39 | 21 05 | 22 07 | 23 08 | 24 08 |
| 30 | 17 43 | 18 07 | 18 35 | 21 14 | 22 19 | 23 24 | 24 26 |
| 35 | 17 39 | 18 05 | 18 34 | 21 19 | 22 26 | 23 33 | 24 36 |
| 40 | 17 34 | 18 01 | 18 33 | 21 24 | 22 35 | 23 43 | 24 48 |
| 45 | 17 28 | 17 58 | 18 32 | 21 31 | 22 44 | 23 55 | 25 02 |
| S 50 | 17 22 | 17 55 | 18 32 | 21 39 | 22 56 | 24 10 | 00 10 |
| 52 | 17 19 | 17 53 | 18 32 | 21 43 | 23 02 | 24 17 | 00 17 |
| 54 | 17 15 | 17 51 | 18 32 | 21 47 | 23 08 | 24 25 | 00 25 |
| 56 | 17 12 | 17 49 | 18 33 | 21 51 | 23 14 | 24 33 | 00 33 |
| 58 | 17 07 | 17 47 | 18 33 | 21 56 | 23 22 | 24 43 | 00 43 |
| S 60 | 17 03 | 17 45 | 18 34 | 22 02 | 23 31 | 24 54 | 00 54 |

| Day | SUN Eqn. of Time 00ʰ | SUN Eqn. of Time 12ʰ | SUN Mer. Pass. | MOON Mer. Pass. Upper | MOON Mer. Pass. Lower | Age | Phase |
|---|---|---|---|---|---|---|---|
| | m s | m s | h m | h m | h m | d | |
| 28 | 01 17 | 01 08 | 12 01 | 14 37 | 02 10 | 03 | ◐ |
| 29 | 00 59 | 00 50 | 12 01 | 15 32 | 03 04 | 04 | |
| 30 | 00 41 | 00 32 | 12 01 | 16 28 | 04 00 | 05 | |

# 1976 SEPTEMBER 3, 4, 5 (FRI., SAT., SUN.)

| G.M.T. | ARIES G.H.A. | VENUS −3.3 G.H.A. | VENUS Dec. | MARS +1.9 G.H.A. | MARS Dec. | JUPITER −2.1 G.H.A. | JUPITER Dec. | SATURN +0.6 G.H.A. | SATURN Dec. |
|---|---|---|---|---|---|---|---|---|---|
| d h | ° ′ | ° ′ | ° ′ | ° ′ | ° ′ | ° ′ | ° ′ | ° ′ | ° ′ |
| 3 00 | 342 15.3 | 160 23.6 | N 0 23.9 | 156 16.3 | S 1 58.8 | 283 25.5 | N19 15.5 | 208 38.8 | N18 01.0 |
| 01 | 357 17.8 | 175 23.3 | 22.6 | 171 17.3 | 1 59.5 | 298 27.8 | 15.5 | 223 40.9 | 00.9 |
| 02 | 12 20.2 | 190 22.9 | 21.3 | 186 18.3 | 2 00.1 | 313 30.2 | 15.5 | 238 43.1 | 00.8 |
| 03 | 27 22.7 | 205 22.6 | ·· 20.0 | 201 19.2 | ·· 00.8 | 328 32.5 | ·· 15.6 | 253 45.3 | ·· 00.7 |
| 04 | 42 25.1 | 220 22.3 | 18.8 | 216 20.2 | 01.5 | 343 34.8 | 15.6 | 268 47.4 | 00.6 |
| 05 | 57 27.6 | 235 21.9 | 17.5 | 231 21.2 | 02.1 | 358 37.1 | 15.6 | 283 49.6 | 00.6 |
| 06 | 72 30.1 | 250 21.6 | N 0 16.2 | 246 22.2 | S 2 02.8 | 13 39.5 | N19 15.6 | 298 51.7 | N18 00.5 |
| 07 | 87 32.5 | 265 21.3 | 14.9 | 261 23.2 | 03.4 | 28 41.8 | 15.6 | 313 53.9 | 00.4 |
| 08 | 102 35.0 | 280 21.0 | 13.6 | 276 24.2 | 04.1 | 43 44.1 | 15.7 | 328 56.1 | 00.3 |
| F 09 | 117 37.5 | 295 20.6 | ·· 12.3 | 291 25.2 | ·· 04.8 | 58 46.4 | ·· 15.7 | 343 58.2 | ·· 00.3 |
| R 10 | 132 39.9 | 310 20.3 | 11.0 | 306 26.1 | 05.4 | 73 48.8 | 15.7 | 359 00.4 | 00.2 |
| I 11 | 147 42.4 | 325 20.0 | 09.8 | 321 27.1 | 06.1 | 88 51.1 | 15.7 | 14 02.6 | 00.1 |
| D 12 | 162 44.9 | 340 19.7 | N 0 08.5 | 336 28.1 | S 2 06.8 | 103 53.4 | N19 15.8 | 29 04.7 | N18 00.0 |
| A 13 | 177 47.3 | 355 19.3 | 07.2 | 351 29.1 | 07.4 | 118 55.7 | 15.8 | 44 06.9 | 18 00.0 |
| Y 14 | 192 49.8 | 10 19.0 | 05.9 | 6 30.1 | 08.1 | 133 58.1 | 15.8 | 59 09.1 | 17 59.9 |
| 15 | 207 52.3 | 25 18.7 | ·· 04.6 | 21 31.1 | ·· 08.7 | 149 00.4 | ·· 15.8 | 74 11.2 | ·· 59.8 |
| 16 | 222 54.7 | 40 18.3 | 03.3 | 36 32.1 | 09.4 | 164 02.7 | 15.8 | 89 13.4 | 59.7 |
| 17 | 237 57.2 | 55 18.0 | 02.0 | 51 33.0 | 10.1 | 179 05.0 | 15.9 | 104 15.6 | 59.7 |
| 18 | 252 59.6 | 70 17.7 | N 0 00.7 | 66 34.0 | S 2 10.7 | 194 07.4 | N19 15.9 | 119 17.7 | N17 59.6 |
| 19 | 268 02.1 | 85 17.4 | S 0 00.5 | 81 35.0 | 11.4 | 209 09.7 | 15.9 | 134 19.9 | 59.5 |
| 20 | 283 04.6 | 100 17.0 | 01.8 | 96 36.0 | 12.0 | 224 12.0 | 15.9 | 149 22.1 | 59.4 |
| 21 | 298 07.0 | 115 16.7 | ·· 03.1 | 111 37.0 | ·· 12.7 | 239 14.4 | ·· 16.0 | 164 24.2 | ·· 59.4 |
| 22 | 313 09.5 | 130 16.4 | 04.4 | 126 38.0 | 13.4 | 254 16.7 | 16.0 | 179 26.4 | 59.3 |
| 23 | 328 12.0 | 145 16.1 | 05.7 | 141 38.9 | 14.0 | 269 19.0 | 16.0 | 194 28.6 | 59.2 |
| 4 00 | 343 14.4 | 160 15.7 | S 0 07.0 | 156 39.9 | S 2 14.7 | 284 21.3 | N19 16.0 | 209 30.7 | N17 59.1 |
| 01 | 358 16.9 | 175 15.4 | 08.3 | 171 40.9 | 15.4 | 299 23.7 | 16.0 | 224 32.9 | 59.0 |
| 02 | 13 19.4 | 190 15.1 | 09.5 | 186 41.9 | 16.0 | 314 26.0 | 16.1 | 239 35.1 | 59.0 |
| 03 | 28 21.8 | 205 14.8 | ·· 10.8 | 201 42.9 | ·· 16.7 | 329 28.3 | ·· 16.1 | 254 37.2 | ·· 58.9 |
| 04 | 43 24.3 | 220 14.4 | 12.1 | 216 43.9 | 17.3 | 344 30.7 | 16.1 | 269 39.4 | 58.8 |
| 05 | 58 26.8 | 235 14.1 | 13.4 | 231 44.9 | 18.0 | 359 33.0 | 16.1 | 284 41.6 | 58.7 |
| 06 | 73 29.2 | 250 13.8 | S 0 14.7 | 246 45.8 | S 2 18.7 | 14 35.3 | N19 16.1 | 299 43.7 | N17 58.7 |
| 07 | 88 31.7 | 265 13.4 | 16.0 | 261 46.8 | 19.3 | 29 37.7 | 16.2 | 314 45.9 | 58.6 |
| S 08 | 103 34.1 | 280 13.1 | 17.3 | 276 47.8 | 20.0 | 44 40.0 | 16.2 | 329 48.1 | 58.5 |
| A 09 | 118 36.6 | 295 12.8 | ·· 18.6 | 291 48.8 | ·· 20.7 | 59 42.3 | ·· 16.2 | 344 50.2 | ·· 58.4 |
| T 10 | 133 39.1 | 310 12.5 | 19.8 | 306 49.8 | 21.3 | 74 44.7 | 16.2 | 359 52.4 | 58.4 |
| U 11 | 148 41.5 | 325 12.1 | 21.1 | 321 50.8 | 22.0 | 89 47.0 | 16.2 | 14 54.6 | 58.3 |
| R 12 | 163 44.0 | 340 11.8 | S 0 22.4 | 336 51.7 | S 2 22.6 | 104 49.3 | N19 16.3 | 29 56.7 | N17 58.2 |
| D 13 | 178 46.5 | 355 11.5 | 23.7 | 351 52.7 | 23.3 | 119 51.7 | 16.3 | 44 58.9 | 58.1 |
| A 14 | 193 48.9 | 10 11.2 | 25.0 | 6 53.7 | 24.0 | 134 54.0 | 16.3 | 60 01.1 | 58.1 |
| Y 15 | 208 51.4 | 25 10.8 | ·· 26.3 | 21 54.7 | ·· 24.6 | 149 56.3 | ·· 16.3 | 75 03.2 | ·· 58.0 |
| 16 | 223 53.9 | 40 10.5 | 27.6 | 36 55.7 | 25.3 | 164 58.7 | 16.3 | 90 05.4 | 57.9 |
| 17 | 238 56.3 | 55 10.2 | 28.9 | 51 56.7 | 26.0 | 180 01.0 | 16.4 | 105 07.6 | 57.8 |
| 18 | 253 58.8 | 70 09.9 | S 0 30.1 | 66 57.6 | S 2 26.6 | 195 03.3 | N19 16.4 | 120 09.7 | N17 57.8 |
| 19 | 269 01.2 | 85 09.5 | 31.4 | 81 58.6 | 27.3 | 210 05.7 | 16.4 | 135 11.9 | 57.7 |
| 20 | 284 03.7 | 100 09.2 | 32.7 | 96 59.6 | 27.9 | 225 08.0 | 16.4 | 150 14.1 | 57.6 |
| 21 | 299 06.2 | 115 08.9 | ·· 34.0 | 112 00.6 | ·· 28.6 | 240 10.3 | ·· 16.4 | 165 16.2 | ·· 57.5 |
| 22 | 314 08.6 | 130 08.6 | 35.3 | 127 01.6 | 29.3 | 255 12.7 | 16.5 | 180 18.4 | 57.5 |
| 23 | 329 11.1 | 145 08.2 | 36.6 | 142 02.5 | 29.9 | 270 15.0 | 16.5 | 195 20.6 | 57.4 |
| 5 00 | 344 13.6 | 160 07.9 | S 0 37.9 | 157 03.5 | S 2 30.6 | 285 17.4 | N19 16.5 | 210 22.7 | N17 57.3 |
| 01 | 359 16.0 | 175 07.6 | 39.2 | 172 04.5 | 31.3 | 300 19.7 | 16.5 | 225 24.9 | 57.2 |
| 02 | 14 18.5 | 190 07.3 | 40.4 | 187 05.5 | 31.9 | 315 22.0 | 16.5 | 240 27.1 | 57.2 |
| 03 | 29 21.0 | 205 06.9 | ·· 41.7 | 202 06.5 | ·· 32.6 | 330 24.4 | ·· 16.6 | 255 29.3 | ·· 57.1 |
| 04 | 44 23.4 | 220 06.6 | 43.0 | 217 07.5 | 33.2 | 345 26.7 | 16.6 | 270 31.4 | 57.0 |
| 05 | 59 25.9 | 235 06.3 | 44.3 | 232 08.4 | 33.9 | 0 29.1 | 16.6 | 285 33.6 | 56.9 |
| 06 | 74 28.4 | 250 05.9 | S 0 45.6 | 247 09.4 | S 2 34.6 | 15 31.4 | N19 16.6 | 300 35.8 | N17 56.8 |
| 07 | 89 30.8 | 265 05.6 | 46.9 | 262 10.4 | 35.2 | 30 33.7 | 16.6 | 315 37.9 | 56.8 |
| 08 | 104 33.3 | 280 05.3 | 48.2 | 277 11.4 | 35.9 | 45 36.1 | 16.7 | 330 40.1 | 56.7 |
| S 09 | 119 35.7 | 295 05.0 | ·· 49.5 | 292 12.4 | ·· 36.6 | 60 38.4 | ·· 16.7 | 345 42.3 | ·· 56.6 |
| U 10 | 134 38.2 | 310 04.6 | 50.7 | 307 13.3 | 37.2 | 75 40.8 | 16.7 | 0 44.4 | 56.5 |
| N 11 | 149 40.7 | 325 04.3 | 52.0 | 322 14.3 | 37.9 | 90 43.1 | 16.7 | 15 46.6 | 56.5 |
| D 12 | 164 43.1 | 340 04.0 | S 0 53.3 | 337 15.3 | S 2 38.5 | 105 45.4 | N19 16.7 | 30 48.8 | N17 56.4 |
| A 13 | 179 45.6 | 355 03.7 | 54.6 | 352 16.3 | 39.2 | 120 47.8 | 16.8 | 45 50.9 | 56.3 |
| Y 14 | 194 48.1 | 10 03.3 | 55.9 | 7 17.3 | 39.9 | 135 50.1 | 16.8 | 60 53.1 | 56.2 |
| 15 | 209 50.5 | 25 03.0 | ·· 57.2 | 22 18.3 | ·· 40.5 | 150 52.5 | ·· 16.8 | 75 55.3 | ·· 56.2 |
| 16 | 224 53.0 | 40 02.7 | 58.5 | 37 19.2 | 41.2 | 165 54.8 | 16.8 | 90 57.4 | 56.1 |
| 17 | 239 55.5 | 55 02.4 | 0 59.8 | 52 20.2 | 41.9 | 180 57.2 | 16.8 | 105 59.6 | 56.0 |
| 18 | 254 57.9 | 70 02.0 | S 1 01.0 | 67 21.2 | S 2 42.5 | 195 59.5 | N19 16.9 | 121 01.8 | N17 55.9 |
| 19 | 270 00.4 | 85 01.7 | 02.3 | 82 22.2 | 43.2 | 211 01.8 | 16.9 | 136 04.0 | 55.9 |
| 20 | 285 02.9 | 100 01.4 | 03.6 | 97 23.2 | 43.8 | 226 04.2 | 16.9 | 151 06.1 | 55.8 |
| 21 | 300 05.3 | 115 01.1 | ·· 04.9 | 112 24.1 | ·· 44.5 | 241 06.5 | ·· 16.9 | 166 08.3 | ·· 55.7 |
| 22 | 315 07.8 | 130 00.7 | 06.2 | 127 25.1 | 45.2 | 256 08.9 | 16.9 | 181 10.5 | 55.6 |
| 23 | 330 10.2 | 145 00.4 | 07.5 | 142 26.1 | 45.8 | 271 11.2 | 16.9 | 196 12.6 | 55.6 |
| Mer. Pass. | h m 1 06.9 | v −0.3 | d 1.3 | v 1.0 | d 0.7 | v 2.3 | d 0.0 | v 2.2 | d 0.1 |

**STARS**

| Name | S.H.A. | Dec. |
|---|---|---|
| | ° ′ | ° ′ |
| Acamar | 315 39.1 | S40 23.6 |
| Achernar | 335 46.9 | S57 21.0 |
| Acrux | 173 40.8 | S62 58.3 |
| Adhara | 255 34.4 | S28 56.3 |
| Aldebaran | 291 21.1 | N16 27.8 |
| Alioth | 166 45.4 | N56 05.3 |
| Alkaid | 153 21.0 | N49 26.0 |
| Al Na'ir | 28 17.9 | S47 04.3 |
| Alnilam | 276 14.5 | S 1 12.9 |
| Alphard | 218 23.5 | S 8 33.4 |
| Alphecca | 126 34.5 | N26 47.8 |
| Alpheratz | 358 11.8 | N28 57.8 |
| Altair | 62 34.9 | N 8 48.6 |
| Ankaa | 353 42.5 | S42 25.7 |
| Antares | 113 00.2 | S26 22.8 |
| Arcturus | 146 21.1 | N19 18.4 |
| Atria | 108 26.8 | S68 59.4 |
| Avior | 234 29.8 | S59 26.0 |
| Bellatrix | 279 01.7 | N 6 19.8 |
| Betelgeuse | 271 31.3 | N 7 24.2 |
| Canopus | 264 08.6 | S52 40.8 |
| Capella | 281 15.3 | N45 58.3 |
| Deneb | 49 49.9 | N45 12.1 |
| Denebola | 183 02.1 | N14 42.2 |
| Diphda | 349 23.3 | S18 06.6 |
| Dubhe | 194 26.2 | N61 52.6 |
| Elnath | 278 47.6 | N28 35.2 |
| Eltanin | 90 58.8 | N51 29.9 |
| Enif | 34 13.9 | N 9 46.3 |
| Fomalhaut | 15 54.1 | S29 44.5 |
| Gacrux | 172 32.2 | S56 59.1 |
| Gienah | 176 21.0 | S17 24.7 |
| Hadar | 149 27.5 | S60 15.8 |
| Hamal | 328 31.7 | N23 21.2 |
| Kaus Aust. | 84 20.3 | S34 23.8 |
| Kochab | 137 19.5 | N74 15.4 |
| Markab | 14 05.5 | N15 05.0 |
| Menkar | 314 43.8 | N 4 00.0 |
| Menkent | 148 40.4 | S36 15.4 |
| Miaplacidus | 221 46.3 | S69 37.2 |
| Mirfak | 309 19.8 | N49 46.6 |
| Nunki | 76 32.3 | S26 19.5 |
| Peacock | 54 02.2 | S56 48.6 |
| Pollux | 244 01.7 | N28 04.9 |
| Procyon | 245 28.8 | N 5 17.1 |
| Rasalhague | 96 32.0 | N12 34.9 |
| Regulus | 208 13.2 | N12 04.9 |
| Rigel | 281 38.7 | S 8 13.6 |
| Rigil Kent. | 140 29.8 | S60 44.5 |
| Sabik | 102 44.2 | S15 41.7 |
| Schedar | 350 11.5 | N56 24.6 |
| Shaula | 96 59.3 | S37 05.3 |
| Sirius | 258 58.3 | S16 41.0 |
| Spica | 159 00.6 | S11 02.3 |
| Suhail | 223 13.1 | S43 20.2 |
| Vega | 80 57.5 | N38 46.1 |
| Zuben'ubi | 137 36.2 | S15 56.7 |

| | S.H.A. | Mer. Pass. |
|---|---|---|
| | ° ′ | h m |
| Venus | 177 01.3 | 13 19 |
| Mars | 173 25.5 | 13 32 |
| Jupiter | 301 06.9 | 5 02 |
| Saturn | 226 16.3 | 10 01 |

# 1976 SEPTEMBER 3, 4, 5 (FRI., SAT., SUN.)

| G.M.T. | SUN G.H.A. | SUN Dec. | MOON G.H.A. | v | MOON Dec. | d | H.P. |
|---|---|---|---|---|---|---|---|
| d h | ° ′ | ° ′ | ° ′ | ′ | ° ′ | ′ | ′ |
| 3 00 | 180 08.7 | N 7 35.2 | 67 46.3 | 7.8 | S18 58.9 | 2.6 | 57.9 |
| 01 | 195 08.9 | 34.2 | 82 13.1 | 7.9 | 18 56.3 | 2.8 | 57.9 |
| 02 | 210 09.1 | 33.3 | 96 40.0 | 8.0 | 18 53.5 | 2.9 | 57.8 |
| 03 | 225 09.3 | ·· 32.4 | 111 07.0 | 8.0 | 18 50.6 | 3.0 | 57.8 |
| 04 | 240 09.5 | 31.5 | 125 34.0 | 8.0 | 18 47.6 | 3.1 | 57.8 |
| 05 | 255 09.7 | 30.6 | 140 01.0 | 8.1 | 18 44.5 | 3.2 | 57.8 |
| 06 | 270 09.9 | N 7 29.7 | 154 28.1 | 8.2 | S18 41.3 | 3.3 | 57.7 |
| 07 | 285 10.1 | 28.7 | 168 55.3 | 8.2 | 18 38.0 | 3.4 | 57.7 |
| 08 | 300 10.3 | 27.8 | 183 22.5 | 8.2 | 18 34.6 | 3.5 | 57.7 |
| F 09 | 315 10.5 | ·· 26.9 | 197 49.7 | 8.3 | 18 31.1 | 3.6 | 57.7 |
| R 10 | 330 10.7 | 26.0 | 212 17.0 | 8.3 | 18 27.5 | 3.8 | 57.7 |
| I 11 | 345 10.9 | 25.1 | 226 44.3 | 8.4 | 18 23.7 | 3.8 | 57.6 |
| D 12 | 0 11.1 | N 7 24.1 | 241 11.7 | 8.4 | S18 19.9 | 4.0 | 57.6 |
| A 13 | 15 11.3 | 23.2 | 255 39.1 | 8.5 | 18 15.9 | 4.0 | 57.6 |
| Y 14 | 30 11.5 | 22.3 | 270 06.6 | 8.6 | 18 11.9 | 4.2 | 57.6 |
| 15 | 45 11.7 | ·· 21.4 | 284 34.2 | 8.6 | 18 07.7 | 4.2 | 57.5 |
| 16 | 60 12.0 | 20.5 | 299 01.8 | 8.6 | 18 03.5 | 4.4 | 57.5 |
| 17 | 75 12.2 | 19.6 | 313 29.4 | 8.7 | 17 59.1 | 4.4 | 57.5 |
| 18 | 90 12.4 | N 7 18.6 | 327 57.1 | 8.8 | S17 54.7 | 4.6 | 57.5 |
| 19 | 105 12.6 | 17.7 | 342 24.9 | 8.8 | 17 50.1 | 4.6 | 57.4 |
| 20 | 120 12.8 | 16.8 | 356 52.7 | 8.8 | 17 45.5 | 4.8 | 57.4 |
| 21 | 135 13.0 | ·· 15.9 | 11 20.5 | 9.0 | 17 40.7 | 4.8 | 57.4 |
| 22 | 150 13.2 | 14.9 | 25 48.5 | 8.9 | 17 35.9 | 5.0 | 57.4 |
| 23 | 165 13.4 | 14.0 | 40 16.4 | 9.1 | 17 30.9 | 5.0 | 57.4 |
| 4 00 | 180 13.6 | N 7 13.1 | 54 44.5 | 9.1 | S17 25.9 | 5.1 | 57.3 |
| 01 | 195 13.8 | 12.2 | 69 12.6 | 9.1 | 17 20.8 | 5.3 | 57.3 |
| 02 | 210 14.0 | 11.3 | 83 40.7 | 9.2 | 17 15.5 | 5.3 | 57.3 |
| 03 | 225 14.2 | ·· 10.3 | 98 08.9 | 9.3 | 17 10.2 | 5.4 | 57.3 |
| 04 | 240 14.4 | 09.4 | 112 37.2 | 9.3 | 17 04.8 | 5.5 | 57.3 |
| 05 | 255 14.6 | 08.5 | 127 05.5 | 9.3 | 16 59.3 | 5.6 | 57.2 |
| 06 | 270 14.8 | N 7 07.6 | 141 33.8 | 9.5 | S16 53.7 | 5.7 | 57.2 |
| 07 | 285 15.0 | 06.6 | 156 02.3 | 9.5 | 16 48.0 | 5.7 | 57.2 |
| S 08 | 300 15.3 | 05.7 | 170 30.8 | 9.5 | 16 42.3 | 5.9 | 57.2 |
| A 09 | 315 15.5 | ·· 04.8 | 184 59.3 | 9.6 | 16 36.4 | 5.9 | 57.1 |
| T 10 | 330 15.7 | 03.9 | 199 27.9 | 9.7 | 16 30.5 | 6.1 | 57.1 |
| U 11 | 345 15.9 | 03.0 | 213 56.6 | 9.7 | 16 24.4 | 6.1 | 57.1 |
| R 12 | 0 16.1 | N 7 02.0 | 228 25.3 | 9.8 | S16 18.3 | 6.2 | 57.1 |
| D 13 | 15 16.3 | 01.1 | 242 54.1 | 9.8 | 16 12.1 | 6.3 | 57.1 |
| A 14 | 30 16.5 | 7 00.2 | 257 22.9 | 9.9 | 16 05.8 | 6.4 | 57.0 |
| Y 15 | 45 16.7 | 6 59.3 | 271 51.8 | 9.9 | 15 59.4 | 6.4 | 57.0 |
| 16 | 60 16.9 | 58.3 | 286 20.7 | 10.0 | 15 53.0 | 6.5 | 57.0 |
| 17 | 75 17.1 | 57.4 | 300 49.7 | 10.1 | 15 46.5 | 6.7 | 57.0 |
| 18 | 90 17.3 | N 6 56.5 | 315 18.8 | 10.1 | S15 39.8 | 6.6 | 56.9 |
| 19 | 105 17.5 | 55.6 | 329 47.9 | 10.2 | 15 33.2 | 6.8 | 56.9 |
| 20 | 120 17.7 | 54.6 | 344 17.1 | 10.3 | 15 26.4 | 6.9 | 56.9 |
| 21 | 135 18.0 | ·· 53.7 | 358 46.4 | 10.3 | 15 19.5 | 6.9 | 56.9 |
| 22 | 150 18.2 | 52.8 | 13 15.7 | 10.4 | 15 12.6 | 7.0 | 56.9 |
| 23 | 165 18.4 | 51.9 | 27 45.1 | 10.4 | 15 05.6 | 7.1 | 56.8 |
| 5 00 | 180 18.6 | N 6 50.9 | 42 14.5 | 10.5 | S14 58.5 | 7.1 | 56.8 |
| 01 | 195 18.8 | 50.0 | 56 44.0 | 10.5 | 14 51.4 | 7.2 | 56.8 |
| 02 | 210 19.0 | 49.1 | 71 13.5 | 10.6 | 14 44.2 | 7.3 | 56.8 |
| 03 | 225 19.2 | ·· 48.2 | 85 43.1 | 10.7 | 14 36.9 | 7.4 | 56.8 |
| 04 | 240 19.4 | 47.2 | 100 12.8 | 10.7 | 14 29.5 | 7.4 | 56.7 |
| 05 | 255 19.6 | 46.3 | 114 42.5 | 10.8 | 14 22.1 | 7.6 | 56.7 |
| 06 | 270 19.8 | N 6 45.4 | 129 12.3 | 10.8 | S14 14.5 | 7.5 | 56.7 |
| 07 | 285 20.0 | 44.4 | 143 42.1 | 10.9 | 14 07.0 | 7.7 | 56.7 |
| 08 | 300 20.3 | 43.5 | 158 12.0 | 10.9 | 13 59.3 | 7.7 | 56.6 |
| S 09 | 315 20.5 | ·· 42.6 | 172 41.9 | 11.0 | 13 51.6 | 7.8 | 56.6 |
| U 10 | 330 20.7 | 41.7 | 187 11.9 | 11.1 | 13 43.8 | 7.8 | 56.6 |
| N 11 | 345 20.9 | 40.7 | 201 42.0 | 11.1 | 13 36.0 | 7.9 | 56.6 |
| D 12 | 0 21.1 | N 6 39.8 | 216 12.1 | 11.2 | S13 28.1 | 8.0 | 56.6 |
| A 13 | 15 21.3 | 38.9 | 230 42.3 | 11.2 | 13 20.1 | 8.0 | 56.5 |
| Y 14 | 30 21.5 | 37.9 | 245 12.5 | 11.3 | 13 12.1 | 8.1 | 56.5 |
| 15 | 45 21.7 | ·· 37.0 | 259 42.8 | 11.4 | 13 04.0 | 8.2 | 56.5 |
| 16 | 60 21.9 | 36.1 | 274 13.2 | 11.4 | 12 55.8 | 8.2 | 56.5 |
| 17 | 75 22.1 | 35.2 | 288 43.6 | 11.5 | 12 47.6 | 8.2 | 56.5 |
| 18 | 90 22.4 | N 6 34.2 | 303 14.1 | 11.5 | S12 39.4 | 8.4 | 56.4 |
| 19 | 105 22.6 | 33.3 | 317 44.6 | 11.5 | 12 31.0 | 8.4 | 56.4 |
| 20 | 120 22.8 | 32.4 | 332 15.1 | 11.7 | 12 22.6 | 8.4 | 56.4 |
| 21 | 135 23.0 | ·· 31.4 | 346 45.8 | 11.7 | 12 14.2 | 8.5 | 56.4 |
| 22 | 150 23.2 | 30.5 | 1 16.5 | 11.7 | 12 05.7 | 8.5 | 56.4 |
| 23 | 165 23.4 | 29.6 | 15 47.2 | 11.8 | 11 57.2 | 8.6 | 56.3 |
| | S.D. 15.9 | d 0.9 | S.D. 15.7 | | 15.6 | | 15.4 |

| Lat. | Twilight Naut. | Twilight Civil | Sunrise | Moonrise 3 | Moonrise 4 | Moonrise 5 | Moonrise 6 |
|---|---|---|---|---|---|---|---|
| ° | h m | h m | h m | h m | h m | h m | h m |
| N 72 | //// | 02 52 | 04 16 | 19 48 | 19 00 | 18 44 | 18 33 |
| N 70 | 01 03 | 03 15 | 04 28 | 18 22 | 18 23 | 18 21 | 18 19 |
| 68 | 01 56 | 03 33 | 04 37 | 17 43 | 17 56 | 18 04 | 18 08 |
| 66 | 02 27 | 03 48 | 04 45 | 17 16 | 17 36 | 17 50 | 17 59 |
| 64 | 02 49 | 03 59 | 04 51 | 16 55 | 17 20 | 17 38 | 17 51 |
| 62 | 03 07 | 04 09 | 04 57 | 16 37 | 17 06 | 17 28 | 17 44 |
| 60 | 03 21 | 04 18 | 05 02 | 16 23 | 16 55 | 17 19 | 17 38 |
| N 58 | 03 32 | 04 25 | 05 06 | 16 11 | 16 45 | 17 11 | 17 33 |
| 56 | 03 42 | 04 31 | 05 10 | 16 01 | 16 36 | 17 05 | 17 29 |
| 54 | 03 51 | 04 36 | 05 13 | 15 51 | 16 28 | 16 59 | 17 24 |
| 52 | 03 59 | 04 41 | 05 16 | 15 43 | 16 21 | 16 53 | 17 21 |
| 50 | 04 05 | 04 46 | 05 19 | 15 36 | 16 15 | 16 48 | 17 17 |
| 45 | 04 19 | 04 55 | 05 25 | 15 20 | 16 02 | 16 38 | 17 10 |
| N 40 | 04 30 | 05 03 | 05 30 | 15 06 | 15 50 | 16 29 | 17 03 |
| 35 | 04 39 | 05 09 | 05 35 | 14 55 | 15 41 | 16 21 | 16 58 |
| 30 | 04 46 | 05 14 | 05 39 | 14 45 | 15 32 | 16 15 | 16 53 |
| 20 | 04 57 | 05 23 | 05 45 | 14 29 | 15 18 | 16 03 | 16 45 |
| N 10 | 05 05 | 05 29 | 05 51 | 14 14 | 15 05 | 15 53 | 16 38 |
| 0 | 05 11 | 05 35 | 05 56 | 14 00 | 14 53 | 15 43 | 16 31 |
| S 10 | 05 15 | 05 40 | 06 01 | 13 46 | 14 41 | 15 33 | 16 24 |
| 20 | 05 18 | 05 44 | 06 06 | 13 32 | 14 28 | 15 23 | 16 17 |
| 30 | 05 20 | 05 48 | 06 12 | 13 15 | 14 13 | 15 11 | 16 08 |
| 35 | 05 20 | 05 50 | 06 15 | 13 05 | 14 05 | 15 04 | 16 04 |
| 40 | 05 20 | 05 52 | 06 19 | 12 54 | 13 55 | 14 57 | 15 58 |
| 45 | 05 20 | 05 54 | 06 23 | 12 40 | 13 43 | 14 48 | 15 52 |
| S 50 | 05 19 | 05 56 | 06 28 | 12 24 | 13 30 | 14 37 | 15 44 |
| 52 | 05 18 | 05 57 | 06 30 | 12 17 | 13 23 | 14 32 | 15 40 |
| 54 | 05 17 | 05 58 | 06 33 | 12 08 | 13 16 | 14 26 | 15 36 |
| 56 | 05 16 | 05 59 | 06 36 | 11 59 | 13 08 | 14 20 | 15 32 |
| 58 | 05 14 | 06 00 | 06 39 | 11 48 | 12 59 | 14 13 | 15 27 |
| S 60 | 05 13 | 06 01 | 06 42 | 11 35 | 12 48 | 14 05 | 15 22 |

| Lat. | Sunset | Twilight Civil | Twilight Naut. | Moonset 3 | Moonset 4 | Moonset 5 | Moonset 6 |
|---|---|---|---|---|---|---|---|
| ° | h m | h m | h m | h m | h m | h m | h m |
| N 72 | 19 39 | 21 02 | //// | 20 47 | 23 23 | 25 23 | 01 23 |
| N 70 | 19 28 | 20 39 | 22 43 | 22 12 | 24 00 | 00 00 | 01 44 |
| 68 | 19 19 | 20 21 | 21 56 | 22 51 | 24 25 | 00 25 | 02 00 |
| 66 | 19 11 | 20 08 | 21 27 | 23 17 | 24 44 | 00 44 | 02 13 |
| 64 | 19 05 | 19 56 | 21 05 | 23 38 | 25 00 | 01 00 | 02 24 |
| 62 | 19 00 | 19 47 | 20 49 | 23 55 | 25 13 | 01 13 | 02 33 |
| 60 | 18 55 | 19 39 | 20 35 | 24 08 | 00 08 | 01 24 | 02 41 |
| N 58 | 18 50 | 19 32 | 20 24 | 24 20 | 00 20 | 01 33 | 02 48 |
| 56 | 18 47 | 19 25 | 20 14 | 24 30 | 00 30 | 01 41 | 02 54 |
| 54 | 18 43 | 19 20 | 20 05 | 24 39 | 00 39 | 01 49 | 02 59 |
| 52 | 18 40 | 19 15 | 19 58 | 24 47 | 00 47 | 01 55 | 03 04 |
| 50 | 18 38 | 19 11 | 19 51 | 24 55 | 00 55 | 02 01 | 03 09 |
| 45 | 18 32 | 19 02 | 19 38 | 00 08 | 01 10 | 02 14 | 03 18 |
| N 40 | 18 27 | 18 54 | 19 27 | 00 22 | 01 23 | 02 24 | 03 26 |
| 35 | 18 23 | 18 48 | 19 19 | 00 34 | 01 33 | 02 33 | 03 33 |
| 30 | 18 19 | 18 43 | 19 12 | 00 44 | 01 43 | 02 41 | 03 39 |
| 20 | 18 13 | 18 35 | 19 01 | 01 02 | 01 59 | 02 55 | 03 49 |
| N 10 | 18 07 | 18 28 | 18 53 | 01 17 | 02 13 | 03 06 | 03 58 |
| 0 | 18 02 | 18 23 | 18 47 | 01 32 | 02 26 | 03 17 | 04 06 |
| S 10 | 17 57 | 18 18 | 18 43 | 01 46 | 02 39 | 03 28 | 04 15 |
| 20 | 17 52 | 18 14 | 18 40 | 02 01 | 02 52 | 03 40 | 04 23 |
| 30 | 17 47 | 18 11 | 18 38 | 02 19 | 03 08 | 03 53 | 04 33 |
| 35 | 17 43 | 18 09 | 18 38 | 02 29 | 03 17 | 04 00 | 04 39 |
| 40 | 17 40 | 18 07 | 18 38 | 02 41 | 03 28 | 04 09 | 04 45 |
| 45 | 17 36 | 18 05 | 18 39 | 02 54 | 03 40 | 04 19 | 04 53 |
| S 50 | 17 31 | 18 03 | 18 40 | 03 11 | 03 54 | 04 31 | 05 02 |
| 52 | 17 28 | 18 02 | 18 41 | 03 19 | 04 01 | 04 36 | 05 06 |
| 54 | 17 26 | 18 01 | 18 42 | 03 27 | 04 09 | 04 42 | 05 10 |
| 56 | 17 23 | 18 00 | 18 44 | 03 37 | 04 17 | 04 49 | 05 15 |
| 58 | 17 20 | 18 00 | 18 45 | 03 48 | 04 27 | 04 57 | 05 21 |
| S 60 | 17 17 | 17 59 | 18 47 | 04 01 | 04 38 | 05 05 | 05 27 |

| Day | SUN Eqn. of Time 00h | SUN Eqn. of Time 12h | SUN Mer. Pass. | MOON Mer. Pass. Upper | MOON Mer. Pass. Lower | Age | Phase |
|---|---|---|---|---|---|---|---|
| | m s | m s | h m | h m | h m | d | |
| 3 | 00 34 | 00 44 | 11 59 | 20 13 | 07 46 | 09 | |
| 4 | 00 54 | 01 04 | 11 59 | 21 05 | 08 39 | 10 | |
| 5 | 01 14 | 01 24 | 11 59 | 21 55 | 09 30 | 11 | |

# 1976 SEPTEMBER 21, 22, 23 (TUES., WED., THURS.)

| G.M.T. | ARIES G.H.A. | VENUS −3.3 G.H.A. | VENUS Dec. | MARS +1.9 G.H.A. | MARS Dec. | JUPITER −2.2 G.H.A. | JUPITER Dec. | SATURN +0.6 G.H.A. | SATURN Dec. |
|---|---|---|---|---|---|---|---|---|---|
| d h | ° ′ | ° ′ | ° ′ | ° ′ | ° ′ | ° ′ | ° ′ | ° ′ | ° ′ |
| 21 00 | 359 59.8 | 157 56.0 | S 8 45.2 | 163 11.9 | S 6 43.7 | 300 40.8 | N19 19.0 | 224 21.5 | N17 29.5 |
| 01 | 15 02.2 | 172 55.6 | 46.5 | 178 12.8 | 44.3 | 315 43.3 | 19.0 | 239 23.7 | 29.4 |
| 02 | 30 04.7 | 187 55.3 | 47.7 | 193 13.8 | 45.0 | 330 45.8 | 19.0 | 254 25.9 | 29.3 |
| 03 | 45 07.2 | 202 54.9 | 48.9 | 208 14.7 | 45.6 | 345 48.3 | 19.0 | 269 28.1 | 29.3 |
| 04 | 60 09.6 | 217 54.5 | 50.1 | 223 15.6 | 46.3 | 0 50.7 | 19.0 | 284 30.3 | 29.2 |
| 05 | 75 12.1 | 232 54.1 | 51.4 | 238 16.6 | 46.9 | 15 53.2 | 19.0 | 299 32.5 | 29.1 |
| 06 | 90 14.6 | 247 53.7 | S 8 52.6 | 253 17.5 | S 6 47.6 | 30 55.7 | N19 18.9 | 314 34.7 | N17 29.1 |
| T 07 | 105 17.0 | 262 53.4 | 53.8 | 268 18.4 | 48.2 | 45 58.2 | 18.9 | 329 36.9 | 29.0 |
| U 08 | 120 19.5 | 277 53.0 | 55.0 | 283 19.4 | 48.9 | 61 00.6 | 18.9 | 344 39.1 | 28.9 |
| E 09 | 135 22.0 | 292 52.6 | 56.3 | 298 20.3 | 49.5 | 76 03.1 | 18.9 | 359 41.3 | 28.9 |
| S 10 | 150 24.4 | 307 52.2 | 57.5 | 313 21.2 | 50.2 | 91 05.6 | 18.9 | 14 43.5 | 28.8 |
| D 11 | 165 26.9 | 322 51.8 | 8 58.7 | 328 22.1 | 50.8 | 106 08.1 | 18.9 | 29 45.7 | 28.7 |
| A 12 | 180 29.3 | 337 51.4 | S 9 00.0 | 343 23.1 | S 6 51.5 | 121 10.6 | N19 18.9 | 44 47.9 | N17 28.7 |
| Y 13 | 195 31.8 | 352 51.1 | 01.2 | 358 24.0 | 52.1 | 136 13.0 | 18.9 | 59 50.1 | 28.6 |
| 14 | 210 34.3 | 7 50.7 | 02.4 | 13 24.9 | 52.8 | 151 15.5 | 18.9 | 74 52.3 | 28.5 |
| 15 | 225 36.7 | 22 50.3 | 03.6 | 28 25.9 | 53.4 | 166 18.0 | 18.9 | 89 54.5 | 28.5 |
| 16 | 240 39.2 | 37 49.9 | 04.9 | 43 26.8 | 54.1 | 181 20.5 | 18.9 | 104 56.7 | 28.4 |
| 17 | 255 41.7 | 52 49.5 | 06.1 | 58 27.7 | 54.8 | 196 23.0 | 18.9 | 119 58.9 | 28.3 |
| 18 | 270 44.1 | 67 49.1 | S 9 07.3 | 73 28.7 | S 6 55.4 | 211 25.4 | N19 18.9 | 135 01.1 | N17 28.2 |
| 19 | 285 46.6 | 82 48.7 | 08.5 | 88 29.6 | 56.1 | 226 27.9 | 18.9 | 150 03.3 | 28.2 |
| 20 | 300 49.1 | 97 48.4 | 09.7 | 103 30.5 | 56.7 | 241 30.4 | 18.8 | 165 05.5 | 28.1 |
| 21 | 315 51.5 | 112 48.0 | 11.0 | 118 31.5 | 57.4 | 256 32.9 | 18.8 | 180 07.7 | 28.0 |
| 22 | 330 54.0 | 127 47.6 | 12.2 | 133 32.4 | 58.0 | 271 35.4 | 18.8 | 195 09.9 | 28.0 |
| 23 | 345 56.5 | 142 47.2 | 13.4 | 148 33.3 | 58.7 | 286 37.8 | 18.8 | 210 12.2 | 27.9 |
| 22 00 | 0 58.9 | 157 46.8 | S 9 14.6 | 163 34.2 | S 6 59.3 | 301 40.3 | N19 18.8 | 225 14.4 | N17 27.8 |
| 01 | 16 01.4 | 172 46.4 | 15.9 | 178 35.2 | 7 00.0 | 316 42.8 | 18.8 | 240 16.6 | 27.8 |
| 02 | 31 03.8 | 187 46.0 | 17.1 | 193 36.1 | 00.6 | 331 45.3 | 18.8 | 255 18.8 | 27.7 |
| 03 | 46 06.3 | 202 45.7 | 18.3 | 208 37.0 | 01.3 | 346 47.8 | 18.8 | 270 21.0 | 27.6 |
| 04 | 61 08.8 | 217 45.3 | 19.5 | 223 38.0 | 01.9 | 1 50.3 | 18.8 | 285 23.2 | 27.6 |
| 05 | 76 11.2 | 232 44.9 | 20.7 | 238 38.9 | 02.6 | 16 52.7 | 18.8 | 300 25.4 | 27.5 |
| 06 | 91 13.7 | 247 44.5 | S 9 22.0 | 253 39.8 | S 7 03.2 | 31 55.2 | N19 18.8 | 315 27.6 | N17 27.4 |
| W 07 | 106 16.2 | 262 44.1 | 23.2 | 268 40.7 | 03.9 | 46 57.7 | 18.7 | 330 29.8 | 27.4 |
| E 08 | 121 18.6 | 277 43.7 | 24.4 | 283 41.7 | 04.5 | 62 00.2 | 18.7 | 345 32.0 | 27.3 |
| D 09 | 136 21.1 | 292 43.3 | 25.6 | 298 42.6 | 05.2 | 77 02.7 | 18.7 | 0 34.2 | 27.2 |
| N 10 | 151 23.6 | 307 42.9 | 26.8 | 313 43.5 | 05.8 | 92 05.2 | 18.7 | 15 36.4 | 27.2 |
| E 11 | 166 26.0 | 322 42.5 | 28.1 | 328 44.5 | 06.5 | 107 07.7 | 18.7 | 30 38.6 | 27.1 |
| S 12 | 181 28.5 | 337 42.2 | S 9 29.3 | 343 45.4 | S 7 07.1 | 122 10.1 | N19 18.7 | 45 40.8 | N17 27.0 |
| D 13 | 196 30.9 | 352 41.8 | 30.5 | 358 46.3 | 07.8 | 137 12.6 | 18.7 | 60 43.0 | 27.0 |
| A 14 | 211 33.4 | 7 41.4 | 31.7 | 13 47.2 | 08.4 | 152 15.1 | 18.7 | 75 45.2 | 26.9 |
| Y 15 | 226 35.9 | 22 41.0 | 32.9 | 28 48.2 | 09.1 | 167 17.6 | 18.7 | 90 47.4 | 26.8 |
| 16 | 241 38.3 | 37 40.6 | 34.1 | 43 49.1 | 09.7 | 182 20.1 | 18.7 | 105 49.6 | 26.8 |
| 17 | 256 40.8 | 52 40.2 | 35.4 | 58 50.0 | 10.4 | 197 22.6 | 18.7 | 120 51.9 | 26.7 |
| 18 | 271 43.3 | 67 39.8 | S 9 36.6 | 73 50.9 | S 7 11.0 | 212 25.1 | N19 18.6 | 135 54.1 | N17 26.6 |
| 19 | 286 45.7 | 82 39.4 | 37.8 | 88 51.9 | 11.7 | 227 27.6 | 18.6 | 150 56.3 | 26.6 |
| 20 | 301 48.2 | 97 39.0 | 39.0 | 103 52.8 | 12.3 | 242 30.0 | 18.6 | 165 58.5 | 26.5 |
| 21 | 316 50.7 | 112 38.6 | 40.2 | 118 53.7 | 13.0 | 257 32.5 | 18.6 | 181 00.7 | 26.4 |
| 22 | 331 53.1 | 127 38.2 | 41.4 | 133 54.6 | 13.6 | 272 35.0 | 18.6 | 196 02.9 | 26.4 |
| 23 | 346 55.6 | 142 37.8 | 42.6 | 148 55.6 | 14.3 | 287 37.5 | 18.6 | 211 05.1 | 26.3 |
| 23 00 | 1 58.1 | 157 37.4 | S 9 43.9 | 163 56.5 | S 7 14.9 | 302 40.0 | N19 18.6 | 226 07.3 | N17 26.2 |
| 01 | 17 00.5 | 172 37.0 | 45.1 | 178 57.4 | 15.6 | 317 42.5 | 18.6 | 241 09.5 | 26.2 |
| 02 | 32 03.0 | 187 36.6 | 46.3 | 193 58.3 | 16.2 | 332 45.0 | 18.6 | 256 11.7 | 26.1 |
| 03 | 47 05.4 | 202 36.3 | 47.5 | 208 59.3 | 16.9 | 347 47.5 | 18.6 | 271 13.9 | 26.0 |
| 04 | 62 07.9 | 217 35.9 | 48.7 | 224 00.2 | 17.5 | 2 50.0 | 18.5 | 286 16.1 | 25.9 |
| 05 | 77 10.4 | 232 35.5 | 49.9 | 239 01.1 | 18.2 | 17 52.5 | 18.5 | 301 18.3 | 25.9 |
| 06 | 92 12.8 | 247 35.1 | S 9 51.1 | 254 02.0 | S 7 18.8 | 32 55.0 | N19 18.5 | 316 20.5 | N17 25.8 |
| 07 | 107 15.3 | 262 34.7 | 52.3 | 269 03.0 | 19.5 | 47 57.5 | 18.5 | 331 22.8 | 25.7 |
| T 08 | 122 17.8 | 277 34.3 | 53.5 | 284 03.9 | 20.1 | 63 00.0 | 18.5 | 346 25.0 | 25.7 |
| H 09 | 137 20.2 | 292 33.9 | 54.8 | 299 04.8 | 20.8 | 78 02.4 | 18.5 | 1 27.2 | 25.6 |
| U 10 | 152 22.7 | 307 33.5 | 56.0 | 314 05.7 | 21.4 | 93 04.9 | 18.5 | 16 29.4 | 25.5 |
| R 11 | 167 25.2 | 322 33.1 | 57.2 | 329 06.7 | 22.1 | 108 07.4 | 18.5 | 31 31.6 | 25.5 |
| S 12 | 182 27.6 | 337 32.7 | S 9 58.4 | 344 07.6 | S 7 22.7 | 123 09.9 | N19 18.5 | 46 33.8 | N17 25.4 |
| D 13 | 197 30.1 | 352 32.3 | 9 59.6 | 359 08.5 | 23.4 | 138 12.4 | 18.4 | 61 36.0 | 25.3 |
| A 14 | 212 32.5 | 7 31.9 | 10 00.8 | 14 09.4 | 24.0 | 153 14.9 | 18.4 | 76 38.2 | 25.3 |
| Y 15 | 227 35.0 | 22 31.5 | 02.0 | 29 10.4 | 24.7 | 168 17.4 | 18.4 | 91 40.4 | 25.2 |
| 16 | 242 37.5 | 37 31.1 | 03.2 | 44 11.3 | 25.3 | 183 19.9 | 18.4 | 106 42.6 | 25.1 |
| 17 | 257 39.9 | 52 30.7 | 04.4 | 59 12.2 | 26.0 | 198 22.4 | 18.4 | 121 44.8 | 25.1 |
| 18 | 272 42.4 | 67 30.3 | S10 05.6 | 74 13.1 | S 7 26.6 | 213 24.9 | N19 18.4 | 136 47.1 | N17 25.0 |
| 19 | 287 44.9 | 82 29.9 | 06.8 | 89 14.1 | 27.3 | 228 27.4 | 18.4 | 151 49.3 | 24.9 |
| 20 | 302 47.3 | 97 29.5 | 08.0 | 104 15.0 | 27.9 | 243 29.9 | 18.4 | 166 51.5 | 24.9 |
| 21 | 317 49.8 | 112 29.1 | 09.2 | 119 15.9 | 28.6 | 258 32.4 | 18.4 | 181 53.7 | 24.8 |
| 22 | 332 52.3 | 127 28.7 | 10.4 | 134 16.8 | 29.2 | 273 34.9 | 18.3 | 196 55.9 | 24.7 |
| 23 | 347 54.7 | 142 28.3 | 11.7 | 149 17.7 | 29.9 | 288 37.4 | 18.3 | 211 58.1 | 24.7 |
| Mer. Pass. | h m 23 52.2 | v −0.4 | d 1.2 | v 0.9 | d 0.7 | v 2.5 | d 0.0 | v 2.2 | d 0.1 |

**STARS**

| Name | S.H.A. | Dec. |
|---|---|---|
| | ° ′ | ° ′ |
| Acamar | 315 39.0 | S40 23.6 |
| Achernar | 335 46.8 | S57 21.1 |
| Acrux | 173 40.8 | S62 58.2 |
| Adhara | 255 34.3 | S28 56.2 |
| Aldebaran | 291 21.0 | N16 27.8 |
| Alioth | 166 45.5 | N56 05.3 |
| Alkaid | 153 21.1 | N49 25.9 |
| Al Na'ir | 28 17.9 | S47 04.4 |
| Alnilam | 276 14.4 | S 1 12.9 |
| Alphard | 218 23.4 | S 8 33.4 |
| Alphecca | 126 34.6 | N26 47.8 |
| Alpheratz | 358 11.7 | N28 57.9 |
| Altair | 62 35.0 | N 8 48.7 |
| Ankaa | 353 42.5 | S42 25.8 |
| Antares | 113 00.3 | S26 22.8 |
| Arcturus | 146 21.2 | N19 18.4 |
| Atria | 108 27.0 | S68 59.4 |
| Avior | 234 29.6 | S59 25.9 |
| Bellatrix | 279 01.6 | N 6 19.8 |
| Betelgeuse | 271 31.2 | N 7 24.2 |
| Canopus | 264 08.4 | S52 40.7 |
| Capella | 281 15.2 | N45 58.3 |
| Deneb | 49 50.0 | N45 12.2 |
| Denebola | 183 02.1 | N14 42.2 |
| Diphda | 349 23.2 | S18 06.7 |
| Dubhe | 194 26.1 | N61 52.5 |
| Elnath | 278 47.5 | N28 35.2 |
| Eltanin | 90 59.0 | N51 29.9 |
| Enif | 34 13.9 | N 9 46.3 |
| Fomalhaut | 15 54.0 | S29 44.6 |
| Gacrux | 172 32.2 | S56 59.0 |
| Gienah | 176 21.0 | S17 24.7 |
| Hadar | 149 27.6 | S60 15.8 |
| Hamal | 328 31.6 | N23 21.2 |
| Kaus Aust. | 84 20.4 | S34 23.8 |
| Kochab | 137 19.8 | N74 15.3 |
| Markab | 14 05.5 | N15 05.0 |
| Menkar | 314 43.7 | N 4 00.0 |
| Menkent | 148 40.5 | S36 15.4 |
| Miaplacidus | 221 46.1 | S69 37.2 |
| Mirfak | 309 19.6 | N49 46.6 |
| Nunki | 76 32.4 | S26 19.5 |
| Peacock | 54 02.3 | S56 48.7 |
| Pollux | 244 01.6 | N28 04.9 |
| Procyon | 245 28.7 | N 5 17.1 |
| Rasalhague | 96 32.1 | N12 34.9 |
| Regulus | 208 13.1 | N12 04.9 |
| Rigel | 281 38.5 | S 8 13.6 |
| Rigil Kent. | 140 29.9 | S60 44.4 |
| Sabik | 102 44.3 | S15 41.7 |
| Schedar | 350 11.5 | N56 24.7 |
| Shaula | 96 59.4 | S37 05.3 |
| Sirius | 258 58.1 | S16 40.9 |
| Spica | 159 00.7 | S11 02.3 |
| Suhail | 223 13.0 | S43 20.2 |
| Vega | 80 57.6 | N38 46.1 |
| Zuben'ubi | 137 36.2 | S15 56.7 |

| | S.H.A. | Mer. Pass. |
|---|---|---|
| | ° ′ | h m |
| Venus | 156 47.9 | 13 29 |
| Mars | 162 35.3 | 13 05 |
| Jupiter | 300 41.4 | 3 53 |
| Saturn | 224 15.4 | 8 58 |

# 1976 SEPTEMBER 21, 22, 23 (TUES., WED., THURS.)

| G.M.T. | SUN G.H.A. | SUN Dec. | MOON G.H.A. | v | Dec. | d | H.P. |
|---|---|---|---|---|---|---|---|
| d h | ° ′ | ° ′ | ° ′ | ′ | ° ′ | ′ | ′ |
| 21 00 | 181 42.7 | N 0 44.6 | 219 21.4 | 9.5 | N10 07.0 | 10.0 | 58.7 |
| 01 | 196 42.9 | 43.6 | 233 49.9 | 9.5 | 9 57.0 | 10.0 | 58.8 |
| 02 | 211 43.2 | 42.6 | 248 18.4 | 9.5 | 9 47.0 | 10.1 | 58.8 |
| 03 | 226 43.4 | 41.7 | 262 46.9 | 9.5 | 9 36.9 | 10.2 | 58.8 |
| 04 | 241 43.6 | 40.7 | 277 15.4 | 9.5 | 9 26.7 | 10.3 | 58.9 |
| 05 | 256 43.8 | 39.7 | 291 43.9 | 9.4 | 9 16.4 | 10.3 | 58.9 |
| 06 | 271 44.0 | N 0 38.7 | 306 12.3 | 9.5 | N 9 06.1 | 10.4 | 58.9 |
| 07 | 286 44.3 | 37.8 | 320 40.8 | 9.4 | 8 55.7 | 10.4 | 59.0 |
| T 08 | 301 44.5 | 36.8 | 335 09.2 | 9.5 | 8 45.3 | 10.6 | 59.0 |
| U 09 | 316 44.7 | 35.8 | 349 37.7 | 9.4 | 8 34.7 | 10.5 | 59.1 |
| E 10 | 331 44.9 | 34.8 | 4 06.1 | 9.4 | 8 24.2 | 10.7 | 59.1 |
| S 11 | 346 45.1 | 33.9 | 18 34.5 | 9.4 | 8 13.5 | 10.7 | 59.1 |
| D 12 | 1 45.4 | N 0 32.9 | 33 02.9 | 9.4 | N 8 02.8 | 10.7 | 59.2 |
| A 13 | 16 45.6 | 31.9 | 47 31.3 | 9.3 | 7 52.1 | 10.9 | 59.2 |
| Y 14 | 31 45.8 | 31.0 | 61 59.6 | 9.4 | 7 41.2 | 10.8 | 59.2 |
| 15 | 46 46.0 | 30.0 | 76 28.0 | 9.3 | 7 30.4 | 11.0 | 59.3 |
| 16 | 61 46.2 | 29.0 | 90 56.3 | 9.4 | 7 19.4 | 11.0 | 59.3 |
| 17 | 76 46.5 | 28.0 | 105 24.7 | 9.3 | 7 08.4 | 11.0 | 59.3 |
| 18 | 91 46.7 | N 0 27.1 | 119 53.0 | 9.3 | N 6 57.4 | 11.1 | 59.4 |
| 19 | 106 46.9 | 26.1 | 134 21.3 | 9.2 | 6 46.3 | 11.2 | 59.4 |
| 20 | 121 47.1 | 25.1 | 148 49.5 | 9.3 | 6 35.1 | 11.2 | 59.4 |
| 21 | 136 47.3 | 24.1 | 163 17.8 | 9.2 | 6 23.9 | 11.2 | 59.5 |
| 22 | 151 47.6 | 23.2 | 177 46.0 | 9.3 | 6 12.7 | 11.4 | 59.5 |
| 23 | 166 47.8 | 22.2 | 192 14.3 | 9.2 | 6 01.3 | 11.3 | 59.5 |
| 22 00 | 181 48.0 | N 0 21.2 | 206 42.5 | 9.2 | N 5 50.0 | 11.4 | 59.6 |
| 01 | 196 48.2 | 20.3 | 221 10.7 | 9.2 | 5 38.6 | 11.5 | 59.6 |
| 02 | 211 48.4 | 19.3 | 235 38.9 | 9.1 | 5 27.1 | 11.5 | 59.6 |
| 03 | 226 48.7 | 18.3 | 250 07.0 | 9.2 | 5 15.6 | 11.5 | 59.7 |
| 04 | 241 48.9 | 17.3 | 264 35.2 | 9.1 | 5 04.1 | 11.6 | 59.7 |
| 05 | 256 49.1 | 16.4 | 279 03.3 | 9.1 | 4 52.5 | 11.6 | 59.7 |
| 06 | 271 49.3 | N 0 15.4 | 293 31.4 | 9.1 | N 4 40.9 | 11.7 | 59.8 |
| W 07 | 286 49.5 | 14.4 | 307 59.5 | 9.1 | 4 29.2 | 11.7 | 59.8 |
| E 08 | 301 49.7 | 13.4 | 322 27.6 | 9.0 | 4 17.5 | 11.7 | 59.8 |
| D 09 | 316 50.0 | 12.5 | 336 55.6 | 9.1 | 4 05.8 | 11.8 | 59.9 |
| N 10 | 331 50.2 | 11.5 | 351 23.7 | 9.0 | 3 54.0 | 11.8 | 59.9 |
| E 11 | 346 50.4 | 10.5 | 5 51.7 | 9.0 | 3 42.2 | 11.9 | 59.9 |
| S 12 | 1 50.6 | N 0 09.5 | 20 19.7 | 8.9 | N 3 30.3 | 11.9 | 59.9 |
| D 13 | 16 50.8 | 08.6 | 34 47.6 | 9.0 | 3 18.4 | 11.9 | 60.0 |
| A 14 | 31 51.1 | 07.6 | 49 15.6 | 8.9 | 3 06.5 | 11.9 | 60.0 |
| Y 15 | 46 51.3 | 06.6 | 63 43.5 | 8.9 | 2 54.6 | 12.0 | 60.0 |
| 16 | 61 51.5 | 05.7 | 78 11.4 | 8.9 | 2 42.6 | 12.0 | 60.1 |
| 17 | 76 51.7 | 04.7 | 92 39.3 | 8.8 | 2 30.6 | 12.0 | 60.1 |
| 18 | 91 51.9 | N 0 03.7 | 107 07.1 | 8.9 | N 2 18.6 | 12.1 | 60.1 |
| 19 | 106 52.1 | 02.7 | 121 35.0 | 8.8 | 2 06.5 | 12.0 | 60.1 |
| 20 | 121 52.4 | 01.8 | 136 02.8 | 8.8 | 1 54.5 | 12.1 | 60.2 |
| 21 | 136 52.6 | N 0 00.8 | 150 30.6 | 8.8 | 1 42.4 | 12.2 | 60.2 |
| 22 | 151 52.8 | S 0 00.2 | 164 58.4 | 8.7 | 1 30.2 | 12.1 | 60.2 |
| 23 | 166 53.0 | 01.2 | 179 26.1 | 8.7 | 1 18.1 | 12.2 | 60.2 |
| 23 00 | 181 53.2 | S 0 02.1 | 193 53.8 | 8.7 | N 1 05.9 | 12.1 | 60.3 |
| 01 | 196 53.5 | 03.1 | 208 21.5 | 8.7 | 0 53.8 | 12.2 | 60.3 |
| 02 | 211 53.7 | 04.1 | 222 49.2 | 8.6 | 0 41.6 | 12.2 | 60.3 |
| 03 | 226 53.9 | 05.1 | 237 16.8 | 8.6 | 0 29.4 | 12.3 | 60.3 |
| 04 | 241 54.1 | 06.0 | 251 44.4 | 8.6 | 0 17.1 | 12.2 | 60.4 |
| 05 | 256 54.3 | 07.0 | 266 12.0 | 8.6 | N 0 04.9 | 12.2 | 60.4 |
| 06 | 271 54.5 | S 0 08.0 | 280 39.6 | 8.5 | S 0 07.3 | 12.3 | 60.4 |
| 07 | 286 54.8 | 09.0 | 295 07.1 | 8.5 | 0 19.6 | 12.2 | 60.4 |
| T 08 | 301 55.0 | 09.9 | 309 34.6 | 8.5 | 0 31.8 | 12.3 | 60.5 |
| H 09 | 316 55.2 | 10.9 | 324 02.1 | 8.5 | 0 44.1 | 12.2 | 60.5 |
| U 10 | 331 55.4 | 11.9 | 338 29.6 | 8.4 | 0 56.3 | 12.3 | 60.5 |
| R 11 | 346 55.6 | 12.9 | 352 57.0 | 8.4 | 1 08.6 | 12.3 | 60.5 |
| S 12 | 1 55.8 | S 0 13.8 | 7 24.4 | 8.3 | S 1 20.9 | 12.2 | 60.5 |
| D 13 | 16 56.1 | 14.8 | 21 51.7 | 8.4 | 1 33.1 | 12.3 | 60.6 |
| A 14 | 31 56.3 | 15.8 | 36 19.1 | 8.3 | 1 45.4 | 12.3 | 60.6 |
| Y 15 | 46 56.5 | 16.7 | 50 46.4 | 8.3 | 1 57.7 | 12.2 | 60.6 |
| 16 | 61 56.7 | 17.7 | 65 13.7 | 8.2 | 2 09.9 | 12.3 | 60.6 |
| 17 | 76 56.9 | 18.7 | 79 40.9 | 8.2 | 2 22.2 | 12.2 | 60.6 |
| 18 | 91 57.1 | S 0 19.7 | 94 08.1 | 8.2 | S 2 34.4 | 12.2 | 60.7 |
| 19 | 106 57.4 | 20.6 | 108 35.3 | 8.2 | 2 46.6 | 12.3 | 60.7 |
| 20 | 121 57.6 | 21.6 | 123 02.5 | 8.1 | 2 58.9 | 12.2 | 60.7 |
| 21 | 136 57.8 | 22.6 | 137 29.6 | 8.1 | 3 11.1 | 12.2 | 60.7 |
| 22 | 151 58.0 | 23.6 | 151 56.7 | 8.0 | 3 23.3 | 12.1 | 60.7 |
| 23 | 166 58.2 | 24.5 | 166 23.7 | 8.0 | 3 35.4 | 12.2 | 60.7 |
| | S.D. 16.0 | d 1.0 | S.D. 16.1 | | 16.3 | | 16.5 |

| Lat. | Twilight Naut. | Twilight Civil | Sunrise | Moonrise 21 | Moonrise 22 | Moonrise 23 | Moonrise 24 |
|---|---|---|---|---|---|---|---|
| ° | h m | h m | h m | h m | h m | h m | h m |
| N 72 | 02 58 | 04 30 | 05 38 | 01 18 | 03 17 | 05 18 | 07 21 |
| N 70 | 03 18 | 04 38 | 05 40 | 01 34 | 03 25 | 05 17 | 07 13 |
| 68 | 03 34 | 04 45 | 05 41 | 01 47 | 03 31 | 05 17 | 07 06 |
| 66 | 03 46 | 04 50 | 05 42 | 01 57 | 03 36 | 05 17 | 07 01 |
| 64 | 03 57 | 04 55 | 05 43 | 02 06 | 03 40 | 05 17 | 06 56 |
| 62 | 04 05 | 04 59 | 05 44 | 02 13 | 03 44 | 05 17 | 06 52 |
| 60 | 04 12 | 05 02 | 05 44 | 02 20 | 03 47 | 05 17 | 06 49 |
| N 58 | 04 18 | 05 05 | 05 45 | 02 25 | 03 50 | 05 17 | 06 46 |
| 56 | 04 24 | 05 08 | 05 45 | 02 30 | 03 52 | 05 17 | 06 43 |
| 54 | 04 28 | 05 10 | 05 46 | 02 35 | 03 54 | 05 17 | 06 41 |
| 52 | 04 32 | 05 12 | 05 46 | 02 39 | 03 56 | 05 17 | 06 39 |
| 50 | 04 36 | 05 14 | 05 46 | 02 42 | 03 58 | 05 17 | 06 37 |
| 45 | 04 43 | 05 18 | 05 47 | 02 50 | 04 02 | 05 17 | 06 33 |
| N 40 | 04 49 | 05 20 | 05 47 | 02 57 | 04 06 | 05 17 | 06 29 |
| 35 | 04 53 | 05 23 | 05 48 | 03 02 | 04 09 | 05 17 | 06 26 |
| 30 | 04 56 | 05 24 | 05 48 | 03 07 | 04 11 | 05 16 | 06 23 |
| 20 | 05 01 | 05 27 | 05 49 | 03 16 | 04 16 | 05 16 | 06 19 |
| N 10 | 05 04 | 05 28 | 05 49 | 03 23 | 04 19 | 05 16 | 06 15 |
| 0 | 05 05 | 05 29 | 05 50 | 03 31 | 04 23 | 05 16 | 06 11 |
| S 10 | 05 04 | 05 29 | 05 50 | 03 38 | 04 27 | 05 16 | 06 07 |
| 20 | 05 02 | 05 28 | 05 50 | 03 45 | 04 31 | 05 17 | 06 03 |
| 30 | 04 58 | 05 26 | 05 50 | 03 54 | 04 35 | 05 17 | 05 59 |
| 35 | 04 55 | 05 24 | 05 49 | 03 58 | 04 38 | 05 17 | 05 57 |
| 40 | 04 51 | 05 22 | 05 49 | 04 04 | 04 41 | 05 17 | 05 54 |
| 45 | 04 46 | 05 20 | 05 49 | 04 10 | 04 44 | 05 17 | 05 51 |
| S 50 | 04 39 | 05 17 | 05 49 | 04 18 | 04 48 | 05 17 | 05 47 |
| 52 | 04 35 | 05 15 | 05 49 | 04 22 | 04 50 | 05 17 | 05 45 |
| 54 | 04 32 | 05 13 | 05 49 | 04 25 | 04 52 | 05 17 | 05 43 |
| 56 | 04 28 | 05 12 | 05 49 | 04 30 | 04 54 | 05 17 | 05 41 |
| 58 | 04 23 | 05 09 | 05 48 | 04 34 | 04 56 | 05 17 | 05 39 |
| S 60 | 04 17 | 05 07 | 05 48 | 04 40 | 04 59 | 05 17 | 05 36 |

| Lat. | Sunset | Twilight Civil | Twilight Naut. | Moonset 21 | Moonset 22 | Moonset 23 | Moonset 24 |
|---|---|---|---|---|---|---|---|
| ° | h m | h m | h m | h m | h m | h m | h m |
| N 72 | 18 05 | 19 13 | 20 43 | 17 27 | 17 18 | 17 10 | 17 01 |
| N 70 | 18 03 | 19 05 | 20 23 | 17 17 | 17 15 | 17 13 | 17 11 |
| 68 | 18 02 | 18 58 | 20 08 | 17 09 | 17 13 | 17 16 | 17 20 |
| 66 | 18 02 | 18 53 | 19 56 | 17 02 | 17 10 | 17 18 | 17 27 |
| 64 | 18 01 | 18 49 | 19 47 | 16 56 | 17 09 | 17 20 | 17 33 |
| 62 | 18 00 | 18 45 | 19 38 | 16 51 | 17 07 | 17 22 | 17 39 |
| 60 | 18 00 | 18 42 | 19 32 | 16 47 | 17 06 | 17 24 | 17 43 |
| N 58 | 18 00 | 18 39 | 19 26 | 16 43 | 17 04 | 17 25 | 17 47 |
| 56 | 17 59 | 18 36 | 19 20 | 16 40 | 17 03 | 17 26 | 17 51 |
| 54 | 17 59 | 18 34 | 19 16 | 16 37 | 17 02 | 17 28 | 17 54 |
| 52 | 17 58 | 18 32 | 19 12 | 16 34 | 17 01 | 17 29 | 17 57 |
| 50 | 17 58 | 18 31 | 19 08 | 16 31 | 17 00 | 17 29 | 18 00 |
| 45 | 17 58 | 18 27 | 19 01 | 16 25 | 16 58 | 17 32 | 18 06 |
| N 40 | 17 57 | 18 24 | 18 56 | 16 21 | 16 57 | 17 33 | 18 11 |
| 35 | 17 57 | 18 22 | 18 52 | 16 17 | 16 56 | 17 35 | 18 15 |
| 30 | 17 57 | 18 21 | 18 48 | 16 13 | 16 54 | 17 36 | 18 19 |
| 20 | 17 56 | 18 18 | 18 44 | 16 07 | 16 52 | 17 38 | 18 26 |
| N 10 | 17 56 | 18 17 | 18 41 | 16 01 | 16 50 | 17 40 | 18 32 |
| 0 | 17 56 | 18 17 | 18 41 | 15 55 | 16 48 | 17 42 | 18 37 |
| S 10 | 17 56 | 18 17 | 18 41 | 15 50 | 16 46 | 17 44 | 18 43 |
| 20 | 17 56 | 18 18 | 18 44 | 15 44 | 16 44 | 17 46 | 18 49 |
| 30 | 17 56 | 18 20 | 18 48 | 15 38 | 16 42 | 17 48 | 18 55 |
| 35 | 17 56 | 18 22 | 18 51 | 15 34 | 16 41 | 17 49 | 18 59 |
| 40 | 17 57 | 18 24 | 18 55 | 15 29 | 16 39 | 17 51 | 19 04 |
| 45 | 17 57 | 18 26 | 19 01 | 15 24 | 16 37 | 17 52 | 19 09 |
| S 50 | 17 57 | 18 30 | 19 08 | 15 18 | 16 35 | 17 54 | 19 15 |
| 52 | 17 58 | 18 31 | 19 11 | 15 15 | 16 34 | 17 55 | 19 18 |
| 54 | 17 58 | 18 33 | 19 15 | 15 12 | 16 33 | 17 56 | 19 21 |
| 56 | 17 58 | 18 35 | 19 20 | 15 08 | 16 32 | 17 57 | 19 24 |
| 58 | 17 58 | 18 38 | 19 25 | 15 04 | 16 30 | 17 59 | 19 28 |
| S 60 | 17 59 | 18 40 | 19 30 | 15 00 | 16 29 | 18 00 | 19 32 |

| Day | SUN Eqn. of Time 00h | SUN Eqn. of Time 12h | SUN Mer. Pass. | MOON Mer. Pass. Upper | MOON Mer. Pass. Lower | Age | Phase |
|---|---|---|---|---|---|---|---|
| | m s | m s | h m | h m | h m | d | |
| 21 | 06 50 | 07 01 | 11 53 | 09 43 | 22 09 | 27 | |
| 22 | 07 12 | 07 22 | 11 53 | 10 36 | 23 02 | 28 | ● |
| 23 | 07 33 | 07 43 | 11 52 | 11 29 | 23 56 | 29 | |

| G.M.T. | ARIES G.H.A. | VENUS −3.4 G.H.A. | VENUS Dec. | MARS +1.9 G.H.A. | MARS Dec. | JUPITER −2.2 G.H.A. | JUPITER Dec. | SATURN +0.6 G.H.A. | SATURN Dec. |
|---|---|---|---|---|---|---|---|---|---|
| d h | ° ′ | ° ′ | ° ′ | ° ′ | ° ′ | ° ′ | ° ′ | ° ′ | ° ′ |
| 27 00 | 5 54.6 | 156 58.0 | S11 38.5 | 165 24.6 | S 8 17.1 | 306 40.9 | N19 17.3 | 229 39.7 | N17 19.9 |
| 01 | 20 57.1 | 171 57.6 | 39.7 | 180 25.5 | 17.7 | 321 43.4 | 17.3 | 244 41.9 | 19.8 |
| 02 | 35 59.5 | 186 57.2 | 40.8 | 195 26.4 | 18.3 | 336 45.9 | 17.3 | 259 44.1 | 19.8 |
| 03 | 51 02.0 | 201 56.8 | ·· 42.0 | 210 27.3 | ·· 19.0 | 351 48.4 | ·· 17.2 | 274 46.4 | ·· 19.7 |
| 04 | 66 04.5 | 216 56.3 | 43.2 | 225 28.2 | 19.6 | 6 51.0 | 17.2 | 289 48.6 | 19.6 |
| 05 | 81 06.9 | 231 55.9 | 44.4 | 240 29.2 | 20.3 | 21 53.5 | 17.2 | 304 50.8 | 19.6 |
| 06 | 96 09.4 | 246 55.5 | S11 45.5 | 255 30.1 | S 8 20.9 | 36 56.0 | N19 17.2 | 319 53.0 | N17 19.5 |
| 07 | 111 11.8 | 261 55.0 | 46.7 | 270 31.0 | 21.6 | 51 58.6 | 17.2 | 334 55.2 | 19.4 |
| 08 | 126 14.3 | 276 54.6 | 47.9 | 285 31.9 | 22.2 | 67 01.1 | 17.2 | 349 57.5 | 19.4 |
| M 09 | 141 16.8 | 291 54.2 | ·· 49.0 | 300 32.8 | ·· 22.8 | 82 03.6 | ·· 17.1 | 4 59.7 | ·· 19.3 |
| O 10 | 156 19.2 | 306 53.7 | 50.2 | 315 33.7 | 23.5 | 97 06.1 | 17.1 | 20 01.9 | 19.2 |
| N 11 | 171 21.7 | 321 53.3 | 51.4 | 330 34.6 | 24.1 | 112 08.7 | 17.1 | 35 04.1 | 19.2 |
| D 12 | 186 24.2 | 336 52.9 | S11 52.5 | 345 35.5 | S 8 24.8 | 127 11.2 | N19 17.1 | 50 06.3 | N17 19.1 |
| A 13 | 201 26.6 | 351 52.4 | 53.7 | 0 36.4 | 25.4 | 142 13.7 | 17.1 | 65 08.6 | 19.1 |
| Y 14 | 216 29.1 | 6 52.0 | 54.9 | 15 37.3 | 26.1 | 157 16.3 | 17.1 | 80 10.8 | 19.0 |
| 15 | 231 31.6 | 21 51.6 | ·· 56.1 | 30 38.2 | ·· 26.7 | 172 18.8 | ·· 17.0 | 95 13.0 | ·· 18.9 |
| 16 | 246 34.0 | 36 51.1 | 57.2 | 45 39.1 | 27.3 | 187 21.3 | 17.0 | 110 15.2 | 18.9 |
| 17 | 261 36.5 | 51 50.7 | 58.4 | 60 40.1 | 28.0 | 202 23.9 | 17.0 | 125 17.4 | 18.8 |
| 18 | 276 39.0 | 66 50.3 | S11 59.5 | 75 41.0 | S 8 28.6 | 217 26.4 | N19 17.0 | 140 19.7 | N17 18.7 |
| 19 | 291 41.4 | 81 49.8 | 12 00.7 | 90 41.9 | 29.3 | 232 28.9 | 17.0 | 155 21.9 | 18.7 |
| 20 | 306 43.9 | 96 49.4 | 01.9 | 105 42.8 | 29.9 | 247 31.5 | 16.9 | 170 24.1 | 18.6 |
| 21 | 321 46.3 | 111 49.0 | ·· 03.0 | 120 43.7 | ·· 30.6 | 262 34.0 | ·· 16.9 | 185 26.3 | ·· 18.5 |
| 22 | 336 48.8 | 126 48.5 | 04.2 | 135 44.6 | 31.2 | 277 36.5 | 16.9 | 200 28.5 | 18.5 |
| 23 | 351 51.3 | 141 48.1 | 05.4 | 150 45.5 | 31.8 | 292 39.1 | 16.9 | 215 30.8 | 18.4 |
| 28 00 | 6 53.7 | 156 47.7 | S12 06.5 | 165 46.4 | S 8 32.5 | 307 41.6 | N19 16.9 | 230 33.0 | N17 18.3 |
| 01 | 21 56.2 | 171 47.2 | 07.7 | 180 47.3 | 33.1 | 322 44.1 | 16.9 | 245 35.2 | 18.3 |
| 02 | 36 58.7 | 186 46.8 | 08.9 | 195 48.2 | 33.8 | 337 46.7 | 16.8 | 260 37.4 | 18.2 |
| 03 | 52 01.1 | 201 46.4 | ·· 10.0 | 210 49.1 | ·· 34.4 | 352 49.2 | ·· 16.8 | 275 39.6 | ·· 18.2 |
| 04 | 67 03.6 | 216 45.9 | 11.2 | 225 50.0 | 35.1 | 7 51.7 | 16.8 | 290 41.9 | 18.1 |
| 05 | 82 06.1 | 231 45.5 | 12.3 | 240 50.9 | 35.7 | 22 54.3 | 16.8 | 305 44.1 | 18.0 |
| 06 | 97 08.5 | 246 45.0 | S12 13.5 | 255 51.8 | S 8 36.3 | 37 56.8 | N19 16.8 | 320 46.3 | N17 18.0 |
| 07 | 112 11.0 | 261 44.6 | 14.7 | 270 52.7 | 37.0 | 52 59.4 | 16.7 | 335 48.5 | 17.9 |
| 08 | 127 13.5 | 276 44.2 | 15.8 | 285 53.6 | 37.6 | 68 01.9 | 16.7 | 350 50.7 | 17.8 |
| T 09 | 142 15.9 | 291 43.7 | ·· 17.0 | 300 54.5 | ·· 38.3 | 83 04.4 | ·· 16.7 | 5 53.0 | ·· 17.8 |
| U 10 | 157 18.4 | 306 43.3 | 18.1 | 315 55.5 | 38.9 | 98 07.0 | 16.7 | 20 55.2 | 17.7 |
| E 11 | 172 20.8 | 321 42.8 | 19.3 | 330 56.4 | 39.5 | 113 09.5 | 16.7 | 35 57.4 | 17.6 |
| S 12 | 187 23.3 | 336 42.4 | S12 20.5 | 345 57.3 | S 8 40.2 | 128 12.0 | N19 16.7 | 50 59.6 | N17 17.6 |
| D 13 | 202 25.8 | 351 42.0 | 21.6 | 0 58.2 | 40.8 | 143 14.6 | 16.6 | 66 01.9 | 17.5 |
| A 14 | 217 28.2 | 6 41.5 | 22.8 | 15 59.1 | 41.5 | 158 17.1 | 16.6 | 81 04.1 | 17.5 |
| Y 15 | 232 30.7 | 21 41.1 | ·· 23.9 | 31 00.0 | ·· 42.1 | 173 19.7 | ·· 16.6 | 96 06.3 | ·· 17.4 |
| 16 | 247 33.2 | 36 40.6 | 25.1 | 46 00.9 | 42.7 | 188 22.2 | 16.6 | 111 08.5 | 17.3 |
| 17 | 262 35.6 | 51 40.2 | 26.2 | 61 01.8 | 43.4 | 203 24.8 | 16.6 | 126 10.7 | 17.3 |
| 18 | 277 38.1 | 66 39.8 | S12 27.4 | 76 02.7 | S 8 44.0 | 218 27.3 | N19 16.5 | 141 13.0 | N17 17.2 |
| 19 | 292 40.6 | 81 39.3 | 28.5 | 91 03.6 | 44.7 | 233 29.8 | 16.5 | 156 15.2 | 17.1 |
| 20 | 307 43.0 | 96 38.9 | 29.7 | 106 04.5 | 45.3 | 248 32.4 | 16.5 | 171 17.4 | 17.1 |
| 21 | 322 45.5 | 111 38.4 | ·· 30.8 | 121 05.4 | ·· 46.0 | 263 34.9 | ·· 16.5 | 186 19.6 | ·· 17.0 |
| 22 | 337 47.9 | 126 38.0 | 32.0 | 136 06.3 | 46.6 | 278 37.5 | 16.5 | 201 21.9 | 16.9 |
| 23 | 352 50.4 | 141 37.5 | 33.2 | 151 07.2 | 47.2 | 293 40.0 | 16.4 | 216 24.1 | 16.9 |
| 29 00 | 7 52.9 | 156 37.1 | S12 34.3 | 166 08.1 | S 8 47.9 | 308 42.5 | N19 16.4 | 231 26.3 | N17 16.8 |
| 01 | 22 55.3 | 171 36.6 | 35.5 | 181 09.0 | 48.5 | 323 45.1 | 16.4 | 246 28.5 | 16.8 |
| 02 | 37 57.8 | 186 36.2 | 36.6 | 196 09.9 | 49.2 | 338 47.6 | 16.4 | 261 30.8 | 16.7 |
| 03 | 53 00.3 | 201 35.7 | ·· 37.8 | 211 10.8 | ·· 49.8 | 353 50.2 | ·· 16.4 | 276 33.0 | ·· 16.6 |
| 04 | 68 02.7 | 216 35.3 | 38.9 | 226 11.7 | 50.4 | 8 52.7 | 16.3 | 291 35.2 | 16.6 |
| 05 | 83 05.2 | 231 34.8 | 40.1 | 241 12.6 | 51.1 | 23 55.3 | 16.3 | 306 37.4 | 16.5 |
| 06 | 98 07.7 | 246 34.4 | S12 41.2 | 256 13.5 | S 8 51.7 | 38 57.8 | N19 16.3 | 321 39.7 | N17 16.4 |
| W 07 | 113 10.1 | 261 34.0 | 42.4 | 271 14.4 | 52.4 | 54 00.4 | 16.3 | 336 41.9 | 16.4 |
| E 08 | 128 12.6 | 276 33.5 | 43.5 | 286 15.3 | 53.0 | 69 02.9 | 16.3 | 351 44.1 | 16.3 |
| D 09 | 143 15.1 | 291 33.1 | ·· 44.6 | 301 16.2 | ·· 53.6 | 84 05.5 | ·· 16.2 | 6 46.3 | ·· 16.3 |
| N 10 | 158 17.5 | 306 32.6 | 45.8 | 316 17.1 | 54.3 | 99 08.0 | 16.2 | 21 48.6 | 16.2 |
| E 11 | 173 20.0 | 321 32.2 | 46.9 | 331 18.0 | 54.9 | 114 10.6 | 16.2 | 36 50.8 | 16.1 |
| S 12 | 188 22.4 | 336 31.7 | S12 48.1 | 346 18.9 | S 8 55.6 | 129 13.1 | N19 16.2 | 51 53.0 | N17 16.1 |
| D 13 | 203 24.9 | 351 31.3 | 49.2 | 1 19.8 | 56.2 | 144 15.6 | 16.2 | 66 55.2 | 16.0 |
| A 14 | 218 27.4 | 6 30.8 | 50.4 | 16 20.7 | 56.8 | 159 18.2 | 16.1 | 81 57.5 | 15.9 |
| Y 15 | 233 29.8 | 21 30.4 | ·· 51.5 | 31 21.6 | ·· 57.5 | 174 20.7 | ·· 16.1 | 96 59.7 | ·· 15.9 |
| 16 | 248 32.3 | 36 29.9 | 52.7 | 46 22.5 | 58.1 | 189 23.3 | 16.1 | 112 01.9 | 15.8 |
| 17 | 263 34.8 | 51 29.4 | 53.8 | 61 23.4 | 58.7 | 204 25.8 | 16.1 | 127 04.1 | 15.8 |
| 18 | 278 37.2 | 66 29.0 | S12 54.9 | 76 24.3 | S 8 59.4 | 219 28.4 | N19 16.0 | 142 06.4 | N17 15.7 |
| 19 | 293 39.7 | 81 28.5 | 56.1 | 91 25.2 | 9 00.0 | 234 30.9 | 16.0 | 157 08.6 | 15.6 |
| 20 | 308 42.2 | 96 28.1 | 57.2 | 106 26.1 | 00.7 | 249 33.5 | 16.0 | 172 10.8 | 15.6 |
| 21 | 323 44.6 | 111 27.6 | ·· 58.4 | 121 27.0 | ·· 01.3 | 264 36.0 | ·· 16.0 | 187 13.0 | ·· 15.5 |
| 22 | 338 47.1 | 126 27.2 | 12 59.5 | 136 27.9 | 01.9 | 279 38.6 | 16.0 | 202 15.3 | 15.4 |
| 23 | 353 49.6 | 141 26.7 | 13 00.6 | 151 28.8 | 02.6 | 294 41.1 | 15.9 | 217 17.5 | 15.4 |
| Mer. Pass. | h m 23 28.6 | v −0.4 | d 1.2 | v 0.9 | d 0.6 | v 2.5 | d 0.0 | v 2.2 | d 0.1 |

| STARS Name | S.H.A. | Dec. |
|---|---|---|
| | ° ′ | ° ′ |
| Acamar | 315 39.0 | S40 23.6 |
| Achernar | 335 46.8 | S57 21.1 |
| Acrux | 173 40.8 | S62 58.2 |
| Adhara | 255 34.3 | S28 56.2 |
| Aldebaran | 291 20.9 | N16 27.8 |
| Alioth | 166 45.5 | N56 05.2 |
| Alkaid | 153 21.1 | N49 25.9 |
| Al Na'ir | 28 18.0 | S47 04.4 |
| Alnilam | 276 14.3 | S 1 12.9 |
| Alphard | 218 23.4 | S 8 33.4 |
| Alphecca | 126 34.6 | N26 47.8 |
| Alpheratz | 358 11.7 | N28 57.9 |
| Altair | 62 35.0 | N 8 48.7 |
| Ankaa | 353 42.5 | S42 25.8 |
| Antares | 113 00.3 | S26 22.8 |
| Arcturus | 146 21.2 | N19 18.4 |
| Atria | 108 27.1 | S68 59.4 |
| Avior | 234 29.6 | S59 25.9 |
| Bellatrix | 279 01.5 | N 6 19.8 |
| Betelgeuse | 271 31.1 | N 7 24.2 |
| Canopus | 264 08.4 | S52 40.7 |
| Capella | 281 15.1 | N45 58.3 |
| Deneb | 49 50.0 | N45 12.2 |
| Denebola | 183 02.1 | N14 42.2 |
| Diphda | 349 23.2 | S18 06.7 |
| Dubhe | 194 26.1 | N61 52.5 |
| Elnath | 278 47.4 | N28 35.2 |
| Eltanin | 90 59.0 | N51 29.9 |
| Enif | 34 14.0 | N 9 46.4 |
| Fomalhaut | 15 54.0 | S29 44.6 |
| Gacrux | 172 32.2 | S56 59.0 |
| Gienah | 176 21.0 | S17 24.7 |
| Hadar | 149 27.7 | S60 15.7 |
| Hamal | 328 31.6 | N23 21.3 |
| Kaus Aust. | 84 20.4 | S34 23.8 |
| Kochab | 137 19.9 | N74 15.3 |
| Markab | 14 05.5 | N15 05.0 |
| Menkar | 314 43.7 | N 4 00.0 |
| Menkent | 148 40.5 | S36 15.3 |
| Miaplacidus | 221 46.0 | S69 37.1 |
| Mirfak | 309 19.6 | N49 46.6 |
| Nunki | 76 32.4 | S26 19.5 |
| Peacock | 54 02.4 | S56 48.7 |
| Pollux | 244 01.6 | N28 04.9 |
| Procyon | 245 28.7 | N 5 17.1 |
| Rasalhague | 96 32.1 | N12 34.9 |
| Regulus | 208 13.1 | N12 04.9 |
| Rigel | 281 38.5 | S 8 13.6 |
| Rigil Kent. | 140 29.9 | S60 44.4 |
| Sabik | 102 44.3 | S15 41.7 |
| Schedar | 350 11.4 | N56 24.7 |
| Shaula | 96 59.5 | S37 05.3 |
| Sirius | 258 58.1 | S16 40.9 |
| Spica | 159 00.7 | S11 02.3 |
| Suhail | 223 13.0 | S43 20.2 |
| Vega | 80 57.6 | N38 46.1 |
| Zuben'ubi | 137 36.3 | S15 56.6 |

| | S.H.A. | Mer. Pass. |
|---|---|---|
| | ° ′ | h m |
| Venus | 149 53.9 | 13 33 |
| Mars | 158 52.7 | 12 56 |
| Jupiter | 300 47.9 | 3 29 |
| Saturn | 223 39.2 | 8 37 |



| G.M.T. | SUN G.H.A. | SUN Dec. | MOON G.H.A. | v | MOON Dec. | d | H.P. |
|---|---|---|---|---|---|---|---|
| d h | ° ′ | ° ′ | ° ′ | ′ | ° ′ | ′ | ′ |
| 30 00 | 182 28.8 | S 2 45.7 | 97 47.2 | 7.2 | S19 01.4 | 2.0 | 58.4 |
| 01 | 197 29.0 | 46.7 | 112 13.4 | 7.3 | 18 59.4 | 2.1 | 58.4 |
| 02 | 212 29.2 | 47.7 | 126 39.7 | 7.3 | 18 57.3 | 2.3 | 58.4 |
| 03 | 227 29.4 | ·· 48.6 | 141 06.0 | 7.3 | 18 55.0 | 2.4 | 58.3 |
| 04 | 242 29.6 | 49.6 | 155 32.3 | 7.4 | 18 52.6 | 2.4 | 58.3 |
| 05 | 257 29.8 | 50.6 | 169 58.7 | 7.5 | 18 50.2 | 2.6 | 58.3 |
| 06 | 272 30.0 | S 2 51.5 | 184 25.2 | 7.5 | S18 47.6 | 2.7 | 58.2 |
| 07 | 287 30.2 | 52.5 | 198 51.7 | 7.6 | 18 44.9 | 2.8 | 58.2 |
| T 08 | 302 30.4 | 53.5 | 213 18.3 | 7.7 | 18 42.1 | 3.0 | 58.2 |
| H 09 | 317 30.6 | ·· 54.4 | 227 45.0 | 7.7 | 18 39.1 | 3.0 | 58.2 |
| U 10 | 332 30.8 | 55.4 | 242 11.7 | 7.8 | 18 36.1 | 3.1 | 58.1 |
| R 11 | 347 31.1 | 56.4 | 256 38.5 | 7.8 | 18 33.0 | 3.3 | 58.1 |
| S 12 | 2 31.3 | S 2 57.4 | 271 05.3 | 7.9 | S18 29.7 | 3.3 | 58.1 |
| D 13 | 17 31.5 | 58.3 | 285 32.2 | 8.0 | 18 26.4 | 3.5 | 58.0 |
| A 14 | 32 31.7 | 2 59.3 | 299 59.2 | 8.0 | 18 22.9 | 3.6 | 58.0 |
| Y 15 | 47 31.9 | 3 00.3 | 314 26.2 | 8.1 | 18 19.3 | 3.6 | 58.0 |
| 16 | 62 32.1 | 01.2 | 328 53.3 | 8.1 | 18 15.7 | 3.8 | 57.9 |
| 17 | 77 32.3 | 02.2 | 343 20.4 | 8.2 | 18 11.9 | 3.9 | 57.9 |
| 18 | 92 32.5 | S 3 03.2 | 357 47.6 | 8.3 | S18 08.0 | 4.0 | 57.9 |
| 19 | 107 32.7 | 04.2 | 12 14.9 | 8.3 | 18 04.0 | 4.1 | 57.8 |
| 20 | 122 32.9 | 05.1 | 26 42.2 | 8.4 | 17 59.9 | 4.2 | 57.8 |
| 21 | 137 33.1 | ·· 06.1 | 41 09.6 | 8.5 | 17 55.7 | 4.2 | 57.8 |
| 22 | 152 33.3 | 07.1 | 55 37.1 | 8.5 | 17 51.5 | 4.4 | 57.7 |
| 23 | 167 33.5 | 08.0 | 70 04.6 | 8.6 | 17 47.1 | 4.5 | 57.7 |
| 1 00 | 182 33.7 | S 3 09.0 | 84 32.2 | 8.7 | S17 42.6 | 4.6 | 57.7 |
| 01 | 197 33.9 | 10.0 | 98 59.9 | 8.7 | 17 38.0 | 4.7 | 57.7 |
| 02 | 212 34.1 | 10.9 | 113 27.6 | 8.8 | 17 33.3 | 4.7 | 57.6 |
| 03 | 227 34.3 | ·· 11.9 | 127 55.4 | 8.9 | 17 28.6 | 4.9 | 57.6 |
| 04 | 242 34.5 | 12.9 | 142 23.3 | 8.9 | 17 23.7 | 5.0 | 57.6 |
| 05 | 257 34.7 | 13.9 | 156 51.2 | 9.0 | 17 18.7 | 5.0 | 57.5 |
| 06 | 272 34.9 | S 3 14.8 | 171 19.2 | 9.0 | S17 13.7 | 5.2 | 57.5 |
| 07 | 287 35.1 | 15.8 | 185 47.2 | 9.2 | 17 08.5 | 5.2 | 57.5 |
| 08 | 302 35.3 | 16.8 | 200 15.4 | 9.2 | 17 03.3 | 5.4 | 57.4 |
| F 09 | 317 35.5 | ·· 17.7 | 214 43.6 | 9.2 | 16 57.9 | 5.4 | 57.4 |
| R 10 | 332 35.7 | 18.7 | 229 11.8 | 9.4 | 16 52.5 | 5.5 | 57.4 |
| I 11 | 347 35.9 | 19.7 | 243 40.2 | 9.4 | 16 47.0 | 5.6 | 57.3 |
| D 12 | 2 36.1 | S 3 20.6 | 258 08.6 | 9.4 | S16 41.4 | 5.7 | 57.3 |
| A 13 | 17 36.3 | 21.6 | 272 37.0 | 9.6 | 16 35.7 | 5.7 | 57.3 |
| Y 14 | 32 36.5 | 22.6 | 287 05.6 | 9.6 | 16 30.0 | 5.9 | 57.3 |
| 15 | 47 36.7 | ·· 23.5 | 301 34.2 | 9.6 | 16 24.1 | 5.9 | 57.2 |
| 16 | 62 36.9 | 24.5 | 316 02.8 | 9.8 | 16 18.2 | 6.0 | 57.2 |
| 17 | 77 37.1 | 25.5 | 330 31.6 | 9.8 | 16 12.2 | 6.2 | 57.2 |
| 18 | 92 37.3 | S 3 26.5 | 345 00.4 | 9.8 | S16 06.0 | 6.1 | 57.1 |
| 19 | 107 37.5 | 27.4 | 359 29.2 | 10.0 | 15 59.9 | 6.3 | 57.1 |
| 20 | 122 37.7 | 28.4 | 13 58.2 | 10.0 | 15 53.6 | 6.4 | 57.1 |
| 21 | 137 37.9 | ·· 29.4 | 28 27.2 | 10.1 | 15 47.2 | 6.4 | 57.1 |
| 22 | 152 38.1 | 30.3 | 42 56.3 | 10.1 | 15 40.8 | 6.5 | 57.0 |
| 23 | 167 38.3 | 31.3 | 57 25.4 | 10.2 | 15 34.3 | 6.6 | 57.0 |
| 2 00 | 182 38.5 | S 3 32.3 | 71 54.6 | 10.3 | S15 27.7 | 6.6 | 57.0 |
| 01 | 197 38.7 | 33.2 | 86 23.9 | 10.3 | 15 21.1 | 6.8 | 56.9 |
| 02 | 212 38.9 | 34.2 | 100 53.2 | 10.4 | 15 14.3 | 6.8 | 56.9 |
| 03 | 227 39.1 | ·· 35.2 | 115 22.6 | 10.5 | 15 07.5 | 6.8 | 56.9 |
| 04 | 242 39.3 | 36.1 | 129 52.1 | 10.5 | 15 00.7 | 7.0 | 56.9 |
| 05 | 257 39.5 | 37.1 | 144 21.6 | 10.7 | 14 53.7 | 7.0 | 56.8 |
| 06 | 272 39.7 | S 3 38.1 | 158 51.3 | 10.6 | S14 46.7 | 7.1 | 56.8 |
| 07 | 287 39.9 | 39.0 | 173 20.9 | 10.8 | 14 39.6 | 7.2 | 56.8 |
| S 08 | 302 40.1 | 40.0 | 187 50.7 | 10.8 | 14 32.4 | 7.2 | 56.7 |
| A 09 | 317 40.3 | ·· 41.0 | 202 20.5 | 10.8 | 14 25.2 | 7.3 | 56.7 |
| T 10 | 332 40.5 | 41.9 | 216 50.3 | 11.0 | 14 17.9 | 7.4 | 56.7 |
| U 11 | 347 40.7 | 42.9 | 231 20.3 | 11.0 | 14 10.5 | 7.4 | 56.7 |
| R 12 | 2 40.9 | S 3 43.9 | 245 50.3 | 11.0 | S14 03.1 | 7.5 | 56.6 |
| D 13 | 17 41.1 | 44.9 | 260 20.3 | 11.1 | 13 55.6 | 7.6 | 56.6 |
| A 14 | 32 41.3 | 45.8 | 274 50.4 | 11.2 | 13 48.0 | 7.6 | 56.6 |
| Y 15 | 47 41.5 | ·· 46.8 | 289 20.6 | 11.3 | 13 40.4 | 7.7 | 56.6 |
| 16 | 62 41.7 | 47.8 | 303 50.9 | 11.3 | 13 32.7 | 7.8 | 56.5 |
| 17 | 77 41.8 | 48.7 | 318 21.2 | 11.4 | 13 24.9 | 7.8 | 56.5 |
| 18 | 92 42.0 | S 3 49.7 | 332 51.6 | 11.4 | S13 17.1 | 7.9 | 56.5 |
| 19 | 107 42.2 | 50.7 | 347 22.0 | 11.5 | 13 09.2 | 7.9 | 56.5 |
| 20 | 122 42.4 | 51.6 | 1 52.5 | 11.6 | 13 01.3 | 8.0 | 56.4 |
| 21 | 137 42.6 | ·· 52.6 | 16 23.1 | 11.6 | 12 53.3 | 8.0 | 56.4 |
| 22 | 152 42.8 | 53.6 | 30 53.7 | 11.7 | 12 45.3 | 8.1 | 56.4 |
| 23 | 167 43.0 | 54.5 | 45 24.4 | 11.7 | 12 37.2 | 8.2 | 56.4 |
| | S.D. 16.0 | d 1.0 | S.D. 15.8 | | 15.6 | | 15.4 |

| Lat. | Twilight Naut. | Twilight Civil | Sunrise | Moonrise 30 | Moonrise 1 | Moonrise 2 | Moonrise 3 |
|---|---|---|---|---|---|---|---|
| ° | h m | h m | h m | h m | h m | h m | h m |
| N 72 | 03 49 | 05 11 | 06 19 | ■ | 17 15 | 16 58 | 16 47 |
| N 70 | 04 01 | 05 15 | 06 16 | 16 29 | 16 32 | 16 32 | 16 31 |
| 68 | 04 11 | 05 17 | 06 13 | 15 46 | 16 03 | 16 13 | 16 18 |
| 66 | 04 19 | 05 20 | 06 11 | 15 17 | 15 42 | 15 57 | 16 08 |
| 64 | 04 25 | 05 21 | 06 09 | 14 55 | 15 24 | 15 44 | 15 59 |
| 62 | 04 31 | 05 23 | 06 07 | 14 37 | 15 10 | 15 33 | 15 51 |
| 60 | 04 35 | 05 24 | 06 05 | 14 23 | 14 58 | 15 24 | 15 44 |
| N 58 | 04 39 | 05 25 | 06 04 | 14 10 | 14 47 | 15 16 | 15 38 |
| 56 | 04 42 | 05 26 | 06 03 | 13 59 | 14 38 | 15 08 | 15 33 |
| 54 | 04 45 | 05 27 | 06 02 | 13 50 | 14 30 | 15 02 | 15 29 |
| 52 | 04 48 | 05 27 | 06 01 | 13 41 | 14 22 | 14 56 | 15 24 |
| 50 | 04 50 | 05 28 | 06 00 | 13 34 | 14 16 | 14 51 | 15 20 |
| 45 | 04 54 | 05 29 | 05 58 | 13 17 | 14 01 | 14 39 | 15 12 |
| N 40 | 04 58 | 05 29 | 05 56 | 13 04 | 13 50 | 14 30 | 15 05 |
| 35 | 05 00 | 05 29 | 05 54 | 12 52 | 13 40 | 14 21 | 14 59 |
| 30 | 05 02 | 05 29 | 05 53 | 12 42 | 13 31 | 14 14 | 14 54 |
| 20 | 05 03 | 05 29 | 05 51 | 12 25 | 13 16 | 14 02 | 14 44 |
| N 10 | 05 03 | 05 28 | 05 49 | 12 10 | 13 02 | 13 51 | 14 36 |
| 0 | 05 02 | 05 26 | 05 46 | 11 56 | 12 50 | 13 40 | 14 29 |
| S 10 | 04 59 | 05 23 | 05 44 | 11 42 | 12 37 | 13 30 | 14 21 |
| 20 | 04 54 | 05 19 | 05 42 | 11 27 | 12 24 | 13 19 | 14 13 |
| 30 | 04 46 | 05 15 | 05 39 | 11 10 | 12 08 | 13 07 | 14 03 |
| 35 | 04 42 | 05 11 | 05 37 | 11 00 | 12 00 | 12 59 | 13 58 |
| 40 | 04 35 | 05 07 | 05 35 | 10 48 | 11 49 | 12 51 | 13 52 |
| 45 | 04 28 | 05 03 | 05 32 | 10 35 | 11 37 | 12 41 | 13 45 |
| S 50 | 04 18 | 04 57 | 05 29 | 10 18 | 11 23 | 12 29 | 13 36 |
| 52 | 04 13 | 04 54 | 05 28 | 10 11 | 11 16 | 12 24 | 13 32 |
| 54 | 04 08 | 04 51 | 05 26 | 10 02 | 11 09 | 12 18 | 13 27 |
| 56 | 04 02 | 04 47 | 05 25 | 09 52 | 11 00 | 12 11 | 13 23 |
| 58 | 03 55 | 04 43 | 05 23 | 09 41 | 10 51 | 12 03 | 13 17 |
| S 60 | 03 47 | 04 38 | 05 21 | 09 29 | 10 40 | 11 55 | 13 11 |

| Lat. | Sunset | Twilight Civil | Twilight Naut. | Moonset 30 | Moonset 1 | Moonset 2 | Moonset 3 |
|---|---|---|---|---|---|---|---|
| ° | h m | h m | h m | h m | h m | h m | h m |
| N 72 | 17 18 | 18 25 | 19 47 | ■ | 21 01 | 23 02 | 24 51 |
| N 70 | 17 22 | 18 22 | 19 35 | 19 56 | 21 43 | 23 26 | 25 06 |
| 68 | 17 25 | 18 20 | 19 26 | 20 39 | 22 11 | 23 45 | 25 17 |
| 66 | 17 27 | 18 18 | 19 18 | 21 07 | 22 32 | 24 00 | 00 00 |
| 64 | 17 29 | 18 16 | 19 12 | 21 29 | 22 49 | 24 12 | 00 12 |
| 62 | 17 31 | 18 15 | 19 07 | 21 46 | 23 03 | 24 22 | 00 22 |
| 60 | 17 33 | 18 14 | 19 03 | 22 00 | 23 14 | 24 31 | 00 31 |
| N 58 | 17 34 | 18 13 | 18 59 | 22 13 | 23 24 | 24 38 | 00 38 |
| 56 | 17 35 | 18 12 | 18 56 | 22 23 | 23 33 | 24 45 | 00 45 |
| 54 | 17 37 | 18 12 | 18 53 | 22 33 | 23 41 | 24 51 | 00 51 |
| 52 | 17 38 | 18 11 | 18 50 | 22 41 | 23 48 | 24 56 | 00 56 |
| 50 | 17 39 | 18 11 | 18 48 | 22 48 | 23 54 | 25 01 | 01 01 |
| 45 | 17 41 | 18 10 | 18 44 | 23 04 | 24 08 | 00 08 | 01 11 |
| N 40 | 17 43 | 18 09 | 18 41 | 23 17 | 24 19 | 00 19 | 01 20 |
| 35 | 17 44 | 18 09 | 18 39 | 23 28 | 24 28 | 00 28 | 01 27 |
| 30 | 17 46 | 18 09 | 18 37 | 23 38 | 24 36 | 00 36 | 01 34 |
| 20 | 17 48 | 18 10 | 18 36 | 23 54 | 24 51 | 00 51 | 01 45 |
| N 10 | 17 51 | 18 12 | 18 36 | 24 09 | 00 09 | 01 03 | 01 55 |
| 0 | 17 53 | 18 14 | 18 38 | 24 22 | 00 22 | 01 14 | 02 04 |
| S 10 | 17 55 | 18 16 | 18 41 | 24 35 | 00 35 | 01 26 | 02 13 |
| 20 | 17 58 | 18 20 | 18 46 | 24 50 | 00 50 | 01 38 | 02 22 |
| 30 | 18 01 | 18 25 | 18 53 | 00 15 | 01 06 | 01 52 | 02 33 |
| 35 | 18 03 | 18 29 | 18 58 | 00 25 | 01 15 | 02 00 | 02 39 |
| 40 | 18 05 | 18 33 | 19 05 | 00 37 | 01 26 | 02 09 | 02 47 |
| 45 | 18 08 | 18 38 | 19 13 | 00 50 | 01 38 | 02 19 | 02 55 |
| S 50 | 18 11 | 18 44 | 19 23 | 01 07 | 01 54 | 02 32 | 03 05 |
| 52 | 18 13 | 18 47 | 19 28 | 01 15 | 02 01 | 02 38 | 03 09 |
| 54 | 18 14 | 18 50 | 19 33 | 01 24 | 02 09 | 02 45 | 03 14 |
| 56 | 18 16 | 18 54 | 19 40 | 01 34 | 02 17 | 02 52 | 03 20 |
| 58 | 18 18 | 18 58 | 19 47 | 01 45 | 02 27 | 03 00 | 03 26 |
| S 60 | 18 20 | 19 02 | 19 55 | 01 58 | 02 39 | 03 09 | 03 33 |

| Day | SUN Eqn. of Time 00h | SUN Eqn. of Time 12h | SUN Mer. Pass. | MOON Mer. Pass. Upper | MOON Mer. Pass. Lower | Age | Phase |
|---|---|---|---|---|---|---|---|
| | m s | m s | h m | h m | h m | d | |
| 30 | 09 55 | 10 05 | 11 50 | 18 09 | 05 42 | 07 | ◐ |
| 1 | 10 14 | 10 24 | 11 50 | 19 02 | 06 36 | 08 | |
| 2 | 10 34 | 10 43 | 11 49 | 19 52 | 07 28 | 09 | |

# 1976 OCTOBER 18, 19, 20 (MON., TUES., WED.)

| Day | G.M.T. d h | SUN G.H.A. | SUN Dec. | MOON G.H.A. | v | MOON Dec. | d | H.P. |
|---|---|---|---|---|---|---|---|---|
| MONDAY | 18 00 | 183 41.7 | S 9 34.9 | 251 18.2 | 10.6 | N11 32.0 | 9.0 | 57.6 |
| | 01 | 198 41.8 | 35.8 | 265 47.8 | 10.6 | 11 23.0 | 9.0 | 57.7 |
| | 02 | 213 42.0 | 36.7 | 280 17.4 | 10.5 | 11 14.0 | 9.1 | 57.7 |
| | 03 | 228 42.1 | ·· 37.6 | 294 46.9 | 10.6 | 11 04.9 | 9.2 | 57.7 |
| | 04 | 243 42.2 | 38.6 | 309 16.5 | 10.6 | 10 55.7 | 9.3 | 57.8 |
| | 05 | 258 42.3 | 39.5 | 323 46.1 | 10.5 | 10 46.4 | 9.3 | 57.8 |
| | 06 | 273 42.4 | S 9 40.4 | 338 15.6 | 10.5 | N10 37.1 | 9.4 | 57.9 |
| | 07 | 288 42.6 | 41.3 | 352 45.1 | 10.5 | 10 27.7 | 9.5 | 57.9 |
| | 08 | 303 42.7 | 42.2 | 7 14.6 | 10.5 | 10 18.2 | 9.5 | 57.9 |
| | 09 | 318 42.8 | ·· 43.1 | 21 44.1 | 10.5 | 10 08.7 | 9.6 | 58.0 |
| | 10 | 333 42.9 | 44.0 | 36 13.6 | 10.5 | 9 59.1 | 9.7 | 58.0 |
| | 11 | 348 43.0 | 44.9 | 50 43.1 | 10.4 | 9 49.4 | 9.7 | 58.1 |
| | 12 | 3 43.1 | S 9 45.8 | 65 12.5 | 10.4 | N 9 39.7 | 9.9 | 58.1 |
| | 13 | 18 43.3 | 46.7 | 79 41.9 | 10.5 | 9 29.8 | 9.8 | 58.1 |
| | 14 | 33 43.4 | 47.6 | 94 11.4 | 10.4 | 9 20.0 | 10.0 | 58.2 |
| | 15 | 48 43.5 | ·· 48.5 | 108 40.8 | 10.3 | 9 10.0 | 10.0 | 58.2 |
| | 16 | 63 43.6 | 49.4 | 123 10.1 | 10.4 | 9 00.0 | 10.1 | 58.3 |
| | 17 | 78 43.7 | 50.4 | 137 39.5 | 10.4 | 8 49.9 | 10.1 | 58.3 |
| | 18 | 93 43.8 | S 9 51.3 | 152 08.9 | 10.3 | N 8 39.8 | 10.2 | 58.3 |
| | 19 | 108 44.0 | 52.2 | 166 38.2 | 10.3 | 8 29.6 | 10.2 | 58.4 |
| | 20 | 123 44.1 | 53.1 | 181 07.5 | 10.3 | 8 19.4 | 10.4 | 58.4 |
| | 21 | 138 44.2 | ·· 54.0 | 195 36.8 | 10.3 | 8 09.0 | 10.3 | 58.5 |
| | 22 | 153 44.3 | 54.9 | 210 06.1 | 10.2 | 7 58.7 | 10.5 | 58.5 |
| | 23 | 168 44.4 | 55.8 | 224 35.3 | 10.3 | 7 48.2 | 10.5 | 58.5 |
| TUESDAY | 19 00 | 183 44.5 | S 9 56.7 | 239 04.6 | 10.2 | N 7 37.7 | 10.5 | 58.6 |
| | 01 | 198 44.7 | 57.6 | 253 33.8 | 10.2 | 7 27.2 | 10.6 | 58.6 |
| | 02 | 213 44.8 | 58.5 | 268 03.0 | 10.1 | 7 16.6 | 10.7 | 58.7 |
| | 03 | 228 44.9 | 9 59.4 | 282 32.1 | 10.2 | 7 05.9 | 10.7 | 58.7 |
| | 04 | 243 45.0 | 10 00.3 | 297 01.3 | 10.1 | 6 55.2 | 10.8 | 58.7 |
| | 05 | 258 45.1 | 01.2 | 311 30.4 | 10.1 | 6 44.4 | 10.8 | 58.8 |
| | 06 | 273 45.2 | S10 02.1 | 325 59.5 | 10.1 | N 6 33.6 | 10.9 | 58.8 |
| | 07 | 288 45.3 | 03.0 | 340 28.6 | 10.0 | 6 22.7 | 10.9 | 58.9 |
| | 08 | 303 45.4 | 03.9 | 354 57.6 | 10.1 | 6 11.8 | 11.0 | 58.9 |
| | 09 | 318 45.6 | ·· 04.8 | 9 26.7 | 10.0 | 6 00.8 | 11.0 | 58.9 |
| | 10 | 333 45.7 | 05.7 | 23 55.7 | 9.9 | 5 49.8 | 11.1 | 59.0 |
| | 11 | 348 45.8 | 06.6 | 38 24.6 | 10.0 | 5 38.7 | 11.1 | 59.0 |
| | 12 | 3 45.9 | S10 07.5 | 52 53.6 | 9.9 | N 5 27.6 | 11.2 | 59.1 |
| | 13 | 18 46.0 | 08.4 | 67 22.5 | 9.9 | 5 16.4 | 11.2 | 59.1 |
| | 14 | 33 46.1 | 09.3 | 81 51.4 | 9.9 | 5 05.2 | 11.3 | 59.1 |
| | 15 | 48 46.2 | ·· 10.2 | 96 20.3 | 9.8 | 4 53.9 | 11.3 | 59.2 |
| | 16 | 63 46.3 | 11.1 | 110 49.1 | 9.8 | 4 42.6 | 11.4 | 59.2 |
| | 17 | 78 46.4 | 12.0 | 125 17.9 | 9.8 | 4 31.2 | 11.4 | 59.3 |
| | 18 | 93 46.6 | S10 12.9 | 139 46.7 | 9.8 | N 4 19.8 | 11.4 | 59.3 |
| | 19 | 108 46.7 | 13.8 | 154 15.5 | 9.7 | 4 08.4 | 11.5 | 59.3 |
| | 20 | 123 46.8 | 14.7 | 168 44.2 | 9.7 | 3 56.9 | 11.5 | 59.4 |
| | 21 | 138 46.9 | ·· 15.6 | 183 12.9 | 9.7 | 3 45.4 | 11.5 | 59.4 |
| | 22 | 153 47.0 | 16.5 | 197 41.6 | 9.6 | 3 33.9 | 11.6 | 59.5 |
| | 23 | 168 47.1 | 17.4 | 212 10.2 | 9.6 | 3 22.3 | 11.6 | 59.5 |
| WEDNESDAY | 20 00 | 183 47.2 | S10 18.3 | 226 38.8 | 9.6 | N 3 10.7 | 11.7 | 59.5 |
| | 01 | 198 47.3 | 19.2 | 241 07.4 | 9.5 | 2 59.0 | 11.7 | 59.6 |
| | 02 | 213 47.4 | 20.1 | 255 35.9 | 9.5 | 2 47.3 | 11.7 | 59.6 |
| | 03 | 228 47.5 | ·· 21.0 | 270 04.4 | 9.5 | 2 35.6 | 11.7 | 59.6 |
| | 04 | 243 47.6 | 21.9 | 284 32.9 | 9.4 | 2 23.9 | 11.8 | 59.7 |
| | 05 | 258 47.7 | 22.8 | 299 01.3 | 9.4 | 2 12.1 | 11.8 | 59.7 |
| | 06 | 273 47.8 | S10 23.7 | 313 29.7 | 9.3 | N 2 00.3 | 11.9 | 59.8 |
| | 07 | 288 47.9 | 24.6 | 327 58.0 | 9.4 | 1 48.4 | 11.8 | 59.8 |
| | 08 | 303 48.1 | 25.5 | 342 26.4 | 9.2 | 1 36.6 | 11.9 | 59.8 |
| | 09 | 318 48.2 | ·· 26.4 | 356 54.6 | 9.3 | 1 24.7 | 11.9 | 59.9 |
| | 10 | 333 48.3 | 27.3 | 11 22.9 | 9.2 | 1 12.8 | 11.9 | 59.9 |
| | 11 | 348 48.4 | 28.2 | 25 51.1 | 9.2 | 1 00.9 | 12.0 | 59.9 |
| | 12 | 3 48.5 | S10 29.1 | 40 19.3 | 9.1 | N 0 48.9 | 12.0 | 60.0 |
| | 13 | 18 48.6 | 30.0 | 54 47.4 | 9.1 | 0 36.9 | 12.0 | 60.0 |
| | 14 | 33 48.7 | 30.8 | 69 15.5 | 9.0 | 0 24.9 | 12.0 | 60.0 |
| | 15 | 48 48.8 | ·· 31.7 | 83 43.5 | 9.0 | 0 12.9 | 12.0 | 60.1 |
| | 16 | 63 48.9 | 32.6 | 98 11.5 | 9.0 | N 0 00.9 | 12.0 | 60.1 |
| | 17 | 78 49.0 | 33.5 | 112 39.5 | 8.9 | S 0 11.1 | 12.1 | 60.1 |
| | 18 | 93 49.1 | S10 34.4 | 127 07.4 | 8.9 | S 0 23.2 | 12.0 | 60.2 |
| | 19 | 108 49.2 | 35.3 | 141 35.3 | 8.9 | 0 35.2 | 12.1 | 60.2 |
| | 20 | 123 49.3 | 36.2 | 156 03.2 | 8.8 | 0 47.3 | 12.1 | 60.2 |
| | 21 | 138 49.4 | ·· 37.1 | 170 31.0 | 8.7 | 0 59.4 | 12.1 | 60.3 |
| | 22 | 153 49.5 | 38.0 | 184 58.7 | 8.7 | 1 11.5 | 12.1 | 60.3 |
| | 23 | 168 49.6 | 38.9 | 199 26.4 | 8.7 | 1 23.6 | 12.1 | 60.3 |
| | | S.D. 16.1 | d 0.9 | S.D. 15.8 | | 16.1 | | 16.3 |

| Lat. | Twilight Naut. | Twilight Civil | Sunrise | Moonrise 18 | Moonrise 19 | Moonrise 20 | Moonrise 21 |
|---|---|---|---|---|---|---|---|
| ° | h m | h m | h m | h m | h m | h m | h m |
| N 72 | 05 13 | 06 31 | 07 44 | 24 31 | 00 31 | 02 27 | 04 27 |
| N 70 | 05 14 | 06 25 | 07 30 | 24 42 | 00 42 | 02 31 | 04 23 |
| 68 | 05 16 | 06 20 | 07 19 | 24 51 | 00 51 | 02 34 | 04 20 |
| 66 | 05 17 | 06 16 | 07 10 | 24 59 | 00 59 | 02 36 | 04 17 |
| 64 | 05 18 | 06 13 | 07 02 | 25 05 | 01 05 | 02 38 | 04 15 |
| 62 | 05 18 | 06 09 | 06 55 | 25 11 | 01 11 | 02 40 | 04 13 |
| 60 | 05 18 | 06 06 | 06 49 | 25 15 | 01 15 | 02 42 | 04 12 |
| N 58 | 05 18 | 06 04 | 06 44 | 00 00 | 01 20 | 02 43 | 04 10 |
| 56 | 05 18 | 06 02 | 06 39 | 00 06 | 01 23 | 02 45 | 04 09 |
| 54 | 05 18 | 05 59 | 06 35 | 00 11 | 01 27 | 02 46 | 04 08 |
| 52 | 05 18 | 05 57 | 06 32 | 00 16 | 01 30 | 02 47 | 04 07 |
| 50 | 05 18 | 05 55 | 06 28 | 00 20 | 01 32 | 02 48 | 04 06 |
| 45 | 05 17 | 05 51 | 06 21 | 00 30 | 01 38 | 02 50 | 04 04 |
| N 40 | 05 16 | 05 47 | 06 15 | 00 38 | 01 43 | 02 51 | 04 02 |
| 35 | 05 14 | 05 44 | 06 09 | 00 44 | 01 47 | 02 53 | 04 01 |
| 30 | 05 12 | 05 40 | 06 05 | 00 50 | 01 51 | 02 54 | 03 59 |
| 20 | 05 08 | 05 34 | 05 56 | 01 01 | 01 58 | 02 56 | 03 57 |
| N 10 | 05 03 | 05 27 | 05 49 | 01 10 | 02 03 | 02 58 | 03 55 |
| 0 | 04 56 | 05 21 | 05 42 | 01 18 | 02 09 | 03 00 | 03 53 |
| S 10 | 04 48 | 05 13 | 05 34 | 01 26 | 02 14 | 03 02 | 03 52 |
| 20 | 04 38 | 05 04 | 05 27 | 01 35 | 02 20 | 03 04 | 03 50 |
| 30 | 04 24 | 04 53 | 05 18 | 01 45 | 02 26 | 03 07 | 03 48 |
| 35 | 04 15 | 04 46 | 05 12 | 01 51 | 02 30 | 03 08 | 03 47 |
| 40 | 04 05 | 04 38 | 05 07 | 01 58 | 02 34 | 03 09 | 03 45 |
| 45 | 03 52 | 04 29 | 05 00 | 02 06 | 02 39 | 03 11 | 03 44 |
| S 50 | 03 35 | 04 17 | 04 51 | 02 15 | 02 45 | 03 13 | 03 42 |
| 52 | 03 27 | 04 11 | 04 47 | 02 19 | 02 47 | 03 14 | 03 41 |
| 54 | 03 17 | 04 05 | 04 43 | 02 24 | 02 50 | 03 15 | 03 41 |
| 56 | 03 07 | 03 58 | 04 38 | 02 29 | 02 53 | 03 16 | 03 40 |
| 58 | 02 54 | 03 50 | 04 33 | 02 35 | 02 57 | 03 18 | 03 39 |
| S 60 | 02 39 | 03 41 | 04 27 | 02 41 | 03 01 | 03 19 | 03 37 |

| Lat. | Sunset | Twilight Civil | Twilight Naut. | Moonset 18 | Moonset 19 | Moonset 20 | Moonset 21 |
|---|---|---|---|---|---|---|---|
| ° | h m | h m | h m | h m | h m | h m | h m |
| N 72 | 15 44 | 16 57 | 18 15 | 15 42 | 15 34 | 15 26 | 15 17 |
| N 70 | 15 58 | 17 03 | 18 14 | 15 29 | 15 27 | 15 26 | 15 24 |
| 68 | 16 10 | 17 08 | 18 12 | 15 18 | 15 22 | 15 26 | 15 29 |
| 66 | 16 19 | 17 12 | 18 12 | 15 09 | 15 18 | 15 26 | 15 34 |
| 64 | 16 27 | 17 16 | 18 11 | 15 01 | 15 14 | 15 26 | 15 38 |
| 62 | 16 34 | 17 19 | 18 11 | 14 55 | 15 11 | 15 26 | 15 41 |
| 60 | 16 40 | 17 22 | 18 11 | 14 49 | 15 08 | 15 26 | 15 44 |
| N 58 | 16 45 | 17 25 | 18 11 | 14 44 | 15 05 | 15 26 | 15 47 |
| 56 | 16 49 | 17 27 | 18 11 | 14 39 | 15 03 | 15 26 | 15 49 |
| 54 | 16 54 | 17 30 | 18 11 | 14 35 | 15 01 | 15 26 | 15 51 |
| 52 | 16 58 | 17 32 | 18 11 | 14 31 | 14 59 | 15 26 | 15 53 |
| 50 | 17 01 | 17 34 | 18 11 | 14 28 | 14 57 | 15 26 | 15 55 |
| 45 | 17 09 | 17 38 | 18 12 | 14 21 | 14 53 | 15 26 | 15 59 |
| N 40 | 17 15 | 17 42 | 18 14 | 14 15 | 14 50 | 15 26 | 16 02 |
| 35 | 17 20 | 17 46 | 18 15 | 14 09 | 14 47 | 15 26 | 16 05 |
| 30 | 17 25 | 17 49 | 18 17 | 14 04 | 14 45 | 15 26 | 16 08 |
| 20 | 17 34 | 17 56 | 18 22 | 13 56 | 14 41 | 15 25 | 16 12 |
| N 10 | 17 41 | 18 02 | 18 27 | 13 49 | 14 37 | 15 25 | 16 16 |
| 0 | 17 48 | 18 09 | 18 34 | 13 42 | 14 33 | 15 25 | 16 19 |
| S 10 | 17 56 | 18 17 | 18 42 | 13 35 | 14 29 | 15 25 | 16 23 |
| 20 | 18 04 | 18 26 | 18 53 | 13 28 | 14 25 | 15 25 | 16 27 |
| 30 | 18 13 | 18 37 | 19 06 | 13 19 | 14 21 | 15 25 | 16 31 |
| 35 | 18 18 | 18 44 | 19 15 | 13 14 | 14 18 | 15 25 | 16 34 |
| 40 | 18 24 | 18 52 | 19 26 | 13 09 | 14 15 | 15 25 | 16 36 |
| 45 | 18 31 | 19 02 | 19 39 | 13 02 | 14 12 | 15 24 | 16 40 |
| S 50 | 18 40 | 19 14 | 19 57 | 12 54 | 14 08 | 15 24 | 16 44 |
| 52 | 18 44 | 19 20 | 20 05 | 12 50 | 14 06 | 15 24 | 16 45 |
| 54 | 18 48 | 19 26 | 20 15 | 12 46 | 14 04 | 15 24 | 16 47 |
| 56 | 18 53 | 19 34 | 20 26 | 12 42 | 14 01 | 15 24 | 16 50 |
| 58 | 18 59 | 19 42 | 20 39 | 12 37 | 13 59 | 15 24 | 16 52 |
| S 60 | 19 05 | 19 51 | 20 54 | 12 31 | 13 56 | 15 24 | 16 55 |

| Day | SUN Eqn. of Time 00h | SUN Eqn. of Time 12h | SUN Mer. Pass. | MOON Mer. Pass. Upper | MOON Mer. Pass. Lower | Age | Phase |
|---|---|---|---|---|---|---|---|
| | m s | m s | h m | h m | h m | d | |
| 18 | 14 47 | 14 52 | 11 45 | 07 30 | 19 55 | 25 | |
| 19 | 14 58 | 15 03 | 11 45 | 08 21 | 20 47 | 26 | |
| 20 | 15 09 | 15 14 | 11 45 | 09 13 | 21 39 | 27 | |

# 1976 OCTOBER 24, 25, 26 (SUN., MON., TUES.)

| Day | G.M.T. d h | SUN G.H.A. | SUN Dec. | MOON G.H.A. | v | MOON Dec. | d | H.P. |
|---|---|---|---|---|---|---|---|---|
| SUNDAY | 24 00 | 183 56.2 | S11 43.2 | 172 51.2 | 5.0 | S14 39.7 | 8.3 | 61.4 |
| | 01 | 198 56.3 | 44.1 | 187 15.2 | 4.9 | 14 48.0 | 8.1 | 61.4 |
| | 02 | 213 56.3 | 44.9 | 201 39.1 | 4.9 | 14 56.1 | 8.1 | 61.3 |
| | 03 | 228 56.4 | ·· 45.8 | 216 03.0 | 4.9 | 15 04.2 | 7.9 | 61.3 |
| | 04 | 243 56.5 | 46.7 | 230 26.9 | 4.8 | 15 12.1 | 7.8 | 61.3 |
| | 05 | 258 56.6 | 47.6 | 244 50.7 | 4.8 | 15 19.9 | 7.7 | 61.3 |
| | 06 | 273 56.7 | S11 48.4 | 259 14.5 | 4.7 | S15 27.6 | 7.6 | 61.3 |
| | 07 | 288 56.7 | 49.3 | 273 38.2 | 4.8 | 15 35.2 | 7.5 | 61.3 |
| | 08 | 303 56.8 | 50.2 | 288 02.0 | 4.7 | 15 42.7 | 7.3 | 61.3 |
| | 09 | 318 56.9 | ·· 51.0 | 302 25.7 | 4.6 | 15 50.0 | 7.2 | 61.3 |
| | 10 | 333 57.0 | 51.9 | 316 49.3 | 4.6 | 15 57.2 | 7.2 | 61.3 |
| | 11 | 348 57.0 | 52.8 | 331 12.9 | 4.6 | 16 04.4 | 7.0 | 61.3 |
| | 12 | 3 57.1 | S11 53.6 | 345 36.5 | 4.6 | S16 11.4 | 6.8 | 61.2 |
| | 13 | 18 57.2 | 54.5 | 0 00.1 | 4.6 | 16 18.2 | 6.8 | 61.2 |
| | 14 | 33 57.3 | 55.4 | 14 23.7 | 4.5 | 16 25.0 | 6.6 | 61.2 |
| | 15 | 48 57.3 | ·· 56.2 | 28 47.2 | 4.5 | 16 31.6 | 6.5 | 61.2 |
| | 16 | 63 57.4 | 57.1 | 43 10.7 | 4.4 | 16 38.1 | 6.4 | 61.2 |
| | 17 | 78 57.5 | 58.0 | 57 34.1 | 4.5 | 16 44.5 | 6.3 | 61.2 |
| | 18 | 93 57.6 | S11 58.8 | 71 57.6 | 4.4 | S16 50.8 | 6.1 | 61.2 |
| | 19 | 108 57.6 | 11 59.7 | 86 21.0 | 4.5 | 16 56.9 | 6.0 | 61.1 |
| | 20 | 123 57.7 | 12 00.6 | 100 44.5 | 4.4 | 17 02.9 | 5.9 | 61.1 |
| | 21 | 138 57.8 | ·· 01.4 | 115 07.9 | 4.3 | 17 08.8 | 5.7 | 61.1 |
| | 22 | 153 57.9 | 02.3 | 129 31.2 | 4.4 | 17 14.5 | 5.6 | 61.1 |
| | 23 | 168 57.9 | 03.1 | 143 54.6 | 4.4 | 17 20.1 | 5.5 | 61.1 |
| MONDAY | 25 00 | 183 58.0 | S12 04.0 | 158 18.0 | 4.3 | S17 25.6 | 5.4 | 61.0 |
| | 01 | 198 58.1 | 04.9 | 172 41.3 | 4.3 | 17 31.0 | 5.2 | 61.0 |
| | 02 | 213 58.1 | 05.7 | 187 04.6 | 4.4 | 17 36.2 | 5.1 | 61.0 |
| | 03 | 228 58.2 | ·· 06.6 | 201 28.0 | 4.3 | 17 41.3 | 4.9 | 61.0 |
| | 04 | 243 58.3 | 07.5 | 215 51.3 | 4.3 | 17 46.2 | 4.9 | 61.0 |
| | 05 | 258 58.4 | 08.3 | 230 14.6 | 4.3 | 17 51.1 | 4.7 | 60.9 |
| | 06 | 273 58.4 | S12 09.2 | 244 37.9 | 4.3 | S17 55.8 | 4.5 | 60.9 |
| | 07 | 288 58.5 | 10.0 | 259 01.2 | 4.3 | 18 00.3 | 4.4 | 60.9 |
| | 08 | 303 58.6 | 10.9 | 273 24.5 | 4.3 | 18 04.7 | 4.3 | 60.9 |
| | 09 | 318 58.6 | ·· 11.8 | 287 47.8 | 4.3 | 18 09.0 | 4.2 | 60.8 |
| | 10 | 333 58.7 | 12.6 | 302 11.1 | 4.3 | 18 13.2 | 4.0 | 60.8 |
| | 11 | 348 58.8 | 13.5 | 316 34.4 | 4.3 | 18 17.2 | 3.9 | 60.8 |
| | 12 | 3 58.8 | S12 14.3 | 330 57.7 | 4.4 | S18 21.1 | 3.7 | 60.8 |
| | 13 | 18 58.9 | 15.2 | 345 21.1 | 4.3 | 18 24.8 | 3.6 | 60.8 |
| | 14 | 33 59.0 | 16.1 | 359 44.4 | 4.3 | 18 28.4 | 3.5 | 60.7 |
| | 15 | 48 59.0 | ·· 16.9 | 14 07.7 | 4.4 | 18 31.9 | 3.3 | 60.7 |
| | 16 | 63 59.1 | 17.8 | 28 31.1 | 4.3 | 18 35.2 | 3.2 | 60.7 |
| | 17 | 78 59.2 | 18.6 | 42 54.4 | 4.4 | 18 38.4 | 3.1 | 60.6 |
| | 18 | 93 59.2 | S12 19.5 | 57 17.8 | 4.4 | S18 41.5 | 2.9 | 60.6 |
| | 19 | 108 59.3 | 20.3 | 71 41.2 | 4.4 | 18 44.4 | 2.8 | 60.6 |
| | 20 | 123 59.4 | 21.2 | 86 04.6 | 4.4 | 18 47.2 | 2.6 | 60.6 |
| | 21 | 138 59.4 | ·· 22.0 | 100 28.0 | 4.5 | 18 49.8 | 2.5 | 60.5 |
| | 22 | 153 59.5 | 22.9 | 114 51.5 | 4.4 | 18 52.3 | 2.4 | 60.5 |
| | 23 | 168 59.6 | 23.8 | 129 14.9 | 4.5 | 18 54.7 | 2.2 | 60.5 |
| TUESDAY | 26 00 | 183 59.6 | S12 24.6 | 143 38.4 | 4.5 | S18 56.9 | 2.1 | 60.4 |
| | 01 | 198 59.7 | 25.5 | 158 01.9 | 4.5 | 18 59.0 | 1.9 | 60.4 |
| | 02 | 213 59.8 | 26.3 | 172 25.4 | 4.6 | 19 00.9 | 1.9 | 60.4 |
| | 03 | 228 59.8 | ·· 27.2 | 186 49.0 | 4.6 | 19 02.8 | 1.6 | 60.4 |
| | 04 | 243 59.9 | 28.0 | 201 12.6 | 4.6 | 19 04.4 | 1.6 | 60.3 |
| | 05 | 258 59.9 | 28.9 | 215 36.2 | 4.7 | 19 06.0 | 1.4 | 60.3 |
| | 06 | 274 00.0 | S12 29.7 | 229 59.9 | 4.7 | S19 07.4 | 1.2 | 60.3 |
| | 07 | 289 00.1 | 30.6 | 244 23.6 | 4.7 | 19 08.6 | 1.2 | 60.2 |
| | 08 | 304 00.1 | 31.4 | 258 47.3 | 4.7 | 19 09.8 | 1.0 | 60.2 |
| | 09 | 319 00.2 | ·· 32.3 | 273 11.0 | 4.8 | 19 10.8 | 0.8 | 60.2 |
| | 10 | 334 00.3 | 33.1 | 287 34.8 | 4.9 | 19 11.6 | 0.7 | 60.1 |
| | 11 | 349 00.3 | 34.0 | 301 58.7 | 4.8 | 19 12.3 | 0.6 | 60.1 |
| | 12 | 4 00.4 | S12 34.9 | 316 22.5 | 4.9 | S19 12.9 | 0.5 | 60.1 |
| | 13 | 19 00.4 | 35.7 | 330 46.4 | 5.0 | 19 13.4 | 0.3 | 60.0 |
| | 14 | 34 00.5 | 36.6 | 345 10.4 | 5.0 | 19 13.7 | 0.2 | 60.0 |
| | 15 | 49 00.6 | ·· 37.4 | 359 34.4 | 5.0 | 19 13.9 | 0.0 | 60.0 |
| | 16 | 64 00.6 | 38.3 | 13 58.4 | 5.1 | 19 13.9 | 0.1 | 59.9 |
| | 17 | 79 00.7 | 39.1 | 28 22.5 | 5.2 | 19 13.8 | 0.2 | 59.9 |
| | 18 | 94 00.7 | S12 40.0 | 42 46.7 | 5.2 | S19 13.6 | 0.3 | 59.9 |
| | 19 | 109 00.8 | 40.8 | 57 10.9 | 5.2 | 19 13.3 | 0.5 | 59.8 |
| | 20 | 124 00.9 | 41.6 | 71 35.1 | 5.3 | 19 12.8 | 0.6 | 59.8 |
| | 21 | 139 00.9 | ·· 42.5 | 85 59.4 | 5.4 | 19 12.2 | 0.8 | 59.8 |
| | 22 | 154 01.0 | 43.3 | 100 23.8 | 5.4 | 19 11.4 | 0.9 | 59.7 |
| | 23 | 169 01.0 | 44.2 | 114 48.2 | 5.4 | 19 10.5 | 1.0 | 59.7 |
| | | S.D. 16.1 | d 0.9 | S.D. 16.7 | | 16.6 | | 16.4 |

| Lat. | Twilight Naut. | Twilight Civil | Sunrise | Moonrise 24 | Moonrise 25 | Moonrise 26 | Moonrise 27 |
|---|---|---|---|---|---|---|---|
| ° | h m | h m | h m | h m | h m | h m | h m |
| N 72 | 05 38 | 06 58 | 08 16 | 11 11 | ■ | ■ | ■ |
| N 70 | 05 37 | 06 49 | 07 57 | 10 25 | 12 26 | 14 00 | 14 35 |
| 68 | 05 36 | 06 41 | 07 42 | 09 55 | 11 39 | 12 59 | 13 46 |
| 66 | 05 35 | 06 35 | 07 30 | 09 33 | 11 08 | 12 24 | 13 15 |
| 64 | 05 34 | 06 30 | 07 20 | 09 15 | 10 46 | 11 59 | 12 52 |
| 62 | 05 33 | 06 25 | 07 12 | 09 01 | 10 28 | 11 39 | 12 33 |
| 60 | 05 32 | 06 21 | 07 04 | 08 49 | 10 13 | 11 23 | 12 18 |
| N 58 | 05 31 | 06 17 | 06 58 | 08 39 | 10 00 | 11 10 | 12 05 |
| 56 | 05 30 | 06 14 | 06 52 | 08 29 | 09 49 | 10 58 | 11 54 |
| 54 | 05 29 | 06 10 | 06 47 | 08 21 | 09 39 | 10 47 | 11 44 |
| 52 | 05 28 | 06 07 | 06 42 | 08 14 | 09 31 | 10 38 | 11 35 |
| 50 | 05 27 | 06 05 | 06 38 | 08 08 | 09 23 | 10 30 | 11 27 |
| 45 | 05 24 | 05 59 | 06 29 | 07 54 | 09 07 | 10 13 | 11 10 |
| N 40 | 05 22 | 05 53 | 06 21 | 07 43 | 08 53 | 09 58 | 10 56 |
| 35 | 05 19 | 05 49 | 06 15 | 07 33 | 08 42 | 09 46 | 10 44 |
| 30 | 05 16 | 05 44 | 06 09 | 07 24 | 08 32 | 09 36 | 10 34 |
| 20 | 05 10 | 05 36 | 05 58 | 07 10 | 08 15 | 09 18 | 10 17 |
| N 10 | 05 03 | 05 28 | 05 49 | 06 57 | 08 00 | 09 02 | 10 01 |
| 0 | 04 55 | 05 19 | 05 41 | 06 46 | 07 47 | 08 47 | 09 47 |
| S 10 | 04 45 | 05 10 | 05 32 | 06 34 | 07 33 | 08 33 | 09 32 |
| 20 | 04 33 | 05 00 | 05 23 | 06 21 | 07 18 | 08 17 | 09 17 |
| 30 | 04 17 | 04 47 | 05 12 | 06 07 | 07 02 | 07 59 | 08 59 |
| 35 | 04 07 | 04 39 | 05 05 | 05 59 | 06 52 | 07 49 | 08 49 |
| 40 | 03 55 | 04 30 | 04 58 | 05 50 | 06 41 | 07 37 | 08 37 |
| 45 | 03 40 | 04 18 | 04 50 | 05 39 | 06 28 | 07 23 | 08 24 |
| S 50 | 03 21 | 04 04 | 04 39 | 05 26 | 06 12 | 07 06 | 08 07 |
| 52 | 03 11 | 03 58 | 04 35 | 05 20 | 06 05 | 06 58 | 07 59 |
| 54 | 03 00 | 03 50 | 04 29 | 05 14 | 05 57 | 06 49 | 07 50 |
| 56 | 02 47 | 03 42 | 04 24 | 05 06 | 05 48 | 06 39 | 07 40 |
| 58 | 02 32 | 03 32 | 04 17 | 04 58 | 05 38 | 06 28 | 07 29 |
| S 60 | 02 13 | 03 21 | 04 10 | 04 49 | 05 26 | 06 15 | 07 16 |

| Lat. | Sunset | Twilight Civil | Twilight Naut. | Moonset 24 | Moonset 25 | Moonset 26 | Moonset 27 |
|---|---|---|---|---|---|---|---|
| ° | h m | h m | h m | h m | h m | h m | h m |
| N 72 | 15 11 | 16 29 | 17 48 | 14 36 | ■ | ■ | ■ |
| N 70 | 15 30 | 16 38 | 17 50 | 15 23 | 15 30 | 16 03 | 17 31 |
| 68 | 15 45 | 16 46 | 17 51 | 15 54 | 16 17 | 17 04 | 18 19 |
| 66 | 15 57 | 16 52 | 17 52 | 16 17 | 16 48 | 17 39 | 18 50 |
| 64 | 16 07 | 16 58 | 17 53 | 16 35 | 17 11 | 18 04 | 19 13 |
| 62 | 16 15 | 17 02 | 17 54 | 16 50 | 17 30 | 18 24 | 19 32 |
| 60 | 16 23 | 17 07 | 17 55 | 17 02 | 17 45 | 18 40 | 19 47 |
| N 58 | 16 29 | 17 10 | 17 56 | 17 13 | 17 58 | 18 54 | 20 00 |
| 56 | 16 35 | 17 14 | 17 57 | 17 23 | 18 09 | 19 06 | 20 11 |
| 54 | 16 40 | 17 17 | 17 58 | 17 31 | 18 19 | 19 16 | 20 20 |
| 52 | 16 45 | 17 20 | 17 59 | 17 39 | 18 28 | 19 25 | 20 29 |
| 50 | 16 50 | 17 23 | 18 00 | 17 46 | 18 36 | 19 33 | 20 37 |
| 45 | 16 59 | 17 29 | 18 03 | 18 01 | 18 53 | 19 51 | 20 53 |
| N 40 | 17 07 | 17 34 | 18 06 | 18 13 | 19 06 | 20 05 | 21 07 |
| 35 | 17 13 | 17 39 | 18 09 | 18 23 | 19 18 | 20 17 | 21 18 |
| 30 | 17 19 | 17 44 | 18 12 | 18 32 | 19 28 | 20 28 | 21 28 |
| 20 | 17 30 | 17 52 | 18 18 | 18 48 | 19 46 | 20 46 | 21 45 |
| N 10 | 17 39 | 18 00 | 18 25 | 19 02 | 20 01 | 21 01 | 22 00 |
| 0 | 17 47 | 18 09 | 18 33 | 19 14 | 20 16 | 21 16 | 22 14 |
| S 10 | 17 57 | 18 18 | 18 43 | 19 27 | 20 30 | 21 31 | 22 28 |
| 20 | 18 06 | 18 29 | 18 55 | 19 41 | 20 45 | 21 46 | 22 43 |
| 30 | 18 17 | 18 42 | 19 11 | 19 57 | 21 03 | 22 04 | 23 00 |
| 35 | 18 23 | 18 50 | 19 22 | 20 06 | 21 13 | 22 15 | 23 09 |
| 40 | 18 31 | 18 59 | 19 34 | 20 16 | 21 25 | 22 26 | 23 20 |
| 45 | 18 39 | 19 11 | 19 49 | 20 29 | 21 38 | 22 40 | 23 33 |
| S 50 | 18 50 | 19 25 | 20 09 | 20 44 | 21 55 | 22 57 | 23 49 |
| 52 | 18 55 | 19 32 | 20 19 | 20 51 | 22 03 | 23 06 | 23 57 |
| 54 | 19 00 | 19 39 | 20 30 | 20 58 | 22 12 | 23 14 | 24 05 |
| 56 | 19 06 | 19 48 | 20 43 | 21 07 | 22 22 | 23 24 | 24 14 |
| 58 | 19 13 | 19 58 | 20 59 | 21 17 | 22 33 | 23 36 | 24 25 |
| S 60 | 19 20 | 20 09 | 21 18 | 21 28 | 22 46 | 23 49 | 24 37 |

| Day | SUN Eqn. of Time 00h | SUN Eqn. of Time 12h | SUN Mer. Pass. | MOON Mer. Pass. Upper | MOON Mer. Pass. Lower | Age | Phase |
|---|---|---|---|---|---|---|---|
| | m s | m s | h m | h m | h m | d | |
| 24 | 15 45 | 15 48 | 11 44 | 13 00 | 00 30 | 01 | |
| 25 | 15 52 | 15 55 | 11 44 | 14 01 | 01 30 | 02 | |
| 26 | 15 58 | 16 01 | 11 44 | 15 02 | 02 32 | 03 | |

## 1976 NOVEMBER 17, 18, 19 (WED., THURS., FRI.)

| G.M.T. | ARIES G.H.A. | VENUS −3.5 G.H.A. | VENUS Dec. | MARS +1.6 G.H.A. | MARS Dec. | JUPITER −2.4 G.H.A. | JUPITER Dec. | SATURN +0.5 G.H.A. | SATURN Dec. |
|---|---|---|---|---|---|---|---|---|---|
| d h | ° ′ | ° ′ | ° ′ | ° ′ | ° ′ | ° ′ | ° ′ | ° ′ | ° ′ |
| 17 00 | 56 10.7 | 142 46.1 | S25 26.4 | 181 21.3 | S19 42.0 | 1 54.3 | N18 13.5 | 276 43.3 | N16 31.5 |
| 01 | 71 13.1 | 157 45.3 | 26.4 | 196 21.9 | 42.5 | 16 57.1 | 13.4 | 291 45.7 | 31.5 |
| 02 | 86 15.6 | 172 44.4 | 26.4 | 211 22.6 | 42.9 | 31 59.9 | 13.3 | 306 48.1 | 31.4 |
| 03 | 101 18.0 | 187 43.5 | ·· 26.4 | 226 23.2 | ·· 43.3 | 47 02.7 | ·· 13.3 | 321 50.5 | ·· 31.4 |
| 04 | 116 20.5 | 202 42.6 | 26.3 | 241 23.8 | 43.8 | 62 05.5 | 13.2 | 336 52.9 | 31.4 |
| 05 | 131 23.0 | 217 41.8 | 26.3 | 256 24.5 | 44.2 | 77 08.3 | 13.1 | 351 55.3 | 31.4 |
| 06 | 146 25.4 | 232 40.9 | S25 26.3 | 271 25.1 | S19 44.6 | 92 11.2 | N18 13.0 | 6 57.7 | N16 31.4 |
| 07 | 161 27.9 | 247 40.0 | 26.3 | 286 25.7 | 45.1 | 107 14.0 | 13.0 | 22 00.1 | 31.4 |
| W 08 | 176 30.4 | 262 39.2 | 26.3 | 301 26.4 | 45.5 | 122 16.8 | 12.9 | 37 02.6 | 31.4 |
| E 09 | 191 32.8 | 277 38.3 | ·· 26.3 | 316 27.0 | ·· 45.9 | 137 19.6 | ·· 12.8 | 52 05.0 | ·· 31.4 |
| D 10 | 206 35.3 | 292 37.4 | 26.3 | 331 27.6 | 46.3 | 152 22.4 | 12.7 | 67 07.4 | 31.4 |
| N 11 | 221 37.8 | 307 36.6 | 26.2 | 346 28.3 | 46.8 | 167 25.2 | 12.7 | 82 09.8 | 31.4 |
| E 12 | 236 40.2 | 322 35.7 | S25 26.2 | 1 28.9 | S19 47.2 | 182 28.0 | N18 12.6 | 97 12.2 | N16 31.4 |
| S 13 | 251 42.7 | 337 34.8 | 26.2 | 16 29.5 | 47.6 | 197 30.9 | 12.5 | 112 14.6 | 31.4 |
| D 14 | 266 45.2 | 352 34.0 | 26.2 | 31 30.1 | 48.1 | 212 33.7 | 12.4 | 127 17.0 | 31.4 |
| A 15 | 281 47.6 | 7 33.1 | ·· 26.2 | 46 30.8 | ·· 48.5 | 227 36.5 | ·· 12.4 | 142 19.5 | ·· 31.3 |
| Y 16 | 296 50.1 | 22 32.2 | 26.1 | 61 31.4 | 48.9 | 242 39.3 | 12.3 | 157 21.9 | 31.3 |
| 17 | 311 52.5 | 37 31.3 | 26.1 | 76 32.0 | 49.3 | 257 42.1 | 12.2 | 172 24.3 | 31.3 |
| 18 | 326 55.0 | 52 30.5 | S25 26.1 | 91 32.7 | S19 49.8 | 272 44.9 | N18 12.1 | 187 26.7 | N16 31.3 |
| 19 | 341 57.5 | 67 29.6 | 26.1 | 106 33.3 | 50.2 | 287 47.7 | 12.1 | 202 29.1 | 31.3 |
| 20 | 356 59.9 | 82 28.7 | 26.0 | 121 33.9 | 50.6 | 302 50.6 | 12.0 | 217 31.5 | 31.3 |
| 21 | 12 02.4 | 97 27.9 | ·· 26.0 | 136 34.5 | ·· 51.0 | 317 53.4 | ·· 11.9 | 232 33.9 | ·· 31.3 |
| 22 | 27 04.9 | 112 27.0 | 26.0 | 151 35.2 | 51.5 | 332 56.2 | 11.8 | 247 36.4 | 31.3 |
| 23 | 42 07.3 | 127 26.1 | 25.9 | 166 35.8 | 51.9 | 347 59.0 | 11.8 | 262 38.8 | 31.3 |
| 18 00 | 57 09.8 | 142 25.3 | S25 25.9 | 181 36.4 | S19 52.3 | 3 01.8 | N18 11.7 | 277 41.2 | N16 31.3 |
| 01 | 72 12.3 | 157 24.4 | 25.9 | 196 37.1 | 52.7 | 18 04.6 | 11.6 | 292 43.6 | 31.3 |
| 02 | 87 14.7 | 172 23.5 | 25.8 | 211 37.7 | 53.2 | 33 07.4 | 11.5 | 307 46.0 | 31.3 |
| 03 | 102 17.2 | 187 22.7 | ·· 25.8 | 226 38.3 | ·· 53.6 | 48 10.3 | ·· 11.5 | 322 48.4 | ·· 31.3 |
| 04 | 117 19.7 | 202 21.8 | 25.8 | 241 38.9 | 54.0 | 63 13.1 | 11.4 | 337 50.9 | 31.3 |
| 05 | 132 22.1 | 217 20.9 | 25.7 | 256 39.6 | 54.4 | 78 15.9 | 11.3 | 352 53.3 | 31.3 |
| 06 | 147 24.6 | 232 20.1 | S25 25.7 | 271 40.2 | S19 54.9 | 93 18.7 | N18 11.2 | 7 55.7 | N16 31.2 |
| 07 | 162 27.0 | 247 19.2 | 25.6 | 286 40.8 | 55.3 | 108 21.5 | 11.2 | 22 58.1 | 31.2 |
| T 08 | 177 29.5 | 262 18.3 | 25.6 | 301 41.4 | 55.7 | 123 24.3 | 11.1 | 38 00.5 | 31.2 |
| H 09 | 192 32.0 | 277 17.5 | ·· 25.5 | 316 42.1 | ·· 56.1 | 138 27.1 | ·· 11.0 | 53 02.9 | ·· 31.2 |
| U 10 | 207 34.4 | 292 16.6 | 25.5 | 331 42.7 | 56.5 | 153 30.0 | 10.9 | 68 05.4 | 31.2 |
| R 11 | 222 36.9 | 307 15.7 | 25.4 | 346 43.3 | 57.0 | 168 32.8 | 10.9 | 83 07.8 | 31.2 |
| S 12 | 237 39.4 | 322 14.9 | S25 25.4 | 1 43.9 | S19 57.4 | 183 35.6 | N18 10.8 | 98 10.2 | N16 31.2 |
| D 13 | 252 41.8 | 337 14.0 | 25.3 | 16 44.6 | 57.8 | 198 38.4 | 10.7 | 113 12.6 | 31.2 |
| A 14 | 267 44.3 | 352 13.1 | 25.3 | 31 45.2 | 58.2 | 213 41.2 | 10.6 | 128 15.0 | 31.2 |
| Y 15 | 282 46.8 | 7 12.3 | ·· 25.2 | 46 45.8 | ·· 58.6 | 228 44.0 | ·· 10.6 | 143 17.5 | ·· 31.2 |
| 16 | 297 49.2 | 22 11.4 | 25.2 | 61 46.4 | 59.1 | 243 46.9 | 10.5 | 158 19.9 | 31.2 |
| 17 | 312 51.7 | 37 10.5 | 25.1 | 76 47.1 | 59.5 | 258 49.7 | 10.4 | 173 22.3 | 31.2 |
| 18 | 327 54.1 | 52 09.7 | S25 25.1 | 91 47.7 | S19 59.9 | 273 52.5 | N18 10.3 | 188 24.7 | N16 31.2 |
| 19 | 342 56.6 | 67 08.8 | 25.0 | 106 48.3 | 20 00.3 | 288 55.3 | 10.3 | 203 27.1 | 31.2 |
| 20 | 357 59.1 | 82 07.9 | 24.9 | 121 48.9 | 00.7 | 303 58.1 | 10.2 | 218 29.6 | 31.2 |
| 21 | 13 01.5 | 97 07.1 | ·· 24.9 | 136 49.5 | ·· 01.2 | 319 00.9 | ·· 10.1 | 233 32.0 | ·· 31.2 |
| 22 | 28 04.0 | 112 06.2 | 24.8 | 151 50.2 | 01.6 | 334 03.7 | 10.0 | 248 34.4 | 31.1 |
| 23 | 43 06.5 | 127 05.3 | 24.8 | 166 50.8 | 02.0 | 349 06.6 | 10.0 | 263 36.8 | 31.1 |
| 19 00 | 58 08.9 | 142 04.5 | S25 24.7 | 181 51.4 | S20 02.4 | 4 09.4 | N18 09.9 | 278 39.2 | N16 31.1 |
| 01 | 73 11.4 | 157 03.6 | 24.6 | 196 52.0 | 02.8 | 19 12.2 | 09.8 | 293 41.7 | 31.1 |
| 02 | 88 13.9 | 172 02.7 | 24.6 | 211 52.6 | 03.2 | 34 15.0 | 09.7 | 308 44.1 | 31.1 |
| 03 | 103 16.3 | 187 01.9 | ·· 24.5 | 226 53.3 | ·· 03.7 | 49 17.8 | ·· 09.7 | 323 46.5 | ·· 31.1 |
| 04 | 118 18.8 | 202 01.0 | 24.4 | 241 53.9 | 04.1 | 64 20.6 | 09.6 | 338 48.9 | 31.1 |
| 05 | 133 21.3 | 217 00.1 | 24.3 | 256 54.5 | 04.5 | 79 23.4 | 09.5 | 353 51.3 | 31.1 |
| 06 | 148 23.7 | 231 59.3 | S25 24.3 | 271 55.1 | S20 04.9 | 94 26.3 | N18 09.4 | 8 53.8 | N16 31.1 |
| 07 | 163 26.2 | 246 58.4 | 24.2 | 286 55.7 | 05.3 | 109 29.1 | 09.4 | 23 56.2 | 31.1 |
| 08 | 178 28.6 | 261 57.5 | 24.1 | 301 56.4 | 05.7 | 124 31.9 | 09.3 | 38 58.6 | 31.1 |
| F 09 | 193 31.1 | 276 56.7 | ·· 24.0 | 316 57.0 | ·· 06.2 | 139 34.7 | ·· 09.2 | 54 01.0 | ·· 31.1 |
| R 10 | 208 33.6 | 291 55.8 | 24.0 | 331 57.6 | 06.6 | 154 37.5 | 09.1 | 69 03.5 | 31.1 |
| I 11 | 223 36.0 | 306 55.0 | 23.9 | 346 58.2 | 07.0 | 169 40.3 | 09.1 | 84 05.9 | 31.1 |
| D 12 | 238 38.5 | 321 54.1 | S25 23.8 | 1 58.8 | S20 07.4 | 184 43.1 | N18 09.0 | 99 08.3 | N16 31.1 |
| A 13 | 253 41.0 | 336 53.2 | 23.7 | 16 59.5 | 07.8 | 199 46.0 | 08.9 | 114 10.7 | 31.1 |
| Y 14 | 268 43.4 | 351 52.4 | 23.6 | 32 00.1 | 08.2 | 214 48.8 | 08.8 | 129 13.1 | 31.1 |
| 15 | 283 45.9 | 6 51.5 | ·· 23.6 | 47 00.7 | ·· 08.6 | 229 51.6 | ·· 08.8 | 144 15.6 | ·· 31.1 |
| 16 | 298 48.4 | 21 50.6 | 23.5 | 62 01.3 | 09.1 | 244 54.4 | 08.7 | 159 18.0 | 31.1 |
| 17 | 313 50.8 | 36 49.8 | 23.4 | 77 01.9 | 09.5 | 259 57.2 | 08.6 | 174 20.4 | 31.1 |
| 18 | 328 53.3 | 51 48.9 | S25 23.3 | 92 02.5 | S20 09.9 | 275 00.0 | N18 08.5 | 189 22.8 | N16 31.0 |
| 19 | 343 55.8 | 66 48.0 | 23.2 | 107 03.2 | 10.3 | 290 02.8 | 08.5 | 204 25.3 | 31.0 |
| 20 | 358 58.2 | 81 47.2 | 23.1 | 122 03.8 | 10.7 | 305 05.6 | 08.4 | 219 27.7 | 31.0 |
| 21 | 14 00.7 | 96 46.3 | ·· 23.0 | 137 04.4 | ·· 11.1 | 320 08.5 | ·· 08.3 | 234 30.1 | ·· 31.0 |
| 22 | 29 03.1 | 111 45.5 | 22.9 | 152 05.0 | 11.5 | 335 11.3 | 08.2 | 249 32.5 | 31.0 |
| 23 | 44 05.6 | 126 44.6 | 22.8 | 167 05.6 | 11.9 | 350 14.1 | 08.2 | 264 35.0 | 31.0 |
| Mer. Pass. | h m 20 08.0 | v −0.9 | d 0.1 | v 0.6 | d 0.4 | v 2.8 | d 0.1 | v 2.4 | d 0.0 |

### STARS

| Name | S.H.A. | Dec. |
|---|---|---|
| | ° ′ | ° ′ |
| Acamar | 315 38.8 | S40 23.9 |
| Achernar | 335 46.8 | S57 21.4 |
| Acrux | 173 40.5 | S62 58.0 |
| Adhara | 255 33.9 | S28 56.3 |
| Aldebaran | 291 20.6 | N16 27.8 |
| Alioth | 166 45.3 | N56 04.9 |
| Alkaid | 153 21.0 | N49 25.6 |
| Al Na'ir | 28 18.2 | S47 04.5 |
| Alnilam | 276 14.0 | S 1 13.0 |
| Alphard | 218 23.1 | S 8 33.5 |
| Alphecca | 126 34.7 | N26 47.6 |
| Alpheratz | 358 11.8 | N28 58.0 |
| Altair | 62 35.2 | N 8 48.6 |
| Ankaa | 353 42.6 | S42 26.0 |
| Antares | 113 00.4 | S26 22.8 |
| Arcturus | 146 21.2 | N19 18.2 |
| Atria | 108 27.5 | S68 59.2 |
| Avior | 234 29.0 | S59 25.9 |
| Bellatrix | 279 01.2 | N 6 19.7 |
| Betelgeuse | 271 30.8 | N 7 24.2 |
| Canopus | 264 07.9 | S52 40.9 |
| Capella | 281 14.7 | N45 58.4 |
| Deneb | 49 50.4 | N45 12.2 |
| Denebola | 183 01.9 | N14 42.0 |
| Diphda | 349 23.3 | S18 06.8 |
| Dubhe | 194 25.6 | N61 52.2 |
| Elnath | 278 47.1 | N28 35.2 |
| Eltanin | 90 59.4 | N51 29.8 |
| Enif | 34 14.1 | N 9 46.4 |
| Fomalhaut | 15 54.2 | S29 44.7 |
| Gacrux | 172 31.9 | S56 58.8 |
| Gienah | 176 20.8 | S17 24.7 |
| Hadar | 149 27.5 | S60 15.5 |
| Hamal | 328 31.5 | N23 21.3 |
| Kaus Aust. | 84 20.6 | S34 23.7 |
| Kochab | 137 20.2 | N74 15.0 |
| Markab | 14 05.6 | N15 05.1 |
| Menkar | 314 43.5 | N 4 00.0 |
| Menkent | 148 40.4 | S36 15.2 |
| Miaplacidus | 221 45.2 | S69 37.1 |
| Mirfak | 309 19.3 | N49 46.8 |
| Nunki | 76 32.7 | S26 19.5 |
| Peacock | 54 02.8 | S56 48.7 |
| Pollux | 244 01.1 | N28 04.8 |
| Procyon | 245 28.3 | N 5 17.0 |
| Rasalhague | 96 32.3 | N12 34.8 |
| Regulus | 208 12.8 | N12 04.7 |
| Rigel | 281 38.2 | S 8 13.7 |
| Rigil Kent. | 140 29.9 | S60 44.2 |
| Sabik | 102 44.4 | S15 41.7 |
| Schedar | 350 11.5 | N56 24.9 |
| Shaula | 96 59.7 | S37 05.2 |
| Sirius | 258 57.7 | S16 41.0 |
| Spica | 159 00.5 | S11 02.4 |
| Suhail | 223 12.6 | S43 20.2 |
| Vega | 80 57.9 | N38 46.0 |
| Zuben'ubi | 137 36.2 | S15 56.6 |

| | S.H.A. | Mer. Pass. |
|---|---|---|
| | ° ′ | h m |
| Venus | 85 15.5 | 14 31 |
| Mars | 124 26.6 | 11 53 |
| Jupiter | 305 52.0 | 23 43 |
| Saturn | 220 31.4 | 5 28 |

## 1976 NOVEMBER 23, 24, 25 (TUES., WED., THURS.)

| G.M.T. | ARIES G.H.A. | VENUS −3.6 G.H.A. | VENUS Dec. | MARS +1.6 G.H.A. | MARS Dec. | JUPITER −2.4 G.H.A. | JUPITER Dec. | SATURN +0.5 G.H.A. | SATURN Dec. |
|---|---|---|---|---|---|---|---|---|---|
| d h | ° ′ | ° ′ | ° ′ | ° ′ | ° ′ | ° ′ | ° ′ | ° ′ | ° ′ |
| 23 00 | 62 05.5 | 140 42.3 | S25 12.5 | 182 49.8 | S20 41.1 | 8 39.4 | N18 02.7 | 282 32.5 | N16 30.9 |
| 01 | 77 08.0 | 155 41.4 | 12.3 | 197 50.4 | 41.5 | 23 42.2 | 02.6 | 297 35.0 | 30.9 |
| 02 | 92 10.4 | 170 40.6 | 12.1 | 212 51.0 | 41.9 | 38 45.0 | 02.6 | 312 37.4 | 30.9 |
| 03 | 107 12.9 | 185 39.8 | ·· 11.9 | 227 51.6 | ·· 42.3 | 53 47.8 | ·· 02.5 | 327 39.8 | ·· 30.9 |
| 04 | 122 15.3 | 200 38.9 | 11.7 | 242 52.2 | 42.7 | 68 50.7 | 02.4 | 342 42.3 | 30.9 |
| 05 | 137 17.8 | 215 38.1 | 11.5 | 257 52.8 | 43.0 | 83 53.5 | 02.3 | 357 44.7 | 30.9 |
| 06 | 152 20.3 | 230 37.2 | S25 11.3 | 272 53.4 | S20 43.4 | 98 56.3 | N18 02.3 | 12 47.2 | N16 30.9 |
| 07 | 167 22.7 | 245 36.4 | 11.1 | 287 54.0 | 43.8 | 113 59.1 | 02.2 | 27 49.6 | 30.9 |
| 08 | 182 25.2 | 260 35.5 | 10.9 | 302 54.6 | 44.2 | 129 01.9 | 02.1 | 42 52.0 | 30.9 |
| T 09 | 197 27.7 | 275 34.7 | ·· 10.7 | 317 55.2 | ·· 44.6 | 144 04.7 | ·· 02.0 | 57 54.5 | ·· 30.9 |
| U 10 | 212 30.1 | 290 33.8 | 10.5 | 332 55.8 | 45.0 | 159 07.5 | 02.0 | 72 56.9 | 30.9 |
| E 11 | 227 32.6 | 305 33.0 | 10.3 | 347 56.4 | 45.4 | 174 10.3 | 01.9 | 87 59.4 | 30.9 |
| S 12 | 242 35.1 | 320 32.2 | S25 10.1 | 2 57.0 | S20 45.7 | 189 13.1 | N18 01.8 | 103 01.8 | N16 30.9 |
| D 13 | 257 37.5 | 335 31.3 | 09.9 | 17 57.6 | 46.1 | 204 15.9 | 01.7 | 118 04.2 | 30.9 |
| A 14 | 272 40.0 | 350 30.5 | 09.7 | 32 58.1 | 46.5 | 219 18.8 | 01.7 | 133 06.7 | 30.9 |
| Y 15 | 287 42.5 | 5 29.6 | ·· 09.5 | 47 58.7 | ·· 46.9 | 234 21.6 | ·· 01.6 | 148 09.1 | ·· 30.9 |
| 16 | 302 44.9 | 20 28.8 | 09.3 | 62 59.3 | 47.3 | 249 24.4 | 01.5 | 163 11.6 | 30.9 |
| 17 | 317 47.4 | 35 28.0 | 09.1 | 77 59.9 | 47.7 | 264 27.2 | 01.4 | 178 14.0 | 30.9 |
| 18 | 332 49.8 | 50 27.1 | S25 08.9 | 93 00.5 | S20 48.0 | 279 30.0 | N18 01.4 | 193 16.5 | N16 30.9 |
| 19 | 347 52.3 | 65 26.3 | 08.7 | 108 01.1 | 48.4 | 294 32.8 | 01.3 | 208 18.9 | 30.9 |
| 20 | 2 54.8 | 80 25.4 | 08.5 | 123 01.7 | 48.8 | 309 35.6 | 01.2 | 223 21.3 | 30.9 |
| 21 | 17 57.2 | 95 24.6 | ·· 08.2 | 138 02.3 | ·· 49.2 | 324 38.4 | ·· 01.1 | 238 23.8 | ·· 30.9 |
| 22 | 32 59.7 | 110 23.8 | 08.0 | 153 02.9 | 49.6 | 339 41.2 | 01.1 | 253 26.2 | 30.9 |
| 23 | 48 02.2 | 125 22.9 | 07.8 | 168 03.5 | 49.9 | 354 44.0 | 01.0 | 268 28.7 | 30.9 |
| 24 00 | 63 04.6 | 140 22.1 | S25 07.6 | 183 04.1 | S20 50.3 | 9 46.9 | N18 00.9 | 283 31.1 | N16 30.9 |
| 01 | 78 07.1 | 155 21.3 | 07.4 | 198 04.7 | 50.7 | 24 49.7 | 00.8 | 298 33.6 | 30.9 |
| 02 | 93 09.6 | 170 20.4 | 07.1 | 213 05.2 | 51.1 | 39 52.5 | 00.8 | 313 36.0 | 30.9 |
| 03 | 108 12.0 | 185 19.6 | ·· 06.9 | 228 05.8 | ·· 51.5 | 54 55.3 | ·· 00.7 | 328 38.4 | ·· 30.9 |
| 04 | 123 14.5 | 200 18.7 | 06.7 | 243 06.4 | 51.8 | 69 58.1 | 00.6 | 343 40.9 | 30.9 |
| 05 | 138 17.0 | 215 17.9 | 06.5 | 258 07.0 | 52.2 | 85 00.9 | 00.6 | 358 43.3 | 30.9 |
| 06 | 153 19.4 | 230 17.1 | S25 06.3 | 273 07.6 | S20 52.6 | 100 03.7 | N18 00.5 | 13 45.8 | N16 30.9 |
| 07 | 168 21.9 | 245 16.2 | 06.0 | 288 08.2 | 53.0 | 115 06.5 | 00.4 | 28 48.2 | 30.9 |
| W 08 | 183 24.3 | 260 15.4 | 05.8 | 303 08.8 | 53.4 | 130 09.3 | 00.3 | 43 50.7 | 30.9 |
| E 09 | 198 26.8 | 275 14.6 | ·· 05.6 | 318 09.4 | ·· 53.7 | 145 12.1 | ·· 00.3 | 58 53.1 | ·· 30.9 |
| D 10 | 213 29.3 | 290 13.7 | 05.3 | 333 10.0 | 54.1 | 160 14.9 | 00.2 | 73 55.6 | 30.9 |
| N 11 | 228 31.7 | 305 12.9 | 05.1 | 348 10.5 | 54.5 | 175 17.8 | 00.1 | 88 58.0 | 30.9 |
| E 12 | 243 34.2 | 320 12.1 | S25 04.9 | 3 11.1 | S20 54.9 | 190 20.6 | N18 00.0 | 104 00.5 | N16 30.9 |
| S 13 | 258 36.7 | 335 11.2 | 04.6 | 18 11.7 | 55.2 | 205 23.4 | 18 00.0 | 119 02.9 | 30.9 |
| D 14 | 273 39.1 | 350 10.4 | 04.4 | 33 12.3 | 55.6 | 220 26.2 | 17 59.9 | 134 05.4 | 30.9 |
| A 15 | 288 41.6 | 5 09.6 | ·· 04.2 | 48 12.9 | ·· 56.0 | 235 29.0 | ·· 59.8 | 149 07.8 | ·· 30.9 |
| Y 16 | 303 44.1 | 20 08.7 | 03.9 | 63 13.5 | 56.4 | 250 31.8 | 59.7 | 164 10.2 | 30.9 |
| 17 | 318 46.5 | 35 07.9 | 03.7 | 78 14.1 | 56.8 | 265 34.6 | 59.7 | 179 12.7 | 30.9 |
| 18 | 333 49.0 | 50 07.1 | S25 03.4 | 93 14.6 | S20 57.1 | 280 37.4 | N17 59.6 | 194 15.1 | N16 30.9 |
| 19 | 348 51.5 | 65 06.2 | 03.2 | 108 15.2 | 57.5 | 295 40.2 | 59.5 | 209 17.6 | 30.9 |
| 20 | 3 53.9 | 80 05.4 | 03.0 | 123 15.8 | 57.9 | 310 43.0 | 59.4 | 224 20.0 | 31.0 |
| 21 | 18 56.4 | 95 04.6 | ·· 02.7 | 138 16.4 | ·· 58.2 | 325 45.8 | ·· 59.4 | 239 22.5 | ·· 31.0 |
| 22 | 33 58.8 | 110 03.7 | 02.5 | 153 17.0 | 58.6 | 340 48.6 | 59.3 | 254 24.9 | 31.0 |
| 23 | 49 01.3 | 125 02.9 | 02.2 | 168 17.6 | 59.0 | 355 51.5 | 59.2 | 269 27.4 | 31.0 |
| 25 00 | 64 03.8 | 140 02.1 | S25 02.0 | 183 18.2 | S20 59.4 | 10 54.3 | N17 59.1 | 284 29.8 | N16 31.0 |
| 01 | 79 06.2 | 155 01.2 | 01.7 | 198 18.7 | 20 59.7 | 25 57.1 | 59.1 | 299 32.3 | 31.0 |
| 02 | 94 08.7 | 170 00.4 | 01.5 | 213 19.3 | 21 00.1 | 40 59.9 | 59.0 | 314 34.7 | 31.0 |
| 03 | 109 11.2 | 184 59.6 | ·· 01.2 | 228 19.9 | ·· 00.5 | 56 02.7 | ·· 58.9 | 329 37.2 | ·· 31.0 |
| 04 | 124 13.6 | 199 58.8 | 01.0 | 243 20.5 | 00.9 | 71 05.5 | 58.9 | 344 39.6 | 31.0 |
| 05 | 139 16.1 | 214 57.9 | 00.7 | 258 21.1 | 01.2 | 86 08.3 | 58.8 | 359 42.1 | 31.0 |
| 06 | 154 18.6 | 229 57.1 | S25 00.5 | 273 21.7 | S21 01.6 | 101 11.1 | N17 58.7 | 14 44.5 | N16 31.0 |
| 07 | 169 21.0 | 244 56.3 | 25 00.2 | 288 22.2 | 02.0 | 116 13.9 | 58.6 | 29 47.0 | 31.0 |
| T 08 | 184 23.5 | 259 55.4 | 24 59.9 | 303 22.8 | 02.3 | 131 16.7 | 58.6 | 44 49.4 | 31.0 |
| H 09 | 199 25.9 | 274 54.6 | ·· 59.7 | 318 23.4 | ·· 02.7 | 146 19.5 | ·· 58.5 | 59 51.9 | ·· 31.0 |
| U 10 | 214 28.4 | 289 53.8 | 59.4 | 333 24.0 | 03.1 | 161 22.3 | 58.4 | 74 54.3 | 31.0 |
| R 11 | 229 30.9 | 304 53.0 | 59.2 | 348 24.6 | 03.5 | 176 25.1 | 58.3 | 89 56.8 | 31.0 |
| S 12 | 244 33.3 | 319 52.1 | S24 58.9 | 3 25.2 | S21 03.8 | 191 27.9 | N17 58.3 | 104 59.2 | N16 31.0 |
| D 13 | 259 35.8 | 334 51.3 | 58.6 | 18 25.7 | 04.2 | 206 30.7 | 58.2 | 120 01.7 | 31.0 |
| A 14 | 274 38.3 | 349 50.5 | 58.4 | 33 26.3 | 04.6 | 221 33.6 | 58.1 | 135 04.1 | 31.0 |
| Y 15 | 289 40.7 | 4 49.7 | ·· 58.1 | 48 26.9 | ·· 04.9 | 236 36.4 | ·· 58.0 | 150 06.6 | ·· 31.0 |
| 16 | 304 43.2 | 19 48.8 | 57.8 | 63 27.5 | 05.3 | 251 39.2 | 58.0 | 165 09.0 | 31.0 |
| 17 | 319 45.7 | 34 48.0 | 57.6 | 78 28.1 | 05.7 | 266 42.0 | 57.9 | 180 11.5 | 31.0 |
| 18 | 334 48.1 | 49 47.2 | S24 57.3 | 93 28.6 | S21 06.0 | 281 44.8 | N17 57.8 | 195 13.9 | N16 31.0 |
| 19 | 349 50.6 | 64 46.4 | 57.0 | 108 29.2 | 06.4 | 296 47.6 | 57.7 | 210 16.4 | 31.0 |
| 20 | 4 53.1 | 79 45.5 | 56.7 | 123 29.8 | 06.8 | 311 50.4 | 57.7 | 225 18.8 | 31.0 |
| 21 | 19 55.5 | 94 44.7 | ·· 56.5 | 138 30.4 | ·· 07.1 | 326 53.2 | ·· 57.6 | 240 21.3 | ·· 31.0 |
| 22 | 34 58.0 | 109 43.9 | 56.2 | 153 31.0 | 07.5 | 341 56.0 | 57.5 | 255 23.7 | 31.0 |
| 23 | 50 00.4 | 124 43.1 | 55.9 | 168 31.5 | 07.9 | 356 58.8 | 57.5 | 270 26.2 | 31.1 |
| Mer. Pass. | h m 19 44.4 | v −0.8 | d 0.2 | v 0.6 | d 0.4 | v 2.8 | d 0.1 | v 2.4 | d 0.0 |

### STARS

| Name | S.H.A. | Dec. |
|---|---|---|
| | ° ′ | ° ′ |
| Acamar | 315 38.8 | S40 23.9 |
| Achernar | 335 46.8 | S57 21.4 |
| Acrux | 173 40.4 | S62 58.0 |
| Adhara | 255 33.8 | S28 56.4 |
| Aldebaran | 291 20.6 | N16 27.8 |
| Alioth | 166 45.2 | N56 04.9 |
| Alkaid | 153 21.0 | N49 25.6 |
| Al Na'ir | 28 18.3 | S47 04.5 |
| Alnilam | 276 14.0 | S 1 13.0 |
| Alphard | 218 23.0 | S 8 33.5 |
| Alphecca | 126 34.7 | N26 47.6 |
| Alpheratz | 358 11.8 | N28 58.0 |
| Altair | 62 35.2 | N 8 48.6 |
| Ankaa | 353 42.6 | S42 26.0 |
| Antares | 113 00.4 | S26 22.8 |
| Arcturus | 146 21.1 | N19 18.2 |
| Atria | 108 27.5 | S68 59.1 |
| Avior | 234 28.9 | S59 25.9 |
| Bellatrix | 279 01.2 | N 6 19.7 |
| Betelgeuse | 271 30.8 | N 7 24.1 |
| Canopus | 264 07.9 | S52 40.9 |
| Capella | 281 14.6 | N45 58.4 |
| Deneb | 49 50.4 | N45 12.2 |
| Denebola | 183 01.8 | N14 42.0 |
| Diphda | 349 23.3 | S18 06.8 |
| Dubhe | 194 25.5 | N61 52.2 |
| Elnath | 278 47.0 | N28 35.2 |
| Eltanin | 90 59.4 | N51 29.8 |
| Enif | 34 14.2 | N 9 46.4 |
| Fomalhaut | 15 54.2 | S29 44.7 |
| Gacrux | 172 31.9 | S56 58.8 |
| Gienah | 176 20.8 | S17 24.7 |
| Hadar | 149 27.5 | S60 15.5 |
| Hamal | 328 31.5 | N23 21.3 |
| Kaus Aust. | 84 20.6 | S34 23.7 |
| Kochab | 137 20.2 | N74 14.9 |
| Markab | 14 05.7 | N15 05.1 |
| Menkar | 314 43.5 | N 4 00.0 |
| Menkent | 148 40.4 | S36 15.2 |
| Miaplacidus | 221 45.1 | S69 37.1 |
| Mirfak | 309 19.2 | N49 46.8 |
| Nunki | 76 32.7 | S26 19.5 |
| Peacock | 54 02.8 | S56 48.7 |
| Pollux | 244 01.1 | N28 04.8 |
| Procyon | 245 28.3 | N 5 17.0 |
| Rasalhague | 96 32.3 | N12 34.8 |
| Regulus | 208 12.7 | N12 04.7 |
| Rigel | 281 38.2 | S 8 13.7 |
| Rigil Kent. | 140 29.9 | S60 44.2 |
| Sabik | 102 44.4 | S15 41.7 |
| Schedar | 350 11.5 | N56 24.9 |
| Shaula | 96 59.7 | S37 05.2 |
| Sirius | 258 57.7 | S16 41.1 |
| Spica | 159 00.5 | S11 02.4 |
| Suhail | 223 12.5 | S43 20.2 |
| Vega | 80 57.9 | N38 46.0 |
| Zuben'ubi | 137 36.2 | S15 56.6 |

| | S.H.A. | Mer. Pass. |
|---|---|---|
| | ° ′ | h m |
| Venus | 77 17.5 | 14 39 |
| Mars | 119 59.4 | 11 47 |
| Jupiter | 306 42.2 | 23 17 |
| Saturn | 220 26.5 | 5 05 |

## 1976 NOVEMBER 23, 24, 25 (TUES., WED., THURS.)

| G.M.T. | | SUN G.H.A. | SUN Dec. | MOON G.H.A. | MOON v | MOON Dec. | MOON d | MOON H.P. |
|---|---|---|---|---|---|---|---|---|
| d h | | ° ′ | ° ′ | ° ′ | ′ | ° ′ | ′ | ′ |
| 23 00 | | 183 24.6 | S20 19.4 | 162 35.2 | 3.9 | S19 15.8 | 0.3 | 60.7 |
| 01 | | 198 24.4 | 20.0 | 176 58.1 | 4.0 | 19 16.1 | 0.2 | 60.7 |
| 02 | | 213 24.2 | 20.5 | 191 21.1 | 4.0 | 19 16.3 | 0.0 | 60.7 |
| 03 | | 228 24.0 | 21.0 | 205 44.1 | 4.0 | 19 16.3 | 0.1 | 60.6 |
| 04 | | 243 23.9 | 21.5 | 220 07.1 | 4.1 | 19 16.2 | 0.3 | 60.6 |
| 05 | | 258 23.7 | 22.0 | 234 30.2 | 4.1 | 19 15.9 | 0.4 | 60.6 |
| 06 | | 273 23.5 | S20 22.6 | 248 53.3 | 4.2 | S19 15.5 | 0.5 | 60.6 |
| 07 | | 288 23.3 | 23.1 | 263 16.5 | 4.2 | 19 15.0 | 0.7 | 60.5 |
| 08 | | 303 23.2 | 23.6 | 277 39.7 | 4.2 | 19 14.3 | 0.8 | 60.5 |
| 09 | TUESDAY | 318 23.0 | 24.1 | 292 02.9 | 4.3 | 19 13.5 | 0.9 | 60.5 |
| 10 | | 333 22.8 | 24.6 | 306 26.2 | 4.4 | 19 12.6 | 1.1 | 60.4 |
| 11 | | 348 22.6 | 25.1 | 320 49.6 | 4.4 | 19 11.5 | 1.2 | 60.4 |
| 12 | | 3 22.4 | S20 25.7 | 335 13.0 | 4.4 | S19 10.3 | 1.4 | 60.4 |
| 13 | | 18 22.3 | 26.2 | 349 36.4 | 4.5 | 19 08.9 | 1.5 | 60.4 |
| 14 | | 33 22.1 | 26.7 | 3 59.9 | 4.6 | 19 07.4 | 1.6 | 60.3 |
| 15 | | 48 21.9 | 27.2 | 18 23.5 | 4.6 | 19 05.8 | 1.8 | 60.3 |
| 16 | | 63 21.7 | 27.7 | 32 47.1 | 4.7 | 19 04.0 | 1.9 | 60.3 |
| 17 | | 78 21.6 | 28.2 | 47 10.8 | 4.7 | 19 02.1 | 2.0 | 60.2 |
| 18 | | 93 21.4 | S20 28.7 | 61 34.5 | 4.8 | S19 00.1 | 2.2 | 60.2 |
| 19 | | 108 21.2 | 29.3 | 75 58.3 | 4.8 | 18 57.9 | 2.3 | 60.2 |
| 20 | | 123 21.0 | 29.8 | 90 22.1 | 4.9 | 18 55.6 | 2.4 | 60.1 |
| 21 | | 138 20.8 | 30.3 | 104 46.0 | 5.0 | 18 53.2 | 2.6 | 60.1 |
| 22 | | 153 20.7 | 30.8 | 119 10.0 | 5.1 | 18 50.6 | 2.6 | 60.1 |
| 23 | | 168 20.5 | 31.3 | 133 34.1 | 5.1 | 18 48.0 | 2.8 | 60.0 |
| 24 00 | | 183 20.3 | S20 31.8 | 147 58.2 | 5.1 | S18 45.2 | 3.0 | 60.0 |
| 01 | | 198 20.1 | 32.3 | 162 22.3 | 5.3 | 18 42.2 | 3.0 | 60.0 |
| 02 | | 213 19.9 | 32.8 | 176 46.6 | 5.3 | 18 39.2 | 3.2 | 59.9 |
| 03 | | 228 19.7 | 33.3 | 191 10.9 | 5.4 | 18 36.0 | 3.3 | 59.9 |
| 04 | | 243 19.6 | 33.8 | 205 35.3 | 5.5 | 18 32.7 | 3.5 | 59.9 |
| 05 | | 258 19.4 | 34.3 | 219 59.8 | 5.5 | 18 29.2 | 3.5 | 59.8 |
| 06 | | 273 19.2 | S20 34.8 | 234 24.3 | 5.6 | S18 25.7 | 3.7 | 59.8 |
| 07 | | 288 19.0 | 35.3 | 248 48.9 | 5.7 | 18 22.0 | 3.8 | 59.7 |
| 08 | | 303 18.8 | 35.8 | 263 13.6 | 5.8 | 18 18.2 | 3.9 | 59.7 |
| 09 | | 318 18.6 | 36.3 | 277 38.4 | 5.8 | 18 14.3 | 4.0 | 59.7 |
| 10 | | 333 18.5 | 36.8 | 292 03.2 | 5.9 | 18 10.3 | 4.1 | 59.6 |
| 11 | WEDNESDAY | 348 18.3 | 37.3 | 306 28.1 | 6.0 | 18 06.2 | 4.3 | 59.6 |
| 12 | | 3 18.1 | S20 37.8 | 320 53.1 | 6.1 | S18 01.9 | 4.4 | 59.6 |
| 13 | | 18 17.9 | 38.3 | 335 18.2 | 6.2 | 17 57.5 | 4.5 | 59.5 |
| 14 | | 33 17.7 | 38.8 | 349 43.4 | 6.2 | 17 53.0 | 4.6 | 59.5 |
| 15 | | 48 17.5 | 39.3 | 4 08.6 | 6.3 | 17 48.4 | 4.7 | 59.5 |
| 16 | | 63 17.3 | 39.8 | 18 33.9 | 6.5 | 17 43.7 | 4.8 | 59.4 |
| 17 | | 78 17.2 | 40.3 | 32 59.4 | 6.5 | 17 38.9 | 4.9 | 59.4 |
| 18 | | 93 17.0 | S20 40.8 | 47 24.9 | 6.5 | S17 34.0 | 5.0 | 59.3 |
| 19 | | 108 16.8 | 41.3 | 61 50.4 | 6.7 | 17 29.0 | 5.2 | 59.3 |
| 20 | | 123 16.6 | 41.8 | 76 16.1 | 6.7 | 17 23.8 | 5.2 | 59.3 |
| 21 | | 138 16.4 | 42.3 | 90 41.8 | 6.9 | 17 18.6 | 5.4 | 59.2 |
| 22 | | 153 16.2 | 42.8 | 105 07.7 | 6.9 | 17 13.2 | 5.4 | 59.2 |
| 23 | | 168 16.0 | 43.3 | 119 33.6 | 7.0 | 17 07.8 | 5.6 | 59.1 |
| 25 00 | | 183 15.8 | S20 43.8 | 133 59.6 | 7.1 | S17 02.2 | 5.6 | 59.1 |
| 01 | | 198 15.6 | 44.3 | 148 25.7 | 7.2 | 16 56.6 | 5.8 | 59.1 |
| 02 | | 213 15.5 | 44.8 | 162 51.9 | 7.3 | 16 50.8 | 5.8 | 59.0 |
| 03 | | 228 15.3 | 45.2 | 177 18.2 | 7.3 | 16 45.0 | 5.9 | 59.0 |
| 04 | | 243 15.1 | 45.7 | 191 44.5 | 7.5 | 16 39.1 | 6.1 | 58.9 |
| 05 | | 258 14.9 | 46.2 | 206 11.0 | 7.5 | 16 33.0 | 6.1 | 58.9 |
| 06 | | 273 14.7 | S20 46.7 | 220 37.5 | 7.7 | S16 26.9 | 6.2 | 58.9 |
| 07 | | 288 14.5 | 47.2 | 235 04.2 | 7.7 | 16 20.7 | 6.4 | 58.8 |
| 08 | | 303 14.3 | 47.7 | 249 30.9 | 7.8 | 16 14.3 | 6.4 | 58.8 |
| 09 | | 318 14.1 | 48.2 | 263 57.7 | 7.9 | 16 07.9 | 6.5 | 58.7 |
| 10 | | 333 13.9 | 48.6 | 278 24.6 | 8.0 | 16 01.4 | 6.5 | 58.7 |
| 11 | THURSDAY | 348 13.7 | 49.1 | 292 51.6 | 8.1 | 15 54.9 | 6.7 | 58.7 |
| 12 | | 3 13.5 | S20 49.6 | 307 18.7 | 8.2 | S15 48.2 | 6.8 | 58.6 |
| 13 | | 18 13.3 | 50.1 | 321 45.9 | 8.2 | 15 41.4 | 6.8 | 58.6 |
| 14 | | 33 13.1 | 50.6 | 336 13.1 | 8.4 | 15 34.6 | 6.9 | 58.5 |
| 15 | | 48 13.0 | 51.1 | 350 40.5 | 8.4 | 15 27.7 | 7.0 | 58.5 |
| 16 | | 63 12.8 | 51.5 | 5 07.9 | 8.5 | 15 20.7 | 7.1 | 58.5 |
| 17 | | 78 12.6 | 52.0 | 19 35.4 | 8.7 | 15 13.6 | 7.2 | 58.4 |
| 18 | | 93 12.4 | S20 52.5 | 34 03.1 | 8.7 | S15 06.4 | 7.2 | 58.4 |
| 19 | | 108 12.2 | 53.0 | 48 30.8 | 8.8 | 14 59.2 | 7.3 | 58.3 |
| 20 | | 123 12.0 | 53.5 | 62 58.6 | 8.9 | 14 51.9 | 7.4 | 58.3 |
| 21 | | 138 11.8 | 53.9 | 77 26.5 | 9.0 | 14 44.5 | 7.5 | 58.3 |
| 22 | | 153 11.6 | 54.4 | 91 54.5 | 9.0 | 14 37.0 | 7.5 | 58.2 |
| 23 | | 168 11.4 | 54.9 | 106 22.5 | 9.2 | 14 29.5 | 7.6 | 58.2 |
| | | S.D. 16.2 | d 0.5 | S.D. 16.5 | | 16.2 | | 16.0 |

| Lat. | Twilight Naut. | Twilight Civil | Sunrise | Moonrise 23 | Moonrise 24 | Moonrise 25 | Moonrise 26 |
|---|---|---|---|---|---|---|---|
| ° | h m | h m | h m | h m | h m | h m | h m |
| N 72 | 07 30 | 09 17 | ■ | ■ | 14 36 | 13 36 | 13 20 |
| N 70 | 07 17 | 08 46 | 11 10 | 12 38 | 12 55 | 12 58 | 12 57 |
| 68 | 07 05 | 08 23 | 09 57 | 11 40 | 12 14 | 12 31 | 12 40 |
| 66 | 06 56 | 08 05 | 09 21 | 11 05 | 11 46 | 12 11 | 12 26 |
| 64 | 06 48 | 07 51 | 08 56 | 10 40 | 11 25 | 11 54 | 12 14 |
| 62 | 06 40 | 07 38 | 08 36 | 10 21 | 11 08 | 11 41 | 12 04 |
| 60 | 06 34 | 07 28 | 08 20 | 10 05 | 10 53 | 11 29 | 11 55 |
| N 58 | 06 29 | 07 18 | 08 06 | 09 51 | 10 41 | 11 19 | 11 47 |
| 56 | 06 23 | 07 10 | 07 54 | 09 39 | 10 31 | 11 10 | 11 41 |
| 54 | 06 19 | 07 03 | 07 44 | 09 29 | 10 21 | 11 02 | 11 35 |
| 52 | 06 14 | 06 56 | 07 35 | 09 20 | 10 13 | 10 55 | 11 29 |
| 50 | 06 10 | 06 50 | 07 27 | 09 12 | 10 05 | 10 49 | 11 24 |
| 45 | 06 01 | 06 37 | 07 10 | 08 54 | 09 49 | 10 35 | 11 14 |
| N 40 | 05 52 | 06 26 | 06 55 | 08 40 | 09 36 | 10 24 | 11 05 |
| 35 | 05 45 | 06 16 | 06 43 | 08 28 | 09 24 | 10 14 | 10 57 |
| 30 | 05 38 | 06 07 | 06 32 | 08 17 | 09 15 | 10 05 | 10 50 |
| 20 | 05 24 | 05 51 | 06 14 | 07 59 | 08 58 | 09 51 | 10 39 |
| N 10 | 05 10 | 05 36 | 05 58 | 07 43 | 08 43 | 09 38 | 10 28 |
| 0 | 04 55 | 05 21 | 05 43 | 07 29 | 08 29 | 09 26 | 10 19 |
| S 10 | 04 39 | 05 05 | 05 28 | 07 14 | 08 15 | 09 14 | 10 09 |
| 20 | 04 19 | 04 48 | 05 11 | 06 58 | 08 00 | 09 01 | 09 59 |
| 30 | 03 54 | 04 26 | 04 52 | 06 40 | 07 43 | 08 46 | 09 47 |
| 35 | 03 38 | 04 13 | 04 41 | 06 30 | 07 33 | 08 37 | 09 40 |
| 40 | 03 18 | 03 57 | 04 28 | 06 18 | 07 22 | 08 27 | 09 32 |
| 45 | 02 53 | 03 38 | 04 13 | 06 04 | 07 09 | 08 16 | 09 23 |
| S 50 | 02 17 | 03 13 | 03 54 | 05 47 | 06 52 | 08 02 | 09 12 |
| 52 | 01 58 | 03 01 | 03 45 | 05 39 | 06 45 | 07 55 | 09 07 |
| 54 | 01 34 | 02 47 | 03 35 | 05 30 | 06 36 | 07 48 | 09 01 |
| 56 | 00 58 | 02 31 | 03 24 | 05 19 | 06 27 | 07 40 | 08 55 |
| 58 | //// | 02 10 | 03 11 | 05 08 | 06 16 | 07 31 | 08 48 |
| S 60 | //// | 01 44 | 02 55 | 04 54 | 06 03 | 07 20 | 08 40 |

| Lat. | Sunset | Twilight Civil | Twilight Naut. | Moonset 23 | Moonset 24 | Moonset 25 | Moonset 26 |
|---|---|---|---|---|---|---|---|
| ° | h m | h m | h m | h m | h m | h m | h m |
| N 72 | ■ | 14 15 | 16 02 | ■ | 14 58 | 17 55 | 19 59 |
| N 70 | 12 22 | 14 47 | 16 16 | 14 51 | 16 39 | 18 32 | 20 20 |
| 68 | 13 35 | 15 09 | 16 27 | 15 49 | 17 19 | 18 58 | 20 36 |
| 66 | 14 11 | 15 27 | 16 37 | 16 24 | 17 46 | 19 17 | 20 49 |
| 64 | 14 37 | 15 42 | 16 45 | 16 48 | 18 07 | 19 33 | 21 00 |
| 62 | 14 57 | 15 54 | 16 52 | 17 08 | 18 24 | 19 46 | 21 09 |
| 60 | 15 13 | 16 05 | 16 59 | 17 24 | 18 38 | 19 57 | 21 17 |
| N 58 | 15 27 | 16 14 | 17 04 | 17 37 | 18 50 | 20 07 | 21 24 |
| 56 | 15 39 | 16 23 | 17 10 | 17 49 | 19 00 | 20 15 | 21 30 |
| 54 | 15 49 | 16 30 | 17 14 | 17 59 | 19 09 | 20 22 | 21 36 |
| 52 | 15 58 | 16 37 | 17 19 | 18 08 | 19 17 | 20 29 | 21 41 |
| 50 | 16 06 | 16 43 | 17 23 | 18 16 | 19 24 | 20 35 | 21 45 |
| 45 | 16 24 | 16 56 | 17 32 | 18 34 | 19 40 | 20 48 | 21 55 |
| N 40 | 16 38 | 17 08 | 17 41 | 18 48 | 19 53 | 20 58 | 22 03 |
| 35 | 16 50 | 17 18 | 17 49 | 19 00 | 20 04 | 21 07 | 22 09 |
| 30 | 17 01 | 17 27 | 17 56 | 19 10 | 20 13 | 21 15 | 22 15 |
| 20 | 17 19 | 17 43 | 18 10 | 19 28 | 20 29 | 21 29 | 22 26 |
| N 10 | 17 35 | 17 58 | 18 23 | 19 43 | 20 43 | 21 40 | 22 34 |
| 0 | 17 50 | 18 13 | 18 38 | 19 58 | 20 56 | 21 51 | 22 43 |
| S 10 | 18 06 | 18 28 | 18 55 | 20 12 | 21 10 | 22 02 | 22 51 |
| 20 | 18 22 | 18 46 | 19 15 | 20 28 | 21 23 | 22 14 | 23 00 |
| 30 | 18 41 | 19 08 | 19 40 | 20 45 | 21 39 | 22 27 | 23 10 |
| 35 | 18 53 | 19 21 | 19 56 | 20 55 | 21 48 | 22 35 | 23 15 |
| 40 | 19 06 | 19 37 | 20 16 | 21 07 | 21 59 | 22 43 | 23 22 |
| 45 | 19 21 | 19 56 | 20 42 | 21 21 | 22 11 | 22 53 | 23 29 |
| S 50 | 19 40 | 20 21 | 21 18 | 21 37 | 22 26 | 23 05 | 23 38 |
| 52 | 19 49 | 20 34 | 21 38 | 21 45 | 22 33 | 23 11 | 23 42 |
| 54 | 19 59 | 20 48 | 22 02 | 21 54 | 22 40 | 23 17 | 23 47 |
| 56 | 20 11 | 21 05 | 22 40 | 22 04 | 22 49 | 23 24 | 23 52 |
| 58 | 20 24 | 21 26 | //// | 22 15 | 22 59 | 23 32 | 23 57 |
| S 60 | 20 40 | 21 53 | //// | 22 27 | 23 10 | 23 40 | 24 04 |

| Day | SUN Eqn. of Time 00ʰ | SUN Eqn. of Time 12ʰ | SUN Mer. Pass. | MOON Mer. Pass. Upper | MOON Mer. Pass. Lower | MOON Age | MOON Phase |
|---|---|---|---|---|---|---|---|
| | m s | m s | h m | h m | h m | d | |
| 23 | 13 39 | 13 30 | 11 46 | 13 43 | 01 13 | 02 | |
| 24 | 13 22 | 13 13 | 11 47 | 14 43 | 02 13 | 03 | |
| 25 | 13 04 | 12 55 | 11 47 | 15 39 | 03 11 | 04 | |

## 1976 NOV. 29, 30, DEC. 1 (MON., TUES., WED.)

| G.M.T. | | ARIES G.H.A. | VENUS −3.6 G.H.A. | VENUS Dec. | MARS +1.6 G.H.A. | MARS Dec. | JUPITER −2.4 G.H.A. | JUPITER Dec. | SATURN +0.5 G.H.A. | SATURN Dec. |
|---|---|---|---|---|---|---|---|---|---|---|
| d h | | ° ′ | ° ′ | ° ′ | ° ′ | ° ′ | ° ′ | ° ′ | ° ′ | ° ′ |
| 29 00 | | 68 00.3 | 138 44.2 | S24 32.4 | 184 13.1 | S21 33.7 | 15 23.3 | N17 52.2 | 288 25.8 | N16 31.5 |
| 01 | | 83 02.8 | 153 43.4 | 32.0 | 199 13.7 | 34.0 | 30 26.1 | 52.1 | 303 28.3 | 31.5 |
| 02 | | 98 05.3 | 168 42.6 | 31.6 | 214 14.3 | 34.3 | 45 28.9 | 52.0 | 318 30.7 | 31.6 |
| 03 | | 113 07.7 | 183 41.8 | 31.3 | 229 14.8 | 34.7 | 60 31.7 | 51.9 | 333 33.2 | 31.6 |
| 04 | | 128 10.2 | 198 41.0 | 30.9 | 244 15.4 | 35.0 | 75 34.5 | 51.9 | 348 35.7 | 31.6 |
| 05 | | 143 12.6 | 213 40.2 | 30.5 | 259 16.0 | 35.4 | 90 37.3 | 51.8 | 3 38.1 | 31.6 |
| 06 | | 158 15.1 | 228 39.4 | S24 30.2 | 274 16.5 | S21 35.7 | 105 40.1 | N17 51.7 | 18 40.6 | N16 31.6 |
| 07 | | 173 17.6 | 243 38.6 | 29.8 | 289 17.1 | 36.0 | 120 42.9 | 51.7 | 33 43.1 | 31.6 |
| 08 | | 188 20.0 | 258 37.8 | 29.4 | 304 17.6 | 36.4 | 135 45.7 | 51.6 | 48 45.6 | 31.6 |
| 09 | MONDAY | 203 22.5 | 273 37.1 | 29.0 | 319 18.2 | 36.7 | 150 48.5 | 51.5 | 63 48.0 | 31.6 |
| 10 | | 218 25.0 | 288 36.3 | 28.6 | 334 18.7 | 37.1 | 165 51.3 | 51.4 | 78 50.5 | 31.6 |
| 11 | | 233 27.4 | 303 35.5 | 28.3 | 349 19.3 | 37.4 | 180 54.1 | 51.4 | 93 53.0 | 31.6 |
| 12 | | 248 29.9 | 318 34.7 | S24 27.9 | 4 19.9 | S21 37.7 | 195 56.9 | N17 51.3 | 108 55.4 | N16 31.6 |
| 13 | | 263 32.4 | 333 33.9 | 27.5 | 19 20.4 | 38.1 | 210 59.7 | 51.2 | 123 57.9 | 31.7 |
| 14 | | 278 34.8 | 348 33.1 | 27.1 | 34 21.0 | 38.4 | 226 02.5 | 51.2 | 139 00.4 | 31.7 |
| 15 | | 293 37.3 | 3 32.3 | 26.7 | 49 21.5 | 38.7 | 241 05.3 | 51.1 | 154 02.8 | 31.7 |
| 16 | | 308 39.8 | 18 31.6 | 26.3 | 64 22.1 | 39.1 | 256 08.1 | 51.0 | 169 05.3 | 31.7 |
| 17 | | 323 42.2 | 33 30.8 | 26.0 | 79 22.7 | 39.4 | 271 10.9 | 50.9 | 184 07.8 | 31.7 |
| 18 | | 338 44.7 | 48 30.0 | S24 25.6 | 94 23.2 | S21 39.7 | 286 13.7 | N17 50.9 | 199 10.3 | N16 31.7 |
| 19 | | 353 47.1 | 63 29.2 | 25.2 | 109 23.8 | 40.1 | 301 16.5 | 50.8 | 214 12.7 | 31.7 |
| 20 | | 8 49.6 | 78 28.4 | 24.8 | 124 24.3 | 40.4 | 316 19.2 | 50.7 | 229 15.2 | 31.7 |
| 21 | | 23 52.1 | 93 27.6 | 24.4 | 139 24.9 | 40.7 | 331 22.0 | 50.7 | 244 17.7 | 31.7 |
| 22 | | 38 54.5 | 108 26.9 | 24.0 | 154 25.4 | 41.1 | 346 24.8 | 50.6 | 259 20.1 | 31.7 |
| 23 | | 53 57.0 | 123 26.1 | 23.6 | 169 26.0 | 41.4 | 1 27.6 | 50.5 | 274 22.6 | 31.8 |
| 30 00 | | 68 59.5 | 138 25.3 | S24 23.2 | 184 26.5 | S21 41.7 | 16 30.4 | N17 50.4 | 289 25.1 | N16 31.8 |
| 01 | | 84 01.9 | 153 24.5 | 22.8 | 199 27.1 | 42.1 | 31 33.2 | 50.4 | 304 27.6 | 31.8 |
| 02 | | 99 04.4 | 168 23.7 | 22.4 | 214 27.7 | 42.4 | 46 36.0 | 50.3 | 319 30.0 | 31.8 |
| 03 | | 114 06.9 | 183 23.0 | 22.0 | 229 28.2 | 42.7 | 61 38.8 | 50.2 | 334 32.5 | 31.8 |
| 04 | | 129 09.3 | 198 22.2 | 21.6 | 244 28.8 | 43.1 | 76 41.6 | 50.2 | 349 35.0 | 31.8 |
| 05 | | 144 11.8 | 213 21.4 | 21.2 | 259 29.3 | 43.4 | 91 44.4 | 50.1 | 4 37.4 | 31.8 |
| 06 | | 159 14.3 | 228 20.6 | S24 20.8 | 274 29.9 | S21 43.7 | 106 47.2 | N17 50.0 | 19 39.9 | N16 31.8 |
| 07 | | 174 16.7 | 243 19.8 | 20.4 | 289 30.4 | 44.1 | 121 50.0 | 49.9 | 34 42.4 | 31.8 |
| 08 | | 189 19.2 | 258 19.1 | 20.0 | 304 31.0 | 44.4 | 136 52.8 | 49.9 | 49 44.9 | 31.9 |
| 09 | TUESDAY | 204 21.6 | 273 18.3 | 19.6 | 319 31.5 | 44.7 | 151 55.6 | 49.8 | 64 47.3 | 31.9 |
| 10 | | 219 24.1 | 288 17.5 | 19.2 | 334 32.1 | 45.1 | 166 58.4 | 49.7 | 79 49.8 | 31.9 |
| 11 | | 234 26.6 | 303 16.7 | 18.8 | 349 32.6 | 45.4 | 182 01.2 | 49.7 | 94 52.3 | 31.9 |
| 12 | | 249 29.0 | 318 16.0 | S24 18.4 | 4 33.2 | S21 45.7 | 197 03.9 | N17 49.6 | 109 54.8 | N16 31.9 |
| 13 | | 264 31.5 | 333 15.2 | 18.0 | 19 33.8 | 46.0 | 212 06.7 | 49.5 | 124 57.2 | 31.9 |
| 14 | | 279 34.0 | 348 14.4 | 17.6 | 34 34.3 | 46.4 | 227 09.5 | 49.4 | 139 59.7 | 31.9 |
| 15 | | 294 36.4 | 3 13.6 | 17.1 | 49 34.9 | 46.7 | 242 12.3 | 49.4 | 155 02.2 | 31.9 |
| 16 | | 309 38.9 | 18 12.9 | 16.7 | 64 35.4 | 47.0 | 257 15.1 | 49.3 | 170 04.7 | 31.9 |
| 17 | | 324 41.4 | 33 12.1 | 16.3 | 79 36.0 | 47.4 | 272 17.9 | 49.2 | 185 07.1 | 32.0 |
| 18 | | 339 43.8 | 48 11.3 | S24 15.9 | 94 36.5 | S21 47.7 | 287 20.7 | N17 49.2 | 200 09.6 | N16 32.0 |
| 19 | | 354 46.3 | 63 10.6 | 15.5 | 109 37.1 | 48.0 | 302 23.5 | 49.1 | 215 12.1 | 32.0 |
| 20 | | 9 48.7 | 78 09.8 | 15.1 | 124 37.6 | 48.3 | 317 26.3 | 49.0 | 230 14.6 | 32.0 |
| 21 | | 24 51.2 | 93 09.0 | 14.6 | 139 38.2 | 48.7 | 332 29.1 | 49.0 | 245 17.0 | 32.0 |
| 22 | | 39 53.7 | 108 08.3 | 14.2 | 154 38.7 | 49.0 | 347 31.9 | 48.9 | 260 19.5 | 32.0 |
| 23 | | 54 56.1 | 123 07.5 | 13.8 | 169 39.3 | 49.3 | 2 34.7 | 48.8 | 275 22.0 | 32.0 |
| 1 00 | | 69 58.6 | 138 06.7 | S24 13.4 | 184 39.8 | S21 49.6 | 17 37.4 | N17 48.7 | 290 24.5 | N16 32.0 |
| 01 | | 85 01.1 | 153 05.9 | 12.9 | 199 40.4 | 50.0 | 32 40.2 | 48.7 | 305 26.9 | 32.0 |
| 02 | | 100 03.5 | 168 05.2 | 12.5 | 214 40.9 | 50.3 | 47 43.0 | 48.6 | 320 29.4 | 32.1 |
| 03 | | 115 06.0 | 183 04.4 | 12.1 | 229 41.5 | 50.6 | 62 45.8 | 48.5 | 335 31.9 | 32.1 |
| 04 | | 130 08.5 | 198 03.6 | 11.7 | 244 42.0 | 50.9 | 77 48.6 | 48.5 | 350 34.4 | 32.1 |
| 05 | | 145 10.9 | 213 02.9 | 11.2 | 259 42.6 | 51.3 | 92 51.4 | 48.4 | 5 36.9 | 32.1 |
| 06 | | 160 13.4 | 228 02.1 | S24 10.8 | 274 43.1 | S21 51.6 | 107 54.2 | N17 48.3 | 20 39.3 | N16 32.1 |
| 07 | | 175 15.9 | 243 01.3 | 10.4 | 289 43.7 | 51.9 | 122 57.0 | 48.3 | 35 41.8 | 32.1 |
| 08 | | 190 18.3 | 258 00.6 | 09.9 | 304 44.2 | 52.2 | 137 59.8 | 48.2 | 50 44.3 | 32.1 |
| 09 | | 205 20.8 | 272 59.8 | 09.5 | 319 44.8 | 52.5 | 153 02.6 | 48.1 | 65 46.8 | 32.1 |
| 10 | | 220 23.2 | 287 59.1 | 09.1 | 334 45.3 | 52.9 | 168 05.3 | 48.0 | 80 49.2 | 32.2 |
| 11 | WEDNESDAY | 235 25.7 | 302 58.3 | 08.6 | 349 45.8 | 53.2 | 183 08.1 | 48.0 | 95 51.7 | 32.2 |
| 12 | | 250 28.2 | 317 57.5 | S24 08.2 | 4 46.4 | S21 53.5 | 198 10.9 | N17 47.9 | 110 54.2 | N16 32.2 |
| 13 | | 265 30.6 | 332 56.8 | 07.7 | 19 46.9 | 53.8 | 213 13.7 | 47.8 | 125 56.7 | 32.2 |
| 14 | | 280 33.1 | 347 56.0 | 07.3 | 34 47.5 | 54.1 | 228 16.5 | 47.8 | 140 59.2 | 32.2 |
| 15 | | 295 35.6 | 2 55.2 | 06.9 | 49 48.0 | 54.5 | 243 19.3 | 47.7 | 156 01.6 | 32.2 |
| 16 | | 310 38.0 | 17 54.5 | 06.4 | 64 48.6 | 54.8 | 258 22.1 | 47.6 | 171 04.1 | 32.2 |
| 17 | | 325 40.5 | 32 53.7 | 06.0 | 79 49.1 | 55.1 | 273 24.9 | 47.6 | 186 06.6 | 32.2 |
| 18 | | 340 43.0 | 47 53.0 | S24 05.5 | 94 49.7 | S21 55.4 | 288 27.7 | N17 47.5 | 201 09.1 | N16 32.3 |
| 19 | | 355 45.4 | 62 52.2 | 05.1 | 109 50.2 | 55.7 | 303 30.4 | 47.4 | 216 11.6 | 32.3 |
| 20 | | 10 47.9 | 77 51.4 | 04.6 | 124 50.8 | 56.1 | 318 33.2 | 47.3 | 231 14.0 | 32.3 |
| 21 | | 25 50.4 | 92 50.7 | 04.2 | 139 51.3 | 56.4 | 333 36.0 | 47.3 | 246 16.5 | 32.3 |
| 22 | | 40 52.8 | 107 49.9 | 03.7 | 154 51.9 | 56.7 | 348 38.8 | 47.2 | 261 19.0 | 32.3 |
| 23 | | 55 55.3 | 122 49.2 | 03.3 | 169 52.4 | 57.0 | 3 41.6 | 47.1 | 276 21.5 | 32.3 |
| Mer. Pass. | | h m 19 20.9 | v −0.8 | d 0.4 | v 0.6 | d 0.3 | v 2.8 | d 0.1 | v 2.5 | d 0.0 |

| STARS Name | S.H.A. | Dec. |
|---|---|---|
| | ° ′ | ° ′ |
| Acamar | 315 38.8 | S40 23.9 |
| Achernar | 335 46.8 | S57 21.4 |
| Acrux | 173 40.3 | S62 58.0 |
| Adhara | 255 33.8 | S28 56.4 |
| Aldebaran | 291 20.6 | N16 27.8 |
| Alioth | 166 45.2 | N56 04.9 |
| Alkaid | 153 21.0 | N49 25.6 |
| Al Na'ir | 28 18.3 | S47 04.5 |
| Alnilam | 276 13.9 | S 1 13.0 |
| Alphard | 218 23.0 | S 8 33.5 |
| Alphecca | 126 34.7 | N26 47.6 |
| Alpheratz | 358 11.8 | N28 58.0 |
| Altair | 62 35.3 | N 8 48.6 |
| Ankaa | 353 42.6 | S42 26.0 |
| Antares | 113 00.4 | S26 22.8 |
| Arcturus | 146 21.1 | N19 18.1 |
| Atria | 108 27.5 | S68 59.1 |
| Avior | 234 28.8 | S59 26.0 |
| Bellatrix | 279 01.2 | N 6 19.7 |
| Betelgeuse | 271 30.7 | N 7 24.1 |
| Canopus | 264 07.8 | S52 40.9 |
| Capella | 281 14.6 | N45 58.4 |
| Deneb | 49 50.4 | N45 12.2 |
| Denebola | 183 01.8 | N14 42.0 |
| Diphda | 349 23.3 | S18 06.8 |
| Dubhe | 194 25.4 | N61 52.2 |
| Elnath | 278 47.0 | N28 35.2 |
| Eltanin | 90 59.4 | N51 29.7 |
| Enif | 34 14.2 | N 9 46.3 |
| Fomalhaut | 15 54.2 | S29 44.7 |
| Gacrux | 172 31.8 | S56 58.8 |
| Gienah | 176 20.7 | S17 24.7 |
| Hadar | 149 27.4 | S60 15.5 |
| Hamal | 328 31.5 | N23 21.3 |
| Kaus Aust. | 84 20.6 | S34 23.7 |
| Kochab | 137 20.1 | N74 14.9 |
| Markab | 14 05.7 | N15 05.1 |
| Menkar | 314 43.5 | N 4 00.0 |
| Menkent | 148 40.3 | S36 15.2 |
| Miaplacidus | 221 45.0 | S69 37.1 |
| Mirfak | 309 19.2 | N49 46.9 |
| Nunki | 76 32.7 | S26 19.5 |
| Peacock | 54 02.8 | S56 48.7 |
| Pollux | 244 01.0 | N28 04.8 |
| Procyon | 245 28.2 | N 5 17.0 |
| Rasalhague | 96 32.3 | N12 34.7 |
| Regulus | 208 12.7 | N12 04.7 |
| Rigel | 281 38.1 | S 8 13.7 |
| Rigil Kent. | 140 29.8 | S60 44.2 |
| Sabik | 102 44.4 | S15 41.7 |
| Schedar | 350 11.5 | N56 25.0 |
| Shaula | 96 59.7 | S37 05.2 |
| Sirius | 258 57.7 | S16 41.1 |
| Spica | 159 00.5 | S11 02.4 |
| Suhail | 223 12.4 | S43 20.2 |
| Vega | 80 57.9 | N38 46.0 |
| Zuben'ubi | 137 36.2 | S15 56.7 |

| | S.H.A. | Mer. Pass. |
|---|---|---|
| | ° ′ | h m |
| Venus | 69 25.8 | 14 47 |
| Mars | 115 27.1 | 11 42 |
| Jupiter | 307 31.0 | 22 50 |
| Saturn | 220 25.6 | 4 42 |

## 1976 DECEMBER 8, 9, 10 (WED., THURS., FRI.)

| G.M.T. | ARIES G.H.A. | VENUS −3.7 G.H.A. | VENUS Dec. | MARS +1.6 G.H.A. | MARS Dec. | JUPITER −2.4 G.H.A. | JUPITER Dec. | SATURN +0.4 G.H.A. | SATURN Dec. | STARS Name | S.H.A. | Dec. |
|---|---|---|---|---|---|---|---|---|---|---|---|---|
| d h | ° ′ | ° ′ | ° ′ | ° ′ | ° ′ | ° ′ | ° ′ | ° ′ | ° ′ | | ° ′ | ° ′ |
| 8 00 | 76 52.6 | 136 05.6 | S22 45.8 | 186 09.0 | S22 39.1 | 25 23.9 | N17 37.5 | 297 23.3 | N16 34.8 | Acamar | 315 38.8 | S40 24.0 |
| 01 | 91 55.0 | 151 04.9 | 45.2 | 201 09.5 | 39.3 | 40 26.7 | 37.4 | 312 25.8 | 34.8 | Achernar | 335 46.9 | S57 21.4 |
| 02 | 106 57.5 | 166 04.2 | 44.6 | 216 10.0 | 39.6 | 55 29.4 | 37.4 | 327 28.3 | 34.9 | Acrux | 173 40.2 | S62 58.0 |
| 03 | 122 00.0 | 181 03.6 | ·· 44.0 | 231 10.5 | ·· 39.9 | 70 32.2 | ·· 37.3 | 342 30.8 | ·· 34.9 | Adhara | 255 33.8 | S28 56.4 |
| 04 | 137 02.4 | 196 02.9 | 43.4 | 246 11.0 | 40.1 | 85 35.0 | 37.2 | 357 33.3 | 34.9 | Aldebaran | 291 20.6 | N16 27.8 |
| 05 | 152 04.9 | 211 02.2 | 42.7 | 261 11.5 | 40.4 | 100 37.7 | 37.2 | 12 35.8 | 34.9 | | | |
| 06 | 167 07.4 | 226 01.6 | S22 42.1 | 276 12.0 | S22 40.7 | 115 40.5 | N17 37.1 | 27 38.3 | N16 34.9 | Alioth | 166 45.1 | N56 04.8 |
| 07 | 182 09.8 | 241 00.9 | 41.5 | 291 12.5 | 40.9 | 130 43.2 | 37.0 | 42 40.8 | 35.0 | Alkaid | 153 20.9 | N49 25.5 |
| W 08 | 197 12.3 | 256 00.2 | 40.9 | 306 13.0 | 41.2 | 145 46.0 | 37.0 | 57 43.3 | 35.0 | Al Na'ir | 28 18.3 | S47 04.5 |
| E 09 | 212 14.8 | 270 59.6 | ·· 40.2 | 321 13.6 | ·· 41.4 | 160 48.8 | ·· 36.9 | 72 45.9 | ·· 35.0 | Alnilam | 276 13.9 | S 1 13.0 |
| D 10 | 227 17.2 | 285 58.9 | 39.6 | 336 14.1 | 41.7 | 175 51.5 | 36.9 | 87 48.4 | 35.0 | Alphard | 218 22.9 | S 8 33.5 |
| N 11 | 242 19.7 | 300 58.2 | 39.0 | 351 14.6 | 42.0 | 190 54.3 | 36.8 | 102 50.9 | 35.1 | | | |
| E 12 | 257 22.1 | 315 57.6 | S22 38.4 | 6 15.1 | S22 42.2 | 205 57.0 | N17 36.7 | 117 53.4 | N16 35.1 | Alphecca | 126 34.6 | N26 47.5 |
| S 13 | 272 24.6 | 330 56.9 | 37.7 | 21 15.6 | 42.5 | 220 59.8 | 36.7 | 132 55.9 | 35.1 | Alpheratz | 358 11.8 | N28 58.0 |
| D 14 | 287 27.1 | 345 56.3 | 37.1 | 36 16.1 | 42.7 | 236 02.6 | 36.6 | 147 58.4 | 35.1 | Altair | 62 35.3 | N 8 48.6 |
| A 15 | 302 29.5 | 0 55.6 | ·· 36.5 | 51 16.6 | ·· 43.0 | 251 05.3 | ·· 36.5 | 163 00.9 | ·· 35.1 | Ankaa | 353 42.7 | S42 26.0 |
| Y 16 | 317 32.0 | 15 54.9 | 35.8 | 66 17.1 | 43.2 | 266 08.1 | 36.5 | 178 03.4 | 35.2 | Antares | 113 00.3 | S26 22.8 |
| 17 | 332 34.5 | 30 54.3 | 35.2 | 81 17.6 | 43.5 | 281 10.8 | 36.4 | 193 06.0 | 35.2 | | | |
| 18 | 347 36.9 | 45 53.6 | S22 34.6 | 96 18.1 | S22 43.8 | 296 13.6 | N17 36.3 | 208 08.5 | N16 35.2 | Arcturus | 146 21.1 | N19 18.1 |
| 19 | 2 39.4 | 60 53.0 | 33.9 | 111 18.6 | 44.0 | 311 16.3 | 36.3 | 223 11.0 | 35.2 | Atria | 108 27.4 | S68 59.1 |
| 20 | 17 41.9 | 75 52.3 | 33.3 | 126 19.2 | 44.3 | 326 19.1 | 36.2 | 238 13.5 | 35.3 | Avior | 234 28.7 | S59 26.0 |
| 21 | 32 44.3 | 90 51.7 | ·· 32.7 | 141 19.7 | ·· 44.5 | 341 21.8 | ·· 36.2 | 253 16.0 | ·· 35.3 | Bellatrix | 279 01.1 | N 6 19.7 |
| 22 | 47 46.8 | 105 51.0 | 32.0 | 156 20.2 | 44.8 | 356 24.6 | 36.1 | 268 18.5 | 35.3 | Betelgeuse | 271 30.7 | N 7 24.1 |
| 23 | 62 49.3 | 120 50.3 | 31.4 | 171 20.7 | 45.0 | 11 27.4 | 36.0 | 283 21.0 | 35.3 | | | |
| 9 00 | 77 51.7 | 135 49.7 | S22 30.8 | 186 21.2 | S22 45.3 | 26 30.1 | N17 36.0 | 298 23.5 | N16 35.3 | Canopus | 264 07.8 | S52 41.0 |
| 01 | 92 54.2 | 150 49.0 | 30.1 | 201 21.7 | 45.5 | 41 32.9 | 35.9 | 313 26.1 | 35.4 | Capella | 281 14.6 | N45 58.5 |
| 02 | 107 56.6 | 165 48.4 | 29.5 | 216 22.2 | 45.8 | 56 35.6 | 35.9 | 328 28.6 | 35.4 | Deneb | 49 50.5 | N45 12.2 |
| 03 | 122 59.1 | 180 47.7 | ·· 28.8 | 231 22.7 | ·· 46.1 | 71 38.4 | ·· 35.8 | 343 31.1 | ·· 35.4 | Denebola | 183 01.7 | N14 41.9 |
| 04 | 138 01.6 | 195 47.1 | 28.2 | 246 23.2 | 46.3 | 86 41.1 | 35.7 | 358 33.6 | 35.4 | Diphda | 349 23.3 | S18 06.8 |
| 05 | 153 04.0 | 210 46.4 | 27.5 | 261 23.7 | 46.6 | 101 43.9 | 35.7 | 13 36.1 | 35.5 | | | |
| 06 | 168 06.5 | 225 45.8 | S22 26.9 | 276 24.2 | S22 46.8 | 116 46.6 | N17 35.6 | 28 38.6 | N16 35.5 | Dubhe | 194 25.3 | N61 52.2 |
| 07 | 183 09.0 | 240 45.1 | 26.3 | 291 24.7 | 47.1 | 131 49.4 | 35.5 | 43 41.1 | 35.5 | Elnath | 278 47.0 | N28 35.2 |
| T 08 | 198 11.4 | 255 44.5 | 25.6 | 306 25.2 | 47.3 | 146 52.2 | 35.5 | 58 43.7 | 35.5 | Eltanin | 90 59.5 | N51 29.7 |
| H 09 | 213 13.9 | 270 43.8 | ·· 25.0 | 321 25.7 | ·· 47.6 | 161 54.9 | ·· 35.4 | 73 46.2 | ·· 35.6 | Enif | 34 14.2 | N 9 46.3 |
| U 10 | 228 16.4 | 285 43.2 | 24.3 | 336 26.2 | 47.8 | 176 57.7 | 35.4 | 88 48.7 | 35.6 | Fomalhaut | 15 54.3 | S29 44.7 |
| R 11 | 243 18.8 | 300 42.5 | 23.7 | 351 26.7 | 48.1 | 192 00.4 | 35.3 | 103 51.2 | 35.6 | | | |
| S 12 | 258 21.3 | 315 41.9 | S22 23.0 | 6 27.2 | S22 48.3 | 207 03.2 | N17 35.2 | 118 53.7 | N16 35.6 | Gacrux | 172 31.7 | S56 58.8 |
| D 13 | 273 23.8 | 330 41.2 | 22.4 | 21 27.8 | 48.6 | 222 05.9 | 35.2 | 133 56.2 | 35.6 | Gienah | 176 20.7 | S17 24.8 |
| A 14 | 288 26.2 | 345 40.6 | 21.7 | 36 28.3 | 48.8 | 237 08.7 | 35.1 | 148 58.7 | 35.7 | Hadar | 149 27.3 | S60 15.5 |
| Y 15 | 303 28.7 | 0 40.0 | ·· 21.0 | 51 28.8 | ·· 49.1 | 252 11.4 | ·· 35.1 | 164 01.3 | ·· 35.7 | Hamal | 328 31.5 | N23 21.3 |
| 16 | 318 31.1 | 15 39.3 | 20.4 | 66 29.3 | 49.3 | 267 14.2 | 35.0 | 179 03.8 | 35.7 | Kaus Aust. | 84 20.6 | S34 23.7 |
| 17 | 333 33.6 | 30 38.7 | 19.7 | 81 29.8 | 49.6 | 282 16.9 | 34.9 | 194 06.3 | 35.7 | | | |
| 18 | 348 36.1 | 45 38.0 | S22 19.1 | 96 30.3 | S22 49.8 | 297 19.7 | N17 34.9 | 209 08.8 | N16 35.8 | Kochab | 137 20.1 | N74 14.9 |
| 19 | 3 38.5 | 60 37.4 | 18.4 | 111 30.8 | 50.1 | 312 22.4 | 34.8 | 224 11.3 | 35.8 | Markab | 14 05.7 | N15 05.1 |
| 20 | 18 41.0 | 75 36.7 | 17.8 | 126 31.3 | 50.3 | 327 25.2 | 34.7 | 239 13.8 | 35.8 | Menkar | 314 43.5 | N 4 00.0 |
| 21 | 33 43.5 | 90 36.1 | ·· 17.1 | 141 31.8 | ·· 50.5 | 342 27.9 | ·· 34.7 | 254 16.4 | ·· 35.8 | Menkent | 148 40.3 | S36 15.2 |
| 22 | 48 45.9 | 105 35.5 | 16.4 | 156 32.3 | 50.8 | 357 30.7 | 34.6 | 269 18.9 | 35.9 | Miaplacidus | 221 44.9 | S69 37.2 |
| 23 | 63 48.4 | 120 34.8 | 15.8 | 171 32.8 | 51.0 | 12 33.4 | 34.6 | 284 21.4 | 35.9 | | | |
| 10 00 | 78 50.9 | 135 34.2 | S22 15.1 | 186 33.3 | S22 51.3 | 27 36.2 | N17 34.5 | 299 23.9 | N16 35.9 | Mirfak | 309 19.2 | N49 46.9 |
| 01 | 93 53.3 | 150 33.6 | 14.4 | 201 33.8 | 51.5 | 42 38.9 | 34.4 | 314 26.4 | 35.9 | Nunki | 76 32.7 | S26 19.5 |
| 02 | 108 55.8 | 165 32.9 | 13.8 | 216 34.3 | 51.8 | 57 41.7 | 34.4 | 329 29.0 | 36.0 | Peacock | 54 02.9 | S56 48.7 |
| 03 | 123 58.3 | 180 32.3 | ·· 13.1 | 231 34.8 | ·· 52.0 | 72 44.4 | ·· 34.3 | 344 31.5 | ·· 36.0 | Pollux | 244 01.0 | N28 04.8 |
| 04 | 139 00.7 | 195 31.6 | 12.4 | 246 35.3 | 52.3 | 87 47.2 | 34.3 | 359 34.0 | 36.0 | Procyon | 245 28.2 | N 5 17.0 |
| 05 | 154 03.2 | 210 31.0 | 11.8 | 261 35.8 | 52.5 | 102 49.9 | 34.2 | 14 36.5 | 36.0 | | | |
| 06 | 169 05.6 | 225 30.4 | S22 11.1 | 276 36.3 | S22 52.7 | 117 52.7 | N17 34.1 | 29 39.0 | N16 36.1 | Rasalhague | 96 32.3 | N12 34.7 |
| 07 | 184 08.1 | 240 29.7 | 10.4 | 291 36.8 | 53.0 | 132 55.4 | 34.1 | 44 41.5 | 36.1 | Regulus | 208 12.6 | N12 04.7 |
| 08 | 199 10.6 | 255 29.1 | 09.7 | 306 37.3 | 53.2 | 147 58.2 | 34.0 | 59 44.1 | 36.1 | Rigel | 281 38.1 | S 8 13.7 |
| F 09 | 214 13.0 | 270 28.5 | ·· 09.1 | 321 37.8 | ·· 53.5 | 163 00.9 | ·· 34.0 | 74 46.6 | ·· 36.1 | Rigil Kent. | 140 29.7 | S60 44.1 |
| R 10 | 229 15.5 | 285 27.9 | 08.4 | 336 38.3 | 53.7 | 178 03.7 | 33.9 | 89 49.1 | 36.2 | Sabik | 102 44.4 | S15 41.7 |
| I 11 | 244 18.0 | 300 27.2 | 07.7 | 351 38.8 | 54.0 | 193 06.4 | 33.8 | 104 51.6 | 36.2 | | | |
| D 12 | 259 20.4 | 315 26.6 | S22 07.0 | 6 39.3 | S22 54.2 | 208 09.2 | N17 33.8 | 119 54.1 | N16 36.2 | Schedar | 350 11.6 | N56 25.0 |
| A 13 | 274 22.9 | 330 26.0 | 06.4 | 21 39.8 | 54.4 | 223 11.9 | 33.7 | 134 56.7 | 36.2 | Shaula | 96 59.6 | S37 05.2 |
| Y 14 | 289 25.4 | 345 25.3 | 05.7 | 36 40.3 | 54.7 | 238 14.7 | 33.7 | 149 59.2 | 36.3 | Sirius | 258 57.6 | S16 41.1 |
| 15 | 304 27.8 | 0 24.7 | ·· 05.0 | 51 40.8 | ·· 54.9 | 253 17.4 | ·· 33.6 | 165 01.7 | ·· 36.3 | Spica | 159 00.4 | S11 02.4 |
| 16 | 319 30.3 | 15 24.1 | 04.3 | 66 41.3 | 55.2 | 268 20.2 | 33.5 | 180 04.2 | 36.3 | Suhail | 223 12.4 | S43 20.3 |
| 17 | 334 32.7 | 30 23.5 | 03.6 | 81 41.8 | 55.4 | 283 22.9 | 33.5 | 195 06.8 | 36.3 | | | |
| 18 | 349 35.2 | 45 22.8 | S22 03.0 | 96 42.3 | S22 55.6 | 298 25.7 | N17 33.4 | 210 09.3 | N16 36.4 | Vega | 80 58.0 | N38 45.9 |
| 19 | 4 37.7 | 60 22.2 | 02.3 | 111 42.8 | 55.9 | 313 28.4 | 33.4 | 225 11.8 | 36.4 | Zuben'ubi | 137 36.1 | S15 56.7 |
| 20 | 19 40.1 | 75 21.6 | 01.6 | 126 43.3 | 56.1 | 328 31.1 | 33.3 | 240 14.3 | 36.4 | | S.H.A. | Mer. Pass. |
| 21 | 34 42.6 | 90 21.0 | ·· 00.9 | 141 43.8 | ·· 56.3 | 343 33.9 | ·· 33.2 | 255 16.8 | ·· 36.4 | | ° ′ | h m |
| 22 | 49 45.1 | 105 20.3 | 22 00.2 | 156 44.3 | 56.6 | 358 36.6 | 33.2 | 270 19.4 | 36.5 | Venus | 57 58.0 | 14 57 |
| 23 | 64 47.5 | 120 19.7 | 21 59.5 | 171 44.8 | 56.8 | 13 39.4 | 33.1 | 285 21.9 | 36.5 | Mars | 108 29.5 | 11 34 |
| | h m | | | | | | | | | Jupiter | 308 38.4 | 22 10 |
| Mer. Pass. | 18 45.5 | v −0.6 | d 0.7 | v 0.5 | d 0.2 | v 2.8 | d 0.1 | v 2.5 | d 0.0 | Saturn | 220 31.8 | 4 06 |

## 1976 DECEMBER 17, 18, 19 (FRI., SAT., SUN.)

| G.M.T. | ARIES G.H.A. | VENUS −3.7 G.H.A. | VENUS Dec. | MARS +1.6 G.H.A. | MARS Dec. | JUPITER −2.3 G.H.A. | JUPITER Dec. | SATURN +0.3 G.H.A. | SATURN Dec. | STARS Name | S.H.A. | Dec. |
|---|---|---|---|---|---|---|---|---|---|---|---|---|
| d h | ° ′ | ° ′ | ° ′ | ° ′ | ° ′ | ° ′ | ° ′ | ° ′ | ° ′ | | ° ′ | ° ′ |
| 17 00 | 85 44.8 | 133 57.1 | S20 09.4 | 187 54.7 | S23 26.9 | 35 14.8 | N17 25.1 | 306 29.6 | N16 40.7 | Acamar | 315 38.9 | S40 24.0 |
| 01 | 100 47.3 | 148 56.6 | 08.6 | 202 55.1 | 27.1 | 50 17.5 | 25.1 | 321 32.1 | 40.8 | Achernar | 335 46.9 | S57 21.5 |
| 02 | 115 49.8 | 163 56.1 | 07.8 | 217 55.6 | 27.3 | 65 20.2 | 25.0 | 336 34.7 | 40.8 | Acrux | 173 40.1 | S62 58.0 |
| 03 | 130 52.2 | 178 55.6 | ·· 06.9 | 232 56.1 | ·· 27.4 | 80 22.9 | ·· 25.0 | 351 37.2 | ·· 40.8 | Adhara | 255 33.7 | S28 56.5 |
| 04 | 145 54.7 | 193 55.1 | 06.1 | 247 56.5 | 27.6 | 95 25.6 | 24.9 | 6 39.8 | 40.9 | Aldebaran | 291 20.6 | N16 27.8 |
| 05 | 160 57.2 | 208 54.5 | 05.3 | 262 57.0 | 27.8 | 110 28.3 | 24.9 | 21 42.3 | 40.9 | | | |
| 06 | 175 59.6 | 223 54.0 | S20 04.4 | 277 57.5 | S23 28.0 | 125 31.0 | N17 24.8 | 36 44.9 | N16 40.9 | Alioth | 166 45.0 | N56 04.8 |
| 07 | 191 02.1 | 238 53.5 | 03.6 | 292 57.9 | 28.1 | 140 33.7 | 24.8 | 51 47.4 | 41.0 | Alkaid | 153 20.8 | N49 25.5 |
| 08 | 206 04.5 | 253 53.0 | 02.8 | 307 58.4 | 28.3 | 155 36.4 | 24.7 | 66 50.0 | 41.0 | Al Na'ir | 28 18.4 | S47 04.5 |
| F 09 | 221 07.0 | 268 52.5 | ·· 01.9 | 322 58.9 | ·· 28.5 | 170 39.1 | ·· 24.7 | 81 52.5 | ·· 41.1 | Alnilam | 276 13.9 | S 1 13.1 |
| R 10 | 236 09.5 | 283 52.0 | 01.1 | 337 59.4 | 28.7 | 185 41.8 | 24.6 | 96 55.1 | 41.1 | Alphard | 218 22.8 | S 8 33.6 |
| I 11 | 251 11.9 | 298 51.5 | 20 00.3 | 352 59.8 | 28.8 | 200 44.5 | 24.6 | 111 57.6 | 41.1 | | | |
| D 12 | 266 14.4 | 313 51.0 | S19 59.4 | 8 00.3 | S23 29.0 | 215 47.2 | N17 24.5 | 127 00.2 | N16 41.2 | Alphecca | 126 34.6 | N26 47.5 |
| A 13 | 281 16.9 | 328 50.5 | 58.6 | 23 00.7 | 29.2 | 230 49.9 | 24.5 | 142 02.7 | 41.2 | Alpheratz | 358 11.9 | N28 58.0 |
| Y 14 | 296 19.3 | 343 50.0 | 57.7 | 38 01.2 | 29.4 | 245 52.6 | 24.4 | 157 05.3 | 41.2 | Altair | 62 35.3 | N 8 48.6 |
| 15 | 311 21.8 | 358 49.5 | ·· 56.9 | 53 01.7 | ·· 29.5 | 260 55.3 | ·· 24.4 | 172 07.8 | ·· 41.3 | Ankaa | 353 42.7 | S42 26.0 |
| 16 | 326 24.3 | 13 49.0 | 56.1 | 68 02.1 | 29.7 | 275 58.1 | 24.3 | 187 10.4 | 41.3 | Antares | 113 00.3 | S26 22.8 |
| 17 | 341 26.7 | 28 48.5 | 55.2 | 83 02.6 | 29.9 | 291 00.8 | 24.3 | 202 12.9 | 41.3 | | | |
| 18 | 356 29.2 | 43 47.9 | S19 54.4 | 98 03.1 | S23 30.0 | 306 03.5 | N17 24.2 | 217 15.5 | N16 41.4 | Arcturus | 146 21.0 | N19 18.1 |
| 19 | 11 31.6 | 58 47.4 | 53.5 | 113 03.5 | 30.2 | 321 06.2 | 24.2 | 232 18.0 | 41.4 | Atria | 108 27.3 | S68 59.0 |
| 20 | 26 34.1 | 73 46.9 | 52.7 | 128 04.0 | 30.4 | 336 08.9 | 24.1 | 247 20.6 | 41.4 | Avior | 234 28.6 | S59 26.1 |
| 21 | 41 36.6 | 88 46.4 | ·· 51.8 | 143 04.5 | ·· 30.6 | 351 11.6 | ·· 24.1 | 262 23.1 | ·· 41.5 | Bellatrix | 279 01.1 | N 6 19.7 |
| 22 | 56 39.0 | 103 45.9 | 51.0 | 158 04.9 | 30.7 | 6 14.3 | 24.0 | 277 25.7 | 41.5 | Betelgeuse | 271 30.7 | N 7 24.1 |
| 23 | 71 41.5 | 118 45.4 | 50.2 | 173 05.4 | 30.9 | 21 17.0 | 24.0 | 292 28.2 | 41.5 | | | |
| 18 00 | 86 44.0 | 133 44.9 | S19 49.3 | 188 05.9 | S23 31.1 | 36 19.7 | N17 23.9 | 307 30.8 | N16 41.6 | Canopus | 264 07.8 | S52 41.1 |
| 01 | 101 46.4 | 148 44.5 | 48.5 | 203 06.3 | 31.2 | 51 22.4 | 23.9 | 322 33.3 | 41.6 | Capella | 281 14.5 | N45 58.5 |
| 02 | 116 48.9 | 163 44.0 | 47.6 | 218 06.8 | 31.4 | 66 25.1 | 23.8 | 337 35.9 | 41.6 | Deneb | 49 50.5 | N45 12.2 |
| 03 | 131 51.4 | 178 43.5 | ·· 46.8 | 233 07.3 | ·· 31.6 | 81 27.8 | ·· 23.8 | 352 38.5 | ·· 41.7 | Denebola | 183 01.6 | N14 41.9 |
| 04 | 146 53.8 | 193 43.0 | 45.9 | 248 07.7 | 31.7 | 96 30.5 | 23.7 | 7 41.0 | 41.7 | Diphda | 349 23.3 | S18 06.8 |
| 05 | 161 56.3 | 208 42.5 | 45.1 | 263 08.2 | 31.9 | 111 33.2 | 23.7 | 22 43.6 | 41.7 | | | |
| 06 | 176 58.8 | 223 42.0 | S19 44.2 | 278 08.6 | S23 32.1 | 126 35.9 | N17 23.6 | 37 46.1 | N16 41.8 | Dubhe | 194 25.2 | N61 52.2 |
| 07 | 192 01.2 | 238 41.5 | 43.3 | 293 09.1 | 32.2 | 141 38.6 | 23.6 | 52 48.7 | 41.8 | Elnath | 278 46.9 | N28 35.3 |
| S 08 | 207 03.7 | 253 41.0 | 42.5 | 308 09.6 | 32.4 | 156 41.3 | 23.6 | 67 51.2 | 41.8 | Eltanin | 90 59.5 | N51 29.6 |
| A 09 | 222 06.1 | 268 40.5 | ·· 41.6 | 323 10.0 | ·· 32.6 | 171 44.0 | ·· 23.5 | 82 53.8 | ·· 41.9 | Enif | 34 14.2 | N 9 46.3 |
| T 10 | 237 08.6 | 283 40.0 | 40.8 | 338 10.5 | 32.7 | 186 46.7 | 23.5 | 97 56.3 | 41.9 | Fomalhaut | 15 54.3 | S29 44.7 |
| U 11 | 252 11.1 | 298 39.5 | 39.9 | 353 11.0 | 32.9 | 201 49.4 | 23.4 | 112 58.9 | 41.9 | | | |
| R 12 | 267 13.5 | 313 39.0 | S19 39.1 | 8 11.4 | S23 33.1 | 216 52.1 | N17 23.4 | 128 01.4 | N16 42.0 | Gacrux | 172 31.6 | S56 58.8 |
| D 13 | 282 16.0 | 328 38.5 | 38.2 | 23 11.9 | 33.2 | 231 54.8 | 23.3 | 143 04.0 | 42.0 | Gienah | 176 20.6 | S17 24.8 |
| A 14 | 297 18.5 | 343 38.1 | 37.3 | 38 12.3 | 33.4 | 246 57.4 | 23.3 | 158 06.6 | 42.1 | Hadar | 149 27.2 | S60 15.5 |
| Y 15 | 312 20.9 | 358 37.6 | ·· 36.5 | 53 12.8 | ·· 33.5 | 262 00.1 | ·· 23.2 | 173 09.1 | ·· 42.1 | Hamal | 328 31.5 | N23 21.3 |
| 16 | 327 23.4 | 13 37.1 | 35.6 | 68 13.3 | 33.7 | 277 02.8 | 23.2 | 188 11.7 | 42.1 | Kaus Aust. | 84 20.6 | S34 23.7 |
| 17 | 342 25.9 | 28 36.6 | 34.8 | 83 13.7 | 33.9 | 292 05.5 | 23.1 | 203 14.2 | 42.2 | | | |
| 18 | 357 28.3 | 43 36.1 | S19 33.9 | 98 14.2 | S23 34.0 | 307 08.2 | N17 23.1 | 218 16.8 | N16 42.2 | Kochab | 137 19.9 | N74 14.8 |
| 19 | 12 30.8 | 58 35.6 | 33.0 | 113 14.6 | 34.2 | 322 10.9 | 23.0 | 233 19.3 | 42.2 | Markab | 14 05.7 | N15 05.0 |
| 20 | 27 33.3 | 73 35.1 | 32.2 | 128 15.1 | 34.3 | 337 13.6 | 23.0 | 248 21.9 | 42.3 | Menkar | 314 43.5 | N 4 00.0 |
| 21 | 42 35.7 | 88 34.7 | ·· 31.3 | 143 15.6 | ·· 34.5 | 352 16.3 | ·· 22.9 | 263 24.5 | ·· 42.3 | Menkent | 148 40.2 | S36 15.2 |
| 22 | 57 38.2 | 103 34.2 | 30.4 | 158 16.0 | 34.7 | 7 19.0 | 22.9 | 278 27.0 | 42.3 | Miaplacidus | 221 44.7 | S69 37.2 |
| 23 | 72 40.6 | 118 33.7 | 29.6 | 173 16.5 | 34.8 | 22 21.7 | 22.8 | 293 29.6 | 42.4 | | | |
| 19 00 | 87 43.1 | 133 33.2 | S19 28.7 | 188 16.9 | S23 35.0 | 37 24.4 | N17 22.8 | 308 32.1 | N16 42.4 | Mirfak | 309 19.2 | N49 46.9 |
| 01 | 102 45.6 | 148 32.7 | 27.8 | 203 17.4 | 35.1 | 52 27.1 | 22.7 | 323 34.7 | 42.4 | Nunki | 76 32.7 | S26 19.5 |
| 02 | 117 48.0 | 163 32.3 | 27.0 | 218 17.9 | 35.3 | 67 29.8 | 22.7 | 338 37.2 | 42.5 | Peacock | 54 02.9 | S56 48.6 |
| 03 | 132 50.5 | 178 31.8 | ·· 26.1 | 233 18.3 | ·· 35.5 | 82 32.5 | ·· 22.7 | 353 39.8 | ·· 42.5 | Pollux | 244 00.9 | N28 04.8 |
| 04 | 147 53.0 | 193 31.3 | 25.2 | 248 18.8 | 35.6 | 97 35.2 | 22.6 | 8 42.4 | 42.6 | Procyon | 245 28.1 | N 5 16.9 |
| 05 | 162 55.4 | 208 30.8 | 24.3 | 263 19.2 | 35.8 | 112 37.9 | 22.6 | 23 44.9 | 42.6 | | | |
| 06 | 177 57.9 | 223 30.4 | S19 23.5 | 278 19.7 | S23 35.9 | 127 40.6 | N17 22.5 | 38 47.5 | N16 42.6 | Rasalhague | 96 32.3 | N12 34.7 |
| 07 | 193 00.4 | 238 29.9 | 22.6 | 293 20.2 | 36.1 | 142 43.3 | 22.5 | 53 50.0 | 42.7 | Regulus | 208 12.6 | N12 04.6 |
| 08 | 208 02.8 | 253 29.4 | 21.7 | 308 20.6 | 36.2 | 157 45.9 | 22.4 | 68 52.6 | 42.7 | Rigel | 281 38.1 | S 8 13.8 |
| S 09 | 223 05.3 | 268 28.9 | ·· 20.8 | 323 21.1 | ·· 36.4 | 172 48.6 | ·· 22.4 | 83 55.1 | ·· 42.7 | Rigil Kent. | 140 29.6 | S60 44.1 |
| U 10 | 238 07.7 | 283 28.5 | 20.0 | 338 21.5 | 36.5 | 187 51.3 | 22.3 | 98 57.7 | 42.8 | Sabik | 102 44.4 | S15 41.7 |
| N 11 | 253 10.2 | 298 28.0 | 19.1 | 353 22.0 | 36.7 | 202 54.0 | 22.3 | 114 00.3 | 42.8 | | | |
| D 12 | 268 12.7 | 313 27.5 | S19 18.2 | 8 22.4 | S23 36.9 | 217 56.7 | N17 22.2 | 129 02.8 | N16 42.8 | Schedar | 350 11.7 | N56 25.0 |
| A 13 | 283 15.1 | 328 27.1 | 17.3 | 23 22.9 | 37.0 | 232 59.4 | 22.2 | 144 05.4 | 42.9 | Shaula | 96 59.6 | S37 05.1 |
| Y 14 | 298 17.6 | 343 26.6 | 16.4 | 38 23.4 | 37.2 | 248 02.1 | 22.1 | 159 07.9 | 42.9 | Sirius | 258 57.6 | S16 41.2 |
| 15 | 313 20.1 | 358 26.1 | ·· 15.6 | 53 23.8 | ·· 37.3 | 263 04.8 | ·· 22.1 | 174 10.5 | ·· 43.0 | Spica | 159 00.3 | S11 02.4 |
| 16 | 328 22.5 | 13 25.6 | 14.7 | 68 24.3 | 37.5 | 278 07.5 | 22.0 | 189 13.1 | 43.0 | Suhail | 223 12.3 | S43 20.3 |
| 17 | 343 25.0 | 28 25.2 | 13.8 | 83 24.7 | 37.6 | 293 10.2 | 22.0 | 204 15.6 | 43.0 | | | |
| 18 | 358 27.5 | 43 24.7 | S19 12.9 | 98 25.2 | S23 37.8 | 308 12.8 | N17 22.0 | 219 18.2 | N16 43.1 | Vega | 80 58.0 | N38 45.9 |
| 19 | 13 29.9 | 58 24.2 | 12.0 | 113 25.6 | 37.9 | 323 15.5 | 21.9 | 234 20.7 | 43.1 | Zuben'ubi | 137 36.1 | S15 56.7 |
| 20 | 28 32.4 | 73 23.8 | 11.1 | 128 26.1 | 38.1 | 338 18.2 | 21.9 | 249 23.3 | 43.1 | | S.H.A. | Mer. Pass. |
| 21 | 43 34.9 | 88 23.3 | ·· 10.3 | 143 26.6 | ·· 38.2 | 353 20.9 | ·· 21.8 | 264 25.9 | ·· 43.2 | | ° ′ | h m |
| 22 | 58 37.3 | 103 22.9 | 09.4 | 158 27.0 | 38.4 | 8 23.6 | 21.8 | 279 28.4 | 43.2 | Venus | 47 01.0 | 15 05 |
| 23 | 73 39.8 | 118 22.4 | 08.5 | 173 27.5 | 38.5 | 23 26.3 | 21.7 | 294 31.0 | 43.2 | Mars | 101 21.9 | 11 27 |
| | h m | | | | | | | | | Jupiter | 309 35.7 | 21 31 |
| Mer. Pass. | 18 10.1 | v −0.5 | d 0.9 | v 0.5 | d 0.2 | v 2.7 | d 0.0 | v 2.6 | d 0.0 | Saturn | 220 46.8 | 3 29 |

| G.M.T. d h | ARIES G.H.A. | VENUS −3.8 G.H.A. | VENUS Dec. | MARS +1.6 G.H.A. | MARS Dec. | JUPITER −2.3 G.H.A. | JUPITER Dec. | SATURN +0.3 G.H.A. | SATURN Dec. |
|---|---|---|---|---|---|---|---|---|---|
| 20 00 | 88 42.2 | 133 21.9 | S19 07.6 | 188 27.9 | S23 38.7 | 38 29.0 | N17 21.7 | 309 33.6 | N16 43.3 |
| 01 | 103 44.7 | 148 21.5 | 06.7 | 203 28.4 | 38.8 | 53 31.7 | 21.6 | 324 36.1 | 43.3 |
| 02 | 118 47.2 | 163 21.0 | 05.8 | 218 28.8 | 39.0 | 68 34.3 | 21.6 | 339 38.7 | 43.4 |
| 03 | 133 49.6 | 178 20.6 | ·· 04.9 | 233 29.3 | ·· 39.1 | 83 37.0 | ·· 21.6 | 354 41.2 | ·· 43.4 |
| 04 | 148 52.1 | 193 20.1 | 04.0 | 248 29.8 | 39.3 | 98 39.7 | 21.5 | 9 43.8 | 43.4 |
| 05 | 163 54.6 | 208 19.6 | 03.1 | 263 30.2 | 39.4 | 113 42.4 | 21.5 | 24 46.4 | 43.5 |
| 06 | 178 57.0 | 223 19.2 | S19 02.3 | 278 30.7 | S23 39.5 | 128 45.1 | N17 21.4 | 39 48.9 | N16 43.5 |
| 07 | 193 59.5 | 238 18.7 | 01.4 | 293 31.1 | 39.7 | 143 47.8 | 21.4 | 54 51.5 | 43.5 |
| 08 | 209 02.0 | 253 18.3 | 19 00.5 | 308 31.6 | 39.8 | 158 50.5 | 21.3 | 69 54.1 | 43.6 |
| M 09 | 224 04.4 | 268 17.8 | 18 59.6 | 323 32.0 | ·· 40.0 | 173 53.1 | ·· 21.3 | 84 56.6 | ·· 43.6 |
| O 10 | 239 06.9 | 283 17.4 | 58.7 | 338 32.5 | 40.1 | 188 55.8 | 21.2 | 99 59.2 | 43.7 |
| N 11 | 254 09.4 | 298 16.9 | 57.8 | 353 32.9 | 40.3 | 203 58.5 | 21.2 | 115 01.7 | 43.7 |
| D 12 | 269 11.8 | 313 16.5 | S18 56.9 | 8 33.4 | S23 40.4 | 219 01.2 | N17 21.1 | 130 04.3 | N16 43.7 |
| A 13 | 284 14.3 | 328 16.0 | 56.0 | 23 33.8 | 40.6 | 234 03.9 | 21.1 | 145 06.9 | 43.8 |
| Y 14 | 299 16.7 | 343 15.6 | 55.1 | 38 34.3 | 40.7 | 249 06.6 | 21.1 | 160 09.4 | 43.8 |
| 15 | 314 19.2 | 358 15.1 | ·· 54.2 | 53 34.7 | ·· 40.8 | 264 09.2 | ·· 21.0 | 175 12.0 | ·· 43.8 |
| 16 | 329 21.7 | 13 14.7 | 53.3 | 68 35.2 | 41.0 | 279 11.9 | 21.0 | 190 14.6 | 43.9 |
| 17 | 344 24.1 | 28 14.2 | 52.4 | 83 35.7 | 41.1 | 294 14.6 | 20.9 | 205 17.1 | 43.9 |
| 18 | 359 26.6 | 43 13.8 | S18 51.5 | 98 36.1 | S23 41.3 | 309 17.3 | N17 20.9 | 220 19.7 | N16 44.0 |
| 19 | 14 29.1 | 58 13.3 | 50.6 | 113 36.6 | 41.4 | 324 20.0 | 20.8 | 235 22.3 | 44.0 |
| 20 | 29 31.5 | 73 12.9 | 49.7 | 128 37.0 | 41.5 | 339 22.6 | 20.8 | 250 24.8 | 44.0 |
| 21 | 44 34.0 | 88 12.4 | ·· 48.8 | 143 37.5 | ·· 41.7 | 354 25.3 | ·· 20.8 | 265 27.4 | ·· 44.1 |
| 22 | 59 36.5 | 103 12.0 | 47.8 | 158 37.9 | 41.8 | 9 28.0 | 20.7 | 280 30.0 | 44.1 |
| 23 | 74 38.9 | 118 11.5 | 46.9 | 173 38.4 | 42.0 | 24 30.7 | 20.7 | 295 32.5 | 44.1 |
| 21 00 | 89 41.4 | 133 11.1 | S18 46.0 | 188 38.8 | S23 42.1 | 39 33.4 | N17 20.6 | 310 35.1 | N16 44.2 |
| 01 | 104 43.9 | 148 10.7 | 45.1 | 203 39.3 | 42.2 | 54 36.0 | 20.6 | 325 37.7 | 44.2 |
| 02 | 119 46.3 | 163 10.2 | 44.2 | 218 39.7 | 42.4 | 69 38.7 | 20.5 | 340 40.2 | 44.3 |
| 03 | 134 48.8 | 178 09.8 | ·· 43.3 | 233 40.2 | ·· 42.5 | 84 41.4 | ·· 20.5 | 355 42.8 | ·· 44.3 |
| 04 | 149 51.2 | 193 09.3 | 42.4 | 248 40.6 | 42.7 | 99 44.1 | 20.5 | 10 45.4 | 44.3 |
| 05 | 164 53.7 | 208 08.9 | 41.5 | 263 41.1 | 42.8 | 114 46.8 | 20.4 | 25 47.9 | 44.4 |
| 06 | 179 56.2 | 223 08.5 | S18 40.6 | 278 41.5 | S23 42.9 | 129 49.4 | N17 20.4 | 40 50.5 | N16 44.4 |
| 07 | 194 58.6 | 238 08.0 | 39.7 | 293 42.0 | 43.1 | 144 52.1 | 20.3 | 55 53.1 | 44.5 |
| T 08 | 210 01.1 | 253 07.6 | 38.7 | 308 42.4 | 43.2 | 159 54.8 | 20.3 | 70 55.6 | 44.5 |
| U 09 | 225 03.6 | 268 07.1 | ·· 37.8 | 323 42.9 | ·· 43.3 | 174 57.5 | ·· 20.2 | 85 58.2 | ·· 44.5 |
| E 10 | 240 06.0 | 283 06.7 | 36.9 | 338 43.3 | 43.5 | 190 00.1 | 20.2 | 101 00.8 | 44.6 |
| S 11 | 255 08.5 | 298 06.3 | 36.0 | 353 43.8 | 43.6 | 205 02.8 | 20.2 | 116 03.3 | 44.6 |
| D 12 | 270 11.0 | 313 05.8 | S18 35.1 | 8 44.2 | S23 43.7 | 220 05.5 | N17 20.1 | 131 05.9 | N16 44.6 |
| A 13 | 285 13.4 | 328 05.4 | 34.2 | 23 44.7 | 43.9 | 235 08.2 | 20.1 | 146 08.5 | 44.7 |
| Y 14 | 300 15.9 | 343 05.0 | 33.2 | 38 45.1 | 44.0 | 250 10.8 | 20.0 | 161 11.0 | 44.7 |
| 15 | 315 18.4 | 358 04.5 | ·· 32.3 | 53 45.6 | ·· 44.1 | 265 13.5 | ·· 20.0 | 176 13.6 | ·· 44.8 |
| 16 | 330 20.8 | 13 04.1 | 31.4 | 68 46.0 | 44.3 | 280 16.2 | 19.9 | 191 16.2 | 44.8 |
| 17 | 345 23.3 | 28 03.7 | 30.5 | 83 46.5 | 44.4 | 295 18.9 | 19.9 | 206 18.7 | 44.8 |
| 18 | 0 25.7 | 43 03.3 | S18 29.5 | 98 46.9 | S23 44.5 | 310 21.5 | N17 19.9 | 221 21.3 | N16 44.9 |
| 19 | 15 28.2 | 58 02.8 | 28.6 | 113 47.4 | 44.7 | 325 24.2 | 19.8 | 236 23.9 | 44.9 |
| 20 | 30 30.7 | 73 02.4 | 27.7 | 128 47.8 | 44.8 | 340 26.9 | 19.8 | 251 26.4 | 45.0 |
| 21 | 45 33.1 | 88 02.0 | ·· 26.8 | 143 48.3 | ·· 44.9 | 355 29.6 | ·· 19.7 | 266 29.0 | ·· 45.0 |
| 22 | 60 35.6 | 103 01.6 | 25.9 | 158 48.7 | 45.0 | 10 32.2 | 19.7 | 281 31.6 | 45.0 |
| 23 | 75 38.1 | 118 01.1 | 24.9 | 173 49.2 | 45.2 | 25 34.9 | 19.6 | 296 34.2 | 45.1 |
| 22 00 | 90 40.5 | 133 00.7 | S18 24.0 | 188 49.6 | S23 45.3 | 40 37.6 | N17 19.6 | 311 36.7 | N16 45.1 |
| 01 | 105 43.0 | 148 00.3 | 23.1 | 203 50.1 | 45.4 | 55 40.2 | 19.6 | 326 39.3 | 45.2 |
| 02 | 120 45.5 | 162 59.9 | 22.1 | 218 50.5 | 45.6 | 70 42.9 | 19.5 | 341 41.9 | 45.2 |
| 03 | 135 47.9 | 177 59.4 | ·· 21.2 | 233 51.0 | ·· 45.7 | 85 45.6 | ·· 19.5 | 356 44.4 | ·· 45.2 |
| 04 | 150 50.4 | 192 59.0 | 20.3 | 248 51.4 | 45.8 | 100 48.3 | 19.4 | 11 47.0 | 45.3 |
| 05 | 165 52.9 | 207 58.6 | 19.4 | 263 51.9 | 45.9 | 115 50.9 | 19.4 | 26 49.6 | 45.3 |
| 06 | 180 55.3 | 222 58.2 | S18 18.4 | 278 52.3 | S23 46.1 | 130 53.6 | N17 19.4 | 41 52.1 | N16 45.4 |
| W 07 | 195 57.8 | 237 57.8 | 17.5 | 293 52.8 | 46.2 | 145 56.3 | 19.3 | 56 54.7 | 45.4 |
| E 08 | 211 00.2 | 252 57.3 | 16.6 | 308 53.2 | 46.3 | 160 58.9 | 19.3 | 71 57.3 | 45.4 |
| D 09 | 226 02.7 | 267 56.9 | ·· 15.6 | 323 53.6 | ·· 46.4 | 176 01.6 | ·· 19.2 | 86 59.9 | ·· 45.5 |
| N 10 | 241 05.2 | 282 56.5 | 14.7 | 338 54.1 | 46.6 | 191 04.3 | 19.2 | 102 02.4 | 45.5 |
| E 11 | 256 07.6 | 297 56.1 | 13.8 | 353 54.5 | 46.7 | 206 06.9 | 19.2 | 117 05.0 | 45.6 |
| S 12 | 271 10.1 | 312 55.7 | S18 12.8 | 8 55.0 | S23 46.8 | 221 09.6 | N17 19.1 | 132 07.6 | N16 45.6 |
| D 13 | 286 12.6 | 327 55.3 | 11.9 | 23 55.4 | 46.9 | 236 12.3 | 19.1 | 147 10.1 | 45.6 |
| A 14 | 301 15.0 | 342 54.9 | 10.9 | 38 55.9 | 47.1 | 251 15.0 | 19.0 | 162 12.7 | 45.7 |
| Y 15 | 316 17.5 | 357 54.4 | ·· 10.0 | 53 56.3 | ·· 47.2 | 266 17.6 | ·· 19.0 | 177 15.3 | ·· 45.7 |
| 16 | 331 20.0 | 12 54.0 | 09.1 | 68 56.8 | 47.3 | 281 20.3 | 19.0 | 192 17.9 | 45.8 |
| 17 | 346 22.4 | 27 53.6 | 08.1 | 83 57.2 | 47.4 | 296 23.0 | 18.9 | 207 20.4 | 45.8 |
| 18 | 1 24.9 | 42 53.2 | S18 07.2 | 98 57.7 | S23 47.5 | 311 25.6 | N17 18.9 | 222 23.0 | N16 45.8 |
| 19 | 16 27.3 | 57 52.8 | 06.2 | 113 58.1 | 47.7 | 326 28.3 | 18.8 | 237 25.6 | 45.9 |
| 20 | 31 29.8 | 72 52.4 | 05.3 | 128 58.5 | 47.8 | 341 31.0 | 18.8 | 252 28.2 | 45.9 |
| 21 | 46 32.3 | 87 52.0 | ·· 04.4 | 143 59.0 | ·· 47.9 | 356 33.6 | ·· 18.8 | 267 30.7 | ·· 46.0 |
| 22 | 61 34.7 | 102 51.6 | 03.4 | 158 59.4 | 48.0 | 11 36.3 | 18.7 | 282 33.3 | 46.0 |
| 23 | 76 37.2 | 117 51.2 | 02.5 | 173 59.9 | 48.1 | 26 38.9 | 18.7 | 297 35.9 | 46.0 |
| Mer. Pass. | 17 58.3 | v −0.4 | d 0.9 | v 0.4 | d 0.1 | v 2.7 | d 0.0 | v 2.6 | d 0.0 |

**STARS**

| Name | S.H.A. | Dec. |
|---|---|---|
| Acamar | 315 38.9 | S40 24.0 |
| Achernar | 335 47.0 | S57 21.5 |
| Acrux | 173 40.0 | S62 58.0 |
| Adhara | 255 33.7 | S28 56.5 |
| Aldebaran | 291 20.5 | N16 27.8 |
| Alioth | 166 44.9 | N56 04.8 |
| Alkaid | 153 20.8 | N49 25.4 |
| Al Na'ir | 28 18.4 | S47 04.5 |
| Alnilam | 276 13.9 | S 1 13.1 |
| Alphard | 218 22.8 | S 8 33.6 |
| Alphecca | 126 34.6 | N26 47.5 |
| Alpheratz | 358 11.9 | N28 58.0 |
| Altair | 62 35.3 | N 8 48.6 |
| Ankaa | 353 42.7 | S42 26.0 |
| Antares | 113 00.3 | S26 22.8 |
| Arcturus | 146 21.0 | N19 18.0 |
| Atria | 108 27.3 | S68 59.0 |
| Avior | 234 28.6 | S59 26.1 |
| Bellatrix | 279 01.1 | N 6 19.7 |
| Betelgeuse | 271 30.7 | N 7 24.1 |
| Canopus | 264 07.7 | S52 41.1 |
| Capella | 281 14.5 | N45 58.5 |
| Deneb | 49 50.5 | N45 12.2 |
| Denebola | 183 01.6 | N14 41.9 |
| Diphda | 349 23.3 | S18 06.8 |
| Dubhe | 194 25.1 | N61 52.1 |
| Elnath | 278 46.9 | N28 35.3 |
| Eltanin | 90 59.5 | N51 29.6 |
| Enif | 34 14.2 | N 9 46.3 |
| Fomalhaut | 15 54.3 | S29 44.7 |
| Gacrux | 172 31.5 | S56 58.8 |
| Gienah | 176 20.6 | S17 24.8 |
| Hadar | 149 27.2 | S60 15.5 |
| Hamal | 328 31.5 | N23 21.3 |
| Kaus Aust. | 84 20.6 | S34 23.7 |
| Kochab | 137 19.9 | N74 14.8 |
| Markab | 14 05.7 | N15 05.0 |
| Menkar | 314 43.5 | N 4 00.0 |
| Menkent | 148 40.2 | S36 15.2 |
| Miaplacidus | 221 44.7 | S69 37.2 |
| Mirfak | 309 19.2 | N49 46.9 |
| Nunki | 76 32.7 | S26 19.5 |
| Peacock | 54 02.9 | S56 48.6 |
| Pollux | 244 00.9 | N28 04.8 |
| Procyon | 245 28.1 | N 5 16.9 |
| Rasalhague | 96 32.3 | N12 34.7 |
| Regulus | 208 12.5 | N12 04.6 |
| Rigel | 281 38.1 | S 8 13.8 |
| Rigil Kent. | 140 29.6 | S60 44.1 |
| Sabik | 102 44.4 | S15 41.7 |
| Schedar | 350 11.7 | N56 25.0 |
| Shaula | 96 59.6 | S37 05.1 |
| Sirius | 258 57.6 | S16 41.2 |
| Spica | 159 00.3 | S11 02.4 |
| Suhail | 223 12.3 | S43 20.3 |
| Vega | 80 58.0 | N38 45.9 |
| Zuben'ubi | 137 36.1 | S15 56.7 |

| | S.H.A. | Mer. Pass. h m |
|---|---|---|
| Venus | 43 29.7 | 15 08 |
| Mars | 98 57.4 | 11 25 |
| Jupiter | 309 52.0 | 21 18 |
| Saturn | 220 53.7 | 3 17 |

1976 DECEMBER 20, 21, 22 (MON., TUES., WED.)

| G.M.T. d h | SUN G.H.A. | SUN Dec. | MOON G.H.A. | v | Dec. | d | H.P. |
|---|---|---|---|---|---|---|---|
| 20 00 | 180 37.6 | S23 25.7 | 196 33.1 | 4.0 | S19 02.9 | 2.0 | 60.7 |
| 01 | 195 37.2 | 25.7 | 210 56.1 | 4.0 | 19 04.9 | 1.9 | 60.7 |
| 02 | 210 36.9 | 25.7 | 225 19.1 | 4.0 | 19 06.8 | 1.7 | 60.7 |
| 03 | 225 36.6 | ·· 25.8 | 239 42.1 | 4.0 | 19 08.5 | 1.5 | 60.7 |
| 04 | 240 36.3 | 25.8 | 254 05.1 | 3.9 | 19 10.0 | 1.5 | 60.7 |
| 05 | 255 36.0 | 25.8 | 268 28.0 | 4.0 | 19 11.5 | 1.3 | 60.7 |
| 06 | 270 35.7 | S23 25.9 | 282 51.0 | 4.0 | S19 12.8 | 1.1 | 60.7 |
| 07 | 285 35.4 | 25.9 | 297 14.0 | 3.9 | 19 13.9 | 1.0 | 60.7 |
| 08 | 300 35.1 | 25.9 | 311 36.9 | 4.0 | 19 14.9 | 0.9 | 60.6 |
| M 09 | 315 34.7 | ·· 25.9 | 325 59.9 | 4.0 | 19 15.8 | 0.7 | 60.6 |
| O 10 | 330 34.4 | 26.0 | 340 22.9 | 4.0 | 19 16.5 | 0.6 | 60.6 |
| N 11 | 345 34.1 | 26.0 | 354 45.9 | 4.0 | 19 17.1 | 0.5 | 60.6 |
| D 12 | 0 33.8 | S23 26.0 | 9 08.9 | 4.0 | S19 17.6 | 0.3 | 60.6 |
| A 13 | 15 33.5 | 26.0 | 23 31.9 | 4.0 | 19 17.9 | 0.2 | 60.6 |
| Y 14 | 30 33.2 | 26.1 | 37 54.9 | 4.1 | 19 18.1 | 0.0 | 60.6 |
| 15 | 45 32.9 | ·· 26.1 | 52 18.0 | 4.0 | 19 18.1 | 0.1 | 60.6 |
| 16 | 60 32.6 | 26.1 | 66 41.0 | 4.1 | 19 18.0 | 0.3 | 60.6 |
| 17 | 75 32.3 | 26.1 | 81 04.1 | 4.1 | 19 17.7 | 0.4 | 60.5 |
| 18 | 90 31.9 | S23 26.2 | 95 27.2 | 4.1 | S19 17.3 | 0.5 | 60.5 |
| 19 | 105 31.6 | 26.2 | 109 50.3 | 4.2 | 19 16.8 | 0.7 | 60.5 |
| 20 | 120 31.3 | 26.2 | 124 13.5 | 4.1 | 19 16.1 | 0.8 | 60.5 |
| 21 | 135 31.0 | ·· 26.2 | 138 36.6 | 4.2 | 19 15.3 | 1.0 | 60.5 |
| 22 | 150 30.7 | 26.2 | 152 59.8 | 4.3 | 19 14.3 | 1.1 | 60.5 |
| 23 | 165 30.4 | 26.2 | 167 23.1 | 4.2 | 19 13.2 | 1.2 | 60.4 |
| 21 00 | 180 30.1 | S23 26.3 | 181 46.3 | 4.3 | S19 12.0 | 1.4 | 60.4 |
| 01 | 195 29.8 | 26.3 | 196 09.6 | 4.3 | 19 10.6 | 1.5 | 60.4 |
| 02 | 210 29.4 | 26.3 | 210 32.9 | 4.4 | 19 09.1 | 1.6 | 60.4 |
| 03 | 225 29.1 | ·· 26.3 | 224 56.3 | 4.4 | 19 07.5 | 1.8 | 60.4 |
| 04 | 240 28.8 | 26.3 | 239 19.7 | 4.5 | 19 05.7 | 1.9 | 60.4 |
| 05 | 255 28.5 | 26.3 | 253 43.2 | 4.4 | 19 03.8 | 2.0 | 60.3 |
| 06 | 270 28.2 | S23 26.3 | 268 06.6 | 4.6 | S19 01.8 | 2.2 | 60.3 |
| 07 | 285 27.9 | 26.3 | 282 30.2 | 4.5 | 18 59.6 | 2.3 | 60.3 |
| T 08 | 300 27.6 | 26.3 | 296 53.7 | 4.6 | 18 57.3 | 2.5 | 60.3 |
| U 09 | 315 27.3 | ·· 26.4 | 311 17.3 | 4.7 | 18 54.8 | 2.6 | 60.2 |
| E 10 | 330 27.0 | 26.4 | 325 41.0 | 4.7 | 18 52.2 | 2.7 | 60.2 |
| S 11 | 345 26.6 | 26.4 | 340 04.7 | 4.8 | 18 49.5 | 2.8 | 60.2 |
| D 12 | 0 26.3 | S23 26.4 | 354 28.5 | 4.8 | S18 46.7 | 3.0 | 60.2 |
| A 13 | 15 26.0 | 26.4 | 8 52.3 | 4.9 | 18 43.7 | 3.1 | 60.2 |
| Y 14 | 30 25.7 | 26.4 | 23 16.2 | 4.9 | 18 40.6 | 3.2 | 60.1 |
| 15 | 45 25.4 | ·· 26.4 | 37 40.1 | 5.0 | 18 37.4 | 3.4 | 60.1 |
| 16 | 60 25.1 | 26.4 | 52 04.1 | 5.0 | 18 34.0 | 3.5 | 60.1 |
| 17 | 75 24.8 | 26.4 | 66 28.1 | 5.1 | 18 30.5 | 3.6 | 60.1 |
| 18 | 90 24.5 | S23 26.4 | 80 52.2 | 5.2 | S18 26.9 | 3.7 | 60.0 |
| 19 | 105 24.1 | 26.4 | 95 16.4 | 5.2 | 18 23.2 | 3.9 | 60.0 |
| 20 | 120 23.8 | 26.4 | 109 40.6 | 5.3 | 18 19.3 | 3.9 | 60.0 |
| 21 | 135 23.5 | ·· 26.4 | 124 04.9 | 5.3 | 18 15.4 | 4.2 | 60.0 |
| 22 | 150 23.2 | 26.4 | 138 29.2 | 5.4 | 18 11.2 | 4.2 | 59.9 |
| 23 | 165 22.9 | 26.4 | 152 53.6 | 5.5 | 18 07.0 | 4.3 | 59.9 |
| 22 00 | 180 22.6 | S23 26.4 | 167 18.1 | 5.5 | S18 02.7 | 4.5 | 59.9 |
| 01 | 195 22.3 | 26.4 | 181 42.6 | 5.6 | 17 58.2 | 4.6 | 59.9 |
| 02 | 210 22.0 | 26.4 | 196 07.2 | 5.7 | 17 53.6 | 4.7 | 59.8 |
| 03 | 225 21.6 | ·· 26.3 | 210 31.9 | 5.8 | 17 48.9 | 4.8 | 59.8 |
| 04 | 240 21.3 | 26.3 | 224 56.7 | 5.8 | 17 44.1 | 4.9 | 59.8 |
| 05 | 255 21.0 | 26.3 | 239 21.5 | 5.9 | 17 39.2 | 5.0 | 59.7 |
| 06 | 270 20.7 | S23 26.3 | 253 46.4 | 6.0 | S17 34.2 | 5.2 | 59.7 |
| W 07 | 285 20.4 | 26.3 | 268 11.4 | 6.0 | 17 29.0 | 5.3 | 59.7 |
| E 08 | 300 20.1 | 26.3 | 282 36.4 | 6.1 | 17 23.7 | 5.3 | 59.7 |
| D 09 | 315 19.8 | ·· 26.3 | 297 01.5 | 6.2 | 17 18.4 | 5.5 | 59.6 |
| N 10 | 330 19.5 | 26.3 | 311 26.7 | 6.3 | 17 12.9 | 5.6 | 59.6 |
| E 11 | 345 19.1 | 26.3 | 325 52.0 | 6.4 | 17 07.3 | 5.7 | 59.6 |
| S 12 | 0 18.8 | S23 26.2 | 340 17.4 | 6.4 | S17 01.6 | 5.8 | 59.5 |
| D 13 | 15 18.5 | 26.2 | 354 42.8 | 6.5 | 16 55.8 | 5.9 | 59.5 |
| A 14 | 30 18.2 | 26.2 | 9 08.3 | 6.6 | 16 49.9 | 6.0 | 59.5 |
| Y 15 | 45 17.9 | ·· 26.2 | 23 33.9 | 6.7 | 16 43.9 | 6.1 | 59.4 |
| 16 | 60 17.6 | 26.2 | 37 59.6 | 6.7 | 16 37.8 | 6.2 | 59.4 |
| 17 | 75 17.3 | 26.2 | 52 25.3 | 6.9 | 16 31.6 | 6.3 | 59.4 |
| 18 | 90 17.0 | S23 26.1 | 66 51.2 | 6.9 | S16 25.3 | 6.5 | 59.3 |
| 19 | 105 16.6 | 26.1 | 81 17.1 | 7.0 | 16 18.8 | 6.5 | 59.3 |
| 20 | 120 16.3 | 26.1 | 95 43.1 | 7.1 | 16 12.3 | 6.6 | 59.3 |
| 21 | 135 16.0 | ·· 26.1 | 110 09.2 | 7.1 | 16 05.7 | 6.7 | 59.2 |
| 22 | 150 15.7 | 26.1 | 124 35.3 | 7.3 | 15 59.0 | 6.7 | 59.2 |
| 23 | 165 15.4 | 26.0 | 139 01.6 | 7.3 | 15 52.3 | 6.9 | 59.2 |
| | S.D. 16.3 | d 0.0 | S.D. 16.5 | | 16.4 | | 16.2 |

| Lat. | Twilight Naut. | Twilight Civil | Sunrise | Moonrise 20 | Moonrise 21 | Moonrise 22 | Moonrise 23 |
|---|---|---|---|---|---|---|---|
| N 72 | 08 26 | 10 57 | ■ | ■ | ■ | 12 07 | 11 42 |
| N 70 | 08 06 | 09 54 | ■ | 10 23 | 11 04 | 11 11 | 11 12 |
| 68 | 07 50 | 09 19 | ■ | 09 20 | 10 12 | 10 38 | 10 50 |
| 66 | 07 36 | 08 54 | 10 35 | 08 45 | 09 40 | 10 13 | 10 33 |
| 64 | 07 25 | 08 34 | 09 52 | 08 20 | 09 16 | 09 54 | 10 19 |
| 62 | 07 16 | 08 18 | 09 24 | 08 00 | 08 57 | 09 38 | 10 07 |
| 60 | 07 07 | 08 04 | 09 02 | 07 43 | 08 42 | 09 25 | 09 56 |
| N 58 | 07 00 | 07 52 | 08 44 | 07 30 | 08 28 | 09 13 | 09 47 |
| 56 | 06 53 | 07 42 | 08 30 | 07 18 | 08 17 | 09 03 | 09 39 |
| 54 | 06 47 | 07 33 | 08 17 | 07 08 | 08 07 | 08 55 | 09 32 |
| 52 | 06 41 | 07 25 | 08 06 | 06 58 | 07 58 | 08 47 | 09 26 |
| 50 | 06 36 | 07 17 | 07 56 | 06 50 | 07 50 | 08 40 | 09 20 |
| 45 | 06 24 | 07 01 | 07 35 | 06 33 | 07 33 | 08 24 | 09 08 |
| N 40 | 06 14 | 06 48 | 07 18 | 06 18 | 07 19 | 08 12 | 08 58 |
| 35 | 06 04 | 06 36 | 07 04 | 06 06 | 07 07 | 08 01 | 08 49 |
| 30 | 05 55 | 06 25 | 06 52 | 05 56 | 06 56 | 07 52 | 08 41 |
| 20 | 05 39 | 06 06 | 06 31 | 05 38 | 06 39 | 07 36 | 08 27 |
| N 10 | 05 23 | 05 49 | 06 12 | 05 22 | 06 23 | 07 21 | 08 16 |
| 0 | 05 06 | 05 32 | 05 55 | 05 07 | 06 09 | 07 08 | 08 05 |
| S 10 | 04 47 | 05 14 | 05 37 | 04 52 | 05 54 | 06 55 | 07 54 |
| 20 | 04 24 | 04 53 | 05 18 | 04 37 | 05 39 | 06 41 | 07 42 |
| 30 | 03 55 | 04 28 | 04 56 | 04 19 | 05 21 | 06 25 | 07 28 |
| 35 | 03 36 | 04 13 | 04 43 | 04 09 | 05 10 | 06 15 | 07 20 |
| 40 | 03 13 | 03 55 | 04 28 | 03 57 | 04 59 | 06 04 | 07 11 |
| 45 | 02 42 | 03 32 | 04 10 | 03 43 | 04 45 | 05 52 | 07 01 |
| S 50 | 01 57 | 03 02 | 03 47 | 03 26 | 04 28 | 05 36 | 06 48 |
| 52 | 01 29 | 02 47 | 03 36 | 03 18 | 04 20 | 05 29 | 06 42 |
| 54 | 00 41 | 02 29 | 03 24 | 03 09 | 04 11 | 05 21 | 06 36 |
| 56 | //// | 02 07 | 03 10 | 02 59 | 04 01 | 05 12 | 06 28 |
| 58 | //// | 01 37 | 02 53 | 02 47 | 03 49 | 05 02 | 06 20 |
| S 60 | //// | 00 47 | 02 32 | 02 34 | 03 36 | 04 50 | 06 10 |

| Lat. | Sunset | Twilight Civil | Twilight Naut. | Moonset 20 | Moonset 21 | Moonset 22 | Moonset 23 |
|---|---|---|---|---|---|---|---|
| N 72 | ■ | 12 59 | 15 30 | ■ | ■ | 14 48 | 17 09 |
| N 70 | ■ | 14 02 | 15 51 | 12 20 | 13 47 | 15 43 | 17 37 |
| 68 | ■ | 14 37 | 16 07 | 13 23 | 14 39 | 16 16 | 17 58 |
| 66 | 13 21 | 15 03 | 16 20 | 13 58 | 15 10 | 16 40 | 18 15 |
| 64 | 14 04 | 15 22 | 16 31 | 14 23 | 15 34 | 16 58 | 18 28 |
| 62 | 14 33 | 15 39 | 16 41 | 14 43 | 15 53 | 17 14 | 18 39 |
| 60 | 14 54 | 15 52 | 16 49 | 15 00 | 16 08 | 17 26 | 18 49 |
| N 58 | 15 12 | 16 04 | 16 56 | 15 13 | 16 21 | 17 37 | 18 57 |
| 56 | 15 27 | 16 14 | 17 03 | 15 25 | 16 32 | 17 47 | 19 05 |
| 54 | 15 40 | 16 23 | 17 09 | 15 36 | 16 42 | 17 55 | 19 11 |
| 52 | 15 50 | 16 32 | 17 15 | 15 45 | 16 51 | 18 03 | 19 17 |
| 50 | 16 00 | 16 39 | 17 21 | 15 53 | 16 59 | 18 10 | 19 22 |
| 45 | 16 21 | 16 55 | 17 32 | 16 11 | 17 16 | 18 24 | 19 34 |
| N 40 | 16 38 | 17 09 | 17 43 | 16 25 | 17 29 | 18 36 | 19 43 |
| 35 | 16 52 | 17 20 | 17 52 | 16 37 | 17 41 | 18 46 | 19 51 |
| 30 | 17 05 | 17 31 | 18 01 | 16 48 | 17 51 | 18 55 | 19 58 |
| 20 | 17 26 | 17 50 | 18 17 | 17 06 | 18 08 | 19 10 | 20 10 |
| N 10 | 17 45 | 18 07 | 18 34 | 17 22 | 18 23 | 19 23 | 20 21 |
| 0 | 18 02 | 18 25 | 18 51 | 17 37 | 18 37 | 19 36 | 20 30 |
| S 10 | 18 20 | 18 43 | 19 10 | 17 51 | 18 51 | 19 48 | 20 40 |
| 20 | 18 39 | 19 03 | 19 32 | 18 07 | 19 06 | 20 01 | 20 50 |
| 30 | 19 01 | 19 28 | 20 02 | 18 25 | 19 23 | 20 16 | 21 02 |
| 35 | 19 14 | 19 43 | 20 20 | 18 35 | 19 33 | 20 24 | 21 09 |
| 40 | 19 29 | 20 02 | 20 43 | 18 47 | 19 44 | 20 34 | 21 16 |
| 45 | 19 47 | 20 24 | 21 14 | 19 02 | 19 58 | 20 45 | 21 25 |
| S 50 | 20 09 | 20 54 | 22 00 | 19 19 | 20 14 | 20 59 | 21 36 |
| 52 | 20 20 | 21 09 | 22 28 | 19 27 | 20 21 | 21 05 | 21 41 |
| 54 | 20 33 | 21 27 | 23 15 | 19 36 | 20 29 | 21 12 | 21 46 |
| 56 | 20 47 | 21 50 | //// | 19 46 | 20 39 | 21 20 | 21 52 |
| 58 | 21 04 | 22 19 | //// | 19 57 | 20 49 | 21 29 | 21 59 |
| S 60 | 21 24 | 23 09 | //// | 20 11 | 21 01 | 21 39 | 22 06 |

| Day | SUN Eqn. of Time 00h (m s) | SUN Eqn. of Time 12h (m s) | SUN Mer. Pass. (h m) | MOON Mer. Pass. Upper (h m) | MOON Mer. Pass. Lower (h m) | Age (d) | Phase |
|---|---|---|---|---|---|---|---|
| 20 | 02 31 | 02 16 | 11 58 | 11 22 | 23 53 | 29 | ● |
| 21 | 02 01 | 01 46 | 11 58 | 12 23 | 24 53 | 00 | |
| 22 | 01 31 | 01 16 | 11 59 | 13 22 | 00 53 | 01 | |

| G.M.T. | ARIES G.H.A. | VENUS −3.8 G.H.A. | VENUS Dec. | MARS +1.6 G.H.A. | MARS Dec. | JUPITER −2.3 G.H.A. | JUPITER Dec. | SATURN +0.3 G.H.A. | SATURN Dec. | STARS Name | S.H.A. | Dec. |
|---|---|---|---|---|---|---|---|---|---|---|---|---|
| d h | ° ′ | ° ′ | ° ′ | ° ′ | ° ′ | ° ′ | ° ′ | ° ′ | ° ′ | | ° ′ | ° ′ |
| 23 00 | 91 39.7 | 132 50.8 | S18 01.5 | 189 00.3 | S23 48.3 | 41 41.6 | N17 18.6 | 312 38.5 | N16 46.1 | Acamar | 315 38.9 | S40 24.0 |
| 01 | 106 42.1 | 147 50.4 | 18 00.6 | 204 00.8 | 48.4 | 56 44.3 | 18.6 | 327 41.0 | 46.1 | Achernar | 335 47.0 | S57 21.5 |
| 02 | 121 44.6 | 162 50.0 | 17 59.6 | 219 01.2 | 48.5 | 71 46.9 | 18.6 | 342 43.6 | 46.2 | Acrux | 173 40.0 | S62 58.0 |
| 03 | 136 47.1 | 177 49.6 | ·· 58.7 | 234 01.7 | ·· 48.6 | 86 49.6 | ·· 18.5 | 357 46.2 | ·· 46.2 | Adhara | 255 33.7 | S28 56.5 |
| 04 | 151 49.5 | 192 49.2 | 57.7 | 249 02.1 | 48.7 | 101 52.3 | 18.5 | 12 48.7 | 46.2 | Aldebaran | 291 20.5 | N16 27.8 |
| 05 | 166 52.0 | 207 48.8 | 56.8 | 264 02.5 | 48.8 | 116 54.9 | 18.4 | 27 51.3 | 46.3 | | | |
| 06 | 181 54.5 | 222 48.4 | S17 55.8 | 279 03.0 | S23 49.0 | 131 57.6 | N17 18.4 | 42 53.9 | N16 46.3 | Alioth | 166 44.9 | N56 04.8 |
| 07 | 196 56.9 | 237 48.0 | 54.9 | 294 03.4 | 49.1 | 147 00.3 | 18.4 | 57 56.5 | 46.4 | Alkaid | 153 20.7 | N49 25.4 |
| T 08 | 211 59.4 | 252 47.6 | 53.9 | 309 03.9 | 49.2 | 162 02.9 | 18.3 | 72 59.1 | 46.4 | Al Na'ir | 28 18.4 | S47 04.5 |
| H 09 | 227 01.8 | 267 47.2 | ·· 53.0 | 324 04.3 | ·· 49.3 | 177 05.6 | ·· 18.3 | 88 01.6 | ·· 46.4 | Alnilam | 276 13.9 | S 1 13.1 |
| U 10 | 242 04.3 | 282 46.8 | 52.0 | 339 04.8 | 49.4 | 192 08.2 | 18.2 | 103 04.2 | 46.5 | Alphard | 218 22.8 | S 8 33.6 |
| R 11 | 257 06.8 | 297 46.4 | 51.1 | 354 05.2 | 49.5 | 207 10.9 | 18.2 | 118 06.8 | 46.5 | | | |
| S 12 | 272 09.2 | 312 46.0 | S17 50.1 | 9 05.7 | S23 49.6 | 222 13.6 | N17 18.2 | 133 09.4 | N16 46.6 | Alphecca | 126 34.5 | N26 47.5 |
| D 13 | 287 11.7 | 327 45.6 | 49.2 | 24 06.1 | 49.8 | 237 16.2 | 18.1 | 148 11.9 | 46.6 | Alpheratz | 358 11.9 | N28 58.0 |
| A 14 | 302 14.2 | 342 45.2 | 48.2 | 39 06.5 | 49.9 | 252 18.9 | 18.1 | 163 14.5 | 46.7 | Altair | 62 35.3 | N 8 48.6 |
| Y 15 | 317 16.6 | 357 44.8 | ·· 47.3 | 54 07.0 | ·· 50.0 | 267 21.5 | ·· 18.1 | 178 17.1 | ·· 46.7 | Ankaa | 353 42.7 | S42 26.0 |
| 16 | 332 19.1 | 12 44.4 | 46.3 | 69 07.4 | 50.1 | 282 24.2 | 18.0 | 193 19.7 | 46.7 | Antares | 113 00.3 | S26 22.8 |
| 17 | 347 21.6 | 27 44.0 | 45.3 | 84 07.9 | 50.2 | 297 26.9 | 18.0 | 208 22.2 | 46.8 | | | |
| 18 | 2 24.0 | 42 43.6 | S17 44.4 | 99 08.3 | S23 50.3 | 312 29.5 | N17 17.9 | 223 24.8 | N16 46.8 | Arcturus | 146 21.0 | N19 18.0 |
| 19 | 17 26.5 | 57 43.2 | 43.4 | 114 08.7 | 50.4 | 327 32.2 | 17.9 | 238 27.4 | 46.9 | Atria | 108 27.3 | S68 59.0 |
| 20 | 32 29.0 | 72 42.8 | 42.5 | 129 09.2 | 50.5 | 342 34.8 | 17.9 | 253 30.0 | 46.9 | Avior | 234 28.6 | S59 26.1 |
| 21 | 47 31.4 | 87 42.5 | ·· 41.5 | 144 09.6 | ·· 50.6 | 357 37.5 | ·· 17.8 | 268 32.5 | ·· 46.9 | Bellatrix | 279 01.1 | N 6 19.7 |
| 22 | 62 33.9 | 102 42.1 | 40.5 | 159 10.1 | 50.8 | 12 40.2 | 17.8 | 283 35.1 | 47.0 | Betelgeuse | 271 30.6 | N 7 24.1 |
| 23 | 77 36.3 | 117 41.7 | 39.6 | 174 10.5 | 50.9 | 27 42.8 | 17.7 | 298 37.7 | 47.0 | | | |
| 24 00 | 92 38.8 | 132 41.3 | S17 38.6 | 189 11.0 | S23 51.0 | 42 45.5 | N17 17.7 | 313 40.3 | N16 47.1 | Canopus | 264 07.7 | S52 41.1 |
| 01 | 107 41.3 | 147 40.9 | 37.6 | 204 11.4 | 51.1 | 57 48.1 | 17.7 | 328 42.9 | 47.1 | Capella | 281 14.5 | N45 58.5 |
| 02 | 122 43.7 | 162 40.5 | 36.7 | 219 11.8 | 51.2 | 72 50.8 | 17.6 | 343 45.4 | 47.2 | Deneb | 49 50.5 | N45 12.1 |
| 03 | 137 46.2 | 177 40.1 | ·· 35.7 | 234 12.3 | ·· 51.3 | 87 53.4 | ·· 17.6 | 358 48.0 | ·· 47.2 | Denebola | 183 01.6 | N14 41.9 |
| 04 | 152 48.7 | 192 39.8 | 34.8 | 249 12.7 | 51.4 | 102 56.1 | 17.6 | 13 50.6 | 47.2 | Diphda | 349 23.4 | S18 06.8 |
| 05 | 167 51.1 | 207 39.4 | 33.8 | 264 13.2 | 51.5 | 117 58.7 | 17.5 | 28 53.2 | 47.3 | | | |
| 06 | 182 53.6 | 222 39.0 | S17 32.8 | 279 13.6 | S23 51.6 | 133 01.4 | N17 17.5 | 43 55.8 | N16 47.3 | Dubhe | 194 25.1 | N61 52.1 |
| 07 | 197 56.1 | 237 38.6 | 31.8 | 294 14.0 | 51.7 | 148 04.1 | 17.5 | 58 58.3 | 47.4 | Elnath | 278 46.9 | N28 35.3 |
| 08 | 212 58.5 | 252 38.2 | 30.9 | 309 14.5 | 51.8 | 163 06.7 | 17.4 | 74 00.9 | 47.4 | Eltanin | 90 59.4 | N51 29.6 |
| F 09 | 228 01.0 | 267 37.9 | ·· 29.9 | 324 14.9 | ·· 51.9 | 178 09.4 | ·· 17.4 | 89 03.5 | ·· 47.4 | Enif | 34 14.2 | N 9 46.3 |
| R 10 | 243 03.5 | 282 37.5 | 28.9 | 339 15.4 | 52.0 | 193 12.0 | 17.3 | 104 06.1 | 47.5 | Fomalhaut | 15 54.3 | S29 44.7 |
| I 11 | 258 05.9 | 297 37.1 | 28.0 | 354 15.8 | 52.1 | 208 14.7 | 17.3 | 119 08.6 | 47.5 | | | |
| D 12 | 273 08.4 | 312 36.7 | S17 27.0 | 9 16.2 | S23 52.2 | 223 17.3 | N17 17.3 | 134 11.2 | N16 47.6 | Gacrux | 172 31.5 | S56 58.8 |
| A 13 | 288 10.8 | 327 36.4 | 26.0 | 24 16.7 | 52.3 | 238 20.0 | 17.2 | 149 13.8 | 47.6 | Gienah | 176 20.5 | S17 24.8 |
| Y 14 | 303 13.3 | 342 36.0 | 25.1 | 39 17.1 | 52.4 | 253 22.6 | 17.2 | 164 16.4 | 47.7 | Hadar | 149 27.1 | S60 15.5 |
| 15 | 318 15.8 | 357 35.6 | ·· 24.1 | 54 17.6 | ·· 52.5 | 268 25.3 | ·· 17.2 | 179 19.0 | ·· 47.7 | Hamal | 328 31.5 | N23 21.3 |
| 16 | 333 18.2 | 12 35.2 | 23.1 | 69 18.0 | 52.6 | 283 27.9 | 17.1 | 194 21.5 | 47.7 | Kaus Aust. | 84 20.6 | S34 23.7 |
| 17 | 348 20.7 | 27 34.9 | 22.1 | 84 18.4 | 52.7 | 298 30.6 | 17.1 | 209 24.1 | 47.8 | | | |
| 18 | 3 23.2 | 42 34.5 | S17 21.2 | 99 18.9 | S23 52.8 | 313 33.2 | N17 17.0 | 224 26.7 | N16 47.8 | Kochab | 137 19.9 | N74 14.8 |
| 19 | 18 25.6 | 57 34.1 | 20.2 | 114 19.3 | 52.9 | 328 35.9 | 17.0 | 239 29.3 | 47.9 | Markab | 14 05.7 | N15 05.0 |
| 20 | 33 28.1 | 72 33.8 | 19.2 | 129 19.7 | 53.0 | 343 38.5 | 17.0 | 254 31.9 | 47.9 | Menkar | 314 43.5 | N 4 00.0 |
| 21 | 48 30.6 | 87 33.4 | ·· 18.2 | 144 20.2 | ·· 53.1 | 358 41.2 | ·· 16.9 | 269 34.5 | ·· 48.0 | Menkent | 148 40.1 | S36 15.3 |
| 22 | 63 33.0 | 102 33.0 | 17.2 | 159 20.6 | 53.2 | 13 43.8 | 16.9 | 284 37.0 | 48.0 | Miaplacidus | 221 44.7 | S69 37.2 |
| 23 | 78 35.5 | 117 32.6 | 16.3 | 174 21.1 | 53.3 | 28 46.5 | 16.9 | 299 39.6 | 48.0 | | | |
| 25 00 | 93 38.0 | 132 32.3 | S17 15.3 | 189 21.5 | S23 53.4 | 43 49.1 | N17 16.8 | 314 42.2 | N16 48.1 | Mirfak | 309 19.2 | N49 46.9 |
| 01 | 108 40.4 | 147 31.9 | 14.3 | 204 21.9 | 53.5 | 58 51.8 | 16.8 | 329 44.8 | 48.1 | Nunki | 76 32.7 | S26 19.5 |
| 02 | 123 42.9 | 162 31.6 | 13.3 | 219 22.4 | 53.6 | 73 54.4 | 16.8 | 344 47.4 | 48.2 | Peacock | 54 02.9 | S56 48.6 |
| 03 | 138 45.3 | 177 31.2 | ·· 12.3 | 234 22.8 | ·· 53.7 | 88 57.1 | ·· 16.7 | 359 49.9 | ·· 48.2 | Pollux | 244 00.9 | N28 04.8 |
| 04 | 153 47.8 | 192 30.8 | 11.4 | 249 23.3 | 53.8 | 103 59.7 | 16.7 | 14 52.5 | 48.3 | Procyon | 245 28.1 | N 5 16.9 |
| 05 | 168 50.3 | 207 30.5 | 10.4 | 264 23.7 | 53.9 | 119 02.4 | 16.7 | 29 55.1 | 48.3 | | | |
| 06 | 183 52.7 | 222 30.1 | S17 09.4 | 279 24.1 | S23 54.0 | 134 05.0 | N17 16.6 | 44 57.7 | N16 48.3 | Rasalhague | 96 32.3 | N12 34.7 |
| 07 | 198 55.2 | 237 29.7 | 08.4 | 294 24.6 | 54.1 | 149 07.7 | 16.6 | 60 00.3 | 48.4 | Regulus | 208 12.5 | N12 04.6 |
| S 08 | 213 57.7 | 252 29.4 | 07.4 | 309 25.0 | 54.2 | 164 10.3 | 16.6 | 75 02.9 | 48.4 | Rigel | 281 38.1 | S 8 13.8 |
| A 09 | 229 00.1 | 267 29.0 | ·· 06.4 | 324 25.4 | ·· 54.3 | 179 13.0 | ·· 16.5 | 90 05.4 | ·· 48.5 | Rigil Kent. | 140 29.5 | S60 44.1 |
| T 10 | 244 02.6 | 282 28.7 | 05.4 | 339 25.9 | 54.4 | 194 15.6 | 16.5 | 105 08.0 | 48.5 | Sabik | 102 44.3 | S15 41.7 |
| U 11 | 259 05.1 | 297 28.3 | 04.4 | 354 26.3 | 54.5 | 209 18.3 | 16.4 | 120 10.6 | 48.6 | | | |
| R 12 | 274 07.5 | 312 27.9 | S17 03.5 | 9 26.7 | S23 54.6 | 224 20.9 | N17 16.4 | 135 13.2 | N16 48.6 | Schedar | 350 11.7 | N56 25.0 |
| D 13 | 289 10.0 | 327 27.6 | 02.5 | 24 27.2 | 54.7 | 239 23.5 | 16.4 | 150 15.8 | 48.6 | Shaula | 96 59.6 | S37 05.1 |
| A 14 | 304 12.4 | 342 27.2 | 01.5 | 39 27.6 | 54.7 | 254 26.2 | 16.3 | 165 18.4 | 48.7 | Sirius | 258 57.6 | S16 41.2 |
| Y 15 | 319 14.9 | 357 26.9 | 17 00.5 | 54 28.1 | ·· 54.8 | 269 28.8 | ·· 16.3 | 180 20.9 | ·· 48.7 | Spica | 159 00.3 | S11 02.4 |
| 16 | 334 17.4 | 12 26.5 | 16 59.5 | 69 28.5 | 54.9 | 284 31.5 | 16.3 | 195 23.5 | 48.8 | Suhail | 223 12.2 | S43 20.3 |
| 17 | 349 19.8 | 27 26.2 | 58.5 | 84 28.9 | 55.0 | 299 34.1 | 16.2 | 210 26.1 | 48.8 | | | |
| 18 | 4 22.3 | 42 25.8 | S16 57.5 | 99 29.4 | S23 55.1 | 314 36.8 | N17 16.2 | 225 28.7 | N16 48.9 | Vega | 80 58.0 | N38 45.9 |
| 19 | 19 24.8 | 57 25.5 | 56.5 | 114 29.8 | 55.2 | 329 39.4 | 16.2 | 240 31.3 | 48.9 | Zuben'ubi | 137 36.0 | S15 56.7 |
| 20 | 34 27.2 | 72 25.1 | 55.5 | 129 30.2 | 55.3 | 344 42.0 | 16.1 | 255 33.9 | 48.9 | | S.H.A. ° ′ | Mer. Pass. h m |
| 21 | 49 29.7 | 87 24.8 | ·· 54.5 | 144 30.7 | ·· 55.4 | 359 44.7 | ·· 16.1 | 270 36.5 | ·· 49.0 | | | |
| 22 | 64 32.2 | 102 24.4 | 53.5 | 159 31.1 | 55.5 | 14 47.3 | 16.1 | 285 39.0 | 49.0 | Venus | 40 02.5 | 15 10 |
| 23 | 79 34.6 | 117 24.1 | 52.5 | 174 31.5 | 55.6 | 29 50.0 | 16.0 | 300 41.6 | 49.1 | Mars | 96 32.1 | 11 23 |
| | | | | | | | | | | Jupiter | 310 06.7 | 21 05 |
| Mer. Pass. | h m 17 46.5 | v −0.4 | d 1.0 | v 0.4 | d 0.1 | v 2.7 | d 0.0 | v 2.6 | d 0.0 | Saturn | 221 01.5 | 3 05 |

1976 DECEMBER 23, 24, 25 (THURS., FRI., SAT.)

| G.M.T. | SUN G.H.A. | SUN Dec. | MOON G.H.A. | v | Dec. | d | H.P. |
|---|---|---|---|---|---|---|---|
| d h | ° ′ | ° ′ | ° ′ | ′ | ° ′ | ′ | ′ |
| 23 00 | 180 15.1 | S23 26.0 | 153 27.9 | 7.4 | S15 45.4 | 7.0 | 59.1 |
| 01 | 195 14.8 | 26.0 | 167 54.3 | 7.5 | 15 38.4 | 7.0 | 59.1 |
| 02 | 210 14.5 | 26.0 | 182 20.8 | 7.6 | 15 31.4 | 7.2 | 59.1 |
| 03 | 225 14.1 | ·· 25.9 | 196 47.4 | 7.7 | 15 24.2 | 7.2 | 59.0 |
| 04 | 240 13.8 | 25.9 | 211 14.1 | 7.8 | 15 17.0 | 7.3 | 59.0 |
| 05 | 255 13.5 | 25.9 | 225 40.9 | 7.8 | 15 09.7 | 7.4 | 59.0 |
| 06 | 270 13.2 | S23 25.8 | 240 07.7 | 8.0 | S15 02.3 | 7.5 | 58.9 |
| 07 | 285 12.9 | 25.8 | 254 34.7 | 8.0 | 14 54.8 | 7.6 | 58.9 |
| T 08 | 300 12.6 | 25.8 | 269 01.7 | 8.1 | 14 47.2 | 7.6 | 58.9 |
| H 09 | 315 12.3 | ·· 25.7 | 283 28.8 | 8.2 | 14 39.6 | 7.7 | 58.8 |
| U 10 | 330 12.0 | 25.7 | 297 56.0 | 8.3 | 14 31.9 | 7.8 | 58.8 |
| R 11 | 345 11.6 | 25.7 | 312 23.3 | 8.3 | 14 24.1 | 7.9 | 58.7 |
| S 12 | 0 11.3 | S23 25.6 | 326 50.6 | 8.5 | S14 16.2 | 8.0 | 58.7 |
| D 13 | 15 11.0 | 25.6 | 341 18.1 | 8.5 | 14 08.2 | 8.0 | 58.7 |
| A 14 | 30 10.7 | 25.6 | 355 45.6 | 8.7 | 14 00.2 | 8.1 | 58.6 |
| Y 15 | 45 10.4 | ·· 25.5 | 10 13.3 | 8.7 | 13 52.1 | 8.1 | 58.6 |
| 16 | 60 10.1 | 25.5 | 24 41.0 | 8.8 | 13 44.0 | 8.3 | 58.6 |
| 17 | 75 09.8 | 25.5 | 39 08.8 | 8.9 | 13 35.7 | 8.3 | 58.5 |
| 18 | 90 09.5 | S23 25.4 | 53 36.7 | 8.9 | S13 27.4 | 8.4 | 58.5 |
| 19 | 105 09.2 | 25.4 | 68 04.6 | 9.1 | 13 19.0 | 8.4 | 58.5 |
| 20 | 120 08.8 | 25.3 | 82 32.7 | 9.2 | 13 10.6 | 8.5 | 58.4 |
| 21 | 135 08.5 | ·· 25.3 | 97 00.9 | 9.2 | 13 02.1 | 8.6 | 58.4 |
| 22 | 150 08.2 | 25.3 | 111 29.1 | 9.3 | 12 53.5 | 8.6 | 58.3 |
| 23 | 165 07.9 | 25.2 | 125 57.4 | 9.4 | 12 44.9 | 8.7 | 58.3 |
| 24 00 | 180 07.6 | S23 25.2 | 140 25.8 | 9.5 | S12 36.2 | 8.7 | 58.3 |
| 01 | 195 07.3 | 25.1 | 154 54.3 | 9.6 | 12 27.5 | 8.8 | 58.2 |
| 02 | 210 07.0 | 25.1 | 169 22.9 | 9.6 | 12 18.7 | 8.9 | 58.2 |
| 03 | 225 06.7 | ·· 25.0 | 183 51.5 | 9.8 | 12 09.8 | 8.9 | 58.2 |
| 04 | 240 06.3 | 25.0 | 198 20.3 | 9.8 | 12 00.9 | 9.0 | 58.1 |
| 05 | 255 06.0 | 24.9 | 212 49.1 | 9.9 | 11 51.9 | 9.0 | 58.1 |
| 06 | 270 05.7 | S23 24.9 | 227 18.0 | 10.0 | S11 42.9 | 9.1 | 58.0 |
| 07 | 285 05.4 | 24.8 | 241 47.0 | 10.1 | 11 33.8 | 9.1 | 58.0 |
| 08 | 300 05.1 | 24.8 | 256 16.1 | 10.2 | 11 24.7 | 9.2 | 58.0 |
| F 09 | 315 04.8 | ·· 24.7 | 270 45.3 | 10.2 | 11 15.5 | 9.2 | 57.9 |
| R 10 | 330 04.5 | 24.7 | 285 14.5 | 10.3 | 11 06.3 | 9.3 | 57.9 |
| I 11 | 345 04.2 | 24.6 | 299 43.8 | 10.4 | 10 57.0 | 9.3 | 57.8 |
| D 12 | 0 03.9 | S23 24.6 | 314 13.2 | 10.5 | S10 47.7 | 9.3 | 57.8 |
| A 13 | 15 03.5 | 24.5 | 328 42.7 | 10.6 | 10 38.4 | 9.5 | 57.8 |
| Y 14 | 30 03.2 | 24.5 | 343 12.3 | 10.6 | 10 28.9 | 9.4 | 57.7 |
| 15 | 45 02.9 | ·· 24.4 | 357 41.9 | 10.7 | 10 19.5 | 9.5 | 57.7 |
| 16 | 60 02.6 | 24.4 | 12 11.6 | 10.8 | 10 10.0 | 9.5 | 57.7 |
| 17 | 75 02.3 | 24.3 | 26 41.4 | 10.9 | 10 00.5 | 9.6 | 57.6 |
| 18 | 90 02.0 | S23 24.2 | 41 11.3 | 11.0 | S 9 50.9 | 9.6 | 57.6 |
| 19 | 105 01.7 | 24.2 | 55 41.3 | 11.0 | 9 41.3 | 9.7 | 57.5 |
| 20 | 120 01.4 | 24.1 | 70 11.3 | 11.1 | 9 31.6 | 9.6 | 57.5 |
| 21 | 135 01.0 | ·· 24.1 | 84 41.4 | 11.2 | 9 22.0 | 9.8 | 57.5 |
| 22 | 150 00.7 | 24.0 | 99 11.6 | 11.2 | 9 12.2 | 9.7 | 57.4 |
| 23 | 165 00.4 | 23.9 | 113 41.8 | 11.4 | 9 02.5 | 9.8 | 57.4 |
| 25 00 | 180 00.1 | S23 23.9 | 128 12.2 | 11.4 | S 8 52.7 | 9.8 | 57.4 |
| 01 | 194 59.8 | 23.8 | 142 42.6 | 11.5 | 8 42.9 | 9.9 | 57.3 |
| 02 | 209 59.5 | 23.7 | 157 13.1 | 11.5 | 8 33.0 | 9.8 | 57.3 |
| 03 | 224 59.2 | ·· 23.7 | 171 43.6 | 11.6 | 8 23.2 | 9.9 | 57.2 |
| 04 | 239 58.9 | 23.6 | 186 14.2 | 11.7 | 8 13.3 | 10.0 | 57.2 |
| 05 | 254 58.6 | 23.5 | 200 44.9 | 11.8 | 8 03.3 | 9.9 | 57.2 |
| 06 | 269 58.2 | S23 23.5 | 215 15.7 | 11.8 | S 7 53.4 | 10.0 | 57.1 |
| 07 | 284 57.9 | 23.4 | 229 46.5 | 11.9 | 7 43.4 | 10.0 | 57.1 |
| S 08 | 299 57.6 | 23.3 | 244 17.4 | 12.0 | 7 33.4 | 10.1 | 57.1 |
| A 09 | 314 57.3 | ·· 23.3 | 258 48.4 | 12.0 | 7 23.3 | 10.0 | 57.0 |
| T 10 | 329 57.0 | 23.2 | 273 19.4 | 12.1 | 7 13.3 | 10.1 | 57.0 |
| U 11 | 344 56.7 | 23.1 | 287 50.5 | 12.1 | 7 03.2 | 10.1 | 56.9 |
| R 12 | 359 56.4 | S23 23.0 | 302 21.6 | 12.3 | S 6 53.1 | 10.1 | 56.9 |
| D 13 | 14 56.1 | 23.0 | 316 52.9 | 12.3 | 6 43.0 | 10.2 | 56.9 |
| A 14 | 29 55.8 | 22.9 | 331 24.2 | 12.3 | 6 32.8 | 10.1 | 56.8 |
| Y 15 | 44 55.5 | ·· 22.8 | 345 55.5 | 12.4 | 6 22.7 | 10.2 | 56.8 |
| 16 | 59 55.1 | 22.7 | 0 26.9 | 12.5 | 6 12.5 | 10.2 | 56.8 |
| 17 | 74 54.8 | 22.7 | 14 58.4 | 12.5 | 6 02.3 | 10.2 | 56.7 |
| 18 | 89 54.5 | S23 22.6 | 29 29.9 | 12.6 | S 5 52.1 | 10.2 | 56.7 |
| 19 | 104 54.2 | 22.5 | 44 01.5 | 12.7 | 5 41.9 | 10.2 | 56.7 |
| 20 | 119 53.9 | 22.4 | 58 33.2 | 12.7 | 5 31.7 | 10.3 | 56.6 |
| 21 | 134 53.6 | ·· 22.3 | 73 04.9 | 12.8 | 5 21.4 | 10.2 | 56.6 |
| 22 | 149 53.3 | 22.3 | 87 36.7 | 12.8 | 5 11.2 | 10.3 | 56.6 |
| 23 | 164 53.0 | 22.2 | 102 08.5 | 12.9 | 5 00.9 | 10.3 | 56.5 |
| | S.D. 16.3 | d 0.1 | S.D. 16.0 | | 15.8 | | 15.5 |

| Lat. | Twilight Naut. | Twilight Civil | Sunrise | Moonrise 23 | Moonrise 24 | Moonrise 25 | Moonrise 26 |
|---|---|---|---|---|---|---|---|
| ° | h m | h m | h m | h m | h m | h m | h m |
| N 72 | 08 27 | 10 58 | ▬ | 11 42 | 11 29 | 11 20 | 11 12 |
| N 70 | 08 07 | 09 55 | ▬ | 11 12 | 11 11 | 11 10 | 11 08 |
| 68 | 07 51 | 09 20 | ▬ | 10 50 | 10 57 | 11 01 | 11 04 |
| 66 | 07 38 | 08 55 | 10 35 | 10 33 | 10 46 | 10 54 | 11 01 |
| 64 | 07 27 | 08 35 | 09 53 | 10 19 | 10 36 | 10 49 | 10 59 |
| 62 | 07 17 | 08 19 | 09 25 | 10 07 | 10 27 | 10 43 | 10 57 |
| 60 | 07 09 | 08 05 | 09 03 | 09 56 | 10 20 | 10 39 | 10 55 |
| N 58 | 07 01 | 07 54 | 08 46 | 09 47 | 10 14 | 10 35 | 10 53 |
| 56 | 06 54 | 07 43 | 08 31 | 09 39 | 10 08 | 10 31 | 10 52 |
| 54 | 06 48 | 07 34 | 08 18 | 09 32 | 10 03 | 10 28 | 10 51 |
| 52 | 06 43 | 07 26 | 08 07 | 09 26 | 09 58 | 10 25 | 10 49 |
| 50 | 06 37 | 07 19 | 07 57 | 09 20 | 09 54 | 10 23 | 10 48 |
| 45 | 06 25 | 07 03 | 07 36 | 09 08 | 09 45 | 10 17 | 10 46 |
| N 40 | 06 15 | 06 49 | 07 20 | 08 58 | 09 37 | 10 12 | 10 44 |
| 35 | 06 06 | 06 37 | 07 06 | 08 49 | 09 31 | 10 08 | 10 42 |
| 30 | 05 57 | 06 27 | 06 53 | 08 41 | 09 25 | 10 04 | 10 41 |
| 20 | 05 40 | 06 08 | 06 32 | 08 27 | 09 15 | 09 58 | 10 38 |
| N 10 | 05 24 | 05 50 | 06 13 | 08 16 | 09 06 | 09 52 | 10 36 |
| 0 | 05 07 | 05 33 | 05 56 | 08 05 | 08 57 | 09 47 | 10 33 |
| S 10 | 04 48 | 05 15 | 05 38 | 07 54 | 08 49 | 09 41 | 10 31 |
| 20 | 04 26 | 04 55 | 05 19 | 07 42 | 08 40 | 09 36 | 10 29 |
| 30 | 03 56 | 04 30 | 04 57 | 07 28 | 08 30 | 09 29 | 10 26 |
| 35 | 03 38 | 04 15 | 04 44 | 07 20 | 08 24 | 09 26 | 10 25 |
| 40 | 03 15 | 03 56 | 04 29 | 07 11 | 08 17 | 09 21 | 10 23 |
| 45 | 02 44 | 03 34 | 04 11 | 07 01 | 08 10 | 09 16 | 10 21 |
| S 50 | 01 58 | 03 04 | 03 49 | 06 48 | 08 00 | 09 10 | 10 18 |
| 52 | 01 31 | 02 49 | 03 38 | 06 42 | 07 56 | 09 08 | 10 17 |
| 54 | 00 44 | 02 31 | 03 25 | 06 36 | 07 51 | 09 05 | 10 16 |
| 56 | //// | 02 09 | 03 11 | 06 28 | 07 46 | 09 01 | 10 15 |
| 58 | //// | 01 39 | 02 54 | 06 20 | 07 40 | 08 58 | 10 13 |
| S 60 | //// | 00 49 | 02 34 | 06 10 | 07 33 | 08 54 | 10 12 |

| Lat. | Sunset | Twilight Civil | Twilight Naut. | Moonset 23 | Moonset 24 | Moonset 25 | Moonset 26 |
|---|---|---|---|---|---|---|---|
| ° | h m | h m | h m | h m | h m | h m | h m |
| N 72 | ▬ | 13 02 | 15 33 | 17 09 | 19 09 | 20 59 | 22 42 |
| N 70 | ▬ | 14 04 | 15 53 | 17 37 | 19 25 | 21 07 | 22 43 |
| 68 | ▬ | 14 39 | 16 08 | 17 58 | 19 38 | 21 13 | 22 45 |
| 66 | 13 24 | 15 05 | 16 22 | 18 15 | 19 49 | 21 19 | 22 46 |
| 64 | 14 06 | 15 24 | 16 33 | 18 28 | 19 57 | 21 24 | 22 46 |
| 62 | 14 35 | 15 40 | 16 42 | 18 39 | 20 05 | 21 27 | 22 47 |
| 60 | 14 56 | 15 54 | 16 51 | 18 49 | 20 11 | 21 31 | 22 48 |
| N 58 | 15 14 | 16 06 | 16 58 | 18 57 | 20 17 | 21 34 | 22 48 |
| 56 | 15 29 | 16 16 | 17 05 | 19 05 | 20 22 | 21 37 | 22 49 |
| 54 | 15 41 | 16 25 | 17 11 | 19 11 | 20 26 | 21 39 | 22 49 |
| 52 | 15 52 | 16 33 | 17 17 | 19 17 | 20 30 | 21 41 | 22 50 |
| 50 | 16 02 | 16 41 | 17 22 | 19 22 | 20 34 | 21 43 | 22 50 |
| 45 | 16 23 | 16 57 | 17 34 | 19 34 | 20 42 | 21 47 | 22 51 |
| N 40 | 16 40 | 17 10 | 17 44 | 19 43 | 20 48 | 21 51 | 22 52 |
| 35 | 16 54 | 17 22 | 17 54 | 19 51 | 20 54 | 21 54 | 22 52 |
| 30 | 17 06 | 17 33 | 18 03 | 19 58 | 20 59 | 21 57 | 22 53 |
| 20 | 17 27 | 17 52 | 18 19 | 20 10 | 21 07 | 22 02 | 22 54 |
| N 10 | 17 46 | 18 09 | 18 35 | 20 21 | 21 15 | 22 06 | 22 54 |
| 0 | 18 03 | 18 26 | 18 52 | 20 30 | 21 21 | 22 09 | 22 55 |
| S 10 | 18 21 | 18 44 | 19 11 | 20 40 | 21 28 | 22 13 | 22 56 |
| 20 | 18 40 | 19 05 | 19 34 | 20 50 | 21 35 | 22 17 | 22 56 |
| 30 | 19 02 | 19 30 | 20 03 | 21 02 | 21 44 | 22 22 | 22 57 |
| 35 | 19 15 | 19 45 | 20 22 | 21 09 | 21 48 | 22 24 | 22 57 |
| 40 | 19 30 | 20 03 | 20 45 | 21 16 | 21 54 | 22 27 | 22 58 |
| 45 | 19 48 | 20 26 | 21 15 | 21 25 | 22 00 | 22 30 | 22 58 |
| S 50 | 20 11 | 20 55 | 22 01 | 21 36 | 22 07 | 22 34 | 22 59 |
| 52 | 20 22 | 21 10 | 22 28 | 21 41 | 22 10 | 22 36 | 22 59 |
| 54 | 20 34 | 21 28 | 23 15 | 21 46 | 22 14 | 22 38 | 23 00 |
| 56 | 20 48 | 21 50 | //// | 21 52 | 22 18 | 22 40 | 23 00 |
| 58 | 21 05 | 22 20 | //// | 21 59 | 22 23 | 22 43 | 23 00 |
| S 60 | 21 25 | 23 10 | //// | 22 06 | 22 28 | 22 45 | 23 01 |

| Day | SUN Eqn. of Time 00ʰ | SUN Eqn. of Time 12ʰ | SUN Mer. Pass. | MOON Mer. Pass. Upper | MOON Mer. Pass. Lower | Age | Phase |
|---|---|---|---|---|---|---|---|
| | m s | m s | h m | h m | h m | d | |
| 23 | 01 01 | 00 46 | 11 59 | 14 18 | 01 50 | 02 | |
| 24 | 00 31 | 00 16 | 12 00 | 15 10 | 02 44 | 03 | |
| 25 | 00 01 | 00 14 | 12 00 | 15 58 | 03 34 | 04 | |

# STAR CHARTS

## NORTHERN STARS

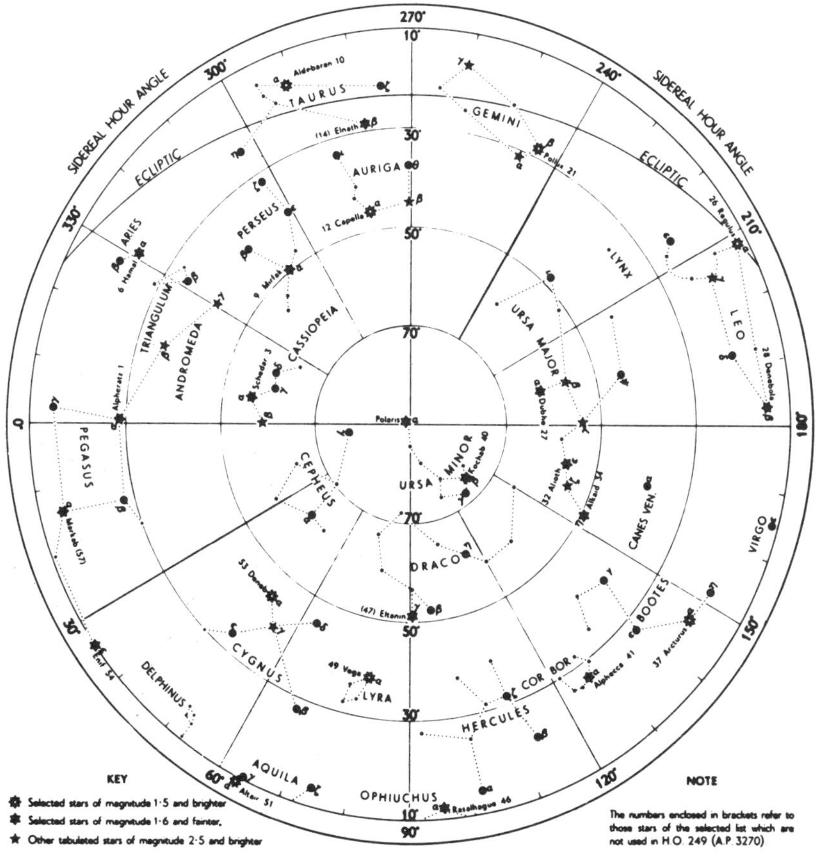


**KEY**

- Selected stars of magnitude 1·5 and brighter
- Selected stars of magnitude 1·6 and fainter.
- Other tabulated stars of magnitude 2·5 and brighter
- Other tabulated stars of magnitude 2·6 and fainter
- Untabulated stars

**NOTE**

The numbers enclosed in brackets refer to those stars of the selected list which are not used in H.O. 249 (A.P. 3270)

### EQUATORIAL STARS (S.H.A. 0° to 180°)

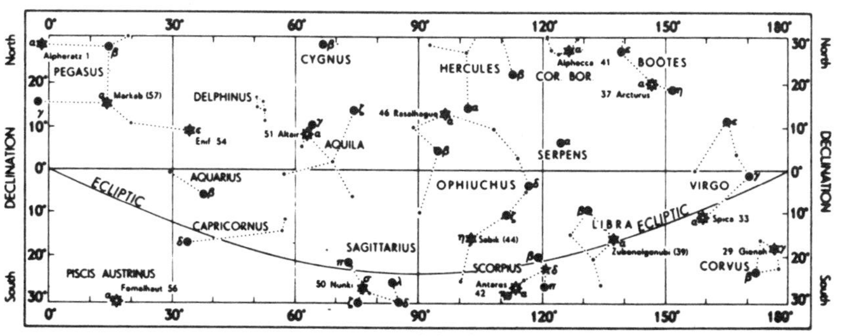


# STAR CHARTS

## SOUTHERN STARS

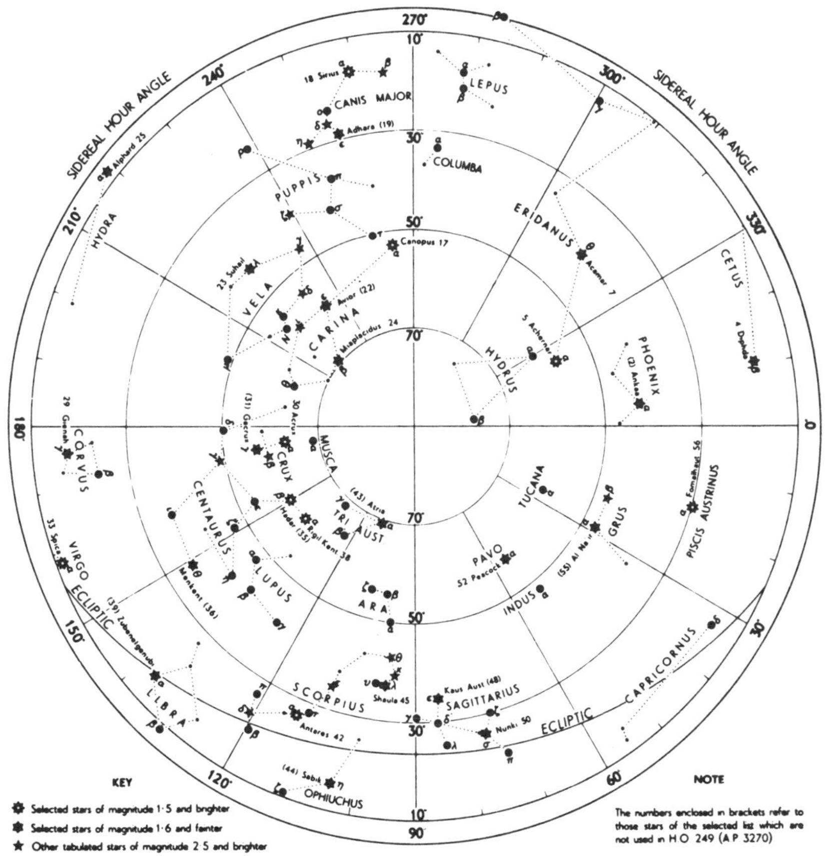


**KEY**

- Selected stars of magnitude 1·5 and brighter
- Selected stars of magnitude 1·6 and fainter
- Other tabulated stars of magnitude 2·5 and brighter
- Other tabulated stars of magnitude 2·6 and fainter
- Untabulated stars

**NOTE**

The numbers enclosed in brackets refer to those stars of the selected list which are not used in H.O. 249 (A.P. 3270)

### EQUATORIAL STARS (S.H.A. 180° to 360°)

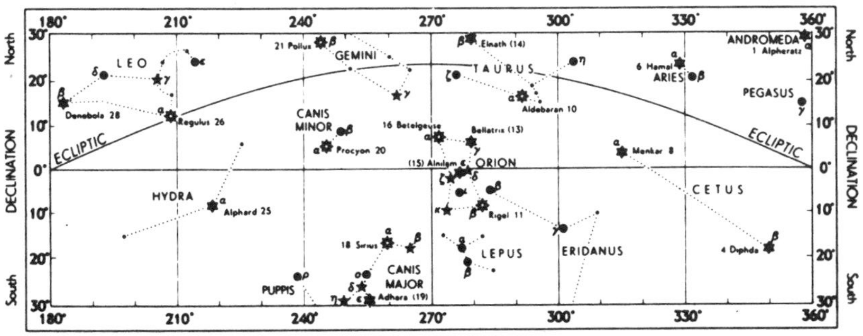

# STARS, 1976 JANUARY—JUNE

| Mag. | Name and Number | | S.H.A. | JAN. | FEB. | MAR. | APR. | MAY | JUNE | Dec. | JAN. | FEB. | MAR. | APR. | MAY | JUNE |
|---|---|---|---|---|---|---|---|---|---|---|---|---|---|---|---|---|
| | | | ° | ′ | ′ | ′ | ′ | ′ | ′ | ° | ′ | ′ | ′ | ′ | ′ | ′ |
| 1·6 | α Geminorum | | **246** | 43·3 | 43·3 | 43·4 | 43·5 | 43·6 | 43·7 | **N. 31** | 56·3 | 56·4 | 56·4 | 56·4 | 56·4 | 56·4 |
| 3·3 | σ Puppis | | **247** | 52·3 | 52·4 | 52·5 | 52·7 | 52·9 | 53·0 | **S. 43** | 15·3 | 15·5 | 15·6 | 15·6 | 15·6 | 15·5 |
| 3·1 | β Canis Minoris | | **248** | 31·7 | 31·7 | 31·8 | 31·9 | 32·0 | 32·0 | **N. 8** | 20·1 | 20·1 | 20·1 | 20·1 | 20·1 | 20·1 |
| 2·4 | η Canis Majoris | | **249** | 12·2 | 12·3 | 12·4 | 12·5 | 12·7 | 12·8 | **S. 29** | 15·5 | 15·7 | 15·7 | 15·7 | 15·7 | 15·6 |
| 2·7 | π Puppis | | **250** | 55·0 | 55·0 | 55·2 | 55·3 | 55·5 | 55·6 | **S. 37** | 03·4 | 03·6 | 03·6 | 03·7 | 03·6 | 03·5 |
| 2·0 | δ Canis Majoris | | **253** | 08·2 | 08·2 | 08·4 | 08·5 | 08·6 | 08·7 | **S. 26** | 21·5 | 21·6 | 21·6 | 21·7 | 21·6 | 21·5 |
| 3·1 | ο Canis Majoris | | **254** | 29·1 | 29·1 | 29·3 | 29·4 | 29·5 | 29·6 | **S. 23** | 48·0 | 48·2 | 48·2 | 48·2 | 48·2 | 48·1 |
| 1·6 | ε Canis Majoris | 19 | **255** | 34·2 | 34·2 | 34·4 | 34·5 | 34·7 | 34·7 | **S. 28** | 56·5 | 56·6 | 56·7 | 56·7 | 56·7 | 56·6 |
| 2·8 | τ Puppis | | **257** | 39·2 | 39·3 | 39·5 | 39·8 | 40·0 | 40·1 | **S. 50** | 35·3 | 35·5 | 35·6 | 35·6 | 35·5 | 35·4 |
| −1·6 | α Canis Majoris | 18 | **258** | 58·1 | 58·2 | 58·3 | 58·4 | 58·5 | 58·6 | **S. 16** | 41·2 | 41·3 | 41·3 | 41·3 | 41·3 | 41·2 |
| 1·9 | γ Geminorum | | **260** | 54·5 | 54·5 | 54·6 | 54·8 | 54·9 | 54·9 | **N. 16** | 25·1 | 25·1 | 25·1 | 25·1 | 25·1 | 25·1 |
| −0·9 | α Carinæ | 17 | **264** | 08·1 | 08·2 | 08·4 | 08·7 | 08·9 | 09·0 | **S. 52** | 41·2 | 41·3 | 41·4 | 41·4 | 41·3 | 41·1 |
| 2·0 | β Canis Majoris | | **264** | 34·8 | 34·9 | 35·0 | 35·2 | 35·3 | 35·3 | **S. 17** | 56·8 | 56·9 | 56·9 | 56·9 | 56·9 | 56·8 |
| 2·7 | θ Aurigæ | | **270** | 28·0 | 28·1 | 28·2 | 28·4 | 28·5 | 28·5 | **N. 37** | 12·7 | 12·7 | 12·7 | 12·7 | 12·7 | 12·6 |
| 2·1 | β Aurigæ | | **270** | 32·7 | 32·8 | 32·9 | 33·1 | 33·2 | 33·2 | **N. 44** | 56·7 | 56·8 | 56·8 | 56·8 | 56·8 | 56·7 |
| Var.‡ | α Orionis | 16 | **271** | 31·4 | 31·4 | 31·5 | 31·7 | 31·7 | 31·7 | **N. 7** | 24·1 | 24·1 | 24·0 | 24·0 | 24·1 | 24·1 |
| 2·2 | κ Orionis | | **273** | 20·2 | 20·3 | 20·4 | 20·6 | 20·6 | 20·6 | **S. 9** | 40·8 | 40·9 | 40·9 | 40·9 | 40·8 | 40·8 |
| 1·9 | ζ Orionis | | **275** | 06·3 | 06·3 | 06·5 | 06·6 | 06·7 | 06·6 | **S. 1** | 57·4 | 57·5 | 57·5 | 57·5 | 57·4 | 57·4 |
| 2·8 | α Columbæ | | **275** | 17·8 | 17·9 | 18·1 | 18·3 | 18·4 | 18·4 | **S. 34** | 05·4 | 05·5 | 05·5 | 05·5 | 05·4 | 05·3 |
| 3·0 | ζ Tauri | | **275** | 56·3 | 56·3 | 56·5 | 56·6 | 56·7 | 56·6 | **N. 21** | 07·7 | 07·7 | 07·7 | 07·6 | 07·6 | 07·6 |
| 1·8 | ε Orionis | 15 | **276** | 14·6 | 14·6 | 14·7 | 14·9 | 14·9 | 14·9 | **S. 1** | 13·1 | 13·2 | 13·2 | 13·2 | 13·1 | 13·1 |
| 2·9 | ι Orionis | | **276** | 25·6 | 25·7 | 25·8 | 25·9 | 26·0 | 26·0 | **S. 5** | 55·6 | 55·7 | 55·7 | 55·7 | 55·7 | 55·6 |
| 2·7 | α Leporis | | **277** | 04·4 | 04·5 | 04·7 | 04·8 | 04·9 | 04·9 | **S. 17** | 50·5 | 50·6 | 50·6 | 50·6 | 50·5 | 50·4 |
| 2·5 | δ Orionis | | **277** | 17·8 | 17·8 | 18·0 | 18·1 | 18·2 | 18·1 | **S. 0** | 19·1 | 19·1 | 19·2 | 19·2 | 19·1 | 19·1 |
| 3·0 | β Leporis | | **278** | 11·3 | 11·3 | 11·5 | 11·6 | 11·7 | 11·7 | **S. 20** | 46·9 | 46·9 | 47·0 | 46·9 | 46·9 | 46·8 |
| 1·8 | β Tauri | 14 | **278** | 47·8 | 47·8 | 48·0 | 48·1 | 48·2 | 48·1 | **N. 28** | 35·3 | 35·3 | 35·3 | 35·3 | 35·2 | 35·2 |
| 1·7 | γ Orionis | 13 | **279** | 01·8 | 01·9 | 02·0 | 02·1 | 02·2 | 02·2 | **N. 6** | 19·6 | 19·6 | 19·6 | 19·6 | 19·6 | 19·6 |
| 0·2 | α Aurigæ | 12 | **281** | 15·5 | 15·6 | 15·8 | 16·0 | 16·1 | 16·0 | **N. 45** | 58·5 | 58·6 | 58·6 | 58·5 | 58·5 | 58·4 |
| 0·3 | β Orionis | 11 | **281** | 38·7 | 38·8 | 39·0 | 39·1 | 39·2 | 39·1 | **S. 8** | 13·9 | 13·9 | 13·9 | 13·9 | 13·9 | 13·8 |
| 2·9 | β Eridani | | **283** | 19·5 | 19·6 | 19·7 | 19·8 | 19·9 | 19·8 | **S. 5** | 07·1 | 07·2 | 07·2 | 07·2 | 07·1 | 07·1 |
| 2·9 | ι Arigæ † | | **286** | 07·9 | 08·0 | 08·2 | 08·3 | 08·4 | 08·3 | **N. 33** | 07·8 | 07·8 | 07·8 | 07·7 | 07·7 | 07·7 |
| 1·1 | α Tauri | 10 | **291** | 21·3 | 21·4 | 21·6 | 21·7 | 21·7 | 21·6 | **N. 16** | 27·7 | 27·7 | 27·7 | 27·6 | 27·6 | 27·7 |
| 3·2 | γ Eridani | | **300** | 46·0 | 46·1 | 46·2 | 46·3 | 46·3 | 46·2 | **S. 13** | 34·7 | 34·8 | 34·8 | 34·7 | 34·6 | 34·5 |
| 3·0 | ε Persei | | **300** | 55·8 | 55·9 | 56·1 | 56·2 | 56·2 | 56·1 | **N. 39** | 56·6 | 56·6 | 56·6 | 56·5 | 56·5 | 56·4 |
| 2·9 | ζ Persei | | **301** | 50·2 | 50·3 | 50·4 | 50·5 | 50·5 | 50·4 | **N. 31** | 48·9 | 48·9 | 48·8 | 48·8 | 48·8 | 48·7 |
| 3·0 | η Tauri | | **303** | 28·7 | 28·8 | 28·9 | 29·0 | 29·0 | 28·9 | **N. 24** | 02·0 | 01·9 | 01·9 | 01·9 | 01·9 | 01·9 |
| 1·9 | α Persei | 9 | **309** | 20·3 | 20·5 | 20·7 | 20·8 | 20·8 | 20·6 | **N. 49** | 46·8 | 46·8 | 46·8 | 46·7 | 46·6 | 46·5 |
| Var.§ | β Persei † | | **313** | 20·4 | 20·6 | 20·7 | 20·8 | 20·8 | 20·6 | **N. 40** | 52·0 | 52·0 | 52·0 | 51·9 | 51·8 | 51·8 |
| 2·8 | α Ceti | 8 | **314** | 44·3 | 44·4 | 44·5 | 44·6 | 44·5 | 44·4 | **N. 3** | 59·7 | 59·7 | 59·7 | 59·7 | 59·8 | 59·8 |
| 3·1 | θ Eridani | 7 | **315** | 39·5 | 39·6 | 39·8 | 39·9 | 39·9 | 39·8 | **S. 40** | 24·3 | 24·3 | 24·2 | 24·1 | 24·0 | 23·8 |
| 2·1 | α Ursæ Minoris † | | **327** | 42·0 | 52·3 | 60·5 | 64·2 | 60·9 | 53·1 | **N. 89** | 09·6 | 09·6 | 09·5 | 09·4 | 09·2 | 09·1 |
| 3·1 | β Trianguli | | **327** | 57·9 | 58·1 | 58·2 | 58·2 | 58·1 | 57·9 | **N. 34** | 52·6 | 52·6 | 52·5 | 52·5 | 52·4 | 52·4 |
| 2·2 | α Arietis | 6 | **328** | 32·4 | 32·5 | 32·6 | 32·6 | 32·6 | 32·4 | **N. 23** | 21·1 | 21·1 | 21·0 | 21·0 | 21·0 | 21·0 |
| 2·2 | γ Andromedæ | | **329** | 23·3 | 23·4 | 23·6 | 23·6 | 23·5 | 23·3 | **N. 42** | 13·1 | 13·1 | 13·0 | 12·9 | 12·9 | 12·9 |
| 3·0 | α Hydri | | **330** | 29·7 | 30·0 | 30·3 | 30·4 | 30·3 | 30·1 | **S. 61** | 41·5 | 41·4 | 41·3 | 41·2 | 41·0 | 40·8 |
| 2·7 | β Arietis | | **331** | 40·0 | 40·1 | 40·2 | 40·2 | 40·1 | 39·9 | **N. 20** | 41·6 | 41·5 | 41·5 | 41·5 | 41·5 | 41·5 |
| 0·6 | α Eridani | 5 | **335** | 47·6 | 47·9 | 48·0 | 48·1 | 48·0 | 47·8 | **S. 57** | 21·8 | 21·7 | 21·6 | 21·4 | 21·3 | 21·1 |
| 2·8 | δ Cassiopeiæ | | **338** | 56·1 | 56·3 | 56·5 | 56·5 | 56·3 | 56·0 | **N. 60** | 07·0 | 06·9 | 06·8 | 06·7 | 06·6 | 06·6 |
| 2·4 | β Andromedæ | | **342** | 54·0 | 54·1 | 54·2 | 54·2 | 54·0 | 53·8 | **N. 35** | 29·8 | 29·8 | 29·7 | 29·6 | 29·6 | 29·6 |
| Var.‖ | γ Cassiopeiæ | | **346** | 10·9 | 11·2 | 11·3 | 11·3 | 11·1 | 10·7 | **N. 60** | 35·6 | 35·5 | 35·4 | 35·2 | 35·2 | 35·1 |
| 2·2 | β Ceti | 4 | **349** | 24·1 | 24·2 | 24·2 | 24·2 | 24·1 | 23·9 | **S. 18** | 07·2 | 07·2 | 07·1 | 07·0 | 06·9 | 06·8 |
| 2·5 | α Cassiopeiæ | 3 | **350** | 12·7 | 12·9 | 13·0 | 12·9 | 12·7 | 12·4 | **N. 56** | 24·7 | 24·6 | 24·5 | 24·4 | 24·3 | 24·3 |
| 2·4 | α Phœnicis | 2 | **353** | 43·5 | 43·6 | 43·7 | 43·6 | 43·5 | 43·2 | **S. 42** | 26·3 | 26·3 | 26·2 | 26·0 | 25·9 | 25·8 |
| 2·9 | β Hydri † | | **353** | 53·0 | 53·5 | 53·8 | 53·7 | 53·4 | 52·7 | **S. 77** | 23·6 | 23·5 | 23·3 | 23·1 | 22·9 | 22·8 |
| 2·9 | γ Pegasi | | **356** | 59·9 | 60·0 | 60·0 | 59·9 | 59·8 | 59·5 | **N. 15** | 03·1 | 03·1 | 03·0 | 03·0 | 03·1 | 03·1 |
| 2·4 | β Cassiopeiæ | | **358** | 01·5 | 01·7 | 01·8 | 01·7 | 01·4 | 01·0 | **N. 59** | 01·4 | 01·3 | 01·2 | 01·0 | 01·0 | 01·0 |
| 2·2 | α Andromedæ | 1 | **358** | 12·7 | 12·8 | 12·8 | 12·7 | 12·6 | 12·3 | **N. 28** | 57·7 | 57·6 | 57·5 | 57·5 | 57·5 | 57·5 |

‡ 0·1—1·2 §2·3—3·5 ‖ Irregular variable; 1973 mag. 2·5 † Not suitable for use with H.O. 214 (H.D. 486)

# STARS, 1976 JULY—DECEMBER

| Mag. | Name and Number | | S.H.A. | JULY | AUG. | SEPT. | OCT. | NOV. | DEC. | Dec. | JULY | AUG. | SEPT. | OCT. | NOV. | DEC. |
|---|---|---|---|---|---|---|---|---|---|---|---|---|---|---|---|---|
| | | | ° | ′ | ′ | ′ | ′ | ′ | ′ | ° | ′ | ′ | ′ | ′ | ′ | ′ |
| 1·6 | *Castor* | | **246** | 43·6 | 43·5 | 43·3 | 43·1 | 42·8 | 42·6 | **N. 31** | 56·4 | 56·3 | 56·3 | 56·2 | 56·2 | 56·2 |
| 3·3 | σ Puppis | | **247** | 53·0 | 52·9 | 52·7 | 52·5 | 52·2 | 52·0 | **S. 43** | 15·3 | 15·2 | 15·1 | 15·1 | 15·1 | 15·3 |
| 3·1 | β Canis Minoris | | **248** | 32·0 | 31·9 | 31·7 | 31·5 | 31·2 | 31·1 | **N. 8** | 20·2 | 20·2 | 20·2 | 20·2 | 20·1 | 20·1 |
| 2·4 | η Canis Majoris | | **249** | 12·7 | 12·6 | 12·4 | 12·2 | 12·0 | 11·8 | **S. 29** | 15·5 | 15·4 | 15·3 | 15·3 | 15·4 | 15·5 |
| 2·7 | π Puppis | | **250** | 55·6 | 55·5 | 55·3 | 55·0 | 54·8 | 54·6 | **S. 37** | 03·4 | 03·2 | 03·2 | 03·1 | 03·2 | 03·4 |
| 2·0 | *Wezen* | | **253** | 08·7 | 08·5 | 08·4 | 08·1 | 07·9 | 07·7 | **S. 26** | 21·4 | 21·3 | 21·2 | 21·2 | 21·3 | 21·4 |
| 3·1 | ο Canis Majoris | | **254** | 29·5 | 29·4 | 29·2 | 29·0 | 28·8 | 28·6 | **S. 23** | 48·0 | 47·9 | 47·8 | 47·8 | 47·9 | 48·0 |
| 1·6 | *Adhara* | 19 | **255** | 34·7 | 34·6 | 34·4 | 34·1 | 33·9 | 33·7 | **S. 28** | 56·4 | 56·3 | 56·2 | 56·3 | 56·3 | 56·5 |
| 2·8 | τ Puppis | | **257** | 40·1 | 40·0 | 39·7 | 39·4 | 39·1 | 38·9 | **S. 50** | 35·2 | 35·1 | 35·0 | 35·0 | 35·1 | 35·3 |
| −1·6 | *Sirius* | 18 | **258** | 58·5 | 58·4 | 58·2 | 58·0 | 57·8 | 57·6 | **S. 16** | 41·1 | 41·0 | 40·9 | 41·0 | 41·0 | 41·2 |
| 1·9 | *Alhena* | | **260** | 54·8 | 54·6 | 54·4 | 54·2 | 54·0 | 53·8 | **N. 16** | 25·1 | 25·1 | 25·1 | 25·1 | 25·1 | 25·1 |
| −0·9 | *Canopus* | 17 | **264** | 09·0 | 08·8 | 08·5 | 08·2 | 07·9 | 07·8 | **S. 52** | 41·0 | 40·8 | 40·7 | 40·8 | 40·9 | 41·0 |
| 2·0 | *Mirzam* | | **264** | 35·2 | 35·1 | 34·9 | 34·6 | 34·4 | 34·3 | **S. 17** | 56·7 | 56·6 | 56·5 | 56·5 | 56·6 | 56·7 |
| 2·7 | θ Aurigæ | | **270** | 28·3 | 28·1 | 27·9 | 27·6 | 27·3 | 27·2 | **N. 37** | 12·6 | 12·6 | 12·5 | 12·5 | 12·6 | 12·6 |
| 2·1 | *Menkalinan* | | **270** | 33·1 | 32·8 | 32·6 | 32·2 | 32·0 | 31·8 | **N. 44** | 56·6 | 56·6 | 56·6 | 56·6 | 56·6 | 56·6 |
| Var.‡ | *Betelgeuse* | 16 | **271** | 31·6 | 31·4 | 31·2 | 31·0 | 30·8 | 30·7 | **N. 7** | 24·1 | 24·2 | 24·2 | 24·2 | 24·2 | 24·1 |
| 2·2 | κ Orionis | | **273** | 20·5 | 20·3 | 20·1 | 19·9 | 19·7 | 19·6 | **S. 9** | 40·7 | 40·6 | 40·5 | 40·6 | 40·6 | 40·7 |
| 1·9 | *Alnitak* | | **275** | 06·5 | 06·3 | 06·1 | 05·9 | 05·7 | 05·6 | **S. 1** | 57·3 | 57·2 | 57·2 | 57·2 | 57·3 | 57·3 |
| 2·8 | *Phact* | | **275** | 18·3 | 18·1 | 17·9 | 17·6 | 17·4 | 17·3 | **S. 34** | 05·1 | 05·0 | 05·0 | 05·0 | 05·1 | 05·3 |
| 3·0 | ζ Tauri | | **275** | 56·5 | 56·3 | 56·1 | 55·8 | 55·6 | 55·5 | **N. 21** | 07·6 | 07·7 | 07·7 | 07·7 | 07·7 | 07·7 |
| 1·8 | *Alnilam* | 15 | **276** | 14·8 | 14·6 | 14·4 | 14·2 | 14·0 | 13·9 | **S. 1** | 13·0 | 12·9 | 12·9 | 12·9 | 13·0 | 13·1 |
| 2·9 | ι Orionis | | **276** | 25·9 | 25·7 | 25·5 | 25·3 | 25·1 | 25·0 | **S. 5** | 55·5 | 55·4 | 55·4 | 55·4 | 55·5 | 55·6 |
| 2·7 | α Leporis | | **277** | 04·8 | 04·6 | 04·4 | 04·1 | 04·0 | 03·9 | **S. 17** | 50·3 | 50·2 | 50·2 | 50·2 | 50·3 | 50·4 |
| 2·5 | δ Orionis | | **277** | 18·0 | 17·8 | 17·6 | 17·4 | 17·2 | 17·1 | **S. 0** | 19·0 | 18·9 | 18·9 | 18·9 | 18·9 | 19·0 |
| 3·0 | β Leporis | | **278** | 11·6 | 11·4 | 11·2 | 11·0 | 10·8 | 10·7 | **S. 20** | 46·6 | 46·5 | 46·5 | 46·5 | 46·6 | 46·7 |
| 1·8 | *Elnath* | 14 | **278** | 48·0 | 47·8 | 47·5 | 47·3 | 47·1 | 46·9 | **N. 28** | 35·2 | 35·2 | 35·2 | 35·2 | 35·2 | 35·3 |
| 1·7 | *Bellatrix* | 13 | **279** | 02·0 | 01·9 | 01·6 | 01·4 | 01·2 | 01·1 | **N. 6** | 19·7 | 19·7 | 19·8 | 19·8 | 19·7 | 19·7 |
| 0·2 | *Capella* | 12 | **281** | 15·8 | 15·6 | 15·2 | 15·0 | 14·7 | 14·5 | **N. 45** | 58·3 | 58·3 | 58·3 | 58·4 | 58·4 | 58·5 |
| 0·3 | *Rigel* | 11 | **281** | 39·0 | 38·8 | 38·6 | 38·4 | 38·2 | 38·1 | **S. 8** | 13·7 | 13·6 | 13·6 | 13·6 | 13·7 | 13·8 |
| 2·9 | β Eridani | | **283** | 19·7 | 19·5 | 19·3 | 19·1 | 18·9 | 18·8 | **S. 5** | 07·0 | 06·9 | 06·9 | 06·9 | 06·9 | 07·0 |
| 2·9 | ι Aurigæ † | | **286** | 08·1 | 07·9 | 07·6 | 07·4 | 07·2 | 07·1 | **N. 33** | 07·7 | 07·7 | 07·7 | 07·7 | 07·7 | 07·8 |
| 1·1 | *Aldebaran* | 10 | **291** | 21·5 | 21·2 | 21·0 | 20·8 | 20·6 | 20·6 | **N. 16** | 27·7 | 27·7 | 27·8 | 27·8 | 27·8 | 27·8 |
| 3·2 | γ Eridani | | **300** | 46·1 | 45·9 | 45·6 | 45·5 | 45·3 | 45·3 | **S. 13** | 34·4 | 34·3 | 34·3 | 34·3 | 34·4 | 34·5 |
| 3·0 | ε Persei | | **300** | 55·9 | 55·6 | 55·3 | 55·1 | 54·9 | 54·8 | **N. 39** | 56·4 | 56·4 | 56·5 | 56·6 | 56·6 | 56·7 |
| 2·9 | ζ Persei | | **301** | 50·2 | 49·9 | 49·7 | 49·5 | 49·3 | 49·2 | **N. 31** | 48·7 | 48·8 | 48·8 | 48·9 | 48·9 | 49·0 |
| 3·0 | *Alcyone* | | **303** | 28·7 | 28·4 | 28·2 | 28·0 | 27·9 | 27·8 | **N. 24** | 01·9 | 01·9 | 02·0 | 02·0 | 02·1 | 02·1 |
| 1·9 | *Mirfak* | 9 | **309** | 20·3 | 20·0 | 19·7 | 19·4 | 19·3 | 19·2 | **N. 49** | 46·5 | 46·5 | 46·6 | 46·7 | 46·8 | 46·9 |
| Var.§ | *Algol* † | | **313** | 20·4 | 20·1 | 19·8 | 19·6 | 19·5 | 19·5 | **N. 40** | 51·8 | 51·8 | 51·9 | 52·0 | 52·1 | 52·2 |
| 2·8 | *Menkar* | 8 | **314** | 44·2 | 44·0 | 43·8 | 43·6 | 43·5 | 43·5 | **N. 3** | 59·9 | 60·0 | 60·0 | 60·0 | 60·0 | 60·0 |
| 3·1 | *Acamar* | 7 | **315** | 39·6 | 39·3 | 39·0 | 38·9 | 38·8 | 38·8 | **S. 40** | 23·7 | 23·6 | 23·6 | 23·7 | 23·8 | 24·0 |
| 2·1 | *Polaris* † | | **327** | 42·3 | 30·8 | 21·2 | 15·3 | 14·6 | 19·3 | **N. 89** | 09·1 | 09·2 | 09·3 | 09·5 | 09·6 | 09·8 |
| 3·1 | β Trianguli | | **327** | 57·7 | 57·4 | 57·2 | 57·0 | 57·0 | 57·0 | **N. 34** | 52·5 | 52·6 | 52·7 | 52·8 | 52·8 | 52·9 |
| 2·2 | *Hamal* | 6 | **328** | 32·1 | 31·9 | 31·7 | 31·6 | 31·5 | 31·5 | **N. 23** | 21·0 | 21·1 | 21·2 | 21·3 | 21·3 | 21·3 |
| 2·2 | *Almak* | | **329** | 23·0 | 22·7 | 22·5 | 22·3 | 22·3 | 22·3 | **N. 42** | 12·9 | 13·0 | 13·1 | 13·2 | 13·3 | 13·4 |
| 3·0 | α Hydri | | **330** | 29·7 | 29·3 | 29·0 | 28·9 | 28·9 | 29·1 | **S. 61** | 40·7 | 40·7 | 40·7 | 40·9 | 41·0 | 41·2 |
| 2·7 | *Sheratan* | | **331** | 39·7 | 39·5 | 39·3 | 39·2 | 39·1 | 39·2 | **N. 20** | 41·6 | 41·7 | 41·7 | 41·8 | 41·8 | 41·9 |
| 0·6 | *Achernar* | 5 | **335** | 47·4 | 47·1 | 46·8 | 46·7 | 46·7 | 46·9 | **S. 57** | 21·0 | 21·0 | 21·1 | 21·2 | 21·3 | 21·5 |
| 2·8 | *Ruchbah* | | **338** | 55·6 | 55·2 | 54·9 | 54·7 | 54·7 | 54·9 | **N. 60** | 06·6 | 06·7 | 06·8 | 07·0 | 07·1 | 07·2 |
| 2·4 | *Mirach* | | **342** | 53·5 | 53·3 | 53·1 | 53·0 | 53·0 | 53·1 | **N. 35** | 29·7 | 29·8 | 29·9 | 30·0 | 30·1 | 30·1 |
| Var.‖ | γ Cassiopeiæ | | **346** | 10·3 | 09·9 | 09·7 | 09·6 | 09·6 | 09·8 | **N. 60** | 35·2 | 35·3 | 35·5 | 35·6 | 35·8 | 35·8 |
| 2·2 | *Diphda* | 4 | **349** | 23·6 | 23·4 | 23·3 | 23·2 | 23·2 | 23·3 | **S. 18** | 06·7 | 06·7 | 06·7 | 06·7 | 06·8 | 06·8 |
| 2·5 | *Schedar* | 3 | **350** | 12·0 | 11·7 | 11·5 | 11·4 | 11·5 | 11·6 | **N. 56** | 24·3 | 24·5 | 24·6 | 24·8 | 24·9 | 25·0 |
| 2·4 | *Ankaa* | 2 | **353** | 42·9 | 42·7 | 42·5 | 42·5 | 42·6 | 42·7 | **S. 42** | 25·7 | 25·7 | 25·7 | 25·8 | 26·0 | 26·0 |
| 2·9 | β Hydri † | | **353** | 51·9 | 51·2 | 50·7 | 50·7 | 51·1 | 51·7 | **S. 77** | 22·8 | 22·8 | 23·0 | 23·1 | 23·3 | 23·3 |
| 2·9 | *Algenib* | | **356** | 59·3 | 59·1 | 59·0 | 59·0 | 59·0 | 59·1 | **N. 15** | 03·2 | 03·3 | 03·4 | 03·5 | 03·5 | 03·5 |
| 2·4 | *Caph* | | **358** | 00·7 | 00·3 | 00·2 | 00·1 | 00·3 | 00·5 | **N. 59** | 01·1 | 01·2 | 01·4 | 01·5 | 01·7 | 01·7 |
| 2·2 | *Alpheratz* | 1 | **358** | 12·1 | 11·9 | 11·7 | 11·7 | 11·8 | 11·9 | **N. 28** | 57·6 | 57·7 | 57·9 | 58·0 | 58·0 | 58·0 |

‡ 0·1—1·2 § 2·3—3·5 ‖ Irregular variable; 1973 mag. 2·5 † Not suitable for use with H.O. 214 (H.D. 486)

# POLARIS (POLE STAR) TABLES, 1976
## FOR DETERMINING LATITUDE FROM SEXTANT ALTITUDE AND FOR AZIMUTH

| L.H.A. ARIES | 0°–9° | 10°–19° | 20°–29° | 30°–39° | 40°–49° | 50°–59° | 60°–69° | 70°–79° | 80°–89° | 90°–99° | 100°–109° | 110°–119° |
|---|---|---|---|---|---|---|---|---|---|---|---|---|
| | $a_0$ | $a_0$ | $a_0$ | $a_0$ | $a_0$ | $a_0$ | $a_0$ | $a_0$ | $a_0$ | $a_0$ | $a_0$ | $a_0$ |
| ° | ° ′ | ° ′ | ° ′ | ° ′ | ° ′ | ° ′ | ° ′ | ° ′ | ° ′ | ° ′ | ° ′ | ° ′ |
| 0 | 0 16·3 | 0 12·2 | 0 09·5 | 0 08·3 | 0 08·8 | 0 10·7 | 0 14·2 | 0 19·0 | 0 25·0 | 0 32·1 | 0 40·0 | 0 48·4 |
| 1 | 15·8 | 11·8 | 09·3 | 08·3 | 08·9 | 11·0 | 14·6 | 19·5 | 25·7 | 32·8 | 40·8 | 49·3 |
| 2 | 15·3 | 11·5 | 09·1 | 08·3 | 09·0 | 11·3 | 15·0 | 20·1 | 26·4 | 33·6 | 41·6 | 50·2 |
| 3 | 14·9 | 11·2 | 09·0 | 08·3 | 09·2 | 11·6 | 15·5 | 20·7 | 27·0 | 34·4 | 42·5 | 51·0 |
| 4 | 14·5 | 10·9 | 08·8 | 08·3 | 09·4 | 11·9 | 15·9 | 21·3 | 27·7 | 35·2 | 43·3 | 51·9 |
| 5 | 0 14·0 | 0 10·6 | 0 08·7 | 0 08·4 | 0 09·5 | 0 12·3 | 0 16·4 | 0 21·9 | 0 28·4 | 0 35·9 | 0 44·1 | 0 52·8 |
| 6 | 13·6 | 10·4 | 08·6 | 08·4 | 09·8 | 12·6 | 16·9 | 22·5 | 29·2 | 36·7 | 45·0 | 53·7 |
| 7 | 13·2 | 10·1 | 08·5 | 08·5 | 10·0 | 13·0 | 17·4 | 23·1 | 29·9 | 37·5 | 45·8 | 54·5 |
| 8 | 12·9 | 09·9 | 08·4 | 08·5 | 10·2 | 13·4 | 17·9 | 23·7 | 30·6 | 38·3 | 46·7 | 55·4 |
| 9 | 12·5 | 09·7 | 08·4 | 08·6 | 10·5 | 13·8 | 18·4 | 24·4 | 31·3 | 39·2 | 47·6 | 56·3 |
| 10 | 0 12·2 | 0 09·5 | 0 08·3 | 0 08·8 | 0 10·7 | 0 14·2 | 0 19·0 | 0 25·0 | 0 32·1 | 0 40·0 | 0 48·4 | 0 57·2 |
| Lat. | $a_1$ | $a_1$ | $a_1$ | $a_1$ | $a_1$ | $a_1$ | $a_1$ | $a_1$ | $a_1$ | $a_1$ | $a_1$ | $a_1$ |
| ° | ′ | ′ | ′ | ′ | ′ | ′ | ′ | ′ | ′ | ′ | ′ | ′ |
| 0 | 0·5 | 0·6 | 0·6 | 0·6 | 0·6 | 0·5 | 0·5 | 0·4 | 0·3 | 0·3 | 0·2 | 0·2 |
| 10 | ·5 | ·6 | ·6 | ·6 | ·6 | ·5 | ·5 | ·4 | ·4 | ·3 | ·3 | ·2 |
| 20 | ·5 | ·6 | ·6 | ·6 | ·6 | ·6 | ·5 | ·5 | ·4 | ·4 | ·3 | ·3 |
| 30 | ·6 | ·6 | ·6 | ·6 | ·6 | ·6 | ·5 | ·5 | ·5 | ·4 | ·4 | ·4 |
| 40 | 0·6 | 0·6 | 0·6 | 0·6 | ·06 | 0·6 | 0·6 | 0·5 | 0·5 | 0·5 | 0·5 | 0·5 |
| 45 | ·6 | ·6 | ·6 | ·6 | ·6 | ·6 | ·6 | ·6 | ·6 | ·5 | ·5 | ·5 |
| 50 | ·6 | ·6 | ·6 | ·6 | ·6 | ·6 | ·6 | ·6 | ·6 | ·6 | ·6 | ·6 |
| 55 | ·6 | ·6 | ·6 | ·6 | ·6 | ·6 | ·6 | ·6 | ·7 | ·7 | ·7 | ·7 |
| 60 | ·6 | ·6 | ·6 | ·6 | ·6 | ·6 | ·7 | ·7 | ·7 | ·8 | ·8 | ·8 |
| 62 | 0·7 | 0·6 | 0·6 | 0·6 | 0·6 | 0·6 | 0·7 | 0·7 | 0·8 | 0·8 | 0·8 | 0·9 |
| 64 | ·7 | ·6 | ·6 | ·6 | ·6 | ·6 | ·7 | ·7 | ·8 | ·9 | 0·9 | 0·9 |
| 66 | ·7 | ·6 | ·6 | ·6 | ·6 | ·7 | ·7 | ·8 | ·8 | 0·9 | 1·0 | 1·0 |
| 68 | 0·7 | 0·6 | 0·6 | 0·6 | 0·6 | 0·7 | 0·7 | 0·8 | 0·9 | 1·0 | 1·0 | 1·1 |
| Month | $a_2$ | $a_2$ | $a_2$ | $a_2$ | $a_2$ | $a_2$ | $a_2$ | $a_2$ | $a_2$ | $a_2$ | $a_2$ | $a_2$ |
| | ′ | ′ | ′ | ′ | ′ | ′ | ′ | ′ | ′ | ′ | ′ | ′ |
| Jan. | 0·7 | 0·7 | 0·7 | 0·7 | 0·7 | 0·7 | 0·7 | 0·7 | 0·7 | 0·7 | 0·7 | 0·7 |
| Feb. | ·6 | ·7 | ·7 | ·7 | ·8 | ·8 | ·8 | ·8 | ·8 | ·8 | ·8 | ·8 |
| Mar. | ·5 | ·5 | ·6 | ·6 | ·7 | ·8 | ·8 | ·8 | ·9 | ·9 | ·9 | ·9 |
| Apr. | 0·3 | 0·4 | 0·4 | 0·5 | 0·6 | 0·6 | 0·7 | 0·8 | 0·8 | 0·9 | 0·9 | 0·9 |
| May | ·2 | ·3 | ·3 | ·4 | ·4 | ·5 | ·6 | ·6 | ·7 | ·8 | ·8 | ·9 |
| June | ·2 | ·2 | ·2 | ·3 | ·3 | ·4 | ·4 | ·5 | ·5 | ·6 | ·7 | ·8 |
| July | 0·2 | 0·2 | 0·2 | 0·2 | 0·2 | 0·3 | 0·3 | 0·3 | 0·4 | 0·5 | 0·5 | 0·6 |
| Aug. | ·4 | ·3 | ·3 | ·3 | ·2 | ·2 | ·3 | ·3 | ·3 | ·3 | ·4 | ·4 |
| Sept. | ·5 | ·5 | ·4 | ·4 | ·3 | ·3 | ·3 | ·3 | ·3 | ·3 | ·3 | ·3 |
| Oct. | 0·7 | 0·7 | 0·6 | 0·5 | 0·5 | 0·4 | 0·4 | 0·3 | 0·3 | 0·3 | 0·3 | 0·2 |
| Nov. | 0·9 | 0·8 | ·8 | ·7 | ·7 | ·6 | ·5 | ·5 | ·4 | ·3 | ·3 | ·3 |
| Dec. | 1·0 | 1·0 | 0·9 | 0·9 | 0·8 | 0·8 | 0·7 | 0·6 | 0·5 | 0·5 | 0·4 | 0·3 |
| Lat. | AZIMUTH | | | | | | | | | | | |
| ° | ° | ° | ° | ° | ° | ° | ° | ° | ° | ° | ° | ° |
| 0 | 0·4 | 0·3 | 0·1 | 0·0 | 359·8 | 359·7 | 359·5 | 359·4 | 359·3 | 359·3 | 359·2 | 359·2 |
| 20 | 0·4 | 0·3 | 0·1 | 0·0 | 359·8 | 359·7 | 359·5 | 359·4 | 359·3 | 359·2 | 359·1 | 359·1 |
| 40 | 0·5 | 0·3 | 0·1 | 359·9 | 359·8 | 359·6 | 359·4 | 359·2 | 359·1 | 359·0 | 358·9 | 358·9 |
| 50 | 0·6 | 0·4 | 0·2 | 359·9 | 359·7 | 359·5 | 359·3 | 359·1 | 358·9 | 358·8 | 358·7 | 358·7 |
| 55 | 0·7 | 0·4 | 0·2 | 359·9 | 359·7 | 359·4 | 359·2 | 359·0 | 358·8 | 358·7 | 358·6 | 358·5 |
| 60 | 0·8 | 0·5 | 0·2 | 359·9 | 359·6 | 359·3 | 359·1 | 358·8 | 358·6 | 358·5 | 358·4 | 358·3 |
| 65 | 0·9 | 0·6 | 0·3 | 359·9 | 359·6 | 359·2 | 358·9 | 358·6 | 358·4 | 358·2 | 358·1 | 358·0 |


# POLARIS (POLE STAR) TABLES, 1976
## FOR DETERMINING LATITUDE FROM SEXTANT ALTITUDE AND FOR AZIMUTH


| L.H.A. ARIES | 120°–129° | 130°–139° | 140°–149° | 150°–159° | 160°–169° | 170°–179° | 180°–189° | 190°–199° | 200°–209° | 210°–219° | 220°–229° | 230°–239° |
|---|---|---|---|---|---|---|---|---|---|---|---|---|
| | $a_0$ | $a_0$ | $a_0$ | $a_0$ | $a_0$ | $a_0$ | $a_0$ | $a_0$ | $a_0$ | $a_0$ | $a_0$ | $a_0$ |
| ° | ° ′ | ° ′ | ° ′ | ° ′ | ° ′ | ° ′ | ° ′ | ° ′ | ° ′ | ° ′ | ° ′ | ° ′ |
| 0 | 0 57·2 | 1 06·0 | 1 14·5 | 1 22·6 | 1 29·9 | 1 36·3 | 1 41·6 | 1 45·6 | 1 48·2 | 1 49·3 | 1 48·9 | 1 47·0 |
| 1 | 58·1 | 06·8 | 15·3 | 23·4 | 30·6 | 36·9 | 42·0 | 45·9 | 48·3 | 49·3 | 48·7 | 46·7 |
| 2 | 58·9 | 07·7 | 16·2 | 24·1 | 31·3 | 37·5 | 42·5 | 46·2 | 48·5 | 49·3 | 48·6 | 46·4 |
| 3 | 0 59·8 | 08·6 | 17·0 | 24·9 | 32·0 | 38·0 | 42·9 | 46·5 | 48·6 | 49·3 | 48·4 | 46·1 |
| 4 | 1 00·7 | 09·4 | 17·8 | 25·6 | 32·6 | 38·6 | 43·3 | 46·8 | 48·8 | 49·3 | 48·3 | 45·8 |
| 5 | 1 01·6 | 1 10·3 | 1 18·6 | 1 26·4 | 1 33·3 | 1 39·1 | 1 43·7 | 1 47·0 | 1 48·9 | 1 49·2 | 1 48·1 | 1 45·5 |
| 6 | 02·5 | 11·1 | 19·4 | 27·1 | 33·9 | 39·6 | 44·1 | 47·3 | 49·0 | 49·2 | 47·9 | 45·1 |
| 7 | 03·3 | 12·0 | 20·2 | 27·8 | 34·5 | 40·1 | 44·5 | 47·5 | 49·1 | 49·1 | 47·7 | 44·8 |
| 8 | 04·2 | 12·8 | 21·0 | 28·5 | 35·1 | 40·6 | 44·9 | 47·8 | 49·2 | 49·1 | 47·5 | 44·4 |
| 9 | 05·1 | 13·7 | 21·8 | 29·2 | 35·7 | 41·1 | 45·2 | 48·0 | 49·2 | 49·0 | 47·2 | 44·0 |
| 10 | 1 06·0 | 1 14·5 | 1 22·6 | 1 29·9 | 1 36·3 | 1 41·6 | 1 45·6 | 1 48·2 | 1 49·3 | 1 48·9 | 1 47·0 | 1 43·6 |
| Lat. | $a_1$ | $a_1$ | $a_1$ | $a_1$ | $a_1$ | $a_1$ | $a_1$ | $a_1$ | $a_1$ | $a_1$ | $a_1$ | $a_1$ |
| ° | ′ | ′ | ′ | ′ | ′ | ′ | ′ | ′ | ′ | ′ | ′ | ′ |
| 0 | 0·2 | 0·2 | 0·2 | 0·3 | 0·4 | 0·4 | 0·5 | 0·6 | 0·6 | 0·6 | 0·6 | 0·5 |
| 10 | ·2 | ·2 | ·3 | ·3 | ·4 | ·5 | ·5 | ·6 | ·6 | ·6 | ·6 | ·5 |
| 20 | ·3 | ·3 | ·3 | ·4 | ·4 | ·5 | ·5 | ·6 | ·6 | ·6 | ·6 | ·6 |
| 30 | ·4 | ·4 | ·4 | ·4 | ·5 | ·5 | ·6 | ·6 | ·6 | ·6 | ·6 | ·6 |
| 40 | 0·5 | 0·5 | 0·5 | 0·5 | 0·5 | 0·6 | 0·6 | 0·6 | 0·6 | 0·6 | 0·6 | 0·6 |
| 45 | ·5 | ·5 | ·5 | ·5 | ·6 | ·6 | ·6 | ·6 | ·6 | ·6 | ·6 | ·6 |
| 50 | ·6 | ·6 | ·6 | ·6 | ·6 | ·6 | ·6 | ·6 | ·6 | ·6 | ·6 | ·6 |
| 55 | ·7 | ·7 | ·7 | ·7 | ·6 | ·6 | ·6 | ·6 | ·6 | ·6 | ·6 | ·6 |
| 60 | ·8 | ·8 | ·8 | ·7 | ·7 | ·7 | ·6 | ·6 | ·6 | ·6 | ·6 | ·6 |
| 62 | 0·9 | 0·8 | 0·8 | 0·8 | 0·7 | 0·7 | 0·7 | 0·6 | 0·6 | 0·6 | 0·6 | 0·6 |
| 64 | 0·9 | 0·9 | ·9 | ·8 | ·8 | ·7 | ·7 | ·6 | ·6 | ·6 | ·6 | ·6 |
| 66 | 1·0 | 1·0 | 0·9 | ·9 | ·8 | ·7 | ·7 | ·6 | ·6 | ·6 | ·6 | ·7 |
| 68 | 1·1 | 1·1 | 1·0 | 0·9 | 0·9 | 0·8 | 0·7 | 0·6 | 0·6 | 0·6 | 0·6 | 0·7 |
| Month | $a_2$ | $a_2$ | $a_2$ | $a_2$ | $a_2$ | $a_2$ | $a_2$ | $a_2$ | $a_2$ | $a_2$ | $a_2$ | $a_2$ |
| | ′ | ′ | ′ | ′ | ′ | ′ | ′ | ′ | ′ | ′ | ′ | ′ |
| Jan. | 0·6 | 0·6 | 0·6 | 0·6 | 0·5 | 0·5 | 0·5 | 0·5 | 0·5 | 0·5 | 0·5 | 0·5 |
| Feb. | ·8 | ·8 | ·7 | ·7 | ·7 | ·6 | ·6 | ·5 | ·5 | ·5 | ·4 | ·4 |
| Mar. | 0·9 | 0·9 | 0·9 | 0·8 | ·8 | ·8 | ·7 | ·7 | ·6 | ·6 | ·5 | ·4 |
| Apr. | 1·0 | 1·0 | 1·0 | 1·0 | 0·9 | 0·9 | 0·9 | 0·8 | 0·8 | 0·7 | 0·6 | 0·6 |
| May | 0·9 | 1·0 | 1·0 | 1·0 | 1·0 | 1·0 | 1·0 | 0·9 | 0·9 | ·8 | ·8 | ·7 |
| June | ·8 | 0·9 | 0·9 | 1·0 | 1·0 | 1·0 | 1·0 | 1·0 | 1·0 | 0·9 | 0·9 | ·8 |
| July | 0·7 | 0·7 | 0·8 | 0·8 | 0·9 | 0·9 | 1·0 | 1·0 | 1·0 | 1·0 | 1·0 | 0·9 |
| Aug. | ·5 | ·6 | ·6 | ·7 | ·7 | ·8 | 0·8 | 0·9 | 0·9 | 0·9 | 1·0 | 1·0 |
| Sept. | ·3 | ·4 | ·4 | ·5 | ·6 | ·6 | ·7 | ·7 | ·8 | ·8 | 0·9 | 0·9 |
| Oct. | 0·3 | 0·3 | 0·3 | 0·3 | 0·4 | 0·4 | 0·5 | 0·5 | 0·6 | 0·7 | 0·7 | 0·8 |
| Nov. | ·2 | ·2 | ·2 | ·2 | ·2 | ·3 | ·3 | ·4 | ·4 | ·5 | ·5 | ·6 |
| Dec. | 0·3 | 0·3 | 0·2 | 0·2 | 0·2 | 0·2 | 0·2 | 0·2 | 0·3 | 0·3 | 0·4 | 0·4 |
| Lat. | AZIMUTH | | | | | | | | | | | |
| ° | ° | ° | ° | ° | ° | ° | ° | ° | ° | ° | ° | ° |
| 0 | 359·2 | 359·2 | 359·2 | 359·3 | 359·4 | 359·5 | 359·6 | 359·7 | 359·9 | 0·0 | 0·2 | 0·3 |
| 20 | 359·1 | 359·1 | 359·2 | 359·2 | 359·3 | 359·5 | 359·6 | 359·7 | 359·9 | 0·0 | 0·2 | 0·3 |
| 40 | 358·9 | 358·9 | 359·0 | 359·1 | 359·2 | 359·3 | 359·5 | 359·7 | 359·9 | 0·1 | 0·2 | 0·4 |
| 50 | 358·7 | 358·7 | 358·8 | 358·9 | 359·0 | 359·2 | 359·4 | 359·6 | 359·8 | 0·1 | 0·3 | 0·5 |
| 55 | 358·5 | 358·6 | 358·7 | 358·8 | 358·9 | 359·1 | 359·3 | 359·6 | 359·8 | 0·1 | 0·3 | 0·6 |
| 60 | 358·3 | 358·4 | 358·5 | 358·6 | 358·8 | 359·0 | 359·2 | 359·5 | 359·8 | 0·1 | 0·4 | 0·6 |
| 65 | 358·0 | 358·1 | 358·2 | 358·4 | 358·6 | 358·8 | 359·1 | 359·4 | 359·8 | 0·1 | 0·4 | 0·7 |

# POLARIS (POLE STAR) TABLES, 1976

## FOR DETERMINING LATITUDE FROM SEXTANT ALTITUDE AND FOR AZIMUTH

| L.H.A. ARIES | 240°–249° | 250°–259° | 260°–269° | 270°–279° | 280°–289° | 290°–299° | 300°–309° | 310°–319° | 320°–329° | 330°–339° | 340°–349° | 350°–359° |
|---|---|---|---|---|---|---|---|---|---|---|---|---|
| | $a_0$ | $a_0$ | $a_0$ | $a_0$ | $a_0$ | $a_0$ | $a_0$ | $a_0$ | $a_0$ | $a_0$ | $a_0$ | $a_0$ |
| ° | ° ′ | ° ′ | ° ′ | ° ′ | ° ′ | ° ′ | ° ′ | ° ′ | ° ′ | ° ′ | ° ′ | ° ′ |
| 0 | 1 43·6 | 1 38·9 | 1 33·1 | 1 26·1 | 1 18·4 | 1 10·0 | 1 01·3 | 0 52·5 | 0 43·9 | 0 35·7 | 0 28·2 | 0 21·7 |
| 1 | 43·2 | 38·4 | 32·4 | 25·4 | 17·6 | 09·2 | 1 00·4 | 51·6 | 43·0 | 34·9 | 27·5 | 21·1 |
| 2 | 42·8 | 37·9 | 31·8 | 24·6 | 16·8 | 08·3 | 0 59·6 | 50·8 | 42·2 | 34·2 | 26·8 | 20·5 |
| 3 | 42·4 | 37·3 | 31·1 | 23·9 | 15·9 | 07·4 | 58·7 | 49·9 | 41·4 | 33·4 | 26·2 | 19·9 |
| 4 | 41·9 | 36·7 | 30·4 | 23·1 | 15·1 | 06·6 | 57·8 | 49·0 | 40·6 | 32·6 | 25·5 | 19·4 |
| 5 | 1 41·4 | 1 36·1 | 1 29·7 | 1 22·3 | 1 14·3 | 1 05·7 | 0 56·9 | 0 48·2 | 0 39·7 | 0 31·9 | 0 24·8 | 0 18·8 |
| 6 | 41·0 | 35·6 | 29·0 | 21·6 | 13·4 | 04·8 | 56·0 | 47·3 | 38·9 | 31·1 | 24·2 | 18·3 |
| 7 | 40·5 | 34·9 | 28·3 | 20·8 | 12·6 | 03·9 | 55·1 | 46·4 | 38·1 | 30·4 | 23·5 | 17·8 |
| 8 | 40·0 | 34·3 | 27·6 | 20·0 | 11·7 | 03·1 | 54·3 | 45·6 | 37·3 | 29·7 | 22·9 | 17·2 |
| 9 | 39·5 | 33·7 | 26·9 | 19·2 | 10·9 | 02·2 | 53·4 | 44·7 | 36·5 | 28·9 | 22·3 | 16·7 |
| 10 | 1 38·9 | 1 33·1 | 1 26·1 | 1 18·4 | 1 10·0 | 1 01·3 | 0 52·5 | 0 43·9 | 0 35·7 | 0 28·2 | 0 21·7 | 0 16·3 |
| Lat. | $a_1$ | $a_1$ | $a_1$ | $a_1$ | $a_1$ | $a_1$ | $a_1$ | $a_1$ | $a_1$ | $a_1$ | $a_1$ | $a_1$ |
| ° | ′ | ′ | ′ | ′ | ′ | ′ | ′ | ′ | ′ | ′ | ′ | ′ |
| 0 | 0·5 | 0·4 | 0·3 | 0·3 | 0·2 | 0·2 | 0·2 | 0·2 | 0·2 | 0·3 | 0·4 | 0·4 |
| 10 | ·5 | ·4 | ·4 | ·3 | ·3 | ·2 | ·2 | ·2 | ·3 | ·3 | ·4 | ·5 |
| 20 | ·5 | ·5 | ·4 | ·4 | ·3 | ·3 | ·3 | ·3 | ·3 | ·4 | ·4 | ·5 |
| 30 | ·5 | ·5 | ·5 | ·4 | ·4 | ·4 | ·4 | ·4 | ·4 | ·4 | ·5 | ·5 |
| 40 | 0·6 | 0·5 | 0·5 | 0·5 | 0·5 | 0·5 | 0·5 | 0·5 | 0·5 | 0·5 | 0·5 | 0·6 |
| 45 | ·6 | ·6 | ·6 | ·5 | ·5 | ·5 | ·5 | ·5 | ·5 | ·5 | ·6 | ·6 |
| 50 | ·6 | ·6 | ·6 | ·6 | ·6 | ·6 | ·6 | ·6 | ·6 | ·6 | ·6 | ·6 |
| 55 | ·6 | ·6 | ·7 | ·7 | ·7 | ·7 | ·7 | ·7 | ·7 | ·7 | ·6 | ·6 |
| 60 | ·7 | ·7 | ·7 | ·8 | ·8 | ·8 | ·8 | ·8 | ·8 | ·7 | ·7 | ·7 |
| 62 | 0·7 | 0·7 | 0·8 | 0·8 | 0·8 | 0·9 | 0·9 | 0·8 | 0·8 | 0·8 | 0·7 | 0·7 |
| 64 | ·7 | ·7 | ·8 | ·9 | 0·9 | 0·9 | 0·9 | 0·9 | ·9 | ·8 | ·8 | ·7 |
| 66 | ·7 | ·8 | ·8 | 0·9 | 1·0 | 1·0 | 1·0 | 1·0 | 0·9 | ·9 | ·8 | ·7 |
| 68 | 0·7 | 0·8 | 0·9 | 1·0 | 1·0 | 1·1 | 1·1 | 1·1 | 1·0 | 0·9 | 0·9 | 0·8 |
| Month | $a_2$ | $a_2$ | $a_2$ | $a_2$ | $a_2$ | $a_2$ | $a_2$ | $a_2$ | $a_2$ | $a_2$ | $a_2$ | $a_2$ |
| | ′ | ′ | ′ | ′ | ′ | ′ | ′ | ′ | ′ | ′ | ′ | ′ |
| **Jan.** | 0·5 | 0·5 | 0·5 | 0·5 | 0·5 | 0·5 | 0·6 | 0·6 | 0·6 | 0·6 | 0·7 | 0·7 |
| **Feb.** | ·4 | ·4 | ·4 | ·4 | ·4 | ·4 | ·4 | ·4 | ·5 | ·5 | ·5 | ·6 |
| **Mar.** | ·4 | ·4 | ·3 | ·3 | ·3 | ·3 | ·3 | ·3 | ·3 | ·4 | ·4 | ·4 |
| **Apr.** | 0·5 | 0·4 | 0·4 | 0·3 | 0·3 | 0·3 | 0·2 | 0·2 | 0·2 | 0·2 | 0·3 | 0·3 |
| **May** | ·6 | ·6 | ·5 | ·4 | ·4 | ·3 | ·3 | ·2 | ·2 | ·2 | ·2 | ·2 |
| **June** | ·8 | ·7 | ·7 | ·6 | ·5 | ·4 | ·4 | ·3 | ·3 | ·2 | ·2 | ·2 |
| **July** | 0·9 | 0·9 | 0·8 | 0·7 | 0·7 | 0·6 | 0·5 | 0·5 | 0·4 | 0·4 | 0·3 | 0·3 |
| **Aug.** | ·9 | ·9 | ·9 | ·9 | ·8 | ·8 | ·7 | ·6 | ·6 | ·5 | ·5 | ·4 |
| **Sept.** | ·9 | ·9 | ·9 | ·9 | ·9 | 0·9 | ·9 | ·8 | ·8 | ·7 | ·6 | ·6 |
| **Oct.** | 0·8 | 0·9 | 0·9 | 0·9 | 0·9 | 1·0 | 0·9 | 0·9 | 0·9 | 0·9 | 0·8 | 0·8 |
| **Nov.** | ·7 | ·7 | ·8 | ·9 | ·9 | 0·9 | 1·0 | 1·0 | 1·0 | 1·0 | 1·0 | 0·9 |
| **Dec.** | 0·5 | 0·6 | 0·7 | 0·7 | 0·8 | 0·9 | 0·9 | 0·9 | 1·0 | 1·0 | 1·0 | 1·0 |
| Lat. | AZIMUTH | | | | | | | | | | | |
| ° | ° | ° | ° | ° | ° | ° | ° | ° | ° | ° | ° | ° |
| 0 | 0·5 | 0·6 | 0·7 | 0·7 | 0·8 | 0·8 | 0·8 | 0·8 | 0·8 | 0·7 | 0·6 | 0·5 |
| 20 | 0·5 | 0·6 | 0·7 | 0·8 | 0·9 | 0·9 | 0·9 | 0·9 | 0·8 | 0·8 | 0·7 | 0·5 |
| 40 | 0·6 | 0·7 | 0·9 | 1·0 | 1·0 | 1·1 | 1·1 | 1·1 | 1·0 | 0·9 | 0·8 | 0·7 |
| 50 | 0·7 | 0·9 | 1·0 | 1·2 | 1·2 | 1·3 | 1·3 | 1·3 | 1·2 | 1·1 | 1·0 | 0·8 |
| 55 | 0·8 | 1·0 | 1·2 | 1·3 | 1·4 | 1·5 | 1·5 | 1·4 | 1·4 | 1·2 | 1·1 | 0·9 |
| 60 | 0·9 | 1·1 | 1·3 | 1·5 | 1·6 | 1·7 | 1·7 | 1·7 | 1·6 | 1·4 | 1·3 | 1·0 |
| 65 | 1·0 | 1·3 | 1·6 | 1·7 | 1·9 | 2·0 | 2·0 | 2·0 | 1·9 | 1·7 | 1·5 | 1·2 |

Latitude = Apparent altitude (corrected for refraction) $-1° + a_0 + a_1 + a_2$

The table is entered with L.H.A. Aries to determine the column to be used; each column refers to a range of 10°. $a_0$ is taken, with mental interpolation, from the upper table with the units of L.H.A. Aries in degrees as argument; $a_1$, $a_2$ are taken, without interpolation, from the second and third tables with arguments latitude and month respectively. $a_0$, $a_1$, $a_2$ are always positive. The final table gives the azimuth of *Polaris*.



# CONVERSION OF ARC TO TIME

| 0°–59° | | 60°–119° | | 120°–179° | | 180°–239° | | 240°–299° | | 300°–359° | | | 0′·00 | 0′·25 | 0′·50 | 0′·75 |
|---|---|---|---|---|---|---|---|---|---|---|---|---|---|---|---|---|
| ° | h m | ° | h m | ° | h m | ° | h m | ° | h m | ° | h m | ′ | m s | m s | m s | m s |
| **0** | 0 00 | **60** | 4 00 | **120** | 8 00 | **180** | 12 00 | **240** | 16 00 | **300** | 20 00 | **0** | 0 00 | 0 01 | 0 02 | 0 03 |
| **1** | 0 04 | **61** | 4 04 | **121** | 8 04 | **181** | 12 04 | **241** | 16 04 | **301** | 20 04 | **1** | 0 04 | 0 05 | 0 06 | 0 07 |
| **2** | 0 08 | **62** | 4 08 | **122** | 8 08 | **182** | 12 08 | **242** | 16 08 | **302** | 20 08 | **2** | 0 08 | 0 09 | 0 10 | 0 11 |
| **3** | 0 12 | **63** | 4 12 | **123** | 8 12 | **183** | 12 12 | **243** | 16 12 | **303** | 20 12 | **3** | 0 12 | 0 13 | 0 14 | 0 15 |
| **4** | 0 16 | **64** | 4 16 | **124** | 8 16 | **184** | 12 16 | **244** | 16 16 | **304** | 20 16 | **4** | 0 16 | 0 17 | 0 18 | 0 19 |
| **5** | 0 20 | **65** | 4 20 | **125** | 8 20 | **185** | 12 20 | **245** | 16 20 | **305** | 20 20 | **5** | 0 20 | 0 21 | 0 22 | 0 23 |
| **6** | 0 24 | **66** | 4 24 | **126** | 8 24 | **186** | 12 24 | **246** | 16 24 | **306** | 20 24 | **6** | 0 24 | 0 25 | 0 26 | 0 27 |
| **7** | 0 28 | **67** | 4 28 | **127** | 8 28 | **187** | 12 28 | **247** | 16 28 | **307** | 20 28 | **7** | 0 28 | 0 29 | 0 30 | 0 31 |
| **8** | 0 32 | **68** | 4 32 | **128** | 8 32 | **188** | 12 32 | **248** | 16 32 | **308** | 20 32 | **8** | 0 32 | 0 33 | 0 34 | 0 35 |
| **9** | 0 36 | **69** | 4 36 | **129** | 8 36 | **189** | 12 36 | **249** | 16 36 | **309** | 20 36 | **9** | 0 36 | 0 37 | 0 38 | 0 39 |
| **10** | 0 40 | **70** | 4 40 | **130** | 8 40 | **190** | 12 40 | **250** | 16 40 | **310** | 20 40 | **10** | 0 40 | 0 41 | 0 42 | 0 43 |
| **11** | 0 44 | **71** | 4 44 | **131** | 8 44 | **191** | 12 44 | **251** | 16 44 | **311** | 20 44 | **11** | 0 44 | 0 45 | 0 46 | 0 47 |
| **12** | 0 48 | **72** | 4 48 | **132** | 8 48 | **192** | 12 48 | **252** | 16 48 | **312** | 20 48 | **12** | 0 48 | 0 49 | 0 50 | 0 51 |
| **13** | 0 52 | **73** | 4 52 | **133** | 8 52 | **193** | 12 52 | **253** | 16 52 | **313** | 20 52 | **13** | 0 52 | 0 53 | 0 54 | 0 55 |
| **14** | 0 56 | **74** | 4 56 | **134** | 8 56 | **194** | 12 56 | **254** | 16 56 | **314** | 20 56 | **14** | 0 56 | 0 57 | 0 58 | 0 59 |
| **15** | 1 00 | **75** | 5 00 | **135** | 9 00 | **195** | 13 00 | **255** | 17 00 | **315** | 21 00 | **15** | 1 00 | 1 01 | 1 02 | 1 03 |
| **16** | 1 04 | **76** | 5 04 | **136** | 9 04 | **196** | 13 04 | **256** | 17 04 | **316** | 21 04 | **16** | 1 04 | 1 05 | 1 06 | 1 07 |
| **17** | 1 08 | **77** | 5 08 | **137** | 9 08 | **197** | 13 08 | **257** | 17 08 | **317** | 21 08 | **17** | 1 08 | 1 09 | 1 10 | 1 11 |
| **18** | 1 12 | **78** | 5 12 | **138** | 9 12 | **198** | 13 12 | **258** | 17 12 | **318** | 21 12 | **18** | 1 12 | 1 13 | 1 14 | 1 15 |
| **19** | 1 16 | **79** | 5 16 | **139** | 9 16 | **199** | 13 16 | **259** | 17 16 | **319** | 21 16 | **19** | 1 16 | 1 17 | 1 18 | 1 19 |
| **20** | 1 20 | **80** | 5 20 | **140** | 9 20 | **200** | 13 20 | **260** | 17 20 | **320** | 21 20 | **20** | 1 20 | 1 21 | 1 22 | 1 23 |
| **21** | 1 24 | **81** | 5 24 | **141** | 9 24 | **201** | 13 24 | **261** | 17 24 | **321** | 21 24 | **21** | 1 24 | 1 25 | 1 26 | 1 27 |
| **22** | 1 28 | **82** | 5 28 | **142** | 9 28 | **202** | 13 28 | **262** | 17 28 | **322** | 21 28 | **22** | 1 28 | 1 29 | 1 30 | 1 31 |
| **23** | 1 32 | **83** | 5 32 | **143** | 9 32 | **203** | 13 32 | **263** | 17 32 | **323** | 21 32 | **23** | 1 32 | 1 33 | 1 34 | 1 35 |
| **24** | 1 36 | **84** | 5 36 | **144** | 9 36 | **204** | 13 36 | **264** | 17 36 | **324** | 21 36 | **24** | 1 36 | 1 37 | 1 38 | 1 39 |
| **25** | 1 40 | **85** | 5 40 | **145** | 9 40 | **205** | 13 40 | **265** | 17 40 | **325** | 21 40 | **25** | 1 40 | 1 41 | 1 42 | 1 43 |
| **26** | 1 44 | **86** | 5 44 | **146** | 9 44 | **206** | 13 44 | **266** | 17 44 | **326** | 21 44 | **26** | 1 44 | 1 45 | 1 46 | 1 47 |
| **27** | 1 48 | **87** | 5 48 | **147** | 9 48 | **207** | 13 48 | **267** | 17 48 | **327** | 21 48 | **27** | 1 48 | 1 49 | 1 50 | 1 51 |
| **28** | 1 52 | **88** | 5 52 | **148** | 9 52 | **208** | 13 52 | **268** | 17 52 | **328** | 21 52 | **28** | 1 52 | 1 53 | 1 54 | 1 55 |
| **29** | 1 56 | **89** | 5 56 | **149** | 9 56 | **209** | 13 56 | **269** | 17 56 | **329** | 21 56 | **29** | 1 56 | 1 57 | 1 58 | 1 59 |
| **30** | 2 00 | **90** | 6 00 | **150** | 10 00 | **210** | 14 00 | **270** | 18 00 | **330** | 22 00 | **30** | 2 00 | 2 01 | 2 02 | 2 03 |
| **31** | 2 04 | **91** | 6 04 | **151** | 10 04 | **211** | 14 04 | **271** | 18 04 | **331** | 22 04 | **31** | 2 04 | 2 05 | 2 06 | 2 07 |
| **32** | 2 08 | **92** | 6 08 | **152** | 10 08 | **212** | 14 08 | **272** | 18 08 | **332** | 22 08 | **32** | 2 08 | 2 09 | 2 10 | 2 11 |
| **33** | 2 12 | **93** | 6 12 | **153** | 10 12 | **213** | 14 12 | **273** | 18 12 | **333** | 22 12 | **33** | 2 12 | 2 13 | 2 14 | 2 15 |
| **34** | 2 16 | **94** | 6 16 | **154** | 10 16 | **214** | 14 16 | **274** | 18 16 | **334** | 22 16 | **34** | 2 16 | 2 17 | 2 18 | 2 19 |
| **35** | 2 20 | **95** | 6 20 | **155** | 10 20 | **215** | 14 20 | **275** | 18 20 | **335** | 22 20 | **35** | 2 20 | 2 21 | 2 22 | 2 23 |
| **36** | 2 24 | **96** | 6 24 | **156** | 10 24 | **216** | 14 24 | **276** | 18 24 | **336** | 22 24 | **36** | 2 24 | 2 25 | 2 26 | 2 27 |
| **37** | 2 28 | **97** | 6 28 | **157** | 10 28 | **217** | 14 28 | **277** | 18 28 | **337** | 22 28 | **37** | 2 28 | 2 29 | 2 30 | 2 31 |
| **38** | 2 32 | **98** | 6 32 | **158** | 10 32 | **218** | 14 32 | **278** | 18 32 | **338** | 22 32 | **38** | 2 32 | 2 33 | 2 34 | 2 35 |
| **39** | 2 36 | **99** | 6 36 | **159** | 10 36 | **219** | 14 36 | **279** | 18 36 | **339** | 22 36 | **39** | 2 36 | 2 37 | 2 38 | 2 39 |
| **40** | 2 40 | **100** | 6 40 | **160** | 10 40 | **220** | 14 40 | **280** | 18 40 | **340** | 22 40 | **40** | 2 40 | 2 41 | 2 42 | 2 43 |
| **41** | 2 44 | **101** | 6 44 | **161** | 10 44 | **221** | 14 44 | **281** | 18 44 | **341** | 22 44 | **41** | 2 44 | 2 45 | 2 46 | 2 47 |
| **42** | 2 48 | **102** | 6 48 | **162** | 10 48 | **222** | 14 48 | **282** | 18 48 | **342** | 22 48 | **42** | 2 48 | 2 49 | 2 50 | 2 51 |
| **43** | 2 52 | **103** | 6 52 | **163** | 10 52 | **223** | 14 52 | **283** | 18 52 | **343** | 22 52 | **43** | 2 52 | 2 53 | 2 54 | 2 55 |
| **44** | 2 56 | **104** | 6 56 | **164** | 10 56 | **224** | 14 56 | **284** | 18 56 | **344** | 22 56 | **44** | 2 56 | 2 57 | 2 58 | 2 59 |
| **45** | 3 00 | **105** | 7 00 | **165** | 11 00 | **225** | 15 00 | **285** | 19 00 | **345** | 23 00 | **45** | 3 00 | 3 01 | 3 02 | 3 03 |
| **46** | 3 04 | **106** | 7 04 | **166** | 11 04 | **226** | 15 04 | **286** | 19 04 | **346** | 23 04 | **46** | 3 04 | 3 05 | 3 06 | 3 07 |
| **47** | 3 08 | **107** | 7 08 | **167** | 11 08 | **227** | 15 08 | **287** | 19 08 | **347** | 23 08 | **47** | 3 08 | 3 09 | 3 10 | 3 11 |
| **48** | 3 12 | **108** | 7 12 | **168** | 11 12 | **228** | 15 12 | **288** | 19 12 | **348** | 23 12 | **48** | 3 12 | 3 13 | 3 14 | 3 15 |
| **49** | 3 16 | **109** | 7 16 | **169** | 11 16 | **229** | 15 16 | **289** | 19 16 | **349** | 23 16 | **49** | 3 16 | 3 17 | 3 18 | 3 19 |
| **50** | 3 20 | **110** | 7 20 | **170** | 11 20 | **230** | 15 20 | **290** | 19 20 | **350** | 23 20 | **50** | 3 20 | 3 21 | 3 22 | 3 23 |
| **51** | 3 24 | **111** | 7 24 | **171** | 11 24 | **231** | 15 24 | **291** | 19 24 | **351** | 23 24 | **51** | 3 24 | 3 25 | 3 26 | 3 27 |
| **52** | 3 28 | **112** | 7 28 | **172** | 11 28 | **232** | 15 28 | **292** | 19 28 | **352** | 23 28 | **52** | 3 28 | 3 29 | 3 30 | 3 31 |
| **53** | 3 32 | **113** | 7 32 | **173** | 11 32 | **233** | 15 32 | **293** | 19 32 | **353** | 23 32 | **53** | 3 32 | 3 33 | 3 34 | 3 35 |
| **54** | 3 36 | **114** | 7 36 | **174** | 11 36 | **234** | 15 36 | **294** | 19 36 | **354** | 23 36 | **54** | 3 36 | 3 37 | 3 38 | 3 39 |
| **55** | 3 40 | **115** | 7 40 | **175** | 11 40 | **235** | 15 40 | **295** | 19 40 | **355** | 23 40 | **55** | 3 40 | 3 41 | 3 42 | 3 43 |
| **56** | 3 44 | **116** | 7 44 | **176** | 11 44 | **236** | 15 44 | **296** | 19 44 | **356** | 23 44 | **56** | 3 44 | 3 45 | 3 46 | 3 47 |
| **57** | 3 48 | **117** | 7 48 | **177** | 11 48 | **237** | 15 48 | **297** | 19 48 | **357** | 23 48 | **57** | 3 48 | 3 49 | 3 50 | 3 51 |
| **58** | 3 52 | **118** | 7 52 | **178** | 11 52 | **238** | 15 52 | **298** | 19 52 | **358** | 23 52 | **58** | 3 52 | 3 53 | 3 54 | 3 55 |
| **59** | 3 56 | **119** | 7 56 | **179** | 11 56 | **239** | 15 56 | **299** | 19 56 | **359** | 23 56 | **59** | 3 56 | 3 57 | 3 58 | 3 59 |

The above table is for converting expressions in arc to their equivalent in time; its main use in this Almanac is for the conversion of longitude for application to L.M.T. (*added* if *west*, *subtracted* if *east*) to give G.M.T. or vice versa, particularly in the case of sunrise, sunset, etc.

0ᵐ INCREMENTS AND CORRECTIONS 1ᵐ

| 0ᵐ s | SUN PLANETS ° ′ | ARIES ° ′ | MOON ° ′ | v or d ′ | Corrⁿ ′ | v or d ′ | Corrⁿ ′ | v or d ′ | Corrⁿ ′ |
|---|---|---|---|---|---|---|---|---|---|
| 00 | 0 00.0 | 0 00.0 | 0 00.0 | 0.0 | 0.0 | 6.0 | 0.1 | 12.0 | 0.1 |
| 01 | 0 00.3 | 0 00.3 | 0 00.2 | 0.1 | 0.0 | 6.1 | 0.1 | 12.1 | 0.1 |
| 02 | 0 00.5 | 0 00.5 | 0 00.5 | 0.2 | 0.0 | 6.2 | 0.1 | 12.2 | 0.1 |
| 03 | 0 00.8 | 0 00.8 | 0 00.7 | 0.3 | 0.0 | 6.3 | 0.1 | 12.3 | 0.1 |
| 04 | 0 01.0 | 0 01.0 | 0 01.0 | 0.4 | 0.0 | 6.4 | 0.1 | 12.4 | 0.1 |
| 05 | 0 01.3 | 0 01.3 | 0 01.2 | 0.5 | 0.0 | 6.5 | 0.1 | 12.5 | 0.1 |
| 06 | 0 01.5 | 0 01.5 | 0 01.4 | 0.6 | 0.0 | 6.6 | 0.1 | 12.6 | 0.1 |
| 07 | 0 01.8 | 0 01.8 | 0 01.7 | 0.7 | 0.0 | 6.7 | 0.1 | 12.7 | 0.1 |
| 08 | 0 02.0 | 0 02.0 | 0 01.9 | 0.8 | 0.0 | 6.8 | 0.1 | 12.8 | 0.1 |
| 09 | 0 02.3 | 0 02.3 | 0 02.1 | 0.9 | 0.0 | 6.9 | 0.1 | 12.9 | 0.1 |
| 10 | 0 02.5 | 0 02.5 | 0 02.4 | 1.0 | 0.0 | 7.0 | 0.1 | 13.0 | 0.1 |
| 11 | 0 02.8 | 0 02.8 | 0 02.6 | 1.1 | 0.0 | 7.1 | 0.1 | 13.1 | 0.1 |
| 12 | 0 03.0 | 0 03.0 | 0 02.9 | 1.2 | 0.0 | 7.2 | 0.1 | 13.2 | 0.1 |
| 13 | 0 03.3 | 0 03.3 | 0 03.1 | 1.3 | 0.0 | 7.3 | 0.1 | 13.3 | 0.1 |
| 14 | 0 03.5 | 0 03.5 | 0 03.3 | 1.4 | 0.0 | 7.4 | 0.1 | 13.4 | 0.1 |
| 15 | 0 03.8 | 0 03.8 | 0 03.6 | 1.5 | 0.0 | 7.5 | 0.1 | 13.5 | 0.1 |
| 16 | 0 04.0 | 0 04.0 | 0 03.8 | 1.6 | 0.0 | 7.6 | 0.1 | 13.6 | 0.1 |
| 17 | 0 04.3 | 0 04.3 | 0 04.1 | 1.7 | 0.0 | 7.7 | 0.1 | 13.7 | 0.1 |
| 18 | 0 04.5 | 0 04.5 | 0 04.3 | 1.8 | 0.0 | 7.8 | 0.1 | 13.8 | 0.1 |
| 19 | 0 04.8 | 0 04.8 | 0 04.5 | 1.9 | 0.0 | 7.9 | 0.1 | 13.9 | 0.1 |
| 20 | 0 05.0 | 0 05.0 | 0 04.8 | 2.0 | 0.0 | 8.0 | 0.1 | 14.0 | 0.1 |
| 21 | 0 05.3 | 0 05.3 | 0 05.0 | 2.1 | 0.0 | 8.1 | 0.1 | 14.1 | 0.1 |
| 22 | 0 05.5 | 0 05.5 | 0 05.2 | 2.2 | 0.0 | 8.2 | 0.1 | 14.2 | 0.1 |
| 23 | 0 05.8 | 0 05.8 | 0 05.5 | 2.3 | 0.0 | 8.3 | 0.1 | 14.3 | 0.1 |
| 24 | 0 06.0 | 0 06.0 | 0 05.7 | 2.4 | 0.0 | 8.4 | 0.1 | 14.4 | 0.1 |
| 25 | 0 06.3 | 0 06.3 | 0 06.0 | 2.5 | 0.0 | 8.5 | 0.1 | 14.5 | 0.1 |
| 26 | 0 06.5 | 0 06.5 | 0 06.2 | 2.6 | 0.0 | 8.6 | 0.1 | 14.6 | 0.1 |
| 27 | 0 06.8 | 0 06.8 | 0 06.4 | 2.7 | 0.0 | 8.7 | 0.1 | 14.7 | 0.1 |
| 28 | 0 07.0 | 0 07.0 | 0 06.7 | 2.8 | 0.0 | 8.8 | 0.1 | 14.8 | 0.1 |
| 29 | 0 07.3 | 0 07.3 | 0 06.9 | 2.9 | 0.0 | 8.9 | 0.1 | 14.9 | 0.1 |
| 30 | 0 07.5 | 0 07.5 | 0 07.2 | 3.0 | 0.0 | 9.0 | 0.1 | 15.0 | 0.1 |
| 31 | 0 07.8 | 0 07.8 | 0 07.4 | 3.1 | 0.0 | 9.1 | 0.1 | 15.1 | 0.1 |
| 32 | 0 08.0 | 0 08.0 | 0 07.6 | 3.2 | 0.0 | 9.2 | 0.1 | 15.2 | 0.1 |
| 33 | 0 08.3 | 0 08.3 | 0 07.9 | 3.3 | 0.0 | 9.3 | 0.1 | 15.3 | 0.1 |
| 34 | 0 08.5 | 0 08.5 | 0 08.1 | 3.4 | 0.0 | 9.4 | 0.1 | 15.4 | 0.1 |
| 35 | 0 08.8 | 0 08.8 | 0 08.4 | 3.5 | 0.0 | 9.5 | 0.1 | 15.5 | 0.1 |
| 36 | 0 09.0 | 0 09.0 | 0 08.6 | 3.6 | 0.0 | 9.6 | 0.1 | 15.6 | 0.1 |
| 37 | 0 09.3 | 0 09.3 | 0 08.8 | 3.7 | 0.0 | 9.7 | 0.1 | 15.7 | 0.1 |
| 38 | 0 09.5 | 0 09.5 | 0 09.1 | 3.8 | 0.0 | 9.8 | 0.1 | 15.8 | 0.1 |
| 39 | 0 09.8 | 0 09.8 | 0 09.3 | 3.9 | 0.0 | 9.9 | 0.1 | 15.9 | 0.1 |
| 40 | 0 10.0 | 0 10.0 | 0 09.5 | 4.0 | 0.0 | 10.0 | 0.1 | 16.0 | 0.1 |
| 41 | 0 10.3 | 0 10.3 | 0 09.8 | 4.1 | 0.0 | 10.1 | 0.1 | 16.1 | 0.1 |
| 42 | 0 10.5 | 0 10.5 | 0 10.0 | 4.2 | 0.0 | 10.2 | 0.1 | 16.2 | 0.1 |
| 43 | 0 10.8 | 0 10.8 | 0 10.3 | 4.3 | 0.0 | 10.3 | 0.1 | 16.3 | 0.1 |
| 44 | 0 11.0 | 0 11.0 | 0 10.5 | 4.4 | 0.0 | 10.4 | 0.1 | 16.4 | 0.1 |
| 45 | 0 11.3 | 0 11.3 | 0 10.7 | 4.5 | 0.0 | 10.5 | 0.1 | 16.5 | 0.1 |
| 46 | 0 11.5 | 0 11.5 | 0 11.0 | 4.6 | 0.0 | 10.6 | 0.1 | 16.6 | 0.1 |
| 47 | 0 11.8 | 0 11.8 | 0 11.2 | 4.7 | 0.0 | 10.7 | 0.1 | 16.7 | 0.1 |
| 48 | 0 12.0 | 0 12.0 | 0 11.5 | 4.8 | 0.0 | 10.8 | 0.1 | 16.8 | 0.1 |
| 49 | 0 12.3 | 0 12.3 | 0 11.7 | 4.9 | 0.0 | 10.9 | 0.1 | 16.9 | 0.1 |
| 50 | 0 12.5 | 0 12.5 | 0 11.9 | 5.0 | 0.0 | 11.0 | 0.1 | 17.0 | 0.1 |
| 51 | 0 12.8 | 0 12.8 | 0 12.2 | 5.1 | 0.0 | 11.1 | 0.1 | 17.1 | 0.1 |
| 52 | 0 13.0 | 0 13.0 | 0 12.4 | 5.2 | 0.0 | 11.2 | 0.1 | 17.2 | 0.1 |
| 53 | 0 13.3 | 0 13.3 | 0 12.6 | 5.3 | 0.0 | 11.3 | 0.1 | 17.3 | 0.1 |
| 54 | 0 13.5 | 0 13.5 | 0 12.9 | 5.4 | 0.0 | 11.4 | 0.1 | 17.4 | 0.1 |
| 55 | 0 13.8 | 0 13.8 | 0 13.1 | 5.5 | 0.0 | 11.5 | 0.1 | 17.5 | 0.1 |
| 56 | 0 14.0 | 0 14.0 | 0 13.4 | 5.6 | 0.0 | 11.6 | 0.1 | 17.6 | 0.1 |
| 57 | 0 14.3 | 0 14.3 | 0 13.6 | 5.7 | 0.0 | 11.7 | 0.1 | 17.7 | 0.1 |
| 58 | 0 14.5 | 0 14.5 | 0 13.8 | 5.8 | 0.0 | 11.8 | 0.1 | 17.8 | 0.1 |
| 59 | 0 14.8 | 0 14.8 | 0 14.1 | 5.9 | 0.0 | 11.9 | 0.1 | 17.9 | 0.1 |
| 60 | 0 15.0 | 0 15.0 | 0 14.3 | 6.0 | 0.1 | 12.0 | 0.1 | 18.0 | 0.2 |

| 1ᵐ s | SUN PLANETS ° ′ | ARIES ° ′ | MOON ° ′ | v or d ′ | Corrⁿ ′ | v or d ′ | Corrⁿ ′ | v or d ′ | Corrⁿ ′ |
|---|---|---|---|---|---|---|---|---|---|
| 00 | 0 15.0 | 0 15.0 | 0 14.3 | 0.0 | 0.0 | 6.0 | 0.2 | 12.0 | 0.3 |
| 01 | 0 15.3 | 0 15.3 | 0 14.6 | 0.1 | 0.0 | 6.1 | 0.2 | 12.1 | 0.3 |
| 02 | 0 15.5 | 0 15.5 | 0 14.8 | 0.2 | 0.0 | 6.2 | 0.2 | 12.2 | 0.3 |
| 03 | 0 15.8 | 0 15.8 | 0 15.0 | 0.3 | 0.0 | 6.3 | 0.2 | 12.3 | 0.3 |
| 04 | 0 16.0 | 0 16.0 | 0 15.3 | 0.4 | 0.0 | 6.4 | 0.2 | 12.4 | 0.3 |
| 05 | 0 16.3 | 0 16.3 | 0 15.5 | 0.5 | 0.0 | 6.5 | 0.2 | 12.5 | 0.3 |
| 06 | 0 16.5 | 0 16.5 | 0 15.7 | 0.6 | 0.0 | 6.6 | 0.2 | 12.6 | 0.3 |
| 07 | 0 16.8 | 0 16.8 | 0 16.0 | 0.7 | 0.0 | 6.7 | 0.2 | 12.7 | 0.3 |
| 08 | 0 17.0 | 0 17.0 | 0 16.2 | 0.8 | 0.0 | 6.8 | 0.2 | 12.8 | 0.3 |
| 09 | 0 17.3 | 0 17.3 | 0 16.5 | 0.9 | 0.0 | 6.9 | 0.2 | 12.9 | 0.3 |
| 10 | 0 17.5 | 0 17.5 | 0 16.7 | 1.0 | 0.0 | 7.0 | 0.2 | 13.0 | 0.3 |
| 11 | 0 17.8 | 0 17.8 | 0 16.9 | 1.1 | 0.0 | 7.1 | 0.2 | 13.1 | 0.3 |
| 12 | 0 18.0 | 0 18.0 | 0 17.2 | 1.2 | 0.0 | 7.2 | 0.2 | 13.2 | 0.3 |
| 13 | 0 18.3 | 0 18.3 | 0 17.4 | 1.3 | 0.0 | 7.3 | 0.2 | 13.3 | 0.3 |
| 14 | 0 18.5 | 0 18.6 | 0 17.7 | 1.4 | 0.0 | 7.4 | 0.2 | 13.4 | 0.3 |
| 15 | 0 18.8 | 0 18.8 | 0 17.9 | 1.5 | 0.0 | 7.5 | 0.2 | 13.5 | 0.3 |
| 16 | 0 19.0 | 0 19.1 | 0 18.1 | 1.6 | 0.0 | 7.6 | 0.2 | 13.6 | 0.3 |
| 17 | 0 19.3 | 0 19.3 | 0 18.4 | 1.7 | 0.0 | 7.7 | 0.2 | 13.7 | 0.3 |
| 18 | 0 19.5 | 0 19.6 | 0 18.6 | 1.8 | 0.0 | 7.8 | 0.2 | 13.8 | 0.3 |
| 19 | 0 19.8 | 0 19.8 | 0 18.9 | 1.9 | 0.0 | 7.9 | 0.2 | 13.9 | 0.3 |
| 20 | 0 20.0 | 0 20.1 | 0 19.1 | 2.0 | 0.1 | 8.0 | 0.2 | 14.0 | 0.4 |
| 21 | 0 20.3 | 0 20.3 | 0 19.3 | 2.1 | 0.1 | 8.1 | 0.2 | 14.1 | 0.4 |
| 22 | 0 20.5 | 0 20.6 | 0 19.6 | 2.2 | 0.1 | 8.2 | 0.2 | 14.2 | 0.4 |
| 23 | 0 20.8 | 0 20.8 | 0 19.8 | 2.3 | 0.1 | 8.3 | 0.2 | 14.3 | 0.4 |
| 24 | 0 21.0 | 0 21.1 | 0 20.0 | 2.4 | 0.1 | 8.4 | 0.2 | 14.4 | 0.4 |
| 25 | 0 21.3 | 0 21.3 | 0 20.3 | 2.5 | 0.1 | 8.5 | 0.2 | 14.5 | 0.4 |
| 26 | 0 21.5 | 0 21.6 | 0 20.5 | 2.6 | 0.1 | 8.6 | 0.2 | 14.6 | 0.4 |
| 27 | 0 21.8 | 0 21.8 | 0 20.8 | 2.7 | 0.1 | 8.7 | 0.2 | 14.7 | 0.4 |
| 28 | 0 22.0 | 0 22.1 | 0 21.0 | 2.8 | 0.1 | 8.8 | 0.2 | 14.8 | 0.4 |
| 29 | 0 22.3 | 0 22.3 | 0 21.2 | 2.9 | 0.1 | 8.9 | 0.2 | 14.9 | 0.4 |
| 30 | 0 22.5 | 0 22.6 | 0 21.5 | 3.0 | 0.1 | 9.0 | 0.2 | 15.0 | 0.4 |
| 31 | 0 22.8 | 0 22.8 | 0 21.7 | 3.1 | 0.1 | 9.1 | 0.2 | 15.1 | 0.4 |
| 32 | 0 23.0 | 0 23.1 | 0 22.0 | 3.2 | 0.1 | 9.2 | 0.2 | 15.2 | 0.4 |
| 33 | 0 23.3 | 0 23.3 | 0 22.2 | 3.3 | 0.1 | 9.3 | 0.2 | 15.3 | 0.4 |
| 34 | 0 23.5 | 0 23.6 | 0 22.4 | 3.4 | 0.1 | 9.4 | 0.2 | 15.4 | 0.4 |
| 35 | 0 23.8 | 0 23.8 | 0 22.7 | 3.5 | 0.1 | 9.5 | 0.2 | 15.5 | 0.4 |
| 36 | 0 24.0 | 0 24.1 | 0 22.9 | 3.6 | 0.1 | 9.6 | 0.2 | 15.6 | 0.4 |
| 37 | 0 24.3 | 0 24.3 | 0 23.1 | 3.7 | 0.1 | 9.7 | 0.2 | 15.7 | 0.4 |
| 38 | 0 24.5 | 0 24.6 | 0 23.4 | 3.8 | 0.1 | 9.8 | 0.2 | 15.8 | 0.4 |
| 39 | 0 24.8 | 0 24.8 | 0 23.6 | 3.9 | 0.1 | 9.9 | 0.2 | 15.9 | 0.4 |
| 40 | 0 25.0 | 0 25.1 | 0 23.9 | 4.0 | 0.1 | 10.0 | 0.3 | 16.0 | 0.4 |
| 41 | 0 25.3 | 0 25.3 | 0 24.1 | 4.1 | 0.1 | 10.1 | 0.3 | 16.1 | 0.4 |
| 42 | 0 25.5 | 0 25.6 | 0 24.3 | 4.2 | 0.1 | 10.2 | 0.3 | 16.2 | 0.4 |
| 43 | 0 25.8 | 0 25.8 | 0 24.6 | 4.3 | 0.1 | 10.3 | 0.3 | 16.3 | 0.4 |
| 44 | 0 26.0 | 0 26.1 | 0 24.8 | 4.4 | 0.1 | 10.4 | 0.3 | 16.4 | 0.4 |
| 45 | 0 26.3 | 0 26.3 | 0 25.1 | 4.5 | 0.1 | 10.5 | 0.3 | 16.5 | 0.4 |
| 46 | 0 26.5 | 0 26.6 | 0 25.3 | 4.6 | 0.1 | 10.6 | 0.3 | 16.6 | 0.4 |
| 47 | 0 26.8 | 0 26.8 | 0 25.5 | 4.7 | 0.1 | 10.7 | 0.3 | 16.7 | 0.4 |
| 48 | 0 27.0 | 0 27.1 | 0 25.8 | 4.8 | 0.1 | 10.8 | 0.3 | 16.8 | 0.4 |
| 49 | 0 27.3 | 0 27.3 | 0 26.0 | 4.9 | 0.1 | 10.9 | 0.3 | 16.9 | 0.4 |
| 50 | 0 27.5 | 0 27.6 | 0 26.2 | 5.0 | 0.1 | 11.0 | 0.3 | 17.0 | 0.4 |
| 51 | 0 27.8 | 0 27.8 | 0 26.5 | 5.1 | 0.1 | 11.1 | 0.3 | 17.1 | 0.4 |
| 52 | 0 28.0 | 0 28.1 | 0 26.7 | 5.2 | 0.1 | 11.2 | 0.3 | 17.2 | 0.4 |
| 53 | 0 28.3 | 0 28.3 | 0 27.0 | 5.3 | 0.1 | 11.3 | 0.3 | 17.3 | 0.4 |
| 54 | 0 28.5 | 0 28.6 | 0 27.2 | 5.4 | 0.1 | 11.4 | 0.3 | 17.4 | 0.4 |
| 55 | 0 28.8 | 0 28.8 | 0 27.4 | 5.5 | 0.1 | 11.5 | 0.3 | 17.5 | 0.4 |
| 56 | 0 29.0 | 0 29.1 | 0 27.7 | 5.6 | 0.1 | 11.6 | 0.3 | 17.6 | 0.4 |
| 57 | 0 29.3 | 0 29.3 | 0 27.9 | 5.7 | 0.1 | 11.7 | 0.3 | 17.7 | 0.4 |
| 58 | 0 29.5 | 0 29.6 | 0 28.2 | 5.8 | 0.1 | 11.8 | 0.3 | 17.8 | 0.4 |
| 59 | 0 29.8 | 0 29.8 | 0 28.4 | 5.9 | 0.1 | 11.9 | 0.3 | 17.9 | 0.4 |
| 60 | 0 30.0 | 0 30.1 | 0 28.6 | 6.0 | 0.2 | 12.0 | 0.3 | 18.0 | 0.5 |

2ᵐ INCREMENTS AND CORRECTIONS 3ᵐ

| 2ᵐ s | SUN PLANETS ° ′ | ARIES ° ′ | MOON ° ′ | v or d ′ | Corrⁿ ′ | v or d ′ | Corrⁿ ′ | v or d ′ | Corrⁿ ′ |
|---|---|---|---|---|---|---|---|---|---|
| 00 | 0 30.0 | 0 30.1 | 0 28.6 | 0.0 | 0.0 | 6.0 | 0.3 | 12.0 | 0.5 |
| 01 | 0 30.3 | 0 30.3 | 0 28.9 | 0.1 | 0.0 | 6.1 | 0.3 | 12.1 | 0.5 |
| 02 | 0 30.5 | 0 30.6 | 0 29.1 | 0.2 | 0.0 | 6.2 | 0.3 | 12.2 | 0.5 |
| 03 | 0 30.8 | 0 30.8 | 0 29.3 | 0.3 | 0.0 | 6.3 | 0.3 | 12.3 | 0.5 |
| 04 | 0 31.0 | 0 31.1 | 0 29.6 | 0.4 | 0.0 | 6.4 | 0.3 | 12.4 | 0.5 |
| 05 | 0 31.3 | 0 31.3 | 0 29.8 | 0.5 | 0.0 | 6.5 | 0.3 | 12.5 | 0.5 |
| 06 | 0 31.5 | 0 31.6 | 0 30.1 | 0.6 | 0.0 | 6.6 | 0.3 | 12.6 | 0.5 |
| 07 | 0 31.8 | 0 31.8 | 0 30.3 | 0.7 | 0.0 | 6.7 | 0.3 | 12.7 | 0.5 |
| 08 | 0 32.0 | 0 32.1 | 0 30.5 | 0.8 | 0.0 | 6.8 | 0.3 | 12.8 | 0.5 |
| 09 | 0 32.3 | 0 32.3 | 0 30.8 | 0.9 | 0.0 | 6.9 | 0.3 | 12.9 | 0.5 |
| 10 | 0 32.5 | 0 32.6 | 0 31.0 | 1.0 | 0.0 | 7.0 | 0.3 | 13.0 | 0.5 |
| 11 | 0 32.8 | 0 32.8 | 0 31.3 | 1.1 | 0.0 | 7.1 | 0.3 | 13.1 | 0.5 |
| 12 | 0 33.0 | 0 33.1 | 0 31.5 | 1.2 | 0.1 | 7.2 | 0.3 | 13.2 | 0.6 |
| 13 | 0 33.3 | 0 33.3 | 0 31.7 | 1.3 | 0.1 | 7.3 | 0.3 | 13.3 | 0.6 |
| 14 | 0 33.5 | 0 33.6 | 0 32.0 | 1.4 | 0.1 | 7.4 | 0.3 | 13.4 | 0.6 |
| 15 | 0 33.8 | 0 33.8 | 0 32.2 | 1.5 | 0.1 | 7.5 | 0.3 | 13.5 | 0.6 |
| 16 | 0 34.0 | 0 34.1 | 0 32.5 | 1.6 | 0.1 | 7.6 | 0.3 | 13.6 | 0.6 |
| 17 | 0 34.3 | 0 34.3 | 0 32.7 | 1.7 | 0.1 | 7.7 | 0.3 | 13.7 | 0.6 |
| 18 | 0 34.5 | 0 34.6 | 0 32.9 | 1.8 | 0.1 | 7.8 | 0.3 | 13.8 | 0.6 |
| 19 | 0 34.8 | 0 34.8 | 0 33.2 | 1.9 | 0.1 | 7.9 | 0.3 | 13.9 | 0.6 |
| 20 | 0 35.0 | 0 35.1 | 0 33.4 | 2.0 | 0.1 | 8.0 | 0.3 | 14.0 | 0.6 |
| 21 | 0 35.3 | 0 35.3 | 0 33.6 | 2.1 | 0.1 | 8.1 | 0.3 | 14.1 | 0.6 |
| 22 | 0 35.5 | 0 35.6 | 0 33.9 | 2.2 | 0.1 | 8.2 | 0.3 | 14.2 | 0.6 |
| 23 | 0 35.8 | 0 35.8 | 0 34.1 | 2.3 | 0.1 | 8.3 | 0.3 | 14.3 | 0.6 |
| 24 | 0 36.0 | 0 36.1 | 0 34.4 | 2.4 | 0.1 | 8.4 | 0.4 | 14.4 | 0.6 |
| 25 | 0 36.3 | 0 36.3 | 0 34.6 | 2.5 | 0.1 | 8.5 | 0.4 | 14.5 | 0.6 |
| 26 | 0 36.5 | 0 36.6 | 0 34.8 | 2.6 | 0.1 | 8.6 | 0.4 | 14.6 | 0.6 |
| 27 | 0 36.8 | 0 36.9 | 0 35.1 | 2.7 | 0.1 | 8.7 | 0.4 | 14.7 | 0.6 |
| 28 | 0 37.0 | 0 37.1 | 0 35.3 | 2.8 | 0.1 | 8.8 | 0.4 | 14.8 | 0.6 |
| 29 | 0 37.3 | 0 37.4 | 0 35.6 | 2.9 | 0.1 | 8.9 | 0.4 | 14.9 | 0.6 |
| 30 | 0 37.5 | 0 37.6 | 0 35.8 | 3.0 | 0.1 | 9.0 | 0.4 | 15.0 | 0.6 |
| 31 | 0 37.8 | 0 37.9 | 0 36.0 | 3.1 | 0.1 | 9.1 | 0.4 | 15.1 | 0.6 |
| 32 | 0 38.0 | 0 38.1 | 0 36.3 | 3.2 | 0.1 | 9.2 | 0.4 | 15.2 | 0.6 |
| 33 | 0 38.3 | 0 38.4 | 0 36.5 | 3.3 | 0.1 | 9.3 | 0.4 | 15.3 | 0.6 |
| 34 | 0 38.5 | 0 38.6 | 0 36.7 | 3.4 | 0.1 | 9.4 | 0.4 | 15.4 | 0.6 |
| 35 | 0 38.8 | 0 38.9 | 0 37.0 | 3.5 | 0.1 | 9.5 | 0.4 | 15.5 | 0.6 |
| 36 | 0 39.0 | 0 39.1 | 0 37.2 | 3.6 | 0.2 | 9.6 | 0.4 | 15.6 | 0.7 |
| 37 | 0 39.3 | 0 39.4 | 0 37.5 | 3.7 | 0.2 | 9.7 | 0.4 | 15.7 | 0.7 |
| 38 | 0 39.5 | 0 39.6 | 0 37.7 | 3.8 | 0.2 | 9.8 | 0.4 | 15.8 | 0.7 |
| 39 | 0 39.8 | 0 39.9 | 0 37.9 | 3.9 | 0.2 | 9.9 | 0.4 | 15.9 | 0.7 |
| 40 | 0 40.0 | 0 40.1 | 0 38.2 | 4.0 | 0.2 | 10.0 | 0.4 | 16.0 | 0.7 |
| 41 | 0 40.3 | 0 40.4 | 0 38.4 | 4.1 | 0.2 | 10.1 | 0.4 | 16.1 | 0.7 |
| 42 | 0 40.5 | 0 40.6 | 0 38.7 | 4.2 | 0.2 | 10.2 | 0.4 | 16.2 | 0.7 |
| 43 | 0 40.8 | 0 40.9 | 0 38.9 | 4.3 | 0.2 | 10.3 | 0.4 | 16.3 | 0.7 |
| 44 | 0 41.0 | 0 41.1 | 0 39.1 | 4.4 | 0.2 | 10.4 | 0.4 | 16.4 | 0.7 |
| 45 | 0 41.3 | 0 41.4 | 0 39.4 | 4.5 | 0.2 | 10.5 | 0.4 | 16.5 | 0.7 |
| 46 | 0 41.5 | 0 41.6 | 0 39.6 | 4.6 | 0.2 | 10.6 | 0.4 | 16.6 | 0.7 |
| 47 | 0 41.8 | 0 41.9 | 0 39.8 | 4.7 | 0.2 | 10.7 | 0.4 | 16.7 | 0.7 |
| 48 | 0 42.0 | 0 42.1 | 0 40.1 | 4.8 | 0.2 | 10.8 | 0.5 | 16.8 | 0.7 |
| 49 | 0 42.3 | 0 42.4 | 0 40.3 | 4.9 | 0.2 | 10.9 | 0.5 | 16.9 | 0.7 |
| 50 | 0 42.5 | 0 42.6 | 0 40.6 | 5.0 | 0.2 | 11.0 | 0.5 | 17.0 | 0.7 |
| 51 | 0 42.8 | 0 42.9 | 0 40.8 | 5.1 | 0.2 | 11.1 | 0.5 | 17.1 | 0.7 |
| 52 | 0 43.0 | 0 43.1 | 0 41.0 | 5.2 | 0.2 | 11.2 | 0.5 | 17.2 | 0.7 |
| 53 | 0 43.3 | 0 43.4 | 0 41.3 | 5.3 | 0.2 | 11.3 | 0.5 | 17.3 | 0.7 |
| 54 | 0 43.5 | 0 43.6 | 0 41.5 | 5.4 | 0.2 | 11.4 | 0.5 | 17.4 | 0.7 |
| 55 | 0 43.8 | 0 43.9 | 0 41.8 | 5.5 | 0.2 | 11.5 | 0.5 | 17.5 | 0.7 |
| 56 | 0 44.0 | 0 44.1 | 0 42.0 | 5.6 | 0.2 | 11.6 | 0.5 | 17.6 | 0.7 |
| 57 | 0 44.3 | 0 44.4 | 0 42.2 | 5.7 | 0.2 | 11.7 | 0.5 | 17.7 | 0.7 |
| 58 | 0 44.5 | 0 44.6 | 0 42.5 | 5.8 | 0.2 | 11.8 | 0.5 | 17.8 | 0.7 |
| 59 | 0 44.8 | 0 44.9 | 0 42.7 | 5.9 | 0.2 | 11.9 | 0.5 | 17.9 | 0.7 |
| 60 | 0 45.0 | 0 45.1 | 0 43.0 | 6.0 | 0.3 | 12.0 | 0.5 | 18.0 | 0.8 |

| 3ᵐ s | SUN PLANETS ° ′ | ARIES ° ′ | MOON ° ′ | v or d ′ | Corrⁿ ′ | v or d ′ | Corrⁿ ′ | v or d ′ | Corrⁿ ′ |
|---|---|---|---|---|---|---|---|---|---|
| 00 | 0 45.0 | 0 45.1 | 0 43.0 | 0.0 | 0.0 | 6.0 | 0.4 | 12.0 | 0.7 |
| 01 | 0 45.3 | 0 45.4 | 0 43.2 | 0.1 | 0.0 | 6.1 | 0.4 | 12.1 | 0.7 |
| 02 | 0 45.5 | 0 45.6 | 0 43.4 | 0.2 | 0.0 | 6.2 | 0.4 | 12.2 | 0.7 |
| 03 | 0 45.8 | 0 45.9 | 0 43.7 | 0.3 | 0.0 | 6.3 | 0.4 | 12.3 | 0.7 |
| 04 | 0 46.0 | 0 46.1 | 0 43.9 | 0.4 | 0.0 | 6.4 | 0.4 | 12.4 | 0.7 |
| 05 | 0 46.3 | 0 46.4 | 0 44.1 | 0.5 | 0.0 | 6.5 | 0.4 | 12.5 | 0.7 |
| 06 | 0 46.5 | 0 46.6 | 0 44.4 | 0.6 | 0.0 | 6.6 | 0.4 | 12.6 | 0.7 |
| 07 | 0 46.8 | 0 46.9 | 0 44.6 | 0.7 | 0.0 | 6.7 | 0.4 | 12.7 | 0.7 |
| 08 | 0 47.0 | 0 47.1 | 0 44.9 | 0.8 | 0.0 | 6.8 | 0.4 | 12.8 | 0.7 |
| 09 | 0 47.3 | 0 47.4 | 0 45.1 | 0.9 | 0.1 | 6.9 | 0.4 | 12.9 | 0.8 |
| 10 | 0 47.5 | 0 47.6 | 0 45.3 | 1.0 | 0.1 | 7.0 | 0.4 | 13.0 | 0.8 |
| 11 | 0 47.8 | 0 47.9 | 0 45.6 | 1.1 | 0.1 | 7.1 | 0.4 | 13.1 | 0.8 |
| 12 | 0 48.0 | 0 48.1 | 0 45.8 | 1.2 | 0.1 | 7.2 | 0.4 | 13.2 | 0.8 |
| 13 | 0 48.3 | 0 48.4 | 0 46.1 | 1.3 | 0.1 | 7.3 | 0.4 | 13.3 | 0.8 |
| 14 | 0 48.5 | 0 48.6 | 0 46.3 | 1.4 | 0.1 | 7.4 | 0.4 | 13.4 | 0.8 |
| 15 | 0 48.8 | 0 48.9 | 0 46.5 | 1.5 | 0.1 | 7.5 | 0.4 | 13.5 | 0.8 |
| 16 | 0 49.0 | 0 49.1 | 0 46.8 | 1.6 | 0.1 | 7.6 | 0.4 | 13.6 | 0.8 |
| 17 | 0 49.3 | 0 49.4 | 0 47.0 | 1.7 | 0.1 | 7.7 | 0.4 | 13.7 | 0.8 |
| 18 | 0 49.5 | 0 49.6 | 0 47.2 | 1.8 | 0.1 | 7.8 | 0.5 | 13.8 | 0.8 |
| 19 | 0 49.8 | 0 49.9 | 0 47.5 | 1.9 | 0.1 | 7.9 | 0.5 | 13.9 | 0.8 |
| 20 | 0 50.0 | 0 50.1 | 0 47.7 | 2.0 | 0.1 | 8.0 | 0.5 | 14.0 | 0.8 |
| 21 | 0 50.3 | 0 50.4 | 0 48.0 | 2.1 | 0.1 | 8.1 | 0.5 | 14.1 | 0.8 |
| 22 | 0 50.5 | 0 50.6 | 0 48.2 | 2.2 | 0.1 | 8.2 | 0.5 | 14.2 | 0.8 |
| 23 | 0 50.8 | 0 50.9 | 0 48.4 | 2.3 | 0.1 | 8.3 | 0.5 | 14.3 | 0.8 |
| 24 | 0 51.0 | 0 51.1 | 0 48.7 | 2.4 | 0.1 | 8.4 | 0.5 | 14.4 | 0.8 |
| 25 | 0 51.3 | 0 51.4 | 0 48.9 | 2.5 | 0.1 | 8.5 | 0.5 | 14.5 | 0.8 |
| 26 | 0 51.5 | 0 51.6 | 0 49.2 | 2.6 | 0.2 | 8.6 | 0.5 | 14.6 | 0.9 |
| 27 | 0 51.8 | 0 51.9 | 0 49.4 | 2.7 | 0.2 | 8.7 | 0.5 | 14.7 | 0.9 |
| 28 | 0 52.0 | 0 52.1 | 0 49.6 | 2.8 | 0.2 | 8.8 | 0.5 | 14.8 | 0.9 |
| 29 | 0 52.3 | 0 52.4 | 0 49.9 | 2.9 | 0.2 | 8.9 | 0.5 | 14.9 | 0.9 |
| 30 | 0 52.5 | 0 52.6 | 0 50.1 | 3.0 | 0.2 | 9.0 | 0.5 | 15.0 | 0.9 |
| 31 | 0 52.8 | 0 52.9 | 0 50.3 | 3.1 | 0.2 | 9.1 | 0.5 | 15.1 | 0.9 |
| 32 | 0 53.0 | 0 53.1 | 0 50.6 | 3.2 | 0.2 | 9.2 | 0.5 | 15.2 | 0.9 |
| 33 | 0 53.3 | 0 53.4 | 0 50.8 | 3.3 | 0.2 | 9.3 | 0.5 | 15.3 | 0.9 |
| 34 | 0 53.5 | 0 53.6 | 0 51.1 | 3.4 | 0.2 | 9.4 | 0.5 | 15.4 | 0.9 |
| 35 | 0 53.8 | 0 53.9 | 0 51.3 | 3.5 | 0.2 | 9.5 | 0.6 | 15.5 | 0.9 |
| 36 | 0 54.0 | 0 54.1 | 0 51.5 | 3.6 | 0.2 | 9.6 | 0.6 | 15.6 | 0.9 |
| 37 | 0 54.3 | 0 54.4 | 0 51.8 | 3.7 | 0.2 | 9.7 | 0.6 | 15.7 | 0.9 |
| 38 | 0 54.5 | 0 54.6 | 0 52.0 | 3.8 | 0.2 | 9.8 | 0.6 | 15.8 | 0.9 |
| 39 | 0 54.8 | 0 54.9 | 0 52.3 | 3.9 | 0.2 | 9.9 | 0.6 | 15.9 | 0.9 |
| 40 | 0 55.0 | 0 55.2 | 0 52.5 | 4.0 | 0.2 | 10.0 | 0.6 | 16.0 | 0.9 |
| 41 | 0 55.3 | 0 55.4 | 0 52.7 | 4.1 | 0.2 | 10.1 | 0.6 | 16.1 | 0.9 |
| 42 | 0 55.5 | 0 55.7 | 0 53.0 | 4.2 | 0.2 | 10.2 | 0.6 | 16.2 | 0.9 |
| 43 | 0 55.8 | 0 55.9 | 0 53.2 | 4.3 | 0.3 | 10.3 | 0.6 | 16.3 | 1.0 |
| 44 | 0 56.0 | 0 56.2 | 0 53.4 | 4.4 | 0.3 | 10.4 | 0.6 | 16.4 | 1.0 |
| 45 | 0 56.3 | 0 56.4 | 0 53.7 | 4.5 | 0.3 | 10.5 | 0.6 | 16.5 | 1.0 |
| 46 | 0 56.5 | 0 56.7 | 0 53.9 | 4.6 | 0.3 | 10.6 | 0.6 | 16.6 | 1.0 |
| 47 | 0 56.8 | 0 56.9 | 0 54.2 | 4.7 | 0.3 | 10.7 | 0.6 | 16.7 | 1.0 |
| 48 | 0 57.0 | 0 57.2 | 0 54.4 | 4.8 | 0.3 | 10.8 | 0.6 | 16.8 | 1.0 |
| 49 | 0 57.3 | 0 57.4 | 0 54.6 | 4.9 | 0.3 | 10.9 | 0.6 | 16.9 | 1.0 |
| 50 | 0 57.5 | 0 57.7 | 0 54.9 | 5.0 | 0.3 | 11.0 | 0.6 | 17.0 | 1.0 |
| 51 | 0 57.8 | 0 57.9 | 0 55.1 | 5.1 | 0.3 | 11.1 | 0.6 | 17.1 | 1.0 |
| 52 | 0 58.0 | 0 58.2 | 0 55.4 | 5.2 | 0.3 | 11.2 | 0.7 | 17.2 | 1.0 |
| 53 | 0 58.3 | 0 58.4 | 0 55.6 | 5.3 | 0.3 | 11.3 | 0.7 | 17.3 | 1.0 |
| 54 | 0 58.5 | 0 58.7 | 0 55.8 | 5.4 | 0.3 | 11.4 | 0.7 | 17.4 | 1.0 |
| 55 | 0 58.8 | 0 58.9 | 0 56.1 | 5.5 | 0.3 | 11.5 | 0.7 | 17.5 | 1.0 |
| 56 | 0 59.0 | 0 59.2 | 0 56.3 | 5.6 | 0.3 | 11.6 | 0.7 | 17.6 | 1.0 |
| 57 | 0 59.3 | 0 59.4 | 0 56.6 | 5.7 | 0.3 | 11.7 | 0.7 | 17.7 | 1.0 |
| 58 | 0 59.5 | 0 59.7 | 0 56.8 | 5.8 | 0.3 | 11.8 | 0.7 | 17.8 | 1.0 |
| 59 | 0 59.8 | 0 59.9 | 0 57.0 | 5.9 | 0.3 | 11.9 | 0.7 | 17.9 | 1.0 |
| 60 | 1 00.0 | 1 00.2 | 0 57.3 | 6.0 | 0.4 | 12.0 | 0.7 | 18.0 | 1.1 |

| $4^m$ | SUN PLANETS | ARIES | MOON | $v$ or $d$ | Corrⁿ | $v$ or $d$ | Corrⁿ | $v$ or $d$ | Corrⁿ |
|---|---|---|---|---|---|---|---|---|---|
| s | ° ′ | ° ′ | ° ′ | ′ | ′ | ′ | ′ | ′ | ′ |
| 00 | 1 00·0 | 1 00·2 | 0 57·3 | 0·0 | 0·0 | 6·0 | 0·5 | 12·0 | 0·9 |
| 01 | 1 00·3 | 1 00·4 | 0 57·5 | 0·1 | 0·0 | 6·1 | 0·5 | 12·1 | 0·9 |
| 02 | 1 00·5 | 1 00·7 | 0 57·7 | 0·2 | 0·0 | 6·2 | 0·5 | 12·2 | 0·9 |
| 03 | 1 00·8 | 1 00·9 | 0 58·0 | 0·3 | 0·0 | 6·3 | 0·5 | 12·3 | 0·9 |
| 04 | 1 01·0 | 1 01·2 | 0 58·2 | 0·4 | 0·0 | 6·4 | 0·5 | 12·4 | 0·9 |
| 05 | 1 01·3 | 1 01·4 | 0 58·5 | 0·5 | 0·0 | 6·5 | 0·5 | 12·5 | 0·9 |
| 06 | 1 01·5 | 1 01·7 | 0 58·7 | 0·6 | 0·0 | 6·6 | 0·5 | 12·6 | 0·9 |
| 07 | 1 01·8 | 1 01·9 | 0 58·9 | 0·7 | 0·1 | 6·7 | 0·5 | 12·7 | 1·0 |
| 08 | 1 02·0 | 1 02·2 | 0 59·2 | 0·8 | 0·1 | 6·8 | 0·5 | 12·8 | 1·0 |
| 09 | 1 02·3 | 1 02·4 | 0 59·4 | 0·9 | 0·1 | 6·9 | 0·5 | 12·9 | 1·0 |
| 10 | 1 02·5 | 1 02·7 | 0 59·7 | 1·0 | 0·1 | 7·0 | 0·5 | 13·0 | 1·0 |
| 11 | 1 02·8 | 1 02·9 | 0 59·9 | 1·1 | 0·1 | 7·1 | 0·5 | 13·1 | 1·0 |
| 12 | 1 03·0 | 1 03·2 | 1 00·1 | 1·2 | 0·1 | 7·2 | 0·5 | 13·2 | 1·0 |
| 13 | 1 03·3 | 1 03·4 | 1 00·4 | 1·3 | 0·1 | 7·3 | 0·5 | 13·3 | 1·0 |
| 14 | 1 03·5 | 1 03·7 | 1 00·6 | 1·4 | 0·1 | 7·4 | 0·6 | 13·4 | 1·0 |
| 15 | 1 03·8 | 1 03·9 | 1 00·8 | 1·5 | 0·1 | 7·5 | 0·6 | 13·5 | 1·0 |
| 16 | 1 04·0 | 1 04·2 | 1 01·1 | 1·6 | 0·1 | 7·6 | 0·6 | 13·6 | 1·0 |
| 17 | 1 04·3 | 1 04·4 | 1 01·3 | 1·7 | 0·1 | 7·7 | 0·6 | 13·7 | 1·0 |
| 18 | 1 04·5 | 1 04·7 | 1 01·6 | 1·8 | 0·1 | 7·8 | 0·6 | 13·8 | 1·0 |
| 19 | 1 04·8 | 1 04·9 | 1 01·8 | 1·9 | 0·1 | 7·9 | 0·6 | 13·9 | 1·0 |
| 20 | 1 05·0 | 1 05·2 | 1 02·0 | 2·0 | 0·2 | 8·0 | 0·6 | 14·0 | 1·1 |
| 21 | 1 05·3 | 1 05·4 | 1 02·3 | 2·1 | 0·2 | 8·1 | 0·6 | 14·1 | 1·1 |
| 22 | 1 05·5 | 1 05·7 | 1 02·5 | 2·2 | 0·2 | 8·2 | 0·6 | 14·2 | 1·1 |
| 23 | 1 05·8 | 1 05·9 | 1 02·8 | 2·3 | 0·2 | 8·3 | 0·6 | 14·3 | 1·1 |
| 24 | 1 06·0 | 1 06·2 | 1 03·0 | 2·4 | 0·2 | 8·4 | 0·6 | 14·4 | 1·1 |
| 25 | 1 06·3 | 1 06·4 | 1 03·2 | 2·5 | 0·2 | 8·5 | 0·6 | 14·5 | 1·1 |
| 26 | 1 06·5 | 1 06·7 | 1 03·5 | 2·6 | 0·2 | 8·6 | 0·6 | 14·6 | 1·1 |
| 27 | 1 06·8 | 1 06·9 | 1 03·7 | 2·7 | 0·2 | 8·7 | 0·7 | 14·7 | 1·1 |
| 28 | 1 07·0 | 1 07·2 | 1 03·9 | 2·8 | 0·2 | 8·8 | 0·7 | 14·8 | 1·1 |
| 29 | 1 07·3 | 1 07·4 | 1 04·2 | 2·9 | 0·2 | 8·9 | 0·7 | 14·9 | 1·1 |
| 30 | 1 07·5 | 1 07·7 | 1 04·4 | 3·0 | 0·2 | 9·0 | 0·7 | 15·0 | 1·1 |
| 31 | 1 07·8 | 1 07·9 | 1 04·7 | 3·1 | 0·2 | 9·1 | 0·7 | 15·1 | 1·1 |
| 32 | 1 08·0 | 1 08·2 | 1 04·9 | 3·2 | 0·2 | 9·2 | 0·7 | 15·2 | 1·1 |
| 33 | 1 08·3 | 1 08·4 | 1 05·1 | 3·3 | 0·2 | 9·3 | 0·7 | 15·3 | 1·1 |
| 34 | 1 08·5 | 1 08·7 | 1 05·4 | 3·4 | 0·3 | 9·4 | 0·7 | 15·4 | 1·2 |
| 35 | 1 08·8 | 1 08·9 | 1 05·6 | 3·5 | 0·3 | 9·5 | 0·7 | 15·5 | 1·2 |
| 36 | 1 09·0 | 1 09·2 | 1 05·9 | 3·6 | 0·3 | 9·6 | 0·7 | 15·6 | 1·2 |
| 37 | 1 09·3 | 1 09·4 | 1 06·1 | 3·7 | 0·3 | 9·7 | 0·7 | 15·7 | 1·2 |
| 38 | 1 09·5 | 1 09·7 | 1 06·3 | 3·8 | 0·3 | 9·8 | 0·7 | 15·8 | 1·2 |
| 39 | 1 09·8 | 1 09·9 | 1 06·6 | 3·9 | 0·3 | 9·9 | 0·7 | 15·9 | 1·2 |
| 40 | 1 10·0 | 1 10·2 | 1 06·8 | 4·0 | 0·3 | 10·0 | 0·8 | 16·0 | 1·2 |
| 41 | 1 10·3 | 1 10·4 | 1 07·0 | 4·1 | 0·3 | 10·1 | 0·8 | 16·1 | 1·2 |
| 42 | 1 10·5 | 1 10·7 | 1 07·3 | 4·2 | 0·3 | 10·2 | 0·8 | 16·2 | 1·2 |
| 43 | 1 10·8 | 1 10·9 | 1 07·5 | 4·3 | 0·3 | 10·3 | 0·8 | 16·3 | 1·2 |
| 44 | 1 11·0 | 1 11·2 | 1 07·8 | 4·4 | 0·3 | 10·4 | 0·8 | 16·4 | 1·2 |
| 45 | 1 11·3 | 1 11·4 | 1 08·0 | 4·5 | 0·3 | 10·5 | 0·8 | 16·5 | 1·2 |
| 46 | 1 11·5 | 1 11·7 | 1 08·2 | 4·6 | 0·3 | 10·6 | 0·8 | 16·6 | 1·2 |
| 47 | 1 11·8 | 1 11·9 | 1 08·5 | 4·7 | 0·4 | 10·7 | 0·8 | 16·7 | 1·3 |
| 48 | 1 12·0 | 1 12·2 | 1 08·7 | 4·8 | 0·4 | 10·8 | 0·8 | 16·8 | 1·3 |
| 49 | 1 12·3 | 1 12·4 | 1 09·0 | 4·9 | 0·4 | 10·9 | 0·8 | 16·9 | 1·3 |
| 50 | 1 12·5 | 1 12·7 | 1 09·2 | 5·0 | 0·4 | 11·0 | 0·8 | 17·0 | 1·3 |
| 51 | 1 12·8 | 1 12·9 | 1 09·4 | 5·1 | 0·4 | 11·1 | 0·8 | 17·1 | 1·3 |
| 52 | 1 13·0 | 1 13·2 | 1 09·7 | 5·2 | 0·4 | 11·2 | 0·8 | 17·2 | 1·3 |
| 53 | 1 13·3 | 1 13·5 | 1 09·9 | 5·3 | 0·4 | 11·3 | 0·8 | 17·3 | 1·3 |
| 54 | 1 13·5 | 1 13·7 | 1 10·2 | 5·4 | 0·4 | 11·4 | 0·9 | 17·4 | 1·3 |
| 55 | 1 13·8 | 1 14·0 | 1 10·4 | 5·5 | 0·4 | 11·5 | 0·9 | 17·5 | 1·3 |
| 56 | 1 14·0 | 1 14·2 | 1 10·6 | 5·6 | 0·4 | 11·6 | 0·9 | 17·6 | 1·3 |
| 57 | 1 14·3 | 1 14·5 | 1 10·9 | 5·7 | 0·4 | 11·7 | 0·9 | 17·7 | 1·3 |
| 58 | 1 14·5 | 1 14·7 | 1 11·1 | 5·8 | 0·4 | 11·8 | 0·9 | 17·8 | 1·3 |
| 59 | 1 14·8 | 1 15·0 | 1 11·3 | 5·9 | 0·4 | 11·9 | 0·9 | 17·9 | 1·3 |
| 60 | 1 15·0 | 1 15·2 | 1 11·6 | 6·0 | 0·5 | 12·0 | 0·9 | 18·0 | 1·4 |

| $5^m$ | SUN PLANETS | ARIES | MOON | $v$ or $d$ | Corrⁿ | $v$ or $d$ | Corrⁿ | $v$ or $d$ | Corrⁿ |
|---|---|---|---|---|---|---|---|---|---|
| s | ° ′ | ° ′ | ° ′ | ′ | ′ | ′ | ′ | ′ | ′ |
| 00 | 1 15·0 | 1 15·2 | 1 11·6 | 0·0 | 0·0 | 6·0 | 0·6 | 12·0 | 1·1 |
| 01 | 1 15·3 | 1 15·5 | 1 11·8 | 0·1 | 0·0 | 6·1 | 0·6 | 12·1 | 1·1 |
| 02 | 1 15·5 | 1 15·7 | 1 12·1 | 0·2 | 0·0 | 6·2 | 0·6 | 12·2 | 1·1 |
| 03 | 1 15·8 | 1 16·0 | 1 12·3 | 0·3 | 0·0 | 6·3 | 0·6 | 12·3 | 1·1 |
| 04 | 1 16·0 | 1 16·2 | 1 12·5 | 0·4 | 0·0 | 6·4 | 0·6 | 12·4 | 1·1 |
| 05 | 1 16·3 | 1 16·5 | 1 12·8 | 0·5 | 0·0 | 6·5 | 0·6 | 12·5 | 1·1 |
| 06 | 1 16·5 | 1 16·7 | 1 13·0 | 0·6 | 0·1 | 6·6 | 0·6 | 12·6 | 1·2 |
| 07 | 1 16·8 | 1 17·0 | 1 13·3 | 0·7 | 0·1 | 6·7 | 0·6 | 12·7 | 1·2 |
| 08 | 1 17·0 | 1 17·2 | 1 13·5 | 0·8 | 0·1 | 6·8 | 0·6 | 12·8 | 1·2 |
| 09 | 1 17·3 | 1 17·5 | 1 13·7 | 0·9 | 0·1 | 6·9 | 0·6 | 12·9 | 1·2 |
| 10 | 1 17·5 | 1 17·7 | 1 14·0 | 1·0 | 0·1 | 7·0 | 0·6 | 13·0 | 1·2 |
| 11 | 1 17·8 | 1 18·0 | 1 14·2 | 1·1 | 0·1 | 7·1 | 0·7 | 13·1 | 1·2 |
| 12 | 1 18·0 | 1 18·2 | 1 14·4 | 1·2 | 0·1 | 7·2 | 0·7 | 13·2 | 1·2 |
| 13 | 1 18·3 | 1 18·5 | 1 14·7 | 1·3 | 0·1 | 7·3 | 0·7 | 13·3 | 1·2 |
| 14 | 1 18·5 | 1 18·7 | 1 14·9 | 1·4 | 0·1 | 7·4 | 0·7 | 13·4 | 1·2 |
| 15 | 1 18·8 | 1 19·0 | 1 15·2 | 1·5 | 0·1 | 7·5 | 0·7 | 13·5 | 1·2 |
| 16 | 1 19·0 | 1 19·2 | 1 15·4 | 1·6 | 0·1 | 7·6 | 0·7 | 13·6 | 1·2 |
| 17 | 1 19·3 | 1 19·5 | 1 15·6 | 1·7 | 0·2 | 7·7 | 0·7 | 13·7 | 1·3 |
| 18 | 1 19·5 | 1 19·7 | 1 15·9 | 1·8 | 0·2 | 7·8 | 0·7 | 13·8 | 1·3 |
| 19 | 1 19·8 | 1 20·0 | 1 16·1 | 1·9 | 0·2 | 7·9 | 0·7 | 13·9 | 1·3 |
| 20 | 1 20·0 | 1 20·2 | 1 16·4 | 2·0 | 0·2 | 8·0 | 0·7 | 14·0 | 1·3 |
| 21 | 1 20·3 | 1 20·5 | 1 16·6 | 2·1 | 0·2 | 8·1 | 0·7 | 14·1 | 1·3 |
| 22 | 1 20·5 | 1 20·7 | 1 16·8 | 2·2 | 0·2 | 8·2 | 0·8 | 14·2 | 1·3 |
| 23 | 1 20·8 | 1 21·0 | 1 17·1 | 2·3 | 0·2 | 8·3 | 0·8 | 14·3 | 1·3 |
| 24 | 1 21·0 | 1 21·2 | 1 17·3 | 2·4 | 0·2 | 8·4 | 0·8 | 14·4 | 1·3 |
| 25 | 1 21·3 | 1 21·5 | 1 17·5 | 2·5 | 0·2 | 8·5 | 0·8 | 14·5 | 1·3 |
| 26 | 1 21·5 | 1 21·7 | 1 17·8 | 2·6 | 0·2 | 8·6 | 0·8 | 14·6 | 1·3 |
| 27 | 1 21·8 | 1 22·0 | 1 18·0 | 2·7 | 0·2 | 8·7 | 0·8 | 14·7 | 1·3 |
| 28 | 1 22·0 | 1 22·2 | 1 18·3 | 2·8 | 0·3 | 8·8 | 0·8 | 14·8 | 1·4 |
| 29 | 1 22·3 | 1 22·5 | 1 18·5 | 2·9 | 0·3 | 8·9 | 0·8 | 14·9 | 1·4 |
| 30 | 1 22·5 | 1 22·7 | 1 18·7 | 3·0 | 0·3 | 9·0 | 0·8 | 15·0 | 1·4 |
| 31 | 1 22·8 | 1 23·0 | 1 19·0 | 3·1 | 0·3 | 9·1 | 0·8 | 15·1 | 1·4 |
| 32 | 1 23·0 | 1 23·2 | 1 19·2 | 3·2 | 0·3 | 9·2 | 0·8 | 15·2 | 1·4 |
| 33 | 1 23·3 | 1 23·5 | 1 19·5 | 3·3 | 0·3 | 9·3 | 0·9 | 15·3 | 1·4 |
| 34 | 1 23·5 | 1 23·7 | 1 19·7 | 3·4 | 0·3 | 9·4 | 0·9 | 15·4 | 1·4 |
| 35 | 1 23·8 | 1 24·0 | 1 19·9 | 3·5 | 0·3 | 9·5 | 0·9 | 15·5 | 1·4 |
| 36 | 1 24·0 | 1 24·2 | 1 20·2 | 3·6 | 0·3 | 9·6 | 0·9 | 15·6 | 1·4 |
| 37 | 1 24·3 | 1 24·5 | 1 20·4 | 3·7 | 0·3 | 9·7 | 0·9 | 15·7 | 1·4 |
| 38 | 1 24·5 | 1 24·7 | 1 20·7 | 3·8 | 0·3 | 9·8 | 0·9 | 15·8 | 1·4 |
| 39 | 1 24·8 | 1 25·0 | 1 20·9 | 3·9 | 0·4 | 9·9 | 0·9 | 15·9 | 1·5 |
| 40 | 1 25·0 | 1 25·2 | 1 21·1 | 4·0 | 0·4 | 10·0 | 0·9 | 16·0 | 1·5 |
| 41 | 1 25·3 | 1 25·5 | 1 21·4 | 4·1 | 0·4 | 10·1 | 0·9 | 16·1 | 1·5 |
| 42 | 1 25·5 | 1 25·7 | 1 21·6 | 4·2 | 0·4 | 10·2 | 0·9 | 16·2 | 1·5 |
| 43 | 1 25·8 | 1 26·0 | 1 21·8 | 4·3 | 0·4 | 10·3 | 0·9 | 16·3 | 1·5 |
| 44 | 1 26·0 | 1 26·2 | 1 22·1 | 4·4 | 0·4 | 10·4 | 1·0 | 16·4 | 1·5 |
| 45 | 1 26·3 | 1 26·5 | 1 22·3 | 4·5 | 0·4 | 10·5 | 1·0 | 16·5 | 1·5 |
| 46 | 1 26·5 | 1 26·7 | 1 22·6 | 4·6 | 0·4 | 10·6 | 1·0 | 16·6 | 1·5 |
| 47 | 1 26·8 | 1 27·0 | 1 22·8 | 4·7 | 0·4 | 10·7 | 1·0 | 16·7 | 1·5 |
| 48 | 1 27·0 | 1 27·2 | 1 23·0 | 4·8 | 0·4 | 10·8 | 1·0 | 16·8 | 1·5 |
| 49 | 1 27·3 | 1 27·5 | 1 23·3 | 4·9 | 0·4 | 10·9 | 1·0 | 16·9 | 1·5 |
| 50 | 1 27·5 | 1 27·7 | 1 23·5 | 5·0 | 0·5 | 11·0 | 1·0 | 17·0 | 1·6 |
| 51 | 1 27·8 | 1 28·0 | 1 23·8 | 5·1 | 0·5 | 11·1 | 1·0 | 17·1 | 1·6 |
| 52 | 1 28·0 | 1 28·2 | 1 24·0 | 5·2 | 0·5 | 11·2 | 1·0 | 17·2 | 1·6 |
| 53 | 1 28·3 | 1 28·5 | 1 24·2 | 5·3 | 0·5 | 11·3 | 1·0 | 17·3 | 1·6 |
| 54 | 1 28·5 | 1 28·7 | 1 24·5 | 5·4 | 0·5 | 11·4 | 1·0 | 17·4 | 1·6 |
| 55 | 1 28·8 | 1 29·0 | 1 24·7 | 5·5 | 0·5 | 11·5 | 1·1 | 17·5 | 1·6 |
| 56 | 1 29·0 | 1 29·2 | 1 24·9 | 5·6 | 0·5 | 11·6 | 1·1 | 17·6 | 1·6 |
| 57 | 1 29·3 | 1 29·5 | 1 25·2 | 5·7 | 0·5 | 11·7 | 1·1 | 17·7 | 1·6 |
| 58 | 1 29·5 | 1 29·7 | 1 25·4 | 5·8 | 0·5 | 11·8 | 1·1 | 17·8 | 1·6 |
| 59 | 1 29·8 | 1 30·0 | 1 25·7 | 5·9 | 0·5 | 11·9 | 1·1 | 17·9 | 1·6 |
| 60 | 1 30·0 | 1 30·2 | 1 25·9 | 6·0 | 0·6 | 12·0 | 1·1 | 18·0 | 1·7 |

| $6^m$ | SUN PLANETS | ARIES | MOON | $v$ or $d$ | Corrⁿ | $v$ or $d$ | Corrⁿ | $v$ or $d$ | Corrⁿ |
|---|---|---|---|---|---|---|---|---|---|
| s | ° ′ | ° ′ | ° ′ | ′ | ′ | ′ | ′ | ′ | ′ |
| 00 | 1 30·0 | 1 30·2 | 1 25·9 | 0·0 | 0·0 | 6·0 | 0·7 | 12·0 | 1·3 |
| 01 | 1 30·3 | 1 30·5 | 1 26·1 | 0·1 | 0·0 | 6·1 | 0·7 | 12·1 | 1·3 |
| 02 | 1 30·5 | 1 30·7 | 1 26·4 | 0·2 | 0·0 | 6·2 | 0·7 | 12·2 | 1·3 |
| 03 | 1 30·8 | 1 31·0 | 1 26·6 | 0·3 | 0·0 | 6·3 | 0·7 | 12·3 | 1·3 |
| 04 | 1 31·0 | 1 31·2 | 1 26·9 | 0·4 | 0·0 | 6·4 | 0·7 | 12·4 | 1·3 |
| 05 | 1 31·3 | 1 31·5 | 1 27·1 | 0·5 | 0·1 | 6·5 | 0·7 | 12·5 | 1·4 |
| 06 | 1 31·5 | 1 31·8 | 1 27·3 | 0·6 | 0·1 | 6·6 | 0·7 | 12·6 | 1·4 |
| 07 | 1 31·8 | 1 32·0 | 1 27·6 | 0·7 | 0·1 | 6·7 | 0·7 | 12·7 | 1·4 |
| 08 | 1 32·0 | 1 32·3 | 1 27·8 | 0·8 | 0·1 | 6·8 | 0·7 | 12·8 | 1·4 |
| 09 | 1 32·3 | 1 32·5 | 1 28·0 | 0·9 | 0·1 | 6·9 | 0·7 | 12·9 | 1·4 |
| 10 | 1 32·5 | 1 32·8 | 1 28·3 | 1·0 | 0·1 | 7·0 | 0·8 | 13·0 | 1·4 |
| 11 | 1 32·8 | 1 33·0 | 1 28·5 | 1·1 | 0·1 | 7·1 | 0·8 | 13·1 | 1·4 |
| 12 | 1 33·0 | 1 33·3 | 1 28·8 | 1·2 | 0·1 | 7·2 | 0·8 | 13·2 | 1·4 |
| 13 | 1 33·3 | 1 33·5 | 1 29·0 | 1·3 | 0·1 | 7·3 | 0·8 | 13·3 | 1·4 |
| 14 | 1 33·5 | 1 33·8 | 1 29·2 | 1·4 | 0·2 | 7·4 | 0·8 | 13·4 | 1·5 |
| 15 | 1 33·8 | 1 34·0 | 1 29·5 | 1·5 | 0·2 | 7·5 | 0·8 | 13·5 | 1·5 |
| 16 | 1 34·0 | 1 34·3 | 1 29·7 | 1·6 | 0·2 | 7·6 | 0·8 | 13·6 | 1·5 |
| 17 | 1 34·3 | 1 34·5 | 1 30·0 | 1·7 | 0·2 | 7·7 | 0·8 | 13·7 | 1·5 |
| 18 | 1 34·5 | 1 34·8 | 1 30·2 | 1·8 | 0·2 | 7·8 | 0·8 | 13·8 | 1·5 |
| 19 | 1 34·8 | 1 35·0 | 1 30·4 | 1·9 | 0·2 | 7·9 | 0·9 | 13·9 | 1·5 |
| 20 | 1 35·0 | 1 35·3 | 1 30·7 | 2·0 | 0·2 | 8·0 | 0·9 | 14·0 | 1·5 |
| 21 | 1 35·3 | 1 35·5 | 1 30·9 | 2·1 | 0·2 | 8·1 | 0·9 | 14·1 | 1·5 |
| 22 | 1 35·5 | 1 35·8 | 1 31·1 | 2·2 | 0·2 | 8·2 | 0·9 | 14·2 | 1·5 |
| 23 | 1 35·8 | 1 36·0 | 1 31·4 | 2·3 | 0·2 | 8·3 | 0·9 | 14·3 | 1·5 |
| 24 | 1 36·0 | 1 36·3 | 1 31·6 | 2·4 | 0·3 | 8·4 | 0·9 | 14·4 | 1·6 |
| 25 | 1 36·3 | 1 36·5 | 1 31·9 | 2·5 | 0·3 | 8·5 | 0·9 | 14·5 | 1·6 |
| 26 | 1 36·5 | 1 36·8 | 1 32·1 | 2·6 | 0·3 | 8·6 | 0·9 | 14·6 | 1·6 |
| 27 | 1 36·8 | 1 37·0 | 1 32·3 | 2·7 | 0·3 | 8·7 | 0·9 | 14·7 | 1·6 |
| 28 | 1 37·0 | 1 37·3 | 1 32·6 | 2·8 | 0·3 | 8·8 | 1·0 | 14·8 | 1·6 |
| 29 | 1 37·3 | 1 37·5 | 1 32·8 | 2·9 | 0·3 | 8·9 | 1·0 | 14·9 | 1·6 |
| 30 | 1 37·5 | 1 37·8 | 1 33·1 | 3·0 | 0·3 | 9·0 | 1·0 | 15·0 | 1·6 |
| 31 | 1 37·8 | 1 38·0 | 1 33·3 | 3·1 | 0·3 | 9·1 | 1·0 | 15·1 | 1·6 |
| 32 | 1 38·0 | 1 38·3 | 1 33·5 | 3·2 | 0·3 | 9·2 | 1·0 | 15·2 | 1·6 |
| 33 | 1 38·3 | 1 38·5 | 1 33·8 | 3·3 | 0·4 | 9·3 | 1·0 | 15·3 | 1·7 |
| 34 | 1 38·5 | 1 38·8 | 1 34·0 | 3·4 | 0·4 | 9·4 | 1·0 | 15·4 | 1·7 |
| 35 | 1 38·8 | 1 39·0 | 1 34·3 | 3·5 | 0·4 | 9·5 | 1·0 | 15·5 | 1·7 |
| 36 | 1 39·0 | 1 39·3 | 1 34·5 | 3·6 | 0·4 | 9·6 | 1·0 | 15·6 | 1·7 |
| 37 | 1 39·3 | 1 39·5 | 1 34·7 | 3·7 | 0·4 | 9·7 | 1·1 | 15·7 | 1·7 |
| 38 | 1 39·5 | 1 39·8 | 1 35·0 | 3·8 | 0·4 | 9·8 | 1·1 | 15·8 | 1·7 |
| 39 | 1 39·8 | 1 40·0 | 1 35·2 | 3·9 | 0·4 | 9·9 | 1·1 | 15·9 | 1·7 |
| 40 | 1 40·0 | 1 40·3 | 1 35·4 | 4·0 | 0·4 | 10·0 | 1·1 | 16·0 | 1·7 |
| 41 | 1 40·3 | 1 40·5 | 1 35·7 | 4·1 | 0·4 | 10·1 | 1·1 | 16·1 | 1·7 |
| 42 | 1 40·5 | 1 40·8 | 1 35·9 | 4·2 | 0·5 | 10·2 | 1·1 | 16·2 | 1·8 |
| 43 | 1 40·8 | 1 41·0 | 1 36·2 | 4·3 | 0·5 | 10·3 | 1·1 | 16·3 | 1·8 |
| 44 | 1 41·0 | 1 41·3 | 1 36·4 | 4·4 | 0·5 | 10·4 | 1·1 | 16·4 | 1·8 |
| 45 | 1 41·3 | 1 41·5 | 1 36·6 | 4·5 | 0·5 | 10·5 | 1·1 | 16·5 | 1·8 |
| 46 | 1 41·5 | 1 41·8 | 1 36·9 | 4·6 | 0·5 | 10·6 | 1·1 | 16·6 | 1·8 |
| 47 | 1 41·8 | 1 42·0 | 1 37·1 | 4·7 | 0·5 | 10·7 | 1·2 | 16·7 | 1·8 |
| 48 | 1 42·0 | 1 42·3 | 1 37·4 | 4·8 | 0·5 | 10·8 | 1·2 | 16·8 | 1·8 |
| 49 | 1 42·3 | 1 42·5 | 1 37·6 | 4·9 | 0·5 | 10·9 | 1·2 | 16·9 | 1·8 |
| 50 | 1 42·5 | 1 42·8 | 1 37·8 | 5·0 | 0·5 | 11·0 | 1·2 | 17·0 | 1·8 |
| 51 | 1 42·8 | 1 43·0 | 1 38·1 | 5·1 | 0·6 | 11·1 | 1·2 | 17·1 | 1·9 |
| 52 | 1 43·0 | 1 43·3 | 1 38·3 | 5·2 | 0·6 | 11·2 | 1·2 | 17·2 | 1·9 |
| 53 | 1 43·3 | 1 43·5 | 1 38·5 | 5·3 | 0·6 | 11·3 | 1·2 | 17·3 | 1·9 |
| 54 | 1 43·5 | 1 43·8 | 1 38·8 | 5·4 | 0·6 | 11·4 | 1·2 | 17·4 | 1·9 |
| 55 | 1 43·8 | 1 44·0 | 1 39·0 | 5·5 | 0·6 | 11·5 | 1·2 | 17·5 | 1·9 |
| 56 | 1 44·0 | 1 44·3 | 1 39·3 | 5·6 | 0·6 | 11·6 | 1·3 | 17·6 | 1·9 |
| 57 | 1 44·3 | 1 44·5 | 1 39·5 | 5·7 | 0·6 | 11·7 | 1·3 | 17·7 | 1·9 |
| 58 | 1 44·5 | 1 44·8 | 1 39·7 | 5·8 | 0·6 | 11·8 | 1·3 | 17·8 | 1·9 |
| 59 | 1 44·8 | 1 45·0 | 1 40·0 | 5·9 | 0·6 | 11·9 | 1·3 | 17·9 | 1·9 |
| 60 | 1 45·0 | 1 45·3 | 1 40·2 | 6·0 | 0·7 | 12·0 | 1·3 | 18·0 | 2·0 |

| $7^m$ | SUN PLANETS | ARIES | MOON | $v$ or $d$ | Corrⁿ | $v$ or $d$ | Corrⁿ | $v$ or $d$ | Corrⁿ |
|---|---|---|---|---|---|---|---|---|---|
| s | ° ′ | ° ′ | ° ′ | ′ | ′ | ′ | ′ | ′ | ′ |
| 00 | 1 45·0 | 1 45·3 | 1 40·2 | 0·0 | 0·0 | 6·0 | 0·8 | 12·0 | 1·5 |
| 01 | 1 45·3 | 1 45·5 | 1 40·5 | 0·1 | 0·0 | 6·1 | 0·8 | 12·1 | 1·5 |
| 02 | 1 45·5 | 1 45·8 | 1 40·7 | 0·2 | 0·0 | 6·2 | 0·8 | 12·2 | 1·5 |
| 03 | 1 45·8 | 1 46·0 | 1 40·9 | 0·3 | 0·0 | 6·3 | 0·8 | 12·3 | 1·5 |
| 04 | 1 46·0 | 1 46·3 | 1 41·2 | 0·4 | 0·1 | 6·4 | 0·8 | 12·4 | 1·6 |
| 05 | 1 46·3 | 1 46·5 | 1 41·4 | 0·5 | 0·1 | 6·5 | 0·8 | 12·5 | 1·6 |
| 06 | 1 46·5 | 1 46·8 | 1 41·6 | 0·6 | 0·1 | 6·6 | 0·8 | 12·6 | 1·6 |
| 07 | 1 46·8 | 1 47·0 | 1 41·9 | 0·7 | 0·1 | 6·7 | 0·8 | 12·7 | 1·6 |
| 08 | 1 47·0 | 1 47·3 | 1 42·1 | 0·8 | 0·1 | 6·8 | 0·9 | 12·8 | 1·6 |
| 09 | 1 47·3 | 1 47·5 | 1 42·4 | 0·9 | 0·1 | 6·9 | 0·9 | 12·9 | 1·6 |
| 10 | 1 47·5 | 1 47·8 | 1 42·6 | 1·0 | 0·1 | 7·0 | 0·9 | 13·0 | 1·6 |
| 11 | 1 47·8 | 1 48·0 | 1 42·8 | 1·1 | 0·1 | 7·1 | 0·9 | 13·1 | 1·6 |
| 12 | 1 48·0 | 1 48·3 | 1 43·1 | 1·2 | 0·2 | 7·2 | 0·9 | 13·2 | 1·7 |
| 13 | 1 48·3 | 1 48·5 | 1 43·3 | 1·3 | 0·2 | 7·3 | 0·9 | 13·3 | 1·7 |
| 14 | 1 48·5 | 1 48·8 | 1 43·6 | 1·4 | 0·2 | 7·4 | 0·9 | 13·4 | 1·7 |
| 15 | 1 48·8 | 1 49·0 | 1 43·8 | 1·5 | 0·2 | 7·5 | 0·9 | 13·5 | 1·7 |
| 16 | 1 49·0 | 1 49·3 | 1 44·0 | 1·6 | 0·2 | 7·6 | 1·0 | 13·6 | 1·7 |
| 17 | 1 49·3 | 1 49·5 | 1 44·3 | 1·7 | 0·2 | 7·7 | 1·0 | 13·7 | 1·7 |
| 18 | 1 49·5 | 1 49·8 | 1 44·5 | 1·8 | 0·2 | 7·8 | 1·0 | 13·8 | 1·7 |
| 19 | 1 49·8 | 1 50·1 | 1 44·8 | 1·9 | 0·2 | 7·9 | 1·0 | 13·9 | 1·7 |
| 20 | 1 50·0 | 1 50·3 | 1 45·0 | 2·0 | 0·3 | 8·0 | 1·0 | 14·0 | 1·8 |
| 21 | 1 50·3 | 1 50·6 | 1 45·2 | 2·1 | 0·3 | 8·1 | 1·0 | 14·1 | 1·8 |
| 22 | 1 50·5 | 1 50·8 | 1 45·5 | 2·2 | 0·3 | 8·2 | 1·0 | 14·2 | 1·8 |
| 23 | 1 50·8 | 1 51·1 | 1 45·7 | 2·3 | 0·3 | 8·3 | 1·0 | 14·3 | 1·8 |
| 24 | 1 51·0 | 1 51·3 | 1 45·9 | 2·4 | 0·3 | 8·4 | 1·1 | 14·4 | 1·8 |
| 25 | 1 51·3 | 1 51·6 | 1 46·2 | 2·5 | 0·3 | 8·5 | 1·1 | 14·5 | 1·8 |
| 26 | 1 51·5 | 1 51·8 | 1 46·4 | 2·6 | 0·3 | 8·6 | 1·1 | 14·6 | 1·8 |
| 27 | 1 51·8 | 1 52·1 | 1 46·7 | 2·7 | 0·3 | 8·7 | 1·1 | 14·7 | 1·8 |
| 28 | 1 52·0 | 1 52·3 | 1 46·9 | 2·8 | 0·4 | 8·8 | 1·1 | 14·8 | 1·9 |
| 29 | 1 52·3 | 1 52·6 | 1 47·1 | 2·9 | 0·4 | 8·9 | 1·1 | 14·9 | 1·9 |
| 30 | 1 52·5 | 1 52·8 | 1 47·4 | 3·0 | 0·4 | 9·0 | 1·1 | 15·0 | 1·9 |
| 31 | 1 52·8 | 1 53·1 | 1 47·6 | 3·1 | 0·4 | 9·1 | 1·1 | 15·1 | 1·9 |
| 32 | 1 53·0 | 1 53·3 | 1 47·9 | 3·2 | 0·4 | 9·2 | 1·2 | 15·2 | 1·9 |
| 33 | 1 53·3 | 1 53·6 | 1 48·1 | 3·3 | 0·4 | 9·3 | 1·2 | 15·3 | 1·9 |
| 34 | 1 53·5 | 1 53·8 | 1 48·3 | 3·4 | 0·4 | 9·4 | 1·2 | 15·4 | 1·9 |
| 35 | 1 53·8 | 1 54·1 | 1 48·6 | 3·5 | 0·4 | 9·5 | 1·2 | 15·5 | 1·9 |
| 36 | 1 54·0 | 1 54·3 | 1 48·8 | 3·6 | 0·5 | 9·6 | 1·2 | 15·6 | 2·0 |
| 37 | 1 54·3 | 1 54·6 | 1 49·0 | 3·7 | 0·5 | 9·7 | 1·2 | 15·7 | 2·0 |
| 38 | 1 54·5 | 1 54·8 | 1 49·3 | 3·8 | 0·5 | 9·8 | 1·2 | 15·8 | 2·0 |
| 39 | 1 54·8 | 1 55·1 | 1 49·5 | 3·9 | 0·5 | 9·9 | 1·2 | 15·9 | 2·0 |
| 40 | 1 55·0 | 1 55·3 | 1 49·8 | 4·0 | 0·5 | 10·0 | 1·3 | 16·0 | 2·0 |
| 41 | 1 55·3 | 1 55·6 | 1 50·0 | 4·1 | 0·5 | 10·1 | 1·3 | 16·1 | 2·0 |
| 42 | 1 55·5 | 1 55·8 | 1 50·2 | 4·2 | 0·5 | 10·2 | 1·3 | 16·2 | 2·0 |
| 43 | 1 55·8 | 1 56·1 | 1 50·5 | 4·3 | 0·5 | 10·3 | 1·3 | 16·3 | 2·0 |
| 44 | 1 56·0 | 1 56·3 | 1 50·7 | 4·4 | 0·6 | 10·4 | 1·3 | 16·4 | 2·1 |
| 45 | 1 56·3 | 1 56·6 | 1 51·0 | 4·5 | 0·6 | 10·5 | 1·3 | 16·5 | 2·1 |
| 46 | 1 56·5 | 1 56·8 | 1 51·2 | 4·6 | 0·6 | 10·6 | 1·3 | 16·6 | 2·1 |
| 47 | 1 56·8 | 1 57·1 | 1 51·4 | 4·7 | 0·6 | 10·7 | 1·3 | 16·7 | 2·1 |
| 48 | 1 57·0 | 1 57·3 | 1 51·7 | 4·8 | 0·6 | 10·8 | 1·4 | 16·8 | 2·1 |
| 49 | 1 57·3 | 1 57·6 | 1 51·9 | 4·9 | 0·6 | 10·9 | 1·4 | 16·9 | 2·1 |
| 50 | 1 57·5 | 1 57·8 | 1 52·1 | 5·0 | 0·6 | 11·0 | 1·4 | 17·0 | 2·1 |
| 51 | 1 57·8 | 1 58·1 | 1 52·4 | 5·1 | 0·6 | 11·1 | 1·4 | 17·1 | 2·1 |
| 52 | 1 58·0 | 1 58·3 | 1 52·6 | 5·2 | 0·7 | 11·2 | 1·4 | 17·2 | 2·2 |
| 53 | 1 58·3 | 1 58·6 | 1 52·9 | 5·3 | 0·7 | 11·3 | 1·4 | 17·3 | 2·2 |
| 54 | 1 58·5 | 1 58·8 | 1 53·1 | 5·4 | 0·7 | 11·4 | 1·4 | 17·4 | 2·2 |
| 55 | 1 58·8 | 1 59·1 | 1 53·3 | 5·5 | 0·7 | 11·5 | 1·4 | 17·5 | 2·2 |
| 56 | 1 59·0 | 1 59·3 | 1 53·6 | 5·6 | 0·7 | 11·6 | 1·5 | 17·6 | 2·2 |
| 57 | 1 59·3 | 1 59·6 | 1 53·8 | 5·7 | 0·7 | 11·7 | 1·5 | 17·7 | 2·2 |
| 58 | 1 59·5 | 1 59·8 | 1 54·1 | 5·8 | 0·7 | 11·8 | 1·5 | 17·8 | 2·2 |
| 59 | 1 59·8 | 2 00·1 | 1 54·3 | 5·9 | 0·7 | 11·9 | 1·5 | 17·9 | 2·2 |
| 60 | 2 00·0 | 2 00·3 | 1 54·5 | 6·0 | 0·8 | 12·0 | 1·5 | 18·0 | 2·3 |

# 8m INCREMENTS AND CORRECTIONS

| 8m s | SUN PLANETS ° ′ | ARIES ° ′ | MOON ° ′ | v or d ′ | Corr ′ | v or d ′ | Corr ′ | v or d ′ | Corr ′ |
|---|---|---|---|---|---|---|---|---|---|
| 00 | 2 00.0 | 2 00.3 | 1 54.5 | 0.0 | 0.0 | 6.0 | 0.9 | 12.0 | 1.7 |
| 01 | 2 00.3 | 2 00.6 | 1 54.8 | 0.1 | 0.0 | 6.1 | 0.9 | 12.1 | 1.7 |
| 02 | 2 00.5 | 2 00.8 | 1 55.0 | 0.2 | 0.0 | 6.2 | 0.9 | 12.2 | 1.7 |
| 03 | 2 00.8 | 2 01.1 | 1 55.2 | 0.3 | 0.0 | 6.3 | 0.9 | 12.3 | 1.7 |
| 04 | 2 01.0 | 2 01.3 | 1 55.5 | 0.4 | 0.1 | 6.4 | 0.9 | 12.4 | 1.8 |
| 05 | 2 01.3 | 2 01.6 | 1 55.7 | 0.5 | 0.1 | 6.5 | 0.9 | 12.5 | 1.8 |
| 06 | 2 01.5 | 2 01.8 | 1 56.0 | 0.6 | 0.1 | 6.6 | 0.9 | 12.6 | 1.8 |
| 07 | 2 01.8 | 2 02.1 | 1 56.2 | 0.7 | 0.1 | 6.7 | 0.9 | 12.7 | 1.8 |
| 08 | 2 02.0 | 2 02.3 | 1 56.4 | 0.8 | 0.1 | 6.8 | 1.0 | 12.8 | 1.8 |
| 09 | 2 02.3 | 2 02.6 | 1 56.7 | 0.9 | 0.1 | 6.9 | 1.0 | 12.9 | 1.8 |
| 10 | 2 02.5 | 2 02.8 | 1 56.9 | 1.0 | 0.1 | 7.0 | 1.0 | 13.0 | 1.8 |
| 11 | 2 02.8 | 2 03.1 | 1 57.2 | 1.1 | 0.2 | 7.1 | 1.0 | 13.1 | 1.9 |
| 12 | 2 03.0 | 2 03.3 | 1 57.4 | 1.2 | 0.2 | 7.2 | 1.0 | 13.2 | 1.9 |
| 13 | 2 03.3 | 2 03.6 | 1 57.6 | 1.3 | 0.2 | 7.3 | 1.0 | 13.3 | 1.9 |
| 14 | 2 03.5 | 2 03.8 | 1 57.9 | 1.4 | 0.2 | 7.4 | 1.0 | 13.4 | 1.9 |
| 15 | 2 03.8 | 2 04.1 | 1 58.1 | 1.5 | 0.2 | 7.5 | 1.1 | 13.5 | 1.9 |
| 16 | 2 04.0 | 2 04.3 | 1 58.4 | 1.6 | 0.2 | 7.6 | 1.1 | 13.6 | 1.9 |
| 17 | 2 04.3 | 2 04.6 | 1 58.6 | 1.7 | 0.2 | 7.7 | 1.1 | 13.7 | 1.9 |
| 18 | 2 04.5 | 2 04.8 | 1 58.8 | 1.8 | 0.3 | 7.8 | 1.1 | 13.8 | 2.0 |
| 19 | 2 04.8 | 2 05.1 | 1 59.1 | 1.9 | 0.3 | 7.9 | 1.1 | 13.9 | 2.0 |
| 20 | 2 05.0 | 2 05.3 | 1 59.3 | 2.0 | 0.3 | 8.0 | 1.1 | 14.0 | 2.0 |
| 21 | 2 05.3 | 2 05.6 | 1 59.5 | 2.1 | 0.3 | 8.1 | 1.1 | 14.1 | 2.0 |
| 22 | 2 05.5 | 2 05.8 | 1 59.8 | 2.2 | 0.3 | 8.2 | 1.2 | 14.2 | 2.0 |
| 23 | 2 05.8 | 2 06.1 | 2 00.0 | 2.3 | 0.3 | 8.3 | 1.2 | 14.3 | 2.0 |
| 24 | 2 06.0 | 2 06.3 | 2 00.3 | 2.4 | 0.3 | 8.4 | 1.2 | 14.4 | 2.0 |
| 25 | 2 06.3 | 2 06.6 | 2 00.5 | 2.5 | 0.4 | 8.5 | 1.2 | 14.5 | 2.1 |
| 26 | 2 06.5 | 2 06.8 | 2 00.7 | 2.6 | 0.4 | 8.6 | 1.2 | 14.6 | 2.1 |
| 27 | 2 06.8 | 2 07.1 | 2 01.0 | 2.7 | 0.4 | 8.7 | 1.2 | 14.7 | 2.1 |
| 28 | 2 07.0 | 2 07.3 | 2 01.2 | 2.8 | 0.4 | 8.8 | 1.2 | 14.8 | 2.1 |
| 29 | 2 07.3 | 2 07.6 | 2 01.5 | 2.9 | 0.4 | 8.9 | 1.3 | 14.9 | 2.1 |
| 30 | 2 07.5 | 2 07.8 | 2 01.7 | 3.0 | 0.4 | 9.0 | 1.3 | 15.0 | 2.1 |
| 31 | 2 07.8 | 2 08.1 | 2 01.9 | 3.1 | 0.4 | 9.1 | 1.3 | 15.1 | 2.1 |
| 32 | 2 08.0 | 2 08.4 | 2 02.2 | 3.2 | 0.5 | 9.2 | 1.3 | 15.2 | 2.2 |
| 33 | 2 08.3 | 2 08.6 | 2 02.4 | 3.3 | 0.5 | 9.3 | 1.3 | 15.3 | 2.2 |
| 34 | 2 08.5 | 2 08.9 | 2 02.6 | 3.4 | 0.5 | 9.4 | 1.3 | 15.4 | 2.2 |
| 35 | 2 08.8 | 2 09.1 | 2 02.9 | 3.5 | 0.5 | 9.5 | 1.3 | 15.5 | 2.2 |
| 36 | 2 09.0 | 2 09.4 | 2 03.1 | 3.6 | 0.5 | 9.6 | 1.4 | 15.6 | 2.2 |
| 37 | 2 09.3 | 2 09.6 | 2 03.4 | 3.7 | 0.5 | 9.7 | 1.4 | 15.7 | 2.2 |
| 38 | 2 09.5 | 2 09.9 | 2 03.6 | 3.8 | 0.5 | 9.8 | 1.4 | 15.8 | 2.2 |
| 39 | 2 09.8 | 2 10.1 | 2 03.8 | 3.9 | 0.6 | 9.9 | 1.4 | 15.9 | 2.3 |
| 40 | 2 10.0 | 2 10.4 | 2 04.1 | 4.0 | 0.6 | 10.0 | 1.4 | 16.0 | 2.3 |
| 41 | 2 10.3 | 2 10.6 | 2 04.3 | 4.1 | 0.6 | 10.1 | 1.4 | 16.1 | 2.3 |
| 42 | 2 10.5 | 2 10.9 | 2 04.6 | 4.2 | 0.6 | 10.2 | 1.4 | 16.2 | 2.3 |
| 43 | 2 10.8 | 2 11.1 | 2 04.8 | 4.3 | 0.6 | 10.3 | 1.5 | 16.3 | 2.3 |
| 44 | 2 11.0 | 2 11.4 | 2 05.0 | 4.4 | 0.6 | 10.4 | 1.5 | 16.4 | 2.3 |
| 45 | 2 11.3 | 2 11.6 | 2 05.3 | 4.5 | 0.6 | 10.5 | 1.5 | 16.5 | 2.3 |
| 46 | 2 11.5 | 2 11.9 | 2 05.5 | 4.6 | 0.7 | 10.6 | 1.5 | 16.6 | 2.4 |
| 47 | 2 11.8 | 2 12.1 | 2 05.7 | 4.7 | 0.7 | 10.7 | 1.5 | 16.7 | 2.4 |
| 48 | 2 12.0 | 2 12.4 | 2 06.0 | 4.8 | 0.7 | 10.8 | 1.5 | 16.8 | 2.4 |
| 49 | 2 12.3 | 2 12.6 | 2 06.2 | 4.9 | 0.7 | 10.9 | 1.5 | 16.9 | 2.4 |
| 50 | 2 12.5 | 2 12.9 | 2 06.5 | 5.0 | 0.7 | 11.0 | 1.6 | 17.0 | 2.4 |
| 51 | 2 12.8 | 2 13.1 | 2 06.7 | 5.1 | 0.7 | 11.1 | 1.6 | 17.1 | 2.4 |
| 52 | 2 13.0 | 2 13.4 | 2 06.9 | 5.2 | 0.7 | 11.2 | 1.6 | 17.2 | 2.4 |
| 53 | 2 13.3 | 2 13.6 | 2 07.2 | 5.3 | 0.8 | 11.3 | 1.6 | 17.3 | 2.5 |
| 54 | 2 13.5 | 2 13.9 | 2 07.4 | 5.4 | 0.8 | 11.4 | 1.6 | 17.4 | 2.5 |
| 55 | 2 13.8 | 2 14.1 | 2 07.7 | 5.5 | 0.8 | 11.5 | 1.6 | 17.5 | 2.5 |
| 56 | 2 14.0 | 2 14.4 | 2 07.9 | 5.6 | 0.8 | 11.6 | 1.6 | 17.6 | 2.5 |
| 57 | 2 14.3 | 2 14.6 | 2 08.1 | 5.7 | 0.8 | 11.7 | 1.7 | 17.7 | 2.5 |
| 58 | 2 14.5 | 2 14.9 | 2 08.4 | 5.8 | 0.8 | 11.8 | 1.7 | 17.8 | 2.5 |
| 59 | 2 14.8 | 2 15.1 | 2 08.6 | 5.9 | 0.8 | 11.9 | 1.7 | 17.9 | 2.5 |
| 60 | 2 15.0 | 2 15.4 | 2 08.9 | 6.0 | 0.9 | 12.0 | 1.7 | 18.0 | 2.6 |

# 9m

| 9m s | SUN PLANETS ° ′ | ARIES ° ′ | MOON ° ′ | v or d ′ | Corr ′ | v or d ′ | Corr ′ | v or d ′ | Corr ′ |
|---|---|---|---|---|---|---|---|---|---|
| 00 | 2 15.0 | 2 15.4 | 2 08.9 | 0.0 | 0.0 | 6.0 | 1.0 | 12.0 | 1.9 |
| 01 | 2 15.3 | 2 15.6 | 2 09.1 | 0.1 | 0.0 | 6.1 | 1.0 | 12.1 | 1.9 |
| 02 | 2 15.5 | 2 15.9 | 2 09.3 | 0.2 | 0.0 | 6.2 | 1.0 | 12.2 | 1.9 |
| 03 | 2 15.8 | 2 16.1 | 2 09.6 | 0.3 | 0.0 | 6.3 | 1.0 | 12.3 | 1.9 |
| 04 | 2 16.0 | 2 16.4 | 2 09.8 | 0.4 | 0.1 | 6.4 | 1.0 | 12.4 | 2.0 |
| 05 | 2 16.3 | 2 16.6 | 2 10.0 | 0.5 | 0.1 | 6.5 | 1.0 | 12.5 | 2.0 |
| 06 | 2 16.5 | 2 16.9 | 2 10.3 | 0.6 | 0.1 | 6.6 | 1.0 | 12.6 | 2.0 |
| 07 | 2 16.8 | 2 17.1 | 2 10.5 | 0.7 | 0.1 | 6.7 | 1.1 | 12.7 | 2.0 |
| 08 | 2 17.0 | 2 17.4 | 2 10.8 | 0.8 | 0.1 | 6.8 | 1.1 | 12.8 | 2.0 |
| 09 | 2 17.3 | 2 17.6 | 2 11.0 | 0.9 | 0.1 | 6.9 | 1.1 | 12.9 | 2.0 |
| 10 | 2 17.5 | 2 17.9 | 2 11.2 | 1.0 | 0.2 | 7.0 | 1.1 | 13.0 | 2.1 |
| 11 | 2 17.8 | 2 18.1 | 2 11.5 | 1.1 | 0.2 | 7.1 | 1.1 | 13.1 | 2.1 |
| 12 | 2 18.0 | 2 18.4 | 2 11.7 | 1.2 | 0.2 | 7.2 | 1.1 | 13.2 | 2.1 |
| 13 | 2 18.3 | 2 18.6 | 2 12.0 | 1.3 | 0.2 | 7.3 | 1.2 | 13.3 | 2.1 |
| 14 | 2 18.5 | 2 18.9 | 2 12.2 | 1.4 | 0.2 | 7.4 | 1.2 | 13.4 | 2.1 |
| 15 | 2 18.8 | 2 19.1 | 2 12.4 | 1.5 | 0.2 | 7.5 | 1.2 | 13.5 | 2.1 |
| 16 | 2 19.0 | 2 19.4 | 2 12.7 | 1.6 | 0.3 | 7.6 | 1.2 | 13.6 | 2.2 |
| 17 | 2 19.3 | 2 19.6 | 2 12.9 | 1.7 | 0.3 | 7.7 | 1.2 | 13.7 | 2.2 |
| 18 | 2 19.5 | 2 19.9 | 2 13.1 | 1.8 | 0.3 | 7.8 | 1.2 | 13.8 | 2.2 |
| 19 | 2 19.8 | 2 20.1 | 2 13.4 | 1.9 | 0.3 | 7.9 | 1.3 | 13.9 | 2.2 |
| 20 | 2 20.0 | 2 20.4 | 2 13.6 | 2.0 | 0.3 | 8.0 | 1.3 | 14.0 | 2.2 |
| 21 | 2 20.3 | 2 20.6 | 2 13.9 | 2.1 | 0.3 | 8.1 | 1.3 | 14.1 | 2.2 |
| 22 | 2 20.5 | 2 20.9 | 2 14.1 | 2.2 | 0.3 | 8.2 | 1.3 | 14.2 | 2.2 |
| 23 | 2 20.8 | 2 21.1 | 2 14.3 | 2.3 | 0.4 | 8.3 | 1.3 | 14.3 | 2.3 |
| 24 | 2 21.0 | 2 21.4 | 2 14.6 | 2.4 | 0.4 | 8.4 | 1.3 | 14.4 | 2.3 |
| 25 | 2 21.3 | 2 21.6 | 2 14.8 | 2.5 | 0.4 | 8.5 | 1.3 | 14.5 | 2.3 |
| 26 | 2 21.5 | 2 21.9 | 2 15.1 | 2.6 | 0.4 | 8.6 | 1.4 | 14.6 | 2.3 |
| 27 | 2 21.8 | 2 22.1 | 2 15.3 | 2.7 | 0.4 | 8.7 | 1.4 | 14.7 | 2.3 |
| 28 | 2 22.0 | 2 22.4 | 2 15.5 | 2.8 | 0.4 | 8.8 | 1.4 | 14.8 | 2.3 |
| 29 | 2 22.3 | 2 22.6 | 2 15.8 | 2.9 | 0.5 | 8.9 | 1.4 | 14.9 | 2.4 |
| 30 | 2 22.5 | 2 22.9 | 2 16.0 | 3.0 | 0.5 | 9.0 | 1.4 | 15.0 | 2.4 |
| 31 | 2 22.8 | 2 23.1 | 2 16.2 | 3.1 | 0.5 | 9.1 | 1.4 | 15.1 | 2.4 |
| 32 | 2 23.0 | 2 23.4 | 2 16.5 | 3.2 | 0.5 | 9.2 | 1.5 | 15.2 | 2.4 |
| 33 | 2 23.3 | 2 23.6 | 2 16.7 | 3.3 | 0.5 | 9.3 | 1.5 | 15.3 | 2.4 |
| 34 | 2 23.5 | 2 23.9 | 2 17.0 | 3.4 | 0.5 | 9.4 | 1.5 | 15.4 | 2.4 |
| 35 | 2 23.8 | 2 24.1 | 2 17.2 | 3.5 | 0.6 | 9.5 | 1.5 | 15.5 | 2.5 |
| 36 | 2 24.0 | 2 24.4 | 2 17.4 | 3.6 | 0.6 | 9.6 | 1.5 | 15.6 | 2.5 |
| 37 | 2 24.3 | 2 24.6 | 2 17.7 | 3.7 | 0.6 | 9.7 | 1.5 | 15.7 | 2.5 |
| 38 | 2 24.5 | 2 24.9 | 2 17.9 | 3.8 | 0.6 | 9.8 | 1.6 | 15.8 | 2.5 |
| 39 | 2 24.8 | 2 25.1 | 2 18.2 | 3.9 | 0.6 | 9.9 | 1.6 | 15.9 | 2.5 |
| 40 | 2 25.0 | 2 25.4 | 2 18.4 | 4.0 | 0.6 | 10.0 | 1.6 | 16.0 | 2.5 |
| 41 | 2 25.3 | 2 25.6 | 2 18.6 | 4.1 | 0.6 | 10.1 | 1.6 | 16.1 | 2.5 |
| 42 | 2 25.5 | 2 25.9 | 2 18.9 | 4.2 | 0.7 | 10.2 | 1.6 | 16.2 | 2.6 |
| 43 | 2 25.8 | 2 26.1 | 2 19.1 | 4.3 | 0.7 | 10.3 | 1.6 | 16.3 | 2.6 |
| 44 | 2 26.0 | 2 26.4 | 2 19.3 | 4.4 | 0.7 | 10.4 | 1.6 | 16.4 | 2.6 |
| 45 | 2 26.3 | 2 26.7 | 2 19.6 | 4.5 | 0.7 | 10.5 | 1.7 | 16.5 | 2.6 |
| 46 | 2 26.5 | 2 26.9 | 2 19.8 | 4.6 | 0.7 | 10.6 | 1.7 | 16.6 | 2.6 |
| 47 | 2 26.8 | 2 27.2 | 2 20.1 | 4.7 | 0.7 | 10.7 | 1.7 | 16.7 | 2.6 |
| 48 | 2 27.0 | 2 27.4 | 2 20.3 | 4.8 | 0.8 | 10.8 | 1.7 | 16.8 | 2.7 |
| 49 | 2 27.3 | 2 27.7 | 2 20.5 | 4.9 | 0.8 | 10.9 | 1.7 | 16.9 | 2.7 |
| 50 | 2 27.5 | 2 27.9 | 2 20.8 | 5.0 | 0.8 | 11.0 | 1.7 | 17.0 | 2.7 |
| 51 | 2 27.8 | 2 28.2 | 2 21.0 | 5.1 | 0.8 | 11.1 | 1.8 | 17.1 | 2.7 |
| 52 | 2 28.0 | 2 28.4 | 2 21.3 | 5.2 | 0.8 | 11.2 | 1.8 | 17.2 | 2.7 |
| 53 | 2 28.3 | 2 28.7 | 2 21.5 | 5.3 | 0.8 | 11.3 | 1.8 | 17.3 | 2.7 |
| 54 | 2 28.5 | 2 28.9 | 2 21.7 | 5.4 | 0.9 | 11.4 | 1.8 | 17.4 | 2.8 |
| 55 | 2 28.8 | 2 29.2 | 2 22.0 | 5.5 | 0.9 | 11.5 | 1.8 | 17.5 | 2.8 |
| 56 | 2 29.0 | 2 29.4 | 2 22.2 | 5.6 | 0.9 | 11.6 | 1.8 | 17.6 | 2.8 |
| 57 | 2 29.3 | 2 29.7 | 2 22.5 | 5.7 | 0.9 | 11.7 | 1.9 | 17.7 | 2.8 |
| 58 | 2 29.5 | 2 29.9 | 2 22.7 | 5.8 | 0.9 | 11.8 | 1.9 | 17.8 | 2.8 |
| 59 | 2 29.8 | 2 30.2 | 2 22.9 | 5.9 | 0.9 | 11.9 | 1.9 | 17.9 | 2.8 |
| 60 | 2 30.0 | 2 30.4 | 2 23.2 | 6.0 | 1.0 | 12.0 | 1.9 | 18.0 | 2.9 |

# 10m INCREMENTS AND CORRECTIONS

| 10m s | SUN PLANETS ° ′ | ARIES ° ′ | MOON ° ′ | v or d ′ | Corr ′ | v or d ′ | Corr ′ | v or d ′ | Corr ′ |
|---|---|---|---|---|---|---|---|---|---|
| 00 | 2 30.0 | 2 30.4 | 2 23.2 | 0.0 | 0.0 | 6.0 | 1.1 | 12.0 | 2.1 |
| 01 | 2 30.3 | 2 30.7 | 2 23.4 | 0.1 | 0.0 | 6.1 | 1.1 | 12.1 | 2.1 |
| 02 | 2 30.5 | 2 30.9 | 2 23.6 | 0.2 | 0.0 | 6.2 | 1.1 | 12.2 | 2.1 |
| 03 | 2 30.8 | 2 31.2 | 2 23.9 | 0.3 | 0.1 | 6.3 | 1.1 | 12.3 | 2.2 |
| 04 | 2 31.0 | 2 31.4 | 2 24.1 | 0.4 | 0.1 | 6.4 | 1.1 | 12.4 | 2.2 |
| 05 | 2 31.3 | 2 31.7 | 2 24.4 | 0.5 | 0.1 | 6.5 | 1.1 | 12.5 | 2.2 |
| 06 | 2 31.5 | 2 31.9 | 2 24.6 | 0.6 | 0.1 | 6.6 | 1.2 | 12.6 | 2.2 |
| 07 | 2 31.8 | 2 32.2 | 2 24.8 | 0.7 | 0.1 | 6.7 | 1.2 | 12.7 | 2.2 |
| 08 | 2 32.0 | 2 32.4 | 2 25.1 | 0.8 | 0.1 | 6.8 | 1.2 | 12.8 | 2.2 |
| 09 | 2 32.3 | 2 32.7 | 2 25.3 | 0.9 | 0.2 | 6.9 | 1.2 | 12.9 | 2.3 |
| 10 | 2 32.5 | 2 32.9 | 2 25.6 | 1.0 | 0.2 | 7.0 | 1.2 | 13.0 | 2.3 |
| 11 | 2 32.8 | 2 33.2 | 2 25.8 | 1.1 | 0.2 | 7.1 | 1.2 | 13.1 | 2.3 |
| 12 | 2 33.0 | 2 33.4 | 2 26.0 | 1.2 | 0.2 | 7.2 | 1.3 | 13.2 | 2.3 |
| 13 | 2 33.3 | 2 33.7 | 2 26.3 | 1.3 | 0.2 | 7.3 | 1.3 | 13.3 | 2.3 |
| 14 | 2 33.5 | 2 33.9 | 2 26.5 | 1.4 | 0.2 | 7.4 | 1.3 | 13.4 | 2.3 |
| 15 | 2 33.8 | 2 34.2 | 2 26.7 | 1.5 | 0.3 | 7.5 | 1.3 | 13.5 | 2.4 |
| 16 | 2 34.0 | 2 34.4 | 2 27.0 | 1.6 | 0.3 | 7.6 | 1.3 | 13.6 | 2.4 |
| 17 | 2 34.3 | 2 34.7 | 2 27.2 | 1.7 | 0.3 | 7.7 | 1.3 | 13.7 | 2.4 |
| 18 | 2 34.5 | 2 34.9 | 2 27.5 | 1.8 | 0.3 | 7.8 | 1.4 | 13.8 | 2.4 |
| 19 | 2 34.8 | 2 35.2 | 2 27.7 | 1.9 | 0.3 | 7.9 | 1.4 | 13.9 | 2.4 |
| 20 | 2 35.0 | 2 35.4 | 2 27.9 | 2.0 | 0.4 | 8.0 | 1.4 | 14.0 | 2.5 |
| 21 | 2 35.3 | 2 35.7 | 2 28.2 | 2.1 | 0.4 | 8.1 | 1.4 | 14.1 | 2.5 |
| 22 | 2 35.5 | 2 35.9 | 2 28.4 | 2.2 | 0.4 | 8.2 | 1.4 | 14.2 | 2.5 |
| 23 | 2 35.8 | 2 36.2 | 2 28.7 | 2.3 | 0.4 | 8.3 | 1.5 | 14.3 | 2.5 |
| 24 | 2 36.0 | 2 36.4 | 2 28.9 | 2.4 | 0.4 | 8.4 | 1.5 | 14.4 | 2.5 |
| 25 | 2 36.3 | 2 36.7 | 2 29.1 | 2.5 | 0.4 | 8.5 | 1.5 | 14.5 | 2.5 |
| 26 | 2 36.5 | 2 36.9 | 2 29.4 | 2.6 | 0.5 | 8.6 | 1.5 | 14.6 | 2.6 |
| 27 | 2 36.8 | 2 37.2 | 2 29.6 | 2.7 | 0.5 | 8.7 | 1.5 | 14.7 | 2.6 |
| 28 | 2 37.0 | 2 37.4 | 2 29.8 | 2.8 | 0.5 | 8.8 | 1.5 | 14.8 | 2.6 |
| 29 | 2 37.3 | 2 37.7 | 2 30.1 | 2.9 | 0.5 | 8.9 | 1.6 | 14.9 | 2.6 |
| 30 | 2 37.5 | 2 37.9 | 2 30.3 | 3.0 | 0.5 | 9.0 | 1.6 | 15.0 | 2.6 |
| 31 | 2 37.8 | 2 38.2 | 2 30.6 | 3.1 | 0.5 | 9.1 | 1.6 | 15.1 | 2.6 |
| 32 | 2 38.0 | 2 38.4 | 2 30.8 | 3.2 | 0.6 | 9.2 | 1.6 | 15.2 | 2.7 |
| 33 | 2 38.3 | 2 38.7 | 2 31.0 | 3.3 | 0.6 | 9.3 | 1.6 | 15.3 | 2.7 |
| 34 | 2 38.5 | 2 38.9 | 2 31.3 | 3.4 | 0.6 | 9.4 | 1.6 | 15.4 | 2.7 |
| 35 | 2 38.8 | 2 39.2 | 2 31.5 | 3.5 | 0.6 | 9.5 | 1.7 | 15.5 | 2.7 |
| 36 | 2 39.0 | 2 39.4 | 2 31.8 | 3.6 | 0.6 | 9.6 | 1.7 | 15.6 | 2.7 |
| 37 | 2 39.3 | 2 39.7 | 2 32.0 | 3.7 | 0.6 | 9.7 | 1.7 | 15.7 | 2.7 |
| 38 | 2 39.5 | 2 39.9 | 2 32.2 | 3.8 | 0.7 | 9.8 | 1.7 | 15.8 | 2.8 |
| 39 | 2 39.8 | 2 40.2 | 2 32.5 | 3.9 | 0.7 | 9.9 | 1.7 | 15.9 | 2.8 |
| 40 | 2 40.0 | 2 40.4 | 2 32.7 | 4.0 | 0.7 | 10.0 | 1.8 | 16.0 | 2.8 |
| 41 | 2 40.3 | 2 40.7 | 2 32.9 | 4.1 | 0.7 | 10.1 | 1.8 | 16.1 | 2.8 |
| 42 | 2 40.5 | 2 40.9 | 2 33.2 | 4.2 | 0.7 | 10.2 | 1.8 | 16.2 | 2.8 |
| 43 | 2 40.8 | 2 41.2 | 2 33.4 | 4.3 | 0.8 | 10.3 | 1.8 | 16.3 | 2.9 |
| 44 | 2 41.0 | 2 41.4 | 2 33.7 | 4.4 | 0.8 | 10.4 | 1.8 | 16.4 | 2.9 |
| 45 | 2 41.3 | 2 41.7 | 2 33.9 | 4.5 | 0.8 | 10.5 | 1.8 | 16.5 | 2.9 |
| 46 | 2 41.5 | 2 41.9 | 2 34.1 | 4.6 | 0.8 | 10.6 | 1.9 | 16.6 | 2.9 |
| 47 | 2 41.8 | 2 42.2 | 2 34.4 | 4.7 | 0.8 | 10.7 | 1.9 | 16.7 | 2.9 |
| 48 | 2 42.0 | 2 42.4 | 2 34.6 | 4.8 | 0.8 | 10.8 | 1.9 | 16.8 | 2.9 |
| 49 | 2 42.3 | 2 42.7 | 2 34.9 | 4.9 | 0.9 | 10.9 | 1.9 | 16.9 | 3.0 |
| 50 | 2 42.5 | 2 42.9 | 2 35.1 | 5.0 | 0.9 | 11.0 | 1.9 | 17.0 | 3.0 |
| 51 | 2 42.8 | 2 43.2 | 2 35.3 | 5.1 | 0.9 | 11.1 | 1.9 | 17.1 | 3.0 |
| 52 | 2 43.0 | 2 43.4 | 2 35.6 | 5.2 | 0.9 | 11.2 | 2.0 | 17.2 | 3.0 |
| 53 | 2 43.3 | 2 43.7 | 2 35.8 | 5.3 | 0.9 | 11.3 | 2.0 | 17.3 | 3.0 |
| 54 | 2 43.5 | 2 43.9 | 2 36.1 | 5.4 | 0.9 | 11.4 | 2.0 | 17.4 | 3.0 |
| 55 | 2 43.8 | 2 44.2 | 2 36.3 | 5.5 | 1.0 | 11.5 | 2.0 | 17.5 | 3.1 |
| 56 | 2 44.0 | 2 44.4 | 2 36.5 | 5.6 | 1.0 | 11.6 | 2.0 | 17.6 | 3.1 |
| 57 | 2 44.3 | 2 44.7 | 2 36.8 | 5.7 | 1.0 | 11.7 | 2.0 | 17.7 | 3.1 |
| 58 | 2 44.5 | 2 45.0 | 2 37.0 | 5.8 | 1.0 | 11.8 | 2.1 | 17.8 | 3.1 |
| 59 | 2 44.8 | 2 45.2 | 2 37.2 | 5.9 | 1.0 | 11.9 | 2.1 | 17.9 | 3.1 |
| 60 | 2 45.0 | 2 45.5 | 2 37.5 | 6.0 | 1.1 | 12.0 | 2.1 | 18.0 | 3.2 |

# 11m

| 11m s | SUN PLANETS ° ′ | ARIES ° ′ | MOON ° ′ | v or d ′ | Corr ′ | v or d ′ | Corr ′ | v or d ′ | Corr ′ |
|---|---|---|---|---|---|---|---|---|---|
| 00 | 2 45.0 | 2 45.5 | 2 37.5 | 0.0 | 0.0 | 6.0 | 1.2 | 12.0 | 2.3 |
| 01 | 2 45.3 | 2 45.7 | 2 37.7 | 0.1 | 0.0 | 6.1 | 1.2 | 12.1 | 2.3 |
| 02 | 2 45.5 | 2 46.0 | 2 38.0 | 0.2 | 0.0 | 6.2 | 1.2 | 12.2 | 2.3 |
| 03 | 2 45.8 | 2 46.2 | 2 38.2 | 0.3 | 0.1 | 6.3 | 1.2 | 12.3 | 2.4 |
| 04 | 2 46.0 | 2 46.5 | 2 38.4 | 0.4 | 0.1 | 6.4 | 1.2 | 12.4 | 2.4 |
| 05 | 2 46.3 | 2 46.7 | 2 38.7 | 0.5 | 0.1 | 6.5 | 1.2 | 12.5 | 2.4 |
| 06 | 2 46.5 | 2 47.0 | 2 38.9 | 0.6 | 0.1 | 6.6 | 1.3 | 12.6 | 2.4 |
| 07 | 2 46.8 | 2 47.2 | 2 39.2 | 0.7 | 0.1 | 6.7 | 1.3 | 12.7 | 2.4 |
| 08 | 2 47.0 | 2 47.5 | 2 39.4 | 0.8 | 0.2 | 6.8 | 1.3 | 12.8 | 2.5 |
| 09 | 2 47.3 | 2 47.7 | 2 39.6 | 0.9 | 0.2 | 6.9 | 1.3 | 12.9 | 2.5 |
| 10 | 2 47.5 | 2 48.0 | 2 39.9 | 1.0 | 0.2 | 7.0 | 1.3 | 13.0 | 2.5 |
| 11 | 2 47.8 | 2 48.2 | 2 40.1 | 1.1 | 0.2 | 7.1 | 1.4 | 13.1 | 2.5 |
| 12 | 2 48.0 | 2 48.5 | 2 40.3 | 1.2 | 0.2 | 7.2 | 1.4 | 13.2 | 2.5 |
| 13 | 2 48.3 | 2 48.7 | 2 40.6 | 1.3 | 0.2 | 7.3 | 1.4 | 13.3 | 2.5 |
| 14 | 2 48.5 | 2 49.0 | 2 40.8 | 1.4 | 0.3 | 7.4 | 1.4 | 13.4 | 2.6 |
| 15 | 2 48.8 | 2 49.2 | 2 41.1 | 1.5 | 0.3 | 7.5 | 1.4 | 13.5 | 2.6 |
| 16 | 2 49.0 | 2 49.5 | 2 41.3 | 1.6 | 0.3 | 7.6 | 1.5 | 13.6 | 2.6 |
| 17 | 2 49.3 | 2 49.7 | 2 41.5 | 1.7 | 0.3 | 7.7 | 1.5 | 13.7 | 2.6 |
| 18 | 2 49.5 | 2 50.0 | 2 41.8 | 1.8 | 0.3 | 7.8 | 1.5 | 13.8 | 2.6 |
| 19 | 2 49.8 | 2 50.2 | 2 42.0 | 1.9 | 0.4 | 7.9 | 1.5 | 13.9 | 2.7 |
| 20 | 2 50.0 | 2 50.5 | 2 42.3 | 2.0 | 0.4 | 8.0 | 1.5 | 14.0 | 2.7 |
| 21 | 2 50.3 | 2 50.7 | 2 42.5 | 2.1 | 0.4 | 8.1 | 1.6 | 14.1 | 2.7 |
| 22 | 2 50.5 | 2 51.0 | 2 42.7 | 2.2 | 0.4 | 8.2 | 1.6 | 14.2 | 2.7 |
| 23 | 2 50.8 | 2 51.2 | 2 43.0 | 2.3 | 0.4 | 8.3 | 1.6 | 14.3 | 2.7 |
| 24 | 2 51.0 | 2 51.5 | 2 43.2 | 2.4 | 0.5 | 8.4 | 1.6 | 14.4 | 2.8 |
| 25 | 2 51.3 | 2 51.7 | 2 43.4 | 2.5 | 0.5 | 8.5 | 1.6 | 14.5 | 2.8 |
| 26 | 2 51.5 | 2 52.0 | 2 43.7 | 2.6 | 0.5 | 8.6 | 1.6 | 14.6 | 2.8 |
| 27 | 2 51.8 | 2 52.2 | 2 43.9 | 2.7 | 0.5 | 8.7 | 1.7 | 14.7 | 2.8 |
| 28 | 2 52.0 | 2 52.5 | 2 44.2 | 2.8 | 0.5 | 8.8 | 1.7 | 14.8 | 2.8 |
| 29 | 2 52.3 | 2 52.7 | 2 44.4 | 2.9 | 0.6 | 8.9 | 1.7 | 14.9 | 2.9 |
| 30 | 2 52.5 | 2 53.0 | 2 44.6 | 3.0 | 0.6 | 9.0 | 1.7 | 15.0 | 2.9 |
| 31 | 2 52.8 | 2 53.2 | 2 44.9 | 3.1 | 0.6 | 9.1 | 1.7 | 15.1 | 2.9 |
| 32 | 2 53.0 | 2 53.5 | 2 45.1 | 3.2 | 0.6 | 9.2 | 1.8 | 15.2 | 2.9 |
| 33 | 2 53.3 | 2 53.7 | 2 45.4 | 3.3 | 0.6 | 9.3 | 1.8 | 15.3 | 2.9 |
| 34 | 2 53.5 | 2 54.0 | 2 45.6 | 3.4 | 0.7 | 9.4 | 1.8 | 15.4 | 3.0 |
| 35 | 2 53.8 | 2 54.2 | 2 45.8 | 3.5 | 0.7 | 9.5 | 1.8 | 15.5 | 3.0 |
| 36 | 2 54.0 | 2 54.5 | 2 46.1 | 3.6 | 0.7 | 9.6 | 1.8 | 15.6 | 3.0 |
| 37 | 2 54.3 | 2 54.7 | 2 46.3 | 3.7 | 0.7 | 9.7 | 1.9 | 15.7 | 3.0 |
| 38 | 2 54.5 | 2 55.0 | 2 46.6 | 3.8 | 0.7 | 9.8 | 1.9 | 15.8 | 3.0 |
| 39 | 2 54.8 | 2 55.2 | 2 46.8 | 3.9 | 0.7 | 9.9 | 1.9 | 15.9 | 3.0 |
| 40 | 2 55.0 | 2 55.5 | 2 47.0 | 4.0 | 0.8 | 10.0 | 1.9 | 16.0 | 3.1 |
| 41 | 2 55.3 | 2 55.7 | 2 47.3 | 4.1 | 0.8 | 10.1 | 1.9 | 16.1 | 3.1 |
| 42 | 2 55.5 | 2 56.0 | 2 47.5 | 4.2 | 0.8 | 10.2 | 2.0 | 16.2 | 3.1 |
| 43 | 2 55.8 | 2 56.2 | 2 47.7 | 4.3 | 0.8 | 10.3 | 2.0 | 16.3 | 3.1 |
| 44 | 2 56.0 | 2 56.5 | 2 48.0 | 4.4 | 0.8 | 10.4 | 2.0 | 16.4 | 3.1 |
| 45 | 2 56.3 | 2 56.7 | 2 48.2 | 4.5 | 0.9 | 10.5 | 2.0 | 16.5 | 3.2 |
| 46 | 2 56.5 | 2 57.0 | 2 48.5 | 4.6 | 0.9 | 10.6 | 2.0 | 16.6 | 3.2 |
| 47 | 2 56.8 | 2 57.2 | 2 48.7 | 4.7 | 0.9 | 10.7 | 2.1 | 16.7 | 3.2 |
| 48 | 2 57.0 | 2 57.5 | 2 48.9 | 4.8 | 0.9 | 10.8 | 2.1 | 16.8 | 3.2 |
| 49 | 2 57.3 | 2 57.7 | 2 49.2 | 4.9 | 0.9 | 10.9 | 2.1 | 16.9 | 3.2 |
| 50 | 2 57.5 | 2 58.0 | 2 49.4 | 5.0 | 1.0 | 11.0 | 2.1 | 17.0 | 3.3 |
| 51 | 2 57.8 | 2 58.2 | 2 49.7 | 5.1 | 1.0 | 11.1 | 2.1 | 17.1 | 3.3 |
| 52 | 2 58.0 | 2 58.5 | 2 49.9 | 5.2 | 1.0 | 11.2 | 2.1 | 17.2 | 3.3 |
| 53 | 2 58.3 | 2 58.7 | 2 50.1 | 5.3 | 1.0 | 11.3 | 2.2 | 17.3 | 3.3 |
| 54 | 2 58.5 | 2 59.0 | 2 50.4 | 5.4 | 1.0 | 11.4 | 2.2 | 17.4 | 3.3 |
| 55 | 2 58.8 | 2 59.2 | 2 50.6 | 5.5 | 1.1 | 11.5 | 2.2 | 17.5 | 3.4 |
| 56 | 2 59.0 | 2 59.5 | 2 50.8 | 5.6 | 1.1 | 11.6 | 2.2 | 17.6 | 3.4 |
| 57 | 2 59.3 | 2 59.7 | 2 51.1 | 5.7 | 1.1 | 11.7 | 2.2 | 17.7 | 3.4 |
| 58 | 2 59.5 | 3 00.0 | 2 51.3 | 5.8 | 1.1 | 11.8 | 2.3 | 17.8 | 3.4 |
| 59 | 2 59.8 | 3 00.2 | 2 51.6 | 5.9 | 1.1 | 11.9 | 2.3 | 17.9 | 3.4 |
| 60 | 3 00.0 | 3 00.5 | 2 51.8 | 6.0 | 1.2 | 12.0 | 2.3 | 18.0 | 3.5 |

| 12ᵐ s | SUN PLANETS ° ′ | ARIES ° ′ | MOON ° ′ | v or d ′ | Corrⁿ ′ | v or d ′ | Corrⁿ ′ | v or d ′ | Corrⁿ ′ |
|---|---|---|---|---|---|---|---|---|---|
| 00 | 3 00·0 | 3 00·5 | 2 51·8 | 0·0 | 0·0 | 6·0 | 1·3 | 12·0 | 2·5 |
| 01 | 3 00·3 | 3 00·7 | 2 52·0 | 0·1 | 0·0 | 6·1 | 1·3 | 12·1 | 2·5 |
| 02 | 3 00·5 | 3 01·0 | 2 52·3 | 0·2 | 0·0 | 6·2 | 1·3 | 12·2 | 2·5 |
| 03 | 3 00·8 | 3 01·2 | 2 52·5 | 0·3 | 0·1 | 6·3 | 1·3 | 12·3 | 2·6 |
| 04 | 3 01·0 | 3 01·5 | 2 52·8 | 0·4 | 0·1 | 6·4 | 1·3 | 12·4 | 2·6 |
| 05 | 3 01·3 | 3 01·7 | 2 53·0 | 0·5 | 0·1 | 6·5 | 1·4 | 12·5 | 2·6 |
| 06 | 3 01·5 | 3 02·0 | 2 53·2 | 0·6 | 0·1 | 6·6 | 1·4 | 12·6 | 2·6 |
| 07 | 3 01·8 | 3 02·2 | 2 53·5 | 0·7 | 0·1 | 6·7 | 1·4 | 12·7 | 2·6 |
| 08 | 3 02·0 | 3 02·5 | 2 53·7 | 0·8 | 0·2 | 6·8 | 1·4 | 12·8 | 2·7 |
| 09 | 3 02·3 | 3 02·7 | 2 53·9 | 0·9 | 0·2 | 6·9 | 1·4 | 12·9 | 2·7 |
| 10 | 3 02·5 | 3 03·0 | 2 54·2 | 1·0 | 0·2 | 7·0 | 1·5 | 13·0 | 2·7 |
| 11 | 3 02·8 | 3 03·3 | 2 54·4 | 1·1 | 0·2 | 7·1 | 1·5 | 13·1 | 2·7 |
| 12 | 3 03·0 | 3 03·5 | 2 54·7 | 1·2 | 0·3 | 7·2 | 1·5 | 13·2 | 2·8 |
| 13 | 3 03·3 | 3 03·8 | 2 54·9 | 1·3 | 0·3 | 7·3 | 1·5 | 13·3 | 2·8 |
| 14 | 3 03·5 | 3 04·0 | 2 55·1 | 1·4 | 0·3 | 7·4 | 1·5 | 13·4 | 2·8 |
| 15 | 3 03·8 | 3 04·3 | 2 55·4 | 1·5 | 0·3 | 7·5 | 1·6 | 13·5 | 2·8 |
| 16 | 3 04·0 | 3 04·5 | 2 55·6 | 1·6 | 0·3 | 7·6 | 1·6 | 13·6 | 2·8 |
| 17 | 3 04·3 | 3 04·8 | 2 55·9 | 1·7 | 0·4 | 7·7 | 1·6 | 13·7 | 2·9 |
| 18 | 3 04·5 | 3 05·0 | 2 56·1 | 1·8 | 0·4 | 7·8 | 1·6 | 13·8 | 2·9 |
| 19 | 3 04·8 | 3 05·3 | 2 56·3 | 1·9 | 0·4 | 7·9 | 1·6 | 13·9 | 2·9 |
| 20 | 3 05·0 | 3 05·5 | 2 56·6 | 2·0 | 0·4 | 8·0 | 1·7 | 14·0 | 2·9 |
| 21 | 3 05·3 | 3 05·8 | 2 56·8 | 2·1 | 0·4 | 8·1 | 1·7 | 14·1 | 2·9 |
| 22 | 3 05·5 | 3 06·0 | 2 57·0 | 2·2 | 0·5 | 8·2 | 1·7 | 14·2 | 3·0 |
| 23 | 3 05·8 | 3 06·3 | 2 57·3 | 2·3 | 0·5 | 8·3 | 1·7 | 14·3 | 3·0 |
| 24 | 3 06·0 | 3 06·5 | 2 57·5 | 2·4 | 0·5 | 8·4 | 1·8 | 14·4 | 3·0 |
| 25 | 3 06·3 | 3 06·8 | 2 57·8 | 2·5 | 0·5 | 8·5 | 1·8 | 14·5 | 3·0 |
| 26 | 3 06·5 | 3 07·0 | 2 58·0 | 2·6 | 0·5 | 8·6 | 1·8 | 14·6 | 3·0 |
| 27 | 3 06·8 | 3 07·3 | 2 58·2 | 2·7 | 0·6 | 8·7 | 1·8 | 14·7 | 3·1 |
| 28 | 3 07·0 | 3 07·5 | 2 58·5 | 2·8 | 0·6 | 8·8 | 1·8 | 14·8 | 3·1 |
| 29 | 3 07·3 | 3 07·8 | 2 58·7 | 2·9 | 0·6 | 8·9 | 1·9 | 14·9 | 3·1 |
| 30 | 3 07·5 | 3 08·0 | 2 59·0 | 3·0 | 0·6 | 9·0 | 1·9 | 15·0 | 3·1 |
| 31 | 3 07·8 | 3 08·3 | 2 59·2 | 3·1 | 0·6 | 9·1 | 1·9 | 15·1 | 3·1 |
| 32 | 3 08·0 | 3 08·5 | 2 59·4 | 3·2 | 0·7 | 9·2 | 1·9 | 15·2 | 3·2 |
| 33 | 3 08·3 | 3 08·8 | 2 59·7 | 3·3 | 0·7 | 9·3 | 1·9 | 15·3 | 3·2 |
| 34 | 3 08·5 | 3 09·0 | 2 59·9 | 3·4 | 0·7 | 9·4 | 2·0 | 15·4 | 3·2 |
| 35 | 3 08·8 | 3 09·3 | 3 00·2 | 3·5 | 0·7 | 9·5 | 2·0 | 15·5 | 3·2 |
| 36 | 3 09·0 | 3 09·5 | 3 00·4 | 3·6 | 0·8 | 9·6 | 2·0 | 15·6 | 3·3 |
| 37 | 3 09·3 | 3 09·8 | 3 00·6 | 3·7 | 0·8 | 9·7 | 2·0 | 15·7 | 3·3 |
| 38 | 3 09·5 | 3 10·0 | 3 00·9 | 3·8 | 0·8 | 9·8 | 2·0 | 15·8 | 3·3 |
| 39 | 3 09·8 | 3 10·3 | 3 01·1 | 3·9 | 0·8 | 9·9 | 2·1 | 15·9 | 3·3 |
| 40 | 3 10·0 | 3 10·5 | 3 01·3 | 4·0 | 0·8 | 10·0 | 2·1 | 16·0 | 3·3 |
| 41 | 3 10·3 | 3 10·8 | 3 01·6 | 4·1 | 0·9 | 10·1 | 2·1 | 16·1 | 3·4 |
| 42 | 3 10·5 | 3 11·0 | 3 01·8 | 4·2 | 0·9 | 10·2 | 2·1 | 16·2 | 3·4 |
| 43 | 3 10·8 | 3 11·3 | 3 02·1 | 4·3 | 0·9 | 10·3 | 2·1 | 16·3 | 3·4 |
| 44 | 3 11·0 | 3 11·5 | 3 02·3 | 4·4 | 0·9 | 10·4 | 2·2 | 16·4 | 3·4 |
| 45 | 3 11·3 | 3 11·8 | 3 02·5 | 4·5 | 0·9 | 10·5 | 2·2 | 16·5 | 3·4 |
| 46 | 3 11·5 | 3 12·0 | 3 02·8 | 4·6 | 1·0 | 10·6 | 2·2 | 16·6 | 3·5 |
| 47 | 3 11·8 | 3 12·3 | 3 03·0 | 4·7 | 1·0 | 10·7 | 2·2 | 16·7 | 3·5 |
| 48 | 3 12·0 | 3 12·5 | 3 03·3 | 4·8 | 1·0 | 10·8 | 2·3 | 16·8 | 3·5 |
| 49 | 3 12·3 | 3 12·8 | 3 03·5 | 4·9 | 1·0 | 10·9 | 2·3 | 16·9 | 3·5 |
| 50 | 3 12·5 | 3 13·0 | 3 03·7 | 5·0 | 1·0 | 11·0 | 2·3 | 17·0 | 3·5 |
| 51 | 3 12·8 | 3 13·3 | 3 04·0 | 5·1 | 1·1 | 11·1 | 2·3 | 17·1 | 3·6 |
| 52 | 3 13·0 | 3 13·5 | 3 04·2 | 5·2 | 1·1 | 11·2 | 2·3 | 17·2 | 3·6 |
| 53 | 3 13·3 | 3 13·8 | 3 04·4 | 5·3 | 1·1 | 11·3 | 2·4 | 17·3 | 3·6 |
| 54 | 3 13·5 | 3 14·0 | 3 04·7 | 5·4 | 1·1 | 11·4 | 2·4 | 17·4 | 3·6 |
| 55 | 3 13·8 | 3 14·3 | 3 04·9 | 5·5 | 1·1 | 11·5 | 2·4 | 17·5 | 3·6 |
| 56 | 3 14·0 | 3 14·5 | 3 05·2 | 5·6 | 1·2 | 11·6 | 2·4 | 17·6 | 3·7 |
| 57 | 3 14·3 | 3 14·8 | 3 05·4 | 5·7 | 1·2 | 11·7 | 2·4 | 17·7 | 3·7 |
| 58 | 3 14·5 | 3 15·0 | 3 05·6 | 5·8 | 1·2 | 11·8 | 2·5 | 17·8 | 3·7 |
| 59 | 3 14·8 | 3 15·3 | 3 05·9 | 5·9 | 1·2 | 11·9 | 2·5 | 17·9 | 3·7 |
| 60 | 3 15·0 | 3 15·5 | 3 06·1 | 6·0 | 1·3 | 12·0 | 2·5 | 18·0 | 3·8 |

| 13ᵐ s | SUN PLANETS ° ′ | ARIES ° ′ | MOON ° ′ | v or d ′ | Corrⁿ ′ | v or d ′ | Corrⁿ ′ | v or d ′ | Corrⁿ ′ |
|---|---|---|---|---|---|---|---|---|---|
| 00 | 3 15·0 | 3 15·5 | 3 06·1 | 0·0 | 0·0 | 6·0 | 1·4 | 12·0 | 2·7 |
| 01 | 3 15·3 | 3 15·8 | 3 06·4 | 0·1 | 0·0 | 6·1 | 1·4 | 12·1 | 2·7 |
| 02 | 3 15·5 | 3 16·0 | 3 06·6 | 0·2 | 0·0 | 6·2 | 1·4 | 12·2 | 2·7 |
| 03 | 3 15·8 | 3 16·3 | 3 06·8 | 0·3 | 0·1 | 6·3 | 1·4 | 12·3 | 2·8 |
| 04 | 3 16·0 | 3 16·5 | 3 07·1 | 0·4 | 0·1 | 6·4 | 1·4 | 12·4 | 2·8 |
| 05 | 3 16·3 | 3 16·8 | 3 07·3 | 0·5 | 0·1 | 6·5 | 1·5 | 12·5 | 2·8 |
| 06 | 3 16·5 | 3 17·0 | 3 07·5 | 0·6 | 0·1 | 6·6 | 1·5 | 12·6 | 2·8 |
| 07 | 3 16·8 | 3 17·3 | 3 07·8 | 0·7 | 0·2 | 6·7 | 1·5 | 12·7 | 2·9 |
| 08 | 3 17·0 | 3 17·5 | 3 08·0 | 0·8 | 0·2 | 6·8 | 1·5 | 12·8 | 2·9 |
| 09 | 3 17·3 | 3 17·8 | 3 08·3 | 0·9 | 0·2 | 6·9 | 1·6 | 12·9 | 2·9 |
| 10 | 3 17·5 | 3 18·0 | 3 08·5 | 1·0 | 0·2 | 7·0 | 1·6 | 13·0 | 2·9 |
| 11 | 3 17·8 | 3 18·3 | 3 08·7 | 1·1 | 0·2 | 7·1 | 1·6 | 13·1 | 2·9 |
| 12 | 3 18·0 | 3 18·5 | 3 09·0 | 1·2 | 0·3 | 7·2 | 1·6 | 13·2 | 3·0 |
| 13 | 3 18·3 | 3 18·8 | 3 09·2 | 1·3 | 0·3 | 7·3 | 1·6 | 13·3 | 3·0 |
| 14 | 3 18·5 | 3 19·0 | 3 09·5 | 1·4 | 0·3 | 7·4 | 1·7 | 13·4 | 3·0 |
| 15 | 3 18·8 | 3 19·3 | 3 09·7 | 1·5 | 0·3 | 7·5 | 1·7 | 13·5 | 3·0 |
| 16 | 3 19·0 | 3 19·5 | 3 09·9 | 1·6 | 0·4 | 7·6 | 1·7 | 13·6 | 3·1 |
| 17 | 3 19·3 | 3 19·8 | 3 10·2 | 1·7 | 0·4 | 7·7 | 1·7 | 13·7 | 3·1 |
| 18 | 3 19·5 | 3 20·0 | 3 10·4 | 1·8 | 0·4 | 7·8 | 1·8 | 13·8 | 3·1 |
| 19 | 3 19·8 | 3 20·3 | 3 10·7 | 1·9 | 0·4 | 7·9 | 1·8 | 13·9 | 3·1 |
| 20 | 3 20·0 | 3 20·5 | 3 10·9 | 2·0 | 0·5 | 8·0 | 1·8 | 14·0 | 3·2 |
| 21 | 3 20·3 | 3 20·8 | 3 11·1 | 2·1 | 0·5 | 8·1 | 1·8 | 14·1 | 3·2 |
| 22 | 3 20·5 | 3 21·0 | 3 11·4 | 2·2 | 0·5 | 8·2 | 1·8 | 14·2 | 3·2 |
| 23 | 3 20·8 | 3 21·3 | 3 11·6 | 2·3 | 0·5 | 8·3 | 1·9 | 14·3 | 3·2 |
| 24 | 3 21·0 | 3 21·6 | 3 11·8 | 2·4 | 0·5 | 8·4 | 1·9 | 14·4 | 3·2 |
| 25 | 3 21·3 | 3 21·8 | 3 12·1 | 2·5 | 0·6 | 8·5 | 1·9 | 14·5 | 3·3 |
| 26 | 3 21·5 | 3 22·1 | 3 12·3 | 2·6 | 0·6 | 8·6 | 1·9 | 14·6 | 3·3 |
| 27 | 3 21·8 | 3 22·3 | 3 12·6 | 2·7 | 0·6 | 8·7 | 2·0 | 14·7 | 3·3 |
| 28 | 3 22·0 | 3 22·6 | 3 12·8 | 2·8 | 0·6 | 8·8 | 2·0 | 14·8 | 3·3 |
| 29 | 3 22·3 | 3 22·8 | 3 13·0 | 2·9 | 0·7 | 8·9 | 2·0 | 14·9 | 3·4 |
| 30 | 3 22·5 | 3 23·1 | 3 13·3 | 3·0 | 0·7 | 9·0 | 2·0 | 15·0 | 3·4 |
| 31 | 3 22·8 | 3 23·3 | 3 13·5 | 3·1 | 0·7 | 9·1 | 2·0 | 15·1 | 3·4 |
| 32 | 3 23·0 | 3 23·6 | 3 13·8 | 3·2 | 0·7 | 9·2 | 2·1 | 15·2 | 3·4 |
| 33 | 3 23·3 | 3 23·8 | 3 14·0 | 3·3 | 0·7 | 9·3 | 2·1 | 15·3 | 3·4 |
| 34 | 3 23·5 | 3 24·1 | 3 14·2 | 3·4 | 0·8 | 9·4 | 2·1 | 15·4 | 3·5 |
| 35 | 3 23·8 | 3 24·3 | 3 14·5 | 3·5 | 0·8 | 9·5 | 2·1 | 15·5 | 3·5 |
| 36 | 3 24·0 | 3 24·6 | 3 14·7 | 3·6 | 0·8 | 9·6 | 2·2 | 15·6 | 3·5 |
| 37 | 3 24·3 | 3 24·8 | 3 14·9 | 3·7 | 0·8 | 9·7 | 2·2 | 15·7 | 3·5 |
| 38 | 3 24·5 | 3 25·1 | 3 15·2 | 3·8 | 0·9 | 9·8 | 2·2 | 15·8 | 3·6 |
| 39 | 3 24·8 | 3 25·3 | 3 15·4 | 3·9 | 0·9 | 9·9 | 2·2 | 15·9 | 3·6 |
| 40 | 3 25·0 | 3 25·6 | 3 15·7 | 4·0 | 0·9 | 10·0 | 2·3 | 16·0 | 3·6 |
| 41 | 3 25·3 | 3 25·8 | 3 15·9 | 4·1 | 0·9 | 10·1 | 2·3 | 16·1 | 3·6 |
| 42 | 3 25·5 | 3 26·1 | 3 16·1 | 4·2 | 0·9 | 10·2 | 2·3 | 16·2 | 3·6 |
| 43 | 3 25·8 | 3 26·3 | 3 16·4 | 4·3 | 1·0 | 10·3 | 2·3 | 16·3 | 3·7 |
| 44 | 3 26·0 | 3 26·6 | 3 16·6 | 4·4 | 1·0 | 10·4 | 2·3 | 16·4 | 3·7 |
| 45 | 3 26·3 | 3 26·8 | 3 16·9 | 4·5 | 1·0 | 10·5 | 2·4 | 16·5 | 3·7 |
| 46 | 3 26·5 | 3 27·1 | 3 17·1 | 4·6 | 1·0 | 10·6 | 2·4 | 16·6 | 3·7 |
| 47 | 3 26·8 | 3 27·3 | 3 17·3 | 4·7 | 1·1 | 10·7 | 2·4 | 16·7 | 3·8 |
| 48 | 3 27·0 | 3 27·6 | 3 17·6 | 4·8 | 1·1 | 10·8 | 2·4 | 16·8 | 3·8 |
| 49 | 3 27·3 | 3 27·8 | 3 17·8 | 4·9 | 1·1 | 10·9 | 2·5 | 16·9 | 3·8 |
| 50 | 3 27·5 | 3 28·1 | 3 18·0 | 5·0 | 1·1 | 11·0 | 2·5 | 17·0 | 3·8 |
| 51 | 3 27·8 | 3 28·3 | 3 18·3 | 5·1 | 1·1 | 11·1 | 2·5 | 17·1 | 3·8 |
| 52 | 3 28·0 | 3 28·6 | 3 18·5 | 5·2 | 1·2 | 11·2 | 2·5 | 17·2 | 3·9 |
| 53 | 3 28·3 | 3 28·8 | 3 18·8 | 5·3 | 1·2 | 11·3 | 2·5 | 17·3 | 3·9 |
| 54 | 3 28·5 | 3 29·1 | 3 19·0 | 5·4 | 1·2 | 11·4 | 2·6 | 17·4 | 3·9 |
| 55 | 3 28·8 | 3 29·3 | 3 19·2 | 5·5 | 1·2 | 11·5 | 2·6 | 17·5 | 3·9 |
| 56 | 3 29·0 | 3 29·6 | 3 19·5 | 5·6 | 1·3 | 11·6 | 2·6 | 17·6 | 4·0 |
| 57 | 3 29·3 | 3 29·8 | 3 19·7 | 5·7 | 1·3 | 11·7 | 2·6 | 17·7 | 4·0 |
| 58 | 3 29·5 | 3 30·1 | 3 20·0 | 5·8 | 1·3 | 11·8 | 2·7 | 17·8 | 4·0 |
| 59 | 3 29·8 | 3 30·3 | 3 20·2 | 5·9 | 1·3 | 11·9 | 2·7 | 17·9 | 4·0 |
| 60 | 3 30·0 | 3 30·6 | 3 20·4 | 6·0 | 1·4 | 12·0 | 2·7 | 18·0 | 4·1 |



| 14ᵐ s | SUN PLANETS ° ′ | ARIES ° ′ | MOON ° ′ | v or d ′ | Corrⁿ ′ | v or d ′ | Corrⁿ ′ | v or d ′ | Corrⁿ ′ |
|---|---|---|---|---|---|---|---|---|---|
| 00 | 3 30·0 | 3 30·6 | 3 20·4 | 0·0 | 0·0 | 6·0 | 1·5 | 12·0 | 2·9 |
| 01 | 3 30·3 | 3 30·8 | 3 20·7 | 0·1 | 0·0 | 6·1 | 1·5 | 12·1 | 2·9 |
| 02 | 3 30·5 | 3 31·1 | 3 20·9 | 0·2 | 0·0 | 6·2 | 1·5 | 12·2 | 2·9 |
| 03 | 3 30·8 | 3 31·3 | 3 21·1 | 0·3 | 0·1 | 6·3 | 1·5 | 12·3 | 3·0 |
| 04 | 3 31·0 | 3 31·6 | 3 21·4 | 0·4 | 0·1 | 6·4 | 1·5 | 12·4 | 3·0 |
| 05 | 3 31·3 | 3 31·8 | 3 21·6 | 0·5 | 0·1 | 6·5 | 1·6 | 12·5 | 3·0 |
| 06 | 3 31·5 | 3 32·1 | 3 21·9 | 0·6 | 0·1 | 6·6 | 1·6 | 12·6 | 3·0 |
| 07 | 3 31·8 | 3 32·3 | 3 22·1 | 0·7 | 0·2 | 6·7 | 1·6 | 12·7 | 3·1 |
| 08 | 3 32·0 | 3 32·6 | 3 22·3 | 0·8 | 0·2 | 6·8 | 1·6 | 12·8 | 3·1 |
| 09 | 3 32·3 | 3 32·8 | 3 22·6 | 0·9 | 0·2 | 6·9 | 1·7 | 12·9 | 3·1 |
| 10 | 3 32·5 | 3 33·1 | 3 22·8 | 1·0 | 0·2 | 7·0 | 1·7 | 13·0 | 3·1 |
| 11 | 3 32·8 | 3 33·3 | 3 23·1 | 1·1 | 0·3 | 7·1 | 1·7 | 13·1 | 3·2 |
| 12 | 3 33·0 | 3 33·6 | 3 23·3 | 1·2 | 0·3 | 7·2 | 1·7 | 13·2 | 3·2 |
| 13 | 3 33·3 | 3 33·8 | 3 23·5 | 1·3 | 0·3 | 7·3 | 1·8 | 13·3 | 3·2 |
| 14 | 3 33·5 | 3 34·1 | 3 23·8 | 1·4 | 0·3 | 7·4 | 1·8 | 13·4 | 3·2 |
| 15 | 3 33·8 | 3 34·3 | 3 24·0 | 1·5 | 0·4 | 7·5 | 1·8 | 13·5 | 3·3 |
| 16 | 3 34·0 | 3 34·6 | 3 24·3 | 1·6 | 0·4 | 7·6 | 1·8 | 13·6 | 3·3 |
| 17 | 3 34·3 | 3 34·8 | 3 24·5 | 1·7 | 0·4 | 7·7 | 1·9 | 13·7 | 3·3 |
| 18 | 3 34·5 | 3 35·1 | 3 24·7 | 1·8 | 0·4 | 7·8 | 1·9 | 13·8 | 3·3 |
| 19 | 3 34·8 | 3 35·3 | 3 25·0 | 1·9 | 0·5 | 7·9 | 1·9 | 13·9 | 3·4 |
| 20 | 3 35·0 | 3 35·6 | 3 25·2 | 2·0 | 0·5 | 8·0 | 1·9 | 14·0 | 3·4 |
| 21 | 3 35·3 | 3 35·8 | 3 25·4 | 2·1 | 0·5 | 8·1 | 2·0 | 14·1 | 3·4 |
| 22 | 3 35·5 | 3 36·1 | 3 25·7 | 2·2 | 0·5 | 8·2 | 2·0 | 14·2 | 3·4 |
| 23 | 3 35·8 | 3 36·3 | 3 25·9 | 2·3 | 0·6 | 8·3 | 2·0 | 14·3 | 3·5 |
| 24 | 3 36·0 | 3 36·6 | 3 26·2 | 2·4 | 0·6 | 8·4 | 2·0 | 14·4 | 3·5 |
| 25 | 3 36·3 | 3 36·8 | 3 26·4 | 2·5 | 0·6 | 8·5 | 2·1 | 14·5 | 3·5 |
| 26 | 3 36·5 | 3 37·1 | 3 26·6 | 2·6 | 0·6 | 8·6 | 2·1 | 14·6 | 3·5 |
| 27 | 3 36·8 | 3 37·3 | 3 26·9 | 2·7 | 0·7 | 8·7 | 2·1 | 14·7 | 3·6 |
| 28 | 3 37·0 | 3 37·6 | 3 27·1 | 2·8 | 0·7 | 8·8 | 2·1 | 14·8 | 3·6 |
| 29 | 3 37·3 | 3 37·8 | 3 27·4 | 2·9 | 0·7 | 8·9 | 2·2 | 14·9 | 3·6 |
| 30 | 3 37·5 | 3 38·1 | 3 27·6 | 3·0 | 0·7 | 9·0 | 2·2 | 15·0 | 3·6 |
| 31 | 3 37·8 | 3 38·3 | 3 27·8 | 3·1 | 0·7 | 9·1 | 2·2 | 15·1 | 3·6 |
| 32 | 3 38·0 | 3 38·6 | 3 28·1 | 3·2 | 0·8 | 9·2 | 2·2 | 15·2 | 3·7 |
| 33 | 3 38·3 | 3 38·8 | 3 28·3 | 3·3 | 0·8 | 9·3 | 2·2 | 15·3 | 3·7 |
| 34 | 3 38·5 | 3 39·1 | 3 28·5 | 3·4 | 0·8 | 9·4 | 2·3 | 15·4 | 3·7 |
| 35 | 3 38·8 | 3 39·3 | 3 28·8 | 3·5 | 0·8 | 9·5 | 2·3 | 15·5 | 3·7 |
| 36 | 3 39·0 | 3 39·6 | 3 29·0 | 3·6 | 0·9 | 9·6 | 2·3 | 15·6 | 3·8 |
| 37 | 3 39·3 | 3 39·9 | 3 29·3 | 3·7 | 0·9 | 9·7 | 2·3 | 15·7 | 3·8 |
| 38 | 3 39·5 | 3 40·1 | 3 29·5 | 3·8 | 0·9 | 9·8 | 2·4 | 15·8 | 3·8 |
| 39 | 3 39·8 | 3 40·4 | 3 29·7 | 3·9 | 0·9 | 9·9 | 2·4 | 15·9 | 3·8 |
| 40 | 3 40·0 | 3 40·6 | 3 30·0 | 4·0 | 1·0 | 10·0 | 2·4 | 16·0 | 3·9 |
| 41 | 3 40·3 | 3 40·9 | 3 30·2 | 4·1 | 1·0 | 10·1 | 2·4 | 16·1 | 3·9 |
| 42 | 3 40·5 | 3 41·1 | 3 30·5 | 4·2 | 1·0 | 10·2 | 2·5 | 16·2 | 3·9 |
| 43 | 3 40·8 | 3 41·4 | 3 30·7 | 4·3 | 1·0 | 10·3 | 2·5 | 16·3 | 3·9 |
| 44 | 3 41·0 | 3 41·6 | 3 30·9 | 4·4 | 1·1 | 10·4 | 2·5 | 16·4 | 4·0 |
| 45 | 3 41·3 | 3 41·9 | 3 31·2 | 4·5 | 1·1 | 10·5 | 2·5 | 16·5 | 4·0 |
| 46 | 3 41·5 | 3 42·1 | 3 31·4 | 4·6 | 1·1 | 10·6 | 2·6 | 16·6 | 4·0 |
| 47 | 3 41·8 | 3 42·4 | 3 31·6 | 4·7 | 1·1 | 10·7 | 2·6 | 16·7 | 4·0 |
| 48 | 3 42·0 | 3 42·6 | 3 31·9 | 4·8 | 1·2 | 10·8 | 2·6 | 16·8 | 4·1 |
| 49 | 3 42·3 | 3 42·9 | 3 32·1 | 4·9 | 1·2 | 10·9 | 2·6 | 16·9 | 4·1 |
| 50 | 3 42·5 | 3 43·1 | 3 32·4 | 5·0 | 1·2 | 11·0 | 2·7 | 17·0 | 4·1 |
| 51 | 3 42·8 | 3 43·4 | 3 32·6 | 5·1 | 1·2 | 11·1 | 2·7 | 17·1 | 4·1 |
| 52 | 3 43·0 | 3 43·6 | 3 32·8 | 5·2 | 1·3 | 11·2 | 2·7 | 17·2 | 4·2 |
| 53 | 3 43·3 | 3 43·9 | 3 33·1 | 5·3 | 1·3 | 11·3 | 2·7 | 17·3 | 4·2 |
| 54 | 3 43·5 | 3 44·1 | 3 33·3 | 5·4 | 1·3 | 11·4 | 2·8 | 17·4 | 4·2 |
| 55 | 3 43·8 | 3 44·4 | 3 33·6 | 5·5 | 1·3 | 11·5 | 2·8 | 17·5 | 4·2 |
| 56 | 3 44·0 | 3 44·6 | 3 33·8 | 5·6 | 1·4 | 11·6 | 2·8 | 17·6 | 4·3 |
| 57 | 3 44·3 | 3 44·9 | 3 34·0 | 5·7 | 1·4 | 11·7 | 2·8 | 17·7 | 4·3 |
| 58 | 3 44·5 | 3 45·1 | 3 34·3 | 5·8 | 1·4 | 11·8 | 2·9 | 17·8 | 4·3 |
| 59 | 3 44·8 | 3 45·4 | 3 34·5 | 5·9 | 1·4 | 11·9 | 2·9 | 17·9 | 4·3 |
| 60 | 3 45·0 | 3 45·6 | 3 34·8 | 6·0 | 1·5 | 12·0 | 2·9 | 18·0 | 4·4 |

| 15ᵐ s | SUN PLANETS ° ′ | ARIES ° ′ | MOON ° ′ | v or d ′ | Corrⁿ ′ | v or d ′ | Corrⁿ ′ | v or d ′ | Corrⁿ ′ |
|---|---|---|---|---|---|---|---|---|---|
| 00 | 3 45·0 | 3 45·6 | 3 34·8 | 0·0 | 0·0 | 6·0 | 1·6 | 12·0 | 3·1 |
| 01 | 3 45·3 | 3 45·9 | 3 35·0 | 0·1 | 0·0 | 6·1 | 1·6 | 12·1 | 3·1 |
| 02 | 3 45·5 | 3 46·1 | 3 35·2 | 0·2 | 0·1 | 6·2 | 1·6 | 12·2 | 3·2 |
| 03 | 3 45·8 | 3 46·4 | 3 35·5 | 0·3 | 0·1 | 6·3 | 1·6 | 12·3 | 3·2 |
| 04 | 3 46·0 | 3 46·6 | 3 35·7 | 0·4 | 0·1 | 6·4 | 1·7 | 12·4 | 3·2 |
| 05 | 3 46·3 | 3 46·9 | 3 35·9 | 0·5 | 0·1 | 6·5 | 1·7 | 12·5 | 3·2 |
| 06 | 3 46·5 | 3 47·1 | 3 36·2 | 0·6 | 0·2 | 6·6 | 1·7 | 12·6 | 3·3 |
| 07 | 3 46·8 | 3 47·4 | 3 36·4 | 0·7 | 0·2 | 6·7 | 1·7 | 12·7 | 3·3 |
| 08 | 3 47·0 | 3 47·6 | 3 36·7 | 0·8 | 0·2 | 6·8 | 1·8 | 12·8 | 3·3 |
| 09 | 3 47·3 | 3 47·9 | 3 36·9 | 0·9 | 0·2 | 6·9 | 1·8 | 12·9 | 3·3 |
| 10 | 3 47·5 | 3 48·1 | 3 37·1 | 1·0 | 0·3 | 7·0 | 1·8 | 13·0 | 3·4 |
| 11 | 3 47·8 | 3 48·4 | 3 37·4 | 1·1 | 0·3 | 7·1 | 1·8 | 13·1 | 3·4 |
| 12 | 3 48·0 | 3 48·6 | 3 37·6 | 1·2 | 0·3 | 7·2 | 1·9 | 13·2 | 3·4 |
| 13 | 3 48·3 | 3 48·9 | 3 37·9 | 1·3 | 0·3 | 7·3 | 1·9 | 13·3 | 3·4 |
| 14 | 3 48·5 | 3 49·1 | 3 38·1 | 1·4 | 0·4 | 7·4 | 1·9 | 13·4 | 3·5 |
| 15 | 3 48·8 | 3 49·4 | 3 38·3 | 1·5 | 0·4 | 7·5 | 1·9 | 13·5 | 3·5 |
| 16 | 3 49·0 | 3 49·6 | 3 38·6 | 1·6 | 0·4 | 7·6 | 2·0 | 13·6 | 3·5 |
| 17 | 3 49·3 | 3 49·9 | 3 38·8 | 1·7 | 0·4 | 7·7 | 2·0 | 13·7 | 3·5 |
| 18 | 3 49·5 | 3 50·1 | 3 39·0 | 1·8 | 0·5 | 7·8 | 2·0 | 13·8 | 3·6 |
| 19 | 3 49·8 | 3 50·4 | 3 39·3 | 1·9 | 0·5 | 7·9 | 2·0 | 13·9 | 3·6 |
| 20 | 3 50·0 | 3 50·6 | 3 39·5 | 2·0 | 0·5 | 8·0 | 2·1 | 14·0 | 3·6 |
| 21 | 3 50·3 | 3 50·9 | 3 39·8 | 2·1 | 0·5 | 8·1 | 2·1 | 14·1 | 3·6 |
| 22 | 3 50·5 | 3 51·1 | 3 40·0 | 2·2 | 0·6 | 8·2 | 2·1 | 14·2 | 3·7 |
| 23 | 3 50·8 | 3 51·4 | 3 40·2 | 2·3 | 0·6 | 8·3 | 2·1 | 14·3 | 3·7 |
| 24 | 3 51·0 | 3 51·6 | 3 40·5 | 2·4 | 0·6 | 8·4 | 2·2 | 14·4 | 3·7 |
| 25 | 3 51·3 | 3 51·9 | 3 40·7 | 2·5 | 0·6 | 8·5 | 2·2 | 14·5 | 3·7 |
| 26 | 3 51·5 | 3 52·1 | 3 41·0 | 2·6 | 0·7 | 8·6 | 2·2 | 14·6 | 3·8 |
| 27 | 3 51·8 | 3 52·4 | 3 41·2 | 2·7 | 0·7 | 8·7 | 2·2 | 14·7 | 3·8 |
| 28 | 3 52·0 | 3 52·6 | 3 41·4 | 2·8 | 0·7 | 8·8 | 2·3 | 14·8 | 3·8 |
| 29 | 3 52·3 | 3 52·9 | 3 41·7 | 2·9 | 0·7 | 8·9 | 2·3 | 14·9 | 3·8 |
| 30 | 3 52·5 | 3 53·1 | 3 41·9 | 3·0 | 0·8 | 9·0 | 2·3 | 15·0 | 3·9 |
| 31 | 3 52·8 | 3 53·4 | 3 42·1 | 3·1 | 0·8 | 9·1 | 2·4 | 15·1 | 3·9 |
| 32 | 3 53·0 | 3 53·6 | 3 42·4 | 3·2 | 0·8 | 9·2 | 2·4 | 15·2 | 3·9 |
| 33 | 3 53·3 | 3 53·9 | 3 42·6 | 3·3 | 0·9 | 9·3 | 2·4 | 15·3 | 4·0 |
| 34 | 3 53·5 | 3 54·1 | 3 42·9 | 3·4 | 0·9 | 9·4 | 2·4 | 15·4 | 4·0 |
| 35 | 3 53·8 | 3 54·4 | 3 43·1 | 3·5 | 0·9 | 9·5 | 2·5 | 15·5 | 4·0 |
| 36 | 3 54·0 | 3 54·6 | 3 43·3 | 3·6 | 0·9 | 9·6 | 2·5 | 15·6 | 4·0 |
| 37 | 3 54·3 | 3 54·9 | 3 43·6 | 3·7 | 1·0 | 9·7 | 2·5 | 15·7 | 4·1 |
| 38 | 3 54·5 | 3 55·1 | 3 43·8 | 3·8 | 1·0 | 9·8 | 2·5 | 15·8 | 4·1 |
| 39 | 3 54·8 | 3 55·4 | 3 44·1 | 3·9 | 1·0 | 9·9 | 2·6 | 15·9 | 4·1 |
| 40 | 3 55·0 | 3 55·6 | 3 44·3 | 4·0 | 1·0 | 10·0 | 2·6 | 16·0 | 4·1 |
| 41 | 3 55·3 | 3 55·9 | 3 44·5 | 4·1 | 1·1 | 10·1 | 2·6 | 16·1 | 4·2 |
| 42 | 3 55·5 | 3 56·1 | 3 44·8 | 4·2 | 1·1 | 10·2 | 2·6 | 16·2 | 4·2 |
| 43 | 3 55·8 | 3 56·4 | 3 45·0 | 4·3 | 1·1 | 10·3 | 2·7 | 16·3 | 4·2 |
| 44 | 3 56·0 | 3 56·6 | 3 45·2 | 4·4 | 1·1 | 10·4 | 2·7 | 16·4 | 4·2 |
| 45 | 3 56·3 | 3 56·9 | 3 45·5 | 4·5 | 1·2 | 10·5 | 2·7 | 16·5 | 4·3 |
| 46 | 3 56·5 | 3 57·1 | 3 45·7 | 4·6 | 1·2 | 10·6 | 2·7 | 16·6 | 4·3 |
| 47 | 3 56·8 | 3 57·4 | 3 46·0 | 4·7 | 1·2 | 10·7 | 2·8 | 16·7 | 4·3 |
| 48 | 3 57·0 | 3 57·6 | 3 46·2 | 4·8 | 1·2 | 10·8 | 2·8 | 16·8 | 4·3 |
| 49 | 3 57·3 | 3 57·9 | 3 46·4 | 4·9 | 1·3 | 10·9 | 2·8 | 16·9 | 4·4 |
| 50 | 3 57·5 | 3 58·2 | 3 46·7 | 5·0 | 1·3 | 11·0 | 2·8 | 17·0 | 4·4 |
| 51 | 3 57·8 | 3 58·4 | 3 46·9 | 5·1 | 1·3 | 11·1 | 2·9 | 17·1 | 4·4 |
| 52 | 3 58·0 | 3 58·7 | 3 47·2 | 5·2 | 1·3 | 11·2 | 2·9 | 17·2 | 4·4 |
| 53 | 3 58·3 | 3 58·9 | 3 47·4 | 5·3 | 1·4 | 11·3 | 2·9 | 17·3 | 4·5 |
| 54 | 3 58·5 | 3 59·2 | 3 47·6 | 5·4 | 1·4 | 11·4 | 2·9 | 17·4 | 4·5 |
| 55 | 3 58·8 | 3 59·4 | 3 47·9 | 5·5 | 1·4 | 11·5 | 3·0 | 17·5 | 4·5 |
| 56 | 3 59·0 | 3 59·7 | 3 48·1 | 5·6 | 1·4 | 11·6 | 3·0 | 17·6 | 4·5 |
| 57 | 3 59·3 | 3 59·9 | 3 48·4 | 5·7 | 1·5 | 11·7 | 3·0 | 17·7 | 4·6 |
| 58 | 3 59·5 | 4 00·2 | 3 48·6 | 5·8 | 1·5 | 11·8 | 3·0 | 17·8 | 4·6 |
| 59 | 3 59·8 | 4 00·4 | 3 48·8 | 5·9 | 1·5 | 11·9 | 3·1 | 17·9 | 4·6 |
| 60 | 4 00·0 | 4 00·7 | 3 49·1 | 6·0 | 1·6 | 12·0 | 3·1 | 18·0 | 4·7 |

| 16m s | SUN PLANETS | ARIES | MOON | v or d | Corrⁿ | v or d | Corrⁿ | v or d | Corrⁿ |
|---|---|---|---|---|---|---|---|---|---|
| | ° ′ | ° ′ | ° ′ | ′ | ′ | ′ | ′ | ′ | ′ |
| 00 | 4 00·0 | 4 00·7 | 3 49·1 | 0·0 | 0·0 | 6·0 | 1·7 | 12·0 | 3·3 |
| 01 | 4 00·3 | 4 00·9 | 3 49·3 | 0·1 | 0·0 | 6·1 | 1·7 | 12·1 | 3·3 |
| 02 | 4 00·5 | 4 01·2 | 3 49·5 | 0·2 | 0·1 | 6·2 | 1·7 | 12·2 | 3·4 |
| 03 | 4 00·8 | 4 01·4 | 3 49·8 | 0·3 | 0·1 | 6·3 | 1·7 | 12·3 | 3·4 |
| 04 | 4 01·0 | 4 01·7 | 3 50·0 | 0·4 | 0·1 | 6·4 | 1·8 | 12·4 | 3·4 |
| 05 | 4 01·3 | 4 01·9 | 3 50·3 | 0·5 | 0·1 | 6·5 | 1·8 | 12·5 | 3·4 |
| 06 | 4 01·5 | 4 02·2 | 3 50·5 | 0·6 | 0·2 | 6·6 | 1·8 | 12·6 | 3·5 |
| 07 | 4 01·8 | 4 02·4 | 3 50·7 | 0·7 | 0·2 | 6·7 | 1·8 | 12·7 | 3·5 |
| 08 | 4 02·0 | 4 02·7 | 3 51·0 | 0·8 | 0·2 | 6·8 | 1·9 | 12·8 | 3·5 |
| 09 | 4 02·3 | 4 02·9 | 3 51·2 | 0·9 | 0·2 | 6·9 | 1·9 | 12·9 | 3·5 |
| 10 | 4 02·5 | 4 03·2 | 3 51·5 | 1·0 | 0·3 | 7·0 | 1·9 | 13·0 | 3·6 |
| 11 | 4 02·8 | 4 03·4 | 3 51·7 | 1·1 | 0·3 | 7·1 | 2·0 | 13·1 | 3·6 |
| 12 | 4 03·0 | 4 03·7 | 3 51·9 | 1·2 | 0·3 | 7·2 | 2·0 | 13·2 | 3·6 |
| 13 | 4 03·3 | 4 03·9 | 3 52·2 | 1·3 | 0·4 | 7·3 | 2·0 | 13·3 | 3·7 |
| 14 | 4 03·5 | 4 04·2 | 3 52·4 | 1·4 | 0·4 | 7·4 | 2·0 | 13·4 | 3·7 |
| 15 | 4 03·8 | 4 04·4 | 3 52·6 | 1·5 | 0·4 | 7·5 | 2·1 | 13·5 | 3·7 |
| 16 | 4 04·0 | 4 04·7 | 3 52·9 | 1·6 | 0·4 | 7·6 | 2·1 | 13·6 | 3·7 |
| 17 | 4 04·3 | 4 04·9 | 3 53·1 | 1·7 | 0·5 | 7·7 | 2·1 | 13·7 | 3·8 |
| 18 | 4 04·5 | 4 05·2 | 3 53·4 | 1·8 | 0·5 | 7·8 | 2·1 | 13·8 | 3·8 |
| 19 | 4 04·8 | 4 05·4 | 3 53·6 | 1·9 | 0·5 | 7·9 | 2·2 | 13·9 | 3·8 |
| 20 | 4 05·0 | 4 05·7 | 3 53·8 | 2·0 | 0·6 | 8·0 | 2·2 | 14·0 | 3·9 |
| 21 | 4 05·3 | 4 05·9 | 3 54·1 | 2·1 | 0·6 | 8·1 | 2·2 | 14·1 | 3·9 |
| 22 | 4 05·5 | 4 06·2 | 3 54·3 | 2·2 | 0·6 | 8·2 | 2·3 | 14·2 | 3·9 |
| 23 | 4 05·8 | 4 06·4 | 3 54·6 | 2·3 | 0·6 | 8·3 | 2·3 | 14·3 | 3·9 |
| 24 | 4 06·0 | 4 06·7 | 3 54·8 | 2·4 | 0·7 | 8·4 | 2·3 | 14·4 | 4·0 |
| 25 | 4 06·3 | 4 06·9 | 3 55·0 | 2·5 | 0·7 | 8·5 | 2·3 | 14·5 | 4·0 |
| 26 | 4 06·5 | 4 07·2 | 3 55·3 | 2·6 | 0·7 | 8·6 | 2·4 | 14·6 | 4·0 |
| 27 | 4 06·8 | 4 07·4 | 3 55·5 | 2·7 | 0·7 | 8·7 | 2·4 | 14·7 | 4·0 |
| 28 | 4 07·0 | 4 07·7 | 3 55·7 | 2·8 | 0·8 | 8·8 | 2·4 | 14·8 | 4·1 |
| 29 | 4 07·3 | 4 07·9 | 3 56·0 | 2·9 | 0·8 | 8·9 | 2·4 | 14·9 | 4·1 |
| 30 | 4 07·5 | 4 08·2 | 3 56·2 | 3·0 | 0·8 | 9·0 | 2·5 | 15·0 | 4·1 |
| 31 | 4 07·8 | 4 08·4 | 3 56·5 | 3·1 | 0·9 | 9·1 | 2·5 | 15·1 | 4·2 |
| 32 | 4 08·0 | 4 08·7 | 3 56·7 | 3·2 | 0·9 | 9·2 | 2·5 | 15·2 | 4·2 |
| 33 | 4 08·3 | 4 08·9 | 3 56·9 | 3·3 | 0·9 | 9·3 | 2·6 | 15·3 | 4·2 |
| 34 | 4 08·5 | 4 09·2 | 3 57·2 | 3·4 | 0·9 | 9·4 | 2·6 | 15·4 | 4·2 |
| 35 | 4 08·8 | 4 09·4 | 3 57·4 | 3·5 | 1·0 | 9·5 | 2·6 | 15·5 | 4·3 |
| 36 | 4 09·0 | 4 09·7 | 3 57·7 | 3·6 | 1·0 | 9·6 | 2·6 | 15·6 | 4·3 |
| 37 | 4 09·3 | 4 09·9 | 3 57·9 | 3·7 | 1·0 | 9·7 | 2·7 | 15·7 | 4·3 |
| 38 | 4 09·5 | 4 10·2 | 3 58·1 | 3·8 | 1·0 | 9·8 | 2·7 | 15·8 | 4·3 |
| 39 | 4 09·8 | 4 10·4 | 3 58·4 | 3·9 | 1·1 | 9·9 | 2·7 | 15·9 | 4·4 |
| 40 | 4 10·0 | 4 10·7 | 3 58·6 | 4·0 | 1·1 | 10·0 | 2·8 | 16·0 | 4·4 |
| 41 | 4 10·3 | 4 10·9 | 3 58·8 | 4·1 | 1·1 | 10·1 | 2·8 | 16·1 | 4·4 |
| 42 | 4 10·5 | 4 11·2 | 3 59·1 | 4·2 | 1·2 | 10·2 | 2·8 | 16·2 | 4·5 |
| 43 | 4 10·8 | 4 11·4 | 3 59·3 | 4·3 | 1·2 | 10·3 | 2·8 | 16·3 | 4·5 |
| 44 | 4 11·0 | 4 11·7 | 3 59·6 | 4·4 | 1·2 | 10·4 | 2·9 | 16·4 | 4·5 |
| 45 | 4 11·3 | 4 11·9 | 3 59·8 | 4·5 | 1·2 | 10·5 | 2·9 | 16·5 | 4·5 |
| 46 | 4 11·5 | 4 12·2 | 4 00·0 | 4·6 | 1·3 | 10·6 | 2·9 | 16·6 | 4·6 |
| 47 | 4 11·8 | 4 12·4 | 4 00·3 | 4·7 | 1·3 | 10·7 | 2·9 | 16·7 | 4·6 |
| 48 | 4 12·0 | 4 12·7 | 4 00·5 | 4·8 | 1·3 | 10·8 | 3·0 | 16·8 | 4·6 |
| 49 | 4 12·3 | 4 12·9 | 4 00·8 | 4·9 | 1·3 | 10·9 | 3·0 | 16·9 | 4·6 |
| 50 | 4 12·5 | 4 13·2 | 4 01·0 | 5·0 | 1·4 | 11·0 | 3·0 | 17·0 | 4·7 |
| 51 | 4 12·8 | 4 13·4 | 4 01·2 | 5·1 | 1·4 | 11·1 | 3·1 | 17·1 | 4·7 |
| 52 | 4 13·0 | 4 13·7 | 4 01·5 | 5·2 | 1·4 | 11·2 | 3·1 | 17·2 | 4·7 |
| 53 | 4 13·3 | 4 13·9 | 4 01·7 | 5·3 | 1·5 | 11·3 | 3·1 | 17·3 | 4·8 |
| 54 | 4 13·5 | 4 14·2 | 4 02·0 | 5·4 | 1·5 | 11·4 | 3·1 | 17·4 | 4·8 |
| 55 | 4 13·8 | 4 14·4 | 4 02·2 | 5·5 | 1·5 | 11·5 | 3·2 | 17·5 | 4·8 |
| 56 | 4 14·0 | 4 14·7 | 4 02·4 | 5·6 | 1·5 | 11·6 | 3·2 | 17·6 | 4·8 |
| 57 | 4 14·3 | 4 14·9 | 4 02·7 | 5·7 | 1·6 | 11·7 | 3·2 | 17·7 | 4·9 |
| 58 | 4 14·5 | 4 15·2 | 4 02·9 | 5·8 | 1·6 | 11·8 | 3·2 | 17·8 | 4·9 |
| 59 | 4 14·8 | 4 15·4 | 4 03·1 | 5·9 | 1·6 | 11·9 | 3·3 | 17·9 | 4·9 |
| 60 | 4 15·0 | 4 15·7 | 4 03·4 | 6·0 | 1·7 | 12·0 | 3·3 | 18·0 | 5·0 |

| 17m s | SUN PLANETS | ARIES | MOON | v or d | Corrⁿ | v or d | Corrⁿ | v or d | Corrⁿ |
|---|---|---|---|---|---|---|---|---|---|
| | ° ′ | ° ′ | ° ′ | ′ | ′ | ′ | ′ | ′ | ′ |
| 00 | 4 15·0 | 4 15·7 | 4 03·4 | 0·0 | 0·0 | 6·0 | 1·8 | 12·0 | 3·5 |
| 01 | 4 15·3 | 4 15·9 | 4 03·6 | 0·1 | 0·0 | 6·1 | 1·8 | 12·1 | 3·5 |
| 02 | 4 15·5 | 4 16·2 | 4 03·9 | 0·2 | 0·1 | 6·2 | 1·8 | 12·2 | 3·6 |
| 03 | 4 15·8 | 4 16·5 | 4 04·1 | 0·3 | 0·1 | 6·3 | 1·8 | 12·3 | 3·6 |
| 04 | 4 16·0 | 4 16·7 | 4 04·3 | 0·4 | 0·1 | 6·4 | 1·9 | 12·4 | 3·6 |
| 05 | 4 16·3 | 4 17·0 | 4 04·6 | 0·5 | 0·1 | 6·5 | 1·9 | 12·5 | 3·6 |
| 06 | 4 16·5 | 4 17·2 | 4 04·8 | 0·6 | 0·2 | 6·6 | 1·9 | 12·6 | 3·7 |
| 07 | 4 16·8 | 4 17·5 | 4 05·1 | 0·7 | 0·2 | 6·7 | 2·0 | 12·7 | 3·7 |
| 08 | 4 17·0 | 4 17·7 | 4 05·3 | 0·8 | 0·2 | 6·8 | 2·0 | 12·8 | 3·7 |
| 09 | 4 17·3 | 4 18·0 | 4 05·5 | 0·9 | 0·3 | 6·9 | 2·0 | 12·9 | 3·8 |
| 10 | 4 17·5 | 4 18·2 | 4 05·8 | 1·0 | 0·3 | 7·0 | 2·0 | 13·0 | 3·8 |
| 11 | 4 17·8 | 4 18·5 | 4 06·0 | 1·1 | 0·3 | 7·1 | 2·1 | 13·1 | 3·8 |
| 12 | 4 18·0 | 4 18·7 | 4 06·2 | 1·2 | 0·4 | 7·2 | 2·1 | 13·2 | 3·9 |
| 13 | 4 18·3 | 4 19·0 | 4 06·5 | 1·3 | 0·4 | 7·3 | 2·1 | 13·3 | 3·9 |
| 14 | 4 18·5 | 4 19·2 | 4 06·7 | 1·4 | 0·4 | 7·4 | 2·2 | 13·4 | 3·9 |
| 15 | 4 18·8 | 4 19·5 | 4 07·0 | 1·5 | 0·4 | 7·5 | 2·2 | 13·5 | 3·9 |
| 16 | 4 19·0 | 4 19·7 | 4 07·2 | 1·6 | 0·5 | 7·6 | 2·2 | 13·6 | 4·0 |
| 17 | 4 19·3 | 4 20·0 | 4 07·4 | 1·7 | 0·5 | 7·7 | 2·3 | 13·7 | 4·0 |
| 18 | 4 19·5 | 4 20·2 | 4 07·7 | 1·8 | 0·5 | 7·8 | 2·3 | 13·8 | 4·0 |
| 19 | 4 19·8 | 4 20·5 | 4 07·9 | 1·9 | 0·6 | 7·9 | 2·3 | 13·9 | 4·1 |
| 20 | 4 20·0 | 4 20·7 | 4 08·2 | 2·0 | 0·6 | 8·0 | 2·3 | 14·0 | 4·1 |
| 21 | 4 20·3 | 4 21·0 | 4 08·4 | 2·1 | 0·6 | 8·1 | 2·4 | 14·1 | 4·1 |
| 22 | 4 20·5 | 4 21·2 | 4 08·6 | 2·2 | 0·6 | 8·2 | 2·4 | 14·2 | 4·1 |
| 23 | 4 20·8 | 4 21·5 | 4 08·9 | 2·3 | 0·7 | 8·3 | 2·4 | 14·3 | 4·2 |
| 24 | 4 21·0 | 4 21·7 | 4 09·1 | 2·4 | 0·7 | 8·4 | 2·5 | 14·4 | 4·2 |
| 25 | 4 21·3 | 4 22·0 | 4 09·3 | 2·5 | 0·7 | 8·5 | 2·5 | 14·5 | 4·2 |
| 26 | 4 21·5 | 4 22·2 | 4 09·6 | 2·6 | 0·8 | 8·6 | 2·5 | 14·6 | 4·3 |
| 27 | 4 21·8 | 4 22·5 | 4 09·8 | 2·7 | 0·8 | 8·7 | 2·5 | 14·7 | 4·3 |
| 28 | 4 22·0 | 4 22·7 | 4 10·1 | 2·8 | 0·8 | 8·8 | 2·6 | 14·8 | 4·3 |
| 29 | 4 22·3 | 4 23·0 | 4 10·3 | 2·9 | 0·8 | 8·9 | 2·6 | 14·9 | 4·3 |
| 30 | 4 22·5 | 4 23·2 | 4 10·5 | 3·0 | 0·9 | 9·0 | 2·6 | 15·0 | 4·4 |
| 31 | 4 22·8 | 4 23·5 | 4 10·8 | 3·1 | 0·9 | 9·1 | 2·7 | 15·1 | 4·4 |
| 32 | 4 23·0 | 4 23·7 | 4 11·0 | 3·2 | 0·9 | 9·2 | 2·7 | 15·2 | 4·4 |
| 33 | 4 23·3 | 4 24·0 | 4 11·3 | 3·3 | 1·0 | 9·3 | 2·7 | 15·3 | 4·5 |
| 34 | 4 23·5 | 4 24·2 | 4 11·5 | 3·4 | 1·0 | 9·4 | 2·7 | 15·4 | 4·5 |
| 35 | 4 23·8 | 4 24·5 | 4 11·7 | 3·5 | 1·0 | 9·5 | 2·8 | 15·5 | 4·5 |
| 36 | 4 24·0 | 4 24·7 | 4 12·0 | 3·6 | 1·1 | 9·6 | 2·8 | 15·6 | 4·6 |
| 37 | 4 24·3 | 4 25·0 | 4 12·2 | 3·7 | 1·1 | 9·7 | 2·8 | 15·7 | 4·6 |
| 38 | 4 24·5 | 4 25·2 | 4 12·5 | 3·8 | 1·1 | 9·8 | 2·9 | 15·8 | 4·6 |
| 39 | 4 24·8 | 4 25·5 | 4 12·7 | 3·9 | 1·1 | 9·9 | 2·9 | 15·9 | 4·6 |
| 40 | 4 25·0 | 4 25·7 | 4 12·9 | 4·0 | 1·2 | 10·0 | 2·9 | 16·0 | 4·7 |
| 41 | 4 25·3 | 4 26·0 | 4 13·2 | 4·1 | 1·2 | 10·1 | 2·9 | 16·1 | 4·7 |
| 42 | 4 25·5 | 4 26·2 | 4 13·4 | 4·2 | 1·2 | 10·2 | 3·0 | 16·2 | 4·7 |
| 43 | 4 25·8 | 4 26·5 | 4 13·6 | 4·3 | 1·3 | 10·3 | 3·0 | 16·3 | 4·8 |
| 44 | 4 26·0 | 4 26·7 | 4 13·9 | 4·4 | 1·3 | 10·4 | 3·0 | 16·4 | 4·8 |
| 45 | 4 26·3 | 4 27·0 | 4 14·1 | 4·5 | 1·3 | 10·5 | 3·1 | 16·5 | 4·8 |
| 46 | 4 26·5 | 4 27·2 | 4 14·4 | 4·6 | 1·3 | 10·6 | 3·1 | 16·6 | 4·8 |
| 47 | 4 26·8 | 4 27·5 | 4 14·6 | 4·7 | 1·4 | 10·7 | 3·1 | 16·7 | 4·9 |
| 48 | 4 27·0 | 4 27·7 | 4 14·8 | 4·8 | 1·4 | 10·8 | 3·2 | 16·8 | 4·9 |
| 49 | 4 27·3 | 4 28·0 | 4 15·1 | 4·9 | 1·4 | 10·9 | 3·2 | 16·9 | 4·9 |
| 50 | 4 27·5 | 4 28·2 | 4 15·3 | 5·0 | 1·5 | 11·0 | 3·2 | 17·0 | 5·0 |
| 51 | 4 27·8 | 4 28·5 | 4 15·6 | 5·1 | 1·5 | 11·1 | 3·2 | 17·1 | 5·0 |
| 52 | 4 28·0 | 4 28·7 | 4 15·8 | 5·2 | 1·5 | 11·2 | 3·3 | 17·2 | 5·0 |
| 53 | 4 28·3 | 4 29·0 | 4 16·0 | 5·3 | 1·5 | 11·3 | 3·3 | 17·3 | 5·0 |
| 54 | 4 28·5 | 4 29·2 | 4 16·3 | 5·4 | 1·6 | 11·4 | 3·3 | 17·4 | 5·1 |
| 55 | 4 28·8 | 4 29·5 | 4 16·5 | 5·5 | 1·6 | 11·5 | 3·4 | 17·5 | 5·1 |
| 56 | 4 29·0 | 4 29·7 | 4 16·7 | 5·6 | 1·6 | 11·6 | 3·4 | 17·6 | 5·1 |
| 57 | 4 29·3 | 4 30·0 | 4 17·0 | 5·7 | 1·7 | 11·7 | 3·4 | 17·7 | 5·2 |
| 58 | 4 29·5 | 4 30·2 | 4 17·2 | 5·8 | 1·7 | 11·8 | 3·4 | 17·8 | 5·2 |
| 59 | 4 29·8 | 4 30·5 | 4 17·5 | 5·9 | 1·7 | 11·9 | 3·5 | 17·9 | 5·2 |
| 60 | 4 30·0 | 4 30·7 | 4 17·7 | 6·0 | 1·8 | 12·0 | 3·5 | 18·0 | 5·3 |



| 18m s | SUN PLANETS | ARIES | MOON | v or d | Corrⁿ | v or d | Corrⁿ | v or d | Corrⁿ |
|---|---|---|---|---|---|---|---|---|---|
| | ° ′ | ° ′ | ° ′ | ′ | ′ | ′ | ′ | ′ | ′ |
| 00 | 4 30·0 | 4 30·7 | 4 17·7 | 0·0 | 0·0 | 6·0 | 1·9 | 12·0 | 3·7 |
| 01 | 4 30·3 | 4 31·0 | 4 17·9 | 0·1 | 0·0 | 6·1 | 1·9 | 12·1 | 3·7 |
| 02 | 4 30·5 | 4 31·2 | 4 18·2 | 0·2 | 0·1 | 6·2 | 1·9 | 12·2 | 3·8 |
| 03 | 4 30·8 | 4 31·5 | 4 18·4 | 0·3 | 0·1 | 6·3 | 1·9 | 12·3 | 3·8 |
| 04 | 4 31·0 | 4 31·7 | 4 18·7 | 0·4 | 0·1 | 6·4 | 2·0 | 12·4 | 3·8 |
| 05 | 4 31·3 | 4 32·0 | 4 18·9 | 0·5 | 0·2 | 6·5 | 2·0 | 12·5 | 3·9 |
| 06 | 4 31·5 | 4 32·2 | 4 19·1 | 0·6 | 0·2 | 6·6 | 2·0 | 12·6 | 3·9 |
| 07 | 4 31·8 | 4 32·5 | 4 19·4 | 0·7 | 0·2 | 6·7 | 2·1 | 12·7 | 3·9 |
| 08 | 4 32·0 | 4 32·7 | 4 19·6 | 0·8 | 0·2 | 6·8 | 2·1 | 12·8 | 3·9 |
| 09 | 4 32·3 | 4 33·0 | 4 19·8 | 0·9 | 0·3 | 6·9 | 2·1 | 12·9 | 4·0 |
| 10 | 4 32·5 | 4 33·2 | 4 20·1 | 1·0 | 0·3 | 7·0 | 2·2 | 13·0 | 4·0 |
| 11 | 4 32·8 | 4 33·5 | 4 20·3 | 1·1 | 0·3 | 7·1 | 2·2 | 13·1 | 4·0 |
| 12 | 4 33·0 | 4 33·7 | 4 20·6 | 1·2 | 0·4 | 7·2 | 2·2 | 13·2 | 4·1 |
| 13 | 4 33·3 | 4 34·0 | 4 20·8 | 1·3 | 0·4 | 7·3 | 2·3 | 13·3 | 4·1 |
| 14 | 4 33·5 | 4 34·2 | 4 21·0 | 1·4 | 0·4 | 7·4 | 2·3 | 13·4 | 4·1 |
| 15 | 4 33·8 | 4 34·5 | 4 21·3 | 1·5 | 0·5 | 7·5 | 2·3 | 13·5 | 4·2 |
| 16 | 4 34·0 | 4 34·8 | 4 21·5 | 1·6 | 0·5 | 7·6 | 2·3 | 13·6 | 4·2 |
| 17 | 4 34·3 | 4 35·0 | 4 21·8 | 1·7 | 0·5 | 7·7 | 2·4 | 13·7 | 4·2 |
| 18 | 4 34·5 | 4 35·3 | 4 22·0 | 1·8 | 0·6 | 7·8 | 2·4 | 13·8 | 4·3 |
| 19 | 4 34·8 | 4 35·5 | 4 22·2 | 1·9 | 0·6 | 7·9 | 2·4 | 13·9 | 4·3 |
| 20 | 4 35·0 | 4 35·8 | 4 22·5 | 2·0 | 0·6 | 8·0 | 2·5 | 14·0 | 4·3 |
| 21 | 4 35·3 | 4 36·0 | 4 22·7 | 2·1 | 0·6 | 8·1 | 2·5 | 14·1 | 4·3 |
| 22 | 4 35·5 | 4 36·3 | 4 22·9 | 2·2 | 0·7 | 8·2 | 2·5 | 14·2 | 4·4 |
| 23 | 4 35·8 | 4 36·5 | 4 23·2 | 2·3 | 0·7 | 8·3 | 2·6 | 14·3 | 4·4 |
| 24 | 4 36·0 | 4 36·8 | 4 23·4 | 2·4 | 0·7 | 8·4 | 2·6 | 14·4 | 4·4 |
| 25 | 4 36·3 | 4 37·0 | 4 23·7 | 2·5 | 0·8 | 8·5 | 2·6 | 14·5 | 4·5 |
| 26 | 4 36·5 | 4 37·3 | 4 23·9 | 2·6 | 0·8 | 8·6 | 2·7 | 14·6 | 4·5 |
| 27 | 4 36·8 | 4 37·5 | 4 24·1 | 2·7 | 0·8 | 8·7 | 2·7 | 14·7 | 4·5 |
| 28 | 4 37·0 | 4 37·8 | 4 24·4 | 2·8 | 0·9 | 8·8 | 2·7 | 14·8 | 4·6 |
| 29 | 4 37·3 | 4 38·0 | 4 24·6 | 2·9 | 0·9 | 8·9 | 2·7 | 14·9 | 4·6 |
| 30 | 4 37·5 | 4 38·3 | 4 24·9 | 3·0 | 0·9 | 9·0 | 2·8 | 15·0 | 4·6 |
| 31 | 4 37·8 | 4 38·5 | 4 25·1 | 3·1 | 1·0 | 9·1 | 2·8 | 15·1 | 4·7 |
| 32 | 4 38·0 | 4 38·8 | 4 25·3 | 3·2 | 1·0 | 9·2 | 2·8 | 15·2 | 4·7 |
| 33 | 4 38·3 | 4 39·0 | 4 25·6 | 3·3 | 1·0 | 9·3 | 2·9 | 15·3 | 4·7 |
| 34 | 4 38·5 | 4 39·3 | 4 25·8 | 3·4 | 1·0 | 9·4 | 2·9 | 15·4 | 4·7 |
| 35 | 4 38·8 | 4 39·5 | 4 26·1 | 3·5 | 1·1 | 9·5 | 2·9 | 15·5 | 4·8 |
| 36 | 4 39·0 | 4 39·8 | 4 26·3 | 3·6 | 1·1 | 9·6 | 3·0 | 15·6 | 4·8 |
| 37 | 4 39·3 | 4 40·0 | 4 26·5 | 3·7 | 1·1 | 9·7 | 3·0 | 15·7 | 4·8 |
| 38 | 4 39·5 | 4 40·3 | 4 26·8 | 3·8 | 1·2 | 9·8 | 3·0 | 15·8 | 4·9 |
| 39 | 4 39·8 | 4 40·5 | 4 27·0 | 3·9 | 1·2 | 9·9 | 3·1 | 15·9 | 4·9 |
| 40 | 4 40·0 | 4 40·8 | 4 27·2 | 4·0 | 1·2 | 10·0 | 3·1 | 16·0 | 4·9 |
| 41 | 4 40·3 | 4 41·0 | 4 27·5 | 4·1 | 1·3 | 10·1 | 3·1 | 16·1 | 5·0 |
| 42 | 4 40·5 | 4 41·3 | 4 27·7 | 4·2 | 1·3 | 10·2 | 3·1 | 16·2 | 5·0 |
| 43 | 4 40·8 | 4 41·5 | 4 28·0 | 4·3 | 1·3 | 10·3 | 3·2 | 16·3 | 5·0 |
| 44 | 4 41·0 | 4 41·8 | 4 28·2 | 4·4 | 1·4 | 10·4 | 3·2 | 16·4 | 5·1 |
| 45 | 4 41·3 | 4 42·0 | 4 28·4 | 4·5 | 1·4 | 10·5 | 3·2 | 16·5 | 5·1 |
| 46 | 4 41·5 | 4 42·3 | 4 28·7 | 4·6 | 1·4 | 10·6 | 3·3 | 16·6 | 5·1 |
| 47 | 4 41·8 | 4 42·5 | 4 28·9 | 4·7 | 1·4 | 10·7 | 3·3 | 16·7 | 5·1 |
| 48 | 4 42·0 | 4 42·8 | 4 29·2 | 4·8 | 1·5 | 10·8 | 3·3 | 16·8 | 5·2 |
| 49 | 4 42·3 | 4 43·0 | 4 29·4 | 4·9 | 1·5 | 10·9 | 3·4 | 16·9 | 5·2 |
| 50 | 4 42·5 | 4 43·3 | 4 29·6 | 5·0 | 1·5 | 11·0 | 3·4 | 17·0 | 5·2 |
| 51 | 4 42·8 | 4 43·5 | 4 29·9 | 5·1 | 1·6 | 11·1 | 3·4 | 17·1 | 5·3 |
| 52 | 4 43·0 | 4 43·8 | 4 30·1 | 5·2 | 1·6 | 11·2 | 3·5 | 17·2 | 5·3 |
| 53 | 4 43·3 | 4 44·0 | 4 30·3 | 5·3 | 1·6 | 11·3 | 3·5 | 17·3 | 5·3 |
| 54 | 4 43·5 | 4 44·3 | 4 30·6 | 5·4 | 1·7 | 11·4 | 3·5 | 17·4 | 5·4 |
| 55 | 4 43·8 | 4 44·5 | 4 30·8 | 5·5 | 1·7 | 11·5 | 3·5 | 17·5 | 5·4 |
| 56 | 4 44·0 | 4 44·8 | 4 31·1 | 5·6 | 1·7 | 11·6 | 3·6 | 17·6 | 5·4 |
| 57 | 4 44·3 | 4 45·0 | 4 31·3 | 5·7 | 1·8 | 11·7 | 3·6 | 17·7 | 5·5 |
| 58 | 4 44·5 | 4 45·3 | 4 31·5 | 5·8 | 1·8 | 11·8 | 3·6 | 17·8 | 5·5 |
| 59 | 4 44·8 | 4 45·5 | 4 31·8 | 5·9 | 1·8 | 11·9 | 3·7 | 17·9 | 5·5 |
| 60 | 4 45·0 | 4 45·8 | 4 32·0 | 6·0 | 1·9 | 12·0 | 3·7 | 18·0 | 5·6 |

| 19m s | SUN PLANETS | ARIES | MOON | v or d | Corrⁿ | v or d | Corrⁿ | v or d | Corrⁿ |
|---|---|---|---|---|---|---|---|---|---|
| | ° ′ | ° ′ | ° ′ | ′ | ′ | ′ | ′ | ′ | ′ |
| 00 | 4 45·0 | 4 45·8 | 4 32·0 | 0·0 | 0·0 | 6·0 | 2·0 | 12·0 | 3·9 |
| 01 | 4 45·3 | 4 46·0 | 4 32·3 | 0·1 | 0·0 | 6·1 | 2·0 | 12·1 | 3·9 |
| 02 | 4 45·5 | 4 46·3 | 4 32·5 | 0·2 | 0·1 | 6·2 | 2·0 | 12·2 | 4·0 |
| 03 | 4 45·8 | 4 46·5 | 4 32·7 | 0·3 | 0·1 | 6·3 | 2·0 | 12·3 | 4·0 |
| 04 | 4 46·0 | 4 46·8 | 4 33·0 | 0·4 | 0·1 | 6·4 | 2·1 | 12·4 | 4·0 |
| 05 | 4 46·3 | 4 47·0 | 4 33·2 | 0·5 | 0·2 | 6·5 | 2·1 | 12·5 | 4·1 |
| 06 | 4 46·5 | 4 47·3 | 4 33·4 | 0·6 | 0·2 | 6·6 | 2·1 | 12·6 | 4·1 |
| 07 | 4 46·8 | 4 47·5 | 4 33·7 | 0·7 | 0·2 | 6·7 | 2·2 | 12·7 | 4·1 |
| 08 | 4 47·0 | 4 47·8 | 4 33·9 | 0·8 | 0·3 | 6·8 | 2·2 | 12·8 | 4·2 |
| 09 | 4 47·3 | 4 48·0 | 4 34·2 | 0·9 | 0·3 | 6·9 | 2·2 | 12·9 | 4·2 |
| 10 | 4 47·5 | 4 48·3 | 4 34·4 | 1·0 | 0·3 | 7·0 | 2·3 | 13·0 | 4·2 |
| 11 | 4 47·8 | 4 48·5 | 4 34·6 | 1·1 | 0·4 | 7·1 | 2·3 | 13·1 | 4·3 |
| 12 | 4 48·0 | 4 48·8 | 4 34·9 | 1·2 | 0·4 | 7·2 | 2·3 | 13·2 | 4·3 |
| 13 | 4 48·3 | 4 49·0 | 4 35·1 | 1·3 | 0·4 | 7·3 | 2·4 | 13·3 | 4·3 |
| 14 | 4 48·5 | 4 49·3 | 4 35·4 | 1·4 | 0·5 | 7·4 | 2·4 | 13·4 | 4·4 |
| 15 | 4 48·8 | 4 49·5 | 4 35·6 | 1·5 | 0·5 | 7·5 | 2·4 | 13·5 | 4·4 |
| 16 | 4 49·0 | 4 49·8 | 4 35·8 | 1·6 | 0·5 | 7·6 | 2·5 | 13·6 | 4·4 |
| 17 | 4 49·3 | 4 50·0 | 4 36·1 | 1·7 | 0·6 | 7·7 | 2·5 | 13·7 | 4·5 |
| 18 | 4 49·5 | 4 50·3 | 4 36·3 | 1·8 | 0·6 | 7·8 | 2·5 | 13·8 | 4·5 |
| 19 | 4 49·8 | 4 50·5 | 4 36·6 | 1·9 | 0·6 | 7·9 | 2·6 | 13·9 | 4·5 |
| 20 | 4 50·0 | 4 50·8 | 4 36·8 | 2·0 | 0·7 | 8·0 | 2·6 | 14·0 | 4·6 |
| 21 | 4 50·3 | 4 51·0 | 4 37·0 | 2·1 | 0·7 | 8·1 | 2·6 | 14·1 | 4·6 |
| 22 | 4 50·5 | 4 51·3 | 4 37·3 | 2·2 | 0·7 | 8·2 | 2·7 | 14·2 | 4·6 |
| 23 | 4 50·8 | 4 51·5 | 4 37·5 | 2·3 | 0·7 | 8·3 | 2·7 | 14·3 | 4·6 |
| 24 | 4 51·0 | 4 51·8 | 4 37·7 | 2·4 | 0·8 | 8·4 | 2·7 | 14·4 | 4·7 |
| 25 | 4 51·3 | 4 52·0 | 4 38·0 | 2·5 | 0·8 | 8·5 | 2·8 | 14·5 | 4·7 |
| 26 | 4 51·5 | 4 52·3 | 4 38·2 | 2·6 | 0·8 | 8·6 | 2·8 | 14·6 | 4·7 |
| 27 | 4 51·8 | 4 52·5 | 4 38·5 | 2·7 | 0·9 | 8·7 | 2·8 | 14·7 | 4·8 |
| 28 | 4 52·0 | 4 52·8 | 4 38·7 | 2·8 | 0·9 | 8·8 | 2·9 | 14·8 | 4·8 |
| 29 | 4 52·3 | 4 53·1 | 4 38·9 | 2·9 | 0·9 | 8·9 | 2·9 | 14·9 | 4·8 |
| 30 | 4 52·5 | 4 53·3 | 4 39·2 | 3·0 | 1·0 | 9·0 | 2·9 | 15·0 | 4·9 |
| 31 | 4 52·8 | 4 53·6 | 4 39·4 | 3·1 | 1·0 | 9·1 | 3·0 | 15·1 | 4·9 |
| 32 | 4 53·0 | 4 53·8 | 4 39·7 | 3·2 | 1·0 | 9·2 | 3·0 | 15·2 | 4·9 |
| 33 | 4 53·3 | 4 54·1 | 4 39·9 | 3·3 | 1·1 | 9·3 | 3·0 | 15·3 | 5·0 |
| 34 | 4 53·5 | 4 54·3 | 4 40·1 | 3·4 | 1·1 | 9·4 | 3·1 | 15·4 | 5·0 |
| 35 | 4 53·8 | 4 54·6 | 4 40·4 | 3·5 | 1·1 | 9·5 | 3·1 | 15·5 | 5·0 |
| 36 | 4 54·0 | 4 54·8 | 4 40·6 | 3·6 | 1·2 | 9·6 | 3·1 | 15·6 | 5·1 |
| 37 | 4 54·3 | 4 55·1 | 4 40·8 | 3·7 | 1·2 | 9·7 | 3·2 | 15·7 | 5·1 |
| 38 | 4 54·5 | 4 55·3 | 4 41·1 | 3·8 | 1·2 | 9·8 | 3·2 | 15·8 | 5·1 |
| 39 | 4 54·8 | 4 55·6 | 4 41·3 | 3·9 | 1·3 | 9·9 | 3·2 | 15·9 | 5·2 |
| 40 | 4 55·0 | 4 55·8 | 4 41·6 | 4·0 | 1·3 | 10·0 | 3·3 | 16·0 | 5·2 |
| 41 | 4 55·3 | 4 56·1 | 4 41·8 | 4·1 | 1·3 | 10·1 | 3·3 | 16·1 | 5·2 |
| 42 | 4 55·5 | 4 56·3 | 4 42·0 | 4·2 | 1·4 | 10·2 | 3·3 | 16·2 | 5·3 |
| 43 | 4 55·8 | 4 56·6 | 4 42·3 | 4·3 | 1·4 | 10·3 | 3·3 | 16·3 | 5·3 |
| 44 | 4 56·0 | 4 56·8 | 4 42·5 | 4·4 | 1·4 | 10·4 | 3·4 | 16·4 | 5·3 |
| 45 | 4 56·3 | 4 57·1 | 4 42·8 | 4·5 | 1·5 | 10·5 | 3·4 | 16·5 | 5·4 |
| 46 | 4 56·5 | 4 57·3 | 4 43·0 | 4·6 | 1·5 | 10·6 | 3·4 | 16·6 | 5·4 |
| 47 | 4 56·8 | 4 57·6 | 4 43·2 | 4·7 | 1·5 | 10·7 | 3·5 | 16·7 | 5·4 |
| 48 | 4 57·0 | 4 57·8 | 4 43·5 | 4·8 | 1·6 | 10·8 | 3·5 | 16·8 | 5·5 |
| 49 | 4 57·3 | 4 58·1 | 4 43·7 | 4·9 | 1·6 | 10·9 | 3·5 | 16·9 | 5·5 |
| 50 | 4 57·5 | 4 58·3 | 4 43·9 | 5·0 | 1·6 | 11·0 | 3·6 | 17·0 | 5·5 |
| 51 | 4 57·8 | 4 58·6 | 4 44·2 | 5·1 | 1·7 | 11·1 | 3·6 | 17·1 | 5·6 |
| 52 | 4 58·0 | 4 58·8 | 4 44·4 | 5·2 | 1·7 | 11·2 | 3·6 | 17·2 | 5·6 |
| 53 | 4 58·3 | 4 59·1 | 4 44·7 | 5·3 | 1·7 | 11·3 | 3·7 | 17·3 | 5·6 |
| 54 | 4 58·5 | 4 59·3 | 4 44·9 | 5·4 | 1·8 | 11·4 | 3·7 | 17·4 | 5·7 |
| 55 | 4 58·8 | 4 59·6 | 4 45·1 | 5·5 | 1·8 | 11·5 | 3·7 | 17·5 | 5·7 |
| 56 | 4 59·0 | 4 59·8 | 4 45·4 | 5·6 | 1·8 | 11·6 | 3·8 | 17·6 | 5·7 |
| 57 | 4 59·3 | 5 00·1 | 4 45·6 | 5·7 | 1·9 | 11·7 | 3·8 | 17·7 | 5·8 |
| 58 | 4 59·5 | 5 00·3 | 4 45·9 | 5·8 | 1·9 | 11·8 | 3·8 | 17·8 | 5·8 |
| 59 | 4 59·8 | 5 00·6 | 4 46·1 | 5·9 | 1·9 | 11·9 | 3·9 | 17·9 | 5·8 |
| 60 | 5 00·0 | 5 00·8 | 4 46·3 | 6·0 | 2·0 | 12·0 | 3·9 | 18·0 | 5·9 |

| 20m s | SUN PLANETS ° ′ | ARIES ° ′ | MOON ° ′ | v or d ′ | Corrⁿ ′ | v or d ′ | Corrⁿ ′ | v or d ′ | Corrⁿ ′ |
|---|---|---|---|---|---|---|---|---|---|
| 00 | 5 00·0 | 5 00·8 | 4 46·3 | 0·0 | 0·0 | 6·0 | 2·1 | 12·0 | 4·1 |
| 01 | 5 00·3 | 5 01·1 | 4 46·6 | 0·1 | 0·0 | 6·1 | 2·1 | 12·1 | 4·1 |
| 02 | 5 00·5 | 5 01·3 | 4 46·8 | 0·2 | 0·1 | 6·2 | 2·1 | 12·2 | 4·2 |
| 03 | 5 00·8 | 5 01·6 | 4 47·0 | 0·3 | 0·1 | 6·3 | 2·2 | 12·3 | 4·2 |
| 04 | 5 01·0 | 5 01·8 | 4 47·3 | 0·4 | 0·1 | 6·4 | 2·2 | 12·4 | 4·2 |
| 05 | 5 01·3 | 5 02·1 | 4 47·5 | 0·5 | 0·2 | 6·5 | 2·2 | 12·5 | 4·3 |
| 06 | 5 01·5 | 5 02·3 | 4 47·8 | 0·6 | 0·2 | 6·6 | 2·3 | 12·6 | 4·3 |
| 07 | 5 01·8 | 5 02·6 | 4 48·0 | 0·7 | 0·2 | 6·7 | 2·3 | 12·7 | 4·3 |
| 08 | 5 02·0 | 5 02·8 | 4 48·2 | 0·8 | 0·3 | 6·8 | 2·3 | 12·8 | 4·4 |
| 09 | 5 02·3 | 5 03·1 | 4 48·5 | 0·9 | 0·3 | 6·9 | 2·4 | 12·9 | 4·4 |
| 10 | 5 02·5 | 5 03·3 | 4 48·7 | 1·0 | 0·3 | 7·0 | 2·4 | 13·0 | 4·4 |
| 11 | 5 02·8 | 5 03·6 | 4 49·0 | 1·1 | 0·4 | 7·1 | 2·4 | 13·1 | 4·5 |
| 12 | 5 03·0 | 5 03·8 | 4 49·2 | 1·2 | 0·4 | 7·2 | 2·5 | 13·2 | 4·5 |
| 13 | 5 03·3 | 5 04·1 | 4 49·4 | 1·3 | 0·4 | 7·3 | 2·5 | 13·3 | 4·5 |
| 14 | 5 03·5 | 5 04·3 | 4 49·7 | 1·4 | 0·5 | 7·4 | 2·5 | 13·4 | 4·6 |
| 15 | 5 03·8 | 5 04·6 | 4 49·9 | 1·5 | 0·5 | 7·5 | 2·6 | 13·5 | 4·6 |
| 16 | 5 04·0 | 5 04·8 | 4 50·2 | 1·6 | 0·5 | 7·6 | 2·6 | 13·6 | 4·6 |
| 17 | 5 04·3 | 5 05·1 | 4 50·4 | 1·7 | 0·6 | 7·7 | 2·6 | 13·7 | 4·7 |
| 18 | 5 04·5 | 5 05·3 | 4 50·6 | 1·8 | 0·6 | 7·8 | 2·7 | 13·8 | 4·7 |
| 19 | 5 04·8 | 5 05·6 | 4 50·9 | 1·9 | 0·6 | 7·9 | 2·7 | 13·9 | 4·7 |
| 20 | 5 05·0 | 5 05·8 | 4 51·1 | 2·0 | 0·7 | 8·0 | 2·7 | 14·0 | 4·8 |
| 21 | 5 05·3 | 5 06·1 | 4 51·3 | 2·1 | 0·7 | 8·1 | 2·8 | 14·1 | 4·8 |
| 22 | 5 05·5 | 5 06·3 | 4 51·6 | 2·2 | 0·8 | 8·2 | 2·8 | 14·2 | 4·9 |
| 23 | 5 05·8 | 5 06·6 | 4 51·8 | 2·3 | 0·8 | 8·3 | 2·8 | 14·3 | 4·9 |
| 24 | 5 06·0 | 5 06·8 | 4 52·1 | 2·4 | 0·8 | 8·4 | 2·9 | 14·4 | 4·9 |
| 25 | 5 06·3 | 5 07·1 | 4 52·3 | 2·5 | 0·9 | 8·5 | 2·9 | 14·5 | 5·0 |
| 26 | 5 06·5 | 5 07·3 | 4 52·5 | 2·6 | 0·9 | 8·6 | 2·9 | 14·6 | 5·0 |
| 27 | 5 06·8 | 5 07·6 | 4 52·8 | 2·7 | 0·9 | 8·7 | 3·0 | 14·7 | 5·0 |
| 28 | 5 07·0 | 5 07·8 | 4 53·0 | 2·8 | 1·0 | 8·8 | 3·0 | 14·8 | 5·1 |
| 29 | 5 07·3 | 5 08·1 | 4 53·3 | 2·9 | 1·0 | 8·9 | 3·0 | 14·9 | 5·1 |
| 30 | 5 07·5 | 5 08·3 | 4 53·5 | 3·0 | 1·0 | 9·0 | 3·1 | 15·0 | 5·1 |
| 31 | 5 07·8 | 5 08·6 | 4 53·7 | 3·1 | 1·1 | 9·1 | 3·1 | 15·1 | 5·2 |
| 32 | 5 08·0 | 5 08·8 | 4 54·0 | 3·2 | 1·1 | 9·2 | 3·1 | 15·2 | 5·2 |
| 33 | 5 08·3 | 5 09·1 | 4 54·2 | 3·3 | 1·1 | 9·3 | 3·2 | 15·3 | 5·2 |
| 34 | 5 08·5 | 5 09·3 | 4 54·4 | 3·4 | 1·2 | 9·4 | 3·2 | 15·4 | 5·3 |
| 35 | 5 08·8 | 5 09·6 | 4 54·7 | 3·5 | 1·2 | 9·5 | 3·2 | 15·5 | 5·3 |
| 36 | 5 09·0 | 5 09·8 | 4 54·9 | 3·6 | 1·2 | 9·6 | 3·3 | 15·6 | 5·3 |
| 37 | 5 09·3 | 5 10·1 | 4 55·2 | 3·7 | 1·3 | 9·7 | 3·3 | 15·7 | 5·4 |
| 38 | 5 09·5 | 5 10·3 | 4 55·4 | 3·8 | 1·3 | 9·8 | 3·3 | 15·8 | 5·4 |
| 39 | 5 09·8 | 5 10·6 | 4 55·6 | 3·9 | 1·3 | 9·9 | 3·4 | 15·9 | 5·4 |
| 40 | 5 10·0 | 5 10·8 | 4 55·9 | 4·0 | 1·4 | 10·0 | 3·4 | 16·0 | 5·5 |
| 41 | 5 10·3 | 5 11·1 | 4 56·1 | 4·1 | 1·4 | 10·1 | 3·5 | 16·1 | 5·5 |
| 42 | 5 10·5 | 5 11·4 | 4 56·4 | 4·2 | 1·4 | 10·2 | 3·5 | 16·2 | 5·5 |
| 43 | 5 10·8 | 5 11·6 | 4 56·6 | 4·3 | 1·5 | 10·3 | 3·5 | 16·3 | 5·6 |
| 44 | 5 11·0 | 5 11·9 | 4 56·8 | 4·4 | 1·5 | 10·4 | 3·6 | 16·4 | 5·6 |
| 45 | 5 11·3 | 5 12·1 | 4 57·1 | 4·5 | 1·5 | 10·5 | 3·6 | 16·5 | 5·6 |
| 46 | 5 11·5 | 5 12·4 | 4 57·3 | 4·6 | 1·6 | 10·6 | 3·6 | 16·6 | 5·7 |
| 47 | 5 11·8 | 5 12·6 | 4 57·5 | 4·7 | 1·6 | 10·7 | 3·7 | 16·7 | 5·7 |
| 48 | 5 12·0 | 5 12·9 | 4 57·8 | 4·8 | 1·6 | 10·8 | 3·7 | 16·8 | 5·7 |
| 49 | 5 12·3 | 5 13·1 | 4 58·0 | 4·9 | 1·7 | 10·9 | 3·7 | 16·9 | 5·8 |
| 50 | 5 12·5 | 5 13·4 | 4 58·3 | 5·0 | 1·7 | 11·0 | 3·8 | 17·0 | 5·8 |
| 51 | 5 12·8 | 5 13·6 | 4 58·5 | 5·1 | 1·7 | 11·1 | 3·8 | 17·1 | 5·8 |
| 52 | 5 13·0 | 5 13·9 | 4 58·7 | 5·2 | 1·8 | 11·2 | 3·8 | 17·2 | 5·9 |
| 53 | 5 13·3 | 5 14·1 | 4 59·0 | 5·3 | 1·8 | 11·3 | 3·9 | 17·3 | 5·9 |
| 54 | 5 13·5 | 5 14·4 | 4 59·2 | 5·4 | 1·8 | 11·4 | 3·9 | 17·4 | 5·9 |
| 55 | 5 13·8 | 5 14·6 | 4 59·5 | 5·5 | 1·9 | 11·5 | 3·9 | 17·5 | 6·0 |
| 56 | 5 14·0 | 5 14·9 | 4 59·7 | 5·6 | 1·9 | 11·6 | 4·0 | 17·6 | 6·0 |
| 57 | 5 14·3 | 5 15·1 | 4 59·9 | 5·7 | 1·9 | 11·7 | 4·0 | 17·7 | 6·0 |
| 58 | 5 14·5 | 5 15·4 | 5 00·2 | 5·8 | 2·0 | 11·8 | 4·0 | 17·8 | 6·1 |
| 59 | 5 14·8 | 5 15·6 | 5 00·4 | 5·9 | 2·0 | 11·9 | 4·1 | 17·9 | 6·1 |
| 60 | 5 15·0 | 5 15·9 | 5 00·7 | 6·0 | 2·1 | 12·0 | 4·1 | 18·0 | 6·2 |

| 21m s | SUN PLANETS ° ′ | ARIES ° ′ | MOON ° ′ | v or d ′ | Corrⁿ ′ | v or d ′ | Corrⁿ ′ | v or d ′ | Corrⁿ ′ |
|---|---|---|---|---|---|---|---|---|---|
| 00 | 5 15·0 | 5 15·9 | 5 00·7 | 0·0 | 0·0 | 6·0 | 2·2 | 12·0 | 4·3 |
| 01 | 5 15·3 | 5 16·1 | 5 00·9 | 0·1 | 0·0 | 6·1 | 2·2 | 12·1 | 4·3 |
| 02 | 5 15·5 | 5 16·4 | 5 01·1 | 0·2 | 0·1 | 6·2 | 2·2 | 12·2 | 4·4 |
| 03 | 5 15·8 | 5 16·6 | 5 01·4 | 0·3 | 0·1 | 6·3 | 2·3 | 12·3 | 4·4 |
| 04 | 5 16·0 | 5 16·9 | 5 01·6 | 0·4 | 0·1 | 6·4 | 2·3 | 12·4 | 4·4 |
| 05 | 5 16·3 | 5 17·1 | 5 01·8 | 0·5 | 0·2 | 6·5 | 2·3 | 12·5 | 4·5 |
| 06 | 5 16·5 | 5 17·4 | 5 02·1 | 0·6 | 0·2 | 6·6 | 2·4 | 12·6 | 4·5 |
| 07 | 5 16·8 | 5 17·6 | 5 02·3 | 0·7 | 0·3 | 6·7 | 2·4 | 12·7 | 4·6 |
| 08 | 5 17·0 | 5 17·9 | 5 02·6 | 0·8 | 0·3 | 6·8 | 2·4 | 12·8 | 4·6 |
| 09 | 5 17·3 | 5 18·1 | 5 02·8 | 0·9 | 0·3 | 6·9 | 2·5 | 12·9 | 4·6 |
| 10 | 5 17·5 | 5 18·4 | 5 03·0 | 1·0 | 0·4 | 7·0 | 2·5 | 13·0 | 4·7 |
| 11 | 5 17·8 | 5 18·6 | 5 03·3 | 1·1 | 0·4 | 7·1 | 2·5 | 13·1 | 4·7 |
| 12 | 5 18·0 | 5 18·9 | 5 03·5 | 1·2 | 0·4 | 7·2 | 2·6 | 13·2 | 4·7 |
| 13 | 5 18·3 | 5 19·1 | 5 03·8 | 1·3 | 0·5 | 7·3 | 2·6 | 13·3 | 4·8 |
| 14 | 5 18·5 | 5 19·4 | 5 04·0 | 1·4 | 0·5 | 7·4 | 2·7 | 13·4 | 4·8 |
| 15 | 5 18·8 | 5 19·6 | 5 04·2 | 1·5 | 0·5 | 7·5 | 2·7 | 13·5 | 4·8 |
| 16 | 5 19·0 | 5 19·9 | 5 04·5 | 1·6 | 0·6 | 7·6 | 2·7 | 13·6 | 4·9 |
| 17 | 5 19·3 | 5 20·1 | 5 04·7 | 1·7 | 0·6 | 7·7 | 2·8 | 13·7 | 4·9 |
| 18 | 5 19·5 | 5 20·4 | 5 04·9 | 1·8 | 0·6 | 7·8 | 2·8 | 13·8 | 4·9 |
| 19 | 5 19·8 | 5 20·6 | 5 05·2 | 1·9 | 0·7 | 7·9 | 2·8 | 13·9 | 5·0 |
| 20 | 5 20·0 | 5 20·9 | 5 05·4 | 2·0 | 0·7 | 8·0 | 2·9 | 14·0 | 5·0 |
| 21 | 5 20·3 | 5 21·1 | 5 05·7 | 2·1 | 0·8 | 8·1 | 2·9 | 14·1 | 5·1 |
| 22 | 5 20·5 | 5 21·4 | 5 05·9 | 2·2 | 0·8 | 8·2 | 2·9 | 14·2 | 5·1 |
| 23 | 5 20·8 | 5 21·6 | 5 06·1 | 2·3 | 0·8 | 8·3 | 3·0 | 14·3 | 5·1 |
| 24 | 5 21·0 | 5 21·9 | 5 06·4 | 2·4 | 0·9 | 8·4 | 3·0 | 14·4 | 5·2 |
| 25 | 5 21·3 | 5 22·1 | 5 06·6 | 2·5 | 0·9 | 8·5 | 3·0 | 14·5 | 5·2 |
| 26 | 5 21·5 | 5 22·4 | 5 06·9 | 2·6 | 0·9 | 8·6 | 3·1 | 14·6 | 5·2 |
| 27 | 5 21·8 | 5 22·6 | 5 07·1 | 2·7 | 1·0 | 8·7 | 3·1 | 14·7 | 5·3 |
| 28 | 5 22·0 | 5 22·9 | 5 07·3 | 2·8 | 1·0 | 8·8 | 3·2 | 14·8 | 5·3 |
| 29 | 5 22·3 | 5 23·1 | 5 07·6 | 2·9 | 1·0 | 8·9 | 3·2 | 14·9 | 5·3 |
| 30 | 5 22·5 | 5 23·4 | 5 07·8 | 3·0 | 1·1 | 9·0 | 3·2 | 15·0 | 5·4 |
| 31 | 5 22·8 | 5 23·6 | 5 08·0 | 3·1 | 1·1 | 9·1 | 3·3 | 15·1 | 5·4 |
| 32 | 5 23·0 | 5 23·9 | 5 08·3 | 3·2 | 1·1 | 9·2 | 3·3 | 15·2 | 5·4 |
| 33 | 5 23·3 | 5 24·1 | 5 08·5 | 3·3 | 1·2 | 9·3 | 3·3 | 15·3 | 5·5 |
| 34 | 5 23·5 | 5 24·4 | 5 08·8 | 3·4 | 1·2 | 9·4 | 3·4 | 15·4 | 5·5 |
| 35 | 5 23·8 | 5 24·6 | 5 09·0 | 3·5 | 1·3 | 9·5 | 3·4 | 15·5 | 5·6 |
| 36 | 5 24·0 | 5 24·9 | 5 09·2 | 3·6 | 1·3 | 9·6 | 3·4 | 15·6 | 5·6 |
| 37 | 5 24·3 | 5 25·1 | 5 09·5 | 3·7 | 1·3 | 9·7 | 3·5 | 15·7 | 5·6 |
| 38 | 5 24·5 | 5 25·4 | 5 09·7 | 3·8 | 1·4 | 9·8 | 3·5 | 15·8 | 5·7 |
| 39 | 5 24·8 | 5 25·6 | 5 10·0 | 3·9 | 1·4 | 9·9 | 3·5 | 15·9 | 5·7 |
| 40 | 5 25·0 | 5 25·9 | 5 10·2 | 4·0 | 1·4 | 10·0 | 3·6 | 16·0 | 5·7 |
| 41 | 5 25·3 | 5 26·1 | 5 10·4 | 4·1 | 1·5 | 10·1 | 3·6 | 16·1 | 5·8 |
| 42 | 5 25·5 | 5 26·4 | 5 10·7 | 4·2 | 1·5 | 10·2 | 3·7 | 16·2 | 5·8 |
| 43 | 5 25·8 | 5 26·6 | 5 10·9 | 4·3 | 1·5 | 10·3 | 3·7 | 16·3 | 5·8 |
| 44 | 5 26·0 | 5 26·9 | 5 11·1 | 4·4 | 1·6 | 10·4 | 3·7 | 16·4 | 5·9 |
| 45 | 5 26·3 | 5 27·1 | 5 11·4 | 4·5 | 1·6 | 10·5 | 3·8 | 16·5 | 5·9 |
| 46 | 5 26·5 | 5 27·4 | 5 11·6 | 4·6 | 1·6 | 10·6 | 3·8 | 16·6 | 5·9 |
| 47 | 5 26·8 | 5 27·6 | 5 11·9 | 4·7 | 1·7 | 10·7 | 3·8 | 16·7 | 6·0 |
| 48 | 5 27·0 | 5 27·9 | 5 12·1 | 4·8 | 1·7 | 10·8 | 3·9 | 16·8 | 6·0 |
| 49 | 5 27·3 | 5 28·1 | 5 12·3 | 4·9 | 1·8 | 10·9 | 3·9 | 16·9 | 6·1 |
| 50 | 5 27·5 | 5 28·4 | 5 12·6 | 5·0 | 1·8 | 11·0 | 3·9 | 17·0 | 6·1 |
| 51 | 5 27·8 | 5 20·6 | 5 12·8 | 5·1 | 1·8 | 11·1 | 4·0 | 17·1 | 6·1 |
| 52 | 5 28·0 | 5 28·9 | 5 13·1 | 5·2 | 1·9 | 11·2 | 4·0 | 17·2 | 6·2 |
| 53 | 5 28·3 | 5 29·1 | 5 13·3 | 5·3 | 1·9 | 11·3 | 4·0 | 17·3 | 6·2 |
| 54 | 5 28·5 | 5 29·4 | 5 13·5 | 5·4 | 1·9 | 11·4 | 4·1 | 17·4 | 6·2 |
| 55 | 5 28·8 | 5 29·7 | 5 13·8 | 5·5 | 2·0 | 11·5 | 4·1 | 17·5 | 6·3 |
| 56 | 5 29·0 | 5 29·9 | 5 14·0 | 5·6 | 2·0 | 11·6 | 4·2 | 17·6 | 6·3 |
| 57 | 5 29·3 | 5 30·2 | 5 14·3 | 5·7 | 2·0 | 11·7 | 4·2 | 17·7 | 6·3 |
| 58 | 5 29·5 | 5 30·4 | 5 14·5 | 5·8 | 2·1 | 11·8 | 4·2 | 17·8 | 6·4 |
| 59 | 5 29·8 | 5 30·7 | 5 14·7 | 5·9 | 2·1 | 11·9 | 4·3 | 17·9 | 6·4 |
| 60 | 5 30·0 | 5 30·9 | 5 15·0 | 6·0 | 2·2 | 12·0 | 4·3 | 18·0 | 6·5 |



| 22m s | SUN PLANETS ° ′ | ARIES ° ′ | MOON ° ′ | v or d ′ | Corrⁿ ′ | v or d ′ | Corrⁿ ′ | v or d ′ | Corrⁿ ′ |
|---|---|---|---|---|---|---|---|---|---|
| 00 | 5 30·0 | 5 30·9 | 5 15·0 | 0·0 | 0·0 | 6·0 | 2·3 | 12·0 | 4·5 |
| 01 | 5 30·3 | 5 31·2 | 5 15·2 | 0·1 | 0·0 | 6·1 | 2·3 | 12·1 | 4·5 |
| 02 | 5 30·5 | 5 31·4 | 5 15·4 | 0·2 | 0·1 | 6·2 | 2·3 | 12·2 | 4·6 |
| 03 | 5 30·8 | 5 31·7 | 5 15·7 | 0·3 | 0·1 | 6·3 | 2·4 | 12·3 | 4·6 |
| 04 | 5 31·0 | 5 31·9 | 5 15·9 | 0·4 | 0·2 | 6·4 | 2·4 | 12·4 | 4·7 |
| 05 | 5 31·3 | 5 32·2 | 5 16·2 | 0·5 | 0·2 | 6·5 | 2·4 | 12·5 | 4·7 |
| 06 | 5 31·5 | 5 32·4 | 5 16·4 | 0·6 | 0·2 | 6·6 | 2·5 | 12·6 | 4·7 |
| 07 | 5 31·8 | 5 32·7 | 5 16·6 | 0·7 | 0·3 | 6·7 | 2·5 | 12·7 | 4·8 |
| 08 | 5 32·0 | 5 32·9 | 5 16·9 | 0·8 | 0·3 | 6·8 | 2·6 | 12·8 | 4·8 |
| 09 | 5 32·3 | 5 33·2 | 5 17·1 | 0·9 | 0·3 | 6·9 | 2·6 | 12·9 | 4·8 |
| 10 | 5 32·5 | 5 33·4 | 5 17·4 | 1·0 | 0·4 | 7·0 | 2·6 | 13·0 | 4·9 |
| 11 | 5 32·8 | 5 33·7 | 5 17·6 | 1·1 | 0·4 | 7·1 | 2·7 | 13·1 | 4·9 |
| 12 | 5 33·0 | 5 33·9 | 5 17·8 | 1·2 | 0·5 | 7·2 | 2·7 | 13·2 | 5·0 |
| 13 | 5 33·3 | 5 34·2 | 5 18·1 | 1·3 | 0·5 | 7·3 | 2·7 | 13·3 | 5·0 |
| 14 | 5 33·5 | 5 34·4 | 5 18·3 | 1·4 | 0·5 | 7·4 | 2·8 | 13·4 | 5·0 |
| 15 | 5 33·8 | 5 34·7 | 5 18·5 | 1·5 | 0·6 | 7·5 | 2·8 | 13·5 | 5·1 |
| 16 | 5 34·0 | 5 34·9 | 5 18·8 | 1·6 | 0·6 | 7·6 | 2·9 | 13·6 | 5·1 |
| 17 | 5 34·3 | 5 35·2 | 5 19·0 | 1·7 | 0·6 | 7·7 | 2·9 | 13·7 | 5·1 |
| 18 | 5 34·5 | 5 35·4 | 5 19·3 | 1·8 | 0·7 | 7·8 | 2·9 | 13·8 | 5·2 |
| 19 | 5 34·8 | 5 35·7 | 5 19·5 | 1·9 | 0·7 | 7·9 | 3·0 | 13·9 | 5·2 |
| 20 | 5 35·0 | 5 35·9 | 5 19·7 | 2·0 | 0·8 | 8·0 | 3·0 | 14·0 | 5·3 |
| 21 | 5 35·3 | 5 36·2 | 5 20·0 | 2·1 | 0·8 | 8·1 | 3·0 | 14·1 | 5·3 |
| 22 | 5 35·5 | 5 36·4 | 5 20·2 | 2·2 | 0·8 | 8·2 | 3·1 | 14·2 | 5·3 |
| 23 | 5 35·8 | 5 36·7 | 5 20·5 | 2·3 | 0·9 | 8·3 | 3·1 | 14·3 | 5·4 |
| 24 | 5 36·0 | 5 36·9 | 5 20·7 | 2·4 | 0·9 | 8·4 | 3·2 | 14·4 | 5·4 |
| 25 | 5 36·3 | 5 37·2 | 5 20·9 | 2·5 | 0·9 | 8·5 | 3·2 | 14·5 | 5·4 |
| 26 | 5 36·5 | 5 37·4 | 5 21·2 | 2·6 | 1·0 | 8·6 | 3·2 | 14·6 | 5·5 |
| 27 | 5 36·8 | 5 37·7 | 5 21·4 | 2·7 | 1·0 | 8·7 | 3·3 | 14·7 | 5·5 |
| 28 | 5 37·0 | 5 37·9 | 5 21·6 | 2·8 | 1·1 | 8·8 | 3·3 | 14·8 | 5·6 |
| 29 | 5 37·3 | 5 38·2 | 5 21·9 | 2·9 | 1·1 | 8·9 | 3·3 | 14·9 | 5·6 |
| 30 | 5 37·5 | 5 38·4 | 5 22·1 | 3·0 | 1·1 | 9·0 | 3·4 | 15·0 | 5·6 |
| 31 | 5 37·8 | 5 38·7 | 5 22·4 | 3·1 | 1·2 | 9·1 | 3·4 | 15·1 | 5·7 |
| 32 | 5 38·0 | 5 38·9 | 5 22·6 | 3·2 | 1·2 | 9·2 | 3·5 | 15·2 | 5·7 |
| 33 | 5 38·3 | 5 39·2 | 5 22·8 | 3·3 | 1·2 | 9·3 | 3·5 | 15·3 | 5·7 |
| 34 | 5 38·5 | 5 39·4 | 5 23·1 | 3·4 | 1·3 | 9·4 | 3·5 | 15·4 | 5·8 |
| 35 | 5 38·8 | 5 39·7 | 5 23·3 | 3·5 | 1·3 | 9·5 | 3·6 | 15·5 | 5·8 |
| 36 | 5 39·0 | 5 39·9 | 5 23·6 | 3·6 | 1·4 | 9·6 | 3·6 | 15·6 | 5·9 |
| 37 | 5 39·3 | 5 40·2 | 5 23·8 | 3·7 | 1·4 | 9·7 | 3·6 | 15·7 | 5·9 |
| 38 | 5 39·5 | 5 40·4 | 5 24·0 | 3·8 | 1·4 | 9·8 | 3·7 | 15·8 | 5·9 |
| 39 | 5 39·8 | 5 40·7 | 5 24·3 | 3·9 | 1·5 | 9·9 | 3·7 | 15·9 | 6·0 |
| 40 | 5 40·0 | 5 40·9 | 5 24·5 | 4·0 | 1·5 | 10·0 | 3·8 | 16·0 | 6·0 |
| 41 | 5 40·3 | 5 41·2 | 5 24·7 | 4·1 | 1·5 | 10·1 | 3·8 | 16·1 | 6·0 |
| 42 | 5 40·5 | 5 41·4 | 5 25·0 | 4·2 | 1·6 | 10·2 | 3·8 | 16·2 | 6·1 |
| 43 | 5 40·8 | 5 41·7 | 5 25·2 | 4·3 | 1·6 | 10·3 | 3·9 | 16·3 | 6·1 |
| 44 | 5 41·0 | 5 41·9 | 5 25·5 | 4·4 | 1·7 | 10·4 | 3·9 | 16·4 | 6·2 |
| 45 | 5 41·3 | 5 42·2 | 5 25·7 | 4·5 | 1·7 | 10·5 | 3·9 | 16·5 | 6·2 |
| 46 | 5 41·5 | 5 42·4 | 5 25·9 | 4·6 | 1·7 | 10·6 | 4·0 | 16·6 | 6·2 |
| 47 | 5 41·8 | 5 42·7 | 5 26·2 | 4·7 | 1·8 | 10·7 | 4·0 | 16·7 | 6·3 |
| 48 | 5 42·0 | 5 42·9 | 5 26·4 | 4·8 | 1·8 | 10·8 | 4·1 | 16·8 | 6·3 |
| 49 | 5 42·3 | 5 43·2 | 5 26·7 | 4·9 | 1·8 | 10·9 | 4·1 | 16·9 | 6·3 |
| 50 | 5 42·5 | 5 43·4 | 5 26·9 | 5·0 | 1·9 | 11·0 | 4·1 | 17·0 | 6·4 |
| 51 | 5 42·8 | 5 43·7 | 5 27·1 | 5·1 | 1·9 | 11·1 | 4·2 | 17·1 | 6·4 |
| 52 | 5 43·0 | 5 43·9 | 5 27·4 | 5·2 | 2·0 | 11·2 | 4·2 | 17·2 | 6·5 |
| 53 | 5 43·3 | 5 44·2 | 5 27·6 | 5·3 | 2·0 | 11·3 | 4·2 | 17·3 | 6·5 |
| 54 | 5 43·5 | 5 44·4 | 5 27·9 | 5·4 | 2·0 | 11·4 | 4·3 | 17·4 | 6·5 |
| 55 | 5 43·8 | 5 44·7 | 5 28·1 | 5·5 | 2·1 | 11·5 | 4·3 | 17·5 | 6·6 |
| 56 | 5 44·0 | 5 44·9 | 5 28·3 | 5·6 | 2·1 | 11·6 | 4·4 | 17·6 | 6·6 |
| 57 | 5 44·3 | 5 45·2 | 5 28·6 | 5·7 | 2·1 | 11·7 | 4·4 | 17·7 | 6·6 |
| 58 | 5 44·5 | 5 45·4 | 5 28·8 | 5·8 | 2·2 | 11·8 | 4·4 | 17·8 | 6·7 |
| 59 | 5 44·8 | 5 45·7 | 5 29·0 | 5·9 | 2·2 | 11·9 | 4·5 | 17·9 | 6·7 |
| 60 | 5 45·0 | 5 45·9 | 5 29·3 | 6·0 | 2·3 | 12·0 | 4·5 | 18·0 | 6·8 |

| 23m s | SUN PLANETS ° ′ | ARIES ° ′ | MOON ° ′ | v or d ′ | Corrⁿ ′ | v or d ′ | Corrⁿ ′ | v or d ′ | Corrⁿ ′ |
|---|---|---|---|---|---|---|---|---|---|
| 00 | 5 45·0 | 5 45·9 | 5 29·3 | 0·0 | 0·0 | 6·0 | 2·4 | 12·0 | 4·7 |
| 01 | 5 45·3 | 5 46·2 | 5 29·5 | 0·1 | 0·0 | 6·1 | 2·4 | 12·1 | 4·7 |
| 02 | 5 45·5 | 5 46·4 | 5 29·8 | 0·2 | 0·1 | 6·2 | 2·4 | 12·2 | 4·8 |
| 03 | 5 45·8 | 5 46·7 | 5 30·0 | 0·3 | 0·1 | 6·3 | 2·5 | 12·3 | 4·8 |
| 04 | 5 46·0 | 5 46·9 | 5 30·2 | 0·4 | 0·2 | 6·4 | 2·5 | 12·4 | 4·9 |
| 05 | 5 46·3 | 5 47·2 | 5 30·5 | 0·5 | 0·2 | 6·5 | 2·5 | 12·5 | 4·9 |
| 06 | 5 46·5 | 5 47·4 | 5 30·7 | 0·6 | 0·2 | 6·6 | 2·6 | 12·6 | 4·9 |
| 07 | 5 46·8 | 5 47·7 | 5 31·0 | 0·7 | 0·3 | 6·7 | 2·6 | 12·7 | 5·0 |
| 08 | 5 47·0 | 5 48·0 | 5 31·2 | 0·8 | 0·3 | 6·8 | 2·7 | 12·8 | 5·0 |
| 09 | 5 47·3 | 5 48·2 | 5 31·4 | 0·9 | 0·4 | 6·9 | 2·7 | 12·9 | 5·1 |
| 10 | 5 47·5 | 5 48·5 | 5 31·7 | 1·0 | 0·4 | 7·0 | 2·7 | 13·0 | 5·1 |
| 11 | 5 47·8 | 5 48·7 | 5 31·9 | 1·1 | 0·4 | 7·1 | 2·8 | 13·1 | 5·1 |
| 12 | 5 48·0 | 5 49·0 | 5 32·1 | 1·2 | 0·5 | 7·2 | 2·8 | 13·2 | 5·2 |
| 13 | 5 48·3 | 5 49·2 | 5 32·4 | 1·3 | 0·5 | 7·3 | 2·9 | 13·3 | 5·2 |
| 14 | 5 48·5 | 5 49·5 | 5 32·6 | 1·4 | 0·5 | 7·4 | 2·9 | 13·4 | 5·2 |
| 15 | 5 48·8 | 5 49·7 | 5 32·9 | 1·5 | 0·6 | 7·5 | 2·9 | 13·5 | 5·3 |
| 16 | 5 49·0 | 5 50·0 | 5 33·1 | 1·6 | 0·6 | 7·6 | 3·0 | 13·6 | 5·3 |
| 17 | 5 49·3 | 5 50·2 | 5 33·3 | 1·7 | 0·7 | 7·7 | 3·0 | 13·7 | 5·4 |
| 18 | 5 49·5 | 5 50·5 | 5 33·6 | 1·8 | 0·7 | 7·8 | 3·1 | 13·8 | 5·4 |
| 19 | 5 49·8 | 5 50·7 | 5 33·8 | 1·9 | 0·7 | 7·9 | 3·1 | 13·9 | 5·4 |
| 20 | 5 50·0 | 5 51·0 | 5 34·1 | 2·0 | 0·8 | 8·0 | 3·1 | 14·0 | 5·5 |
| 21 | 5 50·3 | 5 51·2 | 5 34·3 | 2·1 | 0·8 | 8·1 | 3·2 | 14·1 | 5·5 |
| 22 | 5 50·5 | 5 51·5 | 5 34·5 | 2·2 | 0·9 | 8·2 | 3·2 | 14·2 | 5·6 |
| 23 | 5 50·8 | 5 51·7 | 5 34·8 | 2·3 | 0·9 | 8·3 | 3·3 | 14·3 | 5·6 |
| 24 | 5 51·0 | 5 52·0 | 5 35·0 | 2·4 | 0·9 | 8·4 | 3·3 | 14·4 | 5·6 |
| 25 | 5 51·3 | 5 52·2 | 5 35·2 | 2·5 | 1·0 | 8·5 | 3·3 | 14·5 | 5·7 |
| 26 | 5 51·5 | 5 52·5 | 5 35·5 | 2·6 | 1·0 | 8·6 | 3·4 | 14·6 | 5·7 |
| 27 | 5 51·8 | 5 52·7 | 5 35·7 | 2·7 | 1·1 | 8·7 | 3·4 | 14·7 | 5·8 |
| 28 | 5 52·0 | 5 53·0 | 5 36·0 | 2·8 | 1·1 | 8·8 | 3·4 | 14·8 | 5·8 |
| 29 | 5 52·3 | 5 53·2 | 5 36·2 | 2·9 | 1·1 | 8·9 | 3·5 | 14·9 | 5·8 |
| 30 | 5 52·5 | 5 53·5 | 5 36·4 | 3·0 | 1·2 | 9·0 | 3·5 | 15·0 | 5·9 |
| 31 | 5 52·8 | 5 53·7 | 5 36·7 | 3·1 | 1·2 | 9·1 | 3·6 | 15·1 | 5·9 |
| 32 | 5 53·0 | 5 54·0 | 5 36·9 | 3·2 | 1·3 | 9·2 | 3·6 | 15·2 | 6·0 |
| 33 | 5 53·3 | 5 54·2 | 5 37·2 | 3·3 | 1·3 | 9·3 | 3·6 | 15·3 | 6·0 |
| 34 | 5 53·5 | 5 54·5 | 5 37·4 | 3·4 | 1·3 | 9·4 | 3·7 | 15·4 | 6·0 |
| 35 | 5 53·8 | 5 54·7 | 5 37·6 | 3·5 | 1·4 | 9·5 | 3·7 | 15·5 | 6·1 |
| 36 | 5 54·0 | 5 55·0 | 5 37·9 | 3·6 | 1·4 | 9·6 | 3·8 | 15·6 | 6·1 |
| 37 | 5 54·3 | 5 55·2 | 5 38·1 | 3·7 | 1·4 | 9·7 | 3·8 | 15·7 | 6·1 |
| 38 | 5 54·5 | 5 55·5 | 5 38·4 | 3·8 | 1·5 | 9·8 | 3·8 | 15·8 | 6·2 |
| 39 | 5 54·8 | 5 55·7 | 5 38·6 | 3·9 | 1·5 | 9·9 | 3·9 | 15·9 | 6·2 |
| 40 | 5 55·0 | 5 56·0 | 5 38·8 | 4·0 | 1·6 | 10·0 | 3·9 | 16·0 | 6·3 |
| 41 | 5 55·3 | 5 56·2 | 5 39·1 | 4·1 | 1·6 | 10·1 | 4·0 | 16·1 | 6·3 |
| 42 | 5 55·5 | 5 56·5 | 5 39·3 | 4·2 | 1·6 | 10·2 | 4·0 | 16·2 | 6·3 |
| 43 | 5 55·8 | 5 56·7 | 5 39·5 | 4·3 | 1·7 | 10·3 | 4·0 | 16·3 | 6·4 |
| 44 | 5 56·0 | 5 57·0 | 5 39·8 | 4·4 | 1·7 | 10·4 | 4·1 | 16·4 | 6·4 |
| 45 | 5 56·3 | 5 57·2 | 5 40·0 | 4·5 | 1·8 | 10·5 | 4·1 | 16·5 | 6·5 |
| 46 | 5 56·5 | 5 57·5 | 5 40·3 | 4·6 | 1·8 | 10·6 | 4·2 | 16·6 | 6·5 |
| 47 | 5 56·8 | 5 57·7 | 5 40·5 | 4·7 | 1·8 | 10·7 | 4·2 | 16·7 | 6·5 |
| 48 | 5 57·0 | 5 58·0 | 5 40·7 | 4·8 | 1·9 | 10·8 | 4·2 | 16·8 | 6·6 |
| 49 | 5 57·3 | 5 58·2 | 5 41·0 | 4·9 | 1·9 | 10·9 | 4·3 | 16·9 | 6·6 |
| 50 | 5 57·5 | 5 58·5 | 5 41·2 | 5·0 | 2·0 | 11·0 | 4·3 | 17·0 | 6·7 |
| 51 | 5 57·8 | 5 58·7 | 5 41·5 | 5·1 | 2·0 | 11·1 | 4·3 | 17·1 | 6·7 |
| 52 | 5 58·0 | 5 59·0 | 5 41·7 | 5·2 | 2·0 | 11·2 | 4·4 | 17·2 | 6·7 |
| 53 | 5 58·3 | 5 59·2 | 5 41·9 | 5·3 | 2·1 | 11·3 | 4·4 | 17·3 | 6·8 |
| 54 | 5 58·5 | 5 59·5 | 5 42·2 | 5·4 | 2·1 | 11·4 | 4·5 | 17·4 | 6·8 |
| 55 | 5 58·8 | 5 59·7 | 5 42·4 | 5·5 | 2·2 | 11·5 | 4·5 | 17·5 | 6·9 |
| 56 | 5 59·0 | 6 00·0 | 5 42·6 | 5·6 | 2·2 | 11·6 | 4·5 | 17·6 | 6·9 |
| 57 | 5 59·3 | 6 00·2 | 5 42·9 | 5·7 | 2·2 | 11·7 | 4·6 | 17·7 | 6·9 |
| 58 | 5 59·5 | 6 00·5 | 5 43·1 | 5·8 | 2·3 | 11·8 | 4·6 | 17·8 | 7·0 |
| 59 | 5 59·8 | 6 00·7 | 5 43·4 | 5·9 | 2·3 | 11·9 | 4·7 | 17·9 | 7·0 |
| 60 | 6 00·0 | 6 01·0 | 5 43·6 | 6·0 | 2·4 | 12·0 | 4·7 | 18·0 | 7·1 |

| 24m | SUN PLANETS | ARIES | MOON | v or d | Corrn | v or d | Corrn | v or d | Corrn |
|---|---|---|---|---|---|---|---|---|---|
| s | ° ′ | ° ′ | ° ′ | ′ | ′ | ′ | ′ | ′ | ′ |
| 00 | 6 00·0 | 6 01·0 | 5 43·6 | 0·0 | 0·0 | 6·0 | 2·5 | 12·0 | 4·9 |
| 01 | 6 00·3 | 6 01·2 | 5 43·8 | 0·1 | 0·0 | 6·1 | 2·5 | 12·1 | 4·9 |
| 02 | 6 00·5 | 6 01·5 | 5 44·1 | 0·2 | 0·1 | 6·2 | 2·5 | 12·2 | 5·0 |
| 03 | 6 00·8 | 6 01·7 | 5 44·3 | 0·3 | 0·1 | 6·3 | 2·6 | 12·3 | 5·0 |
| 04 | 6 01·0 | 6 02·0 | 5 44·6 | 0·4 | 0·2 | 6·4 | 2·6 | 12·4 | 5·1 |
| 05 | 6 01·3 | 6 02·2 | 5 44·8 | 0·5 | 0·2 | 6·5 | 2·7 | 12·5 | 5·1 |
| 06 | 6 01·5 | 6 02·5 | 5 45·0 | 0·6 | 0·2 | 6·6 | 2·7 | 12·6 | 5·1 |
| 07 | 6 01·8 | 6 02·7 | 5 45·3 | 0·7 | 0·3 | 6·7 | 2·7 | 12·7 | 5·2 |
| 08 | 6 02·0 | 6 03·0 | 5 45·5 | 0·8 | 0·3 | 6·8 | 2·8 | 12·8 | 5·2 |
| 09 | 6 02·3 | 6 03·2 | 5 45·7 | 0·9 | 0·4 | 6·9 | 2·8 | 12·9 | 5·3 |
| 10 | 6 02·5 | 6 03·5 | 5 46·0 | 1·0 | 0·4 | 7·0 | 2·9 | 13·0 | 5·3 |
| 11 | 6 02·8 | 6 03·7 | 5 46·2 | 1·1 | 0·4 | 7·1 | 2·9 | 13·1 | 5·3 |
| 12 | 6 03·0 | 6 04·0 | 5 46·5 | 1·2 | 0·5 | 7·2 | 2·9 | 13·2 | 5·4 |
| 13 | 6 03·3 | 6 04·2 | 5 46·7 | 1·3 | 0·5 | 7·3 | 3·0 | 13·3 | 5·4 |
| 14 | 6 03·5 | 6 04·5 | 5 46·9 | 1·4 | 0·6 | 7·4 | 3·0 | 13·4 | 5·5 |
| 15 | 6 03·8 | 6 04·7 | 5 47·2 | 1·5 | 0·6 | 7·5 | 3·1 | 13·5 | 5·5 |
| 16 | 6 04·0 | 6 05·0 | 5 47·4 | 1·6 | 0·7 | 7·6 | 3·1 | 13·6 | 5·6 |
| 17 | 6 04·3 | 6 05·2 | 5 47·7 | 1·7 | 0·7 | 7·7 | 3·1 | 13·7 | 5·6 |
| 18 | 6 04·5 | 6 05·5 | 5 47·9 | 1·8 | 0·7 | 7·8 | 3·2 | 13·8 | 5·6 |
| 19 | 6 04·8 | 6 05·7 | 5 48·1 | 1·9 | 0·8 | 7·9 | 3·2 | 13·9 | 5·7 |
| 20 | 6 05·0 | 6 06·0 | 5 48·4 | 2·0 | 0·8 | 8·0 | 3·3 | 14·0 | 5·7 |
| 21 | 6 05·3 | 6 06·3 | 5 48·6 | 2·1 | 0·9 | 8·1 | 3·3 | 14·1 | 5·8 |
| 22 | 6 05·5 | 6 06·5 | 5 48·8 | 2·2 | 0·9 | 8·2 | 3·3 | 14·2 | 5·8 |
| 23 | 6 05·8 | 6 06·8 | 5 49·1 | 2·3 | 0·9 | 8·3 | 3·4 | 14·3 | 5·8 |
| 24 | 6 06·0 | 6 07·0 | 5 49·3 | 2·4 | 1·0 | 8·4 | 3·4 | 14·4 | 5·9 |
| 25 | 6 06·3 | 6 07·3 | 5 49·6 | 2·5 | 1·0 | 8·5 | 3·5 | 14·5 | 5·9 |
| 26 | 6 06·5 | 6 07·5 | 5 49·8 | 2·6 | 1·1 | 8·6 | 3·5 | 14·6 | 6·0 |
| 27 | 6 06·8 | 6 07·8 | 5 50·0 | 2·7 | 1·1 | 8·7 | 3·6 | 14·7 | 6·0 |
| 28 | 6 07·0 | 6 08·0 | 5 50·3 | 2·8 | 1·1 | 8·8 | 3·6 | 14·8 | 6·0 |
| 29 | 6 07·3 | 6 08·3 | 5 50·5 | 2·9 | 1·2 | 8·9 | 3·6 | 14·9 | 6·1 |
| 30 | 6 07·5 | 6 08·5 | 5 50·8 | 3·0 | 1·2 | 9·0 | 3·7 | 15·0 | 6·1 |
| 31 | 6 07·8 | 6 08·8 | 5 51·0 | 3·1 | 1·3 | 9·1 | 3·7 | 15·1 | 6·2 |
| 32 | 6 08·0 | 6 09·0 | 5 51·2 | 3·2 | 1·3 | 9·2 | 3·8 | 15·2 | 6·2 |
| 33 | 6 08·3 | 6 09·3 | 5 51·5 | 3·3 | 1·3 | 9·3 | 3·8 | 15·3 | 6·2 |
| 34 | 6 08·5 | 6 09·5 | 5 51·7 | 3·4 | 1·4 | 9·4 | 3·8 | 15·4 | 6·3 |
| 35 | 6 08·8 | 6 09·8 | 5 52·0 | 3·5 | 1·4 | 9·5 | 3·9 | 15·5 | 6·3 |
| 36 | 6 09·0 | 6 10·0 | 5 52·2 | 3·6 | 1·5 | 9·6 | 3·9 | 15·6 | 6·4 |
| 37 | 6 09·3 | 6 10·3 | 5 52·4 | 3·7 | 1·5 | 9·7 | 4·0 | 15·7 | 6·4 |
| 38 | 6 09·5 | 6 10·5 | 5 52·7 | 3·8 | 1·6 | 9·8 | 4·0 | 15·8 | 6·5 |
| 39 | 6 09·8 | 6 10·8 | 5 52·9 | 3·9 | 1·6 | 9·9 | 4·0 | 15·9 | 6·5 |
| 40 | 6 10·0 | 6 11·0 | 5 53·1 | 4·0 | 1·6 | 10·0 | 4·1 | 16·0 | 6·5 |
| 41 | 6 10·3 | 6 11·3 | 5 53·4 | 4·1 | 1·7 | 10·1 | 4·1 | 16·1 | 6·6 |
| 42 | 6 10·5 | 6 11·5 | 5 53·6 | 4·2 | 1·7 | 10·2 | 4·2 | 16·2 | 6·6 |
| 43 | 6 10·8 | 6 11·8 | 5 53·9 | 4·3 | 1·8 | 10·3 | 4·2 | 16·3 | 6·7 |
| 44 | 6 11·0 | 6 12·0 | 5 54·1 | 4·4 | 1·8 | 10·4 | 4·2 | 16·4 | 6·7 |
| 45 | 6 11·3 | 6 12·3 | 5 54·3 | 4·5 | 1·8 | 10·5 | 4·3 | 16·5 | 6·7 |
| 46 | 6 11·5 | 6 12·5 | 5 54·6 | 4·6 | 1·9 | 10·6 | 4·3 | 16·6 | 6·8 |
| 47 | 6 11·8 | 6 12·8 | 5 54·8 | 4·7 | 1·9 | 10·7 | 4·4 | 16·7 | 6·8 |
| 48 | 6 12·0 | 6 13·0 | 5 55·1 | 4·8 | 2·0 | 10·8 | 4·4 | 16·8 | 6·9 |
| 49 | 6 12·3 | 6 13·3 | 5 55·3 | 4·9 | 2·0 | 10·9 | 4·5 | 16·9 | 6·9 |
| 50 | 6 12·5 | 6 13·5 | 5 55·5 | 5·0 | 2·0 | 11·0 | 4·5 | 17·0 | 6·9 |
| 51 | 6 12·8 | 6 13·8 | 5 55·8 | 5·1 | 2·1 | 11·1 | 4·5 | 17·1 | 7·0 |
| 52 | 6 13·0 | 6 14·0 | 5 56·0 | 5·2 | 2·1 | 11·2 | 4·6 | 17·2 | 7·0 |
| 53 | 6 13·3 | 6 14·3 | 5 56·2 | 5·3 | 2·2 | 11·3 | 4·6 | 17·3 | 7·1 |
| 54 | 6 13·5 | 6 14·5 | 5 56·5 | 5·4 | 2·2 | 11·4 | 4·7 | 17·4 | 7·1 |
| 55 | 6 13·8 | 6 14·8 | 5 56·7 | 5·5 | 2·2 | 11·5 | 4·7 | 17·5 | 7·1 |
| 56 | 6 14·0 | 6 15·0 | 5 57·0 | 5·6 | 2·3 | 11·6 | 4·7 | 17·6 | 7·2 |
| 57 | 6 14·3 | 6 15·3 | 5 57·2 | 5·7 | 2·3 | 11·7 | 4·8 | 17·7 | 7·2 |
| 58 | 6 14·5 | 6 15·5 | 5 57·4 | 5·8 | 2·4 | 11·8 | 4·8 | 17·8 | 7·3 |
| 59 | 6 14·8 | 6 15·8 | 5 57·7 | 5·9 | 2·4 | 11·9 | 4·9 | 17·9 | 7·3 |
| 60 | 6 15·0 | 6 16·0 | 5 57·9 | 6·0 | 2·5 | 12·0 | 4·9 | 18·0 | 7·4 |

| 25m | SUN PLANETS | ARIES | MOON | v or d | Corrn | v or d | Corrn | v or d | Corrn |
|---|---|---|---|---|---|---|---|---|---|
| s | ° ′ | ° ′ | ° ′ | ′ | ′ | ′ | ′ | ′ | ′ |
| 00 | 6 15·0 | 6 16·0 | 5 57·9 | 0·0 | 0·0 | 6·0 | 2·6 | 12·0 | 5·1 |
| 01 | 6 15·3 | 6 16·3 | 5 58·2 | 0·1 | 0·0 | 6·1 | 2·6 | 12·1 | 5·1 |
| 02 | 6 15·5 | 6 16·5 | 5 58·4 | 0·2 | 0·1 | 6·2 | 2·6 | 12·2 | 5·2 |
| 03 | 6 15·8 | 6 16·8 | 5 58·6 | 0·3 | 0·1 | 6·3 | 2·7 | 12·3 | 5·2 |
| 04 | 6 16·0 | 6 17·0 | 5 58·9 | 0·4 | 0·2 | 6·4 | 2·7 | 12·4 | 5·3 |
| 05 | 6 16·3 | 6 17·3 | 5 59·1 | 0·5 | 0·2 | 6·5 | 2·8 | 12·5 | 5·3 |
| 06 | 6 16·5 | 6 17·5 | 5 59·3 | 0·6 | 0·3 | 6·6 | 2·8 | 12·6 | 5·4 |
| 07 | 6 16·8 | 6 17·8 | 5 59·6 | 0·7 | 0·3 | 6·7 | 2·8 | 12·7 | 5·4 |
| 08 | 6 17·0 | 6 18·0 | 5 59·8 | 0·8 | 0·3 | 6·8 | 2·9 | 12·8 | 5·4 |
| 09 | 6 17·3 | 6 18·3 | 6 00·1 | 0·9 | 0·4 | 6·9 | 2·9 | 12·9 | 5·5 |
| 10 | 6 17·5 | 6 18·5 | 6 00·3 | 1·0 | 0·4 | 7·0 | 3·0 | 13·0 | 5·5 |
| 11 | 6 17·8 | 6 18·8 | 6 00·5 | 1·1 | 0·5 | 7·1 | 3·0 | 13·1 | 5·6 |
| 12 | 6 18·0 | 6 19·0 | 6 00·8 | 1·2 | 0·5 | 7·2 | 3·1 | 13·2 | 5·6 |
| 13 | 6 18·3 | 6 19·3 | 6 01·0 | 1·3 | 0·6 | 7·3 | 3·1 | 13·3 | 5·7 |
| 14 | 6 18·5 | 6 19·5 | 6 01·3 | 1·4 | 0·6 | 7·4 | 3·1 | 13·4 | 5·7 |
| 15 | 6 18·8 | 6 19·8 | 6 01·5 | 1·5 | 0·6 | 7·5 | 3·2 | 13·5 | 5·7 |
| 16 | 6 19·0 | 6 20·0 | 6 01·7 | 1·6 | 0·7 | 7·6 | 3·2 | 13·6 | 5·8 |
| 17 | 6 19·3 | 6 20·3 | 6 02·0 | 1·7 | 0·7 | 7·7 | 3·3 | 13·7 | 5·8 |
| 18 | 6 19·5 | 6 20·5 | 6 02·2 | 1·8 | 0·8 | 7·8 | 3·3 | 13·8 | 5·9 |
| 19 | 6 19·8 | 6 20·8 | 6 02·5 | 1·9 | 0·8 | 7·9 | 3·4 | 13·9 | 5·9 |
| 20 | 6 20·0 | 6 21·0 | 6 02·7 | 2·0 | 0·9 | 8·0 | 3·4 | 14·0 | 6·0 |
| 21 | 6 20·3 | 6 21·3 | 6 02·9 | 2·1 | 0·9 | 8·1 | 3·4 | 14·1 | 6·0 |
| 22 | 6 20·5 | 6 21·5 | 6 03·2 | 2·2 | 0·9 | 8·2 | 3·5 | 14·2 | 6·0 |
| 23 | 6 20·8 | 6 21·8 | 6 03·4 | 2·3 | 1·0 | 8·3 | 3·5 | 14·3 | 6·1 |
| 24 | 6 21·0 | 6 22·0 | 6 03·6 | 2·4 | 1·0 | 8·4 | 3·6 | 14·4 | 6·1 |
| 25 | 6 21·3 | 6 22·3 | 6 03·9 | 2·5 | 1·1 | 8·5 | 3·6 | 14·5 | 6·2 |
| 26 | 6 21·5 | 6 22·5 | 6 04·1 | 2·6 | 1·1 | 8·6 | 3·7 | 14·6 | 6·2 |
| 27 | 6 21·8 | 6 22·8 | 6 04·4 | 2·7 | 1·1 | 8·7 | 3·7 | 14·7 | 6·2 |
| 28 | 6 22·0 | 6 23·0 | 6 04·6 | 2·8 | 1·2 | 8·8 | 3·7 | 14·8 | 6·3 |
| 29 | 6 22·3 | 6 23·3 | 6 04·8 | 2·9 | 1·2 | 8·9 | 3·8 | 14·9 | 6·3 |
| 30 | 6 22·5 | 6 23·5 | 6 05·1 | 3·0 | 1·3 | 9·0 | 3·8 | 15·0 | 6·4 |
| 31 | 6 22·8 | 6 23·8 | 6 05·3 | 3·1 | 1·3 | 9·1 | 3·9 | 15·1 | 6·4 |
| 32 | 6 23·0 | 6 24·0 | 6 05·6 | 3·2 | 1·4 | 9·2 | 3·9 | 15·2 | 6·5 |
| 33 | 6 23·3 | 6 24·3 | 6 05·8 | 3·3 | 1·4 | 9·3 | 4·0 | 15·3 | 6·5 |
| 34 | 6 23·5 | 6 24·5 | 6 06·0 | 3·4 | 1·4 | 9·4 | 4·0 | 15·4 | 6·5 |
| 35 | 6 23·8 | 6 24·8 | 6 06·3 | 3·5 | 1·5 | 9·5 | 4·0 | 15·5 | 6·6 |
| 36 | 6 24·0 | 6 25·1 | 6 06·5 | 3·6 | 1·5 | 9·6 | 4·1 | 15·6 | 6·6 |
| 37 | 6 24·3 | 6 25·3 | 6 06·7 | 3·7 | 1·6 | 9·7 | 4·1 | 15·7 | 6·7 |
| 38 | 6 24·5 | 6 25·6 | 6 07·0 | 3·8 | 1·6 | 9·8 | 4·2 | 15·8 | 6·7 |
| 39 | 6 24·8 | 6 25·8 | 6 07·2 | 3·9 | 1·7 | 9·9 | 4·2 | 15·9 | 6·8 |
| 40 | 6 25·0 | 6 26·1 | 6 07·5 | 4·0 | 1·7 | 10·0 | 4·3 | 16·0 | 6·8 |
| 41 | 6 25·3 | 6 26·3 | 6 07·7 | 4·1 | 1·7 | 10·1 | 4·3 | 16·1 | 6·8 |
| 42 | 6 25·5 | 6 26·6 | 6 07·9 | 4·2 | 1·8 | 10·2 | 4·3 | 16·2 | 6·9 |
| 43 | 6 25·8 | 6 26·8 | 6 08·2 | 4·3 | 1·8 | 10·3 | 4·4 | 16·3 | 6·9 |
| 44 | 6 26·0 | 6 27·1 | 6 08·4 | 4·4 | 1·9 | 10·4 | 4·4 | 16·4 | 7·0 |
| 45 | 6 26·3 | 6 27·3 | 6 08·7 | 4·5 | 1·9 | 10·5 | 4·5 | 16·5 | 7·0 |
| 46 | 6 26·5 | 6 27·6 | 6 08·9 | 4·6 | 2·0 | 10·6 | 4·5 | 16·6 | 7·1 |
| 47 | 6 26·8 | 6 27·8 | 6 09·1 | 4·7 | 2·0 | 10·7 | 4·5 | 16·7 | 7·1 |
| 48 | 6 27·0 | 6 28·1 | 6 09·4 | 4·8 | 2·0 | 10·8 | 4·6 | 16·8 | 7·1 |
| 49 | 6 27·3 | 6 28·3 | 6 09·6 | 4·9 | 2·1 | 10·9 | 4·6 | 16·9 | 7·2 |
| 50 | 6 27·5 | 6 28·6 | 6 09·8 | 5·0 | 2·1 | 11·0 | 4·7 | 17·0 | 7·2 |
| 51 | 6 27·8 | 6 28·8 | 6 10·1 | 5·1 | 2·2 | 11·1 | 4·7 | 17·1 | 7·3 |
| 52 | 6 28·0 | 6 29·1 | 6 10·3 | 5·2 | 2·2 | 11·2 | 4·8 | 17·2 | 7·3 |
| 53 | 6 28·3 | 6 29·3 | 6 10·6 | 5·3 | 2·3 | 11·3 | 4·8 | 17·3 | 7·4 |
| 54 | 6 28·5 | 6 29·6 | 6 10·8 | 5·4 | 2·3 | 11·4 | 4·8 | 17·4 | 7·4 |
| 55 | 6 28·8 | 6 29·8 | 6 11·0 | 5·5 | 2·3 | 11·5 | 4·9 | 17·5 | 7·4 |
| 56 | 6 29·0 | 6 30·1 | 6 11·3 | 5·6 | 2·4 | 11·6 | 4·9 | 17·6 | 7·5 |
| 57 | 6 29·3 | 6 30·3 | 6 11·5 | 5·7 | 2·4 | 11·7 | 5·0 | 17·7 | 7·5 |
| 58 | 6 29·5 | 6 30·6 | 6 11·8 | 5·8 | 2·5 | 11·8 | 5·0 | 17·8 | 7·6 |
| 59 | 6 29·8 | 6 30·8 | 6 12·0 | 5·9 | 2·5 | 11·9 | 5·1 | 17·9 | 7·6 |
| 60 | 6 30·0 | 6 31·1 | 6 12·2 | 6·0 | 2·6 | 12·0 | 5·1 | 18·0 | 7·7 |

| 26m | SUN PLANETS | ARIES | MOON | v or d | Corrn | v or d | Corrn | v or d | Corrn |
|---|---|---|---|---|---|---|---|---|---|
| s | ° ′ | ° ′ | ° ′ | ′ | ′ | ′ | ′ | ′ | ′ |
| 00 | 6 30·0 | 6 31·1 | 6 12·2 | 0·0 | 0·0 | 6·0 | 2·7 | 12·0 | 5·3 |
| 01 | 6 30·3 | 6 31·3 | 6 12·5 | 0·1 | 0·0 | 6·1 | 2·7 | 12·1 | 5·3 |
| 02 | 6 30·5 | 6 31·6 | 6 12·7 | 0·2 | 0·1 | 6·2 | 2·7 | 12·2 | 5·4 |
| 03 | 6 30·8 | 6 31·8 | 6 12·9 | 0·3 | 0·1 | 6·3 | 2·8 | 12·3 | 5·4 |
| 04 | 6 31·0 | 6 32·1 | 6 13·2 | 0·4 | 0·2 | 6·4 | 2·8 | 12·4 | 5·5 |
| 05 | 6 31·3 | 6 32·3 | 6 13·4 | 0·5 | 0·2 | 6·5 | 2·9 | 12·5 | 5·5 |
| 06 | 6 31·5 | 6 32·6 | 6 13·7 | 0·6 | 0·3 | 6·6 | 2·9 | 12·6 | 5·6 |
| 07 | 6 31·8 | 6 32·8 | 6 13·9 | 0·7 | 0·3 | 6·7 | 3·0 | 12·7 | 5·6 |
| 08 | 6 32·0 | 6 33·1 | 6 14·1 | 0·8 | 0·4 | 6·8 | 3·0 | 12·8 | 5·7 |
| 09 | 6 32·3 | 6 33·3 | 6 14·4 | 0·9 | 0·4 | 6·9 | 3·0 | 12·9 | 5·7 |
| 10 | 6 32·5 | 6 33·6 | 6 14·6 | 1·0 | 0·4 | 7·0 | 3·1 | 13·0 | 5·7 |
| 11 | 6 32·8 | 6 33·8 | 6 14·9 | 1·1 | 0·5 | 7·1 | 3·1 | 13·1 | 5·8 |
| 12 | 6 33·0 | 6 34·1 | 6 15·1 | 1·2 | 0·5 | 7·2 | 3·2 | 13·2 | 5·8 |
| 13 | 6 33·3 | 6 34·3 | 6 15·3 | 1·3 | 0·6 | 7·3 | 3·2 | 13·3 | 5·9 |
| 14 | 6 33·5 | 6 34·6 | 6 15·6 | 1·4 | 0·6 | 7·4 | 3·3 | 13·4 | 5·9 |
| 15 | 6 33·8 | 6 34·8 | 6 15·8 | 1·5 | 0·7 | 7·5 | 3·3 | 13·5 | 6·0 |
| 16 | 6 34·0 | 6 35·1 | 6 16·1 | 1·6 | 0·7 | 7·6 | 3·4 | 13·6 | 6·0 |
| 17 | 6 34·3 | 6 35·3 | 6 16·3 | 1·7 | 0·8 | 7·7 | 3·4 | 13·7 | 6·1 |
| 18 | 6 34·5 | 6 35·6 | 6 16·5 | 1·8 | 0·8 | 7·8 | 3·4 | 13·8 | 6·1 |
| 19 | 6 34·8 | 6 35·8 | 6 16·8 | 1·9 | 0·8 | 7·9 | 3·5 | 13·9 | 6·1 |
| 20 | 6 35·0 | 6 36·1 | 6 17·0 | 2·0 | 0·9 | 8·0 | 3·5 | 14·0 | 6·2 |
| 21 | 6 35·3 | 6 36·3 | 6 17·2 | 2·1 | 0·9 | 8·1 | 3·6 | 14·1 | 6·2 |
| 22 | 6 35·5 | 6 36·6 | 6 17·5 | 2·2 | 1·0 | 8·2 | 3·6 | 14·2 | 6·3 |
| 23 | 6 35·8 | 6 36·8 | 6 17·7 | 2·3 | 1·0 | 8·3 | 3·7 | 14·3 | 6·3 |
| 24 | 6 36·0 | 6 37·1 | 6 18·0 | 2·4 | 1·1 | 8·4 | 3·7 | 14·4 | 6·4 |
| 25 | 6 36·3 | 6 37·3 | 6 18·2 | 2·5 | 1·1 | 8·5 | 3·8 | 14·5 | 6·4 |
| 26 | 6 36·5 | 6 37·6 | 6 18·4 | 2·6 | 1·1 | 8·6 | 3·8 | 14·6 | 6·4 |
| 27 | 6 36·8 | 6 37·8 | 6 18·7 | 2·7 | 1·2 | 8·7 | 3·8 | 14·7 | 6·5 |
| 28 | 6 37·0 | 6 38·1 | 6 18·9 | 2·8 | 1·2 | 8·8 | 3·9 | 14·8 | 6·5 |
| 29 | 6 37·3 | 6 38·3 | 6 19·2 | 2·9 | 1·3 | 8·9 | 3·9 | 14·9 | 6·6 |
| 30 | 6 37·5 | 6 38·6 | 6 19·4 | 3·0 | 1·3 | 9·0 | 4·0 | 15·0 | 6·6 |
| 31 | 6 37·8 | 6 38·8 | 6 19·6 | 3·1 | 1·4 | 9·1 | 4·0 | 15·1 | 6·7 |
| 32 | 6 38·0 | 6 39·1 | 6 19·9 | 3·2 | 1·4 | 9·2 | 4·1 | 15·2 | 6·7 |
| 33 | 6 38·3 | 6 39·3 | 6 20·1 | 3·3 | 1·5 | 9·3 | 4·1 | 15·3 | 6·8 |
| 34 | 6 38·5 | 6 39·6 | 6 20·3 | 3·4 | 1·5 | 9·4 | 4·2 | 15·4 | 6·8 |
| 35 | 6 38·8 | 6 39·8 | 6 20·6 | 3·5 | 1·5 | 9·5 | 4·2 | 15·5 | 6·8 |
| 36 | 6 39·0 | 6 40·1 | 6 20·8 | 3·6 | 1·6 | 9·6 | 4·2 | 15·6 | 6·9 |
| 37 | 6 39·3 | 6 40·3 | 6 21·1 | 3·7 | 1·6 | 9·7 | 4·3 | 15·7 | 6·9 |
| 38 | 6 39·5 | 6 40·6 | 6 21·3 | 3·8 | 1·7 | 9·8 | 4·3 | 15·8 | 7·0 |
| 39 | 6 39·8 | 6 40·8 | 6 21·5 | 3·9 | 1·7 | 9·9 | 4·4 | 15·9 | 7·0 |
| 40 | 6 40·0 | 6 41·1 | 6 21·8 | 4·0 | 1·8 | 10·0 | 4·4 | 16·0 | 7·1 |
| 41 | 6 40·3 | 6 41·3 | 6 22·0 | 4·1 | 1·8 | 10·1 | 4·5 | 16·1 | 7·1 |
| 42 | 6 40·5 | 6 41·6 | 6 22·3 | 4·2 | 1·9 | 10·2 | 4·5 | 16·2 | 7·2 |
| 43 | 6 40·8 | 6 41·8 | 6 22·5 | 4·3 | 1·9 | 10·3 | 4·5 | 16·3 | 7·2 |
| 44 | 6 41·0 | 6 42·1 | 6 22·7 | 4·4 | 1·9 | 10·4 | 4·6 | 16·4 | 7·2 |
| 45 | 6 41·3 | 6 42·3 | 6 23·0 | 4·5 | 2·0 | 10·5 | 4·6 | 16·5 | 7·3 |
| 46 | 6 41·5 | 6 42·6 | 6 23·2 | 4·6 | 2·0 | 10·6 | 4·7 | 16·6 | 7·3 |
| 47 | 6 41·8 | 6 42·8 | 6 23·4 | 4·7 | 2·1 | 10·7 | 4·7 | 16·7 | 7·4 |
| 48 | 6 42·0 | 6 43·1 | 6 23·7 | 4·8 | 2·1 | 10·8 | 4·8 | 16·8 | 7·4 |
| 49 | 6 42·3 | 6 43·4 | 6 23·9 | 4·9 | 2·2 | 10·9 | 4·8 | 16·9 | 7·5 |
| 50 | 6 42·5 | 6 43·6 | 6 24·2 | 5·0 | 2·2 | 11·0 | 4·9 | 17·0 | 7·5 |
| 51 | 6 42·8 | 6 43·9 | 6 24·4 | 5·1 | 2·3 | 11·1 | 4·9 | 17·1 | 7·6 |
| 52 | 6 43·0 | 6 44·1 | 6 24·6 | 5·2 | 2·3 | 11·2 | 4·9 | 17·2 | 7·6 |
| 53 | 6 43·3 | 6 44·4 | 6 24·9 | 5·3 | 2·3 | 11·3 | 5·0 | 17·3 | 7·6 |
| 54 | 6 43·5 | 6 44·6 | 6 25·1 | 5·4 | 2·4 | 11·4 | 5·0 | 17·4 | 7·7 |
| 55 | 6 43·8 | 6 44·9 | 6 25·4 | 5·5 | 2·4 | 11·5 | 5·1 | 17·5 | 7·7 |
| 56 | 6 44·0 | 6 45·1 | 6 25·6 | 5·6 | 2·5 | 11·6 | 5·1 | 17·6 | 7·8 |
| 57 | 6 44·3 | 6 45·4 | 6 25·8 | 5·7 | 2·5 | 11·7 | 5·2 | 17·7 | 7·8 |
| 58 | 6 44·5 | 6 45·6 | 6 26·1 | 5·8 | 2·6 | 11·8 | 5·2 | 17·8 | 7·9 |
| 59 | 6 44·8 | 6 45·9 | 6 26·3 | 5·9 | 2·6 | 11·9 | 5·3 | 17·9 | 7·9 |
| 60 | 6 45·0 | 6 46·1 | 6 26·6 | 6·0 | 2·7 | 12·0 | 5·3 | 18·0 | 8·0 |

| 27m | SUN PLANETS | ARIES | MOON | v or d | Corrn | v or d | Corrn | v or d | Corrn |
|---|---|---|---|---|---|---|---|---|---|
| s | ° ′ | ° ′ | ° ′ | ′ | ′ | ′ | ′ | ′ | ′ |
| 00 | 6 45·0 | 6 46·1 | 6 26·6 | 0·0 | 0·0 | 6·0 | 2·8 | 12·0 | 5·5 |
| 01 | 6 45·3 | 6 46·4 | 6 26·8 | 0·1 | 0·0 | 6·1 | 2·8 | 12·1 | 5·5 |
| 02 | 6 45·5 | 6 46·6 | 6 27·0 | 0·2 | 0·1 | 6·2 | 2·8 | 12·2 | 5·6 |
| 03 | 6 45·8 | 6 46·9 | 6 27·3 | 0·3 | 0·1 | 6·3 | 2·9 | 12·3 | 5·6 |
| 04 | 6 46·0 | 6 47·1 | 6 27·5 | 0·4 | 0·2 | 6·4 | 2·9 | 12·4 | 5·7 |
| 05 | 6 46·3 | 6 47·4 | 6 27·7 | 0·5 | 0·2 | 6·5 | 3·0 | 12·5 | 5·7 |
| 06 | 6 46·5 | 6 47·6 | 6 28·0 | 0·6 | 0·3 | 6·6 | 3·0 | 12·6 | 5·8 |
| 07 | 6 46·8 | 6 47·9 | 6 28·2 | 0·7 | 0·3 | 6·7 | 3·1 | 12·7 | 5·8 |
| 08 | 6 47·0 | 6 48·1 | 6 28·5 | 0·8 | 0·4 | 6·8 | 3·1 | 12·8 | 5·9 |
| 09 | 6 47·3 | 6 48·4 | 6 28·7 | 0·9 | 0·4 | 6·9 | 3·2 | 12·9 | 5·9 |
| 10 | 6 47·5 | 6 48·6 | 6 28·9 | 1·0 | 0·5 | 7·0 | 3·2 | 13·0 | 6·0 |
| 11 | 6 47·8 | 6 48·9 | 6 29·2 | 1·1 | 0·5 | 7·1 | 3·3 | 13·1 | 6·0 |
| 12 | 6 48·0 | 6 49·1 | 6 29·4 | 1·2 | 0·6 | 7·2 | 3·3 | 13·2 | 6·1 |
| 13 | 6 48·3 | 6 49·4 | 6 29·7 | 1·3 | 0·6 | 7·3 | 3·3 | 13·3 | 6·1 |
| 14 | 6 48·5 | 6 49·6 | 6 29·9 | 1·4 | 0·6 | 7·4 | 3·4 | 13·4 | 6·1 |
| 15 | 6 48·8 | 6 49·9 | 6 30·1 | 1·5 | 0·7 | 7·5 | 3·4 | 13·5 | 6·2 |
| 16 | 6 49·0 | 6 50·1 | 6 30·4 | 1·6 | 0·7 | 7·6 | 3·5 | 13·6 | 6·2 |
| 17 | 6 49·3 | 6 50·4 | 6 30·6 | 1·7 | 0·8 | 7·7 | 3·5 | 13·7 | 6·3 |
| 18 | 6 49·5 | 6 50·6 | 6 30·8 | 1·8 | 0·8 | 7·8 | 3·6 | 13·8 | 6·3 |
| 19 | 6 49·8 | 6 50·9 | 6 31·1 | 1·9 | 0·9 | 7·9 | 3·6 | 13·9 | 6·4 |
| 20 | 6 50·0 | 6 51·1 | 6 31·3 | 2·0 | 0·9 | 8·0 | 3·7 | 14·0 | 6·4 |
| 21 | 6 50·3 | 6 51·4 | 6 31·6 | 2·1 | 1·0 | 8·1 | 3·7 | 14·1 | 6·5 |
| 22 | 6 50·5 | 6 51·6 | 6 31·8 | 2·2 | 1·0 | 8·2 | 3·8 | 14·2 | 6·5 |
| 23 | 6 50·8 | 6 51·9 | 6 32·0 | 2·3 | 1·1 | 8·3 | 3·8 | 14·3 | 6·6 |
| 24 | 6 51·0 | 6 52·1 | 6 32·3 | 2·4 | 1·1 | 8·4 | 3·9 | 14·4 | 6·6 |
| 25 | 6 51·3 | 6 52·4 | 6 32·5 | 2·5 | 1·1 | 8·5 | 3·9 | 14·5 | 6·6 |
| 26 | 6 51·5 | 6 52·6 | 6 32·8 | 2·6 | 1·2 | 8·6 | 3·9 | 14·6 | 6·7 |
| 27 | 6 51·8 | 6 52·9 | 6 33·0 | 2·7 | 1·2 | 8·7 | 4·0 | 14·7 | 6·7 |
| 28 | 6 52·0 | 6 53·1 | 6 33·2 | 2·8 | 1·3 | 8·8 | 4·0 | 14·8 | 6·8 |
| 29 | 6 52·3 | 6 53·4 | 6 33·5 | 2·9 | 1·3 | 8·9 | 4·1 | 14·9 | 6·8 |
| 30 | 6 52·5 | 6 53·6 | 6 33·7 | 3·0 | 1·4 | 9·0 | 4·1 | 15·0 | 6·9 |
| 31 | 6 52·8 | 6 53·9 | 6 33·9 | 3·1 | 1·4 | 9·1 | 4·2 | 15·1 | 6·9 |
| 32 | 6 53·0 | 6 54·1 | 6 34·2 | 3·2 | 1·5 | 9·2 | 4·2 | 15·2 | 7·0 |
| 33 | 6 53·3 | 6 54·4 | 6 34·4 | 3·3 | 1·5 | 9·3 | 4·3 | 15·3 | 7·0 |
| 34 | 6 53·5 | 6 54·6 | 6 34·7 | 3·4 | 1·6 | 9·4 | 4·3 | 15·4 | 7·1 |
| 35 | 6 53·8 | 6 54·9 | 6 34·9 | 3·5 | 1·6 | 9·5 | 4·4 | 15·5 | 7·1 |
| 36 | 6 54·0 | 6 55·1 | 6 35·1 | 3·6 | 1·7 | 9·6 | 4·4 | 15·6 | 7·2 |
| 37 | 6 54·3 | 6 55·4 | 6 35·4 | 3·7 | 1·7 | 9·7 | 4·4 | 15·7 | 7·2 |
| 38 | 6 54·5 | 6 55·6 | 6 35·6 | 3·8 | 1·7 | 9·8 | 4·5 | 15·8 | 7·2 |
| 39 | 6 54·8 | 6 55·9 | 6 35·9 | 3·9 | 1·8 | 9·9 | 4·5 | 15·9 | 7·3 |
| 40 | 6 55·0 | 6 56·1 | 6 36·1 | 4·0 | 1·8 | 10·0 | 4·6 | 16·0 | 7·3 |
| 41 | 6 55·3 | 6 56·4 | 6 36·3 | 4·1 | 1·9 | 10·1 | 4·6 | 16·1 | 7·4 |
| 42 | 6 55·5 | 6 56·6 | 6 36·6 | 4·2 | 1·9 | 10·2 | 4·7 | 16·2 | 7·4 |
| 43 | 6 55·8 | 6 56·9 | 6 36·8 | 4·3 | 2·0 | 10·3 | 4·7 | 16·3 | 7·5 |
| 44 | 6 56·0 | 6 57·1 | 6 37·0 | 4·4 | 2·0 | 10·4 | 4·8 | 16·4 | 7·5 |
| 45 | 6 56·3 | 6 57·4 | 6 37·3 | 4·5 | 2·1 | 10·5 | 4·8 | 16·5 | 7·6 |
| 46 | 6 56·5 | 6 57·6 | 6 37·5 | 4·6 | 2·1 | 10·6 | 4·9 | 16·6 | 7·6 |
| 47 | 6 56·8 | 6 57·9 | 6 37·8 | 4·7 | 2·2 | 10·7 | 4·9 | 16·7 | 7·7 |
| 48 | 6 57·0 | 6 58·1 | 6 38·0 | 4·8 | 2·2 | 10·8 | 5·0 | 16·8 | 7·7 |
| 49 | 6 57·3 | 6 58·4 | 6 38·2 | 4·9 | 2·2 | 10·9 | 5·0 | 16·9 | 7·7 |
| 50 | 6 57·5 | 6 58·6 | 6 38·5 | 5·0 | 2·3 | 11·0 | 5·0 | 17·0 | 7·8 |
| 51 | 6 57·8 | 6 58·9 | 6 38·7 | 5·1 | 2·3 | 11·1 | 5·1 | 17·1 | 7·8 |
| 52 | 6 58·0 | 6 59·1 | 6 39·0 | 5·2 | 2·4 | 11·2 | 5·1 | 17·2 | 7·9 |
| 53 | 6 58·3 | 6 59·4 | 6 39·2 | 5·3 | 2·4 | 11·3 | 5·2 | 17·3 | 7·9 |
| 54 | 6 58·5 | 6 59·6 | 6 39·4 | 5·4 | 2·5 | 11·4 | 5·2 | 17·4 | 8·0 |
| 55 | 6 58·8 | 6 59·9 | 6 39·7 | 5·5 | 2·5 | 11·5 | 5·3 | 17·5 | 8·0 |
| 56 | 6 59·0 | 7 00·1 | 6 39·9 | 5·6 | 2·6 | 11·6 | 5·3 | 17·6 | 8·1 |
| 57 | 6 59·3 | 7 00·4 | 6 40·2 | 5·7 | 2·6 | 11·7 | 5·4 | 17·7 | 8·1 |
| 58 | 6 59·5 | 7 00·6 | 6 40·4 | 5·8 | 2·7 | 11·8 | 5·4 | 17·8 | 8·2 |
| 59 | 6 59·8 | 7 00·9 | 6 40·6 | 5·9 | 2·7 | 11·9 | 5·5 | 17·9 | 8·2 |
| 60 | 7 00·0 | 7 01·1 | 6 40·9 | 6·0 | 2·8 | 12·0 | 5·5 | 18·0 | 8·3 |

## 28ᵐ INCREMENTS AND CORRECTIONS 29ᵐ

| 28ᵐ | SUN PLANETS | ARIES | MOON | v or d | Corrⁿ | v or d | Corrⁿ | v or d | Corrⁿ |
|---|---|---|---|---|---|---|---|---|---|
| s | ° ′ | ° ′ | ° ′ | ′ | ′ | ′ | ′ | ′ | ′ |
| 00 | 7 00·0 | 7 01·1 | 6 40·9 | 0·0 | 0·0 | 6·0 | 2·9 | 12·0 | 5·7 |
| 01 | 7 00·3 | 7 01·4 | 6 41·1 | 0·1 | 0·0 | 6·1 | 2·9 | 12·1 | 5·7 |
| 02 | 7 00·5 | 7 01·7 | 6 41·3 | 0·2 | 0·1 | 6·2 | 2·9 | 12·2 | 5·8 |
| 03 | 7 00·8 | 7 01·9 | 6 41·6 | 0·3 | 0·1 | 6·3 | 3·0 | 12·3 | 5·8 |
| 04 | 7 01·0 | 7 02·2 | 6 41·8 | 0·4 | 0·2 | 6·4 | 3·0 | 12·4 | 5·9 |
| 05 | 7 01·3 | 7 02·4 | 6 42·1 | 0·5 | 0·2 | 6·5 | 3·1 | 12·5 | 5·9 |
| 06 | 7 01·5 | 7 02·7 | 6 42·3 | 0·6 | 0·3 | 6·6 | 3·1 | 12·6 | 6·0 |
| 07 | 7 01·8 | 7 02·9 | 6 42·5 | 0·7 | 0·3 | 6·7 | 3·2 | 12·7 | 6·0 |
| 08 | 7 02·0 | 7 03·2 | 6 42·8 | 0·8 | 0·4 | 6·8 | 3·2 | 12·8 | 6·1 |
| 09 | 7 02·3 | 7 03·4 | 6 43·0 | 0·9 | 0·4 | 6·9 | 3·3 | 12·9 | 6·1 |
| 10 | 7 02·5 | 7 03·7 | 6 43·3 | 1·0 | 0·5 | 7·0 | 3·3 | 13·0 | 6·2 |
| 11 | 7 02·8 | 7 03·9 | 6 43·5 | 1·1 | 0·5 | 7·1 | 3·4 | 13·1 | 6·2 |
| 12 | 7 03·0 | 7 04·2 | 6 43·7 | 1·2 | 0·6 | 7·2 | 3·4 | 13·2 | 6·3 |
| 13 | 7 03·3 | 7 04·4 | 6 44·0 | 1·3 | 0·6 | 7·3 | 3·5 | 13·3 | 6·3 |
| 14 | 7 03·5 | 7 04·7 | 6 44·2 | 1·4 | 0·7 | 7·4 | 3·5 | 13·4 | 6·4 |
| 15 | 7 03·8 | 7 04·9 | 6 44·4 | 1·5 | 0·7 | 7·5 | 3·6 | 13·5 | 6·4 |
| 16 | 7 04·0 | 7 05·2 | 6 44·7 | 1·6 | 0·8 | 7·6 | 3·6 | 13·6 | 6·5 |
| 17 | 7 04·3 | 7 05·4 | 6 44·9 | 1·7 | 0·8 | 7·7 | 3·7 | 13·7 | 6·5 |
| 18 | 7 04·5 | 7 05·7 | 6 45·2 | 1·8 | 0·9 | 7·8 | 3·7 | 13·8 | 6·6 |
| 19 | 7 04·8 | 7 05·9 | 6 45·4 | 1·9 | 0·9 | 7·9 | 3·8 | 13·9 | 6·6 |
| 20 | 7 05·0 | 7 06·2 | 6 45·6 | 2·0 | 1·0 | 8·0 | 3·8 | 14·0 | 6·7 |
| 21 | 7 05·3 | 7 06·4 | 6 45·9 | 2·1 | 1·0 | 8·1 | 3·8 | 14·1 | 6·7 |
| 22 | 7 05·5 | 7 06·7 | 6 46·1 | 2·2 | 1·0 | 8·2 | 3·9 | 14·2 | 6·7 |
| 23 | 7 05·8 | 7 06·9 | 6 46·4 | 2·3 | 1·1 | 8·3 | 3·9 | 14·3 | 6·8 |
| 24 | 7 06·0 | 7 07·2 | 6 46·6 | 2·4 | 1·1 | 8·4 | 4·0 | 14·4 | 6·8 |
| 25 | 7 06·3 | 7 07·4 | 6 46·8 | 2·5 | 1·2 | 8·5 | 4·0 | 14·5 | 6·9 |
| 26 | 7 06·5 | 7 07·7 | 6 47·1 | 2·6 | 1·2 | 8·6 | 4·1 | 14·6 | 6·9 |
| 27 | 7 06·8 | 7 07·9 | 6 47·3 | 2·7 | 1·3 | 8·7 | 4·1 | 14·7 | 7·0 |
| 28 | 7 07·0 | 7 08·2 | 6 47·5 | 2·8 | 1·3 | 8·8 | 4·2 | 14·8 | 7·0 |
| 29 | 7 07·3 | 7 08·4 | 6 47·8 | 2·9 | 1·4 | 8·9 | 4·2 | 14·9 | 7·1 |
| 30 | 7 07·5 | 7 08·7 | 6 48·0 | 3·0 | 1·4 | 9·0 | 4·3 | 15·0 | 7·1 |
| 31 | 7 07·8 | 7 08·9 | 6 48·3 | 3·1 | 1·5 | 9·1 | 4·3 | 15·1 | 7·2 |
| 32 | 7 08·0 | 7 09·2 | 6 48·5 | 3·2 | 1·5 | 9·2 | 4·4 | 15·2 | 7·2 |
| 33 | 7 08·3 | 7 09·4 | 6 48·7 | 3·3 | 1·6 | 9·3 | 4·4 | 15·3 | 7·3 |
| 34 | 7 08·5 | 7 09·7 | 6 49·0 | 3·4 | 1·6 | 9·4 | 4·5 | 15·4 | 7·3 |
| 35 | 7 08·8 | 7 09·9 | 6 49·2 | 3·5 | 1·7 | 9·5 | 4·5 | 15·5 | 7·4 |
| 36 | 7 09·0 | 7 10·2 | 6 49·5 | 3·6 | 1·7 | 9·6 | 4·6 | 15·6 | 7·4 |
| 37 | 7 09·3 | 7 10·4 | 6 49·7 | 3·7 | 1·8 | 9·7 | 4·6 | 15·7 | 7·5 |
| 38 | 7 09·5 | 7 10·7 | 6 49·9 | 3·8 | 1·8 | 9·8 | 4·7 | 15·8 | 7·5 |
| 39 | 7 09·8 | 7 10·9 | 6 50·2 | 3·9 | 1·9 | 9·9 | 4·7 | 15·9 | 7·6 |
| 40 | 7 10·0 | 7 11·2 | 6 50·4 | 4·0 | 1·9 | 10·0 | 4·8 | 16·0 | 7·6 |
| 41 | 7 10·3 | 7 11·4 | 6 50·6 | 4·1 | 1·9 | 10·1 | 4·8 | 16·1 | 7·6 |
| 42 | 7 10·5 | 7 11·7 | 6 50·9 | 4·2 | 2·0 | 10·2 | 4·8 | 16·2 | 7·7 |
| 43 | 7 10·8 | 7 11·9 | 6 51·1 | 4·3 | 2·0 | 10·3 | 4·9 | 16·3 | 7·7 |
| 44 | 7 11·0 | 7 12·2 | 6 51·4 | 4·4 | 2·1 | 10·4 | 4·9 | 16·4 | 7·8 |
| 45 | 7 11·3 | 7 12·4 | 6 51·6 | 4·5 | 2·1 | 10·5 | 5·0 | 16·5 | 7·8 |
| 46 | 7 11·5 | 7 12·7 | 6 51·8 | 4·6 | 2·2 | 10·6 | 5·0 | 16·6 | 7·9 |
| 47 | 7 11·8 | 7 12·9 | 6 52·1 | 4·7 | 2·2 | 10·7 | 5·1 | 16·7 | 7·9 |
| 48 | 7 12·0 | 7 13·2 | 6 52·3 | 4·8 | 2·3 | 10·8 | 5·1 | 16·8 | 8·0 |
| 49 | 7 12·3 | 7 13·4 | 6 52·6 | 4·9 | 2·3 | 10·9 | 5·2 | 16·9 | 8·0 |
| 50 | 7 12·5 | 7 13·7 | 6 52·8 | 5·0 | 2·4 | 11·0 | 5·2 | 17·0 | 8·1 |
| 51 | 7 12·8 | 7 13·9 | 6 53·0 | 5·1 | 2·4 | 11·1 | 5·3 | 17·1 | 8·1 |
| 52 | 7 13·0 | 7 14·2 | 6 53·3 | 5·2 | 2·5 | 11·2 | 5·3 | 17·2 | 8·2 |
| 53 | 7 13·3 | 7 14·4 | 6 53·5 | 5·3 | 2·5 | 11·3 | 5·4 | 17·3 | 8·2 |
| 54 | 7 13·5 | 7 14·7 | 6 53·8 | 5·4 | 2·6 | 11·4 | 5·4 | 17·4 | 8·3 |
| 55 | 7 13·8 | 7 14·9 | 6 54·0 | 5·5 | 2·6 | 11·5 | 5·5 | 17·5 | 8·3 |
| 56 | 7 14·0 | 7 15·2 | 6 54·2 | 5·6 | 2·7 | 11·6 | 5·5 | 17·6 | 8·4 |
| 57 | 7 14·3 | 7 15·4 | 6 54·5 | 5·7 | 2·7 | 11·7 | 5·6 | 17·7 | 8·4 |
| 58 | 7 14·5 | 7 15·7 | 6 54·7 | 5·8 | 2·8 | 11·8 | 5·6 | 17·8 | 8·5 |
| 59 | 7 14·8 | 7 15·9 | 6 54·9 | 5·9 | 2·8 | 11·9 | 5·7 | 17·9 | 8·5 |
| 60 | 7 15·0 | 7 16·2 | 6 55·2 | 6·0 | 2·9 | 12·0 | 5·7 | 18·0 | 8·6 |

| 29ᵐ | SUN PLANETS | ARIES | MOON | v or d | Corrⁿ | v or d | Corrⁿ | v or d | Corrⁿ |
|---|---|---|---|---|---|---|---|---|---|
| s | ° ′ | ° ′ | ° ′ | ′ | ′ | ′ | ′ | ′ | ′ |
| 00 | 7 15·0 | 7 16·2 | 6 55·2 | 0·0 | 0·0 | 6·0 | 3·0 | 12·0 | 5·9 |
| 01 | 7 15·3 | 7 16·4 | 6 55·4 | 0·1 | 0·0 | 6·1 | 3·0 | 12·1 | 5·9 |
| 02 | 7 15·5 | 7 16·7 | 6 55·7 | 0·2 | 0·1 | 6·2 | 3·0 | 12·2 | 6·0 |
| 03 | 7 15·8 | 7 16·9 | 6 55·9 | 0·3 | 0·1 | 6·3 | 3·1 | 12·3 | 6·0 |
| 04 | 7 16·0 | 7 17·2 | 6 56·1 | 0·4 | 0·2 | 6·4 | 3·1 | 12·4 | 6·1 |
| 05 | 7 16·3 | 7 17·4 | 6 56·4 | 0·5 | 0·2 | 6·5 | 3·2 | 12·5 | 6·1 |
| 06 | 7 16·5 | 7 17·7 | 6 56·6 | 0·6 | 0·3 | 6·6 | 3·2 | 12·6 | 6·2 |
| 07 | 7 16·8 | 7 17·9 | 6 56·9 | 0·7 | 0·3 | 6·7 | 3·3 | 12·7 | 6·2 |
| 08 | 7 17·0 | 7 18·2 | 6 57·1 | 0·8 | 0·4 | 6·8 | 3·3 | 12·8 | 6·3 |
| 09 | 7 17·3 | 7 18·4 | 6 57·3 | 0·9 | 0·4 | 6·9 | 3·4 | 12·9 | 6·3 |
| 10 | 7 17·5 | 7 18·7 | 6 57·6 | 1·0 | 0·5 | 7·0 | 3·4 | 13·0 | 6·4 |
| 11 | 7 17·8 | 7 18·9 | 6 57·8 | 1·1 | 0·5 | 7·1 | 3·5 | 13·1 | 6·4 |
| 12 | 7 18·0 | 7 19·2 | 6 58·0 | 1·2 | 0·6 | 7·2 | 3·5 | 13·2 | 6·5 |
| 13 | 7 18·3 | 7 19·4 | 6 58·3 | 1·3 | 0·6 | 7·3 | 3·6 | 13·3 | 6·5 |
| 14 | 7 18·5 | 7 19·7 | 6 58·5 | 1·4 | 0·7 | 7·4 | 3·6 | 13·4 | 6·6 |
| 15 | 7 18·8 | 7 20·0 | 6 58·8 | 1·5 | 0·7 | 7·5 | 3·7 | 13·5 | 6·6 |
| 16 | 7 19·0 | 7 20·2 | 6 59·0 | 1·6 | 0·8 | 7·6 | 3·7 | 13·6 | 6·7 |
| 17 | 7 19·3 | 7 20·5 | 6 59·2 | 1·7 | 0·8 | 7·7 | 3·8 | 13·7 | 6·7 |
| 18 | 7 19·5 | 7 20·7 | 6 59·5 | 1·8 | 0·9 | 7·8 | 3·8 | 13·8 | 6·8 |
| 19 | 7 19·8 | 7 21·0 | 6 59·7 | 1·9 | 0·9 | 7·9 | 3·9 | 13·9 | 6·8 |
| 20 | 7 20·0 | 7 21·2 | 7 00·0 | 2·0 | 1·0 | 8·0 | 3·9 | 14·0 | 6·9 |
| 21 | 7 20·3 | 7 21·5 | 7 00·2 | 2·1 | 1·0 | 8·1 | 4·0 | 14·1 | 6·9 |
| 22 | 7 20·5 | 7 21·7 | 7 00·4 | 2·2 | 1·1 | 8·2 | 4·0 | 14·2 | 7·0 |
| 23 | 7 20·8 | 7 22·0 | 7 00·7 | 2·3 | 1·1 | 8·3 | 4·1 | 14·3 | 7·0 |
| 24 | 7 21·0 | 7 22·2 | 7 00·9 | 2·4 | 1·2 | 8·4 | 4·1 | 14·4 | 7·1 |
| 25 | 7 21·3 | 7 22·5 | 7 01·1 | 2·5 | 1·2 | 8·5 | 4·2 | 14·5 | 7·1 |
| 26 | 7 21·5 | 7 22·7 | 7 01·4 | 2·6 | 1·3 | 8·6 | 4·2 | 14·6 | 7·2 |
| 27 | 7 21·8 | 7 23·0 | 7 01·6 | 2·7 | 1·3 | 8·7 | 4·3 | 14·7 | 7·2 |
| 28 | 7 22·0 | 7 23·2 | 7 01·9 | 2·8 | 1·4 | 8·8 | 4·3 | 14·8 | 7·3 |
| 29 | 7 22·3 | 7 23·5 | 7 02·1 | 2·9 | 1·4 | 8·9 | 4·4 | 14·9 | 7·3 |
| 30 | 7 22·5 | 7 23·7 | 7 02·3 | 3·0 | 1·5 | 9·0 | 4·4 | 15·0 | 7·4 |
| 31 | 7 22·8 | 7 24·0 | 7 02·6 | 3·1 | 1·5 | 9·1 | 4·5 | 15·1 | 7·4 |
| 32 | 7 23·0 | 7 24·2 | 7 02·8 | 3·2 | 1·6 | 9·2 | 4·5 | 15·2 | 7·5 |
| 33 | 7 23·3 | 7 24·5 | 7 03·1 | 3·3 | 1·6 | 9·3 | 4·6 | 15·3 | 7·5 |
| 34 | 7 23·5 | 7 24·7 | 7 03·3 | 3·4 | 1·7 | 9·4 | 4·6 | 15·4 | 7·6 |
| 35 | 7 23·8 | 7 25·0 | 7 03·5 | 3·5 | 1·7 | 9·5 | 4·7 | 15·5 | 7·6 |
| 36 | 7 24·0 | 7 25·2 | 7 03·8 | 3·6 | 1·8 | 9·6 | 4·7 | 15·6 | 7·7 |
| 37 | 7 24·3 | 7 25·5 | 7 04·0 | 3·7 | 1·8 | 9·7 | 4·8 | 15·7 | 7·7 |
| 38 | 7 24·5 | 7 25·7 | 7 04·3 | 3·8 | 1·9 | 9·8 | 4·8 | 15·8 | 7·8 |
| 39 | 7 24·8 | 7 26·0 | 7 04·5 | 3·9 | 1·9 | 9·9 | 4·9 | 15·9 | 7·8 |
| 40 | 7 25·0 | 7 26·2 | 7 04·7 | 4·0 | 2·0 | 10·0 | 4·9 | 16·0 | 7·9 |
| 41 | 7 25·3 | 7 26·5 | 7 05·0 | 4·1 | 2·0 | 10·1 | 5·0 | 16·1 | 7·9 |
| 42 | 7 25·5 | 7 26·7 | 7 05·2 | 4·2 | 2·1 | 10·2 | 5·0 | 16·2 | 8·0 |
| 43 | 7 25·8 | 7 27·0 | 7 05·4 | 4·3 | 2·1 | 10·3 | 5·1 | 16·3 | 8·0 |
| 44 | 7 26·0 | 7 27·2 | 7 05·7 | 4·4 | 2·2 | 10·4 | 5·1 | 16·4 | 8·1 |
| 45 | 7 26·3 | 7 27·5 | 7 05·9 | 4·5 | 2·2 | 10·5 | 5·2 | 16·5 | 8·1 |
| 46 | 7 26·5 | 7 27·7 | 7 06·2 | 4·6 | 2·3 | 10·6 | 5·2 | 16·6 | 8·2 |
| 47 | 7 26·8 | 7 28·0 | 7 06·4 | 4·7 | 2·3 | 10·7 | 5·3 | 16·7 | 8·2 |
| 48 | 7 27·0 | 7 28·2 | 7 06·6 | 4·8 | 2·4 | 10·8 | 5·3 | 16·8 | 8·3 |
| 49 | 7 27·3 | 7 28·5 | 7 06·9 | 4·9 | 2·4 | 10·9 | 5·4 | 16·9 | 8·3 |
| 50 | 7 27·5 | 7 28·7 | 7 07·1 | 5·0 | 2·5 | 11·0 | 5·4 | 17·0 | 8·4 |
| 51 | 7 27·8 | 7 29·0 | 7 07·4 | 5·1 | 2·5 | 11·1 | 5·5 | 17·1 | 8·4 |
| 52 | 7 28·0 | 7 29·2 | 7 07·6 | 5·2 | 2·6 | 11·2 | 5·5 | 17·2 | 8·5 |
| 53 | 7 28·3 | 7 29·5 | 7 07·8 | 5·3 | 2·6 | 11·3 | 5·6 | 17·3 | 8·5 |
| 54 | 7 28·5 | 7 29·7 | 7 08·1 | 5·4 | 2·7 | 11·4 | 5·6 | 17·4 | 8·6 |
| 55 | 7 28·8 | 7 30·0 | 7 08·3 | 5·5 | 2·7 | 11·5 | 5·7 | 17·5 | 8·6 |
| 56 | 7 29·0 | 7 30·2 | 7 08·5 | 5·6 | 2·8 | 11·6 | 5·7 | 17·6 | 8·7 |
| 57 | 7 29·3 | 7 30·5 | 7 08·8 | 5·7 | 2·8 | 11·7 | 5·8 | 17·7 | 8·7 |
| 58 | 7 29·5 | 7 30·7 | 7 09·0 | 5·8 | 2·9 | 11·8 | 5·8 | 17·8 | 8·8 |
| 59 | 7 29·8 | 7 31·0 | 7 09·3 | 5·9 | 2·9 | 11·9 | 5·9 | 17·9 | 8·8 |
| 60 | 7 30·0 | 7 31·2 | 7 09·5 | 6·0 | 3·0 | 12·0 | 5·9 | 18·0 | 8·9 |

## 30ᵐ INCREMENTS AND CORRECTIONS 31ᵐ

| 30ᵐ | SUN PLANETS | ARIES | MOON | v or d | Corrⁿ | v or d | Corrⁿ | v or d | Corrⁿ |
|---|---|---|---|---|---|---|---|---|---|
| s | ° ′ | ° ′ | ° ′ | ′ | ′ | ′ | ′ | ′ | ′ |
| 00 | 7 30·0 | 7 31·2 | 7 09·5 | 0·0 | 0·0 | 6·0 | 3·1 | 12·0 | 6·1 |
| 01 | 7 30·3 | 7 31·5 | 7 09·7 | 0·1 | 0·1 | 6·1 | 3·1 | 12·1 | 6·2 |
| 02 | 7 30·5 | 7 31·7 | 7 10·0 | 0·2 | 0·1 | 6·2 | 3·2 | 12·2 | 6·2 |
| 03 | 7 30·8 | 7 32·0 | 7 10·2 | 0·3 | 0·2 | 6·3 | 3·2 | 12·3 | 6·3 |
| 04 | 7 31·0 | 7 32·2 | 7 10·5 | 0·4 | 0·2 | 6·4 | 3·3 | 12·4 | 6·3 |
| 05 | 7 31·3 | 7 32·5 | 7 10·7 | 0·5 | 0·3 | 6·5 | 3·3 | 12·5 | 6·4 |
| 06 | 7 31·5 | 7 32·7 | 7 10·9 | 0·6 | 0·3 | 6·6 | 3·4 | 12·6 | 6·4 |
| 07 | 7 31·8 | 7 33·0 | 7 11·2 | 0·7 | 0·4 | 6·7 | 3·4 | 12·7 | 6·5 |
| 08 | 7 32·0 | 7 33·2 | 7 11·4 | 0·8 | 0·4 | 6·8 | 3·5 | 12·8 | 6·5 |
| 09 | 7 32·3 | 7 33·5 | 7 11·6 | 0·9 | 0·5 | 6·9 | 3·5 | 12·9 | 6·6 |
| 10 | 7 32·5 | 7 33·7 | 7 11·9 | 1·0 | 0·5 | 7·0 | 3·6 | 13·0 | 6·6 |
| 11 | 7 32·8 | 7 34·0 | 7 12·1 | 1·1 | 0·6 | 7·1 | 3·6 | 13·1 | 6·7 |
| 12 | 7 33·0 | 7 34·2 | 7 12·4 | 1·2 | 0·6 | 7·2 | 3·7 | 13·2 | 6·7 |
| 13 | 7 33·3 | 7 34·5 | 7 12·6 | 1·3 | 0·7 | 7·3 | 3·7 | 13·3 | 6·8 |
| 14 | 7 33·5 | 7 34·7 | 7 12·8 | 1·4 | 0·7 | 7·4 | 3·8 | 13·4 | 6·8 |
| 15 | 7 33·8 | 7 35·0 | 7 13·1 | 1·5 | 0·8 | 7·5 | 3·8 | 13·5 | 6·9 |
| 16 | 7 34·0 | 7 35·2 | 7 13·3 | 1·6 | 0·8 | 7·6 | 3·9 | 13·6 | 6·9 |
| 17 | 7 34·3 | 7 35·5 | 7 13·6 | 1·7 | 0·9 | 7·7 | 3·9 | 13·7 | 7·0 |
| 18 | 7 34·5 | 7 35·7 | 7 13·8 | 1·8 | 0·9 | 7·8 | 4·0 | 13·8 | 7·0 |
| 19 | 7 34·8 | 7 36·0 | 7 14·0 | 1·9 | 1·0 | 7·9 | 4·0 | 13·9 | 7·1 |
| 20 | 7 35·0 | 7 36·2 | 7 14·3 | 2·0 | 1·0 | 8·0 | 4·1 | 14·0 | 7·1 |
| 21 | 7 35·3 | 7 36·5 | 7 14·5 | 2·1 | 1·1 | 8·1 | 4·1 | 14·1 | 7·2 |
| 22 | 7 35·5 | 7 36·7 | 7 14·7 | 2·2 | 1·1 | 8·2 | 4·2 | 14·2 | 7·2 |
| 23 | 7 35·8 | 7 37·0 | 7 15·0 | 2·3 | 1·2 | 8·3 | 4·2 | 14·3 | 7·3 |
| 24 | 7 36·0 | 7 37·2 | 7 15·2 | 2·4 | 1·2 | 8·4 | 4·3 | 14·4 | 7·3 |
| 25 | 7 36·3 | 7 37·5 | 7 15·5 | 2·5 | 1·3 | 8·5 | 4·3 | 14·5 | 7·4 |
| 26 | 7 36·5 | 7 37·7 | 7 15·7 | 2·6 | 1·3 | 8·6 | 4·4 | 14·6 | 7·4 |
| 27 | 7 36·8 | 7 38·0 | 7 15·9 | 2·7 | 1·4 | 8·7 | 4·4 | 14·7 | 7·5 |
| 28 | 7 37·0 | 7 38·3 | 7 16·2 | 2·8 | 1·4 | 8·8 | 4·5 | 14·8 | 7·5 |
| 29 | 7 37·3 | 7 38·5 | 7 16·4 | 2·9 | 1·5 | 8·9 | 4·5 | 14·9 | 7·6 |
| 30 | 7 37·5 | 7 38·8 | 7 16·7 | 3·0 | 1·5 | 9·0 | 4·6 | 15·0 | 7·6 |
| 31 | 7 37·8 | 7 39·0 | 7 16·9 | 3·1 | 1·6 | 9·1 | 4·6 | 15·1 | 7·7 |
| 32 | 7 38·0 | 7 39·3 | 7 17·1 | 3·2 | 1·6 | 9·2 | 4·7 | 15·2 | 7·7 |
| 33 | 7 38·3 | 7 39·5 | 7 17·4 | 3·3 | 1·7 | 9·3 | 4·7 | 15·3 | 7·8 |
| 34 | 7 38·5 | 7 39·8 | 7 17·6 | 3·4 | 1·7 | 9·4 | 4·8 | 15·4 | 7·8 |
| 35 | 7 38·8 | 7 40·0 | 7 17·9 | 3·5 | 1·8 | 9·5 | 4·8 | 15·5 | 7·9 |
| 36 | 7 39·0 | 7 40·3 | 7 18·1 | 3·6 | 1·8 | 9·6 | 4·9 | 15·6 | 7·9 |
| 37 | 7 39·3 | 7 40·5 | 7 18·3 | 3·7 | 1·9 | 9·7 | 4·9 | 15·7 | 8·0 |
| 38 | 7 39·5 | 7 40·8 | 7 18·6 | 3·8 | 1·9 | 9·8 | 5·0 | 15·8 | 8·0 |
| 39 | 7 39·8 | 7 41·0 | 7 18·8 | 3·9 | 2·0 | 9·9 | 5·0 | 15·9 | 8·1 |
| 40 | 7 40·0 | 7 41·3 | 7 19·0 | 4·0 | 2·0 | 10·0 | 5·1 | 16·0 | 8·1 |
| 41 | 7 40·3 | 7 41·5 | 7 19·3 | 4·1 | 2·1 | 10·1 | 5·1 | 16·1 | 8·2 |
| 42 | 7 40·5 | 7 41·8 | 7 19·5 | 4·2 | 2·1 | 10·2 | 5·2 | 16·2 | 8·2 |
| 43 | 7 40·8 | 7 42·0 | 7 19·8 | 4·3 | 2·2 | 10·3 | 5·2 | 16·3 | 8·3 |
| 44 | 7 41·0 | 7 42·3 | 7 20·0 | 4·4 | 2·2 | 10·4 | 5·3 | 16·4 | 8·3 |
| 45 | 7 41·3 | 7 42·5 | 7 20·2 | 4·5 | 2·3 | 10·5 | 5·3 | 16·5 | 8·4 |
| 46 | 7 41·5 | 7 42·8 | 7 20·5 | 4·6 | 2·3 | 10·6 | 5·4 | 16·6 | 8·4 |
| 47 | 7 41·8 | 7 43·0 | 7 20·7 | 4·7 | 2·4 | 10·7 | 5·4 | 16·7 | 8·5 |
| 48 | 7 42·0 | 7 43·3 | 7 21·0 | 4·8 | 2·4 | 10·8 | 5·5 | 16·8 | 8·5 |
| 49 | 7 42·3 | 7 43·5 | 7 21·2 | 4·9 | 2·5 | 10·9 | 5·5 | 16·9 | 8·6 |
| 50 | 7 42·5 | 7 43·8 | 7 21·4 | 5·0 | 2·5 | 11·0 | 5·6 | 17·0 | 8·6 |
| 51 | 7 42·8 | 7 44·0 | 7 21·7 | 5·1 | 2·6 | 11·1 | 5·6 | 17·1 | 8·7 |
| 52 | 7 43·0 | 7 44·3 | 7 21·9 | 5·2 | 2·6 | 11·2 | 5·7 | 17·2 | 8·7 |
| 53 | 7 43·3 | 7 44·5 | 7 22·1 | 5·3 | 2·7 | 11·3 | 5·7 | 17·3 | 8·8 |
| 54 | 7 43·5 | 7 44·8 | 7 22·4 | 5·4 | 2·7 | 11·4 | 5·8 | 17·4 | 8·8 |
| 55 | 7 43·8 | 7 45·0 | 7 22·6 | 5·5 | 2·8 | 11·5 | 5·8 | 17·5 | 8·9 |
| 56 | 7 44·0 | 7 45·3 | 7 22·9 | 5·6 | 2·8 | 11·6 | 5·9 | 17·6 | 8·9 |
| 57 | 7 44·3 | 7 45·5 | 7 23·1 | 5·7 | 2·9 | 11·7 | 5·9 | 17·7 | 9·0 |
| 58 | 7 44·5 | 7 45·8 | 7 23·3 | 5·8 | 2·9 | 11·8 | 6·0 | 17·8 | 9·0 |
| 59 | 7 44·8 | 7 46·0 | 7 23·6 | 5·9 | 3·0 | 11·9 | 6·0 | 17·9 | 9·1 |
| 60 | 7 45·0 | 7 46·3 | 7 23·8 | 6·0 | 3·1 | 12·0 | 6·1 | 18·0 | 9·2 |

| 31ᵐ | SUN PLANETS | ARIES | MOON | v or d | Corrⁿ | v or d | Corrⁿ | v or d | Corrⁿ |
|---|---|---|---|---|---|---|---|---|---|
| s | ° ′ | ° ′ | ° ′ | ′ | ′ | ′ | ′ | ′ | ′ |
| 00 | 7 45·0 | 7 46·3 | 7 23·8 | 0·0 | 0·0 | 6·0 | 3·2 | 12·0 | 6·3 |
| 01 | 7 45·3 | 7 46·5 | 7 24·1 | 0·1 | 0·1 | 6·1 | 3·2 | 12·1 | 6·4 |
| 02 | 7 45·5 | 7 46·8 | 7 24·3 | 0·2 | 0·1 | 6·2 | 3·3 | 12·2 | 6·4 |
| 03 | 7 45·8 | 7 47·0 | 7 24·5 | 0·3 | 0·2 | 6·3 | 3·3 | 12·3 | 6·5 |
| 04 | 7 46·0 | 7 47·3 | 7 24·8 | 0·4 | 0·2 | 6·4 | 3·4 | 12·4 | 6·5 |
| 05 | 7 46·3 | 7 47·5 | 7 25·0 | 0·5 | 0·3 | 6·5 | 3·4 | 12·5 | 6·6 |
| 06 | 7 46·5 | 7 47·8 | 7 25·2 | 0·6 | 0·3 | 6·6 | 3·5 | 12·6 | 6·6 |
| 07 | 7 46·8 | 7 48·0 | 7 25·5 | 0·7 | 0·4 | 6·7 | 3·5 | 12·7 | 6·7 |
| 08 | 7 47·0 | 7 48·3 | 7 25·7 | 0·8 | 0·4 | 6·8 | 3·6 | 12·8 | 6·7 |
| 09 | 7 47·3 | 7 48·5 | 7 26·0 | 0·9 | 0·5 | 6·9 | 3·6 | 12·9 | 6·8 |
| 10 | 7 47·5 | 7 48·8 | 7 26·2 | 1·0 | 0·5 | 7·0 | 3·7 | 13·0 | 6·8 |
| 11 | 7 47·8 | 7 49·0 | 7 26·4 | 1·1 | 0·6 | 7·1 | 3·7 | 13·1 | 6·9 |
| 12 | 7 48·0 | 7 49·3 | 7 26·7 | 1·2 | 0·6 | 7·2 | 3·8 | 13·2 | 6·9 |
| 13 | 7 48·3 | 7 49·5 | 7 26·9 | 1·3 | 0·7 | 7·3 | 3·8 | 13·3 | 7·0 |
| 14 | 7 48·5 | 7 49·8 | 7 27·2 | 1·4 | 0·7 | 7·4 | 3·9 | 13·4 | 7·0 |
| 15 | 7 48·8 | 7 50·0 | 7 27·4 | 1·5 | 0·8 | 7·5 | 3·9 | 13·5 | 7·1 |
| 16 | 7 49·0 | 7 50·3 | 7 27·6 | 1·6 | 0·8 | 7·6 | 4·0 | 13·6 | 7·1 |
| 17 | 7 49·3 | 7 50·5 | 7 27·9 | 1·7 | 0·9 | 7·7 | 4·0 | 13·7 | 7·2 |
| 18 | 7 49·5 | 7 50·8 | 7 28·1 | 1·8 | 0·9 | 7·8 | 4·1 | 13·8 | 7·2 |
| 19 | 7 49·8 | 7 51·0 | 7 28·4 | 1·9 | 1·0 | 7·9 | 4·1 | 13·9 | 7·3 |
| 20 | 7 50·0 | 7 51·3 | 7 28·6 | 2·0 | 1·1 | 8·0 | 4·2 | 14·0 | 7·4 |
| 21 | 7 50·3 | 7 51·5 | 7 28·8 | 2·1 | 1·1 | 8·1 | 4·3 | 14·1 | 7·4 |
| 22 | 7 50·5 | 7 51·8 | 7 29·1 | 2·2 | 1·2 | 8·2 | 4·3 | 14·2 | 7·5 |
| 23 | 7 50·8 | 7 52·0 | 7 29·3 | 2·3 | 1·2 | 8·3 | 4·4 | 14·3 | 7·5 |
| 24 | 7 51·0 | 7 52·3 | 7 29·5 | 2·4 | 1·3 | 8·4 | 4·4 | 14·4 | 7·6 |
| 25 | 7 51·3 | 7 52·5 | 7 29·8 | 2·5 | 1·3 | 8·5 | 4·5 | 14·5 | 7·6 |
| 26 | 7 51·5 | 7 52·8 | 7 30·0 | 2·6 | 1·4 | 8·6 | 4·5 | 14·6 | 7·7 |
| 27 | 7 51·8 | 7 53·0 | 7 30·3 | 2·7 | 1·4 | 8·7 | 4·6 | 14·7 | 7·7 |
| 28 | 7 52·0 | 7 53·3 | 7 30·5 | 2·8 | 1·5 | 8·8 | 4·6 | 14·8 | 7·8 |
| 29 | 7 52·3 | 7 53·5 | 7 30·7 | 2·9 | 1·5 | 8·9 | 4·7 | 14·9 | 7·8 |
| 30 | 7 52·5 | 7 53·8 | 7 31·0 | 3·0 | 1·6 | 9·0 | 4·7 | 15·0 | 7·9 |
| 31 | 7 52·8 | 7 54·0 | 7 31·2 | 3·1 | 1·6 | 9·1 | 4·8 | 15·1 | 7·9 |
| 32 | 7 53·0 | 7 54·3 | 7 31·5 | 3·2 | 1·7 | 9·2 | 4·8 | 15·2 | 8·0 |
| 33 | 7 53·3 | 7 54·5 | 7 31·7 | 3·3 | 1·7 | 9·3 | 4·9 | 15·3 | 8·0 |
| 34 | 7 53·5 | 7 54·8 | 7 31·9 | 3·4 | 1·8 | 9·4 | 4·9 | 15·4 | 8·1 |
| 35 | 7 53·8 | 7 55·0 | 7 32·2 | 3·5 | 1·8 | 9·5 | 5·0 | 15·5 | 8·1 |
| 36 | 7 54·0 | 7 55·3 | 7 32·4 | 3·6 | 1·9 | 9·6 | 5·0 | 15·6 | 8·2 |
| 37 | 7 54·3 | 7 55·5 | 7 32·6 | 3·7 | 1·9 | 9·7 | 5·1 | 15·7 | 8·2 |
| 38 | 7 54·5 | 7 55·8 | 7 32·9 | 3·8 | 2·0 | 9·8 | 5·1 | 15·8 | 8·3 |
| 39 | 7 54·8 | 7 56·0 | 7 33·1 | 3·9 | 2·0 | 9·9 | 5·2 | 15·9 | 8·3 |
| 40 | 7 55·0 | 7 56·3 | 7 33·4 | 4·0 | 2·1 | 10·0 | 5·3 | 16·0 | 8·4 |
| 41 | 7 55·3 | 7 56·6 | 7 33·6 | 4·1 | 2·2 | 10·1 | 5·3 | 16·1 | 8·5 |
| 42 | 7 55·5 | 7 56·8 | 7 33·8 | 4·2 | 2·2 | 10·2 | 5·4 | 16·2 | 8·5 |
| 43 | 7 55·8 | 7 57·1 | 7 34·1 | 4·3 | 2·3 | 10·3 | 5·4 | 16·3 | 8·6 |
| 44 | 7 56·0 | 7 57·3 | 7 34·3 | 4·4 | 2·3 | 10·4 | 5·5 | 16·4 | 8·6 |
| 45 | 7 56·3 | 7 57·6 | 7 34·6 | 4·5 | 2·4 | 10·5 | 5·5 | 16·5 | 8·7 |
| 46 | 7 56·5 | 7 57·8 | 7 34·8 | 4·6 | 2·4 | 10·6 | 5·6 | 16·6 | 8·7 |
| 47 | 7 56·8 | 7 58·1 | 7 35·0 | 4·7 | 2·5 | 10·7 | 5·6 | 16·7 | 8·8 |
| 48 | 7 57·0 | 7 58·3 | 7 35·3 | 4·8 | 2·5 | 10·8 | 5·7 | 16·8 | 8·8 |
| 49 | 7 57·3 | 7 58·6 | 7 35·5 | 4·9 | 2·6 | 10·9 | 5·7 | 16·9 | 8·9 |
| 50 | 7 57·5 | 7 58·8 | 7 35·7 | 5·0 | 2·6 | 11·0 | 5·8 | 17·0 | 8·9 |
| 51 | 7 57·8 | 7 59·1 | 7 36·0 | 5·1 | 2·7 | 11·1 | 5·8 | 17·1 | 9·0 |
| 52 | 7 58·0 | 7 59·3 | 7 36·2 | 5·2 | 2·7 | 11·2 | 5·9 | 17·2 | 9·0 |
| 53 | 7 58·3 | 7 59·6 | 7 36·5 | 5·3 | 2·8 | 11·3 | 5·9 | 17·3 | 9·1 |
| 54 | 7 58·5 | 7 59·8 | 7 36·7 | 5·4 | 2·8 | 11·4 | 6·0 | 17·4 | 9·1 |
| 55 | 7 58·8 | 8 00·1 | 7 36·9 | 5·5 | 2·9 | 11·5 | 6·0 | 17·5 | 9·2 |
| 56 | 7 59·0 | 8 00·3 | 7 37·2 | 5·6 | 2·9 | 11·6 | 6·1 | 17·6 | 9·2 |
| 57 | 7 59·3 | 8 00·6 | 7 37·4 | 5·7 | 3·0 | 11·7 | 6·1 | 17·7 | 9·3 |
| 58 | 7 59·5 | 8 00·8 | 7 37·7 | 5·8 | 3·0 | 11·8 | 6·2 | 17·8 | 9·3 |
| 59 | 7 59·8 | 8 01·1 | 7 37·9 | 5·9 | 3·1 | 11·9 | 6·2 | 17·9 | 9·4 |
| 60 | 8 00·0 | 8 01·3 | 7 38·1 | 6·0 | 3·2 | 12·0 | 6·3 | 18·0 | 9·5 |

| 32m | SUN PLANETS | ARIES | MOON | v or d | Corrn | v or d | Corrn | v or d | Corrn |
|---|---|---|---|---|---|---|---|---|---|
| s | ° ′ | ° ′ | ° ′ | ′ | ′ | ′ | ′ | ′ | ′ |
| 00 | 8 00·0 | 8 01·3 | 7 38·1 | 0·0 | 0·0 | 6·0 | 3·3 | 12·0 | 6·5 |
| 01 | 8 00·3 | 8 01·6 | 7 38·4 | 0·1 | 0·1 | 6·1 | 3·3 | 12·1 | 6·6 |
| 02 | 8 00·5 | 8 01·8 | 7 38·6 | 0·2 | 0·1 | 6·2 | 3·4 | 12·2 | 6·6 |
| 03 | 8 00·8 | 8 02·1 | 7 38·8 | 0·3 | 0·2 | 6·3 | 3·4 | 12·3 | 6·7 |
| 04 | 8 01·0 | 8 02·3 | 7 39·1 | 0·4 | 0·2 | 6·4 | 3·5 | 12·4 | 6·7 |
| 05 | 8 01·3 | 8 02·6 | 7 39·3 | 0·5 | 0·3 | 6·5 | 3·5 | 12·5 | 6·8 |
| 06 | 8 01·5 | 8 02·8 | 7 39·6 | 0·6 | 0·3 | 6·6 | 3·6 | 12·6 | 6·8 |
| 07 | 8 01·8 | 8 03·1 | 7 39·8 | 0·7 | 0·4 | 6·7 | 3·6 | 12·7 | 6·9 |
| 08 | 8 02·0 | 8 03·3 | 7 40·0 | 0·8 | 0·4 | 6·8 | 3·7 | 12·8 | 6·9 |
| 09 | 8 02·3 | 8 03·6 | 7 40·3 | 0·9 | 0·5 | 6·9 | 3·7 | 12·9 | 7·0 |
| 10 | 8 02·5 | 8 03·8 | 7 40·5 | 1·0 | 0·5 | 7·0 | 3·8 | 13·0 | 7·0 |
| 11 | 8 02·8 | 8 04·1 | 7 40·8 | 1·1 | 0·6 | 7·1 | 3·8 | 13·1 | 7·1 |
| 12 | 8 03·0 | 8 04·3 | 7 41·0 | 1·2 | 0·7 | 7·2 | 3·9 | 13·2 | 7·2 |
| 13 | 8 03·3 | 8 04·6 | 7 41·2 | 1·3 | 0·7 | 7·3 | 4·0 | 13·3 | 7·2 |
| 14 | 8 03·5 | 8 04·8 | 7 41·5 | 1·4 | 0·8 | 7·4 | 4·0 | 13·4 | 7·3 |
| 15 | 8 03·8 | 8 05·1 | 7 41·7 | 1·5 | 0·8 | 7·5 | 4·1 | 13·5 | 7·3 |
| 16 | 8 04·0 | 8 05·3 | 7 42·0 | 1·6 | 0·9 | 7·6 | 4·1 | 13·6 | 7·4 |
| 17 | 8 04·3 | 8 05·6 | 7 42·2 | 1·7 | 0·9 | 7·7 | 4·2 | 13·7 | 7·4 |
| 18 | 8 04·5 | 8 05·8 | 7 42·4 | 1·8 | 1·0 | 7·8 | 4·2 | 13·8 | 7·5 |
| 19 | 8 04·8 | 8 06·1 | 7 42·7 | 1·9 | 1·0 | 7·9 | 4·3 | 13·9 | 7·5 |
| 20 | 8 05·0 | 8 06·3 | 7 42·9 | 2·0 | 1·1 | 8·0 | 4·3 | 14·0 | 7·6 |
| 21 | 8 05·3 | 8 06·6 | 7 43·1 | 2·1 | 1·1 | 8·1 | 4·4 | 14·1 | 7·6 |
| 22 | 8 05·5 | 8 06·8 | 7 43·4 | 2·2 | 1·2 | 8·2 | 4·4 | 14·2 | 7·7 |
| 23 | 8 05·8 | 8 07·1 | 7 43·6 | 2·3 | 1·2 | 8·3 | 4·5 | 14·3 | 7·7 |
| 24 | 8 06·0 | 8 07·3 | 7 43·9 | 2·4 | 1·3 | 8·4 | 4·6 | 14·4 | 7·8 |
| 25 | 8 06·3 | 8 07·6 | 7 44·1 | 2·5 | 1·4 | 8·5 | 4·6 | 14·5 | 7·9 |
| 26 | 8 06·5 | 8 07·8 | 7 44·3 | 2·6 | 1·4 | 8·6 | 4·7 | 14·6 | 7·9 |
| 27 | 8 06·8 | 8 08·1 | 7 44·6 | 2·7 | 1·5 | 8·7 | 4·7 | 14·7 | 8·0 |
| 28 | 8 07·0 | 8 08·3 | 7 44·8 | 2·8 | 1·5 | 8·8 | 4·8 | 14·8 | 8·0 |
| 29 | 8 07·3 | 8 08·6 | 7 45·1 | 2·9 | 1·6 | 8·9 | 4·8 | 14·9 | 8·1 |
| 30 | 8 07·5 | 8 08·8 | 7 45·3 | 3·0 | 1·6 | 9·0 | 4·9 | 15·0 | 8·1 |
| 31 | 8 07·8 | 8 09·1 | 7 45·5 | 3·1 | 1·7 | 9·1 | 4·9 | 15·1 | 8·2 |
| 32 | 8 08·0 | 8 09·3 | 7 45·8 | 3·2 | 1·7 | 9·2 | 5·0 | 15·2 | 8·2 |
| 33 | 8 08·3 | 8 09·6 | 7 46·0 | 3·3 | 1·8 | 9·3 | 5·0 | 15·3 | 8·3 |
| 34 | 8 08·5 | 8 09·8 | 7 46·2 | 3·4 | 1·8 | 9·4 | 5·1 | 15·4 | 8·3 |
| 35 | 8 08·8 | 8 10·1 | 7 46·5 | 3·5 | 1·9 | 9·5 | 5·1 | 15·5 | 8·4 |
| 36 | 8 09·0 | 8 10·3 | 7 46·7 | 3·6 | 2·0 | 9·6 | 5·2 | 15·6 | 8·5 |
| 37 | 8 09·3 | 8 10·6 | 7 47·0 | 3·7 | 2·0 | 9·7 | 5·3 | 15·7 | 8·5 |
| 38 | 8 09·5 | 8 10·8 | 7 47·2 | 3·8 | 2·1 | 9·8 | 5·3 | 15·8 | 8·6 |
| 39 | 8 09·8 | 8 11·1 | 7 47·4 | 3·9 | 2·1 | 9·9 | 5·4 | 15·9 | 8·6 |
| 40 | 8 10·0 | 8 11·3 | 7 47·7 | 4·0 | 2·2 | 10·0 | 5·4 | 16·0 | 8·7 |
| 41 | 8 10·3 | 8 11·6 | 7 47·9 | 4·1 | 2·2 | 10·1 | 5·5 | 16·1 | 8·7 |
| 42 | 8 10·5 | 8 11·8 | 7 48·2 | 4·2 | 2·3 | 10·2 | 5·5 | 16·2 | 8·8 |
| 43 | 8 10·8 | 8 12·1 | 7 48·4 | 4·3 | 2·3 | 10·3 | 5·6 | 16·3 | 8·8 |
| 44 | 8 11·0 | 8 12·3 | 7 48·6 | 4·4 | 2·4 | 10·4 | 5·6 | 16·4 | 8·9 |
| 45 | 8 11·3 | 8 12·6 | 7 48·9 | 4·5 | 2·4 | 10·5 | 5·7 | 16·5 | 8·9 |
| 46 | 8 11·5 | 8 12·8 | 7 49·1 | 4·6 | 2·5 | 10·6 | 5·7 | 16·6 | 9·0 |
| 47 | 8 11·8 | 8 13·1 | 7 49·3 | 4·7 | 2·5 | 10·7 | 5·8 | 16·7 | 9·0 |
| 48 | 8 12·0 | 8 13·3 | 7 49·6 | 4·8 | 2·6 | 10·8 | 5·9 | 16·8 | 9·1 |
| 49 | 8 12·3 | 8 13·6 | 7 49·8 | 4·9 | 2·7 | 10·9 | 5·9 | 16·9 | 9·2 |
| 50 | 8 12·5 | 8 13·8 | 7 50·1 | 5·0 | 2·7 | 11·0 | 6·0 | 17·0 | 9·2 |
| 51 | 8 12·8 | 8 14·1 | 7 50·3 | 5·1 | 2·8 | 11·1 | 6·0 | 17·1 | 9·3 |
| 52 | 8 13·0 | 8 14·3 | 7 50·5 | 5·2 | 2·8 | 11·2 | 6·1 | 17·2 | 9·3 |
| 53 | 8 13·3 | 8 14·6 | 7 50·8 | 5·3 | 2·9 | 11·3 | 6·1 | 17·3 | 9·4 |
| 54 | 8 13·5 | 8 14·9 | 7 51·0 | 5·4 | 2·9 | 11·4 | 6·2 | 17·4 | 9·4 |
| 55 | 8 13·8 | 8 15·1 | 7 51·3 | 5·5 | 3·0 | 11·5 | 6·2 | 17·5 | 9·5 |
| 56 | 8 14·0 | 8 15·4 | 7 51·5 | 5·6 | 3·0 | 11·6 | 6·3 | 17·6 | 9·5 |
| 57 | 8 14·3 | 8 15·6 | 7 51·7 | 5·7 | 3·1 | 11·7 | 6·3 | 17·7 | 9·6 |
| 58 | 8 14·5 | 8 15·9 | 7 52·0 | 5·8 | 3·1 | 11·8 | 6·4 | 17·8 | 9·6 |
| 59 | 8 14·8 | 8 16·1 | 7 52·2 | 5·9 | 3·2 | 11·9 | 6·4 | 17·9 | 9·7 |
| 60 | 8 15·0 | 8 16·4 | 7 52·5 | 6·0 | 3·3 | 12·0 | 6·5 | 18·0 | 9·8 |

| 33m | SUN PLANETS | ARIES | MOON | v or d | Corrn | v or d | Corrn | v or d | Corrn |
|---|---|---|---|---|---|---|---|---|---|
| s | ° ′ | ° ′ | ° ′ | ′ | ′ | ′ | ′ | ′ | ′ |
| 00 | 8 15·0 | 8 16·4 | 7 52·5 | 0·0 | 0·0 | 6·0 | 3·4 | 12·0 | 6·7 |
| 01 | 8 15·3 | 8 16·6 | 7 52·7 | 0·1 | 0·1 | 6·1 | 3·4 | 12·1 | 6·8 |
| 02 | 8 15·5 | 8 16·9 | 7 52·9 | 0·2 | 0·1 | 6·2 | 3·5 | 12·2 | 6·8 |
| 03 | 8 15·8 | 8 17·1 | 7 53·2 | 0·3 | 0·2 | 6·3 | 3·5 | 12·3 | 6·9 |
| 04 | 8 16·0 | 8 17·4 | 7 53·4 | 0·4 | 0·2 | 6·4 | 3·6 | 12·4 | 6·9 |
| 05 | 8 16·3 | 8 17·6 | 7 53·6 | 0·5 | 0·3 | 6·5 | 3·6 | 12·5 | 7·0 |
| 06 | 8 16·5 | 8 17·9 | 7 53·9 | 0·6 | 0·3 | 6·6 | 3·7 | 12·6 | 7·0 |
| 07 | 8 16·8 | 8 18·1 | 7 54·1 | 0·7 | 0·4 | 6·7 | 3·7 | 12·7 | 7·1 |
| 08 | 8 17·0 | 8 18·4 | 7 54·4 | 0·8 | 0·4 | 6·8 | 3·8 | 12·8 | 7·1 |
| 09 | 8 17·3 | 8 18·6 | 7 54·6 | 0·9 | 0·5 | 6·9 | 3·9 | 12·9 | 7·2 |
| 10 | 8 17·5 | 8 18·9 | 7 54·8 | 1·0 | 0·6 | 7·0 | 3·9 | 13·0 | 7·3 |
| 11 | 8 17·8 | 8 19·1 | 7 55·1 | 1·1 | 0·6 | 7·1 | 4·0 | 13·1 | 7·3 |
| 12 | 8 18·0 | 8 19·4 | 7 55·3 | 1·2 | 0·7 | 7·2 | 4·0 | 13·2 | 7·4 |
| 13 | 8 18·3 | 8 19·6 | 7 55·6 | 1·3 | 0·7 | 7·3 | 4·1 | 13·3 | 7·4 |
| 14 | 8 18·5 | 8 19·9 | 7 55·8 | 1·4 | 0·8 | 7·4 | 4·1 | 13·4 | 7·5 |
| 15 | 8 18·8 | 8 20·1 | 7 56·0 | 1·5 | 0·8 | 7·5 | 4·2 | 13·5 | 7·5 |
| 16 | 8 19·0 | 8 20·4 | 7 56·3 | 1·6 | 0·9 | 7·6 | 4·2 | 13·6 | 7·6 |
| 17 | 8 19·3 | 8 20·6 | 7 56·5 | 1·7 | 0·9 | 7·7 | 4·3 | 13·7 | 7·6 |
| 18 | 8 19·5 | 8 20·9 | 7 56·7 | 1·8 | 1·0 | 7·8 | 4·4 | 13·8 | 7·7 |
| 19 | 8 19·8 | 8 21·1 | 7 57·0 | 1·9 | 1·1 | 7·9 | 4·4 | 13·9 | 7·8 |
| 20 | 8 20·0 | 8 21·4 | 7 57·2 | 2·0 | 1·1 | 8·0 | 4·5 | 14·0 | 7·8 |
| 21 | 8 20·3 | 8 21·6 | 7 57·5 | 2·1 | 1·2 | 8·1 | 4·5 | 14·1 | 7·9 |
| 22 | 8 20·5 | 8 21·9 | 7 57·7 | 2·2 | 1·2 | 8·2 | 4·6 | 14·2 | 7·9 |
| 23 | 8 20·8 | 8 22·1 | 7 57·9 | 2·3 | 1·3 | 8·3 | 4·6 | 14·3 | 8·0 |
| 24 | 8 21·0 | 8 22·4 | 7 58·2 | 2·4 | 1·3 | 8·4 | 4·7 | 14·4 | 8·0 |
| 25 | 8 21·3 | 8 22·6 | 7 58·4 | 2·5 | 1·4 | 8·5 | 4·7 | 14·5 | 8·1 |
| 26 | 8 21·5 | 8 22·9 | 7 58·7 | 2·6 | 1·5 | 8·6 | 4·8 | 14·6 | 8·2 |
| 27 | 8 21·8 | 8 23·1 | 7 58·9 | 2·7 | 1·5 | 8·7 | 4·9 | 14·7 | 8·2 |
| 28 | 8 22·0 | 8 23·4 | 7 59·1 | 2·8 | 1·6 | 8·8 | 4·9 | 14·8 | 8·3 |
| 29 | 8 22·3 | 8 23·6 | 7 59·4 | 2·9 | 1·6 | 8·9 | 5·0 | 14·9 | 8·3 |
| 30 | 8 22·5 | 8 23·9 | 7 59·6 | 3·0 | 1·7 | 9·0 | 5·0 | 15·0 | 8·4 |
| 31 | 8 22·8 | 8 24·1 | 7 59·8 | 3·1 | 1·7 | 9·1 | 5·1 | 15·1 | 8·4 |
| 32 | 8 23·0 | 8 24·4 | 8 00·1 | 3·2 | 1·8 | 9·2 | 5·1 | 15·2 | 8·5 |
| 33 | 8 23·3 | 8 24·6 | 8 00·3 | 3·3 | 1·8 | 9·3 | 5·2 | 15·3 | 8·5 |
| 34 | 8 23·5 | 8 24·9 | 8 00·6 | 3·4 | 1·9 | 9·4 | 5·2 | 15·4 | 8·6 |
| 35 | 8 23·8 | 8 25·1 | 8 00·8 | 3·5 | 2·0 | 9·5 | 5·3 | 15·5 | 8·7 |
| 36 | 8 24·0 | 8 25·4 | 8 01·0 | 3·6 | 2·0 | 9·6 | 5·4 | 15·6 | 8·7 |
| 37 | 8 24·3 | 8 25·6 | 8 01·3 | 3·7 | 2·1 | 9·7 | 5·4 | 15·7 | 8·8 |
| 38 | 8 24·5 | 8 25·9 | 8 01·5 | 3·8 | 2·1 | 9·8 | 5·5 | 15·8 | 8·8 |
| 39 | 8 24·8 | 8 26·1 | 8 01·8 | 3·9 | 2·2 | 9·9 | 5·5 | 15·9 | 8·9 |
| 40 | 8 25·0 | 8 26·4 | 8 02·0 | 4·0 | 2·2 | 10·0 | 5·6 | 16·0 | 8·9 |
| 41 | 8 25·3 | 8 26·6 | 8 02·2 | 4·1 | 2·3 | 10·1 | 5·6 | 16·1 | 9·0 |
| 42 | 8 25·5 | 8 26·9 | 8 02·5 | 4·2 | 2·3 | 10·2 | 5·7 | 16·2 | 9·0 |
| 43 | 8 25·8 | 8 27·1 | 8 02·7 | 4·3 | 2·4 | 10·3 | 5·8 | 16·3 | 9·1 |
| 44 | 8 26·0 | 8 27·4 | 8 02·9 | 4·4 | 2·5 | 10·4 | 5·8 | 16·4 | 9·2 |
| 45 | 8 26·3 | 8 27·6 | 8 03·2 | 4·5 | 2·5 | 10·5 | 5·9 | 16·5 | 9·2 |
| 46 | 8 26·5 | 8 27·9 | 8 03·4 | 4·6 | 2·6 | 10·6 | 5·9 | 16·6 | 9·3 |
| 47 | 8 26·8 | 8 28·1 | 8 03·7 | 4·7 | 2·6 | 10·7 | 6·0 | 16·7 | 9·3 |
| 48 | 8 27·0 | 8 28·4 | 8 03·9 | 4·8 | 2·7 | 10·8 | 6·0 | 16·8 | 9·4 |
| 49 | 8 27·3 | 8 28·6 | 8 04·1 | 4·9 | 2·7 | 10·9 | 6·1 | 16·9 | 9·4 |
| 50 | 8 27·5 | 8 28·9 | 8 04·4 | 5·0 | 2·8 | 11·0 | 6·1 | 17·0 | 9·5 |
| 51 | 8 27·8 | 8 29·1 | 8 04·6 | 5·1 | 2·8 | 11·1 | 6·2 | 17·1 | 9·5 |
| 52 | 8 28·0 | 8 29·4 | 8 04·9 | 5·2 | 2·9 | 11·2 | 6·3 | 17·2 | 9·6 |
| 53 | 8 28·3 | 8 29·6 | 8 05·1 | 5·3 | 3·0 | 11·3 | 6·3 | 17·3 | 9·7 |
| 54 | 8 28·5 | 8 29·9 | 8 05·3 | 5·4 | 3·0 | 11·4 | 6·4 | 17·4 | 9·7 |
| 55 | 8 28·8 | 8 30·1 | 8 05·6 | 5·5 | 3·1 | 11·5 | 6·4 | 17·5 | 9·8 |
| 56 | 8 29·0 | 8 30·4 | 8 05·8 | 5·6 | 3·1 | 11·6 | 6·5 | 17·6 | 9·8 |
| 57 | 8 29·3 | 8 30·6 | 8 06·1 | 5·7 | 3·2 | 11·7 | 6·5 | 17·7 | 9·9 |
| 58 | 8 29·5 | 8 30·9 | 8 06·3 | 5·8 | 3·2 | 11·8 | 6·6 | 17·8 | 9·9 |
| 59 | 8 29·8 | 8 31·1 | 8 06·5 | 5·9 | 3·3 | 11·9 | 6·6 | 17·9 | 10·0 |
| 60 | 8 30·0 | 8 31·4 | 8 06·8 | 6·0 | 3·4 | 12·0 | 6·7 | 18·0 | 10·1 |



| 34m | SUN PLANETS | ARIES | MOON | v or d | Corrn | v or d | Corrn | v or d | Corrn |
|---|---|---|---|---|---|---|---|---|---|
| s | ° ′ | ° ′ | ° ′ | ′ | ′ | ′ | ′ | ′ | ′ |
| 00 | 8 30·0 | 8 31·4 | 8 06·8 | 0·0 | 0·0 | 6·0 | 3·5 | 12·0 | 6·9 |
| 01 | 8 30·3 | 8 31·6 | 8 07·0 | 0·1 | 0·1 | 6·1 | 3·5 | 12·1 | 7·0 |
| 02 | 8 30·5 | 8 31·9 | 8 07·2 | 0·2 | 0·1 | 6·2 | 3·6 | 12·2 | 7·0 |
| 03 | 8 30·8 | 8 32·1 | 8 07·5 | 0·3 | 0·2 | 6·3 | 3·6 | 12·3 | 7·1 |
| 04 | 8 31·0 | 8 32·4 | 8 07·7 | 0·4 | 0·2 | 6·4 | 3·7 | 12·4 | 7·1 |
| 05 | 8 31·3 | 8 32·6 | 8 08·0 | 0·5 | 0·3 | 6·5 | 3·7 | 12·5 | 7·2 |
| 06 | 8 31·5 | 8 32·9 | 8 08·2 | 0·6 | 0·3 | 6·6 | 3·8 | 12·6 | 7·2 |
| 07 | 8 31·8 | 8 33·2 | 8 08·4 | 0·7 | 0·4 | 6·7 | 3·9 | 12·7 | 7·3 |
| 08 | 8 32·0 | 8 33·4 | 8 08·7 | 0·8 | 0·5 | 6·8 | 3·9 | 12·8 | 7·4 |
| 09 | 8 32·3 | 8 33·7 | 8 08·9 | 0·9 | 0·5 | 6·9 | 4·0 | 12·9 | 7·4 |
| 10 | 8 32·5 | 8 33·9 | 8 09·2 | 1·0 | 0·6 | 7·0 | 4·0 | 13·0 | 7·5 |
| 11 | 8 32·8 | 8 34·2 | 8 09·4 | 1·1 | 0·6 | 7·1 | 4·1 | 13·1 | 7·5 |
| 12 | 8 33·0 | 8 34·4 | 8 09·6 | 1·2 | 0·7 | 7·2 | 4·1 | 13·2 | 7·6 |
| 13 | 8 33·3 | 8 34·7 | 8 09·9 | 1·3 | 0·7 | 7·3 | 4·2 | 13·3 | 7·6 |
| 14 | 8 33·5 | 8 34·9 | 8 10·1 | 1·4 | 0·8 | 7·4 | 4·3 | 13·4 | 7·7 |
| 15 | 8 33·8 | 8 35·2 | 8 10·3 | 1·5 | 0·9 | 7·5 | 4·3 | 13·5 | 7·8 |
| 16 | 8 34·0 | 8 35·4 | 8 10·6 | 1·6 | 0·9 | 7·6 | 4·4 | 13·6 | 7·8 |
| 17 | 8 34·3 | 8 35·7 | 8 10·8 | 1·7 | 1·0 | 7·7 | 4·4 | 13·7 | 7·9 |
| 18 | 8 34·5 | 8 35·9 | 8 11·1 | 1·8 | 1·0 | 7·8 | 4·5 | 13·8 | 7·9 |
| 19 | 8 34·8 | 8 36·2 | 8 11·3 | 1·9 | 1·1 | 7·9 | 4·5 | 13·9 | 8·0 |
| 20 | 8 35·0 | 8 36·4 | 8 11·5 | 2·0 | 1·2 | 8·0 | 4·6 | 14·0 | 8·1 |
| 21 | 8 35·3 | 8 36·7 | 8 11·8 | 2·1 | 1·2 | 8·1 | 4·7 | 14·1 | 8·1 |
| 22 | 8 35·5 | 8 36·9 | 8 12·0 | 2·2 | 1·3 | 8·2 | 4·7 | 14·2 | 8·2 |
| 23 | 8 35·8 | 8 37·2 | 8 12·3 | 2·3 | 1·3 | 8·3 | 4·8 | 14·3 | 8·2 |
| 24 | 8 36·0 | 8 37·4 | 8 12·5 | 2·4 | 1·4 | 8·4 | 4·8 | 14·4 | 8·3 |
| 25 | 8 36·3 | 8 37·7 | 8 12·7 | 2·5 | 1·4 | 8·5 | 4·9 | 14·5 | 8·3 |
| 26 | 8 36·5 | 8 37·9 | 8 13·0 | 2·6 | 1·5 | 8·6 | 4·9 | 14·6 | 8·4 |
| 27 | 8 36·8 | 8 38·2 | 8 13·2 | 2·7 | 1·6 | 8·7 | 5·0 | 14·7 | 8·5 |
| 28 | 8 37·0 | 8 38·4 | 8 13·4 | 2·8 | 1·6 | 8·8 | 5·1 | 14·8 | 8·5 |
| 29 | 8 37·3 | 8 38·7 | 8 13·7 | 2·9 | 1·7 | 8·9 | 5·1 | 14·9 | 8·6 |
| 30 | 8 37·5 | 8 38·9 | 8 13·9 | 3·0 | 1·7 | 9·0 | 5·2 | 15·0 | 8·6 |
| 31 | 8 37·8 | 8 39·2 | 8 14·2 | 3·1 | 1·8 | 9·1 | 5·2 | 15·1 | 8·7 |
| 32 | 8 38·0 | 8 39·4 | 8 14·4 | 3·2 | 1·8 | 9·2 | 5·3 | 15·2 | 8·7 |
| 33 | 8 38·3 | 8 39·7 | 8 14·6 | 3·3 | 1·9 | 9·3 | 5·3 | 15·3 | 8·8 |
| 34 | 8 38·5 | 8 39·9 | 8 14·9 | 3·4 | 2·0 | 9·4 | 5·4 | 15·4 | 8·9 |
| 35 | 8 38·8 | 8 40·2 | 8 15·1 | 3·5 | 2·0 | 9·5 | 5·5 | 15·5 | 8·9 |
| 36 | 8 39·0 | 8 40·4 | 8 15·4 | 3·6 | 2·1 | 9·6 | 5·5 | 15·6 | 9·0 |
| 37 | 8 39·3 | 8 40·7 | 8 15·6 | 3·7 | 2·1 | 9·7 | 5·6 | 15·7 | 9·0 |
| 38 | 8 39·5 | 8 40·9 | 8 15·8 | 3·8 | 2·2 | 9·8 | 5·6 | 15·8 | 9·1 |
| 39 | 8 39·8 | 8 41·2 | 8 16·1 | 3·9 | 2·2 | 9·9 | 5·7 | 15·9 | 9·1 |
| 40 | 8 40·0 | 8 41·4 | 8 16·3 | 4·0 | 2·3 | 10·0 | 5·8 | 16·0 | 9·2 |
| 41 | 8 40·3 | 8 41·7 | 8 16·5 | 4·1 | 2·4 | 10·1 | 5·8 | 16·1 | 9·3 |
| 42 | 8 40·5 | 8 41·9 | 8 16·8 | 4·2 | 2·4 | 10·2 | 5·9 | 16·2 | 9·3 |
| 43 | 8 40·8 | 8 42·2 | 8 17·0 | 4·3 | 2·5 | 10·3 | 5·9 | 16·3 | 9·4 |
| 44 | 8 41·0 | 8 42·4 | 8 17·3 | 4·4 | 2·5 | 10·4 | 6·0 | 16·4 | 9·4 |
| 45 | 8 41·3 | 8 42·7 | 8 17·5 | 4·5 | 2·6 | 10·5 | 6·0 | 16·5 | 9·5 |
| 46 | 8 41·5 | 8 42·9 | 8 17·7 | 4·6 | 2·6 | 10·6 | 6·1 | 16·6 | 9·5 |
| 47 | 8 41·8 | 8 43·2 | 8 18·0 | 4·7 | 2·7 | 10·7 | 6·2 | 16·7 | 9·6 |
| 48 | 8 42·0 | 8 43·4 | 8 18·2 | 4·8 | 2·8 | 10·8 | 6·2 | 16·8 | 9·7 |
| 49 | 8 42·3 | 8 43·7 | 8 18·5 | 4·9 | 2·8 | 10·9 | 6·3 | 16·9 | 9·7 |
| 50 | 8 42·5 | 8 43·9 | 8 18·7 | 5·0 | 2·9 | 11·0 | 6·3 | 17·0 | 9·8 |
| 51 | 8 42·8 | 8 44·2 | 8 18·9 | 5·1 | 2·9 | 11·1 | 6·4 | 17·1 | 9·8 |
| 52 | 8 43·0 | 8 44·4 | 8 19·2 | 5·2 | 3·0 | 11·2 | 6·4 | 17·2 | 9·9 |
| 53 | 8 43·3 | 8 44·7 | 8 19·4 | 5·3 | 3·0 | 11·3 | 6·5 | 17·3 | 9·9 |
| 54 | 8 43·5 | 8 44·9 | 8 19·7 | 5·4 | 3·1 | 11·4 | 6·6 | 17·4 | 10·0 |
| 55 | 8 43·8 | 8 45·2 | 8 19·9 | 5·5 | 3·2 | 11·5 | 6·6 | 17·5 | 10·1 |
| 56 | 8 44·0 | 8 45·4 | 8 20·1 | 5·6 | 3·2 | 11·6 | 6·7 | 17·6 | 10·1 |
| 57 | 8 44·3 | 8 45·7 | 8 20·4 | 5·7 | 3·3 | 11·7 | 6·7 | 17·7 | 10·2 |
| 58 | 8 44·5 | 8 45·9 | 8 20·6 | 5·8 | 3·3 | 11·8 | 6·8 | 17·8 | 10·2 |
| 59 | 8 44·8 | 8 46·2 | 8 20·8 | 5·9 | 3·4 | 11·9 | 6·8 | 17·9 | 10·3 |
| 60 | 8 45·0 | 8 46·4 | 8 21·1 | 6·0 | 3·5 | 12·0 | 6·9 | 18·0 | 10·4 |

| 35m | SUN PLANETS | ARIES | MOON | v or d | Corrn | v or d | Corrn | v or d | Corrn |
|---|---|---|---|---|---|---|---|---|---|
| s | ° ′ | ° ′ | ° ′ | ′ | ′ | ′ | ′ | ′ | ′ |
| 00 | 8 45·0 | 8 46·4 | 8 21·1 | 0·0 | 0·0 | 6·0 | 3·6 | 12·0 | 7·1 |
| 01 | 8 45·3 | 8 46·7 | 8 21·3 | 0·1 | 0·1 | 6·1 | 3·6 | 12·1 | 7·2 |
| 02 | 8 45·5 | 8 46·9 | 8 21·6 | 0·2 | 0·1 | 6·2 | 3·7 | 12·2 | 7·2 |
| 03 | 8 45·8 | 8 47·2 | 8 21·8 | 0·3 | 0·2 | 6·3 | 3·7 | 12·3 | 7·3 |
| 04 | 8 46·0 | 8 47·4 | 8 22·0 | 0·4 | 0·2 | 6·4 | 3·8 | 12·4 | 7·3 |
| 05 | 8 46·3 | 8 47·7 | 8 22·3 | 0·5 | 0·3 | 6·5 | 3·8 | 12·5 | 7·4 |
| 06 | 8 46·5 | 8 47·9 | 8 22·5 | 0·6 | 0·4 | 6·6 | 3·9 | 12·6 | 7·5 |
| 07 | 8 46·8 | 8 48·2 | 8 22·8 | 0·7 | 0·4 | 6·7 | 4·0 | 12·7 | 7·5 |
| 08 | 8 47·0 | 8 48·4 | 8 23·0 | 0·8 | 0·5 | 6·8 | 4·0 | 12·8 | 7·6 |
| 09 | 8 47·3 | 8 48·7 | 8 23·2 | 0·9 | 0·5 | 6·9 | 4·1 | 12·9 | 7·6 |
| 10 | 8 47·5 | 8 48·9 | 8 23·5 | 1·0 | 0·6 | 7·0 | 4·1 | 13·0 | 7·7 |
| 11 | 8 47·8 | 8 49·2 | 8 23·7 | 1·1 | 0·7 | 7·1 | 4·2 | 13·1 | 7·8 |
| 12 | 8 48·0 | 8 49·4 | 8 23·9 | 1·2 | 0·7 | 7·2 | 4·3 | 13·2 | 7·8 |
| 13 | 8 48·3 | 8 49·7 | 8 24·2 | 1·3 | 0·8 | 7·3 | 4·3 | 13·3 | 7·9 |
| 14 | 8 48·5 | 8 49·9 | 8 24·4 | 1·4 | 0·8 | 7·4 | 4·4 | 13·4 | 7·9 |
| 15 | 8 48·8 | 8 50·2 | 8 24·7 | 1·5 | 0·9 | 7·5 | 4·4 | 13·5 | 8·0 |
| 16 | 8 49·0 | 8 50·4 | 8 24·9 | 1·6 | 0·9 | 7·6 | 4·5 | 13·6 | 8·0 |
| 17 | 8 49·3 | 8 50·7 | 8 25·1 | 1·7 | 1·0 | 7·7 | 4·6 | 13·7 | 8·1 |
| 18 | 8 49·5 | 8 50·9 | 8 25·4 | 1·8 | 1·1 | 7·8 | 4·6 | 13·8 | 8·2 |
| 19 | 8 49·8 | 8 51·2 | 8 25·6 | 1·9 | 1·1 | 7·9 | 4·7 | 13·9 | 8·2 |
| 20 | 8 50·0 | 8 51·5 | 8 25·9 | 2·0 | 1·2 | 8·0 | 4·7 | 14·0 | 8·3 |
| 21 | 8 50·3 | 8 51·7 | 8 26·1 | 2·1 | 1·2 | 8·1 | 4·8 | 14·1 | 8·3 |
| 22 | 8 50·5 | 8 52·0 | 8 26·3 | 2·2 | 1·3 | 8·2 | 4·9 | 14·2 | 8·4 |
| 23 | 8 50·8 | 8 52·2 | 8 26·6 | 2·3 | 1·4 | 8·3 | 4·9 | 14·3 | 8·5 |
| 24 | 8 51·0 | 8 52·5 | 8 26·8 | 2·4 | 1·4 | 8·4 | 5·0 | 14·4 | 8·5 |
| 25 | 8 51·3 | 8 52·7 | 8 27·0 | 2·5 | 1·5 | 8·5 | 5·0 | 14·5 | 8·6 |
| 26 | 8 51·5 | 8 53·0 | 8 27·3 | 2·6 | 1·5 | 8·6 | 5·1 | 14·6 | 8·6 |
| 27 | 8 51·8 | 8 53·2 | 8 27·5 | 2·7 | 1·6 | 8·7 | 5·1 | 14·7 | 8·7 |
| 28 | 8 52·0 | 8 53·5 | 8 27·8 | 2·8 | 1·7 | 8·8 | 5·2 | 14·8 | 8·8 |
| 29 | 8 52·3 | 8 53·7 | 8 28·0 | 2·9 | 1·7 | 8·9 | 5·3 | 14·9 | 8·8 |
| 30 | 8 52·5 | 8 54·0 | 8 28·2 | 3·0 | 1·8 | 9·0 | 5·3 | 15·0 | 8·9 |
| 31 | 8 52·8 | 8 54·2 | 8 28·5 | 3·1 | 1·8 | 9·1 | 5·4 | 15·1 | 8·9 |
| 32 | 8 53·0 | 8 54·5 | 8 28·7 | 3·2 | 1·9 | 9·2 | 5·4 | 15·2 | 9·0 |
| 33 | 8 53·3 | 8 54·7 | 8 29·0 | 3·3 | 2·0 | 9·3 | 5·5 | 15·3 | 9·1 |
| 34 | 8 53·5 | 8 55·0 | 8 29·2 | 3·4 | 2·0 | 9·4 | 5·6 | 15·4 | 9·1 |
| 35 | 8 53·8 | 8 55·2 | 8 29·4 | 3·5 | 2·1 | 9·5 | 5·6 | 15·5 | 9·2 |
| 36 | 8 54·0 | 8 55·5 | 8 29·7 | 3·6 | 2·1 | 9·6 | 5·7 | 15·6 | 9·2 |
| 37 | 8 54·3 | 8 55·7 | 8 29·9 | 3·7 | 2·2 | 9·7 | 5·7 | 15·7 | 9·3 |
| 38 | 8 54·5 | 8 56·0 | 8 30·2 | 3·8 | 2·2 | 9·8 | 5·8 | 15·8 | 9·3 |
| 39 | 8 54·8 | 8 56·2 | 8 30·4 | 3·9 | 2·3 | 9·9 | 5·9 | 15·9 | 9·4 |
| 40 | 8 55·0 | 8 56·5 | 8 30·6 | 4·0 | 2·4 | 10·0 | 5·9 | 16·0 | 9·5 |
| 41 | 8 55·3 | 8 56·7 | 8 30·9 | 4·1 | 2·4 | 10·1 | 6·0 | 16·1 | 9·5 |
| 42 | 8 55·5 | 8 57·0 | 8 31·1 | 4·2 | 2·5 | 10·2 | 6·0 | 16·2 | 9·6 |
| 43 | 8 55·8 | 8 57·2 | 8 31·3 | 4·3 | 2·5 | 10·3 | 6·1 | 16·3 | 9·6 |
| 44 | 8 56·0 | 8 57·5 | 8 31·6 | 4·4 | 2·6 | 10·4 | 6·2 | 16·4 | 9·7 |
| 45 | 8 56·3 | 8 57·7 | 8 31·8 | 4·5 | 2·7 | 10·5 | 6·2 | 16·5 | 9·8 |
| 46 | 8 56·5 | 8 58·0 | 8 32·1 | 4·6 | 2·7 | 10·6 | 6·3 | 16·6 | 9·8 |
| 47 | 8 56·8 | 8 58·2 | 8 32·3 | 4·7 | 2·8 | 10·7 | 6·3 | 16·7 | 9·9 |
| 48 | 8 57·0 | 8 58·5 | 8 32·5 | 4·8 | 2·8 | 10·8 | 6·4 | 16·8 | 9·9 |
| 49 | 8 57·3 | 8 58·7 | 8 32·8 | 4·9 | 2·9 | 10·9 | 6·4 | 16·9 | 10·0 |
| 50 | 8 57·5 | 8 59·0 | 8 33·0 | 5·0 | 3·0 | 11·0 | 6·5 | 17·0 | 10·1 |
| 51 | 8 57·8 | 8 59·2 | 8 33·3 | 5·1 | 3·0 | 11·1 | 6·6 | 17·1 | 10·1 |
| 52 | 8 58·0 | 8 59·5 | 8 33·5 | 5·2 | 3·1 | 11·2 | 6·6 | 17·2 | 10·2 |
| 53 | 8 58·3 | 8 59·7 | 8 33·7 | 5·3 | 3·1 | 11·3 | 6·7 | 17·3 | 10·2 |
| 54 | 8 58·5 | 9 00·0 | 8 34·0 | 5·4 | 3·2 | 11·4 | 6·7 | 17·4 | 10·3 |
| 55 | 8 58·8 | 9 00·2 | 8 34·2 | 5·5 | 3·3 | 11·5 | 6·8 | 17·5 | 10·4 |
| 56 | 8 59·0 | 9 00·5 | 8 34·4 | 5·6 | 3·3 | 11·6 | 6·9 | 17·6 | 10·4 |
| 57 | 8 59·3 | 9 00·7 | 8 34·7 | 5·7 | 3·4 | 11·7 | 6·9 | 17·7 | 10·5 |
| 58 | 8 59·5 | 9 01·0 | 8 34·9 | 5·8 | 3·4 | 11·8 | 7·0 | 17·8 | 10·5 |
| 59 | 8 59·8 | 9 01·2 | 8 35·2 | 5·9 | 3·5 | 11·9 | 7·0 | 17·9 | 10·6 |
| 60 | 9 00·0 | 9 01·5 | 8 35·4 | 6·0 | 3·6 | 12·0 | 7·1 | 18·0 | 10·7 |

| 36m s | SUN PLANETS ° ′ | ARIES ° ′ | MOON ° ′ | v or d ′ | Corr ′ | v or d ′ | Corr ′ | v or d ′ | Corr ′ |
|---|---|---|---|---|---|---|---|---|---|
| 00 | 9 00.0 | 9 01.5 | 8 35.4 | 0.0 | 0.0 | 6.0 | 3.7 | 12.0 | 7.3 |
| 01 | 9 00.3 | 9 01.7 | 8 35.6 | 0.1 | 0.1 | 6.1 | 3.7 | 12.1 | 7.4 |
| 02 | 9 00.5 | 9 02.0 | 8 35.9 | 0.2 | 0.1 | 6.2 | 3.8 | 12.2 | 7.4 |
| 03 | 9 00.8 | 9 02.2 | 8 36.1 | 0.3 | 0.2 | 6.3 | 3.8 | 12.3 | 7.5 |
| 04 | 9 01.0 | 9 02.5 | 8 36.4 | 0.4 | 0.2 | 6.4 | 3.9 | 12.4 | 7.5 |
| 05 | 9 01.3 | 9 02.7 | 8 36.6 | 0.5 | 0.3 | 6.5 | 4.0 | 12.5 | 7.6 |
| 06 | 9 01.5 | 9 03.0 | 8 36.8 | 0.6 | 0.4 | 6.6 | 4.0 | 12.6 | 7.7 |
| 07 | 9 01.8 | 9 03.2 | 8 37.1 | 0.7 | 0.4 | 6.7 | 4.1 | 12.7 | 7.7 |
| 08 | 9 02.0 | 9 03.5 | 8 37.3 | 0.8 | 0.5 | 6.8 | 4.1 | 12.8 | 7.8 |
| 09 | 9 02.3 | 9 03.7 | 8 37.5 | 0.9 | 0.5 | 6.9 | 4.2 | 12.9 | 7.8 |
| 10 | 9 02.5 | 9 04.0 | 8 37.8 | 1.0 | 0.6 | 7.0 | 4.3 | 13.0 | 7.9 |
| 11 | 9 02.8 | 9 04.2 | 8 38.0 | 1.1 | 0.7 | 7.1 | 4.3 | 13.1 | 8.0 |
| 12 | 9 03.0 | 9 04.5 | 8 38.3 | 1.2 | 0.7 | 7.2 | 4.4 | 13.2 | 8.0 |
| 13 | 9 03.3 | 9 04.7 | 8 38.5 | 1.3 | 0.8 | 7.3 | 4.4 | 13.3 | 8.1 |
| 14 | 9 03.5 | 9 05.0 | 8 38.7 | 1.4 | 0.9 | 7.4 | 4.5 | 13.4 | 8.2 |
| 15 | 9 03.8 | 9 05.2 | 8 39.0 | 1.5 | 0.9 | 7.5 | 4.6 | 13.5 | 8.2 |
| 16 | 9 04.0 | 9 05.5 | 8 39.2 | 1.6 | 1.0 | 7.6 | 4.6 | 13.6 | 8.3 |
| 17 | 9 04.3 | 9 05.7 | 8 39.5 | 1.7 | 1.0 | 7.7 | 4.7 | 13.7 | 8.3 |
| 18 | 9 04.5 | 9 06.0 | 8 39.7 | 1.8 | 1.1 | 7.8 | 4.7 | 13.8 | 8.4 |
| 19 | 9 04.8 | 9 06.2 | 8 39.9 | 1.9 | 1.2 | 7.9 | 4.8 | 13.9 | 8.5 |
| 20 | 9 05.0 | 9 06.5 | 8 40.2 | 2.0 | 1.2 | 8.0 | 4.9 | 14.0 | 8.5 |
| 21 | 9 05.3 | 9 06.7 | 8 40.4 | 2.1 | 1.3 | 8.1 | 4.9 | 14.1 | 8.6 |
| 22 | 9 05.5 | 9 07.0 | 8 40.6 | 2.2 | 1.3 | 8.2 | 5.0 | 14.2 | 8.6 |
| 23 | 9 05.8 | 9 07.2 | 8 40.9 | 2.3 | 1.4 | 8.3 | 5.0 | 14.3 | 8.7 |
| 24 | 9 06.0 | 9 07.5 | 8 41.1 | 2.4 | 1.5 | 8.4 | 5.1 | 14.4 | 8.8 |
| 25 | 9 06.3 | 9 07.7 | 8 41.4 | 2.5 | 1.5 | 8.5 | 5.2 | 14.5 | 8.8 |
| 26 | 9 06.5 | 9 08.0 | 8 41.6 | 2.6 | 1.6 | 8.6 | 5.2 | 14.6 | 8.9 |
| 27 | 9 06.8 | 9 08.2 | 8 41.8 | 2.7 | 1.6 | 8.7 | 5.3 | 14.7 | 8.9 |
| 28 | 9 07.0 | 9 08.5 | 8 42.1 | 2.8 | 1.7 | 8.8 | 5.4 | 14.8 | 9.0 |
| 29 | 9 07.3 | 9 08.7 | 8 42.3 | 2.9 | 1.8 | 8.9 | 5.4 | 14.9 | 9.1 |
| 30 | 9 07.5 | 9 09.0 | 8 42.6 | 3.0 | 1.8 | 9.0 | 5.5 | 15.0 | 9.1 |
| 31 | 9 07.8 | 9 09.2 | 8 42.8 | 3.1 | 1.9 | 9.1 | 5.5 | 15.1 | 9.2 |
| 32 | 9 08.0 | 9 09.5 | 8 43.0 | 3.2 | 1.9 | 9.2 | 5.6 | 15.2 | 9.2 |
| 33 | 9 08.3 | 9 09.8 | 8 43.3 | 3.3 | 2.0 | 9.3 | 5.7 | 15.3 | 9.3 |
| 34 | 9 08.5 | 9 10.0 | 8 43.5 | 3.4 | 2.1 | 9.4 | 5.7 | 15.4 | 9.4 |
| 35 | 9 08.8 | 9 10.3 | 8 43.8 | 3.5 | 2.1 | 9.5 | 5.8 | 15.5 | 9.4 |
| 36 | 9 09.0 | 9 10.5 | 8 44.0 | 3.6 | 2.2 | 9.6 | 5.8 | 15.6 | 9.5 |
| 37 | 9 09.3 | 9 10.8 | 8 44.2 | 3.7 | 2.3 | 9.7 | 5.9 | 15.7 | 9.6 |
| 38 | 9 09.5 | 9 11.0 | 8 44.5 | 3.8 | 2.3 | 9.8 | 6.0 | 15.8 | 9.6 |
| 39 | 9 09.8 | 9 11.3 | 8 44.7 | 3.9 | 2.4 | 9.9 | 6.0 | 15.9 | 9.7 |
| 40 | 9 10.0 | 9 11.5 | 8 44.9 | 4.0 | 2.4 | 10.0 | 6.1 | 16.0 | 9.7 |
| 41 | 9 10.3 | 9 11.8 | 8 45.2 | 4.1 | 2.5 | 10.1 | 6.1 | 16.1 | 9.8 |
| 42 | 9 10.5 | 9 12.0 | 8 45.4 | 4.2 | 2.6 | 10.2 | 6.2 | 16.2 | 9.9 |
| 43 | 9 10.8 | 9 12.3 | 8 45.7 | 4.3 | 2.6 | 10.3 | 6.3 | 16.3 | 9.9 |
| 44 | 9 11.0 | 9 12.5 | 8 45.9 | 4.4 | 2.7 | 10.4 | 6.3 | 16.4 | 10.0 |
| 45 | 9 11.3 | 9 12.8 | 8 46.1 | 4.5 | 2.7 | 10.5 | 6.4 | 16.5 | 10.0 |
| 46 | 9 11.5 | 9 13.0 | 8 46.4 | 4.6 | 2.8 | 10.6 | 6.4 | 16.6 | 10.1 |
| 47 | 9 11.8 | 9 13.3 | 8 46.6 | 4.7 | 2.9 | 10.7 | 6.5 | 16.7 | 10.2 |
| 48 | 9 12.0 | 9 13.5 | 8 46.9 | 4.8 | 2.9 | 10.8 | 6.6 | 16.8 | 10.2 |
| 49 | 9 12.3 | 9 13.8 | 8 47.1 | 4.9 | 3.0 | 10.9 | 6.6 | 16.9 | 10.3 |
| 50 | 9 12.5 | 9 14.0 | 8 47.3 | 5.0 | 3.0 | 11.0 | 6.7 | 17.0 | 10.3 |
| 51 | 9 12.8 | 9 14.3 | 8 47.6 | 5.1 | 3.1 | 11.1 | 6.8 | 17.1 | 10.4 |
| 52 | 9 13.0 | 9 14.5 | 8 47.8 | 5.2 | 3.2 | 11.2 | 6.8 | 17.2 | 10.5 |
| 53 | 9 13.3 | 9 14.8 | 8 48.0 | 5.3 | 3.2 | 11.3 | 6.9 | 17.3 | 10.5 |
| 54 | 9 13.5 | 9 15.0 | 8 48.3 | 5.4 | 3.3 | 11.4 | 6.9 | 17.4 | 10.6 |
| 55 | 9 13.8 | 9 15.3 | 8 48.5 | 5.5 | 3.3 | 11.5 | 7.0 | 17.5 | 10.6 |
| 56 | 9 14.0 | 9 15.5 | 8 48.8 | 5.6 | 3.4 | 11.6 | 7.1 | 17.6 | 10.7 |
| 57 | 9 14.3 | 9 15.8 | 8 49.0 | 5.7 | 3.5 | 11.7 | 7.1 | 17.7 | 10.8 |
| 58 | 9 14.5 | 9 16.0 | 8 49.2 | 5.8 | 3.5 | 11.8 | 7.2 | 17.8 | 10.8 |
| 59 | 9 14.8 | 9 16.3 | 8 49.5 | 5.9 | 3.6 | 11.9 | 7.2 | 17.9 | 10.9 |
| 60 | 9 15.0 | 9 16.5 | 8 49.7 | 6.0 | 3.7 | 12.0 | 7.3 | 18.0 | 11.0 |

| 37m s | SUN PLANETS ° ′ | ARIES ° ′ | MOON ° ′ | v or d ′ | Corr ′ | v or d ′ | Corr ′ | v or d ′ | Corr ′ |
|---|---|---|---|---|---|---|---|---|---|
| 00 | 9 15.0 | 9 16.5 | 8 49.7 | 0.0 | 0.0 | 6.0 | 3.8 | 12.0 | 7.5 |
| 01 | 9 15.3 | 9 16.8 | 8 50.0 | 0.1 | 0.1 | 6.1 | 3.8 | 12.1 | 7.6 |
| 02 | 9 15.5 | 9 17.0 | 8 50.2 | 0.2 | 0.1 | 6.2 | 3.9 | 12.2 | 7.6 |
| 03 | 9 15.8 | 9 17.3 | 8 50.4 | 0.3 | 0.2 | 6.3 | 3.9 | 12.3 | 7.7 |
| 04 | 9 16.0 | 9 17.5 | 8 50.7 | 0.4 | 0.3 | 6.4 | 4.0 | 12.4 | 7.8 |
| 05 | 9 16.3 | 9 17.8 | 8 50.9 | 0.5 | 0.3 | 6.5 | 4.1 | 12.5 | 7.8 |
| 06 | 9 16.5 | 9 18.0 | 8 51.1 | 0.6 | 0.4 | 6.6 | 4.1 | 12.6 | 7.9 |
| 07 | 9 16.8 | 9 18.3 | 8 51.4 | 0.7 | 0.4 | 6.7 | 4.2 | 12.7 | 7.9 |
| 08 | 9 17.0 | 9 18.5 | 8 51.6 | 0.8 | 0.5 | 6.8 | 4.3 | 12.8 | 8.0 |
| 09 | 9 17.3 | 9 18.8 | 8 51.9 | 0.9 | 0.6 | 6.9 | 4.3 | 12.9 | 8.1 |
| 10 | 9 17.5 | 9 19.0 | 8 52.1 | 1.0 | 0.6 | 7.0 | 4.4 | 13.0 | 8.1 |
| 11 | 9 17.8 | 9 19.3 | 8 52.3 | 1.1 | 0.7 | 7.1 | 4.4 | 13.1 | 8.2 |
| 12 | 9 18.0 | 9 19.5 | 8 52.6 | 1.2 | 0.8 | 7.2 | 4.5 | 13.2 | 8.3 |
| 13 | 9 18.3 | 9 19.8 | 8 52.8 | 1.3 | 0.8 | 7.3 | 4.6 | 13.3 | 8.3 |
| 14 | 9 18.5 | 9 20.0 | 8 53.1 | 1.4 | 0.9 | 7.4 | 4.6 | 13.4 | 8.4 |
| 15 | 9 18.8 | 9 20.3 | 8 53.3 | 1.5 | 0.9 | 7.5 | 4.7 | 13.5 | 8.4 |
| 16 | 9 19.0 | 9 20.5 | 8 53.5 | 1.6 | 1.0 | 7.6 | 4.8 | 13.6 | 8.5 |
| 17 | 9 19.3 | 9 20.8 | 8 53.8 | 1.7 | 1.1 | 7.7 | 4.8 | 13.7 | 8.6 |
| 18 | 9 19.5 | 9 21.0 | 8 54.0 | 1.8 | 1.1 | 7.8 | 4.9 | 13.8 | 8.6 |
| 19 | 9 19.8 | 9 21.3 | 8 54.3 | 1.9 | 1.2 | 7.9 | 4.9 | 13.9 | 8.7 |
| 20 | 9 20.0 | 9 21.5 | 8 54.5 | 2.0 | 1.3 | 8.0 | 5.0 | 14.0 | 8.8 |
| 21 | 9 20.3 | 9 21.8 | 8 54.7 | 2.1 | 1.3 | 8.1 | 5.1 | 14.1 | 8.8 |
| 22 | 9 20.5 | 9 22.0 | 8 55.0 | 2.2 | 1.4 | 8.2 | 5.1 | 14.2 | 8.9 |
| 23 | 9 20.8 | 9 22.3 | 8 55.2 | 2.3 | 1.4 | 8.3 | 5.2 | 14.3 | 8.9 |
| 24 | 9 21.0 | 9 22.5 | 8 55.4 | 2.4 | 1.5 | 8.4 | 5.3 | 14.4 | 9.0 |
| 25 | 9 21.3 | 9 22.8 | 8 55.7 | 2.5 | 1.6 | 8.5 | 5.3 | 14.5 | 9.1 |
| 26 | 9 21.5 | 9 23.0 | 8 55.9 | 2.6 | 1.6 | 8.6 | 5.4 | 14.6 | 9.1 |
| 27 | 9 21.8 | 9 23.3 | 8 56.2 | 2.7 | 1.7 | 8.7 | 5.4 | 14.7 | 9.2 |
| 28 | 9 22.0 | 9 23.5 | 8 56.4 | 2.8 | 1.8 | 8.8 | 5.5 | 14.8 | 9.3 |
| 29 | 9 22.3 | 9 23.8 | 8 56.6 | 2.9 | 1.8 | 8.9 | 5.6 | 14.9 | 9.3 |
| 30 | 9 22.5 | 9 24.0 | 8 56.9 | 3.0 | 1.9 | 9.0 | 5.6 | 15.0 | 9.4 |
| 31 | 9 22.8 | 9 24.3 | 8 57.1 | 3.1 | 1.9 | 9.1 | 5.7 | 15.1 | 9.4 |
| 32 | 9 23.0 | 9 24.5 | 8 57.4 | 3.2 | 2.0 | 9.2 | 5.8 | 15.2 | 9.5 |
| 33 | 9 23.3 | 9 24.8 | 8 57.6 | 3.3 | 2.1 | 9.3 | 5.8 | 15.3 | 9.6 |
| 34 | 9 23.5 | 9 25.0 | 8 57.8 | 3.4 | 2.1 | 9.4 | 5.9 | 15.4 | 9.6 |
| 35 | 9 23.8 | 9 25.3 | 8 58.1 | 3.5 | 2.2 | 9.5 | 5.9 | 15.5 | 9.7 |
| 36 | 9 24.0 | 9 25.5 | 8 58.3 | 3.6 | 2.3 | 9.6 | 6.0 | 15.6 | 9.8 |
| 37 | 9 24.3 | 9 25.8 | 8 58.5 | 3.7 | 2.3 | 9.7 | 6.1 | 15.7 | 9.8 |
| 38 | 9 24.5 | 9 26.0 | 8 58.8 | 3.8 | 2.4 | 9.8 | 6.1 | 15.8 | 9.9 |
| 39 | 9 24.8 | 9 26.3 | 8 59.0 | 3.9 | 2.4 | 9.9 | 6.2 | 15.9 | 9.9 |
| 40 | 9 25.0 | 9 26.5 | 8 59.3 | 4.0 | 2.5 | 10.0 | 6.3 | 16.0 | 10.0 |
| 41 | 9 25.3 | 9 26.8 | 8 59.5 | 4.1 | 2.6 | 10.1 | 6.3 | 16.1 | 10.1 |
| 42 | 9 25.5 | 9 27.0 | 8 59.7 | 4.2 | 2.6 | 10.2 | 6.4 | 16.2 | 10.1 |
| 43 | 9 25.8 | 9 27.3 | 9 00.0 | 4.3 | 2.7 | 10.3 | 6.4 | 16.3 | 10.2 |
| 44 | 9 26.0 | 9 27.5 | 9 00.2 | 4.4 | 2.8 | 10.4 | 6.5 | 16.4 | 10.3 |
| 45 | 9 26.3 | 9 27.8 | 9 00.5 | 4.5 | 2.8 | 10.5 | 6.6 | 16.5 | 10.3 |
| 46 | 9 26.5 | 9 28.1 | 9 00.7 | 4.6 | 2.9 | 10.6 | 6.6 | 16.6 | 10.4 |
| 47 | 9 26.8 | 9 28.3 | 9 00.9 | 4.7 | 2.9 | 10.7 | 6.7 | 16.7 | 10.4 |
| 48 | 9 27.0 | 9 28.6 | 9 01.2 | 4.8 | 3.0 | 10.8 | 6.8 | 16.8 | 10.5 |
| 49 | 9 27.3 | 9 28.8 | 9 01.4 | 4.9 | 3.1 | 10.9 | 6.8 | 16.9 | 10.6 |
| 50 | 9 27.5 | 9 29.1 | 9 01.6 | 5.0 | 3.1 | 11.0 | 6.9 | 17.0 | 10.6 |
| 51 | 9 27.8 | 9 29.3 | 9 01.9 | 5.1 | 3.2 | 11.1 | 6.9 | 17.1 | 10.7 |
| 52 | 9 28.0 | 9 29.6 | 9 02.1 | 5.2 | 3.3 | 11.2 | 7.0 | 17.2 | 10.8 |
| 53 | 9 28.3 | 9 29.8 | 9 02.4 | 5.3 | 3.3 | 11.3 | 7.1 | 17.3 | 10.8 |
| 54 | 9 28.5 | 9 30.1 | 9 02.6 | 5.4 | 3.4 | 11.4 | 7.1 | 17.4 | 10.9 |
| 55 | 9 28.8 | 9 30.3 | 9 02.8 | 5.5 | 3.4 | 11.5 | 7.2 | 17.5 | 10.9 |
| 56 | 9 29.0 | 9 30.6 | 9 03.1 | 5.6 | 3.5 | 11.6 | 7.3 | 17.6 | 11.0 |
| 57 | 9 29.3 | 9 30.8 | 9 03.3 | 5.7 | 3.6 | 11.7 | 7.3 | 17.7 | 11.1 |
| 58 | 9 29.5 | 9 31.1 | 9 03.6 | 5.8 | 3.6 | 11.8 | 7.4 | 17.8 | 11.1 |
| 59 | 9 29.8 | 9 31.3 | 9 03.8 | 5.9 | 3.7 | 11.9 | 7.4 | 17.9 | 11.2 |
| 60 | 9 30.0 | 9 31.6 | 9 04.0 | 6.0 | 3.8 | 12.0 | 7.5 | 18.0 | 11.3 |



| 38m s | SUN PLANETS ° ′ | ARIES ° ′ | MOON ° ′ | v or d ′ | Corr ′ | v or d ′ | Corr ′ | v or d ′ | Corr ′ |
|---|---|---|---|---|---|---|---|---|---|
| 00 | 9 30.0 | 9 31.6 | 9 04.0 | 0.0 | 0.0 | 6.0 | 3.9 | 12.0 | 7.7 |
| 01 | 9 30.3 | 9 31.8 | 9 04.3 | 0.1 | 0.1 | 6.1 | 3.9 | 12.1 | 7.8 |
| 02 | 9 30.5 | 9 32.1 | 9 04.5 | 0.2 | 0.1 | 6.2 | 4.0 | 12.2 | 7.8 |
| 03 | 9 30.8 | 9 32.3 | 9 04.7 | 0.3 | 0.2 | 6.3 | 4.0 | 12.3 | 7.9 |
| 04 | 9 31.0 | 9 32.6 | 9 05.0 | 0.4 | 0.3 | 6.4 | 4.1 | 12.4 | 8.0 |
| 05 | 9 31.3 | 9 32.8 | 9 05.2 | 0.5 | 0.3 | 6.5 | 4.2 | 12.5 | 8.0 |
| 06 | 9 31.5 | 9 33.1 | 9 05.5 | 0.6 | 0.4 | 6.6 | 4.2 | 12.6 | 8.1 |
| 07 | 9 31.8 | 9 33.3 | 9 05.7 | 0.7 | 0.4 | 6.7 | 4.3 | 12.7 | 8.1 |
| 08 | 9 32.0 | 9 33.6 | 9 05.9 | 0.8 | 0.5 | 6.8 | 4.4 | 12.8 | 8.2 |
| 09 | 9 32.3 | 9 33.8 | 9 06.2 | 0.9 | 0.6 | 6.9 | 4.4 | 12.9 | 8.3 |
| 10 | 9 32.5 | 9 34.1 | 9 06.4 | 1.0 | 0.6 | 7.0 | 4.5 | 13.0 | 8.3 |
| 11 | 9 32.8 | 9 34.3 | 9 06.7 | 1.1 | 0.7 | 7.1 | 4.6 | 13.1 | 8.4 |
| 12 | 9 33.0 | 9 34.6 | 9 06.9 | 1.2 | 0.8 | 7.2 | 4.6 | 13.2 | 8.5 |
| 13 | 9 33.3 | 9 34.8 | 9 07.1 | 1.3 | 0.8 | 7.3 | 4.7 | 13.3 | 8.5 |
| 14 | 9 33.5 | 9 35.1 | 9 07.4 | 1.4 | 0.9 | 7.4 | 4.7 | 13.4 | 8.6 |
| 15 | 9 33.8 | 9 35.3 | 9 07.6 | 1.5 | 1.0 | 7.5 | 4.8 | 13.5 | 8.7 |
| 16 | 9 34.0 | 9 35.6 | 9 07.9 | 1.6 | 1.0 | 7.6 | 4.9 | 13.6 | 8.7 |
| 17 | 9 34.3 | 9 35.8 | 9 08.1 | 1.7 | 1.1 | 7.7 | 4.9 | 13.7 | 8.8 |
| 18 | 9 34.5 | 9 36.1 | 9 08.3 | 1.8 | 1.2 | 7.8 | 5.0 | 13.8 | 8.9 |
| 19 | 9 34.8 | 9 36.3 | 9 08.6 | 1.9 | 1.2 | 7.9 | 5.1 | 13.9 | 8.9 |
| 20 | 9 35.0 | 9 36.6 | 9 08.8 | 2.0 | 1.3 | 8.0 | 5.1 | 14.0 | 9.0 |
| 21 | 9 35.3 | 9 36.8 | 9 09.0 | 2.1 | 1.3 | 8.1 | 5.2 | 14.1 | 9.0 |
| 22 | 9 35.5 | 9 37.1 | 9 09.3 | 2.2 | 1.4 | 8.2 | 5.3 | 14.2 | 9.1 |
| 23 | 9 35.8 | 9 37.3 | 9 09.5 | 2.3 | 1.5 | 8.3 | 5.3 | 14.3 | 9.2 |
| 24 | 9 36.0 | 9 37.6 | 9 09.8 | 2.4 | 1.5 | 8.4 | 5.4 | 14.4 | 9.2 |
| 25 | 9 36.3 | 9 37.8 | 9 10.0 | 2.5 | 1.6 | 8.5 | 5.5 | 14.5 | 9.3 |
| 26 | 9 36.5 | 9 38.1 | 9 10.2 | 2.6 | 1.7 | 8.6 | 5.5 | 14.6 | 9.4 |
| 27 | 9 36.8 | 9 38.3 | 9 10.5 | 2.7 | 1.7 | 8.7 | 5.6 | 14.7 | 9.4 |
| 28 | 9 37.0 | 9 38.6 | 9 10.7 | 2.8 | 1.8 | 8.8 | 5.6 | 14.8 | 9.5 |
| 29 | 9 37.3 | 9 38.8 | 9 11.0 | 2.9 | 1.9 | 8.9 | 5.7 | 14.9 | 9.6 |
| 30 | 9 37.5 | 9 39.1 | 9 11.2 | 3.0 | 1.9 | 9.0 | 5.8 | 15.0 | 9.6 |
| 31 | 9 37.8 | 9 39.3 | 9 11.4 | 3.1 | 2.0 | 9.1 | 5.8 | 15.1 | 9.7 |
| 32 | 9 38.0 | 9 39.6 | 9 11.7 | 3.2 | 2.1 | 9.2 | 5.9 | 15.2 | 9.8 |
| 33 | 9 38.3 | 9 39.8 | 9 11.9 | 3.3 | 2.1 | 9.3 | 6.0 | 15.3 | 9.8 |
| 34 | 9 38.5 | 9 40.1 | 9 12.1 | 3.4 | 2.2 | 9.4 | 6.0 | 15.4 | 9.9 |
| 35 | 9 38.8 | 9 40.3 | 9 12.4 | 3.5 | 2.2 | 9.5 | 6.1 | 15.5 | 9.9 |
| 36 | 9 39.0 | 9 40.6 | 9 12.6 | 3.6 | 2.3 | 9.6 | 6.2 | 15.6 | 10.0 |
| 37 | 9 39.3 | 9 40.8 | 9 12.9 | 3.7 | 2.4 | 9.7 | 6.2 | 15.7 | 10.1 |
| 38 | 9 39.5 | 9 41.1 | 9 13.1 | 3.8 | 2.4 | 9.8 | 6.3 | 15.8 | 10.1 |
| 39 | 9 39.8 | 9 41.3 | 9 13.3 | 3.9 | 2.5 | 9.9 | 6.4 | 15.9 | 10.2 |
| 40 | 9 40.0 | 9 41.6 | 9 13.6 | 4.0 | 2.6 | 10.0 | 6.4 | 16.0 | 10.3 |
| 41 | 9 40.3 | 9 41.8 | 9 13.8 | 4.1 | 2.6 | 10.1 | 6.5 | 16.1 | 10.3 |
| 42 | 9 40.5 | 9 42.1 | 9 14.1 | 4.2 | 2.7 | 10.2 | 6.5 | 16.2 | 10.4 |
| 43 | 9 40.8 | 9 42.3 | 9 14.3 | 4.3 | 2.8 | 10.3 | 6.6 | 16.3 | 10.5 |
| 44 | 9 41.0 | 9 42.6 | 9 14.5 | 4.4 | 2.8 | 10.4 | 6.7 | 16.4 | 10.5 |
| 45 | 9 41.3 | 9 42.8 | 9 14.8 | 4.5 | 2.9 | 10.5 | 6.7 | 16.5 | 10.6 |
| 46 | 9 41.5 | 9 43.1 | 9 15.0 | 4.6 | 3.0 | 10.6 | 6.8 | 16.6 | 10.7 |
| 47 | 9 41.8 | 9 43.3 | 9 15.2 | 4.7 | 3.0 | 10.7 | 6.9 | 16.7 | 10.7 |
| 48 | 9 42.0 | 9 43.6 | 9 15.5 | 4.8 | 3.1 | 10.8 | 6.9 | 16.8 | 10.8 |
| 49 | 9 42.3 | 9 43.8 | 9 15.7 | 4.9 | 3.1 | 10.9 | 7.0 | 16.9 | 10.8 |
| 50 | 9 42.5 | 9 44.1 | 9 16.0 | 5.0 | 3.2 | 11.0 | 7.1 | 17.0 | 10.9 |
| 51 | 9 42.8 | 9 44.3 | 9 16.2 | 5.1 | 3.3 | 11.1 | 7.1 | 17.1 | 11.0 |
| 52 | 9 43.0 | 9 44.6 | 9 16.4 | 5.2 | 3.3 | 11.2 | 7.2 | 17.2 | 11.0 |
| 53 | 9 43.3 | 9 44.8 | 9 16.7 | 5.3 | 3.4 | 11.3 | 7.3 | 17.3 | 11.1 |
| 54 | 9 43.5 | 9 45.1 | 9 16.9 | 5.4 | 3.5 | 11.4 | 7.3 | 17.4 | 11.2 |
| 55 | 9 43.8 | 9 45.3 | 9 17.2 | 5.5 | 3.5 | 11.5 | 7.4 | 17.5 | 11.2 |
| 56 | 9 44.0 | 9 45.6 | 9 17.4 | 5.6 | 3.6 | 11.6 | 7.4 | 17.6 | 11.3 |
| 57 | 9 44.3 | 9 45.8 | 9 17.6 | 5.7 | 3.7 | 11.7 | 7.5 | 17.7 | 11.4 |
| 58 | 9 44.5 | 9 46.1 | 9 17.9 | 5.8 | 3.7 | 11.8 | 7.6 | 17.8 | 11.4 |
| 59 | 9 44.8 | 9 46.4 | 9 18.1 | 5.9 | 3.8 | 11.9 | 7.6 | 17.9 | 11.5 |
| 60 | 9 45.0 | 9 46.6 | 9 18.4 | 6.0 | 3.9 | 12.0 | 7.7 | 18.0 | 11.6 |

| 39m s | SUN PLANETS ° ′ | ARIES ° ′ | MOON ° ′ | v or d ′ | Corr ′ | v or d ′ | Corr ′ | v or d ′ | Corr ′ |
|---|---|---|---|---|---|---|---|---|---|
| 00 | 9 45.0 | 9 46.6 | 9 18.4 | 0.0 | 0.0 | 6.0 | 4.0 | 12.0 | 7.9 |
| 01 | 9 45.3 | 9 46.9 | 9 18.6 | 0.1 | 0.1 | 6.1 | 4.0 | 12.1 | 8.0 |
| 02 | 9 45.5 | 9 47.1 | 9 18.8 | 0.2 | 0.1 | 6.2 | 4.1 | 12.2 | 8.0 |
| 03 | 9 45.8 | 9 47.4 | 9 19.1 | 0.3 | 0.2 | 6.3 | 4.1 | 12.3 | 8.1 |
| 04 | 9 46.0 | 9 47.6 | 9 19.3 | 0.4 | 0.3 | 6.4 | 4.2 | 12.4 | 8.2 |
| 05 | 9 46.3 | 9 47.9 | 9 19.5 | 0.5 | 0.3 | 6.5 | 4.3 | 12.5 | 8.2 |
| 06 | 9 46.5 | 9 48.1 | 9 19.8 | 0.6 | 0.4 | 6.6 | 4.3 | 12.6 | 8.3 |
| 07 | 9 46.8 | 9 48.4 | 9 20.0 | 0.7 | 0.5 | 6.7 | 4.4 | 12.7 | 8.4 |
| 08 | 9 47.0 | 9 48.6 | 9 20.3 | 0.8 | 0.5 | 6.8 | 4.5 | 12.8 | 8.4 |
| 09 | 9 47.3 | 9 48.9 | 9 20.5 | 0.9 | 0.6 | 6.9 | 4.5 | 12.9 | 8.5 |
| 10 | 9 47.5 | 9 49.1 | 9 20.7 | 1.0 | 0.7 | 7.0 | 4.6 | 13.0 | 8.6 |
| 11 | 9 47.8 | 9 49.4 | 9 21.0 | 1.1 | 0.7 | 7.1 | 4.7 | 13.1 | 8.6 |
| 12 | 9 48.0 | 9 49.6 | 9 21.2 | 1.2 | 0.8 | 7.2 | 4.7 | 13.2 | 8.7 |
| 13 | 9 48.3 | 9 49.9 | 9 21.5 | 1.3 | 0.9 | 7.3 | 4.8 | 13.3 | 8.8 |
| 14 | 9 48.5 | 9 50.1 | 9 21.7 | 1.4 | 0.9 | 7.4 | 4.9 | 13.4 | 8.8 |
| 15 | 9 48.8 | 9 50.4 | 9 21.9 | 1.5 | 1.0 | 7.5 | 4.9 | 13.5 | 8.9 |
| 16 | 9 49.0 | 9 50.6 | 9 22.2 | 1.6 | 1.1 | 7.6 | 5.0 | 13.6 | 9.0 |
| 17 | 9 49.3 | 9 50.9 | 9 22.4 | 1.7 | 1.1 | 7.7 | 5.1 | 13.7 | 9.0 |
| 18 | 9 49.5 | 9 51.1 | 9 22.6 | 1.8 | 1.2 | 7.8 | 5.1 | 13.8 | 9.1 |
| 19 | 9 49.8 | 9 51.4 | 9 22.9 | 1.9 | 1.3 | 7.9 | 5.2 | 13.9 | 9.2 |
| 20 | 9 50.0 | 9 51.6 | 9 23.1 | 2.0 | 1.3 | 8.0 | 5.3 | 14.0 | 9.2 |
| 21 | 9 50.3 | 9 51.9 | 9 23.4 | 2.1 | 1.4 | 8.1 | 5.3 | 14.1 | 9.3 |
| 22 | 9 50.5 | 9 52.1 | 9 23.6 | 2.2 | 1.4 | 8.2 | 5.4 | 14.2 | 9.3 |
| 23 | 9 50.8 | 9 52.4 | 9 23.8 | 2.3 | 1.5 | 8.3 | 5.5 | 14.3 | 9.4 |
| 24 | 9 51.0 | 9 52.6 | 9 24.1 | 2.4 | 1.6 | 8.4 | 5.5 | 14.4 | 9.5 |
| 25 | 9 51.3 | 9 52.9 | 9 24.3 | 2.5 | 1.6 | 8.5 | 5.6 | 14.5 | 9.5 |
| 26 | 9 51.5 | 9 53.1 | 9 24.6 | 2.6 | 1.7 | 8.6 | 5.7 | 14.6 | 9.6 |
| 27 | 9 51.8 | 9 53.4 | 9 24.8 | 2.7 | 1.8 | 8.7 | 5.7 | 14.7 | 9.7 |
| 28 | 9 52.0 | 9 53.6 | 9 25.0 | 2.8 | 1.8 | 8.8 | 5.8 | 14.8 | 9.7 |
| 29 | 9 52.3 | 9 53.9 | 9 25.3 | 2.9 | 1.9 | 8.9 | 5.9 | 14.9 | 9.8 |
| 30 | 9 52.5 | 9 54.1 | 9 25.5 | 3.0 | 2.0 | 9.0 | 5.9 | 15.0 | 9.9 |
| 31 | 9 52.8 | 9 54.4 | 9 25.7 | 3.1 | 2.0 | 9.1 | 6.0 | 15.1 | 9.9 |
| 32 | 9 53.0 | 9 54.6 | 9 26.0 | 3.2 | 2.1 | 9.2 | 6.1 | 15.2 | 10.0 |
| 33 | 9 53.3 | 9 54.9 | 9 26.2 | 3.3 | 2.2 | 9.3 | 6.1 | 15.3 | 10.1 |
| 34 | 9 53.5 | 9 55.1 | 9 26.5 | 3.4 | 2.2 | 9.4 | 6.2 | 15.4 | 10.1 |
| 35 | 9 53.8 | 9 55.4 | 9 26.7 | 3.5 | 2.3 | 9.5 | 6.3 | 15.5 | 10.2 |
| 36 | 9 54.0 | 9 55.6 | 9 26.9 | 3.6 | 2.4 | 9.6 | 6.3 | 15.6 | 10.3 |
| 37 | 9 54.3 | 9 55.9 | 9 27.2 | 3.7 | 2.4 | 9.7 | 6.4 | 15.7 | 10.3 |
| 38 | 9 54.5 | 9 56.1 | 9 27.4 | 3.8 | 2.5 | 9.8 | 6.5 | 15.8 | 10.4 |
| 39 | 9 54.8 | 9 56.4 | 9 27.7 | 3.9 | 2.6 | 9.9 | 6.5 | 15.9 | 10.5 |
| 40 | 9 55.0 | 9 56.6 | 9 27.9 | 4.0 | 2.6 | 10.0 | 6.6 | 16.0 | 10.5 |
| 41 | 9 55.3 | 9 56.9 | 9 28.1 | 4.1 | 2.7 | 10.1 | 6.6 | 16.1 | 10.6 |
| 42 | 9 55.5 | 9 57.1 | 9 28.4 | 4.2 | 2.8 | 10.2 | 6.7 | 16.2 | 10.7 |
| 43 | 9 55.8 | 9 57.4 | 9 28.6 | 4.3 | 2.8 | 10.3 | 6.8 | 16.3 | 10.7 |
| 44 | 9 56.0 | 9 57.6 | 9 28.8 | 4.4 | 2.9 | 10.4 | 6.8 | 16.4 | 10.8 |
| 45 | 9 56.3 | 9 57.9 | 9 29.1 | 4.5 | 3.0 | 10.5 | 6.9 | 16.5 | 10.9 |
| 46 | 9 56.5 | 9 58.1 | 9 29.3 | 4.6 | 3.0 | 10.6 | 7.0 | 16.6 | 10.9 |
| 47 | 9 56.8 | 9 58.4 | 9 29.6 | 4.7 | 3.1 | 10.7 | 7.0 | 16.7 | 11.0 |
| 48 | 9 57.0 | 9 58.6 | 9 29.8 | 4.8 | 3.2 | 10.8 | 7.1 | 16.8 | 11.1 |
| 49 | 9 57.3 | 9 58.9 | 9 30.0 | 4.9 | 3.2 | 10.9 | 7.2 | 16.9 | 11.1 |
| 50 | 9 57.5 | 9 59.1 | 9 30.3 | 5.0 | 3.3 | 11.0 | 7.2 | 17.0 | 11.2 |
| 51 | 9 57.8 | 9 59.4 | 9 30.5 | 5.1 | 3.4 | 11.1 | 7.3 | 17.1 | 11.3 |
| 52 | 9 58.0 | 9 59.6 | 9 30.8 | 5.2 | 3.4 | 11.2 | 7.4 | 17.2 | 11.3 |
| 53 | 9 58.3 | 9 59.9 | 9 31.0 | 5.3 | 3.5 | 11.3 | 7.4 | 17.3 | 11.4 |
| 54 | 9 58.5 | 10 00.1 | 9 31.2 | 5.4 | 3.6 | 11.4 | 7.5 | 17.4 | 11.5 |
| 55 | 9 58.8 | 10 00.4 | 9 31.5 | 5.5 | 3.6 | 11.5 | 7.6 | 17.5 | 11.5 |
| 56 | 9 59.0 | 10 00.6 | 9 31.7 | 5.6 | 3.7 | 11.6 | 7.6 | 17.6 | 11.6 |
| 57 | 9 59.3 | 10 00.9 | 9 32.0 | 5.7 | 3.8 | 11.7 | 7.7 | 17.7 | 11.7 |
| 58 | 9 59.5 | 10 01.1 | 9 32.2 | 5.8 | 3.8 | 11.8 | 7.8 | 17.8 | 11.7 |
| 59 | 9 59.8 | 10 01.4 | 9 32.4 | 5.9 | 3.9 | 11.9 | 7.8 | 17.9 | 11.8 |
| 60 | 10 00.0 | 10 01.6 | 9 32.7 | 6.0 | 4.0 | 12.0 | 7.9 | 18.0 | 11.9 |

| 40m s | SUN PLANETS ° ′ | ARIES ° ′ | MOON ° ′ | v or d ′ | Corrⁿ ′ | v or d ′ | Corrⁿ ′ | v or d ′ | Corrⁿ ′ |
|---|---|---|---|---|---|---|---|---|---|
| 00 | 10 00·0 | 10 01·6 | 9 32·7 | 0·0 | 0·0 | 6·0 | 4·1 | 12·0 | 8·1 |
| 01 | 10 00·3 | 10 01·9 | 9 32·9 | 0·1 | 0·1 | 6·1 | 4·1 | 12·1 | 8·2 |
| 02 | 10 00·5 | 10 02·1 | 9 33·1 | 0·2 | 0·1 | 6·2 | 4·2 | 12·2 | 8·2 |
| 03 | 10 00·8 | 10 02·4 | 9 33·4 | 0·3 | 0·2 | 6·3 | 4·3 | 12·3 | 8·3 |
| 04 | 10 01·0 | 10 02·6 | 9 33·6 | 0·4 | 0·3 | 6·4 | 4·3 | 12·4 | 8·4 |
| 05 | 10 01·3 | 10 02·9 | 9 33·9 | 0·5 | 0·3 | 6·5 | 4·4 | 12·5 | 8·4 |
| 06 | 10 01·5 | 10 03·1 | 9 34·1 | 0·6 | 0·4 | 6·6 | 4·5 | 12·6 | 8·5 |
| 07 | 10 01·8 | 10 03·4 | 9 34·3 | 0·7 | 0·5 | 6·7 | 4·5 | 12·7 | 8·6 |
| 08 | 10 02·0 | 10 03·6 | 9 34·6 | 0·8 | 0·5 | 6·8 | 4·6 | 12·8 | 8·6 |
| 09 | 10 02·3 | 10 03·9 | 9 34·8 | 0·9 | 0·6 | 6·9 | 4·7 | 12·9 | 8·7 |
| 10 | 10 02·5 | 10 04·1 | 9 35·1 | 1·0 | 0·7 | 7·0 | 4·7 | 13·0 | 8·8 |
| 11 | 10 02·8 | 10 04·4 | 9 35·3 | 1·1 | 0·7 | 7·1 | 4·8 | 13·1 | 8·8 |
| 12 | 10 03·0 | 10 04·7 | 9 35·5 | 1·2 | 0·8 | 7·2 | 4·9 | 13·2 | 8·9 |
| 13 | 10 03·3 | 10 04·9 | 9 35·8 | 1·3 | 0·9 | 7·3 | 4·9 | 13·3 | 9·0 |
| 14 | 10 03·5 | 10 05·2 | 9 36·0 | 1·4 | 0·9 | 7·4 | 5·0 | 13·4 | 9·0 |
| 15 | 10 03·8 | 10 05·4 | 9 36·2 | 1·5 | 1·0 | 7·5 | 5·1 | 13·5 | 9·1 |
| 16 | 10 04·0 | 10 05·7 | 9 36·5 | 1·6 | 1·1 | 7·6 | 5·1 | 13·6 | 9·2 |
| 17 | 10 04·3 | 10 05·9 | 9 36·7 | 1·7 | 1·1 | 7·7 | 5·2 | 13·7 | 9·2 |
| 18 | 10 04·5 | 10 06·2 | 9 37·0 | 1·8 | 1·2 | 7·8 | 5·3 | 13·8 | 9·3 |
| 19 | 10 04·8 | 10 06·4 | 9 37·2 | 1·9 | 1·3 | 7·9 | 5·3 | 13·9 | 9·4 |
| 20 | 10 05·0 | 10 06·7 | 9 37·4 | 2·0 | 1·4 | 8·0 | 5·4 | 14·0 | 9·5 |
| 21 | 10 05·3 | 10 06·9 | 9 37·7 | 2·1 | 1·4 | 8·1 | 5·5 | 14·1 | 9·5 |
| 22 | 10 05·5 | 10 07·2 | 9 37·9 | 2·2 | 1·5 | 8·2 | 5·5 | 14·2 | 9·6 |
| 23 | 10 05·8 | 10 07·4 | 9 38·2 | 2·3 | 1·6 | 8·3 | 5·6 | 14·3 | 9·7 |
| 24 | 10 06·0 | 10 07·7 | 9 38·4 | 2·4 | 1·6 | 8·4 | 5·7 | 14·4 | 9·7 |
| 25 | 10 06·3 | 10 07·9 | 9 38·6 | 2·5 | 1·7 | 8·5 | 5·7 | 14·5 | 9·8 |
| 26 | 10 06·5 | 10 08·2 | 9 38·9 | 2·6 | 1·8 | 8·6 | 5·8 | 14·6 | 9·9 |
| 27 | 10 06·8 | 10 08·4 | 9 39·1 | 2·7 | 1·8 | 8·7 | 5·9 | 14·7 | 9·9 |
| 28 | 10 07·0 | 10 08·7 | 9 39·3 | 2·8 | 1·9 | 8·8 | 5·9 | 14·8 | 10·0 |
| 29 | 10 07·3 | 10 08·9 | 9 39·6 | 2·9 | 2·0 | 8·9 | 6·0 | 14·9 | 10·1 |
| 30 | 10 07·5 | 10 09·2 | 9 39·8 | 3·0 | 2·0 | 9·0 | 6·1 | 15·0 | 10·1 |
| 31 | 10 07·8 | 10 09·4 | 9 40·1 | 3·1 | 2·1 | 9·1 | 6·1 | 15·1 | 10·2 |
| 32 | 10 08·0 | 10 09·7 | 9 40·3 | 3·2 | 2·2 | 9·2 | 6·2 | 15·2 | 10·3 |
| 33 | 10 08·3 | 10 09·9 | 9 40·5 | 3·3 | 2·2 | 9·3 | 6·3 | 15·3 | 10·3 |
| 34 | 10 08·5 | 10 10·2 | 9 40·8 | 3·4 | 2·3 | 9·4 | 6·3 | 15·4 | 10·4 |
| 35 | 10 08·8 | 10 10·4 | 9 41·0 | 3·5 | 2·4 | 9·5 | 6·4 | 15·5 | 10·5 |
| 36 | 10 09·0 | 10 10·7 | 9 41·3 | 3·6 | 2·4 | 9·6 | 6·5 | 15·6 | 10·5 |
| 37 | 10 09·3 | 10 10·9 | 9 41·5 | 3·7 | 2·5 | 9·7 | 6·5 | 15·7 | 10·6 |
| 38 | 10 09·5 | 10 11·2 | 9 41·7 | 3·8 | 2·6 | 9·8 | 6·6 | 15·8 | 10·7 |
| 39 | 10 09·8 | 10 11·4 | 9 42·0 | 3·9 | 2·6 | 9·9 | 6·7 | 15·9 | 10·7 |
| 40 | 10 10·0 | 10 11·7 | 9 42·2 | 4·0 | 2·7 | 10·0 | 6·8 | 16·0 | 10·8 |
| 41 | 10 10·3 | 10 11·9 | 9 42·4 | 4·1 | 2·8 | 10·1 | 6·8 | 16·1 | 10·9 |
| 42 | 10 10·5 | 10 12·2 | 9 42·7 | 4·2 | 2·8 | 10·2 | 6·9 | 16·2 | 10·9 |
| 43 | 10 10·8 | 10 12·4 | 9 42·9 | 4·3 | 2·9 | 10·3 | 7·0 | 16·3 | 11·0 |
| 44 | 10 11·0 | 10 12·7 | 9 43·2 | 4·4 | 3·0 | 10·4 | 7·0 | 16·4 | 11·1 |
| 45 | 10 11·3 | 10 12·9 | 9 43·4 | 4·5 | 3·0 | 10·5 | 7·1 | 16·5 | 11·1 |
| 46 | 10 11·5 | 10 13·2 | 9 43·6 | 4·6 | 3·1 | 10·6 | 7·2 | 16·6 | 11·2 |
| 47 | 10 11·8 | 10 13·4 | 9 43·9 | 4·7 | 3·2 | 10·7 | 7·2 | 16·7 | 11·3 |
| 48 | 10 12·0 | 10 13·7 | 9 44·1 | 4·8 | 3·2 | 10·8 | 7·3 | 16·8 | 11·3 |
| 49 | 10 12·3 | 10 13·9 | 9 44·4 | 4·9 | 3·3 | 10·9 | 7·4 | 16·9 | 11·4 |
| 50 | 10 12·5 | 10 14·2 | 9 44·6 | 5·0 | 3·4 | 11·0 | 7·4 | 17·0 | 11·5 |
| 51 | 10 12·8 | 10 14·4 | 9 44·8 | 5·1 | 3·4 | 11·1 | 7·5 | 17·1 | 11·5 |
| 52 | 10 13·0 | 10 14·7 | 9 45·1 | 5·2 | 3·5 | 11·2 | 7·6 | 17·2 | 11·6 |
| 53 | 10 13·3 | 10 14·9 | 9 45·3 | 5·3 | 3·6 | 11·3 | 7·6 | 17·3 | 11·7 |
| 54 | 10 13·5 | 10 15·2 | 9 45·6 | 5·4 | 3·6 | 11·4 | 7·7 | 17·4 | 11·7 |
| 55 | 10 13·8 | 10 15·4 | 9 45·8 | 5·5 | 3·7 | 11·5 | 7·8 | 17·5 | 11·8 |
| 56 | 10 14·0 | 10 15·7 | 9 46·0 | 5·6 | 3·8 | 11·6 | 7·8 | 17·6 | 11·9 |
| 57 | 10 14·3 | 10 15·9 | 9 46·3 | 5·7 | 3·8 | 11·7 | 7·9 | 17·7 | 11·9 |
| 58 | 10 14·5 | 10 16·2 | 9 46·5 | 5·8 | 3·9 | 11·8 | 8·0 | 17·8 | 12·0 |
| 59 | 10 14·8 | 10 16·4 | 9 46·7 | 5·9 | 4·0 | 11·9 | 8·0 | 17·9 | 12·1 |
| 60 | 10 15·0 | 10 16·7 | 9 47·0 | 6·0 | 4·1 | 12·0 | 8·1 | 18·0 | 12·2 |

| 41m s | SUN PLANETS ° ′ | ARIES ° ′ | MOON ° ′ | v or d ′ | Corrⁿ ′ | v or d ′ | Corrⁿ ′ | v or d ′ | Corrⁿ ′ |
|---|---|---|---|---|---|---|---|---|---|
| 00 | 10 15·0 | 10 16·7 | 9 47·0 | 0·0 | 0·0 | 6·0 | 4·2 | 12·0 | 8·3 |
| 01 | 10 15·3 | 10 16·9 | 9 47·2 | 0·1 | 0·1 | 6·1 | 4·2 | 12·1 | 8·4 |
| 02 | 10 15·5 | 10 17·2 | 9 47·5 | 0·2 | 0·1 | 6·2 | 4·3 | 12·2 | 8·4 |
| 03 | 10 15·8 | 10 17·4 | 9 47·7 | 0·3 | 0·2 | 6·3 | 4·4 | 12·3 | 8·5 |
| 04 | 10 16·0 | 10 17·7 | 9 47·9 | 0·4 | 0·3 | 6·4 | 4·4 | 12·4 | 8·6 |
| 05 | 10 16·3 | 10 17·9 | 9 48·2 | 0·5 | 0·3 | 6·5 | 4·5 | 12·5 | 8·6 |
| 06 | 10 16·5 | 10 18·2 | 9 48·4 | 0·6 | 0·4 | 6·6 | 4·6 | 12·6 | 8·7 |
| 07 | 10 16·8 | 10 18·4 | 9 48·7 | 0·7 | 0·5 | 6·7 | 4·6 | 12·7 | 8·8 |
| 08 | 10 17·0 | 10 18·7 | 9 48·9 | 0·8 | 0·6 | 6·8 | 4·7 | 12·8 | 8·9 |
| 09 | 10 17·3 | 10 18·9 | 9 49·1 | 0·9 | 0·6 | 6·9 | 4·8 | 12·9 | 8·9 |
| 10 | 10 17·5 | 10 19·2 | 9 49·4 | 1·0 | 0·7 | 7·0 | 4·8 | 13·0 | 9·0 |
| 11 | 10 17·8 | 10 19·4 | 9 49·6 | 1·1 | 0·8 | 7·1 | 4·9 | 13·1 | 9·1 |
| 12 | 10 18·0 | 10 19·7 | 9 49·8 | 1·2 | 0·8 | 7·2 | 5·0 | 13·2 | 9·1 |
| 13 | 10 18·3 | 10 19·9 | 9 50·1 | 1·3 | 0·9 | 7·3 | 5·0 | 13·3 | 9·2 |
| 14 | 10 18·5 | 10 20·2 | 9 50·3 | 1·4 | 1·0 | 7·4 | 5·1 | 13·4 | 9·3 |
| 15 | 10 18·8 | 10 20·4 | 9 50·6 | 1·5 | 1·0 | 7·5 | 5·2 | 13·5 | 9·3 |
| 16 | 10 19·0 | 10 20·7 | 9 50·8 | 1·6 | 1·1 | 7·6 | 5·3 | 13·6 | 9·4 |
| 17 | 10 19·3 | 10 20·9 | 9 51·0 | 1·7 | 1·2 | 7·7 | 5·3 | 13·7 | 9·5 |
| 18 | 10 19·5 | 10 21·2 | 9 51·3 | 1·8 | 1·2 | 7·8 | 5·4 | 13·8 | 9·5 |
| 19 | 10 19·8 | 10 21·4 | 9 51·5 | 1·9 | 1·3 | 7·9 | 5·5 | 13·9 | 9·6 |
| 20 | 10 20·0 | 10 21·7 | 9 51·8 | 2·0 | 1·4 | 8·0 | 5·5 | 14·0 | 9·7 |
| 21 | 10 20·3 | 10 21·9 | 9 52·0 | 2·1 | 1·5 | 8·1 | 5·6 | 14·1 | 9·8 |
| 22 | 10 20·5 | 10 22·2 | 9 52·2 | 2·2 | 1·5 | 8·2 | 5·7 | 14·2 | 9·8 |
| 23 | 10 20·8 | 10 22·4 | 9 52·5 | 2·3 | 1·6 | 8·3 | 5·7 | 14·3 | 9·9 |
| 24 | 10 21·0 | 10 22·7 | 9 52·7 | 2·4 | 1·7 | 8·4 | 5·8 | 14·4 | 10·0 |
| 25 | 10 21·3 | 10 23·0 | 9 52·9 | 2·5 | 1·7 | 8·5 | 5·9 | 14·5 | 10·0 |
| 26 | 10 21·5 | 10 23·2 | 9 53·2 | 2·6 | 1·8 | 8·6 | 5·9 | 14·6 | 10·1 |
| 27 | 10 21·8 | 10 23·5 | 9 53·4 | 2·7 | 1·9 | 8·7 | 6·0 | 14·7 | 10·2 |
| 28 | 10 22·0 | 10 23·7 | 9 53·7 | 2·8 | 1·9 | 8·8 | 6·1 | 14·8 | 10·2 |
| 29 | 10 22·3 | 10 24·0 | 9 53·9 | 2·9 | 2·0 | 8·9 | 6·2 | 14·9 | 10·3 |
| 30 | 10 22·5 | 10 24·2 | 9 54·1 | 3·0 | 2·1 | 9·0 | 6·2 | 15·0 | 10·4 |
| 31 | 10 22·8 | 10 24·5 | 9 54·4 | 3·1 | 2·1 | 9·1 | 6·3 | 15·1 | 10·4 |
| 32 | 10 23·0 | 10 24·7 | 9 54·6 | 3·2 | 2·2 | 9·2 | 6·4 | 15·2 | 10·5 |
| 33 | 10 23·3 | 10 25·0 | 9 54·9 | 3·3 | 2·3 | 9·3 | 6·4 | 15·3 | 10·6 |
| 34 | 10 23·5 | 10 25·2 | 9 55·1 | 3·4 | 2·4 | 9·4 | 6·5 | 15·4 | 10·7 |
| 35 | 10 23·8 | 10 25·5 | 9 55·3 | 3·5 | 2·4 | 9·5 | 6·6 | 15·5 | 10·7 |
| 36 | 10 24·0 | 10 25·7 | 9 55·6 | 3·6 | 2·5 | 9·6 | 6·6 | 15·6 | 10·8 |
| 37 | 10 24·3 | 10 26·0 | 9 55·8 | 3·7 | 2·6 | 9·7 | 6·7 | 15·7 | 10·9 |
| 38 | 10 24·5 | 10 26·2 | 9 56·1 | 3·8 | 2·6 | 9·8 | 6·8 | 15·8 | 10·9 |
| 39 | 10 24·8 | 10 26·5 | 9 56·3 | 3·9 | 2·7 | 9·9 | 6·8 | 15·9 | 11·0 |
| 40 | 10 25·0 | 10 26·7 | 9 56·5 | 4·0 | 2·8 | 10·0 | 6·9 | 16·0 | 11·1 |
| 41 | 10 25·3 | 10 27·0 | 9 56·8 | 4·1 | 2·8 | 10·1 | 7·0 | 16·1 | 11·1 |
| 42 | 10 25·5 | 10 27·2 | 9 57·0 | 4·2 | 2·9 | 10·2 | 7·1 | 16·2 | 11·2 |
| 43 | 10 25·8 | 10 27·5 | 9 57·2 | 4·3 | 3·0 | 10·3 | 7·1 | 16·3 | 11·3 |
| 44 | 10 26·0 | 10 27·7 | 9 57·5 | 4·4 | 3·0 | 10·4 | 7·2 | 16·4 | 11·3 |
| 45 | 10 26·3 | 10 28·0 | 9 57·7 | 4·5 | 3·1 | 10·5 | 7·3 | 16·5 | 11·4 |
| 46 | 10 26·5 | 10 28·2 | 9 58·0 | 4·6 | 3·2 | 10·6 | 7·3 | 16·6 | 11·5 |
| 47 | 10 26·8 | 10 28·5 | 9 58·2 | 4·7 | 3·3 | 10·7 | 7·4 | 16·7 | 11·6 |
| 48 | 10 27·0 | 10 28·7 | 9 58·4 | 4·8 | 3·3 | 10·8 | 7·5 | 16·8 | 11·6 |
| 49 | 10 27·3 | 10 29·0 | 9 58·7 | 4·9 | 3·4 | 10·9 | 7·5 | 16·9 | 11·7 |
| 50 | 10 27·5 | 10 29·2 | 9 58·9 | 5·0 | 3·5 | 11·0 | 7·6 | 17·0 | 11·8 |
| 51 | 10 27·8 | 10 29·5 | 9 59·2 | 5·1 | 3·5 | 11·1 | 7·7 | 17·1 | 11·8 |
| 52 | 10 28·0 | 10 29·7 | 9 59·4 | 5·2 | 3·6 | 11·2 | 7·7 | 17·2 | 11·9 |
| 53 | 10 28·3 | 10 30·0 | 9 59·6 | 5·3 | 3·7 | 11·3 | 7·8 | 17·3 | 12·0 |
| 54 | 10 28·5 | 10 30·2 | 9 59·9 | 5·4 | 3·7 | 11·4 | 7·9 | 17·4 | 12·0 |
| 55 | 10 28·8 | 10 30·5 | 10 00·1 | 5·5 | 3·8 | 11·5 | 8·0 | 17·5 | 12·1 |
| 56 | 10 29·0 | 10 30·7 | 10 00·3 | 5·6 | 3·9 | 11·6 | 8·0 | 17·6 | 12·2 |
| 57 | 10 29·3 | 10 31·0 | 10 00·6 | 5·7 | 3·9 | 11·7 | 8·1 | 17·7 | 12·2 |
| 58 | 10 29·5 | 10 31·2 | 10 00·8 | 5·8 | 4·0 | 11·8 | 8·2 | 17·8 | 12·3 |
| 59 | 10 29·8 | 10 31·5 | 10 01·1 | 5·9 | 4·1 | 11·9 | 8·2 | 17·9 | 12·4 |
| 60 | 10 30·0 | 10 31·7 | 10 01·3 | 6·0 | 4·2 | 12·0 | 8·3 | 18·0 | 12·5 |



| 42m s | SUN PLANETS ° ′ | ARIES ° ′ | MOON ° ′ | v or d ′ | Corrⁿ ′ | v or d ′ | Corrⁿ ′ | v or d ′ | Corrⁿ ′ |
|---|---|---|---|---|---|---|---|---|---|
| 00 | 10 30·0 | 10 31·7 | 10 01·3 | 0·0 | 0·0 | 6·0 | 4·3 | 12·0 | 8·5 |
| 01 | 10 30·3 | 10 32·0 | 10 01·5 | 0·1 | 0·1 | 6·1 | 4·3 | 12·1 | 8·6 |
| 02 | 10 30·5 | 10 32·2 | 10 01·8 | 0·2 | 0·1 | 6·2 | 4·4 | 12·2 | 8·6 |
| 03 | 10 30·8 | 10 32·5 | 10 02·0 | 0·3 | 0·2 | 6·3 | 4·5 | 12·3 | 8·7 |
| 04 | 10 31·0 | 10 32·7 | 10 02·3 | 0·4 | 0·3 | 6·4 | 4·5 | 12·4 | 8·8 |
| 05 | 10 31·3 | 10 33·0 | 10 02·5 | 0·5 | 0·4 | 6·5 | 4·6 | 12·5 | 8·9 |
| 06 | 10 31·5 | 10 33·2 | 10 02·7 | 0·6 | 0·4 | 6·6 | 4·7 | 12·6 | 8·9 |
| 07 | 10 31·8 | 10 33·5 | 10 03·0 | 0·7 | 0·5 | 6·7 | 4·7 | 12·7 | 9·0 |
| 08 | 10 32·0 | 10 33·7 | 10 03·2 | 0·8 | 0·6 | 6·8 | 4·8 | 12·8 | 9·1 |
| 09 | 10 32·3 | 10 34·0 | 10 03·4 | 0·9 | 0·6 | 6·9 | 4·9 | 12·9 | 9·1 |
| 10 | 10 32·5 | 10 34·2 | 10 03·7 | 1·0 | 0·7 | 7·0 | 5·0 | 13·0 | 9·2 |
| 11 | 10 32·8 | 10 34·5 | 10 03·9 | 1·1 | 0·8 | 7·1 | 5·0 | 13·1 | 9·3 |
| 12 | 10 33·0 | 10 34·7 | 10 04·2 | 1·2 | 0·9 | 7·2 | 5·1 | 13·2 | 9·4 |
| 13 | 10 33·3 | 10 35·0 | 10 04·4 | 1·3 | 0·9 | 7·3 | 5·2 | 13·3 | 9·4 |
| 14 | 10 33·5 | 10 35·2 | 10 04·6 | 1·4 | 1·0 | 7·4 | 5·2 | 13·4 | 9·5 |
| 15 | 10 33·8 | 10 35·5 | 10 04·9 | 1·5 | 1·1 | 7·5 | 5·3 | 13·5 | 9·6 |
| 16 | 10 34·0 | 10 35·7 | 10 05·1 | 1·6 | 1·1 | 7·6 | 5·4 | 13·6 | 9·6 |
| 17 | 10 34·3 | 10 36·0 | 10 05·4 | 1·7 | 1·2 | 7·7 | 5·5 | 13·7 | 9·7 |
| 18 | 10 34·5 | 10 36·2 | 10 05·6 | 1·8 | 1·3 | 7·8 | 5·5 | 13·8 | 9·8 |
| 19 | 10 34·8 | 10 36·5 | 10 05·8 | 1·9 | 1·3 | 7·9 | 5·6 | 13·9 | 9·8 |
| 20 | 10 35·0 | 10 36·7 | 10 06·1 | 2·0 | 1·4 | 8·0 | 5·7 | 14·0 | 9·9 |
| 21 | 10 35·3 | 10 37·0 | 10 06·3 | 2·1 | 1·5 | 8·1 | 5·7 | 14·1 | 10·0 |
| 22 | 10 35·5 | 10 37·2 | 10 06·5 | 2·2 | 1·6 | 8·2 | 5·8 | 14·2 | 10·1 |
| 23 | 10 35·8 | 10 37·5 | 10 06·8 | 2·3 | 1·6 | 8·3 | 5·9 | 14·3 | 10·1 |
| 24 | 10 36·0 | 10 37·7 | 10 07·0 | 2·4 | 1·7 | 8·4 | 6·0 | 14·4 | 10·2 |
| 25 | 10 36·3 | 10 38·0 | 10 07·3 | 2·5 | 1·8 | 8·5 | 6·0 | 14·5 | 10·3 |
| 26 | 10 36·5 | 10 38·2 | 10 07·5 | 2·6 | 1·8 | 8·6 | 6·1 | 14·6 | 10·3 |
| 27 | 10 36·8 | 10 38·5 | 10 07·7 | 2·7 | 1·9 | 8·7 | 6·2 | 14·7 | 10·4 |
| 28 | 10 37·0 | 10 38·7 | 10 08·0 | 2·8 | 2·0 | 8·8 | 6·2 | 14·8 | 10·5 |
| 29 | 10 37·3 | 10 39·0 | 10 08·2 | 2·9 | 2·1 | 8·9 | 6·3 | 14·9 | 10·6 |
| 30 | 10 37·5 | 10 39·2 | 10 08·5 | 3·0 | 2·1 | 9·0 | 6·4 | 15·0 | 10·6 |
| 31 | 10 37·8 | 10 39·5 | 10 08·7 | 3·1 | 2·2 | 9·1 | 6·4 | 15·1 | 10·7 |
| 32 | 10 38·0 | 10 39·7 | 10 08·9 | 3·2 | 2·3 | 9·2 | 6·5 | 15·2 | 10·8 |
| 33 | 10 38·3 | 10 40·0 | 10 09·2 | 3·3 | 2·3 | 9·3 | 6·6 | 15·3 | 10·8 |
| 34 | 10 38·5 | 10 40·2 | 10 09·4 | 3·4 | 2·4 | 9·4 | 6·7 | 15·4 | 10·9 |
| 35 | 10 38·8 | 10 40·5 | 10 09·7 | 3·5 | 2·5 | 9·5 | 6·7 | 15·5 | 11·0 |
| 36 | 10 39·0 | 10 40·7 | 10 09·9 | 3·6 | 2·6 | 9·6 | 6·8 | 15·6 | 11·1 |
| 37 | 10 39·3 | 10 41·0 | 10 10·1 | 3·7 | 2·6 | 9·7 | 6·9 | 15·7 | 11·1 |
| 38 | 10 39·5 | 10 41·3 | 10 10·4 | 3·8 | 2·7 | 9·8 | 6·9 | 15·8 | 11·2 |
| 39 | 10 39·8 | 10 41·5 | 10 10·6 | 3·9 | 2·8 | 9·9 | 7·0 | 15·9 | 11·3 |
| 40 | 10 40·0 | 10 41·8 | 10 10·8 | 4·0 | 2·8 | 10·0 | 7·1 | 16·0 | 11·3 |
| 41 | 10 40·3 | 10 42·0 | 10 11·1 | 4·1 | 2·9 | 10·1 | 7·2 | 16·1 | 11·4 |
| 42 | 10 40·5 | 10 42·3 | 10 11·3 | 4·2 | 3·0 | 10·2 | 7·2 | 16·2 | 11·5 |
| 43 | 10 40·8 | 10 42·5 | 10 11·6 | 4·3 | 3·0 | 10·3 | 7·3 | 16·3 | 11·5 |
| 44 | 10 41·0 | 10 42·8 | 10 11·8 | 4·4 | 3·1 | 10·4 | 7·4 | 16·4 | 11·6 |
| 45 | 10 41·3 | 10 43·0 | 10 12·0 | 4·5 | 3·2 | 10·5 | 7·4 | 16·5 | 11·7 |
| 46 | 10 41·5 | 10 43·3 | 10 12·3 | 4·6 | 3·3 | 10·6 | 7·5 | 16·6 | 11·8 |
| 47 | 10 41·8 | 10 43·5 | 10 12·5 | 4·7 | 3·3 | 10·7 | 7·6 | 16·7 | 11·8 |
| 48 | 10 42·0 | 10 43·8 | 10 12·8 | 4·8 | 3·4 | 10·8 | 7·7 | 16·8 | 11·9 |
| 49 | 10 42·3 | 10 44·0 | 10 13·0 | 4·9 | 3·5 | 10·9 | 7·7 | 16·9 | 12·0 |
| 50 | 10 42·5 | 10 44·3 | 10 13·2 | 5·0 | 3·5 | 11·0 | 7·8 | 17·0 | 12·0 |
| 51 | 10 42·8 | 10 44·5 | 10 13·5 | 5·1 | 3·6 | 11·1 | 7·9 | 17·1 | 12·1 |
| 52 | 10 43·0 | 10 44·8 | 10 13·7 | 5·2 | 3·7 | 11·2 | 7·9 | 17·2 | 12·2 |
| 53 | 10 43·3 | 10 45·0 | 10 13·9 | 5·3 | 3·8 | 11·3 | 8·0 | 17·3 | 12·3 |
| 54 | 10 43·5 | 10 45·3 | 10 14·2 | 5·4 | 3·8 | 11·4 | 8·1 | 17·4 | 12·3 |
| 55 | 10 43·8 | 10 45·5 | 10 14·4 | 5·5 | 3·9 | 11·5 | 8·1 | 17·5 | 12·4 |
| 56 | 10 44·0 | 10 45·8 | 10 14·7 | 5·6 | 4·0 | 11·6 | 8·2 | 17·6 | 12·5 |
| 57 | 10 44·3 | 10 46·0 | 10 14·9 | 5·7 | 4·0 | 11·7 | 8·3 | 17·7 | 12·5 |
| 58 | 10 44·5 | 10 46·3 | 10 15·1 | 5·8 | 4·1 | 11·8 | 8·4 | 17·8 | 12·6 |
| 59 | 10 44·8 | 10 46·5 | 10 15·4 | 5·9 | 4·2 | 11·9 | 8·4 | 17·9 | 12·7 |
| 60 | 10 45·0 | 10 46·8 | 10 15·6 | 6·0 | 4·3 | 12·0 | 8·5 | 18·0 | 12·8 |

| 43m s | SUN PLANETS ° ′ | ARIES ° ′ | MOON ° ′ | v or d ′ | Corrⁿ ′ | v or d ′ | Corrⁿ ′ | v or d ′ | Corrⁿ ′ |
|---|---|---|---|---|---|---|---|---|---|
| 00 | 10 45·0 | 10 46·8 | 10 15·6 | 0·0 | 0·0 | 6·0 | 4·4 | 12·0 | 8·7 |
| 01 | 10 45·3 | 10 47·0 | 10 15·9 | 0·1 | 0·1 | 6·1 | 4·4 | 12·1 | 8·8 |
| 02 | 10 45·5 | 10 47·3 | 10 16·1 | 0·2 | 0·1 | 6·2 | 4·5 | 12·2 | 8·8 |
| 03 | 10 45·8 | 10 47·5 | 10 16·3 | 0·3 | 0·2 | 6·3 | 4·6 | 12·3 | 8·9 |
| 04 | 10 46·0 | 10 47·8 | 10 16·6 | 0·4 | 0·3 | 6·4 | 4·6 | 12·4 | 9·0 |
| 05 | 10 46·3 | 10 48·0 | 10 16·8 | 0·5 | 0·4 | 6·5 | 4·7 | 12·5 | 9·1 |
| 06 | 10 46·5 | 10 48·3 | 10 17·0 | 0·6 | 0·4 | 6·6 | 4·8 | 12·6 | 9·1 |
| 07 | 10 46·8 | 10 48·5 | 10 17·3 | 0·7 | 0·5 | 6·7 | 4·9 | 12·7 | 9·2 |
| 08 | 10 47·0 | 10 48·8 | 10 17·5 | 0·8 | 0·6 | 6·8 | 4·9 | 12·8 | 9·3 |
| 09 | 10 47·3 | 10 49·0 | 10 17·8 | 0·9 | 0·7 | 6·9 | 5·0 | 12·9 | 9·4 |
| 10 | 10 47·5 | 10 49·3 | 10 18·0 | 1·0 | 0·7 | 7·0 | 5·1 | 13·0 | 9·4 |
| 11 | 10 47·8 | 10 49·5 | 10 18·2 | 1·1 | 0·8 | 7·1 | 5·1 | 13·1 | 9·5 |
| 12 | 10 48·0 | 10 49·8 | 10 18·5 | 1·2 | 0·9 | 7·2 | 5·2 | 13·2 | 9·6 |
| 13 | 10 48·3 | 10 50·0 | 10 18·7 | 1·3 | 0·9 | 7·3 | 5·3 | 13·3 | 9·6 |
| 14 | 10 48·5 | 10 50·3 | 10 19·0 | 1·4 | 1·0 | 7·4 | 5·4 | 13·4 | 9·7 |
| 15 | 10 48·8 | 10 50·5 | 10 19·2 | 1·5 | 1·1 | 7·5 | 5·4 | 13·5 | 9·8 |
| 16 | 10 49·0 | 10 50·8 | 10 19·4 | 1·6 | 1·2 | 7·6 | 5·5 | 13·6 | 9·9 |
| 17 | 10 49·3 | 10 51·0 | 10 19·7 | 1·7 | 1·2 | 7·7 | 5·6 | 13·7 | 9·9 |
| 18 | 10 49·5 | 10 51·3 | 10 19·9 | 1·8 | 1·3 | 7·8 | 5·7 | 13·8 | 10·0 |
| 19 | 10 49·8 | 10 51·5 | 10 20·2 | 1·9 | 1·4 | 7·9 | 5·7 | 13·9 | 10·1 |
| 20 | 10 50·0 | 10 51·8 | 10 20·4 | 2·0 | 1·5 | 8·0 | 5·8 | 14·0 | 10·2 |
| 21 | 10 50·3 | 10 52·0 | 10 20·6 | 2·1 | 1·5 | 8·1 | 5·9 | 14·1 | 10·2 |
| 22 | 10 50·5 | 10 52·3 | 10 20·9 | 2·2 | 1·6 | 8·2 | 5·9 | 14·2 | 10·3 |
| 23 | 10 50·8 | 10 52·5 | 10 21·1 | 2·3 | 1·7 | 8·3 | 6·0 | 14·3 | 10·4 |
| 24 | 10 51·0 | 10 52·8 | 10 21·3 | 2·4 | 1·7 | 8·4 | 6·1 | 14·4 | 10·4 |
| 25 | 10 51·3 | 10 53·0 | 10 21·6 | 2·5 | 1·8 | 8·5 | 6·2 | 14·5 | 10·5 |
| 26 | 10 51·5 | 10 53·3 | 10 21·8 | 2·6 | 1·9 | 8·6 | 6·2 | 14·6 | 10·6 |
| 27 | 10 51·8 | 10 53·5 | 10 22·1 | 2·7 | 2·0 | 8·7 | 6·3 | 14·7 | 10·7 |
| 28 | 10 52·0 | 10 53·8 | 10 22·3 | 2·8 | 2·0 | 8·8 | 6·4 | 14·8 | 10·7 |
| 29 | 10 52·3 | 10 54·0 | 10 22·5 | 2·9 | 2·1 | 8·9 | 6·5 | 14·9 | 10·8 |
| 30 | 10 52·5 | 10 54·3 | 10 22·8 | 3·0 | 2·2 | 9·0 | 6·5 | 15·0 | 10·9 |
| 31 | 10 52·8 | 10 54·5 | 10 23·0 | 3·1 | 2·2 | 9·1 | 6·6 | 15·1 | 10·9 |
| 32 | 10 53·0 | 10 54·8 | 10 23·3 | 3·2 | 2·3 | 9·2 | 6·7 | 15·2 | 11·0 |
| 33 | 10 53·3 | 10 55·0 | 10 23·5 | 3·3 | 2·4 | 9·3 | 6·7 | 15·3 | 11·1 |
| 34 | 10 53·5 | 10 55·3 | 10 23·7 | 3·4 | 2·5 | 9·4 | 6·8 | 15·4 | 11·2 |
| 35 | 10 53·8 | 10 55·5 | 10 24·0 | 3·5 | 2·5 | 9·5 | 6·9 | 15·5 | 11·2 |
| 36 | 10 54·0 | 10 55·8 | 10 24·2 | 3·6 | 2·6 | 9·6 | 7·0 | 15·6 | 11·3 |
| 37 | 10 54·3 | 10 56·0 | 10 24·4 | 3·7 | 2·7 | 9·7 | 7·0 | 15·7 | 11·4 |
| 38 | 10 54·5 | 10 56·3 | 10 24·7 | 3·8 | 2·8 | 9·8 | 7·1 | 15·8 | 11·5 |
| 39 | 10 54·8 | 10 56·5 | 10 24·9 | 3·9 | 2·8 | 9·9 | 7·2 | 15·9 | 11·5 |
| 40 | 10 55·0 | 10 56·8 | 10 25·2 | 4·0 | 2·9 | 10·0 | 7·3 | 16·0 | 11·6 |
| 41 | 10 55·3 | 10 57·0 | 10 25·4 | 4·1 | 3·0 | 10·1 | 7·3 | 16·1 | 11·7 |
| 42 | 10 55·5 | 10 57·3 | 10 25·6 | 4·2 | 3·0 | 10·2 | 7·4 | 16·2 | 11·7 |
| 43 | 10 55·8 | 10 57·5 | 10 25·9 | 4·3 | 3·1 | 10·3 | 7·5 | 16·3 | 11·8 |
| 44 | 10 56·0 | 10 57·8 | 10 26·1 | 4·4 | 3·2 | 10·4 | 7·5 | 16·4 | 11·9 |
| 45 | 10 56·3 | 10 58·0 | 10 26·4 | 4·5 | 3·3 | 10·5 | 7·6 | 16·5 | 12·0 |
| 46 | 10 56·5 | 10 58·3 | 10 26·6 | 4·6 | 3·3 | 10·6 | 7·7 | 16·6 | 12·0 |
| 47 | 10 56·8 | 10 58·5 | 10 26·8 | 4·7 | 3·4 | 10·7 | 7·8 | 16·7 | 12·1 |
| 48 | 10 57·0 | 10 58·8 | 10 27·1 | 4·8 | 3·5 | 10·8 | 7·8 | 16·8 | 12·2 |
| 49 | 10 57·3 | 10 59·0 | 10 27·3 | 4·9 | 3·6 | 10·9 | 7·9 | 16·9 | 12·3 |
| 50 | 10 57·5 | 10 59·3 | 10 27·5 | 5·0 | 3·6 | 11·0 | 8·0 | 17·0 | 12·3 |
| 51 | 10 57·8 | 10 59·6 | 10 27·8 | 5·1 | 3·7 | 11·1 | 8·0 | 17·1 | 12·4 |
| 52 | 10 58·0 | 10 59·8 | 10 28·0 | 5·2 | 3·8 | 11·2 | 8·1 | 17·2 | 12·5 |
| 53 | 10 58·3 | 11 00·1 | 10 28·3 | 5·3 | 3·8 | 11·3 | 8·2 | 17·3 | 12·5 |
| 54 | 10 58·5 | 11 00·3 | 10 28·5 | 5·4 | 3·9 | 11·4 | 8·3 | 17·4 | 12·6 |
| 55 | 10 58·8 | 11 00·6 | 10 28·7 | 5·5 | 4·0 | 11·5 | 8·3 | 17·5 | 12·7 |
| 56 | 10 59·0 | 11 00·8 | 10 29·0 | 5·6 | 4·1 | 11·6 | 8·4 | 17·6 | 12·8 |
| 57 | 10 59·3 | 11 01·1 | 10 29·2 | 5·7 | 4·1 | 11·7 | 8·5 | 17·7 | 12·8 |
| 58 | 10 59·5 | 11 01·3 | 10 29·5 | 5·8 | 4·2 | 11·8 | 8·6 | 17·8 | 12·9 |
| 59 | 10 59·8 | 11 01·6 | 10 29·7 | 5·9 | 4·3 | 11·9 | 8·6 | 17·9 | 13·0 |
| 60 | 11 00·0 | 11 01·8 | 10 29·9 | 6·0 | 4·4 | 12·0 | 8·7 | 18·0 | 13·1 |

| 44ᵐ s | SUN PLANETS ° ′ | ARIES ° ′ | MOON ° ′ | v or d ′ | Corrⁿ ′ | v or d ′ | Corrⁿ ′ | v or d ′ | Corrⁿ ′ |
|---|---|---|---|---|---|---|---|---|---|
| 00 | 11 00·0 | 11 01·8 | 10 29·9 | 0·0 | 0·0 | 6·0 | 4·5 | 12·0 | 8·9 |
| 01 | 11 00·3 | 11 02·1 | 10 30·2 | 0·1 | 0·1 | 6·1 | 4·5 | 12·1 | 9·0 |
| 02 | 11 00·5 | 11 02·3 | 10 30·4 | 0·2 | 0·1 | 6·2 | 4·6 | 12·2 | 9·0 |
| 03 | 11 00·8 | 11 02·6 | 10 30·6 | 0·3 | 0·2 | 6·3 | 4·7 | 12·3 | 9·1 |
| 04 | 11 01·0 | 11 02·8 | 10 30·9 | 0·4 | 0·3 | 6·4 | 4·7 | 12·4 | 9·2 |
| 05 | 11 01·3 | 11 03·1 | 10 31·1 | 0·5 | 0·4 | 6·5 | 4·8 | 12·5 | 9·3 |
| 06 | 11 01·5 | 11 03·3 | 10 31·4 | 0·6 | 0·4 | 6·6 | 4·9 | 12·6 | 9·3 |
| 07 | 11 01·8 | 11 03·6 | 10 31·6 | 0·7 | 0·5 | 6·7 | 5·0 | 12·7 | 9·4 |
| 08 | 11 02·0 | 11 03·8 | 10 31·8 | 0·8 | 0·6 | 6·8 | 5·0 | 12·8 | 9·5 |
| 09 | 11 02·3 | 11 04·1 | 10 32·1 | 0·9 | 0·7 | 6·9 | 5·1 | 12·9 | 9·6 |
| 10 | 11 02·5 | 11 04·3 | 10 32·3 | 1·0 | 0·7 | 7·0 | 5·2 | 13·0 | 9·6 |
| 11 | 11 02·8 | 11 04·6 | 10 32·6 | 1·1 | 0·8 | 7·1 | 5·3 | 13·1 | 9·7 |
| 12 | 11 03·0 | 11 04·8 | 10 32·8 | 1·2 | 0·9 | 7·2 | 5·3 | 13·2 | 9·8 |
| 13 | 11 03·3 | 11 05·1 | 10 33·0 | 1·3 | 1·0 | 7·3 | 5·4 | 13·3 | 9·9 |
| 14 | 11 03·5 | 11 05·3 | 10 33·3 | 1·4 | 1·0 | 7·4 | 5·5 | 13·4 | 9·9 |
| 15 | 11 03·8 | 11 05·6 | 10 33·5 | 1·5 | 1·1 | 7·5 | 5·6 | 13·5 | 10·0 |
| 16 | 11 04·0 | 11 05·8 | 10 33·8 | 1·6 | 1·2 | 7·6 | 5·6 | 13·6 | 10·1 |
| 17 | 11 04·3 | 11 06·1 | 10 34·0 | 1·7 | 1·3 | 7·7 | 5·7 | 13·7 | 10·2 |
| 18 | 11 04·5 | 11 06·3 | 10 34·2 | 1·8 | 1·3 | 7·8 | 5·8 | 13·8 | 10·2 |
| 19 | 11 04·8 | 11 06·6 | 10 34·5 | 1·9 | 1·4 | 7·9 | 5·9 | 13·9 | 10·3 |
| 20 | 11 05·0 | 11 06·8 | 10 34·7 | 2·0 | 1·5 | 8·0 | 5·9 | 14·0 | 10·4 |
| 21 | 11 05·3 | 11 07·1 | 10 34·9 | 2·1 | 1·6 | 8·1 | 6·0 | 14·1 | 10·5 |
| 22 | 11 05·5 | 11 07·3 | 10 35·2 | 2·2 | 1·6 | 8·2 | 6·1 | 14·2 | 10·5 |
| 23 | 11 05·8 | 11 07·6 | 10 35·4 | 2·3 | 1·7 | 8·3 | 6·2 | 14·3 | 10·6 |
| 24 | 11 06·0 | 11 07·8 | 10 35·7 | 2·4 | 1·8 | 8·4 | 6·2 | 14·4 | 10·7 |
| 25 | 11 06·3 | 11 08·1 | 10 35·9 | 2·5 | 1·9 | 8·5 | 6·3 | 14·5 | 10·8 |
| 26 | 11 06·5 | 11 08·3 | 10 36·1 | 2·6 | 1·9 | 8·6 | 6·4 | 14·6 | 10·8 |
| 27 | 11 06·8 | 11 08·6 | 10 36·4 | 2·7 | 2·0 | 8·7 | 6·5 | 14·7 | 10·9 |
| 28 | 11 07·0 | 11 08·8 | 10 36·6 | 2·8 | 2·1 | 8·8 | 6·5 | 14·8 | 11·0 |
| 29 | 11 07·3 | 11 09·1 | 10 36·9 | 2·9 | 2·2 | 8·9 | 6·6 | 14·9 | 11·1 |
| 30 | 11 07·5 | 11 09·3 | 10 37·1 | 3·0 | 2·2 | 9·0 | 6·7 | 15·0 | 11·1 |
| 31 | 11 07·8 | 11 09·6 | 10 37·3 | 3·1 | 2·3 | 9·1 | 6·7 | 15·1 | 11·2 |
| 32 | 11 08·0 | 11 09·8 | 10 37·6 | 3·2 | 2·4 | 9·2 | 6·8 | 15·2 | 11·3 |
| 33 | 11 08·3 | 11 10·1 | 10 37·8 | 3·3 | 2·4 | 9·3 | 6·9 | 15·3 | 11·3 |
| 34 | 11 08·5 | 11 10·3 | 10 38·0 | 3·4 | 2·5 | 9·4 | 7·0 | 15·4 | 11·4 |
| 35 | 11 08·8 | 11 10·6 | 10 38·3 | 3·5 | 2·6 | 9·5 | 7·0 | 15·5 | 11·5 |
| 36 | 11 09·0 | 11 10·8 | 10 38·5 | 3·6 | 2·7 | 9·6 | 7·1 | 15·6 | 11·6 |
| 37 | 11 09·3 | 11 11·1 | 10 38·8 | 3·7 | 2·7 | 9·7 | 7·2 | 15·7 | 11·6 |
| 38 | 11 09·5 | 11 11·3 | 10 39·0 | 3·8 | 2·8 | 9·8 | 7·3 | 15·8 | 11·7 |
| 39 | 11 09·8 | 11 11·6 | 10 39·2 | 3·9 | 2·9 | 9·9 | 7·3 | 15·9 | 11·8 |
| 40 | 11 10·0 | 11 11·8 | 10 39·5 | 4·0 | 3·0 | 10·0 | 7·4 | 16·0 | 11·9 |
| 41 | 11 10·3 | 11 12·1 | 10 39·7 | 4·1 | 3·0 | 10·1 | 7·5 | 16·1 | 11·9 |
| 42 | 11 10·5 | 11 12·3 | 10 40·0 | 4·2 | 3·1 | 10·2 | 7·6 | 16·2 | 12·0 |
| 43 | 11 10·8 | 11 12·6 | 10 40·2 | 4·3 | 3·2 | 10·3 | 7·6 | 16·3 | 12·1 |
| 44 | 11 11·0 | 11 12·8 | 10 40·4 | 4·4 | 3·3 | 10·4 | 7·7 | 16·4 | 12·2 |
| 45 | 11 11·3 | 11 13·1 | 10 40·7 | 4·5 | 3·3 | 10·5 | 7·8 | 16·5 | 12·2 |
| 46 | 11 11·5 | 11 13·3 | 10 40·9 | 4·6 | 3·4 | 10·6 | 7·9 | 16·6 | 12·3 |
| 47 | 11 11·8 | 11 13·6 | 10 41·1 | 4·7 | 3·5 | 10·7 | 7·9 | 16·7 | 12·4 |
| 48 | 11 12·0 | 11 13·8 | 10 41·4 | 4·8 | 3·6 | 10·8 | 8·0 | 16·8 | 12·5 |
| 49 | 11 12·3 | 11 14·1 | 10 41·6 | 4·9 | 3·6 | 10·9 | 8·1 | 16·9 | 12·5 |
| 50 | 11 12·5 | 11 14·3 | 10 41·9 | 5·0 | 3·7 | 11·0 | 8·2 | 17·0 | 12·6 |
| 51 | 11 12·8 | 11 14·6 | 10 42·1 | 5·1 | 3·8 | 11·1 | 8·2 | 17·1 | 12·7 |
| 52 | 11 13·0 | 11 14·8 | 10 42·3 | 5·2 | 3·9 | 11·2 | 8·3 | 17·2 | 12·8 |
| 53 | 11 13·3 | 11 15·1 | 10 42·6 | 5·3 | 3·9 | 11·3 | 8·4 | 17·3 | 12·8 |
| 54 | 11 13·5 | 11 15·3 | 10 42·8 | 5·4 | 4·0 | 11·4 | 8·5 | 17·4 | 12·9 |
| 55 | 11 13·8 | 11 15·6 | 10 43·1 | 5·5 | 4·1 | 11·5 | 8·5 | 17·5 | 13·0 |
| 56 | 11 14·0 | 11 15·8 | 10 43·3 | 5·6 | 4·2 | 11·6 | 8·6 | 17·6 | 13·1 |
| 57 | 11 14·3 | 11 16·1 | 10 43·5 | 5·7 | 4·2 | 11·7 | 8·7 | 17·7 | 13·1 |
| 58 | 11 14·5 | 11 16·3 | 10 43·8 | 5·8 | 4·3 | 11·8 | 8·8 | 17·8 | 13·2 |
| 59 | 11 14·8 | 11 16·6 | 10 44·0 | 5·9 | 4·4 | 11·9 | 8·8 | 17·9 | 13·3 |
| 60 | 11 15·0 | 11 16·8 | 10 44·3 | 6·0 | 4·5 | 12·0 | 8·9 | 18·0 | 13·4 |

| 45ᵐ s | SUN PLANETS ° ′ | ARIES ° ′ | MOON ° ′ | v or d ′ | Corrⁿ ′ | v or d ′ | Corrⁿ ′ | v or d ′ | Corrⁿ ′ |
|---|---|---|---|---|---|---|---|---|---|
| 00 | 11 15·0 | 11 16·8 | 10 44·3 | 0·0 | 0·0 | 6·0 | 4·6 | 12·0 | 9·1 |
| 01 | 11 15·3 | 11 17·1 | 10 44·5 | 0·1 | 0·1 | 6·1 | 4·6 | 12·1 | 9·2 |
| 02 | 11 15·5 | 11 17·3 | 10 44·7 | 0·2 | 0·2 | 6·2 | 4·7 | 12·2 | 9·3 |
| 03 | 11 15·8 | 11 17·6 | 10 45·0 | 0·3 | 0·2 | 6·3 | 4·8 | 12·3 | 9·3 |
| 04 | 11 16·0 | 11 17·9 | 10 45·2 | 0·4 | 0·3 | 6·4 | 4·9 | 12·4 | 9·4 |
| 05 | 11 16·3 | 11 18·1 | 10 45·4 | 0·5 | 0·4 | 6·5 | 4·9 | 12·5 | 9·5 |
| 06 | 11 16·5 | 11 18·4 | 10 45·7 | 0·6 | 0·5 | 6·6 | 5·0 | 12·6 | 9·6 |
| 07 | 11 16·8 | 11 18·6 | 10 45·9 | 0·7 | 0·5 | 6·7 | 5·1 | 12·7 | 9·6 |
| 08 | 11 17·0 | 11 18·9 | 10 46·2 | 0·8 | 0·6 | 6·8 | 5·2 | 12·8 | 9·7 |
| 09 | 11 17·3 | 11 19·1 | 10 46·4 | 0·9 | 0·7 | 6·9 | 5·2 | 12·9 | 9·8 |
| 10 | 11 17·5 | 11 19·4 | 10 46·6 | 1·0 | 0·8 | 7·0 | 5·3 | 13·0 | 9·9 |
| 11 | 11 17·8 | 11 19·6 | 10 46·9 | 1·1 | 0·8 | 7·1 | 5·4 | 13·1 | 9·9 |
| 12 | 11 18·0 | 11 19·9 | 10 47·1 | 1·2 | 0·9 | 7·2 | 5·5 | 13·2 | 10·0 |
| 13 | 11 18·3 | 11 20·1 | 10 47·4 | 1·3 | 1·0 | 7·3 | 5·5 | 13·3 | 10·1 |
| 14 | 11 18·5 | 11 20·4 | 10 47·6 | 1·4 | 1·1 | 7·4 | 5·6 | 13·4 | 10·2 |
| 15 | 11 18·8 | 11 20·6 | 10 47·8 | 1·5 | 1·1 | 7·5 | 5·7 | 13·5 | 10·2 |
| 16 | 11 19·0 | 11 20·9 | 10 48·1 | 1·6 | 1·2 | 7·6 | 5·8 | 13·6 | 10·3 |
| 17 | 11 19·3 | 11 21·1 | 10 48·3 | 1·7 | 1·3 | 7·7 | 5·8 | 13·7 | 10·4 |
| 18 | 11 19·5 | 11 21·4 | 10 48·5 | 1·8 | 1·4 | 7·8 | 5·9 | 13·8 | 10·5 |
| 19 | 11 19·8 | 11 21·6 | 10 48·8 | 1·9 | 1·4 | 7·9 | 6·0 | 13·9 | 10·5 |
| 20 | 11 20·0 | 11 21·9 | 10 49·0 | 2·0 | 1·5 | 8·0 | 6·1 | 14·0 | 10·6 |
| 21 | 11 20·3 | 11 22·1 | 10 49·3 | 2·1 | 1·6 | 8·1 | 6·1 | 14·1 | 10·7 |
| 22 | 11 20·5 | 11 22·4 | 10 49·5 | 2·2 | 1·7 | 8·2 | 6·2 | 14·2 | 10·8 |
| 23 | 11 20·8 | 11 22·6 | 10 49·7 | 2·3 | 1·7 | 8·3 | 6·3 | 14·3 | 10·8 |
| 24 | 11 21·0 | 11 22·9 | 10 50·0 | 2·4 | 1·8 | 8·4 | 6·4 | 14·4 | 10·9 |
| 25 | 11 21·3 | 11 23·1 | 10 50·2 | 2·5 | 1·9 | 8·5 | 6·4 | 14·5 | 11·0 |
| 26 | 11 21·5 | 11 23·4 | 10 50·5 | 2·6 | 2·0 | 8·6 | 6·5 | 14·6 | 11·1 |
| 27 | 11 21·8 | 11 23·6 | 10 50·7 | 2·7 | 2·0 | 8·7 | 6·6 | 14·7 | 11·1 |
| 28 | 11 22·0 | 11 23·9 | 10 50·9 | 2·8 | 2·1 | 8·8 | 6·7 | 14·8 | 11·2 |
| 29 | 11 22·3 | 11 24·1 | 10 51·2 | 2·9 | 2·2 | 8·9 | 6·7 | 14·9 | 11·3 |
| 30 | 11 22·5 | 11 24·4 | 10 51·4 | 3·0 | 2·3 | 9·0 | 6·8 | 15·0 | 11·4 |
| 31 | 11 22·8 | 11 24·6 | 10 51·6 | 3·1 | 2·4 | 9·1 | 6·9 | 15·1 | 11·5 |
| 32 | 11 23·0 | 11 24·9 | 10 51·9 | 3·2 | 2·4 | 9·2 | 7·0 | 15·2 | 11·5 |
| 33 | 11 23·3 | 11 25·1 | 10 52·1 | 3·3 | 2·5 | 9·3 | 7·1 | 15·3 | 11·6 |
| 34 | 11 23·5 | 11 25·4 | 10 52·4 | 3·4 | 2·6 | 9·4 | 7·1 | 15·4 | 11·7 |
| 35 | 11 23·8 | 11 25·6 | 10 52·6 | 3·5 | 2·7 | 9·5 | 7·2 | 15·5 | 11·8 |
| 36 | 11 24·0 | 11 25·9 | 10 52·8 | 3·6 | 2·7 | 9·6 | 7·3 | 15·6 | 11·8 |
| 37 | 11 24·3 | 11 26·1 | 10 53·1 | 3·7 | 2·8 | 9·7 | 7·4 | 15·7 | 11·9 |
| 38 | 11 24·5 | 11 26·4 | 10 53·3 | 3·8 | 2·9 | 9·8 | 7·4 | 15·8 | 12·0 |
| 39 | 11 24·8 | 11 26·6 | 10 53·6 | 3·9 | 3·0 | 9·9 | 7·5 | 15·9 | 12·1 |
| 40 | 11 25·0 | 11 26·9 | 10 53·8 | 4·0 | 3·0 | 10·0 | 7·6 | 16·0 | 12·1 |
| 41 | 11 25·3 | 11 27·1 | 10 54·0 | 4·1 | 3·1 | 10·1 | 7·7 | 16·1 | 12·2 |
| 42 | 11 25·5 | 11 27·4 | 10 54·3 | 4·2 | 3·2 | 10·2 | 7·7 | 16·2 | 12·3 |
| 43 | 11 25·8 | 11 27·6 | 10 54·5 | 4·3 | 3·3 | 10·3 | 7·8 | 16·3 | 12·4 |
| 44 | 11 26·0 | 11 27·9 | 10 54·7 | 4·4 | 3·3 | 10·4 | 7·9 | 16·4 | 12·4 |
| 45 | 11 26·3 | 11 28·1 | 10 55·0 | 4·5 | 3·4 | 10·5 | 8·0 | 16·5 | 12·5 |
| 46 | 11 26·5 | 11 28·4 | 10 55·2 | 4·6 | 3·5 | 10·6 | 8·0 | 16·6 | 12·6 |
| 47 | 11 26·8 | 11 28·6 | 10 55·5 | 4·7 | 3·6 | 10·7 | 8·1 | 16·7 | 12·7 |
| 48 | 11 27·0 | 11 28·9 | 10 55·7 | 4·8 | 3·6 | 10·8 | 8·2 | 16·8 | 12·7 |
| 49 | 11 27·3 | 11 29·1 | 10 55·9 | 4·9 | 3·7 | 10·9 | 8·3 | 16·9 | 12·8 |
| 50 | 11 27·5 | 11 29·4 | 10 56·2 | 5·0 | 3·8 | 11·0 | 8·3 | 17·0 | 12·9 |
| 51 | 11 27·8 | 11 29·6 | 10 56·4 | 5·1 | 3·9 | 11·1 | 8·4 | 17·1 | 13·0 |
| 52 | 11 28·0 | 11 29·9 | 10 56·7 | 5·2 | 3·9 | 11·2 | 8·5 | 17·2 | 13·0 |
| 53 | 11 28·3 | 11 30·1 | 10 56·9 | 5·3 | 4·0 | 11·3 | 8·6 | 17·3 | 13·1 |
| 54 | 11 28·5 | 11 30·4 | 10 57·1 | 5·4 | 4·1 | 11·4 | 8·6 | 17·4 | 13·2 |
| 55 | 11 28·8 | 11 30·6 | 10 57·4 | 5·5 | 4·2 | 11·5 | 8·7 | 17·5 | 13·3 |
| 56 | 11 29·0 | 11 30·9 | 10 57·6 | 5·6 | 4·2 | 11·6 | 8·8 | 17·6 | 13·3 |
| 57 | 11 29·3 | 11 31·1 | 10 57·9 | 5·7 | 4·3 | 11·7 | 8·9 | 17·7 | 13·4 |
| 58 | 11 29·5 | 11 31·4 | 10 58·1 | 5·8 | 4·4 | 11·8 | 8·9 | 17·8 | 13·5 |
| 59 | 11 29·8 | 11 31·6 | 10 58·3 | 5·9 | 4·5 | 11·9 | 9·0 | 17·9 | 13·6 |
| 60 | 11 30·0 | 11 31·9 | 10 58·6 | 6·0 | 4·6 | 12·0 | 9·1 | 18·0 | 13·7 |



| 46ᵐ s | SUN PLANETS ° ′ | ARIES ° ′ | MOON ° ′ | v or d ′ | Corrⁿ ′ | v or d ′ | Corrⁿ ′ | v or d ′ | Corrⁿ ′ |
|---|---|---|---|---|---|---|---|---|---|
| 00 | 11 30·0 | 11 31·9 | 10 58·6 | 0·0 | 0·0 | 6·0 | 4·7 | 12·0 | 9·3 |
| 01 | 11 30·3 | 11 32·1 | 10 58·8 | 0·1 | 0·1 | 6·1 | 4·7 | 12·1 | 9·4 |
| 02 | 11 30·5 | 11 32·4 | 10 59·0 | 0·2 | 0·2 | 6·2 | 4·8 | 12·2 | 9·5 |
| 03 | 11 30·8 | 11 32·6 | 10 59·3 | 0·3 | 0·2 | 6·3 | 4·9 | 12·3 | 9·5 |
| 04 | 11 31·0 | 11 32·9 | 10 59·5 | 0·4 | 0·3 | 6·4 | 5·0 | 12·4 | 9·6 |
| 05 | 11 31·3 | 11 33·1 | 10 59·8 | 0·5 | 0·4 | 6·5 | 5·0 | 12·5 | 9·7 |
| 06 | 11 31·5 | 11 33·4 | 11 00·0 | 0·6 | 0·5 | 6·6 | 5·1 | 12·6 | 9·8 |
| 07 | 11 31·8 | 11 33·6 | 11 00·2 | 0·7 | 0·5 | 6·7 | 5·2 | 12·7 | 9·8 |
| 08 | 11 32·0 | 11 33·9 | 11 00·5 | 0·8 | 0·6 | 6·8 | 5·3 | 12·8 | 9·9 |
| 09 | 11 32·3 | 11 34·1 | 11 00·7 | 0·9 | 0·7 | 6·9 | 5·3 | 12·9 | 10·0 |
| 10 | 11 32·5 | 11 34·4 | 11 01·0 | 1·0 | 0·8 | 7·0 | 5·4 | 13·0 | 10·1 |
| 11 | 11 32·8 | 11 34·6 | 11 01·2 | 1·1 | 0·9 | 7·1 | 5·5 | 13·1 | 10·2 |
| 12 | 11 33·0 | 11 34·9 | 11 01·4 | 1·2 | 0·9 | 7·2 | 5·6 | 13·2 | 10·2 |
| 13 | 11 33·3 | 11 35·1 | 11 01·7 | 1·3 | 1·0 | 7·3 | 5·7 | 13·3 | 10·3 |
| 14 | 11 33·5 | 11 35·4 | 11 01·9 | 1·4 | 1·1 | 7·4 | 5·7 | 13·4 | 10·4 |
| 15 | 11 33·8 | 11 35·6 | 11 02·1 | 1·5 | 1·2 | 7·5 | 5·8 | 13·5 | 10·5 |
| 16 | 11 34·0 | 11 35·9 | 11 02·4 | 1·6 | 1·2 | 7·6 | 5·9 | 13·6 | 10·5 |
| 17 | 11 34·3 | 11 36·2 | 11 02·6 | 1·7 | 1·3 | 7·7 | 6·0 | 13·7 | 10·6 |
| 18 | 11 34·5 | 11 36·4 | 11 02·9 | 1·8 | 1·4 | 7·8 | 6·0 | 13·8 | 10·7 |
| 19 | 11 34·8 | 11 36·7 | 11 03·1 | 1·9 | 1·5 | 7·9 | 6·1 | 13·9 | 10·8 |
| 20 | 11 35·0 | 11 36·9 | 11 03·3 | 2·0 | 1·6 | 8·0 | 6·2 | 14·0 | 10·9 |
| 21 | 11 35·3 | 11 37·2 | 11 03·6 | 2·1 | 1·6 | 8·1 | 6·3 | 14·1 | 10·9 |
| 22 | 11 35·5 | 11 37·4 | 11 03·8 | 2·2 | 1·7 | 8·2 | 6·4 | 14·2 | 11·0 |
| 23 | 11 35·8 | 11 37·7 | 11 04·1 | 2·3 | 1·8 | 8·3 | 6·4 | 14·3 | 11·1 |
| 24 | 11 36·0 | 11 37·9 | 11 04·3 | 2·4 | 1·9 | 8·4 | 6·5 | 14·4 | 11·2 |
| 25 | 11 36·3 | 11 38·2 | 11 04·5 | 2·5 | 1·9 | 8·5 | 6·6 | 14·5 | 11·2 |
| 26 | 11 36·5 | 11 38·4 | 11 04·8 | 2·6 | 2·0 | 8·6 | 6·7 | 14·6 | 11·3 |
| 27 | 11 36·8 | 11 38·7 | 11 05·0 | 2·7 | 2·1 | 8·7 | 6·7 | 14·7 | 11·4 |
| 28 | 11 37·0 | 11 38·9 | 11 05·2 | 2·8 | 2·2 | 8·8 | 6·8 | 14·8 | 11·5 |
| 29 | 11 37·3 | 11 39·2 | 11 05·5 | 2·9 | 2·2 | 8·9 | 6·9 | 14·9 | 11·5 |
| 30 | 11 37·5 | 11 39·4 | 11 05·7 | 3·0 | 2·3 | 9·0 | 7·0 | 15·0 | 11·6 |
| 31 | 11 37·8 | 11 39·7 | 11 06·0 | 3·1 | 2·4 | 9·1 | 7·1 | 15·1 | 11·7 |
| 32 | 11 38·0 | 11 39·9 | 11 06·2 | 3·2 | 2·5 | 9·2 | 7·1 | 15·2 | 11·8 |
| 33 | 11 38·3 | 11 40·2 | 11 06·4 | 3·3 | 2·6 | 9·3 | 7·2 | 15·3 | 11·9 |
| 34 | 11 38·5 | 11 40·4 | 11 06·7 | 3·4 | 2·6 | 9·4 | 7·3 | 15·4 | 11·9 |
| 35 | 11 38·8 | 11 40·7 | 11 06·9 | 3·5 | 2·7 | 9·5 | 7·4 | 15·5 | 12·0 |
| 36 | 11 39·0 | 11 40·9 | 11 07·2 | 3·6 | 2·8 | 9·6 | 7·4 | 15·6 | 12·1 |
| 37 | 11 39·3 | 11 41·2 | 11 07·4 | 3·7 | 2·9 | 9·7 | 7·5 | 15·7 | 12·2 |
| 38 | 11 39·5 | 11 41·4 | 11 07·6 | 3·8 | 2·9 | 9·8 | 7·6 | 15·8 | 12·2 |
| 39 | 11 39·8 | 11 41·7 | 11 07·9 | 3·9 | 3·0 | 9·9 | 7·7 | 15·9 | 12·3 |
| 40 | 11 40·0 | 11 41·9 | 11 08·1 | 4·0 | 3·1 | 10·0 | 7·8 | 16·0 | 12·4 |
| 41 | 11 40·3 | 11 42·2 | 11 08·3 | 4·1 | 3·2 | 10·1 | 7·8 | 16·1 | 12·5 |
| 42 | 11 40·5 | 11 42·4 | 11 08·6 | 4·2 | 3·3 | 10·2 | 7·9 | 16·2 | 12·6 |
| 43 | 11 40·8 | 11 42·7 | 11 08·8 | 4·3 | 3·3 | 10·3 | 8·0 | 16·3 | 12·6 |
| 44 | 11 41·0 | 11 42·9 | 11 09·1 | 4·4 | 3·4 | 10·4 | 8·1 | 16·4 | 12·7 |
| 45 | 11 41·3 | 11 43·2 | 11 09·3 | 4·5 | 3·5 | 10·5 | 8·1 | 16·5 | 12·8 |
| 46 | 11 41·5 | 11 43·4 | 11 09·5 | 4·6 | 3·6 | 10·6 | 8·2 | 16·6 | 12·9 |
| 47 | 11 41·8 | 11 43·7 | 11 09·8 | 4·7 | 3·6 | 10·7 | 8·3 | 16·7 | 12·9 |
| 48 | 11 42·0 | 11 43·9 | 11 10·0 | 4·8 | 3·7 | 10·8 | 8·4 | 16·8 | 13·0 |
| 49 | 11 42·3 | 11 44·2 | 11 10·3 | 4·9 | 3·8 | 10·9 | 8·4 | 16·9 | 13·1 |
| 50 | 11 42·5 | 11 44·4 | 11 10·5 | 5·0 | 3·9 | 11·0 | 8·5 | 17·0 | 13·2 |
| 51 | 11 42·8 | 11 44·7 | 11 10·7 | 5·1 | 4·0 | 11·1 | 8·6 | 17·1 | 13·3 |
| 52 | 11 43·0 | 11 44·9 | 11 11·0 | 5·2 | 4·0 | 11·2 | 8·7 | 17·2 | 13·3 |
| 53 | 11 43·3 | 11 45·2 | 11 11·2 | 5·3 | 4·1 | 11·3 | 8·8 | 17·3 | 13·4 |
| 54 | 11 43·5 | 11 45·4 | 11 11·5 | 5·4 | 4·2 | 11·4 | 8·8 | 17·4 | 13·5 |
| 55 | 11 43·8 | 11 45·7 | 11 11·7 | 5·5 | 4·3 | 11·5 | 8·9 | 17·5 | 13·6 |
| 56 | 11 44·0 | 11 45·9 | 11 11·9 | 5·6 | 4·3 | 11·6 | 9·0 | 17·6 | 13·6 |
| 57 | 11 44·3 | 11 46·2 | 11 12·2 | 5·7 | 4·4 | 11·7 | 9·1 | 17·7 | 13·7 |
| 58 | 11 44·5 | 11 46·4 | 11 12·4 | 5·8 | 4·5 | 11·8 | 9·1 | 17·8 | 13·8 |
| 59 | 11 44·8 | 11 46·7 | 11 12·6 | 5·9 | 4·6 | 11·9 | 9·2 | 17·9 | 13·9 |
| 60 | 11 45·0 | 11 46·9 | 11 12·9 | 6·0 | 4·7 | 12·0 | 9·3 | 18·0 | 14·0 |

| 47ᵐ s | SUN PLANETS ° ′ | ARIES ° ′ | MOON ° ′ | v or d ′ | Corrⁿ ′ | v or d ′ | Corrⁿ ′ | v or d ′ | Corrⁿ ′ |
|---|---|---|---|---|---|---|---|---|---|
| 00 | 11 45·0 | 11 46·9 | 11 12·9 | 0·0 | 0·0 | 6·0 | 4·8 | 12·0 | 9·5 |
| 01 | 11 45·3 | 11 47·2 | 11 13·1 | 0·1 | 0·1 | 6·1 | 4·8 | 12·1 | 9·6 |
| 02 | 11 45·5 | 11 47·4 | 11 13·4 | 0·2 | 0·2 | 6·2 | 4·9 | 12·2 | 9·7 |
| 03 | 11 45·8 | 11 47·7 | 11 13·6 | 0·3 | 0·2 | 6·3 | 5·0 | 12·3 | 9·7 |
| 04 | 11 46·0 | 11 47·9 | 11 13·8 | 0·4 | 0·3 | 6·4 | 5·1 | 12·4 | 9·8 |
| 05 | 11 46·3 | 11 48·2 | 11 14·1 | 0·5 | 0·4 | 6·5 | 5·1 | 12·5 | 9·9 |
| 06 | 11 46·5 | 11 48·4 | 11 14·3 | 0·6 | 0·5 | 6·6 | 5·2 | 12·6 | 10·0 |
| 07 | 11 46·8 | 11 48·7 | 11 14·6 | 0·7 | 0·6 | 6·7 | 5·3 | 12·7 | 10·1 |
| 08 | 11 47·0 | 11 48·9 | 11 14·8 | 0·8 | 0·6 | 6·8 | 5·4 | 12·8 | 10·1 |
| 09 | 11 47·3 | 11 49·2 | 11 15·0 | 0·9 | 0·7 | 6·9 | 5·5 | 12·9 | 10·2 |
| 10 | 11 47·5 | 11 49·4 | 11 15·3 | 1·0 | 0·8 | 7·0 | 5·5 | 13·0 | 10·3 |
| 11 | 11 47·8 | 11 49·7 | 11 15·5 | 1·1 | 0·9 | 7·1 | 5·6 | 13·1 | 10·4 |
| 12 | 11 48·0 | 11 49·9 | 11 15·7 | 1·2 | 1·0 | 7·2 | 5·7 | 13·2 | 10·5 |
| 13 | 11 48·3 | 11 50·2 | 11 16·0 | 1·3 | 1·0 | 7·3 | 5·8 | 13·3 | 10·5 |
| 14 | 11 48·5 | 11 50·4 | 11 16·2 | 1·4 | 1·1 | 7·4 | 5·9 | 13·4 | 10·6 |
| 15 | 11 48·8 | 11 50·7 | 11 16·5 | 1·5 | 1·2 | 7·5 | 5·9 | 13·5 | 10·7 |
| 16 | 11 49·0 | 11 50·9 | 11 16·7 | 1·6 | 1·3 | 7·6 | 6·0 | 13·6 | 10·8 |
| 17 | 11 49·3 | 11 51·2 | 11 16·9 | 1·7 | 1·3 | 7·7 | 6·1 | 13·7 | 10·8 |
| 18 | 11 49·5 | 11 51·4 | 11 17·2 | 1·8 | 1·4 | 7·8 | 6·2 | 13·8 | 10·9 |
| 19 | 11 49·8 | 11 51·7 | 11 17·4 | 1·9 | 1·5 | 7·9 | 6·3 | 13·9 | 11·0 |
| 20 | 11 50·0 | 11 51·9 | 11 17·7 | 2·0 | 1·6 | 8·0 | 6·3 | 14·0 | 11·1 |
| 21 | 11 50·3 | 11 52·2 | 11 17·9 | 2·1 | 1·7 | 8·1 | 6·4 | 14·1 | 11·2 |
| 22 | 11 50·5 | 11 52·4 | 11 18·1 | 2·2 | 1·7 | 8·2 | 6·5 | 14·2 | 11·2 |
| 23 | 11 50·8 | 11 52·7 | 11 18·4 | 2·3 | 1·8 | 8·3 | 6·6 | 14·3 | 11·3 |
| 24 | 11 51·0 | 11 52·9 | 11 18·6 | 2·4 | 1·9 | 8·4 | 6·7 | 14·4 | 11·4 |
| 25 | 11 51·3 | 11 53·2 | 11 18·8 | 2·5 | 2·0 | 8·5 | 6·7 | 14·5 | 11·5 |
| 26 | 11 51·5 | 11 53·4 | 11 19·1 | 2·6 | 2·1 | 8·6 | 6·8 | 14·6 | 11·6 |
| 27 | 11 51·8 | 11 53·7 | 11 19·3 | 2·7 | 2·1 | 8·7 | 6·9 | 14·7 | 11·6 |
| 28 | 11 52·0 | 11 53·9 | 11 19·6 | 2·8 | 2·2 | 8·8 | 7·0 | 14·8 | 11·7 |
| 29 | 11 52·3 | 11 54·2 | 11 19·8 | 2·9 | 2·3 | 8·9 | 7·0 | 14·9 | 11·8 |
| 30 | 11 52·5 | 11 54·5 | 11 20·0 | 3·0 | 2·4 | 9·0 | 7·1 | 15·0 | 11·9 |
| 31 | 11 52·8 | 11 54·7 | 11 20·3 | 3·1 | 2·5 | 9·1 | 7·2 | 15·1 | 12·0 |
| 32 | 11 53·0 | 11 55·0 | 11 20·5 | 3·2 | 2·5 | 9·2 | 7·3 | 15·2 | 12·0 |
| 33 | 11 53·3 | 11 55·2 | 11 20·8 | 3·3 | 2·6 | 9·3 | 7·4 | 15·3 | 12·1 |
| 34 | 11 53·5 | 11 55·5 | 11 21·0 | 3·4 | 2·7 | 9·4 | 7·4 | 15·4 | 12·2 |
| 35 | 11 53·8 | 11 55·7 | 11 21·2 | 3·5 | 2·8 | 9·5 | 7·5 | 15·5 | 12·3 |
| 36 | 11 54·0 | 11 56·0 | 11 21·5 | 3·6 | 2·9 | 9·6 | 7·6 | 15·6 | 12·4 |
| 37 | 11 54·3 | 11 56·2 | 11 21·7 | 3·7 | 2·9 | 9·7 | 7·7 | 15·7 | 12·4 |
| 38 | 11 54·5 | 11 56·5 | 11 22·0 | 3·8 | 3·0 | 9·8 | 7·8 | 15·8 | 12·5 |
| 39 | 11 54·8 | 11 56·7 | 11 22·2 | 3·9 | 3·1 | 9·9 | 7·8 | 15·9 | 12·6 |
| 40 | 11 55·0 | 11 57·0 | 11 22·4 | 4·0 | 3·2 | 10·0 | 7·9 | 16·0 | 12·7 |
| 41 | 11 55·3 | 11 57·2 | 11 22·7 | 4·1 | 3·2 | 10·1 | 8·0 | 16·1 | 12·7 |
| 42 | 11 55·5 | 11 57·5 | 11 22·9 | 4·2 | 3·3 | 10·2 | 8·1 | 16·2 | 12·8 |
| 43 | 11 55·8 | 11 57·7 | 11 23·1 | 4·3 | 3·4 | 10·3 | 8·2 | 16·3 | 12·9 |
| 44 | 11 56·0 | 11 58·0 | 11 23·4 | 4·4 | 3·5 | 10·4 | 8·2 | 16·4 | 13·0 |
| 45 | 11 56·3 | 11 58·2 | 11 23·6 | 4·5 | 3·6 | 10·5 | 8·3 | 16·5 | 13·1 |
| 46 | 11 56·5 | 11 58·5 | 11 23·9 | 4·6 | 3·6 | 10·6 | 8·4 | 16·6 | 13·1 |
| 47 | 11 56·8 | 11 58·7 | 11 24·1 | 4·7 | 3·7 | 10·7 | 8·5 | 16·7 | 13·2 |
| 48 | 11 57·0 | 11 59·0 | 11 24·3 | 4·8 | 3·8 | 10·8 | 8·6 | 16·8 | 13·3 |
| 49 | 11 57·3 | 11 59·2 | 11 24·6 | 4·9 | 3·9 | 10·9 | 8·6 | 16·9 | 13·4 |
| 50 | 11 57·5 | 11 59·5 | 11 24·8 | 5·0 | 4·0 | 11·0 | 8·7 | 17·0 | 13·5 |
| 51 | 11 57·8 | 11 59·7 | 11 25·1 | 5·1 | 4·0 | 11·1 | 8·8 | 17·1 | 13·5 |
| 52 | 11 58·0 | 12 00·0 | 11 25·3 | 5·2 | 4·1 | 11·2 | 8·9 | 17·2 | 13·6 |
| 53 | 11 58·3 | 12 00·2 | 11 25·5 | 5·3 | 4·2 | 11·3 | 8·9 | 17·3 | 13·7 |
| 54 | 11 58·5 | 12 00·5 | 11 25·8 | 5·4 | 4·3 | 11·4 | 9·0 | 17·4 | 13·8 |
| 55 | 11 58·8 | 12 00·7 | 11 26·0 | 5·5 | 4·4 | 11·5 | 9·1 | 17·5 | 13·9 |
| 56 | 11 59·0 | 12 01·0 | 11 26·2 | 5·6 | 4·4 | 11·6 | 9·2 | 17·6 | 13·9 |
| 57 | 11 59·3 | 12 01·2 | 11 26·5 | 5·7 | 4·5 | 11·7 | 9·3 | 17·7 | 14·0 |
| 58 | 11 59·5 | 12 01·5 | 11 26·7 | 5·8 | 4·6 | 11·8 | 9·3 | 17·8 | 14·1 |
| 59 | 11 59·8 | 12 01·7 | 11 27·0 | 5·9 | 4·7 | 11·9 | 9·4 | 17·9 | 14·2 |
| 60 | 12 00·0 | 12 02·0 | 11 27·2 | 6·0 | 4·8 | 12·0 | 9·5 | 18·0 | 14·3 |

| 48m | SUN PLANETS | ARIES | MOON | v or d | Corrn | v or d | Corrn | v or d | Corrn |
|---|---|---|---|---|---|---|---|---|---|
| s | ° ′ | ° ′ | ° ′ | ′ | ′ | ′ | ′ | ′ | ′ |
| 00 | 12 00·0 | 12 02·0 | 11 27·2 | 0·0 | 0·0 | 6·0 | 4·9 | 12·0 | 9·7 |
| 01 | 12 00·3 | 12 02·2 | 11 27·4 | 0·1 | 0·1 | 6·1 | 4·9 | 12·1 | 9·8 |
| 02 | 12 00·5 | 12 02·5 | 11 27·7 | 0·2 | 0·2 | 6·2 | 5·0 | 12·2 | 9·9 |
| 03 | 12 00·8 | 12 02·7 | 11 27·9 | 0·3 | 0·2 | 6·3 | 5·1 | 12·3 | 9·9 |
| 04 | 12 01·0 | 12 03·0 | 11 28·2 | 0·4 | 0·3 | 6·4 | 5·2 | 12·4 | 10·0 |
| 05 | 12 01·3 | 12 03·2 | 11 28·4 | 0·5 | 0·4 | 6·5 | 5·3 | 12·5 | 10·1 |
| 06 | 12 01·5 | 12 03·5 | 11 28·6 | 0·6 | 0·5 | 6·6 | 5·3 | 12·6 | 10·2 |
| 07 | 12 01·8 | 12 03·7 | 11 28·9 | 0·7 | 0·6 | 6·7 | 5·4 | 12·7 | 10·3 |
| 08 | 12 02·0 | 12 04·0 | 11 29·1 | 0·8 | 0·6 | 6·8 | 5·5 | 12·8 | 10·3 |
| 09 | 12 02·3 | 12 04·2 | 11 29·3 | 0·9 | 0·7 | 6·9 | 5·6 | 12·9 | 10·4 |
| 10 | 12 02·5 | 12 04·5 | 11 29·6 | 1·0 | 0·8 | 7·0 | 5·7 | 13·0 | 10·5 |
| 11 | 12 02·8 | 12 04·7 | 11 29·8 | 1·1 | 0·9 | 7·1 | 5·7 | 13·1 | 10·6 |
| 12 | 12 03·0 | 12 05·0 | 11 30·1 | 1·2 | 1·0 | 7·2 | 5·8 | 13·2 | 10·7 |
| 13 | 12 03·3 | 12 05·2 | 11 30·3 | 1·3 | 1·1 | 7·3 | 5·9 | 13·3 | 10·8 |
| 14 | 12 03·5 | 12 05·5 | 11 30·5 | 1·4 | 1·1 | 7·4 | 6·0 | 13·4 | 10·8 |
| 15 | 12 03·8 | 12 05·7 | 11 30·8 | 1·5 | 1·2 | 7·5 | 6·1 | 13·5 | 10·9 |
| 16 | 12 04·0 | 12 06·0 | 11 31·0 | 1·6 | 1·3 | 7·6 | 6·1 | 13·6 | 11·0 |
| 17 | 12 04·3 | 12 06·2 | 11 31·3 | 1·7 | 1·4 | 7·7 | 6·2 | 13·7 | 11·1 |
| 18 | 12 04·5 | 12 06·5 | 11 31·5 | 1·8 | 1·5 | 7·8 | 6·3 | 13·8 | 11·2 |
| 19 | 12 04·8 | 12 06·7 | 11 31·7 | 1·9 | 1·5 | 7·9 | 6·4 | 13·9 | 11·2 |
| 20 | 12 05·0 | 12 07·0 | 11 32·0 | 2·0 | 1·6 | 8·0 | 6·5 | 14·0 | 11·3 |
| 21 | 12 05·3 | 12 07·2 | 11 32·2 | 2·1 | 1·7 | 8·1 | 6·5 | 14·1 | 11·4 |
| 22 | 12 05·5 | 12 07·5 | 11 32·4 | 2·2 | 1·8 | 8·2 | 6·6 | 14·2 | 11·5 |
| 23 | 12 05·8 | 12 07·7 | 11 32·7 | 2·3 | 1·9 | 8·3 | 6·7 | 14·3 | 11·6 |
| 24 | 12 06·0 | 12 08·0 | 11 32·9 | 2·4 | 1·9 | 8·4 | 6·8 | 14·4 | 11·6 |
| 25 | 12 06·3 | 12 08·2 | 11 33·2 | 2·5 | 2·0 | 8·5 | 6·9 | 14·5 | 11·7 |
| 26 | 12 06·5 | 12 08·5 | 11 33·4 | 2·6 | 2·1 | 8·6 | 7·0 | 14·6 | 11·8 |
| 27 | 12 06·8 | 12 08·7 | 11 33·6 | 2·7 | 2·2 | 8·7 | 7·0 | 14·7 | 11·9 |
| 28 | 12 07·0 | 12 09·0 | 11 33·9 | 2·8 | 2·3 | 8·8 | 7·1 | 14·8 | 12·0 |
| 29 | 12 07·3 | 12 09·2 | 11 34·1 | 2·9 | 2·3 | 8·9 | 7·2 | 14·9 | 12·0 |
| 30 | 12 07·5 | 12 09·5 | 11 34·4 | 3·0 | 2·4 | 9·0 | 7·3 | 15·0 | 12·1 |
| 31 | 12 07·8 | 12 09·7 | 11 34·6 | 3·1 | 2·5 | 9·1 | 7·4 | 15·1 | 12·2 |
| 32 | 12 08·0 | 12 10·0 | 11 34·8 | 3·2 | 2·6 | 9·2 | 7·4 | 15·2 | 12·3 |
| 33 | 12 08·3 | 12 10·2 | 11 35·1 | 3·3 | 2·7 | 9·3 | 7·5 | 15·3 | 12·4 |
| 34 | 12 08·5 | 12 10·5 | 11 35·3 | 3·4 | 2·7 | 9·4 | 7·6 | 15·4 | 12·4 |
| 35 | 12 08·8 | 12 10·7 | 11 35·6 | 3·5 | 2·8 | 9·5 | 7·7 | 15·5 | 12·5 |
| 36 | 12 09·0 | 12 11·0 | 11 35·8 | 3·6 | 2·9 | 9·6 | 7·8 | 15·6 | 12·6 |
| 37 | 12 09·3 | 12 11·2 | 11 36·0 | 3·7 | 3·0 | 9·7 | 7·8 | 15·7 | 12·7 |
| 38 | 12 09·5 | 12 11·5 | 11 36·3 | 3·8 | 3·1 | 9·8 | 7·9 | 15·8 | 12·8 |
| 39 | 12 09·8 | 12 11·7 | 11 36·5 | 3·9 | 3·2 | 9·9 | 8·0 | 15·9 | 12·9 |
| 40 | 12 10·0 | 12 12·0 | 11 36·7 | 4·0 | 3·2 | 10·0 | 8·1 | 16·0 | 12·9 |
| 41 | 12 10·3 | 12 12·2 | 11 37·0 | 4·1 | 3·3 | 10·1 | 8·2 | 16·1 | 13·0 |
| 42 | 12 10·5 | 12 12·5 | 11 37·2 | 4·2 | 3·4 | 10·2 | 8·2 | 16·2 | 13·1 |
| 43 | 12 10·8 | 12 12·8 | 11 37·5 | 4·3 | 3·5 | 10·3 | 8·3 | 16·3 | 13·2 |
| 44 | 12 11·0 | 12 13·0 | 11 37·7 | 4·4 | 3·6 | 10·4 | 8·4 | 16·4 | 13·3 |
| 45 | 12 11·3 | 12 13·3 | 11 37·9 | 4·5 | 3·6 | 10·5 | 8·5 | 16·5 | 13·3 |
| 46 | 12 11·5 | 12 13·5 | 11 38·2 | 4·6 | 3·7 | 10·6 | 8·6 | 16·6 | 13·4 |
| 47 | 12 11·8 | 12 13·8 | 11 38·4 | 4·7 | 3·8 | 10·7 | 8·6 | 16·7 | 13·5 |
| 48 | 12 12·0 | 12 14·0 | 11 38·7 | 4·8 | 3·9 | 10·8 | 8·7 | 16·8 | 13·6 |
| 49 | 12 12·3 | 12 14·3 | 11 38·9 | 4·9 | 4·0 | 10·9 | 8·8 | 16·9 | 13·7 |
| 50 | 12 12·5 | 12 14·5 | 11 39·1 | 5·0 | 4·0 | 11·0 | 8·9 | 17·0 | 13·7 |
| 51 | 12 12·8 | 12 14·8 | 11 39·4 | 5·1 | 4·1 | 11·1 | 9·0 | 17·1 | 13·8 |
| 52 | 12 13·0 | 12 15·0 | 11 39·6 | 5·2 | 4·2 | 11·2 | 9·1 | 17·2 | 13·9 |
| 53 | 12 13·3 | 12 15·3 | 11 39·8 | 5·3 | 4·3 | 11·3 | 9·1 | 17·3 | 14·0 |
| 54 | 12 13·5 | 12 15·5 | 11 40·1 | 5·4 | 4·4 | 11·4 | 9·2 | 17·4 | 14·1 |
| 55 | 12 13·8 | 12 15·8 | 11 40·3 | 5·5 | 4·4 | 11·5 | 9·3 | 17·5 | 14·1 |
| 56 | 12 14·0 | 12 16·0 | 11 40·6 | 5·6 | 4·5 | 11·6 | 9·4 | 17·6 | 14·2 |
| 57 | 12 14·3 | 12 16·3 | 11 40·8 | 5·7 | 4·6 | 11·7 | 9·5 | 17·7 | 14·3 |
| 58 | 12 14·5 | 12 16·5 | 11 41·0 | 5·8 | 4·7 | 11·8 | 9·5 | 17·8 | 14·4 |
| 59 | 12 14·8 | 12 16·8 | 11 41·3 | 5·9 | 4·8 | 11·9 | 9·6 | 17·9 | 14·5 |
| 60 | 12 15·0 | 12 17·0 | 11 41·5 | 6·0 | 4·9 | 12·0 | 9·7 | 18·0 | 14·6 |

| 49m | SUN PLANETS | ARIES | MOON | v or d | Corrn | v or d | Corrn | v or d | Corrn |
|---|---|---|---|---|---|---|---|---|---|
| s | ° ′ | ° ′ | ° ′ | ′ | ′ | ′ | ′ | ′ | ′ |
| 00 | 12 15·0 | 12 17·0 | 11 41·5 | 0·0 | 0·0 | 6·0 | 5·0 | 12·0 | 9·9 |
| 01 | 12 15·3 | 12 17·3 | 11 41·8 | 0·1 | 0·1 | 6·1 | 5·0 | 12·1 | 10·0 |
| 02 | 12 15·5 | 12 17·5 | 11 42·0 | 0·2 | 0·2 | 6·2 | 5·1 | 12·2 | 10·1 |
| 03 | 12 15·8 | 12 17·8 | 11 42·2 | 0·3 | 0·2 | 6·3 | 5·2 | 12·3 | 10·1 |
| 04 | 12 16·0 | 12 18·0 | 11 42·5 | 0·4 | 0·3 | 6·4 | 5·3 | 12·4 | 10·2 |
| 05 | 12 16·3 | 12 18·3 | 11 42·7 | 0·5 | 0·4 | 6·5 | 5·4 | 12·5 | 10·3 |
| 06 | 12 16·5 | 12 18·5 | 11 42·9 | 0·6 | 0·5 | 6·6 | 5·4 | 12·6 | 10·4 |
| 07 | 12 16·8 | 12 18·8 | 11 43·2 | 0·7 | 0·6 | 6·7 | 5·5 | 12·7 | 10·5 |
| 08 | 12 17·0 | 12 19·0 | 11 43·4 | 0·8 | 0·7 | 6·8 | 5·6 | 12·8 | 10·6 |
| 09 | 12 17·3 | 12 19·3 | 11 43·7 | 0·9 | 0·7 | 6·9 | 5·7 | 12·9 | 10·6 |
| 10 | 12 17·5 | 12 19·5 | 11 43·9 | 1·0 | 0·8 | 7·0 | 5·8 | 13·0 | 10·7 |
| 11 | 12 17·8 | 12 19·8 | 11 44·1 | 1·1 | 0·9 | 7·1 | 5·9 | 13·1 | 10·8 |
| 12 | 12 18·0 | 12 20·0 | 11 44·4 | 1·2 | 1·0 | 7·2 | 5·9 | 13·2 | 10·9 |
| 13 | 12 18·3 | 12 20·3 | 11 44·6 | 1·3 | 1·1 | 7·3 | 6·0 | 13·3 | 11·0 |
| 14 | 12 18·5 | 12 20·5 | 11 44·9 | 1·4 | 1·2 | 7·4 | 6·1 | 13·4 | 11·1 |
| 15 | 12 18·8 | 12 20·8 | 11 45·1 | 1·5 | 1·2 | 7·5 | 6·2 | 13·5 | 11·1 |
| 16 | 12 19·0 | 12 21·0 | 11 45·3 | 1·6 | 1·3 | 7·6 | 6·3 | 13·6 | 11·2 |
| 17 | 12 19·3 | 12 21·3 | 11 45·6 | 1·7 | 1·4 | 7·7 | 6·4 | 13·7 | 11·3 |
| 18 | 12 19·5 | 12 21·5 | 11 45·8 | 1·8 | 1·5 | 7·8 | 6·4 | 13·8 | 11·4 |
| 19 | 12 19·8 | 12 21·8 | 11 46·1 | 1·9 | 1·6 | 7·9 | 6·5 | 13·9 | 11·5 |
| 20 | 12 20·0 | 12 22·0 | 11 46·3 | 2·0 | 1·7 | 8·0 | 6·6 | 14·0 | 11·6 |
| 21 | 12 20·3 | 12 22·3 | 11 46·5 | 2·1 | 1·7 | 8·1 | 6·7 | 14·1 | 11·6 |
| 22 | 12 20·5 | 12 22·5 | 11 46·8 | 2·2 | 1·8 | 8·2 | 6·8 | 14·2 | 11·7 |
| 23 | 12 20·8 | 12 22·8 | 11 47·0 | 2·3 | 1·9 | 8·3 | 6·8 | 14·3 | 11·8 |
| 24 | 12 21·0 | 12 23·0 | 11 47·2 | 2·4 | 2·0 | 8·4 | 6·9 | 14·4 | 11·9 |
| 25 | 12 21·3 | 12 23·3 | 11 47·5 | 2·5 | 2·1 | 8·5 | 7·0 | 14·5 | 12·0 |
| 26 | 12 21·5 | 12 23·5 | 11 47·7 | 2·6 | 2·1 | 8·6 | 7·1 | 14·6 | 12·0 |
| 27 | 12 21·8 | 12 23·8 | 11 48·0 | 2·7 | 2·2 | 8·7 | 7·2 | 14·7 | 12·1 |
| 28 | 12 22·0 | 12 24·0 | 11 48·2 | 2·8 | 2·3 | 8·8 | 7·3 | 14·8 | 12·2 |
| 29 | 12 22·3 | 12 24·3 | 11 48·4 | 2·9 | 2·4 | 8·9 | 7·3 | 14·9 | 12·3 |
| 30 | 12 22·5 | 12 24·5 | 11 48·7 | 3·0 | 2·5 | 9·0 | 7·4 | 15·0 | 12·4 |
| 31 | 12 22·8 | 12 24·8 | 11 48·9 | 3·1 | 2·6 | 9·1 | 7·5 | 15·1 | 12·5 |
| 32 | 12 23·0 | 12 25·0 | 11 49·2 | 3·2 | 2·6 | 9·2 | 7·6 | 15·2 | 12·5 |
| 33 | 12 23·3 | 12 25·3 | 11 49·4 | 3·3 | 2·7 | 9·3 | 7·7 | 15·3 | 12·6 |
| 34 | 12 23·5 | 12 25·5 | 11 49·6 | 3·4 | 2·8 | 9·4 | 7·8 | 15·4 | 12·7 |
| 35 | 12 23·8 | 12 25·8 | 11 49·9 | 3·5 | 2·9 | 9·5 | 7·8 | 15·5 | 12·8 |
| 36 | 12 24·0 | 12 26·0 | 11 50·1 | 3·6 | 3·0 | 9·6 | 7·9 | 15·6 | 12·9 |
| 37 | 12 24·3 | 12 26·3 | 11 50·3 | 3·7 | 3·1 | 9·7 | 8·0 | 15·7 | 13·0 |
| 38 | 12 24·5 | 12 26·5 | 11 50·6 | 3·8 | 3·1 | 9·8 | 8·1 | 15·8 | 13·0 |
| 39 | 12 24·8 | 12 26·8 | 11 50·8 | 3·9 | 3·2 | 9·9 | 8·2 | 15·9 | 13·1 |
| 40 | 12 25·0 | 12 27·0 | 11 51·1 | 4·0 | 3·3 | 10·0 | 8·3 | 16·0 | 13·2 |
| 41 | 12 25·3 | 12 27·3 | 11 51·3 | 4·1 | 3·4 | 10·1 | 8·3 | 16·1 | 13·3 |
| 42 | 12 25·5 | 12 27·5 | 11 51·5 | 4·2 | 3·5 | 10·2 | 8·4 | 16·2 | 13·4 |
| 43 | 12 25·8 | 12 27·8 | 11 51·8 | 4·3 | 3·5 | 10·3 | 8·5 | 16·3 | 13·4 |
| 44 | 12 26·0 | 12 28·0 | 11 52·0 | 4·4 | 3·6 | 10·4 | 8·6 | 16·4 | 13·5 |
| 45 | 12 26·3 | 12 28·3 | 11 52·3 | 4·5 | 3·7 | 10·5 | 8·7 | 16·5 | 13·6 |
| 46 | 12 26·5 | 12 28·5 | 11 52·5 | 4·6 | 3·8 | 10·6 | 8·7 | 16·6 | 13·7 |
| 47 | 12 26·8 | 12 28·8 | 11 52·7 | 4·7 | 3·9 | 10·7 | 8·8 | 16·7 | 13·8 |
| 48 | 12 27·0 | 12 29·0 | 11 53·0 | 4·8 | 4·0 | 10·8 | 8·9 | 16·8 | 13·9 |
| 49 | 12 27·3 | 12 29·3 | 11 53·2 | 4·9 | 4·0 | 10·9 | 9·0 | 16·9 | 13·9 |
| 50 | 12 27·5 | 12 29·5 | 11 53·4 | 5·0 | 4·1 | 11·0 | 9·1 | 17·0 | 14·0 |
| 51 | 12 27·8 | 12 29·8 | 11 53·7 | 5·1 | 4·2 | 11·1 | 9·2 | 17·1 | 14·1 |
| 52 | 12 28·0 | 12 30·0 | 11 53·9 | 5·2 | 4·3 | 11·2 | 9·2 | 17·2 | 14·2 |
| 53 | 12 28·3 | 12 30·3 | 11 54·2 | 5·3 | 4·4 | 11·3 | 9·3 | 17·3 | 14·3 |
| 54 | 12 28·5 | 12 30·5 | 11 54·4 | 5·4 | 4·5 | 11·4 | 9·4 | 17·4 | 14·4 |
| 55 | 12 28·8 | 12 30·8 | 11 54·6 | 5·5 | 4·5 | 11·5 | 9·5 | 17·5 | 14·4 |
| 56 | 12 29·0 | 12 31·1 | 11 54·9 | 5·6 | 4·6 | 11·6 | 9·6 | 17·6 | 14·5 |
| 57 | 12 29·3 | 12 31·3 | 11 55·1 | 5·7 | 4·7 | 11·7 | 9·7 | 17·7 | 14·6 |
| 58 | 12 29·5 | 12 31·6 | 11 55·4 | 5·8 | 4·8 | 11·8 | 9·7 | 17·8 | 14·7 |
| 59 | 12 29·8 | 12 31·8 | 11 55·6 | 5·9 | 4·9 | 11·9 | 9·8 | 17·9 | 14·8 |
| 60 | 12 30·0 | 12 32·1 | 11 55·8 | 6·0 | 5·0 | 12·0 | 9·9 | 18·0 | 14·9 |



| 50m | SUN PLANETS | ARIES | MOON | v or d | Corrn | v or d | Corrn | v or d | Corrn |
|---|---|---|---|---|---|---|---|---|---|
| s | ° ′ | ° ′ | ° ′ | ′ | ′ | ′ | ′ | ′ | ′ |
| 00 | 12 30·0 | 12 32·1 | 11 55·8 | 0·0 | 0·0 | 6·0 | 5·1 | 12·0 | 10·1 |
| 01 | 12 30·3 | 12 32·3 | 11 56·1 | 0·1 | 0·1 | 6·1 | 5·1 | 12·1 | 10·2 |
| 02 | 12 30·5 | 12 32·6 | 11 56·3 | 0·2 | 0·2 | 6·2 | 5·2 | 12·2 | 10·3 |
| 03 | 12 30·8 | 12 32·8 | 11 56·5 | 0·3 | 0·3 | 6·3 | 5·3 | 12·3 | 10·4 |
| 04 | 12 31·0 | 12 33·1 | 11 56·8 | 0·4 | 0·3 | 6·4 | 5·4 | 12·4 | 10·4 |
| 05 | 12 31·3 | 12 33·3 | 11 57·0 | 0·5 | 0·4 | 6·5 | 5·5 | 12·5 | 10·5 |
| 06 | 12 31·5 | 12 33·6 | 11 57·3 | 0·6 | 0·5 | 6·6 | 5·6 | 12·6 | 10·6 |
| 07 | 12 31·8 | 12 33·8 | 11 57·5 | 0·7 | 0·6 | 6·7 | 5·6 | 12·7 | 10·7 |
| 08 | 12 32·0 | 12 34·1 | 11 57·7 | 0·8 | 0·7 | 6·8 | 5·7 | 12·8 | 10·8 |
| 09 | 12 32·3 | 12 34·3 | 11 58·0 | 0·9 | 0·8 | 6·9 | 5·8 | 12·9 | 10·9 |
| 10 | 12 32·5 | 12 34·6 | 11 58·2 | 1·0 | 0·8 | 7·0 | 5·9 | 13·0 | 10·9 |
| 11 | 12 32·8 | 12 34·8 | 11 58·5 | 1·1 | 0·9 | 7·1 | 6·0 | 13·1 | 11·0 |
| 12 | 12 33·0 | 12 35·1 | 11 58·7 | 1·2 | 1·0 | 7·2 | 6·1 | 13·2 | 11·1 |
| 13 | 12 33·3 | 12 35·3 | 11 58·9 | 1·3 | 1·1 | 7·3 | 6·1 | 13·3 | 11·2 |
| 14 | 12 33·5 | 12 35·6 | 11 59·2 | 1·4 | 1·2 | 7·4 | 6·2 | 13·4 | 11·3 |
| 15 | 12 33·8 | 12 35·8 | 11 59·4 | 1·5 | 1·3 | 7·5 | 6·3 | 13·5 | 11·4 |
| 16 | 12 34·0 | 12 36·1 | 11 59·7 | 1·6 | 1·3 | 7·6 | 6·4 | 13·6 | 11·4 |
| 17 | 12 34·3 | 12 36·3 | 11 59·9 | 1·7 | 1·4 | 7·7 | 6·5 | 13·7 | 11·5 |
| 18 | 12 34·5 | 12 36·6 | 12 00·1 | 1·8 | 1·5 | 7·8 | 6·6 | 13·8 | 11·6 |
| 19 | 12 34·8 | 12 36·8 | 12 00·4 | 1·9 | 1·6 | 7·9 | 6·6 | 13·9 | 11·7 |
| 20 | 12 35·0 | 12 37·1 | 12 00·6 | 2·0 | 1·7 | 8·0 | 6·7 | 14·0 | 11·8 |
| 21 | 12 35·3 | 12 37·3 | 12 00·8 | 2·1 | 1·8 | 8·1 | 6·8 | 14·1 | 11·9 |
| 22 | 12 35·5 | 12 37·6 | 12 01·1 | 2·2 | 1·9 | 8·2 | 6·9 | 14·2 | 12·0 |
| 23 | 12 35·8 | 12 37·8 | 12 01·3 | 2·3 | 1·9 | 8·3 | 7·0 | 14·3 | 12·0 |
| 24 | 12 36·0 | 12 38·1 | 12 01·6 | 2·4 | 2·0 | 8·4 | 7·1 | 14·4 | 12·1 |
| 25 | 12 36·3 | 12 38·3 | 12 01·8 | 2·5 | 2·1 | 8·5 | 7·2 | 14·5 | 12·2 |
| 26 | 12 36·5 | 12 38·6 | 12 02·0 | 2·6 | 2·2 | 8·6 | 7·2 | 14·6 | 12·3 |
| 27 | 12 36·8 | 12 38·8 | 12 02·3 | 2·7 | 2·3 | 8·7 | 7·3 | 14·7 | 12·4 |
| 28 | 12 37·0 | 12 39·1 | 12 02·5 | 2·8 | 2·4 | 8·8 | 7·4 | 14·8 | 12·5 |
| 29 | 12 37·3 | 12 39·3 | 12 02·8 | 2·9 | 2·4 | 8·9 | 7·5 | 14·9 | 12·5 |
| 30 | 12 37·5 | 12 39·6 | 12 03·0 | 3·0 | 2·5 | 9·0 | 7·6 | 15·0 | 12·6 |
| 31 | 12 37·8 | 12 39·8 | 12 03·2 | 3·1 | 2·6 | 9·1 | 7·7 | 15·1 | 12·7 |
| 32 | 12 38·0 | 12 40·1 | 12 03·5 | 3·2 | 2·7 | 9·2 | 7·7 | 15·2 | 12·8 |
| 33 | 12 38·3 | 12 40·3 | 12 03·7 | 3·3 | 2·8 | 9·3 | 7·8 | 15·3 | 12·9 |
| 34 | 12 38·5 | 12 40·6 | 12 03·9 | 3·4 | 2·9 | 9·4 | 7·9 | 15·4 | 13·0 |
| 35 | 12 38·8 | 12 40·8 | 12 04·2 | 3·5 | 2·9 | 9·5 | 8·0 | 15·5 | 13·0 |
| 36 | 12 39·0 | 12 41·1 | 12 04·4 | 3·6 | 3·0 | 9·6 | 8·1 | 15·6 | 13·1 |
| 37 | 12 39·3 | 12 41·3 | 12 04·7 | 3·7 | 3·1 | 9·7 | 8·2 | 15·7 | 13·2 |
| 38 | 12 39·5 | 12 41·6 | 12 04·9 | 3·8 | 3·2 | 9·8 | 8·2 | 15·8 | 13·3 |
| 39 | 12 39·8 | 12 41·8 | 12 05·1 | 3·9 | 3·3 | 9·9 | 8·3 | 15·9 | 13·4 |
| 40 | 12 40·0 | 12 42·1 | 12 05·4 | 4·0 | 3·4 | 10·0 | 8·4 | 16·0 | 13·5 |
| 41 | 12 40·3 | 12 42·3 | 12 05·6 | 4·1 | 3·5 | 10·1 | 8·5 | 16·1 | 13·6 |
| 42 | 12 40·5 | 12 42·6 | 12 05·9 | 4·2 | 3·5 | 10·2 | 8·6 | 16·2 | 13·6 |
| 43 | 12 40·8 | 12 42·8 | 12 06·1 | 4·3 | 3·6 | 10·3 | 8·7 | 16·3 | 13·7 |
| 44 | 12 41·0 | 12 43·1 | 12 06·3 | 4·4 | 3·7 | 10·4 | 8·8 | 16·4 | 13·8 |
| 45 | 12 41·3 | 12 43·3 | 12 06·6 | 4·5 | 3·8 | 10·5 | 8·8 | 16·5 | 13·9 |
| 46 | 12 41·5 | 12 43·6 | 12 06·8 | 4·6 | 3·9 | 10·6 | 8·9 | 16·6 | 14·0 |
| 47 | 12 41·8 | 12 43·8 | 12 07·0 | 4·7 | 4·0 | 10·7 | 9·0 | 16·7 | 14·1 |
| 48 | 12 42·0 | 12 44·1 | 12 07·3 | 4·8 | 4·0 | 10·8 | 9·1 | 16·8 | 14·1 |
| 49 | 12 42·3 | 12 44·3 | 12 07·5 | 4·9 | 4·1 | 10·9 | 9·2 | 16·9 | 14·2 |
| 50 | 12 42·5 | 12 44·6 | 12 07·8 | 5·0 | 4·2 | 11·0 | 9·3 | 17·0 | 14·3 |
| 51 | 12 42·8 | 12 44·8 | 12 08·0 | 5·1 | 4·3 | 11·1 | 9·3 | 17·1 | 14·4 |
| 52 | 12 43·0 | 12 45·1 | 12 08·2 | 5·2 | 4·4 | 11·2 | 9·4 | 17·2 | 14·5 |
| 53 | 12 43·3 | 12 45·3 | 12 08·5 | 5·3 | 4·5 | 11·3 | 9·5 | 17·3 | 14·6 |
| 54 | 12 43·5 | 12 45·6 | 12 08·7 | 5·4 | 4·5 | 11·4 | 9·6 | 17·4 | 14·6 |
| 55 | 12 43·8 | 12 45·8 | 12 09·0 | 5·5 | 4·6 | 11·5 | 9·7 | 17·5 | 14·7 |
| 56 | 12 44·0 | 12 46·1 | 12 09·2 | 5·6 | 4·7 | 11·6 | 9·8 | 17·6 | 14·8 |
| 57 | 12 44·3 | 12 46·3 | 12 09·4 | 5·7 | 4·8 | 11·7 | 9·8 | 17·7 | 14·9 |
| 58 | 12 44·5 | 12 46·6 | 12 09·7 | 5·8 | 4·9 | 11·8 | 9·9 | 17·8 | 15·0 |
| 59 | 12 44·8 | 12 46·8 | 12 09·9 | 5·9 | 5·0 | 11·9 | 10·0 | 17·9 | 15·1 |
| 60 | 12 45·0 | 12 47·1 | 12 10·2 | 6·0 | 5·1 | 12·0 | 10·1 | 18·0 | 15·2 |

| 51m | SUN PLANETS | ARIES | MOON | v or d | Corrn | v or d | Corrn | v or d | Corrn |
|---|---|---|---|---|---|---|---|---|---|
| s | ° ′ | ° ′ | ° ′ | ′ | ′ | ′ | ′ | ′ | ′ |
| 00 | 12 45·0 | 12 47·1 | 12 10·2 | 0·0 | 0·0 | 6·0 | 5·2 | 12·0 | 10·3 |
| 01 | 12 45·3 | 12 47·3 | 12 10·4 | 0·1 | 0·1 | 6·1 | 5·2 | 12·1 | 10·4 |
| 02 | 12 45·5 | 12 47·6 | 12 10·6 | 0·2 | 0·2 | 6·2 | 5·3 | 12·2 | 10·5 |
| 03 | 12 45·8 | 12 47·8 | 12 10·9 | 0·3 | 0·3 | 6·3 | 5·4 | 12·3 | 10·6 |
| 04 | 12 46·0 | 12 48·1 | 12 11·1 | 0·4 | 0·3 | 6·4 | 5·5 | 12·4 | 10·6 |
| 05 | 12 46·3 | 12 48·3 | 12 11·3 | 0·5 | 0·4 | 6·5 | 5·6 | 12·5 | 10·7 |
| 06 | 12 46·5 | 12 48·6 | 12 11·6 | 0·6 | 0·5 | 6·6 | 5·7 | 12·6 | 10·8 |
| 07 | 12 46·8 | 12 48·8 | 12 11·8 | 0·7 | 0·6 | 6·7 | 5·8 | 12·7 | 10·9 |
| 08 | 12 47·0 | 12 49·1 | 12 12·1 | 0·8 | 0·7 | 6·8 | 5·8 | 12·8 | 11·0 |
| 09 | 12 47·3 | 12 49·4 | 12 12·3 | 0·9 | 0·8 | 6·9 | 5·9 | 12·9 | 11·1 |
| 10 | 12 47·5 | 12 49·6 | 12 12·5 | 1·0 | 0·9 | 7·0 | 6·0 | 13·0 | 11·2 |
| 11 | 12 47·8 | 12 49·9 | 12 12·8 | 1·1 | 0·9 | 7·1 | 6·1 | 13·1 | 11·2 |
| 12 | 12 48·0 | 12 50·1 | 12 13·0 | 1·2 | 1·0 | 7·2 | 6·2 | 13·2 | 11·3 |
| 13 | 12 48·3 | 12 50·4 | 12 13·3 | 1·3 | 1·1 | 7·3 | 6·3 | 13·3 | 11·4 |
| 14 | 12 48·5 | 12 50·6 | 12 13·5 | 1·4 | 1·2 | 7·4 | 6·4 | 13·4 | 11·5 |
| 15 | 12 48·8 | 12 50·9 | 12 13·7 | 1·5 | 1·3 | 7·5 | 6·4 | 13·5 | 11·6 |
| 16 | 12 49·0 | 12 51·1 | 12 14·0 | 1·6 | 1·4 | 7·6 | 6·5 | 13·6 | 11·7 |
| 17 | 12 49·3 | 12 51·4 | 12 14·2 | 1·7 | 1·5 | 7·7 | 6·6 | 13·7 | 11·8 |
| 18 | 12 49·5 | 12 51·6 | 12 14·4 | 1·8 | 1·5 | 7·8 | 6·7 | 13·8 | 11·8 |
| 19 | 12 49·8 | 12 51·9 | 12 14·7 | 1·9 | 1·6 | 7·9 | 6·8 | 13·9 | 11·9 |
| 20 | 12 50·0 | 12 52·1 | 12 14·9 | 2·0 | 1·7 | 8·0 | 6·9 | 14·0 | 12·0 |
| 21 | 12 50·3 | 12 52·4 | 12 15·2 | 2·1 | 1·8 | 8·1 | 7·0 | 14·1 | 12·1 |
| 22 | 12 50·5 | 12 52·6 | 12 15·4 | 2·2 | 1·9 | 8·2 | 7·0 | 14·2 | 12·2 |
| 23 | 12 50·8 | 12 52·9 | 12 15·6 | 2·3 | 2·0 | 8·3 | 7·1 | 14·3 | 12·3 |
| 24 | 12 51·0 | 12 53·1 | 12 15·9 | 2·4 | 2·1 | 8·4 | 7·2 | 14·4 | 12·4 |
| 25 | 12 51·3 | 12 53·4 | 12 16·1 | 2·5 | 2·1 | 8·5 | 7·3 | 14·5 | 12·4 |
| 26 | 12 51·5 | 12 53·6 | 12 16·4 | 2·6 | 2·2 | 8·6 | 7·4 | 14·6 | 12·5 |
| 27 | 12 51·8 | 12 53·9 | 12 16·6 | 2·7 | 2·3 | 8·7 | 7·5 | 14·7 | 12·6 |
| 28 | 12 52·0 | 12 54·1 | 12 16·8 | 2·8 | 2·4 | 8·8 | 7·6 | 14·8 | 12·7 |
| 29 | 12 52·3 | 12 54·4 | 12 17·1 | 2·9 | 2·5 | 8·9 | 7·6 | 14·9 | 12·8 |
| 30 | 12 52·5 | 12 54·6 | 12 17·3 | 3·0 | 2·6 | 9·0 | 7·7 | 15·0 | 12·9 |
| 31 | 12 52·8 | 12 54·9 | 12 17·5 | 3·1 | 2·7 | 9·1 | 7·8 | 15·1 | 13·0 |
| 32 | 12 53·0 | 12 55·1 | 12 17·8 | 3·2 | 2·7 | 9·2 | 7·9 | 15·2 | 13·0 |
| 33 | 12 53·3 | 12 55·4 | 12 18·0 | 3·3 | 2·8 | 9·3 | 8·0 | 15·3 | 13·1 |
| 34 | 12 53·5 | 12 55·6 | 12 18·3 | 3·4 | 2·9 | 9·4 | 8·1 | 15·4 | 13·2 |
| 35 | 12 53·8 | 12 55·9 | 12 18·5 | 3·5 | 3·0 | 9·5 | 8·2 | 15·5 | 13·3 |
| 36 | 12 54·0 | 12 56·1 | 12 18·7 | 3·6 | 3·1 | 9·6 | 8·2 | 15·6 | 13·4 |
| 37 | 12 54·3 | 12 56·4 | 12 19·0 | 3·7 | 3·2 | 9·7 | 8·3 | 15·7 | 13·5 |
| 38 | 12 54·5 | 12 56·6 | 12 19·2 | 3·8 | 3·3 | 9·8 | 8·4 | 15·8 | 13·6 |
| 39 | 12 54·8 | 12 56·9 | 12 19·5 | 3·9 | 3·3 | 9·9 | 8·5 | 15·9 | 13·6 |
| 40 | 12 55·0 | 12 57·1 | 12 19·7 | 4·0 | 3·4 | 10·0 | 8·6 | 16·0 | 13·7 |
| 41 | 12 55·3 | 12 57·4 | 12 19·9 | 4·1 | 3·5 | 10·1 | 8·7 | 16·1 | 13·8 |
| 42 | 12 55·5 | 12 57·6 | 12 20·2 | 4·2 | 3·6 | 10·2 | 8·8 | 16·2 | 13·9 |
| 43 | 12 55·8 | 12 57·9 | 12 20·4 | 4·3 | 3·7 | 10·3 | 8·8 | 16·3 | 14·0 |
| 44 | 12 56·0 | 12 58·1 | 12 20·6 | 4·4 | 3·8 | 10·4 | 8·9 | 16·4 | 14·1 |
| 45 | 12 56·3 | 12 58·4 | 12 20·9 | 4·5 | 3·9 | 10·5 | 9·0 | 16·5 | 14·2 |
| 46 | 12 56·5 | 12 58·6 | 12 21·1 | 4·6 | 3·9 | 10·6 | 9·1 | 16·6 | 14·2 |
| 47 | 12 56·8 | 12 58·9 | 12 21·4 | 4·7 | 4·0 | 10·7 | 9·2 | 16·7 | 14·3 |
| 48 | 12 57·0 | 12 59·1 | 12 21·6 | 4·8 | 4·1 | 10·8 | 9·3 | 16·8 | 14·4 |
| 49 | 12 57·3 | 12 59·4 | 12 21·8 | 4·9 | 4·2 | 10·9 | 9·4 | 16·9 | 14·5 |
| 50 | 12 57·5 | 12 59·6 | 12 22·1 | 5·0 | 4·3 | 11·0 | 9·4 | 17·0 | 14·6 |
| 51 | 12 57·8 | 12 59·9 | 12 22·3 | 5·1 | 4·4 | 11·1 | 9·5 | 17·1 | 14·7 |
| 52 | 12 58·0 | 13 00·1 | 12 22·6 | 5·2 | 4·5 | 11·2 | 9·6 | 17·2 | 14·8 |
| 53 | 12 58·3 | 13 00·4 | 12 22·8 | 5·3 | 4·5 | 11·3 | 9·7 | 17·3 | 14·8 |
| 54 | 12 58·5 | 13 00·6 | 12 23·0 | 5·4 | 4·6 | 11·4 | 9·8 | 17·4 | 14·9 |
| 55 | 12 58·8 | 13 00·9 | 12 23·3 | 5·5 | 4·7 | 11·5 | 9·9 | 17·5 | 15·0 |
| 56 | 12 59·0 | 13 01·1 | 12 23·5 | 5·6 | 4·8 | 11·6 | 10·0 | 17·6 | 15·1 |
| 57 | 12 59·3 | 13 01·4 | 12 23·8 | 5·7 | 4·9 | 11·7 | 10·0 | 17·7 | 15·2 |
| 58 | 12 59·5 | 13 01·6 | 12 24·0 | 5·8 | 5·0 | 11·8 | 10·1 | 17·8 | 15·3 |
| 59 | 12 59·8 | 13 01·9 | 12 24·2 | 5·9 | 5·1 | 11·9 | 10·2 | 17·9 | 15·4 |
| 60 | 13 00·0 | 13 02·1 | 12 24·5 | 6·0 | 5·2 | 12·0 | 10·3 | 18·0 | 15·5 |

| 52$^{m}$ | SUN PLANETS | ARIES | MOON | v or d | Corrⁿ | v or d | Corrⁿ | v or d | Corrⁿ |
|---|---|---|---|---|---|---|---|---|---|
| s | ° ′ | ° ′ | ° ′ | ′ | ′ | ′ | ′ | ′ | ′ |
| 00 | 13 00·0 | 13 02·1 | 12 24·5 | 0·0 | 0·0 | 6·0 | 5·3 | 12·0 | 10·5 |
| 01 | 13 00·3 | 13 02·4 | 12 24·7 | 0·1 | 0·1 | 6·1 | 5·3 | 12·1 | 10·6 |
| 02 | 13 00·5 | 13 02·6 | 12 24·9 | 0·2 | 0·2 | 6·2 | 5·4 | 12·2 | 10·7 |
| 03 | 13 00·8 | 13 02·9 | 12 25·2 | 0·3 | 0·3 | 6·3 | 5·5 | 12·3 | 10·8 |
| 04 | 13 01·0 | 13 03·1 | 12 25·4 | 0·4 | 0·4 | 6·4 | 5·6 | 12·4 | 10·9 |
| 05 | 13 01·3 | 13 03·4 | 12 25·7 | 0·5 | 0·4 | 6·5 | 5·7 | 12·5 | 10·9 |
| 06 | 13 01·5 | 13 03·6 | 12 25·9 | 0·6 | 0·5 | 6·6 | 5·8 | 12·6 | 11·0 |
| 07 | 13 01·8 | 13 03·9 | 12 26·1 | 0·7 | 0·6 | 6·7 | 5·9 | 12·7 | 11·1 |
| 08 | 13 02·0 | 13 04·1 | 12 26·4 | 0·8 | 0·7 | 6·8 | 6·0 | 12·8 | 11·2 |
| 09 | 13 02·3 | 13 04·4 | 12 26·6 | 0·9 | 0·8 | 6·9 | 6·0 | 12·9 | 11·3 |
| 10 | 13 02·5 | 13 04·6 | 12 26·9 | 1·0 | 0·9 | 7·0 | 6·1 | 13·0 | 11·4 |
| 11 | 13 02·8 | 13 04·9 | 12 27·1 | 1·1 | 1·0 | 7·1 | 6·2 | 13·1 | 11·5 |
| 12 | 13 03·0 | 13 05·1 | 12 27·3 | 1·2 | 1·1 | 7·2 | 6·3 | 13·2 | 11·6 |
| 13 | 13 03·3 | 13 05·4 | 12 27·6 | 1·3 | 1·1 | 7·3 | 6·4 | 13·3 | 11·6 |
| 14 | 13 03·5 | 13 05·6 | 12 27·8 | 1·4 | 1·2 | 7·4 | 6·5 | 13·4 | 11·7 |
| 15 | 13 03·8 | 13 05·9 | 12 28·0 | 1·5 | 1·3 | 7·5 | 6·6 | 13·5 | 11·8 |
| 16 | 13 04·0 | 13 06·1 | 12 28·3 | 1·6 | 1·4 | 7·6 | 6·7 | 13·6 | 11·9 |
| 17 | 13 04·3 | 13 06·4 | 12 28·5 | 1·7 | 1·5 | 7·7 | 6·7 | 13·7 | 12·0 |
| 18 | 13 04·5 | 13 06·6 | 12 28·8 | 1·8 | 1·6 | 7·8 | 6·8 | 13·8 | 12·1 |
| 19 | 13 04·8 | 13 06·9 | 12 29·0 | 1·9 | 1·7 | 7·9 | 6·9 | 13·9 | 12·2 |
| 20 | 13 05·0 | 13 07·1 | 12 29·2 | 2·0 | 1·8 | 8·0 | 7·0 | 14·0 | 12·3 |
| 21 | 13 05·3 | 13 07·4 | 12 29·5 | 2·1 | 1·8 | 8·1 | 7·1 | 14·1 | 12·3 |
| 22 | 13 05·5 | 13 07·7 | 12 29·7 | 2·2 | 1·9 | 8·2 | 7·2 | 14·2 | 12·4 |
| 23 | 13 05·8 | 13 07·9 | 12 30·0 | 2·3 | 2·0 | 8·3 | 7·3 | 14·3 | 12·5 |
| 24 | 13 06·0 | 13 08·2 | 12 30·2 | 2·4 | 2·1 | 8·4 | 7·4 | 14·4 | 12·6 |
| 25 | 13 06·3 | 13 08·4 | 12 30·4 | 2·5 | 2·2 | 8·5 | 7·4 | 14·5 | 12·7 |
| 26 | 13 06·5 | 13 08·7 | 12 30·7 | 2·6 | 2·3 | 8·6 | 7·5 | 14·6 | 12·8 |
| 27 | 13 06·8 | 13 08·9 | 12 30·9 | 2·7 | 2·4 | 8·7 | 7·6 | 14·7 | 12·9 |
| 28 | 13 07·0 | 13 09·2 | 12 31·1 | 2·8 | 2·5 | 8·8 | 7·7 | 14·8 | 13·0 |
| 29 | 13 07·3 | 13 09·4 | 12 31·4 | 2·9 | 2·5 | 8·9 | 7·8 | 14·9 | 13·0 |
| 30 | 13 07·5 | 13 09·7 | 12 31·6 | 3·0 | 2·6 | 9·0 | 7·9 | 15·0 | 13·1 |
| 31 | 13 07·8 | 13 09·9 | 12 31·9 | 3·1 | 2·7 | 9·1 | 8·0 | 15·1 | 13·2 |
| 32 | 13 08·0 | 13 10·2 | 12 32·1 | 3·2 | 2·8 | 9·2 | 8·1 | 15·2 | 13·3 |
| 33 | 13 08·3 | 13 10·4 | 12 32·3 | 3·3 | 2·9 | 9·3 | 8·1 | 15·3 | 13·4 |
| 34 | 13 08·5 | 13 10·7 | 12 32·6 | 3·4 | 3·0 | 9·4 | 8·2 | 15·4 | 13·5 |
| 35 | 13 08·8 | 13 10·9 | 12 32·8 | 3·5 | 3·1 | 9·5 | 8·3 | 15·5 | 13·6 |
| 36 | 13 09·0 | 13 11·2 | 12 33·1 | 3·6 | 3·2 | 9·6 | 8·4 | 15·6 | 13·7 |
| 37 | 13 09·3 | 13 11·4 | 12 33·3 | 3·7 | 3·2 | 9·7 | 8·5 | 15·7 | 13·7 |
| 38 | 13 09·5 | 13 11·7 | 12 33·5 | 3·8 | 3·3 | 9·8 | 8·6 | 15·8 | 13·8 |
| 39 | 13 09·8 | 13 11·9 | 12 33·8 | 3·9 | 3·4 | 9·9 | 8·7 | 15·9 | 13·9 |
| 40 | 13 10·0 | 13 12·2 | 12 34·0 | 4·0 | 3·5 | 10·0 | 8·8 | 16·0 | 14·0 |
| 41 | 13 10·3 | 13 12·4 | 12 34·2 | 4·1 | 3·6 | 10·1 | 8·8 | 16·1 | 14·1 |
| 42 | 13 10·5 | 13 12·7 | 12 34·5 | 4·2 | 3·7 | 10·2 | 8·9 | 16·2 | 14·2 |
| 43 | 13 10·8 | 13 12·9 | 12 34·7 | 4·3 | 3·8 | 10·3 | 9·0 | 16·3 | 14·3 |
| 44 | 13 11·0 | 13 13·2 | 12 35·0 | 4·4 | 3·9 | 10·4 | 9·1 | 16·4 | 14·4 |
| 45 | 13 11·3 | 13 13·4 | 12 35·2 | 4·5 | 3·9 | 10·5 | 9·2 | 16·5 | 14·4 |
| 46 | 13 11·5 | 13 13·7 | 12 35·4 | 4·6 | 4·0 | 10·6 | 9·3 | 16·6 | 14·5 |
| 47 | 13 11·8 | 13 13·9 | 12 35·7 | 4·7 | 4·1 | 10·7 | 9·4 | 16·7 | 14·6 |
| 48 | 13 12·0 | 13 14·2 | 12 35·9 | 4·8 | 4·2 | 10·8 | 9·5 | 16·8 | 14·7 |
| 49 | 13 12·3 | 13 14·4 | 12 36·2 | 4·9 | 4·3 | 10·9 | 9·5 | 16·9 | 14·8 |
| 50 | 13 12·5 | 13 14·7 | 12 36·4 | 5·0 | 4·4 | 11·0 | 9·6 | 17·0 | 14·9 |
| 51 | 13 12·8 | 13 14·9 | 12 36·6 | 5·1 | 4·5 | 11·1 | 9·7 | 17·1 | 15·0 |
| 52 | 13 13·0 | 13 15·2 | 12 36·9 | 5·2 | 4·6 | 11·2 | 9·8 | 17·2 | 15·1 |
| 53 | 13 13·3 | 13 15·4 | 12 37·1 | 5·3 | 4·6 | 11·3 | 9·9 | 17·3 | 15·1 |
| 54 | 13 13·5 | 13 15·7 | 12 37·4 | 5·4 | 4·7 | 11·4 | 10·0 | 17·4 | 15·2 |
| 55 | 13 13·8 | 13 15·9 | 12 37·6 | 5·5 | 4·8 | 11·5 | 10·1 | 17·5 | 15·3 |
| 56 | 13 14·0 | 13 16·2 | 12 37·8 | 5·6 | 4·9 | 11·6 | 10·2 | 17·6 | 15·4 |
| 57 | 13 14·3 | 13 16·4 | 12 38·1 | 5·7 | 5·0 | 11·7 | 10·2 | 17·7 | 15·5 |
| 58 | 13 14·5 | 13 16·7 | 12 38·3 | 5·8 | 5·1 | 11·8 | 10·3 | 17·8 | 15·6 |
| 59 | 13 14·8 | 13 16·9 | 12 38·5 | 5·9 | 5·2 | 11·9 | 10·4 | 17·9 | 15·7 |
| 60 | 13 15·0 | 13 17·2 | 12 38·8 | 6·0 | 5·3 | 12·0 | 10·5 | 18·0 | 15·8 |

| 53$^{m}$ | SUN PLANETS | ARIES | MOON | v or d | Corrⁿ | v or d | Corrⁿ | v or d | Corrⁿ |
|---|---|---|---|---|---|---|---|---|---|
| s | ° ′ | ° ′ | ° ′ | ′ | ′ | ′ | ′ | ′ | ′ |
| 00 | 13 15·0 | 13 17·2 | 12 38·8 | 0·0 | 0·0 | 6·0 | 5·4 | 12·0 | 10·7 |
| 01 | 13 15·3 | 13 17·4 | 12 39·0 | 0·1 | 0·1 | 6·1 | 5·4 | 12·1 | 10·8 |
| 02 | 13 15·5 | 13 17·7 | 12 39·3 | 0·2 | 0·2 | 6·2 | 5·5 | 12·2 | 10·9 |
| 03 | 13 15·8 | 13 17·9 | 12 39·5 | 0·3 | 0·3 | 6·3 | 5·6 | 12·3 | 11·0 |
| 04 | 13 16·0 | 13 18·2 | 12 39·7 | 0·4 | 0·4 | 6·4 | 5·7 | 12·4 | 11·1 |
| 05 | 13 16·3 | 13 18·4 | 12 40·0 | 0·5 | 0·4 | 6·5 | 5·8 | 12·5 | 11·1 |
| 06 | 13 16·5 | 13 18·7 | 12 40·2 | 0·6 | 0·5 | 6·6 | 5·9 | 12·6 | 11·2 |
| 07 | 13 16·8 | 13 18·9 | 12 40·5 | 0·7 | 0·6 | 6·7 | 6·0 | 12·7 | 11·3 |
| 08 | 13 17·0 | 13 19·2 | 12 40·7 | 0·8 | 0·7 | 6·8 | 6·1 | 12·8 | 11·4 |
| 09 | 13 17·3 | 13 19·4 | 12 40·9 | 0·9 | 0·8 | 6·9 | 6·2 | 12·9 | 11·5 |
| 10 | 13 17·5 | 13 19·7 | 12 41·2 | 1·0 | 0·9 | 7·0 | 6·2 | 13·0 | 11·6 |
| 11 | 13 17·8 | 13 19·9 | 12 41·4 | 1·1 | 1·0 | 7·1 | 6·3 | 13·1 | 11·7 |
| 12 | 13 18·0 | 13 20·2 | 12 41·6 | 1·2 | 1·1 | 7·2 | 6·4 | 13·2 | 11·8 |
| 13 | 13 18·3 | 13 20·4 | 12 41·9 | 1·3 | 1·2 | 7·3 | 6·5 | 13·3 | 11·9 |
| 14 | 13 18·5 | 13 20·7 | 12 42·1 | 1·4 | 1·2 | 7·4 | 6·6 | 13·4 | 11·9 |
| 15 | 13 18·8 | 13 20·9 | 12 42·4 | 1·5 | 1·3 | 7·5 | 6·7 | 13·5 | 12·0 |
| 16 | 13 19·0 | 13 21·2 | 12 42·6 | 1·6 | 1·4 | 7·6 | 6·8 | 13·6 | 12·1 |
| 17 | 13 19·3 | 13 21·4 | 12 42·8 | 1·7 | 1·5 | 7·7 | 6·9 | 13·7 | 12·2 |
| 18 | 13 19·5 | 13 21·7 | 12 43·1 | 1·8 | 1·6 | 7·8 | 7·0 | 13·8 | 12·3 |
| 19 | 13 19·8 | 13 21·9 | 12 43·3 | 1·9 | 1·7 | 7·9 | 7·0 | 13·9 | 12·4 |
| 20 | 13 20·0 | 13 22·2 | 12 43·6 | 2·0 | 1·8 | 8·0 | 7·1 | 14·0 | 12·5 |
| 21 | 13 20·3 | 13 22·4 | 12 43·8 | 2·1 | 1·9 | 8·1 | 7·2 | 14·1 | 12·6 |
| 22 | 13 20·5 | 13 22·7 | 12 44·0 | 2·2 | 2·0 | 8·2 | 7·3 | 14·2 | 12·7 |
| 23 | 13 20·8 | 13 22·9 | 12 44·3 | 2·3 | 2·1 | 8·3 | 7·4 | 14·3 | 12·8 |
| 24 | 13 21·0 | 13 23·2 | 12 44·5 | 2·4 | 2·1 | 8·4 | 7·5 | 14·4 | 12·8 |
| 25 | 13 21·3 | 13 23·4 | 12 44·7 | 2·5 | 2·2 | 8·5 | 7·6 | 14·5 | 12·9 |
| 26 | 13 21·5 | 13 23·7 | 12 45·0 | 2·6 | 2·3 | 8·6 | 7·7 | 14·6 | 13·0 |
| 27 | 13 21·8 | 13 23·9 | 12 45·2 | 2·7 | 2·4 | 8·7 | 7·8 | 14·7 | 13·1 |
| 28 | 13 22·0 | 13 24·2 | 12 45·5 | 2·8 | 2·5 | 8·8 | 7·8 | 14·8 | 13·2 |
| 29 | 13 22·3 | 13 24·4 | 12 45·7 | 2·9 | 2·6 | 8·9 | 7·9 | 14·9 | 13·3 |
| 30 | 13 22·5 | 13 24·7 | 12 45·9 | 3·0 | 2·7 | 9·0 | 8·0 | 15·0 | 13·4 |
| 31 | 13 22·8 | 13 24·9 | 12 46·2 | 3·1 | 2·8 | 9·1 | 8·1 | 15·1 | 13·5 |
| 32 | 13 23·0 | 13 25·2 | 12 46·4 | 3·2 | 2·9 | 9·2 | 8·2 | 15·2 | 13·6 |
| 33 | 13 23·3 | 13 25·4 | 12 46·7 | 3·3 | 2·9 | 9·3 | 8·3 | 15·3 | 13·6 |
| 34 | 13 23·5 | 13 25·7 | 12 46·9 | 3·4 | 3·0 | 9·4 | 8·4 | 15·4 | 13·7 |
| 35 | 13 23·8 | 13 26·0 | 12 47·1 | 3·5 | 3·1 | 9·5 | 8·5 | 15·5 | 13·8 |
| 36 | 13 24·0 | 13 26·2 | 12 47·4 | 3·6 | 3·2 | 9·6 | 8·6 | 15·6 | 13·9 |
| 37 | 13 24·3 | 13 26·5 | 12 47·6 | 3·7 | 3·3 | 9·7 | 8·7 | 15·7 | 14·0 |
| 38 | 13 24·5 | 13 26·7 | 12 47·9 | 3·8 | 3·4 | 9·8 | 8·7 | 15·8 | 14·1 |
| 39 | 13 24·8 | 13 27·0 | 12 48·1 | 3·9 | 3·5 | 9·9 | 8·8 | 15·9 | 14·2 |
| 40 | 13 25·0 | 13 27·2 | 12 48·3 | 4·0 | 3·6 | 10·0 | 8·9 | 16·0 | 14·3 |
| 41 | 13 25·3 | 13 27·5 | 12 48·6 | 4·1 | 3·7 | 10·1 | 9·0 | 16·1 | 14·4 |
| 42 | 13 25·5 | 13 27·7 | 12 48·8 | 4·2 | 3·7 | 10·2 | 9·1 | 16·2 | 14·4 |
| 43 | 13 25·8 | 13 28·0 | 12 49·0 | 4·3 | 3·8 | 10·3 | 9·2 | 16·3 | 14·5 |
| 44 | 13 26·0 | 13 28·2 | 12 49·3 | 4·4 | 3·9 | 10·4 | 9·3 | 16·4 | 14·6 |
| 45 | 13 26·3 | 13 28·5 | 12 49·5 | 4·5 | 4·0 | 10·5 | 9·4 | 16·5 | 14·7 |
| 46 | 13 26·5 | 13 28·7 | 12 49·8 | 4·6 | 4·1 | 10·6 | 9·5 | 16·6 | 14·8 |
| 47 | 13 26·8 | 13 29·0 | 12 50·0 | 4·7 | 4·2 | 10·7 | 9·5 | 16·7 | 14·9 |
| 48 | 13 27·0 | 13 29·2 | 12 50·2 | 4·8 | 4·3 | 10·8 | 9·6 | 16·8 | 15·0 |
| 49 | 13 27·3 | 13 29·5 | 12 50·5 | 4·9 | 4·4 | 10·9 | 9·7 | 16·9 | 15·1 |
| 50 | 13 27·5 | 13 29·7 | 12 50·7 | 5·0 | 4·5 | 11·0 | 9·8 | 17·0 | 15·2 |
| 51 | 13 27·8 | 13 30·0 | 12 51·0 | 5·1 | 4·5 | 11·1 | 9·9 | 17·1 | 15·2 |
| 52 | 13 28·0 | 13 30·2 | 12 51·2 | 5·2 | 4·6 | 11·2 | 10·0 | 17·2 | 15·3 |
| 53 | 13 28·3 | 13 30·5 | 12 51·4 | 5·3 | 4·7 | 11·3 | 10·1 | 17·3 | 15·4 |
| 54 | 13 28·5 | 13 30·7 | 12 51·7 | 5·4 | 4·8 | 11·4 | 10·2 | 17·4 | 15·5 |
| 55 | 13 28·8 | 13 31·0 | 12 51·9 | 5·5 | 4·9 | 11·5 | 10·3 | 17·5 | 15·6 |
| 56 | 13 29·0 | 13 31·2 | 12 52·1 | 5·6 | 5·0 | 11·6 | 10·3 | 17·6 | 15·7 |
| 57 | 13 29·3 | 13 31·5 | 12 52·4 | 5·7 | 5·1 | 11·7 | 10·4 | 17·7 | 15·8 |
| 58 | 13 29·5 | 13 31·7 | 12 52·6 | 5·8 | 5·2 | 11·8 | 10·5 | 17·8 | 15·9 |
| 59 | 13 29·8 | 13 32·0 | 12 52·9 | 5·9 | 5·3 | 11·9 | 10·6 | 17·9 | 16·0 |
| 60 | 13 30·0 | 13 32·2 | 12 53·1 | 6·0 | 5·4 | 12·0 | 10·7 | 18·0 | 16·1 |

| 54$^{m}$ | SUN PLANETS | ARIES | MOON | v or d | Corrⁿ | v or d | Corrⁿ | v or d | Corrⁿ |
|---|---|---|---|---|---|---|---|---|---|
| s | ° ′ | ° ′ | ° ′ | ′ | ′ | ′ | ′ | ′ | ′ |
| 00 | 13 30·0 | 13 32·2 | 12 53·1 | 0·0 | 0·0 | 6·0 | 5·5 | 12·0 | 10·9 |
| 01 | 13 30·3 | 13 32·5 | 12 53·3 | 0·1 | 0·1 | 6·1 | 5·5 | 12·1 | 11·0 |
| 02 | 13 30·5 | 13 32·7 | 12 53·6 | 0·2 | 0·2 | 6·2 | 5·6 | 12·2 | 11·1 |
| 03 | 13 30·8 | 13 33·0 | 12 53·8 | 0·3 | 0·3 | 6·3 | 5·7 | 12·3 | 11·2 |
| 04 | 13 31·0 | 13 33·2 | 12 54·1 | 0·4 | 0·4 | 6·4 | 5·8 | 12·4 | 11·3 |
| 05 | 13 31·3 | 13 33·5 | 12 54·3 | 0·5 | 0·5 | 6·5 | 5·9 | 12·5 | 11·4 |
| 06 | 13 31·5 | 13 33·7 | 12 54·5 | 0·6 | 0·5 | 6·6 | 6·0 | 12·6 | 11·4 |
| 07 | 13 31·8 | 13 34·0 | 12 54·8 | 0·7 | 0·6 | 6·7 | 6·1 | 12·7 | 11·5 |
| 08 | 13 32·0 | 13 34·2 | 12 55·0 | 0·8 | 0·7 | 6·8 | 6·2 | 12·8 | 11·6 |
| 09 | 13 32·3 | 13 34·5 | 12 55·2 | 0·9 | 0·8 | 6·9 | 6·3 | 12·9 | 11·7 |
| 10 | 13 32·5 | 13 34·7 | 12 55·5 | 1·0 | 0·9 | 7·0 | 6·4 | 13·0 | 11·8 |
| 11 | 13 32·8 | 13 35·0 | 12 55·7 | 1·1 | 1·0 | 7·1 | 6·4 | 13·1 | 11·9 |
| 12 | 13 33·0 | 13 35·2 | 12 56·0 | 1·2 | 1·1 | 7·2 | 6·5 | 13·2 | 12·0 |
| 13 | 13 33·3 | 13 35·5 | 12 56·2 | 1·3 | 1·2 | 7·3 | 6·6 | 13·3 | 12·1 |
| 14 | 13 33·5 | 13 35·7 | 12 56·4 | 1·4 | 1·3 | 7·4 | 6·7 | 13·4 | 12·2 |
| 15 | 13 33·8 | 13 36·0 | 12 56·7 | 1·5 | 1·4 | 7·5 | 6·8 | 13·5 | 12·3 |
| 16 | 13 34·0 | 13 36·2 | 12 56·9 | 1·6 | 1·5 | 7·6 | 6·9 | 13·6 | 12·4 |
| 17 | 13 34·3 | 13 36·5 | 12 57·2 | 1·7 | 1·5 | 7·7 | 7·0 | 13·7 | 12·4 |
| 18 | 13 34·5 | 13 36·7 | 12 57·4 | 1·8 | 1·6 | 7·8 | 7·1 | 13·8 | 12·5 |
| 19 | 13 34·8 | 13 37·0 | 12 57·6 | 1·9 | 1·7 | 7·9 | 7·2 | 13·9 | 12·6 |
| 20 | 13 35·0 | 13 37·2 | 12 57·9 | 2·0 | 1·8 | 8·0 | 7·3 | 14·0 | 12·7 |
| 21 | 13 35·3 | 13 37·5 | 12 58·1 | 2·1 | 1·9 | 8·1 | 7·4 | 14·1 | 12·8 |
| 22 | 13 35·5 | 13 37·7 | 12 58·3 | 2·2 | 2·0 | 8·2 | 7·4 | 14·2 | 12·9 |
| 23 | 13 35·8 | 13 38·0 | 12 58·6 | 2·3 | 2·1 | 8·3 | 7·5 | 14·3 | 13·0 |
| 24 | 13 36·0 | 13 38·2 | 12 58·8 | 2·4 | 2·2 | 8·4 | 7·6 | 14·4 | 13·1 |
| 25 | 13 36·3 | 13 38·5 | 12 59·1 | 2·5 | 2·3 | 8·5 | 7·7 | 14·5 | 13·2 |
| 26 | 13 36·5 | 13 38·7 | 12 59·3 | 2·6 | 2·4 | 8·6 | 7·8 | 14·6 | 13·3 |
| 27 | 13 36·8 | 13 39·0 | 12 59·5 | 2·7 | 2·5 | 8·7 | 7·9 | 14·7 | 13·4 |
| 28 | 13 37·0 | 13 39·2 | 12 59·8 | 2·8 | 2·5 | 8·8 | 8·0 | 14·8 | 13·4 |
| 29 | 13 37·3 | 13 39·5 | 13 00·0 | 2·9 | 2·6 | 8·9 | 8·1 | 14·9 | 13·5 |
| 30 | 13 37·5 | 13 39·7 | 13 00·3 | 3·0 | 2·7 | 9·0 | 8·2 | 15·0 | 13·6 |
| 31 | 13 37·8 | 13 40·0 | 13 00·5 | 3·1 | 2·8 | 9·1 | 8·3 | 15·1 | 13·7 |
| 32 | 13 38·0 | 13 40·2 | 13 00·7 | 3·2 | 2·9 | 9·2 | 8·4 | 15·2 | 13·8 |
| 33 | 13 38·3 | 13 40·5 | 13 01·0 | 3·3 | 3·0 | 9·3 | 8·4 | 15·3 | 13·9 |
| 34 | 13 38·5 | 13 40·7 | 13 01·2 | 3·4 | 3·1 | 9·4 | 8·5 | 15·4 | 14·0 |
| 35 | 13 38·8 | 13 41·0 | 13 01·5 | 3·5 | 3·2 | 9·5 | 8·6 | 15·5 | 14·1 |
| 36 | 13 39·0 | 13 41·2 | 13 01·7 | 3·6 | 3·3 | 9·6 | 8·7 | 15·6 | 14·2 |
| 37 | 13 39·3 | 13 41·5 | 13 01·9 | 3·7 | 3·4 | 9·7 | 8·8 | 15·7 | 14·3 |
| 38 | 13 39·5 | 13 41·7 | 13 02·2 | 3·8 | 3·5 | 9·8 | 8·9 | 15·8 | 14·4 |
| 39 | 13 39·8 | 13 42·0 | 13 02·4 | 3·9 | 3·5 | 9·9 | 9·0 | 15·9 | 14·4 |
| 40 | 13 40·0 | 13 42·2 | 13 02·6 | 4·0 | 3·6 | 10·0 | 9·1 | 16·0 | 14·5 |
| 41 | 13 40·3 | 13 42·5 | 13 02·9 | 4·1 | 3·7 | 10·1 | 9·2 | 16·1 | 14·6 |
| 42 | 13 40·5 | 13 42·7 | 13 03·1 | 4·2 | 3·8 | 10·2 | 9·3 | 16·2 | 14·7 |
| 43 | 13 40·8 | 13 43·0 | 13 03·4 | 4·3 | 3·9 | 10·3 | 9·4 | 16·3 | 14·8 |
| 44 | 13 41·0 | 13 43·2 | 13 03·6 | 4·4 | 4·0 | 10·4 | 9·4 | 16·4 | 14·9 |
| 45 | 13 41·3 | 13 43·5 | 13 03·8 | 4·5 | 4·1 | 10·5 | 9·5 | 16·5 | 15·0 |
| 46 | 13 41·5 | 13 43·7 | 13 04·1 | 4·6 | 4·2 | 10·6 | 9·6 | 16·6 | 15·1 |
| 47 | 13 41·8 | 13 44·0 | 13 04·3 | 4·7 | 4·3 | 10·7 | 9·7 | 16·7 | 15·2 |
| 48 | 13 42·0 | 13 44·3 | 13 04·6 | 4·8 | 4·4 | 10·8 | 9·8 | 16·8 | 15·3 |
| 49 | 13 42·3 | 13 44·5 | 13 04·8 | 4·9 | 4·5 | 10·9 | 9·9 | 16·9 | 15·4 |
| 50 | 13 42·5 | 13 44·8 | 13 05·0 | 5·0 | 4·5 | 11·0 | 10·0 | 17·0 | 15·4 |
| 51 | 13 42·8 | 13 45·0 | 13 05·3 | 5·1 | 4·6 | 11·1 | 10·1 | 17·1 | 15·5 |
| 52 | 13 43·0 | 13 45·3 | 13 05·5 | 5·2 | 4·7 | 11·2 | 10·2 | 17·2 | 15·6 |
| 53 | 13 43·3 | 13 45·5 | 13 05·7 | 5·3 | 4·8 | 11·3 | 10·3 | 17·3 | 15·7 |
| 54 | 13 43·5 | 13 45·8 | 13 06·0 | 5·4 | 4·9 | 11·4 | 10·4 | 17·4 | 15·8 |
| 55 | 13 43·8 | 13 46·0 | 13 06·2 | 5·5 | 5·0 | 11·5 | 10·4 | 17·5 | 15·9 |
| 56 | 13 44·0 | 13 46·3 | 13 06·5 | 5·6 | 5·1 | 11·6 | 10·5 | 17·6 | 16·0 |
| 57 | 13 44·3 | 13 46·5 | 13 06·7 | 5·7 | 5·2 | 11·7 | 10·6 | 17·7 | 16·1 |
| 58 | 13 44·5 | 13 46·8 | 13 06·9 | 5·8 | 5·3 | 11·8 | 10·7 | 17·8 | 16·2 |
| 59 | 13 44·8 | 13 47·0 | 13 07·2 | 5·9 | 5·4 | 11·9 | 10·8 | 17·9 | 16·3 |
| 60 | 13 45·0 | 13 47·3 | 13 07·4 | 6·0 | 5·5 | 12·0 | 10·9 | 18·0 | 16·4 |

| 55$^{m}$ | SUN PLANETS | ARIES | MOON | v or d | Corrⁿ | v or d | Corrⁿ | v or d | Corrⁿ |
|---|---|---|---|---|---|---|---|---|---|
| s | ° ′ | ° ′ | ° ′ | ′ | ′ | ′ | ′ | ′ | ′ |
| 00 | 13 45·0 | 13 47·3 | 13 07·4 | 0·0 | 0·0 | 6·0 | 5·6 | 12·0 | 11·1 |
| 01 | 13 45·3 | 13 47·5 | 13 07·7 | 0·1 | 0·1 | 6·1 | 5·6 | 12·1 | 11·2 |
| 02 | 13 45·5 | 13 47·8 | 13 07·9 | 0·2 | 0·2 | 6·2 | 5·7 | 12·2 | 11·3 |
| 03 | 13 45·8 | 13 48·0 | 13 08·1 | 0·3 | 0·3 | 6·3 | 5·8 | 12·3 | 11·4 |
| 04 | 13 46·0 | 13 48·3 | 13 08·4 | 0·4 | 0·4 | 6·4 | 5·9 | 12·4 | 11·5 |
| 05 | 13 46·3 | 13 48·5 | 13 08·6 | 0·5 | 0·5 | 6·5 | 6·0 | 12·5 | 11·6 |
| 06 | 13 46·5 | 13 48·8 | 13 08·8 | 0·6 | 0·6 | 6·6 | 6·1 | 12·6 | 11·7 |
| 07 | 13 46·8 | 13 49·0 | 13 09·1 | 0·7 | 0·6 | 6·7 | 6·2 | 12·7 | 11·7 |
| 08 | 13 47·0 | 13 49·3 | 13 09·3 | 0·8 | 0·7 | 6·8 | 6·3 | 12·8 | 11·8 |
| 09 | 13 47·3 | 13 49·5 | 13 09·6 | 0·9 | 0·8 | 6·9 | 6·4 | 12·9 | 11·9 |
| 10 | 13 47·5 | 13 49·8 | 13 09·8 | 1·0 | 0·9 | 7·0 | 6·5 | 13·0 | 12·0 |
| 11 | 13 47·8 | 13 50·0 | 13 10·0 | 1·1 | 1·0 | 7·1 | 6·6 | 13·1 | 12·1 |
| 12 | 13 48·0 | 13 50·3 | 13 10·3 | 1·2 | 1·1 | 7·2 | 6·7 | 13·2 | 12·2 |
| 13 | 13 48·3 | 13 50·5 | 13 10·5 | 1·3 | 1·2 | 7·3 | 6·8 | 13·3 | 12·3 |
| 14 | 13 48·5 | 13 50·8 | 13 10·8 | 1·4 | 1·3 | 7·4 | 6·8 | 13·4 | 12·4 |
| 15 | 13 48·8 | 13 51·0 | 13 11·0 | 1·5 | 1·4 | 7·5 | 6·9 | 13·5 | 12·5 |
| 16 | 13 49·0 | 13 51·3 | 13 11·2 | 1·6 | 1·5 | 7·6 | 7·0 | 13·6 | 12·6 |
| 17 | 13 49·3 | 13 51·5 | 13 11·5 | 1·7 | 1·6 | 7·7 | 7·1 | 13·7 | 12·7 |
| 18 | 13 49·5 | 13 51·8 | 13 11·7 | 1·8 | 1·7 | 7·8 | 7·2 | 13·8 | 12·8 |
| 19 | 13 49·8 | 13 52·0 | 13 12·0 | 1·9 | 1·8 | 7·9 | 7·3 | 13·9 | 12·9 |
| 20 | 13 50·0 | 13 52·3 | 13 12·2 | 2·0 | 1·9 | 8·0 | 7·4 | 14·0 | 13·0 |
| 21 | 13 50·3 | 13 52·5 | 13 12·4 | 2·1 | 1·9 | 8·1 | 7·5 | 14·1 | 13·0 |
| 22 | 13 50·5 | 13 52·8 | 13 12·7 | 2·2 | 2·0 | 8·2 | 7·6 | 14·2 | 13·1 |
| 23 | 13 50·8 | 13 53·0 | 13 12·9 | 2·3 | 2·1 | 8·3 | 7·7 | 14·3 | 13·2 |
| 24 | 13 51·0 | 13 53·3 | 13 13·1 | 2·4 | 2·2 | 8·4 | 7·8 | 14·4 | 13·3 |
| 25 | 13 51·3 | 13 53·5 | 13 13·4 | 2·5 | 2·3 | 8·5 | 7·9 | 14·5 | 13·4 |
| 26 | 13 51·5 | 13 53·8 | 13 13·6 | 2·6 | 2·4 | 8·6 | 8·0 | 14·6 | 13·5 |
| 27 | 13 51·8 | 13 54·0 | 13 13·9 | 2·7 | 2·5 | 8·7 | 8·0 | 14·7 | 13·6 |
| 28 | 13 52·0 | 13 54·3 | 13 14·1 | 2·8 | 2·6 | 8·8 | 8·1 | 14·8 | 13·7 |
| 29 | 13 52·3 | 13 54·5 | 13 14·3 | 2·9 | 2·7 | 8·9 | 8·2 | 14·9 | 13·8 |
| 30 | 13 52·5 | 13 54·8 | 13 14·6 | 3·0 | 2·8 | 9·0 | 8·3 | 15·0 | 13·9 |
| 31 | 13 52·8 | 13 55·0 | 13 14·8 | 3·1 | 2·9 | 9·1 | 8·4 | 15·1 | 14·0 |
| 32 | 13 53·0 | 13 55·3 | 13 15·1 | 3·2 | 3·0 | 9·2 | 8·5 | 15·2 | 14·1 |
| 33 | 13 53·3 | 13 55·5 | 13 15·3 | 3·3 | 3·1 | 9·3 | 8·6 | 15·3 | 14·2 |
| 34 | 13 53·5 | 13 55·8 | 13 15·5 | 3·4 | 3·1 | 9·4 | 8·7 | 15·4 | 14·2 |
| 35 | 13 53·8 | 13 56·0 | 13 15·8 | 3·5 | 3·2 | 9·5 | 8·8 | 15·5 | 14·3 |
| 36 | 13 54·0 | 13 56·3 | 13 16·0 | 3·6 | 3·3 | 9·6 | 8·9 | 15·6 | 14·4 |
| 37 | 13 54·3 | 13 56·5 | 13 16·2 | 3·7 | 3·4 | 9·7 | 9·0 | 15·7 | 14·5 |
| 38 | 13 54·5 | 13 56·8 | 13 16·5 | 3·8 | 3·5 | 9·8 | 9·1 | 15·8 | 14·6 |
| 39 | 13 54·8 | 13 57·0 | 13 16·7 | 3·9 | 3·6 | 9·9 | 9·2 | 15·9 | 14·7 |
| 40 | 13 55·0 | 13 57·3 | 13 17·0 | 4·0 | 3·7 | 10·0 | 9·3 | 16·0 | 14·8 |
| 41 | 13 55·3 | 13 57·5 | 13 17·2 | 4·1 | 3·8 | 10·1 | 9·3 | 16·1 | 14·9 |
| 42 | 13 55·5 | 13 57·8 | 13 17·4 | 4·2 | 3·9 | 10·2 | 9·4 | 16·2 | 15·0 |
| 43 | 13 55·8 | 13 58·0 | 13 17·7 | 4·3 | 4·0 | 10·3 | 9·5 | 16·3 | 15·1 |
| 44 | 13 56·0 | 13 58·3 | 13 17·9 | 4·4 | 4·1 | 10·4 | 9·6 | 16·4 | 15·2 |
| 45 | 13 56·3 | 13 58·5 | 13 18·2 | 4·5 | 4·2 | 10·5 | 9·7 | 16·5 | 15·3 |
| 46 | 13 56·5 | 13 58·8 | 13 18·4 | 4·6 | 4·3 | 10·6 | 9·8 | 16·6 | 15·4 |
| 47 | 13 56·8 | 13 59·0 | 13 18·6 | 4·7 | 4·3 | 10·7 | 9·9 | 16·7 | 15·4 |
| 48 | 13 57·0 | 13 59·3 | 13 18·9 | 4·8 | 4·4 | 10·8 | 10·0 | 16·8 | 15·5 |
| 49 | 13 57·3 | 13 59·5 | 13 19·1 | 4·9 | 4·5 | 10·9 | 10·1 | 16·9 | 15·6 |
| 50 | 13 57·5 | 13 59·8 | 13 19·3 | 5·0 | 4·6 | 11·0 | 10·2 | 17·0 | 15·7 |
| 51 | 13 57·8 | 14 00·0 | 13 19·6 | 5·1 | 4·7 | 11·1 | 10·3 | 17·1 | 15·8 |
| 52 | 13 58·0 | 14 00·3 | 13 19·8 | 5·2 | 4·8 | 11·2 | 10·4 | 17·2 | 15·9 |
| 53 | 13 58·3 | 14 00·5 | 13 20·1 | 5·3 | 4·9 | 11·3 | 10·5 | 17·3 | 16·0 |
| 54 | 13 58·5 | 14 00·8 | 13 20·3 | 5·4 | 5·0 | 11·4 | 10·5 | 17·4 | 16·1 |
| 55 | 13 58·8 | 14 01·0 | 13 20·5 | 5·5 | 5·1 | 11·5 | 10·6 | 17·5 | 16·2 |
| 56 | 13 59·0 | 14 01·3 | 13 20·8 | 5·6 | 5·2 | 11·6 | 10·7 | 17·6 | 16·3 |
| 57 | 13 59·3 | 14 01·5 | 13 21·0 | 5·7 | 5·3 | 11·7 | 10·8 | 17·7 | 16·4 |
| 58 | 13 59·5 | 14 01·8 | 13 21·3 | 5·8 | 5·4 | 11·8 | 10·9 | 17·8 | 16·5 |
| 59 | 13 59·8 | 14 02·0 | 13 21·5 | 5·9 | 5·5 | 11·9 | 11·0 | 17·9 | 16·6 |
| 60 | 14 00·0 | 14 02·3 | 13 21·7 | 6·0 | 5·6 | 12·0 | 11·1 | 18·0 | 16·7 |

| 56m s | SUN PLANETS ° ′ | ARIES ° ′ | MOON ° ′ | v or d ′ | Corrn ′ | v or d ′ | Corrn ′ | v or d ′ | Corrn ′ |
|---|---|---|---|---|---|---|---|---|---|
| 00 | 14 00·0 | 14 02·3 | 13 21·7 | 0·0 | 0·0 | 6·0 | 5·7 | 12·0 | 11·3 |
| 01 | 14 00·3 | 14 02·6 | 13 22·0 | 0·1 | 0·1 | 6·1 | 5·7 | 12·1 | 11·4 |
| 02 | 14 00·5 | 14 02·8 | 13 22·2 | 0·2 | 0·2 | 6·2 | 5·8 | 12·2 | 11·5 |
| 03 | 14 00·8 | 14 03·1 | 13 22·4 | 0·3 | 0·3 | 6·3 | 5·9 | 12·3 | 11·6 |
| 04 | 14 01·0 | 14 03·3 | 13 22·7 | 0·4 | 0·4 | 6·4 | 6·0 | 12·4 | 11·7 |
| 05 | 14 01·3 | 14 03·6 | 13 22·9 | 0·5 | 0·5 | 6·5 | 6·1 | 12·5 | 11·8 |
| 06 | 14 01·5 | 14 03·8 | 13 23·2 | 0·6 | 0·6 | 6·6 | 6·2 | 12·6 | 11·9 |
| 07 | 14 01·8 | 14 04·1 | 13 23·4 | 0·7 | 0·7 | 6·7 | 6·3 | 12·7 | 12·0 |
| 08 | 14 02·0 | 14 04·3 | 13 23·6 | 0·8 | 0·8 | 6·8 | 6·4 | 12·8 | 12·1 |
| 09 | 14 02·3 | 14 04·6 | 13 23·9 | 0·9 | 0·8 | 6·9 | 6·5 | 12·9 | 12·1 |
| 10 | 14 02·5 | 14 04·8 | 13 24·1 | 1·0 | 0·9 | 7·0 | 6·6 | 13·0 | 12·2 |
| 11 | 14 02·8 | 14 05·1 | 13 24·4 | 1·1 | 1·0 | 7·1 | 6·7 | 13·1 | 12·3 |
| 12 | 14 03·0 | 14 05·3 | 13 24·6 | 1·2 | 1·1 | 7·2 | 6·8 | 13·2 | 12·4 |
| 13 | 14 03·3 | 14 05·6 | 13 24·8 | 1·3 | 1·2 | 7·3 | 6·9 | 13·3 | 12·5 |
| 14 | 14 03·5 | 14 05·8 | 13 25·1 | 1·4 | 1·3 | 7·4 | 7·0 | 13·4 | 12·6 |
| 15 | 14 03·8 | 14 06·1 | 13 25·3 | 1·5 | 1·4 | 7·5 | 7·1 | 13·5 | 12·7 |
| 16 | 14 04·0 | 14 06·3 | 13 25·6 | 1·6 | 1·5 | 7·6 | 7·2 | 13·6 | 12·8 |
| 17 | 14 04·3 | 14 06·6 | 13 25·8 | 1·7 | 1·6 | 7·7 | 7·3 | 13·7 | 12·9 |
| 18 | 14 04·5 | 14 06·8 | 13 26·0 | 1·8 | 1·7 | 7·8 | 7·3 | 13·8 | 13·0 |
| 19 | 14 04·8 | 14 07·1 | 13 26·3 | 1·9 | 1·8 | 7·9 | 7·4 | 13·9 | 13·1 |
| 20 | 14 05·0 | 14 07·3 | 13 26·5 | 2·0 | 1·9 | 8·0 | 7·5 | 14·0 | 13·2 |
| 21 | 14 05·3 | 14 07·6 | 13 26·7 | 2·1 | 2·0 | 8·1 | 7·6 | 14·1 | 13·3 |
| 22 | 14 05·5 | 14 07·8 | 13 27·0 | 2·2 | 2·1 | 8·2 | 7·7 | 14·2 | 13·4 |
| 23 | 14 05·8 | 14 08·1 | 13 27·2 | 2·3 | 2·2 | 8·3 | 7·8 | 14·3 | 13·5 |
| 24 | 14 06·0 | 14 08·3 | 13 27·5 | 2·4 | 2·3 | 8·4 | 7·9 | 14·4 | 13·6 |
| 25 | 14 06·3 | 14 08·6 | 13 27·7 | 2·5 | 2·4 | 8·5 | 8·0 | 14·5 | 13·7 |
| 26 | 14 06·5 | 14 08·8 | 13 27·9 | 2·6 | 2·4 | 8·6 | 8·1 | 14·6 | 13·7 |
| 27 | 14 06·8 | 14 09·1 | 13 28·2 | 2·7 | 2·5 | 8·7 | 8·2 | 14·7 | 13·8 |
| 28 | 14 07·0 | 14 09·3 | 13 28·4 | 2·8 | 2·6 | 8·8 | 8·3 | 14·8 | 13·9 |
| 29 | 14 07·3 | 14 09·6 | 13 28·7 | 2·9 | 2·7 | 8·9 | 8·4 | 14·9 | 14·0 |
| 30 | 14 07·5 | 14 09·8 | 13 28·9 | 3·0 | 2·8 | 9·0 | 8·5 | 15·0 | 14·1 |
| 31 | 14 07·8 | 14 10·1 | 13 29·1 | 3·1 | 2·9 | 9·1 | 8·6 | 15·1 | 14·2 |
| 32 | 14 08·0 | 14 10·3 | 13 29·4 | 3·2 | 3·0 | 9·2 | 8·7 | 15·2 | 14·3 |
| 33 | 14 08·3 | 14 10·6 | 13 29·6 | 3·3 | 3·1 | 9·3 | 8·8 | 15·3 | 14·4 |
| 34 | 14 08·5 | 14 10·8 | 13 29·8 | 3·4 | 3·2 | 9·4 | 8·9 | 15·4 | 14·5 |
| 35 | 14 08·8 | 14 11·1 | 13 30·1 | 3·5 | 3·3 | 9·5 | 8·9 | 15·5 | 14·6 |
| 36 | 14 09·0 | 14 11·3 | 13 30·3 | 3·6 | 3·4 | 9·6 | 9·0 | 15·6 | 14·7 |
| 37 | 14 09·3 | 14 11·6 | 13 30·6 | 3·7 | 3·5 | 9·7 | 9·1 | 15·7 | 14·8 |
| 38 | 14 09·5 | 14 11·8 | 13 30·8 | 3·8 | 3·6 | 9·8 | 9·2 | 15·8 | 14·9 |
| 39 | 14 09·8 | 14 12·1 | 13 31·0 | 3·9 | 3·7 | 9·9 | 9·3 | 15·9 | 15·0 |
| 40 | 14 10·0 | 14 12·3 | 13 31·3 | 4·0 | 3·8 | 10·0 | 9·4 | 16·0 | 15·1 |
| 41 | 14 10·3 | 14 12·6 | 13 31·5 | 4·1 | 3·9 | 10·1 | 9·5 | 16·1 | 15·2 |
| 42 | 14 10·5 | 14 12·8 | 13 31·8 | 4·2 | 4·0 | 10·2 | 9·6 | 16·2 | 15·3 |
| 43 | 14 10·8 | 14 13·1 | 13 32·0 | 4·3 | 4·0 | 10·3 | 9·7 | 16·3 | 15·3 |
| 44 | 14 11·0 | 14 13·3 | 13 32·2 | 4·4 | 4·1 | 10·4 | 9·8 | 16·4 | 15·4 |
| 45 | 14 11·3 | 14 13·6 | 13 32·5 | 4·5 | 4·2 | 10·5 | 9·9 | 16·5 | 15·5 |
| 46 | 14 11·5 | 14 13·8 | 13 32·7 | 4·6 | 4·3 | 10·6 | 10·0 | 16·6 | 15·6 |
| 47 | 14 11·8 | 14 14·1 | 13 32·9 | 4·7 | 4·4 | 10·7 | 10·1 | 16·7 | 15·7 |
| 48 | 14 12·0 | 14 14·3 | 13 33·2 | 4·8 | 4·5 | 10·8 | 10·2 | 16·8 | 15·8 |
| 49 | 14 12·3 | 14 14·6 | 13 33·4 | 4·9 | 4·6 | 10·9 | 10·3 | 16·9 | 15·9 |
| 50 | 14 12·5 | 14 14·8 | 13 33·7 | 5·0 | 4·7 | 11·0 | 10·4 | 17·0 | 16·0 |
| 51 | 14 12·8 | 14 15·1 | 13 33·9 | 5·1 | 4·8 | 11·1 | 10·5 | 17·1 | 16·1 |
| 52 | 14 13·0 | 14 15·3 | 13 34·1 | 5·2 | 4·9 | 11·2 | 10·5 | 17·2 | 16·2 |
| 53 | 14 13·3 | 14 15·6 | 13 34·4 | 5·3 | 5·0 | 11·3 | 10·6 | 17·3 | 16·3 |
| 54 | 14 13·5 | 14 15·8 | 13 34·6 | 5·4 | 5·1 | 11·4 | 10·7 | 17·4 | 16·4 |
| 55 | 14 13·8 | 14 16·1 | 13 34·9 | 5·5 | 5·2 | 11·5 | 10·8 | 17·5 | 16·5 |
| 56 | 14 14·0 | 14 16·3 | 13 35·1 | 5·6 | 5·3 | 11·6 | 10·9 | 17·6 | 16·6 |
| 57 | 14 14·3 | 14 16·6 | 13 35·3 | 5·7 | 5·4 | 11·7 | 11·0 | 17·7 | 16·7 |
| 58 | 14 14·5 | 14 16·8 | 13 35·6 | 5·8 | 5·5 | 11·8 | 11·1 | 17·8 | 16·8 |
| 59 | 14 14·8 | 14 17·1 | 13 35·8 | 5·9 | 5·6 | 11·9 | 11·2 | 17·9 | 16·9 |
| 60 | 14 15·0 | 14 17·3 | 13 36·1 | 6·0 | 5·7 | 12·0 | 11·3 | 18·0 | 17·0 |

| 57m s | SUN PLANETS ° ′ | ARIES ° ′ | MOON ° ′ | v or d ′ | Corrn ′ | v or d ′ | Corrn ′ | v or d ′ | Corrn ′ |
|---|---|---|---|---|---|---|---|---|---|
| 00 | 14 15·0 | 14 17·3 | 13 36·1 | 0·0 | 0·0 | 6·0 | 5·8 | 12·0 | 11·5 |
| 01 | 14 15·3 | 14 17·6 | 13 36·3 | 0·1 | 0·1 | 6·1 | 5·8 | 12·1 | 11·6 |
| 02 | 14 15·5 | 14 17·8 | 13 36·5 | 0·2 | 0·2 | 6·2 | 5·9 | 12·2 | 11·7 |
| 03 | 14 15·8 | 14 18·1 | 13 36·8 | 0·3 | 0·3 | 6·3 | 6·0 | 12·3 | 11·8 |
| 04 | 14 16·0 | 14 18·3 | 13 37·0 | 0·4 | 0·4 | 6·4 | 6·1 | 12·4 | 11·9 |
| 05 | 14 16·3 | 14 18·6 | 13 37·2 | 0·5 | 0·5 | 6·5 | 6·2 | 12·5 | 12·0 |
| 06 | 14 16·5 | 14 18·8 | 13 37·5 | 0·6 | 0·6 | 6·6 | 6·3 | 12·6 | 12·1 |
| 07 | 14 16·8 | 14 19·1 | 13 37·7 | 0·7 | 0·7 | 6·7 | 6·4 | 12·7 | 12·2 |
| 08 | 14 17·0 | 14 19·3 | 13 38·0 | 0·8 | 0·8 | 6·8 | 6·5 | 12·8 | 12·3 |
| 09 | 14 17·3 | 14 19·6 | 13 38·2 | 0·9 | 0·9 | 6·9 | 6·6 | 12·9 | 12·4 |
| 10 | 14 17·5 | 14 19·8 | 13 38·4 | 1·0 | 1·0 | 7·0 | 6·7 | 13·0 | 12·5 |
| 11 | 14 17·8 | 14 20·1 | 13 38·7 | 1·1 | 1·1 | 7·1 | 6·8 | 13·1 | 12·6 |
| 12 | 14 18·0 | 14 20·3 | 13 38·9 | 1·2 | 1·2 | 7·2 | 6·9 | 13·2 | 12·7 |
| 13 | 14 18·3 | 14 20·6 | 13 39·2 | 1·3 | 1·2 | 7·3 | 7·0 | 13·3 | 12·7 |
| 14 | 14 18·5 | 14 20·9 | 13 39·4 | 1·4 | 1·3 | 7·4 | 7·1 | 13·4 | 12·8 |
| 15 | 14 18·8 | 14 21·1 | 13 39·6 | 1·5 | 1·4 | 7·5 | 7·2 | 13·5 | 12·9 |
| 16 | 14 19·0 | 14 21·4 | 13 39·9 | 1·6 | 1·5 | 7·6 | 7·3 | 13·6 | 13·0 |
| 17 | 14 19·3 | 14 21·6 | 13 40·1 | 1·7 | 1·6 | 7·7 | 7·4 | 13·7 | 13·1 |
| 18 | 14 19·5 | 14 21·9 | 13 40·3 | 1·8 | 1·7 | 7·8 | 7·5 | 13·8 | 13·2 |
| 19 | 14 19·8 | 14 22·1 | 13 40·6 | 1·9 | 1·8 | 7·9 | 7·6 | 13·9 | 13·3 |
| 20 | 14 20·0 | 14 22·4 | 13 40·8 | 2·0 | 1·9 | 8·0 | 7·7 | 14·0 | 13·4 |
| 21 | 14 20·3 | 14 22·6 | 13 41·1 | 2·1 | 2·0 | 8·1 | 7·8 | 14·1 | 13·5 |
| 22 | 14 20·5 | 14 22·9 | 13 41·3 | 2·2 | 2·1 | 8·2 | 7·9 | 14·2 | 13·6 |
| 23 | 14 20·8 | 14 23·1 | 13 41·5 | 2·3 | 2·2 | 8·3 | 8·0 | 14·3 | 13·7 |
| 24 | 14 21·0 | 14 23·4 | 13 41·8 | 2·4 | 2·3 | 8·4 | 8·1 | 14·4 | 13·8 |
| 25 | 14 21·3 | 14 23·6 | 13 42·0 | 2·5 | 2·4 | 8·5 | 8·1 | 14·5 | 13·9 |
| 26 | 14 21·5 | 14 23·9 | 13 42·3 | 2·6 | 2·5 | 8·6 | 8·2 | 14·6 | 14·0 |
| 27 | 14 21·8 | 14 24·1 | 13 42·5 | 2·7 | 2·6 | 8·7 | 8·3 | 14·7 | 14·1 |
| 28 | 14 22·0 | 14 24·4 | 13 42·7 | 2·8 | 2·7 | 8·8 | 8·4 | 14·8 | 14·2 |
| 29 | 14 22·3 | 14 24·6 | 13 43·0 | 2·9 | 2·8 | 8·9 | 8·5 | 14·9 | 14·3 |
| 30 | 14 22·5 | 14 24·9 | 13 43·2 | 3·0 | 2·9 | 9·0 | 8·6 | 15·0 | 14·4 |
| 31 | 14 22·8 | 14 25·1 | 13 43·4 | 3·1 | 3·0 | 9·1 | 8·7 | 15·1 | 14·5 |
| 32 | 14 23·0 | 14 25·4 | 13 43·7 | 3·2 | 3·1 | 9·2 | 8·8 | 15·2 | 14·6 |
| 33 | 14 23·3 | 14 25·6 | 13 43·9 | 3·3 | 3·2 | 9·3 | 8·9 | 15·3 | 14·7 |
| 34 | 14 23·5 | 14 25·9 | 13 44·2 | 3·4 | 3·3 | 9·4 | 9·0 | 15·4 | 14·8 |
| 35 | 14 23·8 | 14 26·1 | 13 44·4 | 3·5 | 3·4 | 9·5 | 9·1 | 15·5 | 14·9 |
| 36 | 14 24·0 | 14 26·4 | 13 44·6 | 3·6 | 3·5 | 9·6 | 9·2 | 15·6 | 15·0 |
| 37 | 14 24·3 | 14 26·6 | 13 44·9 | 3·7 | 3·5 | 9·7 | 9·3 | 15·7 | 15·0 |
| 38 | 14 24·5 | 14 26·9 | 13 45·1 | 3·8 | 3·6 | 9·8 | 9·4 | 15·8 | 15·1 |
| 39 | 14 24·8 | 14 27·1 | 13 45·4 | 3·9 | 3·7 | 9·9 | 9·5 | 15·9 | 15·2 |
| 40 | 14 25·0 | 14 27·4 | 13 45·6 | 4·0 | 3·8 | 10·0 | 9·6 | 16·0 | 15·3 |
| 41 | 14 25·3 | 14 27·6 | 13 45·8 | 4·1 | 3·9 | 10·1 | 9·7 | 16·1 | 15·4 |
| 42 | 14 25·5 | 14 27·9 | 13 46·1 | 4·2 | 4·0 | 10·2 | 9·8 | 16·2 | 15·5 |
| 43 | 14 25·8 | 14 28·1 | 13 46·3 | 4·3 | 4·1 | 10·3 | 9·9 | 16·3 | 15·6 |
| 44 | 14 26·0 | 14 28·4 | 13 46·5 | 4·4 | 4·2 | 10·4 | 10·0 | 16·4 | 15·7 |
| 45 | 14 26·3 | 14 28·6 | 13 46·8 | 4·5 | 4·3 | 10·5 | 10·1 | 16·5 | 15·8 |
| 46 | 14 26·5 | 14 28·9 | 13 47·0 | 4·6 | 4·4 | 10·6 | 10·2 | 16·6 | 15·9 |
| 47 | 14 26·8 | 14 29·1 | 13 47·3 | 4·7 | 4·5 | 10·7 | 10·3 | 16·7 | 16·0 |
| 48 | 14 27·0 | 14 29·4 | 13 47·5 | 4·8 | 4·6 | 10·8 | 10·4 | 16·8 | 16·1 |
| 49 | 14 27·3 | 14 29·6 | 13 47·7 | 4·9 | 4·7 | 10·9 | 10·4 | 16·9 | 16·2 |
| 50 | 14 27·5 | 14 29·9 | 13 48·0 | 5·0 | 4·8 | 11·0 | 10·5 | 17·0 | 16·3 |
| 51 | 14 27·8 | 14 30·1 | 13 48·2 | 5·1 | 4·9 | 11·1 | 10·6 | 17·1 | 16·4 |
| 52 | 14 28·0 | 14 30·4 | 13 48·5 | 5·2 | 5·0 | 11·2 | 10·7 | 17·2 | 16·5 |
| 53 | 14 28·3 | 14 30·6 | 13 48·7 | 5·3 | 5·1 | 11·3 | 10·8 | 17·3 | 16·6 |
| 54 | 14 28·5 | 14 30·9 | 13 48·9 | 5·4 | 5·2 | 11·4 | 10·9 | 17·4 | 16·7 |
| 55 | 14 28·8 | 14 31·1 | 13 49·2 | 5·5 | 5·3 | 11·5 | 11·0 | 17·5 | 16·8 |
| 56 | 14 29·0 | 14 31·4 | 13 49·4 | 5·6 | 5·4 | 11·6 | 11·1 | 17·6 | 16·9 |
| 57 | 14 29·3 | 14 31·6 | 13 49·7 | 5·7 | 5·5 | 11·7 | 11·2 | 17·7 | 17·0 |
| 58 | 14 29·5 | 14 31·9 | 13 49·9 | 5·8 | 5·6 | 11·8 | 11·3 | 17·8 | 17·1 |
| 59 | 14 29·8 | 14 32·1 | 13 50·1 | 5·9 | 5·7 | 11·9 | 11·4 | 17·9 | 17·2 |
| 60 | 14 30·0 | 14 32·4 | 13 50·4 | 6·0 | 5·8 | 12·0 | 11·5 | 18·0 | 17·3 |



| 58m s | SUN PLANETS ° ′ | ARIES ° ′ | MOON ° ′ | v or d ′ | Corrn ′ | v or d ′ | Corrn ′ | v or d ′ | Corrn ′ |
|---|---|---|---|---|---|---|---|---|---|
| 00 | 14 30·0 | 14 32·4 | 13 50·4 | 0·0 | 0·0 | 6·0 | 5·9 | 12·0 | 11·7 |
| 01 | 14 30·3 | 14 32·6 | 13 50·6 | 0·1 | 0·1 | 6·1 | 5·9 | 12·1 | 11·8 |
| 02 | 14 30·5 | 14 32·9 | 13 50·8 | 0·2 | 0·2 | 6·2 | 6·0 | 12·2 | 11·9 |
| 03 | 14 30·8 | 14 33·1 | 13 51·1 | 0·3 | 0·3 | 6·3 | 6·1 | 12·3 | 12·0 |
| 04 | 14 31·0 | 14 33·4 | 13 51·3 | 0·4 | 0·4 | 6·4 | 6·2 | 12·4 | 12·1 |
| 05 | 14 31·3 | 14 33·6 | 13 51·6 | 0·5 | 0·5 | 6·5 | 6·3 | 12·5 | 12·2 |
| 06 | 14 31·5 | 14 33·9 | 13 51·8 | 0·6 | 0·6 | 6·6 | 6·4 | 12·6 | 12·3 |
| 07 | 14 31·8 | 14 34·1 | 13 52·0 | 0·7 | 0·7 | 6·7 | 6·5 | 12·7 | 12·4 |
| 08 | 14 32·0 | 14 34·4 | 13 52·3 | 0·8 | 0·8 | 6·8 | 6·6 | 12·8 | 12·5 |
| 09 | 14 32·3 | 14 34·6 | 13 52·5 | 0·9 | 0·9 | 6·9 | 6·7 | 12·9 | 12·6 |
| 10 | 14 32·5 | 14 34·9 | 13 52·8 | 1·0 | 1·0 | 7·0 | 6·8 | 13·0 | 12·7 |
| 11 | 14 32·8 | 14 35·1 | 13 53·0 | 1·1 | 1·1 | 7·1 | 6·9 | 13·1 | 12·8 |
| 12 | 14 33·0 | 14 35·4 | 13 53·2 | 1·2 | 1·2 | 7·2 | 7·0 | 13·2 | 12·9 |
| 13 | 14 33·3 | 14 35·6 | 13 53·5 | 1·3 | 1·3 | 7·3 | 7·1 | 13·3 | 13·0 |
| 14 | 14 33·5 | 14 35·9 | 13 53·7 | 1·4 | 1·4 | 7·4 | 7·2 | 13·4 | 13·1 |
| 15 | 14 33·8 | 14 36·1 | 13 53·9 | 1·5 | 1·5 | 7·5 | 7·3 | 13·5 | 13·2 |
| 16 | 14 34·0 | 14 36·4 | 13 54·2 | 1·6 | 1·6 | 7·6 | 7·4 | 13·6 | 13·3 |
| 17 | 14 34·3 | 14 36·6 | 13 54·4 | 1·7 | 1·7 | 7·7 | 7·5 | 13·7 | 13·4 |
| 18 | 14 34·5 | 14 36·9 | 13 54·7 | 1·8 | 1·8 | 7·8 | 7·6 | 13·8 | 13·5 |
| 19 | 14 34·8 | 14 37·1 | 13 54·9 | 1·9 | 1·9 | 7·9 | 7·7 | 13·9 | 13·6 |
| 20 | 14 35·0 | 14 37·4 | 13 55·1 | 2·0 | 2·0 | 8·0 | 7·8 | 14·0 | 13·7 |
| 21 | 14 35·3 | 14 37·6 | 13 55·4 | 2·1 | 2·0 | 8·1 | 7·9 | 14·1 | 13·7 |
| 22 | 14 35·5 | 14 37·9 | 13 55·6 | 2·2 | 2·1 | 8·2 | 8·0 | 14·2 | 13·8 |
| 23 | 14 35·8 | 14 38·1 | 13 55·9 | 2·3 | 2·2 | 8·3 | 8·1 | 14·3 | 13·9 |
| 24 | 14 36·0 | 14 38·4 | 13 56·1 | 2·4 | 2·3 | 8·4 | 8·2 | 14·4 | 14·0 |
| 25 | 14 36·3 | 14 38·6 | 13 56·3 | 2·5 | 2·4 | 8·5 | 8·3 | 14·5 | 14·1 |
| 26 | 14 36·5 | 14 38·9 | 13 56·6 | 2·6 | 2·5 | 8·6 | 8·4 | 14·6 | 14·2 |
| 27 | 14 36·8 | 14 39·2 | 13 56·8 | 2·7 | 2·6 | 8·7 | 8·5 | 14·7 | 14·3 |
| 28 | 14 37·0 | 14 39·4 | 13 57·0 | 2·8 | 2·7 | 8·8 | 8·6 | 14·8 | 14·4 |
| 29 | 14 37·3 | 14 39·7 | 13 57·3 | 2·9 | 2·8 | 8·9 | 8·7 | 14·9 | 14·5 |
| 30 | 14 37·5 | 14 39·9 | 13 57·5 | 3·0 | 2·9 | 9·0 | 8·8 | 15·0 | 14·6 |
| 31 | 14 37·8 | 14 40·2 | 13 57·8 | 3·1 | 3·0 | 9·1 | 8·9 | 15·1 | 14·7 |
| 32 | 14 38·0 | 14 40·4 | 13 58·0 | 3·2 | 3·1 | 9·2 | 9·0 | 15·2 | 14·8 |
| 33 | 14 38·3 | 14 40·7 | 13 58·2 | 3·3 | 3·2 | 9·3 | 9·1 | 15·3 | 14·9 |
| 34 | 14 38·5 | 14 40·9 | 13 58·5 | 3·4 | 3·3 | 9·4 | 9·2 | 15·4 | 15·0 |
| 35 | 14 38·8 | 14 41·2 | 13 58·7 | 3·5 | 3·4 | 9·5 | 9·3 | 15·5 | 15·1 |
| 36 | 14 39·0 | 14 41·4 | 13 59·0 | 3·6 | 3·5 | 9·6 | 9·4 | 15·6 | 15·2 |
| 37 | 14 39·3 | 14 41·7 | 13 59·2 | 3·7 | 3·6 | 9·7 | 9·5 | 15·7 | 15·3 |
| 38 | 14 39·5 | 14 41·9 | 13 59·4 | 3·8 | 3·7 | 9·8 | 9·6 | 15·8 | 15·4 |
| 39 | 14 39·8 | 14 42·2 | 13 59·7 | 3·9 | 3·8 | 9·9 | 9·7 | 15·9 | 15·5 |
| 40 | 14 40·0 | 14 42·4 | 13 59·9 | 4·0 | 3·9 | 10·0 | 9·8 | 16·0 | 15·6 |
| 41 | 14 40·3 | 14 42·7 | 14 00·1 | 4·1 | 4·0 | 10·1 | 9·8 | 16·1 | 15·7 |
| 42 | 14 40·5 | 14 42·9 | 14 00·4 | 4·2 | 4·1 | 10·2 | 9·9 | 16·2 | 15·8 |
| 43 | 14 40·8 | 14 43·2 | 14 00·6 | 4·3 | 4·2 | 10·3 | 10·0 | 16·3 | 15·9 |
| 44 | 14 41·0 | 14 43·4 | 14 00·9 | 4·4 | 4·3 | 10·4 | 10·1 | 16·4 | 16·0 |
| 45 | 14 41·3 | 14 43·7 | 14 01·1 | 4·5 | 4·4 | 10·5 | 10·2 | 16·5 | 16·1 |
| 46 | 14 41·5 | 14 43·9 | 14 01·3 | 4·6 | 4·5 | 10·6 | 10·3 | 16·6 | 16·2 |
| 47 | 14 41·8 | 14 44·2 | 14 01·6 | 4·7 | 4·6 | 10·7 | 10·4 | 16·7 | 16·3 |
| 48 | 14 42·0 | 14 44·4 | 14 01·8 | 4·8 | 4·7 | 10·8 | 10·5 | 16·8 | 16·4 |
| 49 | 14 42·3 | 14 44·7 | 14 02·1 | 4·9 | 4·8 | 10·9 | 10·6 | 16·9 | 16·5 |
| 50 | 14 42·5 | 14 44·9 | 14 02·3 | 5·0 | 4·9 | 11·0 | 10·7 | 17·0 | 16·6 |
| 51 | 14 42·8 | 14 45·2 | 14 02·5 | 5·1 | 5·0 | 11·1 | 10·8 | 17·1 | 16·7 |
| 52 | 14 43·0 | 14 45·4 | 14 02·8 | 5·2 | 5·1 | 11·2 | 10·9 | 17·2 | 16·8 |
| 53 | 14 43·3 | 14 45·7 | 14 03·0 | 5·3 | 5·2 | 11·3 | 11·0 | 17·3 | 16·9 |
| 54 | 14 43·5 | 14 45·9 | 14 03·3 | 5·4 | 5·3 | 11·4 | 11·1 | 17·4 | 17·0 |
| 55 | 14 43·8 | 14 46·2 | 14 03·5 | 5·5 | 5·4 | 11·5 | 11·2 | 17·5 | 17·1 |
| 56 | 14 44·0 | 14 46·4 | 14 03·7 | 5·6 | 5·5 | 11·6 | 11·3 | 17·6 | 17·2 |
| 57 | 14 44·3 | 14 46·7 | 14 04·0 | 5·7 | 5·6 | 11·7 | 11·4 | 17·7 | 17·3 |
| 58 | 14 44·5 | 14 46·9 | 14 04·2 | 5·8 | 5·7 | 11·8 | 11·5 | 17·8 | 17·4 |
| 59 | 14 44·8 | 14 47·2 | 14 04·4 | 5·9 | 5·8 | 11·9 | 11·6 | 17·9 | 17·5 |
| 60 | 14 45·0 | 14 47·4 | 14 04·7 | 6·0 | 5·9 | 12·0 | 11·7 | 18·0 | 17·6 |

| 59m s | SUN PLANETS ° ′ | ARIES ° ′ | MOON ° ′ | v or d ′ | Corrn ′ | v or d ′ | Corrn ′ | v or d ′ | Corrn ′ |
|---|---|---|---|---|---|---|---|---|---|
| 00 | 14 45·0 | 14 47·4 | 14 04·7 | 0·0 | 0·0 | 6·0 | 6·0 | 12·0 | 11·9 |
| 01 | 14 45·3 | 14 47·7 | 14 04·9 | 0·1 | 0·1 | 6·1 | 6·0 | 12·1 | 12·0 |
| 02 | 14 45·5 | 14 47·9 | 14 05·2 | 0·2 | 0·2 | 6·2 | 6·1 | 12·2 | 12·1 |
| 03 | 14 45·8 | 14 48·2 | 14 05·4 | 0·3 | 0·3 | 6·3 | 6·2 | 12·3 | 12·2 |
| 04 | 14 46·0 | 14 48·4 | 14 05·6 | 0·4 | 0·4 | 6·4 | 6·3 | 12·4 | 12·3 |
| 05 | 14 46·3 | 14 48·7 | 14 05·9 | 0·5 | 0·5 | 6·5 | 6·4 | 12·5 | 12·4 |
| 06 | 14 46·5 | 14 48·9 | 14 06·1 | 0·6 | 0·6 | 6·6 | 6·5 | 12·6 | 12·5 |
| 07 | 14 46·8 | 14 49·2 | 14 06·4 | 0·7 | 0·7 | 6·7 | 6·6 | 12·7 | 12·6 |
| 08 | 14 47·0 | 14 49·4 | 14 06·6 | 0·8 | 0·8 | 6·8 | 6·7 | 12·8 | 12·7 |
| 09 | 14 47·3 | 14 49·7 | 14 06·8 | 0·9 | 0·9 | 6·9 | 6·8 | 12·9 | 12·8 |
| 10 | 14 47·5 | 14 49·9 | 14 07·1 | 1·0 | 1·0 | 7·0 | 6·9 | 13·0 | 12·9 |
| 11 | 14 47·8 | 14 50·2 | 14 07·3 | 1·1 | 1·1 | 7·1 | 7·0 | 13·1 | 13·0 |
| 12 | 14 48·0 | 14 50·4 | 14 07·5 | 1·2 | 1·2 | 7·2 | 7·1 | 13·2 | 13·1 |
| 13 | 14 48·3 | 14 50·7 | 14 07·8 | 1·3 | 1·3 | 7·3 | 7·2 | 13·3 | 13·2 |
| 14 | 14 48·5 | 14 50·9 | 14 08·0 | 1·4 | 1·4 | 7·4 | 7·3 | 13·4 | 13·3 |
| 15 | 14 48·8 | 14 51·2 | 14 08·3 | 1·5 | 1·5 | 7·5 | 7·4 | 13·5 | 13·4 |
| 16 | 14 49·0 | 14 51·4 | 14 08·5 | 1·6 | 1·6 | 7·6 | 7·5 | 13·6 | 13·5 |
| 17 | 14 49·3 | 14 51·7 | 14 08·7 | 1·7 | 1·7 | 7·7 | 7·6 | 13·7 | 13·6 |
| 18 | 14 49·5 | 14 51·9 | 14 09·0 | 1·8 | 1·8 | 7·8 | 7·7 | 13·8 | 13·7 |
| 19 | 14 49·8 | 14 52·2 | 14 09·2 | 1·9 | 1·9 | 7·9 | 7·8 | 13·9 | 13·8 |
| 20 | 14 50·0 | 14 52·4 | 14 09·5 | 2·0 | 2·0 | 8·0 | 7·9 | 14·0 | 13·9 |
| 21 | 14 50·3 | 14 52·7 | 14 09·7 | 2·1 | 2·1 | 8·1 | 8·0 | 14·1 | 14·0 |
| 22 | 14 50·5 | 14 52·9 | 14 09·9 | 2·2 | 2·2 | 8·2 | 8·1 | 14·2 | 14·1 |
| 23 | 14 50·8 | 14 53·2 | 14 10·2 | 2·3 | 2·3 | 8·3 | 8·2 | 14·3 | 14·2 |
| 24 | 14 51·0 | 14 53·4 | 14 10·4 | 2·4 | 2·4 | 8·4 | 8·3 | 14·4 | 14·3 |
| 25 | 14 51·3 | 14 53·7 | 14 10·6 | 2·5 | 2·5 | 8·5 | 8·4 | 14·5 | 14·4 |
| 26 | 14 51·5 | 14 53·9 | 14 10·9 | 2·6 | 2·6 | 8·6 | 8·5 | 14·6 | 14·5 |
| 27 | 14 51·8 | 14 54·2 | 14 11·1 | 2·7 | 2·7 | 8·7 | 8·6 | 14·7 | 14·6 |
| 28 | 14 52·0 | 14 54·4 | 14 11·4 | 2·8 | 2·8 | 8·8 | 8·7 | 14·8 | 14·7 |
| 29 | 14 52·3 | 14 54·7 | 14 11·6 | 2·9 | 2·9 | 8·9 | 8·8 | 14·9 | 14·8 |
| 30 | 14 52·5 | 14 54·9 | 14 11·8 | 3·0 | 3·0 | 9·0 | 8·9 | 15·0 | 14·9 |
| 31 | 14 52·8 | 14 55·2 | 14 12·1 | 3·1 | 3·1 | 9·1 | 9·0 | 15·1 | 15·0 |
| 32 | 14 53·0 | 14 55·4 | 14 12·3 | 3·2 | 3·2 | 9·2 | 9·1 | 15·2 | 15·1 |
| 33 | 14 53·3 | 14 55·7 | 14 12·6 | 3·3 | 3·3 | 9·3 | 9·2 | 15·3 | 15·2 |
| 34 | 14 53·5 | 14 55·9 | 14 12·8 | 3·4 | 3·4 | 9·4 | 9·3 | 15·4 | 15·3 |
| 35 | 14 53·8 | 14 56·2 | 14 13·0 | 3·5 | 3·5 | 9·5 | 9·4 | 15·5 | 15·4 |
| 36 | 14 54·0 | 14 56·4 | 14 13·3 | 3·6 | 3·6 | 9·6 | 9·5 | 15·6 | 15·5 |
| 37 | 14 54·3 | 14 56·7 | 14 13·5 | 3·7 | 3·7 | 9·7 | 9·6 | 15·7 | 15·6 |
| 38 | 14 54·5 | 14 56·9 | 14 13·8 | 3·8 | 3·8 | 9·8 | 9·7 | 15·8 | 15·7 |
| 39 | 14 54·8 | 14 57·2 | 14 14·0 | 3·9 | 3·9 | 9·9 | 9·8 | 15·9 | 15·8 |
| 40 | 14 55·0 | 14 57·5 | 14 14·2 | 4·0 | 4·0 | 10·0 | 9·9 | 16·0 | 15·9 |
| 41 | 14 55·3 | 14 57·7 | 14 14·5 | 4·1 | 4·1 | 10·1 | 10·0 | 16·1 | 16·0 |
| 42 | 14 55·5 | 14 58·0 | 14 14·7 | 4·2 | 4·2 | 10·2 | 10·1 | 16·2 | 16·1 |
| 43 | 14 55·8 | 14 58·2 | 14 14·9 | 4·3 | 4·3 | 10·3 | 10·2 | 16·3 | 16·2 |
| 44 | 14 56·0 | 14 58·5 | 14 15·2 | 4·4 | 4·4 | 10·4 | 10·3 | 16·4 | 16·3 |
| 45 | 14 56·3 | 14 58·7 | 14 15·4 | 4·5 | 4·5 | 10·5 | 10·4 | 16·5 | 16·4 |
| 46 | 14 56·5 | 14 59·0 | 14 15·7 | 4·6 | 4·6 | 10·6 | 10·5 | 16·6 | 16·5 |
| 47 | 14 56·8 | 14 59·2 | 14 15·9 | 4·7 | 4·7 | 10·7 | 10·6 | 16·7 | 16·6 |
| 48 | 14 57·0 | 14 59·5 | 14 16·1 | 4·8 | 4·8 | 10·8 | 10·7 | 16·8 | 16·7 |
| 49 | 14 57·3 | 14 59·7 | 14 16·4 | 4·9 | 4·9 | 10·9 | 10·8 | 16·9 | 16·8 |
| 50 | 14 57·5 | 15 00·0 | 14 16·6 | 5·0 | 5·0 | 11·0 | 10·9 | 17·0 | 16·9 |
| 51 | 14 57·8 | 15 00·2 | 14 16·9 | 5·1 | 5·1 | 11·1 | 11·0 | 17·1 | 17·0 |
| 52 | 14 58·0 | 15 00·5 | 14 17·1 | 5·2 | 5·2 | 11·2 | 11·1 | 17·2 | 17·1 |
| 53 | 14 58·3 | 15 00·7 | 14 17·3 | 5·3 | 5·3 | 11·3 | 11·2 | 17·3 | 17·2 |
| 54 | 14 58·5 | 15 01·0 | 14 17·6 | 5·4 | 5·4 | 11·4 | 11·3 | 17·4 | 17·3 |
| 55 | 14 58·8 | 15 01·2 | 14 17·8 | 5·5 | 5·5 | 11·5 | 11·4 | 17·5 | 17·4 |
| 56 | 14 59·0 | 15 01·5 | 14 18·0 | 5·6 | 5·6 | 11·6 | 11·5 | 17·6 | 17·5 |
| 57 | 14 59·3 | 15 01·7 | 14 18·3 | 5·7 | 5·7 | 11·7 | 11·6 | 17·7 | 17·6 |
| 58 | 14 59·5 | 15 02·0 | 14 18·5 | 5·8 | 5·8 | 11·8 | 11·7 | 17·8 | 17·7 |
| 59 | 14 59·8 | 15 02·2 | 14 18·8 | 5·9 | 5·9 | 11·9 | 11·8 | 17·9 | 17·8 |
| 60 | 15 00·0 | 15 02·5 | 14 19·0 | 6·0 | 6·0 | 12·0 | 11·9 | 18·0 | 17·9 |

# ABBREVIATIONS USED IN THIS TEXT

| | |
|---|---|
| a | intercept or numerical difference between $H_o$ and $H_c$ |
| a | the change of altitude in $1^m$ from the meridian transit |
| $a_0$ $a_1$ $a_2$ | Polaris table corrections |
| A | away |
| AP | assumed position |
| App Alt | apparent altitude |
| C, $C_n$ | course |
| CMG | course made good |
| d | change in declination during one hour (Nautical Almanac) |
| d | change in $H_c$ for $1^\circ$ of declination change (H.O. 229) |
| D | distance |
| Dec | declination |
| Dec Inc | declination increment |
| Dep | departure |
| DLat | difference in latitude |
| DLo | difference in longitude |
| DMG | distance made good |
| DR | dead reckoning |
| DSD | double second difference |
| EP | estimated position |
| GHA | Greenwich hour angle |
| GMT | Greenwich mean time |
| $H_c$ | computed altitude |
| $H_o$ | corrected sextant altitude |
| $H_s$ | sextant altitude |
| H.P. | horizontal parallax |
| Ht. | height |
| IC | index correction |
| K | construction part of H.O. 211 triangle |
| L, Lat | latitude |
| $\lambda$, Lo, Long | longitude |
| LAN | local apparent noon |
| LHA | local hour angle |
| LL | lower limb |
| LOP | line of position |
| m | difference of meridional parts |
| M | meridional parts. On hour angle diagram M = our Meridian |
| NCP | north celestial pole |
| n.m. | nautical miles |
| Net corr | net correction |
| $P_n$ | north pole |
| R | construction part of H.O. 211 triangle |
| RA | right ascension |
| RP | real position |
| R. Fix | running fix |
| S | speed |
| SHA | sidereal hour angle |
| t | meridian angle |
| T | toward |
| Tab Dec | tabular declination |
| UL | upper limb |
| v | change in GHA for one hour (Nautical Almanac) |
| $\Upsilon$ | vernal equinox, first point of Aries |
| W.E. | watch error |
| W.T. | watch time |
| Z | azimuth angle |
| $Z_n$ | azimuth |
| Z.D. | zone description |
| Z.T. | zone time |

The following four forms have been devised and used for the Mystic Seaport Planetarium navigation classes. They may be reproduced for student use but not for resale.

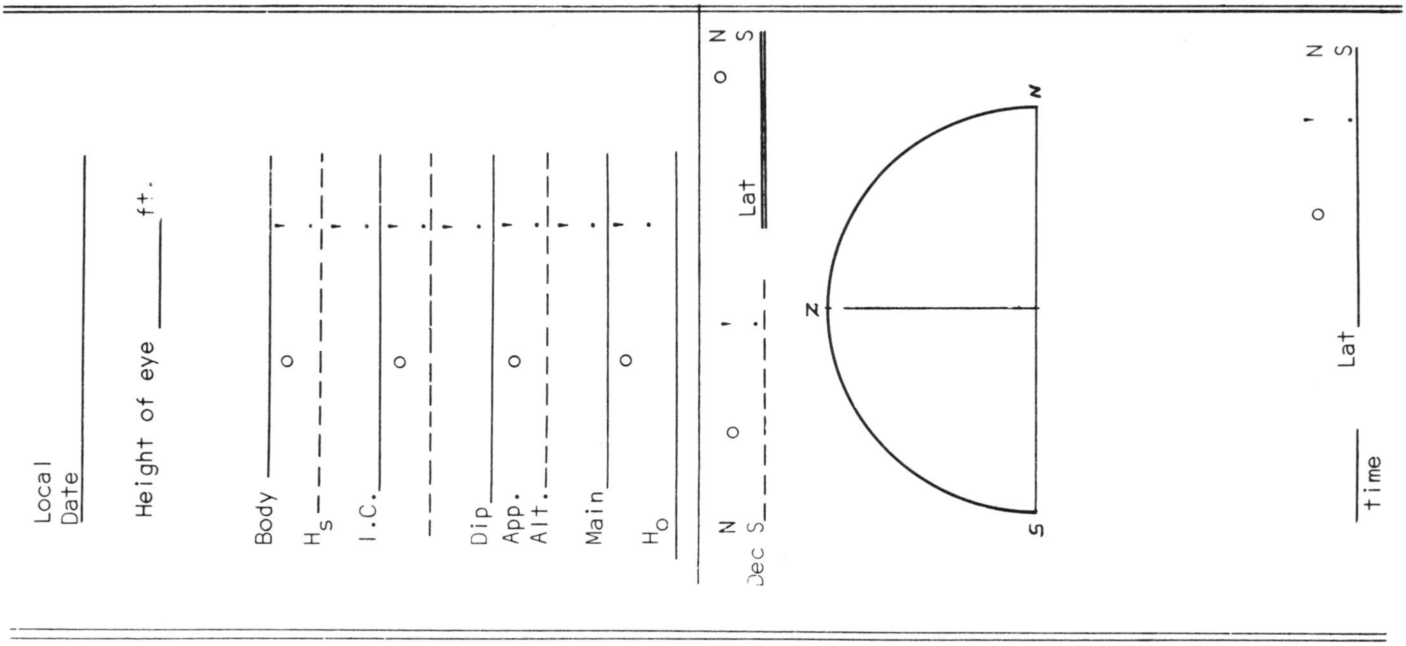

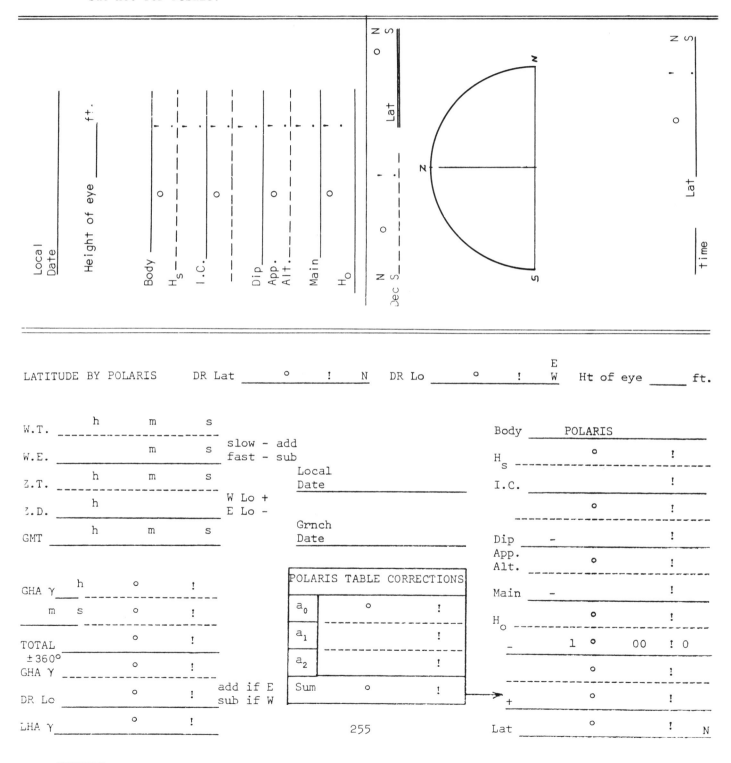

LATITUDE BY POLARIS    DR Lat ____ ° ____ ' N    DR Lo ____ ° ____ ' E/W    Ht of eye ____ ft.

| | | | | |
|---|---|---|---|---|
| W.T. | h | m | s | |
| W.E. | | m | s | slow - add<br>fast - sub |
| Z.T. | h | m | s | |
| Z.D. | h | | | W Lo +<br>E Lo - |
| GMT | h | m | s | |

Local Date ____

Grnch Date ____

| | | | |
|---|---|---|---|
| GHA ϒ | h | ° | ' |
| m s | | ° | ' |
| TOTAL | | ° | ' |
| ±360° GHA ϒ | | ° | ' |
| DR Lo | | ° | ' |
| LHA ϒ | | ° | ' |

add if E
sub if W

| POLARIS TABLE CORRECTIONS | | |
|---|---|---|
| $a_0$ | ° | ' |
| $a_1$ | | ' |
| $a_2$ | | ' |
| Sum | ° | ' |

| | | |
|---|---|---|
| Body | POLARIS | |
| $H_s$ | ° | ' |
| I.C. | | ' |
| | ° | ' |
| Dip | - | ' |
| App. Alt. | ° | ' |
| Main | - | ' |
| $H_o$ | ° | ' |
| - | 1 ° | 00 ' 0 |
| | ° | ' |
| + | ° | ' |
| Lat | ° | ' N |

# SIGHT REDUCTION BY H.O. 229

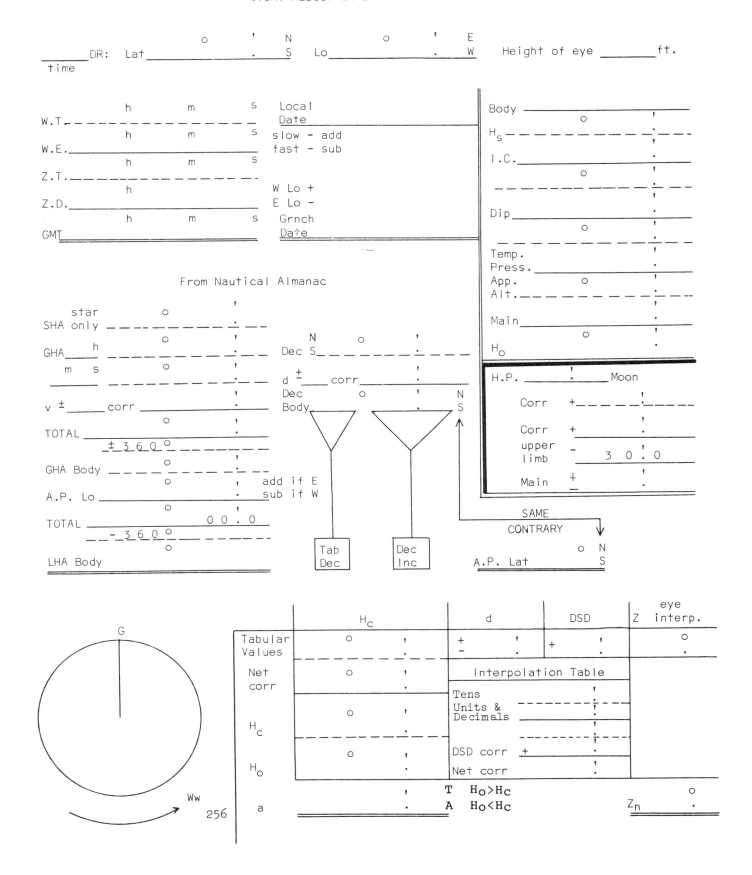

______ DR: Lat ______ ° ' N/S  Lo ______ ° ' E/W  Height of eye ______ ft.
time

| | h | m | s | |
|---|---|---|---|---|
| W.T. | | | | Local Date ______ |
| W.E. | | | | slow - add<br>fast - sub |
| Z.T. | | | | |
| Z.D. | | | | W Lo +<br>E Lo - |
| GMT | | | | Grnch Date ______ |

| Body | ° | ' |
|---|---|---|
| $H_s$ | | |
| I.C. | | |
| | | |
| Dip | | |
| | | |
| Temp.<br>Press. | | |
| App. Alt. | | |
| Main | | |
| $H_o$ | | |

| H.P. ______ ' ______ Moon | | |
|---|---|---|
| Corr | + | |
| Corr | + | |
| upper limb | - | 30.0 |
| Main | $\pm$ | |

From Nautical Almanac

| | ° | ' |
|---|---|---|
| star SHA only | | |
| GHA ___ h | | |
| ___ m s | | |
| v ± ___ corr | | |
| TOTAL | | |
| | ± 360 | |
| GHA Body | | |
| A.P. Lo | | |
| TOTAL | | 00.0 |
| | - 360 | |
| LHA Body | | |

add if E
sub if W

| | ° | ' |
|---|---|---|
| Dec N/S | | |
| d ± ___ corr | | |
| Dec Body | | N/S |

Tab Dec

Dec Inc

SAME
CONTRARY

A.P. Lat ______ ° N/S

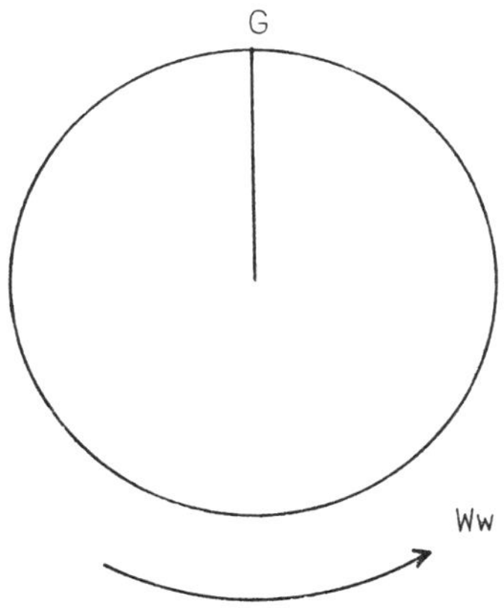


| | $H_c$ | d | DSD | Z | eye interp. |
|---|---|---|---|---|---|
| Tabular Values | ° ' | + / - | + | | ° |
| Net corr | ° ' | Interpolation Table | | | |
| | | Tens | | | |
| | | Units & Decimals | | | |
| $H_c$ | ° ' | | | | |
| | | DSD corr + | | | |
| $H_o$ | ° ' | Net corr | | | |
| a | ' | T $H_o > H_c$<br>A $H_o < H_c$ | | $Z_n$ | ° |

(TIME)

# SIGHT REDUCTION BY H.O. 211

DR: Lat ________ N/S  Lo ________  Ht. of Eye ________ ft.

W.T. h m s
W.E. h m s
Z.T. h m s
Z.D. h  W $L_o+$  E $L_o-$
G.M.T. h m s

Date ________
slow - add
fast - sub

Date ________
(Grnch)

Body ________
$H_s$ ° '
I.C. '
° '
Dip '
° '
Temp.
Press. '
App. Alt. ° '
Main '
$H_o$ ° '

## FROM NAUTICAL ALMANAC

SHA ✲ ° '
GHA ___ h ° '
m s ° '
v ________ corr '
———360° ° '
GHA Body ° '
D R Lo ° '  E+ W-
———360° ° '
LHA Body ° '
t (H.A.) ° '  E W

Dec. Body ° '  N S
R
K ° '  N S
DR Lat ° '  N S
(K ∾ L) ° '
$H_c$ ° '
$H_o$ ° '
a  T $H_o>H_c$  A $H_o<H_c$  mi

K∾L: If different name add
If same name subtract

Dec ° '
d ___ corr '
Dec. Body ° '

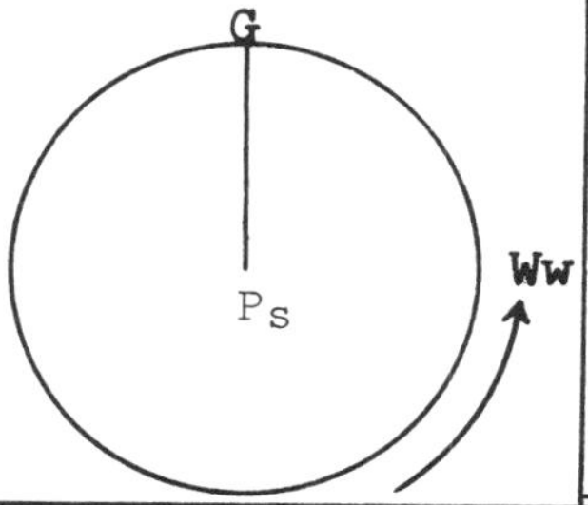


H.P. ________ ' MOON
Corr + '
Corr + '
Upper Limb -30' -
Main ± '

| ADD | SUBTRACT | ADD | SUBTRACT AZIMUTH |
|---|---|---|---|
| A | | | |
| B | A | | |
| A | B | B | A |
| | A | | |
| | | B | |
| | | A | B |
| | | | A |

K & Dec Same Name

See rule top of left page.

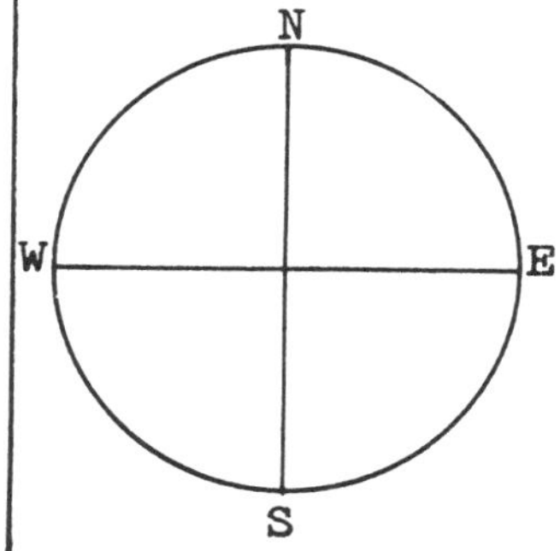


$Z_n$ ° '  Z N/S ° '  E W

See rule - top of right page
Z: N or S, Same as Lat.
E or W, Same as "t"
$Z_n$ if, N & E = Z
N & W = 360° - Z
S & E = 180° - Z
S & W = 180° + Z

POSITION PLOTTING SHEET - MERCATOR PROJECTION

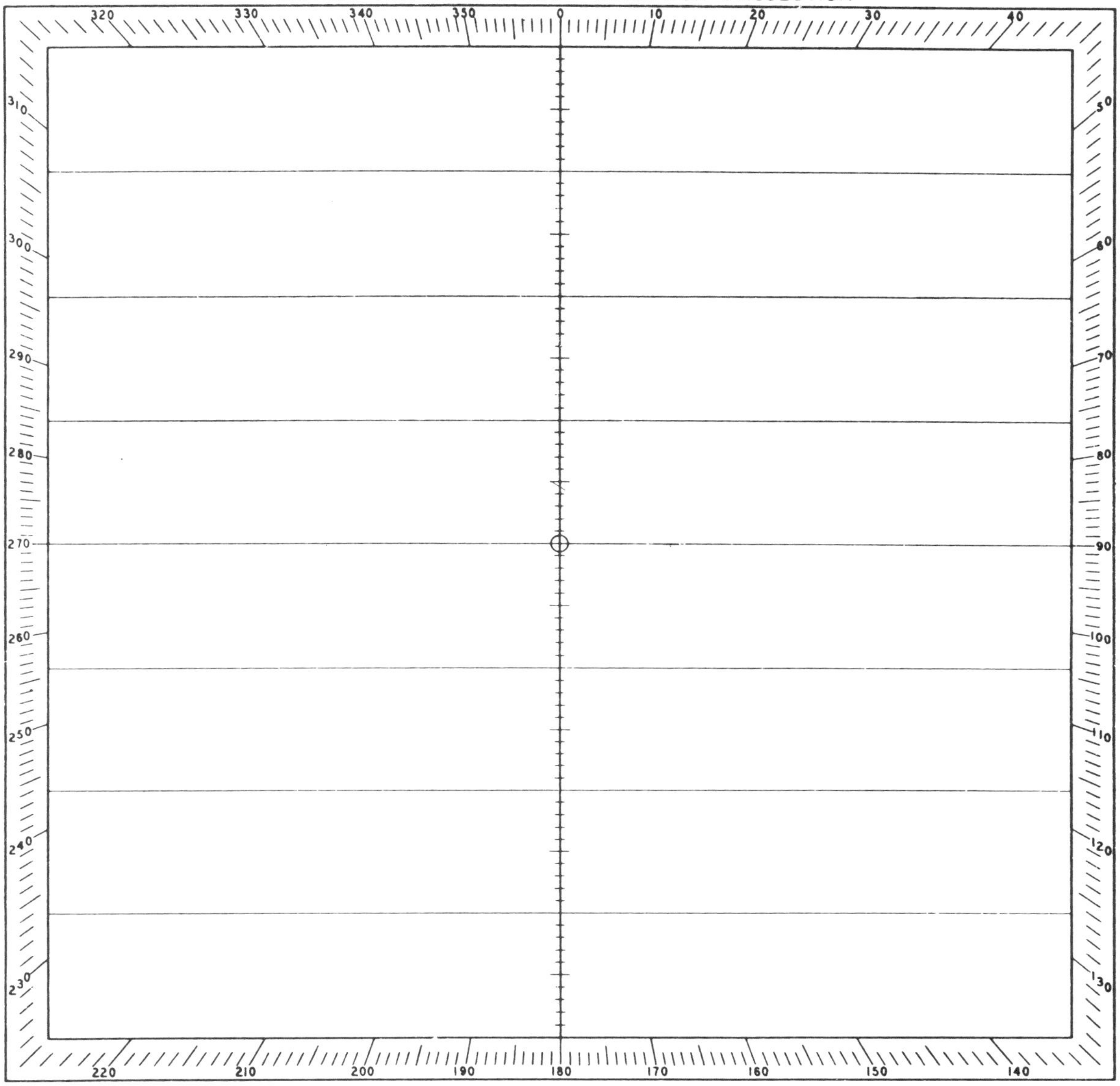


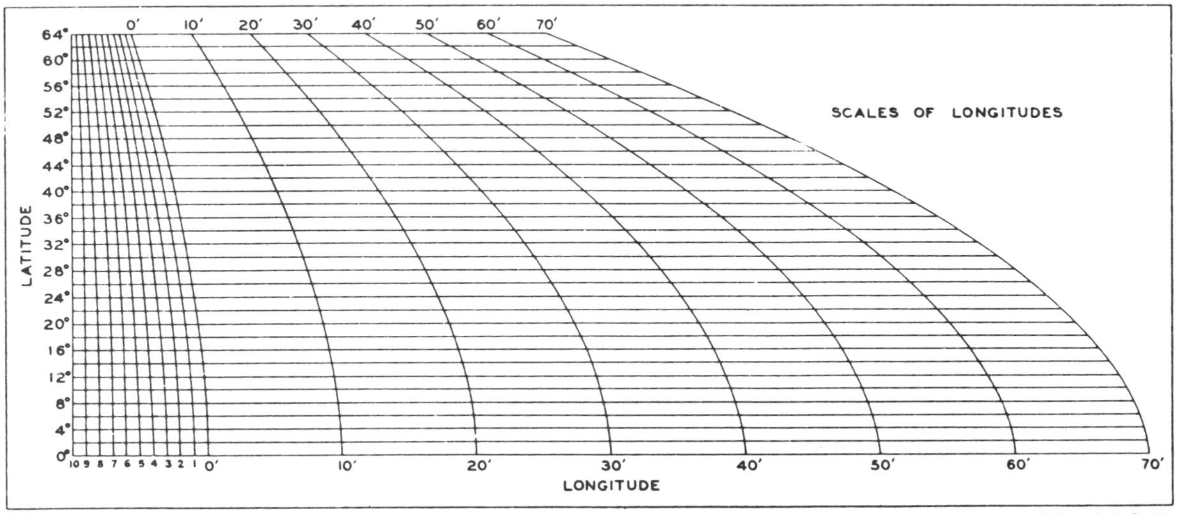


ADAPTED FROM U.S. COAST GUARD FORM. NO.2543

FORM NO. N-E 1941

BIOGRAPHICAL NOTES ON AUTHOR

Susan P. Howell, a native of South Bristol, Maine, graduated from Mount Holyoke College in 1968 with a math and astronomy background. Since that time she has worked for the planetarium at Mystic Seaport with the exception of one year as Planetarium Lecturer at Dickinson College in Carlisle, Pennsylvania. Her duties on the Seaport staff include writing planetarium programs, presenting lectures to school groups and Seaport visitors, and instructing classes in basic celestial navigation, astronomy, piloting and dead reckoning, weather, and advanced celestial navigation, the last three which she introduced into the planetarium class curriculum. She has done part-time work for Sail magazine teaching summer cruises in celestial navigation, for Connecticut College instructing astronomy laboratories, and for Eastern Connecticut State College teaching astronomy. She has written astronomical, meteorological, navigational and biographical articles for The Naturalist's Almanac, Pequot Trails, The Practical Sailor and the Seaport's Log. Outside major interests include sailing, gardening, music, carpentry and horseback riding. She and her husband, David, have three children and live in Hebron, Connecticut.

(Above notes are from the first edition.)

---

In 1983, Susan became Chairman of the Sail Training and Education Committee and Member of the Board of Directors of The American Sail Training Association. It was while serving in this capacity as an Education Officer that she died in the sudden sinking of the British barque Marques during a squall while enroute from Bermuda to Halifax on 3 June 1984.

Original photo by George Hall

# *Index*